District Gazetteers of India Series 131

GAZETTEER
OF THE
BOMBAY PRESIDENCY

District Gazetteers of India Series 131

GAZETTEER
OF THE
BOMBAY PRESIDENCY.

27 VOLUMES (IN 35 BINDINGS)
VOLUME XXVII.

GENERAL INDEX.

EDITED BY
R. E. ENTHOVEN

GYAN

Published by

Gyan Publishing House
5, Ansari Road
Daryaganj, New Delhi-110002
Phone: 011-47034999, 9811692060
E-mail: books@gyanbooks.com

Distribution Network
gyanbooks.com
India, USA, Canada, UK, Australia, France

ISBN: 978-81-212-8560-5 (Set) 27 Volumes (In 35 Bindings)
978-81-212-8492-9 (PB)
First Published, 1904

2nd Impression 2024

Printed at: Gyan Press, Delhi.

GAZETTEER OF THE BOMBAY PRESIDENCY (VOL. XXVII)
Editor: R. E. ENTHOVEN

LIST OF VOLUMES

S. NO.	ISBN NO.	VOLUME	TITLE	AUTHOR	PRICE	PAGES
			ASSAM DISTRICT GAZETTEERS			
1	9788121285926	1st	Cachar	B. C. Allen	600	300
2	9788121285919	2nd	Sylhet	B. C. Allen	750	378
3	9788121285902	3rd	Goalpara	B. C. Allen	400	203
4	9788121285896	4th	Kamrup	B. C. Allen	675	344
5	9788121285889	5th	Darrang	B. C. Allen	725	364
6	9788121285872	6th	Nowgong	B. C. Allen	560	280
7	9788121285865	7th	Sibsagar	B. C. Allen	675	343
8	9788121285858	8th	Lakhimpur	B. C. Allen	690	347
9	9788121285841	9th	Naga Hills and Manipur	B. C. Allen	580	294
10	9788121285834	10th	The Khasi And Jaintia Hills, The Garo Hills And The Lushai Hills	B. C. Allen	675	363
11	9788121285827	11th	The Sadiya and Balipara Frontier Tract	B. C. Allen	375	190
			BENGAL DISTRICT GAZETTEERS			
12	9788121218672	1st	Angul	L. S. S. O'Malley	340	168
13	9788121259637	2nd	Bakarganj	J. C. JACK	970	194
14	9788121218696	3rd	Balasore	L. S. S. O'Malley	450	228
15	9788121259590	4th	Bankura	L. S. S. O'Malley	1000	199
16	9788121218375	5th	Bhagalpur	J. Byrne	390	194
17	9788121218290	6th	Birbhum	L. S. S. O'Malley	300	150
18	9788121259651	7th	Eastern Bengal and Assam - Bogra	J. N. Gupta	940	188
19	9788121218351	8th	Burdwan	J. C. K. Peterson	450	227
20	9788121259538	9th	Calcutta District Gazetteer - Statistics, 1901 - 02		340	68
21	9788121218313	10th	Champaran	L. S. S. O'Malley	410	205
22	9788121259613	11th	Eastern Bengal District Gazetters - Chittagong	L. S. S. O'Malley	1080	216
23	9788121259552	12th	Chota Nagpur Tributary		130	26
24	9788121259415	13th	The Cooch Behar Gazette: Statistics		1460	292
25	9788121218412	14th	Cuttack	L. S. S. O'Malley	490	248
26	9788121261357	15th	Eastern Bengal District Gazetteers Dacca	B. C. Allen	400	207
27	9788121218436	16th	Darbhanga	L. S. S. O'Malley	360	180
28	9789362089335	17th	Darjeeling	L. S. S. O'Malley	500	248
29	9788121259453	18th	Eastern Bengal District Gazetteers - Dinajpur	F. W. Strong	890	178
30	9788121259392	19th	Faridpur	L. S. S. O'Malley	700	140
31	9788121218474	20th	Gaya	L. S. S. O'Malley	540	270
32	9788121214032	21st	Bihar and Orissa District Gazetteer: Hazaribagh	E. Lister	715	234
33	9788121218337	22nd	Hooghly	L. S. S. O'Malley	680	340
34	9788121218191	23rd	Bengal District Gazetteer Howrah	L. S. S. O'Malley	390	199
35	9788121259293	24th	Eastern Bengal and Assam - Jalpaiguri	John F. Gruning	890	178
36	9788121259279	25th	Jessore	L. S. S. O'Malley	960	192
37	9788121259231	26th	Khulna	L. S. S. O'Malley	1100	220
38	9788121259217	27th	Malda	G. E. Lambourn	670	134
39	9788121267854	28th	Manbhum	H. Coupland	600	313
40	9788121218498	29th	Midnapore	L. S. S. O'Malley	500	252
41	9788121218597	30th	Monghyr	L. S. S. O'Malley	560	280
42	9788121259156	31st	Murshidabad	L. S. S. O'Malley	1250	250
43	9788121259576	32nd	Bengal District Gazetteers - Muzaffarpur	L. S. S. O'Malley	940	188
44	9788121259132	33rd	Mymensingh	F. A. Sachse	960	192
45	9788121259118	34th	Nadia	J. H. E. Garrett	1070	214
46	9788121259095	35th	Eastern Bengal and Assam - Noakhali	J. E. Webster	580	115
47	9788121218450	36th	Feudatory States of Orissa	L. E. B. Cobdenramsay	790	395
48	9788121259071	37th	Pabna	L. S. S. O'Malley	710	142
49	9788121218511	38th	Palamau	L. S. S. O'Malley	380	190
50	9788121218634	39th	Patna	L. S. S. O'Malley	500	250
51	9788121218535	40th	Puri	L. S. S. O'Malley	650	328
52	9788121218757	41st	Purnea	L. S. S. O'Malley	440	220
53	9788121258937	42nd	Rajshahi	L. S. S. O'Malley	1080	216
54	9788121256681	43rd	Bihar and Orissa District Gazetteers: Ranchi	M. G. Hallett	1350	278
55	9788121258913	44th	Eastern Bengal and assam - Rangpur	J. A. Vas	890	178
56	9788121218559	45th	Sambalpur	L. S. S. O'Malley	480	242
57	9788121214056	46th	Santal Parganas	L. S. S. O'Malley	940	308
58	9788121218610	47th	Saran	L. S. S. O'Malley	380	190
59	9788121218658	48th	Shahabad	L. S. S. O'Malley	380	190
60	9788121256704	49th	The Gazetteer of Sikhim	H. H. Risley	960	481
61	9788121218573	50th	Singhbhum, Saraikela And Kharsawan	L. S. S. O'Malley	560	280
62	9788121259439	51st	Eastern Bengal District Gazetteers - Tippera	J. E. Webster	730	146
63	9788121259033	52nd	24 Parganas	L. S. S. O'Malley	1420	284

S. NO.	ISBN NO.	VOLUME	TITLE	AUTHOR	PRICE	PAGES
			CENTRAL PROVINCES DISTRICT GAZETTEERS			
64	9789362081728	1st, Vol. A	Akola (Descriptive)	A. E. Nelson, C. Brown	870	436
65	9789362085481	2nd, Vol. A	Amraoti (Descriptive)	S. V. Fitzgerald, A. E. Nelson	1050	524
66	9789362089267	3rd,Vol. A	Balaghat (Descriptive)	R. V. RUSSELL	430	216
67	9789362083494	4th, Vol. A	Betul (Descriptive)	R. V. RUSSELL	610	306
68	9789362085146	5th, Vol. A	Bhandara (Descriptive)	R. V. RUSSELL	580	292
69	9789362088390	6th, Vol. A	Bilaspur (Descriptive)	R. V. RUSSELL	870	434
70	9789362086044	7th, Vol. A	Buldana (Descriptive)	A. E. Nelson	1090	543
71	9789362089014	8th, Vol. B	Chanda (Descriptive)	R. V. RUSSELL	470	234
72	9789362086938	9th	Chhattisgarch Feudatory State	E. A. De Brett	880	440
73	9789362082961	10th	Chhindwara (Descriptive)	R. V. RUSSELL	550	274
74	9789362089342	11th, Vol. A & B	Damoh (Descriptive and Statistical Tables 1891-1901)	R. V. RUSSELL	830	414
75	9789362081230	12th, Vol. A	Durg (Descriptive)	A. E. Nelson	460	232
76	9789362086037	13th, Vol. A	Hoshangabad (Descriptive)	R. V. RUSSELL	860	430
77	9789362086792	14th, Vol. A	Jubbulpore (Descriptive)	A. E. Nelson	950	474
78	9789362089663	15th, Vol. A & B	Mandla (Descriptive and Statistical Tables 1891-1901)	R. V. RUSSELL	370	186
79	9789362086419	16th, Vol. A	Nagpur (Descriptive)	R. V. RUSSELL	790	394
80	9789362080646	17th, Vol. A	Narsinghpur (Descriptive)	R. V. RUSSELL	510	257
81	9789362084835	18th, Vol. A	Nimar (Descriptive)	R. V. RUSSELL	600	299
82	9789362087737	19th, Vol. A	Raipur (Descriptive)	A. E. Nelson	790	396
83	9789362080264	20th, Vol. A	Saugor (Descriptive)	R. V. RUSSELL	570	285
84	9789362081117	21st, Vol. A	Seoni (Descriptive)	R. V. RUSSELL	460	232
85	9789362084965	22nd, Vol. A	Wardha (Descriptive)	R. V. RUSSELL	600	302
86	9789362083401	23rd, Vol. A	Yeotmal (Descriptive)	R. V. RUSSELL	550	277
87	9789362080325	24th, Vol. I, Pt. I	Gwalior (Text and Tables)	R. V. RUSSELL	980	489
88	9789362087133	24th, Vol. I, Pt. II	Gwalior (Maps)	R. V. RUSSELL	400	198
89	9789362086341	24th, Vol. I, Pt. III	Gwalior (Village List)	R. V. RUSSELL	810	406
90	9789362085467	24th, Vol. I, Pt. IV	Gwalior (Photos)	R. V. RUSSELL	1400	698
91	9789362087393	25th, Vol. II	Indore (Text and Tables)	C. E. Luard	1050	524
92	9789362084422	26th, Vol. III	Bhopal (Text and Tables)	C. E. Luard	540	272
93	9789362086815	27th, Vol. IV	Rewah (Text and Tables)	C. E. Luard	500	250
94	9789362087584	28th, Vol. V, Pt. A	Western States - Malwa (Text)	C. E. Luard	1520	762
95	9789362087300	29th, Vol. VI, Pt. A	Eastern States - Bundelkhand (Text)	C. E. Luard	930	463
96	9789362082169	30th, Vol. VI, Pt. B	Eastern States - Bundelkhand (Tables)	C. E. Luard	830	417
			GAZETTEER OF THE BOMBAY PRESIDENCY:			
97	9788121283441	1st, Part I	History of Gujarat	Ed.: James M. Campbell	3220	644
98	9788121285582	1st, Part II	History of the Konkan Dakhan and Southern Maratha Country	Ed.: James M. Campbell	4200	840
99	9788121285568	2nd	Gujarat, Surat and Broach	Ed.: James M. Campbell	2990	598
100	9788121285544	3rd	Kaira and Panch Mahals	Ed.: James M. Campbell	1690	339
101	9788121285520	4th	Ahmedabad	Ed.: James M. Campbell	1860	372
102	9788121285506	5th	Cutch, Palanpur, and Mahi Kantha	Ed.: James M. Campbell	2390	478
103	9788121285483	6th	Rewa Kantha, Narukot, Cambay, and Surat States	Ed.: James M. Campbell	1450	290
104	9788121285469	7th	Baroda	Ed.: James M. Campbell	3260	652
105	9788121285445	8th	Kathiawar	Ed.: James M. Campbell	3790	758
106	9788121285421	9th, Part I	Gujarat Population - Hindus	Ed.: James M. Campbell	3170	636
107	9788121285407	9th, Part II	Gujarat Population - Musalmans and Parsis	Ed.: James M. Campbell	1520	304
108	9788121285384	10th	Ratnagiri and Savantvadi	Ed.: James M. Campbell	2500	501
109	9788121285360	11th	Kolaba and Janjira	Ed.: James M. Campbell	2550	513
110	9788121285346	12th	Khandesh	Ed.: James M. Campbell	3190	638
111	9788121285322	13th Part I	Thana	Ed.: James M. Campbell	2050	413
112	9788121285308	13th Part II	Thana	Ed.: James M. Campbell	1770	357
113	9788121285285	14th	Thana - Places of Interest	Ed.: James M. Campbell	3290	659
114	9788121285261	15th Part I	Kanara	Ed.: James M. Campbell	2340	348
115	9788121285247	15th Part II	Kanara	Ed.: James M. Campbell	1740	348
116	9788121285223	16th	Nasik	Ed.: James M. Campbell	3490	698
117	9788121285209	17th	Ahmadnagar	Ed.: James M. Campbell	3860	772
118	9788121285186	18th Part I	Poona	Ed.: James M. Campbell	2930	586
119	9788121285162	18th Part II	Poona	Ed.: James M. Campbell	2680	537
120	9788121285148	18th Part III	Poona	Ed.: James M. Campbell	2500	503
121	9788121285124	19th	Satara	Ed.: James M. Campbell	3450	692
122	9788121285100	20th	Sholapur	Ed.: James M. Campbell	2730	547
123	9788121285087	21st	Gazetteer of the Bomaby Presidency: Belgaum	Ed.: James M. Campbell	2570	514
124	9788121285063	22nd	Dharwar	Ed.: James M. Campbell	4200	841
125	9788121285049	23rd	Gazetteer of the Bombay Presidency:Bijapur	Ed.: James M. Campbell	3550	712
126	9788121285025	24th	Kolhapur	Ed.: James M. Campbell	2250	450

S. NO.	ISBN NO.	VOLUME	TITLE	AUTHOR	PRICE	PAGES
127	9788121285001	25th	Botany	Ed.: James M. Campbell	2040	408
128	9788121284981	26th, Part I	Materials Towards a Statistical Account of the Town and Island of Bombay - History	Ed.: James M. Campbell	2500	504
129	9788121284967	26th, Part II	Materials Towards a Statistical Account of the Town and Island of Bombay - Trade and Fortifications	Ed.: James M. Campbell	2690	538
130	9788121284943	26th, Part III	Materials Towards a Statistical Account of the Town And Island of Bombay - Administration	Ed.: James M. Campbell	2450	702
131	9788121284929	27th	General Index	Ed.:R. E. Enthoven	2190	428
			MADRAS DISTRICT GAZETTEERS			
132	9788121258814	1st	Anantapur	W. Francis	1140	227
133	9788121258555	2nd	Malabar	C. A Innes & F. B Evans	3010	602
134	9788121258791	3rd	Bellary	W. Francis	1890	377
135	9788121258777	4th	Statistical Appendix For Chingleput		280	56
136	9788121258753	5th	Coimbatore	K. N. Krishnaswami Ayyar	3420	628
137	9788121232814	6th	Madras District Gazetteers District Gazetteer Cuddapah	C. F. Brackenbury	1120	285
138	9788121258715	7th	Statistical Appendix For Ganjam		370	73
139	9788121256766	8th, Vol. 1st	Godavari District Gazetteer	F. R. Hemingway	650	320
140	9788121256803	8th, Vol. 2nd	Godavari District Gazetteer	F. R. Hemingway	160	83
141	9788121258678	9th	Statistical Appendix For Kistna		640	127
142	9788121258654	10th	Statistical Appendix For Kurnool		270	54
143	9788121258616	11th	Madura	W. Francis	1900	379
144	9788121258579	12th	Statistical Appendix For Madura		740	148
145	9788121258630	13th	The Nilgiris	W. Francis	2190	437
146	9788121234276	14th	Madras District Gazetteers Gazetteer Of The Nellore District Brought Upto 1938		1150	386
147	9788121258517	15th	North Arcot		590	118
148	9788121258494	16th, Vol. 1, Part I	Salem	F. J. Richards	1710	343
149	9788121258593	16th, Vol. 1, Part II	Salem	F. J. Richards	1800	360
150	9788121258456	17th	South Arcot	W. Francis	2400	480
151	9788121258470	18th	Statistical Appendix For South Canara		400	80
152	9788121258432	19th, Vol. 1st & 2nd	Tanjore: Main Volume and Statistical Appendix		2070	401
153	9788121258395	20th	Tinnevelly	H. R. Pate	2740	547
154	9788121258418	21st	Statistical Appendix For Tinnevelly		320	64
155	9788121258371	22nd, 1st & 2nd	Trichinopoly: Main Volume and Statistical Appendix	F. R. Hemingway	2440	487
156	9788121241953	23rd	Vizagapatam District Gazetteer	W. Francis	760	385
			PUNJAB DISTRICT GAZETTEERS			
157	9788121255943	1st	Ambala District 1883-84		620	124
158	9788121255967	2nd	Amritsar		1180	236
159	9788121255981	3rd	Delhi		1300	260
160	9788121256001	4th	Ferozepore		950	188
161	9788121256025	5th	Faridkot		350	70
162	9788121256049	6th	Gujranwala 1893-94		1270	254
163	9788121256063	7th	Gujrat	C. E. Luard	1140	228
164	9788121256087	8th	Gurdaspur 1891-92		1260	252
165	9788121256100	9th	Gurgaon 1883-4		1020	203
166	9788121256124	10th	Hazara	H. D. Watson	2290	458
167	9788121256148	11th	Hissar district and Lohar State		1840	367
168	9788121256162	12th	Hoshiarpur		1420	283
169	9788121256186	13th	Jhang		1070	213
170	9788121256209	14th	Jhelam		1010	202
171	9788121256223	15th	Jalandhar District 1883-84		540	108
172	9788121256247	16th, Vol. XIV-A	Jullundur District, with maps and Kapurthala		1990	398
173	9788121256261	17th, Pt. I	Kangra (Proper)		1450	290
174	9788121256285	17th, Pt. II	Kangra (Kulu, Lahual, Spiti)		1800	357
175	9788121256308	18th	Karnal		1930	386
176	9788121256322	19th	Kohat		1540	307
177	9788121256346	20th	The Lahore District 1883-84		1220	244
178	9788121256384	21st	Ludhiana and Maler Kotla		1680	335
179	9788121256407	22nd	Lyallpur		735	147
180	9788121256421	23rd	Mianwali		1170	234
181	9788121256445	24th	Montgomery	P. J. Fagan	1590	318
182	9788121258364	25th	Multan (1901-02)	E. D. Maclagan	2400	480
183	9788121258708	26th	The Rohtak District 1883-84		980	196
184	9788121258746	27th, Vol. III A	Dujana State 1904		500	16
185	9788121256483	28th	Shahpur District		1780	356
186	9788121256506	29th	Simla District		800	159

S. NO.	ISBN NO.	VOLUME	TITLE	AUTHOR	PRICE	PAGES
187	9788121256520	30th	The Chamba State		2040	408
188	9788121256544	31st	The Chenab Colony 1904		1550	310
189	9788121256568	32nd	Kalsia State		270	53
190	9788121256582	33rd	Suket and Mandi		770	154
191	9788121256605	34th	Phulkian States, Patiala Jind And Nabha 1904		2070	414
192	9788121256643	35th	Simla Hill States		2220	443
193	9788121256667	36th	Sirmur		920	183
			RAJPUTANA DISTRICT GAZETTEERS			
194	9789362088994	1st, Vol. I-A & B	Ajmer-merwara (Text and Statistics Tables)	C. C. Watson	1230	246
195	9789362080882	2nd. Vol. II-A & B	Mewar Residency (Text and Statistics Tables)	K.D. Erskine	1700	339
196	9789362088444	3rd, Vol. III-A & B	The Western Rajputana States Residency And The Bikaner Agency	K.D. Erskine	3590	718
			UNITED PROVINCES OF AGRA AND OUDH DISTRICT GAZETTEERS			
197	9789362087560	Vol. I	Agra	H. R. Nevill	2260	452
198	9789362082466	Vol. II	Aligarh	H. R. Nevill	1300	260
199	9789362089779	Vol. III	Allahabad	H. R. Nevill	2050	409
200	9789362081346	Vol. IV	Almora	H. G. Walton	1670	333
201	9789362085658	Vol. V	Azamgarh	D. L. Drake Brockman	1750	349
202	9789362080547	Vol. VI	Bahraich	H. R. Nevill	1410	281
203	9789362085214	Vol. VII	Ballia	H. R. Nevill	1750	350
204	9789362084668	Vol. VIII	Banda	D. L. Drake Brockman	1750	349
205	9789362086518	Vol. IX	Bara Banki	H. R. Nevill	1720	344
206	9789362084101	Vol. X	Bareilly	H. R. Nevill	1640	327
207	9789362086631	Vol. XI	Basti	H. R. Nevill	1610	321
208	9789362083814	Vol. XII	Benares	H. R. Nevill	2290	458
209	9789362086105	Vol. XIII	Bijnor	H. R. Nevill	1820	363
210	9789362081674	Vol. XIV	Budaun	H. R. Nevill	1890	378
211	9789362086891	Vol. XV	Bulandshahr	H. R. Nevill	2100	419
212	9789362081520	Vol. XVI	Cawnpore	H. R. Nevill	2210	442
213	9789362088031	Vol. XVII	Dehra Dun	H. G. Walton	1710	342
214	9789362088710	Vol. XVIII	Etah	E. R. Neave	1600	320
215	9789362082992	Vol. XIX	Etawah	D. L. Drake Brockman	1390	277
216	9789362082220	Vol. XX	Farrukhabad	E. R. Neave	1620	324
217	9789362083869	Vol. XXI	Fatehpur	H. R. Nevill	1890	377
218	9789362085962	Vol. XXII	Fyzabad	H. R. Nevill	1700	339
219	9789362087997	Vol. XXIII	Garhwal	H. G. Walton	1270	254
220	9789362089892	Vol. XXIV	Ghazipur	H. R. Nevill	1600	320
221	9789362085436	Vol. XXV	Gonda	H. R. Nevill	1650	330
222	9789362080271	Vol. XXVI	Gorakhpur	H. R. Nevill	1890	378
223	9789362086129	Vol. XXVII	Hamirpur	D. L. Drake Brockman	1390	277
224	9789362087638	Vol. XXVIII	Hardoi	H. R. Nevill	1680	336
225	9789362081636	Vol. XXIX	Jalaun	D. L. Drake Brockman	1180	236
226	9789362084309	Vol. XXX	Jaunpur	H. R. Nevill	1750	350
227	9789362084187	Vol. XXXI	Jhansi	D. L. Drake Brockman	1960	391
228	9789362089168	Vol. XXXII	Kheri	H. R. Nevill	1650	330
229	9789362086778	Vol. XXXIII	Lucknow	H. R. Nevill	1760	352
230	9789362088635	Vol. XXXIV	Mainpuri	H. R. Nevill	1740	348
231	9789362080424	Vol. XXXV	Meerut	H. R. Nevill	2170	434
232	9789362081087	Vol. XXXVI	Mirzapur	D. L. Drake Brockman	2430	486
233	9789362085443	Vol. XXXVII	Moradabad	H. R. Nevill	1900	380
234	9789362082763	Vol. XXXVIII	Muttra	D. L. Drake Brockman	2140	428
235	9789362089915	Vol. XXXIX	Muzaffarnagar	H. R. Nevill	2260	451
236	9789362086143	Vol. XL	Naini Tal	H. R. Nevill	1890	377
237	9789362086761	Vol. XLI	Partabgarh	H. R. Nevill	1560	312
238	9789362081124	Vol. XLII	Pilibhit	H. R. Nevill	1570	314
239	9789362084453	Vol. XLIII	Rai Bareli	H. R. Nevill	1610	322
240	9789362088284	Vol. XLIV	Rampur	H. R. Nevill	1170	234
241	9789362083654	Vol. XLV	Saharanpur	H. R. Nevill	2190	438
242	9789362083142	Vol. XLVI	Shahjahanpur	H. R. Nevill	1510	302
243	9789362083623	Vol. XLVII	Sitapur	H. R. Nevill	1590	317
244	9789362089939	Vol. XLVIII	Sultanpur	H. R. Nevill	1330	266
245	9789362080851	Vol. XLIX	Unnao	H. R. Nevill	1530	305

GAZETTEER

OF THE

BOMBAY PRESIDENCY.

VOLUME XXVII.

GENERAL INDEX.

UNDER GOVERNMENT ORDERS.

BOMBAY:
PRINTED AT THE GOVERNMENT CENTRAL PRESS.

1904.

OFFICIAL AGENTS FOR THE SALE OF INDIAN OFFICIAL PUBLICATIONS.

In England.

E. Arnold, 41 & 43, Maddox Street, Bond Street, W., London.,

Constable & Co., 16, James Street, Haymarket, W., London.

P. S. King & Son, 2 & 4, Great Smith Street, Westminster, S.W., London.

Kegan Paul, Trench, Trubner & Co., Charing Cross Road, W.C., London.

B. Quaritch, 15, Piccadilly, W., London.

Williams & Norgate, Oxford.

Deighton Bell & Co., Cambridge.

On the Continent.

Friedlander & Sohn, 11, Carlstrasse, Berlin.

Otto Harrassowitz, Leipzig.

Karl W. Hiersemann, Leipzig.

Ernest Leroux, 28, Rue Bonaparte, Paris.

Martinus Nijhoff, The Hague.

In India.

Higginbotham & Co. and **V. Kalyanarama Iyer & Co.,** Madras.

Thacker, Spink & Co., and **W. Newman & Co.,** Calcutta.

S. K. Lahiri & Co., Calcutta.

Thacker & Co. (Ld.), A. J. Combridge & Co., and **Curator, Government Central Book Depot,** Bombay.

D. B. Taraporevala (Ld.), Sons & Co., Bombay.

Sunder Pandurang, Bookseller, etc., Bombay.

Sir James Campbell commenced the *Bombay Gazetteer* in 1873 and issued the last volume in 1901. It was his intention to render the contents of this great work more accessible to the public by the issue of a General Index. Illness, leading to his much deplored death in 1903, stood between the design and its accomplishment. It has been my privilege, under the orders of Government, to supply the missing volume.

Special acknowledgments are due to my Assistant, Mr. N. R. Jog, for valuable aid in preparing the materials.

R. E. ENTHOVEN.

Poona, August 1904.

GENERAL INDEX

TO THE

BOMBAY GAZETTEER SERIES.

A

A-AL: plant cultivated in Berár, Khándesh, Surat and other places, useful for dyeing, XXV, 88, 246; as a food plant, *id.* 162; used in famine, *id.* 200.

Aázam, Prince: son of Aurangzib, IX, pt. ii, 98.

Abáji Purandhare: Báláji Vishwanáth's friend, XIX, 254, 258.

Abáji Sondeo: Shiváji's general in the Konkan and Subhedár of Kalyán (1648), I, pt. ii, 69, 592; takes Kalyán (1648), XIV, 120.

Abars: Skythians, conquer Panjáb and Sindh, (second century B. C.); represented by Jatos and Meds, IX, pt. i, 265 note 2.

Ába Shelukar: Peshwa's Subhedár of Gujarát; levies contributions on the Gáikwár's villages, I, pt. i, 411; is made over to the British Government (1807), *id.* 416; a partizan of Nana Fadnavis, and the Subhedár of Ahmadabad; his campaign against the Peshwa, VII, 200, 201 and note 1, 386.

Abbalabhe: daughter of the Ráshtrakuta King Amoghavarsha I, I, pt. ii, 402.

Abbas: the Prophets' uncle, founder of the Abbási family, IX, pt. ii, 8; shrine of, *id.* 12 note 3.

Abbási-Al-Moátamed-Alalláh: the fifteenth Khalífah (870-891), IX, pt. ii, 3 note 3.

Abbási, Al-Muktadir: the eighteenth Khalífah (908-932), IX, pt. ii, 35 note 1.

Abbaaid: Khalifs. *See* Khalifs.

Abbásis: a Section of Shaikhs, IX, pt. ii, 8 and note 3.

Abbe Reynal: Europeon writer (A. D. 1760), IX, pt. i, p. 78 note 1.

Abbigeri: village in Dhárwár District, XXII, 648.

Abdális: beggars, also called Dafális, who assist exorcists in their performances, IX, pt. ii, 20. *See* Beggars.

Abdalláh: meaning of, IX, pt. ii, 136 note 1.

Abdallis: an Afghan tribe, who took the name of Duranis, IX, pt. i, 459.

Ábdar Khánah: water-room in Musalman dwellings, IX, pt. ii, 92.

Abdasa: sub-division in Cutch, historical references to, V, 2, 131, 138, 146.

Ab-der-Razzak: Persian traveller; his notice of pirates in the India seas (A. D. 1440), XIII, 447; his mention of Honávar (1444), XV, pt. ii, 49, 308; description of Vijayanagar Kingdom, *id.* 99-100.

Abdul-Aziz: Wahhábi leader, IX, pt. ii, 12 note 3. *See* Wahhátis.

Abdul Aziz: Khán of Junnar, in the Poona District; becomes viceroy by a forged order and appoints Jawán Mard Khán his deputy in Gujarát, I, pt. i, 326; his defeat and death at Kim Kathodra, *id.* 328.

Abdul Dalél Khán: Nawáb of Sávanur; is made member of the Bombay Legislative Council (1862), I, pt. ii, 668; XXII, 803-804; son of Abdul Kheir Khán, is installed Nawáb of Sávanur (1877), I, pt. ii, 668.

Abdul Gháfar Khán: son of Abdul Ráuf Khán, the founder of Savanur (1700), I, pt. ii, 666.

Abdul Hakim Khán: son and successor of Majid Khán, Nawáb of Sávanur (1751-1795); declines to acknowledge the supremacy of the Nizám and refuses to surrender an officer of the Peshwa; is attacked by both and becomes the Peshwa's vassal (1756), I, pt. ii, 656-657, 666-667; is gained over by Haidar; at war with the Marathas and the Nizám, with Haidar and Tipu, XXII, 797-802; offends Tipu and becomes a pensioner of the Maráthas at Poona, where he dies (1795), I, pt. ii, 667.

Abdul Kádir: son and prime minister of Ghiássuddin Khilji, I, pt. i, 362; *id.* 364. *See* Násiruddin.

Abdul Kádir Jilani: cenotaph of, X, 464.

Abdul Kádir Muhiyud-Din-Gílani: Mauláná Sayad Saint, IX, pt. ii, 6 note 1 (3); *id.* 50; shrine of, *id.* 56; celebration of his birth-day by Sunnis, *id.* 140.

Abdul Karim: engineer of the emperor Jehángir, repairs buildings at Mándu (1617), I, pt. i, 373.

Abdul Karim: grandson of Bahlol Khán, succeeds to supreme power at Bijápur; opposes the Mughals with vigour, I, pt. ii, 653, 665; attacks Panhálá (1674), XXIV, 314; makes a treaty with the Mughals (1675), I, pt. ii, 653, 665; joins the Mughals and attacks Golkonda; his death (1676), *id.* 654.

Abdul Khán: *see* Abdul Hakim Khán.

Abdul Kheir Khán: adopted son of Abdul Hakim Khán of Sávanur, I, pt. ii, 667; successor of Abdul Dalél Khán, Nawáb of Sávanur; his death (1868), *id.* 668.

Abdulla: brother of Ibráhim A'dil Sháh; plots to depose his brother, is discovered, flies to Goa, marches on Bijápur with the help of the Portuguese and Burhán Nizám of Ahmad-

nagar; is forced to fly to Goa; is killed (1554), I, pt. ii, 643.
Abdolláh: Wahhábi leader; his defeat by Muhammad Ali, Pasha of Egypt (1812); suffers death at Constantioople (1818), IX, pt. ii, 12 note 3. *See* Wahhábis.
Abdulláh: Shiah missionary of the Mustaâlian sect, IX, pt. ii, 26; founder of the sect of Shiah Bohoras in Gujarát (1067), *id.* 3 note 3; *id.* 125; his miracles and success at Cambay and Patan; converts King Sidhraj Jaisingh and his Hindu subjects, *id.* 26. *See* Missionaries.
Abdulláh Khán Uzbak: Akbar's general, reconquers Málwa (1563), I, pt. i, 369.
Abdulláh Maimún: IX, pt. ii, 37.
Abdulláh Wassáf: author of Taziyat-ul-Amsár, I, pt. i, 515 and note 6.
Abdul-Malik: Fifth Umayyad Khalifah (684-705), IX, pt. ii, 1 note 1; *id.* 14 note 3.
Abdul Rahim Khán: son of Bahlol Khán, ancestor of the Sávanur family, I, pt. ii, 665.
Abdul Rahmán: Arab missionary, settled in Malanggad in Thána District, XIV, 220.
Abdul Ráuf Khán: successor of Abdul Karim Khán, enters the service of the Mughals; receives the title of Diler Khán Bahádur Diler Jang and an assignment of twenty-two Máháls; founds Sávanur (1700), I, pt. ii, 655, 665-666; Nawáb of Sávanur (1686-1715), XXII, 793.
Abdul Rehmán: Sunni Bohora, who claimed to be the Imám Mahdi, his disturbance at Mándvi (1810), IX, pt. ii, 60 note 4; *id.* 198 note 5.
Abdul Wahâb: Arab reformer (1700-1800), XXIV, 150.
Abdul Wahbáb: clan, IX, pt. ii, 12 note 3. *See* Wahhábis.
Abdul Wahháb: Founder of the Wahhábi sect; his preachings against religious abuses; his expulsion from his native place; his determination to spread his reforms, IX, pt. ii, 12 note 3. *See* Wahbábis.
Abdur Rashi'd: great ancestor of the Afgháns; is believed to have received the title of Batán from the Prophet, IX, pt. ii, 10 note 4.
Abdur Rehman Sámiri: Muhammadan name of a Malabar Zamorin; converted by Náiatás; his tomb at Zhafar, venerated by the Arabs, IX, pt. ii, 15 note 1.
Abelmoschos esculentus: *bhendi*, very commonly cultivated as a vegetable, XXV, 147; a fibrous plant, *id.* 227.
Abhai Singh: Rájá of Jodhpur, assisted the viceroy of Gujarát against Piláji Gáikwar, VII, 171; governorship of Gujarat offered to, by the Delhi Court; defeated by the late viceroy at Adálej (1730), *id.* 172. *See* Abheysingh.
Abhávni: crop share system in Kolába District, XI, 183 note 3; based on inspection, *id.* 184, 185.
Abhaya Mudrá: attitude at the time of giving a blessing, Káshyap statue at Sopára represented in the, XIV, 331; Kanak statue at Sopára represented in the, *id.* 412-413.
Abhayatilaka: reviser of the Dvyáśraya Kosha, I, pt. ii, 567.
Abhayatilakagani: Jain Monk (1255), revised the Dvyáśraya, I, pt. i, 156.
Abheysingh, Mahárája: fifty-third viceroy of Gujarát (1730-1733), I, pt. i, 310; his defeat by Mubáriz-ul-Mulk, *id.* 311; procures assassination of Piláji Gáikwar and takes Baroda (1732), *id.* 313; is reappointed fifty-fifth viceroy of Gujarát, *id.* 319. *See* Abhaisingh.
Abhidhána Chintámani: work, written by Hemachandra, I, pt. i, 192.
Abhilashitártha Chintámani: work of Someśvara III, the Western Chálukya King, I, pt. ii, 456. *See* Mánasollása.
Abhimanyu: early Ráshtrakúta prince, his copper-plate grant, I, pt. i, 120; I, pt. ii, 384, 386.
Abhir (Abhira): country of the shepherds, Introduction to the History of Konkan, I, pt. ii, x; Western Coast of India from the Tapti to Devgad, traces of Ahirs preserved in IX, pt. i, 265 and note 2; name of a province, I, pt. i, 52.
Abhir (Abhira): tribe, I, pt. i, 52, 64 note 3, 137; cowherds, come into power, I, pt. ii, 177-178; race, destroyed by Kholeśvar, Singhaná's general, *id.* 240; cowherds of ancient Hindu writings, IX, pt. i, 264 note 1; a Bráhman sub-division in Khándesh, their origin and dialect, XII, 52. *See* Ahirs.
Abhira Kings: rulers of North Dakhan (A. D. 416), XVI, 15, 16, 183; mention of, in Násik caves, *id.* 580; inscription of Isvarasena Abhir, *id.* 624.
Abhisara: Tract between Mari and Margala, IX, pt. i, 265.
Abhona: in Násik district, survey settlement of (1869), XVI, 253-257; lapsed to the British, *id.* 646.
Abhpura: hill in Káthiáwár, the scene of the rout of the Vághers (1859), VIII, 10.
Abhyadheka: or Vriddhi Shraddha, IX, pt. i, 41.
Abi: tribe, I, pt. i, 534.
Abington: Captain, his unsuccessful attack on Malanggad (1780), and retreat from, XIII, 506, 507; XIV, 221.
Abir: fragrant powder, found in casket containing images of Buddha at Sopára, its probable composition, XIV, 329, 333, 411 and note 1.
Abiria: name of a province, I, pt. i, 52; *id.* 53 note 1, 137; Upper Sindh and Multán, 537. *See* Abhira; in Sind, identified with Ophir, XIV, 318.
Abisares: ruler of the hills, between Mari and Margala pass, traces of Ahirs preserved in, IX, pt. i, 264-265.
Ablur: village in Dhárwár district, inscription at, I, pt. ii, 306 note 5; 482 and note 1; temple of Vira Somanátha at, *id.* 483; village, temples, inscriptions, XXII, 648.
Aboriginal tillage: in Kolába, XI, 93; in Panch Mahals, III, 232; in Surat, II, 62.
Aborigines: (B. C. 1500) early tribes called dásyus or fiends in the Vedas, and nishadas or original settlers in the Ramáyan; existing chief tribes; Kali Paráj or dusky race, general name of early tribes, IX, pt. i, page x.

Abuti : Bráhman sub-division, IX, pt. i, 4 ; in Cutch, V, 47 ; in Káthiáwár, VIII, 146.

Abrus precatorius: *Gunj*, a climbing shrub, XXV, 217.

A'bu : king of, present with Mularája in the battle with Graharipu, I, pt. i, 160 ; magnificent temple of Neminách built by Vastupála and Tejahpála on, *id.* 199, 202 ; inscription on the temple of Vastupála at, 204 ; Mutiny at, *id.* 439 ; Paramára possession, 470 ; Mount, 532, 534 ; fire-baptism on, IX, pt. i, 433 ; *id.* 449 note 4 ; inscription on, *id.* 450 ; fire pit on, *id.* 480, 486, 490, 493, 501 ; shrine of Amba Bhavani on, *id.* ix, *id.* xi, *id.* 549 ; Jain shrines on, *id.* 550.

A'bu : pond in Kolhápur State, XXIV, 12.

Abú-Bakr-As Siddik : Lawful successor of the Prophet, IX, pt. ii, 125 ; first Khalífah (632-634), *id.* 52 note 1 ; founder of Siddiki family, *id.* 8 ; ancestor of one of the four families of Naiatás who migrated to India (865), *id.* 14 note 3.

Abud the Lame : a Baroda Arab officer, VII, 215 note 3 ; his attempt to embroil Baroda with Sindia and the Peshwa (1812), *id.* 218 ; supports Kánhoji and plunders petty States north of Gujarát (1803), *id.* 296.

Abú Hanífah : second Sunni Imám (700-733), IX, pt. ii, 125.

Abuláma : perhaps Obollah, I, pt. i, 35 ; XIII, 413.

Abulfaraj : Arab writer (A. D. 1243), IX, pt. i, 470 note 1 ; *id.* 477.

Abul Fazl : Akbar's historian (1590), his account of Sultán Bahádur's death, I, pt i, 349, *id.* 371 ; his notice of affinity of Káthis and Ahirs, IX, pt. i, 261 ; *id.* 449 note 4 ; *id.* 450 ; notices in his account of Surat the followers of Zerdusht ; is given charge of the sacred fire by Akbar, IX, pt. ii, 190 ; his mention of Bassein as Bussy (1586), XIV, 30.

Abul Fida : Arab Historian (1273-1343), IX, pt. i, 214 note 1 ; *id.* 474 note 5, IX, pt. ii, 1 note 1 ; his mention of Sanján, XIV, 302 note 2 ; of Sopára, *id.* 321 ; of Thána, *id.* 356 ; his mention of Honávar, XV, pt. ii, 49, 307-308.

Abul Hasan Askari : tenth Shiáh Imám (829), IX, pt. ii, 6 note 1 (1) ; *id.* 125 note 2.

Abú Lúlu : Magian convert to Islám, also known as Bába Shuja-ud-din, IX, pt. ii, 142 ; called Bábá Firúz by the Persians, *id.* 136 ; murders the Khalifah Umar, *id.* 136, *id.* 142.

Abul Mughis : known as Mansúr ; his full name ; spiritual head of the Mansúris, IX, pt. ii, 35 note 1.

Abú Muhammad Askari : eleventh Shiáh Imám (845), IX, pt. ii, 125 note 2 continued on page 126.

Abu Rihán : I, pt. i, 508, *id.* 520. *See* Al Biruni.

Abutilon : *Indicum*, fibrous plant, in Málva, Bengal and Bombay, XXV, 228 ; *tomemtosum*, grows at Surat, Poona, Sholápur and other places, its seeds used as food, in famines, *id.* 194.

Abu Zaid : Arab writer (913), I, pt. i, 525, *id.* 526 note 5, 528, 530 ; *id.* pt. ii, 387.

Abu Zeidal Hasan : author of the second part of Silsilát-ut-Tawárikh, I, pt. i, 505 note 2.

Abyssinian : Language, IX, pt. ii, 11 and note 2.

Abyssinians : immigrants, Introduction to the History of the Konkan, I, pt. ii, xii ; colonists, *id.* 7 ; their establishment in Janjira (1489), *id.* 34 ; sailors, *id.* 62, 69. Habashis ; in Gujarát, Sultan's armies (1531), IX, pt. ii, 3 note 1 ; *id.* 11 ; Agate Workers, in Cambay, VI, 206 note 3. *See* Sidis.

Abyssinian Turks : their alliance with the Rájás of Cochin and Cambay, I, pt. ii, 34.

Abwáb-ul-Makkah : Gates of Makkah, Gujarát ports so called, IX, pt. ii, 3 note 1.

Acacia : *catechu*, a timber tree, found in Gujarát, Dakhan and Konkan, XXV, 68, 244 ; a medicinal plant, *id.* 259 ; a sacred plant, *id.* 291 ; *eburnea*, used for fuel, found in Southern India, Dakhan, and Sind, *id.* 67 ; *fernesiana*, a flowering tree found all over India, *id.* 66 ; *ferruginea*, found in Panch Mahals and Konkan, *id.* 69 ; spirit distilled from, *id.* 211 ; *latronum*, common in Eastern Dakhan and Madras Presidency, *id.* 69 ; *leucophlea*, found in Southern Marátha Country, Sholápur and in other places in India, *id.* 67 ; famine plant, *id.* 199 ; spirit distilled from, *id.* 211 ; fibrous plant, *id.* 232 ; *procera*, common on the ghâts and in Konkan, *id.* 70 ; *suma* found in Konkan, Gujarát and Dakhan, *id.* 68, 244, 259 ; *sundra*, found in the Dakhan and other places, *id.* 68, 244 ; *tomentosa*, common in the Dakhan and Khándesh jungles, *id.* 67.

Acalypha Indica : a famine plant, XXV, 204.

Acanthaceæ : a famine plant, produces a dye, XXV, 202, 248.

Accad : early race, I, pt. i, 174 and note 1.

Accipitrinae : in Ratnágiri, X, 55.

Account books : description of, as kept by bankers and merchants in Ahmadabad, IV, 63 ; in Ahmadnagar, XVII, 298-299 ; in Baroda, VII, 115, 127, 131 ; in Bijápur, XXIII, 346 ; in Káthiáwár, VIII, 206-207 ; in Khándesh, XII, 195 ; in Kolába and Janjira, XI, 103, 426 ; in Násik, XVI, 118 ; in Poona, XVIII, pt. ii, 103 ; in Ratnágiri, X, 159 ; in Thána, XIII, 309 ; in Gujarát, IX, pt. i, 82-88.

Accoutrements : of troops (1779), XXVI, pt. iii, 179-182.

A'cha : I, pt. ii, 219 ; Sinda prince and feudatory of Vikramáditya VI, *id.* 452. *See* A'chagi.

Achæmenean : dynasty (B. C. 350), Panjáb under the, IX, pt. ii, 183 note 4 continued on p. 184.

A'chagi : dependant chief of Vikramáditya VI ; repels the expedition of Vishnuvardhana, I, pt. ii, 219. *See* A'chugi II.

A'chala Sthavira : ascetic, I, pt. ii, 354 note 3.

A'chalbág : stream in Kolába District, XI, 9.

Achaldas : Barber Saint, IX, pt i, p. 233.

A'chama : I, pt. ii, 574. *See* A'chugi II.

A'chára : Arhat, I, pt. ii, 354 note 3. *See* Achala Sthavira.

A'charasa : Kalachurya Someśvara's officer (1173), I, pt. ii, 486.

Achári : *see* Lohár.

A'chárya : priest, I, pt. ii, 571.

A'cháryas : funeral Bráhmans, I, pt. i, 451 ; religious heads of gadis established by Shankar, IX, pt. i, p. 542.

Achhabda : Chicken-pox, IX, pt. i, p. 368; ceremonies performed in an attack of, *id.* 372. *See* Small-pox.
A'chi : I, pt ii, 574. *See* A'chugi II.
Achla : fort in Násik District, its fall (1818), XVI, 414, 441, 447.
Achola : village in Thána District near Sopára with a Portuguese fort, XIV, 342.
A'chra : port in Ratnágiri District, exports and imports of, X, 186 ; description, *id.* 317 ; river, *id* 10 ; quartzite inlier at, *id.* 15 ; defeat of the Bijápur fleet at (1555), I, pt. ii 47.
Achras sapota : (chicu), cultivated for its fruit in Bombay and Dakhan gardens, XXV, 89, 163.
A'chugi : I, pt. ii, 452. *See* A'cha.
A'chugi I : Sinda prince of Yelburga, also called A'cha, I, pt. ii, 573, 574.
A'chugi II : also called A'cha, A'chi, A'chama, son and successor of the Sinda prince Singa II (1122) and feudatory of the Western Chalukya King Vikramáditya VI, I, pt. ii, 573, 574 ; pursues the Hoysalas, *id.* 497, 547 ; takes Goa and seizes the Konkan, *id.* 569.
A'chugi III : son of the Sinda prince Chávunda II (1163), I, pt. ii, 573, 575.
Achyranthes aspera : a famine plant in Rájputána, XXV, 203 ; used as an antidote to snake-bite, *id.* 275 ; a plant sacred to Hindus, *id.* 279, 282, 290, 291.
Achyuta Náyaka : Bráhman petty chief, I, pt. ii, 248 ; governor of Sálsette (1272), *id.* 529.
Achyutapuram : grant of Indravarman at (700), I, pt. ii, 422.
Acknowledgment-book : IX, pt. i, 83. *See* Samadaskat.
Acorus calamus : common to moist places in India, Europe and America, used as medicine, XXV, 262.
Acronychia laurifolia : evergreen timber tree, growing at Talkat Ghát in Bombay and in other parts of India, XXV, 31.
Actephila excelsa : timber tree found at Phonda Ghát and in Konkan, in Bombay and in other parts of India, XXV, 115.
Actinodaphne Hookeri : evergreen, found at Mahábaleshvar, Mátherán and other places in the Bombay Presidency, XXV, 112.
Actinodaphne lanceolata : evergreen, found at Mahábaleshvar, Mátherán and other places in Bombay, XXV, 112.
Actors : IX, pt. i. *See* Bards.
Ad : fort in Násik district, XVI, 441, 447.
A'da : creek in Ratnágiri district, X, 11.
Adad : grain, is sacred to Saturn and Hanuman, is used in spirit-scaring rites, IX, pt. i, 391.
Adálaj : battle of (1730), I, pt. i, 311.
Adálat Mahal : Bijápur palace, XXIII, 620.
A'dam : introduced as avatár or incarnation of the Hindu god Vishnu, IX, pt. ii, 40. *See* Avatárs.
A'dam : Shaikh, Head Mulla of the Bohorás, IX, pt. ii, 33. *See* Bohorá.
A'dam : Muhammadan name of Sundarji, a Sindh Lohána, IX, pt. ii, 51. *See* Sundarji.
Adansonia digitata : timber tree, cultivated in Gujarát and in other parts of India, XXV, 16-17 ; a food-plant, *id.* 147 ; fibrous plant, *id.* 229 ; medicinal plant, 258, 259.
Adar : ninth day of the Pársi month, ninth month of the Pársi year, IX, pt. ii, 216, 217.
Adaragunchi : I, pt. ii, 306, 307 ; inscription at, *id.* 422.
Adar Jasan : high festival day, observances on, IX, pt. ii, 217. *See* Jasans.
Adarni : ceremony pertaining to marriage invitations, IX, pt. ii, 233.
Adavad : place of interest, XII, 225, *id.* 431.
Adbatki : caste in Kánara district, XV, pt. i, 332, 333.
Addayika : I, pt. ii, 507.
A'de : place of interest in Ratnágiri district, X, 317.
Adekavve : wife of Mariyáne, I, pt. ii, 492.
Aden : I, pt. i, 514, *id.* 543. Ships from Thána go to, I, pt. ii, 5 ; horses imported from, *id.* 35; trade centre between India and Egypt, XIII, 409 note 2 ; resting place for ships between India and Suez, *id.* 410 note 5; its commerce with Thána coast (810-1260), *id.* 249 ; (1300-1500) *id.* 441 ; Hindu merchants found in (1300-1500), *id.* 446 ; Thána trade with (1500-1760), *id.* 465 ; opium, vermilion, rose-water and quicksilver imported from, *id.* 467 ; its trade diverted to Mocha (1660-1710), *id.* 486.
Adenanthera pavonina : (*mota gunj*), timber tree found in Bombay, Gujarát and other places, XXV, 65 ; a food-plant, *id.* 154.
A'deran : Atesh, fire of fires, IX, pt. ii. 185 note 2 ; purification and installation of, *id.* 213-214. *See* Fires (sacred).
Adesar : place of interest in Cutch, V, 210.
Adeyára : country, I, pt. ii, 320 note 6.
Adgaon : battle of, between Sindia and the English (1803), XII, 253.
Adhatoda vasica : (Adussa), produces a dye, XXV, 248.
Adhela : *see* Dháman.
Adheváda : village in Káthiáwár, a place of pilgrimage, VIII, 355.
Adhika : intercalary month ; observances in, IX, pt. i, 29, *id.* 185.
Adhikári : hereditary revenue officers, their claim to khoti in Kolába, XI, 172 note 1 ; village superintendent, *id.* 178 ; village and Sub-Divisional Officer's grant of *vatan sanads* to, XIII, 538 ; list of such officers, *id.* 572-573.
Adhirájendradeva : I, pt. ii, 445. *See* Parakesarivarman.
Adhoi : place of interest in Cutch, caves at, V, 210.
Adhyátmopanishad : religious work compiled by Hemachandra, I, pt. i, 193.
Adibanjig, pl. adibanjigaru : a sub-caste of the Lingáyats, traders in the Dhárwár district, XXII, 116 ; in Bijápur, XXIII, 238-239.
Adi-Banjig : *see* Adibanjig.
Adigudd : hill in Belgaum district, XXI, 6.
Adil Khán : Bijápur King, Konkan surrendered to (1636), XIII, 464.
A'dil Khán I : Faruki King of Khándesh (1457-1503), I, pt. ii, 621 ; defeats Mahmud Begada of Gujarát (1499) ; his death (1503), *id.* 622, XII, 245.
A'dil Khán II : Fáruki King of Khándesh, dies (1520), I, pt. ii, 622 ; tries to throw up his allegiance to Faruki, the Gujarát King (1510-1520), XII, 246.

Adil Shahi : dynasty (1490-1686), I, pt. ii, 32; Bijápur Kings (1489-1686); hold Sátára; revolt of Saif Ain-ul-Mulk; Ibráhim Adil Sháh's defeat at Mán (1534-1557); Adil Sháhi Institutions; Marátha Chiefs under them; Shiváji's rebellion; Bijápur captured (1686) by the Mughals; XIX, 228-246; historical references to, XVIII, pt. ii, 224, 238; list of, XXIII, 403 note 1; history of, *id.* 404-435.

Adina cordifolia : timber tree, used for furniture, common throughout the Konkan, XXV, 83.

A'dinátha : temple at Satrunjaya of, I, pt. i, 79 note 3; *see* A'dnátha.

A'dipurána : Jain work, I, pt. ii, 200, 407.

A'disvara : Jain god on Satrunjaya hill, I, pt. i, 177, *id.* 186.

A'ditiána : village and state in Káthiáwár, VIII, 355.

Aditvar : Sunday, IX, pt. i, 393; a ward of Poona City, details of, XVIII, pt. iii, 274, 277-278.

A'ditya : I, pt. ii, 182.

A'dityaśakti : Sendraka prince, I, pt. ii, 292.

A'dityavarman : son of Pulakeśi II, I, pt. ii, 186, 212; his grants, *id.* 343, 367; his wrong genealogy, *id.* 361 note 2; Pallava prince, *id.* 323; Southern Konkan Silahara prince, *id.* 537; Hángal Kádamba prince, *id.* 559.

Adivra : place of interest, X, 317.

Adiyama : feudatory of the Chola King, I, pt. ii, 308, 495, 498; defeated by Gangarája, *id.* 499. *See* Idiyama.

Administration : boards of, formed (1785) in Bombay City, XXVI, pt. iii, 404-408.

Administrative divisions : of Konkan, under Musalmáns, I, pt. ii, 40.

Administrative Sub-divisions : all district volumes, *see* under district name.

Admiral d'Almeida : Portuguese Viceroy, plunders Dábhol (1508), X, 328.

Admiralty : situated in Tank House (1754-61), XXVI, pt. iii, 564-67; in Mr. Whitehill's house at present occupied by Kemp and Co. and the B. B. & C. I. Railway in the Elphinstone Circle (1761-64), *id.* 567-68; in Mr. Hornby's house, the present Great Western Hotel (1764-1800), *id.* 568-571; in Dady's building, Apollo Street, at present occupied by Messrs. Finlay Muir and Co. (1800-1840), *id.* 571; probably in the Marine Lines (1840-1864), *id.* 571; in Bungalow No. 2, Marine Lines (1864-94), *id.* 565.

Admiralty Court : established in Bombay City, XXVI, pt. i, 84.

A'dnáth : temple of, completed, I, pt. i, 186. *See* A'dinátha.

Ado-Bhaváni : Invocation of goddess Bhaváni, IX, pt. ii, p. xxxv; *id.* 507.

Adoni : fort in Karnátak, I, pt. ii, 638, 642; taken by A'li A'dil Sháh, *id.* 645.

Adrack : fresh root of Zinziber Officinale, XXV, 174.

Adtála : village in Káthiáwár, VIII, 370.

Adu : *see* Adrack.

Adula : river in Ahmadnagar District, XVII, 7.

Adnli : Abyssinian port, its trade with India (250), XIII, 419.

A'dur : village in Dhárwár District, I, pt. ii, 281 note 3; inscription at, *id.* 377 and note 2, 411 note 3, 438 note 6, 563 notes 6 and 7; XV, pt. ii, 81, 84; description of, XXII, 648-649.

Adur : *see* Borya.

Adussa : *see* Adhatoda Vasica.

Adventure : Captain Kidd's galley, I, pt. ii, 81.

Advichincher : a wandering tribe in Bijápur, their habits, religion, customs, XXIII, 177-178; in Dhárwár, XXII, 193. *See* also Phase Pardhis.

Advi Gol : wandering medicine sellers in Bijápur, their food, dress, occupation, holidays, ceremonies, XXIII, 102-105.

Adwani : I, pt. ii, 638. *See* Adoni.

Adya : Goddess, shrine of, at Halvad, IX, pt. i, p. 136.

Æchmandra rostrata : famine plant, grows in Bombay, Dakhan and Gujarat, XXV, 200.

Ægippæi : Skythian holy men, IX, pt. i, 438.

Ægle marmelos : (*bel*), wild in Gujarát and the Dakhan, XXV, 35; a food plant, *id.* 148; yields scented oil, *id.* 222; pulp of its fruit taken in diarrhœa, *id.* 259; leaves as fodder, *id.* 277; sacred to Hindus, *id.* 279, 285, 288, 291.

Ælius Gallus : I, pt. i, 536.

Ærva lanata : a species of Amaranth used as a pot herb, XXV, 203.

Æschynomene aspera : grows in Bengal, sunhats made of its pith, XXV, 198.

Æthiopia : the mention of, by Friar Jordanus as a field for missionaries (1322), XIV, 322.

Aethrapati : Zend word for Herbad, IX, pt. ii, 222 note 1.

Affiu : *see* Papaver somniferum.

Afghán : derivation of the name of, IX, pt. ii, 13 note 2; race, *id.* 10 note 4; among Gujarát troops (1572), *id.* 3 note 1.

Afghanistán : I, pt. i, 545; Eastern, original settlement of the Aryas in, I, pt. ii, 135; places in, mentioned by Pánini, *id.* 138, 142.

Afiz Bágh : garden at Junnar in the Poona district, XVIII, pt. iii, 152-153.

Africa : I, pt. i, 535; Indian trade with (B. C. 250), XIII, 404 note 3, (A. D. 500), *id.* 420; ports in, export of rice, etc., to (810-1260), *id.* 429, 430, 431, 433; trade in articles of food and pearls with, import of Negro slaves from (1300-1500), *id.* 444, 445, 446; trade with, in articles of food, etc., decline of the trade with (1500-1670), 465, 466; import of gold from, *id.* 467; amount of trade with, *id.* 519, 520.

Africans : in Konkan, XIII, 64.

African slaves : prehistoric trade with India in, XI, 433 and note 1.

Afringan : portion of the Zend Avesta, IX, pt. ii, 212 note 1.

Afu : *see* Papaver somniferum.

Afzul Khán : Bijápur Commandar, I, pt. ii, 68; sent to arrest the progress of Shiváji (1659); his assassination at Pratápgad and the defeat of his troops near Jávli, *id.* 592; his murder further described (1659), XVIII, pt. ii, 288; XIX, 234-237, XXIII, 430.

Afzulpur : Bijápur hamlet, XXIII, 578.

Agá : Rashid Beg, minister, plunders the Bráhmans of Cambay, is imprisoned and murdered (1766), VI, 228.

Agan : a lark, IX, pt. ii, 99.

Agar : town of Agarvals, IX, pt. i, 70 ; petty state in Rewa Kántha, VI, 142.

Agarah : *see* Achyranthes aspera.

Agarás : Land-holders, of part foreign descent, cease to be a separate community, IX, pt. ii, 11 ; *id.* 15.

Agarkhed : village in Bijápur district, XXIII, 545.

Agarni : ceremony relating to pregnancy ; presents given in, rites relating to, IX, pt. ii, 227-228. *See* Pregnancy.

Agarváls : Vanias in Gujaráth, IX, pt. i, p. xi, note 3, *id.* 70 ; traders in Bijápur, XXIII, 90-91 ; in Khándesh, XII, 61 ; in Poona, XVIII, pt. i, 262-263 ; in Sholápur, XX, 48-50.

Agasa, pl. agasaru : a caste of washermen, in Kánara district, XV, pt. i, 326-327.

Agasale, pl. agasaleru : a caste of goldsmiths. *See* Sonars.

Agáshi : town in Thána district, its timber market I, pt. ii, 36 ; stone found near, XIII, 426 note 3 ; port of, burnt by the Portuguese (1529, *id.* 46 ; taken charge of by the Franciscans (1585), *id.* 57 ; destroyed by Antonio (1532), *id.* 451 ; historic references to, *id.* 443, 456, 459, 465, 485 ; a ship building centre (1550-1600), *id* 468 ; a summer resort (1695), *id.* 483-484 ; description of country round (1727), *id.* 490 ; Du Perron's mention of (1760), *id.* 499 : a Thána port (1800-1812), *id.* 514 ; surveyed (1793-94), *id.* 558 ; its history and its description, XIV, 1-2, 11, 314, 316, 386.

Agáshiv : hill in Sátára district, XIX, 11.

Agastya : sage, I, pt. ii, 135, 136. 222, 322 ; introduced Aryan civilization into the Dakhan, XVI, 181 ; supposed builder of a *tirth* at Nandikeshvar, XXIII, 665 note 9.

A'ga Sultán Muhammad Sháh : Khoját Imám, IX, pt. ii, 48.

Agate : in Ahmadabad, iv, 22 ; in Ahmadnagar. XVII, 16 ; in Bijápur, XXIII, 44, 61 ; in Káthiáwár, VIII, 94 ; in Kaira, III, 15 ; in Poona, XVIII, pt. i, 30 ; in the Indrayani (1803) in Poona, *id.* pt. ii, 285 note 9 ; near Poona city, *id.* pt. iii, 402 note 1 ; manufacture of, in Cambay, VI, 198-200 ; in Rewa Kántha, *id.* 11-12, 57 ; cups in Cambay, *id.* 205 note 1.

Agatharcides : (B. C. 177-100) IX, pt. ii, 1 note 1 ; his mention of Indian trade with Socotra (B. C. 177), XIII, 404 note 3 ; mention of Indian trade with the Persian Gulf, *id.* 411 note 1.

Agtaharkhides : (born 250 A. D.), I, pt. i, 535, *id.* 542

Agati grandiflora : cultivated all over India. *See* Sesbania grandiflora.

Agave : Americana, a famine plant, cultivated in many parts of India, XXV, 205-206 ; a fibrous plant, *id.* 235 ; *cantula*, *id.* 205, 235.

Age details : all district Volumes. *See* Census Details under district name.

Agencies : Bhil political tracts in the Khándesh district, XII, 258, *id.* 260.

Ager : a caste in the Kánara district, XV, pt. i, 360.

A'gha Abdas Salám : Khoját Imám, son of A'gha Islámsháh, excommunicates Imámsháh, IX, pt. ii, 41.

A'gha Abd-us-Salám : writes the Pandyád-i-Jawánmardi for the guidance of his Indian followers, IX, pt. ii, 41, *id.* 48.

A'gha Islámshah : unrevealed Khoját Imám, ancestor of His Highness the Ága Khán ; believed to be Ali's incarnation, IX, pt. ii, 40, *id.* 41.

A'gha Khán : His Highness, title of the unrevealed Imám of the Khojáhs, IX, pt. ii, 41 ; descendant of Ali, *id.* 38 ; his influence over the outlying tribes of the Upper Indus Valley, *id.* 36 note 1, *id.* 45, 46 ; Ágha Sháh Hassan Ali, the first A'gha Khán (1845), *id.* 41.

Agha Muhammad Hussain : Commander of the port of Petlad ; his surrender, I, pt. i, 337.

Aghanáshani : river in Kánara district, XV, pt i, 6.

Agharni : IX, pt. i. *See* Pregnancy.

A'gha Sháh Hassan Ali : His Highness, Khoját Imám (1844) ; the first Ismáilia unrevealed Imám to settle in India (1845), IX, pt. ii, 41. *See* A'gha Khán.

Aghnáshi : village in the Kánara district, XV, pt. ii, 249.

Aghori : Order of Shaiv ascetics, IX, pt. i, 543.

Agiári : Fire-place, IX, pt. ii, 213 ; Fire-temple, *id.* 222 ; list of, *id.* 247-251. *See* Temples (Fire).

Agio Vsital : Fire Demon, IX, pt. i, 422.

Aglaia odorata : a shrub with yellow flowers, cultivated in Bombay gardens, XXV, 43.

Aglaia Roxburghiana : timber tree, found in Southern Konkan, XXV, 42-43.

Agni : Hindu deity, I, pt. ii, 182 ; fire element, IX, pt. i, 356. *See* fire ; deity presiding over light, *id.* 348.

Agnihotra : Fire sacrifice, fire used in, IX, pt. i, 356. *See* fire, *id.* pt. ii, 561.

Agnikulas : Fire clan of Rajputs, I, pt. i, 463, 468 ; four tribes of, raised to be Rajputs by rebirth in fire-pit on Mount Abu, and were Gurjjaras or members of great horde of which Gurjjara was one of the leading elements, IX, pt. i, 480 ; were re-born to help Brahmans, *id.* 449, 483 ; distribution of territory to four tribes, *id.* 449 note 3 ; are greatest of Royal races, *id.* 486 note 8 ; date of their origin, *id.* 486, *id.* 443 ; *id.* 469 note 3 ; *id.* 496 ; history of origin of four tribes—Chohau, *id.* 483 484 ; Parihar, *id.* 484 ; Parmar, *id.* 485 ; Solanki, *id.* 485-487. *See* Gujar.

Agni-kund : Abu fire-pit, IX, pt. i, 490.

Agnimitra : second king of the S'unga dynasty, I, pt. ii, 146-147.

Agniupasi Suryavanshi : children of Bappa, IX, pt. i, 495.

A'gra : fort of, I, pt. i, 368 ; underground passage to, I, pt. ii, 13.

Agraháras : I, pt. ii, 440, 443 and note 4, 448, 449, 450, 561.

Agrakon : port in Kánara district, XV, pt. ii, 260 and note 3 ; historical references to, *id.* 114, 118.

Agrarian crimes : in Ahmadabad, IV, 197 ; in Kaira, III, 121 ; in Surat, II, 202.

Agrarian riots (1874-75) : in Sátára district, XIX, 187-188.

Agreement : between the Peshwa and the Dábháde, I, pt. i, 393; between Rávji Appáji and Mr. Duncan (1802), VII, 206.
Agri : a caste in Thána and Kolába, their subdivisions, origin, food, dress, occupation and condition in Kolába District, XI, 51-54; in Janjira, *id.* 412; in Thána, foreign element in, XIII, 61, 62; their arrival from the South, traces of Lingáyat customs among, *id.* 63; their number and sub-divisions, *id.* 115-117.
Agri : the ministrant of the Lonad temple, XIV, 213.
Agria : a caste of salt makers in Ahmadabad, IV, 36, 117, 119.
A'gri Bágáyat: salt garden-land in Ratnágiri, X, 144.
Agricultural Banks : proposed scheme of, XVIII, pt. ii, 512-513.
Agricultural stock : all district volumes. *See* under district name.
Agriculture : all district volumes. *See* under district name.
Agrinagara : identified with A'gar, I, pt. i, 539.
Agunte : village, I, pt. ii, 365 note 1.
Agya : *see* Kolambi.
Ahada : son of Udaya Vania, high officer in the reign of Kumárapála, I, pt. i, 170; not acknowledging Kumárapála, goes to Arnorája, *id.* 184.
Ahalyábái: Holkar's Queen (1765-1795), modern temple of Somnáth built by, IX, pt. i, 19; *see* Somnáth; account and Násik buildings of, XVI, 513 and note 1.
Ahar : City, I, pt. i, 539; site of the former capital of Gehlots of Udaipur, IX, pt. i, 464.
Aharyas : Gehlots of Udaipur known as, IX, pt. i, 464.
A'havamalla : son of the Kalachurya king Bijjála, I, pt. ii, 228, 471, 477; succeeds his brother; his *biruda,* his epithets, and titles, *id.* 488; records of his time, *id.* 488, 570, 581; his feudatories and officials, *id.* 489, 582.
A'havamalla : *biruda* of Someśvara I, the Western Chálukya king, I, pt. ii, 124, 514; Siláhára prince, XIV, 385.
A'her : gifts at a marriage ceremony, XII, 66.
Ahichchhatra : I, pt. ii, 560 and note 11; Agrahára of, *id.* 561, 576; town, literally means land of Ahis or Nags, IX, pt. i, 15 notes 1 and 2.
Ahichhatras : Prashnora Nagars style themselves thus, IX, pt. i, 15 notes 1 and 2.
Ahihaya : Haihaya family, I, pt. ii, 439 note 2, 451, 457.
Ahi-Khestra : snake-land, an old name for Kánára coast, XV, pt. i, 117 note 1; probable identification of, XV, pt. ii, 83 and notes 2 and 3; the birthplace of Vishvavandya, *id.* 346 and note 1.
Ahir : I, pt. i, 175. *See* Chudásama and A'bhira.
Ahiráni : Khándesh dialect, formation and peculiarities of, XII, 39, *id.* 42-45.
Ahir Bráhmans : a sub-division belonging to the Mádhyandin stock, XVI, 38.
Ahire : village, XVIII, pt. iii, 102.
Ahirgaon : town in Násik District, Trimbakji Denglia captured at (1818), XVI, 414.
Ahirs: Abhirs or cow-herds, class of herdsmen, strength; different accounts of origin; distribution; were once a powerful class; were connected with Shepherd Kings of Khándesh; ruled in Central India and in Nepal, were related to the dynasty of Pal, were universal sovereigns, IX, pt. i, 264; their traces preserved in Abisares, *id.* 264 and note 6, 265 and note 2; their connection traced with snake kings of Gujarát, *id.* 264 note 5; claim Mathura as their first seat, *id.* 265; surnames, *id.* 265 and note 3; appearance, dress, *id.* 265; customs, *id.* 266; their affinity with Kathis, *id.* 261; closely connected with Gujars, strong Gujar element in, *id.* 497, 499. *See* Herdsmen in Baroda, VI, 61-62; in Cutch their origin, history, sub-divisions, character, customs, language, V, 77-80; in Pálanpur, *id.* 290; in the Sátpuda hills, I, pt. ii, 619; settlement of, I, pt. i, 137, 138; shepherds in Káthiáwár, have affinity with Bábriás and through them with the Káthis, theirs ub-divisions, VIII, 130, 131, 134-135; a Hindu tribe in Khándesh, their origin, element in Khándesh, population, XII, 38, 78, 240 and note 4.
Ahirvada : Tract in Central India, IX, pt. i, 264 note 2.
Ahis : or Nags (Serpents), IX, pt. i, 15 note 1; *id.* 264 note 5.
Ahivant : pass, XVI, 130; fort, its description, XVI, 415, 441, 447.
Ahl-I-Hadith : People of the tradition, IX, pt. ii, 12. *See* Wahhábis.
Ahmad : I, pt. ii, 622. *See* Malik Ahmad Behori.
Ahmad : Muhammadan name of Rávji, the Lohana convert, IX, pt. ii, 51. *See* Rávji.
Ahmad : Bahmani, attempts the conquest of Konkan (1422-1435), XIII, 441.
Ahmad : Founder of the Karmation sect; his nickname Karmatah; spreads his new doctrines at Nahrein; his persecution; his flight to Syria, IX, pt. ii, 3 note 3 continued on page 4. *See* Karmatians.
Ahmad I : Ahmadábád King (1411-1441), builds Ahmadábád (1413); defeats the Idár Chief (1414); suppresses a revolt, spreads Islám, sends expedition against Málwa (1417); attacks Chámpáner (1418); his war with Málwa (1422); defeats the Idár Chief (1425); recovers Máhim (1429) and Báglan (1431), I, pt. i, 207 note 1, 215, 219, 235-240; enriches Cambay, VI, 217; his bringing of a keen Musalmán spirit into his Government, IX, pt. ii, 188; (1411-1443), *id.* 6 note 1 (7); spreads Islám by force; converts Rajpúts and other Hindus (1414-1420), *id.* 5 and note 2, *id.* 25 note 1; persecutes Bohorás, *id.* 27 note 1; converts Shiáh Bohorás to the Sunni faith, *id.* 58 note 2; *id.* 125; captures Thána and Mahim, XIV, 357.
Ahmad II : Sultán of Gujarát (1554-1561), loses Cambay, VI, 218; his grants of Rádhanpur and Sami to Fateh Khán Baluch, IX, pt. ii, 17.

Ahmadábád District: Boundaries; sub-divisions, aspect and hills, IV, 1-4; rivers; floods; creeks, lakes, islands, climate; 5-21; minerals, forests, trees, animals, birds, fish, 22-30; population in 1846, 1851 and 1872; census details of 1872, 31-34; details of Hindus, Musalmáns, Parsis and Christians, 35-44; villages, houses, communities, movements, 45-48; soil, irrigation, tillage, holdings, stock, crops, 49-57; peasants, bad seasons, 58-62; capitalists, bills of exchange, Bank of Bombay, insurance, gambling, classes who save, modes of investment, 63-67; borrowers, rates of interest, currency, 68-73; wages, prices, condition of labourers, 74-80; roads, bridges, rest-houses, ferries, shipping, light-houses, post and telegraph offices, 81-85; trade (750-1877), details of the railway and sea trade, present 1877; lines of traffic, condition of traders, 86-105; trade guilds, 106-115; manufactures, 116-141; history, 142; acquisition; staff; state of the district in 1803; villages; Kasbátis; Col. Walker's proposals; Girásiás; Gámetis, Chuvália Kolis; Mr. Elphinstone's changes in 1821; first survey (1820-1826); second survey (1853-1863); Tálukdárs; Parántij Kolis; seasons, development of the district (1846-1877), 143-190; civil and criminal justice in 1803, civil court's statistics, offences, police, jails, 191-199; balance sheet, local funds, municipalities, 200-208; schools, pupils, town and village education, libraries, newspapers, 209-217; plague and pestilence, diseases, hospitals, dispensaries, vaccination, cattle diseases, births and deaths, 218-229; sub-divisions, 230-248; places of interest, 249-356.

Ahmadábád City: Position, IV, 249; history, 249; new city, how founded and named, 249; Asával the old town, 250; chief events under the Ahmadabad Kings (1411-1572), 250; under the Mughal Viceroys (1572-1757), 251-258; state of the city between 1573 and 1600, 252; arrival of the English (1613), 253; and of the Dutch (1618), 253; the city in 1618, 253; in 1626 and 1638, 254; in 1666, 255; time of disorder (1707-1737), 255-257; joint Musalman and Maratha rule (1738-1753), 257; taken by the Marathas (1753), 258; recovered by Momin Khán II (1755), 258; retaken by the Marathas (1757), 258; Maratha rule (1757-1817), 258 260; taken by the British and made over to Fateh Singh Gáikwár (1870), 258, 259; its state in 1781, 259; restored to the Peshwa (1783), 259; famine (1790), 259; the Peshwa's Governor driven out (1800), 259; the Peshwa's share in the city farmed by the Gáikwár (1800-1814), 260; famine and pestilence (1812-1813), 260; Peshwa's management (1814-1817), 260; ceded to the British (1817), 260; its state in 1817, 260; growth of trade (1817-1855), 261; the mutiny year (1857), 261; its state for the last 20 years (1858-1878), 262; trade and manufactures, 306-308; population, 292-294; houses and pols, 294-295; style of living, 295; caste lodges, 295-300; Musalman architecture, 262-266; places of interest and worship, Sidi Bashir's mosque, 267; railway station mosque, 267; city walls, 267-268; Queen's mosque in Sárangpur, 269; Muhammad Ghán's mosque, 269; Ránisipri or Asni's mosque, 269-270; Asa Bhil's mound and mosque, 270; Dastur Khan's mosque, 270; Haibat Khan's mosque, 270; Jáma mosque, 271-272; tombs of Sultán Ahmad and his wives, 272; Dutch factory, 272; English factory, 273; Three gate-ways, 273; Káranj, 273; Malik Shábán's mosque, 274; Azam Khan's palace or the city jail, 274; Bhadar or Citadel, 275-277; Sultán Ahmad's mosque, 276; Mának tower and Mánaknáth Godadia, 276; Sidi Syed's mosque, 276-277; Ibráhim Kuli Khán's tomb, 277; Gáikwár's haveli, 277; Shuját Khán's mosque, 278; Sháh Wajih-ud-din's tomb, 278; Syed Alam's mosque, 278; Queen's mosque in Mirzápur, 278-279; Sháhápur's mosque, 279; Sultán Kutb-ud-din's mosque, 279; Muháfiz Khán's mosque, 279; animal home, pánjrápol, 280; Nav Gaz Pirs, 280; old or Jehángir's mint, 280; Musa Suhág's mosque, 281; Dada Harir's well, 282; Máta Bhaváni's well, 282-283; Shahi Bág, 283; Adálaj well, 284; Miya Khán Chishti's mosque, 284; Achut Bibi's mosque, 284; Darya Khán's tomb, 284; Syed Usman's mosque and tomb, 284; Malik Shábán's lake, 285; Kánkariya lake, 285; Dutch tombs, 285; Malik Alam's mosque, 285; Sháh Alam, 286: Batva, 287; Pirána, 287-290; Bába Lulni's mosque, 290; Mir Abu Turáb's tomb, 290-291; Azám and Mozam Khán's tombs, 291; Sarkhej, 291-292; Chánd Suraj Mehel, 317; Alam Chishti's mosque, 317; Sidi Hálim's mosque, 317; Kazi Muhammad Chishti's mosque, 317; Malik Shábán's mosque, 317; Sháh Ali Rozak's tomb, 318; Chandan Talávdi, 318; Daulat Khán's mosque, 318; Malik Sárang's mosque, 319; Ráni Bibi's tomb, 319; Nawab Sardár Khán's mosque and tomb, 319; Sidi Salim's haveli, 319; Hatising's temple, 280-281; Santidás' temple, 285; other Jain temples, 300-302; Jain convents, *apsarás*, 321, 323-324; Brahman temples, Bhadra Káli, 275; Sadubai Deri, 317; Ram, Krishna, Vithoba, Hanumán and Shiv's temples in the Bhadar, 321; Swámi Narayen, 279-280; Gosai Mahárája's Natvarlál and Shamlál, Ambáji Máta and Mohta Rámji, in the Daryápur division, 322; Kabirpanthi, Dvárkánáthji, Rámsnehi, Ranchhodji and Rádha Vallabhji, in the Khádiya division, 324; Prarthana Samáj temple, 325-327; Pársi fire-temple, 327; Christian churches, 279; fairs, Hindu, 302 - 304, and Musalmán, 304-305; burying and burning grounds, 270-271, 316-317; public offices, 308-309; education, 309-311; Municipality, 311-315; floods (1714-1875), 313; fires (1877), 262; water works, 314; health, 315; hospitals, 315-316; markets, 316; divisions, 317-332; within the

walls, in 1824, 317-320; and in 1879, 320-327; suburbs, 327-331; cantonment, 331-332; *another account of*—built (1413), I, pt. i, 236, *id.* 513; sacked (1583), *id.* 224, 225; manuscript fonnd at, *id.* 205; riot at (1681), death of the leader Abu Bakr by poison, *id.* 286, 287; riots at (1730), *id.* 310; Umábái, widow of Khanderáv Dábhade marches upon, *id.* 314; siege of and capture by the Maráthás and Momin Khán (1737-1738), *id.* 320; prosperity of, *id.* 320; disputes about the government of, between Rangoji and Momin Khán (1738), *id.* 322; disturbances at, between the Musalmáns and the Maráthás, *id.* 325; mutiny of troops at, confinement of Fida-ud-din and Muftakhir Khán at, capture of the city of, by Jawán Mard Khán, *id.* 327; Maráthás in (1743-44), *id.* 327; siege of, by Fakhr-ud-daulah and Ráisinghji of Idár and defeat and capture of the Viceroy at, by Jawán Mard Khán, *id.* 329; expulsion of Khanderáv Gáikwár's deputy Trimbak from, by Rangoji, *id.* 329; siege and capture of, by the Maráthás under Raghunáthráo *id.* 337; minting of coins in the emperor's name stopped at, (1753), *id.* 338; assassination of Rághuji the Marátha deputy at, and expulsion of the Maráthás from, by Momin Khán; Kolis attempt to plunder the Dutch factory at, *id.* 339-340; siege of, by the Maráthás, Sháh Nur intercedes with the Peshwa to settle the affairs of, and fails, surrender of (1758), 341, 342; Sadáshiv Rámchandra is appointed Viceroy at (1760), *id.* 344; state of the parties at, *id.* 390; riot at (1738), *id.* 394; captured by General Goddard (1780), *id.* 409; surrendered to Govindráv Gáikwár by Ába Shelukar, *id.* 411; cession of the fort of, to the English by Gáikwár in 1817, *id.* 428; mutiny at (1857), *id.* 438; disturbances at (14th September 1857), *id.* 440; suppression of the mutiny at, *id.* 442; incident attached to the erection of, by Ahmadshah, IX, pt. i, 243 note 3; Mausoleums of Musalmán saints at, *id.* 168; founded by saints, IX, pt. ii, 3 note 1; chief quarters of Mahdavi Sayads at, *id.* 6 note 1; head-quarters of Músa Suhágs at, *id.* 23; former seat of the head Múlla of Daúdi Bohorás at, *id.* 31 note 4; tombs at, of Músa, *id.* 23, of Jaáfar Shirázi, *id.* 34 note 3, of Pír Muhammadshah, *id.* 35, of Sháh Alam, *id.* 148; mosques at, *id.* 131 note 1; Súba of (Gujarát), *id.* 67; arrival of Memans at, *id.* 51; kings of, exert themselves to spread Islám, *id.* 5 and note 2, 125.

Ahmadabad Kings: rule of (1403-1573), I, pt. i, 207, 209, 210, 234, 264.

Ahmad Ayaz: Governor of Gujarát, I, pt. i, 230.

Ahmad Beg: Nawáb of Broach, IX, pt. ii, 198.

Ahmad Bin Ismáil: Head of the Yaman Sulemani Bohorás, IX, pt. ii, 33.

Ahmad Chalebi: a rich merchant of Surat, assassinated (1730-1736), II, 112.

Ahmad Jaáfar Shirázi: Sayád ancestor of the Shirázi Sayad family of Gujarát, IX, pt. ii, 6 note 1 (6); persuades Sunni Bohorás to keep apart from Shiáh Bohorás (1535), *id.* 26 note 1, *id.* 34; Jaáfari Bohorás take their name after him; his descendants become Pirs of Jaáfari Bohorás, *id.* ii, 34; his power of working miracles; tomb of, at Ahmadábád, *id.* 34 note 3.

Ahmad Kabír: Sayad Saint, ancestor of the Rifái Sayad family of Gujarát, IX, pt. ii, 6 note 1 (3), 23, 140.

Ahmad Khán: *see* Ahmad I.

Ahmad Khán: Holkar officer before Songad (1803), VII, 210-211.

Ahmad Khán Habshi: Commandant of the Surat fort, expelled by the English (1759), I, pt. i, 343.

Ahmad Khattu: of Sarkhez, Sheikh, one of the four saintly founders of Ahmadábád City, IX, pt. ii, 3 note 1.

Ahmadnagar District: boundaries, sub-divisions, aspect, XVII, 1-3; mountains, rivers, *id.* 3-9; geology, climate, *id.* 9-15; minerals, forests, forest management and products, *id.* 16-23; trees, wild animals, game birds, domestic animals, fowls, reptiles, fishes, *id.* 23-45; census details, houses, villages, community, *id.* 46-49; Bráhmans, *id.* 49-64; writers, traders, husbandmen, craftsmen, musicians, servants, shepherds, labourers, depressed classes, beggars, unsettled tribes, Musalmáns, Christians, Pársis, *id.* 64-240; agriculture, soils, seasons, holdings, arable land, stock, crops, field, tools, sowing, manure, irrigation, Government water works, harvesting, storing, fallows, crop changes, crop details, silk, field-plagues, famines, *id.* 241-293; capitalists, saving classes, bankers, bills, currency, money-lenders, rate of interest, borrowers, prices, weights and measures, *id.* 294-325; trade routes, roads, railways, passes, post offices, telegraph, *id.* 326-335; trade (A. D. 247-1884), trade centres, markets, fairs, shopkeepers, pedlers, exports, imports, railway traffic, *id.* 335-346; weaving, copper, glass bangles, *id.* 346-350; early history (B. C. 240-A. D. 1294), Delhi Governors (1318-1347), the Bahmanis (1347-1490), Bairam Khán's revolt (1366), Durga Devi Famine (1396-1407), Ahmad Nizám assumes independence (1490), Nizám Sháhis (1490-1636), Ahmadnagar founded (1494), Ahmad Nizám takes Daulatábád (1499), Burhán Nizám Sháh (1508-1553), hostility with Bijápur (1524-1553), Husain Nizám Sháh (1553-1565), hostility with Bijápur, the siege of Ahmadnagar (1562), Murtaza Nizám Sháh (1565-1588), Mirán Husain Nizám Sháh (1588), Ismael Nizám Sháh (1588-1590), Burhán Nizám Sháh II (1590-1594), his campaign against Bijápur, Ibrahim Nizám Sháh (1594), Ahmad II (1594-1595), Chand Bibi's regency (1595-1599), her defence of Ahmadnagar, treaty with the Mughals (1596), Bahadur Nizám Sháh (1596-1599), Chand Bibi's murder (1599), fall of Ahmadnagar (1599), Murtaza Nizám Sháh II (1599-1631), Malik Ambar's regency (1607-1625), his death (1626), fall of Daulatábád (1632), Sháhaji Bhonsla regent (1632), Mughals (1636-1759), Shiváji's incursions (1650-1680), Aurangzeb's march (1684), Maráthás (1759-1817), battle of Kharda (1795), Ahmadnagar taken by General

Wellesley (1803), Koli Risings (1828), Rágboji Bhángria (1845-1847), Bhagoji Naik, *id.* 350-420; Land Revenue staff, *id.* 421-423; its history, under Malik Ambar, under Maráthás, under British (1818-1884), village staff (1818), land holders (1818-1823), revenue settlement (1818-1822), cesses (1822), survey (1848-1853), revision survey (1880-1884), season reports (1850-1884), *id.* 423-557; civil courts, registration, magistracy, police, *id.* 558-566; revenue and finance, *id.* 567-572; progress of instruction, schools, education details, libraries, *id.* 573-581; hospitals and dispensaries, cattle diseases, cat plague, vaccination, births and deaths, *id.* 582-586; sub-divisional details of Akola, Jámkhed, Karjat, Kopargaon, Nagar, Nevása, Párner, Ráhuri, Sangamner, Shevgaon, Shrigonda, *id.* 587-650; places of interest, *id.* 653-741. (*See* also Ahmadnagar City, *id.* 651-711.)

Ahmadnagar City: capital of the Nizám Sháhi dynasty, I, pt. ii, 32; fort built (1427), I, pt. i, 238; city built (1493-1495) by Malik Ahmad Beheri, I, pt. ii, 621-622, 640; extent of the kingdom (1500), *id.* 622; its King joins a confederacy against Bijápur and is defeated (1524), *id.* 641-642; city occupied by Bahádur Sháh of Gujarát (1528), *id.* 622; King joins another confederacy and is bought off by Bijápur (1536), *id.* 643; its treaty with the Portuguese (1547), *id.* 46; besieged by Ali Adil Sháh and Rámráj of Vijaynagar in 1553 and 1562, *id.* 623, 644; the Ahmadnagar princess Chánd Bibi married to Ali Adil Sháh of Bijápur (1563), its King joins the Musalmán confederacy against Vijaynagar (1564), *id.* 623, 644-645; attacks Goa with the King of Bijápur (1570), *id.* 646; hostilities and agreements with Bijápur (1573), *id.* 645; its King joins a confederacy against Bijápur (1580), *id.* 647; Mughal interference (1588), *id.* 623; marriage alliance between Ahmadnagar and Bijápur, invasions of Bijápur by Burhán Nizám Sháh rebelled in 1592 and 1596, *id.* 648-649; internal factions, Mughals called in, Chánd Bibi's gallant defence, peace with the Mughals and surrender of Berár (1595), *id.* 624, 649; disturbances break out at, and Mughals march against (1596); Chánd Bibi is murdered, the city falls, and the King is taken prisoner (1600); Malik Ambar sets up Murtaza as King, and retakes the city, defeats another Mughal army (1612); is defeated by Mughals and the city surrendered to them (1617), *id.* 624; the King is murdered by Malik Ambar's son (1631), *id.* 625, 650; Sháhji Bhonsla sets up another King and overruns the country, he drives back the Mughals (1634), he comes to terms and surrenders the prince and the kingdom is extinguished (1637), *id.* 625, 650; the town surprised (1657) and sacked (1664) by Shiváji, *id.* 625; battle fought between the Maráthás and Mughals near; recognition of the Marátha claims of *chauth* and *sardeshmukhi* on the district of (1720), *id.* 626; fort, gained by the Peshwa (1759); district acquired by the Peshwa (1760), *id.* 602, 627; fort given to Sindia and Nána Phadnavis imprisoned in 1797, *id.* 628; restored to the Peshwa (1803), *id.* 629; district put under Captain Pottinger (1819), *id.* 631. (*See* also XVIII, pt. ii, 221-249.)

Ahmadnagar: a town in Mahi Kántha of the Marátha history, remains, V, 430-432.

Ahmadnagar Kings: list of, XXIII, 403 note 1.

Ahmad Nizam Shah: founder of the Ahmadnagar dynasty, in charge of Junnar province (1485), takes Shivner and other forts from Maráthás, I, pt. ii, 589, 621; defeated Bahmani troops at Jeur and established his independence (1489); founded Ahmadnagar (1493-1495), captured Daulatábád, reduced the fort of Autur and other places in Sátmálás, assisted Adil Khan of Khándesh against Mahmud Begada of Gujarát; his death (1508), *id.* 621-622.

Ahmad Sháh: son and successor of Emperor Muhammad Sháh, I, pt. i, 332; deposed (1754), *id.* 339.

Ahmad Sháh: grandson and successor of Muzzaffar I of Gujarát (1399-1411), besieges Mándu twice between A. D. 1418 and 1422, I, pt. i, 359; Gujarát king, sends an army to re-take Máhim and Sálsette and reduces the Northern Konkan and Bombay, I, pt. ii, 30.

Ahmad Sháh Abdáli: Afghán King, his forces driven out of the Panjáb by Raghunáth Ráo; he defeats two Marátha contingents (1759) and routs the grand Marátha Army at Pánipat (1761), I, pt. ii, 602.

Ahmad Sháh Bahamani: changes his capital from Gulburga to Bidar in 1426, I, pt. ii, 588.

Ahmad Sháh Wali: Bahamani king, sends two deputations from Cheul to Persia, I, pt. ii, 33.

Ahmed: *see* Ahmad.

Ahmed I: *see* Ahmad I.

Ahmed II: *see* Ahmad II.

Ahmedábád: *see* Ahmadábád.

Ahmedábád Kings: *see* Ahmadábád Kings.

Ahmed Jaáfar Shirázi: *see* Ahmad Jaáfar Shirázi.

Ahmed Kabir: *see* Ahmad Kabir.

Ahmed Khan: *see* Ahmad I.

Ahmed Khan: *see* Ahmad Khan.

Ahmed Khan-Habshi: *see* Ahmad Khan Habshi.

Ahmed Khattu: *see* Ahmad Khattu.

Ahmednagar: *see* Ahmadnagar.

Ahmed Shah: *see* Ahmad Shah.

Ahrimán: Satan, of the Parsi religion, IX, pt. ii, 206 note 1; belief in, *id.* 212. *See* Beliefs (Leading).

Ahunvat: a Gatha Day, IX, pt. ii, 218.

Ahunvat Gátha: IX, pt ii, 240.

Ahupe: hill in Poona District, XVIII, pt. i, 4.

Ahuramazd: the Creator, in the Parsi religion, IX, pt. ii, 212, 217; all knowing Lord, *id.* 211; belief in, *id.* 212; Zoroaster brings the true religion from, *id.* 213; name of, included in the Amsháspands, *id.* 215, 216; first day of the Pársi month, *id.* 217.

Aiávej: a petty state in Káthiáwár, VIII, 355.

Aigals: temple servants in Kánara, their daily life, customs, XV, pt. i, 201.

Aigidioi : early reference to Anjediv, I, pt. i, 546, and XV, pt. ii, 48 note 3; mentioned in the Periplus (A. D. 247), *id.* 78; mentioned by Ptolemy, *id.* 336.

Aihole : village in Bijápur District, inscription at, I, pt. i, 107, *id.* pt. ii, 144, 181 and note 1, 191, 194, 278 note 2, 282 and note 5, 291 note 2, 298 note 2, 300, 309, 313 note 1, 336 note 3; inscription, mention of the three Maharashtras in, *id.* 341 note 2; inscription at, *id.* 342, 344, 345, 346 note 4, 349, 350, 351, 353, 355 note 3, 356, 358, 370 note 5, 372, 376, 431, 463, 541; records of the Yelburga Sindas at, *id.* 573, 576; inscriptions (A. D. 334), XXIII, 546, 682, 685. *See* Aivalli.

Ailanthus : *excelsa*, timber tree, common at Broach, Baroda, and in the Dakhan, XXV, 35, 36; *Malabarica*, timber tree found on the Western ghâts, Khandála and other places, *id.* 36.

Ain : Terminalia tomentosa, timber tree found in many districts, XVIII, pt. i, 41; XXV, 75; produces a dye, *id.* 244.

Ainápur : village in Belgaum District, XXI, 510.

Ainâti : Ali Khan's rate of assessment, XXII, 443, 447 note 3, 448.

Aindri river, I, pt. ii, 337, note 4. *See* Indrayani.

Ain-i-Akbari : Gladwin's, IX, pt. i, 208 note 3; *id.* 433 note 2; *id.* 496 note 3; IX, pt. ii, 14; *id.* 65; *id.* 147.

Ain Mokása : portion of the *chauth*, XVI, 207.

Ainshe : food plant, XXV, 162.

Ain-ul-Mulk : chief partisan of Ismail the rebel brother of Ibráhim Ádil Sháh, II, pt. ii, 648, 649; Bijápur general besieged Bijápur (1553), XXIII, 583; his tomb in Bijápur, *id.* 616.

Ain-ul-mulk Multani : Gujarát Governor (1318), I, pt. i, 229, 230; Governor of Málwa, reinforces Malik Káfur (1306), I, pt. ii, 532.

Airani : hill in Dhárwár District, XXII, 3; village fort, *id.* 649-650.

Áishah : Prophet Muhammad's wife, her dower, IX, pt. ii, 166 note 1.

Aitan : Lingáyat initiation ceremony, XXIV, 129.

Aitareya Bráhmana : Áryas acquainted with Northern India in the time of, I, pt. ii, 138.

Aitawáde Khurd : village in Sátára District, I, pt. ii, 390.

Ai Thansi : sister of small-pox god, stone image of, offerings made to, IX, pt. i, 372.

Aitken, Mr. Russel : designed Bandra slaughter-houses, XIV, 18; surveys the site for Tulsi Lake, *id.* 364.

Aivalli or Aihole : old village in Bijápur District, temples, caves, cell-tombs, inscriptions, XXIII, 378, 545-548, 683-686.

Aiyaparája : Siláhára king, I, pt. ii, 537.

Aiyapdev : Hindu chief, I, pt. ii, 18; Hindu chief (1094), XIII, 425.

Ajan : river in Rewá Kántha, VI, 92; in Baroda, VII, 8.

Ajanta : caves, I, pt. ii, 9; Vákátaka inscription at, *id.* 294 note 4; paintings in, *id.* 352; rock-cut Buddhist caves in, *id.* 354; identified with Ajintha, *id.* 354 note 5, 355; village, *id.* 391 note 6; inscription at, *id.* 431 note 2; believed to contain a painting relating to Nanshirván's embassy to Pulikesi II, and pictures of Parviz and Shirin, IX, pt. ii, 183 note 4 continued on page 184. *See* also XII, 206; position, early references, cave details, temples, monasteries, sculptures and paintings, history, *id.* 480-484; life in India (200-700 A. D.), chiefs, houses, ministers, servants, soldiers, craftsmen, husbandmen, amusements, religion, foreigners, art value of paintings, *id.* 485-495; cave descriptions, *id.* 497-595.

Ájarem : village, Gandaráditya builds a Jain temple at, I, pt. ii, 255.

Ajavarman : defeated by the Ratta chieftain Pittuga, I, pt. ii, 552.

Ajayapála : Chohán king (840), I, pt i, 157.

Ajayapála : Chálukya king (1174-1177), successor of Kumárapála persecuted Jain officers and scholars, is murdered by the door-keeper, I, pt. i, 194-195; said to have been converted to Islám, IX, pt. ii, 26 note 2; said to be the most zealous of Musalmán rulers of Gujarát, *id.* 5 note 1.

Ajepal : shrine of, at Anjár in Cutch, V, 212.

Aji : river in Káthiáwár, VIII, 63.

Ajinthá : *see* Ajanta.

Ajipál : monarch of Kanauj, killed by Nainpál, I, pt. i, 120.

Ajitsingh : son of Mahárája Jasvantsingh of Márwár, causes disturbance (1689-1692), I, pt. i, 288, 289; his plans of rebellion checked (1705), *id.* 294; recovers Jodhpur (1709), *id.* 295, 296; is reconciled with the emperor (1714); gives his daughter to him in marriage, *id.* 297; is appointed forty-seventh viceroy of Gujarát, disagrees with Haidar Kulikhán, *id.* 299-300; is appointed forty-ninth viceroy of Gujarát (1719-1721), *id.* 301.

Ajjana : I, pt. ii, 379 note 1. *See* Ayyana.

Ajmer : village in Káthiáwár, formerly a petty state, VIII, 355.

Ajmir : Mher settlement at, I, pt. i, 136; capital of Chohán kings, *id.* 157, 180; head quarters of Husaini Bráhmans at, IX, pt. ii, 22; saint of, *id.* 6 note 1 (4).

Ajowan : oil plant, cultivated all over India, XXV, 223.

Ajra : forest block in Kolhápur state, XXIV, 22, *id.* 23; town details, position, people, imports, exports, weekly market, history, temples and fair, *id.* 290-291.

Ájurica : old name of Ajra, Somdev composed the Shahdárnav Chandrika at, XXIV, 223.

Ajuriká : Jain temple at, I, pt. ii, 549.

Ajwan : a common food plant, XXV, 161.

Ak : *Calatropis gigantea*, grown on the Western Ghâts, Akbar named after, XXV, 211.

Akabaron : perhaps Khabirun, I, pt. i, 518, 546; perhaps Surat, XVI, 634.

Akalanka : Jain writer, I, pt. ii, 407-408.

Akalankachandra : *see* Akalanka.

Akalankacharita : of spotless behaviour; *biruda* of the Western Chálukya king Satyásraya, I, pt. ii, 432.

Akalankadeva : *see* Akalanka.

Akálavarsha : Ráshtrakuta king of the Gujarát branch, re-establishes himself in the territory of his father Dhruva, I, pt. i, 126.
Akálavarsha : another name of Krishna, the Dakhan Ráshtrakuta king, recovers the disputed area to the south of the Tápti; his grants, I, pt. i, 127-128. *See* Krishna. *Biruda* of Krishna I, I, pt. ii, 390, 399 note 7; of Krishna II, *id.* 410; of Krishna III, *id.* 418-419.
Akalis : Sikh Immortals, gained rank as Bráhmans, IX, pt. i, 438.
Akalkot : origin (1708) of the Rájás of, XX, 289; state, description, boundaries, aspect, rivers, water, geology, climate, rainfall, forests, animals, birds, people, irrigation, crops, money-lending, trade, crafts, land, justice, revenue, schools, dispensary, places, history, XX, 505-510.
A'karávanti : ancient name of Málwa, I, pt. i, 36 and note 1; eastern portion of Málwa, ruled by Gotamíputra, I, pt. ii, 149 and note 4; conquered by Rudradáman, *id.* 160.
Akari : Calotropis gigantea, fibrous plant found in Konkan, XXV, 232.
Akarmásás : Marátha cultivators in Khándesh District, XII, 69; in Thána, XIII, 142-143.
Akarmáshes : *see* Akaramásas.
Akasamukhis : order of Shaiv ascetics, IX, pt. i, 544.
Akash : or Ether, an element, IX, pt. i, 348.
Akas-nim : timber tree, planted in Bombay and Poona, XXV, 104.
Akassi : Agáshi, port under Ahmadsháh, I, pt. ii, 30.
Akbar : Emperor of Delhi (1573-1604), favours the Portuguese, I, pt. ii, 40; interferes in the affairs of the Dakhan and favours the claims of Burhán Martiza's brother (1588), *id.* 623; overruns Khándesh and blockades Asirgad (1599); takes the fort and sends the King of Khándesh prisoner to Hindustán (1600), *id.* 624; struggles with the Sesodiás, I, pt. i, 140, 207, 211, 220; marries Miran Mubárak Khán's daughter at Mándu (1564), *id.* 396; takes Surat in 1573, II, 72; Cambay passes to (1573), VI, 218; conquers Gujarát (1573), VIII, 293; belief about, IX, pt. i, 442; IX, pt. ii, 3 note 1; his quarrel with the Mirzás (1571), *id.* 10; his conquest of Gujarát (1573-1574); slays Jhujhár Khán, *id.* 12; *id.* 14; conversion of, to the Pársi faith (1578), *id.* 190 and note 4, 197 note 2; attempts the capture of Bassein and Daman, XIII, 453; Aurangzib's son, rebels (1697), I, pt. i, 290; sails from Rájápur for Muscat (1686), X, 360, 377.
Akbarpur : the palace at, built by Nasir-ud-din of Málwa (1500-1512), I, pt. i, 365.
Akdia : a petty state and a village in Káthiáwár, VIII, 356.
Akeri : place of interest in Sávantvádi State, X, 463.
Akhalkop : town in Sátára District, temples, fair, XIX, 447-448.
Akham Lobána : of Bráhmanábád, asks help of the King of Hindustán, I, pt. i, 519.
A'khari-cháar-shambah : Sunni holiday, IX, pt. ii, 140. *See* Safar.
Akhatrij : or Akshayatritiya, holiday, IX, pt. i, 23 note 5; *id.* 66; *id.* 157; *id.* 170; *id.* 269; *id.* 313; *id.* 336; day for worship of bull, *id.* 374.
Akhlo : Nandi or godho, Shiv's carrier, IX, pt. i, 374.
Akho : celebrated Soni metaphysician of Ahmadabad, IX, pt. i, 201.
A'khúnd : private house-hold tutor, IX, pt. ii, 176 note 1.
Akika : Sacrifice, rite of, IX, pt. ii, 158. *See* Sacrifice.
Akkádevi : elder sister of the Western Chálukya King of Jayasimha II; governs Kisukad (1021), I, pt. ii, 435, 437; lays siege to the fort of Gokák, *id.* 439; mother of Tôyimadeva, the Hángal Kadamba parince, *id.* 564.
Akka Nágamma : Basav's (1100-68) sister and Vijjal's wife, XXIV, 119.
Ak-khazár : or Fair Khazár, division of Khazárs; said to be white Húnas; their appearance, IX, pt. i, 473.
Akkivat : siege of, by Parasharambhau (1777), XXI, 384; village in Belgaum District, fort at, *id.* 510.
Akkuka : brother of Prachanda, I, pt i, 129.
Akloli : in Thána District, tomb at, XIV, 56; hot springs, *id.* 374.
Akluj : town in Sholápur District, Aurangzeb at, General Wellesley halts at (1803), XX, 288, 407.
Akola : in Ahmadnagar District, sub-divisional survey, XVII, 483-89; sub-divisional details, area, aspect, hills, rivers, soil, climate, cultivation, irrigation, crops, people, roads, markets, trades, crafts, survey, changes, *id.* 587-92; town, temples, *id.* 711-12.
A'kota : village near Baroda City, I, pt. i, 125.
Akráni : pargana in Khándesh District; held by a Rájput after the decline of Musalmán power; taken by the Peshwa (1817); by the English (1818), I, pt. ii, 633; teak forest in, XII, 19; petty division, position, boundaries, aspect, hills, water, climate, people, trade, roads, history, *id.* 421-24; fort, *id.* 431.
Akrurésvara : modern Anklésvara, I, pt. i, 115; I, pt. ii, 314.
Akrut : timber tree, XXV, 121.
Aksáli (Agsali) : caste of goldsmiths in Kánarese districts, XV, pt. i, 258-60.
Akshayatritiya : Hindu holiday, XVIII, pt. i, 243; *see* also Akhatrij.
Akshi : village in Kolába District, its trade with Bombay, temples at, XI, 253.
Akulesvara : I, pt. ii, 314; *see* Akrurésvara.
Akurli : village in Thána District, XIV, 2; carvings and Páli letters at, *id.* 51, 101; a temple at, *id.* 102.
Al : Indian mulberry, a red dye plant, its cultivation, use in dyeing cloths, XII, 24, 163-64, 229; *see* also XXV, 200.
A'láchhala : spirit treatment resorted to by Meman women, IX, pt. ii, page 56 note 4. *See* Memans.
Alaf Khán : I, pt. i, 190; brother of Alá-ud-din Khilji, leads an expedition against Gujarát

and conquers it (1297), invades Somnáth; constructs a Jáma mosque at Anahilaváda with white marble pillars taken from Jain temples, *id.* 205; Governor of Gujarát, re-inforces Malik Káfur; carries Devaladevi to Delhi, I, pt. ii, 532; *see* also IX, pt. ii, 125, 2; VIII, 284; spreads Islam by force; and introduces the Musalmán faith from Anahilavád to Broach, IX, pt. ii, 3-5.

Alakhana: Gurjjara king (890), I, pt. i, 3; cedes Takkades'a, *id.* 468.

Alaktaka Nagari: village, I, pt. ii, 344 note 6.

Alam Ali Khán: deputy Viceroy of the Dakhan, pursues the Nizám, is defeated and slain at Bálápur (1720), I, pt. i, 301.

Alamgir II: Azizuddin, son of Jahándar Sháh, succeeds to the throne of Delhi (1754-59), I, pt. i, 339.

Alam Prabhu: temple at Alta, in Kolhápur State, XXIV, 292.

Alampur: village and a petty State in Káthiáwár, VIII, 356.

Alámút: hill fort of Dailam in Persia; establishment of Hasan Sabáh's power at, IX, pt. ii, 37 and note 5; *id.* 40; *id.* 48.

Alan Albanian: Húna gates, one of the Caspian gates, IX, pt. i, 473 note 4.

Alandatirtha: identified with Alundah, I, pt. ii, 357.

Alande: town, I, pt. ii, 482.

Alandi: village in Poona District, temples, fair, municipality, history, XVIII, pt. iii, 102-104.

Alang: fort in Násik District, XVI, 441, 447, 449.

Alang (Manár): village with a temple in Káthiáwár, VIII, 356.

Alangi: timber tree found in Dakhan and Konkan, XXV, 82.

Alangium Larmarckii: timber tree found in Konkan and Dakhan, XXV, 82; a food plant, *id.* 161; antidote to snake bite, *id.* 274.

Alang Kulang: forts in Ahmadnagar District, XVII, 4; blown up by Captain Mackintosh (1819-20), subordinate to Ratangad (1818), 732, 736.

Alankára Chudámani: work on rhetoric, compiled by Hemachandra, I, pt. i, 193.

A'lap Khán: General of Alá-ud-din Khilji, defeats the Rájput king of Sanján; drives away the Pársis from Sanján (1315), IX, pt. ii, 187; probably Ulugh Khán, brother to Alá-ud-din; may be Alap Khán, brother-in-law to Alá-ud-din, *id.* 187 note 3. *See* Ulgh Khán.

Al A'si: father of Usmán, Governor of Bahrein and Umán (Persian Gulf) in A. D. 636, I, pt. i, 505.

Alá-ud-din: Emperor of Delhi (1296-1315); his excuse for entering the Dakhan (1294), IX, pt. ii, p. 2 note 3; converts Kananj Bráhman priests of Bahucheraji, *id.* 82; desecrates the Somnáth temple, I, i, pt. 190, 207, 229, 512, 515; his General conquers Somnáth Patan (1295-1316), VIII, 284; defeats the Sumras, V, 133; captures and plunders Cambay (1304), VI, 216; IX, pt. ii, 187 and note 3; his power established in Gujarát, XIII, 438; overthrows Devgiri Yádavs, his General sacks Sanján, XIV, 84, 302, defeats Rámdev of Devgiri, *id.* 418; defeats Ballál III, XV, pt. ii, 91; defeats Rámdev of Devgiri, *id.* 93, his death, *id.* 94; *another account*: defeats Rámdev of Devgiri, XXII, 401-402; invades the Dakhan and conquers the Devgiri Yádavs (1294); defeats the Yádav king Rámchandra and his son Sámkara and concludes peace with the former (1294), I, pt. ii, 250-51, 531, 619; murders treacherously his uncle Jalál-ud din and ascends the throne of Delhi (1295), *id.* 531-32; sends an expedition to recover Devaladevi (1306), *id.* 532; sends Malik Káfur and Khwája Háji to reduce the Hoysalas (1310), *id.* 509, 533; is poisoned by Malik Káfur (1316), *id.* 513; Bahmani ruler of Cheul (1347-58), XI, 273.

Alá-ud din II: Bahmani king sends an army into the Konkan (1436), I, pt. ii, 31; captures Burhánpur and besieges the fort of Laling (1437), *id.* 620-21; (1435-57), XXIV, 224.

Alaudinae: order of birds found in the Dakhan and at Dápoli in Ratnágiri District, X, 84.

Alawandi: village, inscription at (1203), I, pt. ii, 502 and note 1.

Alay: clod-crusher, a Kánara field tool, XV, pt. ii, 12.

A'lazikri-His-Salam: IX, pt. ii, 37. *See* Hasan.

Al Bailámán: identified with Bhinmál, expedition against, I, pt. i, 109; *id.* 467.

Alban: Lieutenant, disarms and shoots Mustaphakhán, the Arab leader in revolt at Sunth, I, pt. i, 441.

Albert Edward Institute: Reading room and library in Poona Cantonment, description of, XVIII, pt. iii, 360.

Alberuni (Abu Rihan): Arab writer, I, pt. i, 78 and note, 81, 167 note 1; traveller (970-1039), I, pt. i, 453, 500, 507 and note 9; his mention of Sanján as Subára (1030), XIV, 302 note 4, 321; (1020) mentions Banavas, XV, pt. ii, 265.

Al Biláduri: Ahmed bin Yáhya, surnamed Abu Jáfer, writer of Futuh-ul-Buldán (892), I, pt. i, 505 and note 3, 506, 513 and notes 8 and 9, 520.

Albiruni: *See* Alberuni.

Albizzia: *odoratissima*, its leaves used as fodder, XXV, pt. 278; *procera*, timber tree found in Konkan and Dakhan, *id.* 70; a famine plant, *id.* 199; produces a dye, *id.* 244; used for poisoning fish, *id.* 272; *stipulata*, timber tree, common on ghats, *id.* 70; used as fodder, *id.* 278.

Albuquerque: Portuguese Viceroy, provides wives for his soldiers from the country women; I, pt. ii, 47; establishes customs houses and appoints magistrates, *id.* 52; conciliates the goodwill of the natives, *id.* 58; captures Goa from the Bijápur king (1510), *id.* 641; his notice of Maskat as a ship-building centre (1510), XIII, 470.

Alch: food plant cultivated throughout India, XXV, 174.

Ale: market town in Poona District, fair at, XVIII, pt. III, 104.

Alech: hills in Káthiáwár, VIII, 9-10.

Alem: food plant, cultivated throughout India, XXV, 174.

Aleppo: Balúchis said to have come from, IX, pt. ii, 17.

Aleurites: *Moluccana*, timber and food plant cultivated in many parts of Bombay, XXV, 121, 171; yields good oil, *id.* 220, *triloba*, food plant, yields good oil, *id.* 171, 220.

Alexander: the Great, Macedonian emperor (B.C. 326-325). I, pt. i, 164 note 5, 497, 532, 535, 537, 544-45; invasion by; brings the Greeks in contact with the Hindus, Introduction to the early History of the Dakhan, I, ii; I, pt. ii, 5; connection of the successors of, with Puranic kings and dynasties, *id.* 146; relations of Chandragupta with one of the successors of, *id.* 155, 162; opposed by the Káthis, invades India (B.C. 327), VIII, 128, 272; accepted as god-born conqueror, IX, pt. i, 441; his sacrifices to rivers, IX, pt. i, 445; probable date of his entering India, IX, pt. i, 455; IX, pt. ii, 211 note 2 (9), (10), (11); XIII, 404 note 3.

Alexander Point: at Mátherán in Kolába District, XIV, 237, 280, 281.

Alexandria: mosques at (642-643), IX, pt. ii, 31 note 1. Hindus at (A.D. 135-150), XIII, 414; Hindus settled in (A.D. 500), *id.* 420.

Alfonso Martin: owner of the town Grebondel, I, pt. ii, 64.

Algaroba: food plant, lately introduced in India, XXV, 154.

Alhagi maurorum: plant, its leaves used as fodder, XXV, 278.

Al Hajjáj: (714), I, pt. i, 506.

Al Hind: India, I, pt. i, 505 note 5, 507.

Ali: husband of Fátimah, daughter of the Prophet, IX, pt. ii, 7, *id* 16, *id.* 127; father of Hasan and Husain, *id.* 47, *id.* 136; his family falls a victim to the Umayad Khalífahs of Damascus, *id.* 47 note 1; his titles, *id.* 36 note 3, *id.* 47, *id.* 137; his explanation of Allah, *id.* 41 note 1; Shiáh veneration and Sunni reverence for, *id.* 47; Sayads claim descent from, *id.* 6 note 1, 7; His Highness Ágha Khán traces his descent from, *id.* 38; shrine of, *id.* 47, *id.* 45, *id.* 125; believed to have been incarnated in the person of A'gha Islámsháh, *id.* 40.

Ali: *see* Sháh Ali Adil.

Ali: founder of the Alia Bohora sect (1624), IX, pt. ii, 27, *id.* 33.

Alia Bohorás: *see* Bohoras.

A'li A'dil Sháh: succeeds his father Ibráhim A'dil Sháh on the throne of Bijápur (1557), I, pt. ii, 644; negotiates a treaty of alliance with Vijayanagar and carries on war with Ahmadnagar, *id.* 623, 644; joins the Musalman confederacy against Vijayanagar (1564), and marries the Nizám Sháhi princess Chánd Bibi; overthrow of Vijayanagar (1565), *id.* 623, 644-645; interferes with the internal disputes of Vijayanagar and provokes the jealousy of Ahmadnagar; fails to recover Goa from the Portuguese; takes the fort of Adoni; invades the Southern Marátha country (1573); his conquest south of the Tungbhadra; desertion of Marátha cavalry; second failure to recover Goa (1570), *id.* 645-646; his death (1580), *id.* 647. *See* also XXIII, 416-419; his tomb in Bijápur city, *id.* 613.

A'li A'dil Sháh II: succeeds his father Muhammad A'dil Sháh (1656), I, pt. ii, 651; makes peace with Aurangzib (1657); sends Afzul Khán against Shiváji; takes the field in person against Shiváji; goes to the Karnátak and is attacked by the rebel Sidi Johár; makes humiliating peace with Shiváji (1662); renews hostilities with Shiváji and Aurangzib (1664); makes peace with Aurangzib and buys off Shiváji with an annual payment, *id.* 652-653; his death (1672), *id.* 653. *See* also XXIII, 428-431; tomb of, in Bijápur, *id.* 612.

Ali A'kbar: of Ispahán, governor of Surat and Cambay, I, pt. i, 280; his assassination (1646), *id.* 280.

Alibág: town in Kolába District, I, pt. i, 386; sub-division in Kolába District, I, pt. ii, 96; village exchanges with chief of (1818-1840); its lapse to the British (1840), XI, 159 and note 2, *id.* 190; two Kulkarni families in charge of large groups of salt rice villages, *id.* 177 note 4; condition, revenue system, cost and profit of rice tillage, garden assessment, British changes, survey and assessment of garden and salt rice lands (1840-1852), *id.* 190-196; their effect (1856), *id.* 196; low survey rates introduced (Revdanda, 1857 and Underi 1858), *id.* 176, *id.* 198-201; revision of salt rice lands or Khárápát (1872), *id.* 176, *id.* 210, 211; sub-divisional details; boundaries, area, aspect, climate, water, soil, holdings, rental, stock produce, people, *id.* 1, *id.* 240-242; town, appearance, climate, harbour, trade, water-supply, *id.* 253-255; water works, houses, people, history, objects, *id.* 256-259; Hirákot, Kolába fort, *id.* 260-265, *id.* 469.

Alibág: fort near Kelve, in Thána district, XIV, 2, 98; description of, *id.* 200.

Al Idrisi: Abu Abdallah Muhammad, Arab traveller, author of Nuzhat-ul-Mushták (1100), I, pt. i, 508 and note 10, 509 note 5, 510, 511, 512 and note 1, 516, 517 and note 2, 519, 521, 523, 524, 525, 526, 527, 528, 529, 531, *id.* pt. ii, 4; African traveller, his mention of Sapára (1153), XIV, 321.

Alif Khan: *see* Álaf Khan.

Alifsháis: *see* Benawa Beggars.

Aliga: Portuguese name for the Kálinadi river in Kánara district, XV, pt. ii, 101, 112, 118, 249, 332.

Aligadde: place of interest in Kánara district, XV, pt. ii, 249.

Ali-Iláhiva: a sect, mentioned by Farishtah, IX, pt. ii, 33.

Alikapudan: Sidhi, Turkish traveller, his notice of Bhats as safeguards, IX, pt. i, 210 note 1.

Alinga: appointed second counsellor, I, pt. i, 184. *See* Sajjana.

Alisháh: Gujarát Musalman admiral at Chaul (1528), XIII, 449; defeated by the Portuguese in Bombay harbour, *id.* 450.

Ali Shahid: mosque of, in Bijápur city, XXIII, 632.

Alismaceæ : species of food plants, found in Belgaum and Dhárwár districts, XXV, 183.
Al Istakhri, Abu Is-hák : author of Kitáb-ul-Akálim (951), I, pt. i, 509 note 3, 510 note 1, 511 and notes 3 and 4, 512, 514 and notes 2 and 3, 516 notes 6 and 7, 520 and note 10, 523 ; Aráb writer (951), I, pt. ii, 388 ; places Sapára between Cambay and Sanján, XIV, 321.
Alitker : *see* Sultánkar.
Al Jauhari : Aráb writer (982-999), I, pt. i, 508 note 10, 525, 526.
Alkaris : madder growers, XII, 69.
Al Kazwini : Zakariah Ibu Muhammad, author of A'sar-ul-Bilad (1263-1275), I, pt. i, 509 note 2, 510 and note 1, 516 and note 14, 517 note 1, 529.
Alk Palka : hills in Násik district, captured by Khán Khánán, the Mughal General (1635), XVI, 420 and note 2.
Alla : pass in the Dakhan, I, pt. ii, 608.
Allahábád : inscription of Samudragupta at, I, pt. i, 63, 65 ; pillar inscription at, I, pt. ii, 280, 293, 311, 317 ; prince of tirthás, religiously called Prayag, IX, pt. i, 550 ; place of pilgrimage, *id.* 157 ; *id.* 168 ; *id.* 176 ; *id.* 220.
Allah Band: a sand bank thrown across the Khori (eastern mouth of the Indus), in Cutch, by the earthquake of 1179, V, 10.
Alláh-o-Akbar : (God is Great), IX, pt. ii, 126 ; *id.* 141 ; *id.* 154 ; *id.* 160 note 3 ; *id.* 169.
Allapur : suburb of Bijápur, founded by Yusuf-Adil-Shah, XXIII, 577, 583.
Alla-ud-din : *see* Ala-ud-din.
Alligator : (Magar) said to be ridden by a witch ; god of the Bhils, Varlis, and Dublas, IX, pt. i, 380.
Allitrochades : Bindusára, son of Chandragupta, I, pt. i, 534.
Allium : cepa (kauda), common food plant, XXV, 179 ; *porrum*, not cultivated in Bombay Presidency, *id.* 180 ; *sativum* (lassun), common food plant, *id.* 179.
Allophylus cobbe : food plant, common all over India, XXV, 150.
All Souls Day : IX, pt. ii, 216. *See* Farvardin Jasan.
Alluraka : identified with Alura, I, pt. ii, 370 and note 3.
Al Mahdi : Khalifah (775-785), I, pt. i, 525.
Al Mámun : Abbási Khalifah (813-833), I, pt. i, 506, 520.
Al Masudi : Abul Hasan, Arab traveller (915-944) I, pt. i, 505 note 5, 506 note 8, 510, 512, 513, 514, 516, 518 and note 4, 520, 521, 523, 524, 525, 526, 527, 528, 529, 531, I, pt ii, 4, 387, 388.
Almeida, Francis D. : *See* D'almeida, Francis.
Almel: village in Bijápur District, with temples, mosques and a pond, XXIII, 548-549.
Al Murri : Abdur Rahmán, I, pt. i, 513.
Almustaáli : (1094-1101), younger son of Khalifáh Almustansir-billah ; his dispute with his brother Nazar for succession ; Mustaálians are called after his name, IX, pt. ii, 30 note 1.
Almustansir-Billah : (1036-1094) Khalifáh of Egypt. dispute for the succession to the Khilafat between his two sons Nazár and Almustaáli, IX, pt. ii, 30 note 1.
Al Mutawakkil : I, pt. i, 505 note 3.
Alnávar : village with railway station in Dhárwár District, XXII, 650.
Aloe : *Indica*, XXV, 206; *litoralis*, *id.* 206 ; *perfoliata*, *id.* 206.
Alompra : dynasty of, in Burma, I, pt. ii, 346 note 4
Alor : town in the Punjáb or Sind, I, pt. i, 538.
Alpam : plant in Bombay and Konkan, used as antidote to snake-bite, XXV, 275.
Alpinia cardamomum : food plant found in Kánara, XXV, 176.
Alp Khán, Governor of Gujarát (1310), I, pt. i, 229 note 6 ; Alá-ud-din Khilji's General, (1300-1318), conquers Sanján, XIII, 438 ; sacks Sanján, XIV, 302. *See* Alaf Khan.
Alseodaphne semecarpifolia : timber tree found all along the Western Gháts, XXV, 113.
Alsi : oil-yielding and fibrous plant found in several districts, XXV, 215, 231.
Alstonia scholaris : timber and medicinal plant common in Bombay forests, XXV, 100, 259.
Alta : town in Kolhápur, survey details of, XXIV, 256 ; town details, market, school, temples, mosque, *id.* 291-292.
Alternanthesa sessilis : plant used as pot herb, XXV, 203.
Altmash : Shamsh-ud-din, conquers Sind (1211-1236), V, 132.
Alu : timber and food plant found in several districts, XXV, 87, 182.
Aluka : King of, conquered by Kirtivarman I, I, pt. ii, 281, 345.
Alukas : division of the Nágas, I, pt. ii, 309. *See* Alupas.
Alum, manufacture of, in Cutch, V, 19-20.
Alundah : village near Sátára City on the Sivaganga, tributary of the Nira, I, pt. ii, 357.
Alupa : *see* Alupai.
Alupai : town on the Malabár coast I, pt. ii, 309 note 8.
Alupas : possibly Nágas, I, pt. ii, 281 note 3 ; ruling race of Malabár, *id.* 183 ; conquered by Kirtivarman I (367-597), *id.* 309 and note 8 ; their loyalty secured by Pulakesi II, *id.* 189, 282, 309, 350 ; hereditary servants of the Western Chalukya Kings, *id.* 300 ; King of the, renders obeisance to Vikramáditya VI, *id.* 216, 444 ; defeated by Jayakesin I (1052-53), *id.* 309, 567 ; Parthian chiefs (630), XXIII, 380 and note 4.
Alur : village in Dhárwár District, I, pt. ii, 8 ; inscriptions at, *id.* 282 note 3, 379 note 1, 419, 434, 458 note 2, 527, 564 note 5.
Alura : village in Gujarát, I, pt. ii, 370 note 3.
Aluva : Alupa prince, I, pt. ii, 370.
Aluvas : I, pt. ii, 300, 309 ; defeated by Vinayáditya, son of Vikramáditya I, *id.* 368. *See* Alupas.
Alva : State in Rewa Kantha, VI, 143.

Alysicarpus: *rugosus A. styracifolius*, famine plants found in Poona and other districts, XXV, 198.

Am: very common timber and fruit tree, XXV, 53. *See* Amb.

Ama: Vaisya chief (A.D. 743), Oswals said to have been descended from, IX, p. i, 496.

Amal: food plant cultivated in India and other countries, XXV, 144.

Amála: Bhil State in Khandesh District, XII, 604.

Amalánanda: author of the Vedánta Kalpa Taru, I, pt. ii, 246.

Amalner: sub-division of Khandesh District, its boundaries, area, aspect, climate, water, soil, holdings, survey details, survey results, stocks, crops, people, XII, 2, *id.* 342-348; fort, history, town, *id.* 431.

Amaltas: timber tree common in the Konkan and the Ghâts, XXV, 63.

A'mana: Yádava King, succeeds his father Mahádev (1271), but is dethroned by his cousin Rámadeva, I, pt. ii, 247, 519, 528.

Amánat Khan: military Governor of Surat (1690), I, pt. i, 288. *See* Itimád Khán.

Amara: Place of interest in Cutch, a fair at, V, 210.

Amárabhata: Sanskrit form of A'mbada, I, pt. i, 185 note 3.

Amaraganga: son and successor of the Devagiri Yadava King Mallugi I, pt. ii, 517, 519.

Amaragángeya: I, pt. ii, 235; ancestor of Mallugi, *id.* 516 and note 4.

Amaragol: village in Hubli Táluka, Dhárwár District, inscription at, I, pt. ii, 568 note 5, also XXII, 650.

Amarah: timber tree, common all over India, XXV, 56.

Amarakosa: Sanskrit lexicon, I, pt. ii, 248.

Amara Mallugi: Yádava King, son of Mallugi and successor of Govindarája, I, pt. ii, 235, 516.

Amaranthaceæ: species of food and famine plant, XXV, 169, 203.

Amaranthus: *campestris, frumentaceus, giganteus, paniculatus, polygonoides, spinosus, tristis, viridis*, food plants, XXV, 169; *oleraceus*, sacred plant, *id.* 293.

Amarasimha: lexicographer, I, pt. ii, 142; writer of Namalingaanusasana, *id.* 530.

Amardád: Amshaspánd, seventh day of Pársi month; fifth month of the Pársi year, IX, pt. ii, 217.

Amardád Jasan: high festival day, IX, pt. ii, 217. *See* Jasans.

A'mardáka: branch of Saivism, I, pt. i, 138.

Amargol: *see* Amaragol.

Amarji: dewán of Junágadh (1759-1784), I, pt. i, 70.

Amaryllideæ: species of famine and fibrous plants, XXV, 204, 235.

Amas: no-moon day, IX, p. i, 397.

Amb (amba): mango fruit tree found in all districts, XXV, 53, 150, 250, 279, 284, 289, 291, XVIII, pt. i, 4; worship of, by women, leaves and buds of, held to be the arrows of god Madan, IX, pt. i, 382.

Ambá: village in Nizám's dominions, record at, I, pt. ii, 523; in charge of Singhana's minister Rámadeva, *id.* 524.

Ambá: *see* Vijayambá.

Ambá: hill pass in Ratnágiri, X, 166 and note 2; I, pt. ii, 78; XXIV, 5; blockaded (1700-1701), I, pt. ii, 80, 661.

Ambá: river in Kolábá, XI, 7-8.

Ambá: *see* Amb.

Amba, Ambábái, Amba Bhavani, Ambaji: Hindu goddess, IX, pt. i, 20, *id.* 64, 177, 196, 213; inscription in the temple of, at Kolhápur, I, pt ii, 223-224; description of temple of; pilgrims to temple of, holidays in honour of, XXIV, 309-311; an ancient shrine and a place of pilgrimage in Mahi Kantha, V, 432-433, IX, pt. i, 187; performance of bhavais at, *id.* 223 note 1, 225; visited by Kanbis, *id.* 157; by Gujarát depressed classes, *id.* 333, 341; a favourite deity, the ideal mother, IX, pt. i, pp. xxxv, xxxvi; consort of Shiv, *id.* 220; Durga worshipped at Arasur as, *id.* 301 note 2; shrine of, on Mount Abu, *id.* XI, 549, invocation of, *id.* xxxv.

A'mbada: son of Udayana, rises to eminence in the reign of Kumárapála, I, pt i, 170; fights with Mallikárjuna and in a second fight kills him for which he is honoured with the title of Rájápitámaha, *id* 185-186, 186, 194; refuses submission to Ajayapála in religious matters and is killed in a fight, *id.* 195; general of Kumárapála Solanki, I, pt. ii, 19; defeats Mallikárjuna, *id.* 24; defeats Mallikárjuna, the Konkan King, near Bulsár (1150), XIII, 426, *id.* 436.

Ambadah: timber tree found in Konkan and Malabár, XXV, 56.

Ambadári Ghát: pass in Konkan, I, pt. ii, 77.

Ambádi: brown hemp, its cultivation in Khándesh, XII, 153, *id.* 162; crop of, in Sátára, XIX, 165. *See* also XXV, 147, 226.

Amba Ghát: *see* Amba (pass).

Ambaji: *see* Ambábái.

Ambaka: Sanskrit form of A'mbada, I, pt. i, 185 note 3.

Ambakagráma: village in the Dakhan, I, pt. ii, 398.

Ambáli: village in Baroda with a sacred temple, VII, 553.

Ambálika: Buddhist monastery, its probable site, XIV, 7 note 1; mentioned in inscriptions, *id.* 119, 168, 179.

Ambápátaka: village, grant of, to a Jain temple at Navasári, I, pt. i, 125.

Ambar: Sidi governor of Janjira (1621), XI, 435.

Ambarah: timber and food tree yields gum, common in India, XXV, 56, 151, 250.

Ambardi: stream in Kolhápur, XXIV, 9.

Ambari: *see* Ambádi.

Ambari-Chuka: very common food plant, XXV, 170.

Ambarisha: mythological king, I, pt. ii, 149.

Ambarkhána: in Poona City, house built for Shiváji, XVIII, pt. iii, 331.

Ambarnáth: village and temple in Thána district, XIV, 2; remains at, I, pt. ii, 22, temple of, near Kalyán, record at, *id.* 543 and note 1; *see* also IX, pt. i, 480 note 4, XIII, 66 and XIV, 2-8, 385; Siláhár remains

at, XIII, 428; archæological remains at, XIV, 10; resemblance of the temple with Jogeshvari cave, *id.* 112; and Lonád temple, *id.* 213.
Ambat: timber tree in Konkan and Malabár, XXV, 56.
Ambavli: hill pass in Ratnágiri district, X, 166; a road through, *id.* 178.
Ambegaon: a village in Násik district, Hemadpanti temple at, XVI, 416; village in Poona district, XVIII, pt. iii, 102; survey of, *id.* pt. ii, 455-457.
Ambern: village, inscription at, I, pt. ii, 240, 242.
A'mbenal: pass in Ratnágiri district, XI, 114.
Ambenala: *see* Fitz-gerald pass.
Ambera: Chálukya princess of, grants the village of Periyála to Bráhmans, I, pt. ii, 358 note 1.
Amberee: food plant found on the Gháts, XXV, 56, 151.
Amberi: *see* Amberee.
Ambernáth: *see* Ambarnáth.
Ambgul: food plant, XXV, 171.
Ambhoi: kidney disease, its cure, IX, pt. i, 365.
Ambi, Ambig: a caste of fishermen in Kánara district, their occupations, ceremonies, XV, pt. i, 301-304; in Dhárwár district, XXII, 183-4; in Kolhápur, XXIV, 104.
Ambiká: goddess, temple of, at Kodinár, I, pt. i, 182 and note; image of, at Sopára, XIV, 341.
Ambika: River in the Surat district, IX, pt. ii, 66; in Baroda, VII, 581-582.
Ambira: stream in Kolhápur, XXIV, 9.
A'mbivli: village and cave in Thána district, XIV, 9, 10.
Ambli: *see* Amli.
Amblogyna: food plant, XXV, 169.
Ambo: Saint of the Bharvad peasants, IX, pt. i, 269.
Ambo: *see* Amb.
Ambolgad: fort in Ratnágiri district, X, 317.
Amboli: village in Sávantwádi, future sanitarium, X, 463; hill pass, XXI, 305; XXIV, 5, 6; pass between Trimbak and Mokháda, XIII, 5, 319.
Ambor: timber and food plant found in gardens, XXV, 126, 172.
Ambran: village in Káthiáwár, VIII, 356.
Ambuli: pass in Poona district, XVIII, pt. ii, 151.
Ambuti: food plant, XXV, 148, 196.
Amerdád Sál: chief high day of Pársis, IX, pt. ii, 219. *See* festivals (season).
America: Bombay trade with (1800-1810), XIII, 519, *id.* 520.
A'mbal: I, pt. i, 511. *See* Anahilaváda.
A'mil: sub-divisional officer, I, pt. i, 210, 212; exorcist; services of, used by women to cast out the spirit of barrenness, IX, pt. ii, 147-149; his experiences during the performance of Chilláh or forty days term, *id.* 144.
Amildárs: revenue and judicial officer under Bijápur Kings (1489-1686), XIX, 229-230.
Amin: chief treasurer, I, pt. i, 212, 214; principal Sadar, high judicial appointment, IX, pt. ii, 198 note 5.
Aminbhávi: village in the Dhárwár district, I, pt. ii, 358 note 1; XXII, 440; inscriptions at, *id.* 650.
Amir-al-Umra Malik Aiaz Sultani: unites his squadron with the Turkish fleet (1508), I, pt. ii, 44.
Amiráni Sadah: insurrection of (1346), I, pt. i, 230.
Amir Husan: admiral of the Turkish fleet, I, pt. ii, 44.
Amirkhán: Rághoba's general, I, pt. I, 405.
Amir Khusrau: author of Tarikh-i-Alai, I, pt. i, 515; writer (thirteenth century), IX, pt. ii, 10 note 3; *id.* 65-187 note 3, 188 note 2.
Amir Timur: (1400), introduces Taáziahs, IX, pt. ii, 139 note 1.
Amir-ud-din Nuzahat: Sayad, author of Nuzhat-ul-Akhbár, IX, pt. ii, 50 note 2.
Amjera: village in Gujarát, rising at, I, pt. i, 439.
Amla: timber tree common in the Presidency, XXV, 115, 259.
Amlee: food plant, XXV, 154.
Amli: tamarind tree, XXV, 65, 153, 171, 198; held to be wife of Brahma, much haunted by spirits, and worshiped accordingly, IX, pt i, 382; food plant, XXV, 119.
Amma I: Eastern Chálukya king (918-925), I, pt. ii, 316 note 5, 417.
Amma II: Eastern Chálukya king, coronation of (945), I, pt. ii, 399 note 7, 419 note 2.
Ammaiyyanabhávi: village, I, pt. ii, 358 note 1.
Amma-kudaga: a tribe near the Kaveri river, raised to be Brahmans, IX, pt. i, 436.
Ammanadeva: grandson of Kokkala I, king of Chedi, I, pt. ii, 415.
Ammanayya: Kalachurya Somesvara's officer (1176), I, pt. ii, 486.
Ammania baccifera: a poisonous herb, XXV, 265.
Ammianus Marcellinus: Soldier-historian, IX, pt. i, 437 note 2.
Ammugi: son of the Kalachurya king Sandaraja, I, pt. ii, 468.
A'mod: sub-division of Broach district, boundary; area; aspect; climate; water-supply; soil; assessment; resources; occupancy; value of land produce; population and public health, II, 537, 538; town, *id.* 549; Molesalam, Thákor of, IX, pt. ii, 68.
Amoghavarsha: *biruda* of Vaddiga, I, pt. ii, 418; of Kakka II, *id.* 423.
Amoghavarsha I: Dakhan Ráshtrakuta King, I, pt. i, 123, 124; invades Gujarát, *id.* 125, 126, 128, 525; I, pt. ii, 11, 17, 210; succeeds his father Govind III, *id.* 199, 395, 401; attempts to prevent his accession, *id.* 408 note 4, 409; his *birudas* (honorific titles), *id.* 401; his epithets, crest, hereditary title, and musical instrument, *id.* 402; his conquests, *id.* 199, 402, 403; his Siláhára feudatories, *id.* 404, 405, 541, 542; records of his reign, *id.* 387, 400, 403-408; founds, *id.* 199, and completes the fortification of Mányakheta and makes it his capital, *id.* 403; abdicates in favour of his son Krishna II, *id.* 403; his Jain preceptor, *id.* 200, 407

and notes 4 and 5; his conversion to the Jain faith, *id.* 208; author of the Prásnottara Ratanmáliká, *id.* 200, 403; his successor, *id.* 410 note 2; XIII, 424; mention of, in Kanheri caves, XIV, 148, 173, 177; XV, pt. ii, 84, 85 note 2.
Amoghavarsha II: Ráshtrakuta King, I, pt. ii, 210; succeeds his father Indra III; dies soon after, *id.* 204 and note 1, 414 note 5, 416 notes 4, 5 and 6.
Amoghavarsha III: Ráshtrakuta King, I, pt. ii, 210; succeeds his nephew Govinda IV, *id.* 205-207. *See* Baddiga and Vaddiga.
Amoghavarsha IV: I, pt. ii, 210. *See* Karka II.
Amoghavarshya: mistaken form of Amoghavarsha, I, pt. ii, 416 note 4.
Amoghodaya: Amoghavarsha I, I, pt. ii, 201.
Amoora: *cucullata,* timber tree found on Pár Ghát in Bombay, XXV, 43; *lawii,* found at Khandála and Pár Ghát in Bombay, *id.* 44; *rohituka,* found at Khandála and on the Western Gháts, *id.* 43.
Amorphophallus: *bulbiferous* food plant indigenous to Bengal, XXV, 183; *campanulatus,* (suran), cultivated throughout India for its tuber, *id.* 182, 207; *sylvaticus,* a famine plant, *id.* 208.
Ampelidæ: order of birds in Ratnágiri district, X, 80.
Ampelideæ: species of food plant, XXV, 150.
Amra: food plant, XXV, 151.
Amrabbata: *see* Ambada, I, pt. i.
Amraká: place in Surat district, I, pt. ii, 294.
Amrakárdava: Gupta Chief, I, pt. i. 66.
Amrápur: estate in Rewa Kantha, VI, 151; -táluka in Káthiáwár, VIII, 356-357.
Amratvel: village in Káthiáwár, its history, VIII, 357.
Amravátaka [Amravátavaka]; village in Southern Konkan; grant of, I, pt. ii, 186, 356.
Amrávati: coins at, I, pt. ii, 167; pillar inscription at, I, pt ii, 331.
Amrávati: river in Rewa Kántha, VI, 5.
Amrávati: *see* Medad.
Amr-ibnul A'as: Muslim conqueror of Egypt, constructs the first pulpit built in Islam, IX, pt. ii 131 note 1.
Amriteshvar: temple in Poona city, built by Bajirav I's sister, XVIII, pt. iii, 331.
Amriteshvara: temple of, at Annigere, in Dhárwár district; inscription at, I, pt. ii, 502 note 7, 518 note 3.
Amriteshvara: officer of Vira-Ballála II, Hoysala King (1202), I, pt. ii, 506.
Amritrao: *see* Amrutrao.
Amru: very common famine plant, XXV, 196.
Amru Bin Jamal Taghlabi: Arab Commander of an expedition to Balabha (Porbandar), I, pt. i, 524.
Amrul: common food plant, XXV, 148.
Amrut Ráo: Peshwá's adoptive brother, gives shelter to Mahadji Sindiá's wives; is attacked by Shirzi Ráo Ghatge; appointed to the Government of Poona by Holkar (1802); allows his son to be placed on the throne; retires before General Wellesley (1803); comes to terms with the English, serves with them during the war, and is pensioned; I, pt. ii, 607-609; Bajiráv's half brother, his hostility to Sindia, XVIII, pt. ii, 275, 276; becomes Peshwa (1802), *id.* 282; leaves Poona for Sangamner, *id.* 283.
Amsala: King, of Shrivardhana, I, pt. ii, 520.
Amshaspánds: Immortal Furtherers; Hafta; seven days of the month and seven months of the year named after, IX, pt. ii, 215, 216.
Amsuvarman: inscription of, I, pt. i, 81.
Amulets: faith of women in; objects of, IX, pt. ii, 220. *See* Beliefs (Early).
Amygdaloid: rock in Poona district XVIII, pt. i, 9-13; beds of, in Bijápur district, XXIII, 43.
Amygdalus: *communis* (badam) cultivated in Bombay city, XXV, 154; Persica (peach) cultivated in Dakhan and Mahábaleshvar, *id.* 155.
Anacardiaceæ: a species of timber, fruit and oil-yielding trees, XXV, 53, 150, 216, 250.
Anacárdium occidentale: (cashewnut tree) timber and fruit tree, yields oil and liquor, XXV, 53, 150, 210, 216, 250.
Anagnitra: people keeping no sacred fire, IX, pt. i, 447.
Anahilapattana: Chálukya dynasty of, I, pt. ii, 212, 242. *See* Anahilaváda.
Anahilapura: *see* Anahilaváda.
Anahilaváda: Chávadas of, I, pt. i, 124; foundation of (746), *id.* 466; removal of the capital of Mularája Solanki to, *id.* 139; named after a Bharvád who shows its site; founding of Jain temple at, *id.* 151-152; chronicles, *id.* 156; Mularája's father and uncles stop at, *id.* 156; cavalry parade at, 157; Jain and Mahádev temples at, *id.* 160, 161; lake built by Durlabha at, *id.* 163; invasion by Kulachandra of, *id.* 163-164; Bhima I, king of, at Mahmud's advance abandons it and flies away, *id.* 166; proposed capital of Mahmud of Ghazni, *id.* 168 note 1; Karnameru temple at, *id.* 170; Vikramasimha imprisoned at, *id.* 185; Ambada returns victorious to, *id.* 186; louse-temple at, *id.* 193; sack of (1194), *id.* 229, its different names, *id.* 511; Hindu capital of Gujarát, IX, pt. ii. 26; mosques at, frequented by great number of Musalmán traders, *id.* 2 note 1; Musalmán faith introduced from, to Broach by Alif Khán (1297), *id.* 3-5; kings of, encourage settlement of traders mostly from the Persian Gulf, *id.* 2; give kind treatment to traders, *id.* 2 and note 3; to early Shiáh preachers (1067), *id.* 25; Vaghela Kings of, employ Khorásáni soldiers, *id.* 2 note 3; are said to have been converted to Islam, *id.* 5 note 1; *id.* 26 note 2; *id.* 38; settlers from Gujarát into Thána, XIII, 60; historical references, *id.* 436, 437.
Anahilavada Patan: *See* Anahilavada.
Anahilaváta: Sanskrit form of Anahilaváda, I, pt. i, 151.
Anahillapátaka: I, pt. i, 204. *See* Anahilaváda.
Anáka: *see* Arnorája.
Analde: name of Arnorája, father of Lavanaprasáda, as given in an inscription, I, pt. i, 200.

Analladeva : name of Anarája as given in the Hammiramahákávya, I, pt. i, 182. *See* Arnorája.
Anamale : modern Anamali, I, pt. ii, 298, 299, 499.
Anamdera : place of interest in Rewa Kántha, VI, 157.
Anamirta cocculus : liquor yielding, and poisonous plant, XXV, 210, 264, 272.
Anamkand : in Madras Presidency, inscription at, I, pt. ii, 239 ; laid siege to, by Jagaddeva, *id.* 458 note 2, 462.
Ananassa sativa : (pine-apple) fruit and fibrous plant, XXV, 180, 236.
A'nand : sub-division of Káira District, its area, aspect, climate, soil, holdings, stock, people and health, III, 159-161 ; town in Kaira District, III, 166.
A'nanda : Saint, ancestor of Allivarman of Gantur, I, pt. ii, 334, 386.
A'nanda : Sákyamuni's disciple, XIV. 170.
A'nandapura : ancient name of Vadanagara, I, pt. i, 6 and note 2.
A'nandibái : Angria's mother, her struggle for power, death (1793), XI, 155-156, 265; defeated Joysing outside Hirakot (1793), *id.* 260.
A'nandibái: Raghunáthráo's wife, her share in Naráyanrao's murder, XVIII, pt. ii, 255-256.
A'nand Mahál : palace in Bijápur City, XXIII, 619-620.
A'nand Mogri : battle of, between Damáji Gáikwár and Bánde (1736), VII, 174.
A'nandodbhav : theatre in Poona City, XVIII, pt. iii, 332.
Anandpur : village and a petty State in Káthiáwár, VIII, 367-368.
Anandráv Dhulap : Peshwa's admiral, captures the ship Ranger (1783), I, pt. ii, 107.
Anandráv Gáikwád : heir of Govindráo, I, pt. i, 412 ; (1800-1819), VII, 202-232 ; his disputed succession to the throne (1798), *id.* 384.
Anandráv Pavár : settles at Dhár (A.D. 1734), I, pt. i, 382 ; His Highness Sir, K.C.S.I., C.I.E., Mabárája of Dhár, *id.* 383.
Anandveli : village in Nasik, place of residence of Raghunáth Ráo's family after 1792, I, pt. ii, 628, XVI, 9; Raghunáthrao retired to (1764), *id.* 193; Anandibai dies at (1793), called after Anandibái, *id.* 416, *id.* 536.
Ananta : the hooded serpent, I, pt. ii, 577.
Anantadeva : Siláhara king (1095), I, pt. ii, 18, 539 ; ruler of the Konkan and feudatory of Vikramáditya VI, *id.* 450 ; drives back the Kádambas, *id.* 543-544, 567. *See* Anantapála Bháskaráchárya's grand-nephew, builds a temple of Bhaváni, *id.* 244 ; XIII, 422 note 1 ; copper plate grant by, *id.* 425, 426 ; record of his gift in a Vihár stone (1081), XIV, 379, 403.
Anantamul : medicinal plant, XXV, 260.
Anantapála : Siláhára King. *See* Anantadeva.
Anantapálayya : minister of Vikramaditya VI, I, pt. ii, 341 note 2, 451.
Anantapura : fort of, I, pt. i, 180 note 2.
Anantapura : district in Madras Presidency, I, pt. ii, 524.
Anantavarman : son of Rájendravarman, the Western Ganga king, I, pt. ii, 297.
Anantdeva : *see* Anantadeva.
Anantpal : *see* Anantadev.
Anár : fruit tree, yields dyes, XXV, 80, 156, 246.
Anarája : King of Sákambhari, I, pt. i, 181 and note 3, 182. *See* Arnorája.
A'nartta : ancient division of Gujarát, I, pt. i, 6 ; *id.* 35, 36 ; legendary Gujarát king, *id.* 8.
A'narttapura : *see* A'nandapura.
Anasandra : yields spirit, XXV, 211.
Anaskura : his pass in Ratnágiri District, X, 166; pack bullock traffic through, *id.* 177 ; XXIV, 5.
Anatidæ : family of birds, in Ratnágiri District, X, 97.
Anatinæ : family of birds, in Ratnágiri District, X, 97.
Anaval : village near Surat District, hot springs near, IX, pt. i, 4.
Anávla : a Brahman sub-division, in Rewa Kántha, VI, 23 ; consecrated as Bráhmans by Rám, *id.* 253. *See* Bháthela. In Baroda, money lenders, VII, 111, 577 ; traditional account of their origin, *id.* 582-583. Brahmans in Gujarát, IX, pt. i, 1, *id.* 4 ; landholders and cultivators of south Gujarát, *id.* 1, 4, *id.* 152 ; strength and distribution, *id.* 3 ; origin of name ; are known as Mastans and Bhathelas, explanation of the terms, *id.* 4 and notes 1 and 2 ; traditional origin, created by Ram, other accounts, *id.* 4-5 ; their religion, character, occupation, *id.* 5 ; social divisions into Desai and Bháthela ; position, wealth, and power enjoyed by the Desáis, *id.* 5-6 ; their hális or ploughmen ; condition ; polygamy allowed and practised by, *id.* 6 ; are all grahasths or laymen, *id.* 2, 5.
Anavalobhaná : or longing-soothing, Vedic rite, IX, pt. i, 31 note 3. *See* Garbha Rakshana.
Anavati : village, in Mysore, Haidarali retreats to (1764), I, pt. ii, 658 ; inscription at, *id.* 306 note 5 ; record at, *id.* 516 and note 5, 523.
Anawatti : *see* Anavati.
Andaræ : tribe, mentioned by Pliny, Andhras, I, pt. i, 532, 533.
Anderson : Mr. David, English plenipotentiary at the time of Salbai Treaty (1782), XVIII, pt. ii, 267.
Anderson : Colonel G. S. A., Political Agent, the survey of Kolhapur commenced by (1867), XXIV, 254.
Andersonia macrophylla : timber tree found at Khandála and on the Western Ghats, XXV, 43.
Andheri : Railway station in Thána District ; XIV, 21 ; Kondivti Caves near, 203.
Andhiárus : priests, derivation of the word IX, pt. ii, 222.
Andhra : dynasty, I, pt. ii, 167 ; forced to obey Krishna II, the Ráshtrakuta king, *id.* 201 ; king subdued by Somesvara III, *id.* 221 ; overthrown by Singhana, *id.* 525 ; Kingdom, *id.* 403 note 3 ; country, *id.* 507.
Andhra : or Tailang Brahmans in Gujarát, sub-division of the Dravid group of Brahmans, IX, pt. i, 1 note 1 ; in Kánara District, XV, pt. i, 135.

Andhra : river in Poona District, XVIII, pt. i, 8.

Andhrabhritya : Shátakarni, I, pt. ii, 10 ; Sáliváhana, *id.* 279 note 3 ; Sátaváhana, *id.* 279 note 3 ; of the Puránas, identified with Sátaváhanas of the inscriptions, I, pt. ii, 155-156 ; their chronology, *id.* 157, 168 ; their dynasty, *id.* 158, 162, 279 ; their dates, *id.* 161-162 ; their duration, *id.* 163, 164, 165 ; their rise, *id.* 165 ; political and literary traditions about them, *id.* 169, 172 ; religious, social and economic condition of Maháráshtra under them, *id.* 173-176 ; their extinction, *id.* 177-179, 522 ; appearance of the Sákas in their country, *id.* 317 note 3 ; Dakhan Hindu dynasty probably ruled over Sholápur (B. C. 90-A. D. 300), XX, 275. Their rule in Dhárwár (200 B. C.-200 A. D.), XXII, 390 and note 3. Shátkarni kings probably overlords of Kolába (A. D. 160), XI, 137 and note 4 ; old kings of Khandesh, XII, 238 and note 8, 484 ; Dakhan overlords, of Konkan, XIII, 60 ; Telegu, kings possessed Konkan (B. C. 100), *id.* 409 and note 3 ; driven by the Parthians (A. D. 78) ; Konkan trade with the Red Sea under their rule, *id.* 414 ; XVI, 181, 182 and note 1, 183 ; their history derived from Nasik inscriptions, 611, 614, 620-624.

A'ndhras : the (A. D. 138), I, pt. i, 32, 52 ; king of, at the bridegroom-choosing of Durlabhádevi, *id.* 163, 533 ; Telegu people, monkey soldiers sent to the country of the, I, pt. ii, 137 ; said to be the progeny of the cursed sons of Visvámitra, *id.* 138 ; are subdued by Sahadeva, *id.* 142 ; mentioned in the edicts of Asoka, *id.* 143 ; their war with Jaitrapála or Jaïtugi, *id.* 239 ; place a woman on the throne of Tailángana, *id.* 246 ; territories of the, conquered by Rajarájadeva the Chola king, *id.* 308 ; *see* Tailángas.

Andirika : river, in Nizám's dominions, I, pt. ii, 364.

Andrapava : identified with Darban, I, pt. i, 538.

Andrews, Mr. : acting Resident at Baroda (1846), VII, 267.

Andrews : Major, took Rájder fort (1818), XVI, 196 ; wounded before Málegaon, *id.* 197.

Andrographis paniculata : medicinal herb, XXV, 262.

Androi : Pliny's, probably Andra capital Dharnikot near Gautur, XIII, 409 note 3.

Andropogon : (Holcus) *cernuus, glaber, scandens*, fodder plants, XXV, 276 ; *Iwarancusa, muricatus, nardoides, schœnanthus,* oil yieding plants, *id.* 225.

Andu : Mosque at Bijápur City, XXIII, 630.

Andubar : the Indian, said to have taught religion and the arts to Babylonians, XIII, 404 note 3.

Ane : village in Poona District, XVIII, pt. iii, 104.

Anegadeva : father of Vira Bijjarsa, I, pt. ii, 523.

Anegundi : wood bridge in Kánara District at, XV, pt. ii, 43.

Anegundi : site of Vijayanagar capital, the revenue system of its kings, (1333-1573), XXII, 439-441.

Anekárthanámamálá : Collection of words of more than one meaning, compiled by Hemachandra, I, pt. i, 192.

A'nekere : (Elephant tank), at Hángal in Dhárwár District ; Hoysala king Vira Ballála II, encamps at, I, pt. ii, 505, 563.

A'nesejjeya-Basadi : Jain temple at Lakshmeshwar, I, pt. ii, 371, 483 and note 2.

Anethum sawa : food plant, XXV, 161.

Anga : King of, at the bridegroom-choosing of Durlabhadevi, I, pt. i, 163 ; Western Bengal, king of, conquered by Kirtivarman I, I, pt. ii, 281, 345 ; subjugated by Amoghavarsha I, *id.* 402 ; humbled by Singhana, *id.* 525.

Anganadeva : grandson of Kokkala, king of Chedi, I, pt. ii, 203.

Angar : village, destruction of, by Mr. Ashburner, I, pt. i, 443.

Angarias : treasure-carriers in Káthiáwár, VIII, 203.

Angdeva : a Portugnese body or poll cess on fishermen, XIII, 553.

Angediva : island, *see* Anjidiv.

Anghad : State in Rewá Kántha, VI, 150 ; a village, its tenure, VII, 360-361.

Angiras : I, pt. ii, 287 note 4 ; ancestor of the Pallavás, *id.* 317.

Angiras-a-Háritas : royal family of, I, pt. ii, 277 note 5 ; descendants of Ikshváku from Manu, son of the Sun, *id.* 287 note 4.

Angkor : capital of Cambodia, I, pt. i, 499, 500, 502.

A'ngriás : Tukáji, distinguishes himself in the fleet of Shiváji ; Kánhoji becomes master of all the coast from Bombay to Vijaydurg, makes Vijaydurg his capital and is recognised as independent (1713) ; he is attacked by the English, the Portuguese, and the Dutch between 1717 and 1724 ; his death (1728) ; Sakhoji succeeds Kánhoji and is followed by his brother Sambháji ; Sambháji puts his illegitimate brothers Mánáji and Yesáji in charge of Kolába ; the two illegitimate brothers quarrel and Mánáji with the help of the Peshwa defeats Sambháji ; he is also defeated by the English (1738) ; his death (1748) ; his brother Tuláji succeeds him ; a joint expedition sent by the English and the Maráthás against Tuláji (1755), I, pt. ii, 87-88 ; Orme's account of the expedition, *id.* 89-95 ; Tuláji taken prisoner and confined till his death, *id.* 95 ; Mánáji retains possession of Koláha and remains in alliance with the Peshwa till his death (1759), his son Rághoji succeeds him and dies in 1793 ; Rághoji's rule ; Rághoji's son Mánáji is acknowledged by the Peshwa but is deposed by Daulatráv Sindia (1799) ; a grandson of the last Mánáji succeeds ; the last of the Angriás of the direct and legitimate line dies in 1840 and the State lapses to the British Government, *id.* 96. Sharer in the Sâlshi province, I, pt. ii, 79 ; defeats the Portuguese fleet (1740), *id.* 85 ; their origin, XI, 145 ; Kánhoji I (1698-1731), supremacy of fleet, piracies, death, and character, *id.* 146-149 ; Sakoji and Mánáji I, *id.* 150-151 ; siege of Gheria, *id.* 152-154 ; quarrels in the family, *id.* 155-156 ; Bivalkars' influence and

the extinction of the family, *id.* 157-158; territorial exchanges (1818-1840), *id.* 159 and note 2; lapse of his territory (1840), *id.* 159 and note 2, *id.* 190; revenue system in the eighteenth century, *id.* 171-172; revenue (1818-1839), *id.* 175 note 4; inconvenience caused in early years by the division of jurisdiction among the British, the Pánt-sachiv of Bhor, and the Angriás of Alibág, *id.* 177 and note 2; British lands of north Pen mixed with Angriá's villages (1818-1840), *id.* 179 note 1; revenue system and assessment in his lands before their lapse in 1840, and British changes *id.* 190-196; (1690-1840), *id.* 145-158, *id.* 215, *id.* 217; (1698-1756), X, 195; taxes levied by the, *id.* 216; Tuláji, *id.* 318, 338, 380, 383 note 1; their sea fights with Phond Sávant (1709, 1737), *id.* 440, XIII, 474; Indian pirates, *id.* (1700), 488, 489; Sambháji captures ships and crews in Bombay, 496, 497, 502; Kanhoji Angria, proposed action against; war with (1720), XXVI, pt. i, 150-152; negotiations with (1724), *id.* 158-159; Mánáji Angria, negotiations with, broken off, rupture with, captures Elephanta (1739), *id.* 225-227; helped by, Bombay (1740), *id.* 232. Karanj surrendered to (1739), *id.* 204-205; misunderstanding between Mánaji and Sambhaji, Manaji helped by the English (1734), *id.* 171. Sambháji Angria captures the 'Derby' with 100 prisoners; sues for peace (1735), *id.* 171-174; encounter with his fleet (1739), *id.* 197; takes Alibág (1740), *id.* 231; Tuláji Angria, Gheria taken from; his fleet destroyed (1756), *id.* 304, 305; all his fleet burnt (1756), *id.* pt. iii, 221; Kolába Chief defeated and reconciled by Bálaji Vishvanáth (1713), XVIII, pt. ii, 242.

Angur: fruit plant in the Dakhan, XXV, 150.

Anhilvad, Anhilvar, Anhilwad: *see* Anahilaváda.

Animal Feast: IX, pt. ii., 217. *See* Bahman Jasan.

Animals: domestic and wild, all district volumes, *see* under district name; kept by Musalmáns, domestic, IX, pt. ii, 97-98; pet, *id.* 98-99; birds, *id.* 99; worship of, *see* worship.

Aniruddha: figure and story of, XV, pt. ii, 292 and note 3.

Anishtakarman Háleya: Andhrabhritya king mentioned in Bhágavatpurána, I, pt. ii, 164.

Anisochilus carnosus: food plant, XXV, 168.

Anisomeles Malabarica: food plant found on the gháts, yields medicinal oil, XXV, 169, 224.

Anivárităcharya: food plant found on the gháts, yields medicinal oil, *see* Gunda.

Anjan Arjun: tree, timber and fruit tree in Khándesh and other districts, XII, 24, XXV, 64, 74, 156, 245.

Anjana: division of Kanbis, *see* Kanbis.

Anjaneri: village in Násik District, stone inscription at, I, pt, ii, 235, 236; record at, *id.* 457 note 1, 515.

Anjaneri: range of hills in Násik District, XVI, 6; capital of Abhir Kings (A. D. 416), *id.* 183; hill, fort, village, summer residence of Raghoba Peshwa, remains, *id.* 416-419, 441, 447.

Anjangaon: village in Khándesh District, temple at, XII, 432.

Anjansalaka: ceremony of installing a new idol, performance of, IX pt. i, 111 note 1.

Anjanvel: port and fort, in Ratnágiri District, I, pt. ii, 39; fort, rebuilt by Shiváji, *id.* 68; district taken by the Sidis, *id.* 79; fort, taken by the Peshwa(1756), *id.* 92; *see* also X, 318; customs division, imports and exports of, *id.* 184.

Anjár: town in Cutch, historical reference to, V, 2, 137, 140, 147, 148, 151, 157, 158, 159, 165; description, history, *id.* 210-213.

Anjarla: small port in Ratnágiri District, X, 319.

Anjengo: (Anjanvel? in Ratnágiri District) fort built at by the British (1696); XXVI, pt. i, 111.

Anjidiv: island in Kánara District, XV, pt. i, 2; description fort and history, Vasco de Gama at (1498), *id.* pt. ii, 278, 308; Varthema's description of (1503), *id.* 104; naval attack on, by Bijápur ships (1506), *id.* 105; held by the English troops under Sir Abraham Shipman (1662-1664), *id.* 125; *see* also XIII, 472, and XXVI, pt. i, 10; Fryer's description of (1673), *id.* 127; Sambhaji's attack on (1682), *id.* 131; Du Perron's mention of (1758), *id.* 138.

Anjir: fig tree in Poona and other districts, XVIII, pt. i, 41; XXV, 130, 172.

Anjor: Portuguese sub-division in Thána District, XIII, 456.

Anjumans: local councils of Navsári, constitution, functions and powers of, IX, pt. ii, 244; of Imperial Gujarát, constitution, position, and duties of, *id.* 245. *See* community.

Anka: Ratta feudatory of the Western Chálukya King Somesvara I, I, pt. ii, 439, 551, 553.

Ankadi bandi: a form of tenure in Baroda, VII, 359-360.

Ankai Tankai: pass in Násik District, XVI, 131, 195; fort, history, caves, *id.* 419-424; historic reference, *id.* 430; description, *id.* 441, 444, 447.

Ankalesvara: *see* Anklesvara.

Ankalgi: village in Belgaum District, survey of (1853-1854), XXI, 443-445; temple of Lakshmi at, *id.* 511.

Ankdia: timber tree found in Konkan, XXV, 101.

Ankdo: swallow wort tree, is sacred to the sun; its flowers are favourite offerings to Hanuman and Ganpati; a man's marriage with the bush of, called arkvivaha, IX, pt. i, 383.

Ankevália: village and petty state in Káthiáwár, VIII, 368.

Ankideva: Ratta Chieftain, I, pt. ii, 555.

Anklesvara: Akálavarsha Krishná's Bagumra grant from, I, pt. i, 128; Maráthás defeated at (A. D. 1711), *id.* 297; Town, trade centre, *id.* 549; Pársis found in (1258); copy of the Visperád made at, IX, pt. ii, 186 and note 7; sub-division of Broach, boundary, area, aspect, climate, water-supply, soil, assessment, resources, occu-

pancy, value of land, produce, population, and public health, II, 545-548; temple of, at Saundatti, stone inscriptions at I, pt. ii, 553 and note 5, 554.

Ankola: town in Kánara District, creek of, XV, pt. i, 3; river of, *id.* 7; forests, *id.* 46-48; a travellers' bungalow at, XV, pt. ii, 44; a trade centre (1580-1800), *id.* 55; customs division, *id.* 65, 66, 67, 68; historical references to, *id.* 111, 135, 143, 145, 260; Portuguese trade at, *id.* 115; traveller Frederick at, *id.* 117; marked in a Portuguese map (1570), *id.* 118; taken by Shiváji (1675), *id.* 127; burnt by Shiváji, *id.* 129; Du Perron's mention of, *id.* 138; taken by Haidar (1763), *id* 140; deserted (1799), *id.* 147, condition (1801), *id.* 149; schools at, *id.* 215; sub-division, village, aspect, climate water, soil, stock, people, *id.* 226-227; town, people, trade, fort, history, *id.* 257-259; timber tree in Dakhan and Konkan, XXV, 82, 161.

Ankottáka: modern A'kota, in Baroda territory, I, pt. i, 125; circle of villages, identified with Ankút, I, pt. ii 399.

Ankulesvara: modern Aṅkleśwar, in Broach District, I, pt. ii, 412.

Aṅkút: village near Baroda City, I, pt. ii, 399.

Anna: defeated by Bhillama, I, pt. ii, 238.

Annachhatra: bread-house, at Khopivli in Thána District, XIV, 201 note 3; at Nirmal in the same district, *id.* 293.

Annáji Dattu: goes to Delhi with Shiváji, I, pt. ii, 593; given charge of the Dábhol Subha, *id.* 69; kept in charge of Konkan from Kalyán to Phonda till 1678, *id.* 71; put to death (1680), *id.* 76.

Annajipant: takes Sátára by strategy (1705), XIX, 253.

Annana: food plant very common, XXV, 180.

Annesley: President of Bombay, put in irons (1696), released, XXVI, pt. i, 111-112.

Annigere: town in Navalgund táluka of the Dhárwár District, I, pt. ii. 304; its temples and history, XXII, 650-651; chief town of Belvala three hundred, I, pt. ii, 305 note 1, 405, 432; royal city in charge of Ballaya, *id.* 506; Someśvara IV, Western Chálukya King, establishes himself at, *id.* 465 and note 5; inscription at, *id.* 441, 443 note 2, 464 note 3, 466, 473, 474, 502 and note 7, 504, 505, 518 and note 3, 520; *see* also XV, pt. ii, 89, 92; capital of the Chálukya Kingdom under Tailapa II, I, pt. ii, 222, 223.

Annigeri: *see* Annigere.

Anni-nar: timber tree found in several districts, XXV, 19.

Annius Plocamus: visited Ceylon (A.D. 41-54), I, pt. i, 536.

Ano [Anarája, Arnorája]: Prákrit local name of Anarája, a Chálukya princess, I, pt. i, 181 note 3.

Anogeissus: *latifolius*, timber and dye plant found in Konkan forests, XXV, 76, 244; *pendula*, a shrub found in Rajputána, *id.* 76.

Anomospermum excelsum: timber tree found in Konkan, XXV, 115.

Anona: *reticulata* and *squamosa*, fruit trees, XXV, 143.

Anonaceæ: a species of timber, food, oil-yielding and fibrous plant, XXV, 2, 143, 222, 226.

Anopsingh Bhandári: deputy of the Viceroy Ajitsingh of Gujarát, I, pt. i, 301.

Anquetil Du Perron: French traveller, IX, pt. ii, 183 notes 2, 4, 187 note 2, 189 note 2; his description of West Thána (1757), XIII, 498-499; his description of Agashi, XIV, 2; of Bassien, *id.* 34 note 2; his notice of Dharávi Church, *id.* 55; describes Elephanta Caves, *id.* 87, 92 note 1, 93; his notice of a remarkable Jogi, *id.* 135 note 10; description of Kanheri caves, *id.* 157-162; his notice of Malanggad, *id.* 220 note 9; his mention of Sipala, *id.* 360; visits Kánara (1758), XV, pt. ii, 138; his description of Anjidiv, *id.* 256; mention of Ankola, *id.* 258; of Bhatkal, *id.* 274; of Onor, *id.* 312; of Kárwár river, *id.* 325; mention of Komenta (Kumta), *id.* 327; of Manjguni, *id.* 330; Pir fort (Sadáshivagad), *id.* 340.

Anrája: statue of, at Girnár, I, pt. i, 153.

Ansale: fibrous and food plant, common in Konkan, XXV, 147, 230.

Anseridæ: family of birds, in Ratnágiri, X, 97.

Anshi: village and pass in Kánara District, XV, pt. ii, 39, 40; description of, built in (1860), *id.* 259.

Ansodar: village in Káthiáwár, its history, VIII, 368-369.

Aṅt: fictitious currency; a kind of paper currency, IV, 73; an old credit system in Káthiáwár, VIII, 212.

Ant: is held sacred, IX, pt. i, 380; white, damage to sugar by, IV, 61.

Antáji Bhásker: Marátha leader in Gujarát, I, pt. i, 391.

Antáji Ráje Shirke: Native head of the Sátára police (1857), his disloyalty, XIX, 317.

Antala: King Shrivardhan captured from, I, pt. ii, 238.

Antália: village in Káthiawár, with a sacred temple, VIII, 369, 370.

Antargal: hydrocele, cure of, IX, pt. i, 365.

Antelope: wild, found in Gujarát, the Dakhan and Karnátak, XII, 32; four horned in Kánara, XV, pt. i, 102; the Indian, *id.* 103.

Anthamul: medicinal plant, XXV, 256.

Anthiga: Pallava King, I, pt. ii, 420.

Anthistiria: cymbaria, fodder plants, polystachia, XXV, 276.

Anthocephalus cadamba: timber, food, fodder and sacred plant, found in Konkan, XXV, 83, 161, 278, 290, 291.

Antiaris: timber and fibrous plants, found in Konkan forests, *innoxia*, XXV, 128; *sacoidora*, *id.* 128, 234; *toxicaria*, *id.* 128.

Antidesma: timber and food plants found in Konkan, *diandrum*, XXV, 119, 171; *Ghæsemvilla*, *id.* 119; *paniculata*, *id.* 119; *pubescens*, *id.* 119.

Antio-chus: Greek Prince, I, pt. ii, 146.

Antoninus Pius: Roman Emperor (154-181), Indian envoys sent to, I, pt. i, 542

Antonio de Porto: Franciscan friar (1534), built a cathedral at Chaul, XI, 292 and note 1; his missionary efforts, pulling down of

temples and building of churches (1534-1552), XIII, 460, 461 and note 1; built an orphanage at Agáshi (1535), XIV, 1, built churches in Bassein and Sálsette, *id.* 42; defeats the Buddhist champion of Kanheri, *id.* 135 note 8; his unsuccessful exploration of Kanheri Caves, *id.* 150; built two churches in Karanj, *id.* 192; founded a monastery at Mandapeshvar, *id.* 226; built a cathedral at Thána (1540), *id.* 358.

Antonio De Sylveria: Portuguese Commander in India, I, pt. i, 349.

A'ntora: port in Ratnágiri district, trade of, XI, 265.

Antroli-Chároli: in Surat district, Kakka, the Ráshtrakuta prince's grant at, I, pt. i, 121.

Antukkúra: village, I, pt. ii, 334.

Antur: fort in the Sátmálás, taken by Ahmad Nizám Sháh (1500), I, pt. ii, 622.

Auturli: place of interest in Khándesh district, XII, 432.

Anupa: name of country in the vicinity of the Vindyas, I, pt. i, 36 note 2; ruled by Gotamiputra, I, pt. ii, 149; conquered by Rudradáman, *id.* 160, 161.

Anupama: wife of Tejahpála, I, pt. i, 202.

A'nvad: gorge in Satara district, XIX, 202.

Anval: village in Bijápur district, temples at, XXIII, 550.

Anvaprashana: food-tasting, vedic rite, IX, pt. i, 31 note 3; also called Botan, *id.* 35. *See* Botan.

Anwalla: timber tree cultivated throughout India, XXV, 30.

Aod-i-ballessam: timber tree cultivated throughout India, XXV, 39.

Aola: timber tree found in several districts, yields a die, XXV, 115, 249.

Aonli: timber tree found in several districts, XXV, 115.

Ap: *see* water.

A'pa Ganesh: Peshwa's viceroy of Gujarát (1761), I, pt. i, 345.

Aparáditya: successor of Mallikárjuna, I, pt. i, 186.

Aparáditya I: Siláhára king (1138), I, pt. ii, 15; sends a representative to Kashmir, *id.* 22; inscription of a grant by, XIV, 195; his stone land-grant, *id.* 321; (A. D. 1187) grant of a garden by, *id.* 112; mentioned in an inscription at Bassein, 387; mentioned in a stone (1160), XIII, 426; patron of learning, *id.* 429; the second (1185), 18th Siláhára king, *id.* 422 note 1; land grant stones of (1203, 1238), *id.* 427; was an author, *id.* 429.

Aparáditya II: Siláhára king (1184), I, pt. ii, 15, 539; commentator on Hindu law, *id.* 20 note 3, 22; declares his independence, *id.* 544.

Aparájita: Siláhára king, becomes independent (997), I, pt. ii, 15, 18, 539; his grant at Bhadána, *id.* 414 note 1, 416, 426, 430, 542 and note 6; mentioned in a copper plate, XIII, 424, 425; a copper plate of, XIV, 50, 355 note 5.

Aparajita: that is Unbeaten, the shami tree, IX, pt. i, 386. *See* Shami.

Aparánta: the western seaboard, I, pt. i, 36 and note 8; Northern Konkan, I, pt. ii, 134; Aśoka sends religious ministers to, *id.* 143 and note 1, 146; ruled over by Gotamiputra, *id.* 149; conquered by Rudradáman, *id.* 160, 161; Trikuta, its important town, *id.* 294; Gautamiputra's rule over, XVI, 183 and note 2, 631; Aśoka sent Dharmarakshita to, XIII, 405, 407 note 1; Sopára the capital of, XIV, 319.

Aparántaka: Buddhist saint Moggaliputto sends missionaries to, I, pt. ii, 144; IX, pt. i, 447 note 7. *See* Aparanta.

Aparantakas: I, pt. i, 534.

Aparantika: *see* Aparántaka.

Aparárka: North Konkan Siláhára prince and commentator on Yájñavalkya, I, pt. ii, 229; Silhára ruler (A. D. 1187), XIV, 212. *See* Aparáditya II.

Apasaras: Jain monasteries, IX, pt. i, 110; description of, *id.* 113. *See* Buildings.

Apasta: *see* Avesta.

Apastamba Bráhmans: school of Bráhmans found in Thána district, XIII, 74.

Apir: *Ophir* (?), XIII 404 note 3.

Apium: *graveolens*, food plant found in Punjáb, XXV, 160; *involucratum*, food plant cultivated in Gujarát, *id.* 161; *petroselinum*, food plant cultivated throughout India, *id.* 161.

Apocynaceæ: dye and poisonous plant, XXV, 247, 266.

Apocyneæ; timber and food plant naturalised in Poona and Bombay, XXV, 99, 165.

Apokopa: the Arávallis, I, pt. i, 539.

Apollodotus: Baktrian-Greek king, I, pt. i, 17, 18; his inscriptions, *id.* 535, 544, 545.

Apollo Gate: in Bombay city, clearance made outside of (1758-59), XXVI, pt. ii, 459-462.

Apologos: modern Obolláh (?), I, pt. i, 545; in the Persian Gulf, Indian trade with (A. D. 250), XIII, 418.

Aponogeton monostachyum; food plant in Belgaum and Dhárwár districts, XXV, 183.

Apophyllite: mineral found at Matherán, XIV, 241; in Poona, XVIII, pt. i, 30.

Aporosa Lindleyana: timber tree found in Southern Konkan, XXV, 119.

Appa Desái Nipánikar: Marátha jáhgirdár (1811), I, pt. ii, 610. *See* Nipáni.

Appaji Suru: founder of the Ramdurg State (1680), XXIV, 397.

Appás: laymen of the Banjig division of the Lingayat caste, found in the Karnátak, XV, pt. i, 175.

Appa Sáheb: ex-rája of Nágpur, intrigues (1837) with Pratapsinh, XIX, 311.

Appáyika: Ráshtrakuta prince, put to flight by Pulakeśi II, I, pt. ii, 183, 350.

Appearance: of A'hirs, IX, pt. i, 265; Bajániás, *id.* 503; Bhangiás, *id.* 334; Bharváds, *id.* 267; Bhátiás, *id.* 117 and note 7; Bháts, *id.* 208; Bhaváyás, *id.* 222; Bhils, *id.* 295-296; Brahma-Kshatris, *id.* 56; Brahmans, *id.* 21; Chárans, *id.* 216; Chodhrás, *id.* 312; craftsmen, Bhávsárs, *id.* 177-178; Chhipás, Darjis, *id.* 179; Ghánchis, *id.* 182; Golás, *id.* 183; Kansárás, *id.* 186; Khatris, *id.* 189; Luhárs, *id.* 190; Mochis, *id.* 192; Saláts, *id.* 196; Sonis, *id.* 198; Suthárs, *id.* 202; depressed classes: *id.* 331; Dhedás, *id.* 339; early tribes: *id.* 291; Gámits, *id.* 318;

Káchhiás, *id.* 153; Kanbis, *id.* 155, 163, 164, 168; Káthis, *id.* 257; Káthodiás, *id.* 319; Káyasths, *id.* 60; Khálpás, *id.* 345; Kolis, *id.* 245; Lohánás, *id.* 122; Mángs, *id.* 323; Márwáris, *id.* 103; Mers, *id.* 286; Náikdás, *id.* 325; Patchias, *id.* 172; Rabáris, *id.* 287; Rajputs, *id.* 130; Rávaliás, *id.* 508; Shrávaks, *id.* 98; Vághris, *id.* 513; Vániás, *id.* 74-75; Musalmans of regular classes, IX, pt. ii, 7; Daudi Bohoras, *id.* 28; Khojáhs, *id.* 42; Memans, *id.* 52.

Aprameya: minister of the Chola king Rája Rájadeva (1006), I, pt. ii, 308; defeats the Hoysalas, *id.* 491.

Apta: *Bauhinia racemosa*, timber, fibrous and sacred plant found in the Dakhan, XII, 23; XVIII, pt. i, 42; XXV, 65, 232, 279, 280, 281.

A'ptamimámsá: Jain work by Samantabhadra, I, pt. ii, 406, 407.

Aptamimámsálamkára: commentary on A'ptamimámsá, I, pt. ii, 407.

A'ptoryáma: sacrifice, I, pt. ii, 247.

Aqueducts: in Poona city, XVIII, pt. iii, 327-328.

Aquilinæ: family of birds in Ratnágiri, X, 56-57.

Aquillaria agallocha: tree found in Bengal, XXV, 288.

A'r: snake found in Ratnágiri district, X, 48.

Arabastra, Arabastræ: tribe in Konkan, mentioned by Pliny, I, pt. i, 533, 534.

Arab Guard: at Baroda, disbanded (1803), I, pt. i, 413.

Arabhatta: *see* Ahada.

Arabi: breed of cattle in Poona district, XVIII, pt. i, 56.

Arabia: I, pt. i, 543; trade relations with, and settlements from (A. D. 700-1200), XIII, 403; prehistoric trade of, with Thána, *id.* 404 and note 3; trade in Indian articles through (A. D. 78), *id.* 411 note 1, 412; trade centres in (810-1260), *id.* 429; export of leather to, and import of horses from, *id.* 430, 431; Indian merchants settled in, *id.* 432; export of spices to, development of trade in rice, wheat, etc., with (1300-1500), *id.* 444-445; export of rice, pulse, pearls, etc., to, and imports of dates, raisins, etc., from (1500-1670), *id.* 466-467; trade centres in (1600-1710, *id.* 486; Bombay trade with (1800-1810), *id.* 520; Ophir probably situated in XIV, 318.

Arabian Sea: I, pt. ii, 282 note 5.

Arabic Chronicle: records the communication between Pulikeśin II and Khosru II of Persia, I, pt. ii, 352.

Arabi erundie: oil yielding hedge plant, XXV, 221.

Arable land: all district volumes. *See* under District Name.

Arabs: pre-historic trade relations of, with Thána coast (B. C. 1700), XIII, 404 note 3; their early trade and colonies on Thána coast (B. C. 180-A. D. 500), *id.* 61 and note 1, 417, 420; their early settlements at Cheul, Kalyána and Sopára and on the Malábár coast (B. C. 170-A. D. 100), their early religion, their first expedition to India (636), their conquest of Jaipur and Udepur (705-715), their coquest of Ujjain and attack on Chitor (724), attack Broach (730), their fleets sent against Káthiáwár coast (758-778), take Sindan (830), settle in Gujarát as sailors, soldiers and traders (600-900), IX, pt. ii, 1 note 1, 2; advance of, by sea (636), and through Persia (650-660), I, pt. i, 497; *see* also XIII, 421; plunder Thána (660), XIV, 355; victory of, over the Persians (638, 641), IX, pt. ii, 183; *see* also XIII, 421; treatment of the fire-worshippers of Persia by, IX, pt. ii, 188 note 3; their invasion of and defeat at Navasárika (Navasári) (704-734), I, pt. i, 117; I, pt. ii, 310; their arrival in India (713), IX, pt. i, 455; strong in Canton (758), IX, pt. ii, 183 note 4 continued on page 185; their trade with the Thána coast, the Balhárás friendly to (810-1260) XIII, 431, 432, 434; settlement of at Jeran (1303), in the Persian Gulf, IX, pt. ii, 183 note 3; their piracy on the Konkan coast (1570), sailors in Portuguese ship, I, pt. ii, 61, 62; XIII, 471; plunder rival villages and churches about Bassein (1675), I, pt. ii, 70; XIII, 476, XIV, 32; make a descent from Maskat on Salsette, burn villages, plunder Bandra, and carry the inhabitants into slavery (1694), I, pt. ii, 80; XIII, 481; XIV, 380; massacre Versova inhabitants (1694), XIV, 380; take Vesáva from the Portuguese (1700), XXVI, pt. i, 128; their piracy (1700), XIII, 488; in Baroda State as mercenaries (1793-1805), VII, 199, 201, 203, 207, 209; their usury in Násik district (1802-1818), XVI, 194; their treachery at Málegaon (1818), XVI, 197-198, 450-451; XII, 255, 256, 313; their defeat at Kusur pass (1818), XIII, 523; travellers and geographers, I, pt. ii, 378, 388 note 1; their references to Gujarát (A. D. 851-1350), I, pt. i, 505-531; inhabitants of Gujarát, their two divisions, appearance, dress, character, belong to Shafaii and Hamboli Sunni schools, their personal names, and customs, IX, pt. ii, 16-17; their usury (1802-1818), *id.* 194; their treachery at Málegaon (1818), *id.* 197-198; suppressed, *id.* 314; at Málegaon, *id.* 450-451; historic reference, 456 note 1.

Aráchis hypcgea: food and oil plant, XXV, 151, 217.

A'rádhi: caste of beggars, in Poona District, how recruited, initiation ceremony, XVIII, pt. i, 444-446.

Aradore: river, in the Pánuingal country, I, pt. ii, 378.

Arag: village in Kolhápur, temples, monastery, fair, XXIV, 292-293.

Arák: timber tree found in Gujarát and Konkan, XXV, 98.

Arakere: in Mysore, inscription at, I, pt. ii, 508.

Arakhosioi: people of eastern Afghánistán, I, pt. i, 545.

Arálaya: progenitor of the Chámbhárs, XXIV, 109.

Aralesbwar: village in Hangal táluka of Dhárwár district, inscription at, I, pt. ii, 278 note 2, 284 note 4, 446 note 5, 561 note 8, 564 note 4.

A'ram : river in Násik district, XVI, 10.
Arambha : *see* Dwárka, VIII.
Aran : timber tree found in Sátára, XXV, 49.
Arang : timber tree found in Konkan forests, XXV, 24.
Arangaon : village in Ahmadnagar district, temple at, XVII, 712.
Arar : timber tree, XXV, 85.
Arás : battles of (1723-1775), I, pt. i, 305 ; III, 166 ; battle between Pilaji and Rustam Ali Khan and Bandet Hámid Khan (1725), VII, 170 ; battle at, between the Gáikwár and Raghunáthráo helped by Colonel Keating (1775), *id.* 192-193 ; battle between Haripant Phadke and Fatehsing Gáikwár and Raghunáthráo (1775), XVIII, pt. ii, 259.
Aras : or Haras, piles, cure of, IX, pt. i, 365.
Arasárya : Jain grantor, I, pt. ii, 413.
Arasididi : in Hungand tálnka of the Bijápur district, inscription at, I, pt. ii, 435 and notes 3 and 5, 439 ; minor capital of Vikramáditya VI, *id.* 450 and note 5 ; *see* Vikramapura ; a ruined village, was Chalukya capital, XXIII, 550.
Aratrioi : Arattas of the Mahábhárata, I, pt. i, 545.
Arattas : I, pt. i, 545.
A'rannda : lake in Sávantwádi, X, 389.
Aravali : hills, passes in, IX, pt. i, p. xi.
Arávi : town in Janjira, XI, 460.
Arbail : pass in Kánara district, XV, pt. ii, 39, and note 1, 40 ; traveller's bungalow, *id.* 44 ; road, cotton traffic, *id.* 259.
Arbhavi : village in Belgaum district, XXI, 511.
Arbi errand : poisonous plant, XXV, 269.
Arbitembi : in Kánara district, Arab stronghold at, XV, pt. ii, 260.
Arbitration : settlement of debts by, in Navsári, VII, 120.
Arbitration Court : in Poona city, XVIII, pt. iii, 29-30.
Arbuda : *see* A'bu, I, pt. i, 305.
Arbuthnot : Sir R., resident at Baroda (1845-1847), VII, 267.
Archæological Survey : Introduction to the Early History of the Dakhan, I, pt. ii, p. iii.
Archbishop : of Goa, publicly pounds Buddha's tooth, I, pt. ii, 56.
Archbishopric : creation of, at Goa (1560), I, pt. ii, 56.
Archipelago : Malay, Indian settlers in, I, pt. i, 492.
Ardabæ : tribe on the east of Indus, I, pt. i, 534.
Ardeidae : family of birds in Ratnágiri, X, 94-96.
Ardeshir : second son of Dhanjisha of Surat, descendant of Nek Satkhán, IX, pt. ii, 197 note 2 ; as head of the Surat Police ; his receiving in reward grants of villages from the British Government (1829), *id.* 198 note 5 continued on page 199.
Ardeshir : son of Bahman, makes a copy of the Vandidád in Seistán (1184), is said to have come to Gujarát ; is said to have given the copy of the Vandidád to the Pársis, IX, pt. ii, 189 note 2.
Ardeshir : leader of the Sanján Pársis, his death in fighting against Musalmans (1315), IX, pt. ii, 187.
Ardeshir Nosherván : Kirmán priest, is sent to Delhi to explain the Zoroastrian faith to Akbar (1578), IX, pt. ii, 190 and note 3.
Ardeshir Papakán : Sind chief, I, pt. i, 544, 545.
Ardhanárishvar : sculpture of Shiva and Uma at Elephanta Caves, XIV, 67-69.
Ardháshtama : an old district in Gujarát, I, pt. i, 191.
Ardhel : system of sharing profits from land in Thána district, XIII, 530 ; a form of assessment, *id.* 565.
Ardheli : land tenure in Kánara District. *See* Nagadi.
Ardhelis : under-tenants in Ratnágiri (1818), X, 228, *id.* 232, 234.
Ardibehesht : Amshaspánd, third day of Pársi month, second month of the Pársi year, IX, pt. ii, 217 ; 218 ; leading high day, observances on, *id.* 219. *See* Festivals (Season).
Ardibehesht Jasan : high festival day, observances on, IX, pt. ii, 217. *See* Jasans.
Ardivijaya : grandson of Bruvijaya (660), I, pt. i, 489.
Ardoi : village in Káthiáwár, VII, 370.
Area of districts : all district volumes, *see* under District Name.
Are Banjigs : *see* Adibanjig.
Areca catechu : timber, food and fibrous plant, found in Konkan, XXV, 135, 181, 237.
Areiasanga : Buddhist teacher, established the superiority of contemplation in Buddhist doctrine XIV, 131.
A're Maráthá : a caste of husbandmen found in Kánara district, their religion, ceremonies, customs, daily life, XV, pt. i, 244-245.
A'rer : a caste of husbandmen found in Kánara district, their origin, surnames, religion, condition, ceremonies, customs, XV, pt. i, 213-216 ; *id.* pt. ii, 3 ; Kánarese name for Maráthás, XIII, 415.
Argante : city on the Gujarát coast (?) mentioned by Stephanos (450 A. D.), I, pt. i, 546.
Argaon : battle of (1803), I, pt. ii, 609.
Argemone Mexicana : oil yielding and medicinal plant, XXV, 214, 254.
Arghunos : dynasty of (1519-1543), V, 135.
Arghya : offering of handful of water to the sun, IX, pt. i, 393.
Arhái-Dinká Jhopdá : mosque in Ajmir, originally Sanskrit school, I, pt. i, 180.
Arhat A'chára : great monastery built by, I, pt. i, 79.
Arhats : Buddhist saints, I, pt. ii, 288 ; IX, pt. i, 106.
Ariaka : name for North Konkan, I, pt. i, 540, 544, 546 ; I, pt. ii, p. 538 note 8 ; Ptolemy's Marátha country, XIII, 414-415.
Ariake : *see* Ariaka.
Ariana : is Herát, IX, pt. i, 455.
Arikesari : *see* Arikesarin I.
Arikesarin : or Keśideva, Northern Konkan Siláhára king (1017), I, pt. ii, 538, 539, 542, 543 ; tenth Siláhára king (1017), XIII, 422 note 1 ; mentioned in a copper plate grant

(1095), *id.* 425 and note 3; Siláhára chief (A. D. 1017), a copper plate of, XIV, 401; a copper plate grant by, *id.* 418.
Arikesarin I: son of Yuddhamalla I, Chálukya king of Sapádalakha, I, pt. ii, 212, 380; defeats Mahipála Gurjara king (941), I, pt. i, 466.
Arikesarin II: Chálukya prince, I, pt. ii, 212; son of Yuddhamalla II, and patron of Pampa (941), rules over the Jola country and protects Vijayáditya against Gojjiga, *id.* 380.
Arikeshari: *see* Arikesarin.
Arisæma curvatum: famine plant found in Matheran and other Konkan hills, XXV, 207.
Arishtakarman: Andhrabhritya king, I, pt. ii, 164.
Arishtanemi: Jain temple of, I, pt. i, 184; modern Ahmadábád.
Aristolochia: *Indica*, antidote to snake bite found in Konkan hills, XXV, 275; *rotunda, Pinellia tuberifera,* passed for, *id.* 183.
Aristolochia bracteata: medicinal plant common all over India, XXV, 258.
Arivárana: elephant of Paramesvaravarman I, I, pt. ii, 322 note 8.
Arivarman: Harivarman, spurious grant of, I, pt. ii, 292 note 10.
Arjansukh: village in Káthiáwár, VIII, 370.
Arjun: *see* Anjan.
Arjuna: visit of, to Káthiáwár, I, pt. i, 9; one of the Pándavas, I, pt. ii, 142, 149, 234; king of Málwa destroyed by Singhana, *id.* 239; Yádava king, *id.* 234, 514; Chálukya king of Anahilaváda, *id.* 525 and note 4. *See* Arjunadeva, son of the Chedi king Kokkala I, *id.* 203, 415; XIII, 404.
Arjunadeva: Vághela chief (1262-1274), I, pt. i, 176; succeeds Visaladeva; extension of his kingdom and his inscriptions, *id.* 203-204, 206; Chálukya king of Anahilaváda (1261-1275), overthrown by Singhana, I, pt. ii, 525 note 4.
Arjuna sadra: *see* Anjan.
Arjunáyana: Kshatriya tribe, I, pt. i, 64 note 3; frontier kings, early coin of, I, pt. ii, 293 and note 6.
Arka: fibrous plant, yields fermented drink, found in Konkan, XXV, 211, 232.
Arkakirti: Jain teacher, I, pt. ii, 400.
Arkavarman: son of the Pallava king Simhavarman I, I, pt. ii, 33.
A'rk-Killáh: Bijápur citadel, its history, description, XXIII, 573-576; built out of Hindu temple materials, *id.* 635-636.
Arkmut: food plant, XXV, 152.
Arkvivaha: sun marriage, object of, IX, pt. i, 383. *See* A'nkdo. Performed before marrying a third wife, XVIII, pt. i, 560-561.
Arlekatti: village in Dhárwár district, inscriptions at, XXII, 652.
Arleshvar: village in Dhárwár district, temples and inscriptions at, XXII, 652.
Armagara: probably Cape Ramas, I, pt. i, 542.
Armár: a sailing vessel, XIII, 719.
Armativala: of Kurur, minister of Vira Ballála II, I, pt. ii, 428 note 4; rules at Sátarúr (1195), *id.* 505.
Armenians: in Ahmadabad, IV, 255 note 5; their tombs, *id.* 285; first appearance in Bombay of, XXVI, pt. i, 56-59.
Armesia: silk fabric, manufacture of, in Thána (1585), XIV, 358 and note 6.
Aroái: a hot spring at, in Dharampur state, VI, 257.
Arnála: fort in Thána district, remains of, I, pt. ii, 42; taken by the English (1781), *id.* 105; taken by the Maráthás (1737), XIII, pt. ii, 493; Goddard before (1781), *id.* 507; its state (1818), *id.* 523; its description, history, temples, XIV, 10; seized by the Maráthás (1738), *id.* 34; references to, *id.* 200.
Arnej: village in Ahmadabad district, IV, 332.
Arni: cluster of three stars, forecast of rain at the disappearance of, IX, pt. i. 351.
Arnoràja: son of Dhavala, king of Bhimapalli, helps Bhima II in resisting the power of his nobles (1170-1200), I, pt. i, 196, 197, 198, 206. *See* A'náka.
Arnoràja: king of Sámbhar, I, pt. i, 179, 182, 184; fights with Kumárapála and is defeated, 184, 188. *See* Anarája.
Arnotto: fibrous plant, XXV, 226.
Aroideæ: species of food and famine plants, XXV, 182, 207.
Aromata: Cape Guardafui, I, pt. i, 543.
Aror Dominions: spread of, I, pt. i, 495.
Arrack: free allowance of, to soldiers stopped (1757), XXVI, pt. iii, 130; farmed (1720), *id.* 344; (1737) *id.* 344, 346; (1740) *id.* 347; (1741) *id.* 347-355; (1743) *id.* 358-359; (1746) *id.* 359-363; farmed for Rs. 45,000 (1770), *id.* 493-494; farmed for Rs. 41,000 (1775), *id.* 495-496; farmed (1751-54), *id.* 475-476; farmed to the Bhandaris (1757), *id.* 477-480; (1760) *id.* 482-83; (1765) *id.* 485-489.
Arrás: *see* Aras.
Arrian: (150 A. D.) I, pt. i, 532, 533, 534, 542, 545.
Arrianos: I, pt. i, 546.
Arsacidae: Parthian dynasty, XIII, 410.
Arsaks: same as Arsacidae, XIII, 411 note 2.
Arsalán Sháh: Sultán of Ghazni and Hindustán (1115-1118), IX, pt. ii, 58. *See* Behluno.
A'rsappa Naik: first Sonda chief, family tree of, (1555-1598), XV, pt. ii, 120 and note 3, 121; possessed Banavási, *id.* 266; built temples at Sonda, and endowed a monastery, *id.* 346, 347.
Arsenal: in Poona cantonment, XVIII, pt. iii, 360; in Bombay situated to the east end of the Bandar Warehouse, the present (1894) Custom House (1767), XXVI, pt. iii, 572.
Arsul: timber tree found on the ghâts, XXV, 87.
Artal: village in Dhárwár district, temples, inscriptions at, XXII, 652.
Artaminæ: family of birds in Ratnágiri, X, 71.
Arthrocneuum Indicum: food plant, XXV, 169.
Arthur, Sir George: Governor of Bombay (1842-1846), opened Mahim causeway (1845), XIII, 323.
Arthur's Seat: a point at Mahábaleshvar, XIX, 503-504.

Artichoke : food plant, XXV, 163.
Articles : chief, of Musalmán faith, IX, pt. ii, 126. *See* Beliefs.
Artillery : Portuguese, at Bassein and Chaul, I, pt. ii, 54, and at Korlai, *id.* 55 ; insufficiency of non-commissioned officers in (1779), XXVI, pt. iii, 182-183 ; regulations (1748), *id.* 102-108 ; modifications in (1753), *id.* 118.
Artisans : all district volumes. *See* under district name.
Artist : point at Mátherán, XIV, 233.
Artoarta : unidentified town of Ptolemy, perhaps in Sind, I, pt. i, 538.
Artocarpus : timber tree found in Konkan forests, *hirsuta,* XXV, 128 ; *integrifolia,* timber, fruit and dye plant, cultivated all over India, *id.* 127, 172, 249.
Artocarpus lakoocha : timber, fruit and dye plant, found at Bassein and Karanj, XXV, 127, 172, 249.
Aru : fruit tree cultivated in cooler parts of the Dakhan, XXV, 155.
A'rudra : heavenly mansion, IX, pt. i, 352.
Arum : *bulbifera,* food plant found in Konkan and Malabár, XXV, 183 ; *divaricatum,* famine plant common in Bombay, *id.* 207.
Arundinaria Wightiana : timber, food, famine, and fibrous plant, grows on the gháts, XXV, 136, 188, 209, 238.
Aryabhusan : theatre in Poona city, XVIII, pt. iii, 333.
Aryaka : *see* Ariaka.
Aryan : settlement in the Dakhan, date of, I, pt. ii, 138-141 ; origin of the Ráshtrakútas, *id.* 384.
A'ryans : I, pt. ii, 383 ; Ujlivaran or bright coloured race, chief classes of ; object of worship ; early beliefs, IX, pt. I p. x ; early settlements, land routes by which they entered Gujarát, *id.* p. xi; sacred spots from which the stem castes take their names, *id.* p. xi note 1 ; chief new settlements, *id.* p. xi and note 2 ; later immigrants, *id.* p. xi and note 3 ; social rank, *id.* p. xiv ; their settlement in the Dakhan, I, pt. ii, 135-37 ; their acquaintance with Northern India in the time of the Aitareya Bráhmana and Pánini, *id.* 138; their entrance into the Dakhan in the seventh century, B. C. 141 ; their colony in the Ráshtrakuta dominions, *id.* 207.
A'ryapura : I, pt. ii, 282. *See* Aihole.
A'rya Somvanshi Kshatri : *see* Jingar.
A'rya Tárádevi : Vihára of, at Dambal, I, pt. ii, 452.
Aryávarta : region of the Aryas, I, pt. ii, 135.
Arzan : XXV, 185.
Asa : Bhil Chief of Asawal, the site of Ahmadábád, defeated by Ahmad Sháh (1413-14), I, pt. i, 235 ; gave protection to Rájputs against Gujarát Kings (1403-13), father of Teja whom Ahmadshah loved, IX, pt. i, 243 note 3.
A'sa : Shepherd king builds the fort of Asirgad (1370), I, pt. ii, 619 ; *see* also XII, 243 ; IX, pt. i, 264 : treacherously killed by Malik Nasir Fáruki (1399-1437), XII, 244.
Asá : ancestor of Navsari priests, IX, pt. ii, 221.
Asá : wooden staff in a mosque, IX, pt. ii, 131.
Asaána : timber tree found in Konkan and on the gháts, XXV, 120.
Asádaru : a depressed class, division of the Máng caste in Dhárwár District, XXII, 219.
Asad Beg : Musalmán historian, Akbar's envoy to Bijápur (1604), XXIII, 422 ; his description of Bijápur (1605), *id.* 585.
A'sad Khán : Vazir of Aurangzeb, IX, pt. ii, 196 notes 3.
A'sad Khán : Bijápur General Minister (1512-49), title of Khusrao Turk of Belgaum, I, pt. ii, 641 ; commands the troops of Bijápur and defeats the confederate Kings of Ahmadnagar, Berár, Golkonda, and the regent of Bedar at Sholápur (1524), takes Amir Barid prisoner ; captures Bidar, marches against the Vijayánagar Rája and captures the fort of Ráichur and Mudgal, is appointed guardian of Mallu, son of Ismáil A'dil Sháh (1534), marches to attack Adoni and concludes peace with Vijayánagar, *id.* 642 ; Bijápur Governor of the Konkan (1540), *id.* 39 note 3 ; his overtures to the Portuguese for help, *id.* 40 ; is suspected by Ibráhim A'dil Sháh of being implicated in Abdulla's rebellion, retires to Belgaum, his death (1540), *id.* 643. *See* also XXI, 367-71, 545-46 ; and XXIII, 411-15.
A'sad Khán : Governor of Junnar (1468-74), XVIII, pt. ii, 218-19.
A'saf : Jinn or spirit, minister of the Prophet Soleimán, his magical exploits, IX, pt. ii, 143. *See* Magic.
Asámi : a grant, VII, 354, an inquiry into, by the Inám Commission, amount of such grants (1877-81), 421.
Asan : timber tree found in Konkan, XXV, 62.
A'sandi : district, I, pt. ii, 492.
A'sápála : prince, I, pt. i, 172 and note 1.
A'sápalli : modern Ahmadábád, I, pt. i, 205.
A'saph Jah Nizam-ul-Mulk : Governor of Málwa (1717-21), I, pt. i, 382.
A'sapurná or **A'shapuri** : hope-filler or wish-filler, goddess, guardian mother of Chohúns, IX, pt. i, 484 and note 7.
Asar : Evening prayers, IX, pt. ii, 126 note 3.
Asarás : female ghosts, XVIII, pt. i, 553.
Asardánni : Lady possessed by a jinn, IX, pt. ii, 130. *See* Vows.
A'sar Mahál : relic palace at Bijápur, XXIII, 620-23.
A'sár-ul-Bilád : work by Al-Kazwini, I, pt. i, 510 and note 1.
Asárva : village, site of Ahmadábád, I, pt. i, 329, *id.* 513; *see* Asával.
A'satimaynrapura : town, I, pt. ii, 506.
A'sattigráma : village identified with Ashtagam or Atgam, a few miles to the south-east of Navsári, in Baroda territory, I, pt. ii, 364 note 6.
Asáva : fort in Thána near Máhim, its description, XIV, 11.
Asával : modern Ahmadábád, I, pt. i, 231, 234-35, 508, 509, 510, 512, 513, 518, IV, 250 note 1 ; in the hand of a Bhil Chief, IX, pt. i, 243 note 3, 294 note 5 ; temples at, I, pt. i, 170.
Asawal : *see* Asaval.
Ascetics : Shaiv, seven principal orders of—Dandis, or Sanyasis, IX, pt. i, 542, Paramahansas, Aghoris, Yogis, *id.* 543 ; Jangams

or Lingáyats ; Urdhva Báhus, A'kásamukhis, *id.* 544. Shravak, three classes of — Sádhus, Sádhvis and Gorgis, *id.* 106 09 ; Sadhus : recruited from pious Shravaks, IX, pt. i, 106 ; initiating ceremony, *id.* 106-07 ; dress, *id.* 107 ; daily life, *id.* 107-08 ; movements in the fair season ; duties, *id.* 108 ; Sádhvis : or nuns, recruitment of initiation ; dress, IX, pt. i, 108 ; Gorjis : recruitment of, initiatory ceremony, IX, pt. i, 108 ; dress ; observances by a strict Gorji, *id.* 109.

Asclepiadaceæ : a species of poisonous plants, XXV, 267.

Asclepiadeæ : a species of food, famine and fibrous plants, XXV, 165, 201, 232.

Asclepias : *currassavicá*, medicinal plant, XXV, 256 ; *tuberosa*, food plant, *id.* 165.

Asgund : poisonous plant, XXV, 268.

A'sha : Bhil Chief, slain by Karna, the Chálukya King, 1064-94, I, pt. i, 170.

Ashabs : Prophets' companions, IX, pt. ii, 34.

Ashámat : river in Ratnágiri District, X, 13.

A'shapalli : modern Asával, seat of Bhil Chief, A'sha, I, pt. i, 170. *See* Asával.

A'shápuri : Hindu goddess, IX, pt. i, p. xxxvi ; Northern, chief shrine of in Kachh, worshipped by Jádejás, *id.* 136 ; of Ashnái near Petlad, family deity of Lad Vániás, *id.* 72. *See* Asbápurna.

Ashával : *See* Asaval.

Ashburner : Mr., Assistant Magistrate, Kaira, raises a fort for the protection of the district, I, pt. i, 439 ; suppresses a rising of Thákors at Partábpur, 443-44.

Ashburner : Mr. Luke, alderman of Bombay, and editor of *Bombay Courier*, XIV, 44.

Asheri : caves and fort, in Thána District, I, pt. ii, 12 ; acquisition of the fort of, by the Portuguese (1556), *id.* 48 ; hill, retaken by the Portuguese (1684), *id.* 78, and XIII, 7, 452 ; Portuguese sub-division, *id.* 455, under the Portuguese, *id.* 456, 457, retaken from the Marathás, *id.* 480, undefended state of, *id.* 491 ; the Maráthas defeated at (1738), *id.* 493, the Pindháris pass through (1817), *id.* 522, history of its capture by the Maráthas (1738), XIV, 11, 13, 98 ; *id.* 228, 360, history, references to archæological remains at, *id.* 386.

Ashes : holiness of, among Lingáyats, XXIV, 125 note.

A'shiapal : village in Káthiáwár, VIII, 370.

Ashkal-ul-Bilád : work by Ibni Haukal, I, pt. i, 511.

Ashmaka : Hindu rulers mentioned in Ajanta caves, overlords of Konkan ruling near Vidarbba (600 A. D.), XII, 485, *id.* 593 and note 2.

Ashok, Asok : (Jonesia Asoka) Vipashyi's tree of knowledge, XIV, 331 ; timber and sacred tree planted in gardens, XXV, 2-3, 64, 279, 285.

Ashoka, Aśoka : Mauryan emperor (B. C. 263-229), I, pt. i, 13, 14 ; raises monuments in Buddha's places of rest, 79 ; his rock inscriptions, I, pt. ii, 142 ; his moral edicts, *id.* 143, 285 note 5 ; language used in his time, *id.* 177 ; third Buddhist convocation held in his reign, *id.* 144, 278 note 2 ; extent of his dominions, *id.* 146, 277 ; Ratthas found in the time of, *id.* 194 ; his name modified into Asokavarman, *id.* 324 ; Guttas claim descent from his grandfather, *id.* 579 ; his edicts at Girnár, and at other places (B. C. 42), VIII, 272 ; belief about, IX, pt. i, 441 ; builds two shrines to his name, *id.* 480 note 4 ; *id.* 447 note 7 ; his edict on Sopára hill (B. C. 225), XIII, 404, sent Darmárakshita to Konkan, *id.* 405-06 and note 1, 407 note 1, *see* trade with Egypt, *id.* 409, at the time of ; Buddhism at the time of, XIV, 129 ; his round huts near Gaya, *id.* 206 ; antiquity of his edicts, *id.* 289 ; his edicts at Sopára, *id.* 319, 339-40 ; took away Buddha's relics, *id.* 405, 406, built the Purnamaitráyani *stupa* at Mathura, *id.* 410 ; sent a missionary to Banvási, XV, pt. ii, 77, 264 ; edicts of, mentioning Petnikas of Paithan, XVII, 351 ; edicts of (B. C. 250), XVIII, pt. ii, 212.

Ashrafis : coins, I, pt. i, 342.

Ashrophi : ulcer, a Cambay disease, VI, 183.

Ashta : town in Sátára District, XIX, 448-449.

Ashta : lake in Sholápur District, XX, 223-225 ; battle of (1818), *id.* 294-296 and XVIII, pt. ii, 302 ; village in Sholápur, XX, 407-408.

Ashta : timber tree common in the Presidency, XXV, 65.

Ashta-Mahá-Siddhi : eight great supernatural faculties, I, pt. ii, 579.

Ashtami : village in Kolába District mentioned by Oxenden, XI, 265.

Ashtasahasri : I, pt. ii, 407 ; *see* A'ptamimámsálamkára.

Ashtaśati : commentary on A'ptamimámsá, I, pt. ii, 407.

Ashtgám : I, pt. ii, 310.

Ashti : skirmish at (1818), I, pt. ii, 611, 620.

Ashtpradhán : or eight chief ministers of Shiváji (1674), I, pt. ii, 594 ; Shiváji's eight chief officers, their duties, XIX, 243-244.

A'shurá : Tenth day of Muharram, held sacred by Sunnis, IX, pt. ii, 139.

Ashvattháma : worship of, at Asirgad, XII, 238.

Ashvin : river in Rewa Kántha, VI, 5.

A'śika : ruled over by Gotamiputra, I, pt. ii, 149.

Asinda : identification of, I, pt. i, 539.

Asindro : tree, is worshipped by women, by early tribes, IX, pt. i, 383.

Asini : tribe, on the east of the Indus, mentioned by Megasthenes, I, pt. i, 534.

Asir : goddess, IX, pt. i, 200.

Asirgad : fort ; built by A'sa the shepherd king about 1370, I, pt. ii, 619 ; taken by treachery by Malik Názir the first Khándesh king, *id.* 620 ; surrendered to the Mughals (1600), *id.* 624 ; taken by Nizám-ul-mulk (1720), *id.* 626 ; surrendered to the Peshwa (1760), *id.* 627 ; taken by Colonel Stephenson from Sindia (1803), *id.* 629 ; captured by the English (1819), *id.* 631 ; XII, 38 ; further account of its capture by Malik Nasir, *id.* 238, 241, 242, 244. 248, 252, 253 ; description, history, 574-586.

A'skarn : a Cutch minister (1801-1815), V, 151-152, 157.

Asmá : Names of God, the two classes of, terrible and merciful, IX, pt. ii, 144.

Asmagi : the Aśmakas, I, pt. i, 532, 533.

Aśmaka : ruled over by Gotamiputra, I, pt. ii, 149.

Aśmaka : tribe between the Indus and the Jamna, mentioned by Pliny, I, pt. i, 533.
Asna : timber tree found in several districts, XXV, 75.
Asok : *see* Ashok.
Asoka : *see* Ashoka.
Asokavarman : probably a modification of the name of the Buddhist king Aśoka, I, pt. ii, 324.
Aśokesvar : shrine built by Aśoka, IX, pt. i, 480 note 4.
Aśopálav : tree worshipped by Sita ; is worshipped by women and newly married girls, IX, pt. i, 383.
Aspandád : fifth day of the Pársi month ; twelfth month of the Pársi year, IX, pt. ii, 217, 218.
Aspandád Jasan : high festival day, observances on ; also known as Earth Feast, IX, pt. ii, 217 ; *see* Jasans.
Aspandármad : the earth-spirit or angel, IX, pt. ii, 206.
Aspandiárji Kámdinji : Dastur, high priest of Broach, gives A. D. 716 as the year of the Pársi settlement at Sanján, IX, pt. ii, 185 note 3.
Asparagopsis sarmentosa : food plant, used in medicine, XXV, 180.
Asparagus officinalis : food plant, XXV, 180.
Aspect : physical, of district ; all district volumes ; *see* under district name.
A'śráma : hermitage, I, pt. ii, 135.
A'śrámadeva : temple of, in the Bharukachchha District, I, pt. ii, 315.
A'śrámas : Brahman stages of life, I, pt. i, 116.
Asrelei : timber tree, XXV, 9.
Assale : timber tree found in Goa, XXV, 28.
Assana : food, dye and sacred plant, XXV, 171, 249, 291.
Assar : timber tree found in Konkan and Khándesh, XXV, 104.
Assar Tomb : light-house near Mándvi in the Gulf of Cutch, VIII, 19.
Assassins : the order of the Fidawis, known in Europe as, IX, pt. ii, 37 and note 1.
Assaye : battle of (1802), I, pt. ii, 112, 609 ; XII, 253, *id.* 586-589.
Asses : in Poona, XVIII, pt. i, 65 ; in Sholápur, XX, 18.
Assessment : revenue, all district volumes ; *see* under district name.
Assigned lands : during Musalmán period, I, pt. i, 209, 210, 211, 213, 214.
As Sindh : Indus valley, I, pt. i, 507.
Associations : in Surat, II, 259 ; in Broach, *id.* 530 ; Law, formation of, IX, pt. ii, 244. *See* Community.
Assyrian inscriptions : mention of Káthis in, VIII, 127.
Astakapra : town, identified with Hastakavapra or Hathab, I, pt. i, 539, 544.
Astgám : I, pt. ii, 310. *See* Ashtgám.
Asthada : son of Udaya, rises to a high position under Kumárapála, I, pt. i, 170.
A'sthana : darbar hall, built by Siddharája, I, pt. i, 179.
Astika : Naga chiefs, considered the best of Bráhmans, IX, pt. i, 438.
Astrologer : *see* Joshi.
Astrology : faith in, IX, pt. ii, 220. *See* Beliefs (Early) ; Belief in, of Memans, IX, pt. ii, 56 ; practice of, by Husaini Bráhmans, *id.* 22.
Asuf-Jah : Nizám, brings Multani Mochis to the Dakhan, IX, pt. ii, 77.
Asundi : Village in Dhárwár district, temples, inscriptions, XXII, 652.
Asupala : timber tree cultivated in gardens, XXV, 2.
Asuras : mythic warriors, belief in (A. D. 100-400), XIII, 406.
A'śvaláyana : I, pt. ii, 141.
A'śvalya : hill in Ahmadnagar District, XVII, 4.
A'śvamedha : great horse sacrifice of Pulakeśi I ; I, pt. ii, 181 ; restoration of, by Samudragupta, *id.* 290 note 3.
Aśvatthámaan : ancestor of the Pallavas, I, pt. ii, 317.
Asystacia : Coromandeliana Gangetica, famine plants, very common, XXV, 202.
Atábak Abu Bakr : King (1154-1159), Saádi's patron, I, pt. i, 515 note 4.
A'takúr : in Mysore, inscription at, I, pt. ii, 304, 305, 322 note 8, 418, 421.
Atalantia monophylla : timber and oil-yielding plant common on the ghâts, XXV, 33, 222.
Atárs, Atáris : caste of perfumery makers ; *see* Attars.
Atarsumba : sub-division in Baroda territory, its boundaries, aspect, climate, soil, etc., VII, 590 ; town with a fort, *id.* 591.
Atesh Aderán : *see* Aderán.
Atesh Behrám : the fire of Behrám, IX, pt. i, 185 note 2, *id.* 213 ; purification and installation of, *id.* 214-215 ; temple of, at Sanján, *id.* 185, at Bombay, *id.* 193 note 2 ; Chief temples of, in Gujarát, *id* 214 ; list of, *id.* 215, note 2, 247 ; *see* Fires (sacred), Temples (Fire).
Atesh Dádghán : hearth fire ; is also called Proper-place Fire ; in the Agiári or Daremeher, IX, pt. ii, 213 ; *see* Fires (sacred).
Ateshperest : Pársis so called (1660), IX, pt. ii, 191.
Atgaon : Village in Thána District, old temple at, XIII, 429 ; railway station, XIV, 14 ; remains at, *id.* 10, 307-312.
Athanasius Nikitin : Russian traveller, his description of Poona, Dakhan (1468-1474), XVIII, pt. ii, 218-219.
Atharwa Veda : one of the four Vedas of the Hindus, followed by Husaini Bráhmans, IX, pt. ii, 22.
Athávisi : in Surat, Gáikwári possession delivered to the English (1780), VII, 196-197 ; old division of Surat District, IX, pt. i, 60.
Athni : town and trade centre in Belgaum district, XXI, 314, 511 ; sub-division of, remains with Sháhu (1730), I, pt. ii, 656 ; Survey of (1851-53), XXI, 427-434 : sub-divisional details, boundaries, area, aspect, soil, climate, water stock, crops, people, XXI, 494-497.
Athor : a village in Baroda territory, with a temple to Ganpati, VII, 618.

Athornan: priest, a class of the old Persian community, IX, pt. ii, 213, 222.
A'thravan: IX, pt. ii, 222; *see* Athornan.
Aththávisi: *see* Ath4visi.
Athva: village on the Tápti, I, pt. i, 309; fort, built at, (1730), 310, 331.
Athveth: Khoti labour tax, X, 206 and note 1, 231, 242.
Atigre: pond in Kolhápur State, XXIV, 12.
Atiranachanda: Pallana king, I, pt. ii, 331.
Atiranachandeśvara: temple of, at Saluvankuppam, I, pt. ii, 331.
Atiśaya: horse of Parameśvaravarman I, I, pt. ii, 322 note 8.
Atiśayadhavala: *biruda* of Amoghavarsha I, I, pt. ii, 401.
Atit: a Hindu religious order in Cutch, V, 83-84; their monastery at Anjar, *id.* 212; their graves at Kanthkot, *id.* 225; in Pálanpur, *id.* 291; caste of beggars in Káthiáwár, VIII, 154-155; belong to Nakuliśa order, I, pt. i, 84.
Atkot: village in Káthiáwár, VIII, 370-372.
Átmaling: Shiv's emblem at Gokarna in Kánara district, XV, pt. ii, 290; story of, 29 note 1.
Átmánuśásana: work of Gunabhadra, I, pt. ii, 411.
Atonement: ceremony, XVIII, pt. i, 146-147.
Atri: sage, I, pt. i, 461; son of god Brahman, I, pt. ii, 339, 511.
Atták: timber tree found in Konkan and other places, XXV, 7
Attak-ke-jar: fruit tree, XXV, 146.
Attar: perfume, process of manufacturing, V, 300.
Attarasa: I, pt. ii, 507. *See* Attirája.
Attárs: caste of perfume makers in Khándesh district, XII, 125; in Thána district, XIII, 108, 236; in Ahmadnagar district, XVII, 226; in Poona district, XVIII, pt. i, 492; in Satára district, XIX, 135; in Sholápur district, XX, 198; in Belgaum district, XXI, 205, 206; in Dhárwár district, XXII, 232-233; in Bijápur district, XXIII, 289; in Kolhápur, XXIV, 86, *id.* 148.
Atte Vakkals: a caste of husbandmen in Kánara, XV, pt. i, 248-251.
Attinga: Kánarese queen, XIV, 215 note 1.
Attirája: father of Bolalva, I, pt. ii, 507.
Attivarman: born of the family of the king Kandara, I, pt. ii, 334, 386; grant of, *id.* 384.
Attok: town in the Punjab, I, pt. i, 538.
Atu: fruit tree, XXV, 162.
Atylosia: *Lawii alineate*, food-plants, XXV, 153.
Atyantakáma: *birudas* of Rájásimha, I, pt. ii, 329, and of Narasimha, the Pallava kings, *id.* 331.
Aubkin: Piram, island in the Gulf of Cambay, I, pt. i, 509, 515.
Audich (Audichyas): Sub-caste of Bráhmans found in Gujarát, originally northerners, I, pt. i, 161; grant to, *id.* 172; in Cutch, V, 44; in Rewa Kantha, VI, 23; in Baroda, VII, 54; in Káthiáwár, VIII, 145; said to be immigrants from Upper India, IX, pt. i, 2; strength and distribution, *id.* 3; traditional account of their arrival and settlement in Gujarát; subdivisions; means of livelihood, *id.* 6-7; Mirdhas or official spies in the Pálanpur Superintendency, IX, pt. ii, 18; in Thána district, XIII, 74; in Ahmadnagar, district, XVII, 55; in Poona district, XVIII, pt. i, 163; in Sholápur district, XX, 30.
Audumbari Sálvas: tribe mentioned by Pánini, I, pt. i, 534.
Augromanyus: IX, pt. ii, 212. *See* Ahriman.
Augusta: timber and food plant, XXV, 58, 151.
Augustine Friars: at Bassein in 1634, XIII, 462; their monasteries in Bassein destroyed by whirlwind (1618), XIV, 31; remains of their church and chapel at Bassein, *id.* 40, 43; built a church at Thána (1574), *id.* 358.
Augustus: Indian spices in Rome at the time of (B. C. 36, A. D. 17), XIII, 410 note 3.
Aula: sacred plant, XXV, 279, 284.
Aumti: famine plant, XXV, 202.
Aundh: village in Satára district, and action near (1713), XIX, 449-450, 257; State, *id.* 2, 621-622.
Aundha: hill fort in Ahmadnagar district, Peshwá's out-post blown up by Captain Mackintosh (1819-1820), XVII, 4, 732.
Aundha: natural fort, in Násik district, its history, XVI, 424-425; 441, 447.
Aungier, Gerald: Deputy Governor of Bombay, his embassy to Raigad (1674), XI, 365; observes neutrality between the Sidis and Shivaji, (1673), *id.* 438; his Governorship (1669-1677), XIII, 474, 475, 476; see also XXVI, pt. i, 38; his proposals for levying taxes in Bombay for strengthening defences and building a dock and public offices, etc., *id.* 39-40; his proposals for encouraging trade by persuading artificers to settle in Bombay, *id.* 41-42; for appointing responsible heads of different communities, *id.* 43; and others for the good of the inhabitants, *id.* 43-46; detained at Surat, XXVI, pt. i, 51-52; goes to Bombay (1672), *id.* 53; Bombay, *id.* 54-55; his death, *id.* 78.
Auranga: river in Surat district, II, 27.
Aurangábád: town, in the Nizam's dominions, I, pt. ii, 388, 430, 520, 524; Gazi-ud-din's camp at (1752); his death at; greater part of the province ceded to the Maráthas by the Nizam (1760), *id.* 627; named after Aurangzeb, XVII, 399.
Aurangzeb: Mughal emperor; appointed viceroy of Gujarát (1644), his viceroyalty marked by religious disputes and persecution, recalled (1646), I, pt. i, 280; see also IX, pt. ii, 35 note 1, 63, 5 note 3; appointed Subhedar of Dakhan 1650), I, pt. ii, 625; see also XVII, 399; besieges Bijápur (1656), but raises the siege (1657), I, pt. ii, 651-652; see also XXIII, 429; insulted by Shiváji, XVIII, pt. ii. 227; joins Murad, defeats Jasvantsing and Dara and ascends the throne (1658), I, pt. ii, 68; his interview with the head of the Surat factory and Rustom Manek (1660), IX, pt. ii, 196 note 3; sends Shaiste Khán (1663), and Jaysing and Diler Khan (1665) against Shiváji, XVIII, pt. ii, 229, 231; takes

Shiváji in the imperial service and invites him to Delhi (1666), XVIII, pt. ii, 234; appoints Sidi Yakut of Janjira, Mughal admiral (1670), I, pt. i, 285; despatches a force under Mohabat Khan against Shiváji (1671), I, pt. ii, 594; reduces Vishalgad and Panhála fort (1673), XXIV, 226-227; his campaigns against Udepur and Márwár, imposes *jazya* tax in Gujarát (1679), I, pt, i, 286; his ships ravage Konkan coast (1681), I, pt. ii, 76; comes in person into the Dakhan (1684), *id.* 595, 654; sends his son Muazzim into the Konkan (1684), *id.* 654; imposes the poll tax in the Dakhan (1684), XVIII, pt. ii, 238; fall of Bijápur (1686), I, pt, ii, 595, 655; see also XXIII, 438; fall of Golkonda (1687), I, pt. ii, 595; see also XXIII, 439; gives a sanad to the Sidi, (1689), I, pt. ii, 79; Sambhaji's execution, (1689), *id.* 596; see also XXII. i, 238; Sháhu taken prisoner (1690), I, pt. ii, 596; declares war against the Portuguese (1694) and inflicts cruelties on them, I, pt. ii, 40, 80; fixes his head-quarters at Brahmapuri (1694), *id.* 596; his stay at Masur (Kolhapur State) (1698-1700), XXIV, 361-362; his death, (1707), I, pt. ii, 597; *see* also I, pt. i, 295; XVII, 403; XVIII, pt. ii, 240.

Aurv : story of, XV, pt. ii, 295 note 1.

Austrians: in Surat (1707-1733), II, 116.

Authandi : tapping-knife cess in Thána, XIII, 634, 644

Auto-da-fe : I, pt. ii, 56, 58.

Automula : tribe, I, pt. i, 532; modern Chaul, 533, 534, 540.

Auxoamis: town, mentioned by Ptolemy, identification of, I, pt. i, 539.

Avagána: Afgháns mentioned by Varaha-Mihira (550) under the name of, IX, pt. ii, 10 note 4.

Avala : *see* Avla.

Avalokita : father of Yogesvara, I, pt. i, 126.

Avalokiteshvar : Bodhisattva, XIV, 132 note 5; image of, in Kánheri Caves, *id.* 165; mention of, by Fah Hian and Hiwen Thsang, his various names, his representation in sculpture, *id.* 207 and note 1; statue of, told Shri Harsha the story of his former birth, IX, pt. i, 441.

Avan : tenth day of the Pársi month, eighth month of the Pársi year, IX, pt. ii, 216.

Aván Arduisur: water spirit or angel, IX, pt. ii, 206, 216.

Aván Ardnisur Jasan : high festival day, observances on, IX, pt. ii, 216-217. *See* Jasans.

Avanchapali : village in the Avaretika country, I, pt. ii, 356.

Avang : a mode of insurance, V, 122.

Avanijanáśraya-Pulikeśin : of Gujarát, I, pt. ii, 310, 311, 316, 336 note 3, 375, 376. *See* Pulakeśi.

Avanisimha : I, pt. ii, 324. *See* Vishnu, Pallava king.

Avanita Kongani : Ganga king (454-466), I, pt. ii, 300.

Avanti : king of, at the bridegroom-choosing of Durlabhadevi, I, pt. i, 163; country mentioned by Pánini, I, pt. ii, 138; its position in the Puránas, *id.* 139; mentioned in the Rámáyana, *id.* 142; subjugated by Gotamiputra, *id.* 161; Ujjain, *id.* 395; kingdom, *id.* 403, note 3.

Avápa : footpath near Náná pass in the Thána district, XIII, 316; description of, by Fryer from Khopoli to Ávápe, *id.* 317, 321. *See* also XIV, 286; XVIII, pt. ii, 151.

Avaretiká : country, I, pt. ii, 356.

Avaro : journal account book, IX, pt. i, 83; contents of, *id.* 84. *See* Books (Accounts).

Avars : the, tribe of foreign immigrants, I, pt. i, 75, 44; the Jue-Jue or Juán-Juán horde identified with, a strongly Chinese tribe of the same name, IX, pt. i, 461, 471, 474 note 3. *See* Juán-Juán.

Avartiás: or Avarthiya, inferior section of Káthis, Babriás form sub-division of, IX, pt. i, 261; *id.* 444 note 2; strong Juán-Juán or Avár element in, *id.* 462 note 2. *See* Káthis.

Avás : port in Kolába district, XI, 265.

Avasara I : Southern Konkan Siláhára king, I, pt. ii, 537.

Avasara II : Southern Konkan Siláhára king, I, pt. ii, 537.

Avasara III : Southern Konkan Siláhára king, I, pt. ii, 537.

Avasarpini : age, I, pt. i, 193.

Avatárs [incarnations] : of Vishnu, doctrine of; literal meaning of; Ram and Krishna most worshipped incarnations of Vishnu, IX, pt. i, 530, 531, 532; *see* Vishnu; doctrine of, engrafted on the Ismáilián faith to present it in an inviting form to Vishnu and Shakti worshipping followers; Ádam, the Prophet and others described as avatárs of the gods of the Hindu Pantheon, IX, pt. ii, 40, 48 and note 2.

Avchar : Bhil state in Khándesh district, XII, 604.

Avchitgad : remains of the fort of, in Kolábá district, I, pt. ii, 42; XI, 265-277; ceded to the Peshwa (1754), I, pt. ii, 83; XI, 445.

Avenasativa : food plant grown near Poona, XXV, 187.

Averrhoa : *bilimbi, carambola,* timber and fruit trees, XXV, 30, 148.

Averse : in Kánara district, shrine at, XV, pt. ii, 260.

Avesta : language of the holy books, IX, pt. ii, 204 and note 1; sacred texts, *id.* 211; Sassanian name of the ancient texts, *id.* 211 note 1. *See* Zend Avesta.

Avicennia officinalis: timber and dye plant found in Konkan and Bombay, XXV, 109, 248.

Avighnákara : Buddhist of Ganda (Bengal), I, pt. ii, 405.

Avinita Kongani : Ganga king, I, pt. ii, 292 note 10, 300.

Ávla [Avala] : *Phyllanthus emblica,* a Poona tree, found in Dakhan and Khándesh, XII, 23, XVIII, pt. i, 42; also XXV, 171.

Avlingva : Lingáyat monastery at Shirhatti in Kolhápur state, XXIV, 369-371.

Avliya : Musalmán saint, XXIV, 318.

Ávnu : a mode of Alibág salt rice tillage, XI, 191.

Avolokiteshvar : *see* Padmapáni.

Avra : fort in Ratnágiri district, X, 463.
Avsari Budrukh : town in Poona district, temple, XVIII, pt. iii, 104-105.
Avvalladevi : I, pt. ii, 435, 514. *See* Hamma.
Avveśvara : temple of S'iva in Konkau (?), I, pt. ii, 538.
Awah : fibrous plant found in the Himalayas, XXV, 234.
A'yah : maid servant, IX, pt. ii, 96.
Ayama : minister of Nahapána, I, pt. ii, 149; his inscription, *id.* 158.
Ayodhya : capital of Assam, I, pt. i, 491; modern Oudh, I, pt. ii, 281 note 3; original seat of the Chálukyas, *id.* 339, 340 note 1, 345 note 4; place of pilgrimage, IX, pt. i, 549.
Ayra : a Brahman sub-division in Cutch, V, 47.
Ayurvedarasáyana : commentary on a medical treatise by Vágbhata, I, pt. ii, 249.
Ayya : Lingáyat priest, I, pt. ii, 549; in Kánara district, XV, pt. i, 175, 177.
Ayyana I : Western Chálukya king (935), I, pt. ii, 378; marries the daughter of Krishna, Ráshtrakúta king, *id.* 379 notes 1 and 2, 427.
Ayyana II : Western Chálukya king, I, pt. ii, 435.
Ayyanasinga : 'lion of his father,' Karád Siláhára title, I, pt. ii, 547, 548.
Ayyansing I : *see* Gandaráditya.
Ayyansing II : *see* Vijayáditya.
Ayyapadeva : Pallava king of the Begur inscription, I, pt. ii, 379 and note 2.
Ayyávole : I, pt. ii, 282. *See* Aihole.
Azadirachta Indica : XXV, 40, 196, 215.
A'zam Khán : viceroy of Gujarát (1635-1642), I, pt. i, 278; subdues Kolis and Káthis, robbers in Jhálávada, Káthiáwár, Navángar and Cutch (1639), *id.* 278, and marches against Navánagar (1640); is recalled (1642), *id.* 279.
Azam Khán : Mughal general, at operations against Ahmadnagar, I, pt. ii, 649; laid siege to Bijápur (1631), XXIII, 425.
Azamnagar : origin of the name, XXI, 376 note 8. *See* Belgaum.
A'zam Sháh [Azim Sháh] : son of Aurangzeb, withdraws from the Dakhan and releases Sháhu (1707), I, pt. ii, 597, 598; defeated and slain, I, pt. i, 296; at the siege of Satára (1700), XIX, 250-251; advances against Bijápur, I, pt. ii, 654.
A'zam Tára : name given (1700) to Satára fort after Aurangzeb's son, XIX, 251, 575.
Azán : call to prayer, IX, pt. ii, 154.
Azim : prince, Aurangzeb's son. *See* A'zam Sháh.
Azud-ud-Din : sayad, ancestor of the Kasbátis, IX, pt. ii, 64. *See* Kasbátis.

B

BA'BA' DEV : clay image of a horse and rider, worshipped by Bhils, IX, pt. i, 292.
Bábá Fadke : a Baroda officer (1844), his intrigue, VII, 267, 270.
Bábá Firúz : IX, pt. ii, 136. *See* Abú Lúlú.
Bábághor : agates in Rewa Kántha, VI, 162 note 1; in Cambay, *id.* 207.
Bábá Ghor : Abyssinian saint, object of worship of the Sidís; tomb of, at Ratanpur in Káthiáwár, IX, pt. ii, 12.
Bábáji A'páji : brother of the Baroda minister Ravji A'páji, VII, 200-202, 204-205, 319-322, 324; military minister of the Gáikwár (1805), leaves the command of forces in Káthiáwár and takes part in civil administration at Baroda, I, pt. i, 416.
Bábal : Babylon, I, pt. i, 506.
Bába Náphade : a Baroda courtier, his intrigues, VII, 250, 253, 260-261, 266, 268.
Bába Piáráh : ford in the Nerbada, defeat of the Musalmáns at (1705), I, pt. i, 294; *see* also VII, 167; advance of the Maráthás to (1711), *id.* 297; *see* also VII, 169, 193.
Babar : a caste of cultivators in Khándesh district, XII, 69.
Bábariavád : a sub-division in Káthiáwár, VIII, 5; *see* also I, pt. i, 175, 187.
Bábaro : demon, helps Siddharája in his magical feats, I, pt. i, 174.
Bábá Shujá-ud-dín : IX, pt. ii, 142. *See* Abú Lúlú.
Babblers : class of birds in Ratnágiri district, X, 73.
Báber : Mughal Emperor (1526-1530), entertains the Mirzás at his court, IX, pt. ii, 10.
Babhul : timber tree common in most districts of the Presidency, XXV, 66, 199, 244; *see* also XII, 24, XVIII, pt. i, 42; favourite spirit-haunt, worship of, IX, pt. I, 383.
Bábhulna : pass in Násik district, XVI, 127.
Babington : Stephen, his tomb in the English church at Thána, XIV, 352 and note 2.
Babington Point : Mahábaleshwar, XIX, 506.
Bábis : a Gujarát Musalmán dynasty, VII, 170-171; their power weakened by Damaji, *id.* 183-184, 594, 604-605; *see* also I, pt. i, 286, 300, 301; Sherkhán, VII, 173-174, 176, 183; Jawán Mard Khán, *id.* 176, 177, 179, 183; of Rádhanpur in Gujarát, IX, pt. ii, 12.
Babra : town in Káthiáwár, the supposed capital of Babbruváhan, VIII, 372.
Bábrianagar : fort in Káthiáwár (?) invested by Cháhada, I, pt. i, 187.
Bábriá or Babar : a tribe intermediate between Káthis and A'hirs, VIII, 130, 131; their settlement in Káthiáwár, history, *id.* 132-134; their marriage connections with both tribes, IX, pt. i, 261; herdsmen, closely allied to the A'hirs, *id.* 266; origin of the name, a subdivision of the Avártia section of the Káthis, *id.* 444 note 2; Musalmán prisoners of war enrolled among, *id.* 444.
Bábsur : lake in Mahi Kántha, V, 358.
Babul : *see* Babhul.
Bab-Ul-Abwál : city in the Caucasus, IX, pt. i, 475 note 1, 476 note 1; the sea of, a name for the Caspian, *id.* 477 note 4.
Babur : *see* Babhul.
Baburáv : guardian of Yashvantráv, infant son of Umábái Dábháde, I, pt. i, 396; Sindia's general, seizes Hirákot (1796), the fort at Alibág in Kolábá district (1793-1813), XI, 155-156, 260, 265.

Báburáv Keshav Thákur: builds the Káttyáyani conduit (1792), an old Kolhápur waterwork, XXIV, 305.
Babylon: Musalmán beliefs about the great well in, IX, pt. ii, 143; Thána trade with (B. C. 2500-B. C. 500), XIII, 403.
Babylonians: their connection with India, XIII, 404 note 3.
Báchaladevi: wife of the Western Chálukya king Someśvara I, I, pt. ii, 438.
Báchaládevi: of the Pándya family, wife of Tailapa II the Hángal Kádamba, I, pt. ii, 559, 562.
Báchana: officer of Bhillama and governor of Belvola district (now Dhárwár district?), I, pt. ii, 520.
Báchideva: *see* Báchana.
Báchirája: Singhana's officer in charge of the Karnátak in 1247, I, pt. ii, 524.
Bactrian Greeks: foreign invaders settled in the Dakhan, I, pt. ii, 173.
Bacul mulsari: oil yielding tree, common to the whole of India, XXV, 223.
Bádagi: son of Rája the Yádava king, his various names, I, pt. ii, 513.
Badam: almond tree, in Bombay and Poona, XXV, 154, XVIII, pt. i, 43.
Bádámi: táluka in the Bijápur district, I, pt. ii, 572; town, *id.* 538 note 8; *see* also I, pt. i, 125; acquisition of the country round, by Pulikeśin I, the Western Chálukya king (550), *id.* 335, 382; taken from the Kadambas of Banavási and made his capital by Pulikeśin I, *id.* 181, 344 note 5; XV, pt. ii, 81; Pulikeśin II establishes himself at, *id.* 351, 356; his capital, IX, pt. ii, 183 note 4; Western Chálukyas of, *id.* 278 note 1, 299 note 4, 315, 335 note 1, 336, 378; laid waste by Narasimha Varman I, the Pallava king, *id.* 322, 358, 360; destroyed by the Pallava king Parameśvaravarman, *id.* 362; Kirtivarman I finishes a Vaishnáva cave temple at, *id.* 346; Vijayáditya installs the images of the gods Brahmá, Vishnu and Maheśvara at, *id.* 189, 371; inscription at, *id.* 169, 189, 328 and note 5, 329, 330, 336 note 3, 337 notes 1 and 2, 346 and note 1, 348, 457; besieged and taken by the Maráthás from Tipu (1786), *id.* 661; ceded to the Maráthás by Tipu (1787), *id.* 661; capture of, by Colonel T. Munro in 1817, *id.* 664. *See* Vátápi and Vátápipura. Another account of, survey, XXIII, 469-471; subdivision details, boundaries, area, aspect, soil, climate, water, stock, crops, people, *id.* 529-531; town details, position, caves, inscriptions, fortifications, history, sieges (1786 and 1818), *id.* 550-565, 362, 378, 380, 443, 450.
Badanálu: inscription at, I, pt. ii, 507.
Badarasidhi: apparently Borsad in Baroda state, I, pt. i, 126.
Bádávi: Badámi (?) in Bijápur district, Prákrit equivalent of Sanskrit Vátápi, I, pt. ii, 371.
Baddiga: Ráshtrakúta king. *See* Amoghavarsha III and Vaddiga.
Baddiga: fifth Western Chálukya prince, I, pt. ii, 212, 380.
Badgani: river in Kánara district, XV, pt. i, 7, 8.
Badgi: *see* Badige.
Badgir: wood workers in Bijápur. *See* Badige.
Bad-Gujars or Bir-Gujars: special class of Gujars, meaning of the name; held to be Rájpúts, claim descent from Lav the son of Rám; the divine Krishna born in the class of, IX, pt. i, 476, 482 and notes 9 and 10; high Gujjars, I, pt. i, 464.
Badhái: carpenters in Poona, their food, dress, tools, ceremonies, caste, XVIII, pt. i, 314-316.
Bádhekaris: waste tillers in Ratnágiri district, X, 142, 210.
Bádi: miniature garden carried before the bridegroom's steed, IX, pt. ii, 165 note 3.
Badige: carpenters in Kánara district, XV, pt. i, 261, 262; in Belgaum district, XXI, 132-134; in Dhárwár district, XXII, 145-146; in Bijápur district, *see* Panchála.
Badi-Jamát: *see* Jaáfari Bohorás.
Bádipoddi: harlot, makes grants to the temple of Lokeśvara, I, pt. ii, 394.
Badi-ud-din Madár Sháh: saint of Syria, IX, pt. ii, 22.
Badlee: common fodder plant, XXV, 276.
Bádmer: town, I, pt. i, 470.
Báduer: Mher settlement at, I, pt. i, 136.
Badrikedár: place of pilgrimage on the Ganges, IX, pt. i, 157, 549.
Badr-ud-din: head mulla of the Dáudi Bohorás (1837), IX, pt. ii, 31 note 4.
Badr-ul-Zamán: Maisur general, held Dhárwár for Tipu (1790), XXII, 417.
Badvás: Bhil *bhagats*, devotees and exorcists, held in special reverence by Bhils; incantations; duties; part played by them in exorcism and witchcraft; in *jatárs* or sacrifices; Kajaliya or black Badvás specially skilful in finding out witches, IX, pt. i, 302-303; 307 and note 1. *See* Bhils.
Badvás: Pandharpur priests, trustees of Vithobá's temple, XX, 427, 468.
Baer: timber tree, found all over India, XXV, 49.
Bágadage: country round Bágalkot in Bijápur district, forms a part of Ráshtrakúta Vaddiga's daughter's dowry, I, pt. ii, 304-305, 418; hereditary possession of the Sindas of Yelburga, *id.* 572, 575; ruled over by the Sindas, *id.* 431, 437, 441 note 6, 458, 460, 485, 576, 577.
Bagada-toling: timber tree found in Konkan, XXV, 84.
Bágadige: old name for Bágalkot in Bijápur district, I, pt. ii, 305.
Bágalkot: táluka in Bijápur district, I, pt. ii, 576; survey and sub-divisional details, XXIII, 471-473, 531-533; town, captured by Colonel Munro (1817), *id.* 664; details, history, fort, trade, *id.* 361, 378, 563-564.
Bagasra: town in Káthiáwár, funeral monuments at, history, VIII, 372-373.
Bágbán: Musalmán fruiterer in Thána district, XIII, 236; in Ahmadnagar district, XVII, 229; in Khándesh district, XII, 127; in Poona district, XVIII, pt. i, 499; in Sátára district, XIX, 139; in Sholápur district,

XX, 204; in Belgaum district, XXI, 214; in Dhárwár district, XXII, 240; in Bijápur district, XXIII, 297.
Bagda: place of interest in Cambay, memorial stones, temples and other remains at, V, 213.
Bagdáná: place of interest in Káthiáwár, VIII, 373.
Bágdis: beggars in Belgaum district, XXI, 178.
Báge: *see* Bágadage.
Bágedgudd: hill in Belgaum district, XXI, 8.
Bágenád: *see* Bágadage.
Bágevádi: sub-division in Bijápur district, I, pt. ii, 503; survey and sub-divisional details, XXIII, 488-494, 533-535; Town details and temples at, *id.* 362, 564-565; Basav's place of residence, I, pt. ii, 225; antiquarian references to, *id.* 245; XXI, 513.
Bágewádi: *see* Bágevádi.
Bagha: part of *Zend Avesta*, IX, pt. ii, 211 note 2 (4).
Baghan Yesht: part of *Zend Avesta*, IX, pt. ii, 211 note 2 (15).
Bághbán: *see* Bághán.
Baghdád: Cambay known at (915), I, pt. i, 514; settlers at Chaul from (914), *id.* 516; fleets from, sent to plunder and conquer Gujarát coast, IX, pt. ii, 2; shrine of Abdúl Kadir Giláni at, visited by Memans, *id.* 56.
Bághji: founder of Bhagarávat Gujars, was born with a tiger's head and a man's body, story of his marriage with girls of different castes, IX, pt. i, 487.
Baghla: an Arab lateen rigged vessel, its description, XIII, 352-353, 718.
Bághrah: probably Balhára, his rule at Chitakul (913), XV, pt. ii, 278 and note 2.
Bághvati: tiger town, in Cambay, VI, 183.
Baglán: old tract of land between Surat and Nandurbár, XVI, 4, 188; hiding place of Karnadeva, I, pt. i, 205; *see* also I, pt. ii, 532 and note 2; sub-division in Násik district, sub-divisional details and history, survey introduced into, XVI, 399-407, 250-253; *see* also IX, pt. ii, 67.
Bágmándla: village in Ratnágiri district, ceded to the British (1756), X, 319.
Bágni: village in Sátára district, Musalmán remains at, XIX, 451.
Bágoja: Tippoja's son, architect of the temple at Degámve, I, pt. ii, 569.
Bagumra: village in Baroda territory, copper plate grant from, I, pt. i, 117; plate of Akálavarsha at, *id.* 125; grant of Dhurva II at, *id.* 126; Akálavarsha Krishna's grant at, *id.* 127; Krishna, the Gujarát Ráshtrakúta king's grant at, *id.* 129; Dhurva II's plate at, *id.* 130, 468; copper-plate grant from, I, pt. ii, 312 note 7, 360, 363, 365 note 3, 366, 405, 409, 410, 412 and note 4, 414.
Bagváda: fort in Surat district, capture of, by Shiváji (1672), I, pt. i, 387; by Lieutenant Welsh in 1780, *id.* 409.
Bágvati: village in Kánara district, XV, pt. ii, 260.
Bagwel: Commodore, sails against Sambháji A'ngria's fleet (1738), I, pt. ii, 88.
Báhada: son of Udaya, rises to high position under Kumárapála, I, pt. i, 170; is made chief counsellor, *id.* 184; establishes Báhadapura in Baroda territory, *id.* 186.
Báhadapura: town in Baroda territory, established by Báhada, I, pt. i, 186 note 4. *See* also VII, 557.
Bahádur: *see* Bahádur Sháh.
Bahádur Benda: fort in the Karnátak, captured by Haripanth the Marátha commander-in-chief; recovered by Mysore troops (1787), I, pt. ii, 661.
Bahádurgad: fort in Ahmadnagar district, built by the Mughál governor Khán Jahán (1673), I, pt. ii, 626. *See* also XVII, 400.
Bahádur Giláni: Bahmani officer, revolts and seizes Goa and Kolhápur, XXIV, 225; captures Dábhol and burns Máhim (Bombay) (1493), I, pt. ii, 32; X, 327; takes refuge in Panhála, killed, and his fleet handed over to the Gujarát admiral, I, pt. ii, 33; XXIV, 225. *See* also XXI, 366.
Bahádur Khán: son of a slave girl, claims the chiefship of Junágadh (1811), I, pt. i, 425.
Bahádur Khán: Khán Jehán, thirty-fourth viceroy of Gujarát (1668-1671); sent as viceroy of the Dakhan (1671-1674), I, pt. i, 285.
Bahádur Khán Fáruki: (1596-1599), son and successor of Rája A'li of Khándesh, I, pt. ii, 624; defeated and taken prisoner by A'kbar (1599), XII, 247.
Bahádur Khán Giláni: *see* Bahádur Giláni.
Bahádur Khán Ranmast: Mughal general, enters the Konkan (1684), I, pt. ii, 77.
Bahádurpur: town near Burhánpur, founded by Bahádur Khán Fáruki, XII, 247; plundered and burnt by Sambháji (1685), *id.* 251 note 2.
Bahádur Sháh I: (1707-1712) emperor of Delhi, I, pt. i, 296; his death, *id.* 297; his order to introduce the Shiah epithet "Wasi" in public prayers, IX, pt. ii, 125 note 1.
Bahádur Sháh: Sultán of Gujarát (1525-1535), drives Burhán Sháh from Berár, captures Ahmadnagar and compels Burhán to acknowledge his supremacy (1528-1530), I, pt. ii, 622; *see* also XVII, 363-364; invites Sayád Jamál, ancestor of the Kádiri family, to Gujarát (1530), IX, pt. ii, 6 note 1 (2); Turks and Abyssinians in his army (1531), *id.* 3 note 1; accords an asylum to the Mírzás in Ahmadábád and Broach against the vengeance of Humáyun (1532), *id.* 9; captures Mándu and sends Mehmud II of Málwa prisoner to Gujarát; incorporates Málwa with Gujarát (1526), I, pt. i, 367; takes refuge at Mándu after his defeat at Mandasor, flees from Mándu to Chámpánir, *id.* 367, 368; cedes the town of Bassein to the Portuguese, *id.* 347; *see* also XIII, 451, and XIV, 28, 29; his death (1536), I, pt. i, 348-351.
Bahádurvádi: village in Sátára district, fort at, XIX, 450-451.
Bahál: records at, I, pt, ii, 523.
Bahalim: Indian viceroy of the Ghazni king, I, pt. i, 174 note 1.

Bahámani : dynasty founded about A. D. 1347 at Gulbarga, I, pt. ii, 587, 620, 637 ; extent of its territory (1347), *id.* 620, 637 ; during the Durgádevi famine (1396-1408) the hill forts fall into the hands of Marátha chiefs ; Malek-ul-Tujár is sent to subdue the gháts, and the Konkan (1420), *id.* 588 ; another force is sent by Ala-ud-din into the Konkan (1436), *id.* 31, 588 ; Malek-ul-Tujár is again sent (1451) ; Máhmúd Gáwán, the great minister, makes another effort to subdue the hill country and takes Kelua (1472), and makes a new distribution of the dominions, *id.* 588 ; attacks on the Southern Marátha Country (1406-1472) ; the capture of Belgaum brings the whole country under them (1472), *id.* 638-639 ; famine (1472) ; unjust execution of the prime minister precipitates the fall of (1481), *id.* 639 ; partition of the Dakhan (1491), *id.* 589 ; institutions of, XIX, 227 note 5 ; for other accounts *see* XXI, 362-367 ; XXIII, 397-403 ; their rule, in Thána district, XVII, 353-358, and XIV, 120, 357 ; XIII, 441-442, 551 note 6 ; in Ahmadnagar district, XVII, 353-358 ; in Sátára district, XIX, 225-227 ; in Sholápur district, XX, 276-278 ; in Dhárwár, and wars with Vijayánagar, XXII, 403-405 ; in Kolába district, XI, 142 ; in Khándesh, XII, 243 ; in Násik district, XVI, 535 ; in Kánara district, XV, pt. ii, 94, 95 ; in Ratnágiri district, X, 193 ; in Poona district, XVIII, pt. ii, 215-219.

Bahár : (Bihar) Maráthás in (1742), XIX, 285.

Baharám Gor : Persian king, his visit to India (420-440), XII, 557.

Baharimad : Mevád (?), I, pt. i, 109, 492.

Baharji : title of Báglán chiefs, XVI, 184 and note 8.

Bahárvatia : outlawry practised by Káthiáwár Rájpúts, VIII, 116 and note 1, 117 ; indulged by the chiefs, *id.* 329 ; outlaws, in Kaira district, III, 120 ; in Ahmadábád district, IV, 197.

Bahattara-niyog-Adhipati : official title of Kalyáni Kálachuryas, I, pt. ii, 485, 486, 489, 521, 524.

Bahauddin : Nakshband, saint, IX, pt. ii, 20.

Bahawalpur : town in Sind, I, pt. i, 538.

Báhe : village in Sátára district, temples, fairs, XIX, 452.

Bahedári : *Baroda* guarantee system, in the hands of the Arabs, transferred to the Company (1802), VII, 253-263, 271.

Bahika : the West Panjáb, IX, pt. i, 439 note 5.

Bahikás : apparently the S'akes of the second or first century before Christ ; their priests, admitted to be Bráhmans, IX, pt. i, 439 ; their traces remain in Valkel Bráhmans, *id.* 439 note 5.

Bahír : believed to be the origin of the name Bohora, IX, pt. ii, 24 note 3.

Bahiravgad : two forts of the same name in Ratnágiri district, X, 319.

Bahirgad : fort in Kolhápur, XXIV, 4. *See* also Bahirugad.

Báhirji Náik : Shiváji's spy in Gujarát in 1664, I, pt. i, 386.

Bahiropant : Sháhu's minister (1713), XVIII, pt. ii, 242 ; defeated by Kánhoji Angria, XI, 146.

Bahirugad : chief place of the Shirkes, north of Vishalgad in Kolhápur state, I, pt. ii, 31, 86.

Bahirugad : fort in Thána district, XIV, 14.

Bahirupant Pingle Peshwa : *see* Bahiropant.

Bahlol Khán : founder of the Sávanur family, enters the service of Ahmadnagar and thence passes to Bijápur (1626-1656), I, pt. ii, 665. *See* also XXII, 792.

Bahman : animal guardian, second day of the Pársi month ; eleventh month of the Pársi year, IX, pt. ii, 217.

Bahmani : *see* Bahámani.

Bahman Jasan : high festival day ; observances on, IX, pt. ii, 217. *See* Jasans.

Bahraj : believed to be the origin of the name Bohora, IX, pt. ii, 25, note 1.

Bahrám Sháh : Ghazni king (1116-57), I, pt. i, 174 note 1 ; comes to India (1118) ; kills Muhammad Behlim in the battle of Multán, IX, pt. ii, 58.

Bahrein : island in the Persian Gulf, Arab expeditions from, to Thána coast and Broach (636), I, pt. i, 505, 513, 523 ; I, pt. ii, 14 ; trade of, in horses with Cambay (1100), I, pt. i, 515 ; emporium of Indian trade, XIII, 404 note 3.

Bahrots : *see* Bhats.

Bahruch : *see* Broach.

Bahruj : *see* Broach.

Bahrus : I, pt. i, 520. *See* Broach.

Bahuchara, Bahucharaji : Gujarát Hindu goddess, legend of, temple of, at Salkhanpur in Káthiáwár, VIII, 137 note 1 ; votaries of, IX, pt. ii, 21, 22, 82, favourite deity, IX, pt i, pp. xxxv, xxxvi, *id.* 20, 29 and note 1, 510 ; also known as Becharáji or Becharâ ; originally a Cháran woman, becomes a devi by her self-sacrifice ; probably an old Koli goddess, *id.* p. xxxvi ; 216 note 1, 218, 277 note 1 ; head-quarters of the worship of, in the Chunvál, *id.* 216 note 1, 223 ; home of, shrine of, *id.* pp. ix, xi ; 549 ; cock the carrier of, *id.* 380 ; healing shrine of, frequented by the sick, *id.* 365, 366 ; by pilgrims, *id.* 187 ; special mode of offering an animal to, *id.* 407 ; performances of *bhaváis* or comedies by Bhaváyás at the temple of, *id.* 223 note 1 ; worshippers of, *id.* 182, 213, 506, 507 ; place of pilgrimage, *id.* 157, 187, 225, 336 ; the head lodge or *math* of the Bhárváds at, *id.* 277.

Bahula : fort in Násik district, XVI, 425.

Bahule : village, in Sátára district, temple and fairs at, XIX, 452-53.

Bahuleshvar : village in Khándesh, temple at, XII, 432.

Báhuloda : apparently the modern village of Bholáda, in Gujarát, remission of pilgrim tax at, I, pt. i, 172.

Bahuráh : believed to be the origin of the name Bohora, IX, pt. ii, 24 note 3.

Bahuriband : town in Central Provinces, inscription at, I, pt. ii, 425.

Bahurupi : *see* Bhorpi.

Bahusahaya : *see* Dadda III.

Báhva : tree in Khandesh and Poona districts, XII, 24 ; XVIII, pt. i, 43.

Baidaru : *see* Berad.

Baidjadak : Arabic for ruby, I, pt. i, 517.

Báil Hongal : an old town, in Belgaum, trade centre, a temple, fair, and inscriptions at, XXI, 514 ; also I, pt. ii, 555.

Bailur : village in Kánara district, XV, pt. ii, 147 ; temple and fair at, *id.* 260.

Bailur : hill in Belgaum district, XXI, 7.

Baiones : Peram, I, pt. i, 545.

Baira : pirate boats, I, pt. i, 508 note 4, 521.

Bairágis : religious beggars, in Koláha district, XI, 415 ; in Thana district, XIII, 195 ; in Násik district, XVI, 73 ; in Dhárwár and Kolhápur, XXII, 200, XXIV, 115.

Bairámkhán : Bahamani noble, his revolt (1366), XVII, 354.

Báis : widows of Mahádaji Sindia, ill-treated by Shirzi Ráo Ghátge ; take refuge in Amrutráo's camp and afterwards at Kolhápur ; plunder Sindiá's villages ; driven with the help of Yashvant Ráo Holkar into Burhánpur and thenes to Málwa (1798-1800), I, pt. ii, 607.

Baishi : timber tree on Koukan gháts and at Mahabaleshvar, XXV, 133.

Baisura : Vaishyás, fifth class of Hindu population (912), I, pt. i, 530.

Baithak : sitting room, IX, pt. ii, 92 ; form of gymnastic exercise, *id.* 172.

Baithan : Paithan in Nizám's territory, capital of Pnlumáyi, mentioned by Ptolemy, I, pt. i, 37, 541 ; I, pt. ii, 143, 538 note 8.

Baitkul : creek near Kárwár, XV, pt. ii, 319 ; capture of the 'Monsoon' at (1707), *id.* 134 note 3.

Baïza Bái : daughter of Sirji Ráo Ghátke and widow of Daulatráv Sindia of Gwálior, I, pt. i, 437.

Bajaná : state in Káthiáwár, VIII, 373. *See* also IX, pt. ii, 17.

Bajaniás : rope-dancers, in Káthiáwár, VIII, 159 ; musicians in Gujarát, called *dholis* or drummers, appearance, dress, houses, food, means of livelihood, gangs, IX, pt. i, 503 ; customs, *id.* 503-504.

Bajarbatta : guard against evil-eye, IX, pt. i, 378, 427 and note 1.

Bájazet II : emperor of Turkey, I, pt. ii, 44.

Bájera : *see* Bájri.

Báji Ghorpade : Bijápur chief of Mudhol, his treachery and arrest of Sháhji, I, pt. ii, 592, sent against Shiváji ; surprised and killed by Shiváji at Mudhol (1661), *id.* 593 ; XIX, 232-33 ; XVIII, pt. ii, 229. *See* also XXIV, 393-94.

Báji Mohite : manager (1647) of Supa, XVIII, pt. ii, 226.

Baji Prabhu : commandant of Purandhar, killed in its gallant defence (1665), XVIII, pt. ii, 231.

Bajipur : new town of Bassein, I, pt. ii, 99.

Bájiráv I : second Peshwa (1721-40) ; sets out with an army for Khándesh ; his schemes for the conquest of Málwa ; Holkar and Sindia officers in his army ; his character ; his ambitious scheme of conquest ; is opposed by the Pratinidhi ; his incursions in Málwa ; Nizám-ul-Mulk's fears at the spread of the Marátha power ; war with Trimbakráv Dábháde in Gujarát ; Raghuji Bhonsle ; wars in the Konkan ; Bájiráv's money difficulties ; receives assignment of the revenue of the districts south of the Chambal ; defeats the Mughals near Delhi ; Nádir Sháh sacks Delhi ; Bájiráv receives Khillat from the Delhi emperor ; his critical situation ; his arrangements with Raghuji Bhonsle ; treaty of Mungi-Paithan ; his death, XIX, 267-83. *Briefer accounts of*, I, pt. ii, 599-600 ; XVIII, pt. ii, 243-44 ; empowers Udaji Powár to collect *chauth* in Gujarát (1724), VII, 167 ; sends Udaji Powár to Gujarát to drive away Piláji Gáikwár ; carries on negotiations with the Gujarát viceroy and promises to exclude Piláji, Kántáji and other freebooters from Gujarát, I, pt. i, 308 ; his struggle with Piláji Gáikwár for ascendancy in Gujarát (1729-32), *id.* 171-73 ; discovers the intrigues of Trimbakráv Dábháde ; advances to Baroda and besieges it : raises the siege and on his way to the Dakhan defeats the forces of Trimbakráo and Piláji and kills Trimbakráv (1731), *id.* 393 ; his negotiations with the Nizám (1731), *id.* 312-13 ; is appointed governor of Málwa with Anandráv Powár as his deputy (1734), *id.* 382 ; retakes Ráygad, Tala, and Ghosála ; Avchitgad and Birvádi ceded to (1735), I, pt. ii, 83 ; receives marriage presents from Bombay Government (1740), XXVI, pt. i, 271.

Bájiráv II : ninth Peshwa (1796-1817) ; is imprisoned by Nána in the fort of Junnar (1794) ; his condition ; Náná's intrigues for preventing his accession to the Peshwaship on the death of Mádhavráv (1774-1795) ; Bájiráv asks Sindia's help ; deserts Sindia in favour of Nána : his brother Chimnáji is raised to the Peshwaship by Sindia's minister ; Nána's schemes to restore Bájiráv who is sent to North India by Báloba Tátya, Sindia's minister ; Bájiráv is brought back and installed Peshwa ; appoints Nána his prime minister ; the principles which guide his conduct ; is tired of Sindia and Nána ; Nána's house is plundered and Nána sent to Ahmadnagar fort ; his half-brother Amritráv becomes prime minister ; Sindia plunders (1797) Poona ; disorders in Poona ; Nána is set free and is induced to become Bájiráv's prime minister ; Nána's death ; Bájiráv gratifies his revenge by throwing into confinement Nána's former supporters ; Bájiráv entirely in the hands of Sindia ; his cruelties and general discontent ; Yashwantráv Holkar's brother Vithoji is dragged to death and his nephew is imprisoned at Asirgad ; Yashwantráv marches on Poona and defeats Bajiráv and Sindia ; Bájiráv flees to Sinhgad, thence to Ráygad, Suvarndurg, Revdanda and Bassein ; enters into the treaty of Bassein ; General Wellesley's march to Poona ; Bájiráv is restored ; condition of the Dakhan (1803-1808) ; estimate of Bájiráv's character

by Sir James Mackintosh, Lord Valentia, Mr. Elphinstone, and General Wellesley; his disloyalty to the English; raises a brigade of Native Infantry; Bájiráv's adviser, Trimbakji Denglia; strengthens his force; influence of Trimbakji in Bájiráv's Court; is haunted by the ghost of Náráyanráv Peshwa who was murdered by his father; plants several hundred thousand mango trees, apparently to get rid of the ghost; his intrigues against the English; adjustment of his claims on the Gáikwár; Gangádhar Shástri in Poona; murder of Gangádhar Shástri; Mr. Elphinstone demands the surrender of Trimbakji Denglia; Bájiráv's professions of regard to the English; organizes a league against the English; is warned by Mr. Elphinstone who demands the surrender of Trimbakji; treaty of Poona; measures for crushing the Pendháris; Sir John Malcolm meets Bájiráv at Máhuli; Bápu Gokhale, Bájiráv's chief adviser; Bájiráv attempts to murder Mr. Elphinstone; preparations for the rupture; battle of Kirkee (1817); Bájiráv's defeat; Poona surrendered; Bájiráv's flight; is pursued by General Smith; fight at Koregaon; Sátára proclamation; fall of all the Poona forts; battle of Ashta; Bájiráv's flight; surrenders to Sir John Malcolm, XVIII, pt. ii, 270-303; *briefer accounts of*, Konkan, during the reign of, I, pt. ii. 110-119; kept in confinement with his father and brother; on the death of the young Peshwa wins over Báloba Tátia, Sindia's chief adviser; to forestall Báloba, is seated on the throne by Nána Phadnavis; his younger brother put on the throne by Sindia; Sindia declares for him; is reconciled to Nána Phadnavis and is formally installed Peshwa (1796); imprisons Nána Phadnavis in Ahmadnagar and allows Sindia's troops to levy money from the rich inhabitants of Poona (1797); releases Parashrám Bhán and sends him against the Rája of Sátára; war with Kolhápur (1799-1800), *id.* 606-607; executes Vithoji the brother of Yashwantráo Holkar, and imprisons Mahádev Ráo Ráste (1801); is defeated by Yashwantráo Holkar (1802); flies to Bassein and signs treaty (1802), and returns to Poona escorted by the English (1802-1803), *id.* 110-111, 608, 609; his mismanagement; endeavours to centralise his power and imprisons the Pratinidhi at Mhasvad (1806); his crafty policy, *id.* 609; Mahádeo Ráo Ráste and Appa Desái Nipánikar fail to send their contingents and are deprived of their lands; forms a body of disciplined troops commanded by English officers (1813); raises Trimbakji Denglia and gives his consent to murder Gangádhar Shástri; surrenders Trimbakji to the English (1815); Trimbakji escapes; the inhabitants rise against him; surrenders Trimbakji and signs a new treaty with the English (1817), *id.* 610; war with the Peshwa; battle of Kirkee (1817); battle of Koregaon (1818); his surrender (1819), *id.* 611; circumstances attending his accession; treaty of Bassein; state of the country; orders Bápu Gokhale to chastise Parashurám Shrinivás, the Pratinidhi; his advisers; Trimbakji Denglia's insurrection; Bájiráv's disloyalty; battle of Kirkee; his defeat and pursuit; Sátára surrendered to the British; Mr. Elphinstone's manifesto, XIX, 298-305; appoints his younger brother governor of Gujarát (1796), I, pt. i, 411; state of Thána under (1802), XIII, 512; takes refuge in Suvarndurg (1802), X, 339; builds a palace at Guhágar (1810), *id.* 336; his claims on the Gáikwár (1817), VII, 218-223; appoints Trimbakji Denglia Sar Subha of Ahmadabad (1814), I, pt. ii, 427; visits Pandharpur (1815-1817), *id.* 292-293; his relations with the Gáikwár (1817), VII, 385; his flight (1817-1818), XX, 293-295; XVII, 414-415; his feud with Násik Bráhmans, XVI, 40 note 4.

Bájiráv Ballál: *see* Bájiráv I.

Bájra: *see* Bájri.

Bájri: food plant in several districts, XXV, 185, 208, 276; in Sátára district, XIX, 160.

Bájvá: a village near Baroda, VII, 534.

Bákad: depressed class in Kánara district, XV. pt. i, 360-362.

Bakám: dye-yielding tree in Khándesh, XII, 25, XXV, 243.

Bákar A'li: Pírána saint, his tomb at Pírána worshipped chiefly by Hindus, IX, pt. ii, 76 note 2.

Bákar Fakih: his land reclamation in Bassein, XIII, 282.

Bakarkasáis: Musalmán mutton butchers in Ahmadnagar, Bijápur, Poona, Sátára and Sholápur districts, XVII, 229; XXIII, 297; XVIII, pt. i, 500; XIX, 139-140, XX, 204.

Bakayan: timber tree cultivated in villages, XXV, 41.

Bakkam: *see* Bakám.

Bakkar: place mentioned by Ibni Khurdádbha (A. D. 912), I, pt. i, 520.

Bakkas: contribution levied by the Imám among Khojás, IX, pt. ii, 49.

Bakli: timber tree found in Konkan forests, XXV, 76.

Bakr I'd: *see* Id.

Bakshi: military paymaster under the Mughals, I, pt. i, 214.

Bakshindabaksh: name given to Sinhgad by Aurangzeb, XVIII, pt. ii, 240.

Baksi: variety of wheat, XXV, 189.

Baktria: Balkh, IX, pt. i, 455; country of Zoroaster, *id.* pt. ii, 211; independence of, I, pt. i, 543.

Baktrian Greeks: called Yakshas, I, pt. i, 456 note 1; their connection with India, *id.* 535; known as Baktrianoi, a warlike race, *id.* 545; pictures of, in the Ajantá caves, XII, 494 and note 1, 517.

Bakul: timber tree common in the presidency, XXV, 91; in Poona district, XVIII, pt. i, 44.

Bakuládevi: queen of Chálukya king Bhim I, (1169), I, pt. i, 169, 181.

Bákurhole: stream in Kánara district, XV, pt. i, 6.

Bála: oldest name of the Ghelots or Sisodiis, IX, pt. i, 495.

Bála : sacred plant, XXV, 289.
Bála Behlím Patti : *see* Behlím.
Balabha : Valabhi, modern Porbandar, in Káthiáwár, I, pt. i, 524, 525.
Balabhadra : elder brother of Krishna, I, pt. ii, 142.
Balabhi : Valabhi, modern Porbandar, in Káthiáwár, I, pt. ii, 284 note 4.
Bálachandra : author of *Prábhritsâra*, I, pt. ii, 288.
Bálachari : port in Káthiáwár, VIII, 34, 375.
Báládev : object of worship among Bharváds, name suggests the Bharvád connection with Bálás or Válás, IX, pt. i, 268.
Báládeva : uncle of Basava and prime minister of Bijjala the Kaláchuri king, I, pt. ii, 478 ; marries his daughter to Basáva, *id.* 225, 226.
Báládevas : Jain saints, I, pt. i, 451 note 3.
Baladevayya : officer of the Western Chálukya king Someśvara II, I, pt. ii, 443.
Baláditya : of Magadha, I, pt. i, 75 notes 2 and 5.
Balá-en-lena : taking off of sorrow, a ceremony, IX, pt. ii, 160 note 1.
Bálágam : place of interest in Káthiáwár, VIII, 376.
Balagámi : *see* Balagámve.
Balagámve : old town in Mysore, Pándavas at, I, pt. ii, 278 note 2 ; forms part of Kuntala, *id.* 431 ; chief place in the Banávási district, *id.* 437, 439, 489 ; important seat of Western Chálukya power, *id.* 449 ; inscriptions at, *id.* 228, 281 note 3, 282 note 5, 306 note 5, 339, 341 note 2, 369 and note 3, 428 note 4, 435 note 10, 436, 442 note 4, 443 note 3, 448 note 1, 450 note 2, 451 notes 1 and 2, 455 and note 6, 457 note 5, 458 note 2, 459 note 3, 460, 461, 465, 466, 473, 474, 475, 476, 487, 503 note 3, 505, 524, 529, 538 note 8, 568 note 3, 581 note 3. *See* also XV, pt. ii, 86 note 2.
Bálághát : upland, a natural division of Kánara district, XV, pt. i, 2.
Bálághát : flat elevated country in Ahmadnagar district, XVII, 5.
Bálághát : hill range in Sholápur district, XX, 2.
Balagnur : village in Dhárwár district, inscription at, XXII, 652.
Balah : Alberuni's era of, I, pt. i, 78 note 1 ; starting of era, *id.* 81.
Balai : Ptolemy's name of Gopnáth in Káthiáwár, I, pt. i, 78 note 1.
Báláji : Násik temple, XVI, 507-509.
Báláji : temple of, at Tirupati, IX, pt. i, 549.
Báláji : Peshwas ; *see* Báláji Bájiráv and Báláji Vishvanáth.
Báláji Auji : Parbhu, chitnis of Shiváji, I, pt. ii, 594 ; XIX, 249.
Báláji Bájiráv : third Peshwa (1740-1761) ; office contested by Bápuji Náik Bárámatikar ; success of Báláji ; his money difficulties ; his plans for the government of Málwa ; receives a grant by which the territory conquered from the Pothuguese is conferred on him ; Báláji in North India and Málwa ; his rivalry with Raghuji Bhonsle ; expedition into the Karnátak ; his intrigues about Sháhu's succession ; his conduct towards Sakvarbái, Sháhu's widow ; his usurpation of authority ; removes the capital to Poona ; Rám Rája is confined in Sátára ; Tárábái's attempts to divert the power from the Konkani Bráhmans ; Dámáji Gáikwár is defeated by Báláji ; Báláji effects a settlement with Tárábái ; management of the country ; battle of Pánipat ; Báláji's death, XIX, 283-295 ; *briefer accounts of*, succeeds his father ; improves the civil administration ; death of Sháhu ; usurps the sole authority ; is opposed by Tárábái ; makes Poona the capital of the Marátha empire ; quarrels with his cousin Sadáshivráv ; their reconciliation ; imprisons the Gáikwár and Dábháde families in Lohogad ; his wars with the Mughals supported by the French ; the Mughals attack the Marátha camp at Rájápur, plunder Ránjangaon and destroy Talegaon Dábháde ; Báláji leads an army into Karnátak ; Dámáji is released on condition of paying a tribute to the Peshwa ; expeditions in Gujarát ; comes in contact with the English ; enters into a treaty with the English ; sends an army to Hindustán which breaks the power of Ahmad Abdalli ; leads again an army into the Karnátak ; attitude towards the English ; his intrigues at the Háidarábád Court ; family feuds ; war with the Nizám ; battle of Udgir ; battle of Pánipat, death ; character, XVIII, pt. ii, 244-250 ; *another account :* overcomes opposition and assumes the management of the Marátha empire (1749) ; confirms Rághuji Bhonsle in Berár, Yeshvantráo Dábháde in Gujarát, Fatehsing Bhonsle in Akalkot, and divides Málwa among Holkar, Sindia and Pavár ; Yamáji Sivdeo's insurrection quelled ; takes Dámáji Gáikwár prisoner to Poona (1751), I, pt. ii, 600-601 ; war with the Nizám (1751), *id.* 601 ; greater part of Khándesh and the Gangthari ceded by the Nizám, *id.* 601-602 ; Ráni Tárábái rebels and is besieged in the fort of Sátára ; Dámáji Gáikwár released and Marátha supremacy established in Gujarát (1754) ; Marátha defeat at Pánipat and his death (1761), *id.* 602 ; *another account :* Dr. Trotter sent to treat with (1745), XXVI, pt. iii, 551 ; sends an army into Gujarát and frees Rangoji (1748), I, pt. i, 333 ; confirms Fatehsing at Akalkot, negotiations with Jawán Mard Khán (1750), XX, 290, I, pt. i, 334 ; his victory over the Gáikwár, imprisons Dámáji and compels him to surrender half his rights and conquests (1751), VII, 178, I, pt. i, 334 ; quells the rising at Sángola (1752), XX, 290-291 ; his intrigue against Bussy (1756), *id.* 291 ; Ahmadnagar and Násik ceded to (1759-60) ; death of (1761), VII, 185 ; gives Ajra to Ichalkaranji chief, XXIV, 290.
Báláji Janárdan : *see* Náná Fadnavis.
Báláji Kunjar : Peshwa's commander, defeated at Gárdhond (1801), I, pt. ii, 608.
Báláji Lakshman : sarsubhedár of Khándesh and Bágláu, his treacherous massacre of

Bhils in Ahmadnagar and Khándesh, I, pt. ii, 629.
Bálájipant Nátu: Mr. Elphistone's friend, XVIII, pt. ii, 299.
Báláji Vishvanáth: first Peshwa (1714-1720); accountant of Shrivardhan in Jánjira; writer under Dhanáji; is viewed with jealousy by Dhanáji's son Chandrasen; his flight; his concealment in Pandugad; is released; is again imprisoned by Dámáji Thorát; is released by Sháhu; leads an army against Kánhoji Ángria; settlement with Ángria; is appointed Peshwa (1714); releases the Pant Sachiv, then Thorát's prisoner; receives lands in Poona; his scheme of usurpation; assists the Syed brothers in their scheme of deposing the emperor Feroksher; visits Delhi; receives three imperial grants for Sháhu; settlement of the country; his death, XIX, 254-266; *another account*: kárkún to Dhanáji Jádhav and afterwards the founder of the Peshwa dynasty, negotiates on behalf of Sháhu with Kánhoji Ángria (1713) and invades the Sidi territory, I, pt. ii, 598; besieged by Chandrasen Jádhav in Pándugad, *id.* 598; subdues Krishnaráo Khatáokar and becomes Peshwa (1714); defeats Dámáji Thorát and takes him prisoner; induces Mughal officers to make Poona over to him (1715); takes part in the quarrels at Delhi as an ally of the Sayad ministers (1718); obtains the grant of *chauth* and *sardeshmukhi* of the Dakhan and the sovereignty of the districts south of the Bhimá and north of the Vardha and Tungábhadrá from Poona to Kolhápur, a part of the Karnátak and the Konkan (1720), *id.* 598-599; his death (1721), *id.* 599; *another account*: first Peshwa (1714-1720); early life; his rise; rivalry with Chandrasen, Sháhu's Commander-in-Chief; flees to Sásvad; his perilous condition; is dignified by Sháhu with the title of Sena-kurt or army-agent; is imprisoned by Dámáji Thorat; his release; success against Ángria; is appointed Peshwa; is presented the fort of Purandhar by the Pant Sachiv; goes to Delhi to assist the Sayads; obtains for Sháhu three imperial grants, *chauth*, *sardeshmukhi* and svaráj; receives several districts near Poona in personal jágir; death, XVIII, pt ii, 241-243; *another account*: advances to Ahmadábád and levies tribute (1707), I, pt. i, 295; conciliates Ángria and gives Shrivardhan to him, I, pt. ii, 82; XI, 146, 467; his accession to power (1713), XIII, 489; his negotiations at Delhi respecting Gujarát tribute (1717), I, pt. i, 389; obtains *svarája* from the Emperor (1720), I, pt. ii, 626.
Balál Devi: goddess, originally a Cháran woman, becomes a devi by self-sacrifice, is worshipped at Bákalkua, IX, pt. i, 216 note 1.
Balambha: town, VIII, 376.
Bálambid; village in Dhárwár, temples and inscriptions at, XXII, 652.
Bála Muhammad Sháh: Pirána saint, IX, pt. ii, 69; his tomb at Pirána near Ahmadábád, worshipped by the Shaikhs, *id.* 76 note 2.
Bálánadi: river in Kánara district, XV, pt. i, 5.
Balance Sheet: all district volumes, *see* under District name.
Balanites: *Egyptiaca*, *Roxburghii*, timber trees found in several districts, XXV, 37.
Bálánivav: village in Káthiáwár, VIII, 377.
Balantyne: British agent at Baroda (1812), VII, 217; makes engagements with Káthiáwár chiefs, *id.* 328; his settlement with Rewa Kántha chiefs, *id.* 331.
Bálapatna: port on the Konkan coast mentioned by Ptolemy and in the Periplus, I, pt. ii, 1.
Bálápir: ruined mosque near Dábhol in Ratnágiri district, X, 320.
Bálápur: town in Berára, the battle of, in 1720; defeat of the imperial army by Nizám-ul-Mulk, I, pt. ii, 627; I, pt. i, 301, 389; VII, 168.
Bálárám: river in Pálanpur state, V, 283.
Bálás: or Válás, that is, Valabhis, *see* Válás.
Bálásinor: a Rewa Kántha state, VI, 1, 2; area, boundaries, population, sub-divisions history, family tree, *id.* 137-140; town, *id.* 157; residence of the Bábi family, I, pt. i, 314; captured by Bhagvantráv from Sardár Muhammad Khán Bábi (1760), *id.* 344; VII, 174; recaptured by Sardar Muhammad Khán (1761), I, pt i, 345, VII, 335.
Balav or Balyav: fishing boat, its description, cost, XIII, 344, 719.
Balavarman: Chálukya prince, I, pt. ii, 211, 380, 399.
Bálavúr: modern Bálúr village in Dhárwár district, I, pt. ii, 377-378.
Baldæus: Dutch traveller, his description of Bijápur and Kánara and its ports (1660), XIII, 430; XV, pt. ii, 52, 125, 255, 274, 311, 332; his mention of Rájápur in Konkan, I, pt. ii, 72.
Baldev: Basav's (1100-1168) father-in-law, XXIV, 119.
Baldhoi: táluka in Káthiáwár, VIII, 374.
Baldness: disease, its cure, IX, pt. i, 365.
Bále: stream, in Kolába District, XI, 9.
Balegráma: identified with the modern Belgam Tarhálá in the Násik district, I, pt. ii, 185, 357-358.
Baleh: *see* Valeh.
Báleballi: village in Dhárwár district, temples and inscriptions at, XXII, 652.
Baleocuros: king, mentioned by Ptolemy as Governor of the southern province, identified with Viliváyakura, I, pt. ii, 158, 176. *See* also I, pt. i, 541.
Balesar: village granted by Ráshtrakúta king Dhruv II, I, pt. i, 127. *See* Báleshvar.
Báleshvar: a small town in Baroda, VII, 571.
Báleshvar: range in Ahmadnagar, XVII, 4-5.
Balev: Cocoanut day, leading Hindu holiday, the sea worshipped on, IX, pt. i, 23 note 5; *id.* 170, 173, 336
Baleyapattana: fortress, I, pt. ii, 496.
Balhara: *see* Balhárás.
Balhárás: identified with Ráshtrakútás of Malkhed, I, pt, ii, 209, 387, 388; I, pt. i, 519, 525, 526, 527, 529, 530, 531; IX, pt. ii, 2 note 1; X, 132 note 3; XI, 271; rulers of

Konkan (850-916), I, pt. i, 505, 468, 469, 506, 509, 512, 514, 516, 518; I, pt. ii, 4; X, 193 note 1; XIII, 434 and note 10; rulers of Lár (Gujarát) and Cambay, kind to Arabs, I, pt. ii, 22-23; VI, 214; XIII, 432.
Baliakáka: *see* Saiadkáká.
Balibhadra: Bhakta of the fourth yugá or epoch, IX, pt. ii, 48.
Balidháns: Hindu sacrifice, IX, pt. ii, 48 note 2.
Bálinge: village in Kolhápur state, temple of Káttyáyani at, XXIV, 293.
Baliospermum: *montanum* and *polyandrum*, medicinal and poisonous plants, XXV, 255, 269.
Balipátna: town near Chaul, mentioned by Ptolemy, I, pt. ii, 2.
Bálipoddi: *see* Bádipoddi.
Balipur, Balipura: *see* Balagamve.
Balisa: village, identified with Wanesa in Baroda territory, gift of, I, pt. i, 111; I, pt. ii, 360.
Balkh: province of Afghánistán, I, pt. i, 144, 545; sun-worship introduced into India from, IX, pt. i, 476. *See* Baktria.
Balla: Cutch chief, helps Bhimdev II (1180), V, 132.
Ballakunde: province in Karnátak, I, pt. ii, 434.
Ballál: Kolhápur Siláhára king, inscription of, XXIV, 221; I, pt. ii, 254, 545, 547.
Ballála: king of Malwa, defeated by Kumárapála Chálukya (1143-71), I, pt. i, 185.
allála: prince of the Sántali *mandala*, I, pt. ii, 579, 583.
Ballála I: Hoysála prince, I, pt. ii, 218, 374 note 5; fendatory of the Western Chálukya, king Vikramáditya, VI, *id.* 451, 491, 493; rules at Belápura, *id.* 494; his date (1103), *id.* 495 note 2.
Ballála II, Vira-Ballála, Vira-Ballála II: Hoysála king (1173-1212), I, pt. ii, 493; succeeds his father; his *biruda*, *id.* 501; feudatory of Kalachurya Sankama, *id.* 488, 502; defeats Brahma, the general of Someśvara IV, and puts an end to the Chálukya power, *id.* 223, 466, 502; defeats Bhillama, the Devgiri Yádav king, and establishes himself as an independent king, *id.* 237-38, 502-03; is described as a ruler of Kuntala, *id.* 284 note 2, 520; his conquests, *id.* 503-05, 519, 563; his feudatories and officials, *id.* 505-06, 521, 582; his latest date on record, *id.* 506 and note 2; is said to have acquired his sovereignty by favour of the god Náráyan, *id.* 491; his Vaishnáva minister, *id.* 491, 507; captures Uchchangi and restores Pándya his kingdom, *id.* 319 note 1, 333, 501; his inscription, *id.* 218, 240.
Ballála III, Vira-Ballála III: Hoysála king (1310), I, pt. II, 493; succeeds his father Vira Narasimha III, records of his reign, his titles, is defeated by Malik Káfur and Khwája Háji, *id.* 509, 533; XV, pt. ii, 93; retires to Tonnur after the demolition of Dorasamudra (1327), is liberated and reigns at Behir, I, pt. ii, 510.
Balláladeva: Singhana's (Devgiri Yádav) feudatory I, pt. ii, 523.
Ballálgad: fort in Thána, XIV, 14.
Ballantine, Captain: VIII, 306.
Ballare: in Karnátak, conquered by Vishnuvardhána, I, pt. ii, 497.
Ballávalli: modern Walláwal in the Sávantvádi state, I, pt. ii, 372.
Ballayya: officer of Vira-Ballála II, in charge of Annigere (1208) in Dhárwár district, I, pt. ii, 506.
Ballayyasáhani: Western Chálukya king Someśvara IV's officer, I, pt. ii, 465.
Balleshwar: in Mysore, inscription at, I, pt. ii, 529.
Balligáve: *see* Balagamve.
Bálmer: in Rájputána, I, pt. i, 188, 196, 466.
Bál Mularája: *see* Mularája II.
Balmuri: inscription at, I, pt. ii, 308.
Báloba Tátya: intrigues to put Chimnáji on the throne; is arrested by Sindia (1796), I, pt. ii, 606; released by Sindia (1798), *id.* 607. *See* also XVIII, pt. ii, 271-73.
Bálod-Mers: highest division of Mers, apparently the same as the Bala's or rulers of Valabhi, IX, pt. i, 494 and note 2.
Balra: timber tree, common in the plains in India, XXV, 73.
Balsamo-dendron: *berryi*, plant cultivated as a hedge in India, XXV, 39; *mukul Roseburghii*, aromatic plants, found in Khándesh and other places, *id.* 39; *pubescens*, shrub, found in Sind, *id.* 40.
Balsáne: place of interest in Khándesh, old temples and caves at, XII, 432.
Bálsantoshis: beggars in Sátára district, XX, 181.
Balsár: sub-division of Surat: boundary; area, aspect, climate, water-supply; soil; assessment, resources; occupancy: value of land; produce; population and public health, II, 267-70; town, with a municipality, a trade centre, *id.* 297; Ambada defeated Mallikárjuna at, I, pt. ii, 19; XIII, 426; Pársi houses in (1411), IX, pt. ii, 186 note 6; sacked by the Portuguese (1531), I, pt. i, 347; XIII, 451; Sanjan fire brought to (1741), IX, pt. ii, 193; Vinayáditya Mangalrája's and other grants as, I, pt. i, 108, 123; I, pt. ii, 360 notes 1 and 3, 374.
Baltiás; land-holders, of part foreign descent, cease to be a separate community, IX, pt. ii, 11, 15.
Baltipatna: modern Pale, in Kolába district, I, pt. i, 540.
Balúchi: special community of part foreign descent, IX, pt. ii, 11; descendants of Balúchi immigrants, claim to have come from Aleppo and North Syria; language; appearance, grants from Gujarát Sultáns, clans, wives, calling, character, called the Switzers of the East for their fidelity and devotion; Sunnis in name, *id.* 17; Jath origin of; Hindu wives of, appearance, speak Gujaráti; believe in the Sain Dádá Mahábali; originally Shiáhs, now Sunnis in name, *id.* 17-18.
Bálu Mia: of Sachin, makes over Janjira to the Peshwa (1791), XI, 448.
Bálur: village in Dhárwár, temple and inscriptions at, XXII, 653; inscriptions at, I, pt. ii, 278 note 2, 378.
Balutedárs: village servants, XXIV, 41, 42.

Balvantgad : fort in Thánâ district, XIV, 19.
Balvantráv : Mudhol chief (1856-62), XXIV, 395.
Balvantráv Gáikwár ; Sayájiráo II Gáikwár's rival, VII, 233.
Balvant Rao Phadnávis : the Mutálik of the Pratinidhi, kills Fatehsing Máne (1805), I, pt. ii, 609.
Bálya Acha : Kasamachitra, ruler of Gujarát, I, pt. i, 489.
Bambhan : stream in Káthiáwár, VIII, 63.
Bamboo, bambu : fibrous and food plant, XXV, 188, 238 ; in Khándesh, XII, 24 ; exported to the Persian Gulf, XIII, 431 and note 8.
Bambot : canoe in Thána district, XIII, 721.
Bambu : *see* Bamboo.
Bambusa : XXV, 278.
Bambusa : *arundinacea*, XXV, 137, 187, 188, 208, 238, 277 ; *arundo*, *id.* 136, 188, 209 ; *stricta*, *id.* 137, 188, 209 ; *vulgaris*, *id.* 137, 209.
Bamian : I, pt. i, 497.
Bamma : Sinda prince of Yelburga, I, pt. ii, 573-74.
Bamma, Bammana, Bammarasa, Bammayya, Bammideva, Bammidevarasa, Brahma : Káláchurya king Sonidev or Someśvara's feudatory (1175), I, pt. ii, 46 ; general of Western Chálukya king Someśvara IV, restores Chálukya power, *id.* 464, 466, 484, 486 note 1, 489, 502, 504.
Bammana : *see* Bamma.
Bammanayya : Western Chálukya king Jagadekamalla II's officer (1143), I, pt. ii, 457.
Bammarasa : Vikramáditya VI's officer (1108), I, pt. ii, 452.
Bammarasa : *see* Bamma.
Bammayya : *see* Bamma.
Bammideva : *see* Bamma.
Bammidevarasa : *see* Bamma.
Bammogoura : town in Málwa, I, pt. i, 540.
Bámnoli : village in Sátára district, XIX, 453.
Bámnoli-Gheradategad : Sahyádri spur in Sátára district, XIX, 6.
Bána : poet, I, pt. i, 4 ; I, pt. ii, 138 ; refers to Kálidása in the Harshacharitra, *id.* 144 ; refers to Saptaśatí, *id.* 171, 286 ; race, *id.* 486 ; Śiva's attendant, *id.* 482.
Bana : Al Idrisi's name for Thána, I, pt. ii, 4, 24.
Banagara : identified with Bannu in Sind, I, pt. i, 538.
Banájis : chief family among early Pársi settlers in Bombay, IX, pt. ii, 195.
Banalgay : timber tree found in Konkan and Kánara, XXV, 108.
Banana : a common tropical food plant, XXV, 174.
Banaouasei : modern Banavási in Kánara district, I, pt. i, 541.
Banáras : Benares or Káshi, holy city on the Ganges, I, pt. ii, 133, 509 ; temple of Vishveshvar at, IX, pt. i, 549 ; place of pilgrimage, *id.* 119, 157, 164, 168, 175, 213, 220, 225 ; Imámsháh's conversion of Matia kanbis on their way to, IX, pt. ii, 66.
Banás : river in Pálanpur, V, 283, 315.
Bánásur : traditional builder of Elephanta caves, story of, XIV, 81 note 2.
Banaváse : *see* Banavási.
Banavási, Banaváse, Banaváspura, Vanavási : old town and province in Kánara district, inscriptions, fair and history of, XV, pt. ii, 261-266 ; 45, 48, 75, 77, 79, 80, 81, 82, 84, 85, 86, 87, 88, 90, 92, 115, 152 ; origin of the name, *id.* 261 note 2 ; perhaps the scene of Pándav's exile, *id.* 264 note 4 ; its different spellings and identification with Vaijayanti, *id.* 278 and note 2, 281, 285, 560 ; chief city of the Kadambas, *id.* 16, 285, 286 note 2, 335, 344, 350, 558 ; *see* also XIII, 423 ; conquest of, by Kirtivarman I, I, pt. ii, 181, 285 ; reduced by Pulikeśin II, *id* 183, 350 ; territorial division, governed by the feudatories of the Ráshtrakútas, *id.* 403, 411 and note 3, 420 ; given to Bútuga by Krishna III, *id.* 419, 421 ; province of the Western Chálukya empire, *id.* 431 ; governed by officers of the Western Chálukyas, *id.* 428 note 4, 433, 435, 437, 439, 440, 443, 444 ; Vikramáditya VI, passes some time at, on his march to Malaya, *id.* 216, 444, 447 ; Jayasimha III, appointed viceroy at, *id.* 445, 449, 454 ; governed by Western Chálukya officers, *id.* 450, 451, 452, 561, 580 ; seized and ruled over by the Hoysala Vishnuvardhana, *id.* 497, 499, 501, 505 ; governed by Western Chálukya officers, *id.* 456, 458, 460, 562 : capital of the Western Chálukyas removed to the town, *id.* 223, 461, 466 ; governed by the officers of the Kalachuryas, *id.* 472, 473, 475, 476, 483, 485, 487, 489 ; governed by officers of the Devagiri Yádavas, *id.* 523 ; held by the Gutta Vírat-Vikramáditya II, *id.* 520, 524, 578, 582, 583.
Banavásipuravaradhishvara : hereditary title of the Kádambas of Goa, I, pt. ii, 253, 566 ; of Hángal, *id.* 566.
Banda : a lark in Cutch, its crop ravages, V, 109.
Bánda : district in Bundelkhand, I, pt. ii, 469.
Banda : hereditary bondsman, X, 430.
Bánda : sub-division in Sávantvádi state, X, 387 ; river, *id.* 388 ; town, history, fort, remains, *id.* 463-465.
Bandaga, Bandara : timber tree found on the gháts, XXV, 79.
Bandalike : in Mysore, inscription at, I, pt. ii, 284 note 2.
Bandanikeya Soyideva : Yádava king Rámachandra's feudatory (1282), I, pt. ii, 529.
Bandara : *see* Bandaga.
Bandar Abás : port of, in the Persian Gulf ; early Persian trade passes from Jeran to, IX, pt. ii, 183 note 3. *See* Gombrun.
Bandar boat : a Thana boat, XIII, 344.
Bandarah : timber tree found from Gujarát to Konkan, XXV, 79.
Bandári : *see* Bhandári.
Bandar Pier : Bombay, repairs to (1728), XXVI, pt. ii, 278 ; (1742) *id.* 291 ; (1745) *id.* 292 ; additions to (1754, 1756 and 1760), *id.* 306, 315, 333.

Bandar Sákhri: place of interest in Ratnágiri district, X, 320.

Bánde: Maráthá chiefs in Gujarát (1720), VII, 168-169; alliance with Piláji against the Peshwa (1726), *id.* 171; defeated by the Gáikwár at Anand Mogri (1737), *id.* 174.

Bande Ali: Nawáb of Cambay (1823-1841), VI, 232.

Bándekar: trader caste in Dhárwár district, XXII, 125; in Kánara district, XV, pt. i, 181-182; in Belgaum district, XXI, 99.

Bandevi: house-guardian of Bhatána Gujars, head-quarter of, near Bikánir, IX, pt. i, 483.

Bándhárá: a caste of calico-printers, I, pt. i, 450, craftsmen, converts of the Hindu caste of the same name; Sunnis by religion, IX, pt. ii, 71.

Bandhárás: weirs, remains of old, in Khándesh, XII, 139.

Bandhivár: bondsman's day, Wednesday so called, IX, pt. i, 402.

Bándh Tivra: a teak reserve in Ratnágiri district, X, 32.

Bandhuvarman: son of Vaisavavarman, vassal of Kumáragupta I (436), governs Dasápur, now modern Mandasor in West Malwa, I, pt. ii, 312. *See* also, I, pt. i, 76.

Bandi: bondsman, a caste in Kánara district, XV, pt. i, 333-334.

Band Koli: early tribe, in Thána district, XIII, 167.

Bándra: town in Thána district, its water-supply, population, traffic, XIV, 15-17; industries, slaughter-houses, municipality, *id.* 18-21; churches and orphanage, *id.* 22-25; history, *id.* 26-28; naval fight off (1528), paid tribute to the Portuguese, I, pt. ii, 46, XIII, 451; Portuguese factory at (1532), *id.* 457; Jesuit college at (1675), I, pt. ii, 57; XIII, 476; Portuguese fort at, I, pt. ii, 66; chief place in Sálsette (1695), XIII, 484, 485; demolished (1739), XXVI, pt. i, 201; brick trade at, XIII, 562.

Band Stands: at Poona, XVIII, pt. iii, 360.

Bangad Kásár: a caste of bangle-makers in Koláha district, XI, 63, 131.

Bangalore: grant from, I, pt. ii, 467, 508.

Bánganga: river in Thána district, XIV, 28.

Bánganga, river in Násik district, XVI, 8.

Bángaon: village in Násik district, old temple at, XVI, 425.

Bangár: trader caste in Kánara district, XV, pt. i, 282; in Poona city, XVIII, pt. i, 263-265; husbandmen in Ahmadnagar district, their origin, food, dress, condition, religion, customs, XVII, 85-86.

Bangarbárá: a caste of Musalmán bangle-sellers in Dhárwár, XXII, 233-234.

Bángdi: a caste of blanket-weavers in Ahmadnagar district, XVII, 92 93.

Bangles: manufacture of glass, in Khándesh, XII, 234; in Ahmadnagar district, XVII, 350.

Bangrak: weed, used as pot herb, XXV, 162.

Bania: Bazána or Náráyan, I, pt. i, 511 and note 12.

Bánia: Bráhman, lord of Mankir (Málkhet) ruled in Cambay (915), I, pt. i, 514.

Bania-Banri: food plant, XXV, 166.

Banian: tree, is worshipped on Vat-Sávitri day, IX, pt. i, 47; in Poona district, XVIII, pt. i, 54; Kásbyapa's tree of knowledge, XIV, 331.

Banians: Vánias at Mocha (1612, 1660), XIII, 468 note 10; at Bassara, Bandar Abas (1700), their trade in Arabian Gulf (1800), *id.* 520 and note 3.

Bánia Ránka: a Káthiáwár chief (715), I, pt. i, 525.

Banikop: village in Dhárwár, temple and inscriptions at, XXII, 653.

Banjhárá: a wandering tribe of traders; converts of the Hindu caste of the same name; trade in cattle and wool; supplied grain to Musalmán and English armies; believe in Hindu gods; form a separate community, IX, pt. ii, 85-86.

Banjig: a caste of Lingáyat traders in Kánara, XV, pt. i, 175-180; in Dhárwár district, XXII, 122-123; in Bijápur district, XXIII, 221.

Bankápur: táluka in Dhárwár district, I, pt. ii, 278 note 1, 562 notes 1 and 8, 564 note 2; town, *id.* 411 and note 3; inscription at, *id.* 299 note 3, 440 note 4, 443, 444; conquered by Vishnuvardhana, *id.* 497; fort captured by Firoz Sháh Bahamani in 1406, *id.* 638; capital of Vilápa Rai, taken by Ali Adil Sháh (1575), *id.* 645-646; head-quarters of Abdul Ráuf Khán of Sávanur, *id.* 655; pledged by the Nawáb of Sávanur to meet the pecuniary fine levied by the Peshwa (1756), *id.* 657; taken by Haider Ali (1779), *id.* 659; town, XXII, 389; capture of (1406), *id.* 404; siege of (1575), *id.* 408; survey, *id.* 498-502, 548-551; sub-division, details, boundaries, area, aspect, soil, climate, water, stock, crops, people, *id.* 626-628; town, fort, temples, history, *id.* 653-657; spirit-scarers, *id.* 815.

Banker: Vánia, his private dwelling-house, IX, pt. i, p. xvii; undivided family of, management of the family; place of business or *vakhár*, working of the office, head of the firm, *id.* 79, 81; office establishment, *id.* 79; apprentices or *shikáu chhokrás*, their duties, *id.* 79-80; mental calculation, skill noticed by Ovington; bargain-words used by, *id.* 80; pay and duties of the establishment, *id.* 80-82.

Bankers: all district volumes. *See* under District name.

Bankeyarasa: feudatory of Amoghavarsha I, I, pt. ii, 403.

Bank of Bombay: proposed (1717), established (1720), XXVI, pt. ii, 240-242; state of, in 1744, *id.* 242-244; issue of Bank notes and accepting private deposits by (1770), *id.* 245-249; its branch in the city of Ahmadabad, IV, 65.

Bánkot: port in Ratnágiri district, its trade, climate, history, XI, 320-323; exports and imports of, *id.* 183; trade centre, *id.* 166; boat-building town, *id.* 172; south boundary

of the Nizám Sháhi and north boundary of the Bijápur Konkan, I, pt. ii, 34; its capture by the English (1756), *id.* 92; XI, 159; XXVI, pt. i, 303; the first territorial possession of the English, its management, I, pt. ii, 122; creek, *id.* 173.
Banks: state, Baroda (1829-1870), VII, 407-410.
Bannawassi: *see* Banavási.
Banners: of different royal families, I, pt. ii, 299 note 4.
Banni: grass tract in the Ran, V, 14; a raid into (1820), *id.* 164.
Bannihatti: village in Dhárwár district, inscription at, XXII, 657.
Bannikop: village in Dhárwár district, stone inscriptions of Vijayáditya at, I, pt. ii, 374 note 3.
Bannu: town, I, pt. i, 538.
Bannur: in Mysore, inscription at, I, pt. ii, 500.
Banpuri: village in Sátára district, temple at, XIX, 453-454.
Bans: timber, food and famine plant found in Konkan and other parts, XXV, 137, 187, 188, 208, 209.
Bansa: timber tree found in several districts, XXV, 69.
Bansarovar: desert sea, near Bhinmal in Rájputána, I, pt. i, 455.
Bánsda: Surat state; area, boundaries, aspect, rivers, water-supply, climate, trees, animals, population, soil, crops, tillage, husbandmen, money-lending, currency, wages, roads, port, land trade, fairs, history, land administration, justice, revenue and finance, instruction, health, vaccination; town, VI, 245-253; *see* also IX, pt. i, 129; Pársi settlement in, Sanján fire brought to, IX, pt. ii, 187.
Banshi: a variety of wheat in Khándesh, XII, 150.
Banti: grain grown in Cutch, V, 106.
Bántva: state in Káthiáwár, VIII, 377-378, Marátha tribute from, VII, 318.
Banyan: *see* Banian.
Baobab: timber, food and fibrous plant grown all over India, XXV, 16, 147, 229; in Poona district, XVIII, pt. i, 46.
Bappa: Shaivite or Vaishnava pontiffs, I, pt. i, 84-85, 85 note 1.
Bappa: called Váppa, founder of the Gohils or Sisodiás, is said to have been received into the rank of Kshatriyás, IX, pt. i, 436 note 1, 487 note 3; his migration from Valabhi to Chitor, *id.* 126; captures Chitor, *id.* 494 note 3; founds a kingdom at Chitor, *id.* 495 note 3.
Bappuka: becomes insolent and is killed by Krishna III, I pt. ii, 207.
Bappura: family, I, pt. ii, 349. *See* Batpura.
Bappuvarasa: feudatory chief, I, pt. ii, 417 note 5.
Báptis and Verás: cash cesses in Ahmadabad, IV, 157, 165, 166.
Baptism: fire, on Mount Ábu, IX, pt. i, 433, 434; a popular initiation, *id.* 449 note 4. *See* Fire.
Baptist Chapel: in Poona Cantonment, XVIII, pt. iii, 360.
Bápu Bhángria: Koli rebel, his rising (1844), XVIII, pt. ii, 307-308.
Bápu Gáikwár: half-brother of the Gáikwár, a political refugee at Ahmadabad (1857), I, pt. i, 442.
Bápu Gokhale: nephew and successor of the Peshwa's sarsubhedár Dhondopant Gokhale, I, pt. ii, 663; Bájiráv's commander-in-chief, Patvardhan's lands offered to, XXIV, 348; chastisement of Rámoshis by (1806), XVIII, pt. iii, 37; defeats Pratinidhi Shrinivása near Vasantgad (1806), I, pt. ii, 609; XIX, 299-301; at the battle of Kirkee (1817), XVIII, pt. ii, 300-301; XVIII, pt. iii, 376, 379, 380; XIX, 302, 303; at the action of Pandharpur, XX, 293; his death at Ashti (1818), I, pt. ii, 611; XVIII, pt. ii, 303; XX, 295.
Bápu Mohitey: brother-in-law and Senapati to Malhárráo Gáikwár (1872), VII, 280, 283.
Bápuji Naik Báramatikar: Bálúji, the third Peshwa's rival, VII, 176; XIX, 283-287; Peshwa's revenue farmer in Karnátak (1746), I, pt. ii, 656.
Bápuji Sindia: Dhárwár commandant, I, pt. ii, 663; XV, pt. ii, 146; holds Haliyal and Sámbráni (1799) against the British, *id.* 304, 340.
Bápuráv Lámbia: the Peshwa's sardár I, pt. ii, 116-117; captured Kotaligad fort near Neral (1817), XIII, 522; XIV, 210.
Bar: timber tree, common throughout India, XXV, 129.
Bára: island near Sopára, mentioned by the Arab traveller Al Idrisi (1100), I, pt. i, 529.
Bara: village in Cutch, Gajanji's head-quarters at (1365), V, 135; a fort at, *id.* 136.
Bárabij: or barbig, the moon, a Bhil's oath by, IX, pt. i, 301 and note 3, 396.
Bárada: Porbandar, I, pt. i, 524.
Baradwáj: Hindu sage, I, pt. i, 461.
Baragadam: a famine plant, XXV, 197.
Bara-Ganga: river in Kánara district, XV, pt. i, 7.
Barági: Varáha the Boar, temple of, at Bhinmál, I, pt. i, 451; rest-house of, *id.* 471.
Baráhmas: Ibni Khurádbah's name for Bráhmans, I, pt. i, 530 and note 11.
Báráji: *see* Barági.
Bárakanúr: pass in Madras Presidency, mediæval Barkalúr, I, pt. ii, 298, 299, 499.
Baráke: Dvarka in Káthiáwár, I, pt. i, 538, 544, 546.
Barál Reef: coral reef in the Gulf of Cutch, VIII, 29.
Bárámati: town in Poona district, XVIII, pt. iii, 105; survey of, *id.* pt. ii, 444-445; the Peshwa's camp at, stormed by Fatehsing Mane, I, pt. ii, 608.
Bárána: or Náráyan, great trade centre near Jaipur, a Gurjjara capital, IX, pt. i, 480.
Báran Balians: twelve sacred heaps of rice, worshipped by Vániás on the twelfth day after birth of a child, IX, pt. i, 89.

Bárap, Barapa, Barappa, Dvarap: general of Tailappa II, the Dakhan Chálukya (973-997), establishes himself in South Gujarát, is defeated by Mulráj, I, pt. ii, 23; *see* also *id.* 212-213, 430, 431 note 1, I, pt. i, 157, 158; XIII, 435 and note 4; XIV, 402; his son's daughter married to Vesúka, the Yádava king, I, pt. ii, 514; said to be the general of the king of Kanauj, *id.* 431 note 1.

Barashnum: cleansing ceremony among Pársis, IX, pt. ii, 223 and note 1, 226, 239 note 2.

Barashnum Gah: place of purification, IX, pt. ii, 223, 226.

Bárat: hill in Thána district, XIV, 304; *see* Sanjan Peak.

Báranz: Broach, I, pt. i, 513.

Barbara, Barbaraka: demon, defeated by Siddharája (1094-1143), serves Siddharája after his defeat; his followers forced to become Hindus, IX, pt. i, 443, 444 and note 2; *see* also I, pt. i, 173 and note 3; non-Aryan tribe in South Kathiáwár, possible identity of, with the Greek Barbarians, *id.* 174 note 1, 175.

Barbarei, Barbarikon: town on the Indus mentioned by Ptolemy, I, pt. i, 174 note 1, 538, 544.

Barbaria: caste in Káthiáwár, modern representatives of ancient Barbaraka, I, pt. i, 175.

Barbarigas: tribe defeated by Yadava king Singhana, I, pt. ii, 525.

Barbarikon: *see* Barbarei.

Barbers: in Gujarát, IX, pt. ii, 84, 96-97; in Poona district, XVIII, pt. i, 380-383.

Barbets: class of birds in Khándesh, XII, 35; in Ratnágiri district, X, 67; at Mátherán, XIV, 257.

Barbosa: Portuguese traveller (1514), his description of Chaul, I, pt. ii, 35 and note 4, XIII, 446, XI, 275; his mention of Dánda in Koláha district, XI, 435 note 5, 461 and note 4; his mention of Khárepatan and Sangameshvar in Ratnágiri district, X, 319, 343, 372; his description of Bassein, XIV, 28; his visit to Gujarát, IX, pt. ii, 3 note 1; his mention of Cambay stones, VI, 206; his mention of Chámpáner, I, pt. i, 219; his mention of Vijayánagar horses, XV, pt. ii, 50, 51; his mention of Goa, *id.* 108; his description of Kánara, *id.* 112-114; his account of *jogis*, XIV, 35 note 10; of female attendants of Vijayánagar king, *id.* 215 note 1.

Barcelor: town on the Malabar coast, plundered by Shiváji (1664), I, pt. ii, 68; *see* also XVIII, pt. ii, 231.

Bardá: hills in Káthiáwár, I, pt. i, 87, 135, 136; VIII, 9.

Bardá: Bhil tribe in Khándesh, XII, 83, 102.

Bardai: main division of Mher chiefships, in Káthiáwár (770), I, pt. i, 136.

Bardaxema: Porbandar, I, pt. i, 538.

Bardesanes: Roman traveller (A. D. 154-181), I, pt. i, 542.

Bárdeshkar: a sub-division of the Shenvi Bráhmans in Ratnágiri district, X, 411; in Kánara district, XV, pt. i, 171.

Bárdoli: sub-division of Surat, boundary, area, aspect, climate, water-supply, soil, assessment, resources, occupancy, value of land, produce, population and public health, II, 278-280; town, *id.* 297; *see* also I, pt. i, 130.

Bards and Actors: in Surat and Broach districts, II, 53, 374: in Kaira and Panch Maháls districts, III, 33, 217; in Ahmadábád district, IV, 37; in Cutch, Pálanpur and Mahi Kántha, V, 74-76, 290, 365; in Rewa Kántha, VI, 25; in Gujarát, IX, pt. i, 207; in Ratnágiri district, X, 126; in Sávantvádi state, X, 415; in Khándesh, XII, 76.

Bardur: village in Dhárwar district, temple and inscription at, XXII, 657.

Bárgáma: a sub-division of Rájpípla state in Rewa Kántha, VI, 98.

Bargat: banyan tree, XXV, 129.

Bárgira: a name given to the Maráthás, derivation of the word, XX, 285 note 2; employed by Ali Adil Sháh (1575), against Vijayánagar, their treachery and punishment, I, pt. ii, 646; entertained by Ibráhim Adil Sháh, XXIII, 414; at the siege of Bijápur (1582), *id.* 584; their pay in Shiváji's service, XIX, 241.

Bargose: Broach, I, pt. i, 536.

Bargund: timber, food and dye plant found in several districts, XXV, 102, 166, 248.

Bárhaspatya cycle: a Hindu chronological term, I, pt. ii, 264-267.

Bári: city in Northern India, mentioned by Al Masudi (956), I, pt. i, 518.

Bari: also called Sachak, the procession carrying presents to brides, IX, pt. ii, 165 and note 1.

Bari: pass in Násik district, XVI, 131.

Bari: a caste of husbandmen and betel-leaf-sellers, in Thána district, XIII, 117; in Khándesh district, XII, 62, 79; in Poona district, XVIII, pt. i, 280-283.

Bária: a sub-division of the Kolis. *See* Koli.

Bariktil: food and oil-yielding plant, XXV, 167, 219.

Báriya: a Rewa Kántha state, VI, 1, 2; boundaries, aspect, rivers, hills, climate, products, population, sub-divisions, history, development (1865-1876), family tree of its chiefs, *id.* 115-120; chiefship of Chohán Rajpút, IX, pt. i, 125; place of interest, description, fort, *id.* 157-159.

Barkál: a village in Baroda, with a temple and fair, VII, 554.

Bárkas: coasting craft in Thána district, XIII, 717.

Bárkhandia: pass in Násik district, XVI, 129.

Barking Deer: in Kánara district, XV, pt. i, 101-102.

Barley: food-grain cultivated in Cutch, V, 106; in Ahmadnagar, Poona and Sátára districts, XVII, 267, XVIII, pt. ii, 41, XIX, 163; worship of, in Gujarát, IX, pt. i, 391.

Barli: village near Pátan, in Gujarát, IX, pt. ii, 63.

Barmadeva: Vikramáditya VI's governor of Banavási and Santalige provinces, I, pt. ii, 450.

Barmadevarasa: *see* Bammanayya.

Barmarasa : Banavási chief, founder of a state with Annigeri as its capital (1182), XV, pt. ii, 90.
Barmek : clan name of the ministers of Harún-al-Rashidá (A. D. 792-813), IX, pt. i, 489.
Bárnásáyá : river mentioned in an inscription at Násik, I, pt. ii, 148.
Baroda : state, boundaries, aspect, sub-division, climate, VII, 1-26 ; minerals, forests, trees, silk-worms, domestic and wild animals, game birds, fish, *id.* 27-47 ; census details, Bráhmans, feudal classes, traders, husbandmen, artizans, labouring and wandering classes, aboriginal class, Musalmáns, occupations, village communities, *id.* 48-76 ; soil, agricultural stock, crops, irrigation, etc., in Navsári, Baroda and Kádi divisions, *id.* 77-105 ; bankers, pawn-brokers, village money-lenders, investments, account books, rate of interest, labour-mortgage, grain advances, in Navsári, Baroda, and Kádi divisions, *id.* 106-135 ; the mint, rats of exchange, Bábáshéhi currency, Broach rupee, weights and measures, prices, *id.* 135-141 ; roads, lines of traffic, bridges, railways, exports and imports, sea trade, vessels, railway traffic, manufactures, trade guilds, post and telegraph, *id.* 141-164 ; early Marátha invasions (1705-1721), Piláji Gáikwár (1721-1732), *id.* 165-173 ; Dámáji Gáikwár (1732-1768), *id.* 173-188 ; Govindráv Gáikwár (1768-1771), Sáyáji I (1771-1778), *id.* 188-195 ; Fatesing (1778-1789), Mánáji (Regent) (1789-1793), *id.* 195-198 ; Govindráv (1793-1800), Ánandráv (1800-1819), *id.* 198-213 ; Fatesing (Regent) (1806-1818), *id.* 214-229 ; Sáyájiráv II (1819-1847), *id.* 230-268 ; Ganpatráv (1847-1856), *id.* 268-273 ; Khanderáv (1856-1870), Malhárráv (1870-1875), *id.* 273-284 ; Sáyájiráv III, present Mahárája, family tree, list of residents and Diwans, *id.* 285-289 ; history of Gáikwárs' army, *id.* 290-313 ; history of Gáikwárs' tributes, *id.* 314-339 ; ancient land tenures, alienations, *inám* commission, charitable grants, *id.* 340-354 ; government land tenures, revenue farming system, His Highness Khanderáv's reforms, Sir T. Mádhavráv's reforms, *id.* 354-379 ; history of revenue and finance (1752-1878), *id.* 382-437 ; old system of justice, farmer of revenue, the judge, nature of punishments, central court at Baroda (1802-1833), Sadar Nyayádhishi Court (1845), Huzur Fauzdári Court (1860), Codes (1860-1871), Varishta Court (1871), Baroda law, Sir T. Mádhavráv's reforms (1875-1881), civil courts, magistrates' courts, suits, execution of decrees, working of criminal courts, cost of the department, Sardárs' court, extradition, police, jails, *id.* 438-472 ; government schools, Baroda High School, College (1881), Vernacular College of Science, vernacular schools, instruction, statistics, Sanskrit schools, indigenous schools, libraries, *id.* 473-493 ; climate, epidemics, medical organization under the old system, new system, medical department, hospitals and dispensaries, vaccination, cost of the department, *id.* 493-513 ; sub-divisional details and places of interest, *id.* 514-628 ; copper-plate grants in, I, pt. ii, 282 note 5, 405, 415 ; city, description, gardens, suburbs, state hospital, the Págás, parade ground, tanks, city palace, Nazar-Bag, public sports, temples, holidays, history, *id.* 514-533 ; one-fourth revenue of, assigned to Piláji Gáikwár by Hamid Khán, I, pt. i, 306 ; capture of, by the Maráthás under Mahádaji Gáikwár (1734), *id.* 314-315 ; invested by Govindráv Gáikwár (1775), *id.* 401 ; affairs at, managed by Rávji and Bábáji Appa, *id.* 412 ; affairs of (1803), *id.* 413 ; Marátha conspiracy at (1857), *id.* 442-443 ; Arabs defeated by the English at (1802) ; defeat of Arab mercenaries by the English at (1802), IX, pt. ii, 3 note 2 ; chief quarters of Máhdavi Sayads, *id.* 6 note 1 continued on page 7 ; Gujarát headquarters of Husaini Bráhmans, *id.* 22, 10, 14 ; Karka's grant at, I, pt. i, 122, 124, 125 ; Dhruva's grant at, *id.* 126, 127 ; Kumárapála's visit to, *id.* 183 ; granted by Kumárapála to Katuka, *id.* 184, 235.
Barol : enlargement of spleen, its cure, IX, pt. i, 365.
Baroli : temple at, IX, pt. i, 485.
Bárot : *see* Bhát.
Barr, Colonel : Resident at Baroda (1866-1871), VII, 276-278.
Barracks : in Bombay Island, formed part of the Fort (1676), situated in the vicinity of the Fort (1703), XXVI, pt. iii, 572 ; built near the Mint (1705-08), *id.* 572-73 ; repaired (1736-41), additions to (1753-55), new barracks built (1751-1760), *id.* 573-574 ; on Old Woman's Island for European Troops (1770), *id.* 575 ; repaired (1773), *id.* 576 ; repaired (1741), XXVI, pt. iii, 91-93 ; enlarged (1755) ; *id.* 123 ; rebuilt (1759), *id.* 135-136 ; at Kolába, repaired (1777), *id.* 196.
Barra-sof : food-plant common in the presidency, XXV, 161.
Barrenness : in women, causes of, considered a curse, necessity for having a son on religious grounds, IX, pt. i, 366 and note 1 ; means adopted to get rid of, *id.* 366-367 ; rites, *id.* 367 ; name of male child born after performance of rites to get rid of barrenness, *id.* 367-368 ; horror felt by a Musalmán at, remedies to get rid of, IX, pt. ii, 147-149.
Barringtonia : *acutangula*, timber tree found in Konkan, XXV, 78 ; medicinal plant, *id.* 256 ; used for poisoning fish, *id.* 272 ; *racemosa*, timber tree found in Konkan, *id.* 78.
Bársákh : door-post, setting up ceremony of, IX, pt. i, 204.
Bársi : sub-division in Sholápur district, its boundaries, area, aspect, climate, water, soil, stock, holdings, crops, people, XX, 391-93 ; survey of, *id.* 318-321, 348-352 ; town, a trade centre, its exports, imports, *id.* 408-410.
Bárti : grain in Poona district, XVIII, pt. ii, 36.
Bartle : point at Mátherán, XIV, 233.
Bartlett : Mr., physician engaged for Bombay (1702), XXVI, pt. iii, 545.
Bartondi : *Morinda citrifolia*, a timber tree found in Poona district, XVIII, pt. i, 44 ; XXV, 88, 162, 200, 246.

Bartundi : *see* Bartondi.
Barúgaza : ancient name of Broach, I, pt. i, 18 ; its trade with Paithan and Tagara in the time of the Periplus, I, pt. ii, 174.
Báruh : Broach, I, pt. i, 506, 509, 510, 511, 512, 513, 517, 520.
Baruk : Broach, I, pt. ii, 4.
Barus : identified with Bharuch or Broach, expedition against, I, pt. i, 109, 465, 467, 506, 513.
Bárutgar : a caste of Musalmán firework makers, in the district of Ahmadnagar, XVII, 227 ; Poona, XVIII, pt. i, 493, and Sholápur, XX, 199 ; in Kolhápur territory, XXIV, 148-149.
Baruz : Broach, I, pt. i, 505.
Barvála: town in Ahmadabád district, IV, 332.
Barvala : town in Káthiáwár, VIII, 377.
Barvás : hereditary Bhil sorcerers, XII, 86 note 3.
Bárwi : Verával in Káthiáwár, I, pt. i, 521.
Barya : Poona Arab commandant, supposed builder of old Poona wall (A. D. 1350), XVIII, pt. iii, 272.
Barygaza : Broach, I, pt. i, 535 ; I, pt. ii, 278 note 2, 538 note 8, 619 ; gulf of, I, pt. i, 539, 544 ; exports and imports of, *id.* 545-46.
Bas : timber, food and famine plant found in several districts, XXV, 69, 137, 188, 209.
Basadis : Jain temples, I, pt. ii, 437 note 5.
Basálat Jang : Nizám's general (1774), I, pt. ii, 658.
Basaltic beds : in Bijápur district, XXIII, 41-42.
Basaltic flows : in Belgaum district, XXI, 27-28.
Basalts : columns, balls and dikes in Poona, XVIII, pt. i, 10-12.
Basappa : *see* Basava.
Basarál : inscription at, I, pt. ii, 507.
Basarkod : village in Bijápur district, temples at, XXIII, 565.
Basava, Basavana : founder of the Lingáyat faith (1150), XIII, 110 ; XII, 57, 61 ; XV, pt. ii, 90. Bráhman of Bagevadi, becomes prime minister of the Kaláchurya king Vijjána ; with his nephew founds the Lingáyat sect and spends the king's treasure in supporting the priests of the new sect ; plans the king's death ; his end, I, pt. ii, 225-227 ; incarnation of Nandi, *id.* 478 and note 2 ; declares himself a special Śiva worshipper ; is persecuted by Bráhmans and returns to Kappadi ; is made his prime minister by the Kaláchurya Bijjála, marries Bijjála's sister Nilalochana, *id.* 478-479 ; different versions about his death, *id.* 480-481 ; his early life and doctrines, XXII, 103-105 ; XXIV, 97, 119, 120 ; XXIII, 219, 390-391 ; XVII, 82-83 ; lived at Sangameshvar in Ratnágiri district, X, 119 note 1, 372 ; his temple at Ulvi in Kánara district, XV, pt. ii, 354, and at Haveri in Dhárwár district, I, pt. ii, 459 note 3.
Básavalli : province, I, pt. ii, 449, 454.
Basavana : *see* Basava.
Basava-Purána : sacred book of the Lingáyats, I, pt. ii, 437 note 5, 478, 479, 482 note 2.
Basavi : a caste of Lingáyat prostitutes and temple servants, their occupation, XXII, 191-192.
Basav Ling Ráy : sixth Sonda chief (1697-1745), XV, pt. ii, 120 note 3 ; strengthens his power, *id.* 133 ; his hositily to the English, *id.* 134, 136 ; built Sadásivgad, *id.* 279 ; pulled down Kadra fort, *id.* 317 ; besieged English factory at Kárwár, *id.* 324 ; his land grants to the Terbidi at Sonda, *id.* 347.
Basavrájdurg : island fort. *See* under Honávar.
Básavura : province, I, pt. ii, 439, 443, 450.
Básdev : Krishna, I, pt. i, 519.
Basella : *alba*, *rubra*, food-plants, XXV, 169.
Básgad : hill in Thána district, XIII, 4, 5.
Básharaá : class of beggars following the ordinary Muhammadan law, IX, pt. ii, 19, 20.
Basiles : reputed author of the Periplus, I, pt. i, 542.
Basil thread : worn by Vaniás, IX, pt. i, 89.
Básirája : officer of the Gutta prince Vira Vikramáditya II, I, pt. ii, 582.
Basna : timber tree, cultivated all over India, XXV, 58.
Basra : city of, founded by Khalif Umar, IX, pt. ii, 184 note ; I, pt. ii, 505 note 5.
Bassa : food and famine plant common throughout India, XXV, 188, 209.
Bassari : timber tree common in the Konkan, XXV, 129.
Bassarika : poem, I, pt. i, 546.
Bassein : sub-division of Thána district, its boundaries, area, aspect, climate, water, soil, holdings, rental stock, crops and people of, XIII, 2, 678-680 ; town, its situation and history, XIV, 28-36 ; management, churches and remains, *id.* 37-43 ; archæological remains at, *id.* 386-387 ; its trade, XIII, 358-359 ; Mallikarjuna's inscription at, I, pt. i, 186 ; grants at, i, pt. ii, 512, 513, 514 note 1, 515 ; record at, *id.* 518 ; Portuguese remains and churches at, *id.* 65 ; head-quarters of Devagiri Yádava viceroys (1273), *id.* 25 ; district and port of Gujarát kings (1429), *id.* 30 ; Portuguese factory at (1526), XIII, 449 ; trade centre next in importance to Chaul and Dábhol (1529), I, pt. ii, 36 ; attacked, taken and ceded to the Portuguese (1533-1534), *id.* 46 ; Akbar's attack on (1538), I, pt. i, 453 ; besieged by Gujarát force (1539), I, pt. ii, 46 ; under the Portuguese, their judicial establishment and jail at, its revenue, their fortress, head-quarters of the general of the north (1534-1700), *id.* 52, 53, 54 ; Jesuit seminary established at (1548), *id.* 56 ; persecution of the Hindus at (1555), *id.* 59 ; College of Purification established at (1598), *id.* 57 ; frequented by English and Dutch ships (1620), *id.* 63 ; decline of its importance (1672), *id.* 72 ; invested by Sambhaji (1681), *id.* 78 ; capitulates to the Maráthás (1739), *id.* 84 ; terms of surrender, XXVI, pt. i, 211-213 ; place of residence of Marátha Sar Subhedár, I, pt. ii, 99 ; capture by General Goddard (1780), I, pt. i, 409, XVIII, pt. ii, 266 ; restored to

the Maráthás (1782), i, pt. ii, 106; treaty of (1802), *id.* 111, 608, 628, 663; *see* also i, pt. i, 347, 322, 413, 523, 546; X, 198; VI, 232, 250; XII, 253; XIII, 454, 455, 457, 459, 461, 462, 463, 465, 466, 493, 512, 514, 522, 523, 552; XVII, 410; XVIII, pt. ii, 282-283; condition of (1818), I, pt. ii, 125; history of its land revenue (1730-1862), XIII, 552 note 4, 555 note 3, 558, 560, 563 and note 7, 564 and note 7, 569 note 6, 565, 583, 587, 609-611.

Bassein Road: railway station, inscribed stones at, XIV, 387.

Bassia: *latifolia*, *longifolia*, timber, food, famine and oil-yielding plants, found in several districts, XXV, 90, 164, 201, 211, 213, 219; *wightiana*, timber tree found in several districts, *id.* 91.

Bassia elliptica: timber tree common on the *gháts*, XXV, 90.

Basudeo: god Krishna, his residence at Veraval (Barwi) in Káthiáwár, I, pt. i, 521.

Batan: title, said to be the origin of the name Pathan, IX, pt. ii, 10 note 4.

Batchru: tribe of Bráhmans in Kangra, Panjáb, IX, pt. i, 4 note 2.

Batela: sailing vessel in Thána; its description, cost, XIII, 346-47.

Batēr: bird kept by Gujarát Musalmáns, IX, pt. ii, 98.

Bathing: days sacred for, in rivers, IX, pt. i, 29, 349; in sea, *id.* 349.

Batia: Bet, island on the coast of Káthiáwár, I, pt. i, 506 and note 1.

Batpúra: *see* Bappura.

Batrási: mountain peak in Poona district, XVIII, pt. i, 5.

Bats: at Mátherán, XIV, 258.

Batteyur: village in Madras presidency, I, pt. ii, 369.

Batty: outturn of in Bombay island (1780), XXVI, pt. iii, 452.

Batwa: village in Ahmadábád district, IX, pt. ii, 8 note 1.

Báu: a stone worshipped by Patane Prabhus, XIII, 105 note 1.

Bauchi: food-plant found in Konkan, XXV, 146.

Bauhatti: trading village in Kolhápur state, markets at, XXIV, 388.

Bauhinia: *malabarica*, *purpurea*, *variegata*, *vahlii*, food-plants, XXV, 154; *racemosa*, timber and fibrous plant found in several districts, *id.* 65, 232; a sacred plant, *id.* 279, 280.

Bául: or *khári* rice soil in Ratnágiri district, X, 144.

Baunra: timber tree found in Southern Konkan, XXV, 13.

Báva Ghor: *see* Báwá Ghor.

Baváji: hill in Madras presidency, I, pt. ii, 421.

Bavaladevi: queen of Sovideva, the Kalachuri king; pleases the king with a song and obtains his permission to make a grant of land, I, pt. ii, 227, 471, 484.

Bávan Jináli Dehrás: Shrávak temples, IX, pt. i, 110.

Bávápir: pass in Rewa Kántha, VI, 159.

Bávás: priests of Kánará Koknás, XV, pt. i, 223.

Báva Vála: Káthi freebooter (1820-24), confinement in the Gir of Captain Grant by, IX, pt. i, 254-55 and note 1; song in honor of, *id.* 256 and note 1; *see* also VIII, 124, 125 note 1.

Bávchás: labourers in Khándesh, XII, 79.

Bávda: hill fort in Kolhápur, XXIV, 4, 5; history, *id.* 293; hill pass between Ratnágiri district and Kolhápur state, *id.* 5; village, British Resident's office, Native Infantry camp, schools, markets, fairs, *id.* 294.

Bavdhan: village in Sátára district, temples at, XIX, 454.

Bávi: village in Sholápur district, temples at XX, 410.

Bávisi: a sub-division of Mahi Kantha, V, 355.

Bávkule Váni: a caste of traders in Kánara district, XV, pt. i, 174.

Bávliári: creek in Ahmadábád district, IV, 15; port, *id.* 333.

Bawa: timber tree found in Konkan; a sacred plant, XXV, 63, 289.

Báwá Ghor: Cornelian merchant, his tomb near Ratanpur, VI, 168; a famous Abyssinian merchant, *id.* 206 and note 3; beliefs about Ráyan tree close to, IX, pt. i, 361.

Báwa Hom: Musalmán saint, his tomb near Kalyán, XIV, 397-98 and note.

Báwarchi: Musalmán cook, IX, pt. ii, 96.

Bawárij: Abu Rihan's name for the people of Cutch and Somnáth, I, pt. i, 508; for Medh pirates (1030), *id.* 517, 521; *see* also V, 96, 131; VI, 188.

Bayalunád: conquered by Vishnuvardhana, I, pt. ii, 497.

Bayi: timber tree found in Sind, XXV, 40.

Báyin: third form of divorce among Gujarát Musalmáns, IX, pt. ii, 168.

Bazána: Bánia or Náráyan, old town in Sind, I, pt. i, 511 note 12, 520.

Bazár Gate: in Bombay city; clearance made outside of (1758-59), XXVI, pt. ii, 459-62.

Báz Bahádur: the last of the independent chiefs of Mándu, I, pt. i, 355; Malik Báyázid kills his brother Daulatkhán; the defeat of, by the Gonds; his poetic love for Rupmati or Rupmani; expulsion of, by Pir Muhammad, Akbar's general (1560); his restoration and the death of Pir Muhammad (1561); recapture of Mándu by the Mughals under Abdulláh (1562); the retirement of, to Gondwan (1562); accepts service under the Mughals (1570), *id.* 369-71.

Bázigar: *see* Madári.

Bdellium: gum exported from Ophir (B. C. 1100-850), XIII, 404 note 3; to Egypt (A. D. 150), *id.* 416; to Arabia and China (810-1260), *id.* 430.

Bead Necklace: ceremony of fastening on *tulsi* among Agarváls, XVIII, pt. i, 263.

Beal: author of "*Buddhist Records*" IX, pt. i, 434 notes 3, 4, 5, 6, 437 notes 4, 5.

Beam-harrow: field tool, XVIII, pt. ii, 9.

Bear: found in Khándesh, Belgaum and Rátnagiri districts, XII, 31, XXI, 69, X, 44; superstition about, in Gujarát, IX, pt. i, 378.

Becare: ancient port on the Malabár Coast mentioned by Pliny (A. D. 23-79) and in Periplus (A. D. 150), I, pt. i, 537, 546.

Bechará, Becharáji: *see* Bahucharáji.

Bechraji: a large temple of, in Baroda territory, VII, 609-614; a dispensary, *id.* 508.

Bed: timber tree found on the *gháts*, XXV, 133.

Bed: a depressed class in Kánara district, XV, pt. i, 362-63.

Bedani: (1504) his reference to Pársis at Kábul, IX, pt. ii, 188 note 4.

Bedar (Berad): wandering tribe in Dhárwar district, Musalmán converts, XXII, 184-85, 233; in Belgaum district, XXI, 163-65, 208-09; in Bijápur district, XIII, 91-97, 292; in Ratnágiri, X, 416; in Násik, XVI, 67; in Poona, XVIII, pt. i, 406; in Sholápur, XX, 163-65; in Kolhápur, XXIV, 104; in Mysore, XV, pt. i, 362 note 1.

Bedi: port in Káthiáwár, VIII, 239, 378.

Bedina: food-plant found in Konkan, XXV, 162.

Bedkani: *see* Bidarkanni.

Bednur: old city in Mysore, XV, pt. ii, 121 note 8, 124 and note 6; chiefs of (1560-1763), *id.* 121-22; destroyed by the Portuguese, (1713), *id.* 133, treaty by the English with its chief (1751), *id.* 137; plundered by Haidar (1762), *id.* 139; treaty of (1766), I, pt. ii, 199, 659; destroyed by the Maráthás (1792), XV, pt. ii, 144.

Bedrá: a caste of Musalmán traders in Sholápur, XX, 199.

Bedsa: village in Poona district, caves and Buddhistic inscriptions at (A. D. 100-200), XVIII, pt. ii, 212-13, *id.* pt. iii, 105-108; *see* also I, pt. ii, 143, 144, 176, XIII, 412, 413.

Bedti: river in Kanara district, XV, pt. i, 6.

Bee-eater: the common Indian, a species of birds in Ratnágiri district, X, 63.

Bees: at Mátherán, XIV, 255, in Kánara, XV, pt. i, 104-06; in Belgaum, XXI, 72; in Bijápur district, XXIII, 69.

Begáda: Muhammad, Ahmadábád king, defeated Cutch chief (1472) and converted its people to Islám, V, 135. *See* Mahmud Begádá.

Begam: title among Sayad women, IX, pt. ii, 7.

Begam: lake and tomb in Bijápur city, XXIII, 581, 615.

Begampur: village in Sholápur district, Aurangzeb's daughter's tomb at, XX, 411.

Beggars: all district volumes. *See* Population under district name.

Begúr: inscription at, I, pt. ii, 304, 379 note 2.

Behatti: grant from, I, pt. ii, 469, 489, 526, 527.

Behda, behedo: timber tree found in several districts, XII, 24, XXV, 73.

Behechra: *see* Bahuchara.

Behedin: layman, meaning of, IX, pt. ii, 225 note 1.

Beheramini: vow, rites relating to, IX, pt. ii, 230-31.

Beherja or Pinjál: river in Thána district, XIII, 9.

Behesht: Musalmán heaven, belief in, IX, pt. ii, 212.

Behlim: vow, also called Bálá-Behlim patti; vowed by women to be performed in the beginning of marriages, *satwásas* and *bismillahs*; rites relating to, Phadáli or spirit musician chief actor in the performance of, IX, pt. ii, 150-51.

Behlim: a caste of cultivators, Rájpút converts of the Behlim tribe; originally Turks; cease to form a separate class, IX, pt. ii, 58.

Behman Kekobád Sanjáná: of Navsári, author of the Kissah-i-Sanjan, IX, pt. ii, 183 note 2.

Behráh: believed to be the origin of the name Bohora, IX, pt. ii, 24 note 3.

Behrám: *see* Atesh Behrám.

Behrám: ancestor of the Broach priests, IX, pt. ii, 221.

Behram Gor: Varahram V (A. D. 420-40), Sassanian Persian prince, IX, pt. i, 470 note 2, 471, 472, 474; visits India, 436; marries a Hindu princess; establishes the Gardhabin dynasty, IX, pt. ii, 183 note 4 continued on page 184.

Behrinah: town in Yaman in Lower Arabia, birthplace of missionary Abdulláh; believed to be the origin of the name Bohora, IX, pt. ii, 24 note 4.

Behrúpia, Bahampia: a caste of actors and players, Hindu converts of a mixed class; Sunnis in faith, IX, pt ii, 80.

Beils-chmildia: *fagifolia, Roxburghiana*, timber trees found on the *gháts*, XXV, 112, 111.

Bekri: wood and stream at Mátherán, XIV, 231, 242, 243.

Bel: bili tree, home of Párvati, called Shrivraksha, worship of, IX, pt. i, 383; timber and sacred tree found in several districts, XXV, 35, 148, 279, 285, 288, 291; XII, 24, XVIII, pt. i, 43.

Bela: a trade centre in Cutch, V, 213.

Bela: oil-yielding plant, XXV, 222.

Beladori: Arab writer, I, pt. ii, 4.

Belagáve: *see* Balagámve.

Belapur: fort in Thána district, XIV, 43-4; Portuguese district under Bassein (1560), XIII, 455; lost by the Portuguese (1680), *id.* 479; fortified by Sambháji (1682), I, pt. ii, 77; Portuguese garrison at (1727), XIII, 491; seized by Col. Egerton (1778), ceded by the treaty of Poona (1817), *id.* 522.

Belápur: town in Ahmadnagar district, XVII, 712-13.

Belápura, Belupura, Velápura: modern Belúr in Mysore, I, pt. ii, 298, 491, 498; ruled over by Ballála I, *id.* 494, taken by Permádi I, *id.* 459, 497, 575.

Belatti: I, pt. ii, 504. *See* Bellittage.

Belavdi: village in Belgaum district, with a temple and Chálukya inscription at, XXI, 515.

Beláwal: port in Konkan under Gujarát kings (1400-1500), I, pt. ii, 30.

Belbág: temple in Poona city built by Náná Phadnávis, XVIII, pt. iii, 333-34.

Beldár or Od: a caste of stone-cutters and quarrymen in Ratnágiri district, X, 129; in Kolába district, XI, 63-64; in Janjira, *id.*

415; in Khándesh district, XII, 75; in Thána district, XIII, 135; in Násik district, XVI, 57; in Poona district, XVIII, pt. i, 316-19; in Sátára district, XIX, 80; in Sholápur district, XX, 91-92; in Ahmadnagar district, XVII, 93-95; in Belgaum district, XXI, 162; in Kolhápur state, XXIV, 93.

Beldárvádi : village in Ratnágiri district, X, 346 and note 2.

Belehalli : in the Hángal táluka, Dhárwár district, inscription at, I, pt. ii, 561 note 6, 562 note 7.

Belgal : village in Dhárwár district, inscriptions at, XXII, 657.

Belgali : territorial division under Malked Ráshtrakútas, I, pt. ii, 403.

Belgaon-Kurhe : village with a railway station in Násik district, XVI, 425.

Belgaum : district, boundaries, sub-divisions, aspect, XXI, 1-6; hills, rivers, *id.* 6-13; geology, climate, *id.* 13-51; minerals, forests, trees, domestic animals, wild animals, birds, snakes, fish, *id.* 52-86; census details, Bráhmans, writers, traders, husbandmen, craftsmen, personal servants, shepherds, musicians, labourers, beggars, depressed classes, Musalmáns, Christians, *id.* 87-230; houses, furniture, dress, communities, *id.* 230-34; soil, arable area, holdings, field tools, irrigation, manure, crops, famines, *id.* 235-89; currency, savings, investments, money-lending, interest, borrowers, land mortgage and transfer, wages, prices, weights and measures, *id.* 290-301; roads, passes, bridges, rest-houses, ferries, railways, *id.* 302-12; trade centres, markets, carriers, imports, exports, *id.* 312-26; industries, *id.* 326-52; history: Early Kadambas (A. D. 500), Rattas (850-1250), Devgiri Yádavs (1250-1320), Goa Kadambas (1000-1200), Delhi emperors (1294-1350), the Bahmanis (1347-1489), *id.* 352-67; Bijápur kings (1489-1686), the Mughals (1686-1723), Sátára (1707-30), the Peshwás (1746-76), Mysore (1776-90), Third Mysore War (1790-92), Kolhápur power (1795-99), disorder, Nipáni (1804-16), the British (1818-84), *id.* 367-412; land administration, staff, village officers, survey (1849-61), revision survey (1880-84), season reports (1864-83), alienated villages, *id.* 413-66; civil courts and suits, magistracy, police, offences, jail, *id.* 467-73; revenue, imperial and local, balance sheets *id.* 474-80; schools, pupils, newspapers, libraries, *id.* 481-89; diseases, hospitals, vaccination, cattle diseases, births, and deaths, *id.* 490-94; sub-divisional details, *id.* 495-509; places of interest, *id.* 510-514; sub-division, its aspect, soil, water, climate, crops, people, *id.* 505-07.—*Town*, situation, ponds, streams, climate, divisions, population, houses, trade, markets, municipality, fair, cantonment, gardens, objects, Jain temples, inscriptions, history, *id.* 515-50; grant from, I, pt. ii, 225, 227; district, *id.* 298 note 2, 304, 428, 431, 435, 436 note 1, 439 and note 1, 456, 460, 474, 497, 526, 527, 544, 549, 550, 558, 565, 568; Lingáyats in, *id.* 477; records in, *id.* 523; seat of government of the Rattas, *id.* 550, 556, 557; country round, lost by the Goa Kádambas, *id.* 571; the siege and capture of, by the Bahamani king Muhammad Sháh (1472), *id.* 638; taken by the Nizám (1730), *id.* 656; given to the Peshwah (1756), *id.* 657; siege and capture of, by Colonel T. Munro (1818), *id.* 664.

Belgaum lotal : food-plant common on the *ghàts*, XXV, 174.

Belgaum Tarahalá or Tarálhá : village near Igatpuri, in Násik district, I, pt. ii, 185, 358.

Belgaum walnut : food-plant, XXV, 171.

Belhe : village in Poona, Hemadpanti well at, XVIII, pt. iii, 109.

Belhuttee : *see* Bellittage.

Beli : *see* Bel.

Beliefs : among Gujarát Hindu population, early, IX, pt. i, p. xxxiv; influence of evil eye, *id.* 426, 427, 428; among craftsmen, *id.* 185, 196, 233; husbandmen, *id.* 157, 173. *See* witches; in exorcism, *id.* 137, 38, 293, 417-25; among bards and actors *id.* 213, 220, 225; craftsmen, *id.* 178, 181, 182, 185, 191, 194, 196; husbandmen, *id.* 154, 172, 173, 174. *See* spirits; in omens, *id.* 409-10; good, *id.* 138, 410-11; bad, *id.* 138, 411-13; among bards and actors, *id.* 213, 220, 225; craftsmen, *id.* 178, 181, 182, 185, 191, 194, 196, 205; husbandmen, *id.* 154, 157, 164, 172, 173, 174, 175; personal servants, *id.* 230, 233; Rájpúts, *id.* 137; in soothsaying, among Rájpúts, *id.* 137; in sorcery, among bards and actors, *id.* 213, 220, 225; husbandmen, *id.* 154, 157, 164, 172, 174, 175, 205; personal servants, *id.* 230, 233; in spirits, *id.* 416-17; among Rájpúts, *id.* 137; Kolis, *id.* 247; early tribes, *id.* 292, 301; in spirit-possession, *id.* 415-25; among Kolis, *id.* 247. *See* spirits; in witchcraft, *id.* 302-03, 425-30; among bards and actors, *id.* 220, 225, 230, 233; craftsmen, *id.* 178, 181-82, 185, 191, 194, 196, 205; husbandmen, *id.* 157, 164, 173, 175; Rájpúts, *id.* 137. *See* witches.

Among Musalmán and Pársi population of Gujarát, in astrology, IX, pt. ii, 22, 56; *bhúts* (Hindu ghost), *id.* 142 note 1; charms, *id.* 30, 147, 155; *dákans* (witches), *id.* 142 note 1; in the evil eye, *id.* 142; exorcism, *id.* 30; magic, *id.* 56, 142-45; *omens*, *id.* 22, 30, 145-46; saints, *id.* 17, 22; sorcery, *id.* 56; spirits, *id.* 30, 142; the principal tenets of the Musalmán faith; in the unity of God; in angels; in books; in the scriptures; in prophets; in the resurrection, *id.* 126-27.

Belikeri : bay and river in Kánara district, XV, pt. i, 2, 3, 7; port, its trade, *id.* pt. ii, 65, 66, 67; a health resort, *id.* 266.

Belláry : district and town in Madras, I, pt. ii, 298 note 2, 318, 336, 431, 437, 454, 497, 504; copper-plate grant from, *id.* 319.

Beller : a depressed class in Kánara district, XV, pt. i, 363-64.

Belli-pata : timber tree found in Ratnágiri district, XXV, 15.
Bellittage : possibly Belatti, near Lakshmeshwar, I, pt. ii, 504.
Bell-metal : industry in Násik district, XVI, 153.
Bells : Portuguese, in Násik and Bhimáshankar temples, XVI, 519 and note 1.
Belori : timber tree XXV, 113.
Bel-phal : *see* Bel.
Belubbi : village in Bijápur district, temple at, XXIII, 565-66.
Belupura : *see* Belápura.
Belur : town in Mysore, I, pt. ii, 491; the Hoysala king Balláia I rules at, *id.* 494; Balláia III, when liberated by the Musalmáns, reigns at, *id.* 510; copper-plate grant from, *id.* 490 note 1, 509; record at, 298, 435 note 10, 498.
Belur : village in Bijápur district, temples and inscriptions at, XXIII, 566; victorious camp of Bhillama, I, pt. ii, 519 and note 1.
Beluvala : *see* Belvola.
Belvala : *see* Belvola.
Belvandi Kolhár : village in Ahmadnagar district, temple at, XVII, 713.
Belvankigudd : hill in Belgaum district, XXI, 8.
Belvanki or Old Panhála hill : in Belgaum district, XXI, 551.
Belvantra : village in Dhárwár district, inscriptions at, XXII, 657.
Belvatgi : village in Dhárwár district, temple at, XXII, 657.
Belvatti : old village in Dhárwár district, temple and inscriptions at, XXII, 657.
Belvola : district, I, pt. ii, 219, 298 note 2, 304, 305 note 1, 527; governors of, *id.* 306, 307, 308, 405, 418, 419, 421 422, 428 note 4, 431, 432, 440, 441, 442, 443, 449, 451, 452, 454, 456, 458, 465, 475, 485, 486; country conquered by Vishnuvardhána, *id.* 497; invaded by the Cholas, *id.* 499; governors of, *id.* 506, 520, 573, 574.
Benakatti : stream in Belgaum district, XXI, 13.
Benares : holy city. *See* Banáras.
Benawa : a caste of beggars also called Alifsháhis, drawn from many classes of Muhammadan Sunnis in name, IX, pt. ii, 20-21.
Benda : Bhiwndi creek in Thána district I, pt. i, 540, 542.
Bendi : fibrous plant, XXV, 226.
Bendigeri : village in Belgaum district, record at, I, pt. ii, 526.
Bene-Israel : tribe of Jews in Kolába, Thána, Kánara and Poona districts, XI, 85-86, XIII, 273-74, XV, pt. i, 411; XVIII, pt. i, 506-36; in Janjira state, XI, 421; in Belgaum district, XXI, 229.
Bengal : I, pt. i, 124; original place of Śrigaudas, *id.* 161, 468, 494; Gurjjara Vatsarája's success in, *id.* 527; under Tibet, *id.* 528; king of, son-in-law of Govinda III, *id.* 394, 402; Vikramáditya VI carries his arms as far as, *id.* 442; Maráthás in (1745), XIX, 287.
Bengali badham : timber, food and dye-yielding plant, XXV, 76, 155, 244.
Bengal sage : food-plant, XXV, 168.
Bengan : a very common food-plant, XXV, 167.
Bengi : the land of Vengi, territory of the Eastern Chálukyas, I, pt. ii, 308.
Benhadád : king of Damascus, VIII, 128.
Beni-Israel : *see* Bene-Israel.
Benkankond : village in Dhárwár district, temple and inscriptions at, XXII, 657. *See* also I, pt. ii, 529.
Bennihalla : river in Dhárwár district, XXII, 7.
Beobar : believed to be the origin of the name Bohors, IX, pt. ii, 25 note 1.
Be-pir : term of scorn among Musalmáns, IX, pt. ii, 127 note 2.
Berad : *see* Bedar.
Berar : province, I, pt. ii, 135, 141, 143, 355; surrender of, by the Ahmadnagar king to the Mughals (1595), *id.* 624. *See* Vidarbha.
Berbers : division of Abhir, Introduction to the History of the Konkan, I, pt. ii, p. x, 282 note 5.
Berdi : village in Central Provinces mentioned in a copper-plate grant, I, pt. ii, 420.
Berenice, Berenike : town in Africa on the Red Sea, trade centre in early times (B. C. 25-150 A. D.), XIII, 409 note 2, 410 note 5; *see* also I, pt. i, 535, 536, 543.
Bergera Kœnigii : timber, food and oil-yielding plant, grows on the *gháts*, XXV, 32, 149, 222.
Berkley : Mr., Railway Engineer (1860), XIII, 325.
Berman : or Bráhman, Persians styled their Maghs or excellencies as, IX, pt. i, 440 note 4.
Bernier : his travels (1656), I, pt. ii, 625; on the poverty and revenue of Khándesh (1660), XII, 250 note 4, 590; his description of Bijápur (1671), XXIII, 589.
Bertia : food-plant, XXV, 184.
Beruni : *see* Al Biruni.
Besar : caste mentioned by Al Masudi, I, pt. i, 516 and note 5.
Besharáa : beggars above the ordinary Muhammadan law, IX, pt. ii, 19, 20, 22, 23, 24.
Besná : sitting ceremony of a child, IX, pt. ii, 231.
Bet, Bet Dwarka : island and fort in Káthiáwár, VIII, 9, 31, 67, 242; seized by Vághers, captured and destroyed by the English (1859), I, pt. i, 446-447; place of pilgrimage, IX, pt. i, 10; Chapás established at, *id.* 488 notes 5 and 8.
Bet : timber tree found in Konkan, XXV, 136.
Betálas : demons, I, pt. ii, 579.
Betávad : fort in Khándesh district taken and afterwards evacuated by Dáji Gopál (1817), I, pt. ii, 630; XII, 255; town, *id.* 433.
Beta vulgaris : food-plant cultivated throughout India, XXV, 169.
Betel leaf, betel vine : cultivation of, in Kolába district, XI, 97; in Khándesh district, XII, 174, 175; in Kánara district, XV, pt. ii, 11-12; in Násik district, XVI, 104-105; in Ahmadnagar district, XVII, 276; in Poona district, XVIII, pt. ii, 49; in Dhárwár district, XXII, 303; XXV, 173; in Thána district, XIII, 293, 294.

Betelnut : article of luxury, IX, pt. i, p. xxxiv ; exported to Arab ports and to Ormuz (1300-1500), XIII, 445.
Betel palm : cultivation of, estimated profit from, in Thána district, XIII, 298-301 ; growth of (1514), in Ratnágiri district, X, 175 note 4 ; in Kánara district, XV, pt. ii, 7-9 ; in Poona district, XVIII, pt. i, 53 ; in Kolába district, XI, 97-98 ; in Janjira, *id.* 425 ; in Dhárwár district, XXII, 303.
Betel River : or the Muchkundi in Ratnágiri district, X, 175, 356 note 5.
Betel vine : *see* Betel leaf.
Betgere : village in Dhárwár district ; inscriptions at, I, pt. ii, 410.
Betrothal : rites and observances of, among Brahma-Kshatris, IX, pt. i, 57 ; Bráhmans, *id.* 40 ; Kanbis, *id.* 158 ; Káyasths, *id.* 62 ; Naikdás, *id.* 327 ; Rájpúts, *id.* 141-142 ; Vániás, Meshris, *id.* 89-90 ; Shrávaks, *id.* 100 ; Várlis, *id.* 329 ; rites and ceremonies relating to, costs of, IX, pt. ii, 162, 163 note 1 ; gifts in, *id.* 163 and note 2 ; conditions of, presents in, *id.* 232-233.
Betta : variety of soil in Kánara district, XV, pt. ii, 4.
Bettington : Mr., invested Bádámi (1840), XXIII, 453.
Betul : district in the Central Provinces, I, pt. ii, 386.
Betva : river in Central India, I, pt. ii, 135, 142.
Bevur : village in Bijápur district, temples and inscription at, XXIII, 566.
Bhábhar : state in Pálanpur ; its description, history, V, 281, 338.
Bhábhuya : minister of Bhima II, I, pt. i, 200.
Bhachán : town in Cutch, V, 213.
Bhada : táluka in Káthiáwár, VIII, 379.
Bhadadavayal : old province, I, pt. ii, 439, 492.
Bhádalvádi : reservoir at, in Poona district, XVIII, pt. ii, 27.
Bhadána : in Thána district, grant from, I, pt. ii, 414 note 1, 416 note 5, 426, 430, 538, 542 and note 4.
Bhádar : river in Káthiáwár, VIII, 61.
Bhádar Kántha : tract of country in Káthiáwar, VIII, 4.
Bhádarva : a Rewa Kántha state, VI, 152.
Bhádbhunjá : a caste of grain parchers, Hindu converts, IX, pt. ii, 71 ; in Ratnágiri district, X, 128 ; in Khándesh, XII, 62 ; in Ahmadnagar district, XVII, 95 ; in Poona district, XVIII, pt. i, 319-322 ; Hindu and Musalmán in Sholápur district, XX, 92, 204-205 ; in Bijápur district, XXIII, 298.
Bhádbhut : a place of pilgrimage in Broach district, II, 550-551 ; *see* also IX, pt. i, 549.
Bhádela : a class of Musalmán sailors known as lascars, IX, pt. i, 519, 522.
Bhadgaon : place of interest in Khándesh district, XII, 259 ; description, history and experimental farm at, *id.* 433.
Bhádhar : river in Ahmadábád district, IV, 7 ; *see* also I, pt. i, 160.
Bhadiád : place of fair in Ahmadábád district, IV, 333.
Bhadla : town in Káthiáwár, VIII, 379.
Bhadli : village in Káthiáwár, VIII, 379.
Bhadli : daughter of Ughad, a Márwár astrologer, IX, pt. i, 351.
Bhadli : food-plant found in several districts, XXV, 185 ; XVIII, pt. ii, 36.
Bhádoli : village in Kolhápur state, temple and tomb at, XXIV, 294.
Bhadrak : plant used as vegetable, XXV, 163.
Bhadrakáli : Hindu goddess, inscription in the temple of, at Somnáth Pátan in Káthiawár, I, pt. i, 79 note 3, 81, 190 ; temple of, at Násik, XVI, 520-521 ; at Gokarna in Kánara district, XV, pt. ii, 297.
Bhadrasiddha : Hindu ascetic ; Borsad Bráhmans claim descent from, IX, pt. i, 1, 8 note 1.
Bhadráyani : Buddhist school, XIV, 168 and note 1.
Bhadráyaniya : Buddhist sect, I, pt. ii, 149, 150.
Bhadresar, Bhadresvara : village in Cutch, a well, temple and remains of a mosque at, V, 213-215 ; inscription in a temple near, I, pt. i, 172 ; expedition against the chief of, *id.* 201 ; inscription slab at, *id* 204.
Bhádrod : town in Káthiáwár, VIII, 380.
Bhadron : town, headquarters of a Baroda subdivision, VII, 540.
Bhadula : Siddharáj built a fort at (1094-1143), I, pt. i, 180 note 2.
Bhadva : táluka in Káthiáwár, VIII, 381.
Bhadvana : táluka in Káthiáwár, VIII, 381.
Bhagaladevi, Bhágyavati : wife of the Western Chálukya king Dásavarman (1009), I, pt. ii, 434.
Bhágaladevi, Bhágalambika : wife of Kartivirya II, the Ratta chieftain (1076), I, pt. ii, 551, 554.
Bhagaravát : division of Gujars of Ajmer, history of their origin, IX, pt. i, 487.
Bhagat : a class of holy men among Bhangiás, IX, pt. i, 336 ; Bharváds, *id.* 269 ; Dhedás, *id.* 341 ; depressed classes, *id.* 333 ; early tribes, *id.* 293, 302 ; Golás, *id.* 185 ; Káchhiás, *id.* 154 ; Mochis, *id.* 194 ; Sonis, *id.* 201.
Bhagavadgitá, Bhagvad Gitá : philosophic poem sacred to the Hindus, I, pt. ii, 250, 539 ; IX, pt. I, 532.
Bhagavat : sacred place on the Narmada, I, pt. ii, 412.
Bhágavata Purán : Hindu sacred book, I, pt. ii, 155, 156, 162, 163, 164, 165 ; authoritative text book of Vallabhácháryan and Svámináráyen sects, dedicated to the glorification of Bhagavat or Vishnu, IX, pt. i, 532, 536.
Bhagavati : wife of Dásavarman and mother of Vikramáditya I, later Chálukya king (1008), I, pt. ii, 213.
Bhágbatái : an old Baroda land tenure, VII, 356-357. *See* also Bhágvatái.
Bhágdári : tenure in Baroda territory, VII, 359 ; tenure in Kanba villages in Kaira and Panjáb, IX, pt. i, 491.
Bhagiratha : Kadamba king, I, pt. ii, 286.
Bhágirathi : Kadamba king, Kákusthavarman, I, pt. ii, 286.
Bhágirathi : the Ganges, I, pt. ii, 348.

Bhágoji Náik : leader of the Bhils in Ahmadnagar ; attacks the police under Captain Henry and kills him (1857) ; his band destroyed by Mr. (the late Sir) Frank Souter (1859), I, pt. ii, 632 ; *see* also XVI, 199-202, 204 and note 1 ; XVII, 418-419.
Bhagva Jhenda : Shiváji's saffron coloured banner, XVIII, pt. ii, 229.
Bhagvantgad : fort in Ratnágiri district, X, 323 ; built by the Pant of Bávada, I, pt. ii, 79.
Bhagvantráv : Peshwa's deputy, marches on Cambay ; is surrounded and taken prisoner by Mominkháu ; his release, I, pt. i, 338 ; his engagements with Mominkháu (1754), *id.* 339 ; conquers Bálásinor and levies Peshwa's share of the reveune, *id.* 344.
Bhagvantráv Gáikwár : illegitimate son of Govindráv Gáikwár (1800), VII, 201 ; at Poona (1814), *id.* 219-220.
Bhágvatái : share system of levying land revenue in kind, I, pt. i, 279 ; in Káthiáwár, VIII, 295, 322.
Bhagvat Gita : *see* Bhagavad Gita.
Bhágyavati : *see* Bhágaladevi.
Bhaidhar : mangrove island in Káthiáwár, VIII, 29.
Bhai-koi : timber tree found in several districts, XXV, 21.
Bhaira : timber tree found in the *ghâts*, XXV, 73.
Bhaira Devi : seven Jain princesses (1450-1608), XV, pt. ii, 121 ; one married a Gersappa prince, *id.* 283 ; defeated (600 ?), *id.* 284.
Bhairanmatti : village in Bijápur district ; inscription at, XXIII, 566 ; *see* also I, pt. ii, 437 note 6, 574, 576.
Bhairav : shrine of, I, pt. i, 454 ; Buddhistic guardian, *id.* 458 and note 1 ; image of, at Elephanta Caves, XIV, 73 ; village god, XVIII, pt. i, 289.
Bhairavgad : hill and fort in Sátára district, XIX, 454-455 ; *see* also XXIV, 5.
Bhairwádgi : in the Bágewádi táluka in Bijápur district ; inscriptions at, I, pt. ii, 503.
Bhája : village in Poona district ; caves and inscriptions at, XVIII, pt. iii, 109-114 ; *see* also I, pt. ii, 144, XIII, 412.
Bhákodar : táluka in Káthiáwár, VIII, 381.
Bhaktas : four preachers of the four Hindu *yugás* or epochs, IX, pt. ii, 48.
Bhál : a popular sub-division of Ahmadábád district, IV, 2.
Bhál : tract of country in Káthiáwár, VIII, 4.
Bhál : village in Thána district, Marátha and British rental compared (1817 and 1819), XIII, 568 note 2.
Bhalálá : táluka in Káthiáwár, VIII, 381.
Bhál and Chuvál : route guarded by Bahuchára, IX, pt. i, p. xi.
Bhalásna : state in Mahi Kántha, V, 426.
Bhalgám : *see* Baldhvi.
Bhalgámda : táluka in Káthiáwár, VIII, 382.
Bhálgaon : village in Ahmadnagar district ; temple at, XVII, 713.
Bhallasvámin : Bráhman grantee of a Chálukya prince, I, pt. ii, 191.
Bhálod : a sub-division of Rájpipla, VI, 97.
Bháma : river in Poona district, XVIII, pt. i, 7.
Bhámati : commentary on Samkaráchárya's *Vedántasutrabháshya*, I, pt. ii, 245-246.
Bhambhágiri : lord of, overthrown by Singhana, I, pt. ii, 525.
Bhámbhan : village in Káthiáwár, VIII, 382.
Bhámburda : village near Poona, Vithoji Holkár captured at (1801), XVIII, pt. iii, 361.
Bhamer : fort in Khándesh district ; caves at, XII, 241, 434-435.
Bhammaha : father of Jákavva, king of the Rattas, I, pt. ii, 425 note 2, 428.
Bhamodra Mohota : place of intrest in Káthiáwár, VIII, 382.
Bhámtá : a wandering tribe in Násik district, XVI, 66-67 ; in Sholápur district, XX, 165 ; also found in Poona ; *see* Uchliá.
Bhánd : hook-swinging, a festival among Kánara Habbus, XV, pt. i, 247 and foot-note 1.
Bhand : caste of beggars in Káthiáwár, VIII, 160 ; Hindu converts, buffoons, story-tellers, IX, pt. ii, 81, 165.
Bhandar : central pit in a tower of silence, IX, pt. ii, 240 note 1.
Bhandáragavittage : identified with Bhandárkawte in Sholapur district ; camp of Kirtivarman II at (757), I, pt. ii, 377, 378.
Bhandargad : fort in Thána district, XIV, 219.
Bhandári : officer in a beggar brotherhood, IX, pt. ii, 19.
Bhandári : a caste of cultivators and toddy-drawers, in Ratnágiri district, X, 124, 151, 152, 155, 171 ; in Sávantvádi, *id.* 414, 426 ; in Kolába district, XI, 70 ; in Jánjira, *id.* 412 ; in Thána district, XIII, 149-150 ; foreign element in, *id.* 61, 62 ; traces of Lingáyat customs among, *id.* 63 ; in Kánara district, XV, pt. i, 286-288, XV, pt. ii, 2-3 ; in Poona district, XVIII, pt. i, 393-394 ; in Belgaum district, XXI, 162 ; in Kolhápur state, XXIV, 105 ; in Bombay, to supply a militia of 800 men, XXVI, pt. iii, 494 ; rewarded for this service (1757), *id.* 477-480.
Bhandaria : táluka in Káthiáwár, VIII, 382, 384.
Bhandári Vájantri : a caste of musicians in Kánara district, XV, pt. i, 316-317.
Bhandárkawte : village in the Sholápur district, I, pt. ii, 378.
Bhandir : timber tree found in several districts, XXV, 69.
Bhándup : village with railway station in Thána district, XIV, 44-45, I, pt. ii, 21 ; grant at, *id.* 436, 538, 542 ; distilleries at, XIII, 398 ; Siláhára high road near, *id.* 428 ; estate, *id.* 545-546.
Bhanduri : village in Káthiáwár, VIII, 384.
Bhang : hemp preparation, used as an article of luxury and stimulant, IX, pt. i, p. xxxii.
Bhangárika : old town, I, pt. ii, 525.
Bhangia (Bhangi) : a caste of sweepers ; in Cutch, V, 83 ; in Palánpur, *id.* 291 ; in Máhi Kántha, *id.* 367 ; in Káthiáwár, VIII, 157 ; also called Olgánás, meaning of name, IX, pt. i, 334 note 1 ; census details, *id.* 331, 334 ; their origin, appearance, dress, ornaments, food, *id.* 334 ; occupation ; eclipse,

chief harvest time of, *id.* 335; religion, objects of worship, *bhagats* among, holidays, places of pilgrimage, *chhadi* procession in honour of Záhir Pir, *id.* 335-336 and note 1; customs, *id.* 336-338; prospects, *id.* 338; in Kolába district, XI, 73; in Khándesh district, XII, 128; in Thána district, XIII, 190-191; in Násik district, XVI, 72; in Ahmadnagar district, XVII, 164-165; in Sátára district, XIX, 110; in Belgaum district, XXI, 189-190; in Dhárwár district, XXII, 214; in Kolhápur state, XXIV, 109. *See* Halálkhor.

Bhangra: famine plant common throughout India, XXV, 197.

Bhangrah: medicinal plant, XXV, 260.

Bhanibhan: goddess, IX, pt. i, 205.

Bhánmates: Nát women taking part in acrobatic feats; origin of the name of, IX, pt. ii, 89.

Bhánsáli: a caste of tillers and traders, in Cutch V, 56; in Káthiáwár, VIII, 143; in Gujarát called Vegus; census details, IX, pt. i, 69; origin, *id.* 116 and note 1; in Kolába district, XI, 47; in Thána district, XIII, 108.

Bháungupta: Gupta ruler (511), I, pt. i, 72.

Bhánumati: name of spirit believed to live in Kharsáni plant, IX, pt. i, 385.

Bhánusakti: Sendraka king, I, pt ii, 290-292.

Bhanuvarman: Kádamba king, charter issued by, I, pt. ii, 289 note 3, 291 note 1.

Bhánvad: town in Káthiáwár, VIII, 382.

Bhanvad: pass in Násik district, XVI, 128.

Bhánvár: or Bhánuwásar, Sunday, IX, pt. i, 393.

Bhápsháh: hill in Sátára district, XIX, 12.

Bharádi: a caste of beggars in Poona district, XVIII, pt. i, 446-447; in Khándesh district, XII, 69; in Thána district, XIII, 196; in Nasik district, XVI, 73; in Ahmadnagar district, XVII, 188-191.

Bháradvája: sage, I, pt. ii, 136 (*see* also IX, pt. i, 436 and note 1, 442); *gotra*, *id.* 248; family stock of the Pallavas, *id.* 316, 317, 328.

Bháradvájiyas: school of, I, pt. ii, 140.

Bharam Dev: an object of worship, IX, pt. i, 292.

Bharang: food-plant, XXV, 168.

Bhárangi: in Mysore, inscription at, I, pt. ii, 350 note 8.

Bharant: in Central India, Páli inscription at, I, pt. ii, 277 note 5, 538 note 8.

Bharap: fort on the *gháts* in the Dakhan reduced by Malik Ahmad (1485), I, pt. ii, 32.

Bhárata: the great Hindu epic, Kánarese version of, I, pt. ii, 211; the war described in, *id.* 357 note 3.

Bharatgad: fort in Ratnágiri district, X, 323; built by Phond Sávant (1700), I, pt. ii, 79, 112.

Bháravi: Sanskrit poet, I, pt. ii, 357.

Bhárdori: spirit-laden obstetric cord worn by pregnant women, IX, pt. ii, 148, 149.

Bharejra: place of interest in Káthiáwár, VIII, 384.

Bhargav: a sub-caste of Bráhmans in Thána district, XIII, 78; their origin, strength, divisions, condition, IX, pt. i, 1, 3, 7-8.

Bhárgavrám: Bájiráv I's (1721-1740) spiritual adviser, XIX, 466.

Bharhut: town in Northern India; *stúpa* at, I, pt. ii, 176, XIV, 170.

Bhari: timber tree found in Konkan, XXV, 81.

Bhárkhali: or alienated lands in Baroda, VII, 349.

Bhármal I: Ráo of Cutch (1585-1631), arrival of Dádu Pir in Bhuj in the time of, IX, pt. ii, 41.

Bharoch: Broach, I, pt. ii, 148, 241, 353 note 2, 354.

Bharod: *see* Chávadas, I, pt. i, 464.

Bharthari: a caste of beggars in Rewa Kántha, VI, 25.

Bhartrihari: Sanskrit grammarian, I, pt. ii, 408.

Bharttridáman: nineteenth Kshatrapa (278-294), coins of, I, pt. i, 48.

Bharuch: *see* Bárus.

Bharukachchha: old name for Broach, I, pt. ii, 148, 174, 314 note 6, 316, 403.

Bharukachheva: old name for Broach, I, pt. ii, 354.

Bhárut: hills eight miles east of Sanján in Thána district; Pársis fly to, IX, pt. ii, 187.

Bharvád: a caste of shepherds, in Cutch, V, 81; in Káthiáwár, VIII, 138; in Gujarát, strength and distribution, IX, pt. i, 264, 267; origin, *id.* 267; surnames, *id.* 267 and note 1; appearance, *id.* 267; dress, *id.* 267-268; food, religion, followers of *mátás*, *id.* 268; festival days, customs, *id.* 269; account of Bharvád Jang or shepherd wedding at Khedsara, *id.* 270-285; in Thána district, XIII, 144.

Bhásha: current language, I, pt. ii, 141.

Bháskara: *see* Báchana.

Bháskaráchárya: astronomer and mathematician, I, pt. ii, 239, 244, 521, 526.

Bháskargad: fort in Násik district, XVI, 425.

Bháskarpant: Berár minister, his expedition into Behar (1742), XIX, 285; his second expedition and murder (1745), *id.* 287.

Bháskarráv: rebel chief of Nargund, account of his rising (1858), XXII, 434-438, 779, 787.

Bháskarráv Vithal: Khásgivala under Sayáji II Gaikwár, VII, 236, 262.

Bhat: pass in Násik district, XVI, 130.

Bhat: rice, food plant found in several districts, XXV, 186.

Bhát: a caste, genealogists, I, pt. i, 451 and note 1; in Kaira district, III, 34; as revenue agents, *id.* 91; in Cutch, V, 74-75; as escorts, VI, 194; in Baroda (state), VII, 63; in Káthiáwár, VIII, 135-136; also called *bahrots*, heralds and bards; strength and distribution, IX, pt. i, 207, 208 note 3; origin, accounts of, *id.* 207; traces of Bráhman origin, *id.* 207, 438; settlements or *vádás*; clans or *shákhás*; personal names; surnames; twelve divisions, *id.* 207; appearance; dress, *id.* 208; occupation as genea-

logists, bards, historians of their patron's families, *id.* 208 and note 3; Forbes' account of their yearly tours, *id.* 208-209; other means of earning livelihood, *id.* 209; use as securities, both before and after introduction of British rule, *id.* 209 and note 2, 210 and note 1; *trága* and *dharna*, meaning of, *id.* 210; instances of *trága*, in Nadiád in Kaira district (A. D. 1775), narrated by Mr. James Forbes, in Kanua near Viramgám (A. D. 1806), in Kaira (A. D. 1808), *id.* 211; in Ahmadábád (A. D. 1816), in Nadiád on the introduction of income tax (A. D. 1861), *id.* 212; their influence on lower tribes in Central India, *id.* 210 note 3; condition, *id.* 212; religion, poets, *id.* 213; customs, *id.* 213-214; religious beggars in Ratnágiri district, X, 131, in Sávantvádi, *id.* 418; musicians in Kolába district, XI, 67; in Khándesh district, XII, 77; in Thána district, XIII, 141; in Násik district, XVI, 55; in Poona district, XVIII, pt. i, 447; in Sátára district, XIX, 115-116; beggars in Sholápur district, XX, 181; in Belgaum district, XXI, 178; in Kolhápur state, XXIV, 100.

Bhata: military officer, I, pt. i, 125.

Bhatárka: I, pt. i, 80; founder of the Valabhi dynasty of Gurjjara descent, coins ascribed to (509-520), *id.* 85, 86, 87, 135, 136; IX, pt. i, 479, 492; was a Maitraka, Mihira, or Mer, *id.* 495.

Bhatela: pond at Sopára in Thána district, XIV, 339.

Bhátela: a sub-caste of Bráhmans; *see* AnáváLa.

Bhathán: táluka in Káthiáwár, VIII, 385.

Bháthi: dinners cooked at a house of mourning, IX, pt. ii, 169.

Bháti: a caste of Rájpúts in Káthiáwár, VIII, 115.

Bhati: *see* Kolamb.

Bháti or Bhatti: a tribe of Rájpúts, probably of Turkish origin, IX, pt. i, 129, 446 note 4, 483; said to be Gujars in West Marwár and Játs in the Panjáb, *id.* 483; converted by Muhammad of Ghazni (1001-1030), IX, pt. ii, 81.

Bhátia: town (in Sind?) reduced by Muhammad of Ghazni, I, pt. i, 168.

Bhátia: a caste of traders and husbandmen in Cutch, V, 53; in Pálanpur, *id.* 289; in Káthiáwár, VIII, 149; in Gujarát, strength and distribution, IX, pt. i, p. xi, and note 3, 69, 116 and note 7, 117 and notes 3 and 4; derivation of name, *id.* 116 note 2; *Origin*, claim to be Bháti Rájpúts of Yádava stock, *id.* 116 and note 3, 464; claim descent from Sháliváhan, *id.* 117 note 1; are probably Turks, *id.* 453, 464; *History*, ruling tribe in Jesalmir, their modern head-quarters, *id.* 116 and note 4; their earliest capital at Gajnipur (B.C. 600), *id.* 116; their movements and settlement in Cutch, Káthiáwár, Gujarát, Bombay; *Divisions*, Háláis and Kachhis, sub-divisions into Visás and Dasás, *id.* 117; *nukhs* in, *id.* 117 and note 6; appearance, *id.* 117 and note 7; character, occupation *id.* 118 note 1; *Religion*, are Vaishnavs, *id.* 118; places of pilgrimage, *marjadis* in; *Customs*, Birth; Chhathi worship; Botan, *id.* 119; Betrothal, *id.* 120; Marriage, *id.* 119, 120, 121; in Ratnágiri district, X, 120, 171; in Khándesh district, XII, 62, 194; in Thána district, XIII, 109; in Kánara district, XV, pt. i, 185; in Sholápur district, XX, 50-51; in Belgaum district, XXI, 100; in Poona district, XVIII, pt. i, 266.

Bhatinda: town between Delhi and the Satlaj, IX, pt. ii, 81.

Bhatkal: river in Kánara district, XV, pt. i, 8; forests, *id.* 57-58.

Bhatkal: town in Kánara district, schools at XV, pt. ii, 215; port, people, trade, temples, mosques, tombs, old bridge, history (1321-1862), *id.* 266-275.

Bhatkárka: *see* Bhatárka.

Bhatli: level upland soil in Ratnágiri district, X, 145.

Bhátodi: village in Ahmadnagar, XVII, 713; lake, *id.* 252-254.

Bhátsa: river in Thána district, XIII, 10.

Bhattara, Bhattáraka: title of Chandráditya in the Nerúr grant, I, pt. ii, 352, 368 note 1.

Bhattáraka: attribute of priests of Digambara Jain sect, I, pt. i, 85.

Bhatti: *see* Bháti.

Bhatti Gate Bridge: in Poona city, XVIII, pt. iii, 285.

Bhatti Gujar: special class of Gujars, IX, pt. i, 482.

Bhatvadar: táluka in Kátbiáwár, VIII, 385.

Bhatya: *see* Bhatia.

Bhatyar: a caste of Musalmán cooks in Ahmadnagar district, XVII, 230; in Poona district, XVIII, pt. i, 504; in Sholápur district, XX, 206; in Belgaum district, XXI, 221; in Dhárwár district, XXII, 244; in Bijápur district, XXIII, 302.

Bhau-Bij: holiday, IX, pt. i, 54.

Bháu Khare: Bráhman rebel (1839), XVIII, pt. ii, 307.

Bhaulan: timber tree found on the *gháts*, XXV, 84.

Bhaulingi: Sálva tribe, I, pt. i, 534, 546.

Bháu Punekar; Colonel Phayre's agent at Malhárráv Gáikwár's court, VII, 282.

Bháu Puráuik: minister of Sayájiráv II Gáikwár, VII, 240, 250.

Bháuráv Phanse: Peshwa's general, reduces Konkan to obedience (1776), I, pt. ii, 102.

Bháu Sáheb Pavár: Baroda officer, his intrigues (1857), I, pt. i, 442, 445.

Bháu Shinde: Khanderav Gáikwár's minister (1867), VII, 276-277, 280.

Bháu Singh: Rána of Maltwar, annexes the Akráni country in the Sátpuda mountains, and builds the fort of Roshmal, I, pt. ii, 633.

Bháu Támbekar: minister to Ganpatráo Gáikwár (1852), VII, 270, 272-273.

Bhava: the god Śiva, I, pt. ii, 514.

Bhavabhuti: poet, I, pt. ii, 136.

Bháva Brihaspati: state officer at Somanátha, I, pt. i, 193.

Bhávóis: comedies or plays of common life, performed by Bhávayás, description of, IX, pt. i, 224, 225.
Bhaváji Náik: free-booter (1860), XIV, 312.
Bhavangad: fort in Ratnágiri district, X, 323.
Bhavangad: port in Thána district, XIV, 45.
Bhaváni: temple of, built by Anantdev in Khándesh (1222), I, pt. ii, 244; home goddess of all Gurjjaras, originally a Gurjar woman, became guardian mother by her self-sacrifice, IX, pt. i, 501; image of, *id.* xxxv, p. 272, 292, 363; Sakti worshipped as, *id.* p. xxxv; village goddess, XVIII, pt. i, 298-290; Shivaji's goddess, XVIII, pt. ii, 228; XIX, 546; shrines of, at Sátára and Pratapgad, *id.* 567.
Bhaváni: Poona ward, details of, XVIII, pt. iii, 274-276.
Bhaváni: Shiváji's sword, XVIII, pt. ii, 240 note 4; XIX, 238, 249.
Bhaváni's Temple: in Poona city, XVIII, pt. iii, 334.
Bhavánráo: Pratinidhi deposed by Raghunáthráo (1762), restored to his office (1763), XIX, 296.
Bháva Phán: *dargáh* of, at Islámpur, in Sátára, XIX, 598.
Bhávar: pass in Násik district, XVI, 130.
Bhaváyá: a caste of actors in Cutch, V, 102; in Pálanpur, *id.* 290; or Targálás, performers of Bhaváis or comedies, strength and distribution, IX, pt. i, 207, 222; accounts of origin; appearance, *id.* 222; two divisions as actors, companies or *tolis*; yearly tour, performances at the temple of the goddess Bahnucharáji, *id.* 223 and note 1; Bhaváis, *id.* 224-225; Gujar element traced in, *id.* 481 note 4.
Bhavihál: village in Dhárwár district, temple, inscriptions, XXII, 658; *see* also I, pt. ii, 568 note 6.
Bhávin: a caste of prostitutes in Ratnágiri district, X, 126.
Bhavishya: early Ráshtrakúta prince, I, pt. i, 120; I, pt. ii, 386.
Bhavishya Purána: sacred book, I, pt. i, 465; IX, pt. i, 440, 532; *see* Puráns.
Bhávka: a place of interest in Panch Maháls, III, 303.
Bhávnagar: state in Káthiáwár, its description, history and administration, VIII, 385, 394; city, *id.* 394-397; founded (1723), *id.* 301-302; pays tribute to the Gáikwár (1803), VII, 321, 323; Gohil Rájpút chiefship at, origin of the house, IX, pt. i, 125-126; *see* also I, pt. i, 78; port, its importance, its imports and exports, crops and mill, VIII, 237, 262-265.
Bhávnath: place of interest in Mahi Kántha, the resting place of Bhrigu, a leprosy-curing pond at, V, 433.
Bhávsár: a caste of calico-printers in Cutch, V, 73; in Káthiáwár, VIII, 152; their origin; claim Kshatri or Gurjjara origin; original home, Brij Mathura; movements and settlement in different parts; divisions, IX, pt. i, 177; their calling of calico-printers and dyers; busy times, earnings; religion, *id.* 178; customs, *id.* 179; dyers in Poona district, XVIII, pt. i, 322-325.
Bhavsari: village in Poona district, rude stone enclosures at, XVIII, pt. iii, 114-119.
Bhávsingh: of Viramgám, invites the Maráthás to Viramgám and expels the Kasbátis from the town (1735), I, pt. i, 317; attacks the fort and expels the Maráthás, *id.* 323.
Bhavviràja: minister of Ashmaka chief, built one Ajanta Cave (600 A. D.?), XII, 485.
Bhawani: *see* Bhaváni.
Bhawyyá: a caste of strolling players, converts of the Hindu caste of the same name, Sunnis in religion, IX, pt. ii, 81; Hindu players, *id.* 154 note 2.
Bháyá: prince, mentioned in an inscription, I, pt. ii, 147.
Bháyali: small town in Baroda, VII, 534; its *pátil* helps the Gáikwár (1724), *id.* 169.
Bháyávadar: town in Káthiawár, VIII, 397.
Bháyideva: officer of the Western Chálukya king Someśvara IV, governor of the Kundi province, I, pt. ii, 465, 556.
Bháyndar: port in Thána district with railway station, Portuguese church at, XIV, 45.
Bheckhol: fibrous plant found in Konkan, XXV, 229.
Bhedasgáve: hill in Kánara district, XV, pt. i, 4.
Bhedasgávgudda: Sahyádri peak in Kánara district, XV, pt. ii, 275.
Bhekal: timber tree found in several districts, XXV, 6.
Bhekra: deer, in Ratnágiri district, X, 46.
Bhendá: food-tree very common in the presidency, XXV, 147.
Bhendi: timber and food-tree found in several districts, XXV, 15, 147; *see* also XII, 173; fibrous, medicinal and sacred plant, *id.* 227, 226, 289; a Khándesh green, XII, 173.
Bhen Kolis: *see* Ráj Kolis.
Bhensásur: Buffalo-god, worship of, IX, pt. i, 375.
Bherai: port in Káthiáwár, VIII, 241, 398.
Bherda: food-plant, yields dye and gum, XXV, 155, 244, 251.
Bherdha: *see* Behda.
Bheria: timber tree found in Konkan and Dakhan, XXV, 46.
Bherikibháv: an old commutation rate known as, in Rájpuri, XI, 183.
Bherla: wild sago palm in Kolhápur state, XXIV, 24.
Bhersingi: timber tree found in several districts, XXV, 105-106.
Bhes: timber tree found in Eastern Dakhan, XXV, 69.
Bhesván: town in Káthiáwár, VIII, 398.
Bhiba: food-plant, XXV, 151.
Bhigvan: village in Poona district, XVIII, pt. iii, 119.
Bhikáji: son of Bháu Singh of Maltwar, murders Jangar the Bhil Náik of Chikhli, and is killed by Jangar's son Deváji, I, pt. ii, 633.
Bhikshu: Buddhist mendicant, I, pt. ii, 173.
Bhikshuk: clerick, section of Bráhmans according to calling, privileges of, IX, pt. I, 2 and note 2.

Bhil: early tribe in Gujarát, X; IX, pt. i; strength and distribution, *id.* 290, 294; history of origin of former rule and power, *id.* 294-295; Gujar element in, *id.* 455, 497, 499; divisions, Rájpút clan names among, *id.* 295; Captain Melville's account of Modásá Bhils, *id.* 295 note 1; list of their sub-divisions given by different authors, *id.* 295, note 2; appearance, *id* 295-296; described by Mr. Prescott, Bishop Heber, Major LeGeyt, *id.* 296 note 1; houses, *id.* 296; details given by Major G. Fulljames of Bhil hut, *id.* 296 note 2; Bishop Heber's description of Bhil dwellings, *id.* 296, note 3; furniture, *id.* 297; Major Fulljames' description of Bhil carts, *id.* 297 note 1; Major LeGeyt's list of Bhils' cooking and drinking vessels, *id.* 297 note 2; dress, *id.* 297 and note 4, 298; Bishop Heber's description of their dress, *id.* 297 note 3; ornaments, *id.* 298-299 and note 1; food, *id.* 299-300; occupation as peasants, labourers, watchmen, *id.* 300; Major G. Fulljames' details of their tillage, *id.* 300 note 2; character, *id.* 300; Mr. Prescott's and Mr. Fakirbhái's opinion on Bhil truthfulness, *id.* 300 note 3; their daring aggressions, *id.* 300 and note 4; character of Broach Bhils, of Rájpipla as described by Mr. Pollexfen; their drunkenness, *id.* 301; religion, *id.* 301-305; Devi worship, *id.* 301 and note 2; respect Musalmán shrines, make offerings to Musalmán saints, *id.* 301; reverence the moon called Bárbig and swear by it, *id.* 301 and note 3; spirits and ghosts, the chief objects of their worship, *id.* 301 and notes 4 and 5; classes of men held in special reverence by, Bhagats or Badvás, that is devotees and exorcists; their incantation, *id.* 302-303, 307 and note 1; Bhats or Dholis, minstrels; their duties; *id.* 302, 303-304; Rávals or priests, their duties, *id.* 302, 304-305; animal worship by, *id.* 305; festivals, *id.* 305-307; Holi, *id.* 305; Dasara, Devali, *id.* 306; sacrifices or Játars, description of, *id.* 306-307; customs, naming, shaving, betrothal, *id.* 308; marriage, *id.* 300, 308-309; death, *id.* 309-310; beliefs, witchcraft, evil eye, *id.* 302, 310-311; community, *id.* 311-312; education, *id.* 312; *see* Early Tribes; for details of, in Panch Mahál district, *see* III, 218-222; in Cutch and Mahi Kántha, V, 82, 366; in Pálanpur, *id.* 291; in Rewa Kántha, VI, 26-32, 95 note 1; in Thána district, XIII, 156; in Násik district, XVI, 61, 314; in Ahmadnagar district, XVII, 191-193; in Poona and Sholápur districts, XVIII, pt. i, 406, XX, 165; in Kolába district, XI, 71; in Khándesh, XII, 21, 197-198, 248; raised by Piláji Gáikwár against Baude and Musalmáns (1726), VII, 171, 174; plunder Gangathadi (1803) I, pt. ii, 609; harsh treatment of, by the Maráthás (1806), massacre of, *id.* 629, XII, 254, XVI, 194, XVII, 414, 724; invade Kalyán, hold Bor Ghát (1817), XIII, 522-523, I, pt. ii, 116, 125; agencies of, established (1819), *id.* 631; disturbances in Thána district (1818-1820), XIII, 524; in Khándesh (1818-1825), XII, 257-259; rising of, under Kajarsing (1833-1860) and Tulia Náik (1867-1876), *id.* 309-313; rising of, in Násik district (1858), XVI, 202-204; chiefs in the Dangs, XII, 490, 601.

Bhiláala: a Bhil tribe in Khándesh district, XII, 103.

Bhilama: timber tree found in several districts, XXV, 54.

Bhilápur: village in Baroda, VII, 551-552; battle of, between Bájiráo I and the confederate Marátha chiefs in Gujarát (1731), *id.* 172.

Bhilavdi: town in Sátára district, XIX, 455.

Bhilawa: *see* Bhilama.

Bhil corps: raised (1825-27), XII, 258-259; enlistment, active service, present strength, and duties of, *id.* 317.

Bhildi Máta: goddess, worshipped by Sindhvás, IX, pt. i, p. xxxvi, 347.

Bhilkhand: pass in Násik district, XVI, 130.

Bhillam: Chándor Yádav king (A. D. 915), XIII, 424; married to the daughter of Thána Siláhára king Jhanjha, I, pt. ii, 17.

Bhillam: Devgiri Yádav king (1188-1192); discrepancy in connection with his parentage, I, pt. ii, 516-517; his latest date, titles, *id.* 518 and note 5; wrests portions of Chálukya kingdom from Someśvara IV, *id.* 223, 230, 466, 518; rules over Karnátak; killed in a battle with Hoysálas, *id.* 502, 503, 504, 519; (*see* also XV, pt. ii, 91, 92 and note 1); his officers, *id.* 520, 521, 549, 582; his inscriptions in Sholápur district, XX, 275.

Bhillama I: Yádav king, son of Dhádiyappa, I, pt. ii, 231, 513.

Bhillama II: Yádav prince, vassal of the Western Chálukyas, assists Tailapa in his war with Munja; his grant, I, pt. ii, 232, 233, 425, 430, 433; copper-plate grant of, *id.* 511 and note 7, 513; S'iva worshipper, *id.* 514.

Bhillama III: Yádav king, vassal of the Western Chálukyas, I, pt. ii, 234; marries Hámmá, daughter of Jayasimha II, the Western Chálukya king, *id.* 435, 436, 437, 514, 515.

Bhillama IV: Yádav king, I, pt. ii, 234, 515.

Bhillama V: Yádav king, first of the later dynasty, extends his power over the country ruled by the Chálukyas, I, pt. ii, 235-236; puts to death the Hoysála Yádav prince at Kalyán; founds the town of Devagiri and gets himself crowned; endeavours to extend his power beyond the Krishna, but is defeated by Virá-Ballála, *id.* 237-238.

Bhilmál: *see* Bhinmál.

Bhiloda: village in Mahi Kántha, temple at, V, 433.

Bhilodia: state in Rewa Kántha, VI, 145, IX, pt. i, 124.

Bhilrigad: place of interest in Pálanpur, marble remains at, V, 339.

Bhilsá: town in Central India, ancient Daśárna identified with, I, pt. ii, 142, 147.

Bhim: Solanki, called the Gujar in poems, IX, pt. i, 485.

Bhim: legendary ruler of Bombay, Máhim, takes Asheri fort and Tárápur from Kolis (1280), XIV, 11, 344. *See* Bimb.

Bhima: Devgiri Yádav prince, I, pt. ii, 519; Siláhára king, *id.* 537; Sinda prince, *id.* 577.

Bhima: river in the Dakhan, XVII and XVIII, pt. i, 6, XX, 3-4, XXIII, 9, I, pt. ii, 185, 227, 357, 377 note 4; camp of Kirtivarman II, on the bank of, *id.* 378.

Bhima: stream in Kolába, XI, 7.

Bhima I: Chálukya king (1022-1064), succeeds Durlabhá, leads victorious expeditions against the kings of Sind and Chédi; Kulachandra attacks his capital Anahilaváda; he escapes at the advance of Máhmud of Ghazni (1024), his plates, I, pt. i, 79 note 2, 163-164, 166-167, 169-170, 181; builds the Somanátha temple, *id.* 190, 522.

Bhima I: Western Chálukya king, I, pt. ii, 378.

Bhima II: Chálukya king (1179-1242), succeeds Mularája II; his grants, I, pt. i, 195 and note 3; his nickname Bholo (Simpleton), *id.* 196, 470; Lavanaprasád becomes independent of, I, pt. ii, 242; said to have been converted to Islám by Núr Satágur (1240) IX, pt. ii, 26 note 2; *id.* 38.

Bhima II: Western Chálukya king of Kalyáni, I, pt. ii, 378-379.

Bhimadeva I: I, pt. i, 79 note 2, 181, 190; Karna the king of Chédi, forms a confederacy with, I, pt. ii, 214. *See* Bhima I.

Bhimadeva I: Devagiri Yádav prince, is defeated by Alaf Khán's troops while conveying Devaladevi, I, pt. ii, 532.

Bhimadeva II: Chálukya ruler, I, pt. i, 229. *See* Bhima II.

Bhim Agiáras: holiday, observed by Vághers, IX, pt. i, 523.

Bhimapalli: ancient town in Gujarát, I, pt. i, 196.

Bhimarája: Western Chálukya king, Satyásraya's governor of the Banavási, Sántalige, and Kisukád districts, I, pt. ii, 433.

Bhimarasa: feudatory of Tailapa, I, pt. ii, 430.

Bhimarathi: river, modern Bhima, I, pt. ii, 356, 377.

Bhimasen: king of Bhinmál (953) I, pt. i, 469.

Bhimasena: the Pándav, I, pt. ii, 149.

Bhima series: rocks of the, in Bijápur, XXIII, 36-38.

Bhimáshankar: hill in Poona district, XVIII, pt. i, 4; pass between Thána and Poona districts, its holiness, XIII, 321, 508, XVIII, pt. ii, 151, 211 and note 1; holy village in Poona, Mahádev temple and Portuguese bell at, legends, XVIII, pt. iii, 119-121.

Bhima Simha: husbandman, concealed Kumárapála, I, pt. i, 182; is appointed head of the royal bodyguard, *id.* 184.

Bhimavargya: of the branch of Bhimavarman, I, pt. ii, 325, note 1. *See* Nandivarman.

Bhimavarman: younger brother of Simhavishnu, the Pallava king, I, pt. ii, 324 note 1, 325.

Bhimb: food-plant, XXV, 159.

Bhim Bahádur: Kolhápur Sardár (1804-1805), XXIV, 189.

Bhimdev: first Konkan king, I, pt. ii, 27.

Bhimdev I: Solanki king, his rule in Thána district (A. D. 1022-1072), XIII, 436; in Cutch, V, 131; assumes the title of Rája of Rájas, I, pt. ii, 24. *See* also Bhima I.

Bhimeshvar: temple of, at Ganeshpuri, near Vajrábai, hot springs, XIV, 374.

Bhimgad: hill fort in Belgaum, description, history, XXI, 551-552.

Bhimkata: village in Káthiáwár, VIII, 399.

Bhimkund: a place of pilgrimage in the Panch Mahála, III, 303.

Bhimnáth: scene of a fair in Ahmadábád, IV, 333.

Bhimnáth: shrine of, in Gujarát, IX, pt. i, p. ix.

Bhimora: cave in Káthiáwár, VIII, 399.

Bhimpor: place of interest and fair at, in Sáchin State, VI, 364; temple of, near Dumas, I, pt. i, 403.

Bhimráj: I, pt. ii, 24; *see* Bhimadev I.

Bhimrája: son of Rámdev of Devgir, conquers the Konkan, dispossesses the Náik princes, makes Máhim his capital, and is claimed by Parbhus, Rájpúts and Shudrás, I, pt. ii, 27; *see* Bhimadeva I.

Bhimráv Nádgir: a rebel (1858), XXII, 434-435.

Bhimry: modern Bhiwndi under the Gujarát kings, I, pt. ii, 30.

Bhimságiri: group of temples near Sámángad, in Kolhápur, XXIV, 294.

Bhimthadi: breed of horses, named after the Bhima, XVIII, pt. i, 61-63.

Bhimthadi: sub-division of Poona district, its boundaries, area, aspect, water, climate, stock, crops, people, cultivators, and communications, XVIII, pt. iii, 74-78; survey of, in 1829-1830, *id.* pt. ii, 392; in 1838-1839, *id.* 418, 419, 420, 421, 425, 426; in 1871-72, *id.* 477-481.

Bhinála: pond at Uran, XIV, 191.

Bhingár: town near Ahmadnagar city, XVII, 713-714.

Bhinmal: Shrimal town, I, pt. i, 3 and note 5; expedition against, *id.* 109 and note 2; Gurjjars of, *id.* 115, 469; Chávadás connected with Chápas of, *id.* 139, 155; its king sides with Mularaja, *id.* 160; description of, *id.* 449; people of, *id.* 450; objects in the town, *id.* 451-52; surroundings, *id.* 452-456; of Jalkop, *id.* 456-458; sun temple at, *id.* 459-461; legends, *id.* 461-463; caste legends of, *id.* 463-465; history, *id.* 465-471; origin of the name of, *id.* 466 note 6, 469; inscriptions at, *id.* 471-488; Gurjjar chief of, *id.* 489; affliction of, *id.* 513 note 9, 526; capital of great Gujar dynasty of Márwár, IX, pt. i, 479, 496, 499; Pilo-mo-to of Hiuen Tsiang, *id.* 479; also called Shrimál, *id.* 73; inscriptions, *id.* 59 note 1; powers of Gurjjara rulers of, *id.* 479-480; temple to the sun or Jag Svámi at, *id.* 499.

Bhir: Bir, place in Nizam's dominions, identified with Tagar, I, pt. ii, 538 note 8.

Bhiss: pass in Kolába district, XI, 115.

Bhisti: a caste of water-drawers in Káthiáwár, VIII, 157; in Gujarát, also called Pakhali,

Hindu converts, IX, pt. ii, 89, 96 ; officiating priests in boat offerings, *id.* 152-153, 159 ; in Ratnágiri district, X, 127 ; in Ahmadnagar district, XVII, 227.
Bhisti Bág : palace at Ahmadnagar, built by Malik Ahmad, I, pt. ii, 622.
Bhivanayya : officer of Vikramáditya VI (1098), I, pt. ii, 451.
Bhivgad : port in Thána district, XIV, 45.
Bhiwndi : sub-division in Thána district, its boundaries, area, aspect, climate, water, soil, holdings, rental, stock, crops and people, XIII, 2, 681-683 ; its assessment revised (1840), *id.* 584 ; cost and profit of tillage in (1845), *id.* 588 ; survey assessment (1860), *id.* 606-608 ; town, its situation, population, trade, XIV, 45-46 ; history, animal-house, copper-plate and Jain temple at, *id.* 47-50 ; remains of the tomb of a saint at, I, pt. ii, 41.
Bhoga-Nandi : in Mysore, I, pt. ii, 331, 332 and note 3 ; *see* Nandi.
Bhogáva : river in Ahmadábád, IV, 7.
Bhogávati : capital of the serpent king Vásuki, I, pt. ii, 576, 577, XXIII, 394 and note 5.
Bhogávati : river, in Sholápur district, XX, 4.
Bhogávati : stream in Kolhápur state, XXIV, 9, 10.
Bhogávo : river in Káthiáwár, VIII, 63.
Bhogeshvari or Bhogávati : stream in Kolába district, XI, 7.
Bhogte : village in Násik district, fair at, XVI, 426.
Bhogyádi : system of mortgage, XV, pt. ii, 31.
Bhoi : caste of palanquin-bearers and fishermen in Gujarát, their origin, divisions, appearance, dress, means of livelihood, fishing, IX, pt. i, 504-505 ; religion, holidays, *id.* 505, 519; in Ratnagiri district and Sávantvádi state, X, 128, 415 ; in Kolába, XI, 68 ; in Thána, XIII, 146 ; in Kánara, XV, pt. i, 304-305 ; in Násik, XVI, 57 ; in Ahmadnagar, XVII, 153-157 ; in Poona, XVIII, pt. i, 387-389 ; in Sátára, XIX, 105-106 ; Hindu and Musalmán in Sholápur, XX, 152, 205-206 ; in Belgaum, XXI, 155 ; in Dhárwár, XXII, 185-186 ; in Bijápur, XXIII, 97 ; in Kolhápur state, XXIV, 105 ; in Rewá Kántha, VI, 25 ; in Káthiáwár, VIII, 154 ; *see* Kahár.
Bhoika : town in Káthiáwár, VIII, 399.
Bhoira : cave and fort in Káthiáwár, VIII, 399.
Bhoj : village in Belgaum district, battle at (1773), XXI, 552.
Bhoj : rája of Málwa, IX, pt. i, 485 note 7 ; *see* Bhoja.
Bhoj I : Siláhára king (1098), XXIV, 221 ; *see* Bhoja I.
Bhoj II : Siláhára king (1178-1209), Rája of Panhála, his inscriptions, extension of his territories, building of hill forts, his subjugation of hill tribes, XXIV, 223 ; makes Kolhápur his capital, *id.* 307, 314 ; *see* Bhoja II.
Bhoja : king of Málwa, invades the Dakhan to avenge his uncle's death and defeats the Chálukya king Vikramáditya I ; is in turn attacked and defeated by Vikramáditya's son Jayasimha, I, pt. ii, 213-214 ; writes a commentary on a Smriti, *id.* 228 ; his officers defeat Bhima I, I, pt. i, 163, 164 ; a patron of learning, *id.* 180, 453 note 1.
Bhoja : of Panhála, I, pt. ii, 239-240 ; *see* Bhoja II.
Bhoja I : Kolhápur Siláhára king, I, pt. ii, 254 ; also called Karád Siláhára king, *id.* 545, 547 ; is defeated by Achugi II, *id.* 574.
Bhoja II : Siláhára chief of Kolhápur, I, pt. ii, 227 ; his grant, *id.* 255 ; succeeds his father Vijayárka ; Vijjana Kalachuri attempts to subdue him ; he becomes independent ; is completely subjugated by the Yádava king Singhana, *id.* 256 ; his father is also called Vijayáditya of the Karád family (1190-1206), *id.* 524, 545, 548, 549.
Bhoja Charitra : account of Bhoja, king of Málwa, I, pt. ii, 214.
Bhoják : a Bráhman sub-division, in Cutch, V, 47 ; said to be Magasas, IX, pt. i, 440, 500 ; originally Shrimáli Bráhmans converted to Jain faith, *id.* 8.
Bhojápur : village in Násik district, Khandoba's temple at, XVI, 426.
Bhojas : associated with Petenikas ; rule over portions of the Dakhan and Vidarbha, I, pt. ii, 143 and note 2 ; their country, *id.* 146 ; Kshatriya tribe, *id.* 178.
Bhojas : Hindu kings of the Konkan (A. D. 100), XVIII, pt. ii, 213 and notes 1 and 5.
Bhoja Tirmal Rái : the usurper at Vijayánagar, commits suicide, I, pt. ii, 642.
Bhojávadar : táluka in Káthiáwár, VIII, 399.
Bhojdev : Kolhápur chief (1190), X, 193 ; the great fort builder, *id.* 335.
Bhokar : *Cordia latifolia*, timber and dye plant, found in several districts, XXV, 102, 248, XII, 27, XVIII, pt. i, 43.
Bhokri Digar : place of interest in Khándesh district, XII, 435.
Bhoma : timber tree growing in the *gháts*, XXV, 116.
Bhomvár : Tuesday, IX, pt. i, 401.
Bhondekar : class of Musalmán potters in Khándesh district, XII, 125.
Bhonsla : family name of Shiváji and the Sávants, I, pt. ii, 68 ; of Ellora, *id.* 624.
Bhonsla Rája : sardár and kinsman of the Gáikwár (1857), his intrigues, I, pt. i, 442 ; obtains pardon at the intercession of the Gáikwár, *id.* 443.
Bhonsles : origin of, XVIII, pt. i, 285, XVIII, pt. ii, 223 ; *see* Bhonsla.
Bhopa : *see* Rabari.
Bhopál : town in Central India, I, pt. i, 438.
Bhopaládevi : installed as *pattaráni* or queen regnant of Kumárapála, I, pt. i, 182, 184.
Bhopálgad : hill-fort in Sátára district, XIX, 8 ; taken (1679) by the Mughals, *id.* 285 ; fort details, *id.* 455-456.
Bhopat : Mer Pushkar Bráhmans trace descent through, IX, pt. i, 500.
Bhopatgad : fort in Thána district, XIV, 50.
Bhopi : village Mhár (1828), XIII, 574.
Bhor : state, details, history, XIX, 617-618 ; village exchanges with its chief the Pant Sachiv (1818-1840), XI, 159 and note 2 ; seat of intrigue (1857), XIX, 317.

Bhor: timber, fruit and dye plant, XXV, 49-50, 149, 242; yields gum, *id.* 250.

Bhora: timber tree, XXV, 72.

Bhoránde: pass in Thána district, XIII, 321.

Bhore-goti: timber tree common in the forests, XXV, 50.

Bhorgad: *see* Dhair.

Bhorpi: caste of rope dancers in Ratnágiri district, X, 126; mimics in Thána district, XIII, 141; in Ahmadnagar district, XVII, 177-178; musicians in Kolába district, XI, 67.

Bhose: village in Sátára district, cave temple at, XIX, 456-457.

Bhoti: timber and fibrous plant found in the *ghâts*, XXV, 16, 229.

Bhoursal: timber tree found in the *ghâts*, XXV, 84.

Bhovya: cattle disease, X, 294.

Bhragu: or Bhrigu, sage, father of goddess Mahálakshmi, IX, pt. i, 97; founder of Broach, *id.* p. xi; Bhargavs claim descent from, *id.* 1; *umbar* tree is believed to be resting place of, *id.* 388; *see* also I, pt. i, 461.

Bhraguvar: Friday, IX, pt. i, 402.

Bhrigu: *see* Bhragu.

Bhrigukachha: modern Broach, I, pt. i, 127; *id.* pt. ii, 405; Kumárapála meets a soothsayer at, I, pt. i, 183; *see* Broach.

Bhringi: Shiv's attendant, images of, in Ambaranath and Elephanta Caves, XIV, 69, 70.

Bhruvijaya Savelachála: son of Kasamchitra, king of Gujarát, I, pt. i, 489.

Bhuáváda: place of interest in Káthiáwâr, VIII, 400.

Bhudargad: hill fort in Kolhápur state, XXIV, 7; its position, temples and history, *id.* 294-295; sub-division of Kolhapur state, I, pt. ii, 548.

Bhudargad-Nipáni: hill range in Kolhapur state, XXIV, 7, 9.

Bhuising: groundnut, oil-yielding plant, cultivated in several districts, XXV, 217.

Bhuijada: I, pt. i, 156; *see* Bhuváda.

Bhuj: town, capital of Cutch, its climate, history and buildings, Raos' tombs at, V, 215-218; Prágmalji's palace at, *id.* 172; *see* also *id.* 135, 162; arrival of Pir Dádu at, IX, pt. ii, 41.

Bhujabala Vira Ganga: *biruda* (title) of Vishnuvardhána the Hoysála king, I, pt. ii, 494-500, 501.

Bhujári: caste of grain parchers in Násik district, XVI, 60.

Bhujia: fort in Cutch; snake temple at, V, 64; siege of (1730), *id.* 139; strengthened (1730), *id.* 140; held by the British (1820), *id.* 165; description, *id.* 218.

Bhukháris: chief Sayad family in Gujarát, IX, pt. ii, 6 note 1.

Bhukti: territorial sub-division, I, pt. ii, 397, 398.

Bhuleshvar: temple of, at Nirmal in Thána district, XIV, 293; at Málsiras in Poona, XVIII, pt. iii, 258.

Bhulo: Bharvád *bhagat* or holy man, IX, pt. i, 269.

Bhulokamalla: *biruda* (title) of Somesvara III, I, pt. ii, 221.

Bhumbhái: Punjáb earth-brother, name under which stranger admitted to village community, IX, pt. i, 462.

Bhumbhali: village in Káthiáwár, VIII, 400.

Bhumiás: land-owners, *garásias*, I, pt. i, 215 note 2, 451 note 3.

Bhumilika: I, pt. i, 137; *see* Bhumli.

Bhumli: fort in Káthiáwár, capital of the Mhers, I, pt. i, 136, 137, 138.

Bhunete: *see* Bhutadi.

Bhungali Rája: traditional king of Bárot, perhaps Báglan chief, XIV, 305 and note 1.

Bhupaládevi: *see* Bhopaládevi.

Bhurap: fort in Kolába district, XI, 267.

Bhurt-kasi: food plant growing in Konkan, XXV, 162.

Bhusával: sub-division of Khándesh, its boundaries, area, aspect, climate, water, soil, holdings, survey details, survey results, stock, crops, people, XII, 2, *id.* 348-353; town, *id.* 211, 436.

Bhushangad: hill fort in Sátára district, built by Shiváji (1676), XIX, 457; *see* also I, pt. ii, 595.

Bhusparsh Mudra: earth-touching position of Buddha's image at Sopára, XIV, 330 and note 2.

Bhut: Hindu name for a spirit, belief in, IX, pt. ii, 142 note 1.

Bhuta: Indian corn, cultivated in several districts, XXV, 186.

Bhutadi: form of exercise, IX, pt. ii, 172.

Bhutarya: I, pt. ii, 304 note 4; *see* Butayya.

Bhutás: land-holders of part foreign descent; cease to be a separate community, IX, pt. ii, 11, 15.

Bhut-bhiravi: famine plant, native of Bengal, XXV, 203.

Bhute: a caste of religious beggars in Ratnágiri district, X, 131; in Poona district, XVIII, pt. i, 448; in Sátára district, XIX, 116-117.

Bhut-máta: goddess, originally Cháran woman, sister of Báhuchara, becomes *devi*, is worshipped at Arnej, IX, pt. i, 216 note 1.

Bhuts: male spirits; *see* Spirits.

Bhutya: *see* Bhute.

Bhuvad: place of interest in Cutch, a temple with inscriptions at, V, 219.

Bhuvada: Chálukya king, killa Jayaśekhara, I, pt. i, 150, 157.

Bhuvanáditya: Mularájá's ancestor, I, pt. i, 157.

Bhuvanaikamálla: title or *biruda* of Someśvara II, later Chálukya king, I, pt. ii, 216, 442.

Bhuvás: spirit-scarers; *see* Spirits.

Bhuvátimbi: village in Káthiáwár, VIII, 400.

Bhuyada: another name of Chámunda, I, pt. i, 154, 155.

Bhuymung: groundnut plant, XXV, 151; *see* also Bhuising.

Biadaru: *see* Berad.

Biázi: the Fair, title of the Surat Bohora missionary, IX, pt. ii, 27.
Biba: timber, oil-yielding, dye, gum-yielding and poisonous plant, found in several districts, XXV, 54, 216, 242, 250, 264; XVIII, pt. i, 43.
Bibba: *see* Biba.
Bibi: title among Sheikh women, IX, pt. ii, 8.
Bibi-ki-Sahnak: IX, pt. ii, 151; *see* Earthen Dish.
Bibla: timber and gum-yielding tree found in Konkan, XXV, 62, 251.
Bibva: marking nut tree in Khándesh district; XII, 25; *see* Biba.
Bicha: I, pt. ii, 523; *see* Vichana.
Bichana: viceroy of Singhana in the southern provinces; subdues all the kings and erects a triumphal column on the banks of the Káveri, I, pt. ii, 243, 245.
Bichideva: I, pt. ii, 523; *see* Vichana.
Bichiráya: I, pt. ii, 523; *see* Vichana.
Bid: village in Kolhápur state, temple and inscription at, XXIV, 10, *id.* 295.
Bida: name of Changiz Khán's clan, IX, pt. i, 459.
Bidar: town in Nizám's dominions, I, pt. ii, 17; dismemberment of the kingdom of, *id.* 32; first an old Hindu capital but afterwards the capital of the Bahámani kings (1426), *id.* 588; ceded to the Maráthás by the Nizám in 1760, *id.* 629.
Bidarkanni: village in Kánara district, XV, pt. ii, 275.
Bidarkatti: village in Dhárwár district, temple and inscription at, XXII, 658.
Biddulph: author of the "Tribes of Hindu-kush," IX, pt. ii, 36 note 3, 39 note 4; IX, pt. i, 481 notes 2, 3 and 4.
Bidi: village in Belgaum district, disturbances (1829) at, XXI, 552; survey of (1853-1856), *id.* 445-450.
Bidri: lead and silver work, skill of Musalmáns in, IX, pt. ii, 123.
Bidtihalla: *see* Gangávali.
Bier: Khojáh hymns, IX, pt. ii, 40.
Bier: IX, pt. ii, 240; bearers, *id.* 239; *see* Nasesálárs.
Bigbávni: land tenure in Thána district, XIII, 536, 565.
Bighoti: land tenure in Baroda state, VII, 355, 357.
Bignoniaceæ: a species of timber, food and dye-yielding plants, XXV, 104, 167, 248.
Bignonia xylocarpa: food plant, XXV, 167.
Bihora: state in Rewa Kántha, VI, 144.
Bihruch: modern Broach, I, pt. i, 507.
Bija: timber tree found in Konkan, XXV, 62.
Bija: uncle of Mularája, I, pt. i, 156, 160.
Bijabbe: wife of Maruladeva and mother of Rachcha Ganga, I, pt. ii, 305.
Bijápur: town in Gujarát, I, pt. i, 108; *see* Vijayapura.
Bijápur: district, boundaries, subdivisions, aspect, hills, rivers, climate, XXIII, 1-16; geology, *id.* 16-50; minerals, forests, trees, domestic and wild animals, birds, fish, *id.* 51-70; census details, village communities, *id.* 71-78; Bráhmans, Agarváls, *id.* 78-91; Bedars, Gavandis, Gols, Kabligers, Komtis, Kurubars, Maráthás, Raddis, Rájpúts, wanderers, depressed classes, Lingáyats, true, affiliated, and half, Jains, Musalmáns, *id.* 91-306; husbandmen, soil, arable area, stock, holdings, field tools, irrigation, crops, famines, *id.* 307-337; currency, saving classes, investments, interest, borrowers, labour mortgage, wages, prices, weights and measures, *id.* 338-353; roads, railways, ferries, post and telegraph offices, trade centres, markets, fairs, imports, exports, crafts, *id.* 354-377; Early Chálukyas (550-610), Western Chálukyas (610-760), Ráshtrakutas (760-973), Western Chálukyas (973-1190), *id.* 378-389; Kalachuris (1162-1182), Sindas (1120-1180), Devgiri Yádavs (1150-1310), *id.* 389-395; Delhi emperors (1295-1347), Vijsyánagar (1328-1335), the Bahmanis (1347-1489), *id.* 395-403; the Bijápur kings (1489-1686), Mughals (1686-1723), *id.* 403-440; Nizám (1723-1760), the Peshwás (1760-1778), Mysore (1778-1787), the Peshwás (1787-1818), *id.* 440-450; British (1818-1884), *id.* 450-454; land revenue, alienated villages (1884), revenue (1820-1824), survey (1843-1860), revision survey (1874-1877), season reports (1864-1884), staff, *id.* 455-503; civil courts and suits, registration, magistracy, police, criminal classes, jails, *id.* 504-511; sources of revenue, balance sheets (1865-66 and 1882-1883); local funds, municipalities, *id.* 512-517; schools, readers and writers, libraries, newspapers, *id.* 518-523; hospitals, vaccination, births and deaths, *id.* 524-528; sub-divisional details, *id.* 529-544; places of interest, *id.* 545-681; copper-plate grants in, I, pt. ii, 394, 412, 413, 420, 423 note 5, 431, 432, 435 and notes 3 and 7, 440 and note 5, 443, 450, 459 note 3; *sub-division*, its boundaries, area, aspect, soil, climate, water, stock, crops and people, XXIII, 535-536; survey and revision survey of, *id.* 476-480, 484-491; *city*, its aspect, area, walls, bastions, gates, citadel, divisions, suburbs and water works, *id.* 567-581; history objects, Máhmud's, Ibráhim Roza, Ali, Adil Sháh II's, Ali Adil Sháh I's and other tombs, palaces, mosques, temples and miscellaneous objects, *id.* 581-644; inscription pillar kept in the Government museum at, I, pt. ii, 280 note 4; inscriptions at, *id.* 460, 470, 472, 473, 503, 518, 520, 521 and note 3; records at, *id.* 523, 527, 553, 572, 576; minor capital of Vikramáditya VI, *id.* 450; province of, conferred on Yusuf Adilkhán who declares himself king of (1489), *id.* 32, 639-640; limits of the kingdom of, *id.* 640-641; kings brought in contact with the Portuguese and French (1510), *id.* 641; the defeat at, of the confederate kings of Ahmadnagar, Golkonda, Berár, *id.* 641; confederacy of the kings of Ahmadnagar, Golkonda and Vijayánagar, *id.* 643; treaty between the Portuguese, Ahmadnagar and Vijayánagar against, *id.* 46; reverses, *id.* 643; besieged by Seif-ain-ul-Mulk but saved from capture by the brother of the Rája of Vijayánagar (1556), *id.* 644; plots and counterplots during Ibráhim Adil

Sháh II's time, *id.* 647 ; the siege of, by the joint forces of Ahmadnagar, Golkonda and Berár ; Chánd Bibi raises it by the help of Sháh Abdul Hasan and the Maráthás of the Karnátak, *id.* 647 ; king of, sends help to Chánd Bibi at Ahmadnagar ; his troops come in collision with the Mughals and are defeated ; marriage alliance with the Mughals, *id.* 469 ; paramount power in the Konkan, *id.* 39 ; besieged by Asafkhán, *id.* 650 ; attacked by the Mughals under Aurangzib ; Khán Muhammad, prime minister, won over by the Mughals ; Aurangzib raises the siege to hasten to Hindustán on hearing about his father's illness, *id.* 651-652 ; factions at, assassination of Khán Muhammad and despatch of an army under Afzul Khán against Shiváji, *id.* 652 ; enters into a treaty with the Sidis and the Sávants against Shiváji and makes an attempt to recover the southern part of the Konkan, *id.* 68 ; invasion of, by the Mughals under Jaisingh and Shiváji (1664), *id.* 652 ; *see* also XVIII, pt. ii, 234 ; factions at (1672), *id.* 653; besieged by the Mughals, *id.* 654 ; the siege raised by Shiváji's diversion on the Mughal territory in the Dakhan, *id.* 654 ; besieged by the Mughals under Azim, Aurangzib's second son, and taken (1686), *id.* 654 ; *see* also XVIII, pt. ii, 238 ; the province ceded to the Peshwa (1760) by Nizám Ali, *id.* 627, 657 ; *see* also XXIII, 361, 400, 414, 420, 424, 425, 426, 431, 434, 584, 588, 590 ; XIV, 47, 120 ; XVII, 394.

Bijápur kings : (1489-1686), account of, with reference to their rule in Belgaum district ; Goa captured by the Portuguese from (1510) ; Asad Khán their famous governor of Belgaum (1511-1549) ; war with Ahmadnagar, overthrow of Vijayánagar (1565), an understanding with Ahmadnagar (1570), disorders (1593), war with the Mughals (1631), Marátha raids (1648-1680), fall of Bijápur (1686), XXI, 365-377 ; *another account of* : history, their struggle with Vijayánagar (1520), fall of the latter (1665), siege of Bankápur (1575), sack of Hubli (1673), fall of Bijápur (1686), XXII, 406-409 ; their rule in Ratnágiri and Sávantvádi (1500-1627), X, 195, 439.

Bijayagadh : in the Bharatpur state, record at (372), I, pt. ii, 312.

Bijgarnigudd : hill in Belgaum district, XXI, 9 ; fort, *id.* 552.

Bijja : son of the Kalachurya king Kannama, I, pt. ii, 468, 470 ; *see* Bijjala.

Bijjala : son of the Sinda prince Chávunda II and nephew of the Kalachurya Someśvara, I, pt. ii, 485, 573, 576.

Bijjala : Kalachurya prince, son of Kannama, I, pt. ii, 468 ; Kalachurya king represented to be S'iva's door-keeper, *id.* 227, 406 note 5, 428 note 4, 458, 459 note 1, 460 note 1 ; feudatory of Taila III, *id.* 460 ; usurps the Chálukya kingdom and assumes sovereignty (1162), *id.* 462, 463, 464, 468, 469, 470, 471, 472 ; introduces a reckoning of his town ; his *biruda* (title) and designation, *id.* 474 ; his feudatories and officials, *id.* 475-476, 477 ; revival of S'aiva faith in the time of, assassination of, *id.* 478 (*see* also XV, pt. II, 89, and XXIII, 389-391) ; makes Basáva his minister, *id.* 479, 480, 481 ; laves the feet of Ekántada Rámayya, *id.* 483, 501, 548, 555, 577 ; *see* Vijjala and Vijjana.

Bijjaladeva : Sinda prince, I, pt. ii, 463.

Bijjaladevi : mother of Jagaddeva, I, pt. ii, 568.

Bijjalárání : wife of Vira Someśvara, the Hoysála king, I, pt. ii, 493, 508.

Bijjalaráya Charitra : I, pt. ii, 481.

Bijjana : Kalachurya king, I, pt. ii, 458, 470 ; *see* Bijjala.

Bijmargis, Bijpanthis : religious sect in Gujarát, IX, pt. i, p. xxxvi, 544.

Bijnagar : Vijayánagar, ancient Hindu kingdom, I, pt. ii, 29 ; its *rájás*, *id.* 30 ; its treaty with the Portuguese against Bijápur (1547), *id.* 46 ; its trade with the Portuguese (1565), *id.* 62 ; *see* Vijayánagar.

Bijpanthis : *see* Bijmárgis.

Bijvari : Anegundi (1333-1573) assessment system in Dhárwár district, XXII, 441, 453 and note 4.

Bilaiti-ámbli : food plant, XXV, 154.

Bilama : XXV, 216 ; *see* Biba.

Bilambi : XXV, 242 ; *see* Biba.

Biláspur : district in Central Provinces, I, pt. ii, 384.

Bilejádar : caste of weavers in Dhárwár district, XXII, 163-165.

Bileshvar : village in Káthiáwár, VIII, 400.

Bilgi : hills in Bijápur district, XXIII, 5 ; village, wells and temples at, *id.* 566-567.

Bilgi : village in Kánara district, temples, inscriptions, and history of, XV, pt. ii, 276.

Bilhana : poet (c. 1050 A. D.), I, pt. i, 156 ; author of *Vikrámankadeva Charita*, I, pt. ii, 180, 214, 215, 216, 217 ; Kásmirián Pandit, raised to the dignity of chief pandit, *id.* 219, 221, 281 note 3, 309, 340 note 1, 345, note 4, 440 and note 3, 441, 442, 444, 445 note 3, 449, 450 note 5, 452, 454, 546.

Bilimb : food plant, XXV, 148.

Bilimbi : timber tree, cultivated throughout India, XXV, 30.

Bilimora : town in Baroda, its exports, VII, 571.

Bilkha : place of interest in Káthiáwár, VIII, 401.

Billayya : son of Vira-Balláls II, I, pt. ii, 502.

Billi : XXV, 35 ; *see* Bel.

Bill-Register : *see* Hundini-nondh.

Bills : of exchange in Kolhápur state, XXIV, 192-193 ; in Sátára, XIX, 178-179 ; *see* Hundi.

Billu : timber tree found in several districts, XXV, 46.

Bilsad : Gupta inscription at, I, pt. i, 67.

Bimb or Bhim : traditional chief of Thána : apparently two Bhims, one a Solanki or Gujarát Bhim (A. D. 1022-1072), the other a Devgiri Yádav or Dakhan Bhim (A. D. 1286-1292), XIII, 62, 90, 437 note 2.

Bimbastán : probably Bhiwndi, mention of, in a stone inscription at Koprád, XIV, 210.

Bimbisára : king of Magadha, 550 B. C., XII, 551 and note 1.
Binagara : town mentioned by Ptolemy on the left bank of the Indus, I, pt. i, 538.
Binda : river mentioned by Ptolemy between Sopára and Cheul, I, pt. ii, 2.
Binghi : port in Kánara District, XV, pt. ii, 277; traces of Haidar's paths at, *id.* 39.
Binne Khán : Jamádár of Pálanpur, IX, pt. ii, 65 note 2.
Bir, Bhir : town in Nizám's dominions identified with ancient Tagar, I, pt. ii, 538 note 8.
Biradh : pots, IX, pt. ii, 149; *see* Biradh-Bharna.
Biradh-Bharna : pot-filling ceremony preceding all joyous rites, IX, pt. ii, 149.
Birat : IX, pt. ii; *see* Biradh.
Birda : all district volumes; *see* under District Name.
Birgoug : Viramgám, IX, pt. ii, 24 note 3.
Bir-Gujars : *see* Bad Gujar.
Biriávi Bohorá : IX, pt. ii, 61; *see* Bohorá.
Birkana Ray : king of Belgaum, sends his troops against Goa to retake it (1472), I, pt. ii, 638; besieged and severely defeated at Belgaum; his surrender to Muhammad, Sháh II, *id.* 638, 639.
Bi li-maar : fibrous plant, grows in Konkan, XXV, 237.
Biroba : village god XVIII, pt. i, 289-290.
Birth : rites, ceremonies and observances at, among Bajániás, IX, pt. i, 503; Bhangiás, *id.* 336; Bhátiás, *id.* 119; Bhils, *id.* 308; Brahmakshatris, *id.* 57; Bráhmans, *id.* 33; Golás, *id.* 185; Kanbis, *id.* 157; Kansárás, *id.* 187; Káyasths, *id.* 61, 67; Kolis, *id.* 247; Luhárs, *id.* 191; Pateliás, *id.* 173; Rájputs, *id.* 138-139; Shrávaks, *id.* 99-100; Sonis, *id.* 201; Thoris, *id.* 509; Vániás, *id.* 89; rites and ceremonies relating to, charms and talismans used to secure speedy delivery; expenses connected with, *id.* pt. ii, 154-155, *id.* 156 note 1; rites and ceremonies relating to; news of, giving presents on, *id.* 228; naming of the child, *id.* 229; horoscope of the new-born, *id.* 229-230; Pachori ceremony, Dasori ceremony; the Mother sixth worship, Vadhavo presents, *id.* 229; Joripori presents in the third month after; thanksgiving ceremony of Palli, of Chokhiar, *id.* 230; *see* Customs; customs in Kánara among Havig Bráhmans, XV, pt. i, 124; among Shenvis, *id.* 150-151; among Bhangis, *id.* 178; among Hálvakki Vakkals, *id.* 208; among Konkan Kunbis, *id.* 218; among Jains, *id.* 233-234; among Komárpaiks, *id.* 292; among Ambigs, *id.* 303; among Mukris, *id.* 377; among Native Catholic Christians, *id.* 388; among Christian Reverts, *id.* 398; among Musalmáns, *id.* 405; ceremonies of the Chitpávans, XVIII, pt. i, 112-116; Govardhans, *id.* 161-162; Gujaráti Bráhmans, *id*, 164; Kanoj, *id.* 168; Shenvis, *id.* 176; Tailangs, *id.* 181-182; Dhruv Prabhus, *id.* 186-187; Pátáne Prabhus, *id.* 220-222; Bangárs, *id.* 264; Brahma Kshatris, *id.* 267; Kirdas, *id.* 268; Lingáyats, *id.* 271; Gujarát Vánis, *id.* 275; Báris, *id.* 281; Kunbis, *id.* 296-298; Páhádis, *id.* 310, 311; Badháis, *id.* 315; Beldárs, *id.* 317; Bhadbhunjás, *id.* 320; Bhánsárs, *id.* 323; Buruds, *id.* 325-326; Chámbhárs, *id.* 327, 330; Gaudis, *id.* 331; Ghisádis, *id.* 334-335; Halvais, *id.* 338; Jingars, *id.* 341; Khatris, *id.* 346; Koshtis, *id.* 348; Kumbhárs, *id.* 349; Otaris, *id.* 356; Ráuls, *id.* 360; Sális, *id.* 362-363; Shimpis, *id.* 368, 371; Guravs, *id.* 379; Nhávis, *id.* 381; Gavlis, *id.* 386-387; Bhois, *id.* 388; Kolis, *id.* 392-393; Chhaparbands, *id.* 394-395; Kámáthis, *id.* 396; Lodhis, *id.* 399; Rájputs, *id.* 402-403; Rámoshis, *id.* 415; Vadars, *id.* 427; Vanjáris, *id.* 429; Dhors, *id.* 433; Halálkhors, *id.* 437; Mhárs, *id.* 442; Mangs, *id.* 443-444; Chitrakathis, *id.* 449; Holars, *id.* 453; Jangams, *id.* 454; Sarvade Joshis, *id.* 460; Uchlias, *id.* 470-471; Musalmáns, *id.* 488; Bene-Israels, *id.* 525-528.
Birth and death : ceremonies among Deshástha Bráhmans, XXIV, 47-48, 60; among Maráthás, *id.* 72, 80; among Kunbis, *id.* 91; among Mhárs, *id.* 114; among Lingáyats, *id.* 128, 131, 132; among Jains, *id.* 144-146.
Birth-Day : observances on, IX, pt. ii, 231; celebration of, *id.* 159.
Births and deaths : all district volumes; *see* Health under District Name.
Birund : timber tree, grows in Konkan, XXV, 10.
Birundakaram : Aparájit, his grant, I, pt. ii, 18; (A. D. 997), XIII, 424.
Birvádi : fort in Kolába District, XI, 267-269; built (1648), *id.* 144; ceded to the Maráthás (1734), *id.* 445; *see* also I, pt. ii, 67, 83.
Biryáni : dish among Gujarát Musalmáns, first class public dinner called after, cost of, IX, pt. ii, 113 and note 1.
Bischoffia Javanica : timber tree found in Konkan, XXV, 118.
Bishops : appeal of, to Rome against the Inquisitors, I, pt. ii, 60.
Biskhopra : food plant, XXV, 160.
Bismilláh : initiation rite of, IX, pt. ii, 159, *id.* 160.
Bison : in Ratnágiri district, X, 46; in Kánara district; description, XV, pt. i, 96-99; in Khándesh district, XII, 32.
Bistend : timber tree common in the *ghâts*, XXV, 93.
Bitangad : fort in Násik district on Kalsubái range, XVI, 441, 447.
Bittern : class of birds in Ratnágiri district, X, 96.
Bittideva : I, pt. ii, 494; *see* Vishnuvardhana.
Bittiga : marauder, Hoysala prince Vishnuvardhána, I, pt. ii, 459, 494, 497, 575.
Bittimayya : (1175) officer of Vira Ballála II, I, pt. ii, 505.
Bixa orellana : fibrous and dye plant, XXV, 226, 240.
Bixinæ : a species of food, oil yielding, fibrous, dye and gum-yielding plants, XXV, 146, 214, 226, 240, 250.
Biyábáni : a ghoul, a Musalmán spirit, IX, pt. ii, 142 note 1.

Black: Captain, Political Agent, Rádhanpur, I, pt. i, 441.
Black Bear: in Kánara district; its hunt, XV, pt. i, 95-96.
Black bird: in Ratnágiri district, X, 73.
Blankets: manufacture of, in Ahmadábád district, IV, 139; in Khándesh, XII, 235; in Násik, XVI, 176; 177, in Sátára, XIX, 222-223; in Sholápur, XX, 271-272; in Dhárwár, XXII, 380-381; in Bijapur, XXIII, 372-373.
Blasius: Saint, Amboli Church dedicated to, XIV, 9.
Blight: all district volumes; *see* under District Name.
Blimbu: timber tree cultivated for its acid fruit, XXV, 30.
Blind snakes: in Poona district, XVIII, pt. i, 72.
Blind worms: at Mátherán, XIV, 256.
Blochmán: editor of Ain-i-Akbari, IX, pt. ii, 6 note 1 (5), 14, 147, 159 note 4.
Blood: luckiness of, IX, pt. i, 517 note 1.
Boars: *see* Suidæ.
Boat-offerings: also called Náos; made to the water-spirit in fulfilment of vows; description and rites of; *bhishti* or water-carrier officiates at, IX, pt. ii, 152, 153, 158.
Boats: in Ratnágiri District, X, 171; in Sávantvádi State, *id.* 435.
Bobleshvar: place of interest in Bijápur District, XXIII, 644.
Bocagea Dalzellii: timber tree, grows in Konkan forests, XXV, 4; its sacredness, *id.* 291.
Bocarro: Portuguese chronicler, his description of Chaul harbour, XI, 282.
Bochárva: village in Káthiáwár, VIII, 402.
Boda: timber tree found in several districts, XXV, 79.
Bodaga: famine plant common in the presidency, XXV, 197.
Bodánones: tálukah in Káthiáwár, VIII, 402.
Boddam: Honourable Rawson Hart, President and Governor of Bombay (1784-1787), XXVI, pt. i, 430, *id.* pt. ii, 492; retires (1787), *id.* pt. iii, 408.
Bodhán: place of pilgrimage in Surat, II, 298, IX, pt. i, 12 note 1, 550.
Bodhidharma: a Buddhist leader, XIV, 133; apostle to China, *id.* 409.
Bodhidrum: Buddhist tree of knowledge, XII, 541; object of worship, XIV, 128 note 6, 330, 331, 412, 413.
Bodhisattva: potential Buddha, images of, in Kánheri Caves, XIV, 132 and note 5; potential Buddha, XIII, 408 note 2; a Buddhist title, XII, 533 note 1.
Bodki: hill in Sholápur district, XX, 2.
Bodula: timber tree found in several districts, XXV, 21.
Bodvad: place of interest in Khándesh district, XII, 437.
Bœhemeria nivea: fibrous plant, known as China grass, XXV, 234.
Bœrhaavia diffusa: vegetable and medicinal plant, XXV, 203, 257; *repanda*, food plant, found in several districts, *id.* 203.
Bogár: a caste of traders in Ratnágiri district, X, 413; bangle-sellers in Kánara, XV, pt. i, 273.
Bogda: gorge in Sátára district, XIX, 204.
Boghatirth: Sopára pond, XIV, 339.
Bohora: a Musalmán caste in Cutch, V, 98; in Cambay, VI, 185; in Baroda, VII, 70-71; Musalmán traders in Káthiáwár, VIII, 162; Sunni, of Broach and Surat, are cultivators, IX, pt. i, 152; Shiáhs of the Mustaában branch of the great Ismáili sect, IX, pt. ii, 24, *id.* 30; meaning and derivation of the name, *id.* 24 and notes 2, 3 and 4, *id.* 25 notes 1; name extended to converts from all the unarmed castes, *id.* 25 and note 1; sect founded in Gujarát by missionary Abdulláh (1067), conversions first made in Cambay, Anahilaváda or Pátan, *id.* 26 and note 1; arrival of the religious head of the trading Shiáhs from Yaman with a hand of followers (close of the eleventh century), *id.* 3, *id.* 25 note 2; conversions made by early Shiáh missionaries from the great trading centres (eleventh century), progress of the sect in Gujarát (1130-1380), *id.* 26; sect repressed (1390-1413), *id.* 27; some of the Shiáhs converted to the Sunni faith (1391), *id.* 3 note 3, *id.* 26 note 1; persecutions of, by Sunni rulers (1411-1554), *id.* 27 and note 1; transfer of the seat of the head priest of, from Yaman to Gujarát (1539); find shelter under the British (close of eighteenth century); four schisms from the main body of: Alia Jaáfari, Najoshi and Sulaimáni, *id.* 27; Alia, one of the schisms from the main body of Shiáhs, sect founded by Ali (1624), IX, pt. ii, 27, *id.* 33; Biázi, Arabian converts to the Ismáili faith made by a Bohora missionary called Biázi the Fair, IX, pt. ii, 27; Dáúdi, main body of Shiáhs, settlements of, IX, pt. ii, 28, *id.* 32 note 3; appearance, language, dress and ornaments, *id.* 28; food, *id.* 29; houses, *id.* 29 and note 1; calling, character, condition, *id.* 29; religion, special beliefs regarding the spirits of the dead; Indian beliefs, *id.* 30; their position among Muslim sectaries, *id.* 30 note 1; names, customs, written prayers placed in the hands of the dead, *id.* 31 and note 2; community, religious and social head of, the Mulla, 31 and notes 3 and 4, *id.* 32 and notes 1 to 5; taxes, *id.* 33 and note 1; prospect, *id.* 33; Nágoshi, or non-flesh-eating schisms from the main body of Shiáhs (1789), IX, pt. ii, 27, *id.* 33; Sulaimáni, followers of the Yaman priest Sulaimán, progress of, since 1591, IX, pt. ii, 27, *id.* 33; Sunnis, cultivators or village descendants of Hindu converts made by the Sunni rulers of the province from the unarmed classes (fourteenth and fifteenth centuries), IX, pt. ii, 24, *id.* 25, *id.* 58 and note 2; distribution of, *id.* 58; additions to, both from Hindus and Shiáh Bohorás (1411-1513), *id.* 58 note 2; foreign element in the Broach Bohorás mainly of the Márvádis, *id.* 59 and note 1; appearance, language, food, *id.* 59; dress and ornaments of men, *id.* 59 and notes 2 and 3; of women, *id.* 60 and notes 1

and 2; character, *id.* 60 and notes 3 and 4; condition, *id.* 60; names and surnames, *id.* 59 note 1, and *id.* 60; religion, customs, *id.* 60-61; success of Wahhábi preachers among Broach, Surat, Biriávi Bohorás (1880-1897), *id.* 61; community prospects, *id.* 62; Jaáfari, descendants of the Dáudi Bohorás; named after Sayad Jaáfar Shirázi; their other names; separate from the main body of Shiáhs (1391), IX, pt. ii, 3 note 3, *id.* 26 note 1, *id.* 34; continue to intermarry with the main body till 1535, *id.* 26 note 1, *id.* 34; mostly traders; Arabian traders follow many Arab customs; known as Kabriás; form an organized body, *id.* 34, *id.* 35; Surname, IX, pt. ii, 24 note 2; traders in Kolába, XI, 83-84; in Khándesh, XII, 125; in Thána, XIII, 224, *id.* 239-240, 517; in Násik, XVI, 77; in Ahmadnagar, XVII, 230; traders in Poona, XVIII, pt. i, 497-498; in Sátára, XIX, 137; in Sholápur, XX, 201-202; in Belgaum, their occupation, dress, religion, XXI, 209-210; in Dhárwár, XXII, 235-236; in Kolhápur, XXIV, 150.

Boisar: village in Thána with railway station, XIV, 343 note 4.

Bojgar: a caste of Musalmán beer-sellers in Sholápur, XX, 205; in Belgaum, XXI, 216.

Boks: timber tree, grows in Konkan, XXV, 118.

Bokenal: poisonous plant common on the *ghâts*, XXV, 265.

Bokh: a natural hollow in Ahmadábád district IV, 9.

Bokyápur: deserted village in Dhárwár district; temple at, XXII, 658.

Bolandra: station in Mahi Kántha, V, 428.

Bol-choth: dark fourth of *Shrávan*, sacred to bull worship, IX, pt. i, 374.

Boli Gumbaz: tomb at Bijápur, XXIII, 604-607.

Bolingæ: I, pt. i, 534-546; *see* Bhaulingi.

Bolinj: village in Thána district near Sopára, XIV, 314-315, 316.

Bolpsle: timber tree, grows in Konkan forests, XXV, 49.

Bomanji: son of Rustam Máneck, IX, pt. ii, 196 note 3.

Bombaro: name of a well near Bhinmál, I, pt. i, 453.

Bombax: *Malabaricum*, timber, food and gum-yielding plant, XXV, 17, 147, 250; *pentandrum*, famine plant, *id.* 195.

Bombay: town and island, burnt by the Portuguess (1532), I, pt. i, 347; divides Konkan into north and south, Introduction to the History of the Konkan, I, pt. ii, p. x; Gujarát possession, *id.* 29; its reduction by Ahmad Sháh, *id.* 30; its capture by the Franciscans (1585); intended capture by a dismissed English officer (1667), *id.* 57; its cession to England (1661), *id.* 63; harbour of, *id.* 173; presidency, *id.* 282 note 5, 298 note 2, 537, 538, 567; under the Portuguese (1500-1666); under the British (since 1666); settlement of Pársi families in, IX, pt. ii, 195; as head-quarters of the Pársis (1867), *id.* 198; development of the trade of, due to Pársis, *id.* 195; Pársi success in, *id.* 199; first Kadmi fire-temple established in (1783), *id.* 193 note 2; A'tesh Behráms in, *id.* 247; Agiáris in, *id.* 248-249; towers of silence in, *id.* 252; Sidis in, plunder Bombay (1677-1680), XI, 438-441; attacked by Sidi Kásim (1689), *id.* 442; modern port, XIII, 403; line of road (1026), *id.* 428; temple remains (1050), *id.* 429 and note 1; centre of piracy (1290), *id.* 434; port (1500 and 1514), *id.* 443, 449; pleasant island (1530), *id.* 450; battle of, *id.* 450 note 1; a Portuguese district (1560), *id.* 455; small mart (1590), *id.* 465 and note 4; centre of piracy (1500), *id.* 471 and note 8; ceded to the British (1664), *id.* 472; state (1674), *id.* 474; Portuguese disturbances (1673-77), *id.* 478; Janjira Sidis (1680), proposed Marátha invasion (1682), Keigwin and Child (1683), *id.* 479; President's head-quarters (1687), Child's death (1690), *id.* 480; the Sidis (1690), depressed state (1694-1708), *id.* 481-482; trade and condition (1664-1696), *id.* 485 and note 2; trade and taxes (1700), *id.* 487 and notes 1 and 2; merchants (1700), *id.* 488; town wall finished (1716), recovers from depression (1710-1720); Portuguese wish to buy (1727), *id.* 490, 492 and note 1; Portuguese refugees (1740), *id.* 494; alarm in Bombay, ditch made (1740), *id.* 495, 496; storm (1740), *id.* 496; danger from the Maráthás (1750), Bombay prosperous (1750), *id.* 497 and note 1; new fortifications (1757-1770). *id.* 499-500; Parsons' account (1775), *id.* 501; ship building and docks, danger from Maráthás and French, Vadgaon Convention (1779), *id.* 502-504; scarcity of money (1781), *id.* 509; growth, Forbes' and Franklin's accounts (1783), *id.* 511 and note 2; cotton trade with China (1790-1805), *id.* 511, 519; great fire (1803), *id.* 515; famine (1812), *id.* 513; trade (1800-1810), *id.* 514; state (1800-1810), Lord Valentia (1803), Sir J. Mackintosh (1804-1811), Captain Basil Hall (1812), *id.* 514-517; details of trade (1800-1810), *id.* 518-520; summary of trade (1805-1882), *id.* 526 and note 2; population (1665, 1669-1677, 1716, 1750, 1764, 1780, 1812, 1816, 1826, 1882), *id.* 473, 474, 489, 497 note 1, 499, 500 note 1, 511 note 2, 513, 516 and note 6, 526 and note 3; cession of (1660-1664), XV, pt. ii, 255 and note 7; Mahábaleshvar XIX, 505; acquisition by the English Crown, XXVI, pt. i, 1-21; delay regarding delivery of, *id.* 14; articles of delivery, *id.* 15-20; transferred to Company, *id.* 29-35; the erection of fort, warehouses, public and other buildings in, *id.* 55; its condition (1677), *id.* 59-61; orders of the Court to improve its position, *id.* 81-83; ships stationed at, *id.* 86; plague in (1686), *id.* 101; occupied by the Sidis, released, *id.* 103; its bad health (1706), *id.* 142; measures for the defence of, against Marátha attack (1737), *id.* 182-183; building rules in (1742), *id.* 250-251; its government (1715-1720), *id.* 254-255; its governor rather a tradesman, *id.* 255-256; defence of, against French attack (1746), *id.* 282-283; measures for its defence against a French attack (1756), *id.* 307-316; defence preparations (1759), its

garrison, supply of stores and provisions, *id.* 330-343; its dearness (1759), *id.* 329-330; scarcity of money in Bombay (1760-61), *id.* 343-344; its defences (1771), *id.* 360-363; defence of (1773), *id.* 365-369; proposed garrison for (1773), *id.* 369-371; military stores and provisions at, *id.* 373; fire in (1803), 471 houses burnt, damage to the extent of 40 lákhs, *id.* 431-435; trade of (1676-1803), *id.* pt. ii, 1-205; communications (1702-1788), *id.* 1-16; supplies (1676-1781), *id.* 17-77; prices (1676-1781), *id.* 78-90; trade (1694-1776), *id.* 91-130; industries: weaving, *id.* 131-142; fishing, *id.* 142-164; salt-making, *id.* 164-175; building materials, *id.* 175-186; ships, docks, light-houses, *id.* 186-205; its capital, mint (1671-1778), *id.* 206-231; exchange (1677-1783), *id.* 231-239; bank, (1717-1771), *id.* 239-249; loans (1731-1778), *id.* 249-251; wages (1696-1788), *id.* 251-255; slaves (1677-1780), *id.* 255-267; its currency (1676-1774), *id.* 206-230; mint to coin rupees, pice, etc. (1676), *id.* 206; discount on Bombay rupees (1719), *id.* 211; Bombay rupees legal tender (1733), *id.* 212; coinage of gold (1765-1766), *id.* 220-222; export duty on silver (1770-78), *id* 222-224; more gold rupees (1774), *id.* 229-230; its fortification and building (1664-1803), *id.* 268-507 (*vide* Fortifications and Buildings); the valuation of (1726-1739), *id.* pt. iii, 305-307; survey of (1747), *id.* 416-417; (1772) *id.* 420 and note 5, 421; its bad health (1673), *id.* 542; derivation and meaning of the word, *id.* 644-647; description of (1893), *id.* 647-651.

Bombay Karnátak: Southern Maráthá Country, conquered by the Bahámanis (1406-1472), I, pt. ii, 638-639.

Bombias: leather workers, I, pt. i, 451.

Bomma: feudatory of the later Chálukya dynasty, restores Chálukya power, is defeated by Vira-Ballála, I, pt. ii, 223, 237.

Bommana: torch-bearer, slays Bijjala the Kalachurya king, I, pt. ii, 480.

Bommaya: companion of Jagaddeva in assassinating king Vijjana, I, pt. ii, 226.

Bond: labour mortgage, specimen of, in Ratnágiri, Kanara and Thána districts, X, 162 note 1; XV, pt. ii, 32 note 1, 34; XIII, 311; money-lenders' in Poona district, XVIII, pt. ii, 125.

Bonthadevi: wife of Vikramáditya IV, the Western Chálukya king, I, pt. ii, 296, 380 note 1, 427.

Book: worship, IX, pt. i, 82. *See* Vahipujan.

Books: *Account*, in Gujarát, size and form of, IX, pt. i, 82-83; six kinds of: (1) Cash Book or *Rojmel*, contents of; (2) Bill register or *Hundini-nondh*, contents of, *id.* 83; (3) Journal or *Avaro*, *id.* 83; contents of, *id.* 84; (4) Ledger or *Khátávahi*, *id.* 83; contents of, *id* 84; (5) Acknowledgment book or *Samadaskat*, contents of, *id.* 83; (6) Interest book or *Vyáj-vahi*, *id.* 83; contents of, *id.* 84; other registers or *nondhs* kept by bankers, *id.* 88; native system of entering fractional parts of a rupee in, *id.* 83; special method of calculating interest, *id.* 84-88; new books, worship of, *id.* 82. *See* Vaniás; *sacred*, IX, pt. ii, 211-212; languages of, *id.* 204 and note 1, *id.* 211 and note 1. *See* Zend Avesta; belief in, IX, pt. ii, 126; reading of, by men and women, *id.* 174 and note 2.

Boone: Honourable C., Governor of Bombay (1720), XIII, 489 and note 1; XXVI, pt. ii, 240.

Booth-building: IX, pt. ii, 233. *See* Mandav.

Booth Spirit: worship of, among Patáne Prabhus, XVIII, pt. i, 200.

Bopadeva: native of Berár, Hemádri's protegee, composes works on Vaishnáva doctrines, on grammar, and on medicine, I, pt. ii, 249.

Bopárdi: village in Sátára district, temple, XIX, 457-458.

Boppadevi: wife of Ballála I, I, pt. ii, 493; accomplished in the sciences and in singing and dancing, *id.* 494.

Bor: fruit tree found in several districts, XXV, 291; *see* also XII, 25; XVIII, pt. ii, 44.

Bor: pass between Thána and Poona districts, XIII, 316; XVIII, pt. ii, 152-153; old trade (B. C. 100-A. D. 100) along, *id.* 211.

Bor or Pimpri: a Násik pass, XVI, 129.

Boragineæ: species of timber, famine, fibrous, and dye plants, XXV, 102, 166, 202, 233-248.

Boráh: *see* Bohorá.

Borai: river in Khándesh district, XII, 9; forest, *id.* 20.

Borassus flabelliformis: timber, food, famine, liquor-yielding and fibrous plant, grows in Konkan, XXV, 134, 180, 207, 212, 237.

Bore: the, in the Narbadá, description of, in the Periplus, I, pt. i, 545; in Cambay Gulf, VIII, 47, 48; III, 3.

Borgaon: village in Sátára district, XI, 458.

Borghát: pass, I, pt. ii, 42; opened (1830), *id.* 129; *see* Bor.

Borhi chichanda: timber tree, XXV, 69.

Bori: petty division of Junnar in Poona district, survey of, XVIII, pt. ii, 446-447.

Bori: river in Khándesh district, XII, 8.

Boribyál: village in Poona district, with railway station, XVIII, pt. iii, 121.

Borivli: railway station in Thána district, caves, remains, and inscriptions at, XIV, 50-51; nearest railway station to Kánheri Caves, *id.* 44.

Boro Buddor: town in Jáva, I, pt. i, 489.

Borrowers: all district volumes; *see* under District Name.

Borrur: fodder plant, XXV, 276.

Borsad: sub-division of Kaira, its area, aspect, climate, water, soil, population, health, III, 162-165; town, its fortifications and history, *id.* 166-167; traditional foundation of, IX, pt. i, 8 note 1; fort of, built by Jagjivan Pavár, Marátha leader (1742), I, pt. i, 325; given up by Rangoji to the Musalmáns, *id.* 326; siege and fall of, *id.* 332; besieged by Momin Khán, *id.* 339; recovered by Rangoji from Hariba, adopted son of Khánderáo Gaikwár; re-taken by Khanderáo and Dámáji

Gáikwár (1748), *id.* 396; *see* also VII, 176-177, 183.
Borsádá: a caste of Bráhmans, cultivators, claim descent from Bhadrasiddha, IX, pt. i, 1, 3, 8 note 1, 152; traditional origin of, *id.* 8 note 1; crushed by Mahmud Begada, *id.* 8-9.
Borsadiá: *see* Borsadá.
Bosari: Kumárapála's companion in exile, I, pt. i, 182; appointed viceroy of Láta or South Gujarát, *id.* 184.
Borta: hill range near Bhinmál, I, pt. i, 456.
Borya: port in Ratnágiri district, X, 184, 324.
Boswellia thurifera: *glabra*, timber tree found in several districts, XXV, 38.
Botád: town in Káthiáwár, VIII, 402.
Botan: meaning corresponding to Annaprá-shana, tenth vedic rite, IX, pt. i, 31 note 3, 35; rites, ceremonies and observances of, among Bhátiás, *id.* 119; Brahma-kshatris, *id.* 57; Bráhmans, *id.* 35; Káyasths, *id.* 61, 65; Rájpúts, *id.* 140. *See* customs, IX, pt. ii, 159, and Salt tasting.
Botanical Gardens: at Ganesh Khind in Poona, XVIII, pt. ii, 77-80; XVIII, pt. iii, 361.
Botat: food plant, XXV, 178.
Botata: XXV, 167; *see* Potato.
Botel: sailing vessel in Thána, XIII, 351-352, 718.
Bother: timber tree, grows in Konkan, XXV, 24.
Botku: *see Bother.*
Botsaka: famine plant very common in the Presidency, XXV, 197.
Boudaia: town on the Indus mentioned by Ptolemy, I, pt. i, 538.
Boukephala: modern Jalálpur, in Surát district, I, pt. i, 546.
Boundaries: of the Konkan, Introduction to the History of the Konkan, I, pt. ii, pp. ix-x; of Shiváji's kingdom at his death in 1680, *id.* 595; of the two Marátha kingdoms (1760), *id.* 600; of the Ahmadnagar and Khándesh kingdoms (1500), *id.* 622.
Boundaries: all district volumes; *see* under District Name.
Boundary: Chitpávan worship of, XVIII, pt. i, 129-130.
Bourchier: proclaimed President and Governor of Bombay (1753), XXVI, pt. iii, 373; resigns (1760), *id.* 378; *see* also I, pt. i, 343; XIII, 496; XXVI, pt. i, 305.
Bowides: Persian House of, IX, pt. ii, 20; Sultáns (945-1097), *id.* 136 note 3. *See* Buwaih.
Bowl: fragments of Buddha's begging, at Sopára, account of the relics as related to the Chinese traveller Fah Hian, history of, XIV, 403-410.
Bracelet making: in Cutch, V, 127.
Brachypodidæ: family of birds in Ratnágiri district, X, 74.
Bragantia Wallichii: XXV, 275.
Braham: Mr. C. B., designed John Hay Grant Reservoir near Mazgaon, XIV, 378.
Brahamsiddhánta: work on astronomy by Bráhmagupta, I, pt. i, 453 note 1.
Brahaspati: called Guru, teacher of gods, IX, pt. i, 402. *See* Jupiter.
Brahaspatvár: Thursday, IX, pt. i, 402.
Brahma: Hindu god, inscription in the temple of, on the Chitoda fort, I, pt. i, 188; king of the Indians, *id.* 531; first member of the Hindu trinity or *trimurti*, IX, pt. i, p. xxxvi; the creator called Prajápati, *id.* 531, 14, 15 note 1; married a Gujar girl called Gáyatri, *id.* 490, 502 and note 4; Amli tree said to be wife of, *id.* 382; Khakharo tree said to be home of, *id.* 384; temple to, in Pushkar, *id.* 490, 502 and note 4; at Angkor in Cambodia, at Kolhapur, *id.* 502 note 4; at Khed-Brahma, *id.* p. xxxvi; Brahmadev, the divine Bráhman, deity worshipped in Ajmer; shrines of, in many villages in Western India, IX, pt. i, 502 note 4; XIII, 406; statues of, in Elephanta caves, XIV, 63, 67, 69, 73, 75, 76; in Mandapeshvar caves, *id.* 224; in Chakreshvar temple near Sopára, *id.* 337-338; image at Gokarn, story of, XV, pt. ii, 296 and note 1; Pir Sadr-ud-din, the incarnation of, IX, pt. ii, 40, 48.
Brahmachári: ceremony and rites of making a boy Brahmachári after thread-girding ceremony, IX, pt. i, 37-38. *See* Girding (Bráhmans).
Brahmadeva: I, pt. ii, 180; temple of, at Haveri; inscription at, *id.* 459 note 3; *see* Brahma.
Brahmadvaita: doctrine, I, pt. ii, 407.
Brahmagranthi: Brahmá's knot, IX, pt. i, 37.
Brahmagupta: astronomer (628), his work on astronomy called *Brahmagupta Siddhánta*, I, pt. i, 138, 453 note 1, 467; IX, pt. i, 488.
Brahma Hill: at Sopára, XIV, 315, 323.
Brahma Kshatri: a caste of writers in Káthiáwar, VIII, 146-147; gap between Bráhmans and Kshatriyas filled by, IX, pt. i, 441; class of writers, *id.* 55; history of their origin, their arrival in Gujarát, their settlement at Champáner and Ahmadábád, their migration to other parts of India, descendants of original Kshatri race, *id.* 55 and note 4, 56; appearance, language, *id.* 56; religion, *id.* 56-57; customs, Chhathi worship; Botan, Mudan, devkáj ceremony; betrothals, *id.* 57; marriage, *dahiáni*, presents, marriage rites and ceremonies, *id.* 58-59; pregnancy; death; cloth-water or *kápdepáni* ceremony, *id.* 59; in Násik, XVI, 43; traders, in Poona city, XVIII, pt. i, 266-267.
Brahmakund: Bhahmá's pool in the vicinity of Bhinmál, I, pt. i, 452, 462, 463.
Bráhman: god, I, pt. ii, 317, 340 note 2, 511. *See* Brahmá.
Bráhman: the wall-gazing; *see* Bodhidharma.
Bráhmanábád: town, advance of Chach (631-670) on, I, pt. i, 519.
Brahmanda: *Purán*, I, pt. ii, 166.
Brahmanemidatta: author of *Kathákosá*, I, pt. ii, 410 note 2.
Bráhmanism: in Thána at the time of Purna, XIII, 406; revived (1740), *id.* 66; flourishing condition of, in Dakhan, I, pt. ii, 173; revival of, under the Chálukyas, *id.* 191-192.
Bráhmanjáis: *see* Vidura.

Bráhmans : I, pt. i, 530, 531 ; districts of coincide with the limits of Kirát, "Introduction to the History of the Konkan," I, pt. ii, p. x; children brought up as Christians, *id.* 60 ; made to work like Kolis, *id.* 60 ; fed and married for the increase of merit, *id.* 148, 173 ; slaughtered by the Chola king Rájendra, *id.* 433 ; hostility to, *id.* 477 ; persecute Basava, *id.* 478 ; of Alaude, *id.* 482 ; Bhilláma II and Bhilláma III grant villages to, *id.* 514 ; harassed by Jayakesin I, *id.* 514, 543, 567 ; established in Kuntala, *id.* 560 ; in Talgund, *id.* 561 ; in Surat, II, 51-52 ; in Broach, *id.* 372 ; in Káira and Panch Mahals, III, 29 ; *id.* 216 ; in Ahmadábád, IV, 34 ; in Pálanpur, V, 289 ; in Mahi Kántha, *id.* 363 ; in Rewa Kántha, VI, 22-23 ; settlement in Cambay, *id.* 214 ; plunder of, *id.* 228, in Káthiáwár, VIII, 143-146 ; India, the land of, IX, pt. i, 434 ; Gaud and Dravid groups of ; sub-divisions of groups, *id.* 1 and note 1 ; admission of foreigners into the class and rank of, (1) *before Buddhist times*, practice showing admission of individuals not pure Bráhmans ; instances of individuals who passed as, who assumed and abandoned the position of, *id.* 434 ; marriages with women of any of the four castes allowed ; intermarriages with snake people allowed ; sons of such marriages and sons begotten indiscriminately given rank of Bráhman, priest, or *rishi*, IX, pt. i, 435 ; (2) *since Buddhist times*, practice of marriage with women of lower classes still common, *id.* 435 ; origin of marriage with local women, *id.* 435 note 11 ; marriages of, with daughters of Kshatriyás allowed, *id.* 435 and note 10 ; instances of individuals raised to be, *id.* 436 and note 1 ; admission of entire classes, examples not directly and directly connected with inroads of northern conquerors, *id.* 436-441 ; established instances of outsiders being admitted to be Bráhmans, (i) priests of Bahikás, *id.* 439 ; (ii) priests of Mihirás or white Húnás known as Mágha Bráhmans, *id.* 439-440 ; instances, of Bráhmans whose origin traced to Bráhman-maker Parshurám, of made Bráhmans, of classes which passed as Bráhmans, Akalis, Sikhs or immortals, *id.* 438 ; Bháts, Cháraus, *id.* 438 ; Chitpávans, *id.* 436, 438, 439 ; Haiga Bráhmans, *id.* 439 ; Javlás, *id.* 438 ; Kandoliás, *id.* 440 note 5 ; Karhádes, *id.* 436, 438 ; Nágas, *id.* 438 and note 7 ; Nágars of Gujarát, *id.* 438 and note 9 ; Nának Putras, *id.* 438 ; Paliwals, *id.* 440 ; Saiva Bráhmans, *id.* 438 ; Shenvis or Sárasvats, *id.* 436, 438, 439, 440 and note 5 ; Tulava Bráhmans, *id.* 436 ; *Position, power and influence of*, admitted to be highest class in India, during Buddhist period, IX, pt. i, 434 ; their magical and astrological skill ; their influence in Burma, Siam and Cambodia, *id.* 437 and notes 2 to 7 ; Buddhist definition of Brahmans, Yudhisthira's test of Bráhmans, *id.* 437 ; their position affected by (i) priests and medicine men of new comers admitted as Bráhmans, *id.* 436, 438 ; (ii) new comers adopting as their teachers and priests local tribes or families who were not Bráhmans, *id.* 437, 440 ; (iii) new comers in their wanderings through India, carrying with them large bodies of Bráhmans, *id.* 437, 440-441 ; *Rivalry with Buddhism :* contest for foreign proselytes, *id.* 433, 447 ; *Gujarát :* three groups of *Early, Middle*, and *Modern ; Early* group, mostly pre-Aryan tribes made Bráhmans by early Hindu heroes and demigods, IX, pt. i, 1 and note 2 ; some seem to have come to Gujarát from Dakhan, *id.* 1, 2 ; *Middle* group, mostly immigrants from Upper India, Márwár and Rájpútáná ; *Modern* group, mostly immigrants since the time of Musalmán rule, chiefly Maráthá Bráhmans, *id.* pt. xi, 2 ; *settlement* of groups, *id.* 1-2 ; *Divisions*, names, strength and distribution of leading divisions, *id.* 2-3 ; divisions eat together but do not intermarry, *id.* 2 ; sections of *bhikshuk* or cleric and *grahasth* or laymen in a division, chief differences of sections, *id.* 2 and note 2 ; *gotras* or family stock in a division, *id.* 2 ; account of the leading fifty-four divisions, *id.* 4-21 ; *Appearance, Dress, Ornaments, Food, id.* 21 ; *Occupation* of *Secular* classes, of *religious* classes, *id.* 22 ; Ghámot or *gors*, *id.* 22, 23-24 ; Puranis or readers of holy books, *id.* 22, 24-25 ; Hardás or preachers, *id.* 25-26 ; Shástris, *id.* 22, 26-27 ; Joshis or astrologers, *id.* 22, 27-28 ; Pujáris or temple ministrants, *id.* 22 ; Pilgrim's Priest, *id.* 28 ; Tirthvala or Bather's Priest, *id.* 29 ; Beggars, *id.* 29-30 ; *House work ; condition, id.* 30 ; *Religion,*—followers of Shiv ; worship of household gods ; performance of *sandhyá* or twilight prayer ; *gáyatri* or sun-hymn ; religious training, *id.* 31 ; six duties of Bráhmans enjoined by Shástras, *id.* 22 ; *Customs*, Vedic purifying rites, *id.* 31 and note 3 ; (1) *Rakhadi* or Guard-binding ceremony performed in the fifth month of first pregnancy, *id.* 31-32 ; (2) *Simanta* or Hair-dividing commonly known as *Kholobharvo*, or lap-filling performed between sixth and eighth month of first pregnancy ; rites, ceremonies, and observances of ; performances of *Garbhadhana* or Fœtus-laying rite, of *Punusavana* or Male-making rite, of *Anavalobhana*, or Longing-soothing rite, called *Garbharakshana* or Womb-guarding, *id.* 32 ; of *Simantonnayana* or Hair-parting rite ; (3) *Birth*, First confinement ; preparation for delivery ; the child born ; observances during first ten days after delivery, *id.* 33 ; *Destiny Worship* called *Suashthi-Pujan* on sixth night after birth, common belief about Vidhata writing on child's brow the chief events of its coming life, *id.* 33-34 ; (4) *Naming* or *Namkarma*, rites in, *id.* 34-35 ; (5) *Botan* or Weaving ; (6) Head-shaving or *Chaul*, *id.* 35 ; (7) *Upanayana* or Thread-girding, lucky day for girding the boy ; preparations for girding day ; rice-pounding or *ghana* ceremony, performance of religious ceremonies during girding rite, worship of *gotraj* or family goddess, *id.*

36; *Jatakarma* or birth rite, name-giving rite, *nishkramana* or going out ceremony, ear-slitting ceremony, *annaprashana* or feeding ceremony, ceremony for ascertaining calling or profession, ceremony of tonsure and thread-girding, *id.* 37; ceremony or rite of making a boy a *Brahamáchári, id.* 37-38; *samavartana* or water-pouring rite, *id.* 38; procession, *id.* 38-39; (8) *Viváha* or marriage, importance of marriage to the Bráhmans, *id.* 39 note 1; Marriageable age of girls, choice of husband, form of marriage, *id.* 39; Dowry, *id.* 39-40; Betrothal; marriage day, *id.* 40; preparations, *id.* 40-41; rice-pounding ceremony, minor ceremonies in connection with marriage rite, *Varsoddhara* worship, *Matrika* installing, *id.* 41; *Abhyádhika Shraddha, id.* 41-42; ceremony of *Ukardi notarvi* or Dunghill-asking, *id.* 42; ceremony of *Grahashanti* or Planet-soothing, *id.* 42-43; Procession, *id.* 43; minor observances before marriage service, *id.* 43-44; marriage service, 44-45; after rites and observances, *id* 45-47; (9) Death or funeral ceremonies, called *svargárohana*, dying person, dead body, funeral dirge, breast-beating, *id.* 47; bier, funeral party, pyre, religious part of ceremonies before dead body is burnt, burning of dead body, *id.* 48; after rites; funeral rites of a sanyási, *id.* 49; the widow; mourning; *Shradha* or memorial rites; *sejja* giving on the twelth day after death, object of, *id.* 50-51; *Community, Prospects; Education, id.* 51; *Southern Bráhmans:* Telang, IX, pt. i, 51; Dakhani, names, strength and distribution of, *id.* 51-52; language, food, feast and dinner service, *id.* 52; dress, ornaments, *id.* 53; customs; worship of goddess Gauri; *halad-kanku* presents, *id.* 53-54; in Ratnágiri, X, 111-117; cultivators, *id.* 150, in Savantvádi, *id.* 411; in Kolábá, XI, 43-46, in Janjira, *id.* 411; in Constantinople and Jáva (A. D. 24-57), *id.* 138 note 1; in Thána, XIII, 63 and note 2, 64, 66, 73-87, 411, 461; in Kánara, settled by Parashurám, XV, pt. ii, 76; sedition of, at Trimbak (Násik), XVI, 201, 660.

Bráhmanvádi: village in Ahmadnagar, XVII, 714; survey of, XVIII, pt. ii, 448-450.

Brahman-Vania: upper class of Ujlivaran people so called, IX, pt. i, p. xiv.

Bráhmanvel: place of interest in Khándesh district, XII, 437.

Brahmapuri: village in Sholápur district, temple at, XX, 44; Aurangzeb's camp at (1695), *id.* 288.

Brahmapuri hill: in Kolhápur, temples in honor of the deceased members of the royal family at, XXIV, 312.

Brahmápurush: Bráhman ghost, XVIII, pt. i, 553-554.

Brahma Sámpradáya: cult of Vaishnáv creed, IX, pt. i, 533. *See* Vaishnáv sects.

Brahmásarovar: lake, in the vicinity of Bhinmál, I, pt. i, 454.

Brahmaśriràja: prime minister of the Pallava king Nandivarman, I, pt. ii 325.

Brahma Tekri: Sopara hill, XIII, 408, 409.

Brahma Vaivarta Purán: IX, pt. I, 532. *See* Purans.

Bráhmavaka: family name of Prachanda, I, pt. 1, 129; *see* also I, pt. ii, 413.

Brahmávarta: A'rya's holy land, I, pt. ii, 135.

Brahmayavarája: I, pt. ii, 325. *See* Brahmaśriràja.

Brahmeśvara: site of, I, pt. ii, 482.

Bráhmi: one of the Pleiades, I, pt. ii, 337 note 4.

Brahmoka: food plant, XXV, 162; oil-yielding plant, *id.* 219.

Braid-weaving: in Cutch, V, 126.

Brambanum: capital of Bhruvijaya, king of Java, I, pt i, 489.

Bramee: medicinal herb, XXV, 260.

Branding: of boys among Kunbis, XVIII, pt. i, 300.

Brass and copper: Násik industry, workers, their castes, condition, wages, metal used, articles made, XVI, 145-153; *id.* 486-487.

Brassica: *campestris*, food and oil-yielding plant, XXV, 145, 214; *juncea*, food, oil-yielding and medicinal plant, *id.* 145, 214, 256; *napus*, food, oil-yielding and medicinal plant, *id.* 145, 214, 256; *oleracea*, food plant, *id.* 144; *rapa*, food plant, *id.* 145.

Brass work: industry in Poona district, workmen, tools, process, articles, changes in trade, XVIII, pt. ii, 174, 185.

Breach Candy: creek in Bombay, meaning of, XXVI, pt. iii, 651.

Bread-fruit tree: food plant, XXV, 172.

Breast-beating: by women, at death, among Bráhmans, IX, pt i, 47; Brahmakshatris, *id.* 59; Kanbis, *id.* 162.

Breccia beds: in Belgaum district, XXI, 19; in Bijápur, XXIII, 26.

Brick stupas: at Kanheri, perhaps held the ashes of the priests, XIV, 184.

Brickworks: at Panvel, XIV, 294-295.

Bridge-builders: famous, Khárvás of Ránder and Bhimpore as, IX, pt. i, 519, 521.

Bridge of Ráma: connects Ceylon with the Coromandel Coast, I, pt. ii, 341.

Bridges: all district volumes; *see* under District Name.

Briedelia montana: *B. retusa*, timber, food, dye and fodder plants grow on the *gháts*, XXV, 120, 171, 249, 278.

Briggs: I, pt. ii, 30; Captain, in charge of Khándesh (1819), *id.* 631; Colonel (1827), I, pt. i, 383; General, IX, pt. ii, 3 note 3; *id.* 77; *id.* 85 and note 1, 86 note 1.

Brihadratha: last Maurya king, murdered by his general, I, pt. ii, 115.

Brihaspati: Ganda Bháva, repairs the Somanátha temple, I, pt. i, 189, 190.

Brihaspati: ancestor of the Pallavas, I, pt ii, 317.

Brihat-Katha: a Sanskrit work, I, pt. ii, 170, and note 1.

Brihat-Paralur: village, mentioned in a Devgiri grant, I, pt. ii, 288.

Brihatsamhita: work by Varáha Mihira, I, pt. i, 540; I, pt. ii, 310, 413 note 2; IX, pt. ii, 10 note 7.

Brij Mathura: town in Northern India, the original place of Bhávsárs, IX, pt. i, 177.

Briudão : timber tree, grows on the *ghâts*, XXV, 10.

Brinjal : food plant, cultivated in several districts, XXV, 167, XII, 170.

British : the, intervention for protection of the chiefs of Káthiáwár against the Mulakgiri system, I, pt. i, 421-422 ; secret treaty of the, with Rávji ; reward Rávji with a village, *id.* 413 ; make a fresh treaty with the Gáikwár, consolidating all previous engagements into a single treaty and constitute themselves arbiters in all disputes of the Gaikwár with foreign powers and the Peshwá (1805), *id.* 415 ; Arab mercenaries obstruct the establishment of the power of, in Gujarát (1802), IX, pt. ii, 3 note 2 ; give aid to Muhammadáli, the Pasha of Egypt to put down the power of the Wahhabis (1812), *id.* 12 note 3 ; *id.* 27 ; *id.* 60 note 4 ; Bombay transferred to (1666), Surat transferred to (1759), IX, pt. ii, 195 ; in Ratnágiri (1818-1880), X, 198-199 ; in Sávantvádi (1730-1880), *id.* 441-447 ; administration in Násik (1818-1881), XVI, 195-204, 211-214 ; land history under the, XVIII, pt. ii, 341-513 ; management in Poona district (1817-1882), *id.* 304-305

British Museum : grants and stone inscriptions in, I, pt. ii, 344 note 6, 557.

Broach : district, description, II, 337, 338 ; rivers, *id.* 339-350 ; geology, *id.* 351-352 ; climate, *id.* 353, 354 ; minerals and trees, *id.* 355 ; animals, *id.* 356-367 ; population, *id.* 368-380 ; village communities, *id.* 381-388 ; soil, agricultural stock, produce and area under cultivation, *id.* 389-391 ; details of cotton cultivation. *id.* 392-403 ; cultivation of food crops, *id.* 404-409 ; years of scarcity, *id.* 410, 411 ; roads, rest-houses, and ferries, *id.* 412-413 ; vessels, *id.* 413-418 ; railway stations and bridges, *id.* 419 ; post and telegraph statistics, *id.* 420-421 ; trade in ancient times (64-200 A. D. and in the 17th-19th centuries), *id.* 422-423 ; statistics of trade by land and sea, *id.* 424, 425 ; steam factories, *id.* 426 ; course of the cotton trade, *id.* 427-433 ; chief articles of export and import, *id.* 434-437 ; manufactures, *id.* 438-440 ; craft-guilds, exhibition, *id.* 441-443 ; capitalists, banking arrangements, insurance, currency, and bills of exchange, *id.* 444 447 ; forms of investment and classes of money-lenders and borrowers, *id.* 448-451 ; rates of interest and indebtedness of the cultivating classes, *id.* 452-454 ; transfers, sale value, and mortgages, of land, *id.* 455, 456 ; wages, prices, and weights and measures, *id.* 457-463 ; early history, *id.* 464-467 ; Europeans and Maráthás at Broach, *id.* 468 ; rise of the Nawáb, *id.* 469 ; English expeditions against Broach, *id.* 470 ; capture of Broach, *id.* 471 ; settlement of affairs, *id.* 472 ; acquisition of territory, *id.* 473-475 ; disturbances, *id.* 476, 477 ; administrative changes, *id.* 478-480 ; land tenures, *id.* 481-483 ; history of different settlements of land revenue, *id.* 484-497 ; administration of civil and criminal justice and police, *id.* 498-509 ; revenue and finance, *id.* 510-519 ; local funds and municipalities, *id.* 520-522 ; instruction, libraries, newspapers, and associations, *id.* 523-530 ; chief diseases, dispensaries, vaccination, cattle-disease, and vital statistics, *id.* 531-534 ; sub-divisional accounts, *id.* 535-548 ; places of interest, *id.* 549-569 ; *Sub-division*, its boundaries, area, aspect, climate, water, soil, assessment, crops and people, *id.* 542 544 ; *Town*, its description, history, trade and manufactures, *id.* 551-559 ; Valabhi grants in, I, pt. i, 86 ; Gurjjar dynasty of, *id.* 107, 113 ; Valabhi king's camp of victory at, *id.* 114 ; described by Hiuen Tsang ; port, submitted to Pulakeśi II ; grant at, *id.* 116, 117, 126 ; Dhruva II's Bágumra and Baroda grants made at, 127 ; a soothsayer at, promises Kumárapála the throne, *id.* 183 ; Lavanaprasáda's fight with Singhana at, *id.* 199 ; insurrection at (1325), *id.* 513-514 ; siege and relief of (1347), *id.* 230 ; (1412), *id.* 235 ; plundered by the Maráthás (1675), *id.* 387 ; plundered second time by the Maráthás (1685), *id.* 387-388 ; capture of, by the Mátias and Momnás (1691), *id.* 288 ; siege of, by Dámáji and the Maráthás (1741), *id.* 324, 395 ; defended by the Nizám's lieutenant Nek Alum Khán ; raising of the siege by Dámáji ; concessions of a share in the customs revenues of, to Dámáji by the Nizám, *id.* 324 ; governor of, becomes independent (1752), *id.* 334 ; capture of, by the English (1772), *id.* 401 ; given over to Sindia in 1802, *id.* 410 ; captured by the English from Sindia (1803), ceded to the English by the treaty of Sirje Anjangaon (1803), *id.* 414 ; its different names, *id.* 513, 521, 528, 536, 545, 546 ; Dámáji receives a share in the revenue of (1741), VII, 175 ; Peshwá's share in the revenue of (1751), *id.* 180 ; captured by the British (1772), *id.* 190 ; Raghunáthráv promises a share in its revenues, *id.* 191 ; Gáikwár loses his share in its revenues, *id.* 198 ; lost to the Sindia (1803), *id.* 211 ; town, I, pt. ii, 4 ; Gujarát head-quarters of Ráshtrakútas of Malkhet, *id.* 22 ; district, *id.* 310, 314 note 6, 316, 354 ; district, 403, 412 ; territory round, ravaged by Singhana, *id.* 525, 538 note 8 ; attacked by Arabs (730), IX, pt. ii, 1 and note 1 ; revolt of Momnás at (1691), *id.* 76 ; revolt of Matia Kanbis at, *id.* 67 ; disturbance of Sunni Bohorás at (1857), *id.* 60 note 4 ; Musalmán faith introduced into, from Anabilaváda by Alifkhán, *id.* 3-5 ; city, founded by and hermitage of Rishi Bhrigu, IX, pt. i, p. xi, 7 ; Gurjjara dynasty established at, *id.* XII, 479 ; settlements of Pársis in (1300), IX, pt. ii, 186 ; riot at (1857), *id.* 198 and note 3 ; Pársi martyr of, *id.* 198 ; scholarships in Zend and Pehlevi established at, *id.* 194.

Brocade : weaving of, at Ahmadábád, encouraged by Emperor Aurangzeb (1703), I, pt. i, 292 ; manufacture of, in Surat, II, 179 ; in Kátniáwár, VIII, 260.

Brokers: in Cutch, V, 121; Pársis as, of European trading companies at Surat, IX, pt. ii, 196; in Násik, XVI, 115; in Thána, XIII, 332.

Fromelia auanas: fruit and fibrous plant grown in several districts, XXV, 180, 236.

Bromeliaceæ: a species of fruit and fibrous plant, XXV, 180, 236.

Brooks: Captain, takes Kotaligad fort (1817), constructs Kurla-Sion causeway (1798-1803), XIV, 210, 211.

Brother Islands: in Káthiáwár, VIII, 32.

Brown: Honourable Mr. George, appointed Governor of Bombay (1811), XXVI, pt. iii, 416.

Brown hemp: tillage of, in Poona, XVIII, pt. ii, 45.

Brugueiria: *gymnorniza*, *Rheedii*, dye plants, XXV, 244.

Bruguiera parviflora: timber tree, XXV, 73.

Brumaj: timber tree, found in Konkan forests, XXV, 131.

Bryonia umbellata: food and sacred plant, common in the presidency, XXV, 160, 291.

Bubasir: rock in the Gulf of Cambay, VIII, 29.

Bubuji Khánam: Maráthá princess, I, pt. ii, 641 note 3; grandmother of Mallu and mother of Ismáil A'dil Sháh, *id.* 642.

Bucephala: Jalálpur in Surat district, capital of the Asini, I, pt. i, 534.

Bucerotidæ: order of birds in Ratnágiri district, X, 65.

Buchanan: Dr., references to his work "Mysore and Káuara," XV, pt. ii, 75, 80, 83, 101, 257, 260, 266, 274, 277, 302, 303, 315, 317, 327, 330, 334, 335, 336, 341, 345, 349; condition of Kánara according to his journal (1801), *id.* 147-152.

Buchanania latifolia: timber, food, oil, dye and gum-yielding plant, found in Konkan, XXV, 53, 150, 217, 242, 250.

Buckhool: food plant, XXV, 164.

Buckle: Captain, Political Agent of Rewá Kántha (1857), I, pt. i, 439, 443.

Buck-wheat: food plant, cultivated in Dakhan, XXV, 170.

Budhudker: caste of fortune-tellers in Bijápur and Dhárwár districts, XXIII, 178-180; XXII, 200-201.

Bud-dene: palm tree cess, XIII, 642.

Buddha: idol of, I, pt. i, 531; introduction of, in China, *id.* 530; tooth of, pounded, I, pt. ii, 56; religion of, *id.* 173; *vihára* of, at Dambal, *id.* 452; ninth incarnation of Vishnu, IX, pt. i, 549; IX, pt. ii, 48, XII, 484 note 1; *manushya*, *id.* 492 note 3, 568; *dnyáni*, *id.* 567 note; his creed, *id.* 593 note 1, XIII, 404 note 2, *id.* 406, 407, 408 and note 2; eight images of, in Sopára caves, XIV, 329-331; of Sopára and Ajanta, compared, *id.* 412-413

Buddha: Kalachuri king, conquered and put to flight, by Manglesa (597-602), II, 181, 295, 311, 315, 336, 347, 348 and note 6.

Buddhaghosha: a Suakya friar, mentioned in a Káuheri inscription, XIV, 168.

Buddharája: *See* Buddha.

Buddhavarasa: feudatory of Prabhutavarsha Govindarája of Gujarát, I, pt. ii, 399.

Buddhavarman: Pallava king, I, pt. ii, 325, *see* Buddhavarmarája.

Buddhavarmarája: I, pt. ii, 188.

Buddhavarmman: Chálukya ruler of Kaira, I, pt. i, 108, 110, 111; *see* also I, pt. ii, 359.

Buddhavarmman: Kálachuri prince, I, pt. i, 114; *see* Buddharája.

Buddhism: state religion in Cambodia, I, pt. i, 502; religion in Gujarát, *id.* 530; introduction of, into China, "Introduction to the Early History of the Dakhan," I, pt. ii, p. ii; stronghold of, *id.* 12; flourishing condition of, *id.* 173; prevalence of, though in a declining condition, under the Chálukyas, *id.* 191; under the Ráshtrakútas, *id.* 208; under the later Chálukyas, *id.* 228, 406 and note 5; in the Káuarese country, *id.* 452; period of its rivalry with Bráhmanism, IX, pt. i, 433, 447; admission to Buddhist order first confined to Bráhmans and Kshatryas, *id.* 434; no difficulty to admit foreigners to the highest place in the order, *id.* 433, 447 and note 7; foreign conquerors converted to, *id.* 433, 448, 449; Kanishka, great reviver of Buddhism, *id.* 442, 445 note 5; foreigner's part in spread of, *id.* 445 note 5; foreign converts who claimed a share of Buddhá's relics, *id.* 446 note 1; Mihirakula's determination to stamp it out, *id.* 487; its decline (seventh and eighth century), *id.* 449 note 2; the Buddhist as a magician, *id.* 437 note 6; XIII, 404 note 3, 405, 406, 411, 416; history of, in its four stages (B. C. 450-A. D. 750), XIV, 127, 136; lingerings of, *id.* 127 note 3, 321; flourished in Násik (A. D. 416), traces of, in Násik caves, XVI, 184 and note 1, *id.* 607, 628; influence of, in B. C. 90, XVIII, pt. ii, 212.

Buddhist caves: in Káthiáwár, VIII, 10, 12. *See* Caves.

Buddhists: I, pt. i, 531; I, pt. ii, 406 note 5, 482; remains of, in the neighbourhood of Kolhápur, *id.* 538 note 8; community of, at Kánheri, *id.* 541; records of, *id.* 542 and note 2; settlement of, in Kolába (A. D. 1-100), XI, 137; in Thána, XIII, 66, 413, 414; in Kolhápur, XXIV, 152; Chálukya grant (1095) to, XV, pt. ii, 81.

Buddhist Schools of Art: XII, 497 and note 2.

Budgaon: town in Kolhápur, its details, palace, XXIV, 383.

Budh: son of Soma, the moon, I, pt. ii, 340.

Budhagupta: Gupta king (A. D. 494-500), I, pt. i, 71, 72, 135; overthrown by Toramána, *id.* 136; *see* also I, pt. ii, 369 note 5.

Budhiya: town on the Indus mentioned by the Arabs, I, pt. i, 538.

Budhvár: ward of Poona city, details of, XVIII, pt. iii, 274, 281-282.

Budhvár Palace: in Poona city, XVIII, pt. iii, 334-335.

Budh-Yákub: Sayad ancestor of Uraizi Sayad family, IX, pt. ii, 6 note 1 (7).

Budjari-dha-mun: timber tree, grows on Konkan *ghâts*, XXV, 25.

Buettneria heracea: famine plant common in Konkan, XXV, 195.

Buffalo : offerings of, made to goddesses, by Bhil women during famine, IX, pt. i, 356 ; worship of, as the image of Bhensasur, *id.* 375.
Buffaloes : in Khándesh district, XII, 29 ; in Kánara, XV, pt. i, 80 ; in Ahmadnagar, XVII, 34-35 ; in Poona, XVIII, pt. i, 60 61 ; in Sholápur, XX, 16 ; in Belgaum, XXI, 66-67.
Builders : Gujjaras as, IX, pt. i, 499, 502 note 4.
Builders and building materials : in Bombay (1694-1771), XXVI, pt. ii, 175-186 ; tidal saw mill at Worlee (1761), *id.* 181-186.
Building rules : in Bombay city (1731, 1754, 1787), XXVI, pt. ii, 437, 444-445, 491-493.
Buildings : constructed in Siddharája's time, I, pt. i, 179-180 ; Shrávak's religious *apasaras* or monasteries, *dehras* or temples, description of *dehras*, IX, pt. i, 110-113 ; of *apasaras*, *id.* 113 ; religious, IX, pt. ii, 130-132.
Bujagandanapura : town in Mysore, inscription at, I, pt. ii, 502.
Bujva : a natural hollow, in Ahmadábád district, IV, 9.
Bukhara Mosque : at Bijápur, XXIII, 630-631.
Bukháris : chief Sayad family in Gujarát, IX, pt. ii, 6 note 1 (7), 57, 127 note 2.
Bukkaráya : second Vijayánagar king (1350-1379), XV, pt. ii, 96 notes 2 and 4 ; his inscriptions at Banavasi, *id.* 97, 262 ; at Gokarn, *id.* 97-98, 298-299.
Bulbuls : class of birds in Ratnágiri district, X, 74 ; at Mátherán, XIV, 258.
Bulb vegetables : in Poona, XVIII, pt. ii, 55-57 ; in Kolhápur, XXIV, 180, 181.
Bulki : cattle disease, in Ratnágiri district, X, 461.
Bull : called Nandi, carrier of Shiv, held sacred, days sacred for worship of, rites of worship on Bol-choth, IX, pt. i, 374-375.
Bullocks : in Khándesh, XII, 28.
Bulukas : the Indian Buddhist converts, claim Buddha's relics, IX, pt. i, 446 note 1.
Bun : coffee tree grown in Southern India, XXV, 162.
Bundelkhand : Krishna's son Jagattunga, lived in, I, pt. i, 130 ; I, pt. ii, 396, 469.
Bund Gardens : in Poona cantonment, XVIII, pt. iii, 361-362.
Bunkars : caste of weaver cultivators in Khándesh, XII, 69.
Bunting : class of birds, in Ratnágiri district, X, 84.
Buradasingi : village in the Hubli táluka, inscription at, I, pt. ii, 572.
Burburra : famine plant, wild in several districts, XXV, 197.
Burges : Captain, his mutiny, XXVI, pt. i, 49.
Burhán : Martiza Nizám Sháh's brother ; becomes king of Ahmadnagar by the aid of the Mughals and Ibráhim Ádil Sháh (1590), I, pt. ii, 623 ; dies (1594), *id.* 624.
Burhan : Nizám Sháh (1508-1553), son and successor of Ahmad Nizám Sháh ; overruns Berár (1526), is driven back by Bahádur Sháh of Gujarát (1528) ; acknowledges Bahádur Sháh's supremacy (1530) ; overruns Sholápur and the adjoining five districts (1543), I, pt ii, 622 ; captures Gulbarga and Kalyán (1548), *id.* 590 ; recaptures Sholápur (1549), *id.* 590 ; dies (1553), *id.* 623 ; *another account of :* married to Bijápur princess (1523) ; fails to take Sholápur (1524) ; defeated by Ismáil Ádil Sháh (1531) ; takes Sholápur (1542, 1551), XX, 279-282.
Burhánabád : city near Ahmadnagar, sacked by the Mughals (1595), XVII, 382-383.
Burhánpur : I, pt. ii, 607 ; the capital of Khándesh kings ; built by Malik Názir (1399-1441) ; captured by Alá-ud-din Bahámani (1435), *id.* 620 ; Burhán Nizám Sháh acknowledges Bahádur's supremacy at (1530), *id.* 622 ; capital of the Mughal governor Prince Dániál (1600), *id.* 624 ; visited by Sir Thomas Roe in 1616, by Bernier in 1656, by Taverneir in 1665, *id.* 625 ; plundered by the Maráthás (1675), I, pt. i, 387 ; taken by Nizám-ul-mulk in 1720, I, pt. ii, 626 ; the battle of, in 1720, between Nizám-ul-mulk and the imperial army, *id.* 627 ; sacked by the Maráthás, *id.* 626 ; death of Nizám-ul-mulk at (1748), *id.* 627 ; taken from Sindia by Colonel Stephenson for the Peshwa (1803), *id.* 629 ; place of pilgrimage, IX, pt. i, 168, 170 ; former seat of the head *mulla* of the Dáúdi Bohorás, IX, pt. ii, 31 note 4 ; place of interest, trade centre (1600), XII, 214, 248 ; founded (1400), *id.* 244 ; Sháh Jahán at, *id.* 249 ; terrible famine around, *id.* 250 ; Sháhu plunders the country round (1708), *id.* 251 ; seized by Nizám-ul-mulk, *id.* 252 ; taken by the English (1803), *id.* 253 ; history, description, *id.* 589-592 ; XIII, 467, 505.
Burhán-ud-dín : head *mulla* of the Dáúdi Bohorás (1893), IX, pt. ii, 31 note 4.
Burhán-ud-din : Mysore general at Kittur (1786), XXII, 415.
Burhán-ud-din Kutbi A'lam : Sayad ancestor of the Bukhári Sayad family in Gujarát, IX, pt. ii, 6 note 1 (7).
Burial grounds : in Bombay city, at Mendhana's point (1665-1740), XXVI, pt. iii, 576 ; removed outside town wall (1740), *id.* 576 ; transferred to Sonápur (1760-61), *id.* 577 578 ; another burial ground proposed (1780), *id.* 578-579.
Burial-mounds : Buddhist, in Thána district, XIV, 148 ; Elephanta, *id.* 94 ; view from, *id.* 95 ; Kanheri, *id.* 180-184 ; Kondivti, *id.* 204 ; Sopára, *id.* 325-336.
Burial places : names of, IX, pt. ii, 254.
Burka ; veil-robe, IX, pt. ii, 29. 34.
Burke : Edmund, helps Raghunáthráo Peshwá's agent and his Pársi companion, IX, pt. ii, 196 note 3.
Burma : I, pt. i, 527 ; Bráhmanic influence in, IX, pt. i, 437.
"Burne's Travels into Bokhára :" I, pt. i, 544.
Burning : sentence of, in Bombay (1744), XXVI, pt. iii, 20.
Burnouf : translation of the legend of Purna, a Sopára merchant, in his "Introduction to Buddhism," XIV, 320 and note 7, 394, 410.
Burnt Islands : near Vengurla, X, 173, 324, 378.

Buroudi: Javal Bráhman head-quarters in Ratnágiri district, X, 117; place of interest, *id.* 324.
Burr: Colonel, at the battle of Kirkee (1817), XVIII, pt. ii, 300-301.
Burseraceæ: species of timber, food and dye-yielding plants, XXV, 38, 149, 241.
Bursinopetalum arboreum: timber tree, grows in Ceylon, XXV, 82.
Bursunga: food plant, grows in Konkan *ghâts*, XXV, 149.
Burton: Sir Richard, author of "Alf Leilah wa Leigh" quoted, IX, pt. ii, 10 note 4, 15 note 4, 131 note 3, 160 note 3.
Burud: caste of bamboo mat-makers in Ratnágiri district X, 128; in Khándesh, XII, 121; in Thána, XIII, 150; in Kánara, XV, pt. i, 340-341; in Násik, XVI, 59; in Poona, XVIII, pt. i, 325-326; in Sátára, XIX, 80-81; in Sholápur, XX, 92-93; in Belgaum, XXI, 173-174; in Kolhápur, XXIV, 93-94.
Burud bridge: in Poona city, XVIII, pt. iii, 285.
Burud king: his tower near Sopára, XIV, 323; tradition of, *id.* 327.
Burumb: timber tree found at Khandála, XXV, 44.
Burust: part of the Zend Avesta, IX, pt. ii, 211 note 2 (9).
Bussie: Vasi or settler, a slave, IX, pt. i, 454 note 1.
Bussy: French general, defeats Maráthás on the Ghod (1751), XVIII, pt. ii, 246; Bálaji Peshwa's intrigue against (1752), XX, 291, besieges Sávanur (1755), XXII, 656, 796-798.
Buta: a land tenure in Cutch, V, 178; in Pálanpur, *id.* 304.
Bútarasa: governor of the Kongalnád and Punád districts, I, pt. ii, 303.
Bútayya: I, pt. ii, 304; *see* Satyavákya Kongunivarma-Permanadi-Butaga; *see* Bhútarya.
Butcher's Island: in Bombay harbour, political prisoners confined in (1857), XIX, 318-319; meaning of, XXVI, pt. i, 438-439.
Bute: timber tree, XXV, 24; *see Bother.*
Butea: *frondosa*, timber, food, fibrous, dye, gum-yielding, medicinal, fodder, and sacred plant, XXV, 59, 217, 231, 243, 250, 257, 259, 278, 279, 290, 291; *superba*, dye and gum-yielding plant, found in Northern Konkan, XXV, 243, 250.
Butconinæ: family of birds in Ratnágiri district, X, 57.
Butta: famine plant, XXV, 208.
Buttal: depressed class, in Kánara district, XV, pt. i, 364
Buttarasa: married to a Ráshtrakúta princess (850), I, pt. ii, 303 note 7.
Butterflies: at Mátherán, XIV, 255.
Bútuga: mention of, in the Súdi grant, I, pt. ii, 302 note 2.
Buwaih: Persian house of, its supremacy in Persia (946), IX, pt. ii, 20; *see* Bowides.
Buzantion: identified with Vaijayanti, I, pt. ii, 174.
Buzurg Ali Kaderi: Pír of Mundra, descendant of Pír Eusuf-ud-dín, IX, pt. ii, 50 note 2, 51.
Byadaru: *see* Bedar.
Byad Dásar: caste of husbandmen in Dhárwár district, XXII, 133.
Byádgi: town in Dharwár district, trade centre, XXII, 354, 658.
Byáhatti: town in Dhárwár district, temple, inscriptions and copper plates at, XXII, 658-659.
Byfield: Mr. Thomas, visited (1756) Poona, XVIII, pt. ii, 247.
Byrámji Jijibhái: school at Thána, XIV, 353.
Byrasu Wodeyars: Karkal chiefs of Katkal (1500-1600), XV, pt. ii, 121; division of their territory (1550), *id.* 273; absorbed in Gersappa chief, *id.* 283.
Byzantion: Vaijayanti, I, pt. i, 546; Chiplún, *id.* 540.
Byzantium: I, pt. i, 546; I, pt. ii, 2; probable identification of, with Vijayadurg, X, 192 note 3.

C

CACAY: sacred plant, XXV, 289.
Caciga: king of Bhinmál, successor of Udayasimha, I, pt. i, 471.
Cacteæ: species of food and famine plants, XXV, 160, 199.
Cadam: food plant, XXV, 161.
Cæsalpinea: *coriana*, dye plant, cultivated in Bombay and Poona, XXV, 243; *sappan*, dye plant, grows on Malabár coast, *id.* 243.
Cæsar Frederick: Venetian merchant, his travel to Vijayánagar and its description (1567), XV, pt. ii, 116-118; visits Ankola (1567), *id.* 258; Honávar, *id.* 310; his notice of Cambay trade, VI, 191, 218; description of Ahmadnagar government, XVII, 376.
Cæsi: Kêkayas, tribe between the Indus and the Jamna, mentioned by Pliny, I, pt. i, 533.
Caffi: coffee plant, cultivated in Southern India, XXV, 162.
Cahola-baji: food plant, used as vegetable, XXV, 169.
Cairana: Portuguese sub-division, XIV, 44.
Cajanus Indicus: a food plant, XXV, 153.
Caju: timber tree, found along the coast, XXV, 53; a food plant, *id.* 150.
Cajuri: liquor-yielding tree, XXV, 134-135.
Calamoherpinæ: family of birds in Ratnágiri district, X, 78.
Calamus rotang: timber tree found in Southern *ghát*, XXV, 136.
Calcareous Shales: in Belgaum ditsrict, XXI, 25-26.
Calc-spar: in Bijápur district, XXIII, 61.
Calcutta: capture of (1756), XXVI, pt. i, 321.
Calico-printing: in Surat, II. 179; in Broach, *id.* 441; in Kaira, III, 15; in Ahmadábád, IV, 133; in Khándesh, XII, 230; in Násik, XVI, 175; in Belgaum, XXI, 347-348.
Calicut: visited by the Portuguese, I, pt. ii, 43.
Calingon: Point Godávari mentioned by Pliny, I, pt. i, 533.
Calliana: modern Kalyán, mentioned by Cosmos, I, pt. ii, 3.

Callings: *see* Occupation.
Calophyllum: *angustifolium tomentosum*, timber tree, XXV, 13; *inophillum*, *spurium*, *wightianum*, timber trees, *id.* 12; oil-yielding plants, *id.* 214.
Calosanthes Indica: timber tree, found in Konkan, Khándesh, XXV, 104; yields dyes, *id.* 248.
Calotropis gigantea: yields fermented drinks, found in South India, XXV, 211; fibrous plant, found in Konkan, *id.* 232; medicinal plant, *id.* 260; a sacred plant, *id.* 279, 282, 290, 291; *procera*, a fibrous plant, found in Dakhan and Gujarát, *id.* 233.
Calysaccion longifolium: timber tree found in Konkan and the *gháts*, XXV, 11; yields dyes, *id.* 241.
Cambay: Stambhatirtha, I, pt. i, 123; Kumárapála, repairs to, *id.* 182; Jain temple at, repaired by Kumárapála, 190; plundered by Alaf Khán's army, 205; sack of (1573), 220 and note 2, 224 and note 2, 225 and note 2; sack of (1347), 230, 232, 235; siege of, by Trimbakrao Dábháde, 306; Momin Khán appointed governor of, 311, 317; customs house at, 323; included in the Peshwá's share of tribute (1752), 334; failure of a Marátha attempt on (1753), 338, 398; interview of Rávji of Baroda with Governor Duncan at (1800), 412; Musalmán preacher of, 512, 513; its different names, 514; importation of horses into, 515; underground passage to, I, pt. ii, 13; north boundary of Lár, *id.* 22, 23; port of Gujarát, *id.* 25; gulf of, *id.* 310; *state*: boundaries, rivers, lakes, geology, climate, trees, crops, animals, census details, VI, 181-186; trade, its history (900-1900), imports, exports, *id.* 187, 198; precious stone workers, trade in Cambay stones, trade guilds, other manufactures, *id.* 198-209; money-lending, currency, prices, wages, weights, *id.* 209-210; history, origin of the name, Balharas (913), Chálukyás (942-1240), Vághelás (1240-1304), Ahmadábád kings (1400-1575), Mughals (1573-1730), the nawábs (1730-1880), *id.* 211-233; family tree of its chiefs, *id.* 233; administration of land, justice, police, revenue, post, instruction, *id.* 234-239.
City, its description, buildings and mosques, *id.* 240-241; struggle of the Marátha chiefs at (1725), VII, 170; head-quarters of Momin Khán (1737), *id.* 175; Gáikwár's intended attack on (1794), *id.* 200; settlement of Pársis in, Pársi traders in, relations of the Pársis of, with the Pársis of the Panjáb, IX, pt. ii, 186 and note 1, 188 note 4; copies of the *Vandidád* made at, *id.* 189 note 2; *port*, mosques at, IX, pt. ii, 2 note 1, 131 note 1; arrival of Musalmán missionaries at, *id.* 26 and note 1; arrival of Persian refugés, at (1723), (1726), (1757), *id.* 3 note 2; shrine of Pir Muhammadali at, *id.* 26 note 1; grand Imámbada at, *id.* 132; king of, converted to Islám by Mulla Muhammadali, *id.* 26 note 1; nawábs of, spread the Shiáh faith, *id.* 125; Gulf of, Muhammadan Arab expedition against the ports of (636), *id.* 1 note 1 continued on page 2; trade centre (800-1000), XIII, 429; Ráshtrakúta rule at (950), *id.* 435; mention of by Rashid-ud-din (1310), *id.* 437; Daulatábád trade centres at, (1343), *id.* 440; its dealings with Thána (1300-1500), *id.* 444; Barbosa's description of (1500-1670), *id.* 449; connected with Thána ports (1500 1670), *id.* 465; a large city with trade (1660-1710), *id.* 486.
Cambay Stones: carnelians, agates and other varieties, processes of manufacture, ornaments, polishers, trade guilds, trade, history, VI, 198-207.
Cambodia: note on the settlement of Hindus in, I, pt. i, 498-504; origin of the name Kamboja, *id.* 498 note 4; Bráhmanic dynasty of; inscriptions; embassy from the king of, to China (617), *id.* 499; aloes, *id.* 528; Bráhman influence in, IX, pt. i, 437; Bráhman and Buddhist details introduced into the literature and architecture of, *id.* 441.
Cambulana: a food plant, XXV, 159.
Camels: she-camel called Mátá Meri, or mother, is never ridden, IX, pt. i, 377; in Kathiáwár, VIII, 99; in Poona, XVIII, pt. i, 68; in Belgaum, XXI, 66; in Bijápur, XXIII, 65.
Cammuni: a famine plant, common in tropical parts, XXV, 202.
Camoens: Portuguese poet (1517-1579), mentions Angidiv under the name of Floating Island, XV, pt. ii, 253; celebrates the ravages of De Souza in Bhatkal territory in a poem, *id.* 273 note 3.
Camoleuga: a food plaut, XXV, 159.
Camp: description of a Maráthá, XVIII, pt. ii, 284 note 1; of the Mughal (1695), XXIII, 438-439, 649.
Campanulaceæ: an order of poisonous plants, XXV, 265.
Campbell: Captain, takes Kalyán and keeps it (1780), XIII, 506; *see* also XIV, 121.
Campbell: Mr. John, of Messrs. Scott McClelland & Co., constructed Tulsi Lake, Bombay, XIV, 365.
Campbell: Major-General, ordered up by General Wellesley to keep peace in the Southern Maráthá Country (1803), I, pt. ii, 663.
Campephaginæ: family of birds in Ratnágiri, X, 70.
Cámunda: grandson of Udayasimha (1203-1249), king of Bhinmál, I, pt. i, 471.
Canals: in Ahmadábád, IV, 50; in Ahmadnagar, XVII, 254-258; Mutha and Nira, in Poona, XVIII, pt. ii, 15-24; in Násik district, XVI, 94; in Satára district, XIX, 156; in Belgaum, XXI, 243-244; in Dhárwár, XXII, 263-265.
Canarese prosody: of Nágavarman, I, pt. ii, 344 note 5.
Canarins: black priests from Malabár, I, pt. ii, 86.
Canarium strictum: timber tree, found in Konkan, XXV, 40; yields gums and resins, *id.* 250.

Canathra : *see* Kanathra.
Canavalia : *ensiformis, mollis, Stocksii, turgida, virosa*, food-plants, XXV, 152.
Candragupta : I, pt. i, 532. *See* Chandragupta.
Cane : port, Hisn Ghoráb, on the way from India to Alexandra (A. D. 23-79), I, pt. i, 537.
Cane-work : at Kárwár, XV, pt. ii, 70 ; in Thána jail, XIII, 400.
Canidæ : family of wild animals in Ratnágiri, X, 45.
Cannabis : *Indica, sativa*, plants yielding fermented drinks, XXV, 211 ; fibrous plants, *id.* 233.
Canoes : in Thána, their cost, XIII, 343, 344, 721 ; in Kánara, XV, pt. ii, 61-62.
Canorein : Dr. Fryer's (1675) name for Sálsette island, XIV, 26.
Canthium : *parviflorum*, food plant in Southern Marátha Country, XXV, 162 ; *umbellatum*, timber tree, common in *gháts*, *id.* 87.
Canton : in China, Arabs and Persians in, Mobeds in, IX, pt ii, 185 note.
Cantra : food plant, XXV, 148.
Cape Gooseberry : food plant, XXV, 167.
Cape of Good Hope : discovery of, I, pt. ii, 43 ; gives importance to Madras ports, *id.* 64.
Capital : *see* All District Volumes under District Name.
Capitalia : identified with Mount Abu, I, pt. i, 534.
Capitalist : *see* All District Volumes under District Name.
Capparideæ : an order of timber trees, XXV, 4 ; of food plants, *id.* 145.
Capparis : *aphylla*, XXV, 4, 145 ; *brevispina*, *id.* 145, 291 ; *grandis*, *id.* 5 ; *Murraya*, *id.* 277 ; *Murrayana*, *id.* 145 ; *spinosa*, *id.* 145, 277 ; *Zeylanica*, *id.* 145, 160.
Caprimulgidœ : family of birds in Ratnágiri district, X, 63.
Capsicum frutescens : food plant, XXV, 167.
Captain Moor : description of Jejuri (1792) by, XVIII, pt. iii, 137 ; of Poona, *id.* 409-410.
Carallia integerrima : timber tree, found in *gháts*, XXV, 73.
Caralluma fimbriata : food plant, common in Dhárwár and Dakhan, XXV, 165.
Carambol : food plant, XXV, 148.
Caravel : sixteenth century craft, XIII, 723.
Caraway : food-plant, XXV, 161.
Car ceremony : performed in epidemic scaring, details of, part played by an exorcist in, IX, pt. i, 414-415. *See* Epidemic (Scaring).
Cardamoms : cultivation of, in Kánara, XV, pt. ii, 9-10 ; *see* also XXV, 176.
Cardiospermum Halicacabum : famine plant, XXV, 197.
Careya arborea : timber tree common in Konkan and Indápur, XXV, 78 ; fibrous plant, *id.* 232.
Car Festivals : in Kánara temples, XV, pt. i, 122-123 ; among Habbus, *id.* 247.
Cargo : derivation of the word, XIII, 724.
Caribal : Kárwár, XV, pt. ii, 111, 321.
Carica papaya : food plant, XXV, 157.
Carissa : *carandas, lanceolata, spinarum*, food plants, XXV, 265-266.
Carnac : Captain, Resident at Baroda (1811-1829), Governor of Bombay (1839-1841), VII, 216 (*see* also XIX, 311) ; raises Dhákji Dádaji to the minister's post at Baroda (1819), *id.* 231 ; his advice with regard to Govindráv and Takhatábái Gaikwár (1819), *id.* 232-233 ; settles Baroda affairs (1840), *id.* 249-251 ; his policy towards Navánagar (1811), *id.* 325 ; Gáikwár's claim for Broach revenue on the Peshwá, supported by (1815), *id.* 386.
Carnac, Mr. : accompanies the expedition to Poona (1778), XIII, 503 ; a party to the infamous treaty of Vádgáon (1779), *id.* 504 and note 2 ; *see* also XVIII, pt. ii, 263-264, 266.
Carnelians : precious stone in Cambay, VI, 198, 199 ; *see* also, I, pt. i, 78 note 1.
Carnivora : in Ratnágiri district, X, 44.
Carpentry : in Cutch, V, 125 ; in Baroda, VII, 158.
Carpet-making : in Násik, XVI, 169 ; in Cambay, VI, 208 ; in Khándesh, XII, 232 ; in Belgaum, XXI, 342, 343 ; in Bijápur, XXIII, 372 ; in Thána jail, XIII, 401 ; in Dhárwár, XXII, 378-379.
Carpet snakes : in Poona district, XVIII, pt. I, 78.
Carr : Captain, confined (1686), XXVI, pt. iii, 281.
Carriers : *see* All District Volumes under District Name.
Carrot : food plant grown in several districts, XXV, 161 ; *see* also XVIII, pt. ii, 56 ; XII, 171.
Cartage : rates of, in Panch Maháls, III, 248.
Carthamus tinctorius : food plant, XXV, 163 ; oil-yielding plant, *id.* 218 ; yields dyes, 246.
Carts : in Káthiáwár, VIII, 180 ; kinds of Khándesh, XII, 145 ; making of, *id.* 237 ; the use of (200-700), *id.* 489 note 2 ; in Poona (1836), XVIII, pt. ii, 9-10, 424 ; in Belgaum, XXI, 240 ; in Kolhápur, XXIV, 159.
Carum : *carui, copticum, petroselinum, Roxburghianum*, food plants, XXV, 161 ; *copticum*, oil-yielding plant, *id.* 223.
Caryophyllus aromaticus : food plant cultivated in Bombay, XXV, 156.
Caryota urens : timber tree, found in forests of Mahabaleshwar, Khandála and Konkan, XXV, 135 ; yields fermented drinks, *id.* 212 ; fibrous plant, *id.* 237.
Casaba : district between Bassein and Agáshi, I, pt. ii, 48.
Casearia : *graveolens*, XXV, 81, 265, 272 ; *tomentosa*, *id.* 81, 272 ; *ulmifera*, *id.* 265.
Cash Book : an account book, IX, pt. i, 83. *See* Rojmel.
Cáshi : a village in Thána, a Church at, XIV, 51.
Cashtan : I, pt. i, 530. *See* Chastana.
Caspian gates : three sets of, names of, IX, pt. i, 473 note 4.
Cassia : *alata, fistula, occidentalis, sophra, tora*, medicinal plants, XXV, 254 ; *auriculata, occidentalis, sophra, tora*, famine plants, *id.* 198 ; *auriculata, tora*, plants yielding dyes, *id.* 243, *fistula, florida, glauca, siamea, sumatrana*, timber trees, *id.* 63 ; *sophra, tora*, food plants, *id.* 153 ; *fistula, tora, id.* 289-292.

Cassana plant: vegetable poison, XXV, 270.
Castancda: *see* Castenheda.
Caste: distinguished from a tribe, IX, pt. i, 465; Vena causing confusion of, *id.* 434 note 9; Kanishka and Sakas did away with, *id.* 443 note 1; number of, in Gujarát province, *id.* p. xii; formation of, *id.* pp. xiii-xiv; social rank, *id.* p. xiv; entertainments, *id.* pp. xxv-xxix; process of forming, XIII, 65 note 1; theory and practice with regard to, Buddhist respect for, XIV, 129, 130; Gujar underlayer in Gujarát castes, I, pt. i, 4; legends of, *id.* 463-465.
Castenheda: Portuguese historian (1568), I, pt. i, 349; his mention of Anjidiv Moors, XV, pt. ii, 252.
Castle, Bombay: till 1672 only a fortified square house, enlarged (1672-1675); its strength in 1676-1698, in 1750, description of, in 1755, the fort demolished (1862-65), XXVI, pt. iii, 652-655.
Castor oil: its use in lever complaints (1770), XXVI, pt. iii, 558-559.
Castor seed: tillage of, in Poona district, XVIII, pt. ii, 45; in Sátára, XIX, 165.
Castro: John De, Portuguese viceroy, does not carry out his king's order to persecute Hindus and Musalmáns (1546), I, pt. ii, 59; makes treaties with Ahmadnagar and Bijánagar (1547), *id.* 46.
Casuarina equisetipolia: timber tree, XXV, 132; plant yielding dyes, *id.* 249.
Casuarineæ: an order of timber trees, XXV, 132.
Cat: beliefs about; use of its dung in driving away evil spirits; witches appear in the form of; beliefs about the sight of, IX, pt. i, 377.
Catalan Map: of A. D. 1375, I, pt. ii, 4.
Catavari: a food plant, XXV, 180.
Catechu: manufacture of, in Khándesh, XII, 227; in Kánara, XV, pt. ii, 71-72; near Kárwár (1772), *id.* 141; near Ankola (1801), *id.* 149, 259.
Caterpillars: damage to rice crop in Bombay island by (1736), XXVI, pt. iii, 518-519.
Cathedral: Portuguese, at Cheul, XI, 272; at Thána (1634), XIII, 462; at Bombay (1715), *id.* 489; at Bassein (1533), of St. Joseph, XIV, 29, 38; the remains of a, at Mandapeshvar, *id.* 223-225.
Cathedral cave: at Kánheri, XIV, 122, 166-169.
Cathedral rocks: XIV, 51, 220, 230. *See* Malangad.
Catholic Church: at Kirkee, XVIII, pt. iii, 381; in Bombay (1733), XXVI, pt. iii, 529.
Catholic priests: expelled from Bombay for their treason (1720), XXVI, pt. i, 152-158.
Cat Plague: in Poona (1883), XVIII, pt. iii, 71-72.
Cats: civet and toddy, in Ratnágiri district, X, 45.
Cattle diseases: in Poona district, XVIII, pt. i, 69; in Surat, II, 266; in Broach, *id.* 534; in Ahmadábád, IV, 228; in Ratnágiri, X, 239, 264, 265, 294; in Sávantvádi, *id.* 461; in Kolába, XI, 238; in Khándesh, XII, 338; in Thána, XIII, 669; in Kánara, XV, pt. ii, 221; in Násik, XVI, 342; in Ahmadnagar, XVII, 583-584; in Sátára, XIX, 418-420; in Sholápur, XX, 388; in Belgaum, XXI, 492; in Dhárwár, XXII, 624; in Bijápur, XXIII, 498-499.
Cattle plague: in Cutch, V, 175.
Cattle-pox: plague, its goddess; quieting ceremony of, details of, IX, pt. i, 372.
Caulukya: I, pt. i, 526. *See* Cháulukya.
Causeways: of Elephanta, XIV, 61; Lady Jamsetji, *id.* 18, 21; Sion, *id.* 211 (see also XIII, 323); Máhim and Chembhur, XIII, 322, 517.
Cavalry: Shiváji's, XIX, 240-241.
Cave Architecture: used under the Chálukyas for Puránic religion, I, pt. ii, 192.
Caves: Buddhistic, I, pt. ii, 3; Ajanta, Chandansár, Chiplun, Dábhol, Elephanta, Elura, Gavháne-Velgaum, Jambrug, Jogeshvari, Kánheri, Khed, Kondáne, Kondivte, Kuda, Mágáthan, Mandapeshvar, Pál, Sangameshvar, Váde Pádel, *id.* 9; Bráhmanical (Mandapeshvar and Mágáthan), *id.* 11; Kol, *id.* 12; Kondivte, *id.* 27; at Kánheri and Junnar, *id.* 174, 541, 542; in Káthiáwár, at Bhimora, VIII, 399; on Sána hill, *id.* 647; Chiplun and Kol (B. C. 200-A. D. 50), X, 192, 326; Hasta Dongar, *id.* 370; in Kolába, at Cheul, XI, 301-302; at Pále, *id.* 316, 345-349; at Kuda, *id.* 332-342; on Rámdharan hill, *id.* 377; Kánheri, really Buddhistic, XIII, 404; at Kánheri, Násik, Kárli and Junnar, grants by Yavans to, *id.* 414; at Lonád, *id.* 421; at Kánheri, *id.* 455; Kánheri cave (iii) converted to a church, *id.* 461 note 1; Du Perron's visit to Kánheri, *id.* 498; Forbes visits Kánheri (1774), *id.* 501; in Thána at Ambivli, XIV, 9; list of, *id.* 10; at Dhák, *id.* 55; Elephanta, *id.* 60-94; at Gorakhgad, *id.* 101; Kánheri, *id.* 164-189: at Karanja, *id.* 194; Kondivti, *id.* 202-209; at Lonád, *id.* 213-216; at Mandapeshvar, *id.* 223; at Poinsar, *id.* 299; at Sanjan Peak, *id.* 305; at Virár, *id.* 382-383; on Padan hill, *id.* 389; at Kalyán, *id.* 398; Pulu Sonála, *id.* 401; in Násik, XVI, 417 note 1; Ankai Tankai Bráhmanical, XVI, 421; Jain, *id.* 422-424; Chámbhár Jain, *id.* 426-428; *id.* 422 note 5, 445; Sitá's, *id.* 515; Lakshman's, *id.* 538; Pándulena Buddhist, *id.* 539-639, 644, 661; Buddhist and Bráhmanical in Poona, (A. D. 100-200), XVIII, pt. ii, 212-213; at Bedsa, XVIII, pt. iii, 105-108; Bhája, *id.* 109-114; Gárodi, *id.* 129-130; Junnar, *id.* 163-216; Lohogad, *id.* 351; Ganeshkhind and Pánchálesh var, *id.* 368, 385-386; Sinde, *id.* 440-441; Vehárgaon, *id.* 454-464; in Sátára, at Bhose, XIX, 456; at Devráshtra, *id.* 463-465; at Divashi Khurd, *id.* 466; at Karád, *id.* 477-480; at Kusrud, *id.* 489; at Mahábaleshvar, *id.* 510; on Mallikarjun hill, *id.* 522; on Pándavgad fort, *id.* 536; at Páteshvar, *id.* 540-541; at Rájpuri, *id.* 550; at Shirval, *id.* 588; at Takári and Tamkane, *id.* 589; at Wái, *id.* 613-614; at Gokarn, XV, pt. ii, 293.
Cave Temples: believed to be the work of the Pándavas, I, pt. ii, 27; Vaishnáva, at Vátápi

completed in the time of Kirtivarman, I, *id.* 192, 345.
Cay : Colonel, English commander of the expedition to Poona (1778), XVIII, pt. ii, 263-264.
Cazados : Portuguese married soldiers, I, pt. ii, 55.
Cedrela toona : medicinal plant, XXV, 258; fodder, *id.* 278.
Celastrineæ : an order of timber tree, XXV, 48 ; of oil-yielding plants, *id.* 216 ; of vegetable poisons, *id.* 264.
Celastrus paniculata : oil-yielding plant, common on *gháts* and hilly parts in Konkan, XXV, 216.
Celery : food plant, XXV, 160.
Cells : in Thána, at Elephanta, XIV, 76 ; Jain, at Tungár near Bassein, *id.* 369 ; at Kalyán *id.* 397.
Celosia : *argentea*, food plant, available in rainy season, XXV, 170 ; a sacred plant, *id.* 292 ; a famine plant *cristata*, *id.* 203.
Celtis Roxburghii : timber tree common in the forest of Konkan, XXV, 131.
Cemetery : *see* Graveyards.
Census : details of Gujarát, total population (A. D. 1891-1901), IX, pt. i, pp. vii-ix ; religious sects (A. D. 1872), *id.* 530-531 ; chief divisions of classes, strength and distribution (A. D. 1891), of bards and actors, Bháts, Chárans, Gandbraps, Bhaváyás, Turis, *id.* 207 ; Bráhmans, *id.* 3 ; craftsmen, *id.* 177 ; depressed classes, Bhangias, Dhedas, Garaudas, Khálpas, Sindhvas, *id.* 331 ; early tribes, Bhils, Chodhras, Dhundias, Dublas, Gamtas, Konknas, Náiks, Várlis, *id.* 290 ; Gujar population (A. D. 1881 census), *id.* 481 ; herdsmen, Ahirs, Bharváds, Mers, Rabáris, *id.* 264 ; husbandmen, Káchhias, Kanbis, Mális, Pateliás, Sagars, Sathvaras, *id.* 153 ; Káthis, *id.* 252 ; Kolis, *id.* 237 ; personal servants, Dhobis, Hajáms, Khavás, *id.* 228 ; Rájputs, strength, chiefship, *id.* 123 ; traders, Vánias, Bhansális, Bhátias, Luhánas, *id.* 69 ; writers, Brahamakshatris, Káyasths, Prabhus, *id.* 55 ; Musalmán population, according to occupation (1872 census), IX, pt. ii, 118-121 ; according to sects (1891 census), *id.* 1 ; strength of the Pársis in 1806, 1816, 1817, 1825, 1835, 1852, population according to the census of 1872, 1881, 1891, IX, pt. ii, 183, 199 note 2 ; *see* also All District Volumes under District Name.
Central India : earliest traces of the Ráshtrakútas obtained from, I, pt. ii, 384 ; Kalachuris of, *id.* 396, 468, 469, 470.
Central Provinces : Ráshtrakútas' original place Lattanur, most probably to be found in, I, pt. ii, 384.
Centropodinae : family of birds in Ratnágiri district, X, 68.
Cephalandra Indica : food plant, XXV, 159.
Ceratonia siliqua : food plant, indigenous in Spain, Algeria and Syria, XXV, 154.
Cerbera : *odollam Thevetia*, timber tree common on salt grounds along the coasts, XXV, 99 ; *odollam Thevetia*, vegetable poison, *id.* 266-267.
Cereals : cultivation of, in Poona district, XVIII, pt. ii, 35-41 ; in Kolhápur, XXIV, 164-168.
Ceropegia bulbosa : food plant, XXV, 165.
Cesses : fortification, levied in Bombay (1758), XXVI, pt. ii, 323-324 ; continued (1775), *id.* 400 ; imposed by the Portuguese, I, pt ii, 53 ; in Kolába, XI, 171, 172 and note 3, 173 and note 2, 182 and note 7, 183 note 2, 184 and notes 3 and 5, 185 and note 3, 187 and note 1, 188 and note 1, 191, 196, 453-456 ; Marátha, in Khándesh, XII, 268 ; in Kánara, XV, pt. ii, 137, 157, 158 and footnote 1 ; in Sátára, XIX, 349.
Cessions of territory : to Raghunáthráv by Damáji (1763), VII, 186 ; by the Gáikwár to the British (1802), *id.* 206, 387 ; in 1808, *id.* 213 ; by Anandráv and Fatesing Gaikwár (1817), *id.* 226-227.
Cevul : modern Cheul, XI, 273.
Ceylon : I, pt. ii, 28, 146, 207 ; Hemádri is believed to have taken the Modi-writing from, *id.* 249 ; conquest of, *id.* 324 ; king of, attacked by Vikramáditya VI, *id.* 442, 536 ; Babylonian trade with (B. C. 606-561), XIII, 404 note 3 ; Egyptian trade with (250 A. D.), *id.* 418 ; Indians in (550), *id.* 420 ; cotton, cloth exports to, *id.* 430 ; pearls and cinnamon sent from (1300-1500), *id.* 445 ; trade relations with Thána and Cheul (1500-1670), *id.* 464, 465 ; Portuguese driven by the Dutch from (1656), *id.* 473 ; Vijaya, mythical conqueror of, XIV, 317. *See* Simhála.
Chabbi : village in Dhárwár, temple and inscription at, XXII, 659 ; *see* also I, pt. ii, 307.
Chabhária : *see* Samádhials.
Chábuk Sawár : Musalmán jockey ; horse-trainer, IX, pt. ii, 97-98, 123, 172 note 1.
Chách : ruler in Sind (631-670), I, pt. i, 519.
Chách : disciple of Nur-Satágur, kills Núr-Satágur, IX, pt. ii, 38.
Chachána : táluka, in Káthiáwár, VIII, 402.
Chachiga : Modh Vánia of Dhandhuka, father of Hemachandra, I, pt. i, 191.
Chách Námah : Arabic history of Chách, I, pt. i, 519 ; *see* also IX, pt. ii, 1 note 1, *id.* 69.
Chackrabenda : famine plant, XXV, 194.
Chadawwás : Delhi shoes, IX, pt. ii, 100.
Chádchat : state, in Pálanpur, V, 281, 333 ; *see* also IX, pt. i, 126.
Chaganjang : name of white races in Yunnan (1290), I, pt. i, 501.
Chaganlál : Gujarát name, the word Chaghán seems to remain in, IX, pt. i, 484 note 1 ; *see* Chaghán.
Chaghán : originally meaning white, the name Chohán may perhaps be same as, IX, pt. i, 483 ; the word remains in the Gujarát name Chaganlál, *id.* 484 note 1.
Chaghatai : Tartar-Turkish dialect, IX, pt. ii, 9 note 1.
Chaghtáikhán : son of Changizkhán ; Chughadda Mughals called after him, IX, pt. ii, 9, etc., note 1.
Chahad : pass in Thána district, XIV, 11 note 3.

Cháhada : son of Udaya and younger brother of Báhada, rises to a high position under Kumárapála, I, pt. i, 170 ; leads an expedition against Sámbhár ; title of Rájagharatta conferred on him, grants half a village, *id.* 187.
Chailletiaceæ : an order of timber trees, XXV, 47.
Chailletia gelonioides : timber tree common at Rámghát and Southern Konkan, XXV, 47.
Chain Vipers : snakes in Poona district, XVIII, pt. i, 83.
Chaitya Cave : at Ajanta, inscription on, I, pt. ii, 354 note 3.
Chaityas : temple caves, I, pt. ii, 12 ; Buddhist tombs of worship, *id.* 173.
Chákan : town in Poona, its fort and history, XVIII, pt. iii, 121-123 ; military post (1443), XVIII, pt. ii, 217 ; captured (1490) by Malik Ahmad, *id.* 220 ; (1647) by Shiváji, *id.* 226 ; (1662) by the Mughals, *id.* 230 ; restored (1667) to Shiváji, *id.* 235 ; again captured (1671) by the Mughals, *id.* 236 ; Bábáráv Phadke, commandant of the Peshwa's household troops, imprisoned (1796) in, *id.* 273 ; siege (1818) of, *id.* 303 ; *see* also I, pt. ii, 588, 589, 611.
Chákana : Western Chálukya king Someśvara IV's officer, I, pt. ii, 465.
Chákariát : alienated lands in Baroda, VII, 349.
Chakárzan : widow re-marriage, form of, IX, pt. ii, 238 and note 2.
Chákasman : town in Poona District, temple, XVIII, pt. iii, 123-124.
Chakavál : tribe of Rájpúts, Musalmán prisoners of war enrolled among, by Mulrája II, IX, pt. i, 444.
Cháki : caste of oil-pressers in Cutch, V, 127.
Chákirája : Ganga prince, I, pt. ii, 211, 303 note 1, 400.
Chakki-no-áro : a place of interest in Panch Maháls, III, 303.
Chaklási : town in Kaira district, III, 167.
Chakora : mountain, Gotamiputra ruled over, I, pt. ii, 149.
Chakotar : citron, in Poona district, XVIII, pt. i, 44.
Chakra ; Buddhist wheel cut on Padan hill in Thána district, XIV, 102, 389.
Chakragoṭṭa : in Málwa, laid waste by Ereyanga, I, pt. ii, 494 ; burnt by Vishnuvardhana, *id.* 496 and note 2, 497.
Chakrakota : fortress in Dhárá territory, marched against by Vikramáditya II, also styled VI, I, pt. ii, 215, 442.
Chakravartin : emperor, I, pt. ii, 555.
Chakravartis : Jain saints, I, pt. i, 451 note 3.
Chakreshvar : Sopára lake and temple, XIV, 327, 336.
Cháks : race of sun-worshippers in Kashmír, their conversion to Islám, IX, pt. ii, 39.
Chakwit : food plant, XXV, 169.
Chaladuttaranga : *biruda* (title) of the Ganga Chief Márasimha, I, pt. ii, 305.
Cháli : tenure in Bijápur, XXIII, 469 and note 1.
Chaligeni : tenure-at-will, in Kánara district, XV, pt. ii, 187.
Chálikars : privileged land-holders under Bijápur and Maráthás in Dhárwár, XXII, 442 and note 2, 447-449.
Chalikya or Chálkya : *see* Chaulukya and Chálukya.
Chálisgaon : sub-division of Khándesh district, area, boundaries, aspect, climate, water, soil, holdings, survey details, survey results, stock, crops, people, XII, 2, 353-358 ; *town*, *id.* 254, 437 ; *see* also I, pt. ii, 147, 244.
Chálke : Marátha family name, I, pt. ii, 224.
Chalk marks : Pársi beliefs in, IX, pt. ii, 209 note 2, 229, 231.
Chalkya : *see* Chálukya.
Chalky Shale Beds : in Bijápur district, XXIII, 32-33.
Challesvara : temple of, at Átakur in Mysore, I, pt. ii, 421.
Chalmati : village in Dhárwár district, temple at, XXII, 659.
Chálukya : Dakhan dynasty (A. D. 552-973) of Bádámi, I, pt. i, 156 ; early trace in Gujarát of its rule, come from the Dakhan and establish themselves in Gujarát, their grants, genealogy, *id.* 107-112, 466, 467 ; *see* also I, pt. ii, 178, 277 ; its dominions, *id.* 281, 385 ; dynastic name, *id.* 336 note 3 ; record, *id.* 337 note 2 ; family, *id.* 342, 391 ; stock, *id.* 427 note 3 ; possible origin of the name, XV, pt. ii, 80 ; connection of the dynasty with Kánara, *id.* 80-83. *See* Chálukyas of Bádámi.
Chálukya : dynasty of Kalyána, I, pt. ii, 459, 493, 518 ; progenitor of the Chálukyas, *id.* 278 note 1 ; rule of, in Kánara, XV, pt. ii, 85-89 ; in Khándesh, XII, 241. *See* Chálukyas of Kalyána.
Chálukya-Bhima I : Eastern Chálukya king (888-918), I, pt. ii, 412.
Chálukya Bhima II : Eastern Chálukya king (934-945), I, pt. ii, 417.
Chálukyagiri : mountain, Gauri's temple on, I, pt. ii, 340 and note 4.
Chálukyas : of Kalyána or Kalyáni, I, pt. ii, 143, 211-224, 343, 426-467, 549 ; distinct from the Chálukyas of Bádámi, *id.* 211 ; their connection with the Chálukyas of Bádámi, *id.* 335 note 1, 378 and note 3, 379 ; their genealogy, *id.* 379, 436 ; their crests and banners, *id.* 299 note 4 ; dynasty begins with Vikramáditya IV, *id.* 427 ; Kalyána becomes the capital in the reign of Someśvara I, *id.* 440 ; Vikramáditya II also styled VI is the greatest of their monarchs, who abolishes the Śaka era and establishes his own, *id.* 217 ; their power declines in the reigns of Jagadekamalla and Tailapa II, *id.* 222 ; Bhillama, the Yádava, seizes the northern and eastern portions of the kingdom, *id.* 518 ; Bijjala, the general of Tailapa II, also styled Taila III, usurps the throne, *id.* 222, 472, 475, 501 ; Someśvara IV revives with the help of Brahma or Bomma the sovereignty for a short time at Annigeri, *id.* 223, 463, 489 ; Vira-Ballála II acquires supremacy, and the dynasty ends, *id.* 223.

503; branch of the family in Southern Konkan, *id.* 223; religious and social condition of the people; Buddhism, Jainism, Puránic religion, codification of the civil and religious law, *id.* 228-229; *see* Vikramáditya IV, Taila II, Satyáśraya, Vikramáditya V, Jayasimha II, Someśvara I, Someśvara II, Vikramáditya VI, Someśvara III, Jagadekamalla II, Taila III and Someśvara IV; rule of, in Thána district, XIII, 435; in Dhárwár, XXII, 393-396; in Bijápur, XXIII, 387-389. *See* Chálukya of Kalyána.

Chálukyas of Bádámi: I, pt. ii, 143, 180-192, 277, 280, 281, 287 note 1, 315, 335, 336, 345 note 4, 383, 385, 387, 391; foundation of the dynasty of, *id.* 178, 335 and note 1; various forms of the name, *id.* 336 note 3; legendary origin; Ayodhyá, their original seat, *id.* 339 and notes 2 and 3, 340 and note 1; their genealogy, *id.* 336 and note 2, 337, 381; irregular succession, *id.* 346 note 4; crest and banner and other articles of their royal insignia, *id.* 299 note 4, 341 note 1; use Saka era, *id.* 295; authentic names in the family of, *id.* 342; abeyance and recovery (655) of their sovereignty, *id.* 318, 319, 324, 362, 363; chief enemies of Mahendravarman I, Pallava king, *id.* 316 note 5, 350; their hostilities begin in the reign of Pulikeśin II, *id.* 329, 341; separated into Western Chálukyas of Bádámi and Eastern Chálukyas of Vengi (615), *id.* 335 note 1, 352; Hiuen Tsiang's account of Maháráshtra under them, *id.* 184-185, 353-355; establish a branch in Southern Gujarát, *id.* 186-187, 188, 311; overwhelmed by the Ráshtrakútas, *id.* 190, 336, 378, 385, 389; side branch, comes in power (973), *id.* 190, 336, 378; extent of their kingdom, *id.* 341 note 2, 382; Vishnu, their family god; tolerate and patronise Śaivism and also Jainism and Buddhism, *id.* 191-192, 338; Puranic side of Bráhmanism receives a great development and cave architecture comes to be used for the purposes of Puranic religion, *id.* 192; their record, *id.* 322, 327, 427 note 3; Vengi or Eastern branch of; their territory, *id.* 341 note 2; their king burns the city of Ráshtrakúta Krishna II, *id.* 384 note 4; builds the wall of Málkhed at the desire of Ráshtrakúta Govinda III, *id.* 403; their records, *id.* 310, 336 note 3, 337 note 2, 351, 412, 453. *See* Pulakeśi I, Kirtivarman, Mángalisa, Pulakeśi II, Vishnuvardhana, Jayasimha-Chandráditya, Adityavarman, Vikramáditya I, Vinayáditya, Vijayáditya, Vikramáditya II and Kirtivarman II; their rule in Ratnágiri and Sávantvádi (600 A. D.), X, 192, 193, 372, 439, 465; rulers in Cambay (950), VI, 214; in Násik district, XVI, 184; in Poona district, XVIII, pt. ii, 214 note 1; in Belgaum, XXI, 353 and note 2, 354; in Dhárwár, XXII, 391; in Bijápur, XXIII, 379-386.

Chálukya-Vikramakála: (1076-1077), I, pt. ii, 447. *See* Chálukya-Vikramavarsha.

Chálukya-Vikramavarsha: I, pt. ii, 447, 463.

Chalvádi: caste of beggars in Belgaum district, XXI, 190: Mhár sacristans in Bijápur district, XXIII, 239; caste in Kánara district, XV, pt. i, 364-366; in Dhárwár district, XXII, 186.

Chámaladevi: wife of Tailapa II, the Hángal Kádamba, I, pt. ii, 559, 562.

Chámanda: Ratta of Saundatti, I, pt. ii, 455; officer of Jayakarna, the Western Chálukya king, *id.* 554.

Chámar: caste of curriers in Káthiáwár, VIII, 157.

Chamardi: táluka in Káthiáwár, VIII, 403.

Chambadi: timber tree, common in Bombay and Konkan, XXV, 107.

Chambal: river in Central India, I, pt. ii, 135.

Chambal: timber tree, common in Konkan, XXV, 103.

Chambari: famine plant, XXV, 202.

Chambeli: jasmin, IX, pt. ii, 150.

Chambhar: pass in Kolába district, XI, 115.

Chámbhár: caste of shoe-makers in Ratnágiri district, X, 129, *id.* 141; in Sávantvádi, *id.* 415; in Koláha and Janjira, XI, 64, 414; in Khándesh, XII, 114, 236; in Thána, XIII, 190; in Násik, XVI, 68, 71; in Ahmadnagar, XVII, 165-168; in Poona, XVIII, pt. i, 326-331; in Sátára, XIX, 81-83; in Sholápur, XX, 93; in Belgaum, XXI, 191; in Dhárwár, XXII, 221; in Bijápur, XXIII, 279-280; in Kolhápur, XXIV, 109-110.

Chámbhár lena: Jain caves near Násik, XVI, 426-428, 537.

Chamboli: food plants, XXV, 154.

Chambuli: fibrous plant, common in Khándesh, Thal and other *ghâts*, XXV, 232.

Chámdor: I, pt. ii, 231.

Chameli: timber tree, XXV, 99.

Chamgár: caste of shoe-makers in Kánara district, XV, pt. i, 355.

Champa: timber tree, XXV, 2; a sacred plant, *id.* 289; near the tomb of Saint Mussa at Ahmadábád, its holiness, IX, pt. ii, 123 note 2.

Chámpáner: deserted city in Panch Mahals district, history and remains of, III, 304; attacked by Ahmad I of Gujarát (1418), I, pt. i, 237; taken by Máhmad Begáda and made his capital under the name of Mahummadábád (1484), *id.* 247; *see* also IX, pt. ii, 187 note 3; the Mirzas take possession of, after A. D. 1568, IX, pt. ii, 10; given to Piláji Gáikwár (1725), VII, 170; captured by Bande (1727), *id.* 172; captured by the Maráthás (1728), I, pt. i, 308, 367, 368, 391-392; Násik Támbats said to have come from, XVI, 145. *See* Chapaner.

Champávati: traditional name of Cheul, XI, 269, 270 note 1.

Champavats: Márwár chiefs' claim to be, IX, pt. i, 488.

Champo: sacred tree, worship of, IX, pt. i, 383.

Chámtha: caste of dancers in Káthiáwár, VIII, 159.

Chámunda or Chámund: goddess in Márwár, IX, pt. ii, pp. xxxvi, 16, 136, 205; shrines of, I, pt. i, 449, 457-458; one of the Pleiades, I, pt. ii, 337 note 4.

Chamunda: pass near Ajmer, IX, pt. i, 487.

Chámunda : Chávadá king (A. D. 880-908), I, pt. i, 154, 155 ; son of Mularája Chaulukya, slays in fight Dvárappa and Bárappa, *id.* 159; his reign (A. D. 997-1010) ; instals his son Vallabha ; goes on pilgrimage to Benáres, is insulted by the Málwa king, *id.* 162 ; the family stock of Hemachandra, *id.* 191 ; ruler of Vanthali, killed by his brother-in-law Viradhaval Vághela, *id.* 200.

Chámundaráya : minister ofRáchamalla, the Western Ganga prince, and writer of the *Chámundaráya-Purána*, I, pt. ii, 307, *id.* 332.

Chámundaráya-Purána : written by Chámundaráya, minister ofRáchamallá, the Western Ganga chief, I, pt. ii, 307.

Chánasama : a town in Baroda with a very large Jain temple, VII, 608.

Chánch : island in Káthiáwár, VII, 66 ; vernacular word for piracy derived from, *id.* 403.

Chand : Chohán, bard, IX, pt. i, 484, 486 note 8.

Chánda : ancestor of the Navsári priests, IX, pt. ii, 221.

Chanda : timber tree, common in the *gháts*, XXV, 124.

Chandadanda : officer of Pulikeśi II, takes Puri, I, pt. i, 107 ; *see* also I, pt. ii, 14 ; defeats the Mauryas, XIII, 420.

Chandadanda : Pallava king of Kanchi, defeated by Ravivarman Kadamba, I, pt. ii, 289, 291 note 1, 322.

Chandála : menials, I, pt. i, 531 ; treatment of, by Buddhists, XIV, 129, 130.

Chandaladevi : Chandralekhá, wife of the Western Chálukya Vikramáditya II, also styled VI, I, pt. ii, 218, 449, 546, 547.

Chandaladevi : wife of the Ratta chieftain Lakshmideva I, also called Chandrike and Chandrikádevi, I, pt. ii, 551-556.

Chandalakabbe: wife of the Western Chálukya king Someśvara I, also called Chandrikádevi, I, pt. ii, 438.

Chandan : sandalwood tree, found in several districts, XXV, 133, 204, XVIII, pt. i, 44 ; is held sacred, IX, pt. i, 384.

Chandansár : village in Thána district, caves at, I, pt. ii, 9.

Chandan-Vandan : Mahádev hill spurr in Sátára, XIX, 7 ; twin-forts, *id.* 10 ; taken (1701) by the Mughals, *id.* 252 ; taken (1707) by Sháhu, *id.* 253 ; fort, details, description, history, *id.* 458-460.

Chanda Sáheb : imprisoned in Sátára (1741), XIX, 283-284 note 1, 574, 577.

Chandasri Sátakarni : identified with Chatushparna Sátakarni, I, pt. ii, 156.

Chandavar : old town in Kárwár, its history, Portuguese factory at (1678, 1701), XV, pt. ii, 277, 52, 53, 133, 311 ; seat of a chief (1330-1480), *id.* 98.

Chandávat-Bads : Rájpúts, said to be Gurjjars, IX, pt. i, 495.

Chánd Bibi : daughter of Hussain Nizám Sháh, married to Ali Ádil Sháh of Bijápur (1564), I, pt. ii, 645 ; confined (1471) in the fort of Sátára by Háji Kishwar Khán ; released by Yeklás Khán, *id.* 647 (*see* also XIX, 229, 574) ; defends Ahmadnagar against the Mughals (1595) ; murdered by the soldiers of Ahmadnagar (1600), *id.* 624 ; *see* also XXIII, 420-421, 421 note 3, 424 note 2 ; well of, in Bijápur city, *id.* 638.

Chandela : dynasty in Bundelkhand, I, pt. i, 178.

Chandelás : division of Gujars, IX, pt. i, 487.

Chanderi : fort in Thána district, XIV, 51.

Chandeshwar : shrine of, near Bhinmál, I, pt. i, 452 and note 1.

Chandgad : village in Belgaum district, XXI, 552 ; I, pt. ii, 568 ; hill fort, XXIV, 7.

Chandhari : a village officer in Cutch, V, 101-102.

Chandi : goddess, IX, pt. i, p. xxxv, 138.

Chandidevi : shrine of, near Bhinmál, I, pt. ii, 452.

Chandipáth : Sanskrit work containing prayers to goddess Chandi, IX, pt. i, 138, 532.

Chandia, or Chandish Mahádev : temple of, at Bhinmál, I, pt. i, 462, 463.

Chandkavte : village in Bijápur district, temples at, XXIII, 644-645.

Chánd Khán : illegitimate brother of Sultán Bahádur of Gujarát, is supported by the Portuguese (1532), I, pt. i, 347, 367.

Chánd Khán : name of a vow-receiving *ginn* or spirit, IX, pt. ii, 130.

Chándkhed : village in Poona district, XVIII, pt. iii, 123.

Chándli : *see* Sisáng.

Chándli : hill in Sátára district, XIX, 10.

Chándod Kanyáli : a town, a holy place on the banks of the Narbada in Baroda, VII, 559-560 ; *see* also IX, pt. i, 28, 549.

Chandola : reservoir in Ahmadábád, IV, 17.

Chandor : sub-division of Násik district, its boundaries, area, aspect, climate, water, history, land revenue, stock, holdings, crop and people, XVI, 407-413, 211 ; survey of (1840-1842), *id.* 218-220 ; revision survey (1871-1874), *id.* 257-264 ; town, mints, population, fort and history, *id.* 428-431, 441.

Chandor : hill range and pass in Násik district, XVI, 130 ; I, pt. ii, 355, 512. *See* Sátmálás.

Chandor Yádavs : kings in Násik district (850-1060), XVI, 185, 430.

Chandra : I, pt. ii, 511. *See* Soma Karád Siláhára, *id.* 545.

Chandra : the moon, worshipped as a planet, IX, pt. i, 392.

Chandra : vegetable poison, common in Konkan and Goa, XXV, 267, 274.

Chandráditya : Mularája's ancestor, I, pt. i, 157.

Chandráditya : Pulakeśi or Pulikesin II's second son, I, pt. ii, 185, 186 ; his charter, *id.* 363 ; his wife's grant at Nerúr, *id.* 185, 352, 365 ; and at Kochrem, *id.* 366.

Chandráditya : Kolhápur or Karád Siláhára prince, I, pt. ii, 254, 545, 546.

Chandrádityapura : town, modern Chándor, I, pt. ii, 231, 512 ; *see* also XVI, 185 and note 4, 430.

Chandragad : fort in Kolába district, XI, 269.

Chandragupta : founder of the Maurya dynasty (B.C. 319), I, pt. i, 13-14 ; "Introduction to the Early History of the Dakhan," I, pt. ii, ii ; extent of his dominions, *id.* 155, 157 ;

his relations with the successors of Alexander the Great, *id.* 162, 277, 284; lineage of, *id.* 578, 579, 580, 582, 584.
Chandragupta: Ráshtrakúta officer, I, pt. ii, 413.
Chandragupta I: third Gupta king (A. D. 349-369), I, pt. i, 61, 67; *see* also I, pt. ii, 580.
Chandragupta II: fifth Gupta king (A. D. 396-415), inscriptions, coins, founded Gupta era (291), I, pt. i, 65-67, 86, 129; son and successor of Samudragupta, I, pt. ii, 361 note 3; defeat of stranger leaders by, IX, pt. i, 444, 448, 453; power of the Kushans broken by, *id.* 491.
Chandrajot: physic-nut in Khándesh district, XII, 153.
Chandrakánta: or moon-stone, I, pt. ii, 437, note 5.
Chandralekhá: *see* Chandaládevi.
Chandramauli: moon-crowned, name for Shiv, IX, pt. i. 397.
Chandramil: old town, Chola, king of, XXIV, 219.
Chandraprabha: eighth Jain *tirthankar*, figure of, in Chakreshvar temple at Sopára, XIV, 337.
Chandrapura: identified with Chandávar near Gokarna, I, pt. i, 171 and note 1; *see* also I, pt. ii, 537, 568.
Chandraraja: third Kolhápur Siláhára prince, I, pt. ii, 254.
Chandrarão More: Jávli chief, history of the family (1653), XIX, 230-231; assassinated by Shiváji, *id.* 232-233, 470.
Chandrasen: Kshatriya king of Oudh; Káyasth Prabhus claim descent from, IX, pt. i, 68.
Chandrasen Jádhav: Dhanáji's son, his quarrel with his father's kárkún Báláji Vishvanáth; is defeated at Deur by Haibatráo Nimbálkar under the orders of Sháhu; retires to Kolhápur and thence to Nizám-ul-Mulk and obtains from him Bálki in *jághir*, I, pt. ii, 598; Sháhu's commander-in-chief (1710), XVIII, pt. ii, 241; *see* also XX, 254, 256.
Chandra S'ri: Andhrabhritya prince (208-211), coins of, I, pt. ii, 166, 168.
Chandrauli; *see* Chandrávati.
Chandrávati: in Pálanpur, ruins of an ancient city at, history of, V, 339-341; visited by Kumárapála, I, pt. i, 185, 188; capital of Visaládeva, 204; Parmára possession, 470; settlement of Pársis in, IX, pt. ii, 189.
Chandravansa: clan, started by Vachha, IX, pt. i, 450.
Chándráyan: a moon-vow, details of, IX, pt. i, 400; *see* Planet, Moon.
Chandrika: poisonous plant common in Konkan and Goa, XXV, 267.
Chandrikádevi: wife of the Western Chálukya king Somes'vara I, I, pt. ii, 438. *See* Chandalakabbe.
Chandrikádevi: wife of the Ratta chieftain Lakshmideva I, I, pt. ii, 556. *See* Chandaládevi.
Chandrike: I, pt. ii, 556. *See* Chandaládevi and Chandrikádevi.
Chandrya: pass in Násik district, XVI, 129.
Chandugideva: officer of the Kalachurya king Ahavamalla, I, pt. ii, 487, 489, 570.
Chandúl: Indian lark, IX, pt. ii, 99.
Chandúl: XXV, 234.
Chándvad: old rupee, X, 154.
Changa A'sa: *Dáwar*, religious layman, works miracles, renews and extends the Pársi faith, IX, pt. ii, 187; builds a fire-temple at Navasári for the Sanján fire, *id.* 188; continues the practice of referring religious points to Persian priests, *id.* 189; is appointed Desai of Navasári (1419), *id.* 200 note 1.
Chángadeva: grandson of Bháskaráchárya, founds a *matha* at Pátná for the study of his grand-father's *Siddhántas'iromani* and other works, I, pt. ii, 244, 526.
Chángadeva: councillor of prince Govana of the Nikumbha family, I, pt. ii, 460.
Changadevayya: Vikramáditya VI's officer, I, pt. ii, 450.
Chángdev: place of interest in Khándesh district, XII, 437.
Changis: landholders in Gujarát, special community of part foreign descent, IX, pt. ii, 11, 15.
Changizi: old coin in Surat and other districts worth 8 to 10 annas, I, pt. i, 222 note 2.
Changizkhán: IX, pt. i, 458; raised the name of Bida, his own clan or stock, to the highest rank, *id.* 459; his wise policy towards the conquered in Central Asia, *id.* 460.
Changizkhán; powerful Gujarát noble, protects the Merzás, is assassinated by Sidi Jhujheirkhan (1568), IX, pt. ii, 10, 12.
Changodeva; original name of Hemachandra, I, pt. i, 191.
Chánka: island in Káthiáwár, VIII, 28, 67.
Channa: fodder plant, XXV, 277.
Channabasava: nephew of Basáva, incarnation of Kárttikeya, I, pt. ii, 479; flies to Ulavi, *id.* 480, 481, 484. *See* Chenna Basáva.
Channabasáva-Purána: sacred book of the Lingáyats, I, pt. ii, 435, 437 and note 5 478, 479, 480 and note 5, 481.
Chánod: place of interest in Rewa Kántha, VI, 159-161.
Chápa: family of Bhinmál, I, pt. i, 139, 463 note 2, 526.
Chápa: dynasty, I, pt. i, 138 and note 1; I, pt. ii, 313 note 3. *See* Gurjaras.
Chápa: Chaura, leading Gujar stock name, IX, pt. i, 459, 479; Sanskritised into Chápotkata, *id.* 488, 489; *see* Chávadás.
Chápa: Champa, companion of Vanrája (A. D. 720-780), IX, pt. i, 488 note 5; founder of Chápaner, *id.* 294 note 4, 455 note 1, *id.* 488; by one account was a Bhil, by another account a Vánia, *id.* 294 note 4, 455 note 1, 488 note 5.
Chápadiás: name of Chorvád Shrávaks, IX, pt. i, 488.
Chapanir: Chápaner, in Central Gujarát, called after Chápa its founder, IX, pt. i, 455 note 1, 488; settlement of Brahma-Kshatrias at, capture of, by Mahomed Begáda (A. D. 1484), *id.* 55; seat of a Bhil dynasty, *id.* 294; dynastic seat, *id.* p. ix; *see* also Champaner.
Chápas: *see* Chávadás.

Chăphá : *Michelia champaca*, flowering tree in Poona district, XVIII, pt. i, 45.
Chăphal : village in Sátára district, temple and fair at, XIX, 460-461.
Chaplets : use of, by Málvan and Vengurla women, X, 110 note 1.
Chaplin : Mr., Madras Civilian, under Mr. Mountstuart Elphinstone, I, pt. ii, 665 ; Collector of the Marátha Country, XXII, 432 ; Agent of the Southern Marátha Country, XXI, 413.
Chapman ; Mr. F. S., wounded in a skirmish with Bhágoji (1857), XVI, 200 ; hanged a Trimbak Bráhman for treason, *id.* 660 ; *see* also XVII, 419.
Chápotkata : Gurjjara origin of, I, pt. i, 467 ; Sanskrit form of Cháp or Chávada, *id.* 150 ; meaning strong bow, IX, pt. i, 454, 480, 485 note 9, 488, 489 note 2, 497, 499 ; I, pt. ii, 409 note 1. *See* Cháudas and Chávadás.
Chappal : food plant, XXV, 160.
Char : timber tree, found in several districts, XXV, 53 ; XII, 25 ; XVIII, pt. i, 45.
Charadrid : family of birds in Ratnágiri district, X, 90.
Charai : pass in Násik district, XVI, 128.
Charana : Vedic schools of Bráhmans, I, pt. ii, 148.
Chárans : class of bards and actors in Gujarát, strength and distribution, IX, pt. i, 207, 214 ; origin, different accounts of, created by Shiv, were super-human spirit-beings settled on earth, bardic account, 214 and note 1, 215 ; facts showing that they were donkey graziers ; some of them passed as Bráhmans, *id.* 215, 438 ; traces of Gujar element in, *id.* 488 and note 2, 499 ; divisions, four sections of, *id.* 215 ; appearance ; language, house ; food ; dress ; ornaments, *id.* 216 ; condition, *id.* 216, 220 ; callings as bards, *id.* 217 ; holders of large grants of land and villages, *id.* 217 note 1 ; as husbandmen, *id.* 217 ; as beggars receiving presents at feasts and marriages, instances of the extravagance of their demands and violence in enforcing them, *id.* 217 and note 2 ; as graziers, cattle-sellers, pack-carriers ; their self-sacrifice as guards or *valdvás* to travellers and goods, *id.* 217 note 3 ; as security, *id.* 217 ; as court-poets, *id.* 219 ; *Trága* or self-sacrifice of, *id.* 218 and note 1 ; Mr. Ovan's details of a case of self-scrifice (A. D. 1820), *id.* 218 and note 2 ; beliefs, Cháran women are supposed to have supernatural power ; instances of Cháran women's suicides ; popular goddesses of north Gujarát believed to be the spirits of Cháran women, *id.* 216 and note 1 ; dread of Cháran ghost, *id.* 218-219 ; religion, devotees of goddesses, their chief places of pilgrimage, poets and holy men among, *id.* 220 ; customs, *id.* 220-222 ; in Cutch, V, 75-76 ; in Baroda, VII, 63-64 ; in Káthiáwár, VIII, 136-137 ; husbandmen in Thána, XIII, 18.
Cháran Vanjári ; a caste in Khándesh, XII, 109 ; *see* also Lamán.
Charcoal : live, is used in purification, ix, pt. i, 356 ; in cases of witchcraft, in cattle-plague, *id.* 357 ; making of, in Sholápur, XX, 10.
Chard : food plant, XXV, 180.
Charegaon : village in Sátára district, a trade-centre, XIX, 215, 461.
Charitable institutions : in Surat, II, 328 ; in Broach, *id.* 555.
Charity : duty enjoyed by Musalmán law, IX, pt. ii, 126, 171 note 2 ; secret, among Memans, *id.* 52 and note 4 ; vow to give in, *id.* 127.
Chár-Jumágis : first four Fridays after marriage, IX, pt. ii, 167.
Charkha : táluka in Káthiáwár, VIII, 404.
Charlotte Lake : at Mátherán, XIV, 246.
Charmæ : tribe mentioned by Pliny, I, pt. i, 532, 534.
Charms : as safeguards against spirit attacks, IX, pt. i, 420 ; belief in, IX, pt. ii, 30, 147 : 155 ; used by Mátherán tribes, XIV, 263.
Charoli : food plant, XXV, 150 ; oil-yielding plant, *id.* 217 ; yields dyes, *id.* 242.
Charotar : fertile tract of land in Kaira, III, 2 ; Kanbis' pleasant land, IX, pt. i, 155 and note 1.
Charter, Royal : to suppress interlopers, XXVI, pt. I, 83 ; to establish Admiralty Court in Bombay, *id.* 83-84 ; of year 1693, *id.* 103 ; proclaimed in Bombay (1753), XXVI, pt. i, 301.
Charters : obtained by the English Company from Delhi (1613), II, 76 ; by the Dutch (1618, 1709), *id.* 87, 115 ; by the Portuguese (1707), *id.* 115.
Charthán : place of interest in Khándesh, XII, 438.
Chárubenna : river mentioned in a grant at Chiplúna, I, pt. ii, 356. *See* Várubenná.
Charubhakshana : minor ceremony during marriage rites, IX, pt. i, 45.
Charuli : timber tree, common in Konkan as far as Baroda, XXV, 53.
Chár Yári : IX, pt. ii, 34. *See* Jaáfari Bohorás.
Chás : bird, worship of, IX, pt. i, 157, 382. *See* Kingfisher.
Chashtana : founder of the Káthiáwár Kshatrapas (B. C. 10-A. D. 5), appearance of his coins, XVI, 616-617 ; his date determined, *id.* 619-620.
Chashtana : second Kshatrapa (A. D. 130), coins of pt. i, 29-31, 32, I, pt. ii, 157 : Satrap, *id.* 159 ; relations of Gotamiputra and his successors with, *id.* 160-161, 170.
Chátáli : *see* Satáni.
Chatarapana : Sátakarni prince, his regnal year, I, pt. ii, 152, 154 ; Ándhrabhritya king (A. D. 20), XVIII, pt. ii, 213.
Chatarki : village in Bijápur district, temple, XXIII, 645.
Chatarkot : hill fort in Bundelkhand, I, pt. ii, 396.
Chatarshingi : hill temple near Poona city, fair at, XVIII, pt. iii, 362.
Chatarsingh : *see* Saptashring.
Chát, Habeli : sub-division in Rewa Kántha, VI, 123.
Chatiun : timber tree, common in forests, XXV, 100.
Chatrál : a village in Baroda, VII, 592.
Chatris : pavilion works, I, pt. i, 453.
Chátta : wandering tribe of Hindu converts, IX, pt. ii, 86.

Chatta : Goa Kádamba feudatory of the Western Chálukya king Jayasimha II, I, pt. ii, 436, 459, 565, 567. *See* Shashthadeva I.
Chatta : Hángal Kádamba prince, I, pt. ii, 559, 560, 561.
Chattaladevi : wife of Vijayáditya I, the Goa Kádamba, I, pt. ii, 565, 568 ; mother of Kamaládevi, *id.* 569.
Chattaya : I, pt. ii, 436, 565, 567. *See* Shashthadeva I and Shashthadeva II.
Chattaya : Hángal Kádamba Chatta, I, pt. ii, 559, 560.
Chattaldeva : I, pt. ii, 436. *See* Shashthadeva I.
Chatter : caste of bodice cloth-sellers in Bijápur, XXIII, 239.
Chattimarasa : Kalachurya Bijjala's accountant, I, pt. ii, 473.
Chattuga : Chatta the Hángal Kádamba, I, pt. ii, 559, 560.
Chaturapana : Ándhra king, I, pt. i, 38 ; son of Yajna S'ri, I, pt. ii, 153 ; son-in-law of Rudrádaman, *id.* 161 ; identified with Vásishthiputra Sátakarni, *id.* 167 ; (172), *id.* 168 ; his name engraved in a Nánághát reservoir, XIV, 287 ; his coin found in Sopára, *id.* 333. *See* Chatarapana.
Chaturhán : four-handed, Chohán supposed to be derived from, IX, pt. i, 483.
Chatursing : brother of the Rája of Sátára taken prisoner (1812) and confined till death (1818), I, pt. ii, 114. *See* Chitursing.
Chaturvarga, Chintámni : work by Hemádri, I, pt. ii, 249.
Chatushparna : may be identified with Chaturapana or with Chandaśri, I, pt. ii, 156.
Chaudadámpur : village in Dhárwár district, temples and inscriptions at, XXII, 390, 659; record of the Devagiri Yádavas at, I, pt. ii, 526, 527 and note 1 ; inscription at, *id.* 529 ; records of the Guttas at, *id.* 578, 580, 581, 582 and note 4, 583.
Cháudás : of Anhilwád, I, pt. ii, 409 note 1.
Chaudhárpáda : village in Thána district, XIV, 212.
Chaudhris : pátil's assistants, XIII, 538 ; at Kalyán (1828), *id.* 572 ; a Dakhan name, *id.* 573.
Chaudri : a caste of palm-tappers in Kánara district, XV, pt. I, 293-295.
Chaudri or Bohata ; pass in Thána district, XIII, 5, 319.
Chaugaon ; place of interest in Khándesh, XII, 438.
Chauháns : Rájpúts of Sámbhár, I, pt. i, 468, 469. *See* Chováns.
Chauk : town in Thána district, XIV, 51 ; Goddard's halt at (1781), XIII, 508 ; Mátherán Points, Little and Great, XIV, 232, 233, 237, 238.
Chaukal : village in Konkan, Kolhápur victory at (1806), X, 198.
Chaukuli : Berad village in Sávantvádi state, X, 416.
Chaul : Ptolemy's Semulla, I, pt. ii, 1, 2 ; Cheul, *id.* 2, 7 ; caves, *id.* 12 ; Chemuli, Capital of the Siláháras, *id.* 16 ; Siláhára port, *id.* 21, 543 ; Chemulya, its rulers helped by Avasara II, the Southern Konkan Siláhara, *id.* 537 ; southern boundary of, *id.* 22 ; district laid waste by Malik Kafur, *id.* 29, 533 ; port of the second government of the Dakhan under the Báhmanis, under the Gujarát kings, *id.* 30 ; passes to Ahmadnagar kings, *id.* 33 ; commercial mart, ranked with Surat and Goa, *id.* 34 ; its imports ; horse traffic and silk weavings, *id.* 35 ; its wood carvings, lacquer work, and its description ; its silk manufactures, *id.* 36 ; port, Moors defeated by D'Almeida (1507), *id.* 43-44 ; Musalmán city, destroyed by Shiváji, *id.* 41 ; Portuguese factory (1512-1521); fort built at, by the Portuguese (1523), *id.* 45 ; Portuguese defeated off and at (1521 and 1530), *id.* 46 ; its siege by Ahmadnagar troops and defence by Don Francisco De Mascarenhas (1570), fortification of the Portuguese town built (1570) and (1592), *id.* 49 ; besieged by the Mughals (1612), *id.* 40 ; magistrate's court, judicial establishment and jail in, *id.* 52 ; Portuguese fortress and artillery at, *id.* 52 ; visit of its Patron Saint Xavier to, *id.* 56 ; exports from, *id.* 62 ; port, frequented by the English and Dutch ships without hindrance, *id.* 63, 71 ; besieged by Sambháji (1683), *id.* 77 ; taken by the Maráthás (1741), *id.* 85 ; cession of, to the French, discussed, *id.* 102-103, 174, 282 note 5 ; Balhára dependency, X, 193 note 1 ; a trade centre (1590), XIV, 30 ; its identification, *id.* 52 ; Ahmadnager, troops of, attack Karanja (1571), *id.* 193 ; Thána trade diverted to (1347), *id.* 357 ; negotiations to transfer (1739-1740), XXVI, pt. i, 228, 229, 234-236 ; held in deposit by the English, transferred to the Maráthás, *id.* 238-242. *See* also Cheul.
Chaul : food plant, XXV, 186.
Chaul : head shaving ; *see* Mudana.
Chauler : fort in Násik district, XVI, 431 ; old guns at, *id.* 443, 444.
Chaulukika : I, pt. ii, 340 note 1. *See* Chaulukya.
Chaulukya : Sanskrit form of Chalkya, I, pt. i, 156 ; ruling dynasty of Anáhilváda (A. D. 961-1242) ; invasion of Somanátha by Máhmud of Ghazni, remission of pilgrim-tax ; architectural buildings, ascendancy of Jainism and division of the kingdom among the nobles under the, 156-197 ; kingdom of, 465 ; *see* also I, pt. ii, 340 note 1, 525 note 4 ; or Chálukya, IX, pt. i, 485 and note 7, 486, 501. *See* Solanki.
Chaunda : Yádava governor of the south, I, pt. ii, 245.
Chaundarája Krishna : Yádava king's officer, I, pt. ii, 527. *See* Chaunda.
Chaundi Setti : I, pt. ii, 527. *See* Chaundarája.
Channing : American cotton planter in Dhárwár (1845), XXII, 290.
Chaura *pl.* Cháuras : leading Gurjar stock name, IX, pt. i, 459 : masters of Cutch after the fall of the Sumrás, I, pt. i, 517 ; dynasty, 526 ; Chávadás, origin of the name, IX,

pt. i, 488 ; in Cutch, claim to be *agnikulas*, *id.* 488 note 8 ; their rule, *id.* 489 and note 1. *See* Chávadás.
Chauri : food plant, XXV, 147.
Chausál : timber mart in Násik, XVI, 431.
Chausar : Indian backgammon, IX, pt. ii, 173 and note 3.
Chauth : Marátha contribution, I, pt. i, 388 ; grant of, in the Mughal Subhás of the Dakhan obtained by Sháhu (1719), I, pt. ii, 655 ; the outstanding balances of, claimed by the Maráthás from the Nizám (1794), *id.* 606 ; Piláji gets half of Gujarát (1725), VII, 170 ; promised to the Peshwá (1726), *id.* 171 ; of country north of the Máhi got by the Gáikwár (1737), *id.* 174 ; Marátha claim to one-fourth share of the revenue first levied by Prataprav Gujar in North Násik (1671), XVI, 191 ; Marátha claim to, acknowledged in Násik (1720), *id.* 207 ; Shiváji gets the right of levying, from Bijápur territory (1665), XVIII, pt. ii, 234 ; Rájárám levies in Khándesh and Berár (1699), *id.* 239 ; Chandrasena, sent by Sháhu to collect (1710), *id.* 241 ; grant to levy, in Dakhan from Delhi (1718), *id.* 243 ; levied by Rájárám (1689), XIV, 250 ; by Chandrasena Jádhav, *id.* 256 ; levied in the Dakhan by Sháhu, *id.* 260-261 ; the so-called *chauth* of Angria, *id.* 265 ; levied by Udáji Powár in Málwá, *id.* 268 ; Holkar, Sindia and Powár authorized to levy (1725), *id.* 270 ; Sháhu's claim for, on Haidarábád territory, *id.* 271 ; *chauth* on Gujarát accepted, *id.* 273 ; Bájiráv gets the right of levying, in the Dakhan, *id.* 278 ; given to Báláji Peshwá by the Mughals, *id.* 285 ; Bápuji Náik collects, in Karnátak, *id.* 287.
Cháva : Sinda prince of Yelburga, I, pt. ii, 573, 574.
Chávadás : of Anahilaváda (720-956), I, pt. i, 124 ; of Gurjjara race establish a small chiefship at Panchásar which falls in A. D. 696 ; establish a kingdom at Anahilaváda, their genealogy, 149-155, 463 note 2 ; their settlements, 464, 465, 466 ; feudatories of Bhinmál, 469 ; their affliction, 513 note 9 ; ruling Rájput tribe, IX, pt. i, 480 ; founders of Anahilaváda (A. D. 746) ; once lords of Gujarát ; their present chiefships ; their former rule, their present condition, *id.* 124 ; proofs of their Gurjjara origin, *id.* 488-489 ; other names of—Chápas, Chaurás, *id.* 488 ; Chápas, Chaura, Chávada, a leading Gurjár stock name, *id.* 454, 459, 489 ; Chápotkata meaning strong bow, Sanskritised form of Chápa or Chávda, *id.* 454, 480, 488 ; bardic dates of Chaura settlements at different places confirmed, *id.* 479, 488 ; traces of their rule in Rájputána, in Márwár, in Kachh ; traces of, remain in the name Chápadiás ; Chorwád, *id.* 488 ; given credit of introducing the name Gujarát ; claim the credit of forming fleets, *id.* 489 ; other proofs of Gurjjara origin ; chiefs of Káthiáwár of the seventh and eighth centuries were Gurjjaras of the Chápa family, *id.* 479 ; Chávadás of North Gujarát were Gurjjarás, *id.* 480 note 4 ; Chávadás or Chápas, a branch of the Gurjjaras, as the centre of power at Anahilaváda, *id.* 480 ; a Gujjara king of Bhinmál (A. D. 628), said to belong to the Shri Chápa dynasty, *id.* 488 and note 3. *See* Chápas, Chaurás, Chápotkatás, Chávotakás, and Chávarás.
Chávalidevi : wife of Ballála I, I, pt. ii, 493 ; accomplished in the sciences and in singing and dancing, *id.* 494.
Chaval-ka-bháji : food plant, XXV, 146.
Chaván : Gurjjara surname, I, pt. i, 468.
Chávand : village in Káthiáwár, VIII, 404.
Chávand : hill in Poona district, XVIII, pt. i, 4 ; fort, its history, XVIII, pt. iii, 124-125 ; fall of (1818), XVIII, pt. ii, 303.
Chavaya : famine plant common at Mátherán, Rám Ghát and Khandála, XXV, 204.
Chávdá or Chápotkat : a clan of Gujarát Rájputs in Cutch, V, 67-68 ; in Káthiáwár, VIII, 109, 277.
Chávdi : village office, XIII, 576.
Chavkoni : Akbar's square rupee, X, 154.
Chavli : pulse, its cultivation in Poona, XVIII, pt. ii, 42, 43.
Chávotaka, *pl.* Chávotakas : kingdom of the Chávadas, afflicted by Arab army, I, pt. i, 109 ; identified with Chávadás of Panchásar, I, pt. i, 150, 151, 465, 466, 467 ; king of, defeated by the Tájikás or Arabs, I, pt. ii, 187, 375 and note 7. *See* Chávadás.
Chávre : pass in Kolába district, XI, 115.
Chávunda I : Sinda prince of Yelburga, i, pt. II, 573 ; also called Chaunda, *id.* 574.
Chávunda II : son of Achugi II, the Yelburga Sinda feudatory of Taila III, I, pt. ii, 439, 460, 462 ; marries the Kalachurya princess Siriyádevi, *id.* 470, 473, 573, 575, 576 ; *see* also XXIII, 393-394.
Chavundaládevi : wife of Tailápa, I, the Hangal Kadamba, I pt. ii, 559, 560.
Chávundaráya : I, pt. ii, 428 note 4 ; feudatory of the Western Chálukya king Someśvara, I, *id.* 439.
Chawadánpur : village in Dhárwár district, records of the Guttas at, I, pt, ii, 578. *See* Chandadámpur.
Cháwarás : identified with Chápas of Bhinmál. I, pt. i, 139. *See* Chávadás.
Chaya Sáhiar : Sanján high priest, brings the Sanján fire to Navsári, IX, pt. ii, 188.
Chebbi : I, pt. 307. *See* Chabbi.
Chechi : branch of Gujárs in Punjáb Gujarát ; chief branch of, at Pushkar, IX, pt. i, 489-490.
Chechijna : modern Chinchni (A. D. 100), in Thána district, XIV, 53.
Chedi : era, I, pt. i, 57, 58 and note 1, 114 ; dynasty, 114 ; modern Bundelkhand, *id.* 130, 163 ; its king present at the bride-groom-choosing of Durlabhádevi, *id.* 163 ; its king strangled, *id.* 186-187, 469. *See* Traikutaka and Kalachuri ; king of, I, pt. ii, 179 ; 201, 203 ; humbled by Tailapa, *id.* 212 ; attacked by Someśvara I, *id.* 214, 410, 431 ; country about Jabalpur, *id.* 181, 225, 468 ; dynasty, *id.* 240 ; era, *id.* 293 note 2, 310, 313 note 4, 314 note 1, 360 note 1, 374. *See* Kaláchuri Era ; lords of the race of, *id.* 380 ; *see* Traikutaka and Kaláchuri.

Cheiroftera : sub-order of animals in Ratnágiri dirtrict, X, 43.
Chelas : IX, pt. ii, 19 ; *see* Khádims.
Chellaketana : family, I, pt. ii, 403 and note 2, *id.* 420 ; feudatory chiefs in Kánara (850-950), XV, pt. ii, 84 ; governed Banavási, *id.* 265.
Chelna : village in Káthiáwár, VIII, 404.
Chelvadi : *see* Chalvadi.
Chembur : village in Thána, its attempted identifications with Saimur, Chemula, Symula, Timulla, XIV, 52, 362 ; why not Symulla, XI, 270 note 5 ; causeway and distilleries at, XIII, 323, 398 ; *see* also I, pt. ii, 174.
Chemul : why Cheul, XI, 270 note 5.
Chemula : modern Chaul, I, pt. i, 533, XIII, 423 ; capital of the Siláháras, I, pt, ii, 11, XIV, 52 ; probably capital of Kapardi II, *id.* 148 ; mentioned in Kánheri caves, *id.* 172, 173, 189. *See* Chaul.
Chemuli : modern Chaul, I, pt. ii, 543, XI, 272.
Chemulya : Chaul, I, pt. ii, 537.
Chemwal ; Chaul, I, pt. ii, 282 note 5, 37.
Chena : food plant cultivated in hilly parts throughout India, XXV, 184.
Chenah : *see* Chena.
Cheudiya : port in Kánara district, its trade, XV, pt. ii, 65, 66, 67 ; people, *id.* 277.
Chendni : suburb of Thána, XIV, 346.
Chendurog : cattle throat disease, XV, pt. ii, 221.
Chengiri : kings, subdued by Vishnuvardhana, I, pt. ii, 495 and note 8 ; country ruled over by Vishnuvaradhana, *id.* 499.
Chenna ; S'iva's attendant, I, pt. ii, 482.
Chenna Basava : nephew of Basava, helps Basava in propounding his new doctrine ; after Basava's death surrenders all his property to the king and is admitted into favour ; becomes the sole leader of the Lingáyats and shapes the creed of his sect, I, pt. ii, 227. *See* Channa Basava.
Chennabhairadevi : Bhatkal Jain princess (1450) ; XV, pt. ii, 271, 275 and note 2, 283, 284. *See* Baira Devi.
Chenna hurbara : food plant, XXV, 152.
Chenopodiaceæ : an order of food plant, XXV, 169 ; an order of famine plants, *id.* 203.
Chenopodium : *album*, food plant, XXV, 169 ; *viride*, food plant, *id.* 169.
Chequered Water Snake : in Poona district, XVIII, pt. i, 76-77.
Chera : kingdom of, conquered by Pulikeśi II, I, pt. i, 111, I, pt. ii, 143 ; country about Maisur ruled by the Ganga family, *id.* 183, 189, 197 ; subdued by Krishna III, *id.* 207 ; king made subject to Vikramáditya, *id.* 219 ; defeated by Someśvara II, *id.* 333 ; humbled by Singhana, *id.* 525 ; territory, *id.* 298, 308 ; country ruled over by Vishnuvardhana, *id.* 499 ; kings of, defeated by the Western Chálukya king Jayasimha II, I, pt. ii, 213, 436.
Cherambola : food plant cultivated in gardens, XXV, 171.
Cherphal tephli : oil-yilding plant, XXV, 222.
Cherty Deposits : in Bijápur, XXIII, 45.
Cherupinai : oil-yielding plant, XXV, 214.
Chess : IX, pt. ii, 173 and note 1.
Chestnut : water, *singodás*, food plant, IX, pt. i, 505.
Chethi : timber tree, XXV, 78.
Chetri : caste of husbandmen in Kánara district, XV, pt. i, 341, 344.
Cheul : XI, 142, 143 ; Cheul or Jival, *id.* 143, 144, 146, 151, 155, 156 ; position, various spellings of the name, *id.* 269 and note 1 ; history, traditional, early Hindu, Ptolemy, (150), Kánheri inscriptions (130), Periplus (247), Kosmas (525), Hiuen Tisang (642), Arab travellers, Masudi (915), Muhalhil (941), Al Istakhri (950), Ibu Haukal (976), Al Beruni (1030), Al Idrisi (1130), *id.* 270-272 ; Devgiri Yádavs (1312), Vijayánagar kings (1336-1587), Báhmanis (1347-1490), Nikitins' accounts (1470), Varthema's account (1503-1508), Portuguese appearance at (1505), battle at, between the Portuguese and Musalmáns (1508), Barbosa's account (1514), Portuguese factory at (1516), first Musalmán fort at Korle (1570), Portuguese Cheul besieged (1571), Linschot's account (1583), second successful Musalmán attempt to fortify Korle (1592), battle at Korle and success of the Portuguess (1594), Pyrard's (1602-1608) account, Della Valle's (1623-1625) account, Bocarro's (1634) account, revenue and expenditure (1634), trade (1634), condition (1640-1668), besieged by Sambhái (1683), Coutinho's account (1728), ceded to the Maráthás (1739), the French at (1777), *id.* 273-286 ; description, objects of interest, Portuguese ruins, the castle, the cathedral, the hospital, Jesuit monastery, Church of the Augustinians, St. Barbara's Tower, Dominican Church, St. Xavier's Chapel, *id.* 287-298 ; Hindu and Musalmán objects of interest ; dancing girls' house, Someshwar temples, response-giving Maruti, Buddhist caves, Dattatraya's shrine, Hamam Khana, mosque, Rajkot fort, landing place, Musalmán dome, old tombs, Mahálakshmi temple, battle stones, water palace, Rameshvar temple, Angria's tomb, *id.* 299-310. *See* also I, pt. i, 351, 513, 516, I, pt. ii, 2, 7 ; caves at, *id.* 12 ; under the Bahámani rule (1347-1500), *id.* 620 ; Chitpávan's head-quarters, IX, pt. i, 439 ; beautiful white people of, *id.* 498 note 2 ; early Arab settlsment at, IX, pt. ii, 1 note 1 ; Musalmáns found at, *id.* 2 note 1 ; Pársi settlements in, fire-worshippers and fire temples mentioned at, IX, pt. ii, 186. *See* Chaul.
Chevari : food plant, XXV, 188.
Chevul : identified with Chaul, XIV, 52.
Chhabina : a Thána boat, literally a guard-boat, XIII, 719.
Chhadi-Nom ; mace-ninth, special festival day on dark ninth of Shrávan, sacred to Zahir Pir, IX, pt. i, 336 note 1 ; origin, observances and procession, *id.* 524, 525.
Chhagalaga : king, grandfather of Sanakanika, I, pt. i, 64 note 3, 65.
Chhalala : táluka in Káthiáwár, VIII, 403.

Chhaliar : state in Rewa Kántha, VI, 152.
Chhandánuśásana : work on prosody, compiled by Hemachandra, I, pt. i, 193.
Chhandasa ; obsolete language, I, pt. ii,, 141.
Chhani : a large village in Baroda, VII, 154.
Chhaparband : caste of Musalmán thatchers in Bijápur, XXIII, 296 ; Hindu caste in Poona, XVIII, pt. i, 394-395.
Chhapardhalli : village in Dhárwár, temple at, XXII, 660.
Chhara : a caste of Hindu converts, in Gujarát, labourers, also called Ghágharias, or petticoat people, Moslims in name only, IX, pt. ii, 86.
Chháróli : village in Láta country, I, pt. ii, 392-393.
Chhathe : goddess, worship of, is also called Sathi or Mother Sixth, IX, pt. ii, 229.
Chhathi Pujan : or *Shashthi Pujan.* *See* Destiny Worship.
Chhatisgarh : province, under the eastern branch of the Chedi dynasty, I, pt. ii, 240.
Chhatri : caste of husbandmen in Belgaum, XXI, 106 ; in Kolhápur XXIV, 88. *See* Kshatriya and Killikiatar.
Chhatti : sixth-day celebration after birth, IX, pt. ii, 155.
Chhaya : village in Káthiáwár, VIII, 403.
Chher : place of interest, in Cutch, V, 219.
Chhetri : *see* Mushtiger.
Chhindwára : district in Central Provinces, VI, pt. ii, 420.
Chhipá : caste of calenders, sub-division of Bhavsars, Vaishnavs in religion, IX, pt. i, 179 ; converts of the Gujaráti and Márwádi castes of the same name, Sunnis by religion, IX, pt. ii, 71-72 ; believe in the Bukhari Pir, *id.* 127 note 2.
Chhittarája : Siláhára king (1026), I, pt. ii, 436, 539, 542, 543. *See* Chhittarája Dev.
Chhittarája Dev : eleventh Siláhára king (1025), XIII, 422 note 1 ; mention of, as king of 1,400 Konkan villages in a copper-plate, *id.* 425. *See* also I, pt. ii, 18.
Chhokra : caste of hereditary servants in Mahi Kántha, V, 374.
Chhota Udepur : Rewa Kántha state, VII, 2 ; boundaries, aspect, rivers, hills, climate, crops, population, sub-divisions, history, family tree of its chiefs, 110-115. *See* also IX, pt. i, 125, I, pt. ii, 315 ; defeat of Tatya Topi at, I, pt. i, 445.
Chhuravana : modern Chorawne, in Ratnágiri district, I, pt. ii, 347 note 2.
Chicacole : town in Madras, grants at, I, pt. ii, 297.
Chichli : village in Ahmadnagar, pond at, XVII, 714.
Chichni : town, seized by Bhimrája, I, pt. ii, 27.
Chicken-pox : IX, pt. i, 368, 372. *See* Achhabda.
Chickrassia : timber tree, XXV, 45 ; *Nimmonii tabularis*, XXV, 45 ; *velutina*, *id.* 46.
Chicu : timber tree, cultivated in gardens in various parts, XXV, 89.
Chidrusht : part of the *Zend Avesta*, IX, pt. ii, 211 note 2 (12).
Chiefs : list of, in Káthiáwár, VIII, 314, 703-706 ; in Khándesh and Násik, their states, early history and powers, I, pt. ii, 632, 633.
Chiefships : Rájpút, in Gujarát, IX, pt. i, 123.
Chigri Betkar : *see* Advichincher.
Chikalgaon : village in Kolába district, XI, 310.
Chikalvohol : village in Násik district, Hemádpanti temple and pond at, XVI, 431.
Chikanji : village in Dhárwár district, temple and inscriptions at, XXII, 660.
Chikarya : Vaisya, builds a Jaina temple, I, pt. ii, 201, 413.
Chikhal : a Portuguese tenure in Thána, XIII, 550 ; (1817), *id.* 564.
Chikhli : sub-division of Surat district, II, 285-288 ; town, *id.* 298 ; ceded to the Company (1776), VII, 194-195 ; ceded in 1802, *id.* 206 ; *see* also I, pt. i, 412.
Chikhli : state in Khándesh district, XII, 607.
Chikhli : canal in Sátára district, XIX, 154-155.
Chikhli : village in Kolhápur, market, school, XXIV, 296.
Chikka : father of Bichana, I, pt. ii, 243.
Chikka Bágewadi : village in Belgaum district, record at, I, pt. ii, 526, 527.
Chikkadeva : subordinate of Vichana, I, pt. ii, 524 ; officer of the Gutta prince Joyideva, ii, *id.* 583.
Chikkaketayya : minister of Vira-Narasimha III, I, pt. ii, 509.
Chikka Muddanúr : in the Nizam's dominions, record at, I, pt. ii, 523.
Chikkanarti : village in Dhárwár district, XXII, 660.
Chikkerur : village in Dhárwár district, pond, temples and inscriptions at, XXII, 660.
Chik Kuruvinava : caste of weavers in Bijápur, XXIII, 259-262.
Chiklodar : hill in Pálanpur state, V, 282.
Chikodi : old rupee, X, 154.
Chikodi : sub-division of Belgaum district, its details, boundaries, area, aspect, soil, climate, water, stock, crops, people, *id.* 497-499 ; survey of (1853-54), *id.* 440-443 ; disputes about, I, pt. ii, 657 ; town, XXI, 553.
Chikotra : river in Kolhápur, feeder of the Vedganga, XXIV, 11.
Chikra : timber tree, XXV, 59.
Chiku : food plant, XXV, 163.
Chikurde : village in Sátára, temple, XIX, 461.
Chilam : bowl of a tobacco pipe, IX, pt. ii, 111 note 1.
Chilbinj : timber tree, common in *ghāts*, XXV, 101.
Child, Sir John : Governor and President of Bombay, appointed general and admiral of the Company's sea and land forces (1684), XXVI, pt. i, 92 ; his death (1690), *id.* 103 ; *see* also XIII, 479, 480, X, 361 note 4.
Child-givers : dead saints, trees near the tombs of certain saints, IX, pt. ii, 147-148. *See* Amil.
Child-marriage : origin of the custom of, XVIII, pt. i, 539.
Chilla : timber tree, common in *ghāts*, XXV, 81.

Chillah : period of forty days during which an exorcist learns his incantation, IX, pt. ii, 144.
Chillies : cultivation of, in Ratnágiri district, X, 149; in Khándesh, XII, 169; in Thána, XIII, 294; in Násik, XVI, 105; in Poona, XVIII, pt. ii, 51; in Dhárwár, XXII, 280-281.
Chimalgi : village, in Bijápur district, temples and inscriptions at, XXIII, 645; survey of, *id.* 481.
Chimanájiráv : brother of Bájiráo II, Peshwa, captures Chámpaner, I, pt. i, 309, 322, 391, 392; is appointed Peshwá's subhadár of Gujarát, *id.* 411. *See* Chimnáji Mádhavráv.
Chimangaon : village in Sátára district, temple, XIX, 461.
China Sáheb : brother of Shiváji IV (1837-1866) of Kolhápur, XXIV, 243.
Chimnáji Appa : Peshwá's brother, takes Bassein (1739), I, pt. ii, 84; Marátha general, attacks Jánjira (1731), XI, 149; besieges Bassein (1739), *id.* 151; his conquests in Thána, siege of Bassein (1739), XIII, 493; British negotiations with, *id.* 495; takes Dáhánu (1739), XIV, 54; Kelva-Máhim, *id.* 199; Sirgaon fort, *id.* 313; Tárápur, *id.* 344-345; granted a *jágir* in Supa, reduces Portuguese possessions in the Konkan (1739), XVIII, pt. ii. 243-244; made commander by Sháhu, XIX, 267; captures Bassein, *id.* 280; asks the English to support Mánáji Angria, joins him, *id.* 282-283; his death, *id.* 284; negotiations with (1737), XXVI, pt. i, 187-188; Bassein surrendered to (1739), *id.* 211-213; Captain Inchbird sent to, *id.* 214-216.
Chimnáji Jádhav : Bráhman rebel (1839), XVIII, pt. ii, 307.
Chimnáji Mádhavráv : eighth Peshwa (1796), XVIII, pt. ii, 272-274. *See* Chimnájiráv.
Chimnáji Pandit : opposed to Bájiráv I, taken prisoner by him (1731), VII, 172-173.
Chimolo : perhaps Cheul, XI, 270 and note 1.
China : I, pt. ii, p. ii; army of, marching from Mágadha to Bamian, I, pt. i, 497; vessels coming from, *id.* 513, 522, 528; religion of, *id.* 530; early trade connection of Persia with; Persians going to; fire temples in, IX, pt. ii, 183 note 4 continued on pages 184, 185; first modern Pársi visitor to, *id.* 195 note 2; its trade relation with the Parthians (B. C. 255-235 A. D.), XIII, 413; Western India trade with (150), *id.* 416; Indians in (550), *id.* 420; trade with Thána coast (810-1260), *id.* 429; exports of cotton cloth to, *id.* 430; imports of gold and silver from, *id.* 431; her ships in Thána ports, *id.* 432; exports of gold, silver, silk, porcelain, etc., from (1660-1710), *id.* 487; Bombay trade with (1800-1810), *id.* 519.
Chinch : pass in Násik district, XVI, 130.
Chinch : timber tree, common in hedges in Bombay, XXV, 71; food plant, *id.* 153; famine plant, *id.* 198; oil-yielding plant, *id.* 217, XVIII, pt. I, 45.
Chinchali : village in Dhárwár district, inscription at, I, pt. ii, 422 note 5.
Chinchani : village in Belgaum, lapse of (1836), XXI, 407.
Chinchdidi Mosque : at Bijápur, XXIII, 631-632.
Chinchgaon : hill in Sholápur district, XX, 2-3.
Chinchinda : food plant, XXV, 169.
Chinchkhed : *see* Máheji.
Chinchli : state in Khándesh district, XII, 604.
Chinchli : village in Kolhápur, temple at, XXIV, 276; cattle fair at, *id.* 25, 57.
Chinchni : an old town in Thána district, a dispensary at, XIV, 53, 345.
Chinchoḷi : village in Násik district, I, pt. ii, 515.
Chincholi : village in Ahmadnagar district, XVII, 714.
Chinchona Plantation : at Mahábaleshvar, XIX, 508-509.
Chinchuli : identified with modern Chincholi in Násik district, I, pt. ii, 515.
Chinchvad : rupees, Marátha assessment paid in, XIII, 561.
Chinchvad : town in Poona district, railway station, Dev family and temples at, XVIII, pt. iii, 125-127.
Chinchvalli : I, pt. ii, 364 note 1. *See* Chinchavālya.
Chinchvalya : identified with Chincholy in Nizám's dominions, I, pt. ii, 364 note 1.
Chinese : authors, effects of their writings on Indian history, "Introduction to the Early History of the Dakhan," I, pt. ii; proposal to establish a colony of, in Sálsette (1794), *id.* 123; in Kánára, XV, pt. i, 411; in Poona, XVIII, pt. i, 538; element of the, in Indian architecture (915-1500), XI, 272 note 2, 469.
Chingleput : district in Madras, I, pt. ii, 421.
Chini-badham : food plant, XXV, 151.
Chini Mahal : Bijápur palace, XXIII, 619.
Chini-naranghi : food plant, found in Konkan, XXV, 149.
Chinkilichkhán : *see* Nizám-ul-mulk.
Chin Mulgund : village in Dhárwár district, temple and inscriptions at, XXII, 660.
Chinni : food plant, XXV, 126.
Chinri : reef in Káthiáwár, VIII, 31.
Chintakuntha : village mentioned in a grant found at Haidarábád (Dakhan), I, pt. ii, 364.
Chintámanráo : of Sángli (1800), wounded by Dhundia Wágh, I, pt. ii, 662; helps Colonel Wellesley against Dhundiya Wágh, XXIV, 348; helps in suppressing the rebellion of 1844; his death (1851), *id.* 350, 352.
Chinto Rámchandra Phadnis : leads (1800) the small garrison of Ajra against Harpávda and Bellevádi and storms Ibráhimpur, XXIV, 290.
Chintz : timber tree, XXV, 65.
Chinvat : way to heaven, IX, pt. ii, 211 note 2 (5). *See* Dámdát.
Chionanthus Malabarica : timber tree, common in *ghāts*, XXV, 98.
Chip : pass in Násik district, XVI, 128.
Chiplun : sub-division of Ratnágiri district, details of, account, X, 2, 301-303; trade, (1880), *id.* 180; town, population, trade, manufactures, management, history, rock temples, *id.* 324-326. *See* also I, pt. ii, 9, 173, 186, 337 note 2; Mallikárjun's inscription at,

I, pt. i, 186, 540, 546; Chitpávan head-quarters, I, pt. ii, 27, 35; Pulikeśin II's grant at, *id.* 345, 356.
Chipluna : *see* Chitpavan.
Chipur : village in Baroda, the scene of Muhamad Ghori's success over Prathiráj (1193), VII, 619.
Chipurupalle : grant at, I pt. ii, 357 note 1.
Chirás : memorial stones, IX, pt. i, 363.
Chirchira : timber tree found in Parwar *ghát* and Nilghiries, XXV, 113.
Chiretta : medicinal plant, XXV, 261, 262.
Chirikya : *see* Chaulukyas, I, pt. i.
Chironji : timber tree, XXV, 53.
Chirphal : timber tree, XXV, 31.
Chirput : food plant, XXV, 167.
Chisut : Sufi school, IX, pt. ii, 8 note 3.
Chishtis : chief Sayad family in Gujarát, IX, pt. ii, 5 note 1 (4); branch of the Faruki section of Shaikhs, descendants of Sheik Nizam-ud-din Chishti, *id.* 8 note 2; Hindu converts of the Chishti school, *id.* 8 note 3, 74.
Chitákul : village in Kánara district, probably the Sindábur and Cintacola of mediæval and Portuguese travellers and historians, history, XV, pt. ii, 277-279; trade centre (1500), *id.* 50; mentioned in the Turkish *Seaman's Guide* (1554), *id.* 51; a fort built at (1505), *id.* 103; Varthema's description of (1503), *id.* 104; attacked by Dalboquerque (1510), *id.* 108; mentioned by Barbosa (1514), *id.* 112; paid 400 rice bags to the Portuguese as tribute (1514), *id.* 114; mention of, by Barros (1582), *id.* 118; mentioned by Baldæus, (1660), *id.* 125; Chitakul fort built by Sonda chiefs (1715), *id.* 133.
Chitaldurg : district in Mysore, I, pt. ii, 285 note 5, 443, 454; inscription at, *id.* 457.
Chitará : section of Mochis, XI, pt. i, 194.
Chitári : caste of painters in Ratnágiri, X, 415, 418, 438.
Chitás : Chohán Mers converted to Islám, IX, pt. i, 493.
Chithal : place of interest in Káthiáwár, VIII, 404, 495.
Chitoda : fort in Rájpútána, I, pt. i, 184; inscription of Kumarapála at, *id.* 188. *See* Chitrakuta.
Chitodi : caste of traders in Khándesh, XII, 58.
Chitor : Mauryas of, afflicted by Arab army, I, pt. i, 109 note 1, 513 note 9; visited by Kumárapála in his exile, *id.* 183; defence of, against Arabs, IX, pt. i, 486, 494; capture of, by Bappa, *id.* 494 note 3; Bappa founded a kingdom at, *id.* 495 note 3. *See* also IX, pt. ii, 1 note 1.
Chitpávan : sub-division of Maharáshtra Bráhmans, creation of, I, pt. ii, 27, 113, 245, IX, pt. i, 51; are said to be off-spring of ship-wrecked strangers whom Parasharám purified with fire, *id.* 436, 438, 449, 486; said to be Persian priests, *id.* 439; in Ratnágiri district, their origin, character, peculiarities, X, 111-113; dialect, peculiarities of, *id.* 111 note 4; land-holders, *id.* 138; in Sávantvádi, *id.* 411; in Khándesh, XII, 50-52; in Ahmadnagar, XVII, 59; in Poona, origin, settlement, rise, family stocks, surnames, appearance, language, houses, furniture, food, dress, ornaments, character, occupations, daily life, religion, birth, sixth day, sun-showing, birthday, shaving, thread-girding, marriage, puberty, pregnancy, and death ceremonies, XVIII, pt. i, 99-158; in Sátára, XIX, 54-55; in Dhárwár, XXII, 95-96; in Bijápur district, XXIII, 89; in Kolába and Jánjira, XI, 44, 411; in Thána, XIII, 63, 75-76, 521; in Kánára, XV, pt. i, 128-129; in Násik, XVI, 40; in Belgaum, XXI, 90; in Kolhápur, XXIV, 43.
Chitpol : *see* Chitpávan.
Chitra : vegetable poison, common in Gujarát and Konkan, XXV, 266.
Chitragar : in Dhárwár, *see* Jingár.
Chitragupta : registrar to Dharmarája, judge of the dead, said to be founder of Káyasths, IX, pt. i, 60 and note 2, 67.
Chitrak : vegetable poison, XXV, 266.
Chitrakantha : breed of horses, I, pt i, 111; charger of Vikramáditya I, I, pt. ii, 186, 322 note 8, 358 note 1, 361.
Chitrakathi : caste of picture showers in Kolába district, XI, 73; in Thána XIII, 96; in Ahmadnagar, XVII, 178; in Poona, XVIII, pt. i, 448-450; in Sátára, XIX, 117.
Chitrakot : hill fort in Bundelkhand, I, pt. ii, 396.
Chitrakuta : peak of Abu, I, pt. i, 169; modern Chitor, *id.* 183, 469.
Chitrakuta : fortress, apparently Chitrakot or Chatarkot in Bundelkhand, I, pt. ii, 207, 396, 420.
Chitramáya : Pallava prince killed by Udayachandra, I, pt. ii, 326.
Chitrarathasvámin : spiritual adviser of Vijayánandivarman, I, pt. ii, 333.
Chitrasedu : village in the Toramara country, I, pt. ii, 309; camp of Vinayáditya at, I, pt. ii, 369.
Chitraváha : son of the A'lupa ruler Gunaságara, I, pt. ii, 309, 369.
Chitraván : táluka in Káthiáwár, VIII, 405.
Chitri : river in Kolhápur, tributary of Hiranyakeshi, XXIV, 11.
Chitrod : town in Cutch, V, 219.
Chitrod : deserted village in Káthiáwár, VIII, 687.
Chitrod : town in Rájpútána, IX, pt. i, 70.
Chitroda : sub-division of Nágar Bráhmans, IX, pt. i, 13, 15; of Vániás, Meshri, *id.* 70.
Chittarájdev : Siláhára ruler, his mention at Ambarnáth (A. D. 1027), XIV, 8; his copper-plate found at Bhándúp, *id.* 45.
Chitthá : village revenue statement, XIII, 576.
Chitursing : brother of the rája of Sátára, flies to Kolhápur; defeats and kills Parsharám Bháu with the help of Kolhápur troops, I, pt. ii, 607; seized and imprisoned in the fort of Kánguri (1812) by Trimbakji Dengle, *id.* 610; pursued by Rastia to Kolhápur, XIX, 299; his gallant attack at Pál, *id.* 532. *See* Chatursing.
Chivari : famine plant, XXV, 209.
Chivers : the pirate, taken (1700), XXVI, pt. i, 121.

Chivil : Cheul, XI, 273.
Chivtia : pass in Násik district, XVI, 129.
Chiwari : timber tree found on the *ghâts*, XXV, 136.
Chlerodendrom serratum : food plant, XXV, 168.
Chloris barbata : fodder-plant, XXV, 277.
Chlorite Schists : in Bijápur district, XXIII, 54.
Chlorite Slate : in Kánara district, XV, pt. i, 10.
Chloroxylon Swietenia : timber tree common in Konkan and Dakhan, XXV, 46.
Chobari : place of interest in Cutch, V, 148, 219.
Chobári : táluka in Káthiáwár, VIII, 405.
Chodadeva I : Kulottunga, Eastern Chálukya king (10631-112), I, pt. ii, 333 and note 8. *See* Rájendra-Choda.
Chodas : Cholas, dynasty in Madras, I, pt. ii, 277.
Chodhrá : early tribe, IX, pt. i, p. x ; strength and distribution, *id.* 290, 312 ; chief sub-division, object of worship ; customs, *id.* 312-313 ; husbandmen, *id.* 152.
Chogat : place of interest, in Káthiáwár, VIII, 405.
Chohâns : Rájpút tribe, Ajmer kings, I, pt. i, 157, 463 note 2, 465, 470; lose Bhinmál, *id.* 471 ; ruling Rájpút tribe, representatives of the imperial family of Delhi (A. D. 1191) present possessions, IX, pt. i, 125 ; origin, tribe of Agnikulas re-born in Abu fire-pit to help Bráhmans, *id.* 483-484 ; traces, *id.* 483-484 ; territory given to, *id.* 449 note 3, 484 ; Chohán tree, *id.* 486 note 5 ; said to be Vishnu formed, *id.* 449 note 3 ; said to be created by Brahmá, *id.* 493 ; Asápurana the guardian of, *id.* 484 and note 7 ; in Káthiáwár, VIII, 115 ; rulers of Asir (1220), XII, 242. *See* Agnikulas.
Chok : town in Káthiáwár, VIII, 406.
Chokdi : village in Káthiáwár, VIII, 406.
Chokhar : caste of husbandmen in Thána district, XIII, 118.
Chokhiar : thanksgiving ceremony, rites relating to, IX, pt. ii, 230. *See* Birth.
Chokideva : Hangal Kadamba, I, pt. ii, 559.
Chola : kingdom, conquered by Pulakesi II, I, pt. i, 111; country, I, pt. ii, 281 ; kings of, defeated by Someśvara II, *id.* 333 ; Puránic genealogy, *id.* 342 note 1, 350 ; king of, defeated by Vikramáditya I, *id.* 362 and note 6 ; by Vinayáditya, I, *id.* 368 ; by Vikramáditya II, *id.* 375 ; records, *id.* 431, 433 ; king of, burns Jain temples in Belvola, *id.* 441 ; kingdom, in a state of anarchy, *id.* 445, 489 ; king, *id.* 491, 492, 495, 496 ; feudatories of the Hoysálas, *id.* 498, 499 ; country, ruled over by Vishnuvardhána, *id.* 499 ; kingdom, established by Narasimha II, *id.* 507 ; taken by Vira-Someśvara, *id.* 508 ; king, subdued by Singhana, *id.* 525. *See* Cholas.
Chola : stream in Kolába district, XI, ii.
Cholana-kote : elephant of Rájáditya, the Chola king, I, pt. ii, 322 note 8.
Cholas : country of the, I, pt. ii, 133 ; monkey soldiers directed to go to, *id.* 137 ; descendants of an individual of the Chola tribe, *id.* 139, 140, 142, 143 ; province, lying outside Aśoka's kingdom, *id.* 146 ; country of the, invaded by Pulakeśi II, *id.* 183 ; rebel against and are subdued by Vikramáditya I, *id.* 186 ; king of the, reduced by Vinayáditya and made ally, *id.* 188-189 ; fought with and reduced by Vikramáditya II, *id.* 190 ; army of the, vanquished by the army of Karnátaka, *id.* 194 ; subdued by Ráshtrakúta Krishna III, *id.* 207, and Kaka II, *id.* 423 ; country of the, invaded by Tailapa, the Western Chálukya, *id.* 212 ; beaten by Jayasimha II, *id.* 213, 436 ; king of, conquered by Someśvara I, *id.* 214, 215, 441, 567 ; defeated by Vikramáditya VI, *id.* 215, 442, 444, 494 ; king of the, in alliance with the Goa king, *id.* 216 ; prince of the, makes alliance with Vikramáditya II, also styled VI, and offers him his daughter in marriage, *id.* 216-217 ; revolution in the kingdom of, *id.* 217 ; king of the, made subject to Vikramáditya, *id.* 219, 277, 282, 322, 340 note 2, 350 ; kingdom of the, *id.* 358 note 1 ; king of the, *id.* 378, 389 ; burn Jain temples, *id.* 443, 449, 527. *See* Chola.
Cholera : outbreaks of, in Cutch ; V, 174 ; in Rewa Kántha, VI, 89 ; in Ratnágiri, X, 231, 239, 264, 292 ; in Sávantvádi, *id.* 460 ; in Kolába (1827), XI, 179 ; (1868, 1875), *id.* 212, 213 ; in Khándesh (1818-1880), XII, 337 ; in Thána (1818-1819), XIII, 569, 572 note 9 ; (1819, 1820), *id.* 69 ; (1819, 1820, 1875-1882), *id.* 627, 665-666 ; in Kánara, XV, pt. ii, 218 ; in Násik, XVI, 296-301, 337, 338 ; rites for abatement of, *id.* 520-521 ; temple of goddess of, *id.* 522 ; in Ahmadnagar, XVII, 548, 550, 551, 552, 714 ; in Poona (1819-1820), XVIII, pt. ii, 345, 469, 476, 477, 481, 501, 502, 508, 510 ; in Sátára, XIX, 385, 386, 387, 388, 389 ; in Sholápur, XX, 361, 362, 363, 364, 386 and note 1, 387 ; in Belgaum (1872-1873), XXI, 462 ; (1875-1879), *id.* 463-464 ; (1881-1883), *id.* 464 ; in Dhárwár (1818), XXII, 433 ; (1861-1867), *id.* 589, 590 ; popular belief of its origin, *id.* 622 note 2 ; in Bijápur (1871-1873), XXIII, 499 ; in Kolhápur (1849-1883), XXIV, 285-286 ; at Pánvel, XIV, 296 ; at Thána (1869, 1875, 1877), *id.* 347 ; a shrine to the goddess of, *id.* 417.
Choliya ; king of, conquered by Kirtivarman I, I, pt. ii, 345 ; country, *id.* 346.
Cholke : surname, its derivation, XV, pt. ii, 80 note 4.
Chondhe-Mandhe : pass, in Thána district, XIII, 320.
Chopda : sub-division of Khándesh district, its boundaries, area, aspect, climate, water, soil, holdings, survey details, survey results, stock, crops, people, XII, 2, 358-363 ; town, a great town (1610), *id.* 249 ; plundered by Shiváji (1675), *id.* 251 ; description, trade, buildings, mosques, *id.* 438-439.
Chopri-alu : food plant, XXV, 178.
Choránda, sub-division : in Baroda territory, VII, 535-536.

Chorángla: state in Rewa Kántha, VI, 145.
Chorási: sub-division of Surat district, its details, II, 274-277.
Chorawne: village in the Sangameśvara táluka of the Ratnágiri district, I, pt. ii, 347 note 2.
Chorle: hill pass in Belgaum district, XXI, 306.
Chorle: town in Káthiáwár, VIII, 406; I, pt. ii, 208 and note 3.
Chorvád: town in Kháthiáwár, VII, 406, I, pt. ii, 208 and note 3; Volári betel vine cultivators' settlement at, *id.* 113 and note 3.
Chosroes II: king of Persia (591-628), I, pt. ii, 185. *See* Kosru II.
Chotachund: vegetable poison, common in Konkan and Goa, XXV, 267; vegetable antidote to snake-bite, *id.* 274.
Chotakunwar: famine plant, found on the sea coast of Madras, XXV, 206.
Chotá Udepur; *see* Chhota Udepur.
Chote: name of missionary Shams-ud-din, IX, pt. ii, 39 and note 3.
Chotila: hill and village in Kháthiáwár, VIII, 10, 407.
Chovisá: caste of Bráhmans in Gujárát, IX, pt. i, 9.
Chowar: food plant, very common at Mahábaleshwar, XXV, 175.
Chowdari: food plant, XXV, 153.
Chowli: food plant, XXV, 153.
Chowra: timber tree, common at Khandála and Belgaum, XXV, 28.
Christe Purán. "Metrical Life of Christ," XIII, 68.
Christian element: in Húna horde, IX, pt. i, 476 and note 3.
Christian missions: in Thána (1250-1330), XIII, 727-728; in Bijápur, XXIII, 435 note 3.
Christianity: propagation of, I, pt. ii, 55; practice of, *id.* 56; in Kánara, XV, pt. i, 380.
Christian Reverts: in Kánara, XV, pt. i, 397-400; in Thána, XIII, 117.
Christians: among early Arabs, IX, pt. ii, 1 and note 1, 188 note 4; in Saimur, I, pt. i, 517; at Kalyán (A. D. 150), I, pt. ii, 3 (*see* also IX, pt. ii, 184); condition of, *id.* 53; pirates, *id.* 61; in Kaira, III, 37; in Panch Mahâls, *id.* 226; in Ahmadábád, IV, 42; in Cutch, V, 100; in Rewa Kántha, VI, 35; in Baroda, VII, 72; in Káthiáwár, VIII, 168-169; in Ratnágiri, X, 135; in Sávantvádi, *id.* 420, 426; in Kolába, XI, 66; in Khándesh, XII, 129; in Thána, perhaps (A. D. 100), XIII, 414 notes 2 and 3, *id.* 417 and note 2; Christian Bishop of Kalyán (540), Nestorians in Kalyán and Sopár (1320), friars and converts (1230-1323), *id.* 200, 439, 727-728; present Native Christians, strength, history, appearance, speech, houses, food, dress, ornaments, occupation, condition, *id.* 199-205; religion and customs, *id.* 206-215; in Kánara as proprietary husbandmen, XV, pt. ii, 3; forced to adopt Islám (1795), *id.* 143, 258; in Násik, XVI, 85-87; in Ahmadnagar, XVII, 235-239; in Poona, XVIII, pt. i, 536; in Sátára, XIX, 147; in Sholápur, XX, 211; in Belgáum, XXI, 226-229; in Dhárwár, XXII, 249-251, 745-46; in Bijápur, XXIII, 305-306; missons, *id.* 435 note 3; in Kolhápur, XXIV, 151-152. *See* Native Christians.
Chroniclers: Jain, I, pt. i, 156; Anahilaváda, *id.* 156; Jain, *id.* 179, 201, 202; of Gujarát, I, pt. ii, 213.
Chronology: of the Andhrabhrityas and Śatavahánas, I, pt. ii, 157-168.
Chrosophora plicata: vegetable poison, XXV, 269.
Chrysel, Chrysobora: town on the Jamna mentioned by Pliny, I, pt. i, 533.
Chrysophyllum Roxburghii: timber tree common in Chorla *ghâts* and Suda jungles in Bombay, XXV, 88.
Chuara: food plant, XXV, 181.
Chubári: fort built at, by Siddharája, I, pt. i, 180 note 2.
Chuda: state in Káthiáwár, VIII, 407, IX, pt. i, 127.
Chudáchandra: first ruler of Vanthali, I, pt. i, 138, 139.
Chudákarma: top-knot rite, a vedic rite, IX, pt. i, 31 note 3; *see* Mudan.
Chudásama: invading tribe, originally of the Ábhira tribe, I, pt. i, 137; foreigners (900-940), *id.* 138-139, 175; Rájpúts, probably of Turk origin, IX, pt. i, 125, 446 note 4; their history, their present condition, *id.* 125; in Káthiáwár, VIII, 109, 278. *See* Ahir.
Chudbudke Joshi: caste of hourglass drum astrologers in Kolhápur, XXIV, 115-116.
Chudesar: state in Rewa Kántha, VI, 145.
Chudgar: caste of bracelet-makers in Káthiáwár, VIII, 152.
Chudiwala: caste of bracelet-makers in Gujarát, converts of the Hindu caste of the same name, Sunnis by religion, IX, pt. ii, 72-73.
Chughadda: Indian Mughals, in Gujarát, IX, pt. ii, 9 and note i.
Chuka-ka-bhaji: food plant, XXV, 170.
Chukandar: food plant, XXV, 169.
Chulabi Rumi Khan: Ahmadnagar officer, maker of the great Bijápur gun, XI, 277 note 1.
Chulai: food plant, XXV, 169.
Chulka: water-pot, XV, pt. ii, 80.
Chulkhan: village in Khándesh district, XII, 12.
Chuluka: hand, hollowed for the reception of oblationary water, I, pt. ii, 180.
Chumli Koli: *see* Malhári Koli.
Chunara: Musalmán lime burners, converts of low class Hindus, Sunnis by religion, IX, pt. ii, 72.
Chunári: *see* Sunnágár.
Chunaváliya: division of Kolis, IX, pt. i, 239. *See* Kolis.
Chundadigira: caste of silk-knot-printers in Gujarát, Hindu converts claim Arab descent, Sunnis by religion, IX, pt. ii, 72.
Chunvál: tract of country in Káthiáwár, VIII, 4, I, pt. i, 513, 517, IX, pt. ii, 82.

Churches: revenue and superintendence of the, I, pt. ii, 57; Christian, in Ratnágiri, X, 135 note; in Koláha, Cheul Augustinian, XI, 295; Dominican, *id.* 297, 298; Portuguese, in Thána under Marátha rule, XIII, 203, 476, 494, 507; Jesuit, at Bándrá, Mán, etc., *id.* 206; destroyed by the Mahomedans (1300-1500), *id.* 439; built by Antonio do Porto (1534-1552), *id.* 461; built (1600-1700), *id.* 462; in Bombay (1674), *id.* 474; burnt by Arabs, 1690-1700), *id.* 481; English attack on Bándrá Church (1720), *id.* 493; notice of, by Du Perron (1760), *id.* 499; Protestant Church in Bombay (1766), *id.* 500; ruins of, in Sálsette (1775), *id.* 501; in Thána places of interest, XIV, 2, 9, 12, 13, 15, 22, 23, 27, 32, 36-37, 41, 45, 51, 56, 100, 101, 194, 202, 208, 210, 211, 223, 229, 268, 272, 275, 293, 297, 298, 299, 304, 350, 351, 352, 355, 359, 360, 362, 371, 375, 380, 381, 382, 383; in Kánara, places of interest, XV, pt. ii, 123, 125 132, 133, 136, 138, 141, 250, 251, 258, 277, 310, 311, 325, 327, 338, 342, 350; in Bombay Island, Bombay Episcopal Church built (1676-1718), XXVI, pt. iii, 580-83; the Koláha Chapel opened (1828), *id.* 584; the Portuguese Church (1675-1760), *id.* 584.

Chusra: rocky islet in Káthiáwár, VIII, 30.

Chutavana: battle at, I, pt. ii, 326.

Chuvál: tract of land in Ahmadábád district, IV, 2.

Chuvália: sub-division of Koli caste in Ahmadábád district, IV, 153.

Chuyipaka: in the Talupaká country, grant of, by Prithivimula, I, pt. ii, 334.

Cicca disticha: timber tree cultivated in gardens, XXV, 116; food plant, *id.* 171.

Cicer arietinum: food plant, XXV, 152; fodder, *id.* 277.

Ciconidæ: family of birds in Ratnágiri, X, 94.

Cinammomum: *camphora*, XXV, 288; *iners*, *id.* 111; *zeylanicum*, *id.* 110, 170, 224.

Cinnamon: in Kánara district, XV, pt. i, 30.

Cintacola: modern Chitákul, XV, pt. ii, 249, 277, 279.

Cintra: in Portugal, inscription from Somanátha found at, I, pt. i, 205.

Cipher Numbers: used by Dhárwár money-changers, XXII, 321 and note 1.

Circles: undressed basalt on Brahma hill near Sopára, XIV, 324-325 and note 2, 414.

Circumcision: rite of, IX, pt. ii, 160-161; ceremony of the Musalmáns, XVIII, pt. i, 489; Bene-Israels, *id.* 528-529.

Cisterns: in Elephanta and Kánheri caves, XIV. 94, 123.

Citrullus: *colocynthis*, food plant found in Dakhan, Gujarát and sparsely in Konkan, XXV, 254; *vulgaris*, food plant, *id.* 159.

Citrus: *aurantium*, *decumana*, *limetta*, *medica*, food plants, XXV, 148-149.

Civil establishment: Bombay Island (1789), XXVI, pt. iii, 409-411.

Civilians: in Bombay Island, covenants to be entered into and security given by (1749, 50, 59 and 60), XXVI, pt. iii, 368, 371, 379-80, 383; (1771), *id.* 394; reduction of (1775), *id.* 395-98.

Clan: titles among Bhátiás, IX, pt. i, 117 note 6; names among Káthiáwár Bháts, *id.* 207; Anjana Kanbis, *id.* 163; Pátelias, *id.* 172; Rajpúts, *id.* 124 note 1; or stock elements in the tribe, *id.* 459.

Clan surnames: among Maráthás, XIX, 75-76.

Clare, Lord: resident at Baroda, his relations with Sayáji II, Gáikwár (1829-1832), VII, 242-243, 245-246, 303, 404-406; presents shawls to Framji of Povai (1831), XIV, 299.

Clausena: *Indica*, timber tree found at Panvar Ghát in Bombay, XXV, 33; *simplicifolia*, timber tree found at Talkat Ghát, *id.* 31.

Clay: in Ratnágiri district, X, 31; deposits of white, *id.* 17.

Clay figures: making of, in Poona, XVIII, pt ii, 202-204.

Clay seals: Buddhist, in Edinburgh Museum, XIV, 175 note 1.

Cleistanthes Malabaricus: timber tree found in Konkan and Malabár, XXV, 120.

Clemens: of Alexandria, first to know of Buddhism (A. D. 200), XIV, 125 note 4.

Clement X: Pope, frees Vicars Apostolic and their missionaries from the jurisdiction of the Inquisition at Goa (1673), I, pt. ii, 61.

Cleome viscosa: food plant, XXV, 145.

Clergy: appeal to Rome against the Inquisitors, I, pt. ii, 61.

Climate: of the Konkan, "Introduction to the History of the Konkan," I, pt. ii, X; *see* All District Volumes under District Name.

Clitoria ternatea: medicinal plant, common in hedges, XXV, 254.

Clive: Colonel (Lord), chief in command in the expedition against Gheria (1756), XXVI, pt. i, 304-305; *see* also I, pt. ii, 93, X, 196, 382, XI, 152-153, XIII, 497.

Close: Colonel, resident at Poona, IX, pt. ii, 198 note 5; *see* also XVIII, pt. ii, 289, 282, 285; British agent at the Bassein treaty (1803), XIII, 512.

Cloth; manufacture of, in Surat, II, 178; in Broach, *id.* 438-440; in Kaira, III, 75; in Ahmadábád, IV, 131; in Rewa Kántha, VI, 56-58; in Cambay, export of, *id.* 191, 208; in Kolába, XI, 132; in Poona city, XVIII, pt. i, 26. *See* All District Volumes except Panch Mahals.

Cloves: Portuguese trade in, XV, pt. ii, 272.

Club of Western India: in Poona cantonment, XVIII, pt. iii, 362-363.

Clunes: Captain (1827), his notice of Kasára, XIV, 197; of Khardi, *id.* 201; of Shábápur, *id.* 306; of Sopára, *id.* 322.

Coal: in Ratnágiri district, X, 30; first importation of, in Bombay, XXVI, pt. i, 101; in Cutch, V, 19.

Coari: a class of merchants and shopkeepers in Bassein, IX, pt. ii, 189. *See* Gaura.

Coast: of the Konkan, description of, "Introduction to the History of the Konkan," I, pt. ii, pp. x-xi.

Coats: Dr. (1819), the condition of cultivators in Poona according to, XVIII, pt. ii, 110, 127 note 1.

Cobb: the Rev. Mr., his letter describing Bombay in 1715, XXVI, pt. i, 253-254.

Cobra: worship in Gujarát, IX, pt. i, 154, 172, 220, 288, 379-380; in Poona district, XVIII, pt. i, 81. *See* Serpent.
Cobra's hood: *see* Nágphaui.
Coccinia Indica: food plant, XXV, 159.
Cocculus Indicus: plant yielding fermented drinks, XXV, 210; plant used for poisoning fish, *id.* 272.
Cochin: state, the alliance of its Rájás with Abyssinian Turks and Egyptians, I, pt. ii, 34; its capture by the Dutch (1663), *id.* 64, 282 note 5; Surat Pársis go to; excise farm of, held by a Pársi, IX, pt. ii, 196 and note 2.
Cochineal: insect, XVIII, pt. ii, 64.
Cochlospermum gossypium: timber tree, XXV, 6; plant yielding gums and resins, *id.* 250.
Cocintaga, Cocintana: spelling of Konkan-Tana in the Catalan map (1375), I, pt. ii, 4.
Cock: carrier of goddess Behecharáji, worship of, IX, pt. i, 380-381; is held sacred, IX, pt. ii, 220; the crow of, believed to scare evil spirits, *id.* 220 note 1.
Cockburn: Colonel, English commander, negotiates the convention at Vadgaon (1778), I, pt. ii, 605; *see* also XIII, 503, 504 and note 2; XVIII, pt. ii, 263-264.
Cocoanut: favourite offering to goddesses, IX, pt. i, 385; *see* Nalieri Day; *see* Balev; fall in the price of (1774) in Bombay Island, XXVI, pt. iii, 468-470.
Cocoa-palm: in Ratnágiri, X, 34; tapping licenses, *id.* 35; in Thána, mode of cultivation, cost, profit, XIII, 295-298; in Kánara, XV, pt. i, 58, 59; in Poona, XVIII, pt. i, 49; in Káthiáwár, VIII, 95; in Dharwár, XXII, 303; *see* also XXV, 136, 180.
Cocos nucifera: cocoanut tree, XXV, 136, 180, 212, 221, 237; food plant, *id.* 180; yields fermented liquors, *id.* 212; oil-yielding plant, *id.* 221; fibrous plant, *id.* 237.
Code: a civil and criminal, enacted by Mr. Mountstuart Elphinstone (1827), I, pt. i, 436.
Code of Morals: in Gujarát, IX, pt. ii, 213.
Coffee: *Arabica, Siberica,* XXV, 162; favourite drink among Musalmáns, IX, pt. i, p. xxxiv; cultivation of, in Ratnágiri district, X, 425; in Kánara, XV, pt. ii, 19; experimental cultivation of, near Poona city, XVIII, pt. ii, 63 64.
Coimbatore: surrendered to Vishnuvardhana the Hoysála king, I, pt. ii, 496.
Coin: in the relics of Sopára *stupa,* XIII, 409 and note 1; (A. D. 400), *id.* 419; Siláhára (A. D. 810-1260), *id.* 428 and note 5; of Eucratides (B. C. 155), I, pt. i, 16-17; of Apollodotus, *id.* 18-19; of Menander, *id.* 18-19; of Nahapána, *id.* 24-25; Gupta, *id.* 29; of Chashtana (A. D. 130), *id.* 29-30; Sopára *stupa* or mound, *id.* 38; hoards of, *id.* 48-49, 57, 60; of Samudragupta, five varieties of, *id.* 62-63, 66, 67-68; Gupta, *id.* 70, 71; of king Mahipála, *id.* 138; Hindu sun, *id.* 142; study of the old, "Introduction to the Early History of the Dakkan," I, pt. ii, p. iii; of the Sátavábanas, *id.* p. vi; of lead and copper, discovered at Kolhápur, characters on, *id.* 152; names of princes on the Supára, *id.* 153; dates on the, of the Kshatrapa dynasty, *id.* 157; found at Kolhápur, *id.* 158; of Kshatrapa, at Kolhápur, and of Yajnaśri at Supára, *id.* 161; 385; found at Girnár, VIII, 273; Baktrian, IX, pt. ii, 183 note 4; in the Sopára *stupa* relics, XIII, 409 and note 1; Ráshtrakúta (400 A. D.), found in Bombay and Sálsette, *id.* 419; Siláhára coins (810-1260), *id.* 428 and note 5; Ahmad Báhmani's (A. D. 1440), XIV, 175; Mulgaon, *id.* 400: Portuguese, *id.* 350 note 2 379; Sopára Buddhist, *id.* 332-333; found in Násik, XVI, 183 note 5; Nahapán's (B. C. 10), *id.* 535 note 3; Nahapán and Chastana compared, *id.* 616-618, 619; Kshatrap and a similar coin in Káthiáwár, *id.* 624; Shátkarni (A. D. 160) in Poona district, XVIII, pt. ii, 213.
Coleus: *aromaticus, barbatus,* food plants common in gardens, XXV, 168.
Colláby: port at the entrance into the river of Chaul, I, pt. ii, 102.
College: of the Purification, establishment of, at Basseiu, I, pt. ii, 57; Mahomedan, at Bhiwndi, XIV, 48; ruins of a Christian, at Mandapeshvar, *id.* 225; military, at Máhim, *id.* 380; in Ahmadábád, IV, 217; Portuguese, seven in Thána and four in Bassein, XIII, 462; at Bándra and Bassein, *id.* 476; at Calcutta established (1800), XXVI, pt. iii, 413.
Colloor: ruined village in Madras presidency, I, pt. ii, 299 note 1.
Colocasia antiquorum: food plant, XXV, 182.
Colonists: Pársis as, IX, pt. ii, 200.
Colt: Mr., President at Surat, imprisoned (1701), XXVI, pt. i, 123.
Columbidæ: family of birds in Ratnágiri, X, 86.
Columbinæ: family of birds in Ratnágiri, X, 86.
Columns: basaltic, in Poona district, XVIII, pt. i, 10-11.
Comara: bay on Konkan coast, I, pt. ii, 90.
Combose: Cambodia, I, pt. i, 499.
Combretaceæ: an order of timber trees, XXV, 73, 155, 218, 244; an order of food plants, *id.* 155; an order of oil-yielding plants, *id.* 218; an order of plants yielding dyes, *id.* 244.
Combs: making of, in Poona district, XVIII, pt. ii, 201-202; in Thána district, XIII, 398.
Comet; called Ketu, his friendly and unfriendly influence, IX, pt. i, 405. *See* Planet.
Coming of age: customs, among Havigs, XV, pt. i, 126-127; among Shenvis, *id.* 164; among Uppárs, *id.* 281; among Chetris, *id.* 343; among Musalmáns, *id.* 408.
Commandments: the ten Buddhist, XIV, 139.
Commelynaceæ: an order of famine plants, XXV, 206.
Commelyna communis: famine plant, XXV, 206.
Commerce: *see* All District Volumes under District Name.
Commissions: forms of, to the commander-in-chief, East Indies, to Bombay commander-in-chief, to the Naval commander-in-chief

and other officers (1694-1778), XXVI, pt. iii, 197-202.
Common beet: food plant, XXV, 169.
Common coriander: food plant, XXV, 161.
Common fennel: food plant, XXV, 161.
Common fig: food plant, XXV, 172.
Common green grass snake: in Poona district, XVIII, pt. i, 77.
Common plantain: food plant, XXV, 174.
Common spinach: food plant, XXV, 169.
Communications: between the several provinces under the Andhrabhrityas or Sátaváhanas, I, pt. ii, 177; All District Volumes *see* under District Name.
Company: the United East India, IX, pt. ii, 192 note 3; East India, desirous of becoming Mughal admirals (1733), XXVI, pt. i, 162-163; the old and the new, union of, (1702), XXVI, 139-142; not really united till 1708, *id.* 143.
Compass: mariner's, used by Mozambique Musalmáns (1498), XIII, 471; invention of, probably known to Bráhman astronomers, *id.* 725-726.
Compositæ: an order of food plants, XXV, 162; an order of famine plants, *id.* 200; an order of oil-yielding plants, *id.* 218; an order of plants yielding dyes, *id.* 246.
Conch Shells: rock-cut, on Padan Hill in Thána, XIV, 390.
Conde d'Alvar: thirty-third Portuguese viceroy (1682), XV, pt. ii, 256.
Condiments: cultivation of, in Khándesh, XII, 174; in Poona, XVIII, pt. ii, 50-55.
Confession: of faith, IX, pt. i, 211; of sin, *id.* 223, 232.
Configuration: of the Konkan, "Introduction to the History of the Konkan," I, pt. ii, pp. x-xi.
Confinement: woman's first, Bráhman's, IX, pt. i, 33; Golás, *id.* 185; Kanbis, *id.* 157; 161; Kansárás, *id.* 187; Káyasthas, *id.* 61, 67; Kolis, *id.* 247; Luhárs, *id.* 191; Patelás, *id.* 173; Rájpúts, *id.* 138; Vániás, *id.* 89, 94.
Conglomeratic Rocks: in Belgaum district, XXI, 19.
Coniferæ: timber tree, XXV, 133.
Conirostres: family of birds in Thána district, XIII, 51.
Conjee House: built (1767) in Bombay Island, XXVI, pt. iii, 144.
Conjeveram: town in Madras, I. pt. ii, 140, *id.* 183; capital of the Pallava kings, captured by Vikramáditya I, *id.* 186; Kanchi, *id.* 280; inscriptions at, *id.* 318 note 3, 319 note 3, 325 note 2, 327 note 8, 329 330; visited by Kumárapála in his exile, I, pt. i, 183.
Conocarpus latifolia: timber tree common in Mira hills, Kennery and forests of Konkan, XXV, 76; dyes, *id.* 244.
Conocephalus nivens: fibrous plant common at Mahábaleshwar and Konkan jungles, XXV, 234.
Conspiracy: against the English at Sátára and Poona detected, and the ring-leaders executed, I, pt. ii, 612.
Consumption: *kshaya*, causes and cure of, IX, pt. i, 365.
Convalescent Hospital: on Old Woman's Island, Bombay, proposed (1768), XXVI, pt. iii, 555; opened (1771), *id.* 560.
Convent: Poona city, XVIII, pt. iii, 362.
Convention: of Vadgaon, disallowed by the Bombay Government, I, pt. ii, 605.
Conversion: to Christianity, I, pt. ii, 55; by force (1594), *id.* 59; to the Pársi religion, of Thána Hindus, IX, pt. ii, 189 note 1; of emperor Akbar, *id.* 190; of the Pársis to Hindu and Musalmán faith, *id.* 187 note 4; Portuguese, to Christianity in Thána district, XIII, 63, 201, 460-462.
Converts: Panjábi, I, pt. ii, 57, 58; privileges of, and encouragement to, *id.* 59; Hindu, IX, pt. ii, 3-5; name of the classes of, *id.* 20, 24, 58, 70, 80, 85; accounts of, *id.* 19-90; to Christianity by the Portuguese, XIII, 200, 202, 461, 462; Musalmán in Belgaum, XXI, 196, 197; Christian, *id.* 226, 227.
Convolvulaceæ: an order of food plants, XXV, 166; an order of famine plants, *id.* 202.
Convoy: regulations and rates (1774), in Bombay Island, XXVI, pt. i, 374-375; duty levied (1732), XXVI, pt. iii, 218; shared by captains of ships (1774), XXVI, pt. iii, 250-251.
Conybeare: Mr., proposed the building of Vehár lake, XIV, 376.
Cooke: Humphrey, commissioned to take possession of Bombay, XXVI, pt. i, 13; takes possession, *id.* 21; his convention disavowed, re-called and tried, *id.* 22; *see* also XIII, 472, XV, pt. ii, 256.
Cooperage: Bombay, removed from the Marine Yard (1742), continues in hired houses till 1781, a shed erected for, on the Apollo ground (1781), XXVI, pt. iii, 584-586.
Coorg: state in Madras, I, pt. ii, 299, 341 note 2.
Coorgs: tribe in Mysore, XV, pt. ii, 79.
Coot: class of birds in Ratnágiri, X, 93.
Coote: Lt.-General Sir Eyre, appointed commander-in-chief to the East Indies (1778), XXVI, pt. iii, 201-202.
Copper: East India Company's trade in (1742-1777), XXVI, pt. ii, 127-128.
Copper and Brass: workers in Ahmadábád, IV, 129; work, in Kolába, XI, 130; in Sátára, XIX, 220; in Sholápur, XX, 272; in Dhárwár, XXII, 381.
Copper Casket: Sopára *stupa*, XIV, 331, 332.
Copper Coinage: (1668) introduced into Gujarát by the viceroy Mahábát Khán (1662-1668), I, pt. i, 284.
Copper-plates: Valabhi, description of, I, pt. i, 70-80; of Gujarát Chálukyas, *id.* 108; of the Gurjjaras, *id.* 113, 114; three forged, *id.* 117 note 1, 118, 121; of Bhima I, *id.* 163; found in Káthiáwár, VIII, 275; in Thána district, XIII, 419, 424, 425, 435 and note 4, 437; Siláhára (1026), at Bhándup, XIV, 45; of Aparajit Siláhára (997), at Bhiwndi, *id.* 50; at Elephanta, *id.* 80 note 1, 388; found at Bassein, of Seunachandra Yádava (1069), *id.* 386-387; of Arikeshari Siláhára, found at Thána (1787), *id.* 418; inscribed, in Kánara district, XV, pt. ii, 77, 78, 101, 106, 268, 269, 270, 280 note 1, 298.

Copper Vessels: making of, in Belgaum, XXI, 352.
Copper Work: in Cutch, V, 124.
Coraciadæ: family of birds in Ratnágiri, X, 64.
Coral: in Káthiáwár, VIII, 93; East India Company's trade in (1730-1772), XXVI, pt. ii, 126-127.
Corchorus: *capsularis olitorius*, fibrous plants, XXV, 230; *olitorius, trilocularis*, famine plants, *id.* 195.
Cordia latifolia: timber tree common in Bombay and *ghâts*, XXV, 102.
Cordia Macleodii: timber tree, XXV, 103; *myxa, Rothi, wallichii*, timber trees, *id.* 102; *myxa, Rothi*, food plants, *id.* 166; *myxa*, plant yields dyes, *id.* 248; *Rothi*, fibrous plant, *id.* 233.
Coriandrum sativum: food plant, XXV, 161.
Cormorant: the little, in Ratnágiri, X, 99.
Cornaceæ: an order of food plants, XXV, 161.
Cornwallis: Marquis of (1791-92), IX, pt. ii, 86.
Coromandel: Coast, I, pt. ii, 4.
Coronation: Shiváji's (1674), description of XI, 369-372; *see* also XVIII, pt. ii, 236.
Coroner: appointed in Bombay Island (1701), XXVI, pt. iii, 8.
Correa: Portuguese historian (1512-1550), died at Goa (1550), I, pt. i, 349.
Corvinæ: family of birds in Ratnágiri, X, 81.
Coryat: Tom, English traveller (1670), I, pt. i, 377.
Cosmas Indikopleustes: Greek merchant of the sixth century, I, pt. ii, 3; his description of North India, I, pt. i, 86, 143, 146.
Cotton: in Surat, II, 66; in Broach, varieties grown, *id.* 392; mode and profits of cultivation, *id.* 393; Government efforts to improve cotton by improving cultivation and by preventing adulteration, *id.* 394, 403; course of the cotton trade (1772-1875), *id.* 426-433; cultivation of, in Kaira, III, 50; in Ahmadábád, IV, 55; in Káthiáwár, cultivation and trade, VIII, 185-186, 249, 255; in Ratnágiri, X. 149; spinning and weaving of, *id.* 188; in Khándesh, varieties, improvement (1831-1880), XII, 153-162; export, *id.* 220-222; hand-spinning and weaving of, *id.* 228; trade in, of Thána with Ophir (B. C. 1100-850), XIII, 404 note 3; with Babylon (A. D. 133-246), *id.* 412; to Egypt (A. D. 150), *id.* 416; export of, from Kánara ports, XXV, pt. ii, 55, 57; through Devimane pass, *id.* 80; press, *id.* 30; raw, in Násik, XVI, 101, 137, 498; goods, *id.* 167-168; in Ahmadnagar, XVII, 270-272; in Poona district, XVIII, pt. ii, 46-48; weaving, *id.* 196-198; in Satára, XIX, 165-166, 381 note 1; in Sholápur, XX, 230-231; export trade in, *id.* 264-266; in Belgaum, area, varieties, seed, soil, water, manure, tools, tillage, diseases, yield, cost, experiments, adulteration, XXI, 253-280; exports, trader's system, *id.* 316-326; weaving, *id.* 336-342; in Dhárwár, area, varieties, climate, soil, watering, changes, manure, tillage, crossing, diseases, outturn, improvements and experiments (1819-1883); XXII, 281-302; in Bijápur, XXIII, 321-324; East India Company's trade in (1684-1780), XXVI, pt. ii, 94-95; in Dhárwár (1829-1884), XXII, 359-365, in Belgaum, XXI, 326-328.
Cottonara: Kadattanádu, port in Southern India, mentioned by Pliny, I, pt. i, 537.
Cotton-cloth: exported to Ceylon, Straits and China (810-1260), *id.* XIII, 430.
Cotton Commission: (1863), XXII, 295; (1874), *id.* 299.
Cotton Frauds Act IX (1863): XXII, 295.
Cotton Gins; in Ahmadábád, IV, 102; in Pálanpur, V, 300, 345, 348; in Belgaum, XXI, 326-28.
Cotton presses; in Ahmadábád, IV, 103.
Coturnicinæ: in Ratnágiri, X, 88.
Council Hall: Poona, XVIII, pt. iii, 363-364.
Council rules: (1777), XXVI, pt. iii, 397.
Courten: Sir William, his association incorporated with the East India Company (1638-1639), I, pt. ii, 120; his Company's factories at Kárwár and Bhatkal (1638), XV, pt. ii, 52, 124, 321, 322 and note 4; his Company in Surat, II, 85.
Courtezans: in Dhárwár district, XXII, 189-193; in Kánara district, XV, pt. i, 321-326.
Court martial: power granted to Bombay Council to hold (1754), XXVI, pt. iii, 120-121.
Court of Directors: oppose the creation of large land-holders (1822), XIII, 570; reluctant to part with ownership of soil (1843), *id.* 548.
Court of Justice: Bombay, met in 1670 at Bombay and Máhim Custom Houses, removed to Marine Yard (1675-76), to Mapla Por (1677), to Rámá Kámáti's building (the old Town Hall) (1720), to Mr. Hornby's house, the Present Great Western Hotel or the old High Court (1788), continues to occupy the same till 1879, XXVI, pt. iii, 586-888.
Court of Madrid: sells Indian appointments to the highest bidder, I, pt. ii, 64.
Court of Requests: established in Bombay (1753), XXVI, pt. iii, 29, 33.
Courts: number and working of, in Ratnágiri, X, 267, 268; in Sávantvádi, *id.* 452; *see* All District Volumes under District Name.
Coussmaker: Major, his experiments in *tasár* silk cultivation, XVII, 280. *See* also XVIII, pt. ii, 67-76.
Coutinho: report on Cheul fortification by (1728), XI, 286.
Couvade: practise of the lying-in husband among Pomaliyas of South Gujarát, etc., XVIII, pt. i, 144 note i.
Covellia: *daemonum, glomerata, opositifolia*, timber trees common especially near the sea side, XXV, 131.
Covenants: Bene-Israel's marriage, XVIII, pt. ii, 520 and note 2.
Cowan, Honourable Mr., President and Governor of Bombay (1729-1734), XXVI, pt. iii, 421.
Cowdung: spirit and evil-eye scaring property in, IX, pt. ii, 228 note 2.
Cowherds: in Poona district, XVIII, pt. i, 57, note 2.

Cow-oath : administration of in Bombay Courts (1746), XXVI, pt. iii, 15, 19 ; (1771), *id.* 51.
Cowries : shell money, I, pt. i, 527.
Cows : held to be representative of Kámdughá the heavenly cow ; Kapiládhenu, black cow with a calf, is particularly sacred ; tail, mouth and haunches are held sacred parts of ; *panchgavya* or five cow-gifts, their use in religious ceremonies, sip of her urine taken by pious Hindus, uses of her dung, IX, pt. i, 372 ; *vibhuti* or cowdung-ash ; occasions and ceremony of *gaudán* or gift of a cow ; beliefs among different classes ; object of marrying black heifer with black bull calf ; day sacred for her worship, *id.* 373 ; *gautrál* ceremony, *id.* 373-374 ; worship of, in Shrávan month, IX, pt. i, 374 ; by different classes, *id.* 137, 154, 157, 173, 175, 185, 187, 220, 247 ; in Khándesh, XII, 28 ; in Kánara, XV, pt. i, 79, 80 ; in Ahmadnagar, XVII, 34 ; in Poona, breeds, use, keep, food, disease, sacredness, XVIII, pt. i, 55-60 ; in Sholápur, XX, 15-16 ; in Belgaum, XXI, 67.
Cow-slaughter : at Bhátkal and Kárwár, results of (1670, 1684), XV, pt. ii, 126, 131.
Cradling : Bene-Israel ceremony, XVIII, pt. i, 529.
Craft Guilds : in Khándesh district, XII, 237.
Crafts : in Poona city, XVII, pt. iii, 338 ; *see* All District Volumes under District Name.
Craftsmen : names, strength and distribution, IX, pt. i, 177 ; accounts of the sixteen main classes, *id.* 177-206 ; foreign element traced in some of the classes, *id.* 453, 454 and note 1, 499 ; classes of, Hindu converts as, IX, pt. ii, 71-80. *See* Baudharas, Bhádbhúnjás, Chhipas, *id.* 71 ; Chundadigiras, Chunaras, Chudiwalas, *id.* 72 ; Ghaucis, Kaghzis, *id.* 73 ; Kadias, Kasais, *id.* 74 ; Kharadis, Khatkis, Luhars, Maniars, *id.* 75 ; Monmas, *id.* 76 ; Multanis and Multani Mochis, *id.* 77 ; Nalbands, Panjuigars, *id.* 78 ; Rangrez, Salats, Sonis, *id.* 79 ; Tais, *id.* 80 ; at Mátherán, XIV, 265 ; *see* All District Volumes under District Name.
Cratæva religiosa : timber tree, found all over the Konkan, XXV, 5 ; a sacred plant, *id.* 290.
Crawford : Mr. A. T., Municipal Commissioner, Bombay, bought Panvel brick-works, XIV, 294.
Crawford : Colonel, suggested the damming of Verár stream, XIV, 376.
Creditors : in Kárwár, XV, pt. ii, 30, 31.
Creeks : in Surat, II, 28 ; Broach, *id.* 350 ; in Ahmadábád, IV, 13-15 ; in Káthiáwár, VIII, 64 ; in Ratnágiri, X, 9 ; minor, *id.* 11 ; in Janjirá, XI, 403 ; in Thána, XIII, 11.
Creepers : Mátherán, XIV, 253.
Crew : on *phatemáris* and other boats, XV, pt. ii, 64, 67, 68.
Crime : *see* All District Volumes under District Name.
Crimimal classes : *see* All District Volumes under District Name.
Crinum : *Asiaticum*, XXV, 256, 270 ; *Roxburghii*, *id.* 204 ; *toxicarium*, *id.* 270.
Crocodiles : in Kánara district, XV, pt. i, 95 ; in Belgaum, XXI, 85.
Crocus sativus : food plant, XXV, 177.
Crommelin : Honourable Charles, Governor of Bombay (1760-1767), XXVI, pt. i, 353 ; *see* also XXVI, pt. iii, 378 ; re-called (1766), *id.* 386-387.
Crops : performance of certain rites for the safety of, IX, pt. i, 157 ; tests to find out failure or thriving of, *id.* 354 ; forecasts, *id.* 358, 399.
Crosby : Lieutenant, defeats (1818) a body of Marátha marauders at Poládpur, I, pt. ii, 119.
Crosophora plicata : yields dyes, XXV, 242, 249.
Crosses : discovery of old, Kánara district (1505), XV, pt. ii, 254.
Cross or Gibbet Island : in Bombay harbour, derivation of the name, XXVI, pt. iii, 655-656.
Crotolaria juncea : fibrous plant, XXV, 231 ; sacred plant, *id.* 290.
Croton : *aromaticus, hypoleucas, malabaricum, oblongifolius, reticulatum, tiglium*, timber trees, common in Konkan and Malabár hills, XXV, 120-121 ; *oblongifolius, tiglium*, medicinal plants, *id.* 255 ; *tiglium*, vegetable poison, *id.* 269.
Crow : beliefs about, IX, pt. i, 382.
Crown Lands : under Mughal administration, I, pt. i, 211.
Crow pheasant : in Ratnágiri, X, 68.
Crows : in Ratnágiri district, X, 81.
Cruciferæ : an order of food plants, XXV, 144 ; an order of oil-yielding plants, *id.* 214.
Cryptocarya floribunda : *wightiana*, timber trees common on the Western *ghúts*, XXV, 113.
Crystal casket : Sopára *stupa*, XIV, 335.
Crystalline limestone : in Belgaum district, XXI, 16.
Crystalline sandstone : in Bijápur district, XXIII, 55.
Cuckoo : held sacred, object of worship by women and girls, IX, pt. i, 381 ; in Ratnágiri district, X, 67 ; in Khándesh, XII, 35.
Cuculidae : family of birds in Ratnágiri, X, 67.
Cucumbers : in Khándesh, XII, 172.
Cucumis : *agrestis, cicatrisatus, culta, maderespatanus, melolepo, momordica, pubescens turbonatus, utilissimus*, food plants cultivated on river banks, XXV, 158 ; *trigonus*, medicinal plant, *id.* 255 ; *sativus*, food, oil-yielding and sacred plants, *id.* 159, 218, 279, 285.
Cucurbita : *maxima, melolepo, moschata, ovifera*, food plants, XXV, 160 ; *pepo*, food, oil-yielding and sacred plants, *id.* 160, 218, 279, 285.
Cultirostres : family of birds in Thána district, XIII, 53.
Cultivators : *see* All District Volumes under District Name.
Cuminum cyminum : food plant, XXV, 161.
Cumin seed : food plant, XXV, 161.
Cunha : Nono da, Portuguese viceroy in India (1529), sends an expedition against the island of Diu ; his defeat ; supports Chánd Khán ; sends an embassy to the Court of Humáyun ; makes peace with Sultán Bahádur

(1634); comes to Diu in 1536; murder of Sultán Bahádur at a meeting with (1536), I, pt. i, 347, 348; prohibits the persecution of Hindus by Catholic priests, I, pt. ii, 58.
Cunningham: General, his works quoted, I, pt. i, 86, *id.* 144, 178, 533, 534, 538, I, pt. ii, 296 note 5, *id.* 311, 338 note 7, 353 note 2, 357 note 3, 380 note 1, 410; his "Indian Eras," *id.* 415 note 3, 418, 432 note 8, IX, pt. i, 116 and notes 2 and 3; *id.* 117 note 1; *id.* 265 note 2, *id.* 442; *id.* 470 and notes 4, 5, 6; *id.* 471 and notes 1 and 2; *id.* 474 note 4; *id.* 478 notes 8, ii; *id.* 481; *id.* 482 notes 3, 6; *id.* 495 note 3; *id.* 496; *id.* 497 note 1; *id.* 501 note 3.
Cupania canescens: timber tree common in Konkan, etc., XXI, 50.
Cupid: god, IX, pt. i. *See* Mudan.
Cupressus: *glanca, torulosa,* timber trees, XXV, 133.
Curcuma: *angustifolia, caulina, longa, pseudo-montana,* food plants, XXV, 174-176; yield dye, *id.* 249.
Curing fish: in Thána district, XIII, 58.
Curly hair: theories about Shákyámunis, XII, 492 note 4.
Currency: under Musalmáns, I, pt. i, 222 note 2; in Baroda, VII, 135-140; in Ratnágiri, X, 154; in Sávantvádi, *id.* 429; in Poona, XVIII, pt. ii, 103-104; in Bombay Island (1676-1774), XXVI, pt. ii, 206-230; mint to coin rupees, pice and *bajruks* (1676), *id.* 206; discount on Bombay rupees (1719), *id.* 211; Bombay rupees legal tender (1733), *id.* 212; coinage of gold (1765-66), *id.* 220-222; export duty on silver (1770-78), *id.* 222-24; more gold rupees (1774), *id.* 229-30.
Cursoridae: family of birds in Ratnágiri, X, 90.
Curumbics: Kunbis, I, pt. ii, 53.
Custard apple: tree in Khándesh, XII, 490 and note 1; in Poona, XVIII, pt. i, 53.
Custom and Excise: revenue in Bombay Island (1734-1744), XXVI, pt. iii, 299-300.
Custom duty: of 3½ per cent. in Bombay Island (1676), XXVI, pt. iii, 266; concessions in regard to, to weavers (1676), *id.* 267; reduced (1677), *id.* 267-70; to be reduced (1715), *id.* 294-95; of 9 per cent. reduced (1720), *id.* 323; rates of, on various goods (1744), *id.* 327-29; of one per cent. continued (1747), *id.* 452-53; additional one per cent. for fortification charges (1757), *id.* 453-54; precautions against escape from (1766-71), *id.* 455-58.
Custom House: new, in Bombay (1724), XXVI, pt. ii, 437; situated on Moody Bay, probably near the present Fort Market (1665-1714) at the present Custom House, XXVI, pt. iii, 589-592.
Custom revenue: of Bombay Island (1771-72), XXVI, pt. iii, 458-461.
Customs: among Gujarát Hindus, Bharváds, IX, pt. i, 269; Bhátiás, *id.* 119-121; Bháts, *id.* 213-214; Bhaváyás, *id.* 225; Bráhmans, *id.* 31-50; Brahma-Kshatrias, *id.* 57-59; Chárans, *id.* 220-221; craftsmen, Bhávsárs, *id.* 178; Days, *id.* 181; Ghánchis, *id.* 183; Golás, *id.* 185-186; Kansárás, *id.* 187-188; Luhárs, *id.* 191-192; Mochis, *id.* 194-195; Saláts, *id.* 196-197; Sonis, *id.* 201-202; depressed classes, *id.* 333-334; Bhangiás, *id.* 336-338; Dhedás, *id.* 342-343; Garudás, *id.* 345; Rávaliás, *id.* 508; Thoris, *id.* 509; Vághris, *id.* 517-518; early tribes, Bajániá, *id.* 503-504; Bhils, *id.* 308-311; Chodhrás, *id.* 313; Dhundias, *id.* 314-315; Dubläs, *id.* 317-318; Gamits, *id.* 319, Káthodiás, *id.* 320; Kolgas, *id.* 321; Konknás, *id.* 322; Mángs, *id.* 323; Náikdás, *id.* 327; Várlis, *id.* 329; Vitolias, *id.* 330; Hajáms, *id.* 233-234; husbandmen, Káchhiás, *id.* 154; Kanbis, *id.* 157-163; Ánjana, *id.* 163; Kadvá, *id.* 165; Matia, *id.* 170-171; Patelás, *id.* 173-174; Ságars, *id.* 174-175; Sathvárás, *id.* 176; Káthis, *id.* 257; Káyasths, Bhatnagra, *id.* 67-68; Máthur, *id.* 64-66; Válmik, *id.* 61-64; Kolis, *id.* 247-251; Márwáris, *id.* 104-105; Rabáris, *id.* 289; Rájpúts, *id.* 138-151; Shrávaks, *id.* 99-102; Vániás, *id.* 89-95;—*Betrothals*: details of rites and ceremonies observed in, among Bráhmans, *id.* 40; Rájpúts, *id.* 141-142; Vániás, *id.* 89-90;—*Birth*: details of ceremonies and observances at, among Brahma-Kshatris, *id.* 57; Bráhmans, *id.* 33; Kanbis, *id.* 157; Kolis, *id.* 247; Rájpúts, *id.* 138; Vániás, *id.* 89;—*Botan*: or weaning, that is first feeding, rites observed in, among Brahma-Kshatris, *id.* 57; Bráhmans, *id.* 35; Káyastha, *id.* 61; Rájpúts, *id.* 140;—*Death*: *svargárohana,* details of funeral ceremonies among Bráhmans, *id.* 47-51; Kanbis, *id.* 161-163; Rájpúts, *id.* 148-151; Vániás, *id.* 94-95;—*Destiny-worship*: details of worship among Bhátiás, *id.* 119; Bráhmans, *id.* 33-34; Kanbis, *id.* 157; Káyasths, *id.* 64; Kolis, *id.* 248; Rájpúts, *id.* 139; Vániás, *id.* 89;—Marriage: or *viváha,* ceremonies and observances in, among Bharváds, *id.* 270-285; Bhils, *id.* 308; Bráhmans, *id.* 39-47; Kanbis, *id.* 158-161; *id.* 165; Kolis, *id.* 248-250; Rájpúts, *id.* 141-147; Vániás, *id.* 90-93;—*Mudan* or head shaving: details of rites in among Bráhmans, *id.* 35; Rájpúts, *id.* 140;—*Naming* or *námkarma,* details of rites and ceremonies observed in, among Bráhmans, *id.* 34-35; Rájpúts, *id.* 139;—*Pregnancy*: details of ceremonies performed in, among Bráhmans, *id.* 31-33; Kanbis, *id.* 161; Rájpúts, *id.* 147-148; Vániás, *id.* 93-94;—*Thread-girding*: details of ceremonies performed in, among Brahma-Kshatris, *id.* 57; Bráhmans, *id.* 36-39; Rájpúts, *id.* 141;—among Gujarát Musalmáns, pregnancy, IX, pt. ii, 147-154; birth, *id.* 154-155; naming, *id.* 156-157; sacrifice, fortieth day, *id.* 158; salt-tasting, birth-day, *id.* 159; initiation, *id.* 159-160; circumcision, *id.* 160-161; first Rammazan fast, *id.* 161; present or *hadiya,* *id.* 162; betrothal, *id.* 162-163; marriage, *id.* 163-167; divorce, *id.* 168; death, 168-170; mourning, *id.* 170; among Gujarát Hindu converts, rites and ceremonies relating to pregnancy, *id.* 45; birth, *id.* 46-48; Gotha or Vows, *id.* 48-49; Navzot, 49-50; betrothals, *id.* 50-51; marriage, *id.* 51-57; death, *id.* 57-61. *See* also all District Volumes under name or caste concerned.

Customs : dues in Thána district, abolished (1803), XIII, 562; in Bombay island, increase of (1756), XXVI, pt. iii, 375; revenue from (1760-1779), *id.* 504; receipts and expenditures, all District Volumes. *See* Revenue and Finance under District Name.

Cutch : state, boundaries, divisions, aspects, geology, hills, rivers, lakes, the Ran, and its description, earthquakes (1819, 1844, 1845), climate, V, 1-18; minerals, trees, plants, domestic and wild animals, birds, fish, *id.* 19-37; census details, appearance of the people, dress, *id.* 38-43; Bráhmans, writers, traders, Rájpúts, craftsmen, bards, herdsmen, beggars, depressed classes, Musalmáns, villages, dwellings, village communities, *id.* 43-103; agriculture, field tools, harvests, crops, husbandmen, *id.* 104-109; capitalists, exchange bills, currency, prices, wages, weights and measures, *id.* 110-113; roads, vessels, steamers, harbours, trade (1818, 1835, 1837, 1879), course of trade, brokers, insurance, trade guilts, *id.* 114-122; manufactures, *id.* 122-128; early history (325 B. C.-640 A. D.); the Arabs (711-1020), Samma conquest (1320), Máhmud Begadá's conquest (1472), the Raos (1548-1741), Mughal expeditions (1718-1730), the Raos continued (1741-1801), the rise of Fateh Muhammad (1786), his fall (1801), again in power (1804-1813), British help (1809), disorders (1814), hostility to the British (1814), administrative summaries (1860-1877), *id.* 129-177; land administration, revenue, *id.* 178-180; justice, courts, police, crime, infanticide, Jadeja court, *id.* 181-203; revenue and finance, instruction, readers and writers, libraries, *id.* 204-206; diseases, hospitals, vaccination, cattle disease, *id.* 207-209; places of interest, *id.* 210-253; H. H. Rao's family tree, *id.* 254; Gupta conquest of, I, pt. i, 70; included in Sauráshtra of Ptolemy, XIII, 414. *See* Kachh.

Cyamopsis psoraloides : food plants, XXV, 151.

Cyanotis axillaris : famine plant, XXV, 206.

Cyclone : description of, at Bassein (1618), XIV, 31 and note 4; at Thána (1618), *id.* 359; in Kánara district, XV, pt. i, 8, 9; in Ratnágiri, X, 23-24.

Cyclostemon Indicum : timber tree found in Konkan, Malabár and Kánara, XXV, 119.

Cylicodaphne Wightiana : timber tree common in *ghâts* and Kánara, XXV, 112.

Cyminosma pedunculata : timber tree, XXV, 31.

Cynara : *carduncul us, scolymus,* food plants, XXV, 163.

Cynodon dactylon : famine plant, XXV, 208; sacred plant, *id.* 279, 283, 289, 290.

Cynophishelena : a species of snake in Poona district, XVIII, pt. i, 75.

Cyperaceæ : species of food and famine plants, XXV, 184, 208.

Cypselinæ : family of birds in Ratnágiri, X, 62.

D

DABALA : *see* Chedi.

Dahalwárah : plundered by Mahmúd of Ghazni, apparently Delváda, in Káthiáwár, I, pt. i, 166 and note 2, 523.

Dabchick : class of birds in Ratnágiri, X, 98.

Dabgar : caste of leather workers in Káthiáwár, VIII, 157.

Dábha : state in Mahi Kántha, V, 424.

Dábhi : Rájpút tribe, VIII, 115; peasant proprietors, IX, pt. i, 129.

Dabhoi : sub-division in Baroda, its area, boundaries, aspect, water, soil, holdings, revenue, products, places of interest, VII, 544-545; town and fort, origin and history of, the Diamond Gate at, present condition of, *id.* 545-550; Senápati Dábháde's head-quarters at (1725), *id.* 171; captured by Piláji Gáikwár (1727), *id.* 172; withheld by the Peshwa (1768), *id.* 187; Colonel Keating takes shelter at (1775), *id.* 193; captured by Goddard (1780), treaty at, with the Gáikwár, *id.* 196; ceded to the British (1817), *id.* 226; for its history *see* also I, pt. i, 179, 203, 394, 405, 408; head-quarters of the Mahdavi *sayads* in Gujarát, IX, pt. ii, 6 note 1 continued on 7, 64 note 2.

Dábhol : town in Ratnágiri district, its trade, history and remains, X, 326-331, 166, 175, 195 note 4; derivation of the name, *id.* 326 note 10; sack of, *id.* 195 note 4; district, I, pt. ii, 7; caves, *id.* 9; district, laid waste by Malik Káfur, *id.* 29; port of the first government of the Dakhan under the Bahámanis; under Gujarát kings, *id.* 30; last Musalmán seaport, *id.* 31; visit of Mahmud Sháh to, *id.* 33; commercial mart, ranked with Surat and Goa and the meeting-place of all nations, *id.* 34; its defences, *id.* 35, 39; frequently burnt by the Portuguese, *id.* 41; port destroyed by Francisco d'Almeida, *id.* 45; Portuguese factory, *id.* 48; destruction of, by the Portuguese (1570), *id.* 49; port, frequented by the English and Dutch ships without hindrance, *id.* 63; burnt by Shiváji (1660), *id.* 68; Subha, *id.* 69; given to the Shirke family, *id.* 72; taken by the Peshwa (1756), *id.* 92, 120; creek, *id.* 173, 533; Chaul trade diverted to (1347), XIII, 444; a trade centre (1500-1670), *id.* 448; English factory at (1674), *id.* 476; *see* also XIV, 357.

Dabir : Shiváji's foreign minister, XIX, 243.

Dabistán : Gujarát Bráhmans mentioned in, IX, i, 438.

Dabka : village in Baroda, noted for its game, VII, 542-544.

Dábshilims : ancient royal family of Somnáth, I, pt. i, 168.

Dachanabades : name of the Dakhan in the *Periplus* (247), I, pt. ii, 619.

Dactylo-etenium Ægyptiacum : XXV, 208.

Dádá : commander of Mullugi's troop of elephants, I, pt. ii, 237.

Dádábhái Nauroji: Malhárráv Gáikwár's minister (1874), VII, 282-283.
Dádá Hari: well of, at Ahmadábád, IX, pt. i, 165.
Dádáji Kondadev, or Kondev: Bráhman, manager of Sháhji Bhonsla and tutor of Shiváji, his death (1647), I, pt. ii, 591; *see* also XVIII, pt. ii, 225-226; XVIII, pt. iii, 403; XIX, 242.
Dádáji Raghunáth Deshpánde: a Marátha general, besieged Janjira and attacked Bombay (1682), XI, 441.
Dádáka: minister of Siddharája, I, pt. i, 172.
Dada Máhábali: saint enshrined at Gotarka, in North Gujarát, IX, pt. ii, 17.
Dáda Mián: Ahmadábád *sayad*, honoured by Mirásis, IX, pt. ii, 83.
Dadda I: Gurjjara king of Nándod (580), I, pt. i, 108, 114; first Gurjjara feudatory of Bhinmál Gurjjara kingdom, *id.* 115.
Dadda I: Gurjara chieftain, uproots the Nágas, I, pt. ii, 281 note 3, 312 note 7, 313 note 4; vassal of the Kalachuri king Buddha, *id.* 315.
Dadda II: Gurjara king (620-650), I, pt. i, 56; Gurjjara chief of Nándod, helps the Valabhis, *id.* 85; his grant, *id.* 111, 114, 115, 116.
Dadda II: Gurjara king, I, pt. ii, 312 and note 7, 313; contemporary of Harshavardhána of Kanauj, *id.* 314 and note 1; gives protection to Dharasena IV, king of Valabhi, *id.* 315.
Dadda III: Gurjara king (680), I, pt. i, 114; feudatory of Jayasimha, the Chálukya; first Saiva of his family, adopts the Puránic pedigree traced to Karna, *id.* 116-117; wages war with the kings of the East and West, I, pt. ii, 316; raised to be Kshatriya, IX, pt. i, 449, 479, 480, 486.
Dadeli well: in the vicinity of Bhinmál, I, pt. i, 455.
Dadháluja: state in Mahi Kántha, V, 424; IX, pt. i, 129.
Dadharapur: fort built at, by Siddharája I, pt. i, 180 note 2.
Dadhich: Rishi, son of Brahma, Sárasvats claim descent from, IX, pt. i, 18 note 2; Dadhich Bráhmans take name from, *id.* 9.
Dadhich: sub-caste of Bráhmans, their original stock, IX, pt. i, 9.
Dadhivále Vaidu: caste of bearded doctors in Poona district, XVIII, pt. i, 479.
Dádiseths: chief family among earlier settlers in Bombay, IX, pt. ii, 195.
Dádji Rámoshi: a noted dacoit in Poona district, his life (1773), XVIII, pt. iii, 36 and notes 1 and 2.
Dadmardun: medicinal plant, XXV, 254.
Dádu: Pir, of Sindh Khoján family; invested with mantle of *pir* or saint by the Khoján Imám; conversions by, at Jámnagar (1549), at Bhúj (1585-1594), IX, pt. ii, 41, 48.
Dádu Narsu Kále: land settlement of (1429), in the Dakhan, XVIII, pt. ii, 217; XIX, 226; XX, 277.
Dádupanthis: religious sect in Gujarát, IX, pt. i, XXXVI, 548; *see* Religious Sects.
Dadva: village in Gondal state in Káthiáwár, VIII, 408.
Dæmia extensa: fibrous, medicinal, vegetable plant, antidote to snake-bite, grows in Bombay and Poona, XXV, 233, 257, 274.
Daerd: South Kánara tribe resembling Gujarát Dhedás, IX, pt. i, 338 note 1.
Daf: drum, players on the, IX, pt. ii, 20.
Dáfali: *see* Abdali.
Dagada-Choth: *see* Ganesh Chaturthi.
Dagdi Bándh: Sopára stone dam, XIV, 342.
Dágh-Dena: Branding among Nats, IX, pt. ii, 89 note 1.
Dáhala: Chedi country in Central India, attacked by the Western Chálukya king Someśvara I, I, pt. ii, 214, 293, 411; acquired by the Kálachuri king Krishna, *id.* 468, 469.
Dáhánu: sub-division of Thána district, its boundaries, area, aspect, climate, water, holdings, rental, stock, crops, people, XIII, 2, 671-673; survey of, *id.* 558; a Portuguese district (1560), *id.* 455; town, its description, history, fort, XIV, 53-55; attacked by the Mughals, I, pt. ii, 40; Portuguese fort at, *id.* 66; reduced by the Maráthas, (1739), XXVI, pt. i, 198; XIII, 493.
Dáhanuká: river in Thána district, I, pt. ii, 148; XIV, 54.
Dahiani: presents among Brahma-Kshatris, IX, pt. i, 58.
Dahida: táluka in Káthiáwár, VIII, 408.
Dahisar: place in Thána district, an inscribed stone at, XIV, 388.
Dahithali: village granted to Devaprasáda, son of Kshemarája, for maintenance, I, pt. i, 170; residence of Kumárapála's ancestors, *id.* 181.
Dahivadi: village in Sátára district, an old mansion at, XIX, 461-462.
Dahivali: pass in Koláha district, XI, 115.
Dahivali: village in Thána district, XIV, 55, 196.
Dahivar: *see* Dheri.
Dahnaj: perhaps Kamlej, mentioned by Al Biladuri (892), I, pt. i, 520.
Dáholi: village in Poona district, temple, fair, XVIII, pt. iii, 127.
Dahrasena: Traikútaka king (457), I, pt. i, 55, 58; grant of, I, pt. ii, 294-295.
Dai: missionary, IX, pt. ii, 26, 37; head *mulla*, *id.* 32; midwife, *id.* 154.
Daialam: Persian district, IX, pt. ii, 37, 38.
Daily Life: of towns people in Gujarát, men, IX, pt. i, pp. xix-xxi; women, *id.* p. xxi; of rural population in Gujarát, men, women, *id.* p. xxii; of men among Gujarát Musalmáns of rich class, middle class, poor class, IX, pt. ii, 116-117; of women, of rich class, middle class, poor class, *id.* 117; of Buddhist monks, XIV, 143; *see* also under the caste concerned.
Dairah: settlement of Mahdavis in Pálanpur, IX, pt. ii, 64 and note 1.
Daivadnya Bráhmans: *see* Sonár.
Dáiwá: tribe of Rájpúts, IX, pt. i, 125.
Dáji Gopál: Bráhman rebel, takes the fort of Betávad (1817), I, pt. ii, 630.

Dáji Krishna Pandit: minister of Kolhápur, XXI, 407. *See* Dáji Pandit.

Dáji Pandit: state *kárbhári*, Kolhápur (1838-1843), XXIV, 242; revenue and judicial system under, *id.* 247-248; added a hall to Ambábai's temple at Kolhápur, *id.* 310.

Dákan: Hindu witch, belief in, IX, pt. ii, 142 note 1. *See* Witches.

Dáken: *see* Witches.

Dakhamitra: wife of Ushavadáta, I, pt. ii, 148.

Dakhan: etymology and denotation of the word, I, pt. ii, 133; its trade with the coast under Aśoka, XIII, 409; Kshatraps driven from (124 A. D.), *id.* 412; its export to Egypt (150 A. D.), *id.* 416; grain market for the Konkan, *id.* 561-562; conquered by Vishnuvardhána Chálukya, *id.* 341, 375, 394, 482, 509, 528; invaded by Bhoja, *id.* 214; invaded by Allá-ud-din, *id.* 530-531; invaded by Malik Káfur, *id.* 532; Malik Káfur marches into, for the fourth time (1312), *id.* 533, 619, 568; remains subject to the Delhi emperors till 1345, *id.* 587; establishment of the Bahámani dynasty in (1347), *id.* 587-588, 620, 637; partition of, into Ahmadnagar and Bijápur kingdoms (1491), *id.* 589; Mughals begin to invade (1600), *id.* 590; Todar Mal's revenue system introduced into, under Aurangzib's governorship (1636), *id.* 625; *chauth* and *sardeshmukhi* obtained by the Maráthás on the revenues of (1720), *id.* 626; becomes subject to Nizám-ul-Mulk (1720), *id.* 626-627; passes to the Maráthás, *id.* 627; ravaged by Fatehsing Máne, *id.* 608; conquest of, by the English, 1818, *id.* 361. *See also* I, pt. i, 534, I, pt. ii, 608-609, 619, 626-627.

Dakhan College: established 1857, XVIII, pt. iii, 51; origin, staff and other details, *id.* 56-57; description of, *id.* 364.

Dakhan Education Society: XVIII, pt. iii, 60, 335.

Dakhan Riots: 1875 A. D. in Ahmadnagar, XVII, 318-319; in Poona, XVIII, pt. ii, 119-123; commission or enquiry into, *id.* 123-128.

Dakhan Trap: *see* District Volumes, Geology.

Dakhani Bráhmans: in Gujarát called Maráthá or Maháráshtra Bráhmans; chief classes, strength and distribution, IX, pt. i, 2, 51; language, food, dress, faith, customs, *id.* 52-54. *See* Bráhmans.

Dákhin: female spirit, XVIII, pt. i, 553-554. *See* Dákan.

Dakhinabades: Dakshinápatha or Dakhan, I, pt. i, 545; I, pt. ii, 133, 174.

Dakhinavadha: Dakhan, I, pt. ii, 133.

Dakkhan: I, pt. ii, 133. *See* Dakhan.

Dakkhinábadha: Dakhan, I, pt. ii, 133.

Dákor: town and place of pilgrimage in Kaira district, its temple and lake, story of Krishna's removal from Dwárka to, III, 167-168; Piláji Gáikwár murdered at (1732), VII, 173; place of pilgrimage, IX, pt. i, 28, 119, 157, 164, 173, 175, 225, 247, 333, 336, 341, 347, 549; temple of Krishna, *id.* 10; arrangements for pilgrims, *id.* 28.

Daksha: father-in-law of Shiv, represented with a goat's head, IX, pt. i, 377; his sacrifice said to have been held at Dhulkhed in Bijápur district, XXIII, 378; historical value of the story, *id.* 646 note 3.

Dakshani: caste of cultivators in Khándesh, XII, 69.

Dakshina: Dábháde's charities continued by the Peshwa, XIX, 274.

Dakshina: Sanskrit form of Dakhan, I, pt. ii, 133. *See* Dakhan.

Dakshina Fund: origin of the, XVIII, pt. ii, 244.

Dakshina Mahi: southern kingdom, I, pt. ii, 523.

Dakshina Mahi Mandala: territory of the southern land, I, pt. ii, 500.

Dakshina Mandala: southern territory ruled over by Vira-Ballála II, I, pt. ii, 502.

Dakshinápatha: southern region, old name of Dakhan, I, pt. ii, 133, 140, 157, 160, 161, 174, 187, 280, 339, 482; XVIII, pt. ii, 212.

Dakshina Prize Committee: in Poona city, formed (1838), its funds, how utilised, fellowships established out of its funds, (1857), XVIII, pt. iii, 62-64.

Dakshina-Śiva: Hindu god, I, pt. ii, 386.

Dalál: caste of Musalmán brokers in Ahmadnagar district, XVII, 227.

Dálan: court-yard of a house, IX, pt. ii, 91.

Dalása: hill in Káthiáwár, VIII, 9.

Dalba Bhandári: tried for treason in Bombay island and fined heavily (1720), XXVI, pt. i, 148-149.

Dalbergia: *latifolia*, fodder plant, XXV, 278; *oogeinensis*, used to poison fish, *id.* 272; *sisso*, oil-yielding plant, *id.* 217.

Dálbhát: dish, public dinners, called after; cost of, IX, pt. ii, 113, 114 and note 1.

D'Alboquerqe: Portuguese viceroy (1508-1512), established in Goa (1512), XV, pt. ii, 51; his tenure of office, *id.* 107-112; anchored at Anjidiv (1510), *id.* 255; permitted to fortify Bhatkal (1510), *id.* 272; takes Chitákul, *id.* 279; sails to Honávar, *id.* 309; visits Mirjan, *id.* 332.

Dáldi: a Musalmán caste in Ratnágiri district, X, 134, 155, 171; fishermen, *id.* 101; in Kolába district, XI, 83; in Janjira, *id.* 421.

Dále: caste of cultivators in Khándesh district, XII, 69.

Dálhi: wood-ash tillage in Násik district, XVI, 97; in Ahmadnagar, XVII, 261-262.

Dali: a tenure in Thána district, XIII, 531 note 3, 586.

Dalim, dalimb: Dye-yielding and fruit plant, grows in Poona district, XXV, 246, XVIII, pt. i, 45.

Dalmaj: town in Gujarát, perhaps Kamlej, I, pt. i, 109.

D'Almeida, Francisco: first Portuguese viceroy, fortified Anjidiv, attacks Honávar (1505), XV, pt. ii, 103, 254, 278, 308; his naval victory at Diu (1509), *id.* 105; succeeded by Afonso D'Alboquerque, *id.* 107.

D'Almeida, Lorenzo: son of Francisco D'Almeida, destroys seven vessels of the Moors (1507), I, pt. ii, 43; burns ships in Dábhol

harbour, attacked by the Gujarát and Egyptian fleets and killed in Chaul harbour, *id.* 44.
Dalsingar: *see* Kárangikar.
Dalvádi: Kolis, sub-division of. *See* Kolis.
Dám: coin, I, pt. i, 222 note 2.
Dama: Dáva, Sinda prince of Yelburga, I, pt. ii, 573, 574.
Damadamis: Indian envoy to Antoninus Pius (A. D. 154-181), I, pt. i, 542.
Dámájadasri: twelfth Kshatrapa (236), coins of, I, pt. i, 45; sixteenth Kshatrapa (250-255), coins of, 47.
Damáji: Founder of the Gáikwár family; distinguishes himself at the battle of Bálápur (1720), I, pt. i, 389; created *Samsher Bahádur*, his death (1721), VII, 168; *see* also XIX, 266-267.
Damáji Gáikwár: son of Piláji, stirs Bhils and Kolis to revolt (1733), I, pt. i, 394; levies tribute from the chiefs of Sorath (1738), *id.* 321; attacks Chunval Kolis and burns the Chhaniar village, *id.* 321-322; appoints Rangoji as his deputy in place of Malharráo Khuni (1741), *id.* 323; besieges Broach and receives a share in its customs revenues (1741), *id.* 324, 395; goes to Cambay from Satára, *id.* 326; defeats Peshwa's army but is treacherously seized by the Peshwa and imprisoned (1751), *id.* 397; is released; his negotiations with the Peshwa (1752), *id.* 397, 398; returns to Gujarát and is reconciled to his brother Khanderáo, *id.* 330, 396; captures Kapadvanj and appoints his deputy Shevakrái to collect his share of revenue, *id.* 338; joins the Peshwa's deputy to invest Ahmadábád (1756), *id.* 340; helps the Ráo of Cutch in his expedition against Sind, *id.* 342; defeats Momin Khán at Cambay and recovers Visalnagar, Kheralu, Vadnagar, Bijápur and Pátan, *id.* 345; captures Bálásinor (1761), *id.* 399; accompanies the Peshwa to Delhi and escapes from Pánipat (1761), *id.* 399; marries a daughter of the Gohil chief of Láthi whose dowry in land gives him the standpoint in the heart of Káthiáwár, *id.* 418; his death (1768), *id.* 400; quarrels for succession in his family, *id.* 400; *another account*: joins Tárábai, defeats the Peshwa's officers and takes several forts for her; is encountered and taken prisoner by the Peshwa and sent to Poona, I, pt. ii, 601; (1732-1768) second Gáikwár, recaptures Baroda (1734), his alliance with Momin Khán, rivalry with the Bráhman party, his contest with and defeat by the Peshwa (1749-1751), partition of Gujarát with the Peshwa, his share in Gujarát at the battle of Pánipat (1761), his conquests (1763-1766), sides with Raghunáthráv against the Peshwa Mádhavráv, defeated by the latter at Dhodap in the Dakhan, his death (1768), VII, 173-188; the revenue of his territories, *id.* 387; attacked the Bábis at Visánagar (1763-1764), VII, 605; *see* also XVIII, pt. ii, 245, 246; XIX, 292-293.
Dámáji Pant: revenue officer at Mangalvedha under Bedar kings (1347-1489); tradition of, XXIV, 361 note 1; famine of 1460 called after his name, XX, 277.
Damáji Thorát: Kolhápur partisan, imprisons Báláji Vishvanáth (1414), XIX, 257-258; XVIII, pt. ii, 242; I, pt. ii, 599.
Daman: Portuguese possession in Western India, coins found at, I, pt. i, 58; burned by the Portuguese (1532), *id.* 347; northern boundary of the Konkan, "Introduction to the History of the Konkan," I, pt. ii, IX; district of Ahmadábád kingdom, *id.* 30, 34; *thánadári*, attacked by the Mughals (1582); town, besieged by the Mughals (1612), *id.* 40; its cession to the Portuguese, *id.* 48; jail at, *id.* 52; Portuguese fortress at, *id.* 54; under Gujarát kings (1508), XIII, 443; taken by the Portuguese (1531), *id.* 451; again taken (1558), *id.* 452-453; a fort built at (1533), *id.* 456; pinnaces built at, by the English (1634), *id.* 468; its description (1695) by Gemelli Careri, *id.* 483.
Daman: fibrous plant, XXV, 230.
Damana: river between Thána and Surat districts, I, pt. ii, 148.
Damana: king of Erandapalla, I, pt. ii, 280.
Damanganga: river in Surat district, II, 28; I, pt. ii, 295, 310.
Damanganga: river in Násik district, XVI, 7.
Dámara: Bhima I's general, takes Karna captive, I, pt. i, 163.
Damari: mother of Virasena Abhira, I, pt. ii, 177.
Damaruka: double drum, I, pt. ii, 469.
Dámasena: eleventh Kshatrapa (A. D. 226-236); coins of, I, pt. i, 45.
Damasiri: twenty-third Kshatrapa (A. D. 320); coins of, I, pt. i, 50.
Damayanti: queen-consort of Nalrája, IX, pt. i, 8 note 1.
Damazada: fifth Kshatrapa (A. D. 158-168), coins of, I, pt. i, 39-40.
Dambal: lake in Dhárwár district, XXII, 260.
Dambal: town in Dhárwár district, its temples, fort, inscriptions and history, XXII, 660-665; recovered from Dhundia Vágh by Col. Wellesley (1800), *id.* 424; survey of, *id.* 492-498, 537-547; a great Buddhist temple at, XXIV, 120 note; Buddhistic *vihara* and remains at, I, pt. ii, 228, 406 note 5, 448 note 1, 452, 465.
Dámdát: part of *Zend Avesta*, IX, pt. ii, 211 note 2 (5).
Dámnagar: town in Káthiáwár, VIII, 408; under the Gáikwár, hospital at, VII, 510.
Dámodar: reservoir at Junágad, IX, pt. i, 9.
Dámodara Kadamba: Konnúr inscription of, I, pt. ii, 286 note 1, 291; feudatory of the Cholas, *id.* 495, 498, 499.
Dampel: dye-yielding plant, XXV, 241.
Damurike: Ptolemy's Tamil country, XIII, 415.
Dánakhanda: part of Hemadri's *Chaturvarga Chintamani*, I, pt. ii, 249.
Dancing Girls: *see* Temple Servants, also Kalávant, Murali, Náikin and Saib.
Dancing Girls' Palace: at Cheul, XI, 299-300.
Dand: form of gymnastic exercise, IX, pt. ii, 172.
Dánda: fort near Kelve Máhim in Thána district, XIV, 55, 200; port under Gujarát kings, I, pt. ii, 30.

Dandaguda: city on the Coromondal Coast mentioned by Pliny, I, pt. i, 533.
Dandáhi: village anecdote of its cultivators, I, pt. i, 169.
Dandái: local name of Kadi district, I, pt. i, 208 note 3.
Dandaka: Mularája's uncle, I, pt. i, 156, 160.
Dandaka (forest): the modern Dakhan, I, pt. ii, 135, 142. *See* also XVIII, pt. ii, 211.
Dandakáranya: forest of Dandaka, I, pt. ii, 135, 136; infested by the *rákshasas*, *id.* 137; Aryas settle in, *id.* 138, 141, 142, 231, 247.
Dandápur: village in Dhárwár district, inscription at, I, pt. ii, 417.
Danda-Rájapuri or Rájpuri: town, same as Janjira, I, pt. i, 207 note; XI, 460, 461; ceded to Bijápur (1636), *id.* 143; head-quarters of Southern Konkan under Bijápur, *id.* 144; Mánáji Angria's attack on (1758), *id.* 154; head-quarters of North Konkan under Yádav kings (1250-1318), *id.* 432; under Gujarát kings (1450-1530); taken by Malik Ahmad (1490), *id.* 434; mentioned by Barbosa (1514), *id.* 435; captured by Shiváji (1661), *id.* 436; retaken by the Sidis (1671), *id.* 438; district and port under Ahmad Sháh, I, pt. ii, 30; its siege and capture by Mulk Ahmad (1490), *id.* 32; its capture by Shiváji (1661), *id.* 68, 69; the Dutch prevented admission into the port of (1756), *id.* 122.
Dandi: or *sanyási*, order of Shaiv ascetics, appearance, daily life, philosophic tenets, IX, pt. i, 542-543. *See* Shaivs.
Dandian: poet, I, pt. ii, 144; author of the *Kávyádarśa*, *id.* 170.
Daudigdásar: caste of beggars in Bijápur district, their food, dress and customs, XXIII, 180-184.
Dándis: name of Khándesh after Dániál, son of Akbar, I, pt. ii, 624.
Dandu Dátátri: commander of Ahmadábád garrison (1753), I, pt. i, 338.
Dánes: traders in Surat (1759-1800), II, 149.
Dáng: clan of Rájpúts in Cutch, V, 65; in Gujarát, IX, pt. i, 123.
Dáng: *see* Dangs.
Dángchi: Dang Bhils in Khándesh, XII, 103.
Danger: Mátherán Point, XIV, 233, 238.
Dangi: breed of cattle in Poona, XVIII, pt. i, 56.
Dángi: Kanbis, *see* Kanbis.
Dángs: forest in Khándesh, XII, 21; *see* also I, pt. i, 508; I, pt. ii, 632; states, XII, 597-606; tract in Násik, XVI, 3; hill villages, survey settlement and reports of (1840-1860), *id.* 205 note 1, 214, 217, 230-245; revision survey (1875-1880), *id.* 280-291; in Ahmadnagar, XVII, 2.
Dániál: son of Akbar, storms Ahmadnagar and takes the king prisoner (1600); is appointed governor of Khándesh and Berár, I, pt. ii, 624.
Daniell: Major H., catches Honya rebel, XVIII, pt. ii, 309; XVII, 420; puts down Rámoshi rising (1879), XVIII, pt. iii, 38-39; captures Vásudev Balvant Phadke rebel, XIII, 526, 637-638.
Dániyál: marriage of prince, with Bijápur princess (1604), XXIII, 422. *See* Dániál.
Danka: drum, IX, pt. ii, 20.
Dannayakanákere: village in the Belláry district, I, pt. ii, 437.
Dánpaisa: copper coin in Khándesh (1818), XII, 248 note 5.
Danta: state in Mahi Kántha, its history, V, 413-416; I, pt. i, 464; IX, pt. i, 127; pays tribute to Baroda, VII, 329.
Dantidurga: son and successor of Indra II, the Ráshtrakúta king (753), conquers the last Chálukya king Kirtivarman II, I, pt. ii, 190 (*see* also XV, pt. ii, 82); real founder of the Ráshtrakúta dynasty, his *biruda*, epithets and titles; his conquests and deposition, *id.* 389 and note 5, 194, 195, 210, 377 and note 3, 378, 382, 384, 388, 390, 391, 392, 397 note 1, 399 note 7, 414 note 1; his grant, XV, pt. ii, 84; *see* also *id.* 85 note 2; I, pt. i, 120, 122, 467. *See* Dautivarma II.
Dantiga: Pallava king of Kanchi, conquered by Govinda III (804), I, pt. ii, 198, 332, 395, 397; killed by Krishna III, *id.* 207, 420.
Dantivarma II: Ráshtrakúta king (753), XXIV, 219. *See* Dantidurga.
Dantivarman: of the Gujarát branch of the Málkhed family, I, pt. ii, 413, 414; another name of Dantidurga, *id.* 389.
Dantivarman I: Ráshtrakúta king, I, pt. ii, 194, 388.
Dantivarmman: I, pt. i, 120; son of the Ráshtrakúta prince Karka, his plates, *id.* 125, 127.
Dantivra: village in Thána district; custom office at, XIV, 55.
Dántrana: village in Káthiáwár, the birth-place of Nágbái, her story, VIII, 408-409.
Dantretia: village in Káthiáwár, said to be a port in former times, VIII, 409.
Danugúr: village south of Bangalore, *matha* at, I, pt. ii, 437 note 6.
Dányál: Akbar's son, takes Ahmadnagar (1599), XVII, 386-387, 391. *See* Dániál.
Daphlapur: petty state in Satára district, XIX, 2, 624.
Daphles: chiefs of Jath, XIX, 232.
Dápoli: sub-division of Ratnágiri district, account of, X, 2, 296-299; town, *id.* 331; climate, statistics of, *id.* 26, 27.
Dapuri: village near Poona city, bungalows and gardens at, XVIII, pt. iii, 127-128.
Dárá: Aurangzib's brother, in Cutch (1659), V, 137. *See* Dárá Shikosh.
Darachini: oil-yielding plant and also used as medicine, XXV, 224.
Darapura: a village in Baroda territory, VII, 544.
Dárá Shikoh: prince Muhammad, twenty-seventh viceroy of Gujarát (1648-1652); sent to Káthiáwár, I, pt. i, 280; obtains the transfer of Murád from Gujarát to Berár; is defeated at Dholpur by Murád and Aurangzib; flies to Delhi and thence to Láhore (1658), *id.* 282; his rebellion; is defeated at Ahmadábád; flies to Sind; is taken prisoner (1659), *id.* 282. *See* Dárá.

Darbár : mansion of a Thákor, description of, IX, pt. i, 130-131.
Darbár cave : at Kánheri, XIV, 172-173 ; I, pt. ii, 404.
Darbha : grass, also called Kusha, its holiness, IX, pt. i, 42 note 1 ; its use in religious ceremonies, *id.* 42, 384.
Darbhávati : modern Dabhoi, I, pt. i, 203.
Dardæ : Dards of the Upper Indus, I, pt. i, 533.
Dardam Shirasta : old or standard rates of land revenue in Thána, XIII, 559.
Daremeher : gate of mercy ; fire temple set apart for the rites of the dead, IX, pt. ii, 213, 224, 225, 226.
Dargáh : tomb of a saint, IX, pt. ii, 160.
Darghácha Killa : *see* Sánkshi.
Darhasena : Traikutaka prince, I, pt. ii, 178.
Dari : tribe mentioned by Pliny, I, pt. i, 533.
Darila : possibly Darje Tavar, perhaps north of Daman, I, pt. ii, 49.
Dari Pir : fair in honor of, at Ichalkaranji, XXIV, 298.
Darius Hystaspes : conquers the Punjab (B. C. 510), IX, pt. ii, 183 note 4.
Dariyásha : Musalmán saint of Virpur, direct descendant of Abbás, IX, pt. i, 361.
Darje Tavar : I, pt. ii, 49. *See* Darila.
Darji : caste of tailors in Cutch, V, 72 ; in Káthiáwár, VIII, 151 ; in Gujarát, strength and distribution, IX, pt. i, 177, 179 ; divisions, surnames, *id.* 179 ; work, shop, tools, earnings, Ovington's notice of Surat tailors, *id.* 180 and note 1 ; officiating priests at Bharvád marriages, *id.* 180-181 ; their religion, customs, *id.* 181 ; Musalmán tailors in Ahmadnagar, XVII, 227.
Darmsteter : his opinion that Mághás were Zoroastrians, IX, pt. i, 440 ; IX, pt. ii, 10 note 4.
Dárna : river in Násik district, XVI, 8, 9.
Daro : grass, Ganpati's favourite offering, its worship, IX, pt. i, 384.
Darod : táluka in Káthiáwár, VIII, 411.
Daroghah : official, I, pt. i, 214.
Darshanigudda : hill in Kánara district, XV, pt. i, 4, 5 ; pt. ii, 153, 280-281.
Darshingudda : *see* Darshanigudda.
Daru : name for priests in *Zend Avesta*, IX, pt. ii, 222.
Darud : calling down blessings on the prophet, IX, pt. ii, 147 note 1.
Darur : I, pt. i, 541. *See* Dhárur.
Dárnvalás Bridge : in Poona city, XVIII, pt. iii, 285.
Darvesh : Musalmán beggars in Belgaum, XXI, 223, 224.
Dary : *see* Dheri.
Darya Khán : Gujarát governor (1373), I, pt. i, 231.
Darya Pir : spirit of the Indus, worshiped by the Lohánas, V, 55 ; vows to, by Bhadálás, *id.* 99 ; worship of, IX, pt. i, p. xxv, 22 ; prayed to by Hindu priests to drive away Eusuf-ud-din, IX, pt. ii, 51.
Dása : Śiva's attendant, I, pt. ii, 482.
Dása : Sinda prince of Yelburga, I, pt. ii, 573, 574.
Dasá : section or sub-division in Vániá caste, IX, pt. i, 70 ; in Bhátiás, *id.* 117 ; the division explains the proportion of outside intermixture, *id.* 435.
Dasábái : hill tomb, in honour of Chánd Bibi, in Ahmadnagar district, XVII, 714.
Daságri : caste of husbandmen in Thána district, XIII, 116.
Dasanámi : *see* Atit, I, pt. i.
Dasánapura : Pallava town, I, pt. ii, 318 ; charter issued from, *id.* 321, 322.
Dasapura : town in Málwa, I, pt. ii, 148 ; perhaps Dasora in Málwa, mentioned in Pandu Lena Caves, XVI, 571, 605, 636.
Dásar : a caste in Kánarese district, I, pt. i, 349 ; pt. ii, 414 note 5 ; in Belgaum, XXI, 179-180 ; in Bijápur district, XXIII, 184-187 ; in Dhárwár, XXII, 132-134 ; in Sholápur, XX, 180-182.
Dasara : táluka in Káthiáwár, VIII, 411.
Dasará : Hindu holiday, IX, pt. i, 53, 67, 136, 336 ; day sacred for making offerings to goddesses, *id.* 406 ; day of the autumn equinox, great festival and *játar* or sacrifice offering day among Bhils, IX, pt. i, 305, 306, 307 ; day of rest, *id.* 175 ; day for worship of elephant, *id.* 376 ; horse, *id.* 137, 173, 213, 305, 376 ; chas or king-fisher, *id.* 157, 173, 175, 382 ; peacock, *id.* 381 ; *shami* tree, *id.* 386 ; of grain, *id.* 390 ; *ásindro* leaves given as gold on, *id.* 383 ; buffalo sacrifice on, *id.* 216, 375 ; *see* also XVIII, pt. i, 250-251 ; Sir J. Malcolm's description of, *id.* 294 and note 3, XVIII, pt. ii, 286 note 1, 299 ; procession of, in Satára city, under the Mahárájás, XIX, 658-659.
Dasaratha : Aśoka's grandson (B. C. 210), I, pt. i, 14-15.
Dasaratha : father of Ráma, I, pt. ii, 142.
Dásari : *see* Dásár.
Dasárna : district mentioned in the *Rámáyana*, I, pt. ii, 142.
Dásaru : *see* Dásar.
Dasarupaka : treatise on rhetoric, Dhanika's commentary on, I, pt. ii, 171.
Dásasvámin : Bráhman grantee of the Chálukyas, I, pt. ii, 191.
Dasatáli : moon worship, details of, IX, pt. i, 400. *See* Planet Moon.
Dasavarman : brother and successor of the Western Chálukya king Satyáśraya, I, pt. ii, 213, 433.
Dasavatár : a Khoja religious book, V, 92, 227.
Daśávatára : cave temple of Ellorá, I, pt. ii, 388, 404 ; rock-cut temple of the, I, pt. ii, 194.
Dasera : *see* Dasara.
Dásgaon : pass in Kolába district, XI, 115 ; town, ceded by the Peshwa (1756), *id.* 159 ; details, rock-cut cistern, and hot springs at, its history, *id.* 310-311.
Daśáhár : division of Bráhmans, in Thána district, XIII, 77.
Daskroi : sub-division of Ahmadábád district, its boundaries, area, aspect, climate, water, soil, holdings, rental, stock, produce and people, IV, 232-235.
Dasori : ceremony relating to birth, IX, pt. ii, 229.

Daspatkari : class of reduced peasant-holders, in Ratnágiri district, X, 203.

Dásri : caste of musicians in Kolhápur, XXIV, 100.

Dassoudh : tythes, IX, pt. ii, 41, 49.

Dastarkhán : IX, pt ii, 111. *See* Meals.

Dastur : high priest, office of, duties and position of, IX, pt. ii, 222; as a member of an Anjumán, *id.* 244.

Dastur Dinár : Abyssinian governor of Gulbarga (1485-1498); his defeat and death, I, pt. ii, 589; Bahámani noble (1478), XX, 278.

Dasyus : wild tribes, met by Aryas, I, pt. ii, 137; descendants of Visvámitra from a large portion of, *id.* 138; or fiends, aborigines so called in the *Vedás*, IX, pt. i, x, 448.

Dátár Pir : tomb at Junágadh, healing shrine, IX, pt. i, 366.

Dategad : hill fort in Sátára district, its description, XIX, 10, 462-463.

Date palm : food plant cultivated in several districts, XXV, 181; culture of, in Surat district, profit from, manufacture of sugar from their juice, II, 39-41.

Datha : táluka in Káthiáwár, VIII, 410.

Dattadevi : Gupta queen, I, pt. i, 65.

Dattámitri : town in Sindh, I, pt. ii, 11, 176; mention of, in Sopára and Kánheri caves, XIV, 147, 168.

Dattátraya : shrine of, at Cheul, XI, 287; temple of, at Nirmal, XIV, 293; image of, in Sopára Chakreshvar temple, *id.* 338; foot-prints of, at Tungár, *id.* 367; image and pool at Gokarn, story of, XV, pt. ii, 296 and note 2.

Datura alba : poisonous plant, XXV, 268.

Dáu : Arab vessel, X, 170.

Daud bin Ajabshah : high priest of the Gujarát Bohoras, IX, pt. ii, 27.

Dáudi : *see* Bohora.

Dáud Khán : Faruki king (1503-1510), XII, 245.

Dáud Khán Panni : forty-sixth viceroy of Gujarát (1714-1715); religious riots at Ahmadábád; his introduction of Dakhan Pandits into official posts, I, pt. i, 298, 299; VII, 167; viceroy of the Dakhan, supports Sháhu, XIX, 254-255; is defeated and slain in Khándesh by Hussain Ali Sayid, I, pt. ii, 626.

Daudmare : poisonous plant, XXV, 265.

Daulatábád : town near Aurangábád, in the Nizám's dominions, I, pt. ii, 3, 136, 231, 253 note 2; Devagiri, so named by Muhammad Tughlak, military post at, *id.* 534, 538 note 8; seat of a governor of the Bahámani kings (1347-1500), *id.* 30, 620; rising at (1366), headed by Bahrám Khán, aided by a Yádav chief and the Rája of Báglan, *id.* 620; district under Malik A'hmad (1485), *id.* 32, 621; unsuccessful efforts of Malik A'hmad to secure the fort of (1493), *id.* 621; capture of, by the Mughals (1633), *id.* 625; fort, surrendered to the Maráthás (1760), *id.* 627. *See* also XV, pt. ii, 94, and XVII, 359-360, 397.

Daulatábád : old rupee, X, 154.

Daulat Khán : Shiváji's Musalmán admiral, I, pt. ii, 72.

Daulatráv Gáikwár; British guarantee in his favour (1808), VII, 259-260.

Daulatráv Sindia : successor of Mahádáji Sindia (1794), I, pt. ii, 606; treacherously seizes Nána Phadnávis and A'ba Shelukar (1797), I, pt. i, 411; hostile to the British (1803), XVII, 410; present in the battle of Kharda (1795), XVIII, pt. ii, 270; promises to secure the accession of Bájiráv, *id.* 271; Bájiráv deserts Sindia whose minister sets up Chimnáji in his place, *id.* 272; Nána's negotiations with Sindia who imprisons his minister and procures the accession of Bájiráv, *id.* 273; his influence in Poona, *id.* 274; he plunders (1797) Poona, *id.* 275; family quarrels, *id.* 276-279; Sindia all powerful at Poona, *id.* 280; his wars with Yashvantráv Holkár, who defeats his army at Ujain, *id.* 281; assists Bájiráv in repelling Holkar who is master of Poona, *id.* 282; tries to seize Patvárdhan's *saranjáms*, XXIV, 234-235; builds a temple at Kedáreshvar, *id.* 299.

Dauri : caste of beggars in Sholápur, XX, 182. *See* Davri.

Dáva : I, pt. ii, 574. *See* Dáma.

Davaka : perhaps Dacca, kingdom of, I, pt. i, 64 and note 2.

Davangere : village in Mysore, I, pt. ii, 285 note 5; inscription at, *id.* 319 note 1, 454, 455 note 6, 459 note 3, 462, 528, 529.

Dávar : early tribe in Thána district, XIII, 156, iron smelters at Mátherán, XIV, 250, 264.

Davari : Ratta chieftain, I, pt. ii, 553.

Davidson : Major, resident at Baroda (1856), VII, 273.

Davidson : Mr., his statements of cost and profit of tillage in Bassein, Máhim, Sanjan, Kolvan and Bhiwndi (1845), XIII, 587-589.

Davies : Mr. J. M., his new assessment (1836-1838), I, pt. ii, 129; political agent (1840), XI, 158; his appointment for revision of assessment (1836), *id.* 182; his account of Sánkshi, Rájpuri and Ráygad (1837), *id.* 182-186; his revision of Thána assessment (1836), XIII, 579-583.

Davis : Mr., resident at Baroda (1853), VII, 271.

Davis : English sea captain, mentions Honávar (1590), XV, pt. ii, 310.

Davis : Lieutenant, at the siege of Rájder, XVI, 196; killed (1818) at the siege of Málegaon, *id.* 197.

Davri : caste of beggars in Belgaum district, XXI, 180; in Kolhápur, XXIV, 101. *See* Budbudker and Dauri.

Dawal : common plant, XXV, 265.

Dáwár : *see* Changa A'sa.

Dawla Kura : poisonous plant, grows on the *ghâts*, XXV, 259.

Dayamava : village goddess, in Dhárwár, temples, image, worship and fair of, XXII, 807-812.

Dayárám : poems of, list of Gujarát Bráhmans in, IX, pt. i, 2.

Dáyima : I, pt. ii, 553. *See* Dávari.

Days : week, common beliefs about, Sunday, IX, pt. i, 393, 396; Monday, *id.* 397, 400; Tuesday, *id.* 401-402; Wednesday, Thurs-

day, *id.* 402; Friday, *id.* 402, 403; Saturday, *id.* 403; lucky and unlucky, IX, pt. ii, 146 and notes 2 and 3; of the Pársi month, names of, IX, pt. ii, 215, 216 note 1; (high) festival, *id.* 216-217. *See* Jasans. Leading high, *id.* 218-219. *See* Festivals (Season).

Deacon: Colonel, I, pt. ii, 611; captures Chákan and other forts (1818), XVIII, pt. ii, 302.

Death: rites and ceremonies among Hindus, Bhangiás, IX, pt. i, 337; Bhátiás, *id.* 121; Bhils, *id.* 309-310; Bráhmans, *id.* 47-51; Brahma Kshatris, *id.* 59; depressed classes, *id.* 333; Dhedás, *id.* 343; Dhundiás, *id.* 315-316; Kanbis, *id.* 161-163; Káyasths, *id.* 64; Kolis, *id.* 251; Konknás, *id.* 322; Mochis, *id.* 195; Naikdás, *id.* 328; Rájpúts, *id.* 148-151; Shrávaks, *id.* 102; Vániás, *id.* 94-95; Varlis, *id.* 329; Gujarát Musalmáns, IX, pt. ii, 239; recital of prayers near the dead, *id.* 239-240; bier, *id.* 240; bier-bearers or *nasesálárs*, *id.* 239 and note 2; last look at the dead; carrying of the dead body to the tower of silence, *id.* 210; funeral party, widow of the dead, *id.* 241; *uthamna* or rising from mourning, *id.* 242; feast-giving on, *id.* 207, 243. Pársis bier or *janazahs*, funeral; to help in funeral a *farz* or duty; *ziárat* feast; dinners on; mourning, IX, pt. ii, 168-170. *See* also in All District Volumes under caste concerned.

Dehal: expedition to, I, pt. i, 506, 511, 512, 513; identified with Karáchi or Thatta, *id.* 508 note 2, 514, 517, 521; perhaps Diu, *id.* 523, 547.

DeBarros: Portuguese historian (1570), I, pt. i, 349; his map (1580), XV, pt. ii, 118; mentions Chitákul (Sintacora), *id.* 249, 279; Agrakon (Egorapan), *id.* 260; Bhatkal (Batekala) mentioned in his map, *id.* 274; mentions Honávar, *id.* 310; Mirjan (Mergen), *id.* 332.

Debregeasia longifolia: fibrous plant, found at Mahábaleshvar and Konkan jungles, XXV, 234.

Debtors: *see* Borrowers.

Debur: place in Mysore, stone inscription at, I, pt. ii, 302.

Decadas: (1497-1539) a work by De Barros, a Portuguese historian, his death in (1570), I, pt. i, 349.

Deccan: *see* Dakhan.

Deccan College: *see* Dakhan College.

De Couto: *see* Do Couto.

De Coutto: Portuguese writer and traveller, I, pt. ii, 58.

Deda: a clan of Samma Rájpúts in Cutch, V, 66.

Dedadra: reservoir built by Siddharáj, I, pt. i. 180 note 2.

Dedal: state in Mahi Kántha, V, 426.

Dedán: táluka in Káthiáwár, VIII, 411.

Deda raids: in Cutch (1871), V, 175.

Dedarda: táluka in Káthiáwár, VIII, 411.

Dedhrota: state in Mahi Kántha, V, 427.

Deer: held sacred, IX, pt. i, 378; in Khándesh, XII, 32; at Mátheran, XIV, 259; in Kánara, XIV, pt. i, 100-102.

Deesa: cantonment, town, in Pálanpur, temples and fair at, V, 341-342; contingent hospital at, maintained by the Gáikwár, VII, 508.

Defence works: Bombay (1737) out forts and *galvats* to defend fords; batteries between Warli and Máhim, breast work from custom house to fort; stone work opposite Dhárávi; wall from Rewa to Sion, XXVI, pt. ii, 279-281; forts at Dongri and the Breach (1739), *id.* 282; the Town Ditch (1739-1743), *id.* 283-291.

Degadi: Prachanda's ancestor, I, pt. i, 129.

Degamve: village in Belgaum district, temples and inscriptions at, XXI, 554; *see* also I, pt. ii, 569, 570; ordeal at, *id.* 571.

Deh: tenth month of the Pársi year, IX, pt. ii, 217, 218.

Dehegám: a part in Broach district, its trade, II, 560.

Dehej; part in Broach district, its history and trade, II, 560.

Dehera: *see* Rájdair.

Deheván: an old port and place of importance in Kaira district, III, 168.

Dehgám: sub-division in Baroda, VII, 588-589; town, *id.* 589-590; hospital at, *id.* 507.

Deh Jasan: high festival day, IX, pt. ii, 217. *See* Jasans.

Dehli: gateway platform in front of Rájpút houses, IX, pt. i, 130, 134.

Dehli Siwálik: pillar, inscriptions on, IX, pt. i, 59 note 1.

Dehra: perhaps Dehra Dún, IX, pt. ii, 188 note 4.

Dehrás: temples, Shrávak religious buildings, description; named after Tirthankars; installation of image of Tirthankar; *anjana-salakha* ceremony; ornaments of the image; ministrants and their duties; worship in, IX, pt. i, 110-113.

Dehu: village in Poona district, birth-place of Tukárám, temples and fairs at, XVIII, pt. iii, 129.

Deimachos: ambassador to Chandragupta's son, his work on India, I, pt. i, 534.

Dekkan: *see* Dakhan.

Delali: state in Mahi Kántha, V, 428.

Delamotte: General, English commander, takes Bhudargad and Panhála (1844), XXIV, 295, 315; seizes and dismantles Sámángad (1844), *id.* 319.

Delasseau: Major, political agent of Dhár (1895), I, pt. i, 384.

Dela Valle, Della Valle: traveller, his description of Cambay (1623), VI, 219; his journey from Cambay to Ahmadábád, I, pt i, 224 note 2; traveller (1624), anchors at Kelshi in Ratnágiri, X, 342; mentions the hurricane (1618), and Máhim, XIV, 32 note 1, 199; his description of Cheul, XI, 280-282, 292, 298, 309; *see* also I, pt. ii, 36; his description of Honávar, Gersappa and Ikkeri, XV, pt. ii, 123, 124, 284, 307, 310; mentions Anjidiv, *id.* 255.

Delhi: establishment of Musalmáns at, I, pt. ii, 250; Musalmán kings of, *id.* 509; empire of, *id.* 510; Khilji emperors of, *id.* 530, 531;

Alla-ud-din ascends the throne of, *id.* 532; Malik Kafur returns to (1311); intrigues at (1316), *id.* 533; empire, decline of (1708), *id.* 626; Shiváji's visit to, XVIII, pt. ii, 234; Bájiráv defeats the Mughals near (1736), XIX, 279; fall of (1857), emperor of, in treasonable correspondence with Nawáb of Rádhanpur, I, pt. i, 441.

Delhi Emperors: their rule in Belgaum district (1294-1350), XXI, 361-362; their rule in Ahmadnagar (1318-1347), XVII, 353; of the Dakhan (1318-1347), XVIII, pt. ii, 215.

Delivery: place of, services of midwife at the time of, IX, pt. ii, 228.

Dellori: imprisoned by the inquisition at Daman (1674), I, pt. ii, 52, 58, 60.

Delváda: town in Káthiáwár, VIII, 667; Rájpúts attacked at (1394), I, pt. i, 233 and note 3.

Demaladevi: wife of the Sinda prince Chávanda II, I, pt. ii, 575.

Demetrius: king of the Indians (B. C. 190-165), I, pt. i, 16.

Demi: river in Káthiáwár, VIII, 63.

Dendro-calamus strictus: food, famine, fibrous and fodder plant common in India, XXV, 188, 209, 238, 277.

Deodár: fibrous plant, XXV, 229.

Deoli: suburb of Ahmadnagar, grant from, I, pt. i, 468, 469, 541; I, pt. ii, 304 note 4, 414, 416 note 4, 417, 418, 419 note 1, 420; Charter at, *id.* 422.

Deopali: town, identified with Deoli, I, pt. i, 541.

Depálá: caste of traders in Cutch, V, 56; an offshoot of Lohánás in Káthiáwár, VIII, 149, IX, pt. i, 122.

Deplá: *see* Depala.

Depressed classes: in Gujarát, strength and distribution; chief classes Bhangiás, Dhedás, Garudas, Khalpas, Sindhvás; main causes of uncleanness; appearance; IX, pt. i, 331; food, position, religion, object of worship and reverence, *id.* 332; *bhagats* or holy men, customs, *id.* 333; community, *id.* 334. *See* All District Volumes under District Name.

Dera: sand-hills in Káthiáwár, VIII, 26.

Dera Ismáil Khán: town once in Sind, I, pt. i, 538.

Derangæ: identified with the Telingas, I, pt. i, 534.

Derbhavti: state in Khándesh, XII, 605.

Derby: English ship, taken by Kánhoji Angria (1727), I, pt. ii, 87.

Derdi Jánbáini: state in Káthiáwár, origin of its name, VIII, 412.

Dermal: fort in Khándesh district, XII, 439.

Desái: social division of Anávalá Bráhmans, IX, pt. i, 5, 6; families in Sajodra Bráhmans, *id.* 18; in Brahma-Kshatris, *id.* 57; family of, of Navsári, IX, pt. ii, 244; office of, holders of the office of Poria, *id.* 200 note 1; British guarantee in favour of (1793), VII, 247; title among some of the Dhandhuka village Bohorás, IX, pt. ii, 62; sub-divisional superintendent in Thána district, *vatan* grants to (1881), XIII, 538; position and duties under the Maráthás, *id.* 556; position and duties of, I, pt. i, 210, 212, 223 and note 2; I, pt. ii, 34; revenue contracters in Surat, their present condition, II, 192; their power and exactions, their relation with the government and the cultivator (1800-1816), their office abolished under the settlement of 1817-1822, *id.* 214-220; in Broach, their exactions (1772-1785), *id.* 484-485; of Kárwár and Sonda; ruled north Kánara under Bijápur (1600-1685), XV, pt. ii, 123; give up allegiance to Sambháji (1685), *id.* 131.

Desan: in Idar state in Mahi Kántha, an old temple at, V, 433-434.

Desar: place of interest in Panch Mahâls, with an old temple, III, 309.

Desastha: *see* Deshasth.

Desávál: sub-caste of Bráhmans, IX, pt. i, 2, 9; of Vániás, *id.* 70-71; takes its name from Deesa, V, 341; in Kolába district, XI, 48.

Desembargadores: Portuguese district judges, I, pt. ii, 52; forbidden to have anything to do with Bráhmans and other Hindus (1591), *id.* 59.

Desert snakes: in Poona, XVIII, pt. i, 77.

Deshantris: Saturday oil-beggars, I, pt. i, 451.

Deshasth: a Bráhman sub-division, in Ratnágiri, X, 115; in Sávantvádi, *id.* 411; in Kolába, XI, 44; in Janjira state, *id.* 411; in Khándesh, XII, 51; in Thána, XIII, 63, 77; in Kánara, XV, pt. i, 129-130; in Ahmadnagar, strength, appearance, division, languages, houses, food, dress, calling, religion, daily life, customs, condition, XVII, 50-54; in Poona, XVIII, pt. i, 159-160; in Sátára, XIX, 51; in Sholápur, XX, 26-27; in Belgaum district, XXI, 89-90; in Dhárwár their sub-divisions into Vaishnavs or Mádhva Bráhmans and Smárt Bhágvats, XXII, 56; in Bijápur their sub-divisions Smárts, Vaishnavás and Savâshes, their food, dress, daily life, birth, thread ceremony, marriage, coming of age, and death ceremonies, XXIII, 79-89; in Kolhápur, their character, dress, occupation, customs, birth, death and marriage ceremonies, thread ceremony, marriage, XXIV, 43-60; *see* Dakhani Bráhmans.

Deshával: caste of labourers in Belgaum district, XXI, 165.

Deshi: breed of cattle, in Poona district, XVIII, pt. i, 56.

Deshkulkarnis: district accountants, XI, 177.

Deshmukhs: hereditary revenue officers in Kolába, their remuneration under Musalmán and Marátha governments, XI, 163; under early Hindu rulers, *id.* 169; sub-divisional superintendent in Thána district, *vatan* grants to (1881), XIII, 538; *izat* tenure enjoyed by, *id.* 540; their duties under Musalmáns, *id.* 553; under the Maráthás, *id.* 556.

Deshnur: hill and village in Belgaum district, XXI, 9, 554.

Deshpandes: sub-divisional accountants in Thána, *vatan* grants to (1881), XIII, 538; *izat* tenure enjoyed by, *id.* 540; their duties under the Musalmáns, *id.* 553; under the Maráthás, *id.* 556; hereditary revenue officers in Kolába, XI, 163, 169, 171, 172 note 1, 178, 194. *See* also I, pt. ii, 34.

Desikosa : vocabulary of vernacular words, I, pt. ii, 169.
Desinama-mála : Prakrit work on local and provincial words compiled by Hemachandra, I, pt. i, 193.
Desinga : I, pt. ii, 435. *See* Jayasimha II.
DeSouza : Emanuel, captain of the fort of Diu (1536), I, pt. i, 347.
DeSouza: dispensary at Uraṇ, in Thána district, XIII, 668.
DeSouza : Martin Alonzo, Portuguese viceroy (1542), wasted Bhatkal territory, XV, pt. ii, 114, 273 and note 3.
Destiny : worship of, called *Shashthi Pujan* or *Chhathi Pujan*, worship of Vidhata or goddess of fortune on the sixth day after birth, rites of, among Bhátiás, IX, pt. i, 119 ; Bráhmans, *id.* 33-34 ; Chárans, *id.* 220-221 ; Kanbis, *id.* 157-158 ; Káyasths, *id.* 61, 64, 67 ; Kolis, *id.* 248 ; Lohárs, *id.* 191 ; Rájpúts, *id.* 139 ; Shrávaks, *id.* 100 ; Sonis, *id.* 201 ; Vániás, *id.* 89 ; is observed among other classes, *id.* 57, 61, 100, 105, 154, 170, 173, 174, 176, 178, 181, 183, 185, 188, 194, 196, 205, 213, 225, 226, 233, 289, 329, 330.
Deur : in Bijápur district, inscription at, I, pt. ii, 440 note 5, 521 and note 5.
Deur : village in Sátára district, action near (1713), XIX, 463, 256 ; action at, between Bápu Gokhle and General Smith (1818), *id.* 303.
Dev : river in Rewa Kántha, VI, 5.
Dev : river in Násik district, XVI, 8.
Devachandra : Jain priest, visits Dhandhuka, carries Changodeva to Karnávati, changes his name Somachandra to Hemachandra, I, pt. i, 191.
Devadaithan : village in Ahmadnagar district, temple at, XVII, 714.
Devadatta : a Buddhist monk, XIV, 142.
Devagana : sect of Digambara Jainás, I, pt. ii, 191.
Devagere : *see* Devagiri.
Devagiri : modern Daulatábád, I, pt. ii, 136, 353 note 2, 520 ; identified with Tagara, *id.* 174, 538 note 8 ; Yádavas of, *id.* 230-252, 299 note 4, 466, 509, 511, 512, 549, 555, 557 ; situated in Seunadeta, *id.* 231 ; founded and made capital by Bhillama, *id.* 238 ; capital of the Yádava kings, *id.* 240, 245, 247, 583, 584 ; expedition of Allá-ud-din, against (1294), two invasions of, by Malik Kafur, 1307 and 1312, respectively, against the Yádava kings Rámachandra and Samkara, *id.* 250-251, 530, 531, 532 ; peaks of, *id.* 501-502 ; Yádava kings, inscriptions of, *id.* 503, 505, 506, 508, 523, 526, 528 ; kingdom under Musalmán yoke, *id.* 530 ; Karnaraya of Gujarát flees to, *id.* 532 ; visited by Muhammad Tughlak, *id.* 533 ; name of, changed to Daulatábád by Muhammad Tughlak, *id.* 534.
Devagiri : village in Dhárwár district, copper-plates at, I, pt. ii, 285, 287, 288, XXII, 400-401.
Devagiri Yádave : Dakhan kings, their rule in Thána, grants of (1273-1291), XIII, 60, 437 ; in Kánara (1188-1318), XV, pt. ii, 91-92 ; in Sátára district (1170-1310), XIX, 224-225 ; their rule in Sholápur (1170-1310, XX, 275 ; in Belgaum (1250-1320), XXI, 358 ; their rule in Dhárwár (1187-1320), XXII, 400-401 ; in Bijapur district, XXIII, 394-395 ; in Kolhápur (1180-1300), XXIV, 218.
Deváji : son of Jangar, Bhil Náik of Chikli, surprises and captures the fort of Roshmal and kills Bhikáji, I, pt. ii, 633.
Deváji Takápir or Takpar : lieutenant of Dámáji Gáikwár, defeats Abdul Aziz (1744), I, pt. i, 328 ; *see* also VII, 174, 176, 179.
Devak : totem or marriage gods among Poona population ; among Káchis, XVIII, pt. i, 284 ; among Koshtis, *id.* 348 ; among Lohárs, *id.* 353 ; among Lodhis, *id.* 399 ; among Rámoshis, *id.* 410 ; among Gondhalis, *id.* 452 ; among Sátára Buruds and Sáugors, XIX, 80, 94 ; among Maráthás, XIII, 125, XXIV, 66 ; Marátha worship of, *id.* 75-76 ; a list of, among Marátha, *id.* 414 ; among Koshtis, *id.* 95 ; among Lingáyats, *id.* 130.
Devaladevi : sister of Kumárapála, married to Anarája, king of Sákambhari, I, pt. i, 181-182.
Devaladevi : daughter of Karnadeva, the last Vághela chief, and Kauladevi, the promised bride of the Devagiri prince Śamkara, is captured by Alaf Khán and married to Allá-ud-din's eldest son Khizr Khán, I, pt. i, 205, *id.* pt. ii, 532 ; *see* also I, pt. i, 205.
Devala Mahadevi : wife of the Hoysála king Vira Someśvara, I, pt. ii, 466, 493, 508.
Deválána : village in Násik district, coins from, I, pt ii, 296, 385.
Deválás : Rájpút tribe of Bhinmál, I, pt. i, 465.
Devalgaon : village in Ahmadnagar district, well at, XVII, 714.
Devalia : state in Rewa Kántha, VI, 143.
Devanágari : written character, I, pt. i, 80.
Devanandin : proper name of Pujyapáda, I, pt. ii, 373.
Devanayya : governor of Belvola, I, pt. ii, 405.
Deváng : caste of weavers in Dhárwár, the story of their origin, XXII, 165-167 ; in Kolhápur, XXIV, 95.
Devangaon : village in Bijápur district, temples at, XXIII, 645.
Devaprasáda : son of Kshemarája, I, pt. i, 170 ; recommended by Karna to Siddharája, burns himself on the funeral pile, 171.
Devaputra : Kushán name, I, pt. i, 64 and note 5.
Devarája : early Ráshtrakúta prince, I, pt. i, 120 ; grantor in Dhruva's Baroda grant, *id.* 126, 470 ; *see* also I, pt. ii, 386.
Devarája : Yádava king Mahádeva's officer (1264), I, pt. ii, 528.
Devar Hippargi : village in Bijápur district, inscription, I, pt. ii, 521.
Devar Hubli : village in Dhárwár district, XXII, 665.
Devar Navadgi : village in Bijápur district, Vásudev Balvant Phadke's capture at (1879), XXIII, 645-646.
Devar Rájpúts : I, pt. i, 465. *See* Devla Rájpúts.

Devasakti : Sendraka chief, I, pt. ii, 186, 292, 363.
Devaśri : lady of Udambara village, feeds Kumárapala in exile, I, pt. i, 182, 184.
Devasuri : Svetámbara Jain Ácharya, holds a religious discussion with Kumdachandra, Digámbara Jain Ácharya, I, pt. i, 181 and note 2; Hemácharya's teacher advises Knmárapála to rebuild the Somanátha temple, *id.* 189.
Devasvámin : Bráhman grantee of the Chálukyas, commentator on sacrificial *sútras* and rites, I, pt. ii, 191.
Devavarman : Kadamba prince, I, pt. ii, 290; father of Krishnávarman, *id.* 291 note 2.
Devayani : wife of Yayáti, I, pt. i, 460.
Devayo : village in Gujárat, perhaps Dholka, I, pt. i, 184.
Devbáráv Dalvi : a Koli freebooter (1820), XIII, 634.
Devchand : Cutch minister, murdered (1778), V. 147.
Devda : village in Káthiáwár, VIII, 411.
Devda : hill path in Kolhápur, XXIV, 5.
Devdása : *see* Kshetridása.
Devdatta : Shákyamuni's brother-in-law, XII, 498 note, 560 note.
Devdhan : food plant cultivated throughout India, XXV, 186.
Devdi : *sati* platform, daily worship, visits to, IX, pt. i, 360. *See* Sati.
Devdig : *see* Sappalig.
Devdiváli : holy day, *tulsi* or sweet basil plant married to Vishnu on, IX, pt. i, 23 note 5, 175.
Devendravarman : son of Anantavarman, I, pt. ii, 297; son of Gunárnava, *id.* 297.
Dev Family : of Chinchvád, story of, XVIII, pt. iii, 125-126.
Devgad : river in Ratnágiri district, X, 10.
Devgad : sub-division of Ratnágiri district, account of, X, 2, 311-313; trade (1818), *id.* 177; port, exports and imports of, *id.* 186; town, trade, history, fort, *id.* 332.
Devgad : *see* Oyster Rocks and Sunghiri; also Hareshvar.
Devgadh : Daulatábád, I, pt. i, 229 and note 4; I, pt. ii, 75; seat of Musalmán government (1312), *id.* 620.
Devgiri : *see* Devagiri.
Devimane : pass in Kánara, trade through, XV, pt. ii, 39, 40, 45, 280.
Deviputra : *see* Káyasth Prabhu, XVIII, pt. i, 193.
Devis : goddesses, of North Gujarát, said to be spirits of Cháran women; nine lákhs or nine hundred thousand *mátás* of Pávágadh said to be Charan girls, IX, pt. i, 216 and note 1.
Devjagan : place of pilgrimage in Broach district, II, 561.
Devji : son of Punja the Cutch minister, poisoned (1772), V, 145.
Devji : of Bednor, originally a Gujár, chief divinity of Ajmer Gujars, IX, pt. i, 502.
Devkáj : ceremony, IX, pt. i, 57.
Devkarn : minister of Cutch, slain by Ráo Lákha (1738), V, 140.
Dev Kedár : place in Panch Mahále, III, 310; temple at, *id.* 310.
Devláli : village with railway station in Násik district, barracks at, XVI, 132, 431.
Devlán : village in Násik district, Hemádpanti temple at, XVI, 431-432.
Devli : goddess, IX, pt. i, 363.
Devli : caste of husbandmen in Ratnágiri, X, 126; in Sávantvádi, *id.* 414; in Kánara, XV, pt. ii, 4; in Belgaum district, XXI, 158.
Devlia : táluka in Káthiáwár, VIII, 412.
Dev Mogra : village in Rájpipla in Rewa Kántha, Bhil fair at, VI, 161.
Devnar : an estate in Sálsette, XIII, 545-546.
Devráj : fourth Vijayánagar king (1401-1451), encourages import of horses, XV, pt. ii, 49, 96 and note 4; prosperity of Vijayánagar under, *id.* 98-99.
Devráshta : village in Sátára district, temples and cells at, its pond and tradition of its origin, XIX, 463-465.
Devrukh : place of interest in Ratnágiri district, X, 333.
Devrukha, Devrukhi : sub-division of Bráhmans, I, pt. ii, 113; in Ratnágiri, X, 114; in Sávantvádi, *id.* 411; in Koláha district, XI, 44; in Janjira, *id.* 411; in Khándesh, XII, 52; in Thána, XIII, 77; in Násik, XVI, 40; in Ahmadnagar, XVII, 54-55; in Poona, XVIII, pt. i, 160; in Sátára, XIX, 51-52; in Sholápur, XX, 27-28; in Kolhápur, XXIV, 60-61; *see* Dakhani Bráhmans.
Devs : un-Bráhman spirits, XIII, 65.
Dev Satia : peak in Rewa Kántha, VI, 3.
Devsthali : pass in Koláha and Janjira districts, XI, 6, 115.
Dewachabasni : Wagher chief in command of the fort of Bet, I, pt. i, 447.
Dewarde : village in Sátára district, I, pt. ii, 390.
Dewla Rajpúts : I, pt. i, 462-463.
Dhada : measure in Ratnágiri, size of, X, 164.
Dhadhar : river in Broach district, II, 339; and Baroda state, VII, 18, 193.
Dhádibhadaka : Ráshtrakúta feudatory of Vikramáditya VI, I, pt. ii, 425, 450.
Dhádibhandaka : I, pt. ii, 425, 450. *See* Dhádibhadaka.
Dhádiyama : son of Vaddiga, I, pt. ii, 513. *See* Dhadiyasa.
Dhádiyappa : son of the Yádava king Sennachandra I, I, pt. ii, 231; his various names, *id.* 512, 514.
Dhádiyasa : I, pt. ii, 232, 512-513. *See* Dhádiyappa.
Dhagya : hill in Ahmadnagar district, XVII, 4.
Dhair : hill fort in Násik district, XVI, 441, 641, 642.
Dhák : hill and fort on the border of Thána and Poona districts, XIV, 55; XVIII, pt. i, 3.
Dhákji Dádáji : appointed native agent to the Residency at Baroda (1816), VII, 224; his intrigues (1818), *id.* 231; his fall (1820), *id.* 234-235; appointed a *potedár* (1816); his deceit, *id.* 398.
Dhalanappa : father of Prachanda, I, pt. ii, 413.
Dhálgar : IX, pt. ii, 75. *See* Khátki.
Dháman : snake in Ratnágiri, X, 48.

Dhámaṇ : tree in Khándesh, XII, 25 ; in Poona, XVIII, pt. i, 45.
Dhámankhed : village in Poona district, temples, fairs at, XVIII, pt. iii, 129.
Dhámápur : village in Ratnágiri district, lake at, X, II, 333.
Dhámlej : village in Káthiáwár, VIII, 414.
Dhammarakhito : Yávan evangelist (B. C. 230), I, pt. i, 13.
Dhammiyara : Siláhára king, founder of Walipattana, I, pt. ii, 537.
Dhamni : carriage drawn by bullocks in Khándesh, XII, 145.
Dhamni : fibrous plant, XXV, 229.
Dhámor : Bhil tribe in the Panch Mahála, IX, pt. i, 295 note 2.
Dhan : Mehr of Dhandhuka, I, pt. i, 87 note.
Dhanáji Jádhav : Shiváji's officer, I, pt. ii, 594 ; enters Gujarát and defeats the Musalmáns at Ratanpur and Baba Piaráh ford (1705), I, pt. i, 291 ; appointed *senápati* of the Marátha forces, I, pt. ii, 597 ; supports Shahu (1707), XIX, 253, 254 ; confirmed as *senápati* by Sháhu (1708), I, pt. ii, 598 ;
Dhanakataka, Dhanakot : Dharnikot, near the mouth of the Krishna, I, pt. ii, 11 ; I, pt. i, 533 ; capital of king Satakarni, I, pt. ii, 150, 151, 152, 165. 166, 167.
Dhanamjaya : king of Kusthalapura, I, pt. ii, 280.
Dhándhalpur : village in Káthiáwár, VIII, 413.
Dhándhár : local name of Pálanpur zillah, I, pt. i, 208 note 3.
Dhandh Khant : Khánt Kholi leader, IX, pt. i, 240.
Dhandhuka : Parmára chief of Abu, subdued by Vimala, general of Bhima, I, pt. i, 169.
Dhandhuka : Hemácharya's birth-place, táluka town, I, pt. i, 191 and note 1 ; district under the Vaghelas, *id.* 198, 470.
Dhandhusar : village in Káthiáwár, origin of its name, VIII, 415.
Dhanduka : sub-division of Ahmadábád district, IV, 243-245 ; town, *id.* 333 ; Hemácharya's birth-place, I, pt. i, 191 and note 1 ; district under the Vaghelas, *id.* 198, 470.
Dhanesa : preceptor of Bopadeva, I, pt. ii, 249.
Dhangar : caste of shepherds in Ratnágiri district, X, 40 note 1, 127 ; in Sávantvádi, *id.* 415 ; in Kolába district, XI, 67-68 ; in Janjira, *id.* 414 ; in Khándesh, XII, 78 ; blanket weavers in Khándesh, *id.* 235 ; in Thána, XIII, 144 ; at Mátherán, XIV, 230 note 1, 259, 260 ; in Kánara, XV, pt. i, 295-296 ; in Násik, XVI, 56 ; in Ahmadnagar, XVII, 149-150 ; in Poona, XVIII, pt. i, 384-385 ; husbandmen in Poona, XVIII, pt. ii, 2 ; in Sátára, XIX, 104-105 ; in the Marátha army, *id.* 250 ; in Sholápur, XX, 146-147 ; in Belgaum, XXI, 153-154 ; in Kolhápur, XXIV, 103.
Dhánia : snake in Ratnágiri, X, 50.
Dhanika : commentator of the *Dasárúpaka*, I, pt. ii, 171.
Dhanjisha : of Surat, takes active part in the suppression of Mándvi riot, recognition of his services by the British Government, IX, pt. ii, 198 note 5.
Dhánk : village under Gondal in Káthiáwár, VIII, 414.
Dhanka : a Bhil sub-division in Rewa Kántha, VI, 34, 95 footnote 1.
Dhanora : fort in Khándesh district, XII, 439.
Dhanpál : ancestor of the Udváda, Bulsár, and Sanjan priests, IX, pt. ii, 221.
Dhanur : village in Bijápur district, temples at, XXIII, 646.
Dhányaghata : Amarávati, sacred to Buddha, I, pt. ii, 331.
Dhányaghataka : I, pt. ii, 331 ; *see* Dhányaghata.
Dhányakasrenis : Buddhist corn dealers, I, pt. ii, 173.
Dhár, Dhára : plateau, I, pt. i, 352 ; capital of the old Hindu kings of Málwa, *id.* 357 ; Anandráv Pavár settles at (1754), *id.* 382 ; defeat of Sultán Hoshang by his uncle Muzaffar I of Gujárát (1408), *id.* 358 ; attacked by Siddharája, I, pt. i. 178 ; carving on pillars of a mosque at, *id.* 180 ; capital of Bhoja, sacked by the joint army of Chedi and Gujárát, I, pt. ii, 214, 228 ; prince of, besieged by Singhana, *id.* 240 ; capital of the Paramáras, stormed by Someśvara I, *id.* 441 ; territory, *id.* 442, 525 ; taken by Ereyanga, *id.* 494.
Dhárabad : rent deduction system in Kolába, XI, 173-174, 181.
Dharada : tribe of hillmen name derived, their mention in the *Mahábhárata* by Mánu, by Ptolemy, IX, pt. i, 338 note 1.
Dhárala : armed population of Gujarát, IX, pt. ii, 25 ; swordsmen, Tálabda Kolis, IX, pt. i, 243 and note 3.
Dharampur : state in Surat, area, boundaries, aspect, water-supply, climate, products, population, soil, crops, roads, history, land management, justice, instruction and places of interest, VI, 254-257 ; *see* also IX, pt. i, 129.
Dharamshálas. *See* Rest-houses.
Dharamtar : port in Kolába district, XI, 311-312.
Dharanendra : serpent king, I, pt. ii, 576.
Dharangaon : place of interest in Khándesh district, XII, 251, 254, 259 ; early trade centre, history, a Bhil school at, *id.* 439-441.
Dharanikot : town in Madras, mention of, in Kánheri caves, XIV, 147, 188 ; Gotamiputra II's coins found at, *id.* 148 ; *see* also I, pt. ii, 151, 152, 167. *See* Dharnikot.
Dharanivaráha : Chápa king of Wadhwán (914), I, pt. i, 138, 466, 469 ; king of Chápa race, I, pt. ii, 343 note 5 ; local representative of Mahipála, *id.* 383.
Dharapatta : Valabhi king, devotee of the sun, I, pt. i, 83.
Dharápur : ruined city in Pálanpur state, V, 282.
Dhárapuri : sacked by Karna, I, pt. 163.
Dhárásar : lake in Pálanpur, V, 282.
Dharasena I : Valabhi king, I, pt. i, 114-115.
Dharasena II : Valabhi king, copper-plate of, I, pt. i, 79 note 1 ; spurious grant of, I, pt. ii, 312 note 7.
Dharasena IV : Valabhi king, I, pt. i, 116 ; defeated by Harshavardhana of Kanauj and protected by Gurjjara king Dadda II (648), I, pt. ii, 316.

Dhárás Raya Jayasimha: *See* Jayasimhavarman.

Dhárávarsha: another name of Dhruva I, also of Dhruva II, I, pt. i, 126; *biruda* of Dhruva, I, pt. ii, 197, 393, 409.

Dhárávarsha: Nirupama Dhruvarája, Ráshtrakúta king of the Gujarát branch (834-835), I, pt. ii 383.

Dhárávi: island in Thána district, ruins of a church and fort at, XIV, 55; seized by the Maráthás (1738), *id.* 34; fortified post at (1775), XXVI, pt. ii, 399; basalt columns at, XIII, 466 note 3.

Dhárekaris: peasant-holders in Ratnágiri, X, 138, 139, 156; position and rights of (1880), *id.* 206-209; position and rights of (1818), *id.* 227-234 and note 1; in Kolába, peasant proprietors, their position (1728 1837), XI, 173, 178, 181, 182 note 3, 183 and note 3, 184 and note 1, 453.

Dhareshvar: village in Kánara, temple and copper-plate grants at, XV, pt. ii, 106, 115, 279-280.

Dháreśvara: Bhoja of Dhára, I, pt. ii, 229.

Dhargaon: fort in Khándesh district, XII, 441.

Dhari: state in Rewa Kántha, VI, 152.

Dhari: town in Káthiáwár, with a mosque and a hospital, VIII, 415; *see* also VII, 509.

Dharma: river in Dhárwár district, XXII, 6.

Dharmachakra Mudra: teaching position Buddha's images in, at Sopára, XIV, 331, 412, 413.

Dharmádáya: land alienation for charitable purposes, in Baroda VII, 349-350; charitable grants, *id.* 353.

Dharmakirti: Bhatkal chief tributary to Portugal (1514), XV, pt. ii, 112, 272.

Dharmapála: king of Bengal, I, pt. ii, 394.

Dharmápura: Dambal town, I pt. ii, 448, 465.

Dharmaráj: the Pándava temple dedicated to, at Kále in Kolhápur state, XXIV, 301.

Dharmárája-Ratha: temple of, I, pt. ii, 331.

Dharmarakshita: Aśoka's Konkan missionary (B. C. 225), XIII, 405; sent to Sopára, XIV, 125, 319.

Dharmaura: village in the Bachche province, in Southern Marátha Country, I, pt. ii, 380.

Dharmávatára: *biruda* of the Ganga chief Márasimha, I, pt. ii, 305.

Dharmavolal: modern Dambal, I, pt. ii, 228.

Dharna: fasting at the door, a mode of exacting debts from powerful debtors, VIII, 326; Bhat's means of extorting compliance with his demands, IX, pt. i, 210.

Dharnidhar: place of pilgrimage in Pálanpur state, fair at, V, 300, 342; gateway, I, pt. i, 450 note 1.

Dharnikot: town in Madras; Andhrabhritya capital, I, pt. ii, 11; *see* also XII, 238; XIII, 409 note 3; XVI, 182; XVIII, pt. ii, 212 note 1.

Dhars: tribe, I, pt. i, 533.

Dharuka: village in Káthiáwár, VIII, 416.

Dhárur: town in the Nizám's territory, identified with ancient Tagara, I, pt. ii, 174; *see* also I, pt. i, 541, 545; siege of, by Murtaza Nizam Sháh (1569), XVII, 371.

Dhárwár: district, XXII, 1-822; its boundaries, sub-divisions, aspect, hills, rivers, *id.* 1-8; geology, climate, *id.* 8-17; production, *id.* 18-44; gold and other minerals, forests, trees, domestic animals, wild animals, birds, insects and fish, *id.* 18-44; population, *id.* 45-251; census details, communities, customs, religion, movements, *id.* 45-56; Deshastha, Smárt, Bhágvat, Kanva and other Bráhmans, *id.* 56-101; Lingáyats, Jangams, *id.* 102-115; Jains, Lavánás, Lingáyat Vánis, Márwáris, Telugu Banjigars and other traders, *id.* 115-131; Dásár, Halepaik, Kámáti, Maráthás and other husbandmen, *id.* 132-145; Badiges, Gavandis, Huzars, Ilgerus, and other craftsmen, *id.* 145-163; Bilejádars, Devanga, Lingáyat Gánigars, Khartis and other manufacturers, *id.* 163-179; Gavlis, Kurubars, *id.* 179-183; Ambigs, Bedars, Bhuis, Mathpathis, Lingáyat Basavas, *id.* 183-193; Dombars, Koravárs and other wandering tribes, *id.* 193-198; Marátha Bháts, Budbudkis, Gollárs and other castes of beggars, *id.* 198-213; Bhangis, Dhors, and other depressed classes, *id.* 213-221; Musalmáns, different classes of, *id.* 222-249; Christians, *id.* 250-251; Pársis, *id.* 251; agriculture, *id.* 252-318; husbandmen, soil, holdings, irrigation, reservoirs, canals, manure, field tools, seasons and crops, *id.* 252-318; capital, *id.* 319-340; currency, bankers, insurance, investments, money-lending, interest, land mortgage, wages, weights and measures, and prices, *id.* 319-340; roads, railways, bridges, ferries, post and telegraph, *id.* 341-351; traders, trade centres, markets, fairs, imports and exports, *id.* 351-365; ginning, spinning, carpets, floor cloths, metal works, molasses, oil, ink and other crafts, *id.* 365-388; history, *id.* 389-438; early history, Kadambas (500), Chálukyás (510-760), Ráshtrakútas (760-973), Western Chálukyas (973-1190), Kálachuris (1161-1184), Hoysála Ballála (1137-1210), and Devgiri Yádava (1187-1320), *id.* 389-401; Delhi emperors (1294-1347, Vijayánagar (1335-1344), the Bahmanis (1347-1489), Bijápur kings (1489 1636), *id.* 401-409; Savnúr Naváb (1700), Peshwas (1752-1776), Maisur (1776-1792), the Peshwas (1792-1817), the British (1818-1883), *id.* 410-438; land, acquisition, history, *id.* 439-452; British management, survey (1843-1860), revision survey (1874-1881), and season reports, *id.* 453-594; staff, village servants, alienated villages, *id.* 594-597; justice, *id.* 598-605; civil courts, civil suits, registration, magistracy, crime, police, *id.* 598-603; offences and jails, *id.* 603-605; finance, excise, assessed taxes, and balance sheets, *id.* 606-611; instruction, private schools, girls' schools, readers and writers, school details, newspapers, libraries, and reading rooms, *id.* 611-621; hospitals, dispensaries, vaccination, births and deaths, *id.* 622-625; sub-divisions, *id.* 626-647; Bankapur, its details, *id.* 628-628; Dhárwár, its details, *id.* 628-630; Gadag, its details, *id.* 630-632; Hángal, its details, *id.* 632-634;

Hubli, its details, *id.* 634-636; Kalghatgi, its details, *id.* 636-638; Karajgi, its details, *id.* 638-640; Kod, its details, *id.* 640-642; Navalgund, its details, *id.* 642 644; Ránebennur, its details, *id.* 644 646; Ron, its details, *id.* 646-647; places of interest, *id.* 648-790; inscriptions in I, pt. ii, 460, 465, 466, 473; Lingáyats in, *id.* 477, 478, 482, 489, 496, 497, 502;—*Sub-division*, its boundaries, area aspect, hills, soil, climate, water, stock, crops, people, *id.* 628-630; survey (1848-49), *id.* 518-521; revision survey (1879-80), *id.* 568-577;—*Town*, aspect, fort, divisions, suburbs, population, houses, roads, management, municipality, water-supply, reservoirs, cisterns, wells, markets, industries, objects, memorial, tablets, civil station, cantonment, history, *id.* 666-711; Goa, Kádamba records at, *id.* 566, 569, 572, 573, 574, 578; retaken by the Hindus, *id.* 640; taken by Ali A'dil Sháh from an officer of the Vijayánagar king (1573), *id.* 645; taken by the Mughals under Muazzim, *id.* 654; taken by Fazl-ullah-Khán (1764), taken by the Maráthás, *id.* 658 659; taken by Haidar, *id.* 659; siege of, in 1789; capture of, by the allied forces of the English and the Maráthás (1790), *id.* 661, 662; the commandant of the fort refuses to give up the fort to Trimbakji Dengle, *id.* 663; ceded to the English by the Peshwa (1817), *id.* 664; becomes the head-quarters of the English commissioner Colonel T. Munro (1817), *id.* 664.

Dhasa: town in Káthiáwár, VIII, 416.

Dhátarvari: river in Káthiáwár, VIII, 63.

Dhatura: tree, worship of, IX, pt. i, 40.

Dhau: Arab vessel in Thána, description of, XIII, 353-354, 718; in Kánara, XV, pt. ii, 60, 320, 327.

Dháukorbái: Sáthodra Nagar Bráhman *sati*, IX, pt. i, 358.

Dhauli: in Bengal, inscriptions at, I, pt. ii, 142.

Dhaura: dye and gum-yielding plant, XXV, 244, 251.

Dhauri: dye-yielding plant, common on the *ghâts*, XXV, 245.

Dhau Vála: Vála Rájpút chief of Dháuk, story of his marriage with Umrábái, daughter of Umro-Káthi, his sons by Umrábái-Vála Khumán and Khâchar, the founders of the three noble tribes of Káthis, their descendants called Shákháyáts, IX, pt. i, 252-253.

Dhavad: caste of blacksmiths in Ratnágiri district, X, 415; Musalmán iron smelters in Sátára district, XIX, 140-141; in Kolhápur, XXIV, 18.

Dhávadshi: village in Sátára district, XIX, 466.

Dhaval: priest, son of Shápur Sheheriar, IX, pt. ii, 221.

Dhavala: king of Bhimapalli, I, pt. i, 196; Vághela chief (1160), *id.* 206.

Dhavala: Maurya chief, I, pt. ii, 284; holds the northern part of Málwa (738), *id.* 312.

Dhavalápps: Prachanda's father and general of Krishna Akalavarsha, I, pt. i, 129.

Dhávda: timber tree in Khándesh, XII, 25; in Poona, XVIII, pt. i, 45.

Dhávdá: caste of iron smelters in Ratnágiri, District, X, 30.

Dhavla: pass in Kolába district, XI, 5, 114.

Dhawalagadha: *see* Dholka.

Dháyata: an old settlement in Khándesh, a trade centre (1609), XII, 248, 441.

Dhaysti: dye-yielding plant, common on the *ghâts*, XXV, 245.

Dhebrá: or Dhivar or Dhimars, caste of fishermen in Gujarát, IX, pt. i, 519, 520.

Dhed, Dhedá: depressed class in Gujarát, strength and distribution, IX, pt. i, 331, *id.* 338; claim descent from Kshatris, and strain of Rájpút blood, *id.* 338 and note 1; claims Solanki descent, *id.* 486; defeated foreigners thrown among, *id.* 454; their surnames, Rajpúts, *id.* 338; local, 339; divisions, ancient—Chásia and Kusia, local; appearance; position, *id.* 339; dress, *id.* 340; occupation, former, present, as labourers, as private servants, *id.* 340-341; as butlers, house servants, and grooms, *id.* 339; traces of former slavery, *id.* 340 and notes 1 and 2, 341 and note 1; Surati Dhedas in European service called Láliás, *id.* 339 and note 2; religion—followers of different sects, worship *tulsi* plant, Garudá priests, places of pilgrimage, saints, *id.* 341; their religious meetings or *ochhavs*, *id.* 344 and note 1; customs, *id.* 341-343; community prospects, *id.* 344 and note 2; beliefs of Kaira Dhedás, *id.* 343 and note 1; reference to tradition of Elias the Prophet, *id.* 343 and note 2; prophecies of high future in store for, *id.* 343; in Káthiáwár, VIII, 157; in Thána, XIII, 191.

Dheguji Meghuji: Cloud of Clouds, name of the teacher of Mahars, XXIV, 114.

Dhenukákata: Dhanakataka modern Dharnikot, I, pt. i, 533.

Dhep: form of assessment in Kolába, XI, 168, 170, 171; in Thána, XIII, 531, 536; a measure, *id.* 547, 550 and note 2, 552; unmeasured lump of land, assessment on, *id.* 565; rental how fixed, *id.* 565; not on the quantity of seed, *id.* 565 note 4; (1828), 574; (1845), 587.

Dhephandi: *see* Dhep.

Dhergaon: village in Ahmadnagar district, temple at, XVII, 714-715.

Dheri: old town near Umbargaon in Thána, XIII, 454; XIV, 55, 370.

Dhigván: caste of saddlers in Khándesh, XII, 74.

Dhimar or Dhivar: *see* Dhebrá.

Dhingi: Sind sailing-vessels, XIII, 350-351.

Dhiniki: village in Káthiáwár, forged grants at, I, pt. i, 87, 137.

Dhinodhar: place of interest in Cutch; *see* Kánphatá beggars, penance of their founder at, V, 85, 220.

Dhinoj: a section of Nágar Bráhmans, origin of their tribe, VII, 625.

Dhiro: *bhagat*, poet, IX, pt. i, 213.

Dhobi: washerman, as servant, IX, pt. ii, 96; caste of, in Káthiáwár, VIII, 157; in Gujarát, IX, pt. i, 228-230; in Khándesh, XII, 77; Musalmán in Poona, XVIII, pt. i, 504; in Sátára, XIX, 141; in Sholápur, XX, 206;

in Belgaum, XXI, 221, 222; in Dhárwár district, XXII, 245; in Thána, XIII, 237.
Dhobis' fall: at Mahábaleshwar, XIX, 507.
Dhodambe: village in Násik district, with a temple, XVI, 432.
Dhodap: hill fort in Nasik district, XVI, 210 note 3; approaches, village, ascent, fort, details, history, *id.* 432-436, 441; Rághobá captured in the action at (1768), XVIII, pt. ii, 253.
Dhoddi: Bráhman, Tenna granted to, I, pt. i, 131.
Dhodiá: early tribe in Thána district, XIII, 157.
Dhokalsing: general of Abhaysing, captures Baroda (1732), VII, 173.
Dhoke: village in Ahmadnagar district, caves at, XVII, 715.
Dhola: town in Káthiáwár, VIII, 417.
Dholádri: táluka in Káthiáwár, VIII, 417.
Dholagri: sub-caste of Agris, in Kolába, XI, 51; in Thána, XIII, 116.
Dholarva: táluka in Káthiáwár, VIII, 417.
Dholera: creek and town in Ahmadábád, IV, 15, 334.
Dholi: village in Gujarát, battle at (1735); defeat and death of Sohráb Khán at, I, pt. i, 316; casts of minstrels among the Bhils in Gujarát, IX, pt. i, 302, their duties; their musical instruments, *id.* 303-304; Bajániás, *id.* 503; *see* also IX, pt. ii, 83, 96.
Dholka: sub-division of Ahmadábád, IV, 241-243;—town, *id.* 337; Málavya lake at, built by Siddharája, I, pt. i, 180 note 2; district under the Vághelas, *id.* 198; assigned to Ratansing Bhandári (1735), *id.* 315; defeat of Rangoji by Ratansing Bhandári at (1736), *id.* 317; defeat of the Maráthás at (1741), *id.* 324, 517, VII, 175; ceded to the British (1802), *id.* 207; Ránás of, I, pt. ii, 525. Vairat identified with, IX, pt. i, p. ix, 294.
Dholkot: village near Asirgad, Bájiráo surrenders himself at (1818), I, pt. ii, 630.
Dholpur: town in Rájputáná, battle of (1658), I, pt. i, 282.
Dhom: holy village near Mahábaleshvar in Sátára, temples, XIX, 466-467.
Dhond: town in Poona district, with railway station, trade and temples at, XVIII, pt. iii, 129.
Dhond and Manmád Railway: its construction, XVII, 330-331.
Dhondopant or Dhondu Pant Gokhale: Maráthá governor of the Bombay Karnátak (1796-1800), defeated Dhundia Vágh (1794), XXII, 419; his aggrandizement, *id.* 420; defeated and killed by Dhundia Vágh (1800), *id.* 423; I, pt. ii, 662; XXIV, 347-348; *see* also XXI, 389-392.
Dhondphoda: class of Musalmán quarrymen in Sátára district, XIX, 141.
Dhopeshvar: village in Ratnágiri, with a temple, X, 334.
Dhor: Koli sub-division in Thána, XIII, 159 note 1, 167; caste of tanners in Kánara district, XV, pt. i, 357-358; in Násik, XVI, 72; in Ahmadnagar, XVII, 168-169; in Poona, XVIII, pt. i, 431, 435; in Sátára, XIX, 111; in Sholápur, XX, 170; in Belgaum, XXI, 192; in Dhárwár, XXII, 214; in Bijápur, XXIII, 263-265; in Kolhápur, XXIV, 110-111.
Dhora: Prákrit form of Dhruva, I, pt. ii, 393.
Dhora: river in Ahmadnagar, XVII, 8.
Dhoráji: town and trade centre in Káthiáwár, VIII, 417; seat of the provincial head or *mukhi* of the Memans, IX, pt. ii, 57.
Dhorap: fort in the Ajintha range, defeat of Raghunáthráo Peshwa at (1768), I, pt. i, 400. *See* Dhodap.
Dhorappa: prince, I, pt. ii, 232; indentified with the Ráshtrakúta king Dhruva, *id.* 513.
Dhorasamudra: I, pt. ii, 491 note 4. *See* Dorasamudra.
Dhorja: village in Ahmadnagar, temples at, XVII, 716.
Dhrangad: goddess, IX, pt. i, 205.
Dhrángadra: state in Káthiáwár, its area, rivers, soil, irrigation, climate, domestic and wild animals, population, trade, history of its chiefs, VIII, 418-432;—town, *id.* 432; *see* also IX, pt. i, 127.
Dhrápba: táluka in Káthiáwár, VIII, 418.
Dhrol: state in Káthiáwár, list of its chiefs, VIII, 432-433; *see* also IX, pt. i, 126.
Dhrua: village revenue officers in Cutch, V, 101-102.
Dhruva: Ráshtrakúta king (754-784), dethrones his brother Govinda II, and usurps the sovereignty; defeats the kings of the North and South and imprisons the Ganga king, I, pt. ii, 197-210, 302; defeats the Pallavas, *id.* 331; his *birudas*, epithets and titles, *id.* 393; his conquests, *id.* 393-394, 395-513; Nirupama, *id.* 423 note 2; *see* also I, pt. i, 121, 122.
Dhruva I: (795) Dakhan Ráshtrakúta king, spreads his conquest from South India to Allahábád, I, pt. i, 123; Gujarát Ráshtrakúta king, his war with Dakhan, Ráshtrakúta king Amoghavarsha, *id.* 121, 126, 466.
Dhruva II: (867) Gujarát Ráshtrakúta king opposed by Dakhan Ráshtrakútas, his relations by the Gurjjaras and by a Mihir king, I, pt. i, 121, 126-127, 136.
Dhruva III: of Broach, his grant, I, pt. i, 468.
Dhruvabhatta: surname of Siláditya VII, IX, pt. i, 13.
Dhruvapatu: Valabhi king, I, pt. i, 79.
Dhruvarája: Dhárávarsha Nirupama, of the Gujarát branch of the Málkhed Ráshtrakútas, son of Akálavarsha Subhatunga, I, pt. ii, 404, 405, 408, 409, 414.
Dhruvarájadeva: Gujarát Ráshtrakúta prince, I, pt. ii, 392.
Dhruvasena I: first Valabhi king (526), follower of Vaishnava sect, I, pt. i, 83; his grant, 86, 116.
Dhruv Prabhu: caste of writers in Poona, XVIII, pt. i, 185, 191.
Dhudi: tree, in Khándesh, XII, 25.
Dhud-kulmi: medicinal plant found in Bombay, Konkan and throughout India, XXV, 255.
Dhulaka: town mentioned by Al Idrisi, I, pt. i, 513.

Dhuldhoyá : a Musalmán class in Khándesh, XII, 125 ; meaning dust-washers, in Gujarát as labourers, converts from the Hindu Khatri caste, form a separate body, Sunnis in faith, IX, pt. ii, 86.

Dhulia : sub-division of Khándesh, its boundaries, area, aspect, climate, water, soil, holdings, survey details, survey results, stock, crops and people, XII, 2, 363, 370 ; town, position, population, history, sub-divisions, markets, municipality, buildings, fort, temples, *id.* 441-447.

Dhulkhed : village in Bijápur district, Daksha's sacrifice, and temples at, XXIII, 378, 646-647.

Dhumkhál : a village in Rewa Kántha, remains of a temple at, VI, 161.

Dhumrája : first Paramára sovereign, I, pt. i, 470.

Dhunya : hill in Ahmadnagar district, XVII, 4.

Dhundiá : early tribe in Gujarát, strength and distribution, IX, pt. i, 290, 314 ; derivation of name, appearance, dress, favourite divinities of ; customs—marriage, *id.* 314, death, *id.* 315 ; community, *id.* 316.

Dhundia Vágh : Mahrátta free-booter, his rise ; plunders Dhárwár, but is driven back (1794) ; in prison till 1799 ; released and driven to Dhárwár by Colonel Stevenson ; defeated by Dhondu Pant Gokhale ; enters Kolhápur service ; again master of Dhárwár ; his success ; defeats and kills Gokhale (1800) ; pursued by Colonel Wellesley ; driven out of Dhárwár ; surprised and killed (1800), XXII, 419-425 ; *another account of,* (1790-1800) leader in Tipu's army ; takes service under Kolhápur ; leads plundering incursions into the territories of the English and the Peshwa ; kills Dhondo Pant Ghokhale, is pursued, and killed by General Wellesley (1800, at Kongal I, pt. ii, 662-663 ; *another account,* a Mahrátta free-booter (1799-1800) ; his success, driven from Dhárwár by Colonel Wellesley, and attacked on the banks of the Malprabha, opposite Manoli, pursued by Colonel Stevenson, driven out of Belgaum, his capture and death, XXI, 391-394 ; *see* also XXIII, 446-447 ; XV, pt. ii, 145, 146 note 1 ; XXIV, 356, 711.

Dhundiráj Tátya Sáheb : chief of Sángli, XXIV, 352.

Dhundiya Vágh : *see* Dhundia Vágh.

Dhundshi : town in Dhárwár, centre of trade, XXII, 356, 711.

Dhup : gum-yielding plant, XXV, 250.

Dhyán Mudra : thinking position, Buddha's image in, at Sopára, XIV, 331, 412, 413.

Dia Bahádur : governor of Mándu ; defeated and slain by Malhárráv Holkar (1732), I, pt. i, 382.

Dialectics : Buddhist, a later innovation, XIV, 135.

Diamonds : in Belgaum, XXI, 52 ; East India Company's trade in (1682-1772), XXVI, pt. ii, 109-111.

Dickenson : Captain T., examines the forts in the North Konkan, I, pt. ii, 118 ; XIII, 523.

Didgur : village in Dhárwár district, temple and inscriptions at, XXII, 712.

Didu : a sub-caste of Vániá, IX, pt. i, 71.

Dieruринæ : family of birds in Ratnágiri, X, 71.

Digambara : Jain sect, I, pt. ii, 191, 197, 200, 201, 208, 406 ; means air-clad. also called Ummad, religious sect among Shrávaks, IX, pt. i, 105.

Diggávi, village in the Nizám's dominions, inscription at, I, pt. ii, 434 note 3, 439 note 2.

Diggi : pass in Kánara district, XV, pt. ii, 39, 40, 281.

Dighási : village in Thána district ; basalt dyke at, XIV, 56.

Dighi : village in Khándesh district, XII, 447.

Digraj : village in Kolhápur, temples, mosque, XXIV, 359.

Digvijaya : triumphal progress, I, pt. ii, 455.

Dihor : town in Káthiáwár, VIII, 433.

Dikamali karunga : gum-yielding plant, XXV, 251.

Dikes : basalt in Poona district, XVIII, pt. i, 11-12.

Diksál : village in Poona district, with railway station, XVIII, pt. iii, 129.

Diksha : ceremony among the Lingáyats, XXIV, 129.

Dikshits : the, of Shendurni, I, pt. ii, 633.

Diláwar Khán : Bijápur general, banishes the Abyssinians and becomes regent of Ibráhim Adil Sháh II (1583-1591) ; makes martial alliances with Ahmadnagar and Golkonda ; goes over to Burhán Nizám Sháh (1591) and induces him to attack Bijápur ; falls into the hands of Ibráhim Adil Sháh and is blinded and kept in confinement for life in the fort of Sátára (1592), I, pt. ii, 647-648 ; *see* also XVII, 379 ; XIX, 229, XX, 285 ; at Ahmadnagar, imprisoned in Sátára, 379 ; Mughal general, lays siege to Bijápur (1677), raises it (1679), XXIII, 432-433 ; sent against Shiváji (1665), his unsuccessful siege of Purandhar, Shiváji's surrender to, XVIII, pt. ii, 231-234 ; compelled by Shiváji to raise the siege of Bijápur, I, pt. ii, 654.

Diláwar Khán Ghori : founds an independent kingdom in Málwa, adorns the hills with buildings and strengthens the defences (1387-1405); I, pt. i, 352, 357 ; entertains Muhammad Tughlak (1398), *id.* 358.

Diler Khán : *See* Diláwar Khán.

Dimuri : tribe mentioned by Pliny, I, pt. i, 534.

Dinára : village in Cutch, ruins of a Jain temple at, V, 220.

Dinára : coins, I, pt. i, 66 ; found at Somanátha, *id.* 167, 515 and note 5, 522.

Dinda : sacred plant, XXV, 291.

Dindori : sub-division of Násik district ; survey (1842-43), XVI, 220-222 ; revision survey (1874), *id.* 260-264 (1885), *id.* 281-284, (1880), *id.* 289-291 ; sub-divisional details, area, aspect, climate, water, history, land revenue, stock, holdings, crops, people, XVI, 388, 394 ; town, *id.* 436.

Dindu : fort, in Thána district, XIV, 56.

Dindvána : town in Márwár, IX, pt. i, 71.

Diniká : mother of Ushavadáta, I, pt. ii, 148.

Dinners : public. *See* Entertainment. Feast day, kind of food served at, cost of, IX, pt. ii, 114-115. Public occasions of, form of invitation to, ceremony observed at, kind of food served at, the three chief classes of, *id.* 112-114 ; 169-170 ; XIV, 53, 370.
Diodar : Pálanpur state, V, 335.
Diodar : Vághela Rájpút chiefship, IX, pt. i, 129.
Diodoros : book, I, pt. i, 535, 536.
Dionysius : Greek writer, I, pt. i, 532, 535.
Dioritic Green-Stone : in Bijápur, used for *lings* and grave stones, XXIII, 54-55.
Dioscorea : *aculeata*, *alata*, *bulbifera*, *globosa*, *oppositifolia*, *pentaphylla*, *sativa*, food plants, XXV, 178, 179
Dioscoreæ : species of food plants, XXV, 178.
Dipavamso : Ceylonese chronicle, i, pt. ii, 143.
Dirhams : coins, I, pt. i, 469 note 2, 515 note 5.
Disá (Deesa) : town, military station, gives name to Desáváls, IX, pt. i, 9, 70 ; conspiracy at (1857), I, pt. i, 441 ; *see* Deesa.
Disease : two forms of—endemic and epidemic, is believed to be due to spirit influence, to unfriendly influence of some planet, to anger of some god or goddess ; is believed to be cured by religious rites ; endemic, special treatment adopted in, causes and cures of, consumption or *kshaya* ; dysentery and diarrhœa or *samgrahani* ; eye-diseases, fever or *táv* ; guineaworm or *válo* ; hydrocele or *antargal* ; jaundice or *kamlo* ; kidney diseases or *ambhoi* ; leprosy ; paralysis or *pakshaghát* ; piles or *haras* ; rheumatism ; scrofula or *kanthmál* ; syphilitic eruptions or *visphotak* ; tumour and baldness ; warts or *varsolis* ; enlargement of spleen or *barol* ; IX, pt. i, 365 ; barrenness in woman, its cause and cure, *id.* 366-368 ; small-pox, different names of, *sitala*, epidimic form of, its god, worship of, offerings made to, *id.* 368 ; *saiad*, endemic form of, its god, the specific treatment of person attacked with, *id.* 368, 369, 370 ; offerings made to the god of, IX, pt. i, 371-372 ; cattle-pox, quieting ceremony of, *id.* 372 ; shrines, healing, of goddess Bahucharáji, of goddess Revali, of Dátár Pir, *id.* 366. *See* All District Volumes under Diseases.
Disease Worship : ix, pt. i, 365-372. *See* Disease.
Disorder : in Gujarát (1535-1573), I, pt. i, 220-221, *id.* 225 ; in Kathiáwár (1707), VIII, 297, 298 ; Bhil, in Khándesh (1804), XII, 254 ; (1818-1827) *id.* 257-258 ; in Belgaum (1802), XXI, 394-395 ; in Dhárwár district (1795-1800), XXII, 420 ; (1800-1803) *id.* 426 ; in Bijápur district (1804-1810), XXIII, 447-448.
Dispensaries : in Ahmadnagar, XVII, 582 ; in Sholápur, XX, 386-387 ; at different places in Thána, XIV, 21, 36, 48, 53, 114, 198, 211, 295, 306, 346, 353, 370, 371 ; in Surat district, II, 262 ; in Broach district, *id.* 532 ; in Kaira, II, 141 ; in Panch Maháls, *id.* 290 ; in Ahmadábád district, IV, 227 ; in Cutch, V, 208 ; in Pálanpur, *id.* 315 ; in Mahi Kántha, *id.* 396 ; in Rewa Kántha Agency, VI, 89 ; in Káthiáwár, VIII, 352-353 ; in Kolába district, XI, 237 ; in Janjira, *id.* 460 ; in Khándesh, XII, 339, 451 ; in Thána, XIII, 667-668 ; in Kánara, XV, pt. ii, 218-220 ; in Poona district, XVIII, pt. iii, 67-68 ; in Násik, XVI, 341 ; in Sátára, XIX, 417 ; in Belgaum, XXI, 491 ; in Dhárwár district, XXII, 623 ; in Bijápur district, XXIII, 525 ; in Kolhápur state, XXIV, 288.
Disputes : religious, between the two bodies of priests of Navsári, IX, pt. ii, 192 ; as to the reckoning of the year ; *id.* 193 and note 2, 194.
Distance of Courts : in Násik, XVI, 309.
Distillery : at Mundhva near Poona city, XVIII : pt. iii, 42 ; in Thána district, XIII, 395-398 ; at Bhándúp (1817-1878), XIV, 44 ; at Karanja, *id.* 192 ; at Uran, *id.* 371.
Disturbances : in the Karnátak (1795-1800), I, pt. ii, 662 ; in Surat district, Abdul Rehmán's (1810), salt riots (1844), weights and measures riots (1848), II, 155-157 ; in Broach district, Koli rising (1823), Musalmán riot (1857), *id.* 475-477 ; in Kaira (1826, 1830), III, 120 ; in Panch Maháls (1858), *id.* 254-258 ; at Godhra, (1855), *id.* 314 ; in Ratnágiri (1844-1850), X, 445 ; at Peint in Násik (1857), XVI, 388 ; created by the chief of Nargund, Bhimráo Nadgir, and the *deshmukh* of Surtur (1857-58), XXII, 434-438.
Ditan : village in Ahmadnagar district, temple, fair at, XVII, 716.
Dittelasma rarak : XXV, 252.
Diu : town and island on the coast of Káthiáwár, its history, trade, fort and churches, VIII, 433-434 ; emporium of trade (1514), *id.* 237 ; port and light house at, *id.* 242 ; seat of the local governor (1513-1526), *id.* 289 ; *another account of*, attempts of the Portuguese to obtain a footing on their defeat (1531) ; fortified ; Emanual DeSouza, the governor of ; meeting of the Portuguese viceroy Nono de Cunha and Sultan Bahádur and the death of the latter at, I, pt. i, 220, 347, 349, 350, 351 ; place of call for China ships, *id.* 497 note 1 ; Portuguese naval victory at (1509), XIII, 448 ; fort built at (1535), *id.* 451-452 ; its trade connection with Thána coast (1500-1670), *id.* 565 ; Dutch design on (1656), *id.* 473 ; a great city (1660-1710), *id.* 485 ; *see* also XIV, 29, 344 ; I, pt. ii, 8, XI, 276 and note 7 ; IX, pt. i, 488 ; Pársis' first settlement in, IX, pt. ii, 184.
Div : island in Rewa Kántha, VI, 6.
Diva : pass in Poona district, XVIII, pt. ii, 154.
Divákar Dikshit : rebel, his rising (1824), XIII, 452.
Diváli : holidays, IX, pt. i, 23 note 5, 54, 82, 119, 151, 170, 173, 175, 178, 303, 305, 306, 316, 336 ; festival days among Bhils, *id.* 305-306 ; fire worship on, *id.* 357 ; days for settling accounts by traders, *id.* 82 ; period best suited to subject evil spirits, IX, pt. ii, 145 ; Hindu new year, considered an evil spirit time, *id.* 148 ; Buddhist holiday, XIV, 145 ; among Pátáne Prabhus, XVIII, pt. i, 251-253 ; among Kunbis, *id.* 294-295.

Diván : Mughal chief secretary, I, pt. i, 211, 214.
Divánkhána : public room or parlour, IX, pt. ii, 91, 94.
Diváns : list of Baroda (1743-1882), VII, 288-289.
Diváshikhurd : village in Sátára district, cave and fairs at, XIX, 466.
Divisions : ancient Gujarát, I, pt. i, 6-7 ; of the Konkan, "Introduction to the History of the Konkan," I, pt. ii, p. ix ; theory of origin of, IX, pt. i, pp. xi, xiii, 457, 464 ; among Bráhmans, Bhikshuk and Grahasth, *id.* 2 ; among Vániás, Visás, Dasás, Pancham, or Pánchás, *id.* 70, 435 ; main, among Bhátiás, *id.* 117 ; Bháts, *id.* 207 ; Bhils, *id.* 295 ; Bráhmans, *id.* 3 ; Chárans, *id.* 215 ; Chodrás, *id.* 312 ; Darjis, *id.* 179 ; Dhedás, *id.* 339 ; Dublás, *id.* 316 ; Ghánchis, *id.* 181 ; Hajáms, *id.* 230 ; Kachhiás, *id.* 153 ; Kaubis, *id.* 163 ; Kansárás, *id.* 186 ; Káthis, *id.* 261-262 ; Kolis, *id.* 237, 239 ; Luhárs, *id.* 190 ; Mochis, *id.* 192 ; Náiks, *id.* 324 ; Rabáris, *id.* 287 ; Rájpúts, chief clans, *id.* 123, 124-129 ; tribes and sub-tribes, *id.* 129-130 ; Sonis, *id.* 197 ; Suthárs, *id.* 202 ; Vániás, *id.* 69. *See* also under all caste names.
Divorce : permitted among Bháts, IX, pt. i, 213 ; Chárans, *id.* 221 ; Bhaváyás, *id.* 225 ; Turis, *id.* 226 ; craftsmen, *id.* 179, 181, 186, 188, 195, 201, 206 ; early tribes, Bhils, *id.* 309 ; Náikadás, *id.* 327 ; herdsmen, Bharváds, *id.* 285 ; Rabáris, *id.* 289 ; husbandmen, *id.* 154, 161, 164, 166, 172, 174, 175, 176 ; Kolis, *id.* 250 ; personal servants, Dhobis, *id.* 230 ; Hajáms, 234 ; forms of, among Gujarát Musalmáns looked on with dislike, less resorted to by Indian Musalmáns, IX, pt. ii, 166 and note 1. *See* also under all caste names.
Divorce Act : IX, pt. ii, 238, 244 ; administration of justice under, *id.* 244.
Djymowr : town mentioned by Alberuni, I, pt. ii, 4.
D'Mello : Ayres D'Silva, sent to superintend the work of Bassein fort, I, pt. ii, 49.
Dnyáneshvar : Marátha Bráhman poet and saint (1271-1300), XVII, 352 ; his pillar at Nevása, inscription, *id.* 729 and note 5 ; tomb and temple of at A'landi in Poona district, fair, life, XVIII, pt. iii, 102, 103-104. *See* Jnanesvara.
Dobásh : ship chandler's boat, in Thána, description, cost, XIII, 344, 345.
Dobetala, Dobetela : identification of, X, 373 ; with Sátavli perhaps Sangameshwar, I, pt. ii, 37.
Dock : at Vijaydurg, I, pt. ii, 118 ; in Bombay (1764), XIII, 499 ; three (1766), *id.* 500 ; a dry dock (1775), *id.* 501 ; (1786) *id.* 511 note 2 ; in 1800-1820, *id.* 515, 517, 518 ; (1686-1803), XXVI, pt. ii, 196-203 ; first dock (1686-1750), *id.* 196-197 ; Mazgaon (1769-74), *id.* 199-200 ; the upper, middle and lower old Bombay docks built (1748-1765), XXVI, pt. ii, 516-517 ; the upper and lower Duncan docks : built (1804-1849), *id.* 518-521 ; the Mazgaon docks : the P. and O. small dock, British Indian Company's dock and the P. and O. Ritchie dock, *id.* 521-522 ; second, finished (1760), XXVI, pt. iii, 225.
Dockyard : Surat, Pársi carpenters as managers of ; Bombay, IX, pt. ii, 192 note 3 ; Haidar's Honávar (1763-1783), XV, pt. ii, 139, 141, 312.
Do Conto : Portuguese writer (1600), I, pt. i, 349 ; historian (1603), XIV, 59 note, 64, 72, 74, 75, 79, 81 ; account of Elephanta. *id.* 84 note 6, 90, 92 note 1, 94 ; account of Kánheri, *id.* 149-151, 226.
Dodala : hill range in the vicinity of Bhinmal, I, pt. i, 456.
Dodda-homma : place in Mysore, inscription at, I, pt. ii, 307.
Doddahundi, Doddhundi : village in Mysore, inscription, I, pt. ii, 304 note 1, 303.
Doddaváda : town in Southern Marátha Country, I, pt. ii, 465.
Dodderi : táluka of the Chitaldurg district in Mysore, I, pt. ii, 285 note 5.
Dodhi : famine plant, XXV, 201.
Dodi : fibrous plant, XXV, 233.
Dodimane : pass in Kánara district, XV, pt. ii, 39, 40, 281.
Dodvád : town in Sángli state, XXI, 554 ; details, history, wells and fort at, XXIV, 359-360.
Dog : is believed unclean, beliefs about, IX, pt. i, 377 ; Sháhú's fondness for a, XIX, 519 note 2 ; in Poona district, XVIII, pt. i, 68 ; in Belgaum district, XXI, 66.
Dohad : sub-division of Panch Maháls, its area, aspect, water, soil, stock, products and people, III, 299-301 ; *Town*, its population, trade, history, remains and buildings, *id.* 310-313 ; I, pt. i, 124 ; inscription at, *id.* 175, 179 ; restored by the English to Sindia under the treaty of Sirji Anjangaon (1803), *id.* 414.
Dohara : caste of leather workers in Násik, XVI, 72, 486.
Dokarpa : pass in Kánara district, XV, pt. ii, 39, 40, 281.
Dokhma : IX, pt. ii, 240 note 1. *See* Tower of Silence.
Dol : pass in Násik district, XVI, 130.
Dol : bamboo basket, used for lifting water, XXI, 241.
Dolia : village in Káthiáwár, VIII, 434.
Dolichos : *biflorus*, *uniflorus*, oil-yielding and fodder plants, XXV, 217, 277.
Dolis : bearers of, X, 41.
Dom or Dommi : Mir women, IX, pt. ii, 83 ; women players, *id.* 160 ; female singers, *id.* 164, 166, 174 note 1. *See* Mir.
Dombár : caste of acrobats in Belgaum, XXI, 166 ; in Dhárwár, XXII, 193 ; in Bijápur, XXIII, 187-189 ; in Kolhápur state, XXIV, 31, *id.* 116. *See* Kolhatis.
Dombingaon : *see* Dheguji Meghuji, Mahár *gurus*, XXIV, 114 note 1.
Domer : IX, pt. ii, 166 ; *see* Meher.
Domestic Animals : at Mátherán, XIV, 259 ; *see* All District Volumes under District Name.
Dominicans : Christian friars, I, pt. ii, 55 ; send missionaries to India and do the work of the inquisition ; their jealousy of the Jesuits, *id.* 60 ; at Bassein (1634), XIV, 42 ; Church at Tárápur (1634), *id.* 344 ; their arrival in Thána (1513), XIII, 460 note 7 ; their chapels in Bassein (1634), *id.* 462 ; chapels at Tárápur (1695), *id.* 483.
Dom João IV : (1656) figure of, at Cheul, XI, 291 ; mentioned in a stone inscription at Cheul, *id.* 297.

Dom João de Castro : Portuguese writer (1540), X, 321, 342 ; viceroy (1538), granted lands near Bassein to soldiers, XIII, 455 ; built St. Joseph at Bassein, XIV, 39 ; an Elephanta inscribed stone taken to Europe by, *id.* 80 ; his description of Elephanta and Kánheri caves, *id.* 84, 148-149 ; his coins found at Vehár, *id.* 379 ; his commercial treaty with Vijayánagar (1547), XV, pt. ii, 51, 115, 258, 263.

Dom João de Monoy : Portuguese general, defeated Máhim commandant (1516), XIII, 449.

Dom Lourenço Almeida : Portuguese commander, destroyed Musalmán ships at Cheul (1505), XI, 273 ; killed in a naval engagement at Cheul with Gujarát and Egyptian fleets (1508), *id.* 274 ; *see* D'Almeida, Lorenzo.

Dom Luiz de Athaide : twelfth Portuguese viceroy (1568), took and fortified Honávar, defended Honávar and Goa, XV, pt. ii, 118, 309, 310.

Don : a row boat in Vengurla harbour, X, 171.

Don : river in Bijápur district, XXIII, 9-10 ; richness of its valley, *id.* 3 and note 1, 308 and note 1 ; scheme, *id.* 315-316.

Dongargaon : village in Ahmadnagar district, happy valley, fair, XVII, 716.

Dongargaon : hill in Belgaum district, XXI, 554.

Dongari Koli : early tribe in Thána district, XIII, 168.

Dongri : upland soil in Ratnágiri, X, 145.

Dongri : village in Thána district, Portuguese Church and remains of a college at, XIV, 56.

Dongri Bagáyat : hill garden land, X, 145.

Dongri fort : Bombay, used as a prison (1728), XXVI, pt. iii, 21-22.

Dongri hill : Bombay, fort at, to be demolished (1760), XXVI, pt. ii, 330-332 ; proposal to level the hill (1763), *id.* 349-350 ; importance and plan for the fortification of the hill (1766), *id.* 357-362 ; the fort blown up (1769), *id.* 376-377 ; the new fortification named Fort George.

Doni : *see* Toni.

Donihalla : river in Kánara district, XV, pt. i, 5, 6.

Donkey : carrier of small-pox goddess, IX, pt. i, 154, 376 ; the, in Khándesh, XII, 29 ; in Belgaum, XXI, 66.

Donovan : Colonel, commander of the expedition against Bet (1859), I, pt. i, 446.

Dor : *see* Sursi.

Dorábji Nánábhái : founder of the Patel family, IX, pt. ii, 195.

Dorasamudra : modern Halebid, seat of Government of the Hoysálas transferred to, in the time of Vishnuvardhana (1117 and 1137), I, pt. ii, 491 and note 4 ; Hoysálas of, *id.* 299 note 4, 517, 524, 555 ; capital of the Hoysála kings, *id.* 499, 502, 507, 508, 509 ; besieged by the Sinda king Permádi I, *id.* 459, 497, 575 ; reduced by Sáluna-Tikkamadeva, the Yadava king Rámachandra's officer, *id.* 530 ; conquest of, by Malik Káfur (1310), *id.* 510, 533 ; entirely demolished by the Musalmáns (1327), *id.* 510 ; *see* Dvárasamudra and Dhorasamudra.

Dore Gujar : cultivators, caste of, XII, 67.

Dorepi : Bhil tribe, XII, 102.

Dorevike : a Gosávi sect, X, 419.

Dorka : estate in Rewá Kánthá, VI, 153.

Dorka Mehvás : states in Rewá Kánthá, VI, 1-2.

Dosál Ven : minister (1790) in Cutch, V, 149-150 ; given Mundera port (1801), *id.* 244.

Dounga : perhaps Dugad, I, pt. i, 540.

Dousrong : crushes a revolt in Nepál and establishes his supremacy in Bengal (703), I, pt. i, 501.

Dove : worship of, IX, pt. i, 63, 381 ; in Ratnágiri, X, 86.

Dowasrujd : part of the *Zend Avestá*, IX, pt. ii, 211 note 2 (18).

Dowry : arrangements, among Bhátiás, IX, pt. i, 119 ; Bráhmans, *id.* 39 40 ; Kanbis, *id.* 158.

Dowson : Professor, antiquarian, I, pt. ii, 188 ; IX, pt. ii, 188 note 4.

Drachmæ : Greek coins found in Káthiáwár, I, pt. i, 16, 17, 18.

Dragon worship : in Cambodia, I, pt. i, 502.

Drainage works : in Kaira district, III, 5-10.

Drakhmai : Greek coins, I, pt. i, 535, 545 ; *see* Drachmæ.

Dráksh : grape vine in Násik, XVI, 102.

Dramila : country, I, pt. ii, 213 ; Dravida, *id.* 281 ; princes, relations of Paraméśvaravarman II, oppose succession of Nandivarman and besiege him in Nandipura, *id.* 326, 328 ; king of, conquered by Kirtivarman I, *id.* 345 ; lord of, *id.* 436 ; *see* Dravida and Dravila.

Dramma : distribution of the coin, I, pt. i, 130 ; coin, *id.* 151, 201 ; *see* also I, pt. ii, 21 notes 1 and 6, 203 ; mention of in a Vehár inscription, XIII, 425 note 6 ; granted by Someśvara, *id.* 427 note 3 ; found in Konkan, *id.* 428 ; mention of, in Kánheri inscriptions, XIV, 147 note 2, 173, 177 ; in a Karanja stone, *id.* 195.

Dravid : group of Bráhman sub-castes, divisions of, IX, pt. i, 1 and note 1.

Dravid : sub-caste of Bráhmans in Násik, XVI, 42 ; in Ahmadnagar, XVII, 55 ; in Poona, XVIII, pt. i, 160 ; in Sátára, XIX, 52 ; in Kolhápur, XXIV, 61.

Dravida : country in Madras, I, pt. ii, 281, 318 and note 4.

Dravidas : subdued by Sahadeva, I, pt. ii, 142 ; *see* Cholas.

Dravidian origin : of the Ráshtrakútas, I, pt. ii, 383.

Dravidian element : in Thána names, XIII, 67 note 1.

Dravila : king, subdued by Someśvara III, I, pt. ii, 221 ; Rájendrachoda, *id.* 416 note 6.

Dravira : I, pt. ii, 4 ; *see* Dravida.

Drennan : Mr. J. M., opened a ginning factory at Dhoráji, VIII, 251.

Dress : of men among Gujarát Hindus, IX, pt. i, 22 23 ; of women, *id.* 23-24 ; Káthiáwár and Kachh, *id.* 24 ; of Bharváds, *id.* 267 ; Bhátiás, *id.* 118 ; Bhils, *id.* 297-298 ; Bráhmans, *id.* 21 ; Brahma-Kshatris, *id.* 56 ; craftsmen, *id.* 178, 179, 182, 193, 196, 198 ; Dhedás, *id.* 340 ; Kanbis, *id.* 155 ; Káyasths,

id. 60-61, 64 ; Kolis, *id.* 245-246 ; Márwáris, *id.* 103 ; Pateliás, *id.* 173 ; Rabáris, *id.* 287 ; Rájpúts, *id.* 131-132 ; Shrávaks, ascetics, *id.* 107, 108, 109 ; Vániás, *id.* 75-76 ; of men among Gujarát Musalmáns, of the rich class, IX, pt. ii, 100-101 and note 2 ; change of fashion of, *id.* 100 note 3 ; of the middle class, *id.* 102 and note 1 ; of the poor class, *id.* 102 and note ; of women of the rich class, *id.* 103, 104 note 1 ; of the middle class, *id.* 105, 106 note 1 ; of the poor class, *id.* 106 and note 2 ; of children, *id.* 107 and note 1 continued on page 108 ; of Khojahs, *id.* 42-44 ; of Memans, *id.* 53-55 ; among Pársis, of village men, ordinary, on great occasions ; of townsmen, indoors and out of doors ; of priests ; details and cost of, IX, pt. ii, 201-202 ; of village women, ordinary, on great occasions ; of townswomen ; details and cost of ; of children ; details and cost of, *id.* 203 ; *see* also under caste concerned.

Dress : trade in articles of, with Ceylon, China (800-1200), XIII, 430 ; with Persia, Arabia, (1300-1500), with Malabár and Africa (1500-1670), *id.* 466 and note 6.

Dridhaprahára : Chand or Yádava king, founder of the family, I, pt. ii, 231, 236 ; establishes himself at Srinagara, *id.* 512 ; (A. D. 801 ?), XVI, 185, 430.

Drinks : fermented and distilled, called *tádi* or toddy, chief kinds of ; fermented liquor, process of drawing juice called *tádi* from the wild date-palm *khájuri* ; distilled liquor made from the flower of the *mahuda*, IX, pt. i, pp. 29-30 ; drinking classes, 30-32 ; *see* Food.

Drishadvati : stream, in Northern India, I, pt. ii, 135.

Drona : ancestor of the Pallavas, I, pt. ii, 317.

Drona : preceptor of Pándavs, is said to have wrested the town of Ahichhatra from Drupada, IX, pt. i, 15 note 2.

Dronamma : military officer, mentioned in a Navsári grant, I, pt. i, 125.

Drona-Simha : of Valabhi, appointed to the feudatory province of Káthiáwár (526), I, pt. ii, 312.

Drongos : class of birds in Ratnágiri, X, 71.

Drowning : Shiv's, at Ambarnáth temple, XIV, 5 and note 3.

Drugs : Tháná trade in (800-1260), XIII, 430 ; (1300-1500), *id.* 445 ; (1500-1670), *id.* 467.

Drymoicinæ : family of birds in Ratnágiri, X, 78.

Duarte Barbosa : Portuguese traveller, his description of Goa and the Bahmani kingdom, (1500-1514), XXIII, 407-409.

Dub : sacred plant, XXV, 289, 290.

Dubla : early tribe in Gujarát, IX, pt. i, p. x ; strength and distribution, *id.* 290, 316 ; sub-divisions in, claim strain of Rájpút blood, dress, ornaments, favourite games, work as ploughmen or *hális* ; object of their worship, *id.* 317 ; customs, *id.* 317-318 ; in Tháná, XIII, 158.

Duda : quells a Sumra rising, I, pt. i, 517.

Dudan : river in Rewa Kántha, VI, 92.

Dudhala : táluka in Káthiáwár, VIII, 434.

Dudhe : state in Khándesh, XII, 605.

Dudhel Máta : Milk Mother, her miraculous powers, IX, pt. i, 389.

Dudheshwar : hill in Ahmadnagar district, XVII, 4.

Dudhganga : river in Kolhápur, XXIV, 8, 10-11.

Dudhia : sub-division of Báriya state in Rewa Kanthá, VI, 116.

Dudhpur : estate in Rewa Kántha, VI, 144.

Dudhrej : táluka in Kathiáwár, VIII, 435.

Dudia : grant, I, pt. ii, 279 note 1.

Dudla : poisonous plant, XXV, 268.

Dudley : Mr., brings Lauji, the founder of the Wadia family of Bombay, IX, pt. ii, 192 note 3.

Dudwala : caste of milkmen, converts from Sabalias and Gauli Hindu castes, their other names, Sunnies by faith, form a separate community, IX, pt. ii, 35 ; also called Mansuris, *id.* 35 note 1.

Duelling : among the Malabars (1514), XV, pt. ii, 113 ; in Ahmadnagar (1588), XVII, 361 and note 1.

Dues : among Khojahs IX, pt, ii, 49 note 2.

Dugad : village in Thána, battle of (1780), between the Maráthás and Colonel Hartley, XIV, 56-57 ; *see* also XIII, 507 ; XVIII, pt. ii, 266.

Dugdhamalla : of a branch of the Chálukyas, I, pt. ii, 212 ; son of Narasimha Bhadradeva, *id.* 380.

Duhai : rite mentioned by Al Idrisi, I, pt. i, 531.

Dukalval : caste of begging bards, a class of Mángs in Kolhápur, XXIV, 111.

Dukánvári : a Portuguese cess, XIII, 553.

Duke's Nose : *see* Nágphani.

Dulaka : Dholka, I, pt. i, 509, 517.

Dulandi : outsider, X, 211 ; one-year tenure in Thána (1817), XIII, 564 ; people of two villages, *id.* 565 ; tenure discontinued (1820), *id.* 566.

Dulas : people possessed by the spirit of the martyrs, vows offered to, IX, pt. ii, 128 ; bridegrooms, *id.* 137 ; also persons possessed by the spirit of the bridegroom-elect of Husain's daughter ; the process to gain the inspiration of, *id.* 138 ; *see* Muharram.

Dulka : I, pt. i, 511. *See* Dholka.

Dulya Máruti : temple of, in Poona city, XVIII, pt. iii. 335.

Dumál : villages, in Baroda, formerly granted for military service, their management by Sir T. Mádhavráo, VII, 347-348.

Dumar Lena : Elura cave, XIV, 112 ; Bhairáv's image at, *id.* 73, 74.

Dumas : large village, summer resort of Surat in Sachin state, VI, 265 ; *see* also I, pt. i, 403.

Duncan : Jonathan, governor of Bombay (1802), I, pt. i, 405 ; assumes chief authority in Surat, *id.* 411 ; his interview with Rávji of Baroda, 412 ; arranges about the collection of tribute in Gujárat and Káthiáwár by the employment of a British contingent, *id.* 414 ; (1795-1811), his death and funeral, XXVI, pt. iii, 414-416 ; *see* XXVI, pt. i, 431 ; interferes in Baroda disorders (1801), VII, 204 ; private engagement with Rávji Appáji (1802), *id.* 207.

Duncker: his *History of Antiquity*, XIII, 715.

Dundas: village in Káthiáwár, its antiquity, VIII, 435.

Dung: of ass or donkey, IX, pt. i, 376; cat, dog, *id.* 377; goat, *id.* 377; horse, *id.* 376; monkey, *id.* 378; used in spirit-scaring rites; cow, used in all sacrifical fires, *id.* 372; rat, used in pregnancy ceremony, *id.* 378.

Dunga: Ptolemy's, identified with either Dugad or Tungár hill, XIV, 56, 366 note 1.

Dungar; town of great antiquity in Káthiáwár, VIII, 436.

Dupleix: French general, his negotiations with the supporters of Muzaffar Jang (1750), XXII, 795.

Dûrái Sarái: convention of, between Bájiráv I and Nizám (1738), XIX, 279.

Durand: Colonel, resident at Mhow, driven out by the troops of Holkar; takes refuge in Bhopál, I, pt. i, 438.

Durgá: goddess, her two forms, Káli and Amba Bhaváni; worship of, IX, pt. i, 35, 64, 292, 301 note 2, 532; her nine names, *id.* 420.

Durgábái: regent for Khem Sávant (1813), X, 443.

Durgabhatta: father of Nemáditya, I, pt. i, 125; father of Náráyan, *id.* 125, 126.

Durgádás Rathod: incites prince Akbar to rebellion, I, pt. i, 288; causes disturbances in Márwár (1672), *id.* 289; is reconciled with the emperor (1698), *id.* 290; obtains for Ajitsing pardon and lands in the districts of Jhálor, and Sáchor (1699), *id.* 290; is appointed governor of Pátan (1703), *id.* 291; intrigues against (1703); his escapes, *id.* 291-292; joins Ajitsingh in his rebellion; takes shelter with the Kolis; his disappearance, *id.* 295.

Durgádevi: famine, in Maháráshtra (1396-1408), I, pt. ii, 588; *see* also IX, pt. i, 12; XII, 244 note; XVI, 105; XVII, 305; XVIII, pt. ii, 216; XIX, 226; XX, 277; XXII, 404.

Durgapáli: identified with Junágadh, I, pt. i, 160.

Durgarája: Ráshtrakúta king, pt. ii, 386.

Durgasakti; Sendraka chief, feudatory of the Chálukyas, I, pt. ii, 358 note 1.

Durgásing: Sátára Senapati's adopted (1857) son, removed to Bombay; XIX, 317-319.

Durgavs: village goddess in Dhárwár, her account, worship and fairs, XXVI, 807.

Durlabha: Chaulukya king (A. D. 1010-1022), attends the *swayamvara* or choice-marriage of Durlabhadevi and is selected as groom, builds a lake at Anahilaváda and abdicates, in favour of his nephew Bhima, I, pt. i, 162-163.

Durlabhadevi: sister of Mahendra Rája of Nándol, selected Durlabha, Chaulukya king, at a *swayamvara*, I, pt. i, 162-163.

Durlabhadevi: of the Batpura family, wife of Pulikesin II, I, pt. ii, 344, 348.

Durlabhasarovara: lake, built at Anahiláváda by Durlabha, the Chaulukya king, I, pt. i, 163.

Durlabhassena: nominated king of Somnáth by Mahmud of Ghazni, I, pt. i, 168.

Durva: famine, fodder and sacred plant, XXV, 208, 276, 283, 289.

Durvásarashi: sage, I, pt. i, 461.

Durvinita-Kongani: Gangá chief (481-514), I, pt. ii, 300.

Dushmata, Duzukhta, Duzuvarsta: a section of the code of morals, IX, pt. ii, 213.

Dussála: king of Sákambhari, I, pt. i, 171.

Dustur Dinar: I, pt. ii, 589. *See* Dastur Dinar.

Dutaka: grantor, I, pt. i, 125.

Dutch: the Portuguese and the emperor Jahángir enter into a treaty against (1615), I, pt. ii, 62; their ships frequent the ports of Dábhol, Chaul, and Bassein without hindrance, blockade Goa from 1639 to 1642; build a fortified factory at Vengurla; refuse an invitation from the king of Bijápur to winter their ships at Dábhol and Ortzery (Áchra?); become the strongest European power in the East, and again blockade Goa in 1660, *id.* 63; capture Cochin (1663), and succumb to the English, *id.* 64; successfully defend themselves (1684), *id.* 77-78; attack Vijayádurg but fail (1724), *id.* 87; excluded from the Marátha dominions and prevented from entering into the Dánda-Rájápur (1756), *id.* 122; in Surat as traders (1616-1620), allowed to erect a factory, II, 79 and note 4; provisions of their charter (1688), their trade centres in the East Indies, course of their trade (1618-1658), *id.* 87 and notes 1 and 2, 88; in Surat (1665-1707), *id.* 106-108; (1707-1733), *id.* 115; (1733-1747), *id.* 121-122, (1759-1800), *id.* 150-152; establish a factory at Broach (16-17), *id.* 468; in Ahmadábád (1618-1744), IV, 253, 285; in Sarkhej, *id.* 272, 292; their appearance in Indian seas (1597), XIII, 453; capture Cochin (1663), *id.* 458-459; in Surat, *id.* 465; their rivalry with the Portuguese (1656), *id.* 473; their trade in the Persian Gulf, Ceylon and the Straits (1660-1710), *id.* 486; exclude the English from Japan (1660-1710), *id.* 487; at Honávar (1673), XV, pt. ii, 124, 311; encouraged by Muhammad Adil Sháh, XXIII, 428 note 3.

Duties: on exports from Bombay, Thána and Kalyán, I, pt. II, 81; customs, between Bombay and Sálsette abolished (1803), *id.* 124.

Duties: enjoined by Musalmán law, belief in the principal tenets of the faith; prayers; fast in the month of Ramazan; pilgrimages; alms, IX, pt. ii, 126, 171 note 2.

Dutonda: snake in Ratnágiri, X, 48.

Duzuk: place of punishment after death, belief in, IX, pt. ii, 212.

Dvádiyappa: I, pt. ii, 512. *See* Dhádiyasa.

Dváraká: modern Dwárká, capital of the Yádava dynasty, I, pt. ii, 231, 490, 517. *See* Dwárká.

Dvárap: *see* Bárap.

Dvárappa: king of Látadesa, I, pt. i, 159 and note 1. *See* Bárappa.

Dvárasamudra: modern Halebid, capital of the Hoysála kings, I, pt. ii, 218, 491 note 4; pt. i, 203 note 3; XXI, 359 note 2; plundered by Alla-ud-din's generals (1310), *id.* 361. *See* Dwárká.

Dvárávati: I, pt. ii, 490, 512, 514, 516, 517. *See* Dwárká.

Dvárávatipura: Dwárká, I, pt. ii, 16.

Dvárávati-puravar-adhisvara: supreme lord of Dvárávati, the best of towns, hereditary title of the Hoysálas, I, pt. ii, 490; also of the Yádavas, *id.* 517.

Dvárka: town in Káthiáwár, schools and hospitals at, VII, 488, 509; I, pt. i, 6, 160; Musalmán post at, attack on, orders of the emperor to raze to the ground the temple at *id.* 295; is captured by Vaghers of Okhámandal (1859), *id.* 446; taken by the English, *id.* 448, 461, 546. *See* Dwárká.

Dvárkabái Sáheb: wife of Santáji Ghorpade, temple dedicated to, XXIV, 301.

Dvyásraya: work compiled by Hemachandra, I, pt. i, 137, 156, 159, 162, 163, 170, 171, 173, 182, 185, 193.

Dvyásraya Kosha: I, pt. i, 180, 192; I, pt. ii, 567. *See* Dvyásraya.

Dwaikir: Devagiri, I, pt. ii, 534.

Dwáparyug: third cycle, I, pt. i, 461.

Dwarf Snake: in Poona, XVIII, pt. I, 73.

Dwárká: legendary capital of Krishna, I, pt. ii, 993; in Káthiáwád, *id.* 517; dynastic seat; shrine at, IX, pt. i, p. ix; Aryan settlement at, *id.* p. xi; seat of Shankaráchárya, *id.* 542; place of pilgrimage, *id.* 10, 157, 164, 175, 213, 220, 247, 336, 549; fire-worshipping priests in, IX, pt. ii, 183 note 4. *See* also XIII, 423. *See* Dvárka.

Dwárkánáth: Hindu god, IX, pt. i, 4.

Dwellings: All District Volumes, *see* census details under District Name in Gujarát houses; two classes of, town and village; town, outward appearance; internal arrangement, names and uses of the different rooms; furniture in IX, pt. i, pp. xv-xviii; village, outward appearance; internal arrangements; furniture, *id.* pp. xviii-xix; religious ceremonies in building a new house, door-post or *bársákh* setting up ceremony, tie-beam or *mobh* erection ceremony, housing or *vástu* ceremony, *id.* 204; of Bhils, *id.* 296-297; Kolis, *id.* 245; Rájpúts, *id.* 130-131; Vániás, *id.* 75.

Dyeing: in Kaira, III, 75; in Baroda, 156-157; in Kolába, XI, 133; in Khándesh, process of, XII, 229; in Násik, XVI, 170-175; in Sátára, XIX, 222; in Sholápur, XX, 269; in Belgaum district, XXI, 348-350; in Bijápur district, XXIII, 165-166, 368.

Dye plants: in Kánara, XV, pt. ii, 19.

Dyers: in Cutch, V, 126.

Dyes: mineral, in Cutch, V, 21; grown in Poona district, XVIII, pt. ii, 48; in Kolhápur, XXIV, 172-173.

Dying Princess; picture of the, in Ajanta caves, XII, 496, 546.

Dyke: basalt, at Dighási, Sopára and Trombay, XIV, 56, 342, 362.

Dynasties: Maurya and Chálukya, "Introduction to the Early History of the Dakhan," I, pt. ii, p. ii; Śatavábana, *id.* 151; Puranic; Maurya, *id.* 155; Andhrabhritya, *id.* 156, Kshatrapa, *id.* 157; Andhrabhritya and Śatavábana, *id.* 158; Andhra, *id.* 167; Vijayánagar, *id.* 175.

Dysentery: disease, its cure, IX, pt. i, 365; in Ratnágiri, X, 292; in Sávantvádi, *id.* 461.

E

EAGLES: in Ratnágiri, X, 1856-57; at Netráni island in Kánara, XV, pt. ii, 337.

Ear-boring: Pátáne Prabhu ceremony, XVIII, pt. i, 223-224; Bene-Israel, ceremony, *id.* 531 and notes 1 and 2.

Earth: Prithvi, an element, IX, pt. i, 348; planet, is called Ráhu, worship of, *id.* 403-405. *See* Planet.

Earthen Dish: rite of, IX, pt. ii, 151. *See* Sahnak Kánduri.

Earthen Mounds: in Násik city, at Panchavati, XVI, 516; at Malhár, *id.* 534; at Govardhan Gangápur, *id.* 539-540.

Earth Feast: IX, pt. ii, 217. *See* Aspandád Jasan.

Earth-nut: cultivation of, in Khándesh, XII, 152; in Sátára district, XIX, 165.

Earthquakes: in Surat, II, 316; in Kaira, III, 169; in Ahmadábád district (1819, 1821, 1864), IV, 261; in Cutch, V, 16-17; of 1819, *id.* 163; in Káthiáwár, VIII, 86; causes of, believed to be a sign of widespread sin and wickedness, IX, pt. i, 404; in Khándesh (1854), XII, 13; in Thána district, XIII, 16.

Earth-salt: making of, in Dhárwár district, XXII, 388.

East India Company: I, pt. ii, 61; put to the annual expense of £50,000 to protect their trade against pirates, *id.* 87; Portuguese, government transfers the monopoly of trade to the, *id.* 62; The Dutch Company, *id.* 63 note 5.

Eastwick: Captain (1883), his description of Mándu, I, pt. i, 383.

Ebhálvad: táluka in Káthiáwár, VIII, 436.

Ecclesiastics: power of, in the state under the Portuguese, I, pt. ii, 56.

Echaladevi: wife of the Kalachurya king Bijjála, I, pt. ii, 471, 477; wife of Ereyanga Hoysála, *id.* 492 and note 4, 493; wife of Narasinha I, Hoysála, *id.* 492, 500; wife of Kartavirya IV, the Ratta chieftain, *id.* 551, 557.

Echo: Mátherán Point, XIV, 239.

Eclipse: held sacred by Hindus, I, pt. i, 165 and note 2, 522; beliefs about, XVIII, pt. i, 255; *grahan*, that is seizure, beliefs about, practices observed at solar and lunar, IX, pt. i, 395; object of, gifts made to Bhangiás during, *id.* 335, 395; other observances during, *id.* 395, 396. *See* Planet, Sun.

Eclipta prostrata: (*máká*) weed very common, used as medicine, XXV, 260; a sacred plant, *id.* 292.

Edatore, Ededore: province in Mysore, I, pt. ii, 436, 489.

Edenád: country on the north-east of Banavási. *See* Edevolal, I, pt. ii, 309 and note 8, 547.

Edevolal: in the Banavási province, I, pt. ii, 278 note 2, 369, 370. *See* Edenád.

Edicts: of Aśoka (B. C. 250), found on the confines of his empire, I, pt. i, 14; I, pt. ii,

142, 143, 146; engraved at Sopára, XIII, 404, 405; XIV, 339, 380, 410.
Edlabad: old town in Khándesh district, XII, 447.
Edlabad: deserted village in Dhárwár district, holy well and fair at, XXII, 712.
Education among Hindus of Gujarát: religious, among Bráhmans, IX, pt. i, 31; school, among bards and actors, Bháts, *id.* 214; Chárans, Gandhrapa, *id.* 222; Bhaváyás, *id.* 225; Turis, *id.* 227; Bráhmaus, *id.* 51; craftsmen, Bhávsárs, *id.* 179; Darjis, Galiásras, *id.* 181; Ghánchis, *id.* 183; Golas, Kadiyás, *id.* 186; Kansárás, *id.* 188; Khatris, *id.* 189; Luhárs, *id.* 192; Mochis, *id.* 195; Saláts, *id.* 197; Sonis, *id.* 202; Suthárs, *id.* 206; depressed classes, Bhangiás, *id.* 338; Dhedás, *id.* 344; Garudás, *id.* 345; Khálpás; *id.* 346; early tribes, *id.* 294; Bhils, *id.* 312; Chodhrás, *id* 313; Dhundeás, IX, pt. i, 316; Dublás, *id.* 318; Gámtás, *id.* 319; Káthodias, *id.* 320; Kolgás, *id.* 321; Mángs, *id.* 324; Várlis, *id.* 329; Vitoliás, *id.* 330; herdsmen, Bharváds, *id.* 285; Rabáris, *id.* 289; husbandmen, Káchhiás, *id.* 154; Kanbis, *id.* 163, 164; Patelias, *id.* 174; Ságars, *id.* 175; personal servants, Dhobis, *id.* 230; Hajáms, *id.* 234; traders, Vániás, of *shikáuchhokrás* or apprentices in Vániá-shops, *id.* 79-80, 96; Shrávaks, *id.* 103; Bhatiás, *id.* 121; Lohánás, *id.* 122; writers, Brahma-Kshatris, *id.* 59; Káyasths, *id.* 61, 67, 68; Prabhus, *id.* 68; among Gujarát Pársis, of boys, primary, IX, pt. ii, 209; higher, 203; female, primary and higher, *id.* 204; schools and colleges for, *id.* 203; in Persian, Zend and other languages, *id.* 194, 204; scholarship for Zend and Pehlevi, *id.* 194; religious, of boys and girls of laymen, of the sons of priests, *id.* 209, 210; Madresa and council schools for, *id.* 204. *See* also All District Volumes under District Name.
Educational Cess: in Surat district, II, 247; in Broach district, *id.* 520; Kaira, III, 130; in Panch Mahák, *id.* 282; in Ahmadábád district, IV, 206.
Educational Institutions: in Poona city, XVIII, pt. iii, 55-60, 330-331.
Egerton: Colonel, I, pt. ii, 103; marches against the Maráthás (1778), *id.* 605; *see* also XIII, 503, 504 and note 2, 505; XVIII, pt. ii, 263-264.
Egg-plant: growing of, in Poona district, XVIII, pt. ii, 60.
Egrets: class of birds in Ratnágiri, X, 94.
Egypt: Indian connection with (B. C. 2500-B. C. 500), XIII, 403 and note 1, 404 and note 3; Thána trade with (B. C. 250), *id.* 409; export of sugar cotton, silk and other articles to (A. D. 150), *id.* 416; decline of trade with (300 600), *id.* 420; its trade with Barygaza (Gulf of Cambay) (A. D. 80), I, pt. i, 545, 546.
Egyptians: ally themselves with the rájas of Cochin and Cambay, I, pt. ii, 34; hold the monopoly of the Indian trade and are supported by the local traders against the Portuguese, *id.* 43; their fleet in the Gulf of Cambay (1507), XIII, 448.
Ehretia lœvis: famine plant, XXV, 202; its leaves used as fodder, *id.* 278.
Eidrusis: *sayad* family in Gujarát, IX, pt. ii, 6, note 1.
Eirinon: Gulf of, in Cutch, mentioned by Ptolemy, V, 130; the Ran, I, pt. i, 544.
Ekadhiramangala: village in Madras, I, pt. ii, 325. *See* Kodukolli.
Ekalla Vira: shrine, visited by Vastupála, I, pt. i, 200.
Ekankadi: a Baroda land tenure, VII, 359-360.
Ekántada-Rámayya: Bráhman, starts the revival of Śaivism known as Lingáyatism, I, pt. ii, 406 note 5, 481, 482; cuts off his own head which is restored by the god Śiva; outrages the idol of Jina, is given a *jayapatra* by the Kalachurya Bijjala, *id.* 483; the Western Chálukya king Someśvara IV and the Hángal Kádamba Kamadeva wash the feet of, *id.* 484.
Ekdara: fort in Ahmadnagar district, XVII, 732.
Ekruk: artificial lake near Sholápur city, XX, 225-226; village, *id.* 411.
Eksáli: one-year tenure in Thána district, XIII, 536, 550.
Eksar: village in Thána district, memorial stones art, XIV, 57-59.
Ekvira: goddess, XI, 383 note 1.
Elæo-carpus: *ganitrus* (*rudráksh*), sacred plant, grows on higher *gháts*, rare in Bombay Presidency, XXV, 286; *tuberculatus*, a sacred plant, *id.* 287.
Elæodendron: *glaucum*, grows in Sátára and the Dakhan, an antidote to snake-bite, XXV, 274; *Roxburghia*, grows in the Dakhan, its bark poisonous, used as an antidote to snake-bite, *id.* 264, 274
Elapur: identified with Ellora, Ráshtrakúta king Krishna I, established at, XV, pt. ii, 84.
Elapura: I, pt. ii, 196. *See* Elur, Ellora, *id.* 391 and note 6.
Eldridge: Major, I, pt. ii, 612; reduces the stronghold in Ahmadnagar, *id.* 630; takes Chávand, Jivadhán and other Marátha forts, XVIII, pt. ii, 303.
Eleáchi: pass in Násik district, XVI, 129.
Elements: names of; the universe formed of; beliefs about; names of deities presiding over, IX, pt. i, 348; worship, of water or *ap*, *id.* 348-349; sea, *id.* 349; rivers, *id.* 349-350; ponds, springs, wells, *id.* 350; rain, *id.* 351-353; of fire or *agni*, *id.* 356-357; of wind or *váyu*, *id.* 358; of earth, *id.* 403-405.
Elephant: is held sacred, days sacred for his worship, Ganpati shown with the head of, IX, pt. i, 376; rock-cut, in Elephanta caves, XIV, 59, 92 and note 1; timber-dragging in Kánara, XV, pt. i, 27-28; in Khándesh, XII, 29; domestic, in Belgaum district, XXI, 66.
Elephanta: island in Bombay harbour, probably old Puri, I, pt. i, 107; fortified by Sambháji (1680), XIII, 479; taken by Mánáji Angria (1739), XXVI, pt. i, 227; taken by the Maráthás (1740), *id.* 233; occupied by the

British (1774), XIII, 501 and note 2, 502, 508, I, pt. ii, 101; entered in Milburn's map (1800), XIII, 514.
Elephanta Caves: XIV, 10; description, *id.* 59-61; great cave, *id.* 62; the Trimurti, *id.* 63-65; Siva and Párvati, *id.* 66-67; Ardhanárishvar, *id.* 67-69; Párvati in a pet, *id.* 69-70; Rávan under Kailás, *id.* 70-71; *ling* chapel, *id.* 71-72; marriage of Shiv and Párvati, *id.* 72-73; Bhairáv, *id.* 73-74; Shiv dancing, *id.* 75; Shiv as Maháyogi, *id.* 76; east wing, *id.* 77-79; west wing, *id.* 79-80; history, *id.* 80-88; second and third caves, *id.* 89-90; remains, *id.* 90-93; fourth cave, *id.* 93-94; remains, *id.* 94-97, 386, 388, 400, 402; see also I, pt. i, 458; I, pt. ii, 9, 13, XI, 151; XIII, 412, 498.
Elephant grass: food-plant grows in Dakhan and Konkan, XXV, 183.
Elettaria cardamomum: grows in Kánara and in Madras Presidency, its seeds used as condiment, XXV, 176.
Eleusine Ægyptiaca: very common in rains, a famine plant, XXV, 208.
Eleusine coracana: (*náchani*) a food-plant common on the *gháts*, XXV, 187.
Elia: Prophet, IX, pt. i, 343.
Elias: Dhedás derive the name from Prophet Elia, IX, pt. i, 343 and note 2. *See* Dhedás.
Elias: Prophet, IX, pt. ii, 152. *See* Khizr, Khwajah.
Elisar: king, destroyed Aden, I, pt. i, 543.
Ellichpur: town in Berár, I, pt. ii, 250, 530; ceded to Allá-ud-din by Rámachandra of Devagiri, *id.* 531.
Elliot: Sir Walter, antiquarian, I, pt. ii, 27, 178, 301 note 1, 347 note 2, 427 note 3, 358 note 1, 373 note 1, 441 note 6, 448, 458 note 1, 548, 573 and note 1; XV, pt. ii, 75; his account of Panchâls, XVIII, pt. i, 343.
Elliot: Sir Henry, author of *History of India* quoted, IX, pt. ii, 69, 70.
Ellis Bridge: in Ahmadábád district, IV, 12.
Ellorá: village in Dakhan, cave temples at, I, pt. ii, 388, 619; inscriptions at, *id.* 389, 391 and note 6, 401.
Elphinstone: Lord, governor of Bombay (1857), I, pt. i, 438; improved the road to Mátherán, XIV, 268.
Elphinstone: Mr. Mountsuart, is appointed (1811) resident at Poona; his former services; his plan of life at Poona; upholds Bájiráv's authority over the estate-holders; intrigues of Khusruji, an agent, at the residency; allows Bájiráv to strengthen his force; Gangadhár Shástri in Poona; Mr. Elphinstone's estimate of his character; murder of the Shástri at Pandharpur; Trimbakji's share in the murder; Mr. Elphinstone demands the surrender of Trimbakji; Bájiráv's plans of a general rising of all the Marátha powers; Mr. Elphinstone warns Bájiráv of the danger he was running; demands the surrender of Trimbakji and the immediate delivery of Sinhgad, Purandhar and Ráygad as a pledge; treaty of Poona; the three forts restored to Bájiráv on the suggestion of Sir John Malcolm, who had an interview with Bájiráv at Máhuli; Bájiráv's attempt to murder Mr. Elphinstone; preparations for the battle; battle of Kirkee; his share in the victory; Poona surrendered; Bájiráv's flight; fight at Koregaon; Sátára proclamation; fall of the Peshwá's forts in Poona; Mr. Elphinstone appointed commissioner; settlement of the country; the country between Chándor hills and the Nira river under two collectors, Captains Robertson and Pottinger; Mr. Elphinstone's policy with regard to existing institutions; position of the sardárs; administrative changes; condition of Poona under the British, XVIII, pt. ii, 290-306;—*another account of*: resident at Poona, XIX, 300-301; his manifesto, *id.* 303-305; description of Sátára, *id.* 306; condition of Sátára (1826), *id.* 309; his treaty with the Peshwa (1817), VII, 225; his settlement of Baroda affairs (1820), *id.* 234; his friendly attitude towards Sayájirav II, *id.* 240; mediates between Patvardhan and the Peshwa, XXIV, 349; present at the treaty of Bassein, XIV, 35; his history quoted, I, pt. ii, XI, 29, 37, 99, 115, 116; his report on Khándesh, *id.* 631; his administrative changes in Ahmadábád district, IV, 159; his minutes on Cutch and Mahi Kántha, V, 255-264, 433-455; enacts a civil and criminal code (1827), I, pt. i, 436; his description of Bijápur walls and mosques, XXIII, 568 note 2, 598, 607 note 1, 612 note 1. *See* also I, pt. ix, 665; IX, pt. ii, 198 note 5; XIII, 322 note 2.
Elphinstone Point: Mahábaleshvar, XIX, 503.
Elphinstone Spring: at Mátherán, XIV, 235, 244.
Elumpundale: village, camp of Vinayáditya at (692), I, pt. ii, 369.
Elur, Elura: inscription of Dantidurga at, I, pt. i, 120, 122, 467; Devaladevi captured near, *id.* 205; caves, I, pt. ii, 9; rock-cut temples at, *id.* 194; Siva temples constructed by Krishnarája at, *id.* 195, 208, 391. *See* Elápura and Ellora.
Embassy: Buddhist (A. D. 560), Bráhmans described by, IX, pt. i, 434; Portuguese, to the chief of Honavar (1623), XV, pt. ii, 123-124; Vijayánagar, to the Portuguese (1505), *id.* 103.
Emberizinae: family of birds in Ratnágiri, X, 84.
Embolima: town identified with Amb sixty miles from Attok, I, pt. i, 538.
Embroidery: in Surat district, II, 179; in Cutch, V, 125-126; in Cambay, VI, 208; special skill of Musalmáns in the art of, IX, pt. ii, 123.
Emigration: all district volumes. *See* Census details under District Name.
Emperors: of Delhi, persecutions of Gujarát Bohoras under IX, pt. ii, 27 note 1; Mughal spread of Islám by, *id.* 5; 125.
Encostema (Hippion) orientalis: medicinal plant found in Gujarát, XXV, 262.
Engineering College: *see* Science College.
English: the, their factory at Surat besieged and plundered, I, pt. i, 333; plundered second time, take the fort of Surat with the help

of the Maráthás (1759), *id.* 343; become chief of the affairs of Surat and enter into agreement with Fatesingh Gáikwár (1773), *id.* 401; capture Broach (1772), *id.* 401; capture Thána and Versova fort, *id.* 401; enter into an alliance offensive and defensive with Fatesingh Gáikwár (1780), *id.* 408; operations of, against Sindia and Holkar, *id.* 409; aid Govindráv Gáikwár's party (1802), *id.* 412; settle the treaty of Bassein (1802), *id.* 413; capture Broach and Pávágad, restore Pávágad and Dohad to Sindhia (1803), *id.* 414; enter into a fresh treaty with the Gáikwár and obtain the Gáikwár's share in Ahmadábád, Surat and Kaira (1817), *id.* 428; sovereignty of Gujarát passes into the hands of (1819), *id.* 428; capture Bet and Dwárka (1859), *id.* 446-448;—*another account of:* in the Konkan, I, pt. ii, 20-131; the Portuguese and the Emperor Jehángir enter into a treaty against (1615), *id.* 62; their ships frequent the ports of Dábhol, Chaul, and Bassein without hindrance, *id.* 63; capture Ormuz (1622), and become a great European power in the East, *id.* 64; Bombay ceded to them (1661), *id.* 63; remove their factory from Ahmadábád to Nandurbár in 1670, *id.* 625; enter into a treaty with Shiváji (1680), *id.* 72; make an alliance with Phond Savant against the Angrias (1730), *id.* 88; enter into a formal alliance with the Sidis against the Angrias (1733), *id.* 83, 88; assist in the defence of Bándra (1737), *id.* 84; join the Maráthás to reduce Tuláji Angria (1755), *id.* 88; obtain Bankot (1756), *id.* 92; administration at Bankot, *id.* 122; take part with the Sidis and hoist their flag at Janjira (1760), *id.* 98; take Málwan and Ráiri (1765), *id.* 106; take Thána (1774), *id.* 85; administration of Sálsette, *id.* 122; take part in the quarrel of Raghunáthráo with the Poona ministers and send Colonel Goddard to help him (1778), *id.* 628; join the Maráthás and the Nizám in an offensive alliance against Tipu (1789), *id.* 661; are allowed to have a factory at Sindhudurg (1792), *id.* 108; escort the Peshwa Bájiráv to Poona (1803), and take Suvarndurg for the Peshwa, *id.* 111; take the Peshwá's country, *id.* 611-612, 631, 664-665; conspiracy against, *id.* 612; settlements of, in Surat (1608-1618), II, 74; (1618-1658), *id.* 85; (1658-1707), *id.* 95; (1707-1733), *id.* 113; (1733-1747), *id.* 121; (1759-1800), *id.* 150; capture Surat (1759), *id.* 127; their connection with Broach, *id.* 468; in Ahmadábád district, as traders (1613-1760), IV, 253, 273; as conquerors (1780), *id.* 258; as rulers (1817-1878), *id.* 143; at Cambay, VI, 218, 219, 220-221, 224; in Thána, XIII, 458, 462, 464, 472, 477, 478, 479, 482, 488, 490, 512, 526; in Kánara district (1638-1660), XV, pt. ii, 124-125; (1700-1720), *id.* 134-135; (1782-1883, *id.* 142-153. *See* also IX, pt. ii, 183 note 2, 197 note 2, 203. *See* British.

English and Dutch: at war in Surat, II, 81.

English factors: confined in Surat (1623 and 1701), II, 84, 100; their number, pay, allowances and mode of life, *id.* 86, 101, 105.

English residents: in Bombay (1677), XXVI, pt. iii, 279-280.

English troops: perished at Anjidiv (1662-1664), XV, pt. i, 2.

Entertainments: caste, in Gujarát or public dinners, three classes of: trade, social and religious, IX, pt. i, 25; trade, two kinds of, paid for from guild funds, paid for by one of the members; occasions for, *id.* 25-26; social, three kinds of, given by caste, called Ochhav, observances on, arrangements for; given by individual members, in honour of some family event, compulsory, optional; caste picnics or *ujáni*, *id.* 26-27; religious occasions for, *id.* 27; preparations of, form of invitation to; gatherings; mode of serving food; three kinds of dinners, *id.* 27-29.

Ephthalite: ruling class of White Húnas, I, pt. i, 86, 145; retreat of, to Káshmir (590-642), *id.* 500; Khazars, IX, pt. i, 455, 456, 471. *See* Húnas.

Epics: chronological value of, I, pt. ii, 141; the *Rámáyana*, *Mahábhárata*; contents of, IX, pt. i, 531-532.

Epidemic: fiercer form of disease, IX, pt. i, 365, 368, 413; causes of, *id.* 365, 413; is believed to be cured by religious rites, *id.* 365; Sitala, epidemic form of small-pox, *id.* 368; scaring rites, offerings made to Máta or goddess to appease her wrath during, performance of disease-soothing ceremony or Shánti to stay epidemics, *id.* 368, 413-414; performance of car ceremony to clear the village of cholera and other plagues. *id.* 414-415; other ways to clear the village of plague, *id.* 302 note 1, 415; dread of breaking out of, *id.* 396, 403; in Baroda state (1863-1881), VII, 496-498; in Kolhápur state, XXIV, 285-287.

Epiphany: Feast of the, I, pt. ii, 65, at Verangal, XIV, 383.

Episcopal See: creation of (1534), at Goa, I, pt. ii, 55.

Epitansa: town on the Indus mentioned by Ptolemy, I, pt. i, 538.

Era: of Nahapána: I, pt. i, 26; the Málwa, 28-29, 67; the Samvat, *id.* 29; the Gupta, id. 29; Valabhi, *id.* 81; Traikútaka, *id.* 113; Chedi, *id.* 114; of Sindharája, the Chaulukya king, *id.* 176 and note; the Gupta, the Christian, the Traikútaka, I, pt. ii, 187.

Eradubilkode: tax under the Chálukyas of Badámi, I, pt. ii, 451.

Eraga: I, pt. ii, 505. *See* Ereyanna, Erega, Ereyamma, Ratta king (1010), *id.* 551; feudatory of the Western Chálukya king Jayasimha II, *id.* 553.

Eragrostis cynosuroides: (*darbh*), sacred grass, XXV, 279, 284, 290.

Erambarage: Yelburga in the Nizám's dominions, I, pt. ii, 504, 505; capital of the Sindas of Yelburga, *id.* 573 and note 1, 575, 576.

Eran: temple, Gupta pillar inscription at, I, pt. i, 71; inscription of Samudragupta at, I, pt. ii, 286 note 1; pillar inscription of Budhagupta, *id.* 369 note 5.

Erandi: castor-plant, cultivation of, in Khándesh, XII, 153. *See* Erundee.

Erandol : sub-division of Khándesh district, its boundaries, area, aspect, climate, water, soil, holdings, survey details, survey results, stocks, crops, people, XII, 2, 371-375 ; town, *id.* 448.
Eratosthenes : Greek geographer (275-194 B. C.), I, pt. i, 535, 537.
Erega : of the Ratta family, I, pt. ii, 437.
Ereppa-Vammadi : king, I, pt. ii, 301 note 1.
Ereyamma : Erega, of the Ratta family, I, pt. ii, 437.
Ereyanga : son of Vinayáditya, Hoysála feudatory, takes Whára, lays waste Chakragotta, and breaks the power of Kalinga, I, pt. ii, 492, 493, 494, 500.
Ereyanna : officer of Vira-Ballála II, in charge of Banavási and Santalige (1192), I, pt. ii, 505.
Ereyappa : Western Ganga king, successor of Satyavákya Permanadi (930-931), fights with Viramahendra, I, pt. ii, 304 and note 1, 332, 379 and note 2, 419.
Ereyur : village in Madras, I, pt. ii, 369.
Ereyya : name of Pulikeśin II, I, pt. ii, 351 note 3, 358 note 1.
Erinpur : town in Rájpútána, mutiny at (1857), I, pt. i, 439.
Eriodendron unfractuosum : a common famine and fibrous plant, XXV, 195, 229.
Erithræa Roxburghii : used as tonic, common in cultivated ground after rains, XXV, 262.
Erskine : Mr., the chief of the factory at Cambay (1759), I, pt. i, 343.
Erskine : historian, I, pt. ii, 30.
Erskine : Mr. W., his description of the carved elephant in the Elephanta caves (1813), XIV, 88, 92 note 1, 93.
Erundee : oil-plant cultivated throughout India, XXV, 220, 255.
Ervad : title of under-priest, IX, pt. ii, 225. *See* Herbad.
Erythroxylon monogynum : famine-plant found in Madras and Ceylon, XXV, 195.
Esacinæ : family of birds in Ratnágiri, X, 91.
Escarpments : in Poona hills, XVIII, pt. i, 10.
Esparis : Pársis known as, in Cambay (1536), IX, pt. ii, 189.
Espirito Sancto : Church of, at Koprád in Thána district, XIV, 210.
Esplanade : Bombay, formed (1739-1744), XXVI, pt. ii, 438-440 ; to be made 1,000 yards wide (1771), *id.* 477-478.
Estate-holders : Maráthá *jághirdárs* in Bijápur district, XXIII, 446.
Estates : wards', in Ratnágiri, X, 451 ; Pársi, in Thána district, XIII, 256 and note 2.
Estreldinæ : family of birds in Ratnágiri, X, 83.
Estuarine snakes : in Poona, XVIII, pt. i, 77.
Etagiri : modern Yátagiri, I, pt. ii, 450 and note 2.
Ether : an element, IX, pt. i, 348. *See* Akásh.
Ethiopia : head-lands of, I, pt. i, 536 ; Thána trade with, XIII, 440, 444.
Eucratides : Baktrian king, I, pt. i, 16-17.
Eudaimon Arabia : modern Aden, I, pt. i, 543.
Eudoxos : of Cyzicus (117 B. C.), his voyage to India, I, pt. i, 535.
Eugenia jambolana : very common tree, produces wine, XXV, 211 ; produces a dye, *id.* 245 ; its bark used as medicine, *id.* 259 ; a sacred plant, *id.* 279, 284, 291.
Eulophia compestris : *herbacea, vera,* food-plants found in Konkan, XXV, 176.
Eunuch Nobles : Sidi, of Delhi and Lucknow, IX, pt. ii, 12. *See* Sidis.
Euphorbia : *hirta,* common famine-plant, XXV, 203 ; *nerifolia,* antidote to snake-bite, a sacred plant, *id.* 275, 289 ; *pilulifera,* common famine-plant, *id.* 203 ; *tirucalli,* produces dye, its juice used for poisoning fish, *id.* 248, 268, 273.
Euphorbiaceæ : species of famine-plants, XXV, 203 ; yields oil, *id.* 220 ; produces a dye, *id.* 248 ; its juice a violent poison, *id.* 268.
Euphrates : river, I, pt. i, 514.
Europeans : in Khándesh, XII, 128 ; in Thána, XIII, 446, 458 note 2, 479, 481, 482 ; in Kánara district, XV, pt. i, 411 ; unlicensed, not allowed to stay in Bombay (1779), XXVI, pt. iii, 400.
Eusuf-ud-din Kadiri : *sayad* saint, his descent ; converts Sind ruler of the Samma dynasty ; converts Lohana community with its leader Manekji ; changes the name of the community to Muamin ; retires to Irak ; his descendants become the religious heads of the converted community, IX, pt. ii, 50-51.
Euthydemos : Baktrian Greek king, I, pt. i, 535.
Evesaruthemgeh : fourth watch, IX, pt. ii, 214 note 1. *See* Geh.
Evil Eye : influence of the, XVIII, pt. i, 292, 299, 526 note 1.
Evil spirits : quieting of, at marriage among Pátane Prabhus, XVIII, pt. i, 203 ; belief in, *id.* 553.
Exacumbicolar : medicinal plant found in Konkan, XXV, 262.
Exæcaria insignis : a poisonous plant, XXV, 268.
Exchange bills : in Kolába district, XI, 101-102, 426 ; varieties of, in Khándesh, XII, 192 ; in Thána, XIII, 305 ; in Kánara, XV, pt. ii, 25 ; in Ahmadnagar district, XVII, 297-298 ; in Poona district, XVIII, pt. ii, 102-103 ; in Sholápur district, XX, 240 ; in Belgaum district, XXI, 291 ; in Dhárwár district, XXII, 322 ; in Bijápur district, XXIII, 338. *See* Hundis.
Exchange, rate of : between India and Europe (1703, 1733, 34, 35, 46), 2*s.* 6*d.* the Bombay rupee, XXVI, pt. ii, 231-232 ; 2*s.* 5*d.* and 2*s.* 3*d.* (1766), favourable to bills on Indian presidencies (768), *id.* 232-234 ; bills on the directors limited to £20,000 (1768), extended to £50,000 (1769), orders not to exceed this limit (1772), restricted to £300,000 by Parliament (1774), *id.* 234-39.
Excise : all district volumes. *See* Revenue and Finance under district name.
Excursions : Mátherán, XIV, 283-284.
Exhibition : industrial, held at Broach (1868), II, 443.
Exorcism : belief in, of Gujarát Hindu population, IX, pt. i, 137-138, 293, 417, 425 ;

among Gujarát Musalmáns, IX, pt. ii, 30; practised among Bijápur Gavandis and Kahligers, XXIII, 99, 114-115.

Exorcists: spirit-scarers, called Bhuvás, IX, pt. i, 137; Badvás, *id.* 302, 414; other names of, classes to which they may belong, *id.* 7, 137, 418; Hindu exorcist, his way of mastering a spell to gain control over a spirit, rites to be observed by, *id.* 418; methods adopted by, to find ont spirit, *id.* 137, 419-420; witches, *id.* 302 and note 1, 303; part played by, in small-pox epidemic scaring, *id.* 368; in blood offerings, 406; in car ceremony, *id.* 414-415; employment of, to drive out evil spirits and to cure the effects of the evil eye, IX, pt. ii, 220; XVIII, pt. i, 555-557. *See* Beliefs, Amil and Spirit.

Exotics: in Dhárwár district, XXII, 36-37.

Expeditions: Arab, to India, IX, pt. ii, 1 note 1.

Expenditure: all district volumes. *See* "Balance Sheet" under district name.

Experimental Farm: in Dhárwár district (1873-1877), XXII, 305-306; at Hivra in Poona district (1841), XVIII, pt. ii, 76-77.

Experiments: horticultural, at Povai in Sálsette, XIV, 299; of growing foreign cotton in Belgaum district, XXI, 262-275.

Exports: from Gujarát coasts, I, pt. i, 529; from Skythia, *id.* 544; from Barugaza and Ariaka, I, pt. ii, 2, from Cambay, Broach, and Malabár ports, *id.* 3; from Thána, *id.* 5; iron and pepper, *id.* 37; from Bijnagar, *id.* 62; from Chaul, *id.* 62; of Poona city, XVIII, pt. iii, 203-204. *See* also all district volumes under district name.

Extradition: between the British and Baroda state (1831-1882), VII, 460-464.

F

FACTORIES: English, Dutch and French, in South Konkan (1600-1700), "Introduction to the History of Konkan," I, pt. ii, p. xii; Portuguese, at Chaul (1512-1521), *id.* 45; at Dábhol, *id.* 48; Dutch, *id.* 63; English, French and Dutch, in Ratnágiri district, X, 197, 360, 378, 361 and note 7, 361 note 9, 377 note 1; in Surat district, English, II, 75, 86; Dutch, *id.* 79, 87; Portuguese, *id.* 88; French, *id.* 88; English and Dutch, in Ahmadábád city, IV, 272, 273; Dutch and English, in Cambay, VI, 195, 219, 224, 232; English, in Khándesh, at Dharangaon and Nandurbár, XII, 439, 458; Portuguese and English, at Chaul and Kalyán, XIII, 449, 476; English, in Kánara district, XV, pt. ii, 52, 53, 54, 124, 125, 127, 129, 130, 132, 134-135, 136, 137, 140; at Bhatkal, *id.* 274; at Honávar, *id.* 311, 312; at Kárwar, *id.* 321, 322-325; Portuguese, in Kánara, *id.* 51, 133; at Anjidiv, *id.* 254; at Bhatkal, *id.* 273, 274; at Chandávar, *id.* 277; at Honávar, *id.* 309, 311; at Mirjan, *id.* 333; steam, in Surat and Broach districts, II, 178, 426; leading part of the Pársis in, IX, pt. ii, 199 and note 3; in Kaira, III, 75; in Ahmadábád district, IV, 131; spinning and weaving, in Khándesh, XII, 231, 451; ginning in Khándesh, XII, 232; sugar at Bassein, XIII, 394; plantain drying at Uran, *id.* 395.

Fadali: class of beggars, IX, pt. ii, 20; *see* Abdali.

Fa or Fah, Hian: Chinese traveller (400 A. D.), visits Swat Valley, I, pt. i, 502; his visit to Kánheri caves, I, pt. ii, 3; XIV, 126; story of Buddha's begging bowl as told to, XIV, 403, 408.

Fairy: vows to, IX, pt. ii, 130.

Faizpur: town and cotton mart in Khándesh, XII, 448.

Fajr: dawn, prayers said at, IX, pt. ii, 126 note 3.

Fakhr-ud-Daulah: viceroy of Gujarát, attacks Ahmadábád; is deserted by his supporters Sherkhán Bábi and Ráisinghji of Idar; is defeated and captured by Jawán Mard Khán; intrigues with the Marátha leader Punáji Vithal, I, pt. i, 329; besieges Kapadvanj, *id.* 330; returns to Delhi (1748), *id.* 333; *see* also VII, 176-177.

Fakhr-ud-din: son of Mulla Muhammad Ali, chief of merchants at Surat; is imprisoned by Sayad Acchan; is sent to Bombay in disguise by the chief of the English factory at Surat, I, pt. i, 332.

Fakirs: class of Musalmán religious beggars, IX, pt. ii, 19.

Falcanera Malabarica: poisonous plant, XXV, 268.

Falconidæ: family of birds in Ratnágiri district, X, 55.

Falconinæ: order of birds in Ratnágiri, X, 55.

Falcons: in Ratnágiri, X, 55; in Khándesh, XII, 34; at Mátherán, XIV, 257.

Fal-Kholua: soothsaying, practice of, IX, pt. ii, 56.

Falkland: Mahábaleshvar Point, XIX, 505.

Fallows: in Surat and Broach districts, II, 64, 390; in Kaira and Panch Mahál districts, III, 45, 232; in Ahmadábád district, IV, 53; in Mahi Kántha, V, 369; in Khándesh, XII, 148; in Násik district, XVI, 97; in Ahmadnagar district, XVII, 259; in Poona district, XVIII, pt. ii, 31; in Kolhápur state, XXIV, 164.

Falls: at Gokák in Belgaum district, XXI, 556-561. *See* Waterfalls.

Fámbal: Al Istakhris (951), name for Anahiláváda, I, pt. i, 511.

Family gods: of several Hindu castes; *see* under caste concerned.

Family stocks: of several castes; *see* under caste concerned.

Famine: in Visaldev's time, I, pt. i, 203 and note 5; in Gujarát (1681), 286; (1654), 287; (1698), 290; (1719), 300; (1732), 313; (1747), 332; the Durgádevi (1396), I, pt. ii, 637; in the Karnátak (1472), *id.* 639; (1629), *id.* 649; (1802-1803), in the Dakhan, *id.* 111, 609, 629; in Cutch, Pálanpur and Mahi Kántha, account of, V, 107-108, 295, 371; signs showing approach and appearance of, IX, pt. i, 353, 358, 396, 402, 403; Durgádevi, in the Dakhan, *id.* 12; of 1813 in North Gujarát, Cutch, and Káthiáwár (1813), IX, pt. ii, 51; of 1790, in Gujarát, *id.* 199 note 1;

of 1803 in Bombay island, XXVI, pt. iii, 522-524; account of, in Cutch, Pálanpur and Mahi Kántha, V, 107-108, 295, 371; in Ratnágiri, X, 153, 347, 379; in Thána district, XIII, 302-303, 511-513, 559 note 4, 562; in Kolhápur state of 1876-77, account of, XXIV, 188-191; in Surat and Broach districts, II, 68, 410; in Kaira and Panch Maháls districts, III, 56, 235; in Ahmadábád district, IV, 58; in Rewa Kántha, VI, 40; in Baroda state, VII, 103-105; in Káthiáwár, VIII, 190-198; in Kolába district and Janjira state, XI, 99-100, 425-426; in Khándesh, XII, 182-190; historical references to, *id.* 243, 249, 253; in Thána district, XIII, 302-303, 511-513; in Násik district (1396-1877), XVI, 105-113, 195, 189; in Ahmadnagar district, account of, XVII, 284-293, 396-397; in Poona district (1397-1877), XVIII, pt. ii, 84-96, 224, 285; in Sátára district, XIX, 168-177; in Sholápur district, XX, 231-237; in Belgaum district, XXI, 280-289; in Dhárwár district, XXII, 306-318; in Bijápur district, account of, XXIII, 324-337.

Fantail: bird in Khándesh, XII, 36.

Faraj: Al, son of Uthmán, IX, pt. ii, 1 note 3 continued on page 4.

Fardápur: village in Nizám's territory, XII, 449.

Faredun: victory of, over the sorcerer Zohák, IX, pt. ii, 216, 220 note 1.

Farhat-ul-Mulk: Hindu convert, governor of Gujarát (1376-1391); encourages Hinduism, IX, pt. ii, 5; defeats Sikandarkhán (1388), I, pt. i, 231.

Faria, Faria-y-Souza: Portuguese historian, his mention of Honávar, XV, pt. ii, 105, 308, 309, 310; of Bhatkal, *id.* 272; of Chitakul, *id.* 279; his description of the 1612 storm at Bassein, XIV, 31 note 4; mention of *jogis* by, *id.* 135 note 10. *See* also I, pt. ii, 46; IX, pt. ii, 28 note 1, 135 note 10.

Faridis: branch of the Faruki *shaikhs*, IX, pt. ii, 8 note 2.

Farid-ud-din Shakarganj: *shaikh*, ancestor of the Faridi branch of *shaikhs*, IX, pt. ii, 8 note 2.

Farishtah: Musalmán historian, his work quoted, I, pt. i, 348, 361, 372, 512 notes 2 and 3, IX, pt. ii, 3 note 3, 10 note 4, 25 note 2, 39 and note 2, 50 note 3, 58.

Farm: government model in Khándesh, XII, 178-181.

Farmers: of revenue under Bájiráv II, Peshwa, I, pt. ii, 113; in Baroda state, VII, 440-441.

Farming system: in Baroda state, 362-366, 413-417.

Farming system: Marátha revenue (1804) in Khándesh, XII, 270; in Baroda state, VII, 362-366, 413-417.

Farm stock: in Dhárwár district, XXII, 256-257.

Farrukhsiyar: emperor (1713-1719), I, pt. i, 213; son of Azim-us-shán, second son of Aurangzeb, marches on Delhi and puts Jehándar Sháh to death (1713); remains under the influence of the Sayad brothers; makes treaty with Ajitsing of Márwár and marries his daughter (1715); religious riots in Ahmadábád (1714), *id.* 297-298; his deposition and death (1719), *id.* 300.

Fárs: IX, pt. ii, 183 note 1, 188 note 3; *see* Párs.

Fartak Point: in Arabia, XIII, 410.

Farukis: section of *shaikhs*, of pure foreign descent; two branches of, IX, pt. ii, 8 and notes 2 and 3.

Fárukis: kings of Khándesh (1370-1600), account of, XII, 243-247.

Farukshir: emperor of Delhi, I, pt. ii, 626; *see* Farrukhsiyar.

Farvardin. nineteenth day of the Pársi month, IX, pt. ii, 216; first month of the Pársi year, *id.* 216; commemoration at Surat on the 25th day of, *id.* 186 note 9.

Farvardin Jasan: chief festival day in the month of Farvardin; in the month of Adar; other names of; observances on, IX, pt. ii, 216.

Farvardin Yasht: IX, pt. ii, 194 note 1.

Faski: allowance levied by the landlord in Kolába district (1837), XI, 184.

Fasts: among Gujarát Hindu population, Ashádh sud 11th, IX, pt. i, 23 note 5; A'so vad 8th, *id.* 269: Bol-Choth, *id.* 375; bright fifteenths, *id.* 399; Gokuláshtami, *id.* 23 note 5; Karavdá Choth, *id.* 67; Mondays, *id.* 400-401; Navrátra, *id.* 220; Rámnavmi, *id.* 23 note 5; Sankasht Chaturthi or dark fourths, *id.* 398; Shivarátra, *id.* 23 note 5; observed by a barren woman, *id.* 367; by Bhátiás, *id.* 119; Bháts, *id.* 213; Bhaváyás, *id.* 225; Bhávsárs, *id.* 178; Bráhmans, *id.* 31; Chárans, *id.* 220; Ghanchis, *id.* 182; Golás, *id.* 185; Hajáms, *id.* 233; Káchhiás, *id.* 154; Kadiyás, *id.* 186; Kanbis, *id.* 157; Kansaras, *id.* 187; Mochis, *id.* 194; Rájputs, *id.* 137; Sagars, *id.* 174; Saláts, *id.* 196; Sonis, *id.* 201; Shrávaks, *id.* 114 and note 1; among Gujarát Musalmáns; Ramazan, IX, pt. ii, 127; among Kunbis of Kolhápur, XXIV, 92; of the Bene-Israels, XVIII, pt. i, 509 note 1, 513, 515.

Fasts and Feasts: among Deshastha Bráhmans, of Dhárwár district, XXII, 69-73.

Fatdas: *see* Paváyás.

Fateh Ali: nawáb of Cambay (1789-1823), VI, 231-232.

Fatehgad: village in Cutch, founded by Fateh Muhammad, V, 220, 153.

Fatehgad: fort in Ratnágiri district, X, 337.

Fateh Khán: Baluch, obtains in gift Rádhanpur and Sami, IX, pt. ii, 17.

Fateh Khán; Sidi ruler of Janjira, his struggle with Shiváji (1665-1670), XI, 436; deposed, I, pt. ii, 69.

Fateh Muhammad: minister in Cutch state (1786-1813), V, 149, 155.

Fatehpur: ruined fort at, in Khándesh, XII, 449.

Fateh Sháh: king of Kashmir (1458-1459), Cháks converted to Islám during the reign of, IX, pt. ii, 39.

Fatehsing: founder (1712) of the family of Akalkot rájás, XX, 289-290.

Fatehsing Bhonsle: appointed by Sháhu to the Karnátak, I, pt. ii, 656.

Fatesing Gáikwár (1778-1789): son of Dámáji, VII, 188; takes refuge at Sátára (1751), *id.* 179; raises the tribute of Rájpipla (1764), *id.* 185; seizes Baroda (1769), *id.* 188; becomes *mutálik* to his brother Sayájiráv I (1771-1778), *id.* 189; his treaty with the English (1773), *id.* 190; his conduct in the Marátha war (1779-1782), *id.* 195-198; his death (1782), *id.* 198; military class in his time, *id.* 293; revenue of Baroda in his time, *id.* 383-384, 387; *see* also I, pt. i, 400, 401, 408, 410.
Fatesing II, Gáikwár: (1800-1819), Anandráv's brother, captured by Holkar, ransomed (1803), VII, 210, 211; becomes regent (1806-1818), *id.* 214-229; the army and revenue in his time, *id.* 299, 328, 385.
Fatesing Mane: Yashvantráv Holkar's officer, defeats the Peshwa's officer Báláji Kunjar at Gar-Dhond (1802) I, pt. ii, 108.
Fatiha: opening chapter of the *Kurán*, reading of, IX, pt. ii, 129, 130, 147 and note 1, 150, 151, 157, 163.
Fatih Khán: traitor, at Ahmadnagar, places the state at the mercy of the Mughals (1629), I, pt. ii, 650.
Fatilah: magic wick, IX, pt. ii, 133; *see* Palita.
Fatimah: eldest daughter of the prophet, wife of Ali and mother of Hasan and Husain, IX, pt. ii, 6 note 1, 7, 16, 45, 47; vows to, fast offered by, *id.* 127; offerings made to, in the earthen dish rite, *id.* 151; dower of, *id.* 166 note 1.
Fatimi: dynasty in Egypt (910-1171), founded by Obeidullah, powers of the Ismailians originated with, IX, pt. ii, 47; *see* Obeidullah and Ismailis.
Fatinute Khilafat: raised in Egypt on the basis of opinions analogous to Karmatian by Obeidullah (919), IX, pt. ii, 3 note 3 continued on page 4, *id.* 37; quarrel for succession to (1094), *id.* 30 note 1, 37; *see* Obeidullab.
Faujdárs: Mughal governors of crown domains, I, pt. i, 211; military police, *id.* 214.
Fawalhant: star, IX, pt. ii, 217 note 1.
Fawcett, Mr.: magistrate of Ahmadábád, attempts to reform marriage customs of Leva Kunbis, IX, pt. i, 167.
Fazendars, Fazendeiros: Portuguese landlords, in Thána district, XIII, 459, 552; origin of, I, pt. ii, 53.
Fazl: founds a Jáma mosque at Sindán, I, pt. i, 506, 520.
Fazl-ul-lah: Mauláná, physician of Mahmud Khilji, I, pt. i, 362.
Fazl-ul-lah Khán: Haidar's general in the Karnatak, defeats Gopálráo Patvárdhan, I, pt. ii, 658, XXI, 382; XXII, 411-412.
Feasts: among Gujarát Musalmáns, private, occasions for giving, way of serving at, IX, pt. ii, 112; public, among Daudi Bohoras, *id.* 31 and note 3; among Gujarát Pársis, occasions of, food served at, ways of serving at, cost of, IX, pt. ii, 207 and note 2; fire, *id.* 2, 7.
Feet-washing: Pátáne Prabhu ceremony, XVIII, pt. i, 207-208, 210.
Feherest: priestly genealogies, IX, pt. ii, 225 and note 2.
Felidæ: tigers, etc., in Ratnágiri district, X, 44.
Felspathic Rocks: in Bijápur district, XXIII, 19.
Felt: making of, in Poona district, XVIII, pt. ii, 208-209.
Fergussion: Dr., archæologist, his works quoted (1839), I, pt. i, 383, 491, 499, 500, 504; I, pt. ii, 196, 353 note 2; XIV, 57 note 1, 82, 164.
Fergusson: Sir James, governor of Bombay, XIII, 349.
Ferishta: historian, "Introduction to the History of the Konkan," his works quoted, I, pt. ii, p. ix, 30, 38, 47, 530, 531; (1550-1611), account of, XXIII, 423 and note 1.
Ferns: at Mátheráo, XIV, 251; in Dhárwár district, XXII, 36.
Feroksher: Delhi emperor (1712-1719), XIX, 260-262.
Feronia elephantum: gum-yielding and sacred plant, XXV, 250, 291.
Ferozsháh: nawáb of Kamona and follower of Tátia Topi, I, pt. i, 445.
Ferozsáh Báhmani: I, pt. ii, 36; *see* Ferozsháh Báhmani.
Ferries: *see* All District Volumes under District Name.
Ferryman: Colonel, at Ahmadábád (1857), I, pt. i, 440.
Festivals: among Bhils, IX, pt. i, 305-307; Ráv's procession to snake temple in Bhuj fort, *id.* 136; at Tavra, *id.* 362; among fishers and sailors of South Gujarát, *id.* 524-525; among Gujarát Musalmáns, IX, pt. ii, 217-218; *see* Gahambhárs, Gáthás, Muktád holidays, leading high days among Pársis, IX, pt. ii, 216-217. *See* Jasans. Vaishnáv, in Kánara, XV, pt ii, 347-348.
Feudal classes: in Baroda state, VII, 56-57.
Feudatory states: during Musalmán period, I, pt. i, 209.
Fever: *táv*, its cause and cure, IX, pt. i, 365; in Ratnágiri district, X, 264, 292; in Sávantvádi, *id.* 460; in Khándesh, XXII, 336; in Thána district, XIII, 663-664; in Kánara district, details of; XV, pt. ii, 217-218; in Násik district, XVI, 337.
Fibre plants, Fibres: cultivation of, in Surat and Broach districts, II, 63, 390; in Kaira and Panch Maháls districts, III, 45, 232; in Cutch, V, 106; in Pálanpur, *id.* 294; in Mahi Kántha, *id.* 371; in Ahmadábád district, IV, 53; in Thána district, XIII, 290, 400; in Poona district, XVIII, pt. ii, 46-48; in Kolhápur state, XXIV, 171-172.
Ficoideæ: species of famine plants, XXV, 200.
Fidai: IX, pt. ii; *see* Fidawi.
Fidalgos: Portuguese noblemen, I, pt. ii, 52, 55, 64; their buildings at Bassein, *id.* 65.
Fidáuddin Khán: acts as viceroy (1743); schemes of Rangoji for his assassination; returns to Cambay; defeats Rangoji and becomes sole master of Gujarát (1743), I, pt. i, 326; confined by his troops for arrears of pay, escapes to Agra, *id.* 327; *see* also VII, 176.

Fidawis: order founded by Hasan Sabah, known in Europe as the assassins; meaning of the name, IX, pt. ii, p. 37 and note 2.
Field Names: under Valabhis, I, pt. i, 83.
Field Operations: in Khándesh, XII, 145-147.
Field Plagues: in Ahmadnagar district, XVII, 280-284; in Poona district, XVIII, pt. ii, 80-84.
Field Rites: among Poona Kunbis, XVIII, pt. i, 295-296; in Bijápur district, XXIII, 147-149.
Field Sports: among Gujarát Musalmáns, IX, pt. ii, 172.
Field Tools: in Rewa Kántha and Cambay, VI, 38; in Ratnágiri district, X, 151; in Kolába, XI, 93-94; in Thána district, XIII, 285, 286; in Khándesh, XII, 143; in Kánara district, XV, pt. ii, 12-13; in Násik district, XVI, 92; in Ahmadnagar district, XVII, 246-248; in Poona district, XVIII, pt. ii, 8-10; in Sátára, XIX, 150-151; in Sholápur, XX, 221-222; in Belgaum, XXI, 238-240; in Bijápur, XXIII, 310-312.
Fife: lake, irrigation work in Poona district, XVIII, pt. ii, 17-18.
Fife's Filter: at Mátherán, XIV, 246.
Fighting Classes: in Kolhápur state, XXIV, 65-86.
Filleted Gronnd Snakes: in Poona district, XVIII, pt. i, 73-74.
Fimbristylis Kysoor: famine plant found in Thána and other places, XXV, 208.
Financial Reform: of Mirza Isa Tarkhán, I, pt. i, 279.
Finch: English traveller, his description of Cambay (1611), VI, 219; his remark on Randir Náiatás, a class of seamen (1610), IX, pt. ii, 15 note 2; his notice of Mulher fort in Násik district, XVI, 459.
Firangi: Bijápur bastion, XXIII, 570-571.
Firangi or Frank: name of higher classes of Christians in Thána district, XIII, 199.
Firanjmushk: (sweet basil) oil-yielding aromatic plant, XXV, 224.
Firdusi: author, IX, pt. ii, 183 note 4.
Fire: *agni*, element; believed to be an element of the soul; is used in burning the dead; in sin-cleansing rites, in sacrifices; is Vishvádev or universal lord of Bráhmans, IX, pt. i, 356; worship, *id.* p. xxxv; chief occasions sacred to; Holi, details of worship; Diváli festival, details of worship, *id.* 357; chief days for, *id.* 356; is worshipped in the form of lighted lamps, *id.* 356, 357; *agnihotra* fire, its worship, *id.* 356; offerings, daily offerings made to, by Bráhmans, by trading classes and craftsmen, *id.* 356; made to complete religious ceremonies, *id.* 33, 37, 356; beliefs, 356-357; devotion to the worship of, among foreigners, *id.* 433, 447; fire-worship said to be introduced by White Húnas, *id.* 439; instances of foreigners purified by, and raised to be Bráhmanic Hindus, *id.* 438, 449; baptism, in firepit on Mount Abu, *id.* 433, 434; popular initiation, *id.* 449 note 4; foreign tribes who passed through, *id.* 433; Agnikula tribes raised to be Rájpúts by passing through, *id.* 480, 483; pit on Mount Abu, *id.* 480; object of, *id.* 486; date of, *id.* 486 and note 5, 490, 493, 501; chief object of veneration among Pársis, the sacred, three orders of, IX, pt. ii. 213-215.
Fire: in Bombay (1803), XIII, 516; *see* also XXVI, 431-435; in Panch Maháls district, III, 315; in Ahmadábád district, IV, 262.
Fire Arms: import of, from Venice, XIII, 446 note 2.
Fire Temples: at Chaul in Kolába district, XI, 272, XIII, 250; in Thána district at Sanján (721), XIII, 249; at Kalyán, Thána and Dheri village; XIV, 119, 354, 370; in Poona city, XVIII, pt. iii, 367.
Fire Worship: in Thána district (1300), XIII, 66; introduced in India, *id.* 247 note 3; in Upper India and Sind, *id.* 253 note 4.
Fire Worshippers: in Saimur, I, pt. i, 516.
Firozsháh Bahamani: captures Bankápur (1406), I, pt. ii, 638; (1397-1422), mentioned in an inscription at Miraj in Belgaum district, XXIV, 224 note 1; I, pt. ii, 530; *see* Jalál-ud-din; Sultán, I, pt. i, 514; *see* Malik Kabir.
Firuz Tughlak: emperor of Delhi (1351-1388), his expeditions against Sind and Gujarát, I, pt. i, 231; Sáhu and Saháran, Tánk chiefs in Gujarát converted to Islám by, IX, pt. ii, 70.
Fiscal Administration: of Gujarát, during Musalmán period, I, pt. i, 210.
Fiscus: *carica* (common fig), XXV, 172; *cardifolia*, a sacred tree, *id.* 172, 279, 284, 291; *glomerata (umbar)*, fruit and famine plant, a sacred tree, *id.* 172, 204, 279, 282, 290; *infectoria*, a food and fibrous plant, *id.* 172, 235; *religiosa*, famine, fibrous and sacred plant, *id.* 204, 235, 279, 283, 291.
Fiscus Bengalensis: (banyan) famine and fibrous tree, XXV, 204, 235; its juice used as medicine, *id.* 261; is a sacred tree, *id.* 278, 279, 283, 290, 291.
Fish: in Kaira and Panch Maháls districts, III, 20, 212; in Ahmadábád district, IV, 29; in Cutch, V, 37; in Pálanpur, *id.* 288; in Mahi Kántha, *id.* 362; in Rewa Kántha, VI, 18; in Baroda state, VII, 46-47; in Káthiáwár, VIII, 106-107; in Ratnágiri, kinds of, trade in fins and maws of, saw-fish, oysters, cuttle-fish, whales, fishermen, stakes, boats, nets markets, curing, X, 99-103, in Sávantvádi, *id.* 406; in Kolába district and Janjira state, XI, 37-39, 408-409; in Khándesh, XII, 37; in Kánara district, kinds of, XV, pt. i, 107-112; export of, XV, pt. ii, 58; in Násik district, XVI, 24-25; in Ahmadnagar district, XVII, 41-45; in Poona district, XVIII, pt. i, 87-93; in Sátára district, XIX, 39; in Sholápur district, XX, 18-22; in Belgaum district, XXI, 85-86; in Dhárwár district, XXII, 42-44; in Bijápur district, XXIII, 69-70; in Kolhápur, XXIV, 34; in Surat and Broach, II, 45, 360-362.
Fisheries: in Thána district, XIII, 54-59; in Surat and Broach, II, 45, 362-367; in Bombay island, (1676-1819), XXVI, pt. ii, 142-164.
Fishermen: in Gujarát, fresh-water, Bhois and Machhis, IX, pt. i, 504-505, 519; salt-water, *id.* 519; in Surat and Broach districts,

II, 53, 375 ; in Ahmadábád district, IV, 38 ; in Cutch, V, 81 ; in Mahi Kántha, *id.* 366 ; in Kaira and Panch Mahals districts, III, 34, 218 ; in Baroda state, VII, 47, 62 ; in Káthiáwár, VIII, 154 ; in Ratnágiri district, X, 101 ; in Kolába district and Janjira state, XI, 68-70, 414 ; in Khándesh, XII, 79 ; in Thána district, XIII, 54, *id.* 146-149 ; in Kánara district, XV, pt. i, 300-314 ; in Poona district, XVIII, pt. i, 387, 393 ; in Sátára district, XIX, 105-106 ; in Sholápur district, XX, 151-157.

Fishing : mode of ; nets, IX, pt. i, 504-505 ; in Kolába district and Janjira state, XI, 135, 474-482 ; in Kánara district, XV, pt. i, 111-112.

Fishing Boats : in Thána district, XIII, 58.

Fish Manure : in Bombay island, evil effects from, its use not allowed in spite of pressing applications from inhabitants (1707-1770), XXVI, pt. iii, 510-517.

Fitch : Ralph, traveller (1584), his notice of Cheul in Kolába district, XI, 278 note 5 ; mentions Bassein, XIV, 29 note 4 ; his description of Bijápur city (1583), XXIII, 420.

Fitrah : form of charity in Ramazan, IX, pt. ii, 141.

Fitzgerald : pass between Kolába and Sátára districts, XI, 5, 114 ; XIX, 201.

Fitzgerald Bridge : near Poona, XVIII, pt. ii, 155 ; *id.* pt. iii, 367.

Flacourtia : *cataphracta*, *Ramontchii*, fodder plants, XXV, 277.

Flamingo : class of birds in Ratnágiri district, X, 97.

Fleet : Angria's, description of, XI, 147, I, pt. ii, 89 ; in Bombay island, increase of (1733), XVI, pt. iii, 207-208 ; Gurjjara, formation of, IX, pt. i, 489 and note 1.

Flinty Beds : in Bijápur district, XXIII, 31.

Floating Island : Camoen's, perhaps Anjidiv, XV, pt. ii, 253 and note 4.

Floods : in Kaira district, III, 11 ; in Ahmadábád district, IV, 9-12 ; in Pálanpur state, V, 295 ; in Mahi Kántha, *id.* 372 ; worship of river during, IX, pt. i, 350 ; of water during, *id.* 137 ; dread of, *id.* 402, 403 ; in Khándesh, XII, 9-10 ; in Kánara district, XV, pt. i, 8 ; in Násik district, XVI, 133, 519, 646.

Floor-cloths : weaving of, in Dhárwár district ; XXII, 379-380.

Florikin : class of birds in Ratnágiri district, X, 90.

Flower-peckers : class of brids in Ratnágiri district, X, 69.

Flowers : in Khándesh, XII, 177 ; in Belgaum district, XXI, 65.

Fluellen : antiquarian, I, pt. i, 538.

Fluggea virosa : poisonous and fodder plant, XXV, 269-272.

Fly-catcher : class of birds in Ratnágiri district, X, 71.

Flying Arch Mosque : at Junnar in Poona district, XVIII, pt. iii, 162-163.

Foetus-laying : rite ; *see* Garbhádhána.

Fogs : in Poona district, XVIII, pt. i, 26.

Food : nature of, used by all classes of Gujarát Hindus, IX, pt. i, pp. xxiv-xxv ; by Bharváds, *id.* 268 ; Bhils, *id.* 299-300 ; Bráhmans, *id.* 21 ; depressed classes, *id.* 332 ; early tribes, *id.* 291 ; Kolis, *id.* 246 ; Rájputs, *id.* 134 ; Shrávaks, *id.* 98-99 ; Vániás, *id.* 75 ; of Gujarát Musalmáns, spirit-scaring virtue of ; virtue of driving off visions in, IX, pt. ii, 206 and note 1 ; varieties of ; details of the cost of, *id.* 206-207 and note 1 ; of Pársis, *id.* 108-115 ; of the rich, *id.* 108-109 ; of middle class, of the poor, *id.* 109 ; marketing of, costs of, *id.* 110 ; stimulants, *id.* 110-111 ; meals, *id.* 111-112 ; served at private feasts, *id.* 112 ; at public dinners, *id.* 112-114 ; at feast-day dinners, *id.* 114-115 ; Buddhist rules about, XIV, 142 ; of Matherán tribes, *id.* 261 ; of different castes ; *see* under caste concerned.

Foot Disease : of cattle in Ratnágiri district, X, 294 ; in Sávantvádi, *id.* 461.

Footmarks : rock-cut, at Goregaon, XIV, 102, 389, 390 ; at Virár, *id.* 382.

Forbes : Mr. A. K., author of *Rás Mála*, description of money-lenders starting in life, IX, pt. i, 78 note 3 ; of Bhats' yearly tours, *id.* 208-209 ; of Bhats as security, *id.* 209 and note 2 ; of *trága* and *dharna*, *id.* 210 ; his opinion about Káthis' original place of settlement, *id.* 252 note 1, 295 and notes 1 and 2 ; his work quoted, I, pt. i, 153, 159 note 5, 160, 188, 470.

Forbes : Major, defeats Sindia at Sinor (1781), I, pt. i, 409.

Forbes : Mr. J., author of *Oriental Memoirs*, his visit to Dásgaon (1771), in Kolába district, XI, 14 note 1 ; condition of Kolába district according to, *id.* 155 ; his visit to Kolába fort (1771), *id.* 264 ; visit to Sov hot-spring in Kolába district, *id.* 388 note 1 ; *see* also I, pt. ii, 100 ; his description of Bombay in 1766 and 1774, XIII, 500, 511 ; of Sálsette (1783), *id.* 509 ; his mention of *jogis*, XIV, 135 note 10 ; description of Thána (1774), *id.* 360-361 ; his description of Bombay buildings in 1784, XXVI, pt. ii, 480-487 ; his description of Kárwár (1772), XV, pt ii, 54, 140-141, 325 ; mention of Honávar (1775), *id.* 305, 312, 314 note 1 ; of Mirjan, *id.* 332, 333 ; on the famine of 1803 in Bombay island, XXVI, pt. iii, 524-525 ; (1781), IX, pt. ii, 3 note 2, 29 note 1, 68, 155 note 1 ; his description of Bháts, IX, pt. i, 208 note 3, 209 note 2, 211 ; his description of the Surat Pársis, IX, pt. ii, 197-198 ; on the Mulakgiri systems of the Maráthás in 1775, I, pt. i, 419.

Forbes Royle : Dr., cotton expert, introduced ginning factories in Dhárwár district (1849-1868), XXII, 294-295, 369, 372.

Forced Labour : in Káthiáwár, VIII, 213-214 ; in Kolába district, under Angrias (1814-1840), XI, 216-217.

Ford : Captain John, commandant of the Poona contingent at the battle of Kirkee (1817), XVIII, pt. ii, 291, 295, 297, 300.

Forecastes : of crops, IX, pt. i, 354 ; of harvest, *id.* 390 ; of rain and weather, *id.* 351-354, 354-355.

Foreign Boys : victory of the, at Bijápur (1531), XX, 281.

Foreigners : settlement of, in Gujarát, I, pt. i, 13 ; horde, constitution and gathering, IX, pt. i, 455, 459 ; journey or moving and travel changes, *id.* 455-456, 459-461 ; melting and spread, *id.* 456-457 ; after melting changes, *id.* 457, 463 ; tribe names attached to countries or places, *id.* 455, 459 note 9, 462 note 3 ; stock or clan names of, *id.* 456-457 ; interlacing of tribes and caste divisions, *id.* 457 ; change of tribe names, *id.* 457-458 ; conqueror's tribe names, *id.* 462 ; confusion of castes, *id.* 463-465 ; leading hordes of, names of the seven hordes that entered India between the time of Alexander (B. C. 325) and the time of the Arab Musalmáns (A. D. 713) ; route by which they entered India, *id.* 455 ; their complexity, *id.* 456, 460-461 ; names of foreigners who conquered in Western India (B. C. 250-A. D. 400), *id.* 433 ; names of foreigners who were converted to or aided Buddhism, *id.* 433, 445, 448 ; foreigners who helped Bráhmans and became their champions, *id.* 433, 439, 447, 449 ; admission of, among Bráhmans, before Buddhist period, *id.* 433, 434-435 ; during and after Buddhist period, of individuals, *id.* 435-436 ; of entire classes, *id.* 436-441 ; among Kshatriyas, *id.* 433 ; of individuals, *id.* 441-443 ; of entire classes, *id.* 443-452 ; among traders, *id.* 452-453 ; among lower classes, *id.* 453-455 ; in Gujárat, *id.* p. xii ; arrival in Gujarát of Arab sailors and soldiers (seventh, eighth and ninth century), IX, pt. ii, 1 notes 1, 2 ; traders from Persion Gulf (ninth and tenth century), *id.* 2 and note 1 ; invaders from the north (eleventh and twelfth century), *id* 2 and notes 2 and 3 ; the religious head of Shiah trading Bohoras with a band of followers (close of the eleventh century), *id.* 3 ; soldiers, traders, refugees and slaves (thirteenth to seventeenth centuries), *id.* 3 and note 1 ; the Zanjira Sidis (middle of seventeenth century), *id.* 3 ; Arab mercenaries and Persian political refugees (eighteenth century), *id.* 3 and note 2.

Forest : *see* All District Volumes under District Names.

Forest Tribes : in Kolhápur state, XXIV, 24.

Formula : Buddhist, XIV, 168 and note 3, 174, 394 ; inscribed at Padan hill in Thána district, *id.* 103.

Foro : Portuguese quit-rent in Thána district, XIII, 552.

Fort : (Bombay) improvement within (1803), XXVI, pt. ii, 495-505 ; *see* also Forts.

Fortalezza : Portuguese word for fortresses, I, pt. ii, 54.

Fort George : (fort on Dongri hill) commenced (1770), XXVI, pt. ii, 380 ; *vide* Dongri.

Fortieth Day : after child-birth, thanks-offering to Khwajah Khizr on, IX, pt. ii, 158.

Fortification charges : (Bombay) reduction of (1772), XXVI, pt. iii, 163-167.

Fortifications : Bombay (1753-1780), XXVI, pt. ii, 305-423 ; additions to Bandar Pier and dock (1754, 56 and 60), *id.* 306, 315, 333 ; survey of fortifications and necessary additions (1755), *id.* 306-315 ; survey by Major Mace (1758), the town undefended, a new line from Dongri to Back Bay proposed, *id.* 323-327 ; cess levied (1758), *id.* 323-324 ; progress of the work, Dongri Hill to be fortified, Portuguese church pulled down (1759-60), *id.* 329-332 ; requirements of Bombay defences (1761), *id.* 334-339 ; Captain Werner's report (1762), *id.* 340-341 ; Major Munro's report (1762), *id.* 341-342 ; defence works continued (1762-1763), *id.* 343-350 ; Captain Keating's survey (1764), *id.* 350-354 ; progress of the works, plans for the fortifications of Dongri Hill (1765-1767), *id.* 354-365 ; Lt.-Col. Campbell's survey recommends fortification of Dongri Hill (1768), *id.* 366-376 ; old Dongri fort blown up, progress of the works (1769), *id.* 377-380 ; progress report (1770), *id.* 381-382 ; rules for work, pay-masters' regulations, wages of artizans (1771-1772), *id.* 386-391 ; progress of the works (1772-74), *id.* 391-399 ; fortification cess continued (1775), *id.* 400 ; progress of the works (1776-1777), *id.* 401-406 ; progress of the works (1778-80), *id.* 408-409, 414-423.

Forts : in Ratnágiri district, X, 334, 335 note 5 ; Portuguese, in Thána district, XIII, 456, 457, 490-491, 499, 515, 523 ; XIV, 50, 54, 55, 94, 98, 115, 199-200, 227, 236, 304, 344, 349, 359, 371, 380, 382, 383 ; in Kánara district, XV, pt. ii, 80, 250, 253, 254, 257, 306, 331, 339, 345 ; in Dhárwár district, XXII, 649, 653, 662, 667-668, 713, 723, 730-731, 766, 771 and note 2, 773, 776-777, 780 ; at Bombay (1672-1677), XXVI, pt. ii, 269-271 ; Mahim, Sion and Worlee (1700-1702), *id.* 273-276.

Fortune Tellers : Audichyas, IX, pt. i, 7 ; Vadádrás, *id.* 20, 29.

Fort Victoria : in Ratnágiri district, X, 335.

Fossils : in Belgaum district, XXI, 35 note 2, 36 note 1 ; in Bijápur district, XXIII, 45.

Foulis : Sir James, Bart., appointed commander of Bombay forces (1753), XXVI, pt. iii, 118.

Foulke Grevil : his notice of Cheul (1599), XI, 279 note 5.

Foulkes : Rev. T., published Udayendiram grant, I, pt. ii, 320 notes 2 and 6, 325, 333.

Fowls : in Khándesh, XII, 29 ; in Kánara district, XV, pt. i, 80, 81 ; in Ahmadnagar district, XVII, 39 ; in Poona district, XVIII, pt. i, 68-69 ; in Sholápur district, XX, 18 ; in Belgaum district, XXI, 68.

Fra Mauro : (1450), Italian writer, astronomers on Indian ships according to, XIII, 725.

Framji : son of Rustam Mánek, IX, pt. ii, 196 note 3.

Frámji Kávasji Banaji ; makes first attempt to open steam factory, IX, pt. ii, 199 note 3.

Franciscans : Christian friars, I, pt. ii, 55 ; take possession of the Káuheri and Mandapeshvar caves, destroy the sculptures and build a Church and the Royal College of Sálsette at Mandapeshvar, *id.* 56 ; take charge of Mandapeshvar, Máhim, Bombay, Karanja, Mount Calvary and Agáshi (1585), *id.* 57 ; at Agáshi, Bassein, Tárápur and Thána, in Thána

district, XIV, 1, 41, 42, 344, 351, 358; XIII, 462; the work of conversion confined to (1542), XIII, 461.
François Pyrard: French traveller, his visit to Cheul in Kolába (1601-1608), XVII, 391.
Fra Paolino: Austrian traveller (1775), his mention of Anjidev, XV, pt. ii, 257.
Fravoshis: IX, pt. ii, 216; *see* Frohars.
Frazer: traveller (A. D. 1821), IX, pt. i, 437 note 3.
Frederick: Major, at the battle of Vadgaon near Poona (1779), XVIII, pt. ii, 265; at the siege of Dhárwár (1789), I, pt. ii, 661; Colonel, commander in the third Maisur War (1790-1792), XXI, 387; his death at Dhárwár (1792), XX, 418.
Frederick: Cæsar, traveller (1563-1585), *see* Cæsar Frederick.
Free traders: pirates, I, pt. ii, 61 (1638-1639), *id.* 120; *see* Interlopers.
French: the, their connection with the Konkan, I, pt. ii, 122; obtain a grant of the site of Pondicherry from the Bijápur viceroy (1678), *id.* 641; cession of Cheul to, discussed, *id.* 102, 103, XI, 286-287; in Surat (1620-1800), II, 88, 108, 116, 122, 153; as traders on Thána coast (1500-1670), XIII, 468; their intrigue in Poona (1778), *id.* 502; XVIII, pt. ii, 261, XXVI, pt. i, 421-426; their alliance with the Portuguese (1741), *id.* 276.
French: Captain, resident at Baroda (1849), condemns *báhedári*, VII, 263 note 1; Gáikwár's friendship for, *id.* 270.
French tombs: in Poona cantonment, XVIII, pt. iii, 367.
Frere: Sir Bartle, resident at Sátára (1848), XIX, 312-313; almshouse at Sátára named after, *id.* 567-568; governor of Bombay, IX, pt. i, 118 note 1, XIV, 369.
Friars: martyrdom of, I, pt. ii, 5.
Friday: Shukarwár, sacred to Venus, beliefs about, IX, pt. i, 402, 403, XVIII, pt. i, 240-241; day of rest for all Musalmáns, IX, pt. ii, 117; service on, *id.* 126.
Frigillinæ: birds in Ratnágiri, X, 84.
Fringillidæ: family of birds in Ratnágiri district, X, 83.
Frog: sacred to rain-god, worship of, IX, pt. i, 380; at Mátherán, XIV, 265; living, found in Sopára *stupa*, *id.* 336.
Frohars: believed to be souls of the dead; guardian spirits; Farvárdin Jasan performed in honour of, IX, pt. ii, 216.
Fruits: good, procurable in Bombay (1676), XXVI, pt. ii, 71; a market for (1770), *id.* 72; new market for (1803) *id.* 73-74.
Fruit-trees: in Kolhápur state, XXIV, 184-187; in Surat district, profits of, II, 41; cesses on, in Ratnágiri district, X, 38; cultivation of, in Kánara district, XV, pt. ii, 21-22.
Fruit vegetables: in Poona district, XVIII, pt. ii, 57-60; in Kolhápur state, XXIV, 181-182.
Fryer: English traveller (1673-1675), I, pt. ii, 57, 64, 72; (A.D. 1670), IX, pt. i, 78 note 1; (1674), his account of the Pársis, IX, pt. ii, 191-192 and note 1; his visit to Raygad (1674) in Kolába district, XI, 368 note 2; his journey to Junnar (1675), XIII, 316-317; his description of Bombay (1674), *id.* 474; on the condition of Thána district (1675), *id.* 476-477; his mention of Bándra, XIV, 26; Bassein, *id.* 41; Chembur, *id.* 52 note 3; Elephanta, *id.* 84, 92 note 1, 93; Ghodbandar, *id.* 99; Kalyán, *id.* 120; Kánheri caves, *id.* 151; Mágáthan, *id.* 216 note 1; Murbad, *id.* 285; Náná Ghát, *id.* 286-291; Titvala, *id.* 362; his notice of Kánára pepper trade, XV, pt. ii, 52; description of Kánara coast, *id.* 126-130; notice of Anjidiv, *id.* 256; of Ankola, *id.* 258; of Bhatkal, *id.* 274; of Honávar, *id.* 311; of Kadra, *id.* 317; of Kárwár, *id.* 322; of Mirjan, *id.* 333; of Shiveshvar, *id.* 342; of Sonda, *id.* 348; *see* also XVIII, pt. ii, 150, 236-237; *id.* pt. iii, 227-230.
Fulbái: temple of, resorted to by barren women, IX, pt. i, 368.
Fulgans: fodder plant, XXV, 276.
Fuligulinæ: family of birds in Ratnágiri, X, 98.
Full James: Major-General, his description of Bhil huts, IX, pt. i, 296 note 2; of carts, *id.* 297 note 1; of dress, *id.* 297 note 3; of tillage, *id.* 300 note 2.
Funck: Captain de, appointed Chief Engineer of Bombay island (1753), XXVI, pt. ii, 304; resigns (1758), *id.* 322-323.
Funds: charitable public; sources of; management of; chief uses of, IX, pt. ii, 245; *see* Community.
Funeral: corpseless, among Pátáne Prabhus when dead body not found, XVIII, pt. i, 234-235.
Funeral rites: *see* Death Ceremonies, XVIII, pt. i, 561-564.
Funnel Hill: in Thána district, XIV, 98; *see* Karnála.
Furniture: in town houses, IX, pt. i, 18; in village houses, *id.* XIX; of Bhils, *id.* 297; among Gujarát Musalmáns, IX, pt. ii, 205; among Pársis, kept by the rich, IX, pt. ii, 92-93; by the middle classes, *id.* 94; by the poor, *id.* 95; details of, *id.* 95 note 2. *See* Dwellings.
Fursa: snake, in Ratnágiri district, X, 51-52.

G

GABAT: state in Mahi Kántha, V, 427.
Gabit: a caste of fishermen, in Ratnágiri district, X, 127, 155, 171; in Sávantvádi state, *id.* 406, 415; in Kolába district, XI, 68; in Kánara district, XV, pt. i, 305; in Belgaum district, XXI, 156.
Gabres: people of Fárs, found on the Gujarát coast (1300), IX, pt. ii, 187 note 3, 188 note 3; of Rohilkhand, believed by Professor Dowson to be relics of the old Upper India Pársis; parts of Hind and Sind belonged to (950), *id.* 188 note 4.
Gabri: dialect of the Kábul country, IX, pt. ii, 188 note 4.
Gachchha: sub-sect of Svetambari division of Shrávaks, their beliefs, their spiritnal head, IX, pt. i, 105-106, 109 and note 1; names of, *id.* 109 note 2. *See* also XIV, 319.
Gad: state in Rewá Kántha, VI, 143.

Gáda : gorge in Sátára district, XIX, 202.
Gadada Singayya : officer of Virá-Ballala II (1184), I, pt. ii, 505.
Gadag : sub-division in Dhárwár district, sub-divisional details, XXII, 630-632 ; *see* also I, pt. ii, 416, 422 note 3, 426 note 3, 431, 436 note 2, 529. *Town*, fort, temples, hero-stones, inscriptions and history of, XXII, 390, 712-720 ; trade centre, *id.* 354, I, pt. ii, 304 ; inscriptions at, *id.* 339, 432, 434 and note 3, 438 note 1, 440 note 3, 444 note 3, 447 note 2, 464 note 4, 466, 496, 502, 504, 505, 506 and note 3, 517, 518 and note 4, 520, 524 ; record at, *id.* 503, 526, 558.
Gadália : a caste of blacksmiths in Cutch, V, 103.
Gadankeri : village in Bijápur district, tombs at, XXIII, 647.
Gádáráraghatta : in Gujarát, fight of Naikidevi at, I, pt. i, 195.
Gádavli : feeder of the Kására in Kolhápur state, XXIV, 9.
Gaddaka : inscriptions at, I, pt. ii, 218, 240.
Gaddi : race in the Kángra hills, apparently S'akas, are Kshatriyas including Bráhmans and Rájpúts ; families of, set apart for religious duties, IX, pt. i, 438 note 7.
Gadhákola : place of interest in Káthiáwár, VIII, 437.
Gadháli : taluka in Káthiáwár, VIII, 436.
Gadhda : holy place of Sváminárâyan sect, IX, pt i, 549.
Gadhesing : legend of, VI, 213.
Gadhia : coinage, I, pt. i, 469.
Gadhia : táluka in Káthiawár, VIII, 437.
Gadh-Juno : ancient fortress of Junágadh, called so in poetry, IX, pt. i, 240 note 4.
Gadhka : táluka in Káthiáwár, VIII, 437.
Gadhra : town in Káthiáwár, VIII, 437.
Gadhula : táluka in Káthiáwár, VIII, 438.
Gadhvi : Chárans known as, IX, pt. i, 214.
Gadinglaj : town in Kolhápur state, position, people, fort, temples and fair at, XXIV, 296-297 ; survey details, *id.* 263.
Gádit : a caste of cartmen in Gujarát, IX, pt. ii, 35.
Gadkaris : military subordinates holding lands round forts, I, pt. ii, 73.
Gadnadi : river in Ratnágiri district, X, 389.
Gadri : caste of wool weavers in Khándesh, XII, 76.
Gág : pass, in Násik district, XVI, 130.
Gagan Mahal : Bijápur palace, XXIII, 620.
Gágode : pass in Kolába district, XI, 115.
Gahambárs : religious national festivals among Pársis, IX, pt. ii, 207 ; season feasts, names of, observances during the, *id.* 217-218, 245.
Gahena Bái : wife of Govindráv Gáikwár (1793-1800), VII, 202, 211, 217, 224.
Galu : food plant grown in several districts, XXV, 208.
Gai Kasáb : a caste of beef butchers, in the district of Sátára, XIX, 138-139 ; in Khándesh, XII, 126, 235 ; in Sholápur, XX, 202 ; in Kolhápur state, XXIV, 150 ; in Poona district, XVIII, pt. i, 500 ; in Belgaum district, XXI, 210 ; in Dhárwár district, XXII, 239 ; in Bijápur district, XXIII, 294.
Gáikwár, Gáikwár family : history of (1720-1877), VII, 168-340 ; rise of, VII, 168, XVIII, pt. ii, 244 ; rose to power in Násik district, XVI, 48 note 1 ; dominions of, I, pt. ii, 382 ; dispute with the Peshwa regarding tribute due to him, sends Gangádhar Shástri to negotiate with the Peshwa (1815), *id.* 610 ; dispute with the Peshwa for independence, I, pt. i, 227. *See* Dámáji Gáikwár, Fatesingh Gáikwár, Govindráv Gáikwár, Piláji Gáikwár, and Sayáji Gáikwár.
Gair Dasti : a special tenure in Ratnágiri district, X, 261.
Gaján Mátá : luck or Śri of Parihára, IX, pt. i, 484.
Gajarábái : mother of Kanoji Gáikwár, son of Govindráv, takes refuge at Surat ; applies for assistance to the English as well as to Malhár, son of Khanderáo Gáikwár (1800), I, pt. i, 412.
Gajendragad : ridge and town in Bijápur district, remains of, XXIII, 6, 647-648 ; taken by Hyder, I, pt. ii, 659 ; taken by Haripant from Tipu (1787), *id.* 661.
Gajera : village in Broach district, II, 561.
Gajjar : measurer, overseer in house building, his duties, IX, pt. i, 203.
Gajni : old Cambay, VI, 213 footnote 2.
Gajnis : salt-swamps in Kánara district, XV, pt. ii, 27.
Galagnáth : village in Dhárwár district, temples and inscriptions at, XXII, 720 ; record at, I, pt. ii, 435 ; inscription of 1080 at, Palava's defeat by Vikramáditya at, *id.* 442 note 1.
Galalpati : cess in Ahmadábád district, IV, 93.
Galbat : general term for vessel, XIII, 343, 717.
Galgali : old village in Bijápur district, Aurangzeb's camp at (1695), XXIII, 378, 648-649.
Galiárá : caste of indigo-dyers in Gujarát ; division of Bhávsárs, IX, pt. i, 181.
Galka Choth : holy day, sacred to the moon, worship of the moon on, IX, pt. i, 398.
Galla Dásár : a caste of husbandmen in Dhárwár district, XXII, 132.
Gallinæ : family of birds in Ratnágiri, X, 87.
Gallitalutæ : perhaps Táilakhali Sálva tribe, I, pt. i, 534.
Gallivats : Ángria's vessels, XI, 147.
Galna : fort in Násik district, description, view and history of, XVI, 436-39, 441, 444.
Gama ; Vasco Da, Portuguese viceroy (1524), I, pt. ii, 45.
Gamaliba : ancient town between Ahmadnagar, and Junnar mentioned by Ptolemy, I, pt. i, 541.
Gaman Singh : son of Chaoji Rána of Dhárwái, in Khándesh district I, pt. ii, 633.
Gambhirgad : hill in Thána district, XIII, 6 ; fort, XIV, 98.
Gambhirnáth : rock temple of, near Khandála in Poona district, XVIII, pt. iii, 240-241.
Gambhuta : ancient name of Cambay, I, pt. i, 123.
Gambier : Mr., chief of the English factory at Surat, I, pt. i, 401 ; Rághoba opens negotiations with, XVIII, pt. ii, 258.

Gambling : *váida*, in Ahmadábád district, IV, 66.
Gambling Transactions : in Káthiáwár, VIII, 209-212
Game : beasts and birds (1676-1690), in Kánara district, XV, pt. ii, 129, 132; birds in Ahmadnagar, XVII, 32-33; and Poona, XVIII, pt. i, 70-71.
Gamelli Careri : his visit to Cambay (1695), VI, 220.
Games : indoor, in Gujarát, IX, pt. ii, 173-174.
Gámeti : caste of Hindu converts, holders of *gám* or village, intermarry with Kasbatis, IX, pt. ii, 62; proprietors of villages in Ahmadábád district, IV, 179.
Gámetia : class of Rájpúts, connecting link between lower and higher class Rájpúts, IX, pt. i, 123.
Gaming : prohibited in Bombay (1727), XXVI, pt. i, 261-262.
Gamit, Gamta : early tribe in Gujarát, IX, pt. i, 290, 318-319.
Gámundabbe : queen consort of Govinda III, I, pt. ii, 394.
Gam Vakkal : caste of husbandmen in Kánara district, XV, pt. i, 220.
Gán : caste of players in Ratnágiri district, X, 415.
Ganapati : nephew of Rudradeva of the Kákatiya family, released from prison, and placed on the throne by Jaitrapála, I, pt. ii, 239, 246, 522.
Ganapati : son of Bháskaráchárya's brother Śripati, I, pt. ii, 244.
Ganapatidevarása : Yádava king Maháde v's feudatory (1265), I, pt. ii, 528.
Ganapatinága : Nága chief, conquered by Samudragupta, I, pt. ii, 281 note 3.
Ganas : Śiva's attendants, I, pt. ii, 482.
Gandabhava : *see* Brahaspati.
Gandagiri : ruled by Vishnuvardhána, I, pt. ii, 496.
Gandalrit (Gandháraraahtra) : Burmese word for Yunnan, I, pt. i, 501.
Gandaráditya : Kolhápur or Karád Siláhára chief, feudatory of Someśvara III and Vikramáditya VI, brings the Southern Konkan under Kolhápur rule; feeds a hundred thousand bráhmans; builds jain temples and constructs a tank, I, pt. ii, 254, 255, 256, 452, 456, 545, 547-548; builds temples to Buddha, XIV, 127 note 1.
Gandaraioi : Gandhára, I, pt. i, 545.
Gandasamudra : tank at Irukudi built by Gandaraditya the Kolhápur Silahára chief, I, pt. ii, 255.
Gandevi : sub-division in Baroda territory, VII, 569-570; schools and hospitals in, *id.* 487, 506; town, *id.* 570.
Gandhar, Gandhára : old town in Broach district, its history, II, 561-562; identified with ancient Gadhendrapuri, VI, 213 note 4; I, pt. i, 75; establishment of the power of Kidáras in, *id.* 144, 467, 491; retreat of White Hunas from, to Kashmir, *id.* 500, 545; identified with Kandahar, IX, pt. i, 455.
Gandhári : stream in Kolába district, XI, 10.
Gandharp, Gandhraph : caste of musicians in Gujarát, IX, pt. i, 222; singers, converts from the Hindu caste of the same name, Sunnis in religion, IX, pt. ii, 81-82.
Gándharva : form of widow-marriage among Khándesh Sonárs, XII, 71.
Gandharva : cherub, images of, in Ajanta caves, XII, 493 and *note* 3; XIV, 70, 73 note 1.
Gandharvagad : hill and fort between Kolhápur state and Belgaum district, XXIV, 8; XXI, 554.
Gándhavi : village in Káthiáwár, the temple of Harsad Máta at, VIII, 438-439.
Gandhi : class of perfumers in Khándesh, XII, 62.
Gandhikas : Buddhist druggists, I, pt. ii, 173.
Gándhli : village in Khándesh, XII, 449.
Gandhol : táluka in Káthiáwár, VIII, 438.
Ganeśa : Hindu god, image of, I, pt. i, 163; represented in Elephanta and Sopárá caves, XIV, 70 and note 1, 75, 78, 224, 337, 385; golden image of, found in Sinhgad fort (1818), XVIII, pt. iii, 446 and note 3; name of a Poona ward, details of, *id.* 274, 278. *See* Ganpati.
Ganesh : footpath and pass in Sátára district, XIX, 202, 205.
Ganesh-Chaturthi : Ganpati's fourth, also called *Dagada Choth*, sacred to the moon, worship of Ganpati on, leading holiday, IX, pt. i, 23 note 5, 398. *See* also, XVIII, pt. i, 246 248.
Ganeshgudde : pass in Kánara district, XV, pt. ii, 281, 329, 342.
Ganeshkhind caves : near Poona city, XVIII, pt. iii, 368.
Ganesh Lena caves : at Junnar, XVIII, pt. iii, 204-216.
Ganesh Pula : stream in Ratnágiri district, X, 335.
Ganeshpuri : village in Thána district, hot-springs and a temple at, XIV 374.
Ganesh S. Ojhe : diwán to Khanderáv Gáikwár (1857), VII, 276.
Ganga : *see* Godavari.
Ganga : the river Ganges, I, pt. i, 165 and note 5, 518; I, pt. ii, 196, 338, 371; emblem of, *id.* 396, 416.
Ganga, Gangas : ruling family of the Chera country, I, pt. ii, 183, 189; prince, made captive by Dhruva and retained in custody, *id.* 197, 393; released by Govinda III, but immediately after assumed an attitude of hostility and was again thrown into prison by Govinda III, *id.* 198, 395; forced to obey Krishna II, *id.* 201; subdued by Krishna, *id.* 206; Western, grants, *id.* 291 note 1; from Mysore, *id.* 301 note 1; territory in Mysore, *id.* 346; family, *id.* 443, 452; probably Gangavádi, *id.* 281; *mandala*, *id.* 399, 441;—*another account of* : I, pt. ii, 282; the Western, of Kalinganagara, *id.* 297-309; Eastern, of Kalinganagara, *id.* 299 note 3; their crest, banner, titles, *id.* 299, 300; Western, their history, *id.* 300, 301, 302; conquered by Kirtivarman I (567-598) and by Pulikesin II (608), overthrow of, by the Early Kadamba king Mrigeśvarman, *id.* 300, 301 note 1; Western, musical instruments of, *id.* 327 note 7; of Kalinganagara, 340 notes 2, 3 and 4; Western and Eastern, of Kalinganagara, Puránic genealogies of, *id.* 342 note 1,

350; defeated by Vinayáditya, son of Vikramáditya I, *id.* 341, 368; conquered by Kirtivarman, *id.* 345; dynasty, *id.* 396; tribe, *id.* 411; tribe subdued by Krishna III, *id.* 420; dominions of the, acquired by Vishnuvardhána, *id.* 495; the city of the, burnt by Vishnuvardhána, *id.* 498; *see* also XV, pt. ii, 79 and note 2, 87; XXII, 390 and note 5; XXIII, 380 and note 4.

Gangábái: Nárayanráv Peshwa's widow (1773), XVIII, pt. iii, 36, 408; (1774) her regency, XVIII, pt. ii, 257-258.

Gangadeva: brother of Bhoja I, the Kolhápur or Kárad Siláhára king, I, pt. ii, 254, 545.

Gangádevi: wife of Basava, her marriage, I, pt. ii, 478.

Gangadhara: son of Dádá, commander of Mallugi's troop of elephants, I, pt. ii, 237, 239.

Gangadhar Shástri: appointed agent to the Baroda darbár (1803), VII, 209-210; his rise, *id.* 209 note 1; sent as an agent to Poona, murder of, at Pandharpur (1815), *id.* 218-223; *see* also I, pt. i, 427; I, pt. ii, 610; XIII, 522; XVIII, pt. ii, 294-295; XX, 292-293, 484.

Gangaikonda Cholapuram: capture of, by Vikrámaditya VI, I, pt. ii, 442. *See* Gangákunda.

Ganga Kandarpa: *biruda* or title of the Ganga chief Marasimha, I, pt. ii, 305.

Gangakandarpa Jinendra Mandir: Jain shrine, named after himself by Marasimha Permanandi (968-69), I, pt. ii, 306.

Gangakunda: Chola city, taken by Vikramáditya I, I, pt. ii, 215; conquered by Vikramáditya VI, *id.* 442, 445.

Gangámah: younger brother of Mularája, I, pt. i, 160.

Gangámbá: I, pt. ii, 478. *See* Gangádevi.

Ganga Náráyana: *biruda* or title of Satyavakya Kongunivarma Permanandi Butuga, I, pt. ii, 304.

Gangapádi: I, pt. ii, 298, 341 note 2. *See* Gangavádi.

Ganga Permádi: lord of the Gangamandala and governor of Belvola province, I, pt. ii, 441 and note 4.

Gangápur: old name of Tulapur, in Poona district, XVIII, pt. ii, 224.

Gangápuri: I, pt. ii, 442. *See* Gangákunda.

Gangarája: Vishnuvardhána's minister and promoter of Jain faith, I, pt. ii, 491, 499 and note 5; of the Ganga stock, *id.* 495, 499; attacks Adiyama or Idiyama, defeats the Chola king and places Gangavádi in the hands of the Hoysála prince Vishnuvardhána (1117), *id.* 308-309, 499; attacks Vikramáditya VI's forces at Kannegál and is presented with the territory by Vishnuvardhána for his services, *id.* 499-500.

Gangérasa: I, pt. ii. 308. *See* Gangarája.

Gangaridæ: tribe in Kalinga country, mentioned by Pliny, I, pt. i. 532, 533.

Gangathadi: the Godávari valley, ceded (1752) to the Maráthás, XVII, 404; plundered by Bhils, I, pt. ii, 609.

Gangavádi: province, modern Mysore, I, pt. ii, 297; country, *id.* 298 and note 2, 304, 306, 307; invaded by the Cholas (about 1021), becomes a part of their kingdom, *id.* 308, 341 note 2, 419; territorial division, *id.* 422, 440, 447, 452, 456, 495, 496; province subjugated by Vishnuvardhána, *id.* 496, 497, 498; boundaries of, ruled over by Vishnuvardhána, *id.* 498; Jain temples of, restored by Gangarája, *id.* 499; ruled over by Vira-Ballála II, *id.* 505, 564.

Gangavajra: *biruda* or title of the Ganga chief Márasimha, I, pt. ii, 305.

Gangávali: river in Kánara and Dhárwár districts, XV, pt i, 5, 6; XXII, 8; rock in Kánara, XV, pt. i, 3.

Gangavali: port in Kánara district, temple and fair at, XV, pt. ii, 281-282; its trade, *id.* 66, 67, 68; visited by Fryer (1676), *id.* 129.

Ganges: river, eastern boundary of Kumárapála's kingdom, I, pt. i, 189, 510; water of the, for Somnáth, *id.* 522, 533, 537, 545; river, I, pt. ii, 202; junction of the, *id.* 380, 530; river, is held sacred, IX, part I, 350, 550.

Gangeya: race, I, pt. ii, 297.

Gangimakkalu = children of Gangi: a caste of fishermen in Bijápur district, XXIII, 113-117.

Gang robbery: in Khandesh, XII, 314; in Thána district, XIII, 523, 524, 526, 635; in Kánara district, XV, pt. ii, 200; in Kolhápur state, XXIV, 274.

Gangthari: *see* Gangathadi.

Gangva: a place of pilgrimage in Broach district, II, 562.

Gánig, Ganigar, *pl.* Ganigaru: a caste of Lingayát oilmen in Bijápur district, XXIII, 239-241; in Kánara district, XV, pt. i, 277, 278; in Dhárwár district, XXII, 167.

Ganimardi: hill and village in Belgaum district, XXI, 9, 555.

Ganira: poisonous flower-plant, found in Sind and other places, XXV, 266.

Ganj: Poona ward, details of, XVIII, pt. iii, 274, 279.

Gánja: fibrous plant, yields fermented drink, XXV, 211, 233; hemp, preparation of, IX, pt. i, 32-33; its cultivation in Khándesh, XII, 167; trade in Thána district, XIII, 336; cultivation in Thána district, XIV, 294.

Ganjam: district in Madras, I, pt. ii, 142.

Ganjávadra: táluka in Káthiáwár, VIII, 438.

Ganjibhoyra: village in Ahmadnagar district, temple at, XVII, 716.

Ganod: town in Káthiáwár, VIII, 438.

Ganpati: god of wisdom, is shown with an elephant's head, offerings made to, worship of, IX, pt. i, 35, 64, 136, 213, 332, 336, 341, 362, 376, 378, 383, 409. *See* Ganesh.

Ganpati procession: in Baroda, British troops not to attend (1875), VII, 249.

Ganpati riots: in Kolába district, XI, 450-451.

Ganpati's temple: in Poona city, XVIII, pt. iii, 335-336.

Ganpatráv Gaikwár: H. H. (1847-1856), son of Sayájiráo, his *khatpat* report, his reform due to Captain French, review of his reign VII, 268-273; of Sankheda, his rebellion against the Gáikwár (1801), VII, 206; his death, *id.* 230.

Gansur: medicinal plant, XXV, 255.

Ganthâchor: *see* Uchliá.

Gáokasáb : *see* Gai Kasáb.

Gaonkars : village headmen in Ratnágiri, their position in 1818, X, 222; in Sávantvádi, *id.* 448.

Gaoris; Ptolemy's name for Vaitarna river, in Thána district, XIV, 103, 291.

Garag : village in Dhárwár district, XXII, 720.

Garamli : táluka in Káthiáwár, VIII, 439.

Garasia : class of superior landlords in Gáikwár's dominions, their history and tenure, VII, 341-346, their depredations in Surat and Broach districts, II, 214, 436; their position, I, pt. i, 215 and note 2; Rájpúts, IX, pt. i, 123; of Abu, *id.* 439 note 1.

Gárbat : Mátherán Point, XIV, 231, 232, 237, 238.

Garbhádhána : fœtus-laying, a Vedic rite among Gujarát Hindus, IX, pt. i, 31 note 3; performance of the rite, *id.* 32; *see* also XXIV, 58-59.

Garbha-rakshana : womb-guarding, also called *anavalobhana,* that is longing-soothing, a Vedic rite, IX, pt. i, 31 note 3; performance of the rite, *id.* 32-33.

Garcia d'Orta : Portuguese historian, his remark on Naiatas (1530), IX, pt. ii, 15; his notice of the Pársis, *id.* 189; his notices of Elephanta caves (1550), XIV, 59 note 1, 84, 92 note 1, 149, 226.

Garcinia : *cambogia, purpurea,* and *xanthochymus,* plants yielding a dye, XXV, 241; *indica* and *purpurea,* plants yielding oil, *id.* 213.

Gardabhin : kings, dynasty of, said to have been founded by the Persian prince Behram Gor, IX, pt. ii, 183 note 4.

Garden : victory of the, Ahmad Nizam's victory (1490) at Bhingár near Ahmadnagar so called XVII, 357.

Gardening : at Mátherán, XIV, 250; in Poona district, soil, tillage, field tools, manure, sowing season, flowers, vegetables, plants, grafting, pruning, XVIII, pt. ii, 31-34.

Gardenia lucida : gum-yielding plant, XXV, 251.

Gardens : experimental, in Poona district, XVIII, pt. ii, 76-77; botanical, *id.* 77-80; experimental, in Kaira, iii, 54; in Dhárwar district, XXII, 302-305; in Bombay, coffee garden (1746), Parel garden and green (1750), mulberry trees garden at the Old Secretariat (1845), animal garden on the Old Woman's Island, (1675, 1816,) XXVI, pt. iii, 592-93.

Gar Dhond : village on the Bhima, in Poona district, Balaji Kunjar defeated at, I, pt. ii, 608.

Gardimani : wrestling houses, in Dhárwár district, XXII, 818-820.

Gárgaon : hot spring in Thána district, XIII, 15.

Gargasvámin : Bráhmán grantee of Chálukya prince, I, pt. ii, 191.

Gargoti : town in Kolhápur state, market and school at, XXIV, 297; *see* also I, pt. ii, 548.

Gárgya : disciple of Nakulisá, founder of a branch of Pásupata school, I, pt. i, 84.

Gáriádhar : place of interest in Kháthiáwár, VIII, 439.

Garjjanaka : Sanskrit form of Ghaznavi, I, pt. i, 195.

Gárkhed : village in Khándesh, under-ground temple at, XII, 449.

Garlic : food-plant, XXV, 179; its cultivation in Khándesh, XII, 171; in Poona district, XVIII, pt. ii, 56.

Garmatba : village, Imámshah Pirána residing at, IX, pt. i, 168.

Gárodi Hill : in Poona district, caves and inscriptions at, XVIII, pt. ii, 129-130.

Gárpir : in Poona, European and Musalmán grave-yards at, XVIII, pt. iii, 365, 368-369.

Garrison : in Poona, XVIII, pt. iii, 356; in Bombay (1739), XXVI, pt. iii, 86-88; strength of (1742), *id.* note 1, 95-97; revision of (1743), *id.* 98-101; 2,000 additional sepoys to be raised (1757) for, *id.* 129-130; increase of (1768), *id.* 148-150.

Garruga pinnata : dye and fodder-plant, XXV, 241, 278.

Carton : Captain, defeats the Pendharis (1817), XXII, 430.

Garud : eagle god, I, pt. i, 465; I, pt. ii, 517, 536, 578; IX, pt. i, 4; representation of, in Elephanta and Mandapeshver caves in Thána district, XIV, 67, 68, 69, 70, 75, 76, 224; device of, I, pt. ii, 392.

Gáruda : a depressed class in Káthiáwár, VIII, 157; priests of Dhedás, IX, pt. i, 331; their origin, divisions, customs, *id* 344-345.

Garuda Dhvaja : banner of the Guttas, I, pt. ii, 578.

Garuda lanchhana : crest of Garuda; hereditary title of the Ráshtrakútas, I, pt. ii, 387.

Gárudi : caste of snake-charmers in Thána district, XIII, 197; in Sátára district, XIX, 142; in Belgaum district, XXI, 224; in Kolhápur state, XXIV, iii, 116.

Garud Purán : holy book, when to be read, IX, pt. i, 25.

Garutmat : Garuda, story of his restoration, I, pt. ii, 536.

Gás : village near Sopára in Thána district, XIV, 316, 323, 324, 341.

Gaspar Correa : Portuguese historian (1514-1583), his description of craft in Konkan ports, XIII, 468.

Gasper de Gama : Christian Jew (1505) taken to Europe by the Portuguese, XV, pt. ii, 253-254.

Gates of Makkah : Gujarát ports, IX, pt. ii, 3 note 1; *see* Abwah-ul-makkah.

Gatha : stanza, I, pt. ii, 171.

Gathas : last extra five days of the Pársi year, names of, IX, pt. ii, 218.

Gatkul, Gatkuli : absentee tenure in Thána district, XIII, 550; in Násik district, XVI, 209 and note 4.

Gattavadi : stone inscription at, I, pt. ii, 301 note 1.

Gaud : a Bráhman sub-castes in Cutch, V, 47; in Ratnágiri, X, 426, 450; *see* Shrigauda.

Gaud : group of Bráhman sub-castes of India, sub-divisions of, IX, pt. i, 1 and note 1.

Gauda : Bengal, I, pt. ii, 11, 197; invaded by Vikramáditya, *id.* 215. 400, 405; mentioned in Kánheri caves, XV, 147, 148; *see* also I, pt. i, 124, 466, 468, 469.

Gaudán : gift of a cow, occasion on which to make it, IX, pt. i, 94, 373; *see* Cow.

Gandaráditya : Siláhára king (1109-1136), his inscriptions, XXIV, 221.
Gaudas : humiliated by Krishna II, I, pt. ii, 201.
Gau Ghât : cow-gate near Bhinmál, remains of steps at, I, pt. i, 453
Gaula : country, I, pt. ii, 333 and note 6 ; king of, conquered by Singhana, *id.* 525.
Gauli : *see* Gavli.
Gaulirájás : of Khándesh, probably of the Yádava family, I, pt. ii, 619 ; *see* also IX, pt. i, 264.
Gaundi or Gavandi : caste of masons in Ratnágiri, X, 125, 163 ; in Khándesh, XII, 74 ; in Thána district, XIII, 136 ; Musalmán, in Sátára district, XIX, 141-142 ; in Sholápur, XX, 94-101 ; in Dhárwár, XXII, 140-147 ; in Bijápur, XXIII, 97-101 ; in Kolhápur, XXIV, 94 ; in Kánara district, XV, pt. i, 273-274 ; in Násik district, XVI, 52 ; Hindu and Musalman, in Ahmadnagar district, XVII, 95-97 ; in Poona district, XVIII, pt. i, 331-333 ; Musalmán bricklayers, *id.* 501 ; in Belgaum district, XXI, 217 ; in Dhárwár district, XXII, 241 ; in Bijápur district, XXIII, 298-299.
Gaur : class of merchants and shopkeepers found at Bassein, IX, pt. ii, 189.
Gaura-Mukh : family priest of Ugrasena of Mathura, IX, pt. i, p. 440.
Gauri : a name for Párvati, XVIII, pt. i, 248 ; favourite goddess of Vishnuvardhána Chálukya, I, pt. ii, 340 ; worship of, among Dakhan Bráhmans, IX, pt. i, p. 54.
Gaurkámat : village in Thána, with Hemádpanti remains, XIV, 10, 99.
Gausi : snake in Ratnágiri district, X, 50.
Gautama : Buddha (B. C. 560-480), his origin, IX, pt i, 9, 435, 445 note 5 ; travel through Valabhi country, I, pt. i, 79 ; sage, tank and hermitage of, *id.* 454, 461 ; statue of, in Ajanta caves, XII, 483 note 2 ; Sopára Bodhisattva, XIV, 316 ; his begging bowl, *id.* 329, 403 ; images of, *id.* 132 note 4.
Gautama : Nága king, XIII, 408.
Gautamiputra : Andhra king (A. D. 138), I, pt. i, 32, 38 ; S'atakarni, *id.* 540 ; defeat of Sáh kings by, his date, XII, 239 and note ; defeat of stranger leaders in Dakhan by, IX, pt. i, 448, 453.
Gautrál : cow-worship ceremony, details of, IX, pt. i, 373-374.
Gavandi : *see* Gaundi.
Gávda : caste of cultivators in Ratnágiri district, X, 125.
Gavhane-Velgaum : in Ratnágiri district, caves at, I, pt. ii, 9.
Gávilabbarasi : wife of Narasimha, Chálukya prince, I, pt. ii, 380.
Gavit : *see* Mávchi.
Gavli : a caste of herdsmen in Ratnágiri district, X, 127 ; in Sávantvádi, *id.* 415 ; caste of cow-keepers in Kolába district, XI, 68, 414 ; in Khándesh, XII, 78 ; in Thána district, XIII, 145 ; in Kánara district, XV, pt. i, 296 ; in Násik district, XVI, 57 ; in Ahmadnagar district, XVII, 150-153 ; in Poona district, XVIII, pt. i, 385-387 ; in Sátára district, XIX, 105 ; in Sholápur district, XX, 148-151 ; in Belgaum district, XXI, 154-155 ; in Dhárwár district, XXII, 179-180 ; in Bijápur district, XXIII, 241-244 ; in Kolhápur state, XXIV, 103. *See* Dudwala.
Gavli Rájás : *see* Gaulirájás.
Gáwarawád : in Dhárwár district, record at, I, pt. ii, 443 note 2.
Gawháli : state in Khándesh, XII, 608.
Gayákarna : Kalachuri king, I, pt. ii, 425.
Gayákarna : *see* Karna.
Gayákund : *see* Goni, I, pt. i, 453.
Gáyatri : sun hymn, IX, pt. i, 31 and note 1, 393.
Gáyatri : Gujar girl, taken by Brahma in marriage, IX, pt. i, 490, 502 and note 4.
Gayávál : sub-caste of Bráhmans, IX, pt. i, 9.
Gayer : Sir John, governor of Bombay (1696) ; imprisoned in Surat (1701), XXVI, pt. i, 122-123 ; IX, pt. ii, 196 note 3 ; released, XXVI, pt. i, 124.
Gaz-gaz : tribe of foreign invaders, IX, pt. i, 469.
Gazi-ud-din : Nizám-ul-Mulk's son, advances with a large army against his brother Salábat (1752), is poisoned at Aurangabád, I, pt. ii, 627.
Gedi : place of interest in Cutch, V, 221.
Gedi : táluka in Káthiáwár, VIII, 439.
Gediya : a sub-caste of Kolis. *See* Koli.
Gedrosia, Gedrosoi : name of country east of the Indus, I, pt. i, 546, 537.
Geh : a watch, names of, IX, pt. ii, 214 and note 1, 215 and note 1, 225.
Gehe : portion of the original *Zend Avesta*, IX, pt. ii, 212 note 1.
Gehela : *Randia dumetorum*, a plant in Poona district, XVIII, pt. i, 45.
Gehlot : tribe of Rájpúts ; *see* Sisodiya, name derived from Valabhi king, I, pt. i, 85, 469.
Geiger : Dr., his notice of the star *Sataves*, IX, pt. ii, 217 note 1.
Gejjihalli : village in Dhárwár district, temple and inscriptions at, XXII, 720.
Gell : General, captured the rebel Rághoji Bhangria (1848), XIII, 636-637 ; XVII, 418 ; XVIII, pt. ii, 308.
Gell : Archdeacon, his description of Kalsubái Point in Násik district (1860), XVI, 447.
Gemelli Careri : Italian traveller, Doctor of Laws ; request to him to stay at Goa, writer on Portuguese affairs, his times, I, pt. ii, 51, 52, 59, 65, 128 ; (1695) his account of Malabar pirates, XI, 281 note 1, 285 note 6, *id.* 433 note 1 ; his description of Daman, Bassein and Sálsette, XIII, 483-484 ; his notice of Bindra, XIV, 27 ; of Bassein and its plague (1690), *id.* 33 note 5, 40, 42 ; his description of Kánheri caves, *id.* 152-156 ; his notice of Máhim fort, *id.* 129 ; of Mandapeshvar Church or cave, *id.* 227 ; of Tárápur, *id.* 344 ; of Thána and Versova, *id.* 359, 380, 381 ; his visit to Sambrani, Sonda and other places on Kánara coast, XV, pt. ii, 131-132, 340, 349 ; his travels in Belgaum district (1695), XXI, 377-378 ; his description of Aurangzeb's camp, XXIII, 438-439, 649.

Gemitores: order of birds, in Ratnágiri, X, 85-87; in Thána district, XIII, 51.
Genigar: a class of tenants in Kánara district, XV, pt ii, 185.
Genii: vows to, IX, pt. ii, 130.
Gentianeæ: famine plant found in Konkan, XXV, 201.
Geology: *see* All District Volumes under District Name.
Georgia: Gurjjaras of, IX, pt. i, 469-470.
Geraniaceæ: famine plant, XXV, 196.
Gerjjihalli: village, I, pt. ii, 278 note 2.
Gerrba: in the Persian Gulf, pre-historic emporium of Indian trade, identified with Ophir, XIII, 404 note 3; its trade with India (B. C. 177-A. D. 247), *id.* 411 note 1, 412.
Gersappa: river in Kánara district, XV, pt. i, 3, 5, 7.
Gersappa: village in Kánara district, XV, pt. ii, 98, 109, 110, 112, 114, 117, 121, 124, 147; temples and history of, *id.* 282-284, 309, 310, 318, 325, 356; pass, *id.* 39, 40, 288.
Gersappa Falls: description of, XV, pt. i, 6, 9; *id.* pt. ii, 284-288.
Ghadi: water clock, construction of, marking of time by, IX, pt. i, 27 note 1.
Ghádi: caste of cultivators in Ratnágiri district, X, 124; temple ministrants, *id.* 140; caste of soothsayers in Kánara district, XV, pt. i, 198, 199.
Ghadse, Ghadsi, Ghadshi: caste of musicians in Kolába district, XI, 67; in Thána district, XIII, 141; Marátha *vajantris* in Kánara district, XV, pt. i, 315-316: in Násik district, XVI, 55; in Ahmadnagar district, XVII, 144; in Poona district, XVIII, pt. i, 378; in Sátára district, XIX, 97-98; in Sholápur district, XX, 145; in Belgaum district, XXI, 159; in Kolhápur state, XXIV, 101.
Ghádus: word possessing magical power, IX, pt. ii, 143.
Ghagada: Chávada king (A. D. 908-937), I, pt. i, 154, 155.
Ghair Mahadi: a caste of Musalmáns in Ahmadnagar district, XVII, 231; in Sholápur district, XX, 207; in Belgaum district, XXI, 213, 214.
Ghaisása: family name among Chitpávans, mention of, in 1100 grants, I, pt. ii, 245, 256.
Ghalisása, Ghalisa: family name among Deshasthas, I, pt. ii, 245.
Ghalla: a port of trade, I, pt. i, 537.
Ghámot: family priest, his duties, his source of income, IX, pt. i, 23-24.
Ghána: rice-pounding ceremony, IX, pt. i, 36.
Gháncha: caste of basket-makers in Cutch, V, 74.
Ghánchi: a Musalmán sect in Rewa Kántha, VI, 35; caste of Hindu oilmen, main divisions; Rájput tribal surnames, IX, pt. i, 181; oil-pressing, other professions, religion, early beliefs, customs, *id.* 182-183; Musalmán descendants of converts of the Hindu Pinjára and Ghánchi castes; known as Ghanchi-Bohorás, call themselves Mansuris; Sunnis in religion; curious forms of names of, form a separate body, IX, pt. ii, 73.
Ghánchi-Gola: lower classes of Ujlivarati people in Gujarát so called, IX, pt. i, p. xiv; *see* also I, pt. i, 450.
Ghániger: *see* Ganig.
Gharab: old war vessel of the Maráthás, XIII, 348 note 1; origin of the word, *id.* 717.
Ghárápuri: island in Bombay harbour, I, pt. ii, 9. *See* Elephanta.
Ghargad: fort in Násik district, XVI, 439, 441.
Ghar-Mandala: territory given to the Chohán, IX, pt. i, 484.
Gharvi: state in Khándesh, XII, 605.
Ghásdána: 'forage money,' Maráthá levy, IV, 154; Gáikwár's tribute, amount of, VII, 338-339; XVIII, pt. ii, 241; XIX, 250, 256.
Ghasheti's Bridge: in Poona city, XVIII, pt. iii, 285.
Gháshirám: head of the Poona police (1791), XVIII, pt. iii, 18 note 1, 369, 409; Poona mansion of, *id.* 369; his cruelties (1800), XVIII, pt. ii, 280.
Ghásia: salt, IV, 117.
Ghatandur: pass in Násik district, XVI, 129.
Ghateya-ankakára: feudatory of the Western Chálukya king Vikramáditya V, I, pt. ii, 434.
Ghatghar: village in Thána district, XIV, 236, 290.
Gháti: a caste of labourers in Thána district, XIII, 151.
Gháti: a common weed, a famine plant, XXV, 202.
Ghatola: caste of cultivators in Khándesh, XII, 68.
Ghatorgach: son of Bhimsen Pándav, Saiad Káka is supposed to live in stone bust of, IX, pt. i, 369.
Ghatotkach: caves (500-600 A. D.) near Jinjála in Nizám's dominions, XII, 241, 592-593; *see* also I, pt. ii, 391 note 6.
Ghatotkacha: second Gupta chief, I, pt. i, 61, 67.
Ghat-Path: heart prayer, Khojáh sacrament, IX, pt. ii, 49.
Ghat-Páth-Mantra: prayer of the Shaktipanthis, IX, pt. ii, 48.
Ghatprabha: river in Southern Maráthá Country, XXI, 10; XXIII, 10-11; XXIV, 8, 9, 11.
Ghátsari: hill in Ahmadnagar district, XVII, 4.
Ghauts or Ghats: the Western, I, pt. ii, 282 note 5, 310, 430; laid waste by Vishnuvardhána, *id.* 496; Western Sahyádri mountains, *id.* 537; subjugated by the Hángal Kadamba king Kámadeva, *id.* 563; people of the, dispersed by A'chugi II, *id.* 574.
Ghawn, Ghawat-ghum: common wheat, XXV, 189.
Gházi-ud-din: Khan Bahádur Furuz Jang, forty-third viceroy of Gujarát (1708-1710), his death, confiscation of his property, I, pt. i, 296, 297.
Ghazni: capital of Mahmúd, I, pt. i, 165, 510.
Ghazni Khán: grave of, near Bhinmal, I, pt. i, 455.
Ghazni Khán: Fáruki (1510), his murder, XII, 245.
Ghed: lake in Káthiáwár, VIII, 4, 68.

Gheir Mukallid : IX, pt. ii, 12. *See* Wahhábi.
Ghela : plant, its fruit used as vegetable soap, XXV, 252.
Ghela : river in Káthiáwar, VIII, 63.
Ghela Somnáth : place of interest in Káthiáwar, VIII, 440.
Ghelkhari : estate of, near Navsári, received in grant by Meherji Rana from Akbar, IX, pt. ii, 190.
Ghelo : near Valeh town, probably a river in Valabhi time, I, pt. i, 79.
Ghelot : a Rájpút tribe, VIII, 115; Rájpút peasant proprietors, IX, pt. i, 129. *See* Sisode.
Ghenims : robbers, Maráthás known as, IX, pt. i, 458.
Ghera Khelanga : *see* Kenjalgad.
Gherámia : a Baroda land tenure, VII, 351.
Gheria : *see* Vijaydurg.
Ghermehdi : class of Hindu converts, and foreign Musalmáns who do not believe in Mehdi, also called Mehdevis, followers of Sayad Muhammad Jaunpuri, IX, pt. ii, 62; persecutions of, by Sultán Muzaffar II (1523), by Aurangzeb (1645), *id.* 63; *dáirah* of, at Pálanpur, *id.* 64 and note 1; customs of, *id.* 64.
Ghiásuddin : son and successor of Mahmud Khilji (1469-1499); appoints his son Abdul Kádir, prime minister; builds *Mándu Shádiábád* or abode of joy; invasion of Málwa by Bahlol Lodi (1482); death of, by poison administered by his son and prime minister Nasir-ud-din, I, pt. i, 362-365.
Ghias-ud-Din Tughlak : emperor (1320), I, pt. i, 230.
Ghir : breed of cattle in Poona district, XVIII, pt. i, 56.
Ghisádi : a caste of blacksmiths in Ratnágiri district, X, 125; in Kolába district, XI, 70; in Janjira state, *id.* 413; in Khándesh, XII, 73, 225; in Thána district, XIII, 151; in Násik district, XVI, 52; in Ahmadnagar district, XVII, 97-99; in Poona district, XVIII, pt. i, 333-338; in Sátára district, XIX, 83; in Sholápur district, XX, 101-103; in Belgaum district, XXI, 135-136; in Bijápur district, XXIII, 189-193; in Kolhápur state, XXIV, 106.
Ghisárá : *see* Saikalgar.
Ghod : stream in Kolábá district, XI, 10.
Ghod : river in Poona and Ahmadnagar districts, XVIII, pt. i, 7; XVII, 8-9.
Ghodadev : horse-god, worship of, IX, pt. i, 173, 376.
Ghodásar : state in Mahi Kántha, V, 418.
Ghodbandar (Ghodbunder) : village and port in Thání district, its history, Portuguese remains at, XIV, 99-100, 10; harbour of Buddhist mendicants, I, pt. ii, 173; Portuguese buildings and Portuguese fort at, *id.* 66; taken by the Maráthás (1737), *id.* 84; XIII, 493; attacked by Shiváji (1670), XIII, 475; its trade, *id.* 358.
Ghode : town in Poona district mosque at, XVIII, pt. iii, 130.
Ghodegaon : in Kolába district, XIV, 99; *see* Goregaon.
Ghodepir : object of interest, in Poona city, XVIII, pt. iii, 336.
Ghodnadi : in Poona district (?), battle of (1763), VII, 186; *see* Sirur.
Gholay : place of interest in Cutch, V, 222.
Gholvad : village in Thána district, XIV, 100.
Ghonas : *see* Kándur.
Ghorpade : Poona city ward, details of, XVIII, pt. iii, 274, 279.
Ghorpade : chief of Kápshi and Mudhol, XIX, 231-257, 283-284.
Gorpadi barracks : near Poona, XVIII, pt. iii, 369-370.
Ghos : the tack of a sail, XIII, 722.
Ghosála (Ghosálgad) : fort in Kolaba district, its description, XI, 312-316; ceded to the Maráthás (1736), *id.* 445; taken by the British (1818), *id.* 156, 375; I, pt. ii, 40, 83.
Ghost : Cháran, dread of, IX, pt. i, p. 218-219; belief in, *id.* 186, IX, pt. ii, 220; *see* Beliefs (Early).
Ghotan : town in Ahmadnagar district, temple at, XVII, 716.
Ghotavde : village in Poona district, XVIII, pt. iii, 131.
Ghotga, Ghotge : hill pass in, between Ratnágiri district and Kolhápur state, X, 66; XXIV, 6.
Ghoti : village in Násik district with railway station, XVI, 439.
Ghozz : ancestors of Seljuks and Osmaulis, IX, pt. i, 470 and note 2.
Ghughula : chief of Godhra, attacked by Tejahpála, I, pt. i, 201.
Ghugri : poisonous plant, XXV, 265.
Ghumat Shirol : *see* Shirol.
Ghumli : place of interest in Káthiáwár, VIII, 440; place in the Baroda hills, first capital of Jethvas, IX, pt. i, 126. *See* Bhumli.
Ghunki : village in Kolhápur state, old military station, XXIV, 297.
Ghurjararája : defeated by the Chálukya prince Narasimha, I, pt ii, 380.
Gidar : táluka in Kathiáwar, VIII, 440.
Gidbudki : a class of beggars in Kánara district, XV, pt. i, 349, 350.
Gidhpani : spring on Tungar hill in Bassein, XIV, 368.
Gifts : mentioned in inscriptions of caves, cisterns, pathways, images, in cash and lands, I, pt. ii, 11; during eclipses, IX, pt. i, 335, 395.
Gigasaran : táluka in Káthiáwár, VIII, 440.
Gilan : saint of, IX, pt. ii, 6 note 1 (2).
Gildemeister : traveller, his description of Thána, I, pt. ii, 4.
Gilding : in Cutch, V, 124.
Gimvas : *see* Náchni.
Gingelly seed : crop of, in Sátára district, XIX, 164.
Ginger : cultivation of, in Thána district, XIII, 292-293; in Khándesh, XII, 171.
Gir : hills in Káthiáwár, VIII, 9-10.
Girardinia heterophylla : fibrous plant common in the Himalayas, XXV, 234.
Giras : land tenure in Káthiawár, VIII, 315.
Girásias : in Ahmadábád district, IV, 150; in Káthiáwár, VIII.

Girdhar Bahádur: Rája, Nágar Bráhman, governor of Mándu (1722-1724); defeat of, by Chimnáji Pandit and Udáji Pavár, I, pt. i, 382.
Girinagara: Junágadh, I, pt. i, 14.
Girná: river in Násik and Khándesh districts, XVI, 3, 9; XII, 8; *see* also I, pt. ii, 353 note 2.
Girnár: hill in Káthiáwár, VIII, 11; Aśoka's edicts inscribed on, *id.* 272; coins and inscriptions of the Kshatraps at, *id.* 273; description, *id.* 441-444; inscription of Skandagupta at, I, pt. i, 69-70, 135, 176, 190; I, pt. ii, 142; fair at, I, pt. i, 9; Vastupála's temple at, *id.* 153; temple of Neminátha repaired at, *id.* 176, 177, 186; visited by Hemachandra, *id.* 192; magnificent temple of Neminátha built on, *id.* 199, 202, 231 and note 2, 236; hill, IX, pt. ii, 1 note 1, IX, pt. i, 241 note 1; gives name to Girnára Bráhmans, *id.* 9; place of pilgrimage, *id.* 220, 247; Jain shrines on, *id.* p. ix, 550. *See* Ujjanta.
Girnára: Bráhman sub division, I, pt. i, 70; in Cutch V, 46; in Káthiáwár, VIII, 146; their origin, settlement at Girnár; sub-divisions in, priests of pilgrims, Vaishnav by religion. IX, pt. i, 9.
Girván Parishad: Sanskrit Society in Násik city, XVI, 336.
Gium: *see* Ghawn.
Gizekia pharnccioides: famine plant found in Konkan and Dakhan, XXV, 200.
Glareolidæ: species of birds in Ratnágiri, X, 90.
Glaser: his opinion on Periplus, I, pt. i, 542.
Glasgow: Dr., his derivation of Gurjjara, IX, pt. i, 469.
Glass: manufacture of, in Kaira district, III, 76.
Glass bangles: making of, in Kolába district, XI, 131; in Poona district, XVIII, pt. ii, 198-201; in Dhárwár district, XXII, 385; in Kolhápur state, XXIV, 210.
Glasspool: Lieutenant, blockaded at Peint in Násik district (1857), XVI, 202.
Glosso-cardia Boswellia: famine-plant found in Poona and other places, XXV, 200.
Glycosmispentaphylla: vegetable antidote to snake-bite, found in Southern Konkan, XXV, 274.
Gnessie Rocks: in Belgaum district, XXI, 15-17; in Bijápur district, XXIII, 17-19.
Gnetaceæ: a species of food-plants common on the *gháts*, XXV, 174.
Gnetum scandens: food-plant used for poisoning fish, XXV, 174, 273.
Goa: copper-plate grant of the Western Chálukyas of Bádámi found near, I pt. ii, 181, 355, 356 note 1; Siláhára possession of, *id.* 539, 566; Kádamba chieftain Jayakeśin I, feudatory of Someśvara I (1044-1068), wrests it from the Siláháras and makes it his capital, *id.* 216, 543, 567; makes presents at, to Vikramáditya II also styled VI, *id.* 444; Kádamba heroes of, defeated by Hoysála Vishnuvardhána, *id.* 496, 498; king of, associates with Vishnuvardhána against Vikramáditya II also styled VI; is defeated by Sinda chieftain Áchugi II, and Goa burnt (1117), *id.* 218-219, 453, 569, 574; Kádamba princes of, re-established by Vijayáditya of Karád (1143-1153), *id.* 570; Kádambas of, remain feudatories of the Western Chalukyas of Kalyáni at, *id.* 439, 451, 452, 456, 460; their doubtful position under the Kalachuryas at, *id.* 476, 480; territory near, burnt by a Kalachurya officer (1181), *id.* 489; defeated by Bichana, officer of Singhana (about 1218) at, *id.* 243, 524; Devagiri Yádava feudatories of, *id.* 519; their family perish with Shahsthadeva II at (1257), *id.* 572; grants of the Kádambas of, *id.* 216; charter of, *id.* 572; inscriptions of the Kádambas of, *id.* 436 note 1, 459 note 4; Mádhava appointed governor of, by the Vijayánagar king (1380), *id.* 5, 175, 566 note 7; head-quarters of Konkan, X, 439; captured from the Vijayánagar king by Mahmud Gáwan (1470), I, pt. ii, 32, 638; XXIII, 401, XV, pt. ii, 100; Bijápur possession ranked with Chaul and Dábhol, I, pt. ii, 34; taken by the Portuguese (1510), *id.* 641; Portuguese expedition sent from, to defeat Bijápur troops (1555), *id.* 47; Portuguese magistrates and supreme courts at, *id.* 52; creation of archbishopric at (1560), *id.* 56; Jesuit College at, *id.* 57, 69; unsuccessful attack of the Bijápur king on (1570), *id.* 646; centre of piracy (1500), XIII, 471; ceded to the Portuguese (1511), *id.* 447, XV, pt. ii, 108-111, 117; XXI, 237; the Inquisition established at (1560), XIII, 463; attacked by Bijápur troops (1570), *id.* 453, XXIII, 407, 418, 419; ship-building and trade centre (1530-1670), XIII, 465, 469; besieged by the Dutch (1664), *id.* 473; provisions supplied to, from Sálsette (1675), *id.* 476, 501; decline of trade at (1660-1710), *id.* 486; harassed by Bhonsles (1737), *id.* 493; Sálsette Portuguese retire to (1740), *id.* 494, 495. Pratápsinh's intrigues in, XIX, 310-11; identified with Ophir, XIV, 318; I, pt. i, 517; ancient seat of the Shenvis, IX, pt. i, 439. *See* Gopakapattana, Gopakapura, Gove, and Sindápur.
Goa (Goba): name of a fort, near Harnai in Ratnágiri district, I, pt. ii, 504 note 7; possession of Gujarát king, I, pt. ii. 30.
Goaris: river Vaitarani, in Thána district, mentioned by Ptolemy, I, pt. i, 540, 542.
Goat: offering of; worship; dung used in spirit-scaring, IX, pt. i, 377; in Poona district, XVIII, pt. i, 67-68; offering, *id.* 195 and note 1; in Sholápur district, XX, 17-18; in Belgaum district, XXI, 68.
Gobbur: town in the Nizám's dominions, I, pt. ii, 450; record at, *id.* 523.
Gobru: measles, IX, pt. i, 368, 372.
God: popolar gods worshipped by different classes in Gujarát, IX, pt. i. 35, 36, 531; Baba Dev, *id.* 292; Bharam Dev, *id.* 292; Bhesnágur, *id.* 375; Bheroba, *id.* 292; Bhil Dev, *id.* 321; Brahm, *id.* 322; Brahmá, *id.* 36, 14, 15 note 1, 382, 384, 490, 502 and note 4; Dwárkánáth, *id.* 4; Ganpati; *id.* 64, 136,

213, 332, 336, 341, 362, 376, 378, 383, 409; Godhádev, *id.* 173, 376; Gováldev, *id.* 363; Hanumán, monkey god, *id.* 12, 292, 317, 321, 323, 332, 335, 341, 362, 363, 383, 409; Haria Dev, *id.* 292, 314; Hatakeshvar, golden *ling* emblem of Shiv, *id.* 14, 73; Hatmál, *id.* 247; Indra Dev, *id.* 247, 348, 351; Ithoba, *id.* 292; Kahnamdev, *id.* 363; Kámdev, *id.* 363; Khandoba, *id.* 292; Khatridev, *id.* 292; Khetarpál, *id.* 200, 292, 354; Kotyarkeshvar, *id.* 72; Krishna, *id.* 4, 9, 10, 381, 384, 409; Magardev, *id.* 380; Magaria Dev, *id.* 292; Mahádev, *id.* 292, 317; *see* Shiv; Maoli, *id.* 292; Moktináth, god of salvation emblem of god Shiv, *id.* 12 note 1; Nandikeshvar, *id.* 73; Pálio, *id.* 313; Rádha-Krishná, form of Vishnu, *id.* 118; Rám, *id.* 4, 12 note 1, 292, 313, 332, 345, 383; Ranchhodji, form of Vishnu, *id.* 118; Saiádkáka, *id.* 368; Shámla Dev, *id.* 292, 314, 319, 363; Shámláji, *id.* 73, 96; Shiv, or Mahádev, *id.* 36, 5, 12 note 1, 14, 64, 136, 168, 213, 362, 377, 433, 440; Siddhanáth, Shiv's *ling* raised at Saras, *id.* 12 note 1; Sámadia Dev or Simaris, *id.* 292, 313, 363; Somnáth Mahádev, *id.* 195; Tulshishám (form of Lakshmi and Krishna), *id.* 266; Vágh Dev, *id.* 292, 319, 322; Vaitál Dev, *id.* 292; Vishnu, *id.* 36, 9, 64, 118, 136, 213, 362, 383, 387, 388, 391, 409; belief in the unity of, among Musalmáns, IX, pt. ii, 126.

Godadi: famine-plant common throughout the Presidency, XXV, 197.

Godadji: Cháran poet and holy man, IX, pt. i, 220.

Godaji Dengle: Trimbakji's brother, raises a revolt in Khándesh (1817), dispersed by Lieutenant Davies, I, pt. ii, 630.

Godávari: river in Násik and Ahmadnagar districts, XVII, 6-7; XVI, 7-9, 468; irrigation project, XVI, 95, I, pt. ii, 133, 135, 136, A'ndhras living about the mouth of the, *id.* 138; settlement of the A'ryas along the, *id.* 141, 143, 169, 185, 198, 213, 277; grant by Prithivimula, *id.* 322 note 8; district, grant from, *id.* 334; river, *id.* 341 note 2, 355, 432, 509, 533; held sacred, IX, pt. i, 350, 550.

Godchi: village in Kolhápur state, temple and fair at, XXIV, 297.

Goddard: Colonel, attacked by Sanyasins in Bundelkhand (1778), XIV, 135 note 10 continued on page 136; his skirmishes with Sindia in Gujarát (1779), VII, 197; marches for the first time with an English force across India, I, pt. ii, 628; XVIII, pt. ii, 266-267; his march to Surat, XIII, 505; I, pt. ii, 103; his march through Khándesh (1779), XII, 252, 583, 591; conducts negotiations with Poona on behalf of supreme Government and the Government of Bombay; advances against Dábhoi, I, pt. i, 408; takes Ahmadábád by storm; takes Bassein (1780), I, pt. ii, 104; I, pt. i, 408-409; XIV, 34-35; advances towards Poona; encounters the Marátha army at Khandála and is forced to retreat to Bombay (1781), I, pt. ii, 605, XIV, 201, XIII, 507-508.

Goddesses: popular, worshipped among different classes in Gujarát, IX, pt. i, pp. xxxv, xxxvi; Adya, *id.* 136; Amba, Ambáji or Amba Bhaváni, consort of Shiv, *id.* p. xxxv, 20, 64, 177, 187, 196, 213, 220, 223 note 1, 301 note 2; Ashápuri or Ashápurna, *id.* 72, 136, 484 and note 7; Assir, *id.* 200; Bahucharáji, Bechara, or Becharáji, *id.* p. xxxv, 20, 29 and note 2, 182, 187, 213, 216 note 1, 218, 223 and note 1, 277, 366, 380, 506, 507; Ballál, *id.* 216 note 1; Bhanibhán, *id.* 205; Bhaváni, *id.* 272, 292, 363, 501; Bhildi Máta, *id.* 347; Bhut, *id.* 216 note 1; Chámunda, *id.* 16, 136, 205; Chaudi, *id.* 138; Chaván, *id* 196; Devli, *id.* 319, 363; Dharangad, *id.* 205; Durga, *id.* 64, 292, 301 note 2, 420; Gauri, *id.* 54; Hajár Máta, other name of A'dya Máta, *id.* 137; Hingláj, *id.* 116, 177, 181, 189, 200, 247, 520; Kálika or Kálka, *id.* p. xxxv, 64, 186, 187, 213, 216 note 1, 295, 301 note 2, 493; Kankudi, *id.* 247; Khodiád or Khodiar, *id.* 136, 247, 363, 503; Lakshmiji, *id.* 16; Mahálakshmi of Kolhápur, *id.* 12; of Shrimál, *id.* 73, 97, 98, 200; Mába Máya, *id.* 205; Mahi river, *id.* 247; Mandavri, *id.* 136; Mari Máta, *id.* 323; Mátang, *id.* 205; Meladi, *id.* 247, 335, 363, 417; Momai, *id.* 200; Osia, *id.* 97; Párvati, wife of Shiv, *id.* 14, 164, 165, 196, 220, 381, 383, 385, 388; Randel Máta, *id.* 122; Revali, *id.* 366; Sachái, *id.* 98; Sakti, *id.* p. xxxv; Sámudri, *id.* 71, 74; Saraswati, *id.* 19; Sávitri, Bráhma's wife, *id.* 15, 502; Shikotri, *id.* 336, 363, 520; Sitala Máta, *id.* 368; Solanki, *id.* 205; Umiya or Umia, other name of Párvati, *id.* 164, 165, 226; Vachran, *id.* 205; Vagandevi, *id.* 378; Vágheshvári, *id.* 73, 200 and note 3, 378; Vankal, *id.* 16; Verai, *id.* 205, 247, 363; Vindhya Vásini, *id.* 136; worshippers of, among Bhátiás, *id.* 116; Bharváds, *id.* 268; Bháts, *id.* 213; Bhávsárs, *id.* 178; Brahma Kshatris, *id.* 56; Chárans, *id.* 220; early tribes, *id.* 292; Dublás, *id.* 317; Káchhiás, *id.* 154; Kanbis, *id.* 156; Khatris, *id.* 189; Kolis, *id.* 247; Mochis, *id.* 194; Rabáris, *id.* 288; Rájpúts, *id.* 136; Sárasvats, *id.* 18; Sonis, *id.* 200; Suthárs, *id.* 205; small-pox, offering of vows to, IX, pt. ii, 220. *See* Beliefs (Early).

Godho: Nandi Akhlo, IX, pt. i, 374.

Godhra: sub-division of Panch Mahála, III, 292-294; town, *id.* 313; *see* also I, pt. ii, 315; Valabhi province, *id.* 315, 382; chief of, deserts Lavanaprasáda and joins Málwa chief, I, pt. i, 199, 201; I, pt. ii, 241.

Godhraha or Godraha: *see* Godhra.

Godia Panthis: *see* Religious sects.

God-installing: Pátáne Prabhu ceremony, XVIII, pt. i, 202.

Godrahaka: modern Godhra, I, pt. ii, 315.

Godri: food-plant, wild and cultivated in India, XXV, 178.

Gods' names: XV, pt. i, 117, 121, 129, 130, 131, 134, 137, 169, 174, 175, 194, 198, 202, 213, 230, 246, 284, 288, 298, 301, 318, 375.

Gœwali, Gowali: fibrous plant, XXV, 230.

Gogáve : village, granted to the temple of Virasomanáth, I, pt. ii, 483.
Gogi (Goggi) : Thána Siláhára king gave his daughter in marriage to the king Vesugi, I, pt. ii, 233, 514 note 2; North Konkan Siláhára king, I, pt. ii, 17, 539, 542 note 3; see also XIII, 422 note 1, 424.
Goggi : Chálukya, *mahásamanta*, also called Gugga, I, pt. ii, 380; son of Chaulukya Bárappa, *id.* 514 and note 2.
Gogha or Gogo : sub-division of Ahmadábád district, IV, 246-248; town, *id.* 339; capture of (1347), I, pt. i, 230; contest for the government of, *id.* 314; captured by Momin Khán (1755), *id.* 339; delivered to the Maráthás by Momin Khán (1758), *id.* 342; port, *id.* 440.
Goghla : *see* Diu.
Gogo : *see* Gogha.
Gohatya : derivation of the name, IX, pt. i, 469 note 1.
Gohelvadia : main division of Mher chiefships, I, pt. i, 136.
Gohil : ruling Rájpút tribe, I, pt. i, 217 note 3; name derived from Valabhi king, *id.* 85, 86; also called Gehlots and Sisodiyás; Rána of Udaipur, head of; history of their origin, claim descent from Válas of Valabhipur, IX, pt. i, 125; are foreigners of Mihira tribe of Gujar or White Huna horde, *id.* 125, 443, 452, 479; Bappa said to be founder of, *id.* 436 note 1; are foreigners of not more than 1500 years' standing, *id.* 452; their rule in Mevád, in South Márwár, in Káthiáwár, origin of different houses of, *id.* 125-126; their family goddess, *id.* 136; in Cutch, V, 69; in Káthiáwár, VIII, 114; occupy the coast belt of Káthiáwár, *id.* 282; massacred (1260), *id.* 283-284.
Gohilvad, Gohilváda : sub-division of Káthiáwár, VIII, 5-6; I, pt. i, 208 and note 3; named after Gohils, IX, pt. i, 125.
Goho : son of Abu king, Bhils trace descent from, IX, pt. i, 294.
Gohum : wheat, its chaff used as food in famines, XXV, 208.
Gojjga, Gojjgavallabha : Govind IV, enemy of Vijayáditya, I, pt. ii, 380, 416.
Gokák, Gokage : sub-division of Belgaum district, its details, XXI, 500-501; survey of (1849-1850), *id.* 421-425; revision survey of (1883-1884), *id.* 456-460; *town* and falls, *id.* 555-564; trade centre, *id.* 314; fort of, laid siege to, by Akkádevi, I, pt. ii, 435, 439; taken by Muazzim, *id.* 654; taken by the Peshwa (1754), *id.* 656; hill, XXI, 8; canal, *id.* 243, 244.
Gokala, Gokalla : Siláhára king of Karád, I, pt. ii, 545. *See* Gonka.
Gokarn, Gokran-Mahábaleshvar : town in Kánara district, XV, pt. ii, 44, 56, 75, 77, 82 note 2, 106, 115, 125, 129, 138, 149; I, pt. ii, 452; Mahábaleshvar temple, fair, shrines, pools, and history of, XV, pt. ii, 288-302, 346; place of pilgrimage, IX, pt. i, 549.
Gokarn-mul : medicinal plant, XXV, 254.
Gokhru : famine plant, found in several districts, XXV, 196.
Gokul : town, sacred to Krishna, IX, pt. i, 9; place of pilgrimage, *id.* 119, 157, 176, 220, 549.
Gokuláshtami : Janmáshtami or birth-day of Krishna, fast-day, IX, pt. i, 23 note 5, 175, 336. *See* also XVIII, pt. i, 246.
Gokulnáthji : descendant of Vallabha, IX, pt. i, 536.
Gol : *See* Goll.
Gol : fibrous and gum-yielding plant, XXV, 234, 251.
Golá : caste of rice-pounders and craftsmen, in Gujarát, originally Rájpúts, IX, pt. i, 183 and note 1; tribal surnames, *id.* 183; rice-pounding tools; other professions, as menials, *id.* 184; religion, early beliefs, customs, *id.* 185-186; Lundás or household slaves, their position, *id.* 234.
Golá : a caste of weavers and labourers in Thána district, XIII, 109.
Golak : Bráhman sub-division in Khándesh, XII, 52; in Thána district, XIII, 77; in Násik district, XVI, 41; in Sátára district, XIX, 52; in Sholápur district, XX, 28-30; in Belgaum district, XXI, 90; in Dhárwár district, XXII, 92; in Kolhápur state, XXIV, 61. *See* Govardhan.
Golak : caste of husbandmen and goldsmiths in Kánara district, XV, pt. i, 344, 345, 260.
Gola Ladái : brawl, IX, pt. i, 185 and note 1.
Gold : in Belgaum district, XXI, 52; in Dhárwár XXII, 18-25; working in, *id.* 381.
Gold and Silver Thread : manufacture of, in Surat district, II, 180; in Ahmadábád, IV, 127; in Poona district, XVIII, pt. ii, 191-196.
Gold and Silver Work : in Ahmadábád, IV, 126; in Cutch, V, 122-123; in Koláha district, XI, 131; in Sátára district, XIX, 220.
Goldar : fibrous plant common on the *ghâts*, produces gum, XXV, 229, 250.
Gold Coin : of Permádi, I, pt. ii, 570; of Jayakesin III, *id.* 571.
Gold Flowers : in Sopára *stupa*, XIV, 331, 332 and note 1, 335, 336, 413; XIII, 409.
Gold Foil : making of, in Ahmadábád, IV, 128.
Goldingham : Mr., his notice of Elephanta and its inhabitants (1795), XIV, 59 note 1, 91 note 1.
Goldsmiths : in Kolhápur state, XXIV, 207; secretly imported from Surat into Bombay island (1719), XXVI, pt. i, 258.
Goldstucker : Professor, his examination of the *Vártikas*, I, pt. ii, 140; his list of obsolete words, *id.* 141.
Gold Thread : making of, in Káthiáwár, VIII, 257-258; at Yeola in Násik district, XVI, 162-167.
Golgeri : village in Bijápur district, temple and fair at, XXIII, 649.
Gol Gumaz : *see* Boli Gumhaz.
Golhá : caste of labourers in Khándesh, XII, 79.
Golhanadeva : Ráshtrakúta feudatory of the Kalachuri king Gayákarna, I, pt. ii, 425.
Goli : a female servant or slave in Rájpút houses, IX, pt. i, 147, 235-236; VIII, 118.

Golihalli: village in Belgaum district, with a temple and inscriptions, XXI, 564; *see* also I, pt. ii, 570.
Golkonda Kings: I, pt. ii, 30; list of, XXIII, 403 note 1; in alliance with Shiváji against Bijápur (1676), I, pt. ii, 654; fall of, *id.* 595; XXIII, 436.
Goll, Golla, *pl.* Gollaru: wandering class in Belgaum district, XXI, 167; in Dhárwár district, XXII, 201-203; herdsmen in Kánara district, XV, pt. i, 297; in Bijápur District, XXIII, 102-105.
Gollas: a ruler, I, pt. i, 76; Hun king, *id.* 86, 143.
Goller: *see* Goll.
Gollikudlu: hill in Kánara district, XV, pt. ii, 303.
Gomati: sacred stream, in Kolhápur state, tributary of the Panchganga, XXIV, 10.
Gombrun: IX. pt. ii, 183 note 3, 190. *See* Bandar A'bás.
Gomes: Manuel, Franciscan friar (1575-1590), his conversions in Sálsette, XII, 462.
Gometti: sacred plant, XXV, 291, 292.
Gomka, Gomkala: Kolhápur Siláhára prince, harasses the Konkan, I, pt. ii, 254. *See* Gonka.
Gomma: a Hindu chief (A. D. 990), XIII, 425; *see* also I, pt. ii, 18.
Gommateśvara: colossal image of, at Śárvana Belgola, I, pt. ii, 307 and note 8.
Gomti: old city in Káthiáwár, IX, pt. i, 9.
Gomtivál: Bráhman sub-division, in Rewa Kántha, VI, 23; *see* also IX, pt. i, 9.
Gomvani: village in Thána district, I, pt. ii, 21.
Gonamarása: officer of Jaituji I (1192), I, pt. ii, 521.
Gond: caste of wandering cowherds in Khándesh, XII, 106.
Gondal: state and town, in Káthiáwár, VIII, 444, 445; Muhammad Tughlak's stay at (1349), I, pt. i, 231, 517; *see* also IX, pt. i, 126.
Gondali: an old tribe in Khándesh, XII, 38.
Gondavádi: Jayasimha III's camp at, I, pt. ii, 443, 453.
Gonde: pass in Thána district, XIII, 320.
Gondhal: a kind of dance, X, 131.
Gondhalgár: a caste of beggars in Dhárwár district, XXII, 203-205.
Gondhali: caste of religious beggars in Ratnágiri district, X, 131; in Kolába district, XI, 73; in Janjira state, *id.* 415; in Khándesh, XII, 122; in Thána district, XIII, 197; in Kánara district, XV, pt. i, 354; in Násik district, XVI, 73; in Ahmadnagar district, XVII, 178-179; in Poona district, XVIII, pt. i, 450-452; in Sátára district, XIX, 117; in Sholápur district, XX, 183; in Belgaum district, XXI, 181-182; in Bijápur district, XXIII, 193; in Kolhápur state, XXIV, 116-117.
Gondhegaon: village in Ahmadnagar district, temple at, XVII, 717.
Gondoli: canal in Sátára district, XIX, 153-154.
Gondur: lake in Khándesh, XII, 11.
Gongdikár: caste of husbandmen in Kánara district, XV, pt. i, 253-255.
Goni: tank in the outskirts of Bhinmál, I, pt. i, 453.
Goniwála: a caste of Musalmán grain-sellers in Ahmadnagar district, XVII, 228.
Gonka, Gonkala: Karád Siláhára (1040-1050), I, pt. ii, 545, 546, 547; *see* Gomka.
Gonkadeva, Gonki: feudatory of the Karád Siláháras, I, pt. ii, 548 and note 4.
Gonsala Rodrigues: Jesuit monk, founded a Christian village at Vehár, in Thána district (1560), XIII, 461; XIV, 376 note 1.
Goodfellow: Lieutenant Charles, R. E., at the siege of Bet (1859), I, pt. i, 447, 448.
Gooseberry: fruit-bearing bush in Poona district, XVIII, pt. i, 47.
Gop: place of interest in Káthiáwár, VIII, 10, 445.
Gopakapattana: Goa, I, pt. ii, 543, 566; made capital by the Goa Kádamba Jayakeśin I, *id.* 567.
Gopakapuri: Goa, I, pt. ii, 566.
Gopal: caste of religious beggars in Ratnágiri district, X, 131; in Kolába, XI, 73; in Janjira state, *id.* 415; Mhár beggars in Khándesh, XII, 115, 123; in Násik district, XVI, 74; in Sátára, XIX, 117-118; in Belgaum, XXI, 167; in Kolhápur state, XXIV, 117.
Gopála: chief, I, pt. ii, 417 note 5.
Gopál Atmárám: minister at Baroda (1829-1833), VII, 240.
Gopálgad: *see* Anjanvel.
Gopál Pant A'pte: chief of Ichalkaranji, XXIV, 295.
Gopálráv Mairál: Gáikwár's agent in Poona (1815), XVIII, pt. ii, 294-295; Baroda minister (1838), VII, 266; his death (1872), *id.* 279.
Gopar: valley near Vehár lake in Thána district, XIV, 376.
Goparáshtra: old district, about Násik, I, pt. ii, 185, 357.
Gopi: the founder of Surat city, II, 70.
Gopikábái: Báláji II's wife, XVIII, pt. ii, 248-249.
Gopitaláv: pond near Dwárka, IX, pt. i, 522.
Gopnáth: temple in Káthiáwár, history of, VIII, 445-446; Valabhi records at, I, pt. i, 79; *see* also IX, pt. i, p. ix, 549.
Gopradáns: cow-gifts, XVIII, pt. i, 59 and note 2.
Gopshitta: pass in Kánara district, XV, pt. ii, 39, 302; village, *id.* 150, 302.
Gopya: pass in Kolába district, XI, 114.
Gor: pilgrim's priest, daily life of, IX, pt. i, 28.
Goradás: priests to Bombias at Bhinmál, I, pt. i, 451.
Gorai: village in Thána district, XIV, 101.
Gorakamla, Gorakchinch: fibrous plant, XXV, 229; *see* also XVIII, pt. i, 46.
Gorakh: caste of religious beggars in Ratnágiri district, X, 419 note 1.
Gorakhgad: fort in Thána district, XIII, 523; caves at, XIV, 98, 101.
Gorakh Machhindar: hot-spring in Thána district, XIII, 16.
Gorakhmadhi: place of interest in Káthiáwár, VIII, 446, 447.

Gorakhnáth: hill in Ahmadnagar district, XVII, 5.

Gorakhnáth: grove at Shirála in Sátára district, XIX, 587.

Gorak Imlis: *boobab* trees in Bijápur district, XXIII, 643; *see* Gorakamla.

Gora Ráma: Násik city temple, XVI, 506.

Gorava: Śiva's priest, I, pt. ii, 397.

Gordhan: minister (1750) in Cutch, V, 141-142.

Gordon: General, his embassy to Sháhu's court (1739), XXVI, pt. i, 217; XIII, 495; his description of Poona, XVIII, pt. iii; chief in command of the expedition against Sálsette (1774), XXVI, pt. i, 381-393; captures Thána, XIV, 360; appointed commander-in-chief, Bombay (1774), XXVI, pt. iii, 201.

Gorea: oil-yielding plant found in Dakhan, XXV, 224.

Goregaon: port in Kolába district, XI, 316.

Goregaon: village in Thána district, remains at, XIV, 101-103, 10, 388-395; *khoti* estate of, XIII, 545, 546.

Goreh: village in Thána district, XIV, 103.

Gorgi: class of Shrávak ascetics, IX, pt. i, 108-109.

Gori: caste of Rájpúts, IX, pt. i, 126.

Gorik Chinch: *see* Gorakamla.

Gori Sáheb Pir: tomb of, at Hátkalangda in Kolhápur state, XXIV, 297.

Gor-Katri: Kanishka's great *vihára* at Peshâwar, translated as trader's house, IX, pt. i, 450.

Gorkhodia: class of grave-diggers, of mixed origin, Sunnis in religion, IX, pt. ii, 87.

Gosála: pond at Thána, XIV, 346, 349.

Gosávi, Gosái: in Káthiáwár; *see* Atit; caste of religious beggars, in Ratnágiri district, X, 131; Bhárati Náth and Votári, in Sávantvádi, *id.* 419; in Kolába district, XI, 73; in Khándesh, XII, 122; in Thána district, XIII, 196; in Kánara district, XV, pt. i, 350, 351; in Násik district, XVI, 73, 490; in Ahmadnagar district, XVII, 179; in Poona district, XVIII, pt. i, 452; in Poona city, XVIII, pt. iii, 301-302; in Sátára district, XIX, 118; in Sholápur district, XX, 183-184; in Belgaum district, XXI, 182-184; in Dhárwár district, XXII, 203; in Bijápur district, XXIII, 193-194; in Kolhápur state, XXIV, 117-118; armed bands of, in Hindustán (1459-1830), XIV, 135 note 10.

Gosávi Bridge: in Poona city, XVIII, pt. iii, 285.

Goshirsh: sandalwood, trade in, at Sopára (200 or 300), XIII, 406; XIV, 321.

Gossypium: *accriminatum, arboreum, barbadense, herbaceum, hirsutum, obtusifolium, religiosum, stocksii, vitifolium,* fibrous plants, XXV, 228.

Gossypium: oil-yielding and sacred plant, XXV, 215, 290.

Gosvámi: or Gossinji, lord of cows, title of Vallabhácharya mahárájas, IX, pt. i, 536.

Gotama Buddha: founder of the Buddhist religion, I, pt. ii, 208.

Gotami: mother to Śatkarni, dedicates a cave to Buddhist mendicants, I, pt. ii, 149, 151.

Gotamiputa, Gotamiputra: charter of, I, pt. ii, 150; inscriptions of, *id.* 155; overthrows Sákas, Pahlavas, and Yavanas, and establishes the Satavahana dynasty, *id.* 155, 156, 317; dates of accession and death of, *id.* 157; inscriptions of, *id.* 150, 157, 158, 159; regains the lost provinces, *id.* 160; relations of Nahapána, Chastana, and Rudradáman with, *id.* 160-161; accession and death, *id.* 165-166; inscriptions of, *id.* 166; the only protector of Bráhmans, *id.* 173; his date discussed, XVI, 183 and note 1; mention of, in Násik Pándu Lená caves, *id.* 559, 561, 611, 614; account of, *id.* 620-623. *See* Śatakarni.

Gotamiputra I: Śatakarni king (A. D. 124), XIII, 412.

Gotamiputra II: A'ndhrabhritya king (177-196), I, pt. ii, 10; mentioned in a Kánheri inscription, XIV, 147.

Gotardi: state in Rewa Kánthá, VI, 150.

Gotarka: village in Pálanpur state, fair at, V, 300, shrine of Saint Dádá Mahâhali at, IX, pt. ii, 17.

Gothra: state in Rewa Kántha, VI, 150.

Goths: IX, pt. ii, 230. *See* Vows.

Goting: dye plant, XXV, 244.

Gotraj: family goddess, worship of, in religious ceremonies, IX, pt. i, 31, 32, 36; house goddess, *id.* 93, 94, 100.

Gotras: family stocks, in each Bráhman division; intermarriages among, IX, pt. i, 2; clan badge of Bráhmans, seem to be Bráhman's seal, *id.* 436 and note 1; of Chitpávan Bráhmans, X, 111 note 2; of Shenvis, *id.* 116 note 5, XXI, 91; of Havig Bráhmans, XV, pt. i, 117; of Deshastha Bráhmans, *id.* 129; of Karnátak Bráhmans, *id.* 130; of Karháda Bráhmans, *id.* 132; of Joishis (Kánara), *id.* 133; of Sásashtakárs, *id.* 137; of Shenvis, *id.* 140; of Pednekár Vánis, *id.* 186; of Lohánas, *id.* 187; of Rájpúts, *id.* 193; of Kongers, *id.* 197; of Habbus, *id.* 246; of Pánchâls, *id.* 257; of Gudigars, *id.* 265; of Deshastha Bráhmans, XXIV, 44.

Gourd-offering: Pátáne Prabhu ceremony, XVIII, pt. i, 201-202.

Gouridæ: order of birds in Ratnágiri, X, 87.

Gova: Goa, princes of, re-established by Karád Siláhára Vijayáditya, I, pt. ii, 548, 570. *See* Goa.

Gova fort: at Harnai in Ratnágiri district, X, 335, 337.

Goval: village in Ratnágiri district, X, 335.

Gováldev: worshipped by early tribes, IX, pt. i, 363.

Govalkot: fort in Ratnágiri district, X, 326, 336.

Govana: prince of the Nikumbha family, I, pt. ii, 460.

Govaráshtra: modern Goa, I, pt. ii, 282 note 5.

Govardhan: mountain, story, of, IX, pt. i, 388.

Govardhan: Bráhman sub-division, in Thána district, XIII, 77 note 3; in Poona district, XVIII, pt. i, 160-163; in Násik district, XVI, 26, 41; in Ahmadnagar district, XVII, 55. *See* Golak.

Govardhan, Govardhan-Gangápur: old village in Násik district, waterfall and temple at,

XVI, 538-541; mention of, in Pándu-Lena caves, id. 636-637; head-quarters of the Ándhrabhrityas (B. C. 200-A. D. 200), id. 183; town, mountain and village near Násik, I, pt ii, 136; mordern Násik district, id. 148, 150, 175.

Govattan: village granted to Bráhmans, I, pt. ii, 399.

Gove: Goa, captured by A'chugi II, I, pt. ii, 219, 574; 451-466; Kádambas rule at, id. 570. See Goa.

Government: of the Dakhan, I, pt. ii, 30; of the Dakhan increased to eight, id. 32; of Gujarát, id. 33; and of the Konkan (1648), id. 39; Marátha system of, id. 99; share of, in crops in Kánara district, XV, pt. ii, 156, 176; of traditional Bráhmans, id. 76; of Bombay, constitution of (1750), XXVI, pt. iii, 370.

Government House: at Parel, inscription near, I, pt. ii, 544; in Bombay, formerly situated in the Castle and called Fort House (1757); Mr. John Spencer's house becomes Government House or the New House (1757-1829); transferred to Parel (1829), XXV, pt. iii, 593-95; in Ganeshkhind, near Poona, XVIII, pt. iii, 370-371.

Governor: of Bombay, ordered to live in the Fort (1783), XXVI, pt. i, 269; provided with a coach and four (1739), id. 270; also to act as commander-in-chief (1774), id. pt. iii, 170-171; his emoluments and allowances (1757), id. 375-78.

Governor's Hill: Mátherán, XIV, 232, 234, 235.

Goveśvara: grant made by Shashthadeva II to, I, pt. ii, 572.

Govinda: Gujarát Ráshtrakúta king (827), I, pt. i, 126.

Govinda: fendatory Ráshtrakúta prince ruling in Gujarát, I, pt. i, 121, 122; enters into an alliance with Pulikeśin II, I, pt. ii, 183, 194, 350, 385; indentified by Dr. Bhándárkar with Govind I, id. 386 note 1.

Govinda I: Dakhan Ráshtrakúta king (680), I, pt. i, 120, 121; attacked Pulikeśin II, the Chálukya king, but afterwards became his ally, I, pt. ii, 183, 194, 210, 350 note 2, 386 note 1, 388, 542 note 4. See Govind.

Govinda II: Dakhan Ráshtrakúta king, I, pt. i, 122; succeeds his father; gives himself up to sensual pleasures; his younger brother Dhruva dethrones him, I, pt. ii, 196-197, 210, 393.

Govinda III: Ráshtrakúta king (784-815), I, pt. ii, 11; succeeds his father Dhruva, id. 197, 394; as prince regent dissuades his father from abdicating in his favour, id. 198, 394; is opposed by a confederacy of twelve kings whom he defeats; releases and again imprisons the Ganga king imprisoned by his father, id. 198, 302, 303 note 1, 395; gives the province of Láta to his brother Indraraja, id. 309, 400; levies tribute from the king of Kanchi, id. 198, 331, 395; his *birudas*, epithets, and titles, id. 199, 394; his contemporaries and conquests, id. 198, 395; takes steps to remove the capital to Málkhed and orders the king of Vengi to construct an outer wall to the city, id. 396, 402, 403, 410 note 2; extent of his dominions, id. 199, 396; records of his time, id. 397-401; religious activity of his time, Buddhism and Jainism, id. 406-408;—*another account of:* holds Gujarat as prince regent, completes the conquest of the north and marches to the south; hands the Gujarát kingdom to his brother Indra (827-833), I, pt. i, 123, 466, 468, 528; his grants at Márkinda in Násik district, XVI, 185, 457. See also XIV, 148; XVII, 352.

Govinda IV: Ráshtrakúta king, succeeds his brother Amoghavarsha II, is suspected to have compassed his brother's death, of licentious habits and hence succumbs to an untimely death, I, pt. ii, 204-205, 416-417; genealogy, id. 210; his insignia, id. 338 note 7; his *birudas*, titles and epithets, id. 205, 387, 416; his war with the Eastern Chálukyas, id. 205, 417; records of his time, id. 204-205, 417-418.

Govindámbá: Chedi princess, wife of Jagattunga II, I, pt. ii, 204 and note 2, 296, 414 and note 5, 418.

Govindarája: Yádava king of Seunadesa, I, pt. ii, 235, 236, 516.

Govindarája: Maurya chief (1069), I, pt. ii, 284, 515; Ráshtrakúta prince of a branch collateral to the Málkhed family, id. 386.

Govindarája: *Prabhutavarsha*, Gujarát Ráshtrakúta prince, son of Indrarája the brother of Govinda III, id. 310, 392, 393, 400, 401, 404, 408, 409. See Govinda, Gujarát King.

Govindarája: Gujarát Ráshtrakúta prince, brother of the younger Dhruvarája, id. 409. See Govinda II.

Govindarasa: feudatory of Vikramáditya VI, I, pt. ii, 428 note 4, 451, 580, 581.

Govindaráya: Chálukya prince, I, pt. ii, 467.

Govindás: a fanatic, his rising (1826), III, 120.

Govindavádi: location of, in Mysore, I, pt. ii, 496 and note 4; given to Gangarája by Vishnuvardhána, id. 500.

Govindavarman: Pallava king, I, pt. ii, 325.

Govindavva: Kánarese form of Govindámbá, I, pt. ii, 414 note 5.

Govind Hari Patvardhan: founder of the Patvardhan family, distinguishes himself at the siege of Savanur, I, pt. ii, 657.

Govindrája: brother of Dhruva II (867), I, pt. i, 127.

Govindráv: Pratápsinh's minister, XIX, 309-310.

Govindráv: Gáikwár, son of Dámáji by his first wife; sides with Raghunáthráo and is taken prisoner with him at Dhodap (1768), promises increased tribute and heavy fine for his conduct and is invested with his father's title and estates, I, pt. i, 399-400; grant made in his favour is cancelled (1771); is reinstated by Raghunáthráo (1773), id. 401; invests Baroda (1775), id. 401; leads Rághobá's army, id. 403; secures the favour of Mahádji Sindia and applies to him for restoration, id. 410; takes up the office of regent at Baroda (1793), id. 411; forces Aba Shelukar to surrender Ahmadábád and keeps him in confinement

(1797), *id.* 411; his death[1] (1799), *id.* 412. *See* also VII, 179, 188, 191-194, 195, 197-198, 384, 386-387.
Govindráv: son of Fatesing Gáikwár, his rebellion in Baroda (1829), VII, 243-244.
Govindráv Banduji Gáikwár: his intrigues in Poona (1814-1816), VII, 219, 225.
Govindráv Patvardhan: received (1761) Miraj, XXI, 381. *See* Govind Hari Patvardhan.
Govindráv Rode: Baroda minister (1860-1867), VII, 272, 276.
Govirle: pass in Kolába district, XI, 115.
Gowar: fodder-plant, XXV, 277.
Gowli: fibrous plant, found in Sálsette and on the *gháts*, XXV, 230.
Graal: story of the, its resemblance to Buddha's bowl, XIV, 404, 403.
Grabs: A'ngria's vessels, XI, 147.
Graculidæ: family of birds in Ratnágiri, X, 99.
Graculinæ: order of birds in Ratnágiri, X, 99.
Graham: monument at Khandála of, XVIII, pt. iii, 236 and note 2.
Grahan: *see* Eclipse.
Grahari, Graharipu: king of the Chudásamás I, pt. i, 137; Mlechcha ruler of Sorath, wars with Mularája and is made prisoner, *id.* 160, 164; Abhir of Junágadh, IX, pt. i, 497; *see* also I, pt. i, 139.
Grahas: *see* Planets.
Grahashánti: planet-soothing ceremony, details of, IX, pt. i, 42-43.
Grahasth: laymen, Bráhman section according to calling, IX, pt. i, p. 2 and note 2.
Grain: worship at harvest time, on no-moon day of Shrávan month, in Bhádarva, IX, pt. i, 389; on Dasara festival, on Makar-Sankránt, on first day of Kártik, on Rishi Panchem, *id.* 390; objects and form of worship of adad, barley, gram, maize, Indian millet, rice, sesame, wheat, *id.* 391; worshipped as goddess, worship of seedlings, *id.* 392.
Grain advances: in Ahmadábád district, IV, 70; in Násik district, XVI, 119; in Ahmadnagar district, XVII, 301-302.
Grain stores: in Ahmadnagar district, XVII, 259.
Grallatores: family of birds in Ratnágiri, X, 89-96.
Gram: grain, sacred to Venus, used in offerings, IX, pt. i, 391; cultivation of, in Khándesh, XII, 151; in Násik district, XVI, 110; in Poona district, XVIII, pt. ii, 42; in Sátára district, XIX, 163.
Gramineæ: a species of food, famine, oil-yielding, fibrous and poisonous plants, XXV, 184, 208, 225, 237, 270.
Grand Inquisitor: at Goa, authority of the, I, pt. ii, 58.
Granite: rock in Kánara district, XV, pt. i, 10; in Bijápur district, XXIII, 17-19; pillars and slabs, *id.* 54.
Granitoid Gneiss: in Belgaum district, XXI, 15.
Grant, Captain: account of his confinement by the Káthis under Báva Vála (1820), VIII, 124 note 1; *see* also IX, pt. i, 254-255.
Grant Duff: Captain, historian of the Maráthás, Introduction to the History of the Konkan, I, pt. ii, p. ix, 98; British agent with the young rája of Sátára (1818), *id.* 612; resident at Sátára (1824), XIX, 305, 308.
Grapes, Grape Vine: rearing of, in Khándesh, XII, 177; in Poona district, XVIII, pt. ii, 62-63.
Grás: *see* Giras.
Grásia Schools: in Káthiáwár, VIII, 349.
Grasses: in Belgaum district, XXI, 64; in Dhárwár district, XXII, 36.
Grass oil: manufacture of, in Panch Mahále, III, 250; in Khándesh, XII, 277.
Grave-yards: in Poona, XVIII, pt. iii, 364-366.
Gray, Captain H.: appointed governor of Bombay, XXVI, pt. i, 24; his dispute with the President at Surat regarding navigating passes, *id.* 24-29; hands over Bombay to the Company, *id.* 31.
Great Western Hotel, Bombay: formerly Hornby House built by Governor Hornby (1771), was Admiralty House (1786-1800), was Recorder's Court (1800-1824), was occupied by the Supreme Court (1824-1862), by the High Court till 1879, XXVI, pt. iii, 656-659.
Grebondel: Martin Alfonso's town or seat, near Thána, I, pt. ii, 64.
Greek Baktrian monarchs: in Káthiáwár, VIII, 272, 277.
Greeks: their probable settlements on Thána coast (B. C. 250-A. D. 250), XIII, 403; reasons for such a supposition, *id.* 407 note 1; Ptolemy's information about India derived from, *id.* 414; their trade with Chaul (A. D. 150), *id.* 415; their ships on Thána coast, *id.* 417, 418; at Barygaza, I, pt. i, 546; settled in India (A. D. 150), XI, 37 and note 8; IX, pt. i, 456; *see* Yavans.
Green Island: in Bombay harbour, XIV, 362.
Greens: in Khándesh, XII, 173.
Greenshanks: class of birds in Ratnágiri, X, 93.
Grenadier: company of, raised in Bombay (1759), XXVI, pt. iii, 135.
Grewia: *Asiatica, microcos, polygama,* fibrous plants, XXV, 230; *tiliæ folia,* fodder-plant, *id.* 277.
Grihas: solitary cells in Kánheri caves, I, pt. ii, 10.
Grihasthas: Buddhist ordinary householders, I, pt. ii, 173.
Grimes: Colonel, stationed at Ahmadábád (1857), I, pt. i, 440.
Grislea tomentosa: dye-plant common in the *gháts*, XXV, 245.
Grose, Mr. (1750): English traveller, origin of A'ngria according to, XI, 145 and note 5; the personal appearance of Kánhoji Angria according to, *id.* 149; his description of the Maráthas and of Bombay, XIII, 496-497 and 497 note 1; his mention of Elephanta caves, XIV, 86; his story of the queen of Attiga, *id.* 215 note 1; on Bombay houses and water-supply (1750), XXVI, pt. ii, 444; on Bombay Government, XXVI, pt. iii, 370; on Bombay crops, *id.* 507; on the improved health of Bombay (1750), *id.* 553-554.

Guabres : people of Fárs, IX, pt. ii, 188 note 3; Pársis so called (1660), *id.* 191, 192 note 1. *See* Gabres.
Guarantee System : in Baroda ; *see* Báhedari.
Guard-binding : or guarding, also called Rákhadi, corresponding with Vishnubali, Vedic rite, takes place in fifth month of first pregnancy, IX, pt. i, 31 ; rites and observances of, *id.* 31-32.
Guava : tree, in Poona district, XVIII, pt. i, 50 ; in Násik district, XVI, 103.
Guazuma tomentosa : famine and fibrous plant, common in Bombay, XXV, 195, 229.
Gudalgi : place of interest in Belgaum district, XXI, 565.
Gudehalli : hill and peak in Kánara district, XV, pt. i, 2, 4, 5 ; health resort, *id.* pt. ii, 302, 303.
Gudgeri : town in Kolhápur state, XXIV, 383.
Gudguddápur : village in Dhárwár district, temple, fair, and municipality at, XXII, 720-722.
Gudgudi : village in Dhárwár district, temple and inscriptions at, XXII, 722.
Gudigár : caste of wood-carvers, in Kánara district, XV, pt. i, 265, 266.
Gudigere : Vijayáditya's inscription at, I, pt. ii, 371.
Gudikatti : inscription at, I, pt. ii, 436 note 1, 439 note 1, 567.
Gudipádva : Hindu holiday, XVIII, pt. i, 242.
Gudur : village in Bijápur district, temple at, XXIII, 649.
Gugal : gum-yielding plant, XXV, 250.
Gugga : *see* Goggi.
Gugli : Bráhman sub-division in Cutch, V, 47 ; in Káthiáwár, VIII, 146 ; origin, are funeral priests, IX, pt. i, 439 note 5 ; found in Dwárka, origin of name, *id.* 9-10.
Gugul : gum ceremony among the Lingáyats, XXIV, 129-130 and note.
Guha : *see* Guhasena.
Guhágar : a large village in Ratnágiri district, X, 336 ; Bájiráv II's palace at, I, pt. ii, 114.
Guhala : Siláhára, I, pt. ii, 403 note 3, 545. *See* Guvala I.
Guhalla : Goa Kádamba, I, pt. ii, 565, 567. *See* Guvala.
Guhasena : Valabhi king (A. D. 559-567), I, pt. i, 85 ; follower of Buddha, *id.* 83.
Guild : trading, at Sopára (A. D. 300), XIII, 406 ; mentioned in Yajnavalkya's code (B. C. 300), *id.* 406 note 3 ; *see* also XIV, 321 ; of crafts in Káthiáwár, VIII, 265-266 ; influence and power of, in Gujarát, IX, pt. i, 95.
Guillandina bonducella : oil-yielding plant, XXV, 217.
Guinea worm : disease, its cure, IX, pt. i, 365 ; in Khándesh, XII, 337.
Guizotia : *Abyssinica*, *oleifera*, oil-yielding plants, XXV, 219.
Gujar or Gurjjara : a tribe, I, pt. i, 2-3, 58 ; central Asian tribe that entered India during first 500 years after Christ ; different meanings and derivations of the name, IX, pt. i, 469 and note 1 ; identification of the tribe, suggested to be Skythian or Turk, *id.* 469 and notes 2 and 3 ; of Georgian origin, *id.* 469 and notes 4 to 6, 470 note 1 ; Ghazz, *id.* 470 and note 2 ; Kushána or Gushána, *id.* 470 and notes 3 to 6 ; Kedáras, *id.* 471 and note 2 ; Jue-Jue or Juán-Juán, *id.* 471 ; proved to be Khazárs and therefore same as White Húnas and Mihiras of fifth century Horde, *id.* 434, 471-477, 492 ; formed part of Great Horde of which Juán-Juán or White Húnas were leading elements, *id.* 455, 471 ; history ; traces beyond India, *id.* 477-478 ; in India, probable date of arrival ; Western Indian Gurjjaras in power (A. D. 400), *id.* 470 note 6 ; no reference to Gurjjaras in India until after close of Kushan power (A. D. 400), *id.* 470 ; their arrival during last quarter of fifth or first quarter of sixth century (A. D. 470-520), *id.* 471 ; Gurjjaras probably entered India about middle of fifth century, *id.* 455, 479 ; settlements and rule, Valabhi dynasty (A. D. 490 or A. D. 525) believed to be Gurjjaras, earliest known mention under name Gurjjara (A. D. 590-606) ; head-quarters in South Márwár, Bhinmál their capital, powers during 8th and 9th century, *id.* 479 ; settlement in the Punjáb (A. D. 890), wide-spread power all over Rájpútána (A. D. 1030), *id.* 480 ; settlements made by rulers of sub-tribe or stock-name of Chapa at Somnáth, Wadhván and Anahilaváda the capital of Bombay-Gujarát, *id.* 479 ; at Broach (A.D. 675-700), *id.* p. xii, 479-480 ; decline of power at Bhinmál (A. D. 950) ; movements and fresh settlements in South Márwár and in North-East Khándesh ; capital passed from Bhinmál to Anahilaváda (A. D. 961), *id.* 480 ; strength of Gujar population, *id.* 480 ; distribution of Gujar population of North-West India ; classes of : (*a*) classes known as Gujars, their head-quarters in the Punjáb, strength, spread, *id.* 481 ; limit of their country, *id.* 482 ; (*b*) special classes of Gujars—Bad or Bir Gujars, *id.* 482 ; the Bhatis of West Márwár, *id.* 483 ; (*c*) classes admitted to be of Gujar stock—Agnikulas, Chohán, *id.* 483-484 ; Parihár, *id.* 484 ; Parmárs, *id.* 485 ; Solanki, *id.* 485-487, 496 ; Bhagarávats, Chandelás, *id.* 487 ; Chárans, *id.* 488 ; Chápas or Chávdás, *id.* 488-489 ; Chechi, *id.* 489-490 ; Jhálás, Kalheniás, Khadwa or Khária, *id.* 490 ; Kors, Kusane, *id.* 491 ; Lavas or Lors, *id.* 491-492 ; Mers, *id.* 492-494 ; Nágaris, Nekadis, Rájpúts, *id.* 494 ; Rinds, *id.* 495 ; Sisodiás, *id.* 495-496 ; (*d*) Lost Gujars, Gujarát Kanbis, *id.* 496 ; Márwár Osváls, *id.* 496-497 ; Ratnágiri Karhádes, *id.* 496, 497-498 ; other minor classes, Ahirs, Bhils, Tanks, *id.* 497 ; results, effect of Gujar layer that overspread the population of Gujarát and Káthiáwár between fifth and thirteenth centuries : *among early and wandering tribes :* Ahirs, Bharváds, Bhils, Chárans, Kolis and Rabáris ; *builders,* Sompura ; *cultivators,* Kadva and Leva Kanbis ; *sailors,* Chávdás, Gohils and Meds ; *traders,* Osváls and Shrimális, *id.* 499 ; Nágar, *id.* 501 ; *Bráhmans,* Bhátela, Bhojak, Dákot, Gujar, Karháde, Mer, Nágar, Pushkar, Shevak, *id.* 500-501 ; have given their

name to the province; formed Gujar subdivisions in most Gujarát castes, IX, pt. i, p. xii and note 3; Gujjars as a god, instances remain in great Mihirakula, Culuk, Solanki, guardian Bhaváni, *id.* 501; Gujar girl Gáyatri, Devji of Bednor in Márwár, Jain, Tirthankars and Siddhas, *id.* 502 and note 4; caste of traders in Ratnágiri district, X, 120, 171; cultivators in Khándesh, XII, 62-68; money-lenders in Sholápur, XX, 242; Rájpút clans in Cutch, V, 67.

Gujarát: boundaries and extent, I, pt. i, 1; the name, *id.* 2-5; Ráshtrakútas in, *id.* 119-134; invaded by Alaf Khán, *id.* 205 note 2; under the Mughals (A. D. 1573-1760), *id.* 221-225; under the rule of Aurangzib (1644-1647), *id.* 280; Shiváji's inroads in (1664-1670), *id.* 284, 386; predatory inroads of the Maráthás, their growth, their power, and their supremacy in, *id.* 385; expeditions of Khanderáo Dábháde in (1700-1711), *id.* 388; administration of, left entirely in the hands of the Gáikwár family after the treaty of Sálbái, *id.* 410, 411; under the management of Aba Shelukar (1796-1797), *id.* 411; farmed to Gáikwár by the Peshwa (1799), *id.* 411; renewal of the farm of, to Bhagwantráo Gáikwár for ten years (1804), *id.* 415; appointment of Trimbakji Dengle as *sar-subha* of Ahmadábád, *id.* 427; Peshwá's rights passed to the British (1819), *id.* 385; disturbances (1857-1859), *id.* 433-448; disarming (1857), *id.* 444; gateway, *id.* 452, 459; Bráhmans, 463; Hindu enterprise by sea to Jáva, *id.* 492 note 3; conquest and settlement of Jáva and Cambodia (603), *id.* 496; earliest Arab references to, *id.* 505, 508, 511; conquest of (1300), *id.* 512, 514, 515, 517, 526, 529; religion in, *id.* 530; people of, *id.* 531, 532. *See* Juzr. *Another account of:* North, held by Valabhi kings (605-766), I, pt. ii, 336; Western Chálukya branch established in South (671), *id.* 186-187; Ráshtrakúta branch in, *id.* 392; Govinda III establishes another branch of the Ráshtrakútas in, *id.* 310, 400; Marasimha Ganga leads an expedition into, at the orders of Krishna III, *id.* 306; Tailapa II, and Vikramáditya II's expeditions into, *id.* 212 and 219; establishment of the overlordship of, in the Konkan (1151), *id.* 24; Singhana's invasion of (1231), *id.* 240-242, 525; king of, subdued by Mahádeva, the Yádava king, *id.* 246; inclusion of Cambay, Somnáth, and Konkan Thána in (1310), *id.* 25; the coast belonging to the kingdom of, falls to the Portuguese, *id.* 38; district in the Panjáb, *id.* 313 note 3;—*another account of:* limits, IX, pt. i, 7; population, details, *id.* 7, 8; divisions, North and South, *id.* 8-9; aborigines, *id.* 10; Aryans, *id.* 10-11; foreigners, *id.* 12; darkening and revival, *id.* 433; arrival of foreigners in, IX, pt. ii, 1-3; arrival of missionaries and learned men in, *id.* 3 and note 3, 6 note 1, 26, 38, 40; arrival and settlement in, of foreign Musalmán families, *id.* 3 note 1; of chief *sayad* families, *id.* 6 note 1; of the Mirzás, *id.* 10; of Memons, *id.* 51; conquest of, by Alikhán (1297), *id.* 2; by Záfarkhán (1371), *id.* 3 note 3; by Humáyun (1535), *id.* 9; by Akbar (1573-74), *id.* 12; decadence of the sultánate of (1554-1561), *id.* 17; immigration from, into Thána district, XIII, 60; trade with, *id.* 414, 429, 444, 465, 519 and note 1.

Gujarát or Gujaráthi Bráhmans: in Kolába district and Janjira state, XI, 44, 411; in Thána district, XIII, 78; in Násik district, XVI, 43; in Ahmadnagar district, XVII, 55-57; in Poona district, XVIII, pt. i, 163-166; in Sátára district, XIX, 53; in Sholápur district, XX, 30-31; in Belgaum district, XXI, 90; in Kolhápur state, XXIV, 61-62.

Gujaráti: modern mother tongue of the Pársis, IX, pt. ii, 203, 209; language, IX, pt. i, 14-15; development of, *id.* 486; trade language at Cheul (915), XI, 272 and note 1.

Gujarát Irregular Horse: raised (1839), VII, 249-250, 305-306.

Gujarátis: expel the Mughal governors of Humáyun from their charges (1536), IX, pt. ii, 10; in Acheen, Banda and Java (1599-1601), II, 80.

Gujarát Jain: a caste of traders in Ahmadnagar district, XVII, 65-67.

Gujarát Kings: in Kolába district and Janjira state, XI, 142, 435.

Gujarát Rajpúts: in Cutch, V, 67-69.

Gujarát Váni: caste of traders in Janjira state, XI, 411; in Thána district, XIII, 112; in Kánara district, XV, pt. i, 188, 189; in Ahmadnagar district, XVII, 67-69; in Poona district, XVIII, pt. i, 273-277; money-lenders, XVIII, pt. ii, 98-99; in Sátára district, XIX, 57-58; in Sholápur district, XX, 51-52; in Belgaum district, XXI, 101; in Bijápur district, XXIII, 105-106; in Kolhápur state, XXIV, 86.

Gujari: milk-selling people, IX, pt. i, 482; weekly market, *id.* 499.

Gujaru: name of cattle-owning people, IX, pt. i, 481.

Gujjar: Meshri Vánias, seem to be Gujjaras or Gujars, originally Rájpúts, IX, pt. i, 71, 499 and note 3.

Gujjiga: I, pt. ii, 380. *See* Gojjiga.

Guláb: rose, yields oil, XXV, 222.

Gul-abbass, gul-bhaji: famine and flowering plant, XXV, 203.

Gulancha, gulvel: medicinal plant found in Konkan, XXV, 261.

Gulbarga: town in Nizám's dominions; Tagara identified with, I, pt. ii, 538 note 8; capital of one of the four governments of the Bahámani kingdom, *id.* 30, 580; annexed to the Bijápur dominions (1504), *id.* 582.

Guledgudd: hill and town in Bijápur district, XXII, 6, 649-650.

Gulf of Cambay: description, points, lighthouses, banks, tides, rivers, ports, silting, survey, VIII, 35-60; silting of, VI, 195 note 2, 214 notes 1 and 6.

Gulf of Cutch: position, direction, foreshore, depth of water, tides, wind and weather, south-west monsoon, north-east monsoon,

gales, passages, meteorological observations, light-houses, towns and ports, VIII, 12-34.
Guli-gaozaban : oil-yielding plant, XXV, 224.
Gul-jafri : flowering and dye-plant, XXV, 247.
Gul-kandar : fibrous plant, produces gum, found iu Konkan, XXV, 229, 250.
Gulla : *see* Mihirgulla.
Gullavelendavu : village granted to a Bráhman by Vinayáditya, I, pt. ii, 369.
Gulleau : Fryer's name for Kalyán, XIV, 362.
Gulls : class of birds in Ratnágiri, X, 98.
Gulsunde : village in Thána district, XIV, 104.
Gumástás : clerks in Vánia banker's office, IX, pt. i, 79-80.
Gumra : village, identified with Bagumra, I, pt. ii, 203.
Gumtara : fort in Thána district, XIV, 104, 373.
Guna : maker of Guna pass in Nánághát, story of, XIV, 287.
Gunabhadra : Jain author of *Uttara-Purána*, I, pt. ii, 200, 202 ; pupil of Jinasena, *id.* 407, 408, 411 ; *biruda* of Mahendravarman I, *id.* 328 ; Pallava king, *id.* 331.
Guuádhya : poet, minister of Satavábana, I, pt. ii, 170-171.
Gunaduttaranga Butuga : marries Abbalabbá, daughter of Amoghavarsha, I, pt. ii, 303 note 7, 402. *See* Butarasa.
Gunaka Vijayáditya III : Eastern Chálukya king (844-888), burns Málkhed, I, pt. ii, 384 note 4, 411-412.
Gunamati : Bodhisattva, author, I, pt. i, 79.
Gunaságara : Alupa ruler, I, pt. ii, 309.
Gunda : place of interest in Káthiáwár, VIII, 447 ; Kshatrapa inscription at, I, pt. i, 42.
Gunda Anivaritacharya : architect who built the temple of Lokeśvara-Virupaksha at Pattadakal, receives the fillet or badge of honour *mumeperjerepu-patta* and the name of Tribhuvanácharya from Vikramáditya II, I, pt. 376.
Gundert, Dr. : author of Malayálam dictionary, I, pt. ii, 282 note 5.
Gundiali : táluka in Káthiáwár, VIII, 448.
Gundi Koliak : place of interest in Káthiáwár, VIII, 448.
Gundilkatta : pass in Kánara district, XV, pt. ii, 39, 40, 303.
Gundiyáli : place of interest in Cutch, V, 222.
Gundur : in Dhárwár district, inscription at, I, pt. ii, 306, 307, 423.
Gundvále : site of an old town in Kánara district, XV, pt. ii, 44, 303.
Gunj : village in Thána district, XIV, 104.
Gunj : oil-yielding plant, XXV, 217.
Gunjála : hill in Ahmadnagar district, XVII, 5.
Gunpowder : use of, XXIII, 398 and note 3 ; manufacture of, in Khándesh, XII, 237.
Gunpowder Factory : Poona, buildings, powder varieties, ingredients, XVIII, pt. iii, 371-372, 465-476.
Gunpowder Mill : in Bombay island, built (1677), XXVI, pt. iii, 186 ; a new mill on Old Woman's Island (1734-1747), *id.* 186-187 ; powder house (1766), *id.* 189 ; reserve store of (1763), *id.* 190 ; powder-works removed to Mazgaon (1766-1769), *id.* 192-195.
Guns : old, on Násik forts, XVI, 443, 458 ; in Bijápur city, XXIII, 638-643 ; East India Company's trade in (1677), XXVI, pt. ii, 128.
Gunthli : place of interest in Cutch, V, 132, 133, 222.
Guntri : fort in Cutch seized by Sammas, I, pt. i, 139, 518.
Guntur : district in Madras, copper-plate grant from, I, pt. ii, 319, 384, 386.
Gunvantgad : Sahyádri spur and hill fort in Sátára district, XIX, 7, 10, 468.
Gunvanti : village in Kánara, temple at, XV, pt. ii, 99, 290 note 1.
Gupta, Guptas : Hindu dynasty, Early, in Málwa, their fall (A. D. 484), I, pt. ii, 312, 388 note 7 ; their rule in Gujarát (410-484), I, pt. i, 60-73 ; their connection with Káthiáwár, VIII, 273 ; epoch of their era, I, pt. i, 29, 58, 67, 81, 87, 110 ; I, pt ii, 13, 293 note 7, 360 note 1 ; note on, *id.* 258-265 ; their inscriptions, *id.* 279, 280 ; at Nánághát, XIV, 289 ; records, I, pt. ii, 359 note 1 ; race and lineage, *id.* 580, 581 ;— Later, their rule in Magadha (Behár), I, pt. i, 73, 77 ; supposed to have ruled Kuntala, I, pt. i, 284 note 2.
Guptanvaya Bhukánta : Gupta title, I, pt. ii, 580, 581.
Guptavamsa Trinetra : Gupta title, I, pt. ii, 580, 581.
Guptigupta : village saints of, I, pt. ii, 400.
Gur, Guru : class of spiritual teachers among Havig and Karnátak Bráhmans, XV, pt. i, 121, 131 ; among Shenvis, *id.* 147-149 ; among Banjigs, *id.* 177 ; among Rájpúts, *id.* 194 ; among Torke Nádors, *id.* 225 ; in Belgaum district, XXI, 118 ; in Dhárwár district, XXII, 108.
Gurat : fodder plant, XXV, 276.
Gurav : a caste of temple ministrants in Ratnágiri district, their sub-divisions and condition, X, 119, 126, 140, 141, 222 ; in Kolába district and Janjira state, XI, 67, 412 ; in Khándesh, XII, 76 ; in Thána district, XIII, 142 ; in Kánara district, XV, pt. i, 199, 200 ; in Násik district, XVI, 54 ; in Poona district, XVIII, pt. i, 378-379 ; in Sátára district, XIX, 98-101 ; husbandmen, in Belgaum district, XXI, 106, 107 ; in Bijápur district, XXIII, 265-267 ; Lingáyat priests, in Kolhápur state, XXIV, 101 ; in Sholápur district, XX, 145.
Gurav Pimpri : village in Ahmadnagar district, temple at, XVII, 717.
Gurgi : Indian millet variety, XII, 149.
Gurjar : a caste of traders in Násik district, XVI, 46 ; in Dhárwár district, XXII, 116.
Gurjar Mandala : Kumárápala called Lord of, IX, pt. i, 470 note 5.
Gurjaras, Gurjjara : I, pt. ii, 312-316, their lineage and pedigree, *id.* 312-313 ; establish themselves by ejecting the Nágas, *id.* 313 ; probably of the Chápa race and their kingdom, an off-shoot of the Punjáb Gurjara kingdom, *id.* 313 note 3 ; extent of their territory and the subordinate position of their princes ; their territory becomes a buffer state between the kingdoms of Valabhi and Bádámi, *id.*

315; conquered by Pulikeśin II, *id.* 183, 282, 350, 359; help the Valabhi king against Harshavardhana (about 648); wage war with the king of Valabhi (706-736), *id.* 316; destroyed by the Tájikas and their territory annexed to Láta by the Chálukya prince Avanijanásraya Pulikeśin (about 736), *id.* 187, 311, 316, 375 and note 3 (of Bhinmál, *see* page 117, pt. i); fled before Govinda III, *id.* 198, 396; their leader put to flight by Indraràja, *id.* 400; put to flight by Dhruvarája, *id.* 409 and note 1; frightened by Krishna II, *id.* 201; followers of the Chálukya king Mulrája, defeated by Krishna III, *id.* 420; conquered by Kakka II, *id.* 423; terrified by Hoysála Vira-Ballála, *id.* 333; repulsed by Singhana, *id.* 517; defeated by Bhillama, *id.* 520; subdued by Singhana, *id.* 524, 525; defeated by Krishna, *id.* 527. *Another account of*: kingdoms, I, pt. i, 3-4; foreign tribe, Valabhis believed to be Gurjjaras, *id.* 97; defeated by Arabs, *id.* 109; establish themselves at Nándod (580-808), *id.* 113; territory, *id.* 113; copper-plate grants, *id.* 113-114; family tree, *id.* 114; give up sun-worship and their name for Saivism and Puránic pedigree, *id.* 116; march against Dhruva II, *id.* 127; Chávdás said to belong to them, *id.* 127 note 2, 458, 463; origin of, *id.* 464; of Broach, *id.* 465, 466; their appearance in India and earliest notice, *id.* 467, 468; migration of, *id.* 469; are defeated by Prabhákaravardhana (600-606), *id.* 490; retain Broach, Valabhi and Bhinmál, *id.* 490; their relation with Mihiras or Meds, *id.* 490, 526. *See* Juzr.

Gurjjararáta: province of Gujarát, name derived from Valabhi kings, I, pt. i, 85.

Gurjjaras: fire-worshipping, IX, pt. ii, 183 note 4. *See* Mihiras.

Gurkhá: military tribe, IX, pt. i, 452.

Guroh: company of Muharram dirge singers, IX, pt. ii, 138 note 1 continued on page 139.

Guru: *see* Jupiter.

Guru-Govind: caste-levelling Sikh hero (A. D. 1680), IX, pt. i, 437 note 7.

Gurungs: military tribe, IX, pt. i, 452.

Guruvár: Thursday, IX, pt. i, 402.

Gurva: *see* Gurav.

Gurvad: hill in Sholápur district, XX, 2, 3.

Gurz: iron spike used by Rafái beggars, IX, pt. ii 23.

Gushtasp: king, IX, pt. ii, 183 note 4; Zoroaster proclaims his religion in the court of, *id.* 219; his conversion to the Zoroastrian faith, *id.* 211 note 2 (11).

Gutiwail: food-plant, found in Konkan and Dakhan, XXV, 179.

Gutta I: Gutta prince, son of Mágutta, I, pt. ii, 579.

Gutta II: Gutta prince, son of Vira Vikramáditya I, I, pt. ii, 579, 582, 583.

Gutta III: Gutta prince, son of Vikramáditya III; feudatory of the Yádava king Mahádeva, I, pt. ii, 528, 579, 583, 584.

Guttal: town, in Dhárwár district, temples, reservoir and inscriptions at, XXII, 722; capital of the Guttas, record at, I, pt. ii, 578.

Guttas: of Guttal, I, pt. ii, 578-584, 428 note 4, 498; claim descent from the early Gupta kings, *id.* 580, 581; their pedigree, *id.* 579; their crest and banner, *id.* 299 note 4, 578; their family god, *id.* 578; feudatories, *id.* 428 note 4; Chálukya feudatories, *id.* 466; Kalachurya feudatories, *id.* 487, 488, 489; either Yádava or Hoysála feudatories, *id.* 520-521; humbled by Bichana, the general of Singhana, *id.* 243; Singhana's feudatories, *id.* 524; their records, *id.* 578, 579, 580.

Guttavolal: I, pt. ii, 466; capital of the Guttas, *id.* 520, 524, 528, 578, 582, 583. *See* Guttal.

Gutti: capital of the Pandyas, I, pt. ii, 519, 524.

Gutti: dye-plant, XXV, 242.

Guttiferæ: a species of plants yielding concrete oils and a dye, XXV, 213, 214, 241.

Guttolal: Guttavolal, I, pt. ii, 578.

Guvaka: first Chohán king, the reign of, I, pt. i, 158 note 1.

Guvala: Goa Kádamba prince and feudatory of Vikramáditya VI, I, pt. ii, 451, 568.

Guvala I: Kolhápur or Karád Siláhára prince, succeeds his brother Gomka, I, pt. ii, 254, 257, 545, 547.

Guvala II: Kolhápur or Karád Siláhára prince, succeeds his father Márasinha, I, pt. ii, 254, 257, 545.

Guzar: name among commanders of native craft from Makran coast, IX, pt. i, 482 note 6.

Gwálior: treaty of (1844), XII, 260.

Gymkhana: Poona, XVIII, pt. iii, 372.

Gymnasium: military, in Poona cantonment, XVIII, pt. iii, 373.

Gymnastics: among Gujarát Musalmáns, IX, pt. ii, 172.

Gymnema sylvestre: vegetable antidote to snake-bites, XXV, 275.

Gypsies: European, names and origin; history, distribution and language; perhaps partly descended from the Sanghárs or Sanganians, the famous Gujarát pirates (A. D. 600-1300), XIII, 713-715.

Gypsum: in Cutch, V, 21.

H

HABA: hill in Cutch, V, 79, 135, 165, 166.

Habashis: Abyssinians (Negroes) in Gujarát troops (1572), IX, pt. ii, 3 note 1, 11. *See* Sidis.

Habbu: a caste of husbandmen in Kánara district, XV, pt. i, 136, 245-248.

Habib Ulla: divine, goes to Bijápur (1460), XXIII, 582.

Habsán: *see* Janjira.

Habshi: Abyssinian ruler of Janjira, his jurisdiction, I, pt. ii, 38. *See* Sidi.

Hadád: lake in Mahi Kántha, V, 358.

Hadal: female spirit, XVIII, pt. i, 553, 554.

Hadálaka: village in Káthiáwár, I, pt. i, 202.

Hadapsar: village in Poona district, I, pt. ii, 608.

Haddala: village on the road from Dholka to Dhandhuka, copper-plate found at, I, pt. i, 138; I, pt. ii, 343 note 5.

Hádia: a tenure in Baroda state, VII, 352.
Hadinád: district ruled over by Armativala, I, pt. ii, 505.
Hadmatia: táluka in Káthiáwár, VIII, 448.
Hadokht: portion of the original *Zend Avesta*, IX, pt. ii, 212 note 1; 220.
Hadol: state in Mahi Kántha, V, 425.
Hadramaut: southern province of Arabia, the Biblical Hazarmaveth; Arabs come from, IX, pt. ii, 15 note 4.
Hadrami: Arab inhabitant of Hadramaut, his character, IX, pt. ii, 15 note 4.
Hadsar: fortified hill in Poona district, XVIII, pt. i, 4; history of, XVIII, pt. iii, 131.
Hadu Karanda: food-plant common in the presidency, XXV, 179.
Hádvalli: old town in Kánara district, XV, pt. ii, 303.
Hadya: present given to child's teacher, IX, pt. ii, 162.
Hæmatite: beds, stone and schists, in Bijápur district, XXIII, 18, 54.
Hæmatopodidæ: a species of birds in Ratnágiri, X, 91.
Háfiz = protector: title; ability to recite the *Kurán* by heart is the chief qualification for obtaining; other qualifications; consideration shown to, IX, pt. ii, 134.
Hafta-Amsháspands: *see* Amsháspands.
Hagaratage, Hagarattage, Hagaritige: place in the Nizám's dominion, record at, I, pt. ii, 523; old province managed by Parisaśetti, *id.* 522, 524, 528, 556.
Haibatráo Nimbálkar: an officer of Sháhu, defeats Chandrasen Jádhava, I, pt. ii, 598; his march on Sátára (1714), XVIII, pt. ii, 242; *see* also XIX, 256, 258.
Haidarábád: town, in Sind, I, pt. i, 511, 517, 538, 546.
Haidarábád: in the Nizám's dominions, grant of Pulikeśin II (612) at, I, pt. ii, 17, 337 note 2, 344, 351 and note 4, 356, 538 note 8; grant of Vikramáditya I at, *id.* 328 note 3, 329 note 5, 352, 361, 364; enriched by the eastern trade, *id.* 17.
Haidar A'li: his rise similar to the Peshwa; expels the Peshwa's troops from the districts pledged to the Peshwa (1759); gets Basálat Khán to invest him with the title of Nawáb of Sira, a district in the possession of the Maráthás (1761); defeats the Nawáb of Savánur, an ally of the Maráthás (1764); is defeated by the Peshwa Mahádev Ráo and pursued across the Tungabhadra by Raghunáth Ráo; makes the treaty of Bednur and relinquishes claims on Savánur; buys off the Peshwa's attack on Mysore (1767); avails himself of the opportunity afforded by the question of disputed succession to the Peshwa's throne and regains the territory south of the Tungabhadra; agrees to support Raghunáth Ráo, and is invited by him to take possession of the Southern Marátha Country (1776); strengthens his hold on the newly conquered country by a marriage alliance with the Nawáb of Savánur (1779); his death (1782), I, pt. ii, 658-660; conquers Bednur (1763), XV, pt. ii, 54, 139; conquers the district of Kánara, *id.* 132; descent and origin of, *id.* 138 note 9; defeats Sonda chief; defeated by the Peshwa (1761-1767), *id.* 140; his civil administration in Kánara, *id.* 142; makes Honávar his port, *id.* 312; destroys Sonda (1764), *id.* 349; his alliance with Raghunathráo Peshwa, XXIV, 345; defeated by Mádhavráo Peshwa (1764, 1767), XVIII, pt. ii, 252; again attacked by the Peshwa (1770), *id.* 254; his possessions in Belgaum district, XXI, 382-385; overruns Dhárwár (1764); is driven back (1765); again master of Dhárwár (1776-1782), XXII, 411-414; master of South Bijápur, XXIII, 442; war with (1769), XXVI, pt. i, 359-360; his alliance with the Nizám and the Maráthás, VII, 197.
Haidar Khán: mosque of, in Bijápur city, XXIII, 632.
Haidar Kuli Khán: appointed *fauzdar* of Sorath and Gohilvád, VIII, 300; fiftieth viceroy of Gujarát; disorder in Ahmadábád (1721); his leniency to Bábis of Gujarát; frees the emperor from the tyranny of the Sayads (1721); is honoured with a title and the governorship of Gujarát (1721-22), I, pt. i, 302; subdues Kolis of Chunvál, shows signs of independence and is re-called (1722), *id.* 303.
Haig: General, antiquarian, I, pt. i, 538.
Haiga: *see* Havigo.
Haiga: snake-land, North Kánara coast, so called, XV, pt. ii, 76, 88.
Haigunda: village in Kánara district, remains of, sacrificial altars at, XV, pt. ii, 303.
Haihaya, Haihayas: a Kshatriya tribe, I, pt. i, 58; of Central India, their rise to power (about 249) and extent of their sway, I, pt. ii, 179; subdued by Vinayáditya and made steadfast allies of the Western Chálukya crown (692-695), *id.* 189, 225, 296, 368; their princesses marry a Western Chálukya king, an Eastern Chálukya king, Ráshtrakúta kings, and a Western Chálukya king of Kalyáni, *id.* 190, 201, 203, 296, 374, 410, 414 and note 4, 415; Kalachuryas of Kalyáni claim some connection with, *id.* 469. *See* Kalachuris of Central India.
Haimakhadda: Hema's pit, I, pt. i, 193.
Haiminámamála: string of names composed by Hemachandra, I, pt. i, 192.
Hair combs: manufacture of, in Panch Maháls, III, 250.
Hair-cutting: *see* Mudan.
Hair-parting: ceremony among Chitpávan Bráhmans, XVIII, pt. i, 146.
Haital: identified with Yethál, I, pt. i, 145.
Haive: *see* Hayve.
Haj: *see* Pilgrimage.
Hajám: a caste of barbers, IX, pt. i, 228; other names, *id.* 230 note 1; main divisions; surnames, *id.* 230; shaving and nail-paring their chief employment; appliances, *id.* 231, 232; as village torch-bearers, *id.* 231; as *dholis* or drum-beaters; as bleeders; women as midwives; social position; their priests; religion; saints, *id.* 233; customs, *id.* 233-234; in Káthiáwár, VIII, 156; in Thána district, XIII, 244; in Ahmadnagar district, XVII, 232; in Sátára district, XIX, 142-143;

in Dhárwár district, XXII, 246; in Bijápur district, XXIII, 302; *see* Valand.
Hajári: *Mátá*, goddess of Vághelás, is known by the name Ádyamáta, IX, pt. i, 137.
Háji: pilgrim to Makkah, IX, pt. ii, 56.
Háji Husain: tomb of, in Bijápur city, XXIII, 615.
Háji Kishwar Khán: Bijápur noble, murders Kámil Khán and succeeds him; gets Mustápha Khán assassinated; confines Chánd Bibi in the fort of Sátára; is compelled to fly through a confederacy of Abyssinian officers, I, pt. ii, 647.
Hajrat: lamp reflection test used in spirit possession, details of, IX, pt. i, 419.
Hajrat Ráje Bágh Savár: *see* Avliya.
Hajuri: caste, in Gujarát, IX, pt. i, 234.
Háka: cattle fair, at Bándra, XIV, 20.
Hákam: brother of Usmán, second Khalifáh, I, pt. i, 505; sends an expedition to Debal and Broach, *id.* 505, 506, 513.
Hakim: Musalmán physician, qualifications of, IX, pt. ii, 122 and note 1; in Bijápur district, XXIII, 292-293; entertained by Baroda Government, in old days, VII, 499-501.
Hákushri, Hakusiri, Hakusri: Shátakarni king, statue of, in Nánághát cave, XIV, 288 and note 2; XII, 239 note 3; I, pt. ii, 147; XVI, 590, 611, 614.
Hála: Andhrabhritya prince, confounded with Aristakarman of the *Vishnu Purána*, I, pt. ii, 164; same as Śáliváhana, *id.* 169; author of Saptasati, *id.* 171.
Halá: a branch of Samma Rájpúts in Cutch, V, 66.
Halad, Haldi: turmeric, cultivation of, in Khándesh, XII, 164, 171; food and dye-plant, XXV, 174, 249.
Halad-kanku, Kunku: turmeric and red powder; distribution or presents, IX, pt. i, 54; turmeric vermilion ceremony among Deshashtha Bráhmans, XXIV, 57-58.
Halakú Khán: Tartar, his massacre of the Ismáilia population of Persia, IX, pt. ii, 41.
Halálkhor: a caste of scavengers in Kánara district, XV, pt. i, 368, 369; in Poona district, XVIII, pt. i, 435-439, 505; in Sholápur district, XX, 171, 207; in Belgaum ditrict, XXI, 189, 190, 222, 223; in Dhárwár district, XXII, 246.
Halálkhor's Bridge: in Poona city, XVIII, pt. iii, 285.
Háláni Jadejás: descendants of Haloji of Mundra (1716), in Cutch, V, 137, 138.
Hálár: sub-division of Kathiáwár, VIII, 4-6; tributary to the Gáikwár (1786), VII, 317; attacked by Fate Muhammad, *id.* 324; *see* also I, pt. i, 208 and note 3.
Halasige: province governed by Barmadevarasa (1143), I, pt. ii, 458; seized by Vishnuvardhána, *id.* 497; province governed by Máyidevapandita (1226), *id.* 523; original territory of the Kádambas of Goa, *id.* 565. *See* Palasige.
Halavur, Hallavar: governed by a Pándya official named Iśvara of the Sinda family (1165), I, pt. ii, 476, 577, 486.
Haláyudha: author of an artificial poem "Kavirahasya," I, pt. ii, 208.
Haláyudha: Śiva's attendant, I, pt. ii, 482.
Halcyonidæ: species of birds in Ratnágiri, X, 64.
Haldarvas: place of interest in Mahi Kántha, V, 434.
Haldipur: town in Kánara district, XV, pt. ii, 148, 303.
Halebid: town in Mysore, I, pt. ii, 218; the Hoysála Yádavas of, *id.* 237; inscription at, *id.* 490 note 2, 491. *See* Dorasamudra.
Halekot: *see* Shiveshvar.
Hálemár: a caste of shoemakers in Násik district, XVI, 72.
Halenda: town in Káthiáwár, VIII, 449.
Halepáik: a caste of palm-tappers in Kánara district, XV, pt. i, 284-286; XV, pt. ii, 2, 149; in Dhárwár district, XXII, 134-135.
Half caste: Portuguese, origin of, I, pt. ii, 47.
Hali: caste of bondsmen, ploughmen to Anávalas, IX, pt. i, 5 and note 2, 6; among Kolis, *id.* 244; among Dublas, *id.* 317; in Surat district, II, 197-199.
Haliyál: town in Kánara district, history, Duke of Wellington's stay at, XV, pt. ii, 304; traveller's bungalow, schools, and dispensaries at, *id.* 147, 216, 219; deadly attack of fever at (1664), *id.* 218.
Haliyun: food-plant, XXV, 180.
Halkhurd: village in Thána district, cave at, XIV, 10, 105.
Hall: Captain, his mention of Bombay (1812), XIII, 515 note 2, 516 note 6, 517; his notice of Elephanta caves, XIV, 59 note 1, 92 note 1; Major, captures (1818) Ráygad, XI, 156.
Hallaharadat-koppa: Ráyadevarasa rules at (1199), I, pt. ii, 506.
Hallavur: *see* Halavur.
Hallegere: copper-plate grant at, I, pt. ii, 301 note 1, 302.
Halleija, Halleyaga: pious Lingáyat, blinded and put to death by Vijjana, I, pt. ii, 226, 479, 480.
Háller Vájantri: a caste of musicians in Kánara district, XV, pt. i, 317.
Halleyaga: *see* Halleija.
Hallian: *Eriodendrum anfructuosum*, dye and timber tree in Poona district, XVIII, pt. i, 46.
Hallur: Kánarese for 'village of the tooth,' I, pt. ii, 318 note 12; place of interest in Dhárwár district, XXII, 722.
Hallur: village in Bijápur district, temples and inscriptions at, XXIII, 650.
Hálol: petty division of the Panch Mahúls, III, 297-298; town, *id.* 316.
Hálria: táluka in Káthiáwár, VIII, 449.
Halsangi: place of interest in Bijápur district, XXIII, 651.
Halsi, Halasige: town in Belgaum district, XXI, 565; copper-plates found at, I, pt. ii, 285, 288, 565; inscription at, *id.* 570; XV, pt. ii, 78, 79. *See* Palásika.
Halva: early rice crop in Ratnágiri, X, 147.
Halvad: place of interest in Káthiáwár, VIII, 449.

Halvái: a caste of sweet-meat makers in Khándesh, XII, 62; in Thána district, XIII, 151; in Násik district, XVI, 60, 483; in Poona district, XVIII, pt. i, 338-339.
Halvakki Vakkal: a sub-caste of the Vakkals or husbandmen in Kánara district, XV, pt. i, 202-203.
Hamajor: a form of salutation, IX, pt. ii, 219.
Hamál Khán: grave in honour of, near Bhinmál, I, pt. i, 455.
Hamaspethmedem: sixth *Gahambár*, falling during the last five days of the year, IX, pt. ii, 218. *See* Gahambárs.
Hambal: Al, Sunni *imám* (780), IX, pt. ii, 125 note 2, 126.
Hambali: one of the four Sunni schools, IX, pt. ii, 16, 126 note 1.
Hambirráv: the title of Hasáji Mohite, Shiváji's commander, his march on Burhánpur, I, pt. i, 387.
Hamgi: village in Dhárwár district, XXII, 722.
Hamid Beg: appointed governor of Broach (1754), I, pt. i, 339.
Hamid Khádir: tomb of, in Bijápur city, XXIII, 615.
Hamid Khán: uncle of Nizám-ul-Mulk, deputy viceroy of Gujarát (1722), I, pt. i, 303; joins his forces with Kántáji Kadam, and defeats and kills Shujáat Khán near Ahmadábád; takes up his quarters at Sháhi Bágh and gets possession of all Ahmadábád except the city; attempt of Ibráhim Kuli, son of Shujáat Khán, to assassinate him, 304-305; defeated by Rustam Ali at Arás (1723), *id.* 305, 213; assigns one-fourth share of the territory north of the Mahi to Kántáji and a corresponding interest in the territory south of Mahi to Pilaji, *id.* 305; unites his forces with the Maráthas under Kántáji and Piláji and marches on Ahmadábad; defeat of, at Sojitra; second defeat, *id.* 307; *see* also VII, 169-171.
Hamid Khán: Bijápur general, kills Ain-ul-Mulk and takes Ismael, the king's brother, prisoner, I, pt. ii, 648-649.
Hamilton: author of 'New Account,' and traveller, IX, pt. ii, 192 note 4; his description of Cambay (1720); VI, 220; his description of Rájápur harbour and Málvan, X, 341, 351, 360; his notice of Kolába fort, XI, 263; mention of slave trade, *id.* 433 note 1; notice of the Sidi in Bombay, *id.* 442 and note 2; mention of Danda Rájpuri, *id.* 461 and note 9; Captain (1700-1720), his map of the Thána coast, XIII, 485; his notice of Bassein, XIV, 33; of Dahanu, *id.* 54; of Elephanta, *id.* 86, 92 note 1, 93; of Kánheri caves, *id.* 156; of Karanja, *id.* 193; of Thána, *id.* 359; his account of Kánara district, XV, pt. ii, 135; his notice of Anjidiv, Ankola, Bhatkal, Honávar, *id.* 256, 258, 274, 307, 311; of Kárwár, Mirján, and Shiveshvar fort, *id.* 324, 333, 342.
Hamirji: jám (1530) of Cutch, V, 135.
Hamjaman: probably Sanján, a Siláhára possession, I, pt. ii, 16; *see* also XIV, 302, 418.
Hámmá: daughter of the Western Chálukya king Jayasimha II and wife of the Yádava prince Bhillama III, I, pt. ii, 435, 514.
Hammám; bath-room, IX, pt. ii, 131.
Hammira: conquered by a boy general of Singhana, I, pt. ii, 240.
Hammiramahákávya: Sanskrit work, I, pt. i, 157, 159, 171, 182, 184.
Hammiras: Musalmáns, defeated by Singhana, I, pt. ii, 525.
Hammuka: king of Sind, invaded by Bhima I, I, pt. i, 163.
Hampe, Hampi: town, in Belláry district, I, pt. ii, 369, 431; site of the Pampá lake at, *id.* 142.
Hámph: place of interest in Rewa Kántha, VI, 112, 161.
Hamsa: river in Kánara district, XV, pt. ii, 265 and note 4.
Hamyaman: probably Sanjáu, XIII, 423, 425, 426, 428; I, pt. ii, 18, 542, 543.
Hanafi: one of the four Sunni schools, IX, pt. ii, 56, 126 note 1.
Hanam: breed of cattle in Poona district, XVIII, pt. i, 57.
Hanáwal: Janáwal, apparently Chunvál or Jháláwar, I, pt. i, 510, 513, 517.
Hanbar: a caste of husbandmen in Kánara district, XV, pt. i, 237-239; in Belgaum district, XXI, 107; in Bijápur district, XXIII, 106-109; in Kolhápur state, XXIV, 94.
Handarike: in Nizam's dominions, inscription at, I, pt. ii, 339 and note 6.
Hande Kurab: *see* Hande Vazir.
Hande Vazir or Hande Kurab: a caste of shepherds in Bijápur district, XXIII, 244.
Handeyava, *pl.* Handeyavaru: a caste of Lingáyat Kabligers in Bijápur district, XXIII, 244.
Hanga: river in Ahmadnagar district, XVII, 9.
Hángal: sub-division in Dhárwár district, its boundaries, area, aspect, climate, water, stock, crops and people, XXII, 632-634; survey of, *id.* 551-555; town, fort, temples, inscriptions and history of, *id.* 389, 722-725; capital of Kadamba Taila II, XV, pt. ii, 88; Pándavas' possible stay at, *id.* 264 note 4; its ancient names, I, pt. ii, 558; included in Kuntala, *id.* 431; hereditary possession of a branch of the Kádambas, *id.* 558; Kádambas of, a branch of the Goa Kádamba family, *id.* 498; Kádambas of, as Western Chálukya feudatories, *id.* 435, 437, 439, 450, 456, 458, 465, 466, 486; of the Kálachuryas of Kalyáni, *id.* 475, 482; Ekántada Ramayya worshipped at, by the Kádamba chief of, *id.* 484; besieged and taken by Vishṇuvardhana Hoysála, *id.* 502; fort of, reduced by Vira-Balláḷa Hoysála, *id.* 504, XV, pt. ii, 91; Kádambas of, as feudatories of the Hoysálas, I, pt. ii, 506; Kádambas of, do not recognise the sovereignty of Bhillama the Devagiri Yádava king or his son, *id.* 519; annexed to his kingdom by the Hoysála king Vira-Balláḷa II (about 1196); inscriptions found in, *id.* 419, 458 note 1, 505, 560, 562, 563, 564 notes

4 and 5; *see* also I, pt. ii, 458, 476, 485, 496, 497, 499, 501, 505, 506, 538, 568.
Haujamana: probably Sanján, next in importance to Puri, I, pt. ii, 19, 542, 543.
Haumant, Haunmant: hill pass between Ratnágiri and Kolhápur state, X, 166; XXIV, 6.
Hanmant: pass in Násik district, XVI, 131.
Hanmantráv: agent of Raghunáthrao Peshwa, visits England, IX, pt. ii, 196 note 3.
Haumat Singh: son of Gaman Singh of the Akráni pargana, I, pt. ii, 633.
Hannikeri: village in Belgaum district, XXI, 567; unpublished inscriptions at, I, pt. ii, 384 note 4, 556.
Hánsot: town in Broach district, II, 563.
Hansráj: commandant of Mándvi (1801) in Cutch, V, 151, 152, 153.
Hansráj: grandson of Lohána, named Táj Muhammad on his conversion to Islám, IX, pt. ii, 51.
Hansthal: creek in Káthiáwár, VIII, 64.
Hanumán: progenitor of Porbandar chiefs, I, pt. i, 135.
Hanumán, Hanumant, Hanumat: the Hindu monkey-god, IX, pt. i, p. xxxv, 12 and note 1, 292, 317, 321, 323, 332, 335, 341; nature of offerings made to, *id.* 362, 363, 383, 409; shrine of, at Gumándev, Dábhoda, and Bhimpor, visited by pilgrims, *id.* 549, IX, pt. ii, 220; shrines of, at Sopára, XIV, 337, 367, 372, 373; at Tungár, Vada and Vajirgad in Thána district, XIV, 337, 367, 372, 373; inscription at the temples at Managoli, I, pt. ii, 521 and note 4; at Khánápur in Kolhápur, *id.* 555 and note 2; *see* also I, pt. ii, 299 note 4, 517, 560.
Hanumandas Báva: a Bharvád saint, IX, pt. i, 271.
Hánumgala: *see* Hangal.
Hápa: state in Mahi Kánta, V, 427.
Hippalus: south-west wind, I, pt. i, 536, 537, 543.
Haptairing: leading constellation of the north, IX, pt. ii, 217 note 1.
Hara: a branch of Chohána, IX, pt. i, 484.
Harakantra: caste of fishermen in Kánara district, XV, pt. i, 306, 307.
Haralahalli, Haralhalli: village in Dhárwár district, temples, inscriptions, and inscribed copper-plate at, XXII, 725; Yádava grant (1238) at, I, pt. ii, 576 note 4, 558; record of the Guttas at, *id.* 518, 581-583.
Haran Shikári: black buck hunters in Kolhápur state, XXIV, 31.
Harapála, Haripáldev, Harpál, Harpaldev, Hirpáldev: son-in-law of Rámachandra the Yádava king of Devagiri, takes advantage of the disorder at Delhi to drive away the Mahomedan governors, but is taken prisoner and inhumanly flayed alive by Mubárik (1318), I, pt. ii, 27, 252, 519, 533; *see* also XV, pt. ii, 94; I, pt. ii, 29, 620.
Haraph: river in Rewa Kántha, VI, 115.
Harasur: in the Nizam's dominions, inscription at, I, pt. ii, 457 note 5, 461 and note 2, 468 and note 3.
Harayali, Hariali, harryali, huriali: famine and fodder-plant, XXV, 208, 276; XXIV, 27; sacred to Ganpati, XXV, 289.
Hárbhánji: chief of Limbdi, pays tribute to the Peshwá (1753), I, pt. i, 337.
Harbhara: gram, in Ratnágiri, X, 148.
Harbhat bin Bálambhat: founder of the Patvardhan states (1714), XXIV, 343.
Harbours: *see* Ports.
Harda: myrabolam tree in Poona district, XVIII, pt. i, 46.
Hardás: the preacher, literal meaning of, his mode of preaching, IX, pt. i, 25-26; priest in Ratnágiri, X, 418.
Hardvár: place of pilgrimage on the bank of the Ganges, IX, pt. i, 549.
Hárej: sub-division in Baroda territory, VII, 596; town, *id.* 606.
Hareshapura, Harishapura: town in Mysore, I, pt. ii, 370.
Hareshvar: town in Kolábá district, XI, 461.
Hargápur: hill in Belgaum district, XXI, 6.
Haria Dev: Hindu deity, IX, pt. i, 292, 314.
Hariáli: *see* Harayáli.
Hariána: place of interest in Káthiáwar, VIII, 449.
Hariba: adopted son of Khanderáo Gaikwár, attacks Rangoji's deputy and kills him; his expulsion by Rangoji from Borsad, I, pt. i, 331.
Hariba Dáda: adviser of Malhárráo Gáikwár (1871), VII, 279-280.
Hari Ballál Kelkar: *killedár* of Suvarndurg, I, pt. ii, 111.
Hari Bhatki: Baroda banker (1800), VII, 260.
Harick, Harik: food-plant, XXV, 184; in Ratnágiri, X, 146; in Kolába, XI, 97; in Thána, XIII, 289; in Poona, XVIII, pt. ii, 39.
Harihar: in Mysore, included in Kuntála, I, pt. ii, 431; inscription at, *id.* 281 note 3, 285 note 5, 456 note 2, 460, 462, 464, 468, 469, 470, 472, 487, 490 note 2, 504 and note 1, 506, 507 and note 2, 529, 530, 546 note 5, 558 note 6, 564 note 3, 577; spurious grant, *id.* 299 note 3; grant of Vinayáditya at (694), *id.* 300, 309, 370.
Harihar: Dandanáyak of Addayida, hereditary minister of Hoysála kings Narasinha II and Vira Someśvara, I, pt. ii, 507, 508.
Harihar I: first Vijayánagar king (1336-1350), XV, pt. ii, 96 and note 4, 97; land system of, *id.* 156, 157; I, pt. ii, 175.
Harihar II: third Vijayánagar king (1379-1401), XV, pt. ii, 96 note 4, 98, 299.
Hariharadevarasa: Kalachurya Sankama's feudatory, I, pt. ii, 488.
Hariharesvara: god at Kaulur, I, pt. ii, 488; inscription at the temple of, at Harihar, *id.* 504 note 1, 507 note 2.
Harik: *see* Harick.
Harikesarin: Hángal Kádamba ruler of the Banavási province under Vikramáditya VI, I, pt. ii, 440, 560, 563; *see* also XV, pt. ii, 87.
Harilál: native agent in the Baroda residency (1843), VII, 267.
Harililá: abstract of *Bhágavata* by Bopadeva, I, pt. ii, 249.
Hari Makáji: Koli dacoit (1879) in Poona district, XVIII, pt. iii, 38.

Haripal: Siláhára ruler, mention of, in inscriptions at Káranjon, Sopára, Agáshi, Borivli, and Utan in Thána district, XIV, 195, 339, 385, 388, 419.
Haripála: minister of Siddharája, I, pt. i, 173; grandfather of Kumárapála, *id.* 181.
Haripáldev: sixteenth Siláhára king (1150), XIII, 422 note 1, 426.
Haripant Phadke: Peshwa's minister (1773), XVIII, pt. ii, 255-57, 259; one of the ministers of the regency in (1774), I, pt. ii, 604; assembles his forces at Talegaon Dabhade to fight the English (1774), *id.* 605; succeeds to the command of the Marátha army, *id.* 105; enters Gujarát and compels Govindráv and Rághobá to raise the siege at Baroda, I, pt. i, 402; opposes Colonel Keating in Gujarát (1775), VII, 192-193; marches against Tipu (1786), I, pt. ii, 661.
Haripur: sacred village in Kolhápur state, XXIV, 383.
Harischandra: *bhakta* or preacher of the second *yugá* or cycle, IX, pt. ii, 48.
Harischandragad: range and hill fort between Ahmadnagar and Poona districts, rainbow phenomenon and caves at, XVII, 5-6, 717-719; XVIII, pt. i, 3; XVI, 447.
Harish: fort in Násik district, XVI, 439, 441, 443 note 1, 447.
Harishpura: *see* Hareshapura.
Harita, Hárita: Chálukya hero, I, pt. ii, 180, 278 note 1, 339 note 7, 340 note 1.
Hárita, Háritas, Háriti, Haritiputra, Haritiputras: *gotra* of the ancestors of the Western Chálukyas of Bádámi, I, pt. ii, 277 note 5, 337; *gotra* of the original ancestors of the Kádambas, *id.* 277 note 5, 286, 287 note 3; *see* also *id.* 211, 337 note 2, 279; XV, pt. ii, 77 note 9, 78, 80.
Haritha: special holiday meal among Arabs, IX, pt. ii, 16.
Háriti: *see* Hárita.
Haritiputra, Haritiputras: *see* Hárita.
Haritiputra Satakarni or Shátakarni: early Banavási king (A. D. 50-100), XV, pt. ii, 77 and note 1, 261, 265; *see* also I, pt. ii, 277.
Haritiputra Saunaka: king mentioned in an inscription in Rewá state in Central India, I, pt. ii, 277 note 5.
Harivamśa: *Purána* of Digámbara Jains, I, pt. ii, 197, 394, 407.
Harivarma: early Kádamba king (A. D. 550?), XV, pt. ii, 79 note 1, 82; I, pt. ii, 289; grants of, *id.* 289 note 3.
Harivarman: Ganga king (A. D. 248), I, pt. ii, 300, 301 note 1.
Hariya Bráhman: descendant of Hariyáji, I, pt. i, 460 and note 3.
Harkárás: messengers, I, pt. i, 214.
Harli: foot-path in Sátára district, XIX, 202.
Harnái: port in Ratnágiri district, X, 171; imports and exports of, *id.* 184; town, *id.* 336; forts, *id.* 337; forts built by Sháhu but taken by Angria, I, pt. ii, 81.
Harogop: village in Dhárwár district, temple and inscription at, XXII, 726.
Harpál, Harpáldev: *see* Harapála.
Harpharan: a Parthian or Persian, mention of, in Kárli inscriptions, XIII, 413.
Har Rámji: a Solanki, marries a Chohán princess, IX, pt. i, 487.
Harrea Kaddu: poisonous plant, XXV, 265.
Harriers: class of birds in Ratnágiri district, X, 57.
Harris: Honourable Mr. Bartholomew, president and governor of Bombay (1690-1694), XXVI, pt. ii, 516; XXVI, pt. i, 103.
Harrison's Spring: at Mátherán, XIV, 245.
Harryali: *see* Harayali.
Harsha, Harshadeva, S'ri Harshavardhána: ruler of Magadh (607), belief about his former existence, IX, pt. i, 441-442; proof of his being a foreigner, *id.* 444 and note 4; Turka and White Húnas beaten by, *id.* 448, 453, 479; king of Kanauj (607-648), I, pt. i, 56, 57, 115, 116; invades the south and is resisted by Pulikeśin II on the Narmada, I, pt. ii, 183, 325 note 3, 350, 351 and note 4, 353, 355, 378, 389; called Siláditya by Hwan Thsang, *id.* 184, 353; defeats Dharasena IV of Valabhi, *id.* 316; *see* also *id.* 314 note 1; XV, pt. ii, 81.
Harshacharita: Sanskrit work by the poet Bána, I, pt. i, 114; *see* also I, pt. ii, 144, 171.
Harshadeva: *see* Harsha.
Harshapura: identified with Harsol, I, pt. i, 129; territorial division, I, pt. ii, 413.
Harshavardhána: *see* Harsha.
Harsol: town in Ahmadábád district, IV, 345; capital of Prachand (A. D. 910), I, pt. i, 129.
Harsol: village in Násik district, disturbances in (1857-59), XVI, 201, 202.
Harsola: sub-caste of Bráhmans, IX, pt. i, 2, 10; of Meshri Vániás, *id.* 71.
Harsutá: temple of, at Verával, I, pt. i, 203.
Hart: point at Mátherán, XIV, 232, 234.
Hartála: lake, in Khándesh district, XII, 142, 11, 140; village, *id.* 449.
Hartálika: goddess, worship of, among Bráhmans, XXIV, 56-57.
Hartley: Captain, English commander (1779) in the expedition against Poona, XVIII, pt. ii, 265, XIII, 504; defeats the Maráthás at Dugad, *id.* 507, XIV, 56, I, pt. ii, 104, 605; relieves Kalyán, XIV, 121; relieves Captain Abington, *id.* 221.
Harut: angel of high estate, first teacher of magic, his trial in the world, his eternal damnation, IX, pt. ii, 142-143. *See* Márut.
Harvest: forecasts, rites to ascertain, IX, pt. i, 390.
Hás: chapters of the *Yesna*, IX, pt. ii, 222.
Hasáji Mohitá: his gallant services in a battle near Panhála with the Bijápur troops (1672), I, pt. ii, 594; plunders Broach (1675), I, pt. i, 387. *See* Hambirráv.
Hasan: Ala Zikri, son of Ali, the martyr, second Shiah *imám*, IX, pt. ii, 45, 47, 125 note 2, 127, 129, 133, 136, 139; his *salám*, fourth successor of Hassan Sabáh; promulgates new doctrines; transfers the Imámate from the Fátimites to himself; declares himself the Unrevealed Imám (1163); is believed to have sent the first missionary to India; His Highness Agá Khán traces his descent fom Ali through, IX, pt. ii, 37, 48; *see* Nazárians.

Hasan Bin Ismáil: (1872), head of the Sulaimani Bohorás, IX, pt. ii, 33.
Hasan Gangu: founded (1347) the Brahmani kingdom, XVIII, pt. ii, 215 and note 5; *see* also XII, 243; XIX, 225-226.
Hasan Muhammad Khán: author of *Mirât-i-Ahmedi* (1730), I, pt. i, 310.
Hasan Sabáh: Ismáilian missionary; founds the order of Fidawis; supports Nazár's claim to the Egyptian succession; makes the power of the Ismáilians supreme in Persia; concentrates his powers at Alamut; ceases to act as *dái* and political emissary of the Fátimites; makes himself known by the title Shaikh-ul-Jabal, his death (1124); powers of the Ismáilias under his two immediate successors, IX, pt. ii, 37, 48. *See* Nazárians.
Haslar: a depressed class in Kánara district, XV, pt. i, 367, 368; in Dhárwár district, XXII, 135-136.
Hastimalla; Ganga prince and vassal of the Chola king Parántaka I, I, pt. ii, 299 note 4.
Hastinagara, Hastinápur: town north of Peshávar, capital of ancient Gandhára, I, pt. i, 490.
Hastinávatipur: Anegundi village in Kánara district, XV, pt. ii, 262 and note 5.
Hastivarman: king of Vengi, I, pt. ii, 280.
Hátakeshvar: golden *ling* of Shiv installed at Vadnagar, IX, pt. i, 14, 73.
Hateshvar Mahádev: Nágar Bráhmans' special guardian at Vadnagar; destruction of the temple of, I, pt. i, 289.
Hátgad: fort in Násik district, XVI, 440, 441, 458.
Hatgar: *see* Hatkar and Devang.
Hatgegad Arle: a spur of the Sahyádris in Sátára district, XIX, 6.
Háthab: place of interest in Káthiáwár, VIII, 449.
Háthasni: táluka in Káthiáwár, VIII, 451.
Hathila: place of interest in Káthiáwár, VIII, 450, 451.
Háthisa: village in Surat district, origin of the name, IX, pt. i, 12 note 1.
Háthmati: river in Mahi Kántha, V, 357.
Hátim: of Tái, Arab hero, famous for his generosity, IX, pt. ii, 80.
Hátkalangda: tributary of the Panchganga, in Kolhápur state, XXIV, 10; town, headquarters of the Alta sub-division, local legend, fair, tomb of Gori Sáheb Pir, temples, and inscriptions at, *id.* 297.
Hatkar: a caste of cultivators in Khándesh, XII, 69; in Sholápur district, XX, 87; weavers in Belgaum district, 136-138; in Bijápur district, XXIII, 267-270; in Kolhápur state, XXIV, 95; in Kánara, XV, pt. i, 366-367.
Hátkeshvar: peak, in Poona district, XVIII, pt. i, 4.
Hátmal: worship of, by Kolis, IX, pt. i, 247.
Hatra: ruins of, in Mesopotamia, XIII, 413.
Hats: making of, in Dhárwár district, XXII, 380.
Hattikankan: *see* Kuruba.
Hatti-Mattur: village in Dhárwár district, XXII, 726; inscription at, I, pt. ii, 416, 428 note 4.
Hattis: hills in Khándesh, XII, 5.
Hátwárás: weekly Markets—*see* Markets.
Hauzi-Shápur: water cistern in Bijápur, I, pt. ii, 647.
Havála: crop assignment, XXII, 475, 469 and note 8.
Haváldár, Haváldárs: Mughal village officer, I, pt. i, 212; Marátha district officer, I, pt. ii, 100; in Thána (1741), XIII, 556; land allotments to, *id.* 568 and note 2; village threshing-floor-keepers (1828), *id.* 574.
Haváldári: cess on lands in Baroda state, VII, 379.
Hávangeh: first watch, IX, pt. ii, 214 note 1.
Havangi, Havanige: village in Dhárwár district, temple, inscriptions, XXII, 726; *see* also I, pt. ii, 562 note 4.
Havasbhávi: village in Dhárwár district, hero-stone at, XXII, 726.
Haveli: sub-division, in Rewa Kántha, VI, 116.
Haveli: sub-division of Poona district, details, boundaries, area, aspect, water, climate, stock, crops, people, communications, XVIII, pt. iii, 78-81; survey of, XVIII, pt. ii, 431-432, 488-495; forest reserves in, XVIII, pt. i, 36.
Havelock: Mr., sent to Janjira (1870), XI, 449-450.
Háveri: tank in Dhárwár district, XXII, 259-260; town, trade centre, *id.* 355-356, 726-727; inscription at, I, pt. ii, 459 note 3, 461, 473, 474.
Havig or Havik: sub-caste of Bráhmans in Kánara district, XV, pt. i, 116-128; XV, pt. ii, 1-2.
Hawkins: English merchant, his visit to Burhánpur (1609), XII, 248.
Hawks: in Ratnágiri district, X, 55.
Hayve: probably North Kánara, I, pt. ii, 282 note 5; ruled over by a Western Chálukya prince, *id.* 437; by a Goa Kádamba prince, *id.* 452; by a governor of the Kalachuryas, *id.* 489; country ruled over by Vishnuvardhána, *id.* 499, 568. *See* Payve.
Házi Muhammad Khán: governor of Mándu (1568), I, pt. i, 370.
Hazrat Ali: Shiáh holiday on the 21st day of Ramazán, IX, pt. ii, 140.
Hazrat-khuld Makáni: title of the emperor Aurangzeb, IX, pt. ii, 67.
Házráts: vows made to genii or fairies, rites relating to, IX, pt. ii, 130.
Head-shaving: *see* Mudan.
Head Tax: the repeal of (1719), I, pt. i, 301.
Healing plants: in Kolhápur state, XXIV, 409-413.
Health: of Bombay, remedies to improve (1708), XXVI, pt. iii, 543; improved (1750), *id.* 553-554; public, in Baroda state, VII, 50, 494-515.
Heaven-climbing: rites. *See* Death.
Hebbál: village in Bijápur district, temples at, XXIII, 651; inscription at, I, pt. ii, 304, 305, 306, 418.
Heber: Bishop, his account of the interview of the resident with Sayáji II, Gáikwár (1825), VII, 240; his account of Bhils, IX, pt. i, 237 note 2, 242, 296 notes 1 and 3, 306;

his mention of Bombay, XIII, 2; travels to Khandála, *id.* 318, 571; his description of the fort of Bassein, XIV, 35; of Elephanta caves, *id.* 88, 92 note 1; of Kánheri caves, *id.* 163; of Khopivli, *id.* 201; of Panvel, *id.* 296; his travels in Poona district, XVIII, pt. ii, 152, 375, 376; his description of Poona (1825), XVIII, pt. iii, 23 note 1, 423; on the condition of Sátára, XIX, 309; his account of Surat Pársis, IX, pt. ii, 198 note 4.

Hebli: town in Dhárwár district, XXII, 440, 727.

Hedu: *Nauclea cordifolia*, tree in Poona district, XVIII, pt. i, 46.

Hedyoti, umbellata: dye-plant common on the gháts, XXV, 242.

Heggade: officer of the Banavási province, I, pt. ii, 473, 476, 485.

Heggeri: village in Dhárwár district, temple, inscriptions, XXII, 727.

Hejjunka: tax levied by Hoysála queen (1203), I, pt. ii, 502.

Hekataios: Greek writer, his mention of India, I, pt. i, 532, 546.

Helav: a caste of beggars in Bijápur district, XXIII, 270-271; in Dhárwár district, XXII, 206.

Helianthus annuus: oil-yielding plant, XXV, 219.

Helicteres isora: fibrous plant, XXV, 229.

Heliotrope: mineral and stone in Poona district, XVIII, pt. i, 13, 30.

Helmia bulbifera: food-plant, common in the presidency, XXV, 179.

Helot: craftsmen called Tajika, IX, pt. i, 454 note 1.

Helvák: village in Sátára district, trade of, XIX, 468-469; survey of, *id.* 379-380.

Hemachandra, Hemácharya: Jain devotee and chronicler (A. D. 1089-1173), I, pt. i, 156; patronised by Siddharája, *id.* 180; his teacher, *id.* 181 note 2; tells Kumárapála his future, *id.* 182-183; birth and education, *id.* 191; becomes Kumárapála's religious adviser, *id.* 192-193; his works and death, *id.* 193; author of Prákrit Grammar, I, pt. ii, 161 note 1, 169, 288 note 1; of *Dvyásrayakosha*, *id.* 567; said to have been converted to Islám, IX, pt. ii, 26 note 2; his rejection of a *palanquin*, I, pt. i, 179, 183; his convent, *id.* 188.

Hemádideva: of the Nikumbha family, officer of Jaitugi I, I, pt. ii, 521.

Hemádpant, Hemadri: Bráhman minister of the Devagiri Yádava kings Mahádeva and Rámachandra, I, pt. ii, 230, 243, 528, 530; patron of learning and a zealous builder, introduces a style of architecture named after him and the *Modi* or current form of Maráthi writing, *id.* 248-249, 528; gives a pedigree and a brief history of the Devagiri Yádavas, *id.* 230, 511 note 8, 512, 513, 514, 515, 520, 522, 525, 528; author of *Vratakhand*, *id.* 136, 239. *See* also, XVI, 186 and note 2; XII, 242 note 1, 449; XXIII, 545 note 2; XVIII, pt. ii, 214 note 3.

Hemádpanti: style of architecture introduced by Hemádpant, I, pt. ii, 528, 619.

Hemádpanti Remains: in Khándesh district, XII, 449; in Poona district, XVIII, pt. iii, 109, 148 and note 1, 218, 259, 343, 402, 425-427, 439, 448; in Sholápur district, XX, 275 and note 2.

Hemádri: *see* Hemádpant.

Hemis-desmus Indicus: medicinal plant, XXV, 260.

Hemmádideva: prince of Másavádi, I, pt. ii, 501.

Hemmaragál: village in Mysore, inscription at, I, pt. ii, 509.

Hemmeyanáyaka: Singhana's governor of Banavási (1215), I, pt. ii, 523.

Hemp: preparations from, *bháng*, *yákudi* or *májam*, *gánja*, uses of, IX, pt. i, pp. xxxii-xxxiii; cultivation of, in Kaira and Panch Mahals districts, III, 54, 234; in Ratnágiri district, X, 149; in Sávantvádi, *id.* 425; in Kolába district, XI, 97; in Poona district, XVIII, pt. ii, 48. *See* Gánjá.

Henjeru: chief driven out by Vishnuvardhána, I, pt. ii, 496.

Henna: seed of, is burnt to drive away evil spirits, IX, pt. ii, 155 and note 1.

Henry: Captain, police officer, killed by Bhils under Bhágoji Náik (1857), I, pt. ii, 632; XVI, 199-200, 534 note 1, XVII, 418.

Heptanesia: islands, identified by Lassen with the islands of Bombay and Sálsette, I, pt. ii, 2; I, pt. i, 542.

Herakleia: Markianosof, I, pt. i, 546.

Herat: *see* Ariana.

Herbad: Pársi under-priest, lower sacerdotal order of the priests; other names of, IX, pt. ii, 222 and note 1; qualifications of, *id.* 222; ordination of, *id.* 223-225; titles of, *id.* 225.

Herbert: Sir Thomas, English traveller in India (1626), his description of Haft Manzar or Victory Pillar at Mandu, I, pt. i, 361; his description of Mandu, *id.* 381; writes on the history and religion of the Pársis, IX, pt. ii, 190; his description of Dabhol, X, 330 note 1; his mention of temples in Sálsette, XIV, 151, 302.

Herdsmen: in Gujarát, chief divisions of, strength and distribution, IX, pt. i, 264; chief classes—Ahirs, *id.* 264-266; Bábriás, *id.* 266; Bharváds, *id.* 267-285; Mers, *id.* 285-286; Rabáris, *id.* 286-289; in Surat and Broach districts, II, 374; in Kaira and Panch Mahals districts, III, 34, 218; in Ahmadábád district, IV, 38; in Cutch, V, 77-81; in Pálanpur, *id.* 290; in Mahi Kántha, *id.* 366; in Rewa Kántha, VI, 25; in Baroda state, VII, 61-62; in Ratnágiri district, X, 127; in Khándesh district, XII, 78.

Herebidri: village in Dhárwár district, temple, inscriptions at, XXII, 727.

Hereditary officers: in Kolába district, absence of, XI, 177; became revenue farmers or *khots*, *id.* 177-178; in Thána district, *deshmukhs* and others, XIII, 538, 553, 554, 556; cease to be of use, *id.* 563; their *izáfat* villages, *id.* 564; made nominal proprietors by the Maráthás, *id.* 565; (1828), *id.* 572-573; in Násik district, XVI, 209 and notes 3 and 6, 211; in Ahmadnagar district, XVII,

436-437; in Poona district (1820-21), XVIII, pt. ii, 366-367; in Dhárwár district, XXII, 464-465.
Herla: village in Kolhápur state, old military station, temples and inscription at, XXIV, 298.
Hermolaos: geographer, I, pt. i, 546.
Herodotos: Greek historian, makes mention of India, I, pt. i, 532.
Heroné: reef on the east of the Gulf of Barygaza, I, pt. i, 539, 545.
Herons: class of birds in Ratnágiri district, X, 94-96.
Herur: probably Belúr in the Bijápur district, I, pt. ii, 519 and note 1.
Herur: village in Dhárwár district, temple and hero-stone at, XXII, 727.
Hetkari: a caste of Maráthás from Málvan, I, pt. ii, 73; husbandmen, in Thána district, XIII, 119; in Násik district, XVI, 49; in Shiváji's army, XVIII, pt. ii, 231-232; XIX, 239.
Hewár: famine-plant, found in Sholápur and other districts, XXV, 199.
Hewitt: Major, at the siege of Sholápur (1818), XX, 297-298.
Hibiscus cannabinus: fibrous plant, XXV, 226; *esculentus*, *furcatus*, *mutabilis*, *sabdariffa*, *id.* 227; *surratensis*, fibrous plant, *id.* 227; *rosasinensis*, sacred plant, *id.* 289; *tiliaceus*, famine and fibrous plant, *id.* 194, 227.
High Court: Bombay, formerly called the Chief Court, occupies the present building (1879), XXVI, pt. iii, 588.
Hijáz: Al, Arabs of, IX, pt. ii, 17.
Hijda: caste of beggars, emasculated male votaries of the goddess Behechra, IX, pt. ii, 21-22; process of the emasculation of, *id.* 21, 154 and note 2; in Násik district, XVI, 55; *see* Pavaiya.
Hikal: medicinal plant, XXV, 254.
Hikulamba: village, grant of, to Bráhmans, I, pt. ii, 372.
Hill forts: in Baroda state, VII, 7, 8; in Násik district, estates granted to their commandants in Marátha times, XVI, 210 and note 3; subdued by the British, *id.* 210; details, description, history, remains, *id.* 441-444.
Hills: beliefs about their sacredness among Bráhmans, Vaishnavs, early tribes, Shrávaks or Jains, IX, pt. i, 388; the sacred hills near the Mahi Kántha village of Satlásan, Dudhel Máta or Milk Mother stone on the top of, worship of the stone-mother by women who cannot suckle their infants, *id.* 388-389; Násik hills of Sálher and Mulher; worship of a heap of cow-dung called Govardhan mountain; occasions and different forms of worship of, *id.* 389; all district volumes, *see* under district name.
Hill Tribes: at Mátherán, XIV, 259-264; *see* Aboriginal Tribes.
Himálayas: Aryás settle south of, I, pt. ii, 135, 142, 207.
Himantopodidæ: a species of birds in Ratnágiri, X, 93.
Himmat Bahádur: Kolhápur *sardár*, XXIV, 189, 299, 303.
Himmatgad: fort in Ratnágiri district, taken and its name changed to Fort Victoria (1755), I, pt. ii, 92.
Himmatráv: minister of the *rája* of Jávli (1653), XIX, 233.
Hind: Persian name for India, Sind not included in (A. D. 951), I, pt. i, 511; dress of the kings of (968), *id.* 529; described to Hajjaj by Ibu-i-Kiriyyah, IX, pt. ii, 1 note 1.
Hindorna: táluka in Káthiáwár, VIII, 451.
Hindu era: *Śaka*, how converted into Christian era, I, pt. ii, 335 and note 2.
Hinduráv Ghátge: (1813) builds a new fort at Kágal, XXIV, 300.
Hindus: settlement of, in different countries of the world in early times, XIII, 403, 404 note 3; the Parthians in Thána marry with (A. D. 78), *id.* 411; found in Alexandria (150), XI, 138 and note 1; merchants on Thána coast (150), XIII, 416-417; (500), *id.* 420; (810-1260), *id.* 431; (1300-1500), *id.* 446; divided into seven castes (A. D. 951), I, pt. i, 530; kings of, accede to the throne at the age of forty (951 A. D.), *id.* 531; punished by Jai Ráj (A. D. 1211) for destroying a mosque at Cambay, *id* 512, 529; religious persecution of, under the Portuguese (1530-1670), XIII, 462; settled in distant lands as traders (1500-1670), *id.* 468; (1670-1800), *id.* 488; (1800-1810), *id.* 520.
Hinganbet: *Balanites Ægyptiaca*, tree, in Poona district, XVIII, pt. i, 46; in Khándesh district, XII, 25.
Hinganghát: cotton variety, in Khandesh, XII, 154, 160, 161.
Hingláj: Hindu goddess, IX, pt. i, p. xxxvi, 116, 177, 181, 189, 200, 247, 506, 508, 520; shrine of, *id.* 549; temple of, at Cheul, XI, 302.
Hingne Khurd: village in Poona district, temple and fair at, XVIII, pt. iii, 131.
Hingne's mansion: in Násik city, XVI, 494-495.
Hingolgad: place of interest in Káthiáwár, VIII, 452.
Hiouan Thsang: *see* Hiuen Thsang.
Hippalus: Greek sailor (A. D. 47), discovers monsoon winds, XIII, 410.
Hippargi: a village in the Sindagi táluka, in Bijápur district, inscription at, I, pt. ii, 435 note 7, 503; temples, inscriptions and fair at, XXIII, 378, 651-652; survey of, *id.* 465-467.
Hipparkhos: Eratosthene's critic, follows Megasthenes in giving geographical position (B. C. 130), I, pt. i, 535.
Hippkura, Hippocura, Hippokoura: identified with Ghodegaon in Kolába district, XI, 10, 138; XIV, 99; I, pt. i, 540; probably either Karhád or Kolhápur, I, pt. ii, 176; XXIV, 218; perhaps Kuda, I, pt. i, 540; possibly Hippargi, *id.* 541.
Hirakot: fort in Alibág town, XI, 254; sieges of, *id.* 155, 156, 260.

Hirakot: Thána fort, its description, XIV, 346, 347, 353.
Hiran: river, in Baroda territory, VII, 13; in Káthiáwár, VIII, 63.
Hirandodi: famine-plant, XXV, 201.
Hirandori: fibrous plant, XXV, 233.
Hiranya, Hiranyavarman: Pallava prince, succeeds Govindavarman, I, pt. ii, 325 and note 2, 327.
Hiranyagarbha: god Brahmá, springs from the navel of Vishnu, I, pt. ii, 339, 334, 342, 344; festival of, *id.* 367, 386; *see* Bráhman.
Hiranya Kasipu: demon, I, pt. i, 120.
Hiranyakeshi: river, in Kolhápur state, XXIV, 8, 9, 11.
Hiranyavarman: *see* Hiranya.
Hirda: dye-plant, XXV, 244. *See* Harda.
Hire-Bágewádi: village, grant of, I, pt. ii, 527.
Hire Básur: village in Dhárwár district, temple, inscriptions and cave at, XXII, 727.
Hirebendigeri: village in Dhárwár district, temple and inscriptions at, XXII, 728.
Hirehalla: river, in Dhárwár district, XXII, 7.
Hirehalli: village in Dhárwár district, XXII, 728.
Hire-Handigol: village, in the Dhárwár distirct, inscription at, I, pt. ii, 422 note 3.
Hire-Kerur: village, in Dhárwár district, pond, temples and inscriptions at, XXII, 728; *see* also I, pt. ii, 562 note 4.
Hirekumbhi: hill in Belgaum district, XXI, 9, 567.
Hirekurvinava: a class of weavers in Dhárwár district, XXII, 168-169; *see* Kuruvinshetti.
Hire-Muddanur: in the Nizám's dominions, inscription at, I, pt. ii, 448 note 3, 457 note 7.
Hirewadawatti: inscription at, I, pt. ii, 501.
Hiriyadeva: Gutta prince, son of Vikramáditya III, I, pt. ii, 579, 584.
Hiriya-Handigol: grant of the village of, I, pt. ii, 520.
Hiriya Savanayya: Kalachurya Áhavamallas' officer, I, pt. ii, 489.
Hirpál; ancestor of the Jhálas, IX, pt. i, 127.
Hirpáldev: *see* Harapála.
Hirundinidæ: order of birds in Ratnágiri, X, 61.
Hirundininæ: sub-order of birds in Ratnágiri, X, 61.
Hirur: village in Dhárwár district, temple, inscription, XXII, 728; I, pt. ii, 436 note 1.
Hirur: village in Bijápur district, temple, XXIII, 652.
Hisámuddin Parmár: Gujarát governor, and his subsequent imprisonment, I, pt. i, 230 and note 1; IX, pt. ii, 69.
Hisham bin Abdul Malik: Khalif (724-743), expedition sent against Broach in the reign of, I, pt. i, 506, 513, 520.
Hislop: General Sir Thomas, captures Holkar's fort of Thálner (1818) in Khándesh, I, pt. ii, 630; *see* also XII, 255, 474; XVI, 195.
Hisn Ghorab: I, pt. i, 537.
History: all district volumes; *see* under district name.
Hittalmardi: hill and place of interest in Belgaum district, XXI, 9, 567.
Hittites: Káthis, IX, pt. i, 258.
Hiuen Tsiang, Hiwen Thsang: Chinese traveller and pilgrim (A. D. 612-640), I, pt. i, 3, 7, 77; his description of the Valabhis, *id.* 79, 85, 111, 115; notices Broach kingdom, *id.* 116, 143, 465, 466, 467, 489, 490, 499, 502, 540; *see* also (629-645), I, pt. ii, 3, 318 note 4; his name also spelt as Hwhan Thsang, "Introduction to the History of the Dekkan," *id.* p. ii; gives Moholocha for Maháráshtra, *id.* 145; refers to the composition of a brief Sanskrit Grammar, *id.* 171; his visit to Maháráshtra and his account of Pulakeśi II and his kingdom, *id.* 184, 185, 353-354, 431 note 2; his account of Buddhism, *id.* 191; refers to Harshavardhána's expedition into the Dakhan, *id.* 350; his visit to the court of Harshavardhána, *id.* 353; his probable mention of Cheul as Chimolo (642), XI, 141, 270; Bráhman and Buddhist (650) monasteries in Persia according to, XIII, 432; his mention of Kalyán, XIV, 119; Kanheri not known to, *id.* 126; his mention of Bráhman colleges, *id.* 135; *see* also IX, pt. i, 434, 444 note 4, 450.
Hivar: *see* Hiwar.
Hivre Budrukh: village in Poona district, temple and fair at, XVIII, pt. iii, 132.
Hiwar: fibrous plant, found in Dakhan, XXV, 232, XII, 25, XVIII, pt. i, 46.
Hodavda: village of, near Sávantvádi, X, 439.
Hodges: Honourable M. Thomas, appointed president and governor of Bombay (1767), XXVI, pt. iii, 387-388; XXVI, pt. i, 353.
Hodgson: Brian, on the spread of Hinduism in Nepal, IX, pt. i, 451, 452 note 2, 454 note 1.
Hoggevaddi: pass in Kánara district, XV, pt. ii, 39, 40, 304-305.
Hog Island: in Bombay harbour, XIII, 11; ceded to the British by the treaty of Surat (1774), *id.* 501, 502; its possession confirmed (1782), *id.* 508; I, pt. ii, 101; hydraulic lift at, XIV, 105-107.
Hog Island: in Kánara district, XV, pt. i, 3. *See* Jalikund.
Hokkáyantra: the mariner's compass, its use by Hindu sailors, XIII, 726.
Holal: I, pt. ii, 497. *See* Polaln.
Holalamarasa: I, pt. ii, 473. *See* Holalarája.
Holalarája: father of Kalachurya Bijjala's feudatory, Kesava, I, pt. ii, 473.
Holalugunda: province, I, pt. ii, 465.
Holár: a caste of beggars, in Kolába district, XI, 73; Máng beggars, in Khándesh district, XII, 123; caste of musicians in Sátára district, XIX, 101-102; beggars in Poona district, XVIII, pt. i, 452-453; musicians in Sholápur district, XX, 145-146.
Holarrhana antidysenterica: medicinal plant, XXV, 259.
Holayá: a depressed class in Kánara district, XV, pt. i, 369-370; in Dhárwár district, XXII, 214-216; in Belgaum, XXI, 192-193; in Bijápur, XXIII, 213-216.

Holayar: chiefs, their supposed rule in Kánara, XV, pt. ii, 81 note 2.
Holcus: *saccharatus*, food-plant, cultivated in several districts, XXV, 208; *sorghum*, cultivated in Karnátic, *id.* 186; *spicatus*, food-plant cultivated in several districts, *id.* 185, 208.
Holdings: all district volumes. *See* Agriculture under district name.
Holedásar: a caste of beggars in Bijápur district, XXIII, 194.
Holi: burning pile, offerings to, IX, pt. ii, 220; chief fire-worship day, the Fágan full-moon at spring equinox, observances, IX, pt. i, 305, 357; fire-worship of, *id.* 357; festival, observed as holiday, *id.* 23 note 5, 119, 170, 171, 173, 175, 178, 182, 184, 185, 226, 336, 364.
Holiá: *see* Holayá.
Holianveri: village in Dhárwár district, temple and inscription at, XXII, 728.
Holidays: chief, observed by Bhangias, IX, pt. i, 336; Bhils, *id.* 305-307; Káyasths, *id.* 66; Rájpúts, *id.* 236; Shrávaks, *id.* 113-115; other classes, *id.* 119, 157, 169-170, 173, 175, 213, 226, 269; Akhátrij or Akshaya-tritiya, Ashádh sud 11th, Balev or Cocoanut Day, Bháu-Bij, Bol-Choth, Dasara, Dev-Diváli, Diváli, Diváso, Ganesh-Chaturthi, Holi, Janma Ashtami or Gokal Ashtami, Kajlitrij or Javkájli, Karvada-Choth, Nágpanchmi, Navrátri, Noli-nom, Rámnavmi, Rishipanchmi, Saukránt, Shivrátri or Maha Shivrátri, Shrávan Mondays, Silisatem, Vághbáras; for details *see* particular names; observed by Kánara population, XV, pt. i, 146, 177, 193, 206, 207, 215, 218, 231, 244, 290, 386; kept by Poona district population, XVIII, pt. i, 168, 241-255, 292-295, 414, 513-515; among Sátára Kunbis, XIX, 64; kept by Kolhápur state population, XXIV, 71, 88, 92, 108, 138.
Holi disturbance: in Thána district (1840), XIII, 525.
Holigarna Arnottiana: gum-yielding plant, XXV, 250.
Ho-li-sha-fa-tán-na: Chinese for Harshavardhána of Kanauj, I, pt. ii, 353.
Holkar: Marátha chief, given a share in the revenues of Málwá (1750), XIX, 291; assembles his forces at Talegaon Dábháde to fight the English (1778), I, pt. ii, 105, 605; origin of the family, XVIII, pt. ii, 244; XIX, 268.
Holkar's Bridge: near Poona city, XVIII, pt. iii, 373.
Holkar's Temple: near Poona city, XVIII, pt. iii, 373.
Holoja: father of Tippoja, the architect, I, pt. ii, 569.
Holostemma Rheedii: fibrous plant, XXV, 233.
Holy Cross: Church of, at Kurla, XIV, 211.
Holy Days: among Gujarát Musalmáns, IX, pt. ii, 136-142, general Muharram, *id.* 137-139; Ramazán id, Bakr id, *id.* 141; Shiah: tenth of Safar, *id.* 139; nineteenth and twenty-first of Ramzán, *id.* 140; eighteenth of Zilhaji, IX, pt. ii, *id.* 141; twenty-eighth of Zilhaji, *id.* 142. Sunni: thirteenth of Safar, *id.* 139; last Wednesday of Safar; twelfth of Rabi-ul-awwal; eleventh of Rabi-us-Sáni; eleventh of Rajab; fourteenth of Shában, *id.* 140. Gujarát Musalmán: seventeenth of Rabi-ul-awwal, *id.* 140; Khojáh, *id.* 41, 49, 50 and note 1.
Holy Magi: Churches of, at Gorai and Yerangal in Thána district, XIV, 101, 383.
Holy Office: the, interprets wrongly the Portuguese king's orders, I, pt. ii, 60.
Hom: Persian plant, is believed to be the Vedic *soma*, IX, pt. ii, 228 note 1, 231; a branch of the, presented to Surat Pársis by Jamasp, *id.* 194 note 1.
Homba: pass in Násik district, XVI, 129.
Hombal: village in Dhárwár district, temples and inscriptions at, XXII, 728.
Hombucha: in the Nagar district, Mysore, I, pt. ii, 458.
Home water: preparation of, early beliefs regarding, IX, pt. ii, 228 and note 1.
Hom Yast: hymn in praise of *hom*, IX, pt. ii, 228.
Hon: a coin, a tenure in Thána district, XIII, 531.
Honalli Math: Smart monastery at Sonda, XV, pt. ii, 345-346.
Honávar: sub-division of Kánara district, villages, aspect, climate, water, soil, stock, survey details, people, *id.* 232-234; town, bar, position, description, management, trade, manufactures, fort, Rámtirth, Basavrájdurg and history of, *id.* 255, 258, 272, 274, 278, 305-315, 327, 330, 336.
Honey: in Bánsda state, varieties of, VI, 253; Kánara forest produce, XV, pt. i, 30; export of, from Kánara district, XV, pt. ii, 58; production of, in Kolhápur state, XXIV, 24-25.
Honey-sipping: Pátáne Prabhu ceremony, XVIII, pt. i, 210.
Honeysuckers: class of birds, in Ratnágiri district, X, 69.
Honi: poisonous plant, XXV, 268.
Honia Náik: a Koli freebooter (1874-1876), XIII, 526, 637. *See* Honya.
Honuur: near Kágal, inscription at, I, pt. ii, 547.
Honots: tribe, perhaps a trace of Húnás, I, pt. i, 465.
Honwád: town in Bijápur district, inscription, I, pt. ii, 438 note 4, 440.
Honya: Bhágoji, Koli rebel (1873), XVII, 420; (1873), XVIII, pt. ii, 309. *See* Honia Naik.
Hoopoes: class of birds in Ratnágiri, X, 69.
Hopea racemosa: a dye-plant, XXV, 247.
Hor: *see* Honi.
Hordes: of foreigners, constitution of, IX, pt. i, 455, 459; start and progress of, *id.* 455-456, 459-460; melting of, *id.* 456-457, 461; later changes in, *id.* 457, 463-465; tribe names among, *id.* 455, 458 note 4, 459 note 9, 462 note 3; stock names among, *id.* 456, 457, 462, 463-465; interlacing of tribe and caste divisions, *id.* 457, 459, 463, 464, 465; *see* Foreigner.

Hordeum hexastychon : food-plant, cultivated in several districts, XXV, 189.
Hormazdiar : priest, grandson of Shapur Sheheriar, IX, pt. ii, 221.
Hornbills : class of birds in Ratnágiri, X, 65.
Hornblende : rock in Kánara district, XV, pt. i, 10 ; in Bijápur district, XXIII, 18.
Hornby : Honourable Mr., William, governor of Bombay (1776-1784), XXVI, pt. ii, 228, XVIII, pt. ii, 261 ; his minute on Maráthá affairs (1777), *id.* 266, XXVI, pt. i, 410-413 ; his alliance with the Gáikwár (1779), XIII, 509 ; his departure (1784), XXVI, pt. iii, 401 ; *see* also I, pt. i, 408 ; XIII, 504.
Horne : Honourable Mr. John, (1734-1739), XXVI, pt. ii, 439.
Horns : export of, from Kánara district, XV, pt. ii, 58.
Horn work : in Ratnágiri, X, 188 ; in Sávantvádi, *id.* 437 ; in Kánara, XV, pt ii, 70.
Horoscope : drawn by Bráhmans, among Gujarát Hindus, IX, pt. ii, 154 note 3 ; among Parsis, preparation of, IX, pt. ii, 229 ; consultation of, *id.* 220, 229-230, 232 ; *see* also XVIII, pt. i, 195.
Horse, horses : held sacred, causes of his sacredness ; believed to be the only teatless animal, days sacred for the worship of, worship of clay horse, IX, pt. i, 375-376 ; trade in (535-1714), in Kánara district, XV, pt. ii, 49 and note 7, 50, 51, 53 and note 5, 108, 111, 112, 115, 133, 272 ; importation of, into Chaul harbour, I, pt. ii, 35 ; import of, from Persia and Arabia into Konkan ports (810-1260), XIII, 431 ; (1300-1500), *id.* 444 ; (1500-1670), *id.* 468 ; in Káthiáwár, VIII, 97-98, 311, 312 ; in Khándesh, XII, 28 ; in Ahmadnagar district, XVII, 35-36 ; in Poona district, use, breed, trade, ponies, horse-breeding department, shows, food, disease, worship, unlucky peculiarities, XVIII, pt. i, 61-65 ; in Sátára district, XIX, 37 ; in Belgaum district, XXI, 66 ; dealing in, chief trade of the Kábulis, IX, pt. ii, 14.
Horse Gram : pulse, crop in Poona district, XVIII, pt. ii, 42.
Horse-shoe : Lord. *See* Nál Sáheb.
Horti : village in Bijápur district, temple at, XXIII, 652-653.
Hoságame : waste lands, XV, pt. ii, 167 and note 5, 184.
Hosala : probably Hoysála Yádava Narasimha, I, pt. ii, 238.
Hosanád : old province under the Kálachuryas, I, pt. ii, 484.
Hosengeh : fifth watch, IX, pt. ii, 214 note 1. *See* Geh.
Hoshalli : village in Dhárwár district, temple and inscriptions at, XXII, 728.
Hoshang Sháh Ghori : sultán of Málwa (1405-1432), the establisher of Mándu's greatness ; goes to Jajnagar (Jaipur) in Cuttack in Orissa (1421) ; returns to Mándu at the news of the siege of Mándu by Ahmad Sháh of Gujarát in 1422 ; prosperity of Málwa and extension of his power by his minister Malik Mughis Khilji and Máhmúd Khán, his son ; his death, I, pt. i, 358-359.
Hospitallers : order of monks, their arrival in India (1681), XIII, 460 note 7 ; remains of their church at Bassein, XIV, 41.
Hospitals : the first, in Bombay founded (1675-76), XXVI, pt. iii, 542-543 ; its staff and management (1738), *id.* 547-49 ; additions to (1740), *id.* 549 551 ; staff in 1772, *id.* 560-61 ; statistics (1774-1776), *id.* 562 ; in Thána district, XIII, 666 ; XIV, 40, 350, 352 ; in Násik district, XVI, 340 ; at Dhárwár, XXII, 622 ; in Kaira and Panch Maháls districts, III, 140, 290 ; in Ahmadábád district, IV, 225 ; in Cutch, V, 208 ; in Mahi Kántha, *id.* 370 ; in Káthiáwár, VIII, 352, 353 ; statistics of, in Ratnágiri, X, 293 ; Sávantvádi, *id.* 461 ; in Khándesh district, XII, 339 ; in Ahmadnagar district, XVII, 582 ; in Sátára district, XIX, 416 ; in Sholápur district, XX, 380 ; in Belgaum district, XXI, 490 ; in Bijápur district, XXIII, 525 ; in Kolhápur, XXIV, 287, 288 ; in Poona district, XVIII, pt. iii, 66-68.
Hosur : near Bangalore, grant at, I, pt. ii, 302 note 2, 358 note 1, 361 note 2.
Hosur : village in Kánara district, XV, pt. ii, 315-316.
Hosur : village in Dhárwár district, temples and inscriptions at, XXII, 728-729.
Hotgi : town in Sholápur district, railway station, XX, 267, 411-412.
Hot-springs : in Káira and Panch Maháls districts, III, 13, 195 ; in Ratnágiri, X, 21, 361-362 ; in Kolábá district, XI, 13, 388 ; in Khándesh, XII, 12 ; in Thána district, XIII, 15-16 ; at Sativli, Vajrábi, and Veholi in Thána district, XIV, 343, 373, 379.
Hottur : in Dhárwár district, inscription at, I, pt. ii, 433, 435 note 6, 564 note 2.
Household fire : *see* Atesh Dádghan.
Houses : of Pársis in Gujarát, town, village ; furniture in, IX, pt. ii, 205 ; observances on the occasions of building, *id.* 225-226 ; of Gujarát Musalmáns, of the rich, IX, pt. ii, 91 and notes 1 and 2, 92-93 ; of the middle class, *id.* 94 ; of the poor, *id.* 95 ; Daudi Bohorás, *id.* 29 and note 1 ; for Company's servants in Bombay (1671), XXVI, pt. ii, 431 ; purchase of, for office accommodation (1762), *id.* 468-470 ; purchase of, for marine offices and stores (1766), *id.* 472-473 ; for Europeans within the Town Wall, (1771), *id.* 478 ; within the Town Wall removed (1770), *id.* 475-476 ; *see* also Census. Details under all district names.
House tax : levied in Bombay island (1680-1683), XXVI, pt. iii, 274-276.
Hové : Dr., Polish traveller, his description of Sálsette (1787), XIII, 509-510 ; I, pt. ii, 123 ; his notice of Dharávi, Elephanta caves, Ghodbandar, Kánheri caves, Karanja, Kelve Máhim, and Sanján, in Thána district, XIV, 55, 88, 99, 162, 193, 199, 302 ; on Bombay Marine (1788), XXVI, pt. iii, 256 ; on the factory at Bankot (1789), I, pt. ii, 122.
Hoya : *pendula*, *viridiflora*, fibrous plants, XXV, 233.
Hoysála, Hoysála Balláls, Hoysálas : of Dorasamudra, I, pt. ii, 490-510 ; the various

forms of the name; claim Yádava descent, *id.* 490, 517; origin of the name, *id.* 490; their family goddess; Velápura or modern, Belur is the town with which the family is first connected; seat of Government transferred to Dorasamudra by Vishnuvardhána; originally Jains and subsequently converted to the Vaishnáva faith; the earliest mention in an inscription of A. D. 1006, *id.* 491; their family, *id.* 451; their genealogical tree, *id.* 493; their crest and banner, *id.* 299 note 4; their kingdom, *id.* 484; northern boundary of, *id.* 503; as feudatories of the Western Chálukyas of Kalyáni, *id.* 428 note 4, 439, 451, 494, 498; rise under Vishnuvardhána and besiege and take Hángal but are prevailed against by the Sinda chieftain Áchagi or Áchugi II, *id.* 218-219, 237, 453, 497, 562, 574; continue as Western Chálukya feudatories, *id.* 456; again become aggressive and again defeated by the Sindas under Permádi I, *id.* 459, 497, 497, 575; declare their independence under Vira-Ballála II, *id.* 501; dispute with the Devagiri Yádavas the possession of the southern provinces of the Chálukya empire, *id.* 466, 519, 521, 524, 555, 583; defeat the Yádavas near Gadag (1191), *id.* 504, 520; Musalmáns under Malik Káfur and Khwájá Háji lay waste their kingdom and their power as a dynasty is practically extinguished (1310), *id.* 509-510, 533; their kingdom annexed to the Delhi empire (1327), *id.* 510; probably overlords of Ratnágiri district (1250), X, 193; their rule in Kánará (1039-1310), XV, pt. ii, 86, and note 3, 88, 90-91, 265; in Dhárwár district (1137-1210), XXII, 399-400; in Bijápur, XXIII, 391 and note 5; in Belgaum district, XXI, 359 and note 2. *See* Vinayáditya, Ereyanga, Ballála I, Vishnuvardhána Narasimha I, Vira-Ballála II, Narasimha II, Vira-Someśvara, Vira-Narasimha III, Vira-Ballála III.

Hoysana: Hoysála, I, pt. ii, 490.

Hubli: sub-division of Dhárwár district, boundaries, area, aspect, soil, climate, water, stock, crops, people, survey of, XXII, 634-636; 487-490; town, position, divisions, forts, sub-divisions, population, houses, roads, trade, cotton mill, shops, markets, management, municipality, water-supply, dispensary, schools, library, place of worship, old temple, inscription, monasteries, mosques, cemeteries, history, *id.* 729-761; trade centre, *id.* 354; weaving centre (1650-1660), XV, pt. ii, 52, 125; sacked by Shiváji (1672), *id.* 126; *see* also I, pt. ii, 307, 549, 572, 594, 653, 654.

Hugár: flower-seller, in Dhárwár district, XXII, 147-148. *See* Gurav.

Hukáli: hill in Kánara district, XV, pt. i, 4, 5.

Hukáligudda: hill in Kánara district, XV, pt. ii, 316.

Hukeri: old rupee in Ratnágiri district, X, 154.

Hukeri: place of interest in Belgaum district, XXI, 567-569; under Delhi emperors (1347), *id.* 359 and note 2; held by a Desai (1689), *id.* 377.

Hukkah: tobacco pipe, IX, pt. ii, 111 and note 2.

Hulgur: village, incription at, I, pt. ii, 459 note 3, 461, 526, 527.

Hulgur: village in Dhárwár district, fair at, XXII, 761-762; inscriptions at, I, pt. ii, 459 note 3, 461, 526, 527.

Huli: village in Belgaum, temple, fort, and history of, XXI, 569-571, 393; I, pt. ii, 432; inscription at, *id.* 474, 475 and note 1; hill, XXI, 9.

Huligere: old province in Dhárwár district I, pt. ii, 304 note 6, 458, 466, 485, 486; shrine of Somanátha at, *id.* 482; seized by Vishnuvardhána, *id.* 497; governed by Mallideva (1295-96), *id.* 530. *See* Puligere.

Hulihalli: village in Dhárwár district, temples and inscriptions, XXII, 762; records of the Guttas at, I, pt. ii, 578, 582 and note 1.

Hulla, Hullapa, Hullamayya, Hullayya: Narasimha I's minister, promoter of the Jain faith, I, pt. ii, 491, 499, 501, 505.

Hulluniyatirtha: Someśvara III encamps at I, pt. ii, 455.

Hul-már: land measure, in Dhárwár under Anegundi kings (1333-1573), XXII, 440 and note 2.

Hultsch, Hultzsch: Dr., archælogist, his views quoted, I, pt. i, 129 note 3; I, pt. ii, 282 note 5, 297 note 8, 298 notes 1 and 3, 316 and note 5, 317 note 1, 318 notes 3, 11 and 12, 322, 323 and note 1, 324 and note 3, 325 notes 3 and 6, 326, 327 note 8, 328 note 1, 329 notes 2 and 4, 330, 331, 343 notes 2 and 5, 362 note 2, 403 note 3, 408 note 4, 409 note 1, 412 note 4, 413, 443 note 5, 445 notes 1, 2 and 3, 446 note 2, 507.

Human offerings or sacrifices: to place-spirits, when building, XX, 527; formerly offered by Karhád Bráhmans, XIX, 54; offered to the place-spirit to the site of Sátára fort, *id.* 574; at Panhála in Kolhápur state, XXIV, 230-231, 314.

Humata, Hukhta, Huvrasta: a section of the code of morals of Zoroaster, IX, pt. ii, 213.

Humáyun: emperor of Dehli, Portuguese alliance with (1532), XIII, 451; (1539-1556), I, pt. i, 220; defeats Sultán Bahádur of Gujarát (1534) at Mandasor; captures the fort of Songad, retires to Mándu from Gujarát (1535), returns to Agra (1535-36), *id.* 367, 368; his visit to Cambay city (1535), XI, 217; entertainment of the Mirzas at the court of, IX, pt. ii, 9-10.

Humba: pass in Thána district, XIII, 5, 320.

Humbad: a caste of traders in Khándesh district, XII, 58.

Humcha: in Mysore, chiefs of (A. D. 560), XV, pt. ii, 80, 82; *see* Hombucha.

Hume: Mr., his description of Netráni (1875) in Kánara district, XV, pt. ii, 336-337.

Humgaon: village in Thána district, XIV, 107-108.

Hun: coin variety, I, pt. i, 219 note 2, 222 note 2; in Dhárwár, XXII, 319 note 4, 440 and note 4.

Hun, Huna, Hunas or Huns: White, their arrival and power in Northern India (A. D. 450-520), I, pt. i, 74-76; their conflict with Skandha Gupta (454-470), *id.* 69, 73; their defeat in Central India (530), *id.* 86; their

power identified with Maitraka power in Northern India, were sun-worshippers, Multán their capital, Maitrakás, Mihiras and Mers formed part of their horde, *id.* 141-146; "Guzır" or "Gurjar" derived from Khazar clan of White Huns, IX, pt. i, 456, 472; their king defeated by the Ráshtrakúta king Kakka II (971), I, pt. ii, 423; king of, at the *svayamvara* of Durlabhadevi (1000), I, pt. i, 163; trace of the name near Bhinmál at present, *id.* 465, 467; *Black*: of the North Caspian called Ugrians, their rise to power (375), overlorded Khazar, IX, pt. i, 456, 473-474. *See* also White Hunas and Mihira Gurjjara.

Hunál: one of the Huna sub-divisions, I, pt. i, 465.

Hunashikatti: record of A. D. 1131 at, I, pt. ii, 455 note 4.

Hunda, Hundábandi: a tenure, in Thána district, XIII, 550 and note 2, 551 note 5; *hunda* an unmeasured plot of land, *id.* 565; *hon* probably for *hunda*, *id.* 565 note 7; (1828), *id.* 574; in Murbád (1837), *id.* 583 note 1; (1845), *id.* 587; old-tenure in Kolába district, XI, 168, 170.

Hundi: bills of exchange, three kinds of—*Dhanijog*, *Sháhjog*, *Nishájog*, meaning of; their entry in *Hundini-Nondh*, IX, pt. i, 83; in Kaira district, III, 58; in Ahmadábád district, IV, 65; in Cutch, V, 110; in Ratnágiri, X, 154; in Sávantvádi, *id.* 429; in Kánara district, XV, pt. ii, 25.

Hundiatum Náik: chief of the Bárgirs, harasses the Bijápur camp, I, pt. ii, 646.

Hundini-Nondh: bill register, an account book, IX, pt. i, 83.

Hungund: sub division in Bijápur district, its boundaries, area, aspect, climate, water, stock, crops, and people, XXIII, 537-538; *Town*, legends of, remains in, *id.* 653 and note 1; inscription at, I, pt. ii, 348 note 8, 435, 562 note 1.

Huni: sub-division of Márwár Kúnbis, I, pt. i, 465.

Hunnur: village in Kolhápur state, XXIV, 388.

Huns: *see* Hun.

Hunur: hill in Belgaum district, XXI, 6, 571-572.

Hupri: village in Kolhápur state, market, temples and fair at, XXIV, 298.

Hura: *Symplocos racemosa*, timber and dye-yielding plant, in Poona district, XVIII, pt. i, 46.

Hura crepitans: a poisonous plant, XXV, 270.

Hurlikop: village in Dhárwár district, temple and inscriptions at, XXII, 762.

Hurmuz: island in the Persian Gulf, horse trade from (A. D. 1145), I, pt. i, 515.

Hurricame: *see* Storms.

Hursul: land tenure in Dhárwár under the Maráthás, XXII, 448.

Hurtu: or Hargaivádi, Vágher's favourite game, IX, pt. i, 278 and note 2.

Huryalli: *see* Harayali.

Husain: son of A'li and Fatimah, third Shiah *imám*, martyr, IX, pt. ii, 22, 45, 47, 62, 125 note 2, 127, 129, 133, 136 and note 3, 139; shrine of, *id.* 47.

Husaini Bráhmans: religious beggars, followers of the Atharwa Veda, call themselves after Husain the prophet's grandson, follow some of the practices of the Hindu faith, means of livelihood of, beliefs among them; their head-quarters, IX, pt. ii, 22. *See* Sahadev Joshis.

Husain Khán Battangi: authorised to enlist persons from dangerous classes (1857), I, pt. i, 439.

Husain Miyan: Fateh Muhammad's son (1813), V, 155, 156, 157, 158.

Husain Nizám Sháh: succeeds his father Burhán of Ahmadnagar (1553), I, pt. ii, 623; makes peace with Ibráhim of Bijápur, *id.* 643; becomes involved in war with A'li A'dil Sháh of Bijápur and Rámráj of Vijayánagar; is severely defeated at Kalyán; Ahmadnagar besieged (1562); retreat of the allies; combines with A'li A'dil Sháh of Bijápur against the king of Vijayánagar and marries his sister Chand Bibi to the former (1563), *id.* 623; his death, *id.* 623.

Husain Sháh: a Sind ruler (1522-1544), his expedition to Cutch (1530), V, 135.

Husain-ud-din: chief *mulla* of Dáudi Bohorás (1882), IX, pt. ii, 31 note 4.

Husain-ud-din: chief *mulla* of Dáudi Bohorás (1893), IX, pt. ii, 31 note 4.

Husbandmen: in Gujarát, professional, Anávalás, IX, pt. i, 1, 4, 152; Káchhiás, Kanbiás, *id.* 153; Kolis, *id.* 152; Mális, Pateliás, Ságara, Sathvarás, *id.* 153; classes partly or wholly depending upon cultivation, A'hirs of Kachh, Bohorás, Sunni, of Surat and Broach, Borsada Bráhmans, Visnagra, Nágar Bráhmans, Ságodra Bráhmans, Oavál Vániás, Rájpúts; classes working as field labourers or partly depending on tillage, Bhangiás, Chodrás, Dhedás, Dhundiás, Dublas, *id.* 152; census details of professional husbandmen, *id.* 153; account of Káchhiás, *id.* 153-154; Kanbis, *id.* 154-171; Kolis, *id.* 237-251; Mális, *id.* 172; Pateliás, *id.* 172-174; Ságara, *id.* 174-175; Sathvarás, *id.* 175-176; all district volumes, *see* under district name.

Husein: sultan of Khurásán, ancestor of the Mirzas entertained at the Mughal court, IX, pt. ii, 10.

Huskárum: part of the *Zend Avesta*, IX, pt. ii, 211 note 2 (19).

Husparum: part of the *Zend Avesta*, IX, pt. ii, 211 note 2 (17).

Hussain A'li Saiad: defeats and kills Dáud Khán, governor of the Dakhan in Khándesh (1716), I, pt. ii, 626.

Husukuru: in Mysore, inscription at, I, pt. ii, 303.

Hutchinson: Captain, political agent of Bhopáwár, hangs the *rája* of Amjera (1857), I, pt. i, 439.

Hutox: craftsmen, a class of the old Persian community, IX, pt. ii, 213.

Huvina-Báge: probably Ráybág in the Kolhápur state, I, pt. ii, 569 and note 7.

Huvina-Sigalli, Huvinsigly: village in Dhárwár district, temple and inscriptions at, XXII, 762; record at, I, pt. ii, 526 note 7.

Hnvishka : Kushán king (A. D. 100-123), I, pt. i, 37.
Huvvalli : in the Kuhundi country, I, pt. ii, 527. *See* Mugut Khán Hubli.
Huyigol : village in Dhárwár district, inscriptions at, XXII, 762.
Hwan Thsang, Hwhan Thsang : *see* Hiuen Tsiang.
Hyæna : in Kánara district, XV, pt. i, 94.
Hyder Ali : *see* Haidar Ali.
Hydnocarpus Wightiana : oil-yielding and Hmedicinal plant used to poison fish, XXV, 214, 260, 272.
Hydraotes : the Rávi in the Panjáb, I, pt. i, 534.
Hydrocele : *see* Antargal.
Hydrocotyle Asiatica : medicinal plant, XXV, 260.
Hymenodictyon excelsum : fodder-plant, XXV, 278.
Hypasis : the Bias in the Panjáb, I, pt. i, 533.

I

IBÁ : river, I, pt. ii, 148.
Iberia : district of Skythia, I, pt. i, 544.
Ibis : class of birds in Ratnágiri district, X, 96.
Ibisinæ : sub-family of birds in Ratnágiri, X, 96.
Ibn Asir, Ibni Asir : Arab historian, author of *Tárikh-i-Kámil* (1160-1232), his description of Somnath and its destruction, I, pt. i, 165, 522-523 ; his mention of Porbandar, *id.* 524 ; *see* also IX, pt. ii, 3 note 3.
Ibn Batuta, Ibni Batuta : African traveller (1340), his mention of Thána, XIV, 215 note 1, 356, 357 ; I, pt. ii, 3, 5 ; visits Daulatábád (1342), XIII, 440 ; I, pt. ii, 534 ; his mention of Cambay (1342), VI, 216 ; his notice of Anjidiv, Chitákul, Honávar and Sidhápur in Kanara district, XV, pt. ii, 252, 278, 308, 343 ; his mention of Náiatas, IX, pt. ii, 14 note 3.
Ibn Haukal, Ibni Haukal or Ibn-i-Haukal : Arab traveller and geographer (943-976), I, pt. ii, 388 ; his references to towns Fámhal, Kámhal, Anahilavada and Kambáya, I, pt. i, 507, 511 and notes 5, 6, 7, 8, 510 note 1, 514 and notes 6, 7, 8, 516 and notes 8, 9, 10, 518, 519, 521, 523, 526, 527, 528, 529 ; IX, pt. ii, 2 note 1 ; exclusiveness of Hindus according to, IX, pt. i, 450 note 7, 470 note 2 ; his reference to the dress of infidels, IX, pt. ii, 183 note 3, 187 note 1 ; his reference to towns in Fárs, *id.* 188 note 3 ; places Sopára between Cambay and Sanján, XIV, 321.
Ibni-Khaldun : (1332-1405), mentions certain words possessing peculiar power, IX, pt. ii, 143.
Ibni Khallikan, Ibni Khalli Khán : author of the biographical dictionary, I, pt. i, 522 note 4 ; his reference to Mirhan, the ancestor of Al Isbáháni, IX, pt. ii, 68 note 1.
Ibni Khurdadbah, Ibn Khurdadba : Arab writer (912), held high office at Baghdad, I, pt. ii, 387 ; I, pt. i, 506 and note 7 ; his reference to Juzr as the fourth in rank of the kings of India, *id.* 468, 509 note 5 ; his reference to Anahilavada, *id.* 512 ; reference to Bárah, *id.* 513 and note 10 ; his reference to Kol, *id.* 519, 520 ; includes places in Gujarát among cities in Sind, *id.* 527, 528, 530 ; referred to by Al Biruni, *id.* 531.
Ibni-Kiriyyah : describes India, IX, pt. ii, 1 note 1 continued on p. 2.
Ibráhim : *see* Ibráhim Nizám Sháh.
Ibráhim : father of A'li, the founder of the A'lia Bohora sect, IX, pt. ii, 33.
Ibrahim : Ghaznivide (1079), attacks a colony, of Persian fire-worshippers at Dehra, IX, pt. ii, 188 note 4.
Ibráhim A'dil Sháh I : king of Bijápur (1534-1557), abjures the Shia tenets of his family, employs the Dakhanis, substitutes Maráthi for Persian in the state accounts (1534), I, pt. ii, 642 ; is defeated by the *rája* of Vijayánagar, *id.* 643 ; his death (1557), *id.* 644 ; *another account of :* administrative reforms ; wars with Vijayánagar and Ahmadnagar ; attack on Bijápur ; battle of Urchan ; internal disorders ; Abdulla's rebellion ; death of Asadkhán ; Bijápur reverses, XXIII, 413-416 ; mention of, in Panhála inscription, XXIV, 314 ; *see* also XIX, 228-229.
Ibráhim A'dil Sháh II : nephew and successor of A'li A'dil Sháh (1580-1626), I, pt. ii, 647 ; plots and counterplots during the minority of, *id.* 647 ; asserts his independence (1591), *id.* 648 ; harasses the invading army of Burhán Nizám Sháh and compels him to sue for peace (1592), *id.* 648 ; his campaign into the Karnátak and Malabár, *id.* 648 ; his campaign against Ahmadnagar ends in the defeat and death of Ibráhim Nizám Sháh, *id.* 649 ; marries his daughter to Dánial, son of Akbar, *id.* 649 ; resists the consolidation of Ahmadnagar by Malik Amber ; his death, *id.* 649 ; *another account of :* internal disorders, attack on Bijápur, the Mughals in Ahmadnagar, Mughal alliance, condition (1604), change of capital, siege of Bijápur (1624), XXIII, 420-424 ; his conversion to Hinduism, *id.* 636.
Ibráhimi : gold coin, I, pt. i, 219 note 2, 222 note 2.
Ibráhim Khán : fortieth viceroy of Gujarát (1705), I, pt. i, 293 ; forty-second viceroy (1706), *id.* 295 ; resigns (1708), *id.* 296.
Ibráhim Khán : *nawáb* of Janjira (1848-1879), his quarrel with his *sardárs*, dethroned by them, Ganpati riots in his state, his death (1879), XI, 449-452.
Ibráhim Miyan : Fateh Muhammad's son (1813), unfriendly to the British, his death, V, 155, 156, 157.
Ibráhim Nizám Sháh : son and successor of Burhán Nizám Sháh, defeated and killed in an action with the Bijápur troops (1594), I, pt. ii, 624, 649.
Ibráhim Roza : tomb of Ibráhim II in Bijápur city, XXIII, 608-611 ; I, pt. ii, 649.
Ichalkaranji : town and state in Kolhápur territory, temples, mosque and fairs at, XXIV, 278 ; survey of, *id.* 254-255.

Ichthyophthalmite: mineral found near Poona city, XVIII, pt. i, 13.

Iconoclasm: Portuguese, XIII, 462.

I'd: festival of sacrifice on the tenth day of Zilhajj month, observances of, IX, pt. ii, 141; feasts and prayers on, *id.* 115, 126, 127, 132, 135, 136; Ramazán, festival at the end of Ramazán fast on the first day of Shawwál month, observances of, *id.* 141; feasts and prayers on, *id.* 115, 126, 127, 132, 135, 136; Shiáh festival on account of Pir Dádú's investiture, observed by Khojahs only, *id.* 41.

Idsiturai Nád: Ededore district, I, pt. ii, 436.

Idar: state in Mahi Kántha, its description, population, trade, V, 398-399; history, legends, Gehlot rulers (800-970), Parihar rulers (1000-1200), *id.* 400; Ráthod supremacy (1250), IX, pt. i, 128; Musalmán supremacy (1300), V, 398; Záfarkhán defeats the *rája* of (1393), I, pt. i, 232, 233; siege of (1398), V, 398-399; references to the *rája* of, I, pt. i, 218, 226, 236, 237; defeat of the chief of (1425), *id.* 238; Ahmadnagar fort built (1427), V, 401-403; Idár taken, again taken by the Musalmáns (1514), recovered from them (1540), tributary to Akbar, *id.* 403-404; taken by Murád (1656), regained (1658), retaken by Musalmáns; death of the chief of, I, pt. i, 286; regained and retaken (1679), V, 398-399; regained (1718); Jodhpur chiefs (1731); unsuccessful attack on, by Jawán Mard Khán (1735), I, pt. i, 315; Rehvar Rájpúts (1742), V, 405-406; Maráthá ascendancy (1766), Idar family divided (1790), enforces tribute from neighbouring chiefs (1800-1804), dispute about Báyad (1823-1833), British supervision (1833), Ahmadnagar lapses to Idár (1848); genealogical tree of its chiefs, *id.* 406-409; (for Maráthá ascendancy *see* also VII, 184-185, 328); land tenures, justice, *id.* 410-411; revenue, *id.* 392, 411; instruction, health, *id.* 412. *Town,* history and objects of interest in, *id.* 432-437; identified with Ophir, XIV, 318.

Iddat: term of three months after divorce, IX, pt. ii, 168.

I'dgáh: Sunni prayer place to hold I'd or festival service, also called *namázgáh,* IX, pt. ii, 127 note 1, 130, 132 141.

Idgah: prayer place in Bijápur city, XXIII, 635, 639.

Id-i-Ghadir: great Shiah holiday on the eighteenth of Zilhajj, IX, pt. ii, 141.

Idigur: district, I, pt. ii, 400.

Idiots: number of, in Surat and Broach districts, II, 50, 370; in Kaira and Panch Máhals districts, III, 27, 214; in Ahmadábád district, IV, 33; in Rewa Kántha, VI, 21; *see* Census Details.

Idiyama: Chola feudatory, attacked by Gangarája (1117), I, pt. ii, 308, 495, 498, 499; *see* Adiyama.

Idol ornaments: manufacture of, in Ahmadábád district, IV, 129.

Idols: search for, in Hindu houses by the Portuguese, I, pt. ii, 59; stones used in making, IX, pt. i, 362; stones for, found near Poona city, XVIII, pt. i, 29.

Idol-worshippers: among early Arabs, IX, pt. ii, 1 note 1.

Idrisi: *see* Al Idrisi.

Idul-Fitr: *see* Id-ur-Ramazán.

Iganmaraimangala: village, I, pt. ii, 327.

Igatpuri: sub-division of Násik district, its area, aspect, climate, water, history, land revenue, stock, holdings, crops and people, XVI, 370-374; origin of the name, *id.* 444 note 1; copper-plate grants found in, I, pt. ii, 185; town, railway station and workshops at, XVI, 444-445.

Iggali: in Mysore, inscription at, I, pt. ii, 304.

Ihtam-fazashat: name possessing special powers, IX, pt. ii, 143.

Ihtam-karashat: name possessing special powers, IX, pt. ii, 143.

Ijára: revenue farming system in Kaira and Panch Mahála, III, 89, 262.

Ijpura: state in Mahi Kántha, V, 429.

Ikhlas Khán: son of Takarib Khán, I, pt. ii, 596.

Ikshváku: son of Manu, son of the sun, I, pt. ii, 277 note 1; king of Ayodhya, *id.* 287 note 4.

Ilachi: cardamom, grown in Kánara district, XXV, 176.

Iláo: copper-plate grant found at, I, pt. i, 146 note 3, 117.

Ilgar, *pl.* Ilgaru: a caste of palm-juice sellers in Belgaum district, XXI, 167; in Bijápur district, XXIII, 109-112; in Dhárwár district, XXII, 148-149.

Ilheos Queimados: burnt rocks, Introduction to the History of the Konkan, I, pt. ii, p. xi.

Ilkal: town in Bijápur district, details of temples and flood at (1882), XXIII, 653-654.

Illupi: famine-plant, grows at Dhárwár, XXV, 201.

Il Morro: Korlai rock, I, pt. ii, 50.

Ilol: state in Mahi Kántha, V, 421.

Ilval: demon at Bádámi in Bijápur district, story of, XXIII, 378.

Imad-ud-din: a Hadramant saint, IX, pt. ii, 15 note 4.

Imád-ul-Mulk: governor of Khándesh (1346), XII, 243.

Imámbádas: Shiáh private mourning chapels, IX, pt. ii, 131, 132; recitals of elegies at, *id.* 132, 133.

Imáms: leaders of the Prophet's family, IX, pt. ii, 3 note 3 continued on page 4; religious leaders, *id.* 131; Shiáh, *id.* 125 note 2; Sunni, *id.* 125 note 2, 126; concealed, *id.* 48.

Imámsháh, Imámsháh Piráná: Musalmán saint of Piráná, founder of Piráná sect, IX, pt. i, 546; miracles, Matia Kanbis and Káchhiás become his followers, *id.* 154, 167, 168; founds a new sect in Gujarát, IX, pt. ii, 40; works miracles and makes many converts, *id.* 3 note 3 continued on page 4, 66, 76 and note 1; denounces the Khojáh practice of tythe gahtering and is excommunicated, *id.* 41; his death (1512); his followers among Matia Kanbis, *id.* 66; among Momnás, *id.* 76;

shrine of, at Karamthah, *id.* 3 note 3 continued on page 4.
Imám-ud-din: Sayad, son of Imám Sháh, Pirána Pir, died at Karamthah, IX, pt. ii, 3 note 3 continued on page 4.
Imlach: Colonel, takes Siddhagad, Bhagvantgad and Achra (1818), I, pt. ii, 118.
Immadi: Nolombadhirája II, the Pallava king (977), I, pt. ii, 332.
Immadi or Immadi Bijjal: son of Vijjana, orders Basava to be arrested, I, pt. ii, 227, 481.
Immigrants: into Konkan, Pársis, Jews, Abyssinians, and Arabs, Introduction to the History of the Konkan, I, pt. ii, p. xii; Bene-Israels and Pársis, *id.* 7; all district volumes, *see* under district name.
Imodi Sadáshiv: seventh Sonda chief (1745-1763), XV, pt. ii, 120 note 3; unfriendly to the Maráthás (1750), *id.* 136; driven by Haidar's general, *id.* 140; inscription of, *id.* 348, 349 and note 10.
Imperata (saccharum) spontanea: fodder plant, XXV, 277.
Imports: into Skythia, I, pt. i, 544; into Chaul from Mecca, Aden and Ormuz, I, pt. ii, 35; into Bijnagar, *id.* 62; all district volumes, *see* trade under district name.
Impotency: believed to be cured by bath in Mán Sarovar, IX, pt. i, 366; *see* also XVIII, pt. i, 93.
Inám: free tenure in Baroda state, Khanderáv's commission on, VII, 350, 352-353.
Inám commission: fanatical spirit excited by the proceedings of, I, pt. i, 436.
Inám villages: Marátha system of conferring, XIX, 264-265.
Incarnations: *see* Avatárs.
Incense: found in Cutch, V, 21.
Inchbird: Captain, chief of forces sent to Underi (1733), XXVI, pt. i, 166; deputed to confer with Chimnaji, the Marátha general (1739), *id.* 214-215; XIII, 495; entrusted with the transfer of Chaul to the Maráthas (1739-40), XXVI, pt. i, 229, 234-236, 238-242; sent to the Maráthas (1741), *id.* 247.
Income tax riots: in Thána district (1860), XIII, 525.
Indápur; sub-division in Poona district, its boundaries, area, aspect, water, climate, stock, crops, people, cultivators and communications, XVIII, pt. iii, 82-84; survey of, *id.* pt. ii, 389-392, 394, 396, 414, 425, 435, 471-475. *Town,* details and history of, XVIII, pt. iii, 132.
Indargad: fort taken by Lieutenant Welsh (1780), I, pt. i, 409.
Inde: *see* Indi.
Indhyádri: range of hills north of the Dakhan, I, pt. ii, 354 note 2.
Indi: sub-division of Bijápur district, its boundaries, area, aspect, soil, climate, water, stock, crops and people, XXIII, 538-540; survey and revision survey of, *id.* 460-464, 484-491. *Town,* people and inscriptions at, *id.* 378, 654-655; trade centre, *id.* 360; *see* also I, pt. i, 541.
India: frontier of, IX, pt. i, 446 note 4; religious sects of, I, pt. i, 530; home of wisdom, *id.* 531; ruled over by Singhana, the Yádava king, I, pt. ii, 525; early connection of, with Persia, IX, pt. ii, 183 note 4.
Indian Antiquary: establishment of the, Introduction to the Early History of the Dakhan, I, pt. ii, p. iii.
Indian Archipelago: I, pt. i, 536.
Indian Gazelle: in Kánara district, XV, pt. i, 103.
Indian lilac: *limb,* tree in Poona district, XVIII, pt. i, 50.
Indian millet: cultivation of, in Ahmadábád, district, IV, 54; in Násik district, XVI, 99; in Ahmadnagar district, XVII, 262-264; in Poona district, XVIII, pt. ii, 39-40; in Belgaum district, XXI, 248; in Dhárwár district, XXII, 273-274; in Bijápur district, XXIII, 319-320.
Indian mulberry: tree in Khándesh district, XII, 163.
Indian rat-snake: in Poona district, XVIII, pt. i, 75.
Indian rock-snake: in Poona district, XVIII, pt. i, 79-80.
Indian settlements and influence: both Buddhist and Bráhman, out of India, IX, pt. I, 437, 441, 446 and note 4.
Indigo: cultivation of, in Broach district, II, 407; in Kaira district, III, 53; in Ahmadábád district, IV, 58; in Cambay, VI, 183; in Khándesh, XII, 164, 479; import of, *id.* 227.
Indigofera: *cardifolia, glandulosa, linifolia,* famine plants, found in several districts, XXV, 197; *tinctoria,* a dye-plant, *id.* 242.
Indo-China: conversion of, to Buddhism (B. C. 240); immigration to, of Sákas or Yávanas from Tamluk or Ratnavati on the Hughli (A. D. 100), I, pt. I, 499.
Indo-Parthians: dynasty (A. D. 100), XIII, 411 note 2.
Indori: village in Poona district, XVIII, pt iii, 102.
Indo-Skythia: I, pt. i, 537, 538, 539.
Indra: Vedic deity presiding over sky-water, IX, pt. i, 247, 348; over rain, his powers, *id.* 351; *see* also I, pt. ii, 180.
Indra or Indravarman: Adhirája of the Ganga dynasty of Kaliganagara, I, pt. ii, 334.
Indra: Ráshtrakúta king (A. D. 500), son of Krishna, conquered by Jayasimha I, the Chalukya king of Bádámi, I, pt. i, 120; I, pt. ii, 342.
Indra, Indrarája: Ráshtrakúta prince, founder of Gujarát branch, I, pt. i, 121, 123-124; brother of Govind III, put in charge of Láta, I, pt. ii, 194, 199, 309, 382, 393, 397, 400, 408.
Indra I: Ráshtrakúta king, son of Dantivarman I, I, pt. i, 120, 121; I, pt. ii, 388.
Indra II: son and successor of the Ráshtrakúta king Karka, marries a Chálukya princess, I, pt. ii, 389.
Indra II: Ráshtrakúta king (850), mentioned in Kánheri inscription, XIV, 148.
Indra III: Ráshtrakúta king (915), succeeds his grandfather Krishna II, his grant of

villages and other charities, I, pt. ii, 203, 210; son of Jagattunga II, marries Vijámba, the grand-daughter of Kokkalla I, *id.* 296, 383, 414 notes 1 and 5; his *biruda* or title, *id.* 415; records regarding him, *id.* 415-416, 416 and note 5, 428 note 4; his grants found at Navsári, I, pt. i, 128, 130, 516.
Indra IV: grandson of Krishna III, the Ráshtrakúta king (973), I, pt. ii, 307 and note 1, 422; crowned by the Ganga prince Marasimha, to continue the Ráshtrakúta family, *id.* 306, 424; his death (982), *id.* 425.
Indra Bhattáraka: Eastern Chálukya king, (663), I, pt. ii, 334.
Indradáman, Indradatta: *see* Indravarman.
Indragad: fort in Thána district, XIII, 506; XIV, 10, 98, 108.
Indrai: fort in Násik district, XVI, 441, 445, 447.
Indrája: holiday among Pávrás in Khándesh, XII, 100.
Indrakeśidevarasa: Kálachurya Someśvara's feudatory, I, pt. ii, 486.
Indráni: one of the Pleiades, I, pt. ii, 337 note 4.
Indrapura: Indore, I, pt. ii, 196.
Indrarája: Siláhára king, I, pt. ii, 537.
Indratta: Bráhman, said to have passed into dead body of king Nanda, IX, pt. i, 437 note 2.
Indravarman: *see* Indra.
Indravarman, Indradáman or Indradatta: Traikutaka king (700), I, pt. ii, 295 note 1, 297.
Indravarman: Satyásraya Dhruvarája, the Western Chálukya chief (643), I, pt. ii, 311, 349.
Indráyani: river in Poona district, XVIII, pt. i, 7.
Indrayeen: medicinal plant, found in several districts, XXV, 254, 255.
Indrayudha: contemporary of Govinda III, I, pt. ii, 395.
Indu: the moon, I, pt. ii, 511; *see* Soma.
Indulgencies: the ten Buddhist, XIV, 137 note 2.
Indur: I, pt. ii, 196; *see* Indrapura.
Indus: river, I, pt. i, 517, 533, 534, 537, 538, I, pt. ii, 576.
Industries: all district volumes, *see* under district name.
Infanticide: formerly prevalent among Kanbis in Ahmadábád district, IV, 36; in Cutch, V, 64, 134, 184-187; in Pálanpur, *id.* 309; in Mahi Kántha, *id.* 891; prohibited in Baroda territory (1850). VII, 270; among Káthiáwár Rájpúts, VIII, 112-113; female, among Kanbis, IX, pt. i, 166, 167; among Rájpúts, *id.* 141.
Infanticide Act: applied to Kadva Kanbis, IX, pt. i, 165; to Leva Kanbis, *id.* 167, 168.
Infirmities: all district volumes, *see* under district name.
Infra-trappean Rocks: in Belgaum district, XXI, 26; in Bijápur district, XXIII, 38-39.
Ingadulcis: oil-yielding plant, XXV, 217.
Ingaleshvar: *see* Ingleshvar.
Ingalgundi: village in Dhárwár district, temple and inscription at, XXII, 762.
Ingali: in the Nizám's dominions, record of A. D. 1210 at, I, pt. ii, 522, 523.
Ingaligi: in the Nizám's dominions, inscription in the Jain temple at, I, pt. ii, 448 note 6.
Ingleshvar or Ingaleshvar: village in Bijápur district, temples, caves and inscriptions at, XXIII, 655-656; *see* also I, pt. ii, 455 note 5, 472 note 2, 527, 528.
Ingunige: village managed by Jakkaladevi, I, pt. ii, 448.
Initiation: *see* Bismillah.
Initiation ceremony: of the Mánbhávs, XVII, 183; of the Arádhis, XVIII, pt. i, 444-445; of Jangams, *id.* 454: of Uchlias, *id.* 465-466; of Lingáyat priests, XXIII, 230-233.
Inns: kept by women (1474), XV, pt. i, 120 note 1.
Inquisition: established in Goa (1560), XIII, 201, 463; its working, *id.* 202; prisoners of, I, pt. ii, 52, 56; jurisdiction of, *id.* 57; managed by the Dominicans, *id.* 60; tyranny of, *id.* 61; abolition (1775) and restoration (1779) of, *id.* 61.
Inquisitors: sent from Europe (1560), I, pt. ii, 56; Dominicans impress the native with dread and overawe their own clergy who appeal to Rome against them, *id.* 60-61.
Insane: number of, in Surat and Broach districts, II, 50, 370; in Kaira and Panch Mahále, III, 27, 214; in Ahmadábád district, IV, 33; in Thána district, XIII, 668; *see* Census Details.
Inscribed stones: at Akshi and Chaul in Kolába district, XI, 253, 272, 471.
Inscriptions: of Goa Kádambas, I, pt. i, 172 note 3; of Naravarman, *id.* 173; of Madanavarman, *id.* 178, 203-204; at Bhinmál, *id.* 471-488; in Káthiáwár, VIII, 273, 274, 282, 283; in Kolába district and Janjira state, XI, 253, 257, 266 and note 1, 291 and notes 3, 5 and 6, 295 and notes 1 and 4, 296 and notes 1 and 2, 298 and notes 1 and 2, 300 and note 1, 303 notes 1, 2 and 3, 304 notes 1 and 2, 331, 332 and note 1, 333, 334, 342, 356; in Thána district, XIII, 407 note 1, 408, 409, 412, 413, 420, 424, 428, 437; XIV, 8, 9, 10, 13, 16 note 1, 21, 38-43, 48 notes 1 and 2, 55, 58, 103, 104, 105, 111, 112 and note 2, 115 note 3, 118, 119, 127, 146, 148, 166, 167, 169, 171, 172, 173, 174, 175, 177, 178, 179, 183, 184, 185, 186, 187 note 1, 188, 189, 196, 198, 206, 209, 210, 211, 212, 225 and note 2, 229, 286, 287, 288, 289, 291, 293, 303, 314, 319, 320, 324, 339, 350, 355, 356, 363, 372, 379, 385, 386, 387, 388, 389, 390, 391-394, 395, 396, 399 and note 2, 400, 401, 402, 418, 419; in Kánara district, XV, pt. ii, 75, 77, 78, 82, 84, 88, 93, 96, 97, 101, 106, 107, 115, 120, 121, 261-264, 265, 267-270, 276, 280 and note 1, 298 and note 3, 335, 348; in Násik district, XVI, 419, 424, 435, 436, 437 and note 1, 438 note 8, 445, 449 and note 4, 458, 461 and note 1, 504, 505, 507, 510, 517, 532, 535, 542, 630, 643, 660; in Poona district, on the Mutha Canal, XVIII, pt. ii, 20; on the Nira Canal, *id.* 23-24; on the Mátoba tank, *id.* 25-26; on the Shirsuphal tank, *id.* 27; on the Bhádalvádi tank,

id. 27; at Nána pass (B. C. 90-A. D. 30), *id.* 212; Shatkarni (B. C. 90), *id.* 212 and note 1; other Buddhist (A. D. 100-200), *id.* 212-213; in Sholápur district, XX, 275 note 2; in Belgaum district, XXI, 354, 356, 357-360, 367.
Insectivora: order of animals, in Ratnágiri district, X, 44.
Insects: in Dhárwár district, XXII, 41-42.
Insessores: family of birds in Ratnágiri, X, 61-84; in Thána district, XIII, 49.
Instruction: all district volumes, *see* under district name.
Insurance: in Ahmadábád district, IV, 65; in Cutch, V, 122; in Káthiáwár, VIII, 207-208; in Kánara district, XV, pt. ii, 25; in Násik district, XVI, 115; in Ahmadnagar district, XVII, 299; in Poona district, XVIII, pt. ii, 105-106; in Dhárwár district, XXII, 322; in Kolhápur state, XXIV, 192.
Intercalary month: in a Hindu year, IX, pt. i, 349; why found necessary, XVIII, pt. i, 241 and note 1. *See* Adhika.
Interest: rate of, in Dakhan, under the Andhrabrityás, I, pt. ii, 176; in Surat district, II, 202; in Broach district, *id.* 452; in Kaira and Panch Maháls districts, III, 60, 237; in Ahmadábád district, IV, 71; in Cutch, V, 111; in Pálanpur, *id.* 297; in Mahi Kántha, *id.* 374; in Rewa Kántha, VI, 41; in Baroda territory, VII, 116, 127, 131-133, 420; in Káthiáwár, VIII, 206; in Ratnágiri district and Sávantvádi state, X, 159, 429; in Kolába district and Janjira state, XI, 104, 426; in Khándesh district, XII, 195; in Thána district, XIII, 309; in Kánara district, XV, pt. ii, 28, 29; in Násik district, XVI, 117; in Ahmadnagar district, XVII, 300-301; in Poona district, XVIII, pt. ii, 107-108; in Sátára district, XIX, 183-184; in Sholápur district, XX, 249; in Belgaum district, XXI, 294; in Dhárwár district, XXII, 326; in Bijápur district, XXIII, 346-347; in Kolhápur state, XXIV, 194; native system of calculating, in Gujarát, entry in *Viyaj-Vahi*, IX, pt. i, 85-88.
Interest Book: *See* Viyaj-Vahi.
Inter-trappean Beds: in Bijápur district, XXIII, 45; in Belgaum district, XXI, 30-31.
Inthapatha-puri: Indraprastha, capital of Cambodia, I, pt. i, 499.
Inundations: *see* Floods.
Investments: forms of, in Surat district, II, 183, 184; in Broach district, *id.* 448, 449; in Kaira and Panch Maháls district, III, 57, 236; in Ahmadábád district, IV, 67; in Cutch, V, 110; in Pálanpur, *id.* 297; in Mahi Kántha, *id.* 373; in Baroda territory, VII, 112-115, 126-127; in Káhiáwár, VIII, 200; in Ratnágiri district, X, 156-159; in Sávantvádi, *id.* 428; in Kolába district, XI, 102-103; in Thána district, XIII, 307; in Kánara district, XV, pt. ii, 25-28; in Násik district, XVI, 114, 115; in Ahmadnagar district, XVII, 296-297; in Sátára district, XIX, 179-180; in Belgaum district, XXI, 291, 292; in Dhárwár district, XXII, 323-324; in Bijápur district, XXIII, 344.
Iomanes: the Yamuna, I, pt. i, 533.
Iora: class of birds in Ratnágiri district, X, 75.
Ipomœa: *hederacea*, medicinal plant, XXV, 255; *pes-capræ*, sacred plant, *id.* 285-286; *reniformis, sepiaria*, famine-plants, *id.* 202; *turpethum*, medicinal plant, *id.* 255.
Ippi: famine-plant found at Dhárwár, XXV, 201.
Irán: *see* Persia.
Ireninae: family of birds in Ratnágiri, X, 76 note 1.
Irideæ: a species of food-plants, XXV, 177.
Iridige: country, I, pt. ii, 282 note 5, 347 note 2; territory in the Konkan forming the Sávantvádi state and the Ratnágiri district, Mahásaptama or the great seventh, one of the divisions of the seven Konkans, *id.* 372, 538.
Irivabedanga, Irivabedangadeva, or Irivabedeng: Satyáśraya, I, pt. ii, 341 note 2, 426; *biruda* or title of the Western Chálukya king Satyáśraya, *id.* 414 note 1, 431, 432, 433, 434, 514, 537, 567.
Irivabedang Márasimha: chief of Manalur family, I, pt. ii, 437.
Iriva Nolambádhiráj: also called Ghateya-Ankakara, Western Chálukya king Vikramáditya V's vassal, I, pt. ii, 333.
Irmadi: *see* Immadi.
Iron: in Kaira and Panch Maháls, III, 15, 197; in Cutch, V, 19, 124; in Rewa Kántha, VI, 11; smelting of, in Káthiáwár, VIII, 90-91; in Ratnágiri district, X, 29; export of, *id.* 175; at Mátherán, XIV, 241, 266; in Kánara district, XV, pt. i, 19; working of, in Sátára district, XIX, 220-221; smelting, *id.* 28-29; in Belgaum district, XXI, 52-53; in Dhárwár district, XXII, 25; in Bijápur district, XXIII, 51-53; in Kolhápur state, XXIV, 18; smelting of, *id.* 18-19, 208; working of, in Sholápur district, XX, 273.
Iron clay: formation of, in Ratnágiri district, X, 396; rock in Poona district, XVIII, pt. i, 12; *see* Laterite rock.
Iron Flail: of the Puranic hero Krishna, legend of the, I, pt. i, 10 and note 2.
Iron Pots: making of, in Poona district, XVIII, pt. ii, 206-207.
Irrigation: all district volumes; *see* under district name.
Irukudi: village in Miraj state, I, pt. ii, 255.
Irumgola: town or province (?), power of, broken by the Hoysála king Vishnuvardhana, I, pt. ii, 496.
Isáji-nimaz: night prayer of the Khojáhs, IX, pt. ii, 49.
Isápur: town near Lohogad in Poona district, fall of (1818), XVIII, pt. ii, 303; *see* also XI, 156.
Isbaháni: Al, famous Hafiz and historian, IX, pt. ii, 68 note 1.
Ishá: night prayer, IX, pt. ii, 126 note 3.
Ishrak: prayer following the morning prayer, IX, pt. ii, 126 note 3.
Ishvar Bárot: Cháran poet, author of *Harirás*, IX, pt. i, 220.

Islám : Mer converts to, I, pt. i, 141 ; spread of (1414), *id.* 236-237 ; precepts of, taught in Kambaya, *id.* 514, 530.
Islámábád : military post (1674) of the Mughals, in Mahi Kántha, I, pt. i, 285 ; *see* Sádra.
Islámábád : modern Kalyán, Musalmán remains at, I, pt. ii, 41.
Islámnagar : *see* Navánagar.
Islámpur, Uran-Islámpur : in Sátara district, lake, trade centre and town, XIX, 158, 215, 597-600.
Islands : in Surat district, II, 9 ; in Broach district, *id.* 342, in Ahmadábád district, IV, 20 ; in Cutch, V, 13-14 ; in Káthiáwár, VIII, 8, 66, 67 ; in Sávantvádi state, X, 388, 389 ; in Thána district, XIII, 2, 11.
Ismáel : successor of Mirán Nizám Sháh, defeated and deposed by Burhán, Mortiza Nizám Sháh's brother (1590), I, pt. ii, 623.
Ismáil : brother of Ibráhim A'dil Sháh II, taken in battle and afterwards put to death (1596) by Hámid Khán, I, pt. ii, 648.
Ismáil : Sidi, minister of the Bábis of Rádhanpur (1820), IX, pt. ii, 12.
Ismáil : son of Muhammad, son of the sixth Shiáh *imám* Jaaffar Sadik ; the last of the revealed *imáms* according to the Ismailians ; IX, pt. ii, 47, 48 ; his dispute with his uncle about the succession to the imámate (765) ; his supporters called Ismáilis, *id.* 30 note 1.
Ismáil A'dil Sháh : son and successor of Yusuf A'dil Khán (1510), I, pt. ii, 641 ; defeats near Bijápur the kings of Ahmadnagar, Golkonda and Berar, and takes Máhmud Sháh Bahamani II and his son A'hmad prisoners ; marries his sister to A'hmad as previously settled, *id.* 641 ; tries to recover Raichur and Mudgal from the Vijayánagar *rája* ; his defeat with great loss, his death (1534), *id.* 642 ; *another account of :* second Bijápur king (1510-1534), imprisoned by Kamál Khán (1510), defeats Burhan Nizám of Ahmadnagar (1524), defeats him a second time (1531), XX, 279-281 ; *another account of :* his minority ; threatened usurpation by the regent Kamál Khán ; death of Kamál Khán ; war with Ahmadnagar, Golkonda, Berar and Vijayánagar ; A'sad Khán appointed commander-in-chief, his character, XXIII, 410-413 ; *see* also X, 329.
Ismáilian, Ismáili : sect of Shiáhs, called after Ismáil, grandson of the sixth Shiáh *imám*, IX, pt. ii, 30 note 1 ; also known as Seveners (because they reckon seven *imáms*) and Ismáilians, *id.* 47 ; separation of, from the main body of Shiáhs (765), *id.* 30 note 1 ; power of, originated with the foundation of the Fatimi dynasty by Obeidullah (910), *id.* 47 ; Ismáilia doctrines first publicly taught at Mahdia (910), at Cairo (953-975), *id.* 48 ; rise of, in Persia from the beginning of the eleventh century ; power of, established at Alamut (1072-1092), by Hassan Sabáh, missionary and political emissary of the Fatimites, *id.* 37 ; division of, into two parties (1094), Nazárians and Mustaálians, *id.* 30 note 1, 36. ; Hasan Sabah supports the Nazárian cause, and ceases to be a missionary (1094) ; the Nazárian form of the sect becomes supreme in Persia, *id.* 37 ; *see* also XIII, 223 note 2.
Ismáil Muhammad : the collector of customs at Cambay in 1741, I, pt. i, 323.
Ismi-Aazám : great name, knowledge of, necessary in high magic, first possessed by the prophet Soleiman, IX, pt. ii, 143.
Isná-Asharis : division of Shiáhs, also known as Twelvers, believe in twelve *imáms*, IX, pt. ii, 47 ; supporters of Musi Kázim the seventh *imám*, *id.* 30 note 1.
Ispandiyár : prince, son of Gushtasp, persuades the emperor of India to adopt fire-worship, IX, pt. ii, 183 note 4.
Istakhlre : Al, IX, pt. ii, 188 note 4.
Istarer, *pl.* Istareru : a caste of silk-weavers and dyers, in Dhárwár district, XXII, 169-170.
Istáv : rising rental, land tenure in Thána district, XIII, 555, 561 note 7 ; leases granted by Ahmadnagar kings in Kolába district, XI, 167.
Istáva kauls : improvement leases in Ratnágiri district, X, 157.
Iśvara, Iśvarapotarája, or Iśvarapotavarman : Parameśvaravarman I, Pallava king, I, pt. ii, 327, 329 note 5, 362 ; *see* Parameśvaravarman I.
Iśvara : prince of the Sinda family, I, pt. ii, 476, 485, 577.
Iśvara : the Hindu god S'iva, I, pt. ii, 469 ; inscription at the temple of, at Tilawalli, *id.* 524 note 1 ; inscription at the temple of, at Chandadampur, *id.* 582 note 4.
Iśvaradatta : Kshatrapa ruler (230-250), coins of, I, pt. i, 51-52 ; ruler, *id.* 57, Abhira chief, comes from Sindh, gains a victory over the Kshatrapas, conquers the western coast and makes Trikuta his capital (249-250), I, pt. ii, 294.
Iśvarapotarája : *see* Iśvara.
Iśvarapotavarman : *see* Iśvara.
Iśvarasena : Abhira king, I, pt. i, 52.
Itgi : village in Kánara district, temple and fair at, XV, pt. ii, 316.
Itimad Khán : regent (1560) in Cambay, VI, 218 ; *see* also IX, pt. ii, 10.
Itola : village in Baroda territory, VII, 535.
Itria Gadhala : táluka in Káthiáwár, VIII, 452.
Itsaka : famine plant, common in India, XXV, 206.
Itsing : Chinese pilgrim ; Bhartrihari's death in A. D. 650 according to, I, pt. ii, 408.
Itvad : state in Rewa Kántha, VI, 152.
Ivatta : *see* Ahivant.
Ive or Ives : traveller, his mention of Bombay (1757), XIII, 499 ; surgeon on Admiral Watson's ship, his account of the capture of Gheria, I, pt. ii, 88, 89 ; his description of A'ngria's fleet (1755), X, 382.
Ivory : East India Company's trade in (1736-1742), XXVI, pt. ii, 128-129.
Ivory bracelets : manufacture of, in Ahmadábád district, IV, 139.
Izáfat : land tenure in Thána district, historical review of, XIII, 534, 539 and note 3, 540-544.
Izáfa Taufer : extra cesses levied by Sávnur *nawábs* (1752), XXII, 443.

Izáfat Khots: revenue farmers in Kolába district and Janjira state, XI, 163, 453.
Izárdárs: farmers of revenue in Baroda state, civil and criminal powers of, VII, 440-441.
Izeshne: *see* Yashna.
Izni: office in a brotherhood of beggars, IX, pt. ii, 19.
Izz-ud-din: name of a head *mulla* of Dáudi Bohorás (1817), IX, pt. ii, 31 note 4.

J

JAAFAR: Shirázi *sayad*. *See* Ahmed Jáafar Shirazi.
Jaafar-Al-Mansur: Abbási Khalifáh (754-775), I, pt. i, 524.
Jaáfari Bohorá. *See* Bohorá.
Jaáfar Muthanna: Sáyad, ancestor of the Bukharis, IX, pt. ii, 6 note 1 (1).
Jaáfar Sádik: sixth Shiáh *imám*, his death (765), dispute for the succession among his heirs, IX, pt. ii, 30 note 1, 47, 125 note 2.
Jab: food plant, grown in Gujarát and Dakhan, XXV, 189.
Jabalpur: district and town in Central Provinces, I, pt. ii, 176, 181, 410, 425, 527; Visaladeva retires to, for help, I, pt. i, 203.
Jabwa: state in Central India, *rája* of, shelters Captain Hutchinson, I, pt. i, 439.
Jaca, jack-tree: found in several districts, XXV, 172; *see* also XVIII, pt. i, 51; X, 37, 39.
Jacana: the pheasant-tailed, in Ratnágiri district, X, 93.
Jáchikadeva: king, copper-plate of, I, pt. i, 136.
Jack: *see* Jaca.
Jacob, Sir George LeGrand: Political Agent in Káthiáwár, VIII, 199, 308: Political Agent at Kolhápur (1858), XXIV, 308.
Jacqnemont: Victor, French traveller, his visit to Poona, description of Dakhan agriculturists (1832), XVIII, pt. ii, 64 note 5, 112; XVII, 306-307; XVIII, pt. iii, 423-424; died (1832), I, pt. ii, 130.
Jád, Jádar: a caste of weavers, in Kánara district XV, pt. i, 277; in Belgaum district, XXI, 138, 139.
Jádam: same as Yádava, I, pt. i, 139.
Jádar: *see* Jád.
Jádav: caste of Rájpúts, peasant proprietors in Káthiáwár, VIII, 115, 267-271; *see* also IX, pt. i, 129.
Jádav Rána, Jádi Rána: Yádav chief of Sanjan (640), allows the Pársis to settle, XIII, 249, 421; I, pt. ii, 14; IX, pt. ii, 185.
Jádejá: Rájpút ruling tribe, sway in Cutch, Káthiáwár, and other places; claim descent from Yádav stock; are believed to be immigrant Turks, IX, pt. i, 126, 446 note 4; their family deity A'shápuri, *id.* 136; peculiarity of practice of female infanticide among, explanation of practice, *id.* 141; *see* also I, pt. i, 137; Rájpúts in Cutch, V, 57-65, 134; in Káthiáwár, VIII, 111-113.
Jádeja Court: a special court in Cutch, V, 188-203.
Jádhavs: Yádavs of Devagiri or Daulatábád, I, pt. ii, 587.
Jádi Rána: *see* Jádav Rána.
Jádoji: son of Umábái Dábháde, I, pt. i, 314.
Jadvi: Bhil headman, VI, 32.
Jáfarábád: port in Káthiáwár, VIII, 240, 452; taken by the Sidis (1759), XI, 447.
Jagadala Purushottama: governor of the Taragale province under Singhana, I, pt. ii, 523.
Jagaddeva or Jag Dev: chief, general of Siddharája, I, pt. i, 172 and note 3.
Jagaddeva: Thribhuvanamalla, of the Sántara family, feudatory of the Western Chálukya king Jagadekamalla II; I, pt. ii, 458 and note 2, 494; power of, destroyed by Vishnuvardhana, *id.* 495, 568.
Jagadekamalla: title assumed by some of the Chálukya kings of Kalyáni, I, pt. ii, 211; *biruda* of Jayasimha the Chálukya king, *id.* 213, 435; *see* also X, 193; *biruda* of Permádi I, I, pt. ii, 575.
Jagadekamalla II: I, pt. ii, 455 note 6; son and successor of the Western Chálukya king Someśvara III, *id.* 222 and note 3, 456 and note 2; his *biruda* or title and records of his reign; his feudatories and officials, *id.* 457 and notes 3 and 5. 458; Perma, *id.* 319 note 1, 459 note 3, 472.
Jagadekavira: *biruda* on title of the Ganga chief Márasimha, I, pt. ii, 305.
Jagalpet: village in Kánara district, XV, pt. ii, 316.
Jagannáth: called Puri, sacred to Buddha, place of pilgrimage in Orissa, IX, pt. i, 119, 157, 168, 225, 549.
Jagannáth Láldás: a rich Surat merchant, broker of the Company, becomes a Marátha commander (1738), II, 112 note 1.
Jagatjhampaka: world guardian, another name of Durlabha, Chálukya king, I, pt. i, 162.
Jagatsen: gives Shrimál to Gujarát Bráhmans, I, pt. i, 463.
Jagatsvámi: I, pt. i, 460, 463. *See* Jagsvámi.
Jagattunga: *see* Jagattunga, II.
Jagattung I: Ráshtrakúta king I, pt. ii, 210; *see* Govind III.
Jagattunga II: Ráshtrakúta king, son of Akálavarsha Krishna II, I, pt. ii, 202, 210, 414; Dr. Bhandárkar holds that he married but one princess of the Haihaya race, *id.* 203, 204 note 2; Dr. Fleet holds that he married two princesses of the Haihaya race, *id.* 296, 374 note 5, 414 note 5; died without ascending the throne, *id.* 202, 414 note 1; *see* also I, pt. i, 128, 130.
Jagattunga III: Ráshtrakúta prince, brother of Krishna III, I, pt. ii, 420, 422.
Jag Dev: *see* Jagaddeva.
Jageshvar: shrine and cistern of, I, pt. i, 453.
Jago: John de St., Portuguese apostate in the service of Sultán Bahádur of Cambay (1536), I, pt. i, 350.
Jagpálráv: Phaltan chief, XIX, 231.
Jágrau: *see* Jagri.
Jagri: class of dancers in North Gujarát, IX, pt. i, 512 note 1.
Jágria: caste of tape-weavers in Cutch, V, 82.

Jagsom: king of Káshmir, I, pt. i, 460, 461, 464; probably builder of the temple at Bhinmál, *id.* 460.
Jag Swámi: or sun, temple of, at Bhinmál, IX, pt. i, 499; I, pt. i, 451, 456, 459, 463, 471.
Jahángir: Mughal emperor (1605-1627), Portuguese treaty with (1614), I, pt. ii, 62; XIII, 454; visits Mandu in 1617; receives English ambassador Sir T. Roe at Mandu, I, pt. i, 361, 372-377; his visit to Ahmadábád (1617), V, 136; exerts to spread Islám (1618), IX, pt. ii, 5, 125; persecutes (1618) Ahmadábád Jains, *id.* 5 note 3; makes a grant of Ratnágiri near Navsári to Mulla Jamasp, IX, pt. ii, 197 note 2.
Jahángir Khán: Bahamani general (1485), XVII, 357.
Jaház: sailing vessel, in Thána district, XIII, 718.
Jahez: wife's property among Musalmáns, goes with her own divorce, IX, pt. ii, 165 note 2.
Jahla: son of Dáda, I, pt. ii, 237; Bhillama's general, *id.* 238, 239.
Jahlana: author of *Suktimuktávali*, I, pt. ii, 245.
Jái: a caste of bastard Bráhmans in Ahmadnagar district, XVII, 57-58.
Jaichand: *rája* of Kanauj, takes to wife an Afghán woman who causes his death, IX, pt. ii, 39.
Jaikadeva: Mehr king, his grant, I, pt. i, 87; another name of Jáchikadeva, *id.* 137; his grant at Morbi, *id.* 139; copper-plate of, *id.* 81.
Jaikop: properly Jakshkop, I, pt. i, 454 and note 1; lake near Bhinmál, *id.* 455, 456-458, 471.
Jail or jails: Portuguese, at Bassein, Chaul, and Daman, I, pt. ii, 52; in Bombay island, the Mapla Par used as (1687), transferred to Dongri Fort (1728-1769), temporarily removed to Moody's house (1739), removed to the Marine Yard (1769-1798), the Umarkhádi jail built (1804), XXVI, pt. iii, 608-611; all district volumes, *see* under district name.
Jaimur: Arab rendering of Chaul, XI, 271.
Jain, Jains: religion, IX, pt. i, 105-110, doctrines, daily life, customs, XXIV, 133-146; holidays, IX, pt. i, 113-115; places of pilgrimage, *id.* 550; temples, *id.* 110-113; temples in the Annigere province, I, pt. ii, 441; burnt by Cholás in the reign of Someśvara, I, *id.* 443; temples of the Gangávádi province restored by Gangarája, *id.* 499-501; religion of the Hoysálas, *id.* 491; saints Párasnáth and Mahávir in Kolhápur state, XXIV, 134; overthrow of, by Ekántada Rámayya, I, pt. ii, 406 note 5, 437 note 5, 483; persecution by the Lingáyats, *id.* 479, 482; of Ahmadábád, persecuted by emperor Jehángir (1618), IX, pt. ii, 5 note 3; at Cambay (1241), VI, 215; at Chaul (1584), XI, 278 note 5; a caste in Baroda state, VII, 67; in Bijápur district, XXIII, 280-282; in Kolhápur state, strength and distribution of, XXIV, 133; traders in Ratnágiri district, X, 119; in Sávantvádi, *id.* 413; in Sátára district, XIX, 58; in Dhárwár district, XXII, 116-119; in Belgaum district, XXI, 102, 103; goldsmiths in Khándesh district, XII, 72; tailors, *id.* 74; husbandmen in Kánara district, XV, pt. i, 229-236; of the Digambara sect I, pt ii, 191.
Jainápur: village in Bijápur district, temples at, XXIII, 656-657.
Jaina Purána: consecration of the, I, pt. ii, 201-202.
Jainendravyákarana: work by Pujyapáda, a Jain teacher, I, pt. ii, 371.
Jainism: under the Chálukyas, three kings of this dynasty favour it by repairs to temples and grant of villages; it holds its sway in the Southern Marátha Country only, I, pt. ii, 191; under the Ráshtrakútas, *id.* 208; under the Chálukyas, *id.* 228, 406, 435; traces of, in Ratnágiri district, X, 119.
Jain Shimpis: a class of tailors in Ahmadnagar district, XVII, 99, 103.
Jain Temples: in Belgaum city, XXI, 539-542.
Jaiphal: oil-yielding plant, XXV, 214.
Jaipur: identification of, with Náráyan, I, pt. i, 511 note 12, 520; conquest of, by Muhammad, son of Kásim, IX, pt. ii, 1 note 1.
Jai Ráj: king referred to by historian Ufi, I, pt. i, 512.
Jaishekar: Chávda king of Panchásar (A. D. 700), Gurjar lord, IX, pt. i, 488 note 3.
Jaising: Aurangzeb's general, invades Bijápur (1664), I, pt. ii, 652.
Jaitapala: *see* Jaitugi I.
Jaitasimha: *see* Jaitrasimha.
Jaitrapála: *see* Jaitugi I.
Jaitrapála: I, pt. ii, 244; *see* Jaitugi II.
Jaitrasimha or Jaitasimha: minister of Bhillama, defeated at Lakkundi by Vira-Ballála II, I, pt. ii, 238, 502, 503, 520.
Jaitugi I or Jaitrasimha: son and successor of Bhillama, the Devagiri-Yádava king (1191-1210), I, pt. ii, 238, 504, 519, 521; records of his time, his titles, epithets, officers, *id.* 503, 521 and note 1; kills king Rudra of the Tailangas and places his nephew on the throne, *id.* 239, 522; makes Bháskarachárya's son Lakshmidhara his chief *pandit*, *id.* 239, 526, 582; XV, pt. ii, 92 and note 1, 93.
Jaitugi II or Jaitrapála: Devagiri-Yádava prince, son of Singhana, dies before his father, I, pt. ii, 519, 526, 244.
Jajalladeva: I, pt. ii, 240, 525 and note 2; *see* Jajjalla.
Jajjaka: minister of Akálavarsha Krishna, I, pt. i, 128.
Jajjalla or Jajalladeva: king defeated by Singhana, I, pt. ii, 239, 525 and note 2; of the eastern branch of the Chedi dynasty, *id.* 240.
Jakaladevi, Jákavva, Jákavve: daughter of Bhammaha and wife of Taila II, i, pt. ii, 425, 428 note 1.
Jakhán: place of interest in Cutch, V, 223, 224.
Jákhan: táluka in Káthiáwár, VIII, 453.
Jakhanácharya: Kánarese architect, XV, pt. ii, 261; story of his temples, XXII, 390 and note 2, 650.
Jakhinvádi: *see* Karád.

Jakkaladevi : daughter of Tikka and wife of the Western Chálukya king Vikramáditya VI, i, pt. ii, 428, 448.
Jakkalamádevi : *see* Jákaladevi.
Jal : I, pt. i, 456 ; *see* Pilu.
Jalál Khán : governor of Navalgund, brother-in-law of Alla-ud-din Bahamani II, raises the standard of revolt (1454) at Navalgund, I, pt. ii, 638.
Jalálpor : sub-division of Surat, II, 281-284. *Town, id.* 298.
Jalálpur : town in Káthiáwár, VIII, 453 ; *see* also I, pt. i, 534, 546.
Jalál-ud-din : first Khilji emperor of Delhi, I, pt. ii, 530 ; treacherously murdered by Allá-ud-din, *id.* 531.
Jalal-ud-din : Malikshah, king of Persia (1074-1092) ; orders the preparation of a calendar, IX, pt. ii, 193 note 2.
Jaláludin Akbar : emperor Akbar, IX, pt. ii, 10.
Jálamangala : village in the Idigur district, I, pt. ii, 400.
Jálandhar : demon, slain by Vishnu, IX, pt. i, 387 ; *see* Vranda.
Jalankuhe : village, I, pt. ii, 386.
Jalgaon : place of interest in Khándesh, cotton trade centre, XII, 451-452.
Jalgaon : town in Ahmadnagar district, XVII, 720.
Jalgár : a caste of gold washers, in Dhárwár district, XXII, 22-24, 149-150.
Jalhaná ; daughter of Arnorája, marries Kumárapála, I, pt. i, 185.
Jalia : táluka in Káthiáwár, VIII, 453-454.
Jalikond, Jálikund : island in Kánara district, XV, pt. ii, 316 ; XV, pt. i, 3.
Jalmandirs : water pavilions in Sátára city, XIX, 566.
Jalmukhi : a poisonous shrub, XXV, 265.
Jálu-Vasantgad : Sahyádri spur in Sátára district, XIX, 6.
Jám : title of the chiefs of Jádeja tribe, I, pt. i, 215 and note 2.
Jamá : fixed sum of land revenue, I, pt. i, 212.
Jamábandi : yearly rent settlement, XIII, 575.
Jamadagni : sage, I, pt. ii, 282 note 5.
Jamalgota : medicinal and poisonous plant, found in the Indian Peninsula, XXV, 255, 269.
Jamál Khán : a military officer of Ahmadnagar, defeats and executes Mirza Khán and his foreigners (1588), XVII, 377.
Jamál Pathri : *sayad*, ancestor of Kádiri, *sayad* family in Gujarát, IX, pt. ii, 6 note 1 (2).
Jamál-ud-din : Honávar chief (1342), XV, pt. ii, 92, 308.
Jamasp : Persian priest ; visits Gujarát (1720) ; makes efforts to increase the knowledge of the Pársis in their sacred books ; leaves a copy of a Zend-Pehlevi *Vandidád* ; establishes centres of Zend-Pehlevi scholarships ; makes a present of the true Hom plant and Farvardin Yasht to Surat Pársis, IX, pt. ii, 193 note 2, 194 and note 1.
Jamasp : *mulla*, priest of Navsári, visits Delhi (1619), receives a grant of Ratnágiri near Navsári from the emperor Jahángir, IX, pt. ii, 197 note 2.
Jamáti : a class of Musalmáns in Ratnágiri district, X, 133 ; in Kolába district ; *see* Konkani.
Jamát-kháná : assembly lodge of Khojáhs, IX, pt. ii, 45.
Jamátkhána : Bohorás' meeting house in Poona city, XVIII, pt. iii, 334.
Jamáwal : tribe in Cashmere, I, pt. i, 460, 464.
Jámb : rose apple-tree in Poona district, XVIII, pt. i, 46.
Jamba : Bania minister of Vanarája, I, pt. i, 152.
Jámhavá : village, south of Baroda, I, pt. ii, 399.
Jámbhli : feeder of the Kásári in Kolhápur state, XXIV, 9.
Jámbhul, Jámhul : *Syzigium jambolanum*, wine produced from its fruit, XXV, 211 ; produces a dye, *id.* 245 ; a sacred plant, *id.* 279, 284, 291.
Jámboti : hill and place of interest in Belgaum district, XXI, 7, 572-573.
Jámbrug : village in Thána district, with a cave and temple, XIV, 9, 108-110 ; *see* also I, pt. ii, 9.
Jámbu : a caste of Bráhmans from the Dakhan, IX, pt. i, 1, 10 ; in Thána district, XIII, 78 ; in Ahmadnagar district, XVII, 58. *See* Holyá.
Jámbu : place of interest in Káthiáwár, VIII, 454.
Jámbughoda : head-quarters of Nárukot state in Panch Mahála, VI, 178.
Jámbul : *see* Jambhul.
Jambulni : hills in Poona district, XVIII, pt. i, 4.
Jambumáli : river in ancient Gujarát, I, pt. i, 160.
Jambusar : sub-division of Broach district, II, 535-536 ; town, *id.* 563-564 ; IX, pt. i, 10 ; I, pt. ii, 359 and note 5 ; Bráhmans of, mentioned as grantees, I, pt. i, 111 ; attacked and plundered by Mominkhán (1755), *id.* 339.
Jámbutke : village in Násik district, XVI, 445.
Jambuváda, Jambuvávika : a village near Baroda, I, pt. i, 125.
Jambuvávika, Jambva : stream in Baroda territory, VII, 14 ; I, pt. ii, 399.
Jámda : water works in Khándesh district, XII, 140, 141.
Jámdagni : Hindu sage I, pt. i, 461.
James : Commodore Sir Henry, his naval fight with Tuláji Angria near Gheria (1755), XI, 152 ; takes the forts of Suvarnadurg and Bánkot in Ratnágiri district (1757), XIII, 497 ; *see* also I, pt. ii, 90.
Jámi-ul-Hikáyát : work of Muhammad Ufi, I, pt. i, 512 and note 5.
Jamkhandi : Southern Marátha state, description, production, people, agriculture, capital, trade, justice, finance, health, instruction, places, XXIV, 386-388 ; *Town*, details, trade, centre, temple and fair at, *id.* 388.
Jámkhed : sub-division of Ahmadnagar district, its survey, XVII, 524-528 ; its area, aspect, hills, soils, climate, rainfall, cultivation, crops,

people, roads, trade and crafts, *id.* 593-597 ; *Town*, *id.* 720.
Jammau Jati : Hindu-Musalmán saint of Northern India, IX, pt. ii, 17.
Jamua : the river Yamuna, I, pt. i, 518 ; is held sacred, IX, pt. i, pp. 350, 550.
Jamnábái, Her Highness : wife of His Highness Khanderáv Gáikwár, retires to Poona (1871), returns to Baroda (1875), VII, 279, 285.
Jámnagar : *see* Navánsgar.
Jámner : sub-division in Khándesh district, its boundaries, area, aspect, climate, water, soil, holdings, history, survey details, survey results, stock, crops, people, XII, 2, 375-379 ; *Town*, *id.* 452.
Jampal, jempal, jepal : medicinal and poisonous plant, XXV, 255, 269.
Jáms : Gujarát chiefs, I, pt. i, 139.
Jamsetji Bund : near Poona city, XVIII, pt. iii, 374.
Jamsetji Jijibhái : Lady, builds Máhim causeway, XIII, 323 ; XIV, 21-22.
Jamshed : Behedin, Persian layman, arrives in Gujarát (1736), brings to the notice of the Surat Pársis the wrong reckoning of the year, IX, pt. ii, 193 note 2.
Jamshed : third king of the Peshdádian dynasty, new year's day fixed by, IX, pt. ii, 219.
Jamshed Kekobád : priest, writes in Persian verse an account of the Surat Pársis (1711), IX, pt. ii, 196 note 3.
Jamshedi Naoroz : leading high day ; Jamshed's New Day, IX, pt. ii, 219.
Jám Sihta : Samma chief of Little Cutch, I, pt. i, 518.
Janábái : Vithoba's devotee, XX, 465.
Janái : Hindu village goddess, XVIII, pt. i, 290.
Janamejaya : Gotamiputra compared to, I, pt. ii, 149.
Jananáthapura : modern Malingi, burnt by Vishnuvardhana, I, pt. ii, 497.
Janárdana : son of Gangádhara, teaches Singhana the art of managing elephants, I, pt ii. 239, 245.
Janárdana : title of Hindu god Vishnu, I, pt. ii, 507.
Janáśraya : grant of, I, pt. i, 56.
Janavallabha : *biruda* or title of Govinda III, I, pt. ii, 394.
Janáwal, Janwal, Junáwal : Chunvál or Virangam, notice of, by Al Idrisi, I, pt. i, 509, 513.
Janázah : bier, IX, pt. ii, 168 note 6 ; title of the hymn written by Imámsháh of Pirana, *id.* 40.
Jandur : Ránder town, mention of, by Al Idrisi, I, pt. i, 509 note 4, 520.
Jang : Bharvád, or shepherd wedding, account of, held at Khedsara (April 1895), fixing of day for, IX, pt. i, 270 ; cutting of branches and stem of Khijaro tree for marriage post ; images in post, *id.* 270-272 ; setting up of post, *id.* 272-273 ; arrival of guests, preparations for three feasts, *id.* 273 ; selection of leading bride and bridegroom for wedding, *id.* 273-274 ; first feast, *id.* 274-275 ; second feast, *id.* 275-278 ; third feast, *id.* 278 ; Pavaiyá's play of *Kalas Bharna*, *id.* 279 280 ; wedding of senior bridegroom, *id.* 281-283 ; of other bridegrooms, *id.* 283 ; absorption or *nirvána* of pillar, *id.* 284-285.
Jangam : Lingáyat priests, I, pt. ii, 479, 481, 226 ; IX, pt. i, 544 ; in Ratnágiri district, X, 131, 141 ; in Sávantvádi, *id.* 413 ; in Kolába, district, XI, 74, 412 ; in Thána district, XIII, 197 ; in Kánara district, XV, pt. i, 175, 177 ; in Násik district, XVI, 74 ; in Poona district, XVIII, pt. i, 454-455 ; in Sátára district, XIX, 59, 118-119 ; in Sholápur district, XX, 184-185 ; in Dhárwár district, XXII, 108-115 ; in Bijápur district, XXIII, 220-221.
Jangameśvara : Hindu god, I, pt. ii, 480.
Janghi : port in the Gulf of Cambay, VIII, 454.
Jangira : *see* Janjira.
Jangli Jaygad : fort in Sátára district, XIX, 5, 469.
Janjira : state in Kolábá district, description, boundaries, sub-divisions, aspect, rivers, creeks, geology, climate, XI, 401-403 ; minerals, forests, domestic animals, wild animals, snakes, birds, fish, *id.* 404-408 ; census details, Hindus, Musalmáns, Beni-Isráels, village communities, movements, *id.* 409-423 ; agricultural population, irrigation crops, bad years, *id.* 424-425 ; interest, currency, money-lenders, mortgages, wages, prices, *id.* 426-427 ; roads, post offices, ferries, vessels, steamers, trade centres, markets, fairs, shopmen, carriers, imports, exports, crafts, *id.* 428-431 ; history, *id.* 432-451 ; land, justice, revenue, instruction, health, *id.* 452-460. *Town*, *id.* 460-467 ; fort, *id.* 462-464 ; identified with Puri, I, pt. i, 107 ; island, *id.* 207 note 1 ; fort, residence of Sidi admirals of Bijápur, *id.* 285, 546 ; identified with Ptolemy's Zizerus, XIII, 410 note 6 ; *another account of* : Arabic name for rocky island, its occupation by Abyssinians, I, pt. ii, 34 ; capital of the Sidis, laid siege to by Shiváji every year from 1661 to 1678, *id.* 68, 69 ; put under the protection of the Mughals, *id.* 69, 70, 71 ; laid siege to by Sambháji (1682), *id.* 77 ; proposal to establish an English factory at (1668), *id.* 121.
Janjiras : island forts, I, pt. ii, 75.
Jankojiráo Sindia : adopted son of Báizábái, widow of Dowlatráv Sindia, I, pt. i, 437.
Janmákshar, Janmotri : birth paper, IX, pt. i, 27.
Janmaranhalli : village, original site of Sávanur, I, pt. ii, 666.
Jannasvámin : Bráhman grantee, I, pt. ii, 191.
Jánoji Bhonsle : Berár ruler, confirmed in his father's position (1753), XVIII, pt. ii, 247 ; his hostility to Peshwa Mádhavrao (1769), *id.* 253 ; partisan of Rághoba, I, pt. i, 399 ; ravages the country round Poona and makes peace with the Peshwa, I, pt. ii, 603.
Jánoji Nimbálkar : Karmála chief (1752), XX, 291, 412.
Ján Sáheb : great Urdu poet, author of the *Rekhtah Zabán*, IX, pt. ii, 130 note 2.
Janwal : *see* Janáwal.
Japal erundi : oil-yielding plant, XXV, 221.

Japnndi : *see* Jasvand.
Járá : place of interest in Cutch, V, 144, 224.
Jarasht : part of the *Zend Avesta,* IX, pt. ii, 211 note 2 (14).
Jariya : goldsmiths, origin of, I, pt. i, 464.
Jarod : sub-division in Baroda territory, VII, 536-537.
Jaságri : a caste of palm-juice drawers in Thána district, XIII, 116 ; *see* Agri.
Jasans : monthly feasts, names of, observances during, IX, pt. ii, 216-217.
Jásar : hill in Pálanpur state, V, 281-282.
Jasdan : state in Káthiáwár, VIII, 455-456 ; Kshatrapa inscription at, I, pt. i, 43.
Jasminum : *latifolium* and *sambæ,* sweet-scented oil produced from, XXV, 223.
Jasques or Jask : in the Persian Gulf, IX, pt. ii, 192 note 4.
Jasvaud : flowering plant, sacred to Ganpati, XXV, 289, 285, 279.
Jasvantráo Holkar : succeeds to power at Indore, ravages Khándesh, occupies Poona, his treaty with the British (1806), XII, 253.
Jasvantsingh, Jasvantsingh Ráthor : Mahárája, viceroy of Málwa (1657), thirty-second viceroy of Gujarát (1659-1662), I, pt. i, 282 ; sent from Gujarát by Aurangzeb to join prince Muázzam against Shiváji in the Dakhan (1662), *id.* 283, 387, XVIII, pt. ii, 230-231 ; thirty-fifth viceroy of Gujarát (1671-1674), sent to Kábul (1674), I, pt. i, 285.
Jat : warlike tribe in the Punjáb, Sind and, Rájputána, claim to be Yádavs, IX, pt. i, 441 ; rise of the tribe, *id.* 452, 453 and note 3, 454 and note 2, 464, 465 ; a caste of cultivators, I, pt. i, 451 ; persecution of, by Bráhmanist Chách (642), *id.* 498 ; a Musalmán sub-division in Cutch, V, 97 ; cattle dealers in Káthiáwar, VIII, 167 ; in Khándesh district, XII, 70 ; in Násik district, XVI, 59 ; a class of Musalmáns in Bijápur district, XXIII, 297.
Jatá Chola : lineage, I, pt. ii, 580.
Játakas : Buddhist birth-stories, XIV, 145.
Játars : sacrifices performed by Bhils, IX, pt. i, 306-307.
Jatávarman : Pándya king, takes S'rirangam from Someśvara, I, pt. ii, 508.
Jath : state in Sátára district, its history, XIX, 2, 622-624.
Jatha : earliest known land tenure in Poona district, XVIII, pt. ii, 313-317.
Jati : a caste of Jain ascetics in Káthiáwár, VIII, 156.
Jatiga I : founder of the Kolhápur or Karád-Siláhara dynasty, I, pt. ii, 254, 545, 546.
Jatiga II : fourth Kolhápur or Karád-Siláhára prince, I, pt. ii, 254, 545, 546.
Jatinga Rámeśvara : hill in Chitaldurg district, record at, I, pt. ii, 443 ; inscription at, *id.* 454.
Jatiyas : tanners in Bhinmál, I, pt. i, 451.
Játkarma : birth-rite, the sixth of the Vedic rites, IX, pt. i, 31 note 3 ; performance of, during girding ceremony, *id.* 37.
Jatmáli : pass in Násik district, XVI, 129.
Ját Márvádi : a class of cultivators in Khándesh district, XII, 61.
Jatropha : *curcas,* oil-yielding, dye, medicinal and poisonous plant, XXV, 221, 248, 255, 269 ; *manihot, multifida,* poisonous plants, *id.* 269, 270.
Jatvár, Jatwár : tract of country in Káthiáwár, VIII, 4, *see* also I, pt. i, 208 and note 3.
Jaudheja : corruption of Yaudheya, and corrupted into Jádeja, I, pt. i, 137.
Jaugad : in Madras, rock inscription at, I, pt. ii, 142.
Jaulia : story of the peak in Khándesh district, XII, 12 note 2.
Jaundice : *see* Kamlo.
Jaundri, jowári : food-plant, XXV, 186.
Jáuvla : *see* Javla.
Jauzhans : *yojanas,* I, pt. i, 525.
Jáva : island, early Hindu settlements in, I, pt. i, 489 ; traditions of expeditions by sea to, *id.* 490, 491 note 5, 492 ; mention of Gandhára and Láta in the legends of, *id.* 497 ; emigration to, of refugees from the defeats of Prabhákaravardhana and Shriharsha of Magadha (600-642), *id.* 497 ; appearance and condition of Hindu settlers in, *id.* 498 ; introduction of Bráhman and Buddhist details into literature and architecture of, IX, pt. i, 441 ; Hindu king of, *id.* 451 ; its trade with Thána coast (500-1810), XIII, 420, 429, 470, 520.
Jávada : corruption of Chávada, I, pt. i, 150.
Jával : a Bráhman sub-division in Ratnágiri district, X, 117 ; landholders, *id.* 138 ; in Kolába district, XI, 44 ; in Thána district, XIII, 79 ; in Poona district, XVIII, pt. i, 166-167.
Javaniké Náráyana : I, pt ii, 509. *See* Perumáledeva.
Jávda : place of interest, in Khándesh district, XII, 452.
Jávji : Koli chief in Peshwa's service, revolts, restored to rank (1760), XVII, 404-406.
Javla : or Javala, family name of great Toramána and Mirakula, IX, pt. i, 459 ; leading stock name, of sixth century White Hunas, *id.* 438 ; *see* also I, pt. i, 146, 465.
Javlá : a caste of Shenvi Bráhmans, traditional origin of, IX, pt. i, 438 ; sub-division of Punjáb Gujars, *id.* 490.
Javli : sub-division of Sátára district, its area, aspect, climate, agriculture and people, XIX, 423-425 ; survey of, *id.* 369-372 ; village, history of, *id.* 469-470 ; origin of its chiefs, *id.* 230-231 ; captured and its chief murdered by Shiváji (1653), *id.* 233, XVIII, pt. ii, 227.
Javus : fodder-plant, XXV, 278.
Jawán Mard Khán Bábi : his unsuccessful attempt on Idar and negotiations with the Maráthás, I, pt. i, 315 ; proclaims himself deputy viceroy of Gujarát, *id.* 326 ; assumes charge of the city of Ahmadábád and persuades the troops to release Fidá-ud-din, drives the viceroy to Cambay and invites Abdul Aziz Khán of Junnar, *id.* 327, 328 ; reconciles himself with his brother Safdar Khán Bábi of Rádhanpur and imprisons Fakhr-ud-dauláh and his family, *id.* 329 ; appoints Janárdanpant in place of Rangoji,

id. 331 ; enters into negotiations with Bálájiráv Peshwa (1750), *id.* 334 ; joins the Maráthás against Momin Khán, *id.* 340, 342, 345.
Jawhár : state in Thána district, its description, area, water, climate, products, population, agriculture, trade, history, administration, revenue, instruction, and health, XIII, 698-709 ; ruled by a Hindu chief (1341), *id.* 440 ; genealogical table of its chiefs, *id.* 706 ; *Town, id.* 709-710 ; recognition of the dynasty of (1341), I, pt. ii, 30 ; Koli state rises into importance, XVII, 354 ; I, pt. ii, 67 ; most of its possessions taken by the Maráthás, *id.* 86 ; its *rája* confirmed (1782), *id.* 106.
Jawla : *see* Jháwla.
Jay : pass in Násik district, XVI, 130.
Jayabbe : younger sister of Nitimárga of the Ganga family and mother of the Pallava king Mahendrádhirája (930-940), I, pt. ii, 332.
Jayabhata I : Gurjjara king (605-620), I, pt. i, 114, 115 ; *see* also I, pt. ii, 313 note 4.
Jayabhata II : Gurjjara chief of Nándod, helps Valabhis, I, pt. i, 85 ; (650-675), *id.* 116.
Jayabhata III : Gurjjara king of Nándod, his copper-plates, I, pt. i, 56, 108 ; (706-734), *id.* 114, 116 ; his grants, *id.* 117 ; deprived of his dominions by Dantidurga, *id.* 122 ; Gurjjara king, his grants, I, pt. ii, 314 ; vassal of the Kalachuri king Buddha, *id.* 315 ; subdues the king of Valabhi (736), *id.* 316, 375 note 3.
Jayab Mukne : founder of the Jawhár family, I, pt. ii, 30.
Jayadáman : son of Saka Chashtana, founder of Káthiáwár Kshatrapas (A. D. 140-143) ; becomes Hindu, IX, pt. i, 442 ; defeated by Gotamipurta, I, pt. ii, 161, 170 ; coins of, I, pt. i, 33-34.
Jayadeva : permits Pársis to settle in India, I, pt. ii, 8.
Jayadeva-pandita : Bráhman grantee, son of Rámadeváchárya of Mulasamgha, I, pt. ii, 373.
Jayadhavalá : important work on the philosophy of the Digambara Jainas, I, pt. ii, 200.
Jayadhavalatiká : Jain work (837), mentions Amoghavarsha and Jinasena, I, pt. ii, 407 note 5.
Jayáditya : the sun-god, I, pt. ii, 404 ; present of a village named Thurnávi in Kotipur near Broach to the temple of, I, pt. i, 126.
Jayaduttaramga : *biruda* or title of Satyavakya-Konganivarma-Permanadi-Butuga, I, pt. ii, 304.
Jayagad : *see* Jaygad.
Jayakarna : Western Chálukya prince, I, pt. ii, 449 ; son of Vikramáditya VI, *id.* 455, 554.
Jayakeśin : of the Manalur family (1038-39), feudatory of the Western Chálukya king Jayasimha II, I, pt. ii, 437.
Jayakeśin I, Jayakeśi I : Kadamba king of Chandrapura, son of Shasthadeva ; marries his daughter to Karna, burns himself on the funeral pyre, I, pt. i, 170 and note 5 ; *another account :* I, pt. ii, 309 ; Goa Kádamba prince (1052-53) and feudatory of the Western Chálukya king Someśvara I, *id.* 439, 565 ; brings presents to Vikramáditya VI, *id.* 216, 444 ; seizes a part of the Konkan from the Siláháras and makes Goa his capital, *id.* 216, 543, 567, 568.
Jayakeśin II : Goa Kádamba king, I, pt. i, 172 note 3 ; his reign (1119-1125), I, pt. ii, 449, 565, 568 ; feudatory of Vikramáditya VI, *id.* 452, 456, 458 note 2 ; holds the whole Konkan, *id.* 544 ; encroaches on the territory of the North Konkan Siláháras, *id.* 548, 568 ; attempts to overthrow the Chálukya supremacy, is defeated and put to flight by Áchugi II and Permádi I ; marries Mailaladevi, daughter of Virkramáditya VI, *id.* 569 ; is defeated by Hoysála Vishnuvardhana, *id.* 496, 569 ; *see* also XV, pt. ii, 82 note 3, 88.
Jayakeśin III : Goa Kádamba king (1187-1211), I, pt. ii, 486, 565 ; his gold coin, *id.* 566, 570 ; the Goa Kádambas lose Venugráma under, *id.* 571.
Jayanátha : of Uchchakalpa, feudatory prince, I, pt. ii, 293.
Jayant : traditional Kádamba founder of Goa (978), XV, pt. ii, 82 ; I, pt. ii, 286 note 2, 566.
Jayantapála : Vastupála's son, raises a shrine over the ashes of his father (1237), I, pt. i, 202.
Jayantasimha : Chálukya noble (1224), I, pt. i, 196.
Jayanti, Jayantipur : town, one of the names of Banavási, I, pt. ii, 278 note 2, 461, 560 ; viceroy of, *id.* 175.
Jayanti : sacred stream, tributary of the Panchganga, in Kolhápur state, XXIV, 10.
Jayantidevi : goddess, temple of, built by Karna (1064-1094) at Asával, I, pt. i, 170.
Jayanti Madhukeśvara : family god of the Hángal Kádambas, I, pt. ii, 560.
Jayantipura : *see* Jayanti.
Jayapatra : certificate of success, I, pt. ii, 483.
Jayaśekhara : Chávada king of Panchásar (696), killed by Bhuvada, I, pt. i, 150, 156.
Jayasimha : I, pt. ii, 559 ; *see* Jayavarman II.
Jayasimha I, Jayasimha : Western Chálukya king of Bádámi (500), I, pt. ii, 178, 181, 185, 296, 335 note 1 ; conquers the Ráshtrakúta king Indra and restores the power of the Chálukyas, *id.* 181, 339, 340, 342, 343 ; I, pt. i, 120 ; identification of, I, pt. ii, 360 note 3, 385.
Jayasimha II, Jayasimha : brother and successor of Vikramáditya V the Western Chálukya king (669-680), I, pt. i, 111, 117 ; I, pt. ii, 229, 213-214, 222, 234, 333, 339, 341 note 2, 428 note 4 ; his *biruda* and records of his time, *id.* 278 note 1, 435 ; marries his daughter to Bhillama III, his great general, *id.* 234, 435, 514 ; breaks the confederacy of Málava and subdues the Cheras and Cholas, *id.* 213-214, 436 ; his feudatories and officials, *id.* 436, 437 note 5, 438, 515, 553, 563, 567, 577.
Jayasimha III, Jayasimha : son of Someśvara I, the Western Chálukya king (1072), XXIV, 219, I, pt. ii, 333, 349 ; governor of Tardavadi in the reign of his father, *id.* 367, 428 note 4, 438, 440, 441, 443, 444 ; appointed viceroy of Banavási by the Western Chálukya king

Vikramáditya VI, *id.* 217, 445, 449, 452; his full designation, *id.* 453; his rebellion and dismissal, *id.* 454; Miraj inscription of, *id.* 282 note 3.

Jayasimha IV: Chalukya prince, governs Banvási (1079-1081), XV, pt. ii, 88.

Jayasimhavarman: third son of Kirtivarman I, the Chálukya king, I, pt. ii, 349.

Jayasimhavarman or Jayasimhavarmman: Dharásraya (A. D. 666-693), younger brother of Vikramáditya Satyásraya I; drives out the Gurjjars and founds the Chálukya power in Láta (South Gujarát), I, pt. i, 107, 108, 110; I, pt. ii, 186-187; feudatory of the Chálukyas, *id.* 357, 364 and note 4, 370, 374, 376.

Jayásraya: succeeds Jayasimha as king of Southern Gujarát, I, pt. ii, 187, 374. *See* Mangalarasa.

Jayasraya: *biruda* or title of Nágavardhana Tribhuvanásraya, I, pt. ii, 357.

Jaychand: son of the Shrimál king Deal, is converted to Jain faith by Ratansuri, IX, pt. i, 97.

Jaygad: port in Ratnágiri district, exports and imports of, X, 184; town and fort, *id.* 340-341; identification of, *id.* 340 note 3; fort rebuilt by Shiváji, I, pt. ii, 68, 75; mention of, *id.* 2, 39, 74, 75.

Jaykeshi II: *see* Jayakesin II.

Jaykheda: village in Násik district, XVI, 445; survey introduced in, *id.* 253-257.

Jáyphal: wild nutmeg, in Poona district, XVIII, pt. i, 46.

Jayrám Sávant: regent at Sávantvádi (1737-1753), X, 441.

Jayshikhri: king of Panchásar in Pálanpur state (697), V, 345.

Jaysing: Angria (1793-1796), his struggle for power, XI, 155-156, 260, 265.

Jaysingh: *see* Jagadekamalla.

Jaysinha: *see* Jayasimha.

Jaytápur: port in Ratnágiri district, imports and exports of, X, 185; history, objects of interest, *id.* 341; burnt by the Sidis (1676), I, pt. ii, 71.

Jaziah or jizia: capitation tax, I, pt. i, 213; imposition of, by Aurangzeb, *id.* 286; imposed (1684), XVIII, pt. ii, 238.

Jazirah: Arabic term for island, IX, pt. ii, 1 note 1.

Je Ambe: war cry and Holi shout of Gujarát, IX, pt. i, p. xxxv.

Jedugur: identified with Jedda in the Sorab táluka, Shimogá district, Mysore, I, pt. ii, 369.

Jehándársháh: Abul Fateh Muiz-ud-din, son and successor of Bahádur Sháh I of Delhi (1712-1713), I, pt. i, 297.

Jejuri: holy village in Poona district, Khandoba's temple, fairs, pilgrims, priests, trade and history of, XVIII, pt. iii, 132-139; Yasvantráv Holkar's march towards (1801), XVIII, pt. ii, 281.

Jempal or Jepál: *see* Jampal.

Jeran: island of, in the Persian Gulf, settlements of the Arabs in (1303); a great trading centre; taken by the Portuguese (1508), by the Persians and English (1622), IX, pt. ii, 183 note 3. *See* Ormuz, New.

Jerbáj: horse disease, in Cutch, V, 209.

Jerbáth: a cattle disease, in Cutch, V, 396.

Jesa: leader of Khánt Kolis, helps emperor Muhammad Tughlák (A. D. 1330) in his capture of Junágad, receives for Khánts grant of the hill of Girnár from the emperor, IX, pt. i, 240 and note 4.

Jesalmir: town, its founder, IX, pt. i, 446 note 4; Mhers settle at, I, pt. i, 136; Jain temple at, *id.* 161 note 1.

Jesar: state in Rewa Kántha, VI, 150.

Jesar: place of interest in Káthiáwár, VIII, 456.

Jesar and Turi: shrine of, at Anjár in Cutch, story of, V, 212-213.

Jesuit monastery: at Chaul, XI, 294.

Jesuits: their rise (1542), XIII, 460 note 7; established at Bassein and Bándra (1548), *id.* 201; conversions by, *id.* 461, 462; their Church at Parel, and college at Bándra (1674), *id.* 474, 476; their schools at Bándra, XIV, 21; their college at Bándra (1675), *id.* 22, 26, 32; their college destroyed (1722), *id.* 27; their connection with Bándra, XIV, 21, 22, 26, 27, 32; with Bassein, *id.* 41, 42; with Thána, *id.* 359; called Paulistines, I, pt. ii, 56; assist a dismissed English officer to capture Bombay (1667), *id.* 57; do the work of conversion, their jealousy of the Dominicans, *id.* 60; pursue a policy of concession and tyranny, *id.* 61.

Jesus: mention of, by Ahmed, IX, pt. ii, 3 note 3.

Jetalsar: village in Káthiáwár, VIII, 457.

Jethimal: division of Modh Bráhmans, wrestlers in Native states, IX, pt. i, 12.

Jethvá: Rájpút tribe, I, pt. i, 139; Porbandar chiefs, *id.* 135; foreign tribe, *id.* 139-140; identified with Játs, *id.* 145; their movements and establishment at Porbandar; claim descent from Makardhvaj, son of Hanumán; are said to be Mers; derivation of name, IX, pt. i, 126-127; their family deity Vindhyavásini; festival of Ráv's procession to snake-temple; are sun-worshippers; are also *smarts*; worship the cow; their visit to local temple of Shiv and Shakti on high days, *id.* 136-137; in Káthiáwár, VIII, 110, 278.

Jetiga: sea spirit at Netráni island, in Kánara district, XV, pt. ii, 336 note 2.

Jetpur: place of interest in Mahi Kántha, V, 437.

Jetpur: sub-division of Chota Udepur state, in Rewa Kántha, VI, 112.

Jetpur: state and town in Káthiáwár, VIII, 457, 458.

Jetsur Khâchar: Káthi chief of Jasdan, notorious free-booter, IX, pt. i, 254.

Jetugi: Siláhára ruler (1255), XIV, 402.

Jeur: town in Ahmadnagar district, XVII, 720.

Jews: in Saimur, I, pt. i, 516; immigrants, "Introduction to the History of the Konkan," I, pt. ii, p. xii; of Cochin, *id.* 7; forbidden to exercise their religion within the towns, *id.*

60; pirates, *id.* 61; among early Arabs, IX, pt. ii, 1 note 1; at Bándra, Bassein, Kalyán, Khalápur, Panvel and Thána, XIV, 16, 28, 113, 201, 294, 347, 354; in Násik district, XVI, 85; in Belgaum district, XXI, 229; in Kolhápur state, XXIV, 152; in Poona district; *see* Bene-Israels.
Jews' Graveyard: in Poona city, XVIII, pt. iii, 374.
Jeyar: village with a temple and fair, in Rewa Kántha, VI, 161.
Jhábugám: sub-division of Chota Udepur state in Rewa Kántha, VI, 112.
Jhadesvara: town-gate, Broach, I, pt. ii, 314.
Jhád Jhádora: garden tax in Kolába district, XI, 170 note 3.
Jhagadia: sub-division of Rájpipla state in Rewa Kántha, VI, 97.
Jhahir Pir: *see* Záhir Pir.
Jhái: village in Thána district, XIV, 110.
Jhál: marriage ceremony among Khándesh Kunbis, XII, 66.
Jhálá: Rájpút caste, confined to east Káthiáwár; origin; derivation of name; name suggested to be Jauvla stock title of White Huna leaders; first capital of the clan at Pardi, next at Kuva, established at Halvad, removed to Dhrángadra; their present chiefships, IX, pt. i, 127; their family deity Ádya Máta, *id.* 136; *see* also I, pt. i, 139, 140, 206 note; in Káthiáwár, VIII, 111, 281.
Jhálábápji: object of worship among Bharváds, IX, pt. i, 268.
Jhálávád: province established in Rájputána by the Jhálá Rájpúts of Káthiáwár, I, pt. i, 140, 208 note 3.
Jhálávád, Jhálávár: sub-division of Káthiáwár, VIII, 3, 6; Rájpúts of, defeated by Zafar Khán (1394), I, pt. i, 233 and note 3, 517.
Jhalindar: ancient name of Jhálor, I, pt. i, 229.
Jhálod: petty division of the Panch Maháls, III, 301-302; *Town, id.* 316.
Jhálor: town, well-known fort and trade centre in Márwár, IX, pt. i, 10, 71; *see* also I, pt. i, 229 and note 5, 449, 454.
Jhálora: sub-caste of Bráhmans, said to have come from Márwár and Rájputána, IX, pt. i, p. xi note 3, 2, 10; VániásMeshri, *id.* 71; in Cutch, V, 48, 51.
Jhálоris: Muhammadan rulers of Pálanpur (1370-1854), V, 318; *see* also I, pt. i, 301.
Jhamar: táluka in Káthiáwar, VIII, 459.
Jhámka: táluka in Káthiáwar, VIII, 458.
Jhámpdi: Hindu goddess, female spirit, IX, pt. i, 417.
Jhámpodar: táluka in Káthiáwár, VIII, 459.
Jhán: dye-yielding plant, found in Sind and Cutch, XXV, 240; in Khándesh district, XII, 25.
Jhanda: a Pathán fakir, propitiated at marriage time among Modh Bráhmans in Cutch, V, 45 and note 4.
Jhanjha: of the Ráshtrakúta lineage, his daughter married by the Yádava king Bhillamal II, I, pt. ii, 425, 513.
Jhanjha: fifth Thána Siláhára king (916), XIII, 422 note 1; rules at Chaul, and over Lár at the time of Al Masudi, *id.* 424, 435; *see* also I, pt. ii, 23, 232, 233, 539, 542 note 3; I, pt. i, 129, 516; XI, 271 and note 3.
Jhánjhmer: place of interest in Káthiáwár, VIII, 459.
Jhánsa: custom of exacting debt by a threat, VIII, 326.
Jhára or Jharakar: a class of Musalmán dust-sifters in Ahmadnagar district, XVII, 232; in Sátára district, XIX, 143; in Bijápur district, XXIII, 299; in Belgaum district, XXI, 217; in Poona district, XVIII, pt. i, 379.
Jhári Ghárkhadi: state in Khándesh district, XII, 605.
Jhárola: caste of traders in Rewa Kántha, VI, 24.
Jhaveri Nálchand: agent of the Baroda conspirators in the Kaira district (1857), I, pt. i, 442.
Jháwla: division of Panjáb Gujjars, I, pt. i, 146.
Jhikádri: place of interest in Káthiáwár, VIII, 459.
Jhinjhuváda: town in Káthiáwár, VIII, 459, 460; fort of, said to to have been built by Siddharája, I, pt. i, 180 note 2.
Jholi: *see* Tythe-gathering Wallet.
Jholikavihára: cradle temple, built by Kumárapála at Dhandhuka, I, pt. i, 190.
Jhorega: village in the Násik district; Hemadpanti temple at, XVI, 445.
Jhujhárkhán: Sidi Gujarát noble, kills Changizkhán, IX, pt. ii, 12.
Jhunjhuna: Siddi's rattle, IX, pt. ii, 12 and note 2.
Jijibái: Shiváji's mother, XIV, 220; taken prisoner (1630), XVIII, pt. ii, 224; lives in Poona, *id.* 225; *see* also XVIII, pt. iii, 226.
Jijibái: widow of Sambháji II of Kolhápur (1712-1760) and regent (1760-1772) of Shiváji III (1760-1812), XXIV, 230-231.
Jimutaketu: king of the Vidyádharas and father of Jimutaváhana, I, pt. ii, 253, 356.
Jimutavahán: mythical founder of the Siláháras, XIII, 422 note 4, 424; son of Jimutaketu, king of the Vidyádharas and originator of the Siláháras, I, pt. ii, 253; lineage, *id.* 439, 443, 450, 476, 523; legend about, *id.* 536 and note 2; lineage of, *id.* 548.
Jin: Musalmán spirit, IX, pt. i, 417.
Jina: image of, broken by Ekántada Rámayya, I, pt. ii, 482, 483.
Jina Bhattáraka: shrine of, inside the Jain temple known as Saukha Jinálaya, I, pt. ii, 373.
Jinadevi: goddess, *kuldevi* of Bháti Gujars, IX, pt. i, 483, 493.
Jinaprabhasuri: Jain sage and writer (1300), I, pt. i, 6, 15, 78; author of the *Tirtha-Kalpa, id.* 176, 182 note 1; author of the *Násaka-Kalpa*, I, pt. ii, 512; *see* also XIV, 319.
Jinasena: composer of the *Harivamsa Purána* of the Jainas, I, pt. ii, 197; compiler of a part of the first half of the *Mahá Purána, id.* 200, 394, 406, 407 and notes 4 and 5, 408.

Jindáran : class of foreign Patháns in Pálanpur state, hold lands under military tenure, IX, pt. ii, 8 note 3.
Jinendra : I, pt. ii, 288 ; temple of, at Ádur in Dhárwár district, *id.* 377.
Jinendrabuddhi : another name of Pujyapáda, I, pt. ii, 373.
Jingar : a caste of saddlers in Ratnágiri district, X, 129 ; in Sávantvádi, *id.* 415, 418, 437 ; in Kolába district, XI, 64 ; in Jánjira state, *id.* 413 ; in Thána district, XIII, 136 ; in Násik district, XVI, 52 ; in Ahmadnagar district, XVII, 193 ; in Poona district, XVIII, pt. i, 339-343 ; in Dhárwár district, XXII, 151 ; in Bijápur district, XXIII, 112-113 ; in Kolhápur state, XXIV, 94 ; wood-workers in Kanára district, XV, pt. i, 266-268 ; in Belgaum district, XXI, 139, 140 ; in Sholápur district, their origin, settlement, customs, etc., XX, 103-118 ; *see* Dhigván.
Jinji (Gingee) : fort in Madras, taken by Shiváji (1676) ; siege of, by the Mughals under Zhulfikár Khán, I, pt. ii, 596.
Jir : in Bijápur district ; *see* Gurav.
Jiral Kamsali : state in Rewa Kántha, VI, 145.
Jirbátan : town, mentioned by Al Idrisi, between Ceylon and the mainland of India, I, pt. i, 509.
Jire-Gavaudi : class of masons, in Sholápur district, XX, 94-97.
Jire-Padhár : hill, in Sátára district, XIX, 11.
Jirnanagara : I, pt. ii, 175 ; *see* Junnar.
Jiti : *see* Jayanti.
Jitpur : town in Gujarát founded by Zafar Khán, battle of (1391), I, pt. i, 232 and note 2 ; fort at, built by Ahmed Sháh (1420), *id.* 238.
Jitpur-Anantpura : reservoir at, built by Siddharáj, I, pt. i, 180 note 2.
Jivadáman : sixth Kshatrapa (178), coins of, I, pt. i, 40-41.
Jivan-Seth : minister (1764) of Cutch, V, 143, 144.
Jivát-khána : insect room of a Jain *panjrápol*, V, 397.
Jivdhan : fort and hill between Thána and Poona districts, XIV, 98, 110 ; story of the goddess at, *id.* 382 ; *see* also XVIII, pt. i, 3, and XVIII, pt. iii, 139-140 ; its fall (1818), XVIII, pt. ii, 303.
Jizia : *see* Jaziah.
Jnanadeva, Jnáneśvara : Marátha saint, writer of a Maráthi commentary on the *Bhagavadgitá* (1290-1291), worshipped at Alandi in the Poona district, I, pt. ii, 249, 250 and note 1, 530 ; XVIII, pt. iii, 102, 103, 104 ; *see* Dnyaneshvar.
Joar, jondla : *see* Jaundri.
Jodhpur : town in Rájputána, I, pt. i, 463.
Jodhpur : town in Káthiáwár, VIII, 461.
Jodi-Basavanapura : inscription at, I, pt. ii, 508.
Jodiya : fort and port in Káthiáwár, VIII, 24, 239, 461.
Jog : river in Ratnágiri district, X, 11, 99.
Jogadeva : Singhana's officer (1222), I, pt. ii, 523.
Jogama : Kálachurya king, I, pt. ii, 225, 468, 469, 470, 471.
Jogamarána or Jogamarasa : of the Suryavamsa, I, pt. ii, 448.
Joger, *pl.* jogeru : a class of beggars in Bijápur district, XXIII, 194-196 ; in Dhárwár district, XXII, 208-209.
Jogeshvari : cave in Sálsette island, XIV, 10, 51, 110-112, 136, 162 ; *see* also, I, pt. ii, 9.
Jogi : a caste of wandering beggars in Káthiáwár, VIII, 159 ; in Ratnágiri, X, 131 ; in Kolába district, XI, 74 ; in Kánara district, XV, pt. i, 351-353 ; in Násik district, XVI, 74 ; ascetics, inhabit Kánheri caves, I, pt. ii, 13 ; as soldiers (1503-1509), XIV, 135 note 10 ; story of, at Mandapeshvar in Thána district, *id.* 226-227.
Jogigudd : hill in Belgaum district, XXI, 6, 573.
Jog Svámi : Yaksh of Parihar Rájput tribes, comes to Bhinmál, I, pt. i, 465.
Jogtin : a class of beggars in Poona district, XVIII, pt. i, 455.
Johári : a caste of jewellers in Kolába district, XI, 47, 48 ; in Thána district, XIII, 198 ; in Násik district, XVI, 55 ; in Poona district, XVIII, pt. i, 455-456 ; in Sholápur district, XX, 185-186.
Joher Pir : Musalmán saint venerated by Poona Halálkhors, story of his life, XVIII, pt. i, 437.
John de Nueva : Portuguese admiral, his visit to Anjidiv (1501), XV, pt. ii, 254.
John of Monte Corvins : missionary sent to India and China by the Pope (1292), XIII, 433, 727.
Joishi : *see* Joshi.
Jokharis : leechmen, IX, pt. ii, 84.
Jokideva : I, pt ii, 559 ; *see* Chokideva.
Jola : old province included in Dhárwár district, I, pt. ii, 211.
Joma : *see* Joyideva I.
Jomma : *see* Joyideva I.
Jonesia Asoca : sacred plant XXV, 285.
Jordanus : Franciscan friar, his visit to Thána and description of Sopára (1322), XIV, 321-322, 356 ; his account of Pársis in Thána, IX, pt. ii, 189 note 1 ; XIII, 251 ; Thána under the Delhi emperors, *id.* 439 ; his mention of Bhatkul in Kánara district, XV, pt. ii, 49, 271.
Joripori : presentation, literal meaning of, IX, pt. ii, 230.
Josaphat : legend of Barlaam and, XIV, 151 and note 1.
Joshi : a caste of beggars in Kolába district, XI, 74 ; fortune-tellers, in Thána district, XIII, 198 ; in Násik district, XVI, 74 ; in Sátára district, XIX, 119 ; in Belgaum district, XXI, 184, 185.
Joshi : sub-caste of Bráhmans in Kánara district, XV, pt. i, 133 ; astrologer, prepares *janmotri*, his other duties, IX, pt. i, 27-28.
Jotiba's hill : in Kolhápur state, XXIV, 20 ; position, temples, holy pools and fairs at, *id.* 299, 300.
Jovideva : *see* Joyideva II.
Jow : *see* Jab.

Joyideva I : of the Gutta family (1181), I, pt. ii, 489; son of Vira-Vikramáditya I, *id.* 579; feudatory of the Kálachurya king Ahavamalla, *id.* 581, 582, 583.

Joyideva II : of the Gutta family (1238), Singhana's feudatory, I, pt. ii, 524; son of Vira-Vikramáditya II, *id.* 579, 583.

Joyideva III : Gutta prince, son of Vikramáditya III, I, pt. ii, 579, 584.

Juán-Juán : a tribe of Eastern Tártárs, IX, pt. i, 471; called Jue-Jue or Avárs, *id.* 455, 461, 469; sink their own name and continue the honoured title of Kushán, *id.* 462; invaders of India from the north, *id.* 469; their movements, driven by the Turks from Central China (A.D. 350), passed north and drove the Kedaras out of Balkh (A. D. 380), attacked Persians and were worsted by Behrám Gohr, *id.* 456, 471, 474; reinforced by Ephthalites or White Hunas in the Oxus Valley and conquered Persia, *id.* 456, 471, 472, 474; associated with contingents from Kushán, Kedaras, *id.* 461; swept into India through Kábul Valley (fifth century), *id.* 433, 455, 461, 469, 471; said to have held a subordinate position in the great White Huna invasion; Indianised into Gujjara or Gurchar the cow-herd, *id.* 446; identification of Gujjara with, not proved, *id.* 471; introduced Buddhist and Bráhman details into the literature and architecture of their settlements in Java, Siam and Cambodia, *id.* 441; strong fire reverence element in, *id.* 447.

Judges : Portuguese, I, pt. ii, 52.

Jue-Jue : *see* Juán-Juán.

Jugal : place of interest in Belgaum district, XXI, 573.

Jugglers : IX, pt. i, 20, 29, 225.

Jugs : rock-cut, on Padan hill in Thána district, XIV, 102, 391.

Juláha : a caste of Musalmán weavers in Thána district, XIII, 225, 245-246, 388-390; *see* Momna.

Julapengudd : hill in Belgaum district, XXI, 6, 573.

Julian : emperor, his war with Sápor, IX, pt. i, 473.

Julwah : unveiling of the bride, IX, pt. ii, 164.

Jumkha : estate, in Rewa Kántha, VI, 151.

Jumná : *see* Jamna.

Junagad or Junágad : state in Káthiáwár, its boundaries, soil, climate, forests, population, ports, history, land-tenures, justice and police, VIII, 462-486, 287-289; *town*, origin of the name, history of its chiefs, *id.* 487-501; Mauryan capital of Gujarát, I, pt. i, 14; establishment of Ahir kingdom at, *id.* 138; capital of Chudásama ruler, *id.* 176; independent ruler of, *id.* 206 note 1, 236; taken by Mahmud Begada and made his capital under the name of Mustafábád (1472), *id.* 245-246; disputed succession (1811), *id.* 425; British aid invoked at (1816), *id.* 427, 538; pays tribute to the Gáikwár, VII, 321-322; inscriptions at, I, pt. ii, 159, 160, 281 note 3, 317; *see* also IX, pt. i, p. xi, 125, 240 note 4.

Junaid : Sind governor of Khalif Hásham, his expeditions, I, pt. i, 109, 467; sends expeditions against Gujarát, *id.* 506, 513, 520.

Juna Kot : *see* Pándhri.

Junanara : *see* Junnar.

Junápadár : táluka in Káthiáwár, VIII, 502.

Junápunpála : hill in Belgaum district, XXI, 8, 550.

Junásávar : place of interest in Káthiáwár, VIII, 502.

Junawal : *see* Junáwal.

Jungly annanas : famine plant, XXV, 205.

Jungly badam : fibrous plant, XXV, 229.

Junjhárráv Ghátge : Málavdi chief (1612), XIX, 231.

Junnaid : *see* Junaid.

Junnar : sub-division of Poona district, its boundaries, area, aspect, water, climate, cultivators, crops, stock, people, communications, traffic, XVIII, pt. iii, 84-89; survey of, *id.* pt. ii, 384-389, 451-454, *town*, description, hills, sub-divisions, people, houses, shops, trade, capital, crafts, municipality, water-supply, *id.* pt. iii, 140-146; objects, gates, old wells, temples, Musalmán remains merchant's tomb, Afiz Bágh, *id.* 142-152, Shivner hill, fort, details, upper hill, view, flying arch mosque, *id.* 153-162; Buddhist caves at, Mánmoda (I-XLV), Bhimáshankar group (I-X), inscriptions 1-3; Ambika group (XI-XXIX), inscriptions 4-18; Bhutling group (XXX-XLV), inscription 19, *id.* 163-184; Shivner (I-L), east face group (I-XXXVII), inscriptions 20-26; west face group (XXXVIII-XLIII); south face group (XLIV-L), inscriptions 28-29, *id.* 184-201; Tulja (I-XI), *id.* 201-204; Ganesh Lena (I-XXVI), inscriptions 30-35, 204-216; XVIII, pt. ii, 212-213; XIII, 411 note 3, 414; trips, Kukdi Valley, Nána pass, inscription (B. C. 100), statues (B. C. 100), pass, details, XVIII, pt. iii, 216-224; history, *id.* 224-231; early trade centre (B. C. 90-A. D. 30), XVIII, pt. ii, 211; XIV, 286; *another account of*; head-quarters of the Malik-al-Tujár's army, I, pt. ii, 31; district under Malik Ahmad, *id.* 32; inscriptions at, *id.* 49, 155, 158; capital of the Maháráshtra, *id.* 160; identified with Tagara, *id.* 174, XIII, 419, 423 note 4; XVIII, pt. ii, 211 note 2; capital of Nahapána, I, pt. ii, 175, 176; XVIII, pt. ii, 213 and note 10; in Poona district, *id.* 538 note 8; head-quarters of the Musalmán garrison in 1451, *id.* 588; rock temples of, *id.* 619; under the Bahamani kings (1347-1500), *id.* 620; second head province of the Bahamani dominions (1489), *id.* 621; *see* also XVIII, pt. ii, 217, 218, 219, 220; made the seat of the Nizám Sháhi government (1607), XVII, 392; seized by Sháháji (1632), XIII, 464; plundered (1657) by Shiváji, XVIII, pt. ii, 228; Fryer's visit to, XIII, 476; XIV, 362; Bájiráv confined in (1794), XVIII, pt. ii, 270.

Jupiter : planet, called Guru or Brihaspati, IX, pt. i, 402.

Juran : place of interest in Cutch, V, 224.

Jurananagar : *see* Junnar.

Jurz : *see* Juzr.

Jusri Máta : yoke goddess, worship of, in cattle-pox, IX, pt. i, 372.

Justice : Mughal administration of, I, pt. i, 213.

Justices : in Bombay island, to try petty civil cases (1670), XXVI, pt. iii, 1-2 ; presided over by a judge (1675), *id.* 2-3.
Jute : famine and fibrous plant, common throughout India, XXV, 195, 230.
Juzr : Gujarát and Gurjjaras, expedition against, I, pt. i, 109, 465, 467, 468, 469, 505, 506, 508, 526, 527 ; Gujar, I, pt. ii, 22.
Jvála-Mukhi : Bhojak priests of, IX, pt. i, 440.

K

KAABA : in Arabia, holy well at, IX, pt. ii, 171.
Kabaligár : a caste of beggars, in Dhárwár district, XXII, 209-210 ; in Bijápur district, XXIII, 113-117.
Kábás : people of Kábulistán, settled at Dwárka, IX, pt. i, 522.
Kábávaliyá : a class of Mahomedan Khárvás ; their origin ; are enterprising sailors, IX, pt. i, 522.
Kabber : a caste of husbandmen, I, pt. ii, 414 note 5 ; in Bijápur district, XXIII, 271-274.
Kabher : a caste of fishermen in Kánara district, XV, pt. i, 307-309.
Kabir : religious reformer of India, founder of Kabirpanthi religious sect, IX, pt. i, 539.
Kabirpanthi : a religious sect instituted by Kabir, IX, pt. i, 539.
Kabir-ud-din : *pir*, fourth Ismáilia missionary (1448), visits the *imám* at Deilam, IX, pt. ii, 40, 49 note 1.
Kábirun : perhaps a town on the Káveri, Musalmáns in, I, pt. i, 518.
Kabir wad : sacred banyan tree near Sukaltirth in Broach district, II, 355 ; place of pilgrimage, IX, pt. i, 549.
Kabisa : intercalary month in every 120th year ; last performance of the, IX, pt. ii, 193 note 2.
Kabliger : *see* Kabaligár.
Kabnur : *see* Hátkalangda.
Kabriá : section of Jaafari Bohorás, origin of the name, IX, pt. ii, 35.
Kábul : Bráhmanism supreme in (600-700 A. D.), IX, pt. i, 449 note 2 ; hordes of foreigners entered India first through the valley of, *id.* 455, 456 ; Turk rulers of, claim Kanishka as an ancestor, *id.* 462, 489 note 2.
Kábuli : special community of part foreign descent in Gujarát ; Afghán settlers from Kábul, appearance, character, chiefly horse-dealers, Sunni in religion, form a separate community, IX, pt. ii, 13-14 ; in Bijápur district, XXIII, 289.
Kábur : village in Belgaum district, XXI, 573.
Kabutris : Nat women, taking part in acrobatic feats, origin of the name, IX, pt. ii, 89.
Kacch : migration of Summas to, I, pt. i, 139 ; Bhima's copper-plate in, 163 ; stone inscription from, *id.* 203, 508 ; references to by Al Biruni, *id.* 513 note 9, 517, 521, 530, 534, 538. *See* Cutch.
Kacchella : identified with Cutch, I, pt. i, 109.
Kácha : coins, I, pt. i, 62 note 2.
Káchan : pass in Násik district, XVI, 130.
Káchári : a caste of glass bangle-makers in Poona district, XVIII, pt. i, 343-344.
Kachchha : modern Cutch, I, pt. i, 36 and note 5 ; country, mentioned by Pánini, I, pt. ii, 138.
Kachchhella : king, destroyed by the army of the Tájikas, I, pt. ii, 187, 375 and note 5.
Kachchi, Kachchippedu : Tamil name for Káñchi, I, pt. ii, 318 note 3.
Kachera : food and famine plant, grows in Thána district, XXV, 184, 208.
Kacheshvar : temple of, at Kopargaon in Ahmadnagar district, story of, XVII, 723 and note 4.
Kachh : Jádeja Rájpút chiefship, IX, pt. i, 126. *See* Cutch.
Kachhi, Káchi, Káchhiá : caste of market gardeners in Gujarát, professional husbandmen ; census details ; sub-divisions, other pursuits, IX, pt. i, 153 ; followers of different religious sects : holy men among, early beliefs, animal worship, customs, *id.* 154 ; in Kolába district, XI, 64 ; in Khándesh district, XII, 74 ; in Thána district, XIII, 119 ; in Poona district, XVIII, pt. i, 283-284 ; in Káthiáwár, VIII, 143.
Kachhigad : village in Káthiáwár, VIII, 502.
Kachivi : village in Dhárwár district, temples and inscriptions at, XXII, 762.
Kachna : hill fort in Násik district, XVI, 441, 442, 445-446.
Kachu : food plant, grows in all districts, XXV, 182.
Kadab : grant from (813), I, pt. ii, 303, 380 ; copper-plate grant of, *id.* 399 and note 7.
Kadakol : village in Dhárwár district, inscription at (1246), I, pt. ii, 522.
Kadalundi : near Bepur, I, pt. i, 546.
Kadam : Marátha surname, XIII, 63 note 4.
Kadam or Kadamb : plant used as tooth-brush by Hindus, XXV, 291 ; believed to be immortal, sacred to Krishna, worship of, IX, pt. i, 384.
Kádamba : *see* Kádambas.
Kadambale : country, ruled over by Vishnuvardhana, I, pt. ii, 499.
Kádambari : Bána's work, I, pt. i, 114 ; I, pt. ii, 138 note 3.
Kádambas, Kadamba : of Goa, I, pt. ii, 564-575 ; belong to the same original stock with the Kádambas of Hángal, *id.* 566 ; their traditional progenitor, *id.* 286 note 2, 566 ; their family and hereditary title, *id.* 566 ; their crest and banner, *id.* 299 note 4, 566 ; their musical instrument, *id.* 327 note 7, 566 ; under Jayakeśin I wrest a portion of the Konkan from the Siláháras and make Goa their capital, *id.* 216, 543, 567 ; extent of their Konkan possessions, *id.* 282 note 5, 347 note 2 ; their prince makes a present to the Chálukya king Vikramáditya II also styled VI, *id.* 444 ; are defeated by Hoysala Vishnuvardhana, *id.* 496, 498 ; associate with Vishnuvardhana against Vikramáditya II also styled VI, and are defeated by the Sinda chieftain A'chugi or A'chugi II (1117), *id.* 218-219, 453, 569, 574 ; re-established by Vijayáditya of Karád (1143-1153), *id.* 548, 570 ; feudatories of the Western Chálukyas of Kalyáni, *id.* 437, 439, 451, 452, 456, 460, 568 ; their doubtful position under

the Kálachuryas, *id.* 476, 480; their territory burnt by a Kálachurya officer (1181), *id.* 489; defeated by Bicha, an officer of Singhana (about 1218), *id.* 243, 524; Devagiri Yádava feudatories, *id.* 519; their family perish with Shashthadeva II (1257), *id.* 572; their grants, *id.* 216; their inscriptions, *id.* 357 note 3, 436 note 1, 459 note 4. *See* also Kádamba of Goa (1007-1250), XV, pt. ii, 82 and note 3; XXI, 358 note 9, 359-360.

Of Hángal, I, pt. ii, 558-564; assert genealogical connection with the Kadamba kings of Banavási, possess the hereditary right to rule the Hánumgal (Hángal) district, *id.* 558; their genealogy, *id.* 559, 560; the head of their genealogy, *id.* 286 note 2; their traditional origin, *id.* 560-561; branch of the Goa Kádamba family, *id.* 498; their family deity, *id.* 278 note 2; their crest and banner, *id.* 299 note 4; their musical instrument, *id.* 327 note 7; Western Chálukya feudatories, *id.* 435, 437, 439, 450, 456, 458, 465, 466, 486; Kálachurya feudatories, *id.* 475, 482; Hoysala feudatories, *id.* 506; do not recognise the sovereignty of Bhillama the Devagiri Yádava or his son, *id.* 519; subjugated by the Hoysala king Vira-Ballála II and their territory annexed to his kingdom (1196), *id.* 563; *see* also Hángal chiefs (1068-1203), XXII, 401.

Of Banavási, I, pt. ii, 16, 285-291; the four important seats of their power, *id.* 285 and notes 5 and 6; their Bráhman origin, their *gotra* or clan and the origin of their name; their ancestor Mayurasarman applies himself to war and obtains a territory on the shore of the Western Ocean from the Pallavas, and his great-grandson Raghu places the power of the family on a firm and wide footing, *id.* 286; under Mrigesavarman they overturn the Ganga family and destroy the Pallavas, *id.* 288; their pedigree, *id.* 289; the sixth century is the probable period of their rule, *id.* 291 and note 1; king of, conquered by Vishnuvardhana the Chálukya prince, *id.* 341; Jayasinha I and Ranarája hold office under them, *id.* 343; Pulakesi I defeats them and takes Bádámi from them, *id.* 343, 344; their confederacy is broken by Kirtivarman I, the Western Chálukya king of Bádámi, *id.* 181, 285, 335, 345 and note 4, 346; reduced by Pulakesin II, *id.* 183, 350; their copper-plate grants, *id.* 174; their inscriptions, *id.* 322; genealogical tree of the dynasty, XV, pt. ii, 79 note 1.

Kadána: state in Rewa Kántha, VI, 1, 2; physical aspect, soil, population and history of, *id.* 154-155. *Town, id.* 162.

Kadappa: origin of the *nawábs* of, XXII, 793.

Kadarmandalgi: village in Dhárwár district, temple and inscriptions at, XXII, 762-763.

Kádaroli: in the Sampgaon táluka, record at, I, pt. ii, 568.

Kádava: king destroyed by Narasimha II, I, pt. ii, 507.

Kadavi nai: medicinal plant, XXV, 262.

Kadboli: snake in Ratnágiri district, X, 50.

Kaddan: pulses in Ratnágiri, X, 147.

Kaddu kankri: medicinal plant found in several districts, XXV, 254.

Kadegaon: village in Sátára district, XIX, 470-471.

Kadepur: village in Sátára district, temple at, XIX, 471.

Kadesia: victory of the Arabs over the Persians at (638), IX, pt. ii, 1 note 1, 183, I, pt. i, 505 note 5.

Kadi: division in Baroda state, VII, 20-23, 587; its agriculture, *id.* 92-102; roads, *id.* 143-145; trade, *id.* 151-152; capital, *id.* 128-135; health, *id.* 494-495; sub-division, *id.* 591-595.

Town, id. 593-594; schools and hospital at, *id.* 486, 506; campaign against (1802), *id.* 205-206, 391; I, pt. i, 412; grant from, *id.* 203, 231.

Kadia: a caste of Musalmán bricklayers in Gujarát; converts from the Hindu caste of the same name, Sunnis in religion; followers of the Pirána saint Imám Sháh, IX, pt. ii, 74; in Khándesh district, XII, 126; in Sholápur district, XX, 206; also called Chunára, IX, pt. i, 186.

Kadiáli: táluka in Káthiáwár, VIII, 502.

Kádiris: chief *sayad* family in Gujarát, IX, pt. ii, 6 note 1 (2).

Kadiwál: a Musalmán sect in Cutch, V, 92.

Kadme: village in Kánara district, XV, pt. ii, 135, 317.

Kadmigudda: peak in Kánara district, XV, pt. i, 3.

Kadmis: a division of the Pársi community, origin of, IX, pt. ii, 193 note 2, 194.

Kadoda: town on the banks of the Tápti, I, pt. ii, 203.

Kadoli: state in Mahi Kántha, V, 426.

Kadphises: Chinese-Turk ruler, his intention to weld his Baktrian subjects with his new Hindu subjects by common religion, IX, pt. i, 442; Kujula Kadphises and Vema Kadphises, *id.* 456 note 3.

Kadra: village in Kánara district, fort, fair, history, XV, pt. ii, 39, 127, 128, 133, 150, 317-318, 328, 342, 343.

Kadri: *see* Satáni.

Kadroli: village in Belgaum district, temple and inscription at, XXI, 573-574.

Kadur: district in Mysore, I, pt. ii, 441.

Kadur: village in Dhárwár district, XXII, 763.

Kadus: market town in Poona district, shrine at, fair at, XVIII, pt. iii, 231-232.

Kaduvapanepu: village, I, pt. ii, 369.

Kádva: river, in Násik district, XVI, 8, 9.

Kadva: a division of the Kanbi caste; *see* under Kanbi.

Kadvád: *see* Kárwár.

Kadva-Kunbi: caste of weavers in Násik district, XVI, 53.

Kadvál: sub-division in Rewa Kántha, VI, 112.

Kadve Gujar: a class of cultivators in Khándesh district, XII, 67.

Kadvi: feeder of the Várna in Kolhápur state, XXIV, 9.

Kadwa: *see* Kadva.

Kafi Khan: Musalmán historian (1680-1735), his description of Bassein and Daman, XIII,

428 and note 9; his description of Bombay, *id.* 485 note 2.
Kafshgar: a caste of Musalmán shoemakers, in Poona district, XVIII, pt. i, 493; in Sholápur district, XX, 199.
Káfnr: Hazár Dinári, minister and general of Ala-ud-din, I, pt. i, 515.
Kágal: town in Kolhápur state, its details, fort, history, temple and fair, XXIV, 300-301; survey of, *id.* 255-256; *see* also I, pt. ii, 547.
Kaginelli or Kágneli: village in Dhárwár district, temples and inscriptions at, XXII, 763; *see* also I, pt. ii, 529.
Kágvad: village in Belgaum district, XXI, 574; survey of, *id.* 450-452.
Kágvádar: táluka in Káthiáwár, VIII, 502.
Kagzi or Kaghzi: caste of paper-makers, in Gujarát, Hindu converts, Sunnis in religion, followers of the Chishtis of Ahmadábád, IX, pt. ii, 73-74; in Násik district, XVI, 81; in Bijápur district, XXIII, 290, 291; in Kolhápur state, XXIV, 149.
Kahár: a caste of fishermen in Khándesh district, XII, 79; in Násik district, XVI, 57; in Ahmadnagar district, XVII, 157-159; in Kolhápur state, XXIV, 105.
Kahir-Kirpa: a spur of the Sahyadris in Sátára district, XIX, 7.
Káhnam Dev: a Hindu god, IX, pt. i, 363.
Káhupur-Ishvariá: táluka in Káthiawár, VIII, 502.
Kai: oil-yielding plant, XXV, 214.
Kaiga: pass in Kánara district, XV, pt. ii, 39, 40, 317.
Kaikádi: early tribe in Násik district, XVI, 65, 315-317; in Belgaum district, XXI, 168; in Ahmadnagar district, XVII, 103-106; in Sátára district, XIX, 108; in Bijápur district, XXIII, 196; in Kolhápur state, XXIV, 107-108; in Poona district, XVIII, pt. i, 406-408; in Sholápur district, XX, 165-166.
Kaikhosbru: Herbad, stranger from Persia, makes copies of the *Vandidád* from the Cambay copy, IX, pt. ii, 189 note 2.
Kailana: Hindu goddess, IX, pt. i, 493.
Kailás: Ellora cave, XV, pt. ii, 84; XVI, 136; I, pt. ii, 391, 482.
Kailása: mountain abode of god S'iva, I, pt. ii, 196.
Kailássá: river west of Kalyán, I, pt. ii, 353 note 2.
Kailásanátha: temple of, at Conjeeveram, I, pt. ii, 319 note 3, 327 note 8; inscription in the temple of, *id.* 330.
Kaineitai: Island of St. George, near Goa, I, pt. i, 546; Hog Island and perhaps Netráni in Kánara, XV, pt. ii, 48 note 3, 78, 336 and note 6.
Kaioji: son of Mirzan Khosru Beg, watch-repairer to Bájiráv Peshwa; goes to Bhávnagar, makes a clock for the chief, his descendants enjoy high reputation in Káthiáwár, IX, pt. ii, 197 note 2.
Kaira: plant, its twigs used as tooth brushes by Hindus, XXV, 291.
Kaira district: III, 1-180; description, 1; rivers, 2-5; drainage, 5-10; floods, 11, 12; geology, 13; climate, 14; minerals and trees, 15; animals, 16-24; census details, 25-28; Hindu castes, 29-35; Musalmáns, Pársis and Christians, 36-38; dwellings and communities, 39; migrations, 40, 41; soil, 42; irrigation, holdings and stock, 43-44; crops, 45; details of cultivation, 46-55; peasants, bad seasons, 56; capitalists, forms of investment, 57; moneylenders, 58, 59; borrowers, 60; rates of interest, grain advances and currency, 61; bankruptcy, mortgages and wages, 62; prices, 63, 64; weights and measures, 65-67; roads, 68; rest-houses, ferries and bridges, 69; post and telegraph figures, 70; land trade, 71; railway traffic, 72-74; manufactures, 75, 76; history, 77; acquisition, administrative changes and revenue staff, 78, 79; land management in 1803; Maliks, alienated lands, Government lands, village organization, 80-91; land management (1803-1830), 92-101; condition of the district (1825-1830), 102-104; land system in 1854, 105-107; survey of the district (1863-1867), 108-112; seasons, 113-114; development of the district, 115; civil and criminal justice, 116-119; police and crime, 120-124; revenue and finance, 125-129; local funds and municipalities, 130-131; schools, libraries, newspapers, 132-139; diseases, hospitals, dispensaries, vaccination, births and deaths, 140-142; sub-divisional accounts, 143-165; places of interest, 166-180; mention of, I, pt. ii, 413, 456 note 1.
Kaira Town: III, 168; Ráshtrakúta town, I pt. ii, 383; copper-plate and charters found at, *id.* 313 note 5; grants of Vijáyarája and Vijayavarman, *id.* 359, 360 note 3, 365 note 3; grant of, I, pt. ii, 110, 467, 518 and note 3; battle near (1802), VII, 192; cession of, to the British (1803), *id.* 207.
Kairana: Portuguese sub-division in Thána district, XIII, 456.
Kaitabha: demon destroyed by god Janárdana, I, pt. ii, 507.
Kaitabhesvara: temple of, at Anawatti, record at, I, pt. ii, 516 note 5.
Kaithal: modern representative of *Yajur Veda*, I, pt. i, 534.
Káitu: eleventh-day funeral ceremony, IX, pt. i, 10.
Kaiyo: name of Bhil race, IX, pt. i, 294.
Kajar Singh: leader of the Bhils in the Sátpuda hills in Khándesh (1857), I, pt. ii, 632; XII, 262, 310.
Káji Alá-ud-din: builder of the Nágothna bridge, I, pt. ii, 42.
Kaji Ibrahim: chief judge of the Moors (1694) in Bombay island, XXVI, pt. iii, 7.
Kajirda: hill pass between Ratnágiri district and Kolhápur state, X, 166, 178; XXIV, 5.
Kájli-trij: or Jav-kajli, barley-grain holiday, IX, pt. i, 66.
Kájra: poisonous plant, found in Konkan, XXV, 267.
Káju; oil, liquor and gum-yielding plant found in Konkan, XXV, 210, 216, 250; *see* also 38, 39; XVIII, pt. i, 47.
Kajubái: goddess, worshipped by Khándesh Bráhmans, XII, 51, 53.

Kajur : food plant indigenous to Arabia, XXV, 181.

Kajuri : food, famine and liquor-yielding plant found in several districts, XXV, 181, 206-212.

Káka : Kakupur, town near Bithur in Northern India, I, pt. i, 64 note 3.

Káka : or devotee, officiators of Matia Kanbis, IX, pt. i, 168.

Kákábalia : or Káko Balio, small-pox god, IX, i, 292, 363.

Kákadi : *see* Kákdi.

Kákadkhila : sub-division, in Rewa Kántha, VI, 117.

Kákáji : Raghunáth Mahipatráv, a Baroda courtier, cousin of Ravji Appaji, VII, 202, 212, 215.

Kákáji : outlaw, plunders villages and burns the Catholic Church of Remedi (1690), I, pt. ii, 80.

Kakamari : intoxicating and poisonous plant, XXV, 210, 264 ; used to poison fish, *id.* 272.

Kákápuris : sons of slaves, said to have come from Márwár, merged into the Bohora community, IX, pt. ii, 62.

Kákar : ruined town in Pálanpur, temple at, V, 342.

Kákar : a caste of Musalmán messengers, in Belgaum district, XXI, 211 ; in Dhárwár district, XXII, 238-239 ; in Bijápur district, XXIII, 294.

Kákara : village, perhaps Kákrej, I, pt. i, 152.

Kákateya, Kákatiya, Kakatya : dynasty of Tailangana, I, pt. ii, 222, 239, 522 ; records and legend, *id.* 340 notes 2 and 4 ; prince, Prola, *id.* 462 and note 2 ; chiefs (1070-1320) of Varangal in Nizam's dominions, XV, pt. ii, 89 note 3.

Kakdi : sacred plant, XXV, 279 ; worshipped by women, its fruit used in snake-worship, *id.* 285 ; *see* also IX, pt. i, 384.

Kakhandki : village in Bijápur district, grave of Mahipati and fair at, XXIII, 657.

Kakka I : founder of the first Gujarát Ráshtrakúta kingdom, I, pt. i, 467 ; king of Malkhed (705) patronises the old Vedic religion, I, pt. ii, 194, 388.

Kakka II : Ráshtrakúta king of Malkhed (972), Khotika's successor, I, pt. ii, 207 ; his Karda grant, *id.* 208, 387 ; his *birudas*, epithets, titles, and wars with the Gurjaras, Cholas, Hunas, and Pándyas, *id.* 423, 425 note 2 ; is overthrown by the Western Chálukya Taila II (973-974), *id.* 208, 306, 307, 385, 424, 426 ; overthrown by Aparájita Siláhára, *id.* 430 ; his grants, I, pt. i, 122.

Kakka III, Kakkala : Ráshtrakúta king of Málkhed, I, pt. i, 120.

Kakkala : I, pt. ii, 18, 207, 211, 256, 423, 542 note 4. *See* Karka II, also Kakka II, Kakka III, I, pt. i, 120.

Kakkalla : overthrown by Singhana, I, pt. ii, 525 and note 3. *See* Kakkula.

Kakkara : I, pt. ii, 423 ; (972), *see* Kakka II of Malkhed Ráshtrakúta.

Kakkarája I : prince of the first Gujarát Ráshtrakúta family, I, pt. ii, 392. *See* Kakka I.

Kakkarája II : last king of the first Gujarát Ráshtrakúta branch (757), I, pt. ii, 382, 389 ; his grant, *id.* 359, 757 ; possibly Ráhappa whom Krishna I defeated, *id.* 392 ; his descendants rebel and are defeated, *id.* 408 and note 4, 409.

Kakkula : monarch, deprived of his sovereignty by Singhana, I, pt. ii, 239 ; identified with Kakkala, *id.* 240.

Kákrez : name of a sub-division near Rádhanpur, I, pt. i, 208 note 3.

Kakri : oil-yielding plant, XXV, 218.

Kakun : food plant cultivated in hilly parts, XXV, 184.

Kakur : village in Dhárwár district, inscription at, XXII, 763.

Kákustha, Kákusthavarman : Kádamba king, I, pt. ii, 285, 286 ; his grant, *id.* 287 and note 6, 291 and notes 1 and 2.

Kál : stream in Kánara district, XV, pt. i, 6.

Kala : king of, subdued by Vishnuvardhana, I, pt. ii, 495.

Kálá : festival at Pandharpur, XX, 466.

Kalabhai Sorabji : son-in-law of Nek sat Khán visits Delhi, receives in grant an estate in Rander, IX, pt. ii, 197 note 2.

Kalabhra, Kalabhras : nation or people in Southern India, allies of Badámi Chalukyas, I, pt. ii, 189 ; overthrown by Vikramáditya I, *id.* 362 ; defeated by Vinayáditya, *id.* 368 ; reduced by Vikramáditya II, *id.* 190, 375.

Kala buch-nag : poisonous plant, XXV, 270.

Kála Chabutra : platform at Junnar built (1657) over the heads of Koli rebels, XVIII, pt. ii, 228.

Kálachchuris : Kalachuris, I, pt. ii, 293.

Kalachuri era : I, pt. ii, 364 ; foundation of, *id.* 294 ; same as the Chedi era, *id.* 293, 295, 310, 313, 314 note 1, 360, 374 ; used in Western Chálukya grants from Láta, *id.* 295, 311 ; *see* also I, pt. i, 57. *See* Haihaya Kalatsuri, Traikuta, Chedi and Traikutaka.

Kalachuris, Kálachuris, Kalachuryas : of Chedi, vanquished by Mangalisa (597-608), I, pt. ii, 181, 293 and note 1, 347 and note 1 ; conquered by Govinda III, *id.* 396 ; protected by Krishna III, *id.* 420 ; claim to be descendants of Sahasrarjuna and are possibly referred to as Arjunáyanas, *id.* 293 ; Pandit Bhagvánlal's theory about them and their era, *id.* 294-295 ; their princesses marry Western and Eastern Chalukya and Ráshtrakúta princes, *id.* 296, 374, 380, 410, 414, 418, 427 ; *see* also XV, pt. ii, 89 and note 4 ; their rule in the valley of the Narbada (500-600), I, pt. i, 114.

Of Kalyáni, I, pt. ii, 225-228, 468-469 ; their original seat, *id.* 225 ; a later offshoot of the Kalachuris of Chedi, *id.* 225, 296 ; founder of the branch, *id.* 225 ; their lineage, *id.* 468-469 ; analogy between the names Chalukya and Chálukya, Kadamba and Kádamba, and Kalachuri and Kalachurya, *id.* 469-470 ; their genealogical list, *id.* 471 ; their crest

and banner, *id.* 299 note 4, 469; their musical instrument, *id.* 469; Western Chálukya feudatories, *id.* 296, 456, 458, 460, 462, 470; usurp the sovereignty (1162), *id.* 296; a portion of their territory seized by the Western Chálukya king Someśvara IV and a portion by the Yádavas of Devagiri, *id.* 228, 489, 505; the dynasty becomes extinct (1183), *id.* 228, 489; revival of the worship of Śiva in the time of, *id.* 225-227, 477-484; *see* also XXII, 397-398; XXIII, 389-392; their rule at Banavási, XV, pt. ii, 265; *see* Bijjala, Sovideva, Samkama, Áhavamalla and Singhana.

Kaladana: medicinal plant, cultivated throughout India, XXV, 255.

Kaládgi: town in Bijápur district, XXIII, 657-658; formerly district head-quarters, *id.* 455.

Kaláigar: a caste of Musalmán tin-smiths, in Ahmadnagar district, XVII, 228; in Poona district, XVIII, pt. i, 494; in Sátára district, XIX, 136; in Sholápur district, XX, 200; in Belgaum district, XXI, 207; in Dhárwár district, XXII, 234; in Bijápur district, XXIII, 291; in Násik district, XVI, 57.

Kala-inderjao: dye-yielding plant, XXV, 248.

Kalaka: food and famine plant, cultivated in several districts, XXV, 108, 209.

Kala-kuda: dye-yielding plant, XXV, 247.

Kalál: a caste of distillers in Kolába district, XI, 70; in Poona district, XVIII, pt. i, 397-398; in Sholápur district, XX, 157; in Bijápur district, XXIII, 117; in Khándesh district, XII, 62; in Násik district, XVI, 60; in Belgaum district, XXI, 168, 169; in Kolhápur state, XXIV, 106; in Kánara district, XV, pt. i, 293.

Kálaledevi: wife of Narasimha II, I, pt. ii, 493, 507.

Kalamb: *Nauclea parvifolia*, timber tree, in Poona district, XVIII, pt. i, 47; in Khándesh district, XII, 25.

Kalamb: village in Poona district, XVIII, pt. iii, 232.

Kálambapattana: city, visited by Kumárapala, I, pt. i, 183 and note 1.

Kalambhom: village in Thána district, XIV, 112.

Kalambhras: *see* Kalabhra.

Kalameśvara: temple of, at Hulgur, inscription at, I, pt. ii, 459 note 3, 526 note 4; temple of, at Renadál, *id.* 528 note 1.

Kala-miri: food plant, indigenous to Malabár, XXV, 173.

Kálan: a caste of distillers in Thána district, XIII, 152; in Kolába district, XI, 71.

Kálánandigad: hill fort in Belgaum district, XXI, 574-575 note 7.

Kalandars: monks, their initiatory rites, IX, pt. ii, 22.

Kalanjar or Kalinjar: city in Bundelkhand, I, pt. ii, 468, 469; I, pt. i, 57 and note 4; fort, *id.* 178; I, pt. ii, 207, 225, 420, 469; Kaláchuri possession, I, pt. i, 469.

Kalanki: Vishnu's last incarnation as a horseman, IX, pt. i, 376.

Kálápaka: *see* Kátantra.

Kála-Rám: Násik temple, XVI, 516-518.

Kalas, Kalas-Budruk: village in Poona district, XVIII, pt. iii, 232; grant at, I, pt. ii, 231, 436, 512, 513, 514.

Kalas, Kaláspur: village in Dhárwár district, market, temple and inscriptions at, XXII, 763; I, pt. ii, 416.

Kalas-Budruk: *see* Kalas.

Kalátil: oil-yielding plant, cultivated in several districts, XXV, 219.

Kálatiyá: sub-caste of Bráhmans in Gujarát, IX, pt. i, 10.

Kalatsuri: Sanskritsed name of Kalachuris, I, pt. ii, 293; conquered by Mangaleśa (597-602), *id.* 295, 348 note 6. *See* Kalachuris.

Kálávad: town in Káthiáwár, VIII, 503.

Kálavanga: village, I, pt. ii, 288.

Kalávant, Kalávantin: a caste of courtezans, in Kánara district, XV, pt. i, 321-325; in Belgaum district, XXI, 159-162; in Bijápur district, XXIII, 244; in Ratnágiri district, X, 126.

Kalávini: river identified with Káveri, I, pt. i, 185 and note 4.

Kálavli, Kaláwali: river in Ratnágiri district, X, 10; I, pt. ii, 347 note 2.

Kálayavana: legendary Dakhan hero, I, pt. i, 9.

Kálbhairav: temple of, at Gokarn, XV, pt. ii, 292.

Kalbhávi: village in Belgaum district, inscription at, I, pt. ii, 299 note 4.

Káldurg: hill in Thána district, XIII, 7; fort, XIV, 11 note 3, 98, 112.

Kále: village in Sátára district, school at, XIX, 471.

Kále: village in Kolhápur state, local legend and temple at, XXIV, 301.

Kálegaon-Jakinvádi: Sahyádrispur, in Sátára district, XIX, 7.

Kále Kunbi: *see* Konkan Kunbi.

Kalen jiree: medicinal plant, common in waste places near villages, XXV, 257.

Kalghatgi: sub-division of Dhárwár district, boundaries, area, aspect, soil, hills, climate, water, stock, crops and people of, XXII, 636-638; *Town, id.* 764.

Kalhana: author of the *Rájatarangini*, IX, pt. i, 438.

Kalhenia: division of Panjáb Gurjjaras, IX, pt. i, 490.

Kalhole: village in Belgaum district, inscribed stone at, I, pt. ii, 557.

Kali: evil deity, I, pt. ii, 426.

Káli: Mátá or goddess, favourite deity, her nature, IX, pt. i, pp. xxxv, xxxvi; also known as Kálika or Kálka, *id.* 216 note 1, 493; form of Durga at Pávágad, *id.* 301 note 2; shrine of, *id.* p. xi, 34, 186, 187, 213, 295, 549; *see* also *id.* pt. ii, 21.

Kalianrai: massacred the Pársis and restored Cambay to the Hindus (947), VI, 216.

Kaliballaha: Prákrit form of Kalivallabha, I, pt. ii, 393.

Kálichitri: system of pounding cattle in Ahmadábád district, IV, 196.

Kálidása: Sanskrit poet, author of the *Meghaduta*, I, pt. ii, 142; author of the *Setubandha, id.* 144, 357.

Kalideva : of Ammaiyyanabhávi, I, pt. ii, 358 note 1.
Kálidurga : fortress of the Pándyas, I, pt. ii, 327.
Kálige : in the Nizam's dominion, inscription at, I, pt. ii, 339, 444 note 4, 445, 468 and note 4.
Kálika : *yogi* of Ujjain, I, pt. i, 174.
Kalika : *see* Káli.
Kalikat : on Malatár Coast, Thána trade with, XIII, 429, 444, 465, 470, 486.
Kalimah : profession of faith among Sunnis and Shiáhs, IX, pt. ii, 46.
Kálinadi : river in Kánara district, XV, pt. i, 2, 3, 4, 5.
Kalindaverman : Pallava king, I, pt. ii, 324.
Kalinga : country, corresponds to the Northern Circars, I, pt. ii, 139 ; between the rivers Godávari and Maháuadi, *id.* 341 note 2 ; one of the traditional nine kingdoms, *id.* 403 note 3 ; mentioned by Pánini, *id.* 138, 139 ; mentioned in the *Rámayana*, *id.* 142 ; eastern boundary of Aśoka's kingdom, *id.* 146 ; conquered by Kirtivarman I (567-598), *id.* 281, 345 ; subdued by Pulakeśi II, *id.* 183, 350 ; subjugated by Dantidurga, *id.* 194, 389 ; reduced to obedience by Krishna II, *id.* 201 ; conquered by Rájarájadeva the king of Chola (1006), *id.* 308 ; subjugated by Achagi II for Vikramáditya II, the Western Chálukya king, *id.* 219 ; power of, broken by Ereyanga Hoysala, *id.* 494 ; humbled by Singhana the Devagiri Yádava, *id.* 525.
Kalinganagara : modern Kalingapatam on the east coast of Madras, I, pt. ii, 297 ; capital of the Eastern Gangas, *id.* 299 note 3 ; Gangas of, *id.* 334 ; records and traditions of the Gangas of, *id.* 340 notes 2, 3 and 4.
Kalingattu Parani : work, composed in the reign of the Eastern Chálukya king Kulottunga Chodadeva I of Kalinganagara (1063-1112), I, pt. ii, 342 note 1.
Káli-Paraj : *i. e.*, dusky race, general name of early tribes in Gujarát, IX, pt. i, p. x ; in Surat states, VI, 246, 255 ; in Baroda state, VII, 30-31, 65-66, 117-118.
Kalivallabha : *biruda* or title of the Ráshtrakúta king Dhruva, I, pt. ii, 393.
Kali-Vikrama : Western Chálukya king Vikramáditya VI, I, pt. ii, 446 and note 1.
Kali-Vitta : of the Chella-Ketana family, I, pt. ii, 420.
Káliya-Ballála : Yádava king, I, pt. ii, 235 ; successor of Amaramallagi, *id.* 516.
Káliyámardan : god Krishna, temple of, at Tungár, XIV, 367.
Kaliyammarasa : Western Chálukya king Someśvara II's officer, I, pt. ii, 443 ; Vikramáditya VI's governor of Básavura province, *id.* 450 ; Kalachurya Bijjala's officer, *id.* 476.
Kaliyuga : fourth cycle of Hindus, I, pt. i, 6, 461 ; I, pt. ii, 248, 357 note 3, 566 and note 8.
Kaliyur : in Mysore, inscription at, I, pt. ii, 308, 491.
Kálka : *see* Káli.
Kalkutgár : a caste of stone-workers. *See* Pánchál.
Kallabbarasi : wife of Butuga, I, pt. ii, 305.
Kallada : port mentioned by Pliny, I, pt. i, 537.
Kalla Mahomed : dye plant, XXV, 249.
Kállamma : Jain deity, XXIV, 95.
Kallesvaradeva : of Kittur, god, I, pt. ii, 571.
Kalliana or Kalliena : *see* Kalyan in Thána.
Kalligeris : probably Galgali, I, pt. i, 541.
Kallukeri : in Dhárwár, record at, I, pt. ii, 526, 527, 528 and note 2.
Kallukutig : a caste of masons in Kánara district, XV, pt. i, 274, 275.
Kalmádu : place of interest in Khándesh, XII, 452.
Kálol : sub-division of Panch Maháls, III, 295-296. *Town*, *id.* 317.
Kálol : sub-division in Baroda state, VII, 590-591. *Town*, *id.* 591.
Kalpasutra : life of Mahávira, IX, pt. i, 114 and note 2.
Kalpole : village in Belgaum district, Jain temple and fair at, XXI, 575.
Kalsubái : hill, in Násik district, origin of its name, XVI, 446-447, 441 ; in Ahmadnagar district, XVII, 3-4.
Kaltar : tenure in Baroda state, VII, 356-357.
Kaltigudda : hill in Kánara district, XV, pt. i, 4, 5 ; XV, pt. ii, 318.
Kálu : river in Thána district, XIII, 10 ; XIV, 361.
Káluhhár : river, in Káthiáwár, VIII, 63.
Kaluka : father of Jajjaka, I, pt. i, 128.
Kálumbhar : island in Káthiáwár, VIII, 27.
Kálundri : river in Thána district, XIII, 10, 11.
Kalusha : Kanoja Bráhman and favourite minister of Sambháji (1680-1689), I, pt. ii, 596 ; appointed in the place of Annaji Datto, farms out districts, *id.* 76 ; tries to save Sambháji and is wounded, *id.* 79 ; added cesses and raised the land rent, XI, 171 ; *see* also XVIII, pt. ii, 238 ; XIX, 246-247.
Kalvan : sub-division in Násik district, details, area, aspect, climate, water, history, land revenue, stock, holdings, crops, people, XVI, 394-399. *Town*, *id.* 447.
Kálvár : village in Thána district, inscription at, XIV, 396.
Kalvari : a caste of traders in Belgaum district, XXI, 103-104.
Kalvini : I, pt. ii, 24. *See* Káveri.
Kalyán : village in Dhárwár district, tomb and inscriptions at, XXII, 764 ; record at, I, pt. ii, 278 note 1, 339 note 4.
Kalyán : sub-division of Thána district, its boundaries, area, aspect, climate, water, soil, holdings, rental, stock, crops, people, XIII, 2, 688-690. *Town* its description, population, trade, fortifications, temples, Musalmán remains, fire temples and history of, XIV, 10, 113-121 ; taken by Shiváji's officer (1674), *id.* 33 ; mentioned in Kánheri caves, *id.* 147, 166, 168, 174, 175, 177, 178, 179, 186, 187, 218 ; mound and other relics at, *id.* 386, 396-399, 401 ; *another account of* : seaport in the Thána district, embargo laid on the use of, I, pt. ii, 538 note 8 ; place of great commercial importance, *id.* 174 ; district, *id.* 7, 17,

29, 37; formerly called Islámábád, *id.* 41; under Gujarát sultáns, *id.* 30; belongs to Ahmadnagar, *id.* 49; town, got possession of by Shiváji, *id.* 67, 68, 69, 70; utterly ruined (1672), *id.* 72; district, extension of, *id.* 100; district, surveyed and assessed in cash (1771-1790), *id.* 108; district, invaded by Bhils and Rámoshis (1817), *id.* 116; *see* also I, pt. i, 86, 547; early Arab settlement at, IX, pt. ii, 1 note 1; *another account of*: ravaged by the Mughals (1682-1707), XIII, 555; surveyed (1771-1772), 558; re-surveyed (1788-1789), *id.* 558; cesses added, *id.* 560; *bigha* cash rate, *id.* 561; cash rental, *id.* 566; farmer's rates, 566 note 2; (1835), 578, 579; assessment revised (1837), *id.* 583-584, 600 note 2; results, *id.* 585; survey assessment introduced (1859), *id.* 599-602; one of the *pránts* under the Peshwás, *id.* 600 note 1.

Kalyána: modern Kalyáni in the Nizám's dominions, I, pt. ii, 234, 427 and note 3; founded by Someśvara I the Western Chálukya king, *id.* 215, 427, 440; burnt by the Chola king, *id.* 350 note 8; entered into by Vikramáditya II also styled VI after his brother's deposition, *id.* 217, 445; Vikramáditya does not reign at, *id.* 446; still continues to be the capital, *id.* 449; Tailapa II flies to, from Annigeri (1157), *id.* 222; ceases to be the capital of the Western Chálukyas, *id.* 461; capital of the Kalachuryas, *id.* 225, 476, 485, 487; Basava welcomed to, *id.* 479; religious revolution at, *id.* 225; Basava reinstated as minister and Vijjana assassinated at, *id.* 226; represented as Śiva's *kailása* or heaven, *id.* 227; lived in by Vijñáneśvara, *id.* 229; sovereignty of, obtained by Bhillama the Devagiri Yádava king, *id.* 238, 520; seat of Vijjal (1156-1167), Jain king of the Kalachuri family, XXIV, 119; capital of Chálukya kingdom, I, pt. i, 86, 150; XV, pt. ii, 86, 89, 90.

Kalyánakataka: city of Kanauj, its king attacks Panchásar in Pálanpur state, V, 345 note 2; capital of Buvada, Cháulukya king, I, pt. i, 150; capital of king Permádi, *id.* 173.

Kalyánapura: *see* Kalyána.

Kalyánasakti: priest of Mulasthánadeva, I, pt. ii, 571.

Kalyangad: *see* Nándgiri.

Kalyankatak: *see* Kalyanakataka.

Káma, Kámadev: god of love, legend of, XV, pt. ii, 249 note 2; I, pt. ii, 577; IX, pt. i, 363.

Káma: Kávana, father of Brahma, Someśvara IV's general, I, pt. ii, 464.

Kámadeva: father of Hemádri, I, pt. ii, 248.

Kámadeva: Hángal Kádamba prince and feudatory of the Western Chálukya king Someśvara IV (1181-1203), I, pt. ii, 465, 559, 482; feudatory of Vira-Ballála II the Hoysala king, *id.* 506; washes the feet of Ekántada Rámayya, *id.* 484; fights against the Hoysala forces, *id.* 563; Pándya chieftain of Nolambavádi, rebels and is reduced by Vira-Ballála II, *id.* 505.

Kámadeva: father of Kamaládevi, wife of the Goa Kádamba Permádi, I, pt. ii, 569.

Kámadeva: Kávana, brother-in-law of Shashthadeva II, I, pt. ii, 572.

Kámadeva: Hindu god of love; *see* Káma.

Kamadhia: táluka in Káthiáwár, VIII, 503.

Kámáji Homaji: a Broach Pársi martyr, IX, pt. ii, 198.

Kamala: dye plant, XXV, 248.

Kamaládevi: wife of the Goa Kádamba Sivachitta Permádi, I, pt. ii, 565; builds the temple at Degámve, *id.* 569.

Kamala-Náráyana Mahálakshmi: god and goddess, temple of, at Degámve, built by Kamaládevi, wife of the Goa Kádamba Permádi, I, pt. ii, 569.

Kamálgad: a spur of the Sahyádris with hill-fort in Sátára district, XIX, 5-6, 9, 471, 509-510.

Kamálias: literal meaning of the name, descendants of Kanauj Bráhmans, worshippers of Bahucheráji, converted by the emperor Ala-ud-din (1297), worship Bahneheráji, Musalmáns in name only, IX, pt. ii, 82.

Kamál Khán: regent at Bijápur during the minority of Ismáel, aspires to supplant his master and is assassinated (1511), I, pt. ii, 589, 641.

Kámalpur: táluka in Káthiáwár, VIII, 503.

Kamál-ud-din: Gáikwár's military officer, VII, 202, 205, 229, 517.

Káman: probably Kámarúpa, that is Assam, inland state, I, pt. i, 528.

Káman: Portuguese sub-division near Bassein, XIII, 456, 457, 490.

Kámandurg: village and fort in Thána district, XIV, 98, 121; hill, XIII, 6.

Kamane: identified with Kamlej, I, pt. i, 539.

Kamángar: a caste of shield painters in Cutch, V, 127.

Kámarupa: *see* Káman.

Kámasutra: institutes of love, written by Vátsyáyana, I, pt. ii, 171.

Kamat: land tenure in Dhárwár district, XXII, 462 and note 5.

Kamathada-Mallisetti: officer of Vira-Ballála II (1203), I, pt. ii, 506.

Kámáthi: a caste of husbandmen, in Thána district, XIII, 119; in Belgaum district, XXI, 108; in Dhárwár district, XXII, 136-137; in Kolába district, XI, 70; in Násik district, XVI, 59; in Ahmadnagar district, XVII, 159-160; in Poona district, XVIII, pt. i, 395-397; in Sholápur district, XX, 158-160.

Kamáti militia: formed (1757) in Bombay island, XXVI, pt. ii, 316-320; disbanded (1759), *id.* 328.

Kámátri: slaughterer at Bándra, XIV, 18.

Kamávisdár: Marátha revenue officer, I, pt. i, 212 note 1; in Baroda, VII, 370; in Ratnágiri, X, 220; in Kolába, XI, 170; in Thána, XIII, 564, 569, 575; in Násik district, XVI, 209, 210.

Kam-Baksh: Aurangzeb's son, governor of Sholápur, XX, 289; of Bijápur, XXIII, 440, 592-593; tries to revive the Mughal empire but is defeated and killed, I, pt. ii, 655.

Kambay: I, pt. i, 518. *See* Cambay.

Kambaya, Kambáyah or Kambáyat: modern Cambay, Arab references to (976-1350), I, pt. i, 507, 508, 509, 511, 514, 515, 520, 523, 528, 529, 531; northern boundary of the Balhára kingdom, I, pt. ii, 388.
Kambhár: caste of iron-workers: *see* Pánchál.
Kamboja: Kábul, I, pt. i, 491, 498 and note 4.
Kambojas: name of a non-Áryan people, I, pt. ii, 139.
Kambu: offshoot of the Afghán stock, IX, pt. ii, 14.
Kámdev: *see* Káma.
Kámdeva: second Kadamba chief (1184), XV, pt. ii, 90-91. *See* Kámadeva.
Kámdhenu: village in Dhárwár district, temple and weir at XXII, 764.
Kámdín Padam: *dastur* of Broach, IX, pt. ii, 190 note 2.
Kámdugha: heavenly cow, her sacredness, IX, pt. i, 372.
Kameras: I, pt. ii, 368. *see* Kavera.
Kámbal: I, pt. i, 507, 511, 514. *See* Anahilaváda.
Kamigara: town, I, pt. i, 538.
Kamil Khán: Dakhani, one of the managers of the state during the minority of Ibráhim Ádil Sháh II, killed by Háji Kishwar Khán, I, pt. ii, 647.
Kamkar: Konkan, boundary of Balhára's kingdom, I, pt. i, 519; *id.* pt. ii, 388.
Kámlej: district, I, pt. i, 108; expedition against, *id.* 109, 130, 520.
Kámli: a caste of husbandmen in Thána district, XIII, 122.
Kamlo: jaundice, its cure, IX, pt. i, 365.
Kammal: flower, the abode of goddess Lakshmi, XXV, 289.
Kammanijja: modern Kámlej, I, pt. i, 130; I, pt. ii, 415.
Kammár: a caste of blacksmiths in Dhárwár district, XXII, 151-152.
Kammara, Kammayyarasa: Sindá prince of Bágadage, I, pt. ii, 576.
Kammarawádi: in the Nizám's dominions, I, pt. ii, 452.
Kammoni: village, identified with Kim, I, pt. i, 539, 545.
Kámpila: town near Vijayanagar, *rája* of, I, pt. i, 230 and note 2.
Kamrakh: gooseberry tree in Poona district, XVIII, pt. i, 47.
Kamrej: in Baroda territory, near Surat, I, pt. ii, 370.
Kamsa: defeated by Krishna, I, pt. i, 178.
Kámtekot: fort in Ratnágiri district, X, 342.
Kámtha: pass in Koláha district, XI, 5, 114.
Kámthi: stream in Koláha district, XI, 10.
Kámti: a caste in Kánara district; *see* Mali.
Kámti: village in Ahmadnagar district, XVII, 721.
Kámuhul: I, pt. i, 511, 514. *See* Anahilaváda.
Kámvadeva, Kámvadevaráya: prince of the Chalukya family and chief of the Konkan, I, pt. ii, 223, 224, 466, 467; donor of the Rájápur grant, *id.* 253.
Kan: fodder plant, found in Sind, XXV, 277.
Kánabhuti: a spirit, I, pt. ii, 170.
Kánáda: a caste of graziers, in Thána district, XIII, 145; in Khándesh district, XII, 105; in Násik district, XVI, 49.
Kánada: a class of Bráhmans, in Násik district, XVI, 43; in Ahmadnagar district, XVII, 58.
Kanaddeva Rása: historical work, I, pt. i, 129.
Kánagopa: Pallava king, I, pt. ii, 324.
Kanak: *see* Kanishka.
Kanakamuni: fifth Buddha image of, at Sopára, XIV, 331, 412.
Kanakdurg: fort in Ratnágiri district, X, 337, 342.
Kanaksen: founder of the Skythian era (78), I, pt. i, 453, 464; founder of Vadnagar, possibly a grandson of Kushán king Kanishka, IX, pt. i, 15 note 1; sat on Krishna's throne at Dwárka; the same as Kanishka; Chávdás and other Rájpút tribes claim origin from, *id.* 462, 495. *See* Kanishka.
Kánalda: place of interest in Khándesh district, XII, 452.
Kánam: local name for Jambusar, I, pt. i, 208 note 3.
Kanara district: its boundaries, sub-divisions and physical aspect, XV, pt. i, 1-4; hills and rivers, *id.* 4-8; geology, *id.* 9-11; climate, *id.* 11-18; minerals, *id.* 19-20; forests, forest administration, forest products and forest trees, *id.* 21-79, 417-448; domestic and wild animals, *id.* 79-104; bees, snakes and fish, *id.* 104-113; census details, *id.* 114-116; Bráhmans, *id.* 116-174; traders, *id.* 174-192; warlike classes, *id.* 193-198; temple servants, *id.* 199-201; husbandmen, *id.* 202-256; craftsmen and manufacturers, *id.* 257-284; shepherds and fishermen, *id.* 295-314; musicians and courtezans, *id.* 315-326; servants, carriers, labourers, beggars, depressed classes and other castes, *id.* 327-380; Native Catholic Christians, *id.* 380-395; Portuguese or East Indians, *id.* 395-396; Christian reverts, *id.* 397-400; Musalmáns, *id.* 400-411; Pársis and other castes, communities, *id.* 411-415; agriculture: stock, soil, spice gardens, field tools, crops, XV, pt. ii, 2-23; capital, currency, investments, land and labour mortgage, weights and measures, *id.* 24-38; early trade routes, roads, post and telegraph, light-houses, *id.* 39-48; history of trade (A. D. 100-1800), *id.* 48-56; traders, trade centres, fairs, exports and imports, sailing vessels and ports, *id.* 56-69; crafts, *id.* 69-74; *History*: early Kadambas, (450-560), early Chálukyas (560-760), second Kadambas (750-1050), second Chálukyas (973-1192), Hoysálas (1117-1137), Kalachuris (1160), Devgiri Yadavs (1188-1318), Vijayanagar kings (1330-1580), the Portuguese (1560-1600), Bijápur kings (1600-1670), the English (1638-1660), Sonda and Bednur chiefs, Haidar Ali (1763-1782), condition in the 19th century, *id.* 75-153; land administration under Sonda and Bednur, under Mysore (1763-1799), under the Company, settlements of Munro (1800), Read (1800-1816), Harris (1817-1822), under Stokes and Viveash (1833), Mr. Maltby

(1838), Bombay survey introduced (1862-1882), *id.* 154-182; land tenures, season reports, *id.* 183-193; administration of justice (1802-1816), changes, civil courts and suits (1870-1881), registration, magistracy, offences, jails, *id.* 194-202; revenue and finance, balance sheet, receipts from stamps, excise, law, items of expenditure, provincial revenue, *id.* 203-209; instruction, private and other schools, readers and writers, village and town schools, *id.* 210-216; health: fevers, hospitals, vaccination, birth and death statistics, cattle diseases, *id.* 217-222; sub-divisional details, *id.* 223-248; places of interest, *id.* 249-356; *see* also I, pt. ii, 298 note 2, 388, 646.

Kánara kings: their rule in Konkan, XI, 142.

Kanarese: non-Áryan language, I, pt. ii, 137, 477; districts or Southern Marátha Country, *id.* 344 note 6, 431, 454 note 5, 509, 572; Buddhism in, *id.* 452.

Kanási: village in Khándesh district, temple at, XII, 453.

Kanaswa: place in Málwa, inscription at (A. D. 738-739); the term Káyasth used in, IX, pt. i, 59 note 1; I, pt. ii, 284.

Kanathra: perhaps Kare-Netráni in Kánara district, XV, pt. ii, 336 and note 6.

Kanauj or Kanoja: town in United Provinces, I, pt. ii, 314 note 1, 350, 384; battle of, I, pt. i, 150; king of, I, pt. ii, 183, 215, 431 note 1; I, pt. i, 507, 508, 519.

Kanbi: origin of the name, I, pt. i, 4; class of professional husbandmen in Gujarát; subdivisions, strength and distribution, IX, pt. i, 153, 154, 163, derivation and meaning of the name, *id.* 154 and note 1; origin, race belonging to the White Húna tribe of Gurjjaras or Mihiras, *id.* 155, 491, 492, 496, 499; foreign element in, *id.* 453, 499; dress, *id.* 155; occupation, condition, *id.* 156; religion: various sects; faith in early beliefs; superstitious beliefs in cultivation; animal worship; places of pilgrimage, *id.* 156-157; Customs—birth, Chhathi worship, *id.* 157; *kanthi* wearing; bethrothals, dowry, *id.* 158; marriage, *ghána* ceremony, *laganpatri*, *grahashánti* ceremony. *id.* 159; wedding ceremony, *id.* 160; widow-marriage, polygamy, divorce; pregnancy, *id.* 161; death ceremonies, *shráddha* ceremonies, *id.* 161-163; Communities, *id.* 163.

Anjana: Rájpút names, clans of; followers of various religious sects; faith in early beliefs; places of pilgrimage; widow marriage and divorce allowed in, *id.* 163-164.

Dángi: hill Kanbis, said to be originally Anjana, *id.* 164

Kadva: strength and distribution, *id.* 153, 164; origin, *id.* 164; trace of Gujar origin, *id.* 496, 499; three sub-divisions in Surat, divisions of Kulia and Akulia in South Gujarát, professional divisions of artisans and peasants, *id.* 164; curious marriage customs of, application of the Infanticide Act to, widow marriage and divorce allowed among, *id.* 165-166; appear in Rájpútána as Kháría Gujars, *id.* 490.

Leva: strength and distribution, *id.* 153, 166; trace of Gujar origin, *id.* 491, 492, 499; social division of Pátidárs and Kanbis; Kulia and Akulia divisions of Pátidárs; position and influence of Pátidárs before British rule, *id.* 166; perquisites levied by Pátidárs, *id.* 166 note 2; marriage customs, application of the Infanticide Act to, reforms in marriage customs, *id.* 167.

Matia: Piràna, strength and distribution, *id.* 153, 167; said to be originally Levás, miracles of Imám Sháh of Piràna, their adoption of his faith, *id.* 167-168; followers of the Atharva Veda; their sacred book *Shikshapatri*; Káka or devotee; three religious divisions, *id.* 168; rite of sin removing or *lahe-utarni* ceremony, *id.* 169; half Musalmán half Hindu holidays, their places of pilgrimage, *id.* 169-170; half Hindu half Musalmán customs, widow marriage and divorce allowed in, *id.* 170-172; Vaishnav Matiás, form of worship, formation into a separate caste, *id.* 168; in Kaira, III, 31; in Cutch, Pálanpur and Mahi Kántha, V, 69-70, 289-290, 292, 364; in Rewa Kántha, VI, 24; in Baroda, VII, 59-60, 61, 619; in Káthiáwár, VIII, 142-143, 176.

Kauchan: pass in Násik district, XVI, 128, 130.

Kanchgár: a caste of brass-workers; *see* Pánchál.

Kánchi: modern Conjevaram, I, pt. ii, 280; capital of the Dravida, the country of the Pallavas, *id.* 190, 281; its various spellings, *id.* 318 note 3; Pallava king of, captured by the Early Gupta king Samudragupta, *id.* 319; kings of, seek to overthrow Mayurasarman, prince of the Kádamba family, *id.* 286; king of, overthrown by the Kádamba king Ravivarman, *id.* 291 note 1, 322; besieged by the Western Chálukya king Pulakesi II (609), *id.* 183, 324, 329, 350 and note 8; taken by Vikramáditya I, *id.* 362; captured by Vikramáditya II, *id.* 190, 327-328, 375, 376; king of, defeated by Kirtivarman II, *id.* 377; subjugated by the Ráshtrakúta king Dantidurga, *id.* 194, 197, 389; conquered by Govinda III, *id.* 331-332, 395, 397; taken by Krishna III, *id.* 419; missionary tour to, of the Digambara Jain author Samantabhadra, *id.* 407; Chola capital, taken by the Western Chalukya king Someśvara I, *id* 215, 350 and note 8, 441, 567; plundered by Vikramáditya II also styled VI, *id.* 442; rebellion at, put down by Vikramáditya II also styled VI, *id.* 217, 445; taken by Hoysala Vishnuvardhana. *id.* 494, 498; Pándya capital, lord of, feudatory of the Kalachuryas of Kalyáni, *id.* 486; visited by Kumarapála, I, pt. i, 183; also known as Kanchipura, I, pt. ii, 140, 183, 199, 320 and note 6.

Kanchineglur: village in Dhárwar district, inscription at, XXII, 764.

Kánchipura: *see* Kánchi.

Kánchiváyil: village in the Madras Presidency, I, pt. ii, 320 note 6, 327.

Kanchugár: *see* Kásár.

Kandahar : *see* Gándbára.

Kandakadevi : wife of Amoghavarsha III, I, pt. ii, 205.

Kándalgaon : village in the Ratnágiri district, charter from, I, pt. ii, 347 note 2 ; copper-plate grant from, *id.* 358 note 1.

Kandalgaon : village in Sholápur district, XX, 412.

Kándáli : town in Madras, grant of Rája Prithivimula, issued from, I, pt. ii, 334.

Kandaná : river, identified with Kanhaná, I, pt. ii, 420.

Kandara or Kandhara : Attivarman descended from, I, pt. ii, 334.

Kandári : village in Khándesh district, temple at, XII, 453.

Kandavalábára : country, I, pt. ii, 364.

Kandavára : in Mysore, inscription at, I, pt. ii, 332.

Kandhár : a village north of Broach, I, pt. i, 525.

Kandhár : town in Nizám's dominions, identified with Kandhárapura, the capital of Ratta chief Lakshmidev I (1208-9), XXI, 357.

Kandhára : *see* Kanhara.

Kandhara : *see* Kandara.

Kandhárapura : unidentified town, Ráshtrakúta king Krishna III said to be the lord of, I, pt. ii, 384 note 4, 419, 556.

Kandjy : town mentioned by Alberuni, I, pt. ii, 4.

Kandoi : a Vánia sub-division in Cutch, V, 52.

Kandol, : village in Káthiáwár, IX, pt. i, 10 ; palace of, I, pt. i, 180 note 2 ; hill in Káthiáwár, VIII, 10.

Kandolia, Kandoliya : a sub-caste of Bráhmans in Gujarát, immigrants from Upper India, IX, pt. i, 2, 10 ; created to hold sacrifice, *id.* 440 note 5 ; in Cutch, V, 48 ; in Káthiáwár, VIII, 48.

Kandori : poisonous plant common in Bombay, XXV, 269.

Kandorna : town in Káthiáwár, VIII, 503.

Kándra : stream, in Kolhápur state, XXIV, 9.

Kandugul : village in the Kanna country, I, pt ii, 364.

Kandul : fibrous plant, XXV, 229 ; yields gum, *id.* 250.

Kándur : snake in Ratnágiri district, X, 50-51.

Kanduri : earthen dish rite. *See* Shanak.

Kane : modern Hisn Ghnráb, I, pt. i, 543.

Kaner : táluka in Káthiáwár, VIII, 504.

Kaner : poisonous plant, grows in Sind, XXV, 266.

Kaneri : village in Kolhápur state, Lingáyat monastery and temple at, XXIV, 301.

Kanerkhed : village in Sátára district, XIX, 411.

Kangai : fibrous plant, XXV, 228.

Kangári : depressed class, in Kánara district, XV, pt. i, 373, 374 ; in Násik district, XVI, 61.

Kangi, Kangia : food plant, XXV, 178.

Kangua : wrist-bands of the bride and bridegroom, IX, pt. ii, 164.

Kangoi, Kangu : food plant, XXV, 184.

Kángo : a sub-caste of Bráhmans in Thána district, XIII, 79.

Kángori : fort in Kolába district, XI, 323 ; I, pt. ii, 114.

Kangra : food plant cultivated on *ghâts*, XXV, 184, 187.

Kangui : oil-yielding plant common on the *ghâts* and in Konkan, XXV, 216.

Kanguvarman : Kadamba king, son of Mayurasárman, I, pt ii, 286.

Kanhada : I, pt. i, 181. *See* Krishnadeva.

Kanhana : river in Central Provinces, I, pt. ii, 420. *See* Kandaná, Kandavá.

Kanhara, Kanhára or Kandhára : Prákrit name of Krishna the Yádava king, I, pt. ii, 244, 526.

Kanher : village in Thána district, XIV, 399.

Kanhera : fort in Khándesh district, XII, 443.

Kanheri : fort in Thána district, XIV, 191.

Kanheri : caves in Thána district, XIV, 10, 51, 52, 101, 119 ; situation and aspect, *id.* 121-123 ; history, *id.* 124-127 ; Buddhism, *id.* 128-136 ; life at Kanheri, *id.* 137-146 ; inscriptions, *id.* 147 ; notices, *id.* 148-164 ; details, caves, *id.* 1-2, 164-165 ; cave, *id.* 3, 166-168 ; *stupas*, *id.* 169-171 ; caves *id.* 4-9, 171-172 ; caves, *id.* 10-15, 172-175 ; caves, *id.* 16-21 ; stone dam, *id.* 175-176 ; caves, *id.* 22-28, 176 ; caves, *id.* 87-78, 176-177 ; caves, *id.* 29-35, 177-178 ; caves, *id.* 36-38, 179 ; galleries, *id.* 38-41 ; stone *stupa*, *id.* 179-184 ; caves, *id.* 42-49, 185 ; caves, *id.* 50-56, 186 ; caves, *id.* 57-66, 186-187 ; caves, *id.* 67-76, 188 ; caves, *id.* 89-102 ; worship, fairs, *id.* 189-190, 320, 363, 364, 389 ; *another account of* : Buddhistic caves, I, pt. ii, 3, 9, 13, 174, 176, 202 ; caves of, taken possession of and the sculptures destroyed by the Franciscans, *id.* 56 ; inscriptions at, *id.* 151, 153, 161, 167, 200, 202, 208, 253, 279 note 1, 294 and note 7, 404, 405, 541, 542 ; cave monasteries at, *id.* 173, 178 ; *chaitya* caves at, *id.* 178. *See* Krishnagiri ; trace of the Pársis in India (10th century) in Pehlevi writings in, IX, pt. ii, 186 and note 2 ; Arjun's visit to, XIII, 404 and note 2 ; Shátakarni remains, *id.* 412 ; mention of Yavans at, *id.* 414 ; a copper-plate found at, *id.* 419 ; one cave turned into a church by Antonio do Porto (1532-1552), *id.* 461 note 1 ; Du Perron's visit to (1760), *id.* 498 ; visit of Forbes to (1774), *id.* 501 ; Macneil's account of, *id.* 509 note 5 ; *see* also I, pt. i, 126, 128.

Kanheri : seat of Sidhgiri in Sátára district, XXIV, 94.

Kanhira : fort in Násik district, XVI, 441, 448.

Kánhoba : Musalmán-Hindu saint, shrine and history of, XVII, 726-727.

Kánhoji Angria I : (1690-1731), review of his reign, XI, 145-149 ; becomes the greatest power in the Konkan, possesses the coast from Sávantwádi to Bombay and extends his authority to Kalyán (1707-1713), I, pt. ii, 81 ; goes over to Sháhu (1713) and invades the Sidi's territories, *id.* 82 ; specimen of his letter, XI, 148 note 2 ; mention of, XIII, 482, 492 ; X, 195 ; XIX, 257, 277.

Kanhoji Angria II : recognized chief of Kolába (1839) by the British, XI, 157.

Kánhoji Gáikwár: son of Govindráv by a Rájputáni princess of Dharampur, kept in confinement during Govindráo's time; manages to secure the government for his idiot brother Anandráo (1800), again kept in confinement by his Arab guard, I, pt. i, 412; collects an army, obtains possession of Anandráo and is subdued by the English (1803), *id.* 413; holds Baroda (1793), VII, 199-200; his intrigues, 203-204, 209, 217-218, 295-296.

Kaniar: tract of land in Ahmadábád district, IV, 2.

Kanika: that is Kanishka, king of the Gushán, IX, pt. i, 470 note 3. *See* Kanishka.

Kanir: flowering plant, its flowers used in worshiping Ganpati, XXV, 289.

Kanishka: great Kushan king; founder of Saka era (A. D. 78), I, pt. ii, 158 note 1; I, pt. i, 22, 33, 37, 64 note 5, 453, 462 note 3; IX, pt. i, 461; great reviver of Buddhism, *id.* 455 note 5; his fight with the dragon, *id.* 441; worked out broader Buddhism, *id.* 442; overthrew caste privileges and divisions, *id.* 443 note 1; his great *vihár* at Peshâwar, *id.* 450; adopted Greek gods and Greek coins and legends, *id.* 456 note 3; believed to be Kauksen, *id.* 462, 495; Kanika same as, *id.* 470 note 3; Shálivahán, same as, *id.* 443 note 1. *See* Kanak.

Kanjar: a caste of Musalmán poulterers, in Ahmadnagar district, XVII, 232; in Sholápur district, XX, 207-208; in Dhárwár district, XXII, 246-247; in Bijápur district, XXIII, 303; in Belgaum district, XXI, 215.

Kánjarda: táluka in Káthiáwár, VIII, 504.

Kanjari: caste of beggars in Ahmadnagar and Sátára districts, XVII, 179-180, XIX, 83 84.

Kanji: I, pt. ii, 318 note 3. *See* Káñchi.

Kánji: Chunvália Koli robber, subdued by A'zam Khán, viceroy (1635-1642), I, pt. i, 278; Koli chief of Chhaniar, *id.* 321.

Kankai: ancient town in Káthiáwár, now deserted, temple of a *mátá* at, VIII, 687.

Kankan: Konkan, I, pt. ii, 3, 4.

Kánkar: village near Dholka, Dámáji's brother Pratápráv died at (1737), I, pt. i, 318.

Kankar: limestome, XII, 16.

Kánkariya: reservoir in Ahmadábád district, IV, 17.

Kánkasiali: táluka in Káthiáwár, VIII, 504.

Kankeshvar: village in Ratnágiri district, temple at, X, 342.

Kankeshvar: hill in Kolába district, XI, 2, 6, 316-318; temple on, *id.* 319-323.

Kankrála: fort in Násik district, XVI, 441, 448.

Kánkrej: state in Pálanpur, V, 288, 331.

Kankudi: Hindu goddess, IX, pt. i, 247.

Kanmadi: village in Belgaum district, temples and fair at, XXI, 575.

Kanna: district, I, pt. ii, 365.

Kanna: Ratta chieftain, I, pt. ii, 441 note 1, 553-554. *See* Kannakaira II.

Kannada: Kánara, XV, pt. i, note 2; I, pt. ii, 388.

Kannakaira I: Ratta feudatory, I, pt. ii, 551, 553.

Kannakaira II: Ratta prince and feudatory of Vikramáditya VI, I, pt. ii, 450; also called Kanna (1069-1076), *id.* 551, 553.

Kannama: Kalachuri king, son of Sagararasa, I, pt. ii, 468, 469.

Kannanur: in the Chola kingdom, I, pt. ii, 507; capital of Vira-Someśvara, *id.* 508.

Kannara: son of the Kalachuri king Sandarája, I, pt. ii, 468.

Kánnav: *see* Kánva.

Kannawa: converted Sindh Lohána; carries Memans to Bhuj at the invitation of Ráo Khengár (1548-1584); is honoured with the title of Shet or Squire by the Ráo, IX, pt. ii, 51.

Kannegál: forces of Vikramáditya VI attacked at, by Gangarája, I, pt. ii, 500.

Kanneshvar: village in Dhárwár district, inscriptions at, XXII, 764; I, pt. ii, 433.

Kannigeri: village in Kánara, saw-mill at, XV, pt. ii, 74 and note 1, 356.

Kannura-Basappa: temple of, at Nágávi in the Gadag táluka, I, pt. ii, 422 note 3.

Kanodar: village in Pálanpur state, V, 342.

Kanoja, Kanojia or Kananj: sub-caste of Gaud Bráhmans, in Gujarát, IX, pt. i, 1 note 1; in Ratnágiri district, X, 117; in Thána, XIII, 79; in Kánara district, XV, pt. i, 172, 173; in Násik district, XVI, 42; in Poona district, XVIII, pt. i, 167-171; in Dhárwár district, XXII, 93-95; in Bijápur district, XXIII, 89; in Sátára district, XIX, 53; in Sholápur district, XX, 31-32; in Kolhápur state, XXIV, 62; worshippers of Bahucheraji converted to Islám by Ala-ud-din, IX, pt. ii, 82. *See* also I, pt. i, 161.

Kánoji Tákpar: Gáikwár's lieutenant, I, pt. i, 330; goes with Fakhr-ud-daulah into Sorath and captures the town of Vanthali; retires to Dholka and expels Muhammad Jánbáz; joins Rangoji and marches on Sánand, *id.* 331, 396.

Kanora: state in Rewa Kántha, VI, 151.

Kánphata, Kanphate: a class of Shaiv *jogis*, IX, pt. i, 543; in Ratnágiri district, X, 131; in Sávantvádi, *id.* 419 note 1; in Kolába district, XI, 415; in Khándesh district, XII, 124; in Násik district, XVI, 74; in Poona district, XVIII, pt. i, 456-457; in Belgaum district, XXI, 185; in Cutch, V, 85-88; in Kánara district, XV, pt. i, 353, 354.

Káns: *mulla*, a Broach Pársi priest, goes to Persia with his son Peshotan, the first Kadmi *dastur*, IX, pt. ii, 193 note 2.

Kánsa: feeder of the Várna in Kolhápur state, XXIV, 9.

Kansára: a caste of Gujaráti copper-smiths, Pávágad their original home, origin, surnames, traces of Rájput blood; sub-divisions, family goddess, IX, pt. i, 186; workers in metal; religion; places of pilgrimage, *id.* 187; customs; trade guild, *id.* 188; in Cutch, V, 71; in Káthiáwár, VIII, 150.

Kánta: variety of honey bee in Kolhápur state, XXIV, 24, 25.

Kanta: *see* Kangi.

Kántáji Kadam, Kántáji Kadam Bánde: officer of the Peshwa, enters Gujarát and levies tribute for the first time (1723), I, pt. i, 304, 310, 317, 390; takes Chámpáner, *id.* 391; harasses Gujárát, *id.* 394; defeats Piláji Gáikwár near Cambay and levies contribution in the city (1725), VI, 221.

Kántela : old village in Káthiáwár, temples and inscription at, VIII, 504.
Kántelun : *see* Srinagar.
Kánthadi : an ascetic, I, pt. i, 161.
Kanthádurg : I, pt. i, 158. *See* Kanthkot.
Kántharia : táluka in Káthiáwár, VIII, 505.
Kánthi : old name for the shore of Cutch, IX, pt. i. 240 note 2; gulf of, mentioned by Ptolemy, I, pt. i, 538.
Kanthi : *basil* thread, IX, pt. i, 89.
Kanthika : coast tract, from Balsár northward, or between Bombay and Cambay, I, pt. i, 123, 126.
Kanthkot : fort in Cutch, I, pt. i, 158, 204, 235 and note 2; its history, the sun and other temples in, V, 224-225.
Kanthmál : scrofula, its cure, IX, pt. i, 365.
Kantra : fort in Násik district, XVI, 441, 448.
Kantrodi : village in Káthiáwár, its claim to antiquity, *sati* memorials and inscriptions at, VIII, 505.
Kanu : tree in Khándesh district, XII, 25.
Kánungos : Mughal accountants, I, pt. i, 212.
Kánva : Puránic dynasty, overthrown by Sipraka, I, pt. ii, 155.
Kánva : school of the White Yajurveda, I, pt. ii, 207.
Kanva, Kánnav : a sub-caste of Bráhmans in, Sátára district, XIX, 53; in Dhárwár district, XXII, 92 93; in Bijápur district, XXIII, 89; in Kolhápur state, XXIV, 62; in Násik district, XVI, 41; *see* also I, pt. ii, 162, 163, 164, 165.
Kanvail : fibrous plant, XXV, 231.
Kanvalli : village in Dhárwár district, temples and inscriptions at, XXII, 764.
Kanvári : village in Rewá Kantha, I, pt. i, 443.
Kánváyana : *see* Kánva.
Kanvisidgeri : village in Dhárwár district; temple and inscriptions at, XXII, 764.
Kánwa : town in Broach district, place of pilgrimage, II, 565.
Kányakubja : modern Kanauj, I, pt. i, 79, 161; king of, put to flight by Someśvara I, I, pt. ii, 215.
Kanyeil : dye plant, common on the *gháts*, XXV, 242.
Kaola : sacred food plant, XXV, 291.
Kaoli : plant found in several districts, used as antidote to snake-bites, XXV, 275.
Kapadvanj, Kápadwanj : sub-division of Kaira district, III, 143-145. *Town*, *id.* 117; Ráshtrakúta possession of (909), I, pt. ii, 383; copper-plate grant at, *id.* 413; grant at, I, pt. i, 123, 129; reservoir built at, by Siddharája, *id.* 180 note 1; battle of (1725), *id.* 307; capture of, by the Maráthás (1736), *id.* 317; Fakhr-ud-daula meets Raisingji of Idar at, *id.* 329; siege of, raised by Holkar (1746), *id.* 330; taken by Dámáji from Sher Khán (1753), *id.* 338; Piláji Gáikwár defeated at (1725), VII, 171.
Kapáleshvar : Násik temple, XVI, 513-514.
Kapáleśvar : the god Śiva, I, pt. ii, 358; temple of, at Konvalli on the Mahi, I, pt. i, 127.
Kápálikeśvara : the god S'iva, temple of, near Igatpuri, I, pt. ii, 185, 192.
Kapardi : Kumárapála's chief minister after the date of Udayana, I, pt. i, 190; becomes Ajayapála's minister, is thrown in a cauldron of boiling oil, *id.* 194.
Kapardi I : I, pt. ii, 17. *See* Kapardin I.
Kapardi II : *see* Kapardin II.
Kápardikadvipa : territorial division, north of Revatidvipa, or Kavadidvipa, I, pt. ii, 347 note 2, 543, 544; king of, slain by the Goa Kádamba Jayakeśin I, *id.* 567, 568.
Kapardin I, Kápardi I : Northern Konkan Siláhára king, I, pt. ii, 200, 539, 541, 543, 567, 17.
Kapardin II, Kapardi II : son of Pullasakti the Siláhára king of Northern Konkan (851 and 877-78), I, pt. ii, 11, 17, 405, 406, 539; feudatory of Amoghavarsha I, *id.* 542, 543, 567; III, 422 note 1, 424; XIV, 148, 173, 177.
Kapas, Kappás, Kápus : cotton plant, yields oil, XXV, 215, 228.
Kápdepáni : cloth water-ceremony during death rites, IX, pt. i, 59.
Kápdi : a hindu religious order, in Cutch, V, 84-85; in Khándesh district, XII, 123; in Thána district, XIII, 199; at Somanáth, I, pt. i, 156.
Kapela : *see* Kamala.
Kápika : identified with Kávi, I, pt. i, 126; I, pt. ii, 404.
Kapil : seer, IX, pt. i, 10.
Kapil : a sub-caste of Bráhmans, in Thána district, XIII, 78; in Gujarát, IX, pt. i, 1, 10.
Kapiládhenu : black cow, her sacredness, IX, pt. i, 372.
Kápilakot : Mularája slew Lákha in a combat at, I, pt. i, 160.
Kapila-Sangam : confluence in the Bijápur district, I, pt. ii, 497.
Kapilátirth : Gokarn pool, XV, pt. ii, 297.
Kapili : modern Kampili on the Tungabhadrá, I, pt. ii, 454.
Kápishthala : mountain mentioned in the *Puránas*, I, pt. i, 534.
Kaple : wheat variety, XXV, 189.
Kapol, Kapol Vánia : a caste of traders, in Káthiáwár, VIII, 149; in Gujarát, IX, pt. I, 71; in Kolába district, XI, 48; in Thána district, XIII, 112.
Kappadevarasa : feudatory of the Western Chálukya king Jagadekamalla II, I, pt. ii, 457.
Kappadi : village, Basava goes to, I, pt. ii, 478; and returns from, *id.* 479.
Kappas, Kápus : *see* Kapas.
Kappatgudd : hill range in Dhárwár district, XXII, 4.
Kápshi : valley and town in Kolhápur state, temple and mosque at, XXIV, 11, 301.
Kápsi : fibrous plant, grows in Konkan jungles, XXV, 234.
Kapurchand Bhansáli : leading merchant of Ahmadábád, murder of, by Anopsing Bhandári, I, pt. i, 302.
Kapurthála : monuments in Násik city, XVI, 510.

Kápurvádi : village near Ahmadnagar, I, pt. ii, 622.

Karabena : river, mentioned in an inscription at Násik, I, pt. ii, 148.

Karáchi : Roman trade with (A. D. 50), XIII, 404 note 3, 410.

Karád : sub-division in Sátárá district, details of, XIX, 425-427; survey of, *id.* 375-378; *Town*, temples, forts, mosque, inscription, trade, caves, and history of, *id.* 472-480; coin-hoard found at, I, pt. i, 48-49; *another account of*: I pt. ii, 390, 407, 538 note 8; visited by Sahadeva, *id.* 142; mentioned in the *Mahábhárata* under the name Karahátaka, *id.* 175; may be Hippocura of Ptolemy, *id.* 176; Kshatrapa coins found in a village near, *id.* 177; capital of the Sindas (1000-1025), *id.* 577-578; Síláháras of, *id.* 254, 544-549; Western Chálukya king Vikramáditya II goes to, and marries Chandaladevi, *id.* 217, 546; Síláháras of, feudatories of the Western Chálukyás of Kalyáni, *id.* 439, 452, 456, 460, 498; do not recognise the sovereignty of the Yádava kings Bhillama and his son, *id.* 519; subdued by Singhana the Devagiri Yádava king, *id.* 524; differences between the Síláháras of, and those of the North Konkan, *id.* 543, 567; prince of, reinstates the Síláhára princes of the North Konkan, *id.* 570; prince of, repulsed by Sinda Achugi II, *id.* 574; discovery of coins near, *id.* 157.

Karád : a Vánia sub-division in Cutch, V, 51.

Karáda Sarovar : lake near Bhinmál, I, pt. i, 453.

Karadgi : village in Dharwar district, XXII, 764.

Karádh : *see* Karád.

Karádi : a caste of husbandmen in Thána district, XIII, 123.

Karádia : lower class of Rájputs, IX, I, 123.

Karahákada : old name of Karad, I, pt. ii, 176; XIX, 224, 480.

Karahakata : another name of Karád, I, pt. ii, 538 note 8.

Karaháta : modern Karád territorial division, I, pt. ii, 298 note 2; *Town, id.* 476, 538 note 8; province, capital of the Karád Síláháras, *id.* 546, 577, 578. *See* Karád.

Karahátaka : modern Karhád, visited by Sahadeva, I, pt. ii, 142, 175, 217, 390, 407, 538 note 8. *See* Karád.

Karahátaka : a Karháde (Karád) Bráhman, I, pt. ii, 256.

Karahátakundi : district, under Gomka the Síláhára prince of Kolhápur, I, pt. ii, 254 and note 3.

Karaiteshvar : *ling* of, near Bhinmál, I, pt. i, 453 and note 2.

Karájang : Yunnán (1290), I, pt. i, 501.

Karajgi : sub-division in Dhárwár district, its boundaries, area, aspect, soil, hills, climate, water, stock, crops, people, XXII, 638-640; *Town, id.* 764-765; *see* also I, pt. ii, 578.

Karajika : village, I, pt. ii, 391 note 6.

Káraktál : ruined town in Ahmadábád district, IV, 345.

Karáli : sub-division in Rewa Kántha, VI, 112.

Karália : Musalmán potters in Gujarát, converts from the Hindu caste of Kumbhárs, Sunnis in name, IX, pt ii, 36.

Karambaka Vihára : temple built by Kumárapála at Pátan, I, pt. i, 190

Karamdivadejaphitadeulaváda : village, I, pt. ii, 390.

Karamthali : village eight miles south of Ahmadábád, shrine of Imámsháh at, IX, pt. ii, 3 note 3.

Karan : *see* Karan Ghelo.

Karan : Solanki king (1072-1094), XIII, 436; I, pt. ii, 24.

Karanas : writers or accountants, I, pt. ii, 473.

Karan Ghelo : Vághela ruler of Gujarát (1296-1304), I, pt. i, 229; IX, pt. i, 127; defeated by the Musalmáns (1297), I, pt. i, 512.

Karanj : *Pongamia glabra*, tree in Poona district, XVIII, pt. i, 47.

Karanja : island, in Bombay harbour, description, history, objects of interest, XIV, 191-195; remains at, *id.* 399; island, I, pt. ii, 9; port, paid tribute to the Portuguese, *id.* 46; south boundary of the Portuguese district under Bassein, *id.* 54; its capture by the Franciscans (1585), *id.* 57; its capture by Sambháji (1683), *id.* 77; its re-capture by the Portuguese (1684), *id.* 78; civil and judicial administration in, *id.* 124; offered by its inhabitants to the English, surrendered to Angria (1739), XXVI, pt. i, 204-205; taken by the Maráthas (1740), *id.* 233; captured (1774), *id.* 383-384; resident appointed (1774), XIII, 562, 566; condition (1774 and 1819), *id.* 562, 563 and note 3.

Karanjapatra : village near the town of Hareshapura, camp of Vinayáditya at (694), I, pt. ii, 370.

Karanjawade : village, I, pt. ii, 390.

Káranjikar, Káranjkár : a caste of fountain makers, in Sholápur district, origin, settlement, appearance, house, food, dress, calling, condition, religion, customs, community, XX, 103-118; in Sátára district, XIX, 84-85. *See* Jingar.

Karanjon : village in Thána district, XIV, 195.

Káravana : modern Kárván, chief shrine of Lakulíśa and temple of Chámundádevi at, I, pt. i, 83 and note 1.

Karavdáchoth : water-jug fourth, IX, pt. i, 67; worship of the moon on, *id.* 398.

Karavera : *see* Kaver.

Karavi : poisonous plant, grows in the Dakhan, XXV, 267.

Karavir : *see* Karvir.

Karavira Máhátmya : local *Purána*, I, pt. ii, 538 note 8.

Karbala : place of Shiah pilgrimage, IX, pt. ii, 12 note 3, 30, 47, 126, 171; martyrs of, *id.* 128, 133, 138; story of the massacre at, *id.* 139.

Kárbhári : *pátil's* assistant in Thána district, XIII, 560; (1817), *id.* 564; Mhár (1828), *id.* 574.

Karbi : dry jowar stalk used as fodder, XXV, 186, 276.
Karda : old sub-division of Ahmadnagar district, survey of, XVII, 504-510 ; plate of, I, pt. i, 128-130 ; grant at, I, pt. ii, 195, 199, 201, 203, 204, 205, 206, 207, 208, 209, 387, 402, 414 and note 5, 418, 423.
Kardai : food and oil-yielding plant, XXV, 163, 218.
Kardama : village on the south of Pulikara, I, pt. ii, 373.
Karddamaka : family, the queen of Sátakarni belongs to the, I, pt. ii, 153 ; dynasty, XIV, 172.
Karde : market town in Poona district, trade centre, XVIII, pt. iii, 232.
Kardi : village in Bijápur district, temples and inscriptions at, XXIII, 658-659.
Kardigudd : hill in Belgaum district, XXI, 8.
Kardla : battle of (1794), Gáikwár's share in, VII, 200.
Kardu : a Koli stronghold in Ratnágiri district, X, 128.
Karel : village in Ratnágiri district, I, pt. ii, 356.
Kárelliká : village, may possibly be Karel, I, pt. ii, 355, 356.
Karen : tree, worshipped to appease planet *Mangal*, IX, pt. i, 384.
Karenitran : *see* Jáli Kund.
Karen Pahlavs : mention of, in the *Periplus* as ruling in Sind, I, pt. i, 544, 545.
Kare Vakkal : a caste of husbandmen in Kánara district, XV, pt. i, 221.
Káreya : sect of the Jains, I, pt. ii, 550, 552.
Kargudari : village in Kánara district, XV, pt. ii, 82 ; inscriptions at, I, pt. ii, 529, 560, 562.
Karha : river in Poona district, XVIII, pt. i, 9.
Karhád : *see* Karád.
Karháda : a caste of Bráhmans, in Gujarát, modern immigrants, IX, pt. i, 2, 497 note 8 ; said to be shipwrecked strangers, made Bráhmans by Parshurám, *id.* 436, 438, 497 ; stranger element shown in, *id.* p. xii note 3, 497, 498 ; Gujar origin of Ratnágiri Karhadás, *id.* 498 and note 5, 500 ; in Ratnágiri district, X, 114 ; Sávantvádi, *id.* 411 ; in Kolába district, XI, 45 ; in Khándesh, XII, 52 ; in Thána district, XIII, 79 ; in Kánara district, XV, pt. i, 132, 133 ; in Násik district, XVI, 40 ; in Ahmadnagar district, XVII, 58-59 ; in Poona district, XVIII, pt. i, 171-172 ; in Sátára district, XIX, 53-54 ; in Sholápur district, XX, 32-33 ; in Belgaum district, XXI, 90 ; in Dhárwár district, XXII, 95 ; in Bijápur district, XXIII, 89 ; in Kolhápur state, XXIV, 62.
Kári : river in Rewa Kantha, VI, 6.
Karia : Salávat, a caste of masons, I, pt. i, 451.
Kariána : táluka in Káthiáwár, VIII, 505.
Karidas : Dhed religious teacher, IX, pt. i, 333.
Karikal : town in the Tanjore district, I, pt. ii, 323.
Karim-ud-din : father of Imámsháh of Pirana, IX, pt. ii, 3 note 3.
Karim-ud-din : governor of Bijápur (1316-1320), XXIII, 396, 582 ; mosque of, in Bijápur city, *id.* 632-634.
Karjála : village in Káthiáwar, the story of its chief Merji Vája, VIII, 506.
Karjan : river in Rewa Kántha, VI, 2, 5, 92.
Karjan : village in Baroda territory, VII, 536 ; dispensary at, *id.* 505.
Karjat : sub-division of Thána district, its boundaries, area, aspect, climate, water, soil, holdings, rental, stock, crops, people, XIII, 2, 695-697 ; village in Thána district with railway station, XIV, 196.
Karjat : sub-division in Ahmadnagar district, details, area, aspect, hills, rivers, water-supply, soil, rainfall, crops, people, roads, railways, markets, crafts, survey, condition, changes, XVII, 597-602 ; *Town*, temple, *id.* 720 ; *see* also I, pt. ii, 399.
Karjika : village granted by Ushavadáta, I, pt. ii, 149.
Karka : I, pt. ii, 194, 388 ; *see* Kakka I of Málkhed Ráshtrakúta.
Karka I : Ráshtrakúta king of the 2nd Gujarát branch (812-821), accepts the overlordship of Dakhan dynasty, helps Amoghavarsha in establishing his supremacy and receives in return a portion of country south of the Tápti ; his grants, I, pt. i, 124-125 ; grant of (812-813), I, pt. i, 466, 468. *See* Kakka II.
Karkamb : town in Sholápur district, XX, 412.
Karkara : I, pt. ii, 423, 426. *See* Kakka II of the Malkhed Ráshtrakúta branch.
Karkarája : Suvarnavarsha Lateśvara, son of Indrarája the Ráshtrakúta of Gujarát, I, pt. ii, 310, 393, 400, 401 and note 1, 402, 408 ; reduces to obedience the rebellions Ráshtrakútas, *id.* 409 ; issues the Baroda grant, *id.* 199. *See* Karka I of 2nd Gujarát Ráshtrakúta branch.
Karkarája : Ráshtrakúta king, I, pt. ii, 18 ; (972), XIII, 425. *See* Kakka II, of Malkhed Ráshtrakútas.
Karkasvámin : Bráhman grantee of the Chálukya king, commentator on sacrificial rites, and *sutras*, I, pt. ii, 191.
Kark Sankránti : sacred day, IX, pt. i, 384.
Karle, Karli : village in Poona district with railway station, XVIII, pt. iii, 232 ; great caves at (B. C. 100) built by Banvási merchant, XV, pt. ii, 77, 264 ; caves at, I, pt. ii, 10, 391 note 6 ; XVIII, pt. iii, 455-464 ; Buddhist inscriptions at, XVIII, pt. ii, 212 ; inscriptions in the cave and temple at, I, pt. ii, 144, 148, 150, 151, 155, 166, 175, 176 ; XIII, 411 note 3, 412, 413, 414, 503 ; XIV, 209, 319 ; Colonel Egerton marches to (1778), I, pt. ii, 605 ; XVIII, pt. ii, 264.
Karli : river in Ratnágiri district and Sávantwadi state, X, 10 ; I, pt. ii, 47.
Kárli : pass in Kolába district, XI, 115, 377, 378.
Karmábáve : lake in Mahi Kántha, V, 358.
Karmad : táluka in Káthiáwár, VIII, 506.
Karmála : sub-division in Sholápur district, details, boundaries, area, aspect, climate, water, soil, stock, holdings, crops, people, XX, 393-396 ; survey of, *id.* 324-327, 353-358 ; *Town*, details, fort, temple, history, *id.* 412-413.

Kármaneya Ahára, Kármaneyáhára: country identified with Kámrej near Surat, I, pt. ii, 370, 376; I, pt. i, 108.
Karmántapura: town, I, pt. ii, 406.
Karmatian: caste of followers of Saint Ahmed of Nahrein; derivation of the name; origin of the sect; principal tenets of the sect; spread of the doctrines of, east to India and west to Africa and Spain; in the west the sect dies of inanition, in the east destroyed by Mahmud Ghaznavi and Muhammad bin Sám (1175), IX, pt. ii, 3 note 3 continued on page 4; a caste of Musalmán heretics in Cutch V, 58 note 1, 132 note 1, 134.
Karna: Puranic king, I, pt. i, 4; *Mahábhárata*, hero, *id.* 85, 86, 116.
Karna: son and successor of Bhima I, the Chaulukya king (1064-1094), I, pt. i, 169, 170-171; marries Mayanalladevi, I, pt. ii, 567-568.
Karna: king of Chedi, pays tribute to Bhima I, I, pt. i, 163; marches against Kumárapála and dies on the way, *id.* 186 and note 5, 187.
Karna: Kalachuri king of Kalyáni, I, pt. ii, 468; deposed and slain by Someśvara I, *id.* 214, 441.
Karna: Yádava prince, son of Mallugi, I, pt. ii, 517, 519.
Karna: Chálukya prince (A. D. 650), built the temple of Karneshvar at Sangameshvar, X, 192 note 5, 372 and note 1.
Karnadeva, Karnadeva II: last Vághela king (1296-1304), flees before Musalmáns to Devagiri, dies a fugitive, I, pt. i, 205-206; mention of, I, pt. ii, 532 note 1. *See* Karnaraya.
Karnadeva: prince of the Southern Konkan Chálukya family, I, pt. ii, 224.
Karnáditya: ancestor of Ráji, the Chalukya king, I, pt. i, 157.
Karnál: district of Panjáb, I, pt. i, 534.
Karnal, Karnala: hill fort, in Thána district, XIV, 98, 196, 400, XIII, 8; the seat of Devagiri viceroy (1270-1300), *id.* 437; Gujarát commander at the fort of (1540), *id.* 443; taken by Burhán Nizám (1540), *id.* 452; lost by the Maráthás (1670), *id.* 475; taken by Col. Prother (1818), *id.* 522; *another account of:* head-quarters of the Devagiri Yádava viceroys, I, pt. ii, 25; fortress, taken by the Portuguese (1540), *id.* 48; and captured by Shiváji, *id.* 69.
Karnáli: holy village on the Narbada in Baroda territory, VII, 553; schools at, *id.* 486.
Karnameru: temple at Anahilaváda, built by Karna the Chaulukya king, I, pt. i, 170.
Karnapuri: district, I, pt. ii, 421.
Karnaráya: of Gujarát, is defeated and his wife taken into Allauddin's harem (1297), flies with his daughter Devaladevi to Baglán, is again defeated by Alaf Khán and flies to Devagiri, I, pt. ii, 532 and note 1.
Karna Ságara: lake made by Karna the Chaulukya king, I, pt. i, 170.
Karnáta, Karnátaka or Karnátakas: country, I, pt. ii, 518; governed by Ganga Permanadi, *id.* 308; king of, subdued by the Yádava king Singhana, *id.* 517; king of, defeated by Bhillama, *id.* 520; and by Mahádeva, *id.* 528; king of, I, pt. i, 203 and note 3; army of, defeated by Dantidurg, I, pt. ii, 194; army of Kirtivarman II, *id.* 377; provinces under Báchirája, *id.* 524; laid waste by Malik Kafur, *id.* 533; attacked by the Bahamani kings (1347-1489), I, pt. ii, 638; brought under the Musalmáns by Máhmud Gawán, the prime minister of the Bahamani kings (1472), *id.* 638, 639; the invasion of Áli Ádil Sháh (1573), 645; absorbed within a decade after the battle of Tálikot into the Bijápur kingdom (1575), *id.* 645; campaign of Ibrahim Ádil Sháh II in, *id.* 648; Shiváji's campaign in, opposed unsuccessfully by Áli Ádil Sháh II in person, *id.* 652; in charge of Abdul Karim the ancestor of the Sávanur Nawábs (1672), *id.* 653; Shiváji's famous expedition into (1676), *id.* 654; under Fateh Sing Bhonsla, an officer of Sháhu, *id.* 656; Maratha expeditions into (1740), XIX, 283; (1746), *id.* 287; Báláji II's expeditions (1752, 1755, 1757), XVIII, pt. ii, 246, 247, 248; invasion of, by the Nizám (1774), I, pt. ii, 658; invasion of, by Haidar in 1776, *id.* 659; disturbances in 1795 and 1800, *id.* 662; falls into the hands of the confederates, the Peshwa, the Nizám, and the English (1790), *id.* 662; condition of (1803), *id.* 663.
Karnátaka: a sub-caste of Bráhmans, IX, pt. i, 1 note 1, 51; in Kánara district, XV, pt. i, 130-131.
Karnávati: city founded by Karna the Chaulukya king and made his capital; temple of Udaya Varáha at, I, pt. i, 170; modern Ahmadábád, *id.* 181; Hemachandra's birthplace, *id.* 191.
Karneśvara: god Mahádeva in Asával, I, pt. i, 170.
Karnul: district of the Carnatic, I, pt. ii, 186, 336; copper-plate grant from, *id.* 343, 351, 363, 364, 365 note 1, 367, 369.
Károd: a place of pilgrimage in Broach district, II, 565.
Károl: táluka in Káthiáwár, VIII, 506.
Károli: village in Thána district, Jain temple at, XIV, 50.
Karpatavánijya: territorial division, identified with Kápadwanj, I, pt. ii, 413.
Kárpatika: I, pt. ii, 156. *See* Kápdi.
Karpuratilaka: elephant, brought by Simharája, the Yádava king, from Láñjipura, I, pt. ii, 235, 516.
Karra: Kaira, I, pt. i, 518.
Karrah Manikpur: on the Ganges, governed by Allá-ud-din, I, pt. ii, 530, 531.
Karranji Hati: Rána of Nagar Párkar rises in revolt, subdued by Colonel Evans, I, pt. i, 448.
Kársai: *khot* exactions, X, 213.
Kárshápana: coin mentioned in an inscription, I, pt. ii, 148, 176; mentioned in Kanheri inscriptions, XIV, 147 note 2, 174, 177.
Kartaláb Khán: viceroy, suppresses the mutiny at Ahmadábád (1688), I, pt. i, 288.
Kárta Máruti: Násik temple, XVI, 515-516.
Kártavirya: I, pt. ii, 410. *See* Sahasrárjuna.

Kártavirya I: Ratta prince of Saundatti (980), I, pt. ii, 428; feudatory of the Western Chálukya kings Someśvara I and Taila II, *id.* 439, 553.
Kártavirya II: Ratta king (1069-1076), I, pt. ii, 551; feudatory of the Western Chálukya kings Someśvara II and Vikramáditya VI, *id.* 443, 451, 554.
Kártavirya III: Ratta chieftain (1143), I, pt. ii, 551; feudatory of the Western Chálukya kings Jagadekamalla II and Taila III, *id.* 460, 475.
Kártavirya IV: Ratta chieftain of Saundatti, son of Laksmideva I (1199-1218), I, pt. ii, 551, 556, 557, 571.
Kartikeya, Karttikeya: god of war and Śiva's son, I, pt. ii, 287 note 1, 337 and note 4, 338, 479; god, favours Sarvavarman with the first *sutra* of a new grammar, I, pt. ii, 170-171; family god of the Chálukyas, *id.* 180; of the Kadambas, *id.* 287 note 1; image of, at Elephanta and Sopára caves, XIV, 69, 75, 337.
Karttrika: Mr. Fleet reads Kártipur for, I, pt. i, 64 and note 2.
Karunj: oil-yielding plant, XXV, 217.
Kárur: village south-east of Multán, battle of, I, pt. i, 143, 496.
Karusa: country mentioned by Pánini, I, pt. ii, 138 and note 4; situation of, assigned in the *Purános*, *id.* 139.
Karusha: disciple of Nakuliśa, I, pt. i, 84.
Karván: *see* Karávana.
Kárván: holy village in Baroda territory, its sanctity according to *Purans*, VII, 550-551; holy tank at, *id.* 19; mention of, I, pt. ii, 314.
Karvand: *Carissa carandas*, creeper in Poona district, XVIII, pt. i, 47.
Karvir, Karavi or Karavira: ancient name of Kolhápur, XXIV, 1, 306; survey details of, *id.* 257-260; *see* also X, 372; I, pt. ii, 538 note 8.
Kárwár: sub-division of Kánara district, its details, XV, pt. ii, 223-226; town, harbour, people, trade, management, and history of, *id.* 315, 318-325; travellers bungalow at, *id.* 44; pepper trade at (500-1400), *id.* 49; rise of, under Bijápur (1600), muslin trade at (1650-1660), *id.* 52; left by the English (1720), *id.* 53; trade centre, *id.* 56; imports and exports of, *id.* 65, 66, 67; bay and forest, in Kánara district, XV, pt. i, 2, 38-39.
Kárwár Cotton Company: its experiments to grow American and Egyptian cotton varieties in Dhárwár district, XXII, 301.
Kárya: in Mysore, inscription at, I, pt. ii, 305.
Karyat: medicinal plant, XXV, 262.
Kás: a tenure, in Thána district, XIII, 531 and note 2, 550 and note 2, 617; in Násik district, XVI, 208 and note 3.
Kásahrada: territorial division, I, pt. ii, 404; leading town, *id.* 413.
Kasái or Kasáb: a caste of butchers, in Gujarát, believe themselves of Rájpút origin, two classes of, Sunnis in religion, form a separate community, IX, pt. ii, 74-75; Musalmán, in Thána district, XIII, 238; in Belgaum district, XXI, 218; in Kánara district, XV, pt. i, 345-346.
Kasákudi: village, I, pt. ii, 322; Pallava grant at, *id.* 316 note 5, 319 note 3; copper-plate grant from, *id.* 323; records at, *id.* 326, 376.
Káśákula, Kásakula: country on the bank of the Tápti, I, pt. ii, 359, 392; division, I, pt. i, 110.
Kásalpura: state in Mahi Kántha, V, 428.
Kasamachitra: ruler in Gujarát, sends an expedition to Jáva (603), I, pt. i, 489.
Kásam Khán: thirtieth viceroy of Gujarát (1657-1659), I, pt. i, 282.
Kasapayyanáyaka: governor of Banawási under the Kalachurya Bijjala, I, pt. ii, 460, 472, 475.
Kásár: a caste of brass-smiths, I, pt. i, 450; in Ratnágiri district, X, 126; in Kolába district, XI, 63, 413; in Khándesh district, XII, 74, 244; in Thána district, XIII, 136; in Kánara district, XV, pt. i, 260, 261; in Násik district, XVI, 51, 145; in Ahmadnagar district, XVII, 106; in Poona district, XVIII, pt. i, 344-345; in Sátára district, XIX, 85; in Sholápur district, XX, 118; in Belgaum district, XXI, 140; in Kolhápur state, XXIV, 95, 207-208.
Kására: village in Thána district, with railway station, XIV, 197.
Kásarde: village in Kolhápur state, temple and legend of, XXIV, 302.
Kásáre: village in Ahmadnagar district, XVII, 721.
Kásári: stream in Kolhápur state, XXIV, 9, 10.
Kasba: Poona city ward, details of, XVIII, pt. iii, 274, 276-277.
Kashan, Kasbin: a caste of Musalmán dancing-girls in Násik district, XVI, 84, 85; in Belgaum district, XXI, 225; in Dhárwár district, XXII, 192-193, 248-249; in Bijápur district, XXIII, 304-305. *See* Kalávant.
Kásbandi: *see* Kás.
Kasbátis: town holders, of part foreign descent, IX, pt. ii, 15; Rájpút converts; origin of, *id.* 64; classes of, of Dholka, *id.* 64 note 3; appearance of, character of, Sunnis in religion, *id.* 64; marriages of, names and customs of, *id.* 65; in Baroda territory, VII, 351; in Ahmadábád district, IV, 147; of Pátan (1748), I, pt. i, 333; Musalmán sailors of Gogha, IX, pt. i, 519, 521.
Kasebin: *see* Kasban.
Kásegaon: village in Sátára district, XIX, 480-481.
Kásegaon: village in Sholápur district, temple, XX, 413.
Kaseli: village granted by Bhoja II, the Kolhápura Siláhára, I, pt. ii, 256.
Káshi: *see* Benáres.
Káshikápdi: a caste of traders in Sholápur district, XX, 52. *See* Tirmali.
Káshmir, Kásmir: state, I, pt. i, 165, 460, 527, 546; chronicle of, "Introduction to the Early History of the Dekkan," I, pt. ii, p. i, 243; history of, *id.* 281 note 3.
Kashyap: *see* Kásyapa.
Káshyapa: sixth Buddha, XIV, 125 note 1, 170 note 4; image of, *id.* 331, 412.

Káśi : king of, present with Mularája in the battle with Grahariрu, I, pt. i, 160 ; present at the *svayamvara* of Durlabhadevi, *id.* 163 ; killed in a battle by Singhana, I, pt. ii, 240, 525.

Kásim : nephew of Husain, bridegroom-elect of Śákinah, daughter of Husain ; slaughter of, spirit of, believed to possess the *dulas* in Muharram, IX, pt. ii, 138.

Kasim : Sidi governor of Janjira and Mughal admiral (1670-1707), XI, 437-442.

Kásim Barid : Bahamani chief, I, pt. ii, 640.

Kasla Pagi : state in Rewa Kántha, VI, 152.

Káśmiradevi : wife of Tribhuvanapála, I, pt. i, 181.

Káśmiras : defeated by Yashovarman, I, pt. i, 469.

Kaspeiros : Káśmir city, I, pt. i, 546.

Kassumba : dye plant, XXV, 246-247.

Kastarias : Kshatriyas, I, pt. i, 531.

Kást, Kásth, Kayastha : a sub-caste of Bráhmans in Násik district, XVI, 41 ; in Sátára district, XIX, 54 ; in Poona district, XVIII, pt. i, 172-174.

Kasthi Koli : *see* Solesi Koli.

Kasumb : oil-yielding plant, XXV, 218.

Kásurdi : reservoir at, in Poona district, XVIII, pt. ii, 24.

Kásyapa, Kashyapa : a *gotra* or exogamous division of the Bráhmans, I, pt. ii, 278 ; note 1 ; name derived from a sage, *id.* 340 note 2 ; I, pt. i, 461.

Katachchuris : Kalachuris, I, pt. ii, 282, 293-296.

Katak : city on the east coast, I, pt. ii, 142.

Kataka : fortified part of Daulatábád, I, pt. ii, 534.

Kátantra : grammar, legend regarding the compilation of, I, pt. ii, 170-171.

Kátári : a caste of wood-turners, in Kolába district, XI, 64 ; in Thána district, XIII, 136 ; in Násik district, XVI, 53 ; in Poona district, XVIII, pt. i, 345-346.

Katariya : Kshatriya, I, pt. i, 530.

Katáriya : place of interest, in Cutch, V, 225-226.

Kátavdi : *see* Kátkari.

Katbu : *see* Kiliket.

Kate's point : at Mahábaleshvar, XIX, 506.

Kath : catechu, prepared from acacia tree, XXV, 244.

Katbákosa : Sanskrit work, I, pt. ii, 410 note 2.

Ka-Thakur : early tribe in Thána district, XIII, 180.

Kathalya : gum-yielding tree, grows in the Dakhan, XXV, 250.

Káthar : a caste of traders in Khándesh district, XII, 59.

Kathária : táluka in Káthiáwár, VIII, 520.

Katharigad : hill-fort in Belgaum district, XXI, 9.

Katbás : extracts from *Puráns*, IX, pt. i, 25.

Kathásaritságara : Sanskrit work, I, pt. i, 78 ; I, pt. ii, 170.

Káthi : state in Khándesh district, XII, 609.

Kathi : food plant wild and cultivated throughout India, XXV, 184.

Káthi : legendary origin of, IX, pt. i, 252 note 1 ; probably wanderers from Central Asia, said to have entered Káthiáwár about A.D. 1400 ; marriage of Dhan Vála, Rájpút chief of Dhánk with their leader Umro's daughter ; rise of three tribes of Vála Kháchar and Khumán out of the marriage, *id.* 252-253 ; for many generations Dhan Vála Káthis as plunderers round Than, their earth hunger, acquisition of Jasdan, Chital, and other territory ; gradual reformation, establishment of order in Jetpur, in Chital, *id.* 253 ; in Jasdan, *id.* 254 ; disturbance of Gir hill Káthis, their leader Báva Vála, capture and imprisonment of Captain Grant in the hills, *id.* 254, 255 and note 1 ; subjugation of Khuman and Kháchar tribes ; existing possessions, *id.* 256 ; history of, in Forbes *Rás Mála*, *id.* 252 note 1 ; by Colonel Watson, said to have come from Asia Minor, *id.* 258 ; from Nepál, *id.* 260 ; probable date of their entrance into Káthiáwár, *id.* 259-260, 261-262 ; Dewan Ranchodji's account of, *id.* 262 ; sub-divisions, Shákháyats and Avartiás, meaning of names, *id.* 253, 259, 261 ; intermarriages among, *id.* 252 note 1 ; affinity with Ahirs, *id.* 261 ; Religion ; Customs, *id.* 257 ; in Káthiáwár, VIII, 122-132, 278, 289-291 ; in Cutch, V, 131, 132 ; *see* also I, pt. i, 209, 217 note 3.

Káthia : a caste of wood-workers, I, pt. i, 450.

Kathiará : caste of fuel-sellers in Gujarát, Hindu converts, IX, pt. ii, 67.

Kathiás : of South Panjab, Káthis seem to be, IX, pt. i, 462.

Káthiavada, Káthiáwada or Káthiáwár Province : description : boundaries, sub-divisions, states, aspect, hills, VIII, 1-12 ; Gulf of Cutch, description of its coasts, tides and harbours, *id.* 12-35 ; Gulf of Cambay ; description, Tapti Light, Broach Point, Mal Bank, Gopnath Point, etc., silting, survey, *id.* 35-60 ; rivers, creeks, harbours, wells, lakes, Little Ran, history of Little Ran, Ran of Cambay, geology, rainfall, climate, *id.* 60-89 ; products : iron, stones, salt, pearls, forests, cocoa-palm, wild date-palm, domestic animals, wild animals, birds, fish, *id.* 90-107 ; population : census details, Rájpúts, and their subdivisions : the Jhálás, the Jádejás, Parmárs ; Kathis, their sub-divisions and history ; Ahirs, Kolis, Bráhmans, Writers, Merchants, Vániás, Bhatiás, Lobanas, manufacturers, sailors, fishers, beggars, wandering classes, Musalmáns, Vághers, native Christians, villages, houses, communities, *id.* 108-174 : agriculture : soil, husbandmen, seasons, field tools ; crops : cotton, wheat, etc. ; famines (1559-1879), *id.* 175-198 ; capital : investments, currency, bankers, money-lenders, borrowers, insurance, weather wagers, forced labour, wages, prices, measures, *id.* 199-218 ; trade : old routes, roads, railways, bridges, ferries, vessels, lighthouses, ports, fairs, markets, imports and exports, crafts, gold thread, knot-printing, brocades, salt, guilds, strikes, *id.* 219-266 ; history : early history, Krishna, Alexander, Kshatraps, Guptas, Valabhis, Mahomed of Ghazni (1024), Mulraj (942), Muhammad and Firoz Tugh-

lak (1347, 1351), Zufar Khan, viceroy of Gujarát (1391), Sultán Mahmud Begada (1439-1513), Muzafar II (1513-1526), Portuguese gain Diu (1536), Akbar conquers Gujarát (1573), Aurangzeb, viceroy (1644), disorder in Gujarát (1707), Marátbas in south Gujarát (1704), their invasion (1722), Pilaji Gaikwár gains Baroda (1727), Colonel Walker (1807-8), British Paramount (1820), reforms (1863-1882), political agents (1820-1880), chieftains of the 1st four classes, *id.* 267-314; land administration, *id.* 315-323; justice, old ways of obtaining justice, piracy, want of jail, chief court established (1831), Rájasthánic court, agency courts, state courts, police, jails, *id.* 324-336; revenue and finance: revenue (1808-1881), improvement cess, transit duties, local funds, *id.* 337-342; instruction, *id.* 343-349; health, *id.* 350-354; states and places of interest, *id.* 355-701; history: southern boundary of Chandragupta's dominions and western boundary of Aśoka's dominions, I, pt. ii, 146; Kshatrapas of, *id.* 153, 157; the name, I, pt. i, 208, 209; Gupta sway in, *id.* 135; arrival of Mers in, *id.* 140 and note 5; disturbance in (1692), *id.* 288; settlement of tribute by Colonel Walker, *id.* 416; state of (1807), *id.* 416; the revenue raid system in, *id.* 417; Bháts and Chárans in, *id.* 420 421; the habit of taking securities in all engagements in, *id.* 420; Peshwa's share of tribute in, *id.* 422-423; cession of the share to the English for military expenses, *id.* 423-424; disturbances in (1811), *id.* 425, 526, 534, 538. *See* also I, pt. ii, 312, 317, 336, 383, 490, 515, 517; VII, 174; Arab fleet sent against the coast of (758-778), IX, pt. II, 1 note 1; Memana in, *id.* 51; Sidi immigration into, XIII, 64.

Kathiawadi: a caste of potters in Násik district, XVI, 60.

Káthiawar: division of Soráth, VIII, 5; I, pt. I, 208 and note 3, 209.

Kathivadar; port in Káthiáwár, VIII, 241.

Káthkari, Káthodi, Kathodia or Katkari: an early tribe, in Kolába district, XI, 71-72, 415; in Thána district, XIII, 64, 158-165, 284, 523; at Mátherán, XIV, 259; in Kánara district, XV, pt. i 346, 347; in Poona district, XVIII, pt. i, 408, in Ratnágiri district, X, 43, 130; in Khándesh district, XII, 25; in Násik district, XVI, 65; in Sholápur district, XX, 166; in Gujarát, IX, pt. i, 290, 319-320; village servants in Cutch, V, 101, 102.

Kátho: catechu, manufacture of, in Rewa Kántha, VI, 57.

Kathodi or Kathodia: *see* Káthkari.

Káthor: village in Baroda territory, schools and hospital at, VII, 487, 506, 575.

Káthrota: táluka in Káthiáwár, VIII, 507.

Katiri: gum-yielding plant, XXV, 250.

Katkari: *see* Kathkari.

Katkol: hill in Kolhápur state, temples, monastery and fair at, XXIV, 4, 302

Katli Imám Ali: Shiáh holiday, IX, pt. ii, 140.

Kátoria: táluka in Káthiáwár, VIII, 507.

Katosan: state in Mahi Kántha, V, 421.

Kátpitiás: sellers of old furniture and house building materials, IX, pt. i, 205.

Katra: an insect, V, 295.

Kátraj: village in Poona district, reservoir at, XVIII, pt. ii, 28; pass, *id.* 154.

Kátsávar: tree in Khándesh district, XII, 25.

Katta: I, pt. ii, 551. *See* Kartavirya I, II and III.

Kattageri: village in Bijápur district with railway station, temples, inscriptions and ponds at, XXIII, 659.

Kattai: a caste of leather workers in Ahmadnagar district, XVII, 107-109.

Káttama: I, pt. ii, 555. *See* Kartavirya III.

Kattguta: land tenure in Dhárwár district, XXII, 447 and note 6, 462.

Katuban: a special tenure in Ratnágiri district, X, 261.

Katuka: Bania, gives parched grain to Kumárapála on credit, I, pt. i, 183; is given Baroda, *id.* 184.

Katumukha: 'harsh-sounding' musical instrument of Pallava Nandipotavarman taken by Vikramáditya II, I, pt. ii, 327, 374.

Kátur: táluka in Káthiáwár, VIII, 507.

Kátyáyana: his acquaintance with southern nations; notices Pánini's omission in explaining Pándya, I, pt. ii, 139, 140; familiarity of North Áryas with the southern countries in the time of, chronological relations with Patañjali and Pánini of, *id.* 140, 141.

Kaula: fort in Kolába district, XI, 324.

Kaula: oil-yielding plant, XXV, 218.

Kauládevi: wife of Karnadeva, taken captive by Alaf Khán and admitted into the Sultán's harem (1297), I, pt. i, 205; I, pt. ii, 532.

Kaulur: in the Nizám's dominions, inscription at, I, pt. ii, 488, 501, 502.

Kaumára: forest in the extreme south, I, pt. ii, 202.

Kaumári: one of the Pleiades, I, pt. ii, 337 note 4.

Kaundinya: a *gotra* or exogamous division of Bráhmans, I, pt. ii, 278 note 1.

Kaunti: famine plant, found in several districts, XXV, 195.

Káusa: *see* Padamdurg.

Kausámbi: capital of the king of the Vatsas, I, pt. ii, 197.

Kanthem: grant from, I, pt. ii, 282, 367, 378 note 3, 293, 339 note 1, 342, 343 note 5, 345 note 4, 346 note 4, 347 notes 1 and 2, 349 note 4, 361 note 2, 378 and note 3, 385, 425 note 2, 426, 434.

Kavadidvipa: I, pt. ii, 282 note 5; northern part of the Konkan, *id.* 298 note 2, 347 note 2; province, *id.* 452; evidently Kápardikadvipa, *id.* 544; ruled by the Goa Kádamba Jayakeśin II, *id.* 568. *See* Kápardikadvipa.

Kavali: *See* Kandul.

Kavalya: pass in Kolába district, XI, 6, 115.

Kávana: Káma, father of Brahma the general of Someśvara IV, I, pt. ii, 464.

Kávana or Kávanayya: Kalachurya Sankama's officer, I, pt. ii, 487, 489.

Kavandanyapur: old name of Kavlápur, XXIV, 360.

Kavánt: sub-division in Rewa Kántha, VI, 112.
Kávar Sain: Bráhman minister of Burhán Nizám (1508-1553), XVII, 363, 365; XVIII, pt. ii, 222.
Kavás Bhumias: servants, I, pt. i, 451.
Kávasji Nánábhai Dávar: opens the first steam factory in Western India, IX, pt. ii, 199 note 3.
Kávasji Rustomji: watch-maker, visits Delhi, receives the title of Mirzan Khosru Beg and a grant of land, IX, pt. ii, 197 note 2.
Kavath: wood-apple tree in Poona district, XVIII, pt. i, 47.
Kávdiácher: a great mangrove tree in Cutch, V, 224.
Kávera, *pl.* Káveras: king of, made tributary to the Chálukya crown, I, pt. ii, 189; defeated by Vinayáditya the son of Vikramáditya I, *id.* 368.
Káveri: river in Rewa Kántha, I, pt. i, 518, 546; VI, 6; river, I, pt. ii, 24; crossed by Pulikeśi II, *id.* 183, 243, 299, 331, 350, 524.
Kávi: a place of pilgrimage in Broach district, II, 566; Govind III's grant at, I, pt. i, 123, 125, 126; grant found at, I, pt. ii, 195, 197, 198, 315, 401, 403, 404, 408, 409.
Kávi Jang: Nizám's commandant of Ahmadnagar fort (1759), XVII, 404.
Kavirahasya: poem, I, pt. ii, 208.
Kavit, Kavitha: plant, its twigs used as toothbrushes by Hindus, XXV, 291; medicinal plant, found in Dakhan, *id.* 255.
Kavithasádhi: modern Kosád, I, pt. i, 128; I, pt. ii, 412.
Kavlápur: village in Kolhápur state, temples at, XXIV, 360.
Kávnai: fort in Násik district, XVI, 441, 448.
Kavte: market village in Poona district, XVIII, pt. iii, 232.
Kavtha: village in Kolhápur state, temples at, XXIV, 383.
Kávyádarsa: Sanskrit work, I, pt. ii, 170.
Kávyaprakása: Sanskrit work on rhetoric, I, pt. ii, 171.
Kawndal: fruit, XXV, 281.
Káyastha: *see* Kást.
Kayastha, Kayasth Prabhu: a class of writers, early reference to, IX, pt. i, p. xi note 3, 59 note 1; claim descent from Chitragupta, *id.* 60 and note 2; three branches of, in Gujarát; *Válmik*, settlement, influence and position under the Mughal, British and Gáikwár rule; dress, *id.* 60, 61; Vaishnavs by religion, customs, *id.* 61, 63; *Máthur*, dress, religion, *id.* 64; customs, elephant worship, *id.* 65; special holidays, *id.* 66, 67; *Bhatnagra*, descent, Vaishnavs by religion, customs, *id.* 67-68; I, pt. i, 461; in Cutch, V, 48; in Kolába district, XI, 46, 411; in Thána district, XIII, 63 note 1, 87-89, 428; in Násik district, XVI, 43; in Ahmadnagar district, XVII, 65; in Poona district, XVIII, pt. i, 192-193; in Sátára district, XIX, 57; in Sholápur district, XX, 44-45; in Belgaum district, XXI, 99; in Kolhápur state, XXIV, 64.
Káyat: a Hindu tribe in Khándesh district, XII, 55.
Káyatia: a sub-caste of Bráhmans in Rewa Kántha, VI, 23.
Kayávatára: village, modern Kárván, I, pt. ii, 314.
Kázi: position and duties of, I, pt. ii, 213, 214, 530; office of, functions of, under Muhammadan rule; present functions of, position of, among the community, IX, pt. ii, 135; office of, in Surat, Broach and Ahmadábád, *id.* 135 note 2; Musalmán head in Ratnágiri, X, 132 note 2, 141; in Cambay, VI, 236; office of, re-established by Báláji Bájiráv, I, pt. ii, 97.
Kázi-ul-Kuzzah: Mughal appellate *kazi*, I, pt. i, 213.
Kazwini: writer (1265), his description of Cheul, XI, 272 note 2.
Keatinge: Lt.-Colonel, captures Vesáva and Karanja (1774), I, pt. i, 101; XXVI, pt. i, 383-384, 387-388; XIV, 380; sent to help Rághuba, I, pt. i, 402; joins Rághuba at Darmaj or Dora near Cambay (1775), *id.* 403; negotiates with Fatehsing, *id.* 405; receives orders to leave Rághuba, *id.* 405; his campaign in Gujarát against the Peshwa (1775), VII, 172-174.
Keatinge: Colonel, political agent in Káthiáwár, drives the Káthis from Gir (1865), VIII, 308, 365.
Kecara: food plant, XXV, 177.
Kedáras: invading horde of foreigners also called Little Yuechi (A. D. 380), IX, pt. i, 446, 455; passed down by Chitral and Swát to Peshäwar (A. D. 390), *id.* 470; conquests in Western India, *id.* 433; staunch adherence of, to Buddhism, *id.* 448; Gujar identification with, *id.* 469, 470; retreat of, to Káshmir, I, pt. i, 500; settle with Tibetans in Yunnan in the ninth century, *id.* 501.
Kedáreśvara: temple in Kumáon repaired by Ganda Brihaspati, I, pt. i, 190.
Kedarites: *see* Kedaras.
Kedarji Gáikwár: Dámáji's cousin, receives one-third of the revenues of Surát for his aid from Sayad Achchan, I, pt. i, 332; regent during the imprisonment of Dámáji (1751), VII, 179.
Kedgaon: village with railway station in Poona district, XVIII, pt. iii, 242-243.
Keigwin: Captain, his revolt (1683), holds Bombay for and petitions the king, XXVI, pt. i, 88-89; his surrender, *id.* 95; XIII, 478, 479.
Keir: Sir William Grant, takes the forts of Nivti and Ráiri, I, pt. ii, 127.
Kekat Kádupáda: state in Khándesh district, XII, 605.
Kekobad: son of Meherji, visits Delhi, receives a grant of land, IX, pt. ii, 197 note 2.
Kel, Kela: plantain, worship of, IX, pt. i, 384; XXV, 279, 284; food plant, *id.* 174; in Poona district, XVIII, pt. i, 48.
Kel: hill pass in Belgaum district, XXI, 306.
Kela: *see* Kel.
Keladi Basavappa Náik: Bednur chief (1713), XV, pt. ii, 133.
Kelambapattana: probably modern Kolam or Quilon, I, pt. i, 183 note.

Kelanpur : village in Baroda territory, VII, 534-535.
Kelasi : a caste of barbers in Kánara district, XV, pt. I, 329, 330.
Kelavadi : province, I, pt. ii, 441 note 6, 458, 460, 485 ; ruled over by the Sindas of Yelburga, *id.* 572, 575, 576.
Keleyabbe, Keleyaladevi : wife of Vinayáditya, I, pt. ii, 492.
Kelhapana : chief of Nador, I, pt. i, 193.
Kelodi : *see* Kelavádi.
Kelshi : creek and port in Ratnágiri district, exports and imports of, X, 11, 183, 342.
Kelvádi : village in Bijápur district, temples and inscription at, XXIII, 659 ; head-quarters of Sinda province of the same name for which *see* Kelavádi.
Kelváli Sonápur : Sahyádri spur in Sátára district, XIX, 6.
Kelva Máhim : town in Thána district, history and forts, XIV, 197-201 ; seized by Bhimrája, I, pt. ii, 27 ; remains of a Portuguese Church at, *id.* 65 ; destroyed by the Portuguese (1531), XIII, 451 ; Portuguese fort at (1533), *id.* 456 ; its trade with Malabár Coast (1500-1670), *id.* 465 ; Hamilton's mention of (1680), *id.* 485 ; condition of its fort (1727), *id.* 491 ; captured by the Maráthás (1739), *id.* 493.
Kelwádi : *see* Kelavádi.
Kemajju : identified with Kimoj or Kimaj, I, pt. ii, 315.
Kembhávi : in the Nizám's dominions, I, pt. ii, 439 ; inscription in a temple at, *id.* 440 note 8, 460.
Kemkem : Konkan, I, pt. ii, 3.
Kena : famine plant, XXV, 206.
Kendattimadivála : inscription at, I, pt. ii, 332.
Kendormánya : village granted by Mangalésa, I, pt. ii, 348.
Kendur : market town in Poona district, tomb and fair at, XVIII, pt. iii, 232.
Kengali : province governed by the feudatory of Vikramáditya I, I, pt. ii, 333, 434.
Kenjalgad : hill-fort in Sátára district, XIX, 9, 481-482.
Kennedy : Col., takes Mandangad (1818), I, pt. ii, 116 ; takes the forts of Rámgad and Pálgad and purchases the possession of Rasalgad, *id.* 117 ; takes Anjanvel, Govalkot, Bairamgarh, and Bháwangarh (1818), *id.* 118.
Kennett : Major, takes (1818) the fort of Nawapura, I, pt. ii, 117.
Kenoj Mata : Hindu goddess, IX, pt. i, 485.
Keprobotras : *see* Keralaputra.
Ker : a Musalmán sub-division in Cutch, V, 100.
Kera : village in Cutch, ruins of a Hindu temple, a mosque and fort at, V, 226.
Keradu : inscriptions near the ruined town of, I, pt. i, 188.
Kerakang, Keranj : *see* Kangni.
Kerákot : fort in Cutch, V, 133.
Kerala : country, modern Malabár, I, pt. ii, 143, 444 ; the people of, *id.* 216 ; forms part of Dakshinápatha, *id.* 133 ; monkey-soldiers are directed to go to, *id.* 137 ; people subdued by Sahadeva the Pándava, *id.* 142 ; come in contact with the Western Chalukyas, *id.* 282 ; made allies by Pulikeśin II, *id.* 183, 350 ; repeatedly defeated by the Pallava king Narsimhavarman I, *id.* 322 ; humbled by Vikramáditya I, *id.* 186, 362 ; reduced by Vikramáditya II, *id.* 190, 194, 375 ; conquered by Govinda III the Ráshtrakúta king, *id.* 396 ; conquered by the Western Chalukya king Vikramáditya II, subdued by the Devagiri Yádava king Singhana, *id.* 525 ; *another account of* : Malabár district, I, pt. ii, 280, 281, 282 and note 5 ; king of, conquered by the Chalukyas of Bádami, *id.* 345, 346, 362 note 6, 368, 375 ; humbled by Vishnuvardhana, *id.* 496 ; slain by Vikramáditya VI, the Western Chálukya king of Kalyáni, *id.* 362, 378, 442, 444.
Keralaputa : king of the Pándyas, mentioned in Aśoka's inscriptions, I, pt. ii, 277.
Keralaputra : Cera king mentioned in the *Periplus*, I, pt. i, 546.
Keralas : *see* Kerala.
Kerálu : deserted village in Gujarát, inscription at, I, pt. i, 196, 470.
Keratahi : one of the seven ancient divisions of Konkan, I, pt. ii, 282 note 5.
Keri : river in Káthiáwár, VIII, 63.
Kerks : pirates (A. D. 890) from Cutch, XIII, 433, 711 note 2.
Kern : Dr., places Kálidása in the first half of the sixth century, I, pt. ii, 144, 162.
Kerur : town in Bijápur district, fort, and temples at, XXIII, 659-660.
Kerváda : *thakor* of, IX, pt. ii, 68.
Kesáva : Nágara Bráhman minister of Karnadeva, slain, I, pt. i, 205 note 2.
Késava : Brahmana chief of the Káshyapa *gotra*, performs an *Aptoryáma* sacrifice, I, pt. ii, 247.
Kéśava : Kánarese poet, I, pt. ii, 344.
Kéśava : son of Holalarája, governs the Banavási province as a feudatory of the Kalachurya Bijjala, I, pt. ii, 473.
Kéśava : Kámvadeváraya's minister, I, pt. ii, 566.
Kesava : god Vishnu, I, pt. ii, 581.
Kesavabhattayya : I, pt. ii, 465. *See* Kesirájayya.
Kesavadeva : Hindu god, grants made to, by a Chalukya queen, I, pt. ii, 449.
Kesaváditya deva : The Western Chálukya king Someśvara II's officer, I, pt. ii, 443.
Kesava Mahajani : minister of Kamvadeva and donor of a copper-plate grant, I, pt. ii, 223.
Kesava Rája : Śiva's attendant, I, pt. ii, 482.
Kesavasvamin : Bráhman grantee of a Chálukya prince, commentator on sacrificial *sutras* and rites, I, pt. ii, 191.
Kesera : village in Pálanpur state, an old temple at, V, 342.
Keshidev : Siláhára king (1203-1238), XIII, 422 note 1 ; his two land grants, 427 and note 2 ; *see* also I, pt. ii, 20, and XIV, 212, 419.
Kesideva : I, pt. ii, 539, 542. *See* Arikesarin.
Kesimayya : officer of Áhavamalla the Kalachurya king, I, pt. ii, 428 note 4.
Kesimayya : Jagadekamalla II's officer. *See* Kesirája.

Kesimayya : Bijjala's officer, I, pt. ii, 458, 473. *See* Kesiraja and Kesava.

Kesimayya : Bolikeya, Kalachurya Somesvara's governor of the Tardavádi, Hanumgal and Banavási provinces, I, pt. ii, 485, 486.

Kesin : demon, destroyed by Krishna, I, pt. ii, 343 note 5.

Kesirája : the Western Chálukya king Jagadekamalla II's governor of the Belvola, Palasige, and Panumgal provinces, I, pt. ii, 458.

Kesirája : Bijjala's officer, I, pt. ii, 473. *See* Kesava and Kesimayya, Bijjala's officer.

Kesirájayya : Kesavabhattayya, the Western Chálukya king Someśvara IV's officer I, pt. ii, 465.

Kesirájayya : Kalachurya Sankama's governor of Banavási, I, pt. ii, 487.

Kesod : town in Káthiáwár, its history, VIII, 507-508.

Kesri : fibrous plant, XXV, 226.

Kesria : táluka in Káthiáwár, VIII, 507.

Kessar : *see* Kecara.

Kesuvolala : modern Pattadakal in the Hungund táluka of the Bijápur district, I, pt. ii, 348.

Ketaladevi : wife of the Western Chálukya king Someśvara I, i, pt. ii, 438, 440.

Ketaladevi : wife of Vira-Ballála II, i, pt. ii, 493, 502.

Ketaladevi : wife of the Hángal Kádamba Kámadeva, I, pt. ii, 559, 560.

Ketalaputras : country of (Chera or Kerala), mentioned in Aśoka's edicts, I, pt. ii, 143. *See* Kerala.

Ketalaputta : province, out-lying Aśoka's dominions, I, pt. ii, 146. *See* Kerala.

Ketarasa : Kadamba king I, pt. ii, 285 note 5, 564.

Ketu : planet according to Hindu astronomy, IX, pt. i, 392 note 1. *See* Comet.

Keuda, Keura : oil-yielding and fibrous plant, XXV, 225, 236 ; a sacred plant used in the worship of Śiva, *id.* 279, 285 ; one of the five arrows of Cupid, *id.* 289.

Keur : famine plant, found in Konkan, XXV, 207.

Keura : *see* Keuda.

Kevai : Hindu goddess, *kuldevi* of Bhati Gujars, IX, pt. i, 483.

Kevaldás : Hajám saint of Pálanpur, IX, pt. i, 233.

Kevál Náik : Náikda Bhil leader, surrender of (1859), I, pt. i, 446.

Kevikuls : tenants-at-will in Sávantvádi state, X, 450.

Khábirun : probably Kávi on the Mahi, noticed by Al Biruni (970), I, pt. i, 513 ; perhaps same as Akabaron of Periplus, *id.* 546.

Khachar : pass in Kolába district, XI, 115.

Khachara : race, I, pt. ii, 439, 443, 450, 452, 476, 523.

Khadáit Váni : a caste of traders in Kolába district, XI, 48.

Khadakvásla : lake at, in Poona district, XVIII, pt. ii, 17-18.

Khadál : state in Mahi Kántha, V, 419.

Khadár Pir : Musalmán saint, tomb of, near Porbandar, IX, pt. i, 522.

Khadarpur : village in Káthiáwár, VIII, 508.

Khadát : village near Prántij, Khadáyatás named after, IX, pt. i, 10, 72.

Khadáyata : sub-caste of Bráhmans in Rewa Kántha, VI, 23-24 ; said to be immigrants from Upper India, IX, pt. i, 2, 10 ; sub-caste of Vániás, *id.* 72.

Khadgaon : village in Ahmadnagar district, pond at, XVII, 721.

Khadgávaloka : *biruda* or title of Dantidurga, I, pt. ii, 389.

Khádim : disciple order in a Musalmán brotherhood, IX, pt. ii, 19.

Khadir : island in Cutch, V, 13, 227.

Khádiyu : quarter of Ahmadábád city occupied by Bráhma-Kshatris, IX, pt. i, 55.

Khadkála : sub-divisional head-quarters with railway station in Poona district, XVIII, pt. iii, 232-233.

Khadki or Kharki : (Aurangábád) founded by Malik Ambar (1607), XVII, 392 ; *see* also I, pt. ii, 624.

Khadki : local breed of bullocks in Kolhápur state, XXIV, 25.

Khadwa : or *Kadva* class of Gujarát *Kanbis*, appears in Rájpútána as Kharia Gujars, IX, pt. i, 490.

Khætvo datha : chapters of the *Zend Avesta* on marriages between near relatives, IX, pt. ii, 211 note 2 (18).

Khafif : son of Singhar, I, pt. i, 517.

Kháfi Khán : Musalmán historian, "Introduction to the History of the Konkan," I, pt. ii, p. ix, 38, 60, 69, 73 ; (1680-1735), his testimony of Shiváji's character, XI, 145 note 3, 364 and notes 1 and 2, 372 note 1, 436, 437.

Khagaráta : race, stock name of Nahapána, IX, pt. i, 497 ; annihilated by Gotamiputra, I, pt. ii, 149, 155, 160.

Khair : *Acacia catechu*, timber tree, in Poona district, XVIII, pt. i, 48 ; in Khándesh, XII, 25 ; in Kánara, XV, pt. i, 60.

Khairát or Khairiyat Khán : Habsi governor of Janjira (1670-1696), takes Anjanvel, X, 318 ; builds two forts at Harnai, *id.* 337 ; captures Dánda Rajpuri (1670), XI, 437, 438 ; defends Janjira against Sambháji (1682), *id.* 441 ; his tomb, *id.* 464.

Khájah : *see* Khwájah.

Khájana, Khajjana : marshy land, I, pt. ii, 185.

Khajuráho : inscription from, I, pt. i, 469.

Khajuri : fibrous plant, XXV, 237 ; in Poona district, XVIII, pt. i, 48.

Khákhar : holy plant, IX, pt. i, 37 note 1.

Khakharáta : I, pt. ii, 155. *See* Khagaráta.

Khákharo : bastard teak, believed to be home of Bráhma, worship of, IX, pt. i, 384.

Khakhi : a Hindu religious order in Rewa Kántha, VI, 25.

Khákhrechi : town in Káthiáwár, VIII, 508.

Khálápur : village in Thána district, XIV, 201 ; XIII, 508 ; survey assessment introduced (1855) into, *id.* 591-594.

Khaláti : coast lands in Ratnágiri district, X, 151 note 1.

Khalifáhs or Khalifs : Umayayd, of Damascus, hostility of, towards, Ali's family, IX, pt. ii, 47 note 1 ; Abbasid, family of the ; religious strictness of, *id.* 183 note 4, 185.

Khalif Hashám : (724-743), expeditions of Arabs in the reign of, I, pt. i, 109.
Khalif Omar : his probable expedition to Thána (636), I, pt. ii, 4.
Khalifs : *see* Khalifahs.
Khálpa : depressed class in Gujarát, other names, origin and customs, IX, pt. i, 331, 345-346.
Khálsáh : crown domain, I, pt. i, 209, 214.
Khalsi : in the Himalayas, rock inscription at, I, pt. ii, 142.
Khámatki : pass in Sátára district, XIX, 7, 201.
Khambáit, Khambát : I, pt. i, 514. *See* Cambay.
Khambátini : vow, rites relating to, IX, pt. ii, 231.
Khambhála : táluka in Káthiáwár, VIII, 508.
Khambhália or Khambhaliya : town in Káthiáwár, VIII, 509; head-quarters of the Navánagar chiefs between 1671-1707, I, pt. i, 285.
Khámbhiyás : memorial stones, IX, pt. i, 363.
Khambhiáv : táluka in Káthiáwár, VIII, 510.
Khambhoi : in Gujarát, West of Pátan, battle of (1391), I, pt. i, 232 and note 2.
Khán : reservoir in Ahmadábád district, IV, 19.
Khán : title among Pathâns, IX, pt. ii, 11.
Khána : evening meal, IX, pt. ii, 109.
Khánah : Khojáh religious lodge, first establishment of, by Pir Sadruddin, IX, pt. ii, 40.
Khanahzád Khán : son of the viceroy of Gujarát (1723-1730); defeats Piláji Gáikwár and other Maráthás (1725), obtains the title of Ghálib Jang, I, pt. i, 307.
Khánam : title of Mughal women, IX, pt. ii, 9.
Khánápur : in the Kolhápur state, inscription at, I, pt. ii, 555.
Khánápur : sub-division in Sátara district, details of, XIX, 427-430; survey of, *id.* 361 363. *Town, id.* 482.
Khánápur : sub-division of Belgaum district, details, boundaries, area, aspect, soil, climate, water, stock, crops, people of, XXI, 508-509. *Town, id.* 576; local story, and tombs at, XXIII, 660-661; *see* also I, pt. ii, 565; Goa Kadamb record at, *id.* 566-570.
Khánápur-Mudhol : hill range in Kolhápur state, XXIV, 7.
Khandahat : fort between Somnáth and the desert attacked by Mahmúd of Ghazni, I, pt. i, 167.
Khandála : town in Poona district with railway station, description, houses, stock, people, trade, Mr. Graham's monument, trips, XVIII, pt. iii, 233-241; occupied by Captain Stuart (1778), XIII, 502; Goddard's halt at (1779), *id.* 507; *see* also XVIII, pt. ii, 263; inscriptions at, I pt. ii, 605, XI, 324.
Khándáu : a caste of money-lenders in Baroda territory, VII, 111.
Khandaraballaba : probably Ráshtrakúta king Krishna III, I, pt. ii, 418 note 8.
Khandás : people of Khándesh, XII, 1 note 2, 38 note 3.
Khandás Patel : of Baroda, his Arab guarantee transferred to the British (1795), VII, 558.
Khánde Khárvi : a caste of fishermen and sailors in Kánara district, XV, pt. i, 309, 310.
Khanderáv Dábháde : Marátha free-booter, his exactions as Rajáram's deputy in Báglán, makes incursions into the Surat district (1699), his expeditions in Gujarát (1700-1711); his defeat at Ankleshvar by the Mughals (1711), defeats the army sent against him under Zulfikár Beg by the Delhi authorities (1716); his outpost between Surat and Burhánpur (1716); is appointed Senápati by Rája Shábu, I, pt. i, 388-389; *see* also I, pt. ii, 599, 626; XIX, 260, XII, 251; *another account of* : his incursions in Gujarát (1712), fights with Chandrasena Jadhava near Ahmadnagar (1716), created Senápati by Sháhu, accompanies the Peshwa to Delhi (1720), empowered to collect tributes in Gujarát and Báglán, fights against the Nizám at Bálápur, his death (1721), VII, 167-168; *see* also XIX, 266.
Khanderáv Gáikwár : brother of Damáji, demands his share; negotiates with Jawan Murd Khán; appoints Dádu Morár his deputy at Ahmadábád and goes to Sorath, I, pt. i, 326, 327; confines Raugoji and Fakhr-ud-daulah; appoints Trimbak Pandit his deputy, *id.* 329; is appointed his brother's deputy in Gujarát, *id.* 332, 340; Nadiad and Borsad conferred as *jagir* on (1747), VII, 176-177, 187, 189, 191-193, 195, 594.
Khanderáv Gáikwár : H. H. (1857-1870), his character, his ministers, VII, 273-278; his proposal to reduce the contingent army (1856), *id.* 306; his reforms, *id.* 366-371; his banks, *id.* 408-409; opens a hospital at Baroda (1858), *id.* 501.
Khanderáv Raste : *sarsubhadár* of the Konkan, I, pt. ii, 110.
Khanderi : Kennery island in Kolába district, lighthouse and history of, XI, 324-327, 472-473; taken and fortified by Shiváji (1679), *id.* 145, 440; I, pt. ii, 71-72; XXVI, pt. i, 80; attacked by the English (1719), XI, 147; taken by Jaysing Angriá's wife (1799), *id.* 156; *see* also XIII, 478, 489, 501.
Khandesh District : origin of, I, pt. ii, 231; description : boundaries, sub-divisions, aspect, hills, rivers, floods, irrigation, soil, geology, hot-springs, earthquakes, climate, XII, 1-15; production : minerals, forests and forest produce, trees, domestic animals, wild animals, birds, *id.* 16 37; population : Ahir element in, Ahirani language, census details, Bráhmans, writers, traders, husbandmen, craftsmen, *sonárs, sutárs, lohárs, shimpis*, manufacturers, bards and actors, personal servants, shepherds, fishers, labourers, unsettled tribes : Bhils, Pávrás, Vanjaris, Chárans, Láds, depressed classes, beggars; Musalmáns, Christians, *id.* 49-129; houses, village communities, movements, *id.* 129-135; agriculture : holdings, stock, irrigation, waterworks, wells, field tools, crops, cotton improvement (1831-1880), Bombay hemp, indigo, turmeric, tobacco, poppy, sugarcane, garden crops, Government Farm, silk, blight, locusts, famines, *id.* 136-190; capital : capitalists, insurance, exchange bills, saving classes, traders, account books, currency, interest, money-lenders, land mortgages, labour mortgage, wages (1788-1880), prices (1788-1879), weights and measures, *id.* 190-205; trade : routes (B. C. 100-A. D. 1880), passes, railway, bridges, ferries, trade

(1820-1840), trade centres, markets, fairs, imports, exports, *id.* 206-223; crafts: gold, copper, iron, stone, pottery, lime, indigo, catechu, grass oil, cotton spinning and weaving, dyeing, calico printing, steam spinning and weaving, carpets, gold and silver thread, blanket weaving, etc., *id.* 223-237; history: early Hindus (1600 B. C.-1300 A. D.), Musalmáns (1295-1760), under Delhi Governors (1323-1370), the Farukis (1370-1600), the Mughals (1600-1760), the Maráthás (1760-1818), *id.* 238-254; the British (1818-1880), Malegaon siege, *id.* 255-256; Bhil disorders (1818, 1821-25), Bhil corps (1825-27), *id.* 256-260; survey riots (1852), the mutinies (1857), *id.* 261-263. Land administration: staff (1880), *id.* 264-266; history: early Hindus, Mughals, the Maráthás, *id.* 266-272; British management, *id.* 272-303; hereditary officers, village staff, landholders (1818), revenue settlement (1821), *id.* 274-281; revenue system (1828), *id.* 283-285; survey (1852-1870), survey results (1855-78), *id.* 292-296; season reports (1852-1880), *id.* 298-303; justice: civil, under the Maráthás, under British Government (1818-1880), *id.* 304-308; criminal justice, criminal tribes, the Bhils, Kajarsing (1833-1860), Tulia Naik (1867-1876), Arabs and Pendharis, *id.* 309-314; police, crimes (1874-78), (1845-49), Bhil police corps, jails, *id.* 315-319; revenue and finance: account heads, land revenue, stamps, excise, customs, etc., balance sheets (1824-25, 1878-79), *id.* 320-325; local funds, municipalities, *id.* 326-328; instruction: schools, cost, private schools, girls' schools (1864), pupils by caste (1879), school returns (1855-79), newspapers, libraries, *id.* 320 335; health: climate, diseases, cattle diseases, small-pox, hospitals and dispensaries, vaccination, births and deaths, *id.* 336-341; sub-divisions: Amalner, its details, *id.* 342-348; Bhusával, its details, *id.* 348-353; Chalisgaon, its sub-divisional deaths, *id.* 351-358; Chopda, its sub-divisional details, *id.* 358-363; Dhulia, its sub-divisional details, *id.* 363-370; Erandol, its sub-divisional details, *id.* 370-375; Jamner, its sub-divisional details, *id.* 375-379; Nandurbár, its sub-divisional details, *id.* 379-386; Nasirábád, *id.* 386-392; Pachora, *id.* 392-396; Pimpalner, *id.* 396-400; Savda, *id.* 400-409; Shaháda, *id.* 409-413; Shirpur, *id.* 413-417; Taloda, *id.* 417-421; Akráni, *id.* 421-424; Virdel, *id.* 424-430; places of interest, *id.* 431-594; states, *id.* 597-613; *see* also I, pt. ii, 278 note 2, 355, 374, 399, 423, 430, 460, 515, 521, 522; kingdom of, founded by Malik Nazir the eldest son of Malik Rája (1399), *id.* 620.

Khándesh kings: (1399-1596), list of, XVII, 359 note 3.

Khándia: táluka in Káthiáwár, VIII, 511.

Khandoba: Hindu god, XVIII, pt. i, 290, 413, 414; temple of, at Pál in Sátára district, XIX, 529-532.

Khandodi: famine plant, XXV, 201.

Khandoji Mánkar: Marátha commander, takes Chaul (1741), I, pt. ii, 85; first *subhadár* of Sálsette, *id.* 99.

Khandul: *Sterculia urens*, timber tree in Poona district, yields fibre, XVIII, pt. i, 47.

Khángi villages: private estates of the Gáikwár, VII, 347-348.

Khán Jahán: Mughal general, sends (1670) ships to help the Sidis, I, pt. ii, 69, XI, 437; cantons at Pedgaon on the Bhima and fortifies it (1673), I, pt. ii, 626; reduces Poona (1685), XVIII, pt. ii, 238.

Khán Jahán or Jahán Lodi: Mughal general sent against Ahmadnagar (1612), XVII, 392; unsuccessfully besieges Mándu (1628), I, pt. i, 381; takes refuge in Báglán, is pursued and slain (1628), I, pt. ii, 624-625.

Khán Khánán: Mughal general (1596-1599), besieges Ahmadnagar (1595), XVII, 383, 384, 386; defeats Malik Ambar, *id.* 390.

Khán Muhammad: prime-minister of Bijápur (1657), I, pt. ii, 652.

Khánpur: sub-division in Rewa Kántha, VI, 123.

Khan Sarovar: reservoir at Pattan in Gáikwár's territory, VII, 604.

Khánt: a sub-caste of Kolis, IX, pt. i, 444.

Khán Zamán: imperial general, ordered to join the Bijápur troops, I, pt. ii, 38.

Khápri: blight in Ahmadábád district, IV, 61.

Khár: salt rice land or Khárapat villages of Alibág, XI, 194 note 1.

Kharádi: class of Musalmán wood-turners, in Belgaum district, XXI, 207-208; in Gujarát, converts from the Hindu caste of the same name, Sunnis in faith, IX, pt. ii, 75. *See* Dhigvan.

Khárághoda: salt works, in Ahmadábád district, salt how made, stored, and distributed; out-turn and sale, IV, 119-124; *see* also XIII, 370.

Kharak: caste of husbandmen in Káthiáwár, VIII, 205 note 1.

Kharaosti: Kshatrapa prince, I, pt. i, 23.

Khárápát: salt reclaimed land, in Kolába district, XI, 91, 166, 167 and notes 1, 2, 3. *See* Shilotri.

Kharas: village in Káthiáwár, inscription found at, VIII, 515-516.

Kharás: vow, rites relating to, IX, pt. ii, 231.

Kharásni: vow, rites relating to, IX, pt. ii, 231.

Kharda: town and fort in Ahmadnagar district, XVII, 721-722; battle of, between the Nizám and the Peshwa (1794), *id.* 406-409; *see* also I, pt. ii, 606; XVIII, pt. ii, 270; XX, 292.

Khardi: village in Thána district, with railway station, XIV, 201.

Kharedi: town in Káthiáwár, VIII, 513.

Khárepatan: river in Ratnágiri district, I, pt. ii, 37.

Khárepátan: town in Ratnagiri district, history, fort and remains of, X, 342-343; trade of (1818), *id.* 177; *see* also I, pt. ii, 41, 206, 207; grant at, *id.* 203, 205, 254, 255, 341 note 2, 414 note 1, 416 note 4, 422 note 1, 426, 431, 433, 536 and note 2, 542, 543, 538.

Khárepathár: plateau in Poona district, XVIII, pt. i, 6.

Khari : river in Gujarát, III, 5 ; IV, 6 ; V, 357.

Khári : *see* Baul.

Kharia : Gujar, class of Gujarát Kadva Kanbis appears in Rájpútána as ; considered lower, IX, pt. i, 490.

Kharia-nág : *see* Kala buch nág.

Kharif : early season, XVIII, pt. ii, 3.

Khari-nimb : oil-yielding plant, XXV, 222.

Khariphron : mouth of the Indus, I, pt. i, 538.

Kharkadi : village in Ahmadábád district, shrine of Bálan Sháh at, story of his life, VIII, 511-512.

Kharki : *see* Khadki.

Kharoli : *inám* village of Khandoji Mánkar, I, pt. ii, 85.

Kharoshi : village in Belgaum district, temple, and fair at, XXI, 576.

Khár Pátil : a caste of husbandmen in Thána district, XIII, 123.

Kharsáni : milkbush, worshipped for favour of spirit Bhánumati, IX, pt. i, 385.

Kharsedji Jamsedji Modi : of Cambay, enjoys a high position in the Peshwa's court under the British Government (1809), receives presents of land in Cambay, IX, pt. ii, 198 note 5.

Kharsedji Rustomji Káma : Mr., gives the year of the arrival of the Pársis at Sanjan, IX, pt. ii, 185 note 3.

Khárva or Khárvi : caste of sea-farers, in Gujarát, IX, pt. i, 519 ; strength, *id.* 520 and note 1 ; claim Koli and Rájpút origin, *id.* 519, 520 and note 2 ; divisions and branches, *id.* 519, 520 ; Rájpút and Gujarát surnames ; history and traditions, *id.* 520-521 ; Cutch and Káthiáwár, three divisions, *id.* 519, 520 ; Cambay, *id.* 519 ; South Gujarát, divisions, Surati, Hánsoti, Khambháti ; appearance, dress, food, character, occupation — sailors, builders of bridges, house building, tile-turning ; other pursuits ; earnings ; religion, *id.* 521 ; customs, *id.* 522 ; in Cutch, V, 81 ; in Káthiáwár, VIII, 153 ; in Ratnágiri district, X, 128 ; in Koláha district, XI, 68, 414 ; in Thána district, XIII, 147 ; in Kánara district, XV, pt. i, 310, 311.

Khárvat : salt rice-land in Ratnágiri district, X, 144.

Khárvela : early Orissa king (B. C. 100), XVI, 613.

Kharvi : *see* Kharva.

Khás : the military of Nepál, originally a small clan, history of its origin, its rise, admitted to be Hindus, IX, pt. i, 451, 452 and note 2, 463 note 2.

Khasa : king of Kumaon, I, pt. i, 190.

Khasás : tribe defeated by Yaśovarmman, I, pt. i, 469.

Khás Khán : general of Sultán Násir-ud-din Kahácbah, I, pt. i, 512.

Khát : newly-created man by Karan, the *Mahábhárat* hero, the Káthis claim descent from, IX, pt. i, 252 note 1.

Khatara : famine plant found in the Konkan, XXV, 201.

Khatarváda : Thána suburb, XIV, 346.

Khatáv : sub-division in Sátára district, XIX, 430-432 ; survey of, *id.* 356-358 ; village, temple at, *id.* 482-483.

Khátá-Vahi : ledger, contents of, IX, pt. i, 83, 84.

Khateli : caste of peasant-holders in Ratnágiri district, X, 450.

Khátgaon : village in Khándesh district, temple at, XII, 453.

Khátgun : village in Sátára district, fair at, XIX, 483-484.

Khatia : caste of Musalmáns of part foreign descent, IX, pt. ii, 11, 15.

Khatib : Musalmán preacher in Gujarát, duties of, IX, pt. ii, 133 ; in Ratnágiri, X, 141.

Khátik : caste of butchers, I, pt. i, 451 ; in Kolába district, XI, 71, 414 ; in Thána district, XIII, 152 ; in Násik district, XVI, 59 ; in Ahmadnagar district, XVII, 153 ; in Sholápur district, XX, 161 ; in Bijápur district, XXIII, 169-173 ; in Kolhápur state, XXIV, 106.

Khatki : tanners in Gujarát, Hindu converts ; two classes of, IX, pt. ii, 75 ; mutton butchers in Khándesh district, XII, 126, 235.

Khatna : circumcision, rite of, IX, pt. ii, 160 and note 3.

Khát Puja : earth worship before foundation stone is laid, details of, IX, pt. i, 404.

Khatrás : funeral memorial stones, IX, pt. i, 363 ; offerings made to, *id.* 407.

Khatri : an important class in Northern India, and Sindh, supposed to be of foreign origin, IX, pt. i, 450, 453 ; in Gujarát, class of weavers, of Brahma-kshatri stock, *id.* 188-189 and note 1 ; weaving, *id.* 189 ; in Cutch, V, 94 ; in Káthiáwár, VIII, 152 ; in Kolába district, XI, 64, 131 ; in Thána district, XIII, 133 ; in Násik district, XVI, 53 ; in Ahmadnagar district, XVII, 109-112 ; in Poona district, XVIII, pt. i, 346-347 ; in Sholápur district, XX, 118-119 ; in Dhárwár district, XXII, 170-171 ; in Kolhápur state, XXIV, 95.

Khatri Dev : pillar of wood, worship of, IX, pt. i, 292.

Khatta : dish, public dinners called after ; cost of, IX, pt. ii, 113, 114 and note 1.

Khattab : father of Umár, the second Khalifah, I, pt. i, 505 ; IX, pt. ii, 1 note 1.

Khatti : Káthis described as, IX, pt. i, 258.

Khatu, Khatun : title of Pathán women, IX, pt. ii, 11.

Khatvánga Dhvaja : club banner of Pallava Nandipotavarman, taken by Vikramáditya II, I, pt. ii, 375.

Khavás : in Gujarát, male slaves, personal attendants of Rájpút chiefs, influence over them, IX, pt. i, 147 and note 1 ; other names, recruitment ; position, *id.* 234-235 ; appearance ; persons raised to power among, *id.* 236 ; in Káthiáwár, VIII, 118, 119 ; in Cutch, V, 76-77 ; in Pálanpur, *id.* 290 ; in Mahi Kántha, *id.* 365 ; usurp government of Navánagar, dispersed by British contingent (1814), I, pt. i, 427.

Khavásans : female servants in Rájpút houses, position, IX, pt. i, 235-236.

Khávda : place of interest in Cutch, V, 227-228.

Khawas Khán : son of Khán Muhammad, the traitorous prime minister, becomes regent of

Bijápur (1672), I, pt. ii, 653; his negotiations with the Mughals to hold Bijápur as a dependent province of the empire (1675), his assassination (1679), *id.* 653; *see* also XXIII, 431-432; tomb of, in Bijápur city, *id.* 614.

Khazánah-i-Amirah: imperial treasury, I, pt. i, 213.

Khazára: tribe of foreign invaders; various forms and variations of the name, IX, pt. i, 471-472; same as White Hunas, *id.* 472, 473; points of their resemblance with White Hunas, *id.* 470 note 1; settlements at Farghana coincide with White Huna settlements, *id.* 472 note 1; two elements of, Ak-Khazar or Fair Khazar and Kára Khazar or Dark Khazar; description of two elements, history, *id.* 473-474; White Khazars found settled in North Persia (close of the fifth century), *id.* 474; their movement to join White Hunas of Badeghiz with whom they passed conquering into India, *id.* 469, 475-476; Gurjjara became the name of, by which the bulk of the great sixth century horde was known, *id.* 434, 446, 449, 455, 456, 461, 469, 470, 476. *See* Gujar.

Khed: sub-division of Poona district, its boundaries, area, aspect, climate, water, crops, stock, people, cultivators, communications, XVIII, pt. iii, 89-92; survey of, XVIII, pt. ii, 392-393, 458, 461. *Town,* details, Dilávarkhán's tomb, temples and fairs at, XVIII, pt. iii, 241-242; action at (1708), XVIII, pt. ii, 240.

Khed: sub-division in Ratnágiri district, X, 2, 299; town, history and rock temples at, *id.* 344; caves at, I, pt. ii, 9.

Kheda: or Kaira, head-quarters of Kaira district, IX, pt. i, 10; grant of, I, pt. i, 108, 115, 116, 125, 126, 518. *See* Kaira.

Kheda: money subscription among Memans, IX, pt. ii, 57.

Khedával: a sub-caste of Bráhmans in Rewa Kántha, VI, 23; in Gujarát, IX, pt. i, 1; origin of name; chief settlements; traditional origin; divisions *baj* and *bhitra* into, origin of divisions, *id.* 10-11; in Thána district, XIII, 78; in Poona district, XVIII, pt. i, 163.

Khedbrahma: village in Mahi Kántha, temple of Brahma at, V, 437; place of pilgrimage, IX, pt. I, 549, p. xxxvi.

Khediapur: village in Kolhápur, Singhana's inscription at, I, pt ii, 240.

Khedrapur: Yádav inscription (1213) at, I, pt. ii, 523, 524, 558.

Khela: *see* Kela.

Khelna: hill fort in Kolhápur state, XXIV, 4; (Vishálgad) I, pt. ii, 31; unsuccessfully besieged by Malik-ul-Tujár (1451), *id.* 588.

Khem Sávant I: Vádi chief (1670), X, 440.

Khem Sávant II: Vádi chief (1675-1709), X, 440.

Khem Sávant III: Vádi chief (1755-1803), X, 441-442; attacks the remains of the Portuguese armies, I, pt. ii, 85, 108; death of (1803), *id.* 112; *see* also XXI, 384.

Khem Sávant IV: Vádi chief (1812-1840), X, 443-445.

Khengár: king of Sorath, killed by Siddharája, I, pt. i, 176.

Khengar: Ráo of Kachh (1548-1584); invites the Sindh Memans to come and settle at Bhuj; honors the head of the Memans with the title of '*shet*' or squire, IX, pt. ii, 51.

Khengar IV: Chudásama king of Junágadh (1279-1333), repairs Somanátha after its desecration by Alá-ud-din Khilji, I, pt. i, 190.

Kheni: Koli rebel (1657) of north-west of Poona against Musalmán rule, XVIII, pt. ii, 227-228.

Kherádi Surmal: a Bhil teacher, V, 366.

Kheráli: táluka in Káthiáwár, VIII, 513.

Kherálu: sub division in Baroda state, VII, 621-625. *Town, id.* 622.

Kheráváda: state in Mahi Kántha, V, 426.

Kherdi: town in Káthiáwár, its history, VIII, 513.

Khersonesos: the peninsula of Goa, I, pt. i, 541, 546.

Khertalab Khán: brother and successor of Nek Alam Khán II of Broach (1751), his death, I, pt. i, 338, 339.

Khervádi: village in Násik district, XVI, 449.

Khetáhára: country, present Khed táluka of the Ratnágiri district, I, pt. ii, 355, 356 note 1; identified with Kittur in the Belgaum district by K. T. Telang, *id.* 356 note 1.

Khétaka or Khetakahára: modern Kaira, mentioned in the Valabhi records, I, pt. ii, 356 note 1, 382, 404, 413. *See* also I, pt. i, 115, 128; province of the Valabhi chiefs (760), I, pt. ii, 315, 316, 382.

Khetrapál: guardian spirit, IX, pt. i, p. xxxv, 200; god of boundaries, *id.* 292, 354.

Khetri: caste of husbandmen in Belgaum district, XXI, 106.

Khichdi: food and money gifts to Bráhmans in Baroda state, VII, 354.

Khidrápur: village in Kolhápur state, temples, inscriptions and fair at, XXIV, 302-303.

Khijaro or Khijda: *sami* tree, its use in building marriage pillar of Bharváds, IX, pt. i, 269, 270; its dread, *mamo* or maternal uncle spirit living in, *id.* 270 and note 3.

Khijdia: táluka in Káthiáwár, VIII, 513-514.

Khikri: a caste of shepherds in Kolába district, XI, 67.

Khiláphat: *see* Fátimite Khiláphat.

Khilari: breed of cattle in Poona district, XVIII, pt. i, 55.

Khiligila, Khiligiladurga or Khiligili: another name for Panhála, I, pt. ii, 254; Síláhára prince Márasimha rules at, *id.* 439; *see* also *id.* 547.

Khilji: emperors of Delhi, I, pt. ii, 509, 531.

Khilji: special community of part foreign descent in Gujarát, IX, pt. ii, 11, 15.

Khillat: dress of honour, XIX, 281 note 1.

Khimo: Dheda saint, IX, pt. i, 341.

"Khing" = Rider: plants the banner of Islám on Táragadh the hill fort of Ajmir, IX, pt. ii, 6 note 1 (7).

Khirdi: reservoir in Násik district, XVI, 95.

Khizar Khán : prince, son of Alá-ud-din Khilji and husband of Devaladevi, I, pt. i, 205 ; *see* also I, pt. ii, 532.
Khizr : Khwájáh, water-spirit, also called Prophet Elias, offerings made to, IX, pt. ii, 152, 158 and note 3.
Khizr Khán : *see* Khizar Khán.
Khmers : Panjáb and Káshmir settlers in Jáva and Cambodia, I, pt. i, 500 note 6, 502.
Khodiad Máta : Hindu goddess, shrine at Rájápur near Sihor, worshipped by Gohils, IX, pt. i, p. xxxvi, 136, 247, 363, 503.
Khodsi : village in Kolhápur state, temple and fair, at, XXIV, 303.
Khodu : village in Káthiáwár, inscription at, VIII, 514-515.
Khojáh : Musalmán sect in Gujarát, Hindu converts to the Nazárian division of the great Ismáili sect; literal meaning of, "honourable converts;" settlements and divisions of, IX, pt. ii, 36 ; first conversions of, by Nur Satgur in Gujarát during the time of Solanki Bhim II (1179-1242), *id.* 38 ; conversions of, in Cutch and Káthiáwár (1200) by Ramde, a converted Tuvar Rájpút, *id.* 40 ; additions to the community of, from the converted Lohána tribe of the Afgháns (1430) ; from the converted Cháks of Kashmir (1496), *id.* 39 ; conversions of Káthiáwár Lohánas by Pir Dádu (1549), conversions at Bhuj by Pir Dádu, *id.* 41 ; *khánah* or religious lodge of, first established by, and tythe-gathering first introduced among, by Pir Sadr-ud-din (1430), theory of the *avatárs* of the gods of the Hindu Pantheon introduced among, by Pir Sadr-ud-din, *id.* 40 ; scriptures of, *id.* 40-41 ; Agha-Khán, the religious head of the, *id.* 41 ; appearance of, *id.* 42 ; dress of, *id.* 42-44 ; ornaments, character, and calling of, *id.* 44 ; customs among : *chhatti* or sixth day celebration, *id.* 44 ; marriage, *id.* 45 ; death, *id.* 46 ; follow the Hindu law of inheritance, *id.* 47 ; religion of, *id.* 46-49 ; form of worship, *id.* 48 ; prayers counting the names of, the *pirs*, the sacrament or heart-prayer ; taxes paid by, id. 49 ; holidays observed by, *id.* 49-50 and note 1 ; in Cutch, V, 91-92 ; in Káthiáwár, VIII, 163 ; in Kolába district, XI, 81.
Khokada : hill and village in Sátára district, XIX, 11.
Khokara : hill in Káthiáwár, VIII, 11.
Khokati : famine plant, XXV, 204.
Khokhar : village in Cutch, inscription at, I, pt. i, 204.
Khokhar : caste of Rájpút converts of the Khokhar tribe in Gujarát, derivation of the name of, origin of, mention of, in *Ain-i-Akbari*, in the *Tárikh-i-Alái*, in *Tabakát-i-Násiri* ; claim Afghán extraction, said to have been represented in Afghánistan by the existence of a *kheyl* (tribe) of the name of, IX, pt. ii, 65.
Khokhari : town in Kolába district, XI, 464.
Khokhri : village in Káthiáwár, VIII, 514.
Khokra : village in Cutch, temple at, V, 228.
Kholeśvara : Bráhman chief and general in the service of Singhana the Yádava king, reduces the Gujarát kings Málava and Abhíra, I, pt. ii, 240, 242, 243, 525.
Khollas : the seven, country under Gandarádítya, I, pt. ii, 255.
Kholobharvo : lap-filling, a pregnancy ceremony among Gujarát Hindus, IX, pt. i, 31, 32.
Khombhátri : a caste of Musalmán dyers in Cutch, V, 126.
Khondeshvar : hill in Poona district, XVIII, pt. i, 5.
Khondmir : *sayad*, companion of Sayad Muhammad Jaunpuri, his defeat by Muzaffar II, IX, pt. ii, 63.
Khopivli or Khopoli : village in Thána district, XIV, 201 ; arrival of Poona expedition to (1778), XIII, 503 ; Goddard's halt at (1781), *id.* 507 ; railway at, *id.* 600, 624 note 1 ; *see* also XVIII, pt. ii, 266.
Khordád : Amshaspad ; sixth day of the Pársi month ; third month of the Pársi year, IX, pt. ii, 217.
Khordád Jasan : chief festival day of Pársis, observances on, IX, pt. ii, 217.
Khordád Sál : leading festive day, believed to be the anniversary of the birth of Zoroaster ; observances on, IX, pt. ii, 219.
Khorshed Kámdin : Sanjan high priest, brings the Sanján fire to Navsári, IX, pt. ii, 188.
Khosás : marauders from Sind, their depredations in Cutch (1786-1819), V, 150, 159, 163, 164, 168 ; in Pálanpur, *id.* 302, 303, 341.
Khosru : dynastic title of Persian kings, I, pt. ii, 388.
Khosru II : of Persia, interchange of letters and presents between, and Pulikeśin II (625-626), I, pt. ii, 352 ; painting of his embassy in the Ajanta caves, XII, 485, 494, 513 ; *see* also XV, pt. ii, 81.
Khots : superior land-holders in Kolába district, revenue farmers (1882), XI, 163-166, 203, 207, (appendix) 473-474 ; villages managed by them (1882), *id.* 161, 162 and note 1 ; forbidden to interfere beyond their strict duties and powers by the Maráthás, *id.* 171 ; their origin, titles and position, *id.* 172 and note 1, 173, 174, 177, 178 and notes 1, 2, 4 and 5 ; *khoti* villages managed by Government accountants, *id.* 181 ; farmed or *khoti* villages in Sankshi, Rájpuri and Raygad (1837), *id.* 182-185 ; *khots*, demands and extortions, *id.* 186, 187, 188 ; general body of land-holders reduced to dependence and poverty by the *khots* (1856), *id.* 197, 453 ; in Thána, XIII, 545, 556 ; grants to (1502), I, pt. ii, 33, 106 ; of Sálsette, *id.* 124, 126 ; in Ratnágiri district, X, 137 ; castes of (1880), *id.* 138, 156 ; position and privileges of (1880), *id.* 204-206 ; position and caste of (1818), *id.* 225-227 ; terms of *khoti* agreements, *id.* 205 note 2.
Khoti : farming tenure in Thána, XIII, 534.
Khotika, Khottiga, Khottigadeva or Khottigadeva Nityavarsha : Ráshtrakúta king, succeeds his brother Krishna III, I, pt. ii, 205-207, 210, 306, 307, 387 ; his *birudas*, titles, epithets and wars with Paramára kings of

Málwa, *id.* 422 and note 3; records regarding him, *id.* 422-423, 424 note 1, 426, 432.
Khowsey : fibrous plant found in Konkan, XXV, 229.
Khubladha : fort in Kolába district, XI, 395, 396.
Khudash-bae-zan : an early form of marriage, IX, pt. ii, 238 note 2.
Khuddika : village in Ratnágiri district, mentioned in a grant, I, pt. ii, 347 note 2.
Khums : subscription among Dáudi Bohorás, IX, pt ii, 33 and note 1.
Khun : port in Ahmadábád district, IV, 345.
Khuntáváda : town in Káthiáwár, VIII, 516-517.
Khurasan : I, pt. i, 168.
Khurdu : timber tree in Khándesh district, XII, 25.
Khurshid Ráni : mother of Nasir-ud-din Khilji (1500-1512), I, pt. i, 365.
Khushálchand Ambaidas : banker in Baroda, guarantee-holder from the British (1801), VII, 258.
Khushálchand Shet : chief merchant of Ahmadábád (1748), I, pt. i, 333.
Khushnáwaz : White Húna emperor (460-500), I, pt. i, 76.
Khus-khus : oil-yielding plant, XXV, 225.
Khusro Turk : defends Ismael Ádil Khán and is rewarded with the *jahágir* of Belgaum, I, pt. ii, 641.
Khwája Gáwán : Bráhmani minister (1463-1481), short account of, XXI, 365 and note 3. *See* Muhammad Gáwan.
Khwájah : Persian form of the Turkish word *khojah*; meaning of, IX, pt. ii, 36 note 1; title, literal meaning of, given to Brahmakshatris on their conversion to Islám, *id.* 39.
Khwája Háji : general of Alla-ud-din, sent with Malik Káfur to reduce Dorasamudra (1310), I, pt. ii, 509; sets out to subdue the king of Warangal and reduce the Hoysalas, *id.* 533.
Khwája Jahán : Bahamani noble in charge of Purenda (1497), I, pt. ii, 589; *see* also XX, 278, 279-280; mosque of, in Bijápur city, XXIII, 634.
Khwája Muhammad Gáwán : I, pt. ii, 639. *See* Muhammad Gáwán.
Kidaras : division of Baktrian Yuetchi, I, pt. i, 144.
Kidd : Captain, English pirate, plunders a Bombay vessel off Rájápur (1697), I, pt. ii, 80.
Kidney-disease : *see* Ambhoi.
Kids : worship of, offerings of, IX, pt. i, 57.
Kie-chá : I, pt. i, 116. *See* Kheda.
Kiggatnád or Kiggatnádu : village in Coorg, inscription at, I, pt. ii, 303, 307; inscribed stones at, *id.* 299.
Kihim : place of interest in Kolába district, XI, 327-328.
Kikar : plant, its seeds eaten in famines, XXV, 199.
Kikli : village in Sátára district, temple at, XIX, 484-485.
Kikvi : market village in Poona district, XVIII, pt. iii, 243 244.
Kilegaon : village in Kolhápur state, fair at, XXIV, 383.
Kiligala, Kiligiladurga : *see* Khiligila.
Killidars : keeper of Vániá's shops, IX, pt. i, 79, 80.
Killiketar or Killikiatar : caste of beggars, in Belgaum district, XXI, 185-187; in Dhárwár district, XXII, 152-153; in Bijápur district, XXIII, 196-201.
Kim : I, pt. i, 545. *See* Kammoni.
Kim : river in Gujarát, II, 6, 346; VI, 6; VII, 8, 576; I, pt. ii, 310, 314; southern boundary of the Gurjara country, *id.* 315, 336, 347, 359 and notes 3 and 5, 370 note 3.
Kimaj : *see* Kimoj.
Kim Kathodra : town in Broach district, battle of (1744), I, pt. i, 328; customs station, its revenue made over to the English by the Baroda minister Rávji (1803), *id.* 414. *See* Ankleshvar.
Kimoj : village in Broach district, identified with Kemajju, I, pt. ii, 315.
King : divine origin of, worship of, belief in king-worship among different nations, IX, pt. i, 441 and note 1, 442 and note 3; worshippers, sect of, *id.* 441 note 1.
Kingfisher : English ship, engaged in the siege of Vijaydurg (1756), I, pt. ii, 94.
Kingfisher : bird, in Ratnágiri, X, 64; in Khándesh, XII, 34; in Gujarát called Nilkhanth or Chás, believed to be an incarnation of Shiv, worship of, IX, pt. i, 382.
Kinhai : village in Sátára district, temple at, XIX, 485-486.
Kini : village in Kolhápur state, temples at, XXIV, 303.
Kinjál : dye-yielding plant, XXV, 244.
Kinkeri : place of interest in Ratnágiri district, X, 465.
Kinnars : heavenly musicians, paintings of, in Ajanta caves, XII, 493 and note 3.
Kinye : famine and dye-yielding plant, found in several districts, XXV, 199, 244.
Kippur : Bene-Israel fast-day, XVIII, pt. i, 514.
Kir : *Capparis aphylla*, tree, I, pt. i, 461.
Kirád : a caste of traders in Poona district, XVIII, pt. i, 267-270.
Kiraita, Kiraittem : *see* Karyat.
Kiramar : medicinal plant, XXV, 258.
Kirán-us saadain : historical work, IX, pt. ii, 10 note 3.
Kirastanvs : vernacular name for native Christians; *see* Christians.
Kirat : division of Abhir, "Introduction to the History of the Konkan," I, pt. ii, p. ix.
Kiratakupa : *see* Keradu.
Kirdias : special community of part foreign descent in Gujarát, IX, pt. ii, 11, 15.
Kirdaár : renewed tillage, tenure in Thána district, XIII, 544 note 2.
Kirgeri : village in Dhárwár district, temple at, XXII, 765.
Kiriya : language spoken at Málkhet, I, pt. i, 519; language of the Balhára country, I, pt. ii, 388.
Kiriya-Kereyur : *agrahára* of, I, pt. ii, 449.
Kirkee : village near Poona city, I, pt. ii, 657; battle of (1817), *id.* 630; *see* also X, 198; XII, 254; XVII, 414; XVIII, pt. ii, 300-301; XIX, 301; battlefield and description of the

battle, XVIII, pt. iii, 374-381, 421; barracks at, *id.* 374; Cantonment, *id.* 357-359.
Kirli: state in Khándesh district, XII, 606.
Kirman: in Persia, merchants of, IX, pt. ii, 183 note 3; priests called from, to explain the Pársi religion to the emperor Akbar, *id.* 190; passage to India through, *id.* 1 note 3.
Kirmira: plant found in Southern Konkan, used as antidote to snake-bite, XXV, 274.
Kirpál: a caste of Christian reverts in Thána district, XIII, 149.
Kirtans: thanksgiving songs, IX, pt. i, 25.
Kirtideva I: *see* Kirtivarman II.
Kirtideva II: Hángal Kádamba, I, pt. ii, 559.
Kirtikaumudi: Sanskrit work compiled by Someśvara, I, pt. i, 159, 174, 178, 179, 194, 195, 196, 198, 199; *see* also I, pt. ii, 213, 241, 525 note 5.
Kirti Náráyana: *biruda* or title of Govinda III, I, pt. ii, 394.
Kirtirája: brother of Gomka the Kolhápur Siláhára prince, I, pt. ii, 254, 545.
Kirtirája: Chaulukya, grandson of Bárappa and king of Láta, his grant at Surat, I, pt. i, 159.
Kirtivarma: *see* Kirtivarman I.
Kirtivarman I or Kirttivarma I: fourth Chalukya prince (567-597), successor of Pulikeśin I, I, pt. ii, 328; his *biruda* or title, *id.* 351 note 3; subdues the Nalas, the Mauryas of North Konkan, and the Kadambas of Banavási, *id.* 13, 181, 182, 285, 335-336; breaks the confederacy of the Kadambas, *id.* 291 note 2; conquers the Gangas, *id.* 300, 309; date of his succession to the throne, *id.* 344 and note 7; adorns Vátápi with buildings and temples, Vaishnava cave temples, appoints Satyáśraya Dhruvarája Indravarman his governor in the Konkan (590); enlargement of the Chalukya power by, *id.* 345 and note 4, 346 note 4, 349, 356; Bádámi cave inscription of (578), *id.* 357, 365, 377 note 2; also styled Kirtiráj, *id.* 345. *See* also I, pt. i, 107; XIII, 420; XV, pt. ii, 80, 81.
Kirtivarman I: Hangal Kádamba, I, pt. ii, 559.
Kirtivarman II or Kirttivarma II: Satyáśraya Nripasimha (746-757), last Western Chalukya king, I, pt. ii, 190, 379, 389; son and successor of Vikramáditya II, *id.* 374; his copperplate, *id.* 190; conquered by Dantidurga, *id.* 194, 211, 212; grant of, *id.* 339 note 3; Pattadakal inscription of, *id.* 374; his *birudas*, epithets, and titles, *id.* 376-377; breaks the power of the Pallavas, *id.* 190, 377; grants villages to a Bráhman (757), *id.* 377; overthrow of the Western Chálukya sovereignty in the time of, by the Ráshtrakútas, *id.* 190, 377; loses the northern provinces of his dominions before the date of the Pattadakal inscription (754), *id.* 378, 391, 397, 427 note 3; *see* also XV, pt. ii, 82; XXIII, 386.
Kirtivarman II, Kirtideva I or Kirttideva: Hángal Kádamba prince (1068-1078) and feudatory of the Western Chálukya kings Someśvara I and Vikramáditya VI, I, pt. ii, 439, 450, 559, 561; *see* also XV, pt. ii, 82, 83 note 8, 262 and note 2.
Kirtivarman III: Western Chálukya king of Kalyáni, I, pt. ii, 378, 379.
Kirttikaumudi: I, pt. ii, 213, 241, 525 note 5; *see Kirtikaumudi.*
Kirttipála: brother of Kumárapála, I, pt. i, 181.
Kirttirája: Parmár king, I, pt. i, 160.
Kirttistambha: reservoir built by Siddharáj, I, pt. i, 180 note 2.
Kirttivarma I: *see* Kirtivarman I.
Kirukágámási: village in the Edevolal district, I, pt. ii, 309, 370.
Kiruvalli: village in the Pánumgál district, I, pt. ii, 377.
Kirvalegudd: hill in Belgaum district, XXI, 8, 576.
Kirvant: *see* Kramvant.
Kis, Kish: probably Kich-Makrán, island of, I, pt. i, 514, 515.
Kishánbivao: gateway of Bhinmál, I, pt. i, 450 note 1.
Kishkindha: visited by Sahádeva, its situation in the *Puránas*, I, pt. ii, 142.
Kishwar Khán: Bijápur general, I, pt. ii, 645; ambassador at the court of Rám Rája (1557), XX, 284; killed (1569), XVII, 371.
Kissah-i-Sanjan: poetic account of the Pársis, IX, pt. ii, 183 and note 2, 187 and notes 2, 3; XIII, 247 and note 1.
Kisukád: territorial division, I, pt. ii, 305, 418, 419, 421, 430, 431, 433, 435, 437, 439, 440, 441 and note 6, 443; ruled over by the Sindas of Yelburga, *id.* 452, 458, 460, 485, 488, 572, 574, 575, 576.
Kisuvolal: modern Pattadakal, city, I, pt. ii, 305, 348 note 8, 358 note 1, 365 note 1, 572, 575. *See* Kesuvolal.
Kitábul Akálim: *Book of Climes*, work of Al Istakhri, I, pt. i, 506 note 9.
Kitolo: last Kushán king, I, pt. i, 75; ruler of Yuetchi, *id.* 144.
Kittur: town in Belgaum district, inscription, fort, history and risings at, XXI, 576-581; origin of the *desai* of, *id.* 377; seized by Tipu (1786), *id.* 385, 386; *another account of*: I, pt. ii, 356 note 1; inscription at, *id.* 570 note 8, 571; the most southerly portion of Ismael Ádil Sháh's kingdom, *id.* 640; besieged by Tipu (1785), *id.* 660; ceded to the Peshwa by Tipu, retaken by the Mysore troops (1787), *id.* 661; state founded by two Lingáyat brothers Malla and Chakka, revolt and capture (1824), *id.* 668-670.
Kiu-che-Lo: Northern Gurjjara kingdom (A. D. 620), I, pt. i, 3; Chinese form of Gurjjara, *id.* 466, 489; *see* also IX, pt. i, 479.
Kiwani: fibrous plant, XXV, 229.
Klaudios Ptolemaios: of Alexandria (161-180), Roman traveller, his geography of India, I, pt. i, 537.
Knot-printing: industry in Káthiáwár, VIII, 258-259.
Koa: Kábul river, I, pt. i, 537.
Koari or Koarigad: fort in Poona district, details and history of, reduced by Malik Ahmad (1486), captured by the British (1818), XVIII, pt. iii, 243; *id.* pt. ii, 303; I, pt. ii, 32.

Kocharem : *see* Kochrem.
Kochchnraka : *see* Kochra.
Kochharva : goddess in Asával, I, pt. i, 170.
Kochin : town on Malabár Coast, Thána trade with (1500-1670, 1660-1710), XIII, 465, 486 ; *see* also I, pt. i, 533.
Kochra, Kochrem, Kocharem or Kocheburaka : village in Ratnágiri district, mentioned in a grant (A. D. 600), X, 192 note 4, 439 note 1 ; *see* also I, pt. ii, 185, 363, 366.
Kod : sub-division of Dhárwár district, details, boundaries, area, aspect, soil, hills, climate, water, stock, crops, people, XXII, 640-642 ; survey of, *id.* 512-517, 559-568 ; *see* also I, pt. ii, 460 note 3, 504, 563 ; village, *id.* 765.
Kod, Koda : ancient tribe in Northern India, settled at Sopára (A. D. 150), XIII, 409 and note 1 ; their relation with the Kol aud Goud tribes of Central India, *id.* 730 ; mentioned in Sopára cave, XIV, 325, 341, 414, 415, 416.
Kodagus : Coorgs, tribe in Mysore, XV, pt. ii, 79.
Kodárgudda : cape in Kánara district, XV, pt. i, 2.
Kodibág : timber store in Kánara district, XV, pt. ii, 61, 325.
Kodikop : village in the Dhárwár district, records at, I, pt. ii, 457, 573, 574, 575.
Kodinár : town and parganah in Káthiáwár, VII, 518-520 ; temple of Ambika at, I, pt. i, 182 and note 1 ; Mula Dwárka, Aryans settle at, IX, pt. i, p. xi.
Kodkani : village in Kánara district, XV, pt. ii, 325. *See* Gersappa.
Kodmagi : village in Dhárwár district, temples and inscriptions at, XXII, 765.
Kodoli : village in Kolhápur state, weaving industry, temples and fair at, XXIV, 303.
Kodra, Kodri : food plant, grown in Konkan, XXV, 184 ; produces poisonous effects, *id.* 270.
Kodrana : town mentioned by Ptolemy, I, pt. i, 538.
Kodroa-kora : fodder plant, XXV, 276.
Kodukolli : village near Conjevaram, I, pt. ii, 325.
Koel : *see* Cuckoo.
Kohala : sacred plant, its worship, XXV, 279, 285.
Kohat : town mentioned by Ptolemy, I, pt. i, 538.
Kohistán : hills of, last *kabisa* performed at, IX, pt. ii, 193 note 2.
Kohoj : hill in Thána district, XIII, 7.
Koili : village in Káthiáwár, Tarnetar monastery at, history of, VIII, 517-518.
Koina : *see* Koyna.
Koiri : rocks in Poona district, XVIII, pt. i, 4.
Koistel : oil-yielding plant, XXV, 214.
Koj : fort in Thána district, XIV, 98, 201.
Kokalla or Kokkala I : Kalachuri prince of the Western branch of Chedi dynasty, gives his daughter in marriage to the Ráshtrakúta king Krishna II, I, pt. ii, 201, 203, 240, 296, 380, 410, 415.
Kokalmir : in Central India, Mher settlement at, I, pt. i, 136.
Kokam : Indian mangosteem, dye-yielding plant, XXV, 241 ; grows in Ratnágiri, X, 37, 39.
Kokamthán : village in Ahmadnagar district, temple at, XVII, 722.
Kokanasth : a sub-caste of Bráhmans. *See* Chitpávan.
Kokangaon : village in Ahmadnagar district, temple at, XVII, 723.
Kokatnur : village in Belgaum district, temple and fair at, XXI, 582 ; grant from, I, pt. ii, 468-469.
Kokir : a casto of Christian masons in Ratnágiri district, X, 31.
Kokkala, Kokkalla, Kokkalla I : *see* Kokalla.
Kokna : a caste of husbandmen in Kánara district, XV, pt. i, 221-224.
Kol : town, perhaps in Cutch, I, pt. i, 519 and note 4, 520.
Kol : village in Ratnágiri district, rock temples at, X, 344.
Kol : village in Kolába district, caves at, XI, 349 ; *see* also I, pt. ii, 12.
Kolába : fort near Alibag, history of, XI, 260-265 ; I, pt. ii, 39 ; fort rebuilt by Shiváji, *id.* 68 ; Shiváji's former naval head-quarters, *id.* 75 ; Ángria's principal place of arms, *id.* 79 ; invested by Sidis (1701), XXVI, pt. i, 133 ; state lapses to the British Government (1840), I, pt. ii, 129.
Kolába District : description : boundaries, sub-divisions, aspect, hills, rivers, reservoirs, geology, hot springs, climate, XI, 1-15 ; production : forests and forest produce, creepers, liquor-yielding trees, domestic animals, wild animls, birds, fish, *id.* 16-39 ; population : census details, Bráhmans, writers, merchants, husbandmen, craftsmen, shepherds, fishers, unsettled tribes, depressed classes, beggars, Musalmáns, communities, *id.* 40-88 ; agriculture : soil, salt lands, irrigation, field tools, crops, bad seasons, *id.* 89-100 ; capital : currency, exchange bills, money-lenders, interest, borrowers, land-mortgage, wages, prices, weights and measures, *id.* 101-110 ; trade : roads, passes, bridges, ferries, rest-houses, trade centres, imports, exports, vessels, ports, crafts, copper and brass work, palm-tapping, salt making, *id.* 111-135 ; history : early history, local rulers (A. D. 100), Mauryas (500), Siláháras (810-1260), Yadavs (1200-1300), Vijayanagar kings (1377), *id.* 136-142 ; Musalmáns : the Bahámanis (1347-1489), Gujarát kings (1509), the Portuguese (1507-1660), the Mughals, Bijápur, the Maráthás (1650-1690), the Ángrias (1690-1840), Kanhoji Ángria (1690-1731), Manaji Ángria (1733-1759), Raghoji (1759-1793), Manaji Ángria (1793-1817), the British (1818-1882), *id.* 136-158 ; land administration : staff, sub-divisional officers, village servants ; tenures ; *khots*, Shilotridárs, history : early Hindus, Malik Ambar, the Maráthás, the British, assessment revision (1837), survey (1837-1857), Nagothna *khoti* system (1860) ; season reports (1868-1881), *id.* 159-214 ; justice : under Ángrias (1814-1840), judicial staff

(1853-1882), debtors, magistracy, police, *id.* 215-221; revenue and finance: land revenue, excise, forests, etc., balance sheets (1852-53 and 1880-81), local funds, municipalities, *id.* 222-229; instruction, private schools, girls' schools, school returns, town schools, village schools, libraries and newspapers, *id.* 230-235; health: climate, diseases, infirmities, cattle diseases, births and deaths, *id.* 236-239; *sub-divisional details*, *id.* 240-252; places of interest, *id.* 253-398; district surveyed and assessed in grain (1784-85), I, pt. ii, 109, 282 note 5, 298 note 2, 537, 543; caves in, *id.* 9.

Koláhala: king, founder of the city of Koláhalapura, I, pt. ii, 297, 340 note 3.

Koláhalapura: modern Kolár in Mysore, I, pt. ii, 297.

Kolai: village in Thána district, XIV, 202.

Kolak: river in Broach district, II, 27.

Kolaka: town north of the western mouth of the Indus, I, pt. i, 538.

Kolála: *see* Kolar.

Kolálapura: town taken by Vishnuvardhana, I, pt. ii, 496.

Kolam or Bháti: pass between Thána and Poona districts, XIII, 321, XVIII, pt. ii, 152.

Kolambapattana: probably modern Quilon, I, pt. i, 183 note 1.

Kolambi: variety of honey bee in Kolhápur state, XXIV, 24.

Kolápoor: Kolhápur city, I, pt. ii, 538 note 8.

Kolár or Koláia: town in Mysore, I, pt. ii, 297, 298, 300; fortress at, *id.* 496.

Kolara: fodder plant, XXV, 276.

Koláramma: inscription at the temple of, at Kolar, I, pt. ii, 297.

Koláti: *see* Kolháti.

Kole: village in Sátára district, fair at, XIX, 486.

Koledhair: fort in Násik district, XVI, 441, 449.

Kolenuru: province, I, pt. ii, 465.

Kolgaon: town in Ahmadnagar district, temple at, XVII, 723.

Kolghás: early tribe in Gujarát, IX, pt. i, 320-321.

Kolhápur: state, sub-divisions boundaries, physical aspect, hills and rivers, XXIV, 1-12; geology and climate, *id.* 13-17; mineral products, forests, forest administration, forest produce, *id.* 18-25; domestic and wild animals, snakes, fish and birds, *id.* 25-34; census details, communities, *id.* 35-42; Bráhmans, fighting classes, husbandmen, crafts, servants, shepherds, labourers and depressed classes, *id.* 42-115; beggars, Lingáyats and Jains, *id.* 115-146; Musalmáns and Christians, *id.* 147-152; agriculture, holdings, stock, soil, crops, field tools, manure, irrigation, crop details, famines, *id.* 153-191; currency, bills, land-mortgage, weights and measures, prices, *id.* 192-197; trade: roads, passes, ferries, post and telegraph, trade centres, fairs, imports and exports, *id.* 198-207; crafts, *id.* 207-217; history: early history, Siláháras (1050-1120), Musalmán period (1347-1700), Maráthás, Shiváji II (1700-1712), Sambhaji II (1712-1760), Shiváji III (1760-1812), Shambhu (1812-1821), Sháhaji (1821-1837), Shiváji IV (1837-1866), Rájárám (1866-1870), Shiváji V (1870-1883), Sháhu (the present *rája*), *id.* 218-246; land administration, revenue history (1867-1884), survey (1869-1882), season reports, *id.* 247-265; administration of justice, *panchâyats*, changes since 1845, civil courts and suits, magistracy, police and jails, *id.* 266-277; finance, *id.* 278-280; schools, libraries and newspapers, *id.* 281-284: health: diseases, epidemics, hospitals, births and deaths, *id.* 285-289; places of interest, *id.* 290-323; mention of, I, pt. ii, 390, 544; "Introduction to the Early History of the Deccan," *id.* p. iv; districts of, *id.* 254; Lingáyats in, *id.* 478; Sháhu's war in (1709), XIX, 254; partition treaty with (1730), *id.* 273; the state, at war with Sátára, XXI, 379-380; power, *id.* 390-391; risings in (1844), *id.* 407-408; *city*, origin of the name of, XXIV, 1; old historic place, *id.* 218, 306; see of Dheguji Meghuji, *id.* 114; town details, area and boundaries, aspect, climate, water-supply, *id.* 303-305; history, *id.* 306-308; municipality, schools, *id.* 309; temples, Ambábai's, *id.* 310; Vithoba's, Temblai's, *id.* 311; Mahákáli's, Phirangái's, Ellamma's underground shrines, monasteries, *id.* 311-312; coins with the names of princes on, found at, I, pt. ii, 152, 158, 161, 166, 167; flourishing inland town under the Andhrabhrityas or Satavábanas, *id.* 175, 176; Jayasimha II the Western Chalukya king's camp at, *id.* 214, 436; Siláhára dynasty of, *id.* 253-257; probably Tagarapura, *id.* 538 and note 8; chief of, filled with fear at the success of Sidhrája (1094-1143), *id.* 24; replaces the dethroned kings of Thána (1151), *id.* 25; won over by Vijjana, *id.* 222, 475; Vijjana's expedition to, *id.* 227, 481; Siláhára chief of, places idols of Buddha, Śiva and Arhat on the margin of a tank at, *id.* 228; annexation to the Yádava dominions of the kingdom of, *id.* 240, 524; inscription at, *id.* 224, 240, 467, 523, 524, 527, 529, 549; temple of Mahálakshmi at, *id.* 546; devastated by the Mughals (1636), *id.* 650; Tárábái established at (1710), *id.* 81; *rája* of, attacks the possessions of the Patvardhan family and levies tribute as far south as Kittur; is defeated near Sávanur by the *sar-subhadár*, *id.* 662; fights with Sávantwádi, *id.* 112, 663; peace with the *rája* of (1800), *id.* 608; Gotamiputra Shatkarni's coins found at, XIV, 148; Kumárapála's visit to, I, pt. i, 183.

Kolhápur Rájás: genealogy of, XXIV, 246.

Kolhápur Siláhárás: (1055-1125), XXI, 218-223; family tree, *id.* 220.

Kolhár: town in Ahmadnagar district, fair at, XVII, 725.

Kolhati or Kolati: caste of tumblers, in Ahmadnagar district, XVII, 180-181; in Belgaum, XXI, 169-170; in Násik, XVI, 54;

in Khándesh, XII, 123; in Thána, XIII, 199; in Poona, XVIII, pt. i, 457-459; in Sátára, XIX, 119-120; in Sholápur, XX, 186-187. *See* also Dombári.

Koli: strength and distribution, IX, pt. i, 237; meaning of name, *id.* 237 and note 1, 455 note 2; origin, said to be aboriginals of plains or civilised Bhils; said to be of same stock as Rájpúts, *id.* 237 and note 2; said to be Mehiras or Mehrs, that is Gujars, *id.* 237-238, 455 and note 2, 499; intermediate layer between Ujli Varan and Káli Paraj races, *id.* p. x; lower classes of Musalmán prisoners allotted to the caste of, *id.* 444; Rájpút marriages with, *id.* 238 and note 2, 239 and note 1; list of Rájpút Koli Thákardás or lordlings of Northern Gujarát, *id.* p. x, 238 and note 2; main divisions of, distribution, sub-divisions, *id.* 239 and note 2; appearance, house, dress, *id.* 245; food, *id.* 246; occupation—robbers and thieves, Surat Talabdás as husbandmen, other pursuits, *id.* 246-247; religion, goddess-worship, animal-worship, followers of various sects, their places of pilgrimage, *id.* 247; customs, birth, *chhathi* worship, *id.* 248; marriage, four forms of, ceremonies in, *id.* 248-250; divorce, polygamy, *id.* 250; death, social position, *id.* 251; sailors and fishers, *id.* 519, 523-524.

Bária: origin and history, *id.* 244.

Chunváliyás: also called Jahángriás, name, sub-divisions, wild race, once the terror of Gujarát, body of organised plunderers, in revolt. (A. D. 1819 and 1825), *id.* 239 and notes 3 to 5, 240 and note 1.

Dalvádis: properly Talváris, look like Kanbis, *id.* 244.

Gediyás: considered highest tribe of Kolis, *id.* 244-245.

Khánts: borderers, wild tribe, their chiefs known as Mer, their early leaders Dháudh Khánt, Pátal Khánt, Jesa or Jesing, their achievements, *id.* 240 and notes 2 to 4, 241 and note 1.

Pátanvádiyás: meaning of name, *id.* 241 and note 2; high spirited and daring tribe, successful soldiers and robbers by land and sea, *id.* 241; successes by land (A. D. 1535 and 1705); expeditions and victories by sea in early years as pirates in the Gulf of Cambay, their reputation as skilled and daring seamen, *id.* 241 note 3; worst points, Mahi Kántha Kolis hired to commit burglaries in Surat, *id.* 242 and note 3; good points, *id.* 242 and note 4; Bishop Herber's description of, *id.* 242-243; attempts to plunder in Kaira (A. D. 1832-1835) peaceful husbandmen, *id.* 243.

Shiáls: once noted pirates, *id.* 245.

Talabdás: also called Dharálás, meaning of name, their origin, *id.* p. x, 243 and notes 2 and 3; Rájpút marriages with; sub-divisions, *id.* 243 and note 4; peaceful husbandmen, Colonel William's description of, *id.* 244.

Valákiyás: strain of Bhil blood in, *id.* 245 and note 1; *see* also I, pt. ii, 125; give trouble in North Konkan, *id.* 127; partizans of early Gáikwárs, VII, 171, 174; raise a rebellion, I, pt. i, 138; in Kaira district, III, 32; in Cutch, V, 70; in Pálanpur, *id.* 289, 290, 292; in Mahi Kántha, *id.* 364; in Rewa Kántha, VI, 32-33; in Cambay, *id.* 189; in Káthiáwár, VIII, 139-142; in Ratnágiri district, X, 127, 128, 131, 171; in Kolába district, XI, 68-70, 414; garrison of Janjira (1490), *id.*, 434; in Khándesh district, XII, 79; in Thána district, XIII, 165-174; dialect of, *id.* 68, 69 note 1; origin of the word, *id.* 165 note 3; in Kánara district, XV, pt. i, 311; in Násik district, XVI, 21, 26; corps of, *id.* 200, 204; village watchmen (1882), *id.* 207, 314-315; in Ahmadnagar district, divisions, houses, food, dress, calling, condition, beliefs, customs, XVII, 193-208; risings (1760-1798), *id.* 404-406; (1828), *id.* 416-417; corps (1858), *id.* 419; in Poona district, XVIII, pt. i, 389-393; their condition under Bahmani rule (1347-1490), XVIII, pt. ii, 218; their risings (1657), *id.* 227-228; (1839-1844), *id.* 307-308; XVIII, pt. iii, 38-39; in Sátára district, XIX, 106; in Sholápur district, XX, 152-157; in Belgaum district, XXI, 157-158; in Kolhápur state, XXIV, 106-107.

Koli Kalyan: village in Thána district, XIV, 202.

Koli Khaláti: petty division in Thána, XIII, 578.

Koli rájás: I, pt. ii, 30, 70; XVII, 353-354.

Koli Thákardas: *see* Thákardás.

Kolla, Kollagiri: Quilon, I, pt. ii, 341 note 2; country, ruled over by Vishnuvardhana, *id.* 499; *see* also *id.* 497 and note 2.

Kollápura: ancient name of Kolhápur, I, pt. ii, 538. *see* Kolhápur.

Kollipáke: unidentified place, I, pt. ii, 437 and note 6.

Kólmándla: town in Janjira state, XI, 464.

Kolsinda, Kolsunda: wild dogs in Ratnágiri district, X, 45; in Thána district, XIII, 45 and note 3; in Kolhápur state, XXIV, 32.

Kolur: village in Dhárwár district, temple, inscriptions at, XXII, 765.

Kolvan: sub-division of Thána, XIII, 585-586, 588; survey assessment introduced (1865), *id.* 616-619; styled Shahapur (1866), *id.* 528.

Kolvo: Cháran *bhagat* of Dwárka, IX, pt. i, 220.

Komála: village in Kolába district, ceded to the British (1756), XI, 159.

Komárpáik: a caste of husbandmen in Kánara district, XV, pt. i, 288-293; XV, pt. ii, 2.

Komkam: Konkan, I, pt. ii, 3.

Komti, Komtig: caste of traders, in Kolába district, XI, 48; in Násik district, XVI, 59; in Ahmadnagar district, XVII, 69-71; in Poona district, XVIII, pt. i, 270; in Sátára district, XIX, 58-59; in Sholápur district, settlement, divisions, appearance, house, food, dress, calling, condition, religion, customs, community, XX, 52-75; in Belgaum district, XXI, 104; in Dhárwár district, XXII, 130-131; in Bijápur district, XXIII, 118-121; in Kolhápur state, XXIV, 86, 87; in Kánara district, XV, pt. i, 189, 190.

Konagal: village in the Southern Marátha Country, battle of (1800), I, pt. ii, 663.

Konay : stream in Kánara district, iron bridge on, XV, pt. ii, 43.
Konay : light-house in Kánara district, XV, pt. ii, 47.
Kondáji Náik : a Rámoshi free-booter (1827), XIII, 634-635.
Kondal : Gondal, I, pt. i, 517.
Kondali : *see* Gondali.
Kondána : *see* Kondhána.
Kondáne : village in Thána district, caves at, XIV, 208, 210 ; *see* also I, pt. ii, 9.
Kondhána or Kondana : modern Sinhgad fort, XVIII, pt. ii, 215 ; captured (1647) by Shiváji, *id.* 226, 591.
Kondivti : hot-springs at, in Kolába district, XI, 13.
Kondivti or Kondivte caves : in Thána district, XIV, 10, 202-208, 381 ; I, pt. ii, 9, 27.
Kondli : village in Kánara district, XV, pt. ii, 45, 325.
Kongali : in the Gangavádi province, fortress at, I, pt. ii, 496.
Kongalnád : district, I, pt. ii, 303.
Konganivarman : alleged founder of the Western Ganga dynasty, I, pt. ii, 301 note 1.
Kongas : slain by Vishnuvardhana, I, pt. ii, 496.
Konger : a warlike class in Kánara district, XV, pt. i, 197, 198.
Kongnoli : town in Belgaum district, XXI, 581.
Kongu : territory, I, pt. ii, 298 ; fortress at, *id.* 496 ; country, ruled over by Vishnuvardhana, *id.* 499, 501, 505.
Kongudesa Rájákkal : Tamil chronicle published by Mr. Rice, I, pt. ii, 300, 301 note 1.
Konherráo Patvardhan : Peshwa's general defeated by Haidar (1776), I, pt. ii, 659.
Konkan : its boundaries and divisions into Tal-Konkan and Ghát-Mátha, "Introduction to the History of the Konkan," I, pt. ii, p. ix ; climate, aspect, and people, *id.* pp. x-xii ; tradition of its creation, *id.* 26 ; extent of, and territories included in its ancient divisions ; its seven divisions, *id.* 282 note 5, 298 note 2 ; its earliest mention, *id.* 1 ; its various spellings, *id.* 3 ; Mauryas of, *id.* 541 ; were dispossessed of, by the Western Chalukya king Kirtivarman I (566-598), *id.* 282, 335, 336 ; Satyásraya-Dhruvarája Indravarman appointed governor of (590), *id.* 345 ; overwhelmed by Pulikeśin II (609-642), *id.* 283, 350 ; Southern Konkan was acquired by Sanaphulla Síláhára under the Ráshtrakúta king Krishna I (754-782), *id.* 537 ; under the Ráshtrakútas and Western Chálukyas, *id.* 26 ; conquered by the Chola king Rájarájadeva, *id.* 308 ; passed into the hands of the Síláháras of North Konkan (1017), *id.* 538 ; Síláháras of North Konkan rule the whole Konkan as feudatories of the Western Chálukyas, *id.* 436, 439, 450, 498 ; some portion of North Konkan held by the Karád Síláhára king Gonka (1040-1050), *id.* 546-547 ; Konkan nine-hundred or Goa territory identified with Revatidvipa, *id.* 347 note 2 ; is wrested from the Síláháras of North Konkan by Kádamba Jayakeśin I (1051), *id.* 566, 567 ; under the Kolhápur or Karád Síláhára prince Gandaráditya, *id.* 255, 547 ; Síláhára princes of North Konkan reinstated by the Karád Síláhára prince Vijayaditya (1143-1153), *id.* 548 ; North Konkan invaded and included among his eighteen districts by Kumárpál of Anahilaváda, *id.* 24 ; subjugated by the Hángal Kádamba Kámadeva, *id.* 563 ; Síláháras of, become independent, *id.* 544 ; Goa Kádambas become independent in, *id.* 476, 486, 568 ; seized upon by the Sinda prince Áchugi II, *id.* 219, 574 ; Goa Kádambas are defeated in, by Áchugi II's son Permádi I, *id.* 569, 575 ; some success obtained in, by the Devagiri Yádava king Krishna, *id.* 246, 527 ; annexed to the kingdom of the Devagiri Yádavas, *id.* 247, 528 ; Devagiri Yádava governors appointed in, *id.* 25, 529-530 ; under Devagiri Yádavas, *id.* 26, 29 ; Mubárik I (1318) extends his garrison to, *id.* 29 ; North, reduced by Ahmad Sháh, *id.* 30 ; its invasion by the Bahamani king Alá-ud-din II, *id.* 31 ; district, put under Junnar, *id.* 32 ; its division between Ahmadnagar and Bijápur and government by Gujarát, *id.* 33 ; transfers of its Ahmadnagar portion to Bijápur (1636), over-running of its northern part by Sháhji Bhonsla, and its survey, *id.* 38 ; its administrative divisions and government by Bijápur, *id.* 39 ; North, passed to the Mughals (1572), and held by the Portuguese, *id.* 40 ; military establishment in, *id.* 54 ; attains its highest importance under Shiváji, *id.* 67 ; Shiváji extends his power to (1648), *id.* 67 ; Southern, its three powers, *id.* 68 ; Northern, suffers from the armies of the Mughals (1684), *id.* 77 ; its condition during the twenty-seven years which elapsed between the deaths of Shiváji and Aurangzeb, *id.* 81 ; its inclusion in the Marátha *svaráj* (1720) and its division between Rájárám and Sháhu, *id.* 82 ; condition of, *id.* 97-99, its management under the last Peshwa, *id.* 113 ; North, ceded to the English (1817), *id.* 115 ; its condition in 1818, *id.* 125 ; Southern, its condition in 1818, *id.* 125, 126 ; military force in, *id.* 127, 128 ; North and South, joined together (1830), *id.* 128 ; its future, *id.* 131. *Another account of :* Aśoka sends a Buddhist preacher to (B. C. 225), XIII, 405-406, 407 ; enriched by Western trade (B. C. 100), *id.* 409-410 and note 5 ; Andhrás driven from (A. D. 1-100), *id.* 411 ; conquered by Gautamiputra (A. D. 124), *id.* 412 ; known to the Greeks (135), *id.* 414 ; Ptolemy's mention of, *id.* 415 ; recovered by the Kshatraps (178), *id.* 417 ; places in, mentioned in the *Periplus*, *id.* 418 ; ruled over by the Síláháras (810-1260), *id.* 421-422 ; Ráshtrakútas of Malkhed overlords of (700-900), *id.* 434 ; over-run by a Marátha impostor (1776), *id.* 502 ; Goddard's operations in (1778-1781), *id.* 506 ; *see* also I, pt. i, 5 note 1, 524, 527, 528, 534 ; I, pt. ii, 310, 412, 452, 456, 460.
Konkanapura : I, pt. ii, 353 note 2.
Konkanasth : a sub-caste of Bráhmans ; *see* Chitpávan.

Konkani : a wandering tribe, in Khándesh district, XII, 105 ; in Thána district, XIII, 174-175 ; in Násik district, XVI, 47.

Konkanig Bráhman : *see* Sásashtakár Bráhman.

Konkani Madival : a caste of washermen in Kánara district, XV, pt. i, 327, 328.

Konkani Musalmán : tribe, descendants of Arab settlers, I, pt. ii, 7 ; in Ratnágiri district, immigrants from Persia (700), X, 104, 132, 171 ; in Thána, XIII, 64, 232-234 ; in Kolába district, XI, 81-83 ; in Janjira state, *id.* 419 ; in Násik district, XVI, 77.

Konkan Kelasi : a caste of barbers, in Kánara district, XV, pt. i, 330.

Konkan Khárvi : a caste of fishermen in Kánara district, XV, pt. i, 310, 311.

Konkan Kumbár : a caste of potters in Kánara district, XV, pt. i, 270, 271.

Konkan Kunbi : a class of husbandmen in Kánara district, XV, pt. i, 216, 220.

Konkans : the Seven, XV, pt. ii, 75 note 4, 86 ; *see* Konkan.

Konkan-Tana or Thána : its various spellings, I, pt. ii, 3 ; part of Gujarát, *id.* 25.

Konknás : early tribe in Gujarát, IX, pt. i, p. x, 290, 321-322.

Konkner : village in Thána district, hot-springs at, XIII, 15.

Konkonga : country, surrendered to Vishnuvardhana, I, pt. ii, 496.

Konnur : village in Belgaum district, cell tombs at, XXI, 582-584 ; I, pt. ii, 431 ; inscription at, *id.* 286 note 1, 406 note 4, 553, 554, 555.

Konnur : village in Dhárwár district, temple at, XXII, 765.

Konvalli : village on the south bank of the Mahi, I, pt. i, 127.

Kopál : captured by Haidar, I, pt. ii, 659 ; taken by the Nizám's troops (1790), *id.* 662.

Ko-Parakesarivarman : another name of Rájendrachola, I, pt. ii, 341 note 2.

Kopargaon : sub-division in Ahmadnagar district, details, area, aspect, soil, rivers, water-supply, rainfall, cultivation, crop, people, roads, railway, markets and survey changes, XVII, 602-607. *Town,* Raghunáthráv Peshwa's palace and cenotaph and temple at, *id.* 723, 724 ; Raghunáthráv's place of residence after the treaty of Sálbái in 1782 ; his death at, I, pt. ii, 628 ; scene of the treacherous murders of Bhils by Báláji Lakshman, *id.* 629 ; *see* also I, pt. i, 410 ; XVIII, pt. ii, 267.

Kopineshvar : temple of, in Thána town, XIV, 346, 354.

Koppa : on the river Tungá, I, pt. ii, 441. *See* Koppam.

Koppal : in the Nizám's dominions, I, pt. ii, 501.

Koppam : on the Perárn river, Western Chalukya king Someśvara I conquered by the Chola king Rájendradeva at, I, pt. ii, 441.

Koppana : town, capital of Someshvar Sovideva, I, pt. ii, 486.

Koppeśvara : grant of a village to the temple of, I, pt. ii, 240.

Koprad : village in Thána district, inscriptions at, XIV, 210, 342.

Koptos : town on the Nile, I, pt. i, 535, 536.

Kora : *see* Kongni.

Kora : village in Cutch, II, 228.

Ko-Rájarája-Rájakesarivarman : Chola king, Irivahedanga-Satyáśraya's opponent, I, pt. ii, 341 note 2, 433. *See* Nurmadi-Chola, Rájarája-deva, Rajendra.

Kora kong : fodder plant, XXV, 276.

Koral : parganah, ceded to the British by the Gáikwár (1775), the cession confirmed (1779), VII, 194, 195 ; town on the north bank of the Narmada, I, pt. ii, 314.

Korál : gorge in Sátára district, XIX, 203.

Koral : food plant, XXV, 292.

Koranhatti : village in Dhárwár district, old weir at, XXII, 765.

Korár : a depressed class, in Kánara district, XV, pt. i, 370, 371 ; in Dhárwár district, XXII, 194-195.

Korav : a caste of musicians in Kánara district, XV, pt. i, 319.

Korchar, *pl.* Korcharn : a caste of labourers, in Belgaum district, XXI, 172, 173 ; in Kánara district, XV, pt. i, 336-338 ; in Bijápur district, XXIII, 201-202.

Koregaon : village in Ahmadnagar district, temples at, XVII, 724.

Koregaon : village in Poona district, battle (1818), obelisk, inscription, XVIII, pt. iii, 244-247. *See* also I, pt. ii, 611 ; XVIII, pt. ii, 302.

Koregaon : sub-division in Sátára district, details of, XIX, 432-434 ; survey of, *id.* 359-362. *Town, id.* 486-487.

Koregaon : village in Sholápur district, XX, 413 ; lake at, *id.* 222.

Korhala : old town in Ahmadnagar district, XVII, 724.

Kori : eastern mouth of the Indus in Cutch, V, 9, 10, 145. *See* also I, pt. i, 538.

Kori : a coin in Cutch, V, 111.

Korılla : modern Koral on the Narmada, I, pt. ii, 314.

Koriya : Kánarese dialect, spoken at Malked and Haidarábád (900), XIII, 67.

Korlai : island fort in Kolába district, description and history of, XI, 328-332 ; rock of, I, pt. ii, 38 ; the name Il Morro given by the Portuguese and other Europeans to, attempts to build a fort on, capture of (1594), *id.* 50 ; artillery at, *id.* 55 ; Portuguese fort at, *id.* 66.

Kormar, *pl.* Kormaru : a caste of carriers in Kánara district, XV, pt. i, 338.

Korondi : pass in Poona district, XVIII, pt. ii, 153.

Korrud : fodder plant, found in Southern Marátha Country, XXV, 276.

Kors : second name of the tribe of Kushans, IX, pt. i, 470, 471 ; subordinate traders of Sind, Khatri caste, seem more likely to be Lohánás or Bhátiás, *id.* 491.

Korti : old sub-division in Ahmadnagar district, survey of, XVII, 515-520.

Korvi : caste of musicians, in Belgaum district, XXI, 170-172 ; in Bijápur district, XXIII, 202-205 ; in Kolhápur state, XXIV, 31, 108.

Kosád: village in Surat district, I, pt. i, 128, I, pt. ii, 412.
Kosala: country, mentioned by Pánini, I, pt. ii, 138; its position assigned in the *Purdnas, id.* 139; king of, surrenders himself to Pulakeśi II, *id.* 183; king of, subdued by Dantidurga, *id.* 194, 389; umbrella of the king of, carried away by Dhruva, *id.* 197; kingdom of, *id.* 403 note 3.
Kosalas: people or nation of Kosala, I, pt. i, 469; I, pt. ii, 282, 350.
Kosam: town near Allahábád, I, pt. ii, 197.
Koshti: a caste weavers, in Ratnágiri district, X, 125; in Sávantvádi, *id.* 415; in Khándesh district, XII, 76; in Thána district, XIII, 133; in Násik district, XVI, 53; in Ahmadnagar district, XVII, 112-114; in Poona district, XVIII, pt. i, 347-349; in Sátára district, XIX, 85-86; in Sholápur district, XX, 119; in Dhárwár district, XXII, 172-178; in Bijápur district, XXIII, 245-247; in Kolhápur state, XXIV, 95.
Koshusaruh: part of the *Zend Avesta*, IX, pt. ii, 211 note 2 (10).
Kosmas Indikopleustes: Greek merchant and monk, author of *Topographia Christiana* (530-550), I, pt. i, 547; Persians the chief traders in India, IX, pt. ii, 183 note 4 continued on page 184; his description of Kalyán as the centre of trade and the seat of a king, Nestorian Christians at, XIII, 200, 419, 420; his notice of Sibor (Chembur or Sopára), XI, 270; *see* also XIV, 52, 119, 320; Persian horses imported into Kánara ports (535), XV, pt. ii, 49.
Kostus: *see* Putchuk.
Kot: sub-caste of Bráhmans in Kánara, XV, pt. i, 133.
Kota: village in Káthiáwár, VIII, 520.
Kota: cow-killing tribe on Nilgiris, IX, pt. i, 469 note 1.
Kotai: village in Cutch, the temple of the sun at, V, 228-229.
Kotaligad: fort in Thána district, history of, XIV, 98, 210; caves at, *id.* 10; see also XIII, 522, 523.
Kotegár: a depressed class, in Kánara district, XV, pt. i, 371-373; in Dhárwár district, XXII, 217-218.
Koteshvar: a small seaport in Cutch, temples at, V, 229-231.
Koteyur: village in ancient Belvola country, I, pt. ii, 421.
Kothal: village in Ahmadnagar district, temple at, XVII, 724-725.
Kothára: town in Cutch, temple of Shantináth at, V, 231-232.
Kothi: river in Násik district, XVI, 11.
Kothia: sailing vessel in Thána district, XIII, 349-350, 719.
Kothligad: fort in Koláha district, XI, 151.
Kothlisánt: money payment to landholders as compensation, VII, 352.
Kothulmukunji: village in Ahmadnagar district, temples at, XVII, 725.
Kothur: village in Násik district, temple at, XVI, 449.
Kotieba: Arab commander, checks Chinese advance (709), I, pt. i, 501.
Kotipur: village in Gujarát, temple of the sun at, I, pt. i, 126; I, pt. ii, 404.
Kotl-tirth: Gokarn pool, XV, pt. ii, 292 and note 2.
Kotra or Kotra Sángáni: town and petty state in Káthiáwár, family tree of its chief, its history, VIII, 520-523; pays tribute to the Gáikwár (1784, 1785, 1786), VII, 317.
Kotri: táluka in Káthiáwár, VIII, 523.
Kotta Harivatsa: Jayasimha described as the chastiser of, I, pt. ii, 386.
Kotta Mandala: Aprameya described as the lord of, I, pt. ii, 491.
Kottatti: in Mysore, inscription at, I, pt. ii, 307 note 7.
Kotul: town in Ahmadnagar district, XVII, 725
Kotumachgi: village in Dhárwár district, temple and inscriptions at, XXII, 765.
Kotumba: boats in Broach, mentioned in the *Periplus*, I, pt. i, 545.
Kotur: inscription at, I, pt. ii, 380.
Kot Vakkal: a caste of husbandmen in Kánara district, XV, pt. i, 228, 229.
Kotvál: Mhár village servant in Thána (1828), XIII, 574; city police inspector, I, pt. i, 214.
Kotvál Chávdi: old police office, in Poona city, XVIII, pt. iii, 337.
Kotyarkeshvar: of Khadát Mahudi, family deity of Khadáyatás, IX, pt. i, 72.
Kouresch: miswriting for Harsha, IX, pt. i, 444 note 4.
Kovaiya: táluka in Káthiáwár, VIII, 523.
Kovaláka: capital of the Ganga kings, I, pt. ii, 298, 303 and note 3. *See* Kolábalapura.
Kovatur: modern Coimbatore, uprooted by Vishnuvardhana, I, pt. ii, 496.
Kowta: gum-yielding plant, XXV, 250.
Kowti-oil: *see* Koistel.
Koyatur: modern Coimbatore, fortress at, I, pt. ii, 496.
Koyimuttur: modern Coimbatore, I, pt. ii, 496.
Koyna: river in Sátára district, XIX, 15; *see* also I, pt. ii, 546; its confluence with the Krishna, *id.* 142.
Koyta: sickle assessment in Thána district, XIII, 565.
Kozolakadaphes: Indo-Skythian king, I, pt. i, 536.
Kraknchchhanda: fourth Buddha, image of, at Sopára, XIV, 331, 413.
Kramvant: a caste of Bráhmans, in Koláha district, XI, 45; in Thána district, XIII, 79; in Ratnágiri district, X, 115.
Krankoch: village in Káthiáwár, temple of Kodiar Máta at, VIII, 523.
Kriat: *see* Karyat.
Krishna: incarnation of Vishnu, IX, pt. i, p. xxxvi, 530; as philosopher and expounder of the eclectic school, *id.* 532; worshipped by Vallabhácháris, *id.* 535; hero of the *Mahábhárata*, *id.* 531; peacock his favourite bird, *id.* 381; *kadamb* tree sacred to, *id.* 384; offerings of flowers to, *id.* 409; said to be born in Bad-Gujars, *id.* 482; his defeat in Dwárka, his people retired west and north to Gajni and Samarkand after his defeat, *id.* 446 note 4; Kanaksen sit on the throne of, at Dwárka, *id.* 4, 9, 10, 462; mythic king

of Dwárka, account of, as given in *Bhágavat Purána*, VIII, 267-272; legendary connection of, with Dwárika, I, pt. i, 8-11; his image at Verával, *id.* 81; claimed by the Chudásamás as their ancestor, *id.* 139, 178; builds the Somanátha temple, *id.* 190; claimed by Gurjjaras as their ancestor, *id.* 464; see also I, pt. ii, 142, 343 note 5, 490, 517.

Krishna: king of Sátaváhana race, I, pt. ii, 147; was 2nd in the dynasty according to the *Puránas*, *id.* 155, 163; dates of his accession and death, *id.* 166; mention of, in a Násik cave, XVI, 592, 611; his date (B. C. 110), *id.* 614; also called Krishnaraja, I, pt. ii, 154. *See* also XII, 239.

Krishna or Krishnarája: Ráshtrakúta king (375-400), contemporary of Chalukya king Jayasimha I, I, pt. ii, 178, 295-296; *see* also I, pt. i, 120.

Krishna: Devagiri Yádava king, I, pt. ii, 244-246, 467; (1247-1260), *id.* 519; Prákrit forms of his name, record of his time, his titles and eipthets, his officers, *id.* 252, 526, 527; also styled Krishna Kandhara, *id.* 508; his connection with Kánara, XV, pt. ii, 92-93.

Krishna: founder of the Kalachuri family of Chedi, I, pt. ii, 225; kills a cannibal king at Kálañjara and acquires the Dahala country, *id.* 468, 469.

Krishna: Yádav king Ramachandra's viceroy in the Konkan, I, pt. ii, 248; also styled Krishnadeva (1289), *id.* 529.

Krishna: Kadamba prince, I, pt. ii, 290 note 2.

Krishna: Nága king, his visit to Sopára, XIII, 408.

Krishná: river in the Dakhan, XIX, 13-14; XXI, 10; XXIII, 7-9; XXIV, 8, 9, 11; I, pt. ii, 133, 185, 334 note 2, 442, 497, 524, 547; confluence of the Koyna and the, *id.* 546; of the, and the Tungabhadra, *id.* 186; of the Malaprabha and the, *id.* 227; and the Malaprabhá, northern boundary of the Hoysala kingdom, *id.* 503, 504, 506.

Krishna I: Ráshtrakúta king (754-782) also styled Krishnaraja, I, pt. ii, 195-196, 382, 385; deposes his nephew Dantidurga, *id.* 389; his *birudas* or titles, *id.* 390; his conquests and grant, constructs a temple of Śiva at Ellora, *id.* 391, 392, 393, 399 note 7, 400, 408 and note 4, 409, 413; fav urs Sanaphulla the first Siláhára king, *id.* 537; his supposed conquest of Yellapur in Kánara district, XV, pt. ii, 84, 85 note 2.

Krishna II: Ráshtrakúta prince (888-912), I, pt. ii, 379 note 2; succeeds his father, marries a Chedi princess, *id.* 201, 296; subdues the neighbouring princes, constructs Jain temples, consecrates the Jaina *Purána*, *id.* 201-202, 210; northern limit of his dominions, *id.* 383; his city burnt, *id.* 384 note 4; his *birudas*, epithets, *id.* 410: his wars with the Eastern Chalukyas, *id.* 411-412 and note 1; records regarding him, *id.* 412-414 and note 1; his connection with Kánara district, XV, pt. ii-84, 85 note 2.

Krishna III: (Krishnarájadeva) Ráshtrakúta king (940-956), succeeds his father Amoghavarsha III, I, pt. ii, 205, 418; his *birudas*, titles, and epithets, *id.* 418-419; his wars, *id.* 207, 305, 332 note 6, 383, 419-420; his feudatories, *id.* 231, 233, 236, 256, 420, 550, 552; records regarding him, *id.* 207, 420-422, 427 note 3; also styled Krishna-Kandhara, *id.* 419, 556; *see* also I, pt. i, 469.

Krishnabenna: river Krishna, I, pt. ii, 334 and note 2.

Krishna Canal: in Sátára district, XIX, 155-156.

Krishnadeva: Yádava governor; *see* Krishna.

Krishnadeva: cavalry general of Siddharája and brother-in-law of Kumárapála, I, pt. i, 181, 182; helps Kumárapála to secure the throne, *id.* 183; insults Kumárapála, *id.* 184.

Krishnagiri: modern Kanheri, mount, I, pt. ii, 404, 405, 541; *see* also XIII, 412.

Krishnaji; foster son of Kántáji, captures the fort of Chámpáner (1728), I, pt. i 308.

Krishnaji: auther of the *Ratnamála*, I, pt. ii, 409 note 1.

Krishna-Kandhara: *see* Krishna III and Krishna of Devagiri.

Krishnapura: unidentified city of Krishna II, I, pt. ii, 384 note 4.

Krishnarája: Paramára king, I, pt. i, 470.

Krishnarája: *see* Krishna, Ráshtrakúta king.

Krishnarája: *see* Krishna I.

Krishnarája: father of Samkaragana, chief of Western India why not Ráshtrakúta Krishna (375-400), I, pt. ii, 295-296; Kálachuri king, *id.* 385.

Krishnarája: Akálavarsha, of the Gujarát branch of the Málkhed family, son of Dantivarman, I, pt. ii, 412, 413, 414.

Krishnarája: Ráshtrakúta king (A. D. 375-400), XIV, 400.

Krishnarájadeva: I, pt. ii, 411 note 1, 500. *See* Krishna III.

Krishna Ráy: ninth Vijayanagar king (1508-1542), XV, pt. ii, 96 note 4, 105-106, 272, 299; *see* also XXII, 400 and note 2.

Krishnaráo Khatáokar: Bráhman plunderer (1713), I, pt. ii, 599; XIX, 257, 483.

Krishnarav: mámlatdár of Sampgaon, suppressed the rising of Kittur (1829), XXI, 404-405.

Krishna Vallabha: Krishna II, I, pt. ii, 201.

Krishnavarman I: Kadamba king, I, pt. ii, 290 and notes 2 and 3, 291 notes 1 and 2; Hángal Kádamba, *id.* 559.

Krishna-Vena, Krishnaveni: river Krishna, I, pt, ii, 219, 237, 437 note 6, 497, 504.

Krishnavenna, Krishnaverna: river Krishna, I, pt. ii, 344 note 2, 369, 547.

Krish-tel: oil-yielding plant, cultivated in several districts, XXV, 219.

Kritavirya: lord of Mahishmatipattana, lineage of, I, pt. ii, 439 note 2.

Kredtyas: Un-Indian Buddhist converts, claim Budha's relics, IX, pt. i, 446 note 1.

Kshaharáta: *see* Khagaráta.

Kshaharáta Nahapána: foreign king, I, pt. ii, 148, 155. *See* Nahapána.

Kshatrapa: title of a king, I, pt. ii, 155.

Kshatrapa, Kshatrapas: dynasty of (B. C. 70-A. D. 398); the name, I, pt. i, 20 and note 1, 21; Northern and Western, *id.* 22-54, 65, 66;

dynasty of, *id.* 464 ; I, pt. ii, 157 ; ruling over part of the Dakhan, *id.* 177 ; blood relationship of Sátaváhanas with, *id.* 161 ; Western, kings in Western India in the early centuries, *id.* 294 ; destruction of the power of, *id.* 295 note 1 ; their era, *id.* 294 ; their rule in Káthiáwár, VIII, 272-273 ; meaning of; claimed to be Kshatriyas, IX, pt. i, 445 and note 7 ; Buddhist, converted to Bráhmanism, *id.* 441 ; settlement of, in Thána district, XIII, 60, 61 ; *see* also XI, 140, XIII, 411, 412, 417 ; XVI, 183 and note 4, 614-620.

Kshatri : a caste of writers in Khándesh district, XII, 54 ; in Cutch, V, 48-49.

Kshatriya : a caste of husbandmen in Bijápur district, XXIII, 121.

Kshatriyas : ruling or warrior class, admission, of foreigners into, of individual conquerors Hindu theories helping such admission, IX, pt. i, 441 ; king-worship, sect of king worshippers, its text, *id.* 441 note 1 ; instances of an individual conqueror or a private foreigner admitted as, *id.* 441-443 ; instances of admission of conqueror's tribe or horde among, *id.* 443-445 ; instances of the form of name, making admission easy, *id.* 445-446 ; instances of certain invaders, who entered India as allies being accepted as, *id.* 447 ; instances of certain of the invaders by devotion to Bráhmans obtaining position as, *id.* 448-450 ; modern instances of classes gaining rank among, *id.* 451-452 ; instances of foreign tribes gaining rank among Rájpúts, Agnikulas, *id.* 433, 449 ; Sisodiás or Gohels, *id.* 443, 452 ; Chukwas in the Chittagong Hills, *id.* 451 ; Gurkhás, Khás, Játa, *id.* 451-452 ; Maráthás, *id.* 442 note 6 continued on page 443, 452 ; foreign invaders who aided the Bráhmans, admitted as, *id.* 433 ; Yavanas, Pahlavas, *id.* 445 ; Kushan, Jue-Jue, Khazár, Turk, White Huna, *id.* 447, 449 ; Gurjaras, *id.* 448, 459 ; upper class of Musalmán captives of war (A. D. 1094-1143, A. D. 1177-1179), *id.* 443-444 ; Agnikulás recognized as, I, pt. i, 463 note 2, 465 ; mentioned by Ibni Khurdádbah, *id.* 530, 531 ; humbled by Gotamiputra, I, pt. ii, 149.

Kshaya : *see* Consumption.

Kshemarája : Chávadá king (841-880) of Anahilaváda, I, pt. i, 127 note 2, 154, 155 ; *see* also I, pt. ii, 409 note 1.

Kshemarája : son of Bhima I, Chaulukya king of Anahilaváda, I, pt. i, 169, 170, 181.

Kshemendra : author of the *Brihatkathá*, I, pt. ii, 170.

Kshetrapáls : number of, at Bhinmál, I, pt. i, 461.

Kshetridása : caste of beggars in Dhárwár district, XXII, 207-208.

Ktesias : (B. C. 400), his mention of a race of Pygmies (Bhils), in India, I, pt. i, 532.

Ktesiphon : in Central Asia, XIII, 412.

Kuba : táluka in Káthiáwár, VIII, 524.

Kubera : king of Devaráshtra, I, pt. ii, 280.

Kubera : Hindu god, painting of, in Ajanta caves, XII, 493 and note 2.

Kuber Panth : a Hindu sect, IX, pt. i, 548.

Kubja-Vishnuvardhana : Western Chálukya prince Vishnuvardhana, I, pt. ii, 349 and note 3.

Kublai Khán : great Manchu emperor of China, his policy towards his subjects, IX, pt. i, 442.

Kuda : *see* Kuta.

Kuda : village in Káthiáwár, VIII, 524.

Kuda : plant, its twigs used as tooth-brushes, XXV, 291.

Kuda Caves : in Kolába district, description, caves I-III, XI, 332-333 ; IV-V, *id.* 334 ; VI, *id.* 335-337 ; VII-XII, *id.* 339 ; XIII-XV, *id.* 340 ; XVI-XIX, *id.* 341 ; XX-XXVI, *id.* 342 ; *see* also I, pt. ii, 9, 12, 173, 174 ; inscriptions at, *id.* 143, 175, 176, 538 note 8.

Kudal : sub-division in Sávantvádi state, X, 387. *Town*, history and fort of, *id.* 465 ; Yadava district, I, pt. ii, 29 ; Savants of, *id.* 68.

Kudali : hoe assessment in Thána, XIII, 531 note 3, 551 note 2, 565.

Kudáli : river in Sátára district, XIX, 14.

Kudaldámvád : old name of Kurandvád in Kolhápur state, grant at, XXIV, 223.

Kudáldeshkar : a sub-caste of the Shenvi Bráhmans, in Ratnágiri district, X, 411 ; in Kánara district, XV, pt. i, 178.

Kudali-Sangameśvara : Basava goes to, from Kalyána, I, pt. ii, 479 ; Basava absorbed into the god of, *id.* 480 and note 1.

Kudamalanádu : identified with Coorg, I, pt. ii, 341 note 2.

Kudási : *see* Tilári.

Kudavakkáligar : a caste of husbandmen in Dhárwár district, XXII, 137-138 ; in Bijápur, XXIII, 247.

Kudbuda Joshi : a caste of beggars in Sholápur district, XX, 187-188.

Kudchi : village in Belgaum district, fair at, XXI, 584.

Kudem : *see* Kuda Caves.

Kudla : village in Dhárwár district, XXII, 765-766.

Kudlápura : stone inscription at, I, pt. ii, 301 note 1.

Kudu : grain, I, pt. ii, 78.

Kuduhára : country, I, pt. ii, 333.

Kudus : village in Thána district, XIV, 210.

Kudva : peak in Poona district, XVIII, pt. i, 5.

Kudvakkalger : *see* Kudavakkáligar.

Kudyát : rice soil in Ratnágiri district, X, 144.

Kufis : *see* Konkani Musalmáns.

Kuhandi : old district corresponding to Belgaum, XXI, 354 and note 1, 358 ; governed by Sámiyára of the Rundranila-Saindraka family, I, pt. ii, 344 note 6, 527 ; governed by the Rattas, *id.* 549.

Kukar : village in Baroda state, VII, 554.

Kukar : fibrous plant, grows along the *ghdts*, XXV, 229 ; yields gum, *id.* 250.

Kukarda : sub-division in Rewa Kántha, VI, 98.

Kukdeshvar : Hemadpanti temple of, at Pur in Poona district, XVIII, pt. iii, 424-428.

Kukdi : river, in Ahmadnagar district, XVII, 9 ; in Poona district, XVIII, pt. i, 8.

Kukkanur: district, in the Nizám's dominions, I, pt. ii, 304, 333, 432, 435; inscriptions at, *id.* 433, 456 note 2, 460, 469, 487; grant of, by the Kalachurya Singhana, *id.* 489, 527.
Kukrej: village in Rewa Kántha, popularly identified with Kambhavati Nagari of Chovan days, VI, 162.
Kukura: name of a province, I, pt. i, 36 and note 7; ruled by Gotamiputra, I, pt. ii, 149.
Kukurmunda: place of interest in Khándesh district, XII, 256, 453.
Kulachandra: general of the Málwa king, invades and sacks Anahilaváda city, I, pt. i, 163-164.
Kulachuri: *see* Kalachuris.
Kulagere: in Mysore, inscription at, I, pt. ii, 303.
Kulambi: *see* Kunbi.
Kulámmali: Quilon, apparently on the Malabár Coast, maritime island, I, pt. i, 509 and note 2.
Kulang: fort in Násik district, XVI, 441, 447, 449.
Kularag, Kulárgi: peasant-held, a Thána tenure, XIII, 545; proprietary holders, *id.* 551; *see* Dharekari.
Kulasekharánka: vanquished by the Sinda prince Permadi I, I, pt. ii, 459.
Kulbarga, Kulburagi: proposed identification of, with *Tagar*, I, pt. ii, 538 note 8 continued on page 540.
Kuli: country of Sind, I, pt. i, 520.
Kuli: food plant, grows in several districts, XXV, 180, 292.
Kuligeri: in the Nizám's dominions, record at, I, pt. ii, 527, 528.
Kulith: oil-yielding and fodder plant, XXV, 217, 277; in Ratnágiri, X, 147; in Sátára, XIX, 163.
Kulkáji: hill in Sátára district, XIX, 12.
Kulkarnis: hereditary village accountants, I, pt. ii, 34; in Ratnágiri, X, 140, 202; (1818), *id.* 222; in Sávantvádi, *id.* 448; in Kolába district, XI, 161 and notes 1 and 2, 171, 172 note 1, 177 and note 4, 452; in Thána district, XIII, 538, 552; Deshpándes or sub-divisional *kulkarnis* (1828), *id.* 572-573; village *kulkarnis* unknown (1828), *id.* 574; in Násik district (1882), XVI, 207; (1818), *id.* 209 and note 5.
Kulmar, *pl.* Kulmaru: caste of iron-workers in Belgaum district, XXI, 108.
Kulottunga Cho-dadeva I: Eastern Chálukya king, I, pt. ii, 342 note 1; inscription of, *id.* 442 note 3, 445. *See* Rájiga.
Kulthi: *see* Kulith.
Kuluhára: I, pt ii, 333. *See* Kuduhára.
Kulvádi: *see* Áre Marátha.
Kumadvati: river in Dhárwár district, XXII, 6-7.
Kumáirs: I, pt. i, 500. *See* Khmers.
Kumaki; waste land in Kánara, XV, pt. ii, 271.
Kumáon: temple in, repaired by Ganda Brihaspati, I, pt. i, 190.
Kumar: famine plant, cultivated in Bombay gardens, XXV, 206.
Kumára-Mangala-Vellattur: village, I, pt. ii, 327.
Kumáradevi: Gupta queen (*c.* 360, A. D.), I, pt. i, 61 and note 4.
Kumáragupta I: sixth Gupta king (A. D. 416-453), inscriptions, coins, I, pt. i, 66, 67, 68, 69, 74, 78 note 1, 86; *see* also I, pt. ii, 580; I, pt. i, 29.
Kumáragupta II: Gupta king, I, pt. i, 74.
Kumáranádu: falls into the hands of Vishnuvardhana, I, pt. ii, 496.
Kumárapala, Kumárpal: Chálukya king (1143-1174), I, pt. i, 156, 170, 176; his ancestry, *id.* 179, 181; his death planned by Siddharája; goes into exile; his wanderings; coins issued in his name by Pratápasimha; is chosen king, *id.* 182-183; rewards his friends in exile; his wars with the kings of Sámbhar, Málwa, the Konkan, and Suráshtra, *id.* 184-187; traditions regarding his Sesodia Ráni, *id.* 188; extent of his kingdom; construction of the temple of Somanáth; his vow to keep apart from women and eschew flesh and wine, *id.* 189; his Jain benefactions; is credited with building 1,444 temples; scholars at his court, *id.* 190; dies, *id.* 194; his general defeats Mallikarjuna of Konkan, XIII, 426, 436, 437; said to have been converted to Islám, IX, pt. ii, 26 note 2; *see* also VIII, 283.
Kumárapálacharita: life of Kumárapála in Sanskrit, I, pt. i, 149 note 1, 170, 177 note 1, 178, 182, 185, 186; written about 1150, IX, pt. ii, 24 note 3.
Kumárapálaprabandha: history of Kumárapála in Sanskrit, I, pt. i, 149 note 1, 173, 183, 194.
Kumárapáleśvara: temple of, I, pt. i, 172.
Kumarbij: famine plant, grows on the coast of Madras, XXV, 206.
Kumárika: *see* Sarasvati.
Kumárika Kshetra: old name for Cambay, its origin, VI, 211, 216 note 2.
Kumárila: a Bhatta, first of the religious founders or apostles, IX, pt. i, 533; *see* also I, pt. ii, 408.
Kumárpál: *see* Kumárapála.
Kumba: fibrous plant, XXV, 232.
Kumbal: food plant, grows on the *ghát*s, XXV, 174; its leaves used for poisoning fish, *id.* 273.
Kumbar: *see* Kumbhár.
Kumbarna: village in Mahi Kántha, marble temple at, V, 438.
Kumbaru Point: in Janjira state, XI, 464-465.
Kumbha: *rána* of Chitor, defeated by Muhammad Khilji (1443), I, pt. i, 361.
Kumbha: pass in Kolába district, XI, 6, 115; I, pt. ii, 38.
Kumbhár, Kumbar: a caste of potters in Gujarát, other names, IX, pt. i, 189 and note 2; tools, pottery, *id.* 189-190; in Kánara district, XV, pt. i, 269-271; in Cutch V, 73, 94; in Káthiáwár, VIII, 151; in Ratnágiri district, X, 126, 141; in Sávantvádi, *id.* 415; in Kolába district, XI, 64; in Janjira state, *id.* 413; in Khándesh district, XII, 74, 144, 225; in Thána, XIII, 137; their Kriyás or obsequies, *id.* 138; in Násik district, XVI, 51; in Ahmadnagar district, XVII, 106-107; in Poona district, XVIII, pt. i, 349-351; in

Sátára district, XIX, 86-87; in Sholápur district, XX, 119-120; in Belgaum district, XXI, 141; in Dhárwár district, XXII, 153-155; in Bijápur district, XXIII, 247-252; in Kolhápur state, XXIV, 95-96. *See* also I, pt. i, 451.
Kumbhárdegudd : hill in Belgaum district, XXI, 9, 585.
Kumbháre : a caste of cultivators in Khándesh district, XII, 68.
Kumbhari : village in Ahmadnagar district, temple at, XVII, 725.
Kumbhárli : hill pass between Ratnágiri and Sátára districts, I, pt. ii, 35; opened (1830), *id.* 129; X, 166, 169, 324; XIX, 202.
Kumbhi : stream in Kolhápur state, XXIV, 9, 10.
Kumbhoj : village in Kolhápur state, market, temples and tomb at, XXIV, 312, 313.
Kumbi : *see* Kathalya.
Kumbia : *see* Kumba.
Kumbli : *see* Kumbal.
Kumkar : Konkan, I, pt. i, 506.
Kummata : taken by Vira-Ballála, I, pt. ii, 505.
Kumri : wood-ash tillage in Kánara district, XV, pt. i, 24, 35; XV, pt. ii, 14, 173, 188-189; in Belgaum district, XXI, 56, 245; in Kolhápur state, XXIV, 21.
Kumta : river in Kánara district, XV, pt. i, 7.
Kumta : sub-division in Kánara district, villages, aspect, climate, water, soil, stock, survey details, people, XV, pt. ii, 227-232; *town,* road-stead, position, people, trade, light-house, management, history, *id.* 326-327; imports and exports of, *id.* 65, 66, 68, 69; historical references to, *id.* 114, 133, 138, 149; schools at, *id.* 215, 216; hospitals at, *id.* 219; *see* also XV, pt. i, 3.
Kumuda : *see* Khatara.
Kumudabhatta : grantor in the Kávi grant, I, pt. i, 126.
Kumudachandra : Digámbara Jain from Karnátaka, his religious discourse with Devasuri and defeat, I, pt. i, 181.
Kumudvat : country mentioned by Pánini, I, pt. ii, 139.
Kunád : district ruled by Armativala, I, pt. ii, 505.
Kunam : a caste of traders in Ahmadnagar district, XVII, 72-74.
Kunbi : a caste of cultivators, in Ratnágiri district, X, 121, 151; in Kolába district and Janjira state, XI, 54-62, 412; in Khándesh, XII, 39, 62-67, 136, 600; in Thána district, XIII, 124-129, 409 note 1, 477; in Násik district, XVI, 26, 27; in Ahmadnagar district, XVII, 86-89; in Poona district, origin, family names, appearance, language, house, house-goods, food, dress, ornaments, character, occupation, condition, daily life, religion, beliefs, holidays, field rites, customs, community, XVIII, pt. i, 284-309; XVIII, pt. ii, I; in Sátára district, XIX, 64-65; in Belgaum district, XXI, 109-124; in Bijápur district, XXIII 121; in Kolhápur state, XXIV, 88 92.
Kunchigár : *see* Kámáti.
Kunda : a weed, XII, 146 note 1.
Kundakadevi : wife of Vaddiga, I, pt. ii, 418.
Kundal : pass in Kánara district, XV, pt. ii, 39, 40, 327.
Kundal : village in Sátára district, caves at, XIX, 465, 487-488.
Kundalika : river in Kolába district, XI, 8, 9.
Kundamarasa : feudatory of the Western Chálukya king and ruler of the Banavási, Sántalige, and Hayne provinces, I, pt. ii, 437.
Kundargi : village in Bijápur district, temple at, XXIII, 661.
Kundgol : town in Kolhápur state, market at, XXIV, 388.
Kundi : village in the Sangameshvar táluka of the Ratnágiri district, I, pt. ii, 348 note 4; country, *id.* 298 note 2, 428, 431, 439, 443, 455, 460, 465, 546; Kuhundi province, governed by the Rattas of Saundatti, *id.* 549, 553, 556, 558.
Kundi : hill pass between Ratnágiri district and Kolhápur state, X, 166; XXIV, 5.
Kundivátaka : possibly Kundi, I, pt. ii, 348 and note 4.
Kundla : town in Káthiáwár, famous for its saddles, VIII, 524.
Kundli : village in Ahmadábád district, a petty state, VIII, 524.
Kundliála : táluka in Káthiáwár, VIII, 525.
Kundur : old Ráshtrakúta district, I, pt. ii, 358 note 1, 403, 432.
Kungari : stream in Belgaum district, XXI, 13.
Kunimallihalli : village near Bankápur in Dhárwár, inscription at, I, pt. ii, 411 note 3.
Kunjál : hill fort in Ahmadnagar district, XVII, 5.
Kunkanás : Surat Nagar Bráhmans, I, pt. i, 5 note 1.
Kunkari Valánjn : a caste of traders in Khándesh district, XII, 59.
Kunkáváv : village in Káthiáwár, VIII, 525.
Kunkumamahádevi : sister of Vijayáditya, builds a Jain temple at Lakshmeshwar called Anesejjeyabasadi, I, pt. ii, 371.
Kunkumbhi : village in Belgaum district, shrines at, arrival of the Ganges at, XXI, 585.
Kunságar : village in Baroda territory, the ruins of a great reservoir at, VII, 609.
Kuntal : old province in Carnatic divisions of, XV, pt ii, 86 note 1; consisting of parts of Mysore, Madras, Nizám's dominions and of Dhárwar district, XXII, 397 and note 1; also parts of Bijapur district, XXIII, 387 note 5; kingdom, I, pt. ii, 216, 403 note 3; country, *id.* 482, 549, 561; Southern Marátha Country, *id.* 238; limits of, *id.* 431 and note 2; ruled by the Nandas, the Gupta family, the Maurya kings, the Rattas, the Chálukyas, Bijjala of the Kalachurya family, and the Hoysala king Vira-Ballala II, *id.* 284 note 2, 462, 503; in Maháráshtra, *id.* 355 note 3.
Kuntala : name of Saliváhana, I, pt. ii, 169.
Kuntala Sátakarni : kills his queen Malayavati in amorous sport, I, pt. ii, 171-172.
Kuntanhashalli : village in Dhárwár district, XXII, 766.
Kuntaváda : Kootwar village south of Miraj, I, pt. ii, 547.

Kuntoji: village in Bijápur district, temple at, XXIII, 661.
Kupanapura: town, Chandriká Devi, the daughter of the lord of, I, pt. ii, 556.
Kupi: *see* Khokati.
Kupicha Dongar: place of interest in Ratnágiri district, X, 465.
Kuppatur: in Mysore, inscription at, I, pt. ii, 284 note 2, 326, 523, 561 note 6.
Kura: village, temple of Pinákapani at, I, pt. ii, 323.
Kuraish: family of *sháikhs*, three branches of, Abbásis, Fárukis, Siddikis, IX, pt. ii, 8; name of the noble Arab tribe Prophet Muhammad belonged to; tribal name assumed by Hindu and other converts to Islám, *id.* 8 note 3; special community of part foreign descent *id.* 11, 15.
Kurak: dye plant, XXV, 241.
Kuram: grant from, I, pt. ii, 319 note 2, 322, 323, 324 note 3, 329, 343 note 5.
Kuramba: shepherd tribe in Kánara district, XV, pt. ii, 83 and note 1. *See* Kuruba.
Kurchaka: Jain sect, I, pt. ii, 288, 289.
Kurda: fort, *see* Vishrámgad.
Kurdápur: village in Dhárwár district, temple at, XXII, 766.
Kurdu: a head-quarter of old local chiefs in Kolába district, XI, 142.
Kurdu: sacred plant, XXV, 292.
Kurgi: popular land measure in Dhárwár district, XXII, 441 and note 5, 459.
Kurhád: pick-axe, assessment in Thána district, XIII, 565.
Kurhádkhurd: village in Khándesh district, temple at, XII, 454.
Kurkumb: village in Poona district, temples at, XVIII, pt. iii, 247.
Kurla: village in Thána district with railway station, XIV, 210-211, mill, XIII, 391; estate, *id.* 545.
Kurli: village in Dakhan, Shiváji's general Nilaji Kátkar's victory at (1678), XIX, 245.
Kurma: food plant, XXV, 181.
Kurmagad: island in Kánara district, history of, XV, pt. ii, 328; *see* also XV, pt. i, 2.
Kuroo nai: *see* Kadavi nai.
Kursáli: a caste of bastards in Bijápur district, XXIII, 252.
Kurtakoti, Kurtkoti: village in Dhárwár district, temples, inscriptions, copper-plate at, XXII, 766; I, pt. ii, 304; grant from, *id.* 327 note 4, 329 note 5, 365 note 1, 462.
Kuru: king of, present at the *svayamvara* or choice marriage of Durlabhadevi, I, pt. i, 163.
Kuruba, *pl.* Kurubaru: a caste of shepherds, in Kánara district, XV, pt. i, 298-300; in Dhárwár district, XXII, 180-182; in Bijápur district, XXIII, 121-124.
Kurugod: fort near Belláry, reduced by Vira-Ballála II, I, pt. ii, 504.
Kurukshetra: holy place, I, pt. i, 161.
Kurumarathi: Kurumarathya, village, I, pt. ii, 356.
Kurundaka: investiture festival at, I, pt. i, 130 and note 3; identified with modern Kadoda on the bank of the Tápti, I, pt. ii, 203, 415.
Kurundvád Junior: state under Kolhápur, description, trade and justice in, XXIV, 385-386.
Kurundvád Senior: state under Kolhápur, description, people, capital, trade, justice, finance, instruction, health, town details, XXIV, 384-385.
Kurus: at war with Yasovarmman, I, pt. i, 469.
Kurutakunte: *see* Kurtakoti.
Kuruvinshetti, Kurvinsheti: a caste of grocers in Bijápur district, XXIII, 252-253; weavers in Dhárwár district, XXII, 171-172.
Kuśa, Kush: son of Ráma of the solar race incarnation of Vishnu, I, pt. i, 119; Gurjjaras claim descent from, IX, pt. i, 471.
Kusada: snake in Ratnágiri district, X, 50.
Kusal: a depressed class in Kánara district, XV, pt. i, 370.
Kusaldevar: rock in Kánara district, XV, pt. i, 3.
Kusane: division of Gurjjaras, IX, pt. i, 470, 491.
Kusásthali: name of Dwárka, I, pt. i, 8.
Kush: *see* Kuśa.
Kush: sacred plant, XXV, 279, 290.
Kushán: capital of Ta-Gaz-Gaz in Farghána, IX, pt. i, 470 note 2.
Kushan, Kusháns: horde of foreigners (B. C. 130), IX, pt. i, 455; called Great Yuechi; *id.* 469; elements in the horde of, that entered India (B. C. 50), *id.* 456; Sakas and Kusháns practically the same; Greek influence on, before their start (B. C. 120), *id.* 456 note 3; conquered in Western India, *id.* 433; suggested relationship with Kush, descendants of Indians not likely, *id.* 445, 446; fire reverencing element in, *id.* 447; Gujars' identification with, *id.* 461, 462, 469, 470; dynasty, I, pt. i, 464; warlike race, *id.* 456 note 1, 544, 545.
Kushasthali: a sub-caste of Bráhmans in Kánara district, XV, pt. i, 168-171.
Kushgal: *see* Kusugal.
Kuśika: disciple of Nakulisa, founder of a branch of Paśupata school, I, pt. i, 84.
Kusrud: village in Sátára district, caves at, XIX, 489.
Kussan: medicinal plant, XXV, 261.
Kussar: oil-yielding plant, XXV, 223.
Kussim: *see* Kussan.
Kusti: sacred cord worn by Pársis, IX, pt. ii, 201, 208, 227; investing the child with, *id.* 231 and note 2; prayer, *id.* 208 note 1, 241.
Kusugal: village in Dhárwár district, cotton experiments at fort, XXII, 297-299, 766-767; captured by the Peshwa, the Nizám and the British (1790), I, pt. ii, 662.
Kusumb: tree in Khándesh district, XII, 26.
Kusumeśvara: camp of Siláditya, son of Jayasimhavarman at, I, pt. ii, 187, 370.
Kusur: pass between Thána and Poona districts, XIII, 322, 508, 523; XVIII, pt. ii, 152.
Kuta: an attribute meaning prominent, I, pt. i, 119.
Kuta: family or group, I, pt. ii, 178.
Kuthi-Alam Sháh Sheikh Jiva: a saint, IX, pt. ii, 63.

Kutb Sháhi Kings: (1512-1687), list of, XVII, 357 note 2.
Kutb-ud-din: Mughal general in Gujarát, captures Navánagar and annexes the territory (1664), I, pt. i, 283.
Kutb-ud-din, Kutb-ud-din Eibak: Delhi emperor (1194), I, pt. i, 229; advances to Kol, *id.* 519 and note 4; defeats Karan Vághela, *id.* 512; invader of Gujarát (1194), IX, pt. ii, 2 note 2; conqueror of the Khokhars (1202), *id.* 65.
Kutb-ud-din: Shiáh missionary (1400), ancestor of the Pirána saints, Shiáh faith spread by, in Gujarát, IX, pt. ii, 125.
Kutb-ud-din Sháh: king of Gujarát, defeats Mehmud Khilji of Málwa (1453), I, pt. i, 362.
Kutiana: town in Káthiáwár, identified with ancient Kundinpur, famous for its bards, Persian inscription at, called Muzafarábád by Musalmáns, VIII, 525-526.
Kutla: probably Kothligad, given to the Peshwa, I, pt. ii, 88.
Kutlei Khanum: minister of Cambay (1783), VI, 230.
Kutra: *inám* village of the Shirke family, I, pt. ii, 86.
Kuttar: pass in Násik district, XVI, 130.
Kutumahámáyi: Hindu goddess, temple of, at Kadra in Kánara district, XV, pt. ii, 317.
Kutumbin: old name for cultivators, I, pt. i, 4.
Kuva: village in Káthiáwár, ruins at, VIII, 526.
Kuvádva: village in Káthiáwár, famous for its lime-stone, VIII, 527.
Kuvalála: I, pt. ii, 298. *See* Koláhalapura.
Kuvars: princes, I, pt. i, 215 note 2.
Kuveshi: pass in Kánara district, XV, pt. ii, 39, 40, 328.
Kuvi: Jain A'chárya, his lineage, I, pt. ii, 400.
Kwaan: *see* Kiwani.
Kwau-tsz'-tsai: Chinese for Bodhisattva, I, pt. ii, 354.
Kyásanur: village, in the Hángal táluka of the Dhárwár district, included in the Edevolal district, I, pt. ii, 278 note 2; inscription at, *id.* 420, 447 note 1, 529, 562 note 5, 564 note 4; XV, pt. ii, 84.
Kydia calicyna: fibrous plant, XXV, 229.

L

LAB: lip saliva of a *pir* or saint, IX, pt. ii, 127 note 2.
Labbay, Labbey: class of Musalmáns in Kolhápur, XXIV, 150; in Belgaum district, XXI, 211, 212; in Dhárwár district, XXII, 236-237; in Bijápur district, XXIII, 295.
Labhána: *see* Lamán.
Labiatæ: species of famine and oil-yielding plants, XXV, 203, 224.
Labourers: all district volumes, *see* under district name.
Labour mortgage: in Ratnágiri, X, 162; in Sávantvádi, *id.* 430; in Kolába district, XI, 106, 427; in Khándesh, XII, 199; in Kánara district, XV, pt. ii, 32 and note 1, 33-34; in Násik district, XVI, 121-122; in Ahmadnagar district, XVII, 303-304; in Belgaum district, XXI, 296, 297; in Dhárwár district, XXII, 329-330; in Bijápur district, XXIII, 349-350; in Thána district, XIII, 310-311; in Sátára district, XIX, 189-190; in Sholápur district, XX, 245; in Kolhápur state, XXIV, 195.
Lac, Lac bracelets: manufacture of, in Panch Maháls, III, 249; in Khándesh district, XII, 223; in Rewá Kántha, VI, 53.
Lachchhiyavvá, Lakshmi, Lasthiyavvá: wife of Bhillama II, I, pt. ii, 232, 513, 425.
Lád or Lád Váni: a sub-caste of Meshri Vánias in Gujarát, take their name from Látdesh; Ashapuri their family deity; Lád women noted for taste in dress, IX, pt. i, 72; in Rewá Kántha, VI, 24; in Kolába district, XI, 272 note 1; in Khándesh, XII, 56, 112; in Dhárwár district, XXII, 119-121; in Thána district, XIII, 63, 112; in Kánara district, XV, pt. i, 184, 185; in Ahmadnagar district, XVII, 71, 72.
Lád: a sub-caste of Vanjáris in Násik district, XVI, 62-63.
Lád, Ládkasáb, Lád Suryavanshi: a sub-caste of mutton-sellers, in Belgaum district, XXI, 194; in Dhárwár district, XXII, 241-242, 156.
Ladávi: dialect in Thána district (900-1100), XIII, 67.
Ladchi: pass in Násik district, XVI, 128.
Laddho-kachro: Khavas of Gondal, IX, pt. i, 236.
Ladhubha: cousin of Ráo Bharmal II (1814-1819) of Cutch, murdered by the Ráo (1818), V, 156, 161.
Lád Kalál: *see* Kalál.
Ládkoshti: a sub-caste of Koshtis in Kolhápur, XXIV, 95.
Ládsakka: caste of traders, in Khándesh, XII, 57-58; in Násik, XVI, 46.
Lád Sultáni: *see* Bakar Kasáb.
Ládvani: *see* Lád.
Lae-lih: Toramána's father, I, pt. i, 74-76.
Lág, Lágrog: cattle foot-disease, X, 461; XV, pt. ii, 221.
Lagenandra toxicaria: poisonous plant found in Belgaum and South Konkan, XXV, 270.
Lagenaria vulgaris: poisonous plant, XXV, 265.
Lagerstræmia parviflora: dye plant found in Kánara, XXV, 245.
Laghiyastraya: Jain work, I, pt. ii, 407.
Lagrog: *see* Lag.
Lahawar: Lahori Bandar, I, pt. i, 509.
Lahi-Utarni: sin-removing ceremony among Matia Kanbis, IX, pt. i, 169.
Lahud: class of Hindus, I, pt. i, 530.
Lai: dye plant found in Sind and Cutch, XXV, 240.
Lakandi: fibrous plant, XXV, 231.
Lakarhára: a caste of Musalmán wood-sellers in Násik district, XVI, 79.
Lakdi Pul: bridge in Poona city, XVIII, pt. iii, 284.
Lákdiya: walled town in Cutch, V, 232.
Lake Fife: in Poona district, description of, XVIII, pt. iii, 382-384.
Lake Formations: in Bijápur district, XXIII, 47-49.
Lakes: all district volumes, *see* under district name.

Lakh: village in Ahmadnagar district, XVII, 725; canal, *id.* 256-257.
Lákhá: son of Phula, king of Cutch, slain by Mularája, I, pt. i, 160.
Lákha: a Sind chief of Samma Rájpút tribe (1300), V, 132.
Lákha Jádeja: Cutch chief (1350-1365), V, 134.
Lakhám Sávant: (1641-1655), chief of Sávantvádi, X, 440.
Lákhan: pass in Násik district, XVI, 130.
Lákhápádar: táluka in Káthiáwár, VIII, 527.
Lákha Phuláni: Samma Rájpút chief conquered and ruled in Cutch (1320-1340), V, 133.
Lakhera, Lakheri: a caste of lac bracelet-makers in Ahmadnagar district, XVII, 114-116; in Poona district, XVIII, pt. i, 351-352; in Sholápur district, XX, 121; in Khándesh, XII, 74, 234; in Násik district, XVI, 53.
Lakhmidás: minister in Cutch state (1815), V, 157, 164.
Lakhmideva: *see* Lakshma.
Lakhmidevayya, Lakhmideva, Lakshmidhara: Kalachurya Sankama's officer (1178), I, pt. ii, 487.
Lakhpat: town and fort in Cutch, V, 232-233; sub-division of Cutch, *id.* 2; historical references to, *id.* 142, 148, 150, 151, 152, 165.
Lakhtar: state in Káthiáwár, VIII, 527, 528; IX, pt. i, 127.
Lakkundi: village in Dhárwár district, temples and inscriptions at, XXII, 390, 767-770; I, pt. ii, 228, 496; battle of and inscription at, *id.* 238, 504, 520; Vira-Ballála II's camp at, *id.* 505; Jaitugi I defeated at (1192), XV, pt. ii, 92.
Lakmaya: officer of Hoysala king Narasimha I, I, pt. ii, 501.
Lakmideva: *see* Lakhmidevayya.
Lakshamithala: Lakshmi's settlement, I, pt. i, 452.
Lakshavarmman: mentioned in a stone inscription from Khajuraho, I, pt. i, 469.
Lakshma, Lakhmideva, Lakshmidhara: officer of Vira-Ballála II (1197), I, pt. ii, 506; put to flight by A'chugi II, *id.* 219.
Lakshmádevi: queen of Vikramáditya VI, I, pt. ii, 428 note 4, 448.
Lakshmádevi, Lakumádevi: wife of Vishnuvardhana, I, pt. ii, 493, 494.
Lakshmana: father of Banthádevi the wife of Vikramáditya IV, I, pt. ii, 427; Kalachurya A'havamalla's officer, *id.* 489.
Lakshmangar's panth: religious sect in Gujarát, IX, pt. i, 548.
Lakshmarasa: feudatory of the Western Chálukya king Someśvara II, I, pt. ii, 443.
Lakshmeshvar: town of the Miraj (senior) state in Dhárwár district, school, temples and inscriptions at, XXIV, 381; XXII, 390; I, pt. ii, 304 note 6, 372-373; its old name Huligere, *id.* 482; Puligere, *id.* 563; and Pulikaranagara, *id.* 524; Jain temple called Anesejjeya-basadi built by Kunkumamahádevi, sister of the Western Chalukya king Vijayáditya at, *id.* 371; temple of Somanáth at, *id.* 482; inscription at, *id.* 209, 292 and note 10, 304 note 6, 305, 336 note 3, 368, 372, 373 note 5, 375, 394, 419, 420, 455 note 6, 529, 569, 431.
Lakshmi: daughter of king of Chedi married to Jagattunga son of Krishna, I, pt. i, 130; I, pt. ii, 203, 216, 414.
Lakshmi: younger sister of Mahendra married to Nága Rája, I, pt. i, 163.
Lakshmi: Hindu goddess of fortune drawn out of the ocean, I, pt. ii, 195 and note 8; temple of, *id.* 460; IX, pt. i, p. xxxv, 16.
Lakshmi: *see* Lachchhiyavva.
Lakshmi: sister of Ráma, a Bráhman chief, I, pt. ii, 242.
Lakshmi: Buddhist goddess, XIV, 129, 141.
Lakshmi: village goddess in Belgaum district, origin of the worship of, XXI, 133-134.
Lakshmi Bai: mistress of Malháraráv Gáikwár, VII, 282.
Lakshmideva: commander of Krishna of Devagiri, I, pt. ii, 245.
Lakshmideva: father of Lakshmidevi, wife of Vijayáditya II, Goa Kádamba prince, I, pt. ii, 569.
Lakshmideva I: Ratta chieftain, I, pt. ii, 551; also called Lakshmana and Lakshmidhara, *id.* 556.
Lakshmideva II: Ratta king (1228), I, pt. ii, 551: son of Kártavirya IV, *id.* 557-558.
Lakshmidevi: wife of Sena II, Ratta chieftain, I, pt. ii, 551, 555.
Lakshmidevi: wife of the Goa Kádamba Vishnuchitta Vijayáditya II, I, pt. ii, 565, 569.
Lakshmidhara: *see* Lakshma, I, pt. ii, 487, 506.
Lakshmidhara: son of Bháskaráchárya, in the service of Jaitrapála the Yádava king, I, pt. ii, 239, 521, 526.
Lakshmidhara: lion of Bhambhágiri, reduced by Singhana, I, pt. ii, 239-240, 525.
Lakshmipáladevarasa: governor of Nágarakhanda district under Singhana (1241), I, pt. ii, 524.
Lakshmisen: Jain pontiff, XXIV, 95.
Lakuliśa: founder of Páśupata sect, chief shrine at Kárávana, I, pt. i, 83, 84. *See* Nakuliśa.
Lakumádevi: *see* Lakshmádevi.
Lála: meaning of the term, IX, pt. i, 61 and note 1.
Lálbeg: Musalmán saint, IX, pt. i, 336.
Lal-chitra: poisonous plant, grows in Southern Konkan, XXV, 266.
Láldás: Mandvi saint, object of Bhansali's reverence, IX, pt. i, 116.
Lálguli Falls: in Kánara district, XV, pt. ii, 328-329; XV, pt. i, 9.
Lalia: a blacksmith of Ahmadábád, possessed the philosopher's stone, story of, VI, 123.
Láliad: táluka in Káthiáwár, VIII, 528.
Láliás: Dhedas in European service, known as, IX pt. i, 339 note 2.
Laling: fort in Khándesh district, chief fort of the Fárukis, history of, XII, 244, 245, 256, 454; forest, *id.* 20.
Lalitadevi: wife of Vastupála, I, pt. i, 202.
Lalitankura: *biruda* or title of Mahendravarman I, I, pt. ii, 328.
Laljhan: dye plant found in river beds in Dakhan, XXV, 241.

Lál-langoti Koli: *see* Solesi Koli.
Lalliya: the Sáhi (chief) of Ohind near Swát, I, pt. i, 468.
Lálo: Soni *bhagat*, IX, pt. i, 201.
Lálpur: town in Káthiáwár, VIII, 528.
Lálthán: village in Thána district, XIV, 343.
Lalvádi: snake-charmer, IX, pt. i, 14.
Lamán or Lambáni: a caste of carriers, in Ahmadnagar district, XVII, 160-162; in Belgaum district, XXI, 124, 125; in Bijápur district, XXIII, 205-210; in Kolhápur, XXIV, 108; in Kánara, XV, pt. i, 338-340. *See* also Vanjári.
Lamb: Mr., chief of the English factory at Surat; sends Mulla Fakhr-ud-din in disguise to Bombay, I, pt. i, 332; his suicide, *id.* 333.
Lámdhár: hill in Káthiáwár, VIII, 11.
Lámgha: a Vanjári sub-division in Khándesh district, XII, 107, 113.
Lanauli: *see* Lonavali.
Lánchhana: crest, I, pt. ii, 469, 517.
Land, Land administration, survey and tenures: all district volumes, *see* under district name.
Land: value of, in Bombay island (1755), XXVI, pt. i, 302; measurement and rent (1757), XXVI, pt. iii, 417-418; sale of, forbidden (1717), *id.* 301.
Land Assessment: under Valabhi, I, pt. i, 82, 83.
Land assignments: to Marátha officers, XIX, 265.
Land produce: in Bombay island, estimated value of, a tax of 10 per cent. on (1758-1759), XXVI, pt. iii, 454-455; remission of the tax (1774), *id.* 470-471.
Land revenue: in Bombay island (1538-1668), XXVI, pt. iii, 257; agreement with regard to (1672-1674), *id.* 258-262; (1728-1744), *id.* 298-299; (1744-1781), *id.* 501-503.
Landscape: point at Mátherán, XIV, 233, 239.
Land Tax: under Mughals, I, pt. i, 212.
Land tenures: *see* under Land.
Lang, Colonel W.: political agent in Káthiáwár (1835-1836), VIII, 308.
Langha: a caste of Musalmán beggars in Káthiáwár, VIII, 164.
Langhas: singers, IX, pt. ii; *see* Mirs.
Language: details of, all district volumes, *see* "Census details" under district name.
Languages: Sanskrit, I, pt. ii, 136-137; Maráthi, *id.* 136; Kánarese, Telegu, Támil, *id.* 137; IX, pt. ii, 194, 204 and note 1, 211 and note 1.
Laniadæ: family of birds in Ratnágiri district, X, 69.
Lánja: *see* Lanje.
Lanja Bijiráo: Bhatti prince, son-in-law of Siddharája, I, pt. i, 174 note 1.
Lánje, Lánja: town in Ratnágiri district, remains at, X, 129, 345; I, pt. ii, 41.
Lanjigesara: village, identical with Lanjisvara, I, pt. ii, 348 and note 2.
Lanjipura: probably Tanjore, I, pt. ii, 235, 516. *See* Tranjipura.
Lanjisvara: modern Nandikeshwar, I, pt. ii, 346, 348 note 2.
Lanka: *see* Ceylon.
Lapsed states: in the Karnátak, I, pt. ii, 668-670.
Lapwing: class of birds in Ratnágiri district, XI, 91.
Lár, Lár Desh: old name for South Gujarát, governed by Jhanja (916), Balhára, overlord of, I, pt. ii, 22, 23 and note 1; X, 271, XIII, 434; Rander and Broach capitals of (1034), I, pt. i, 520, 524; the seat of a Gueber prince (1600), *id.* 194 note 1. *See* Lát.
Lár, Lari, Lariya, Lariayyah or Larwi: Gujaráti dialect, spoken in Thána ports, at Cheul, Sopára and Thána (916), XIII, 112, 431, 434; XI, 272 note 1; I, pt. i, 516, 523, 524; XIV, 321.
Láran: country mentioned by Alberuni, I, pt. ii, 4.
Lari: *see* Lár.
Laridæ: family of birds in Ratnágiri, X, 98.
Larika or Larike: *see* Lát or Lár.
Larinæ: sub-family of birds in Ratnágiri, X, 98.
Lariya or Lariyyah: *see* Lár.
Lark: in Ratnágiri district, X, 84.
Larwi: sea, Indian Ocean, I, pt. ii, 510; for language *see* Lár.
Lásalgaon: town in Násik district, XVI, 450.
Lascar: Bombay sailors, XIII, 521; origin of the word, *id.* 716; IX, pt. i, 519, 521.
Lasiosiphon eriocephalus: poisonous plant found on the *gháts*, XXV, 268.
Lassun: food plant cultivated in several districts, XXV, 179.
Lasthiyavvá: *see* Lachchhiyavva.
Lásur: village in Khándesh, formerly a flourishing town, the seat of a chief, XII, 257, 454.
Láta: ancient name of Central and Southern Gujarát, I, pt. i, 5 note 1, 6, 7 and note 5, 116, 117; South Gujarát, I, pt. ii, 23; one of the seven divisions of the Konkan, *id.* 282 note 5; boundaries of, *id.* 5, 22, 310, 315; one of the traditional nine kingdoms, *id.* 403 note 3; various spellings of, *id.* 1; part of the dominions of the Kalachuri kings, *id.* 295, 310; Western Chálukya king Mangalesa (about 602) acquires the sovereignty of, by overthrowing the Kalachuri kings Samkaragana and Buddha, *id.* 311, 347; governed by Satyásraya Dhruvarája Indravarman (611), *id.* 311; subdued by Pulakesin II, *id.* 183, 350; held by Vijayavarmarája, first Gujarát prince of the Chálukya family (643), *id.* 311; was in charge of Sendraka Prithivivallabha-Nikumbhallasakti (654), *id.* 311, 361; placed in the hands of a prince of the Western Chalukya stock (670), *id.* 311; Avanijanásraya Pulikesin includes the Gurjara territory into (736), *id.* 311, 316; passes into the hands of the Ráshtrakútas, distinct from the Málkhed family, *id.* 382, 392; subdued by the Málkhed Ráshtrakúta Dantidurga (753), *id.* 194, 382, 389; portion of taken by Krishna I, *id.* 382, 393; conquered and given as a feudatory province to his brother Indra by Govind III (783-784), *id.* 199, 382, 393, 400; king of, humbled by Krishna II, *id.* 201; ruled over by

the Ráshtrakúta feudatory Jhanjha of the North Konkan Siláhára family, *id.* 23 and note 1; seized by Bárappa (975), *id.* 213, 430, 514; king of, defeated by Hoysala Vishnuvardhana (1117-1137), *id.* 496, 497; chief of, leaves the side of Lavanaprasáda and joins the princes of Márvár, *id.* 241; subdued by the Devagiri Yádava kings Bhillama (1187-1191), Singhana (1210-1247), and Mahádeva (1260-1271), *id.* 520, 525, 528; *see* also I, pt. i, 122, 199, 465, 467, 468. *See* Lár.

Látadesh: *see* Láta.

Látaka: *see* Láta.

Latalaura: *see* Lattalur.

Látas: kings of Láta, I, pt. ii, 282, 309, 350, 520; I, pt. i, 465, 467.

Lateen sail: its apparent Indian origin, XIII, 724.

Laterite: Konkan, in Ratnágiri district, X, 18; stone, *id.* 31; in Sávantvádi, *id.* 397; at Mátherán, XIV, 241; in Kánara district, XV, pt. i, 10; in Bijápur district, XXIII, 45-47. *See* Iron clay.

Látesvara: Suvarnavarsha Karkarája, son of Indrarája, I, pt. ii, 310, 400.

Láth: village under Gondal in Káthiáwár, VIII, 528.

Láthi: state in Káthiáwár, VIII, 528-529; *see* also IX, pt. i, 125-126.

Lathyrus sativus: poisonous plant, XXV, 264.

Latin Friars: in Thána district (500-600), XIII, 66, 200, 439, 462.

Latitores: birds in Thána district, XIII, 53.

Latta: same as Ratta, I, pt. i, 7.

Lattalur, Lattalaura: the first Ráshtrakúta town, I, pt. ii, 384 and notes 4 and 5; original city of the Rattas, I, pt. i, 7.

Lattanur: I, pt. ii, 387, 402, 552. *See* Lattalur.

Launi: another name for the Kori, the eastern mouth of the Indus, I, pt. i, 538.

Lauraceæ: species of oil-yielding plants, XXV, 224.

Laut Mir: Red Sea, I, pt. i, 492.

Lava: son of Ráma, Bir-Gujars claim descent from, IX, pt. i, 482; said to be the founder of the Ráthor tribe of Rajpúts, IX, pt. ii, 39.

Lavád: arbitration court in Ahmadábád district, IV, 194.

Lavána: caste of traders, in Khandesh district, XII, 62; in Dhárwár district, XXII, 121-122.

Lavanaprasáda: I, pt. i, 196, 197; Vághela chieftain (1200-1233), minister of Bhim II, rules at Anáhilaváda in his sovereign's name, *id.* 199; his war with the Devagiri Yádavs and the Márwár chief; his abdication in favour of his son Viradhavala, *id.* 198, 200, 206; *another account of*: chief of the Vaghela branch of the Chalukya family of Anáhilwád, marches to meet the army of Singhana, but being deserted by the chiefs of Godhra and Láta concludes a treaty with him, I, pt. ii, 241, 525.

Lavandula Burmanni: oil-yielding aromatic plant common in the Dakhan, XXV, 224.

Lávanyaprasáda: *see* Lavanaprasáda.

Lavas: or Lors, Ajmer Gujars, origin of connection with Gujarát Kanbis, IX, pt. i, 491, 492.

Lavji Nasarvánji Vadia: foreman in the Surat Dockyard; Bombay Dockyard built under the supervision of; first Pársi master builder, IX, pt. ii, 192 note 3.

Low, Honourable Mr.: president and governor of Bombay (1739-1742), XXVI, pt. i, 217.

Lawrence: Major-General, assists Násir Jang (1748), XXII, 794.

Lawsonia alba (inermis): a very common dye plant, XXV, 245.

Lazima haks: perquisites in Thána district abolished (1866), XIII, 538.

Lead: in Panch Mahál district, III, 197.

Leaf-printing: with gold foil, in Ahmadábád district, IV, 129.

Lea macrophylla: sacred plant, XXV, 291.

Leasehold: tenure; *see* Land.

Leather: manufacture of, in Cambay, VI, 188 note 7, 191 note 9; in Khándesh, XII, 236; in Sátára district, XIX, 223; in Dhárwár district, XXII, 387-388; in Sholápur district, XX, 274; Lingáyat dislike to, XXIV, 124 note 1, 211.

Leather workers: in Ahmadábád district, IV, 139; in Cutch, V, 82; in Pálanpur, *id.* 291; in Mahi Kántha, *id.* 367; in Rewa Kántha, VI, 25; in Ratnágiri district, X, 129; in Sávantvádi, *id.* 415; in Khándesh, XII, 114; in Kánara district, XV, pt. i, 355.

Leave-taking: Pátáne Prabhu ceremony, XVIII, pt. i, 212.

Leguminosæ: species of famine, oil-yielding, fibrous and poisonous plants, XXV, 197-199, 217-218, 231-232, 242-244, 264.

Lekhapanchásika: work containing forms of letters, deeds, patents, etc., I, pt. ii, 241 and note 4, 525 notes 5 and 7.

Lemon: tree in Poona district, XVIII, pt. i, 48.

Lenás: dwelling caves, I, pt. ii, 12.

Lendas Da Asia: (A. D. 1497-1539), work of Correa, a Portuguese writer (1512-1550), I, pt. i, 349.

Lendeyarasa: feudatory of Indra, III, I, pt. ii, 416.

Lentil: pulse, cultivation of, in Poona district, XVIII, pt. ii, 43.

Leopard Cat: in Kánara district, XV, pt. i, 94.

Leper hospital: at Ratnágiri, X, 293.

Lepers: in Surat and Broach districts, II, 50, 370; in Kaira and Panch Mahál districts, III, 27, 289; in Ahmadábád district, IV, 33; in Rewa Kántha, VI, 21; in Thána district, XIII, 668; in Belgaum district, XXI, 491.

Leprosy: disease, its cure, IX, pt. i, 365; in Ratnágiri district, X, 292; in Khándesh, XII, 337; supposed cure of, XVII, 367 note 1.

Leptadenia reticulata: famine plant common near the sea, XXV, 201.

Lester: General, in command of Belgaum troops (1857), 410-411.

Leucas aspera: famine plant, XXV, 203.

Lenke: (Laccadives ?), pirate haunts, I, pt. i, 546; Ptolemy's name for Lákhadiv islands (?), XV, pt. ii, 48 note 3.

Leva : division of Gujarát Kanbis ; *see* Kanbis, I, pt. i, 4-5.
Leyden : poet and scholar, his desire to rank Europeans among Kshátriyas, IX, pt. i, 442 note 6 continued on p. 443.
Li : Chinese linear measure, I, pt. ii, 184 ; I, pt. i, 79.
Liákat Ali : Maulawi takes part in the 1857 mutiny, travels in Gujarát as Wáhhabi missionary after the mutiny, makes many converts, is arrested and transported for life, IX, pt. ii, 13, 175.
Libi : dye plant cultivated in Bombay and Poona, XXV, 243.
Library, Libraries : Deccan College, I, pt. ii, 248 ; in Surat and Broach districts, II, 258, 529 ; in Kaira and Panch Mahál districts, III, 139-289 ; in Ahmadábád district, IV, 217 ; in Cutch, V, 206 ; in Pálanpur, *id.* 314 ; in Mahi Kántha, *id.* 395 ; in Rewa Kántha, VI, 88 ; in Baroda state, VII, 493 ; in Ratnágiri district, X, 290 ; in Sávantvádi state, *id.* 459 ; in Kolába district, XI, 235 ; in Khándesh, XII, 335 ; in Thána district, XIII, 661-662 ; at Mátheran and Kalyán, XIV, 273, 346 ; in Kanara district, XV, pt. ii, 216 ; in Násik district, XVI, 384 ; in Ahmadnagar district, XVII, 581 ; in Poona district, XVIII, pt. iii, 61-62 ; in Poona city, *id.* 331 ; in Sátára district, XIX, 414-415 ; in Sholápur district, XX, 374-375 ; in Belgaum district, XXI, 488-489 ; in Dhárwár district, XXII, 620 ; in Bijápur district, XXIII, 523 ; in Kolhápur, XXIV, 284.
License-tax : returns in Poona district, XVIII, pt. ii, 97 ; in Sátára district, XIX, 178.
Lichchhavis : of Tirhut, dynasty of the, their origin, I, pt. i, 61 and note 4, 63 ; *see* also IX, pt. i, 446 note 1.
Life-boat : in Kolaba district, XI, 125.
Light : element, deity presiding over, IX, pt. i, 348. *See* Tejas.
Light-houses : in Surat district, II, 165 ; in Ahmadábád district, IV, 84 ; in Cutch, V, 117, 243 ; in Káthiáwár, VIII, 234-236 ; in Ratnágiri district, X, 172, 318, 341, 368, 378 ; in Koláha district, XI, 126 ; in Thána district, XIII, 516 ; in Kánara district, XV, pt. ii, 47, 321, 327, 338 ; at Kolába, construction of (1769-72), XXVI, pt. ii, 204.
Ligustrum : *Neilgherense robustum,* used for fermenting toddy, XXV, 211.
Likhi : state in Mahi Kántha, V, 427.
Liládevi : sister of Sámantasimha, married to Ráji, I, pt. i, 157.
Liladevi : queen of Bhima II, daughter of Chohán, chief Samarasimha, I, pt. i, 197.
Lilávati : site of an old town in Panch Mahál district, III, 317.
Liliaceæ : species of food, famine and fibrous plants, XXV, 179-180, 206, 236.
Lilia Mohota : village in Káthiáwár, VIII, 529.
Limach : Hindu goddess, shrine in Pattan, IX, pt. i, 230, 233.
Limb : *see Limdo.*
Limbdi : *see* Limdi.
Limbdo, Limb : *nim*-tree, regarded as home of Vishnu, worship of, in attack of small-pox ; juice of, drunk on first of Chaitra, IX, pt. i, 385 ; in Poona district, XVIII, pt. i, 50 ; medicinal plant, XXV, 258.
Limbhai : village in Mahi Kántha, V, 438.
Limda : táluka in Káthiáwár, VIII, 529.
Limdi or Limbdi : state in Káthiáwár, VIII, 529 ; IX, pt. i, 127.
Lime, Limestone : in Ratnágiri district, X, 14, 31 ; manufacture of, in Khándesh, XII, 225 ; in Kánara district, XV, pt. i, 10, 20 ; in Dhárwár district, XXII, 26 ; in Kolhápur state, XXIV, 20-21 ; in Sholápur district, XX, 273 ; in Ahmadábád district, IV, 22 ; in Pálanpur state, V, 285 ; in Rewa Kántha, VI, 11 ; in Ahmadnagar district, XVII, 17 ; in Poona district, XVIII, pt. i, 30-31 ; in Sátára district, XIX, 30 ; in Belgaum district, XXI, 23-25, 54 ; in Bijápur district, XXIII, 27-28, 35, 57-58.
Limnanthemum cristatum : famine plant, common in Konkan, XXV, 201.
Limodra : town in Rájpipla state in Rewa Kántha, temple and fair at, Cambay agate trade at, VI, 162, 206.
Limpangaon : village in Ahmadnagar district temples and ponds at, XVII, 725-726.
Limyrike : Ptolemy's name for Malabár Coast, I, pt. i, 543 ; Támil country, *id.* 546 ; XV, pt. ii, 48, 265, 307.
Lineæ : species of famine, oil-yielding and fibrous plants, XXV, 195-196, 215, 231.
Ling, Lingam : phallus of Shiv, IX, pt. i, p. xxxv, 531, 541 ; dropping of water over, *id.* 348, 355 ; I, pt. ii, 226, 477 ; worship of the, I, pt. i, 521, 522 ; spirit-scaring power of, and origin of wearing of, among Lingáyats, XXIV, 118 and note 2 ; mention of, I, pt. i, 461 ; at Elephanta, Sháhapur and Ambarnath, XIV, 91, 95, 96, 97, 309, 310, 385 ; at Gokarn, XV, pt ii, 290-298.
Ling : poisonous plant, XXV, 264.
Linga : pass in Kolába district, XI, 6, 115.
Lingána : fort in Kolába district, built by Shiváji (1648), XI, 144, 269, 343 ; I, pt. ii, 67.
Lingánuśásana : a work on genders compiled by Hemachandra, I, pt. i, 193.
Lingawant : Lingáyat, I, pt. ii, 477.
Lingáyat : a Shaiv sectarian community, with many sub-divisions, in the southern districts of the presidency, I, pt. ii, 464 ; chief characteristics of the faith and practices of, *id.* 477 and note 5 ; their numerical strength, *id.* 477-478 ; *puránas* of, *id.* 478-481 ; establishment of the sect, *id.* 484 ; their attacks chiefly directed against the Jains, *id.* 225, 479 ; title of their priest, *id.* 549 ; in Ratnágiri district, X, 118 ; in Sávantvádi, *id.* 413 ; in Kolába district, XI, 49, 142 ; in Khándesh, XII, 56, 61 ; in Thána district, XIII, 110 ; in Kánara district, their faith and rise, XV, pt. ii, 89-90 ; in Násik district, XVI, 46 ; in Poona district, XVIII, pt. i, 270-272 ; in Belgaum district, XXI, 149, 150 ; in Dhárwár district, their strength and distribution ; Basav's life and parentage ; doctrines and practices ; comparison of Lingáyatism and Jainism ; priest-

hood, XXII, 102-115; in Bijápur district, their doctrines, XXIII, 225-230; customs, *id.* 230-238; true, *id.* 220-238; affiliated, *id.* 238-259; half, *id.* 259-280; in Kolhápur state, strength and distribution; Basav's life, doctrines; sects, daily life, customs, XXIV, 118-133; in Sátára district, XIX, 59-60; in Sholápur district, XX, 75-80.

Lingáyat Burud: a caste of basket-makers in Ahmadnagar district, XVII, 116-118.

Lingáyat Gánig: a caste of oilmen in Kánara district, XV, pt. i, 278.

Lingáyatism: compared with Jainism, XXII, 107-108.

Lingáyat Kelasi: a caste of barbers in Kánara district, XV, pt. i, 331.

Lingáyat Kumbár: a caste of potters in Kánara district, XV, pt. i, 271-272.

Lingáyat Madival: a caste of cloth-cleaners in Kánara district, XV, pt. i, 328.

Lingáyat math: description of a, XXIV, 122-123.

Lingáyat Váni: *see* Banjig.

Ling chapel: in Elephanta caves, XIV, 71-72, 77.

Ling fruit: (*kanduri*), its holiness, IX, pt. ii, 151 note 1.

Lingthali: village near Kárván in the Gáikwár's territory, place of *lingas*, I, pt. i, 84 note.

Lingvant: *see* Lingáyat.

Linschot, Linschoten: Hugues de, Dutch traveller (1583-1596), his mention of Chaul (1583), XI, 278 and notes 1 and 2; his notice of Elephanta, XIV, 59 note 1, 84, 92 note 1; his notice of pepper trade at Honávar, XV, pt. ii, 52, 119, 274, 310; his notice of Jaitapur in Ratnágiri, X, 279; mention of, I, pt. ii, 36, 60.

Linseed: *Linum usitatissimum*, oil-yielding and fibrous plant, cultivated in several districts, XXV, 215, 231; in Khándesh district, XII, 152; in Poona district, XVIII, pt. ii, 45; in Sátára district, XIX, 164.

Lions: in Káthiáwár, VIII, 100, 101.

Liquor: in Khándesh, XII, 227; shops, licenses, farming system, toddy, *id.* 321; distilleries at Karanj and Uran in Thána district, XIV, 191, 371; in Kánara district, shops, manufacture of, classes who drink, system, XV, pt. ii, 35, 204, 205; in Surat and Broach districts, shops, II, 241, 515; manufacture of, in Násik district, XVI, 322, 323.

Liquor-yielding trees: in Kolába district, XI, 27-30; in Kánara district, XV, pt. i, 58-60.

Litter: Banavási marble inscriptions on, XV, pt. ii, 263-264.

Little: Captain, English officer at the siege of Dhárwár (1789), I, pt. ii, 661; English commander sent against Tipu (1790), XXI, 386; XXII, 417.

Lizard: unholiness of, IX, pt. i, 380.

Loahe: wine drawn from trees, I, pt. ii, 5.

Loans; by the East India Company to native merchants (1731-1760), XXVI, pt. iii, 249-250; by the Company's servants to country powers forbidden (1766), *id.* 385-386.

Lobelia nicotianæfolia: poisonous plant, XXV, 265.

Local funds: all district volumes, *see* "Revenue and Finance" under district name.

Locusts: in Cutch, V, 173, 175; in Pálanpur, *id.* 296; in Mahi Kántha, *id.* 371; in Ahmadábád district, IV, 61; in Ratnágiri district, X, 426; in Kolába district, XI, 213; in Khándesh, XII, 182; in Thána district, XIII, 517, 627; in Násik district, (1882), XVI, 211, 301-303; in Ahmadnagar district, XVII, 281-284; ravages of, in Poona district, XVIII, pt. ii, 80-82, 424, 432, 476, 502, 511, 512; in Sátára district, XIX, 385-388; in Belgaum district (1865), XXI, 461; (1875-1876), *id.* 463; (1873-1880), *id.* 464; in Kolhápur state, XXIV, 188.

Lodh, lodhra: dye and sacred plant found on the *ghâts*, XXV, 247, 286.

Lodhi: a caste of cultivators in Khándesh, XII, 70; in Thána district, XIII, 153; in Poona district, XVIII, pt. i, 398-401; in Sholápur district, XX, 161.

Lodhika: táluka in Káthiáwár, VIII, 535.

Lodhva: Ahir village in Káthiáwár, VIII, 534.

Lodra: village in Ahmadábád district, gathering of *thákurs* at (1857), I, pt. i, 443.

Lodwick: Colonel, resident at Sátára (1835), XIX, 309-310; monument of, at Mahábleshwar, *id.* 504, 505.

Lodwick Point: *see* Mahábleshwar.

Loganiaceæ: species of poisonous plants, XXV, 267.

Lohagad or Lohogad: fort in Poona district, details, description, history, XVIII, pt. iii, 247-256; state prison of Ahmadnagar kings (1564), XVIII, pt. ii, 222; captured by Shiváji (1648), I, pt. ii, 592-593; again captured by Moropant (1670), *id.* 594; retaken by Mughals, XVIII, pt. ii, 236; taken by Angria (1713), XI, 146; Gáikwár and Dabhade families imprisoned (1751) in, XVIII, pt. ii, 245; taken by the British (1818), *id.* 303, XI, 156.

Lohagráma: village near Ramapuri, I, pt. ii, 417.

Lohána: caste of traders in Gujarát, IX, pt. i, p. xi note 3; strength and distribution, *id.* 69, 121; name, *id.* 121 and notes 1 and 2; divisions, religion, *id.* 122; said to be of Afghán origin, *id.* 453 and note 1; of Káthiáwár, conversions by Pir Dádu of, to the Khojáh sect, IX, pt. ii, 41; Panjáb, the Afghán tribe of, legendary origin of, conversions of, into the Khojáh sect, *id.* 39; Sindh *nukhs* or divisions of, *id.* 50 note 4; conversions by Eusuf-ud-din of, to the Sunni faith, form a community of Memans, *id.* 50-51. *See* Khojáhs and Memans; in Ratnágiri district, X, 121, 171; in Cutch, V, 54-56; in Pálangur state, *id.* 289; in Káthiáwár, VIII, 149; in Thána district, XIII, 111; in Kánara district, XV, pt. i, 187; in Poona district, XVIII, pt. i, 273; in Sholápur district, XX, 85.

Lohar, Luhar: a caste of iron workers in Gujarát, claim descent from Pithvo; created by Párvati; tribal and local surnames; six

divisions,' IX, pt. i, 190; craft, shop, tools, religious sects, *id.* 191; customs, *id.* 191-192; immigrants from Sind, Sunnis in faith, IX, pt. ii, 75; a caste of blacksmiths, I, pt. i, 451; in Cutch, V, 72; in Káthiáwár, VIII, 151; in Ratnágiri district, X, 125-141; in Koláha district, XI, 413; in Khándesh, XII, 73, 224; in Thána district, XIII, 138; in Kánara district, XV, pt. i, 263-265; in Násik District, XVI, 51, 484; in Ahmadnagar district, XVII, 118-119; in Poona district, XVIII, pt. i, 352-353; in Sátára district, XIX, 87-88; in Sholápur district, XX, 121-122; in Belgaum district, XXI, 141, 142; in Kolhápur state, XXIV, 96.

Lohára: village in Koláha district, monumental pillars at, XI, 343.

Lohara: village in Khándesh district, Hemadpanti temple at, XII, 455.

Lohára: *see* Wai.

Lohasvámin: Bráhman grantee of Chalukya prince, I, pt. ii, 191.

Lohkot: taken to be Láhore, IX, pt. i, 491; fort of, in Káshmir, *id.* 491 and note 6.

Lohogad: *See* Lohagad.

Lokábaliki: a caste of Lingáyat traders in Dhárwár district, XXII, 123-124.

Lokade: *see* Lokáditya.

Lokadeyarasa: *see* Lokáditya.

Lokáditya: Pallava king, *biruda* or title of Ugradanda-Parmeśvaravarman I, I, pt. ii, 330.

Lokáditya, Lokade, Lokadeyarasa: Banavási governor (A. D. 897), feudatory of Krishna II, I, pt. ii, 411 and note 3.

Lokáditya: Gokarn chief (750), XV, pt. ii, 83, 299.

Loka Mahádevi: Háihaya or Kalachuri princess, wife of Vikramáditya II (733-747), I, pt. ii, 190, 296; temple of Shiva built by, at Pattadakal, *id.* 374 and note 5, 414 note 4.

Lokandi: dye plant common on the *gháts*, XXV, 242.

Lokapálesvara: *see* Lokesvara.

Lokápura: province governed by the Western Chálukyas, I, pt. ii, 465.

Lokasena: pupil of Gunabhadra, consecrates the Jain *Purána*, I, pt. ii, 201-202.

Lokesvara, Lokapalesvara: Shiva's temple at Pattadakal in the Bijápur district, I, pt. ii, 190; built by Lokamahádevi, wife of Vikramáditya II, *id.* 372, 374 and note 5, 377; inscriptions at the temple of, *id.* 376, 394; inscription at the temple of, at Handarike in the Nizám's dominions, *id.* 339 and note 6.

Lokhera: river in the Ahmadnagar district, XVII, 8.

Lokkigundi: modern Lakkundi, I, pt ii, 228, 496 and note 6; conquered by Vishnuvardhana, *id.* 497; Bhilláma's forces destroyed by Vira-Ballála II at, *id.* 505.

Lokvant: a division of Lingáyats, origin of the name of, XXIV, 123 note.

Loliyana: village in Káthiáwár, its history, VIII, 535.

Lonad: village in Thána district, description of, inscription, temple and cave at, XIV, 211-216; probable representation of Mauryan court in its caves, XIII, 421; a Siláhára town, *id.* 423, 429; I, pt. ii, 16; remains at, *id.* 22.

Lonári: caste of carriers in Násik district, XVI, 58; saltmen in Belgaum district, XXI, 125, 126; in Bijápur district, XXIII, 124; cement-makers in Khándesh, XII, 75, 225, 229 note 1; in Sátára district, XIX, 88; in Sholápur district, XX, 122-123; in Poona district, XVIII, pt. i, 353; in Ahmadnagar district, XVII, 119-121; in Kolhápur state, XXIV, 31, 107.

Lonavali: town with railway station in Poona district, XVIII pt. iii, 256.

Lonch: hills in Káthiáwár, VIII, 11.

Londári: a caste of cultivators in Khándesh, XII, 63.

Loni: caste of cultivators in Khándesh, XII, 68.

Lonibare: month of the Indus, mentioned by Klaudios Ptolemaios, I, pt. i, 568.

Loni Kalbhar: village with railway station in Poona district, XVIII, pt. iii, 256; Holkar's camp at, I, pt. ii, 608.

Loni Kand: village in Poona district, description of township (1820), XVIII, pt. iii, 256-258.

Lonkagachha: sub-sect of Svetámbari Shrávaks, IX, pt. i, 105-106.

Loranthaceæ: species of food plants, XXV, 174.

Lord: Mr., an English chaplain, writes an account of the Pársis (1620), IX, pt. ii, 190.

Lotheshvar: village in Baroda state, VII, 615.

Loti: village in Pálanpur state, temple and fair at, V, 342.

Lotia: IX, pt. ii, 28 note 1. *See* Dáudi Bohora.

Louisa: point at Mátherán, XIV, 239-240.

Lonse temple: at Anabilváda, I, pt. i, 193.

Love bird: *karta*, in Ratnágiri district, X, 66.

Lovibond: Mr., British agent (1775) to Fatesing Gáikwár, VII, 194.

Lucas: Sir G., appointed governor of Bombay, XXVI, pt. i, 23; death of, *id.* 24.

Ludovico Varthema: travels from Gujarát to Cheul (1503), I, pt. ii, 31.

Luhar: *see* Lohar.

Luhára: village, engagement of the Maráthás with the Kolis at, I, pt. i, 338.

Lumcherri: Bijápur gun, XXIII, 638.

Lunapála: Vastupála's chief supporter, shrine, I, pt. i, 200 note 2.

Lunar Asterisms: XXII, 271.

Lunar (Somvansi) Race: movement of from Dwárka to the west and north to Gijni and Samarkand after defeat of Krishna; said to have founded Jesalmir on their return to India, IX, pt. i, 446 note 4; race, I, pt. ii, 383, 389, 468, 578; Yádavas belong to the, *id.* 512.

Lunáváda: state in Rewa Kántha, VI, 1, 2; its area, boundaries, rivers, hills, climate, population, sub-divisions, history and family tree of its chiefs, *id.* 121-131; Solanki Rájpút chiefship, IX, pt. i, 129; its tribute to the Gáikwár (1812-1883), VII, 334-335; *Town*, palace of the chief at, VI, 163-164; disturb-

ance at, crushed by Lieutenant Albau, I, pt. i, 441.
Lunda : a caste of hereditary servants in Káira district, III, 63. *See* Gola.
Lunghia : táluka in Káthiáwár, VIII, 535.
Luni : river in Márwár, I, pt. i, 538.
Luniga : chief, mentioned by Forbes, I, pt. i, 470.
Lushington Falls : in Kánara district, XV, pt. i, 6, 9 ; XV, pt. ii, 329, 352.
Lutrinæ : otters, etc., in Ratnágiri district, X, 44.
Luykin : Captain (1830), suppresses Koli rising in Ahmadnagar district, XVII, 417.
Lynx : in Khándesh, XII, 31 ; in Kánara district, XV, pt. i, 34.
Lyra : constellation of, IX, pt. ii, 217 note 1.
Lythraceæ : species of dye and poisonous plants, XXV, 245-246, 265.

M

MAAKA : a sacred plant, XXV, 292.
Maar : fibrous plant, XXV, 237.
Macan : Colonel, his engagement with Bhágoji, (1857), XVI, 200.
Macca Mosque : at Bijápur, XXIII, 628-629.
Máchál : hill in Ratnágiri district, X, 4, 8, 345 ; I, pt. ii, 28.
Machandragad, Machhindragad : fort in Sátára district, temple remains and history of, XIX, 489-490, 308 ; built by Shiváji in 1676, I, pt. ii, 595.
Máeharda : place of interest, in Káthiáwár, VIII, 542.
Machhi : a caste of sea-farers in Gujarát, strength, name, divisions, origin, IX, pt. i, 519 ; character, occupation, beliefs, *id.* 520 ; Musalmáns, Hindu converts of Bhoi and Kharva castes, two divisions of—the Inland and the Coast, Sunnis in faith separate classes of the two divisions of, IX, pt. ii, 87 ; in Thána district, XIII, 147, 719 ; in Rewa Kántha, VI, 25 ; in Káthiáwár, VIII, 154.
Machhindragad : rock in Thána district, XIV, 101.
Machhindragad : *see* Machandragad.
Machhlis : Nát women, take part in acrobatic feats ; meaning of the name of, IX, pt. ii, 89.
Machhu : river in Káthiáwár, VIII, 62.
Machhukántha : sub-division of Káthiáwár, VIII, 4.
Machhvá, Machvá : a small boat, in Ratnágiri district, X, 171 ; in Sávantvádi, *id.* 435 ; also called *suvál*, in Thána district, XIII, 345, 719 ; in Kánara district, XV, pt. ii, 60-63.
Machigudd : hill in Belgaum district, XXI, 9.
Machnur : village in Sholápur district, fort at, XX, 413.
Machundri : river in Káthiáwár, VIII, 63.
Machva : *see* Machhva.
Mackintosh : Captain, suppresses the rising of Kolis (1828) in Thána district, XIII, 635 ; suppresses the Koli rising in Ahmadnagar district (1829), XVII, 417.
Mackintosh : Sir James, succeeds Sir William Syer in the post of Recorder of Bombay (1804), XXVI, pt. iii, 688 ; his description of Poona (1805), XVIII, pt. iii, 419-420 ; XVIII, pt. ii, 287-288 ; in Poona (1808), *id.* 289-290 ; his visit to Bijápur (1808), XXIII, 594-597 ; his visit to Kalyán and Panvel (1810), XIV, 121, 296.
Mackivy : small twining medicinal plant, XXV, 260.
MacMurdo : British agent to Fateh Muhammad (1813), V, 154 ; goes to Bhuj (1814), *id.* 156 ; attacked by Vághad banditti (1815), *id.* 157 ; appointed resident at Bhuj (1816), *id.* 159 ; his description of Cutch (1818), *id.* 160-161 ; his description of Sodha Parmar women (1819), IX, pt. i, 128.
MacNeale : Captain, captured (1729) by Ángria, XI, 149.
Maçudi : *see* Masudi.
Madagajendralánchhana : crest of the Western Gangas, I, pt. ii, 299.
Madag Lake : in the Dhárwár district, XXII, 260-263.
Madalámbiká : mother of Basava, I, pt. ii, 478.
Madanapála : brother of Karna's mother, his death, I, pt. i, 172.
Madanarájni : wife of Lavanaprasáda, I, pt. i, 198.
Madanavarmman : Chandela king of Mahobaka, modern Mahoba, his inscription ; his surrender to Siddharája ; his hospitality, I, pt. i, 178-179.
Madanbhánvi : village in Dhárwár district, temples and inscriptions at, XXII, 770.
Madangad : fort in Násik district, XVI, 450.
Madar : a plant used in dying, XXV, 246.
Madari : a caste of homeless wandering beggars in Gujarát, origin of the name of ; their peculiar way of asking alms, IX, pt. ii, 22-23 ; Hindu converts, wandering tribe of players, followers of Saint Sháh Madar, worship Musalmán saints and Hindu gods ; Sunnis in name, follow Hindu customs and form a separate community, *id.* 171 ; in Belgaum, XXI, 224.
Mádevi : wife of Kártavirya IV, the Ratta chieftain, I, pt. ii, 551, 557.
Mádevi : wife of Áchugi II the Sinda prince, I, pt. ii, 573, 574.
Madgad : fortified hill in Janjira state, XI, 402, 465 ; in charge of the Peshwa (1744), *id.* 445.
Madh : village in Cutch, allum manufactured at, temple of Áshápura Máta and caves at, V, 84, 233-234.
Madh : village in Thána district, temple of Ganpati at, XIV, 216.
Madh : village in Poona district, XVIII, pt. iii, 258.
Madh : fortified island north of Bombay, XIV, 379.
Mádha : sub-division of Sholápur district, its boundaries, area, aspect, climate, water, soil, stock, holdings, crops and people, XX, 396-398 ; survey of, *id.* 304-309, 334-341. *Town*, fort and temple at, *id.* 413.

Madhariputa, Madhariputra: Andhrabhritya king, I, pt. ii, 11, 156, 167, 177; dates of the reign of, *id.* 168; mentioned in Kanheri caves, XIV, 147 179; I, pt. ii, 153, 152 and note 1. *See* Sakasena.

Mádhava: Nágar Bráhman, minister of Karnadeva, invites Muhammadans into Gujarát; is appointed civil minister of Alaf Khán, I, pt. i, 205 and note 2.

Mádhava II: Ganga king, marries the sister of Krishnavarman the Kadamba king, I, pt. ii, 291 note 1.

Madhavacharya: Orissa Bráhman, founder of *Brahma Sampradaya*, IX, pt. i, 534.

Mádhavácharya: Vijayanagar minister (1370) of Harihara, XV, pt. ii, 96 and note 3, 262 and note 3; I, pt. ii, 175.

Mádhavasena: cousin of the king of Vidarbha, his capture by the general of the king, I, pt. ii, 147.

Mádhavayya: Kalachurya Someśvara's officer (1713), I, pt. ii, 486.

Madhavayya: Vira-Ballála II's governor of Belvola (1207), I, pt. ii, 506.

Madhavgar's Panth: religious sect in Gujarát, IX, pt. i, 546.

Mádhavpur: place of interest in Káthiáwár, VIII, 285, 535.

Mádhavráv I: son and successor of Báláji Bájiráv Peshwa (1761-1772), I, pt. i, 399; *id.* pt. ii, 602; Nizám Áli advances against, within fourteen miles of Poona (1761), *id.* 602-603; disagreement with Raghunáthráv; defeat of the army of, by Raghunáthráv with the help of the Nizám; the Nizám burns Poona (1763) but is defeated by the Marátha army; recovers the management of the government, *id.* 603; his campaign against Haidar (1764-1766); capture of Dhárwár; treaty of Bednur (1766), *id.* 658-659; by A. D. 1766 retrieves the position of the state, *id.* 98; suppresses the revolt of Raghunáthráv (1768) and imprisons him till the close of his reign; war with Jánoji Bhonsla of Berár, *id.* 603; I, pt. i, 400; captures Govindráo Gáikwár, VII, 187; during his reign the administration reaches its highest excellence, I, pt. ii, 603; his death (1772), *id.* 659; *see* also XV, pt. ii, 140, 335; XVIII, pt. iii, 406-407, 452; refuses to cede Sálsette (1766), XIII, 498; his reforms, XVIII, pt. ii, 253; partial to the Patwardhans, XXIV, 344-345; *another account of:* fourth Peshwa (1761-1772); succeeds his father; Raghunáthráv becomes regent; war with the Nizám; quarrels with Raghunáthráv who defeats Mádhavráv; Raghunáthráv in power, places Mádhavráv in confinement; Raghunáthráv's unpopular measures; war with the Nizám who plunders Poona; battle of Rakisbon; war with Haidar Ali; success of Mádhavráv; Mr. Mostyn, the envoy from the Bombay government, at Poona; Mádhavráv defeats Raghunáthráv at Dhodap and takes him prisoner; his measures against Jánoji; sends an army to Málwa; improves the civil government of the country; sends an army against Haidar Ali in the Karnátak; his death; character, XVIII, pt. ii, 250-254.

Mádhavráv II: seventh Peshwa (1774-1795); minority; internal disorders; the ministry combine and act against Raghunáthráv who is helped by the English; treaty of Purandhar; French intrigues in Poona; rivalry amongst the ministers; Nána Fadnavis; English expedition; convention of Vadgaon; General Goddard's march; treaty of Salbái; Mahádji Sindia in power; war with the Nizám; Nána's height of prosperity; Mádhavráv's death, XVIII, pt. ii, 258-271; *see* also I, pt. ii, 606, 628, 662; XVIII, pt. iii, 411.

Mádhavráv Gáikwár: brother of Piláji, takes Baroda (1734) from Sher Khán Bábi the governor, I, pt. i, 394.

Mádhavráv, Raja Sir T.: appointed minister of Baroda (1875), his early life, his work in Baroda, VII, 285-286; his reforms in land administration, *id.* 371-379; abolishes Baroda state banks, *id.* 410; extract from his first report on Baroda finance, *id.* 418-419; his financial reforms, *id.* 419-437; judicial reforms, *id.* 446; creates an educational department, *id.* 474; starts a medical department, *id.* 501.

Mádhavráv Rastia: *see* Mahadevráv Raste.

Madhi: place of pilgrimage in Ahmadnagar, Kánhoba's shrine, buildings and fair at, XVII, 726-727.

Madhukeshvar: family god of the Hángal Kadambas, I, pt. ii, 278 note 2; XV, pt. ii, 87; temple with inscriptions at, *id.* 77, 261-266.

Mádhu Ling Naik: fourth Sonda chief (1638-1674), XV, pt. ii, 120 note 3, 123, 130.

Madhurántaka II: I, pt. ii, 436. *See* Rájendra-Choladeva and Parakesarivarman.

Madhurapura: held by Vishnuvardhana, I, pt. ii, 497.

Madhuvati: river in Rewa Kántha, VI, 6.

Madhuveija, Madhuveyya: Lingáyat, blinded by the Kalachurya Bijjála or Vijjana, I, pt. ii, 226, 479, 480.

Mádhva Bráhmans: in Dhárwár district, position, names, appearance, houses, food, dress, ornaments, occupation, daily life, religion, customs, XXII, 56-90.

Madhvachari: religious sect in Gujarát, IX, pt. i, 181, 530.

Madhvacharya Pontiffs: list of (1197-1883), XXII, 59.

Madhvi: *pátil's* assistant (1817) in Thána district, XIII, 563; (1828), *id.* 573.

Madhya: pass in Kolába district, XI, 5, 114.

Madhyadeśa: country between the Ganges and the Jamna, I, pt. i, 161, 428.

Mádhyandin Bráhmans: in Násik district, XVI, 37-39; in Kolhápur, XXIV, 62-63.

Madi: a food plant cultivated in low shady land in Goa, Kánara and Sonda, XXV, 181.

Mádig, Mádigar, *pl.* Mádigaru: caste of tanners, in Kánara, XV, pt. i, 358, 359; in Bijápur district, XXIII, 216-219; in Dhárwár, XXII, 218-219; in Belgaum district, XXI, 194-195.

Madinah: Sunni place of pilgrimage, IX, pt. ii, 47, 56, 171; I, pt. i, 204.

Madinayya: in Banvási province, I, pt. ii, 563.

Mádirája: Basava's father, resident of Bágevadi in Bijápur, I, pt. ii, 225, 478.

Mádraka : tribe, I, pt. i, 64 and note 3 ; king of, conquered by Kirtivarman I, I, pt. ii, 281, 345.
Madras : taken by the French (1746), XXVI, pt. i, 281, 283-284 ; capture of (1754), *id.* 321 ; Pársis as merchants in (1780) ; tower of silence in (1790), IX, pt. ii, 195.
Madrasi : a class of servants in Belgaum district, XXI, 151.
Madrási Bráhmans : in Thána district, XIII, 80.
Madura : district in Madras presidency, I, pt ii, 133, 141, 277 ; town, capital of Pandyan chiefs (1252), XV, pt ii, 94, 156 ; I, pt. i, 546.
Mæsa Indica : *atki* ; a plant for poisoning fish, XXV, 272.
Maga : a caste of Bráhmans, sun-worshippers, I, pt. i, 142, 450.
Magadha : kingdom of Aśoka in, I, pt. ii, 142 ; king of, forced to obey Krishna II, *id.* 201 ; is subdued by Someśvara III, *id.* 221 ; is conquered by Kirtivarman I, *id.* 281, 345 ; pays homage to Amoghavarsha, *id.* 402 ; is humbled by Singhana, *id.* 525 ; called Behár, Gupta rule in (7th century), I, pt. i, 73, 77.
Mágadhi : Prakrit dialect, I, pt. ii, 136.
Mágani : revenue village groups under Sonda chiefs, XV, pt. ii, 155.
Maganlál : agent of Bápu Gáikwár, a political refugee at Ahmadábád, I, pt. i, 443.
Magar : *see* Alligator.
Magara, Makara : kingdom uprooted by Narasimha II, I, pt. ii, 507.
Mágáthan : deserted village in Thána district, Buddhist caves and tombs at, XIV, 216-218 ; mentioned in Kanheri caves, *id.* 124, 147 ; I, pt. ii, 9 ; Portuguese church at, *id.* 66.
Magdam Pir : fair in honor of, at Ichalkaranji in Kolhápur state, XXIV, 298.
Magh, Magha : Sanskrit poet, Shrimáli Bráhman, IX, pt. i, 19 ; I, pt. i, 453 note 1.
Magha or Magian : tribe made Bráhmans, IX, pt. i, 440 note 4, 500 ; priestly class of South Marwar, said to be Mihira Bráhmans, *id.* 439 ; their origin ; suggested to be Zoroastrians or Mobeds ; worship of Mihireshwar introduced by, priests to Oswals and other Marwar Shrávaks, *id.* 440 and note 4 ; Gurjar element in, *id.* 500 ; people delighting in fire-worship, IX, pt. ii, 187 note 3 ; of Tughlikhpur, *id.* 188 note 4 ; among early Arabs, *id.* 1 note 1 ; captives of Timur (1398), *id.* 188 note 4.
Maghrib : Sunni prayer at dusk, IX, pt. ii, 49, 126 note 3.
Magi : Bráhmani, mention of, by Ptolemy (150) ; religion of, IX, pt. ii, 183 note 4 continued on page 184.
Magic : belief in, IX, pt. ii, 56, 142 ; practice of, forbidden by the *Kurán* ; resorted to chiefly by women ; its aims ; first teachers of, Harut and Marut, *id.* 142-143 ; two kinds of, *ruhani* or divine and *shaitani* or satanic ; sub-divisions of the divine—*ulavi* the high, and *suffi* the low ; high magic is commoner, requires ceremonial purity and is practised by good men for good ends ; consists in the knowledge of Ismi Aazam ; the knowledge of the name first known to the Prophet Suleiman ; other charmed words and names possessing magical powers, *id.* 143-144 ; performance of *chillah* to secure efficacy in the art of, *id.* 144 ; *satanic* or black magic strictly forbidden, depends on the agency of genii and evil spirits, requires impurity of body and mind, Gujarát ways of acquiring it more gruesome than the Arábian ; Diwali time (Hindu Kartika) chosen to learn, *id.* 145 ; skill in, of Indian Bráhmans, of Buddhists, of Tartars, of the Hyrkanian wizard, IX, pt. i, 437 and notes 2 to 6 ; faith in, IX, pt. ii, 220 ; of Buddhists, XIV, 133.
Magistracy : all district volumes, *see* Justice under District Name.
Mágod Falls : in Kánara district, XV, pt. i, 6, 9 ; *id.* pt. ii, 329.
Magodi : state in Mahi Kántha, V, 422 ; village with memorial stones, *id.* 428.
Magona : state in Mahi Kántha, V, 428.
Magor : military tribe, become Hindus, IX, pt. i, 452.
Magpie : in Ratnágiri district, X, 82.
Magrabu : medicinal plant, XXV, 260.
Mágutta : Gutta king, I, pt. ii, 579, 580.
Magyás : of Málwa, believed by Professor Dowson to be relics of the old Upper India Pársis, IX, pt. ii, 188 note 4.
Mahábaleshvar : temple of, at Gokarn, XV, pt. ii, 289-291.
Mahábaleshvar, Mahableshwar : hill station in Sátára district, XIX, 9 ; description, roads, geology, water, climate, animals, population, history, points, temples, etc., *id.* 490-513 ; defeat of Afzul Khán's army at, by Shiváji, I, pt. ii, 592.
Mahábat Khán : thirty-third viceroy of Gujarát (1662-1668), suppresses the rebellion of the Chunvál Kolis headed by a Baluchi personating Dára Shikoh (1664), I, pt. i, 283.
Mahábhárat : the epic poem of the heroic age, Krishna its hero, IX, pt. i, 531 ; *Bhagvadgita* included in, *id.* 532 ; authority in, of Bráhman marriage with any of the four castes, *id.* 435, 445 note 3, 447, 448 ; reference to Kánheri in, XIV, 124 note 1 ; how recast, *id.* 131 ; mention of Sopára in, *id.* 316 ; mention of Gokarn in, XV, pt. ii, 298. *See* also I, pt. ii, 133, 135, 175, 278 note 2 ; I, pt. i, 545, XIII, 404.
Mahábháshya : Patanjali's commentary on Pánini's grammar, I, pt. ii, 135, 141.
Mahábhoja : "the great Bhoja," mention of, in ancient inscriptions, I, pt. ii, 143 ; princess, *id.* 173.
Mahád : sub-division of Kolába district, its boundaries, area, aspect, climate, water, soil, holdings, rental, stock, produce, people, XI, 1, 250-252 ; included in old Ráygad, sub-division, *id.* 159, 186, 196. *Town*, communities, history, trade, *id.* 343-345 ; *see* also *id.* 150 ; Pále and Kol caves near, *id.* 345-349 ; flourishes under Shiváji, *id.* 72 ; caves at, *id.* 173, 174 ; treaty of (1795), *id.* 110 ; XVIII, pt. ii, 273.
Mahad : a food plant, XXV, 180.
Mahádaji Gáikwár : *see* Maloji.

Mahádájipant Purandhare: Báláji Peshwa's agent, XVIII, pt. ii, 244-246.

Mahádaji Sindia: (1763-1794), Marátha leader, peremptorily ordered to leave Poona (1763), XVIII, pt. ii, 253; joins Nána Fadnavis at Purandhar (1778), *id.* 263; Broach promised to (1779), *id.* 266; sent against Kolhápur (1779), XXI, 384; receives the town of Broach from the English (1782), I, pt. i, 410; in possession of Delhi and the person of the emperor (1789); marches to Poona to support Nána Fadnavis; I, pt. ii, 605-606; his rivalry with Nána Fadnavis, his death and character (1794), XVIII, pt. ii, 269; *id.* pt. iii, 410-411.

Mahádáyi: ravine in Belgaum district, XXI, 9; stream, *id.* 13.

Mahádev: *see* Shiva.

Mahádeva: officer of the Western Chálukya kings Someśvara III, Jagadekamalla II and Taila III, I, pt ii, 456, 457, 460.

Mahádeva: Devagiri Yádava king (1260-1271), I, pt. ii, 230; succeeds his brother Krishna, *id.* 246, 252, 527; records of his reign, *id.* 527-528, 583, 584; defeats the kings of Láta, Karnáta, Tailanga, Konkan and Anhilwád, *id.* 246-247, 528; his feudatories and officials, *id.* 248, 528.

Mahádevarasa: Kalachurya Bijjála's governor of the Banvási province, I, pt. ii, 473.

Mahádevgad: fort in Ratnágiri district, X, 465.

Máhádevi: *see* Mádevi.

Mahádev Koli: *see* Koli.

Mahádevpura: place of interest in Káthiáwár, VIII, 536.

Mahádevráv Ráste: Poona *sardár*, released by Bájiráv (1802), I, pt. ii, 110; *jahgir* restored to (1817), *id.* 611.

Mahágaon: village in Thána district, XIV, 11.

Mahágiri: suburb of Thána, XIV, 346.

Mahágutta: *see* Mágutta.

Mahája: pass in Násik district, XVI, 128.

Mahájan: trade guild in Ahmadábád district, IV, 106; council of leading men among Márwaris, IX, pt. i, 105; Sonis, *id.* 200; Vániás, *id.* 95; trading class at Bhinmal, I, pt. i, 450.

Mahájan: respectable family among Ratnágiri Vanis, X, 118.

Mahákál: *see* Kondivti.

Mahákála: of Ujjayani, family god of the Guttas, I, pt. ii, 578.

Mahákáli: Hindu goddess, IX, pt. i, p. xxxv.

Mahákántára: country along the south of the Narbada, I, pt. ii, 280.

Mahákshatrap: dynasty, mentioned in Kánheri caves, XIV, 172. *See* Kshatrapa.

Mahákuta: ruined town in Bijápur district, pillar inscriptions at, I, pt. ii, 285, 293, 295, 300, 309, 328, 336 note 3, 338 and note 1, 342, 343, 344, 345, 347, 348, 372, 417 note 5. *See* Nandikeshvar.

Mahálakshmi: Hindu goddess, IX, pt. i, p. xxxv; of Kolhápur, *id.* 12; inscription at the temple of, at Kolhápur, I, pt. ii, 467; ancient shrine of, at Kolhápur, *id.* 538 note 8; family deity of the Karad Siláháras, *id.* 546; Shri, of Shrimal, daughter of the sage Bhrigu, IX, pt. i, 73, 97, 98, 200; temple of, at Bhinmal, I, pt. i, 451, 471; worship of, XXIV, 57; temple of, near Dahánu, XIV, 218-219.

Mahálakshmi: hill in Thána district, XIII, 7.

Mahalakshmi: in Bombay island, breach at, stopped (1720-1728), XXVI, pt. iii, 316-319; reclaimed lands let (1738-1742), *id.* 319-321.

Maháiingpur leading town in Mudhol state, temple and fair at, XXIV, 393.

Mahálkari: petty sub-divisional officer under the Collector, XIII, 529; under the Maráthás, *id.* 555-556; his powers; his attendants and armed messengers, revenue farmer, *id.* 559-560, 561, 563 note 4; in Khándesh, XII, 265; in Poona district, XVIII, pt. ii, 311; introduction of, in the Dakhan (1835-1838), *id.* 416.

Mahálunge: market village in Poona district, XVIII, pt. iii, 258.

Mahalungi: river in Ahmadnagar district, XVII, 7-8.

Mahámalla: Pallava *biruda* or title, I, pt. ii, 328 and note 3.

Máha-Máya, Mahammáyi: Hindu goddess, IX, pt. i, p. xxxv, 205; temple of, at Kukkanur, inscription at, I, pt. ii, 456 note 2, 460 note 6, 469 note 3.

Mahánad: father of Mallikárjun, I, pt. ii, 24.

Mahánadi: river in Orissa and Madras, I, pt. ii, 341 note 2, 347 note 2, 358 note 1, 389.

Mahánaka: Gujarát princess, married to a Kányakubja king, I, pt. i, 151.

Mahánámya: great name-telling Vedic rite, IX, pt. i, 31 note 3; performance of, *id.* 38.

Mahápral: town, in Ratnágiri district, X, 345.

Mahápurána: Jain work, I, pt. ii, 407.

Mahar: title of respect among Gujars, IX, pt. i, 493.

Mahár: *See* Mhár.

Mahárája: title of the descendants of Vallabha, the religious head of the Vallabháchári sect, IX, pt. i, 56, 61, 89, 536.

Mahárájabhuvan: Jain temple at Sidhapur, I, pt. i, 172.

Mahárájasarva: *biruda* or title of Amoghavarsha, I, pt. ii, 401 and note 4, 404, 408.

Maháráshtra: region in which Maráthi is spoken except the Konkan; limits of, I, pt. ii, 134, 587; country about the Godávari, *id.* 135; number of villages contained in, *id.* 298 note 2, 341 note 2, 355 note 3, 431 note 2; proof of subjugation of, by the Áryas, *id.* 136; associated with Mahishmati in the *Puránas*, *id.* 140, 141; not referred to in the *Rámáyana* and the *Máháhbárata*, *id.* 142; referred to in books and inscriptions, etymology of the name of, Sanskrit name of, *id.* 143; Varáhamihira mentions it as a southern country, *id.* 144; referred to in the *Puránas*, *id.* 145; political history of, *id.* 146; governed by Pulumáyi, *id.* 151; under the sway of the Kshatrapa dynasty, *id.* 157; ruled by Nahapána, *id.* 160; Yajnaśri's reign in, *id.* 166; dates of the later Sataváhana kings in, *id.* 168, 169; the religious, social and economic condition of, under the Andhra-

bhrityas or Satavâhanas, *id.* 173-176; establishment of the supremacy of Pulikeśin II, *id.* 311; visited by Hwan Thsang, *id.* 184, 353-354 and note 3, 619; overthrow of Chálukya power by Ráshtrakútas in, *id.* 190; Chálukyas of Kalyána rise to power in, Devagiri Yádavas follow Chálukyas; Musalmáns invade (1294), *id.* 587; the Yádava dynasty is extinguished (1312), *id.* 533, 587, 619; becomes a province of the Musalmán empire of Delhi, *id.* 619; Musalmán nobles of the empire revolt and establish a dynasty in (1344-1347), *id.* 588, 520; the Durgádevi famine in (1396-1408), *id.* 588; under the Bahamani dynasty (1347-1500), *id.* 620; southern boundary of Viradhavala's kingdom, I, pt. i, 201; Moggaliputto sends missionaries to, *id.* 143. *See* Dakhan and Maráthás.

Maháráshtra Bráhmans: sub-division of Dravid Bráhmans, IX, pt. i, note 1.

Maháráshtrakas: three countries constituting the, I, pt. ii, 183; captured by Pulikeśin II, *id.* 350.

Maháráshtri: Prakrit dialect, I, pt. ii, 136, 144, 171.

Maháráshtris: Maráthás of the Dakhan, I, pt. ii, 277.

Mahárathi: male donor, mentioned in inscriptions at Karli, I, pt. ii, 144 and note 2; name for the Great Rattas or Ratta kings of the Dakhan and Karnátak (760-973), XVIII, pt. ii, 213 note 1.

Mahárathini: female donor, mentioned in inscriptions at Karli, I, pt. ii, 144.

Mahárattha: *see* Maháráshtra.

Mahárog: cattle disease, XV, pt. ii, 221.

Mahá Sarasvati: Hindu goddess, IX, pt. i, p. xxxv.

Mahasena: mythical Sopára king, XIV, 319.

Maháshivaratra: Shiva's Night, Hindu holiday, IX, pt. i, 23 note 5.

Máhátmyas: that is glory-describing tracts, IX, pt. i, 533.

Mahávamsa: Ceylonese chronicle, I, pt. ii, 143, 278 note 2, 324; IX, pt. i, 445; XIII, 405.

Mahávir, Mahávirasvámi: (B. C. 527), last *tirthankara* of Jain Shrávaks, IX, pt. i, 110, 114 and note 2; XXIV, 133, 134; I, pt. i, 193.

Mahâwanso: *see* Mahávamsa.

Mahâwat: a caste of Musalmán elephant-drivers, in Poona district, XVIII, pt. i, 495-496; in Sátára district, XIX, 17; in Sholápur district, XX, 200; in Bijápur district, XXIII, 293; in Kolhápur state, XXIV, 149.

Máháyana: later Buddhist sect, XII, 491.

Mahdavi: a schism of Sunni *sayads*, followers of Rajo Shahid, the chief leader of, the Gujarát followers of, chief quarters in Gujarát of, IX, pt. ii, 6 note 1 continued on page 7. *See* Ghermehdi.

Mahdi, Mehdi, Al Mahdi: the coming *imám*, the last of the *imáms*, IX, pt. ii, 40, 48; title claimed by Sayad Muhammad Jaunpuri, *id.* 3 note 3, 62; by Obeidullah, *id.* 48; by a Sunni Bohora Abd-ur-Rehman, *id.* 60 note 4.

Maheji: village in Khándesh, a large annual fair at, XII, 455-456.

Mahendra: *rája* of Nadol, holds a *svayamvara* or choice marriage of his sister, I, pt. i, 162, 163.

Mahendra: king of Kosala, I, pt. ii, 280.

Mahendra: *see* Mahendravarman.

Mahendra: king of Pishtapura, I, pt. ii, 280; mentioned in the Allahábád pillar inscription, *id.* 350 note 6.

Mahendragiri: mountain in Southern Marátha Country, I, pt. ii, 340 note 4, 149.

Mahendravarman I: Pallava king, I, pt. ii, 316 note 5; successor of Simhavishnu, defeats the Chalukyas of Bádámi at Pullalura, *id.* 324 and note 1, 328, 331; is defeated by Pulikeśin II and compelled to take refuge in Káñchi, *id.* 329, 350 and notes 7 and 8.

Mahendravarman II: Pallava king, I, pt. ii, 322; son of Narasimhavarman I, *id.* 324 and note 3, 327, 329 note 5, 362.

Mahendravarman III: Pallava king Narasimhavarman II's son, erects a temple called Mahendravarmeśvara, I, pt. ii, 330.

Mahendravarmeśvara, Mahendreśvara: temple of, near the Rajásimheśvara temple, I, pt. ii, 330.

Máhendri: I, pt. ii, 337 note 4. *See* Indráni.

Maheśa: progenitor of Jnáneśvara, I, pt. ii, 250.

Mahesh: the prophet introduced as, IX, pt. ii, 40. *See* Avatars.

Maheshwar Mahádev: shrine of, at Bhinmal, I, pt. i, 454.

Maheśvara: Nága king of the early Gupta period, I, pt. ii, 281 note 3.

Maheśvara: father of Bháskarácharya, I, pt. ii, 526 and note 1.

Maheśvarácharya: grantee in the Haddála copper-plate, I, pt. i, 138.

Maheśvaradevarasa: Kalachurya Someśvara's officer, I, pt. ii, 486.

Máheśvari: one of the Pleiades, I, pt. ii, 337 note 4.

Máhi: river in Gujarát, I, pt. i, 124, 467, 513; I, pt. ii, 199, 241, 310, 311, 315, 336, 348 note 5, 383, 389, 404, 525; II, 339; III, 2, 192; VI, 3; VII, 19; Raghunáthráv defeated on the banks of (1775), *id.* 192; family goddess of Mahi Kántha Kolis, IX, pt. i, p. xxxv, 247.

Mahia: a turbulent tribe in Káthiáwár, claim Káthi origin, IX, pt. i, 263; VIII, 139.

Mahidhara: son of Dáda, commander of Bhillama's troop of elephants, I, pt. ii, 237, 238.

Mahidpur: in Central India, battle of (1817), XII, 254.

Mahi Kántha Agency: boundaries, sub-divisions, aspect, hills, rivers, ponds, geology, climate, etc., V, 355-359; mineral products, trees, domestic and wild animals, *id.* 360-362; population: husbandmen, craftsmen, unsettled tribes, Musalmáns, *id.* 363-368; agriculture: holdings, crops, blights, floods, etc., *id.* 369-372; capitalists, debtors and creditors, mortgage of labour, interest, currency, etc., *id.* 373-374; weights and measures, *id.* 374-375; trade: roads, manufactures, craftsmen, trade guilds and markets, *id.* 377-380; history: early Hindus, Musalmáns (1412-1700), Maráthás (1750-1811), disturb-

ances (1833-1836, 1858, 1867), *id.* 380-385; land administration: revenue system, *id.* 386-387; justice: police, infanticide, widow burning and prisons, *id.* 386-391; revenue and finance, *id.* 392-393; instruction: schools, girls' schools and libraries, *id.* 394-395; health, *id.* 396-97; states under; Idar, its boundaries, aspect, rivers, hills, population, trade, history, land tenures, justice, police, jail, revenue, instruction and health, *id.* 398-412; Pol state, *id.* 412; Danta, its history, *id.* 413-416; Malpur state, *id.* 417; Mansa, *id.* 417-418; Mohanpur, Ghodasar, Amliyara, Punadra, Khadel, Pethapur and other small states, *id.* 418-429; places of interest, *id.* 430-442; Elphinstone's minute on, *id.* 442-455; Gáikwár's tribute from the chiefs of, VII, 328-332; Colonel Walker's tribute system introduced in (1808), I, pt. i, 424; genealogical tree of the chiefs of, V, 409.

Máhim: port in Bombay island, I, pt. i, 207 note 1; capital of Bhimrája, I, pt. ii, 27; its occupation, *id.* 29; its capture by Malik-ul-Tujár, *id.* 30; town attacked by the Mughals, *id.* 40; its capture by the Franciscans (1585), *id.* 57; sack of (1493), X, 194; occupied by Mubárik I (1317-1321), XIII, 438; taken by the Gujarát king (1430), *id.* 442; trade centre (1500-1670), *id.* 465; in 1664, *id.* 474; occupied by the Sidi (1690), *id.* 481; its fort strengthened (1701), XXVI, pt. i, 138.

Mahim: *see* Kelve-Mahim.

Mahim: sub-division of Thána district, details of, XIII, 2, 673-675; surveyed (1793-1794), *id.* 558; its assessment revised (1837), *id.* 583; cost and profit of tillage in (1845), *id.* 588; survey assessment (1863), *id.* 611-614.

Mahimandangad: fort in Sátára district, XIX, 513.

Mahimangad: hill fort in Sátára district, description and history of, XIX, 12, 513-515.

Mahimangad-Panhála: Mahádev hill spur in Sátára district, XIX, 8.

Mahimatgad: hill fort in Kolhápur state, XXIV, 4.

Mahim causeway: in Thána district, XIII, 323.

Mahindri: the river Máhi, I, pt. i, 510.

Mahipála, Mahipáladeva: Chudásama ruler of Káthiáwár (917), his coins, I, pt. i, 138, 466, 469; I, pt. ii, 383.

Mahipala: brother of Kumárapála, I, pt. i, 181; father of Ajayapála, Chaulukya king, *id.* 194.

Mahipalgad: hill fort in Belgaum district, XXI, 7; place of interest, *id.* 585.

Mahipatgad: fort in Ratnágiri district, X, 4, 345.

Mahishakas, Mahishmat: Southern Country, I, pt. ii, 135; Maháráshtra, *id.* 140.

Máhishmati, Mahishmatipattana, Mahishmatipura: lord of, I, pt. ii, 439 and note 2, 450, 457, 523.

Máhlung: *citras medica,* fruit tree in Poona district, XVIII, pt. i, 49.

Mahmud, Mahmud Adil Sháh, etc.: *see* Muhammad, Muhammad Adil Sháh, etc.

Mahóba: province in Bundelkhand, I, pt. i, 178.

Mahommed: *see* Muhammad.

Mahrat Desh: the Marátha country, I, pt. i, 524.

Mahrespand Jasan: chief highday, Zoroaster proclaims his religion on, IX, pt. ii, 219.

Mahuda: *see* Moha.

Mahudha: town in Kaira district, III, 173.

Máhul: seaport in Thána district, XIV, 219.

Mahuli: hill and fort in Thána district, XIII, 7; Hindu chiefship at (1453), *id.* 442; held by Jawhár chief (1626), *id.* 454; lost to the Mughals (1670), *id.* 475; reduced by Malik Ahmed (1485), I, pt. ii, 32, 39; captured by Shiváji, *id.* 69; Dickinson's survey of, its history, XIV, 219-220.

Mahuli: fort in Násik district, XVI, 489; delivered to Khán Zamán (1636), *id.* 656, 660.

Máhuli: village in Sátára district, temples at, XIX, 516-519; Sir John Malcom at (1807), *id.* 301; Bájiráv at (1818), *id.* 302; XVIII, pt. ii, 298.

Máhura: I, pt. i, 519. *See* Mathura.

Mahuvá: sub-division in Baroda territory, VII, 578-580. *Town, id.* 580.

Mahuva: port and town in Káthiáwár, VIII, 238, 536, 537.

Máhyár: Herbad, brings copy of the *Vandidád* from Yezd in Persia to Uch in India, IX, pt. ii, 186 note 1, 189 notes 2 and 3.

Mailaladevi: Western Chálukya king Someśvara I's wife, I, pt. ii, 438, 440.

Mailaladevi: Ratta chieftain Sena I's wife, I, pt. ii, 551, 553.

Mailaladevi: Gutta prince Vikramáditya III's wife, I, pt. ii, 579, 583, 584.

Mailalamahádevi: daughter of the Western Chálukya king Vikramáditya VI and wife of the Goa Kádamba Jayakeśin II, I, pt. ii, 449, 565, 569.

Mailalatirtha: founder of the Káreya sect of the Jains, I, pt. ii, 550, 552.

Mailárayya: Kalachurya Bijjala's governor of Tardavádi, I, pt. ii, 460, 473.

Maimatgad: fort in Ratnágiri district, X, 346.

Mairál: Bapu, Baroda courtier, accompanies Gangádhar Shástri to Poona (1815), VII, 222.

Mairinja: modern Miraj, I, pt. ii, 254 and note 3, 546.

Máis: Máhi river, I, pt. i, 544.

Maithila: sub-division of Gaud Bráhmans, IX, pt. i, 1 note 1.

Maithilas: people mentioned in the Chandel stone inscription, I, pt. i, 469.

Maitland: Captain (1759), brings the Sidi to terms at Surat, XI, 447.

Maitrakas: tribal name of Mehrs, I, pt. i, 75 and note 6, 87-88; identified with Mhers, *id.* 135, 136, 141, 142 and note 2; Mihiras, Meds, or Mers, IX, pt. i, 486, 492. *See* Mihiras.

Maitráyani: a sub-division of the Bráhmans in Khándesh, XII, 52; in Násik, XVI, 41.

Maitreya: disciple of Nakuliśa, founder of a branch of Pásupata school, I, pt. i, 84.

Maitreya: Bodhisattva, XIII, 408 note 2; or the coming Buddha, XIV, 132 note 5; image

of, at Sopára, *id.* 329, 330 and note 1, 403, 410, 412.
Majam : river in Mahi Kántha, V, 357.
Májam : preparation of *bhang*, IX, pt. i, p. xxxiii.
Majevadi : town in Káthiáwár, VIII, 537-538. *See* also I, pt. i, 176.
Májgaon : rock in Poona district, XVIII, pt. i, 4.
Májháli : village in Kánara district, XV, pt. ii, 330.
Májid Khán : successor of Abdul Gháfar of Sávanur (1721-1751) ; signs a treaty with the Peshwa (1746), I, pt. ii, 656 ; yields territory in the Karnátak to the Peshwa (1747), *id.* 665 ; takes part in the contests for the Nizám's throne ; his intrigues with the French ; conspires first in favour of and afterwards against Muzaffar Jang ; his death (1751), *id.* 666.
Majmudárs ; district accountants, I, pt. i, 212, 213 note 2 ; in Broach, II, 485, 512.
Major : author, his account of India in the 15th century, IX, pt. ii, 14 note 3.
Mák : the dewy land, a tract in Cutch, V, 75 note 2, 106.
Maka : food as well as medicinal plant, XXV, 186, 260.
Makanpur : near Cawnpur, tomb of Saint Badi-ud-din Madarsháh at, IX, pt. ii, 22, 64.
Makara : fish, tribal badge of the Mehrs, I, pt. i, 87, 135.
Makara : Magara kingdom, uprooted by Narasimha II, I, pt. ii, 507.
Makaradhvaja : chief of Mehrs, his fights with Mayuradhvaja, I, pt. i, 87 ; ancestor of Mher chiefs of Porbandar, *id.* 135 ; founder of Jethvás, IX, pt. i, 127.
Makarandgad : hill in Ratnágiri district, X, 4.
Mákarappi : village mentioned in a Haidarábád grant, I, pt. ii, 356.
Makar Nimbori : *wild citron*, fruit in Poona district, XVIII, pt. i, 49.
Makar-Sankrant : Hindu holiday, IX, pt. i, 394 ; XVIII, pt. i, 254.
Makarvalli : village in Dhárwár, inscriptions at, XXII, 770.
Makávatinagara : Ghar Mandala, territory given to Chohâns, IX, pt. i, 484.
Makhan Devi : Hindu goddess, story about lamp burning at Ratanpur, IX, pt. i, 361.
Makka, Makkah : Sunni place of pilgrimage, IX, pt. ii, 30, 47, 56, 126, 171 ; temple at, captured by Sadu Wahhabi (1803), *id.* 12 note 3 ; wall in a mosque, *id.* 131 ; I, pt. i, 204, 514, 520.
Mákni : place of interest in Rewa Kántha, VI, 164.
Mako : a common weed found in tropical and temperate parts, XXV, 202.
Makrán : coast of, described by Arab travellers, I, pt. i, 508, 511, 516.
Makrandgad : hill fort in Sátára district, temple of Mallikarjun at, XIX, 5, 9, 509, 519-520.
Makranis : foreigners from the Makran coast in Gujarát, Sunnis by faith, IX, pt. ii, 18.
Makri : an oil-yielding plant, XXV, 222.
Makta : *see* Khand.
Maktab : Mulla's school, IX, pt. ii, 132.
Maktum : concealed *imáms* of the Ismáilias, IX, pt. ii, 48.
Makur-limbo : a medicinal oil-yielding plant, XXV, 222.
Makuteśvaranátha : the god Shiva, grants made to the temple of, I, pt. ii, 348 and note 7.
Makwánás : special community of part foreign descent in Gujarát, IX, pt. ii, 11 ; Hindu converts from Makwana tribe of Rájpúts or Kolis, marriages among, distinct community of, Sunni in faith, *id.* 65-66 ; Rájpúts, peasant proprietors, IX, pt. i, 130 ; same as Jhálás, I, pt. i, 140 ; in Mahi Kántha, V, 419 ; in Káthiáwár, VIII, 115.
Mala : kings, apparently of the Malapas, subdued by Vishnuvardhana, I, pt. ii, 495.
Mala : hill pass in Ratnágiri district, X, 166.
Mala : village in Sátara district, XIX, 520.
Malabár : I, pt. ii, 4, 66, 133, 140 ; province, held by the Alupa race, *id.* 183 ; the Syrians settle on the coast of, *id.* 189 ; district, *id.* 280, 282 note 5 ; Ibráhim Ádil Sháh's campaign into, *id.* 648 ; Arabs on the coast of (B. C. 177-100), IX, pt. ii, 1 note 1 ; spread of the Pársis along, *id.* 195 ; ports of, I, pt. i, 515, 529, 537 ; imports of sandalwood to Sopára from (300 A. D.), XIII, 406 ; its trade with Thána ports (810-1260), *id.* 429, 430, 431, 434 ; (1300-1500), *id.* 440 ; centre of trade with China and Archipelago, *id.* 444 ; imported bamboos, *id.* 445 ; (1500-1670), *id.* 465 ; exports of grain to Bombay (1833-1836), *id.* 577 note 5, 579 ; identified with Ophir, XIV, 318.
Malabár Hill : in Bombay city, state of, in 1664, XIII, 474.
Malabari-elachi : food plant, XXV, 176.
Malabaris : Musalmán traders in Násik district, XVI, 79.
Malabár Point : derivation of the name, X, 342 note 4 ; XXXVI, pt. iii, 667. *See* Shri-Gundi.
Malabars : pirates in the Indian Seas, XIII, 484.
Malacca : Thána trade with (A. D. 150), XIII 416 ; (810-1260), *id.* 429 ; Hindus found in (1300-1500), *id.* 446 ; (1530-1670), *id.* 464, 465 ; (1660-1710), *id.* 486.
Malachra : *capitata* or *rotundifolia*, fibrous plant, XXV, 227.
Malád : an estate, in Thána district, XIII, 545.
Máladeva : chief minister of Arjunadeva and Sárangadeva, I, pt. i, 204.
Malakshâh : (1070-1092) Saljuki emperor, IX, pt ii, 37.
Maladevi : *see* Malala Mahádevi.
Malalu : sandy soil in Kánara district, XV, pt. ii, 4.
Málan : river in Káthiáwár, VIII, 63.
Malang : a Musalmán ascetic school, XIV, 221.
Malanggad : fort in Thána district, XIII, 8 ; attempted capture of (1780), *id.* 506 ; shrine of Háji Abd-ul-Rahman at, history, description, XIV, 220-223.
Malapas : people of the Malenád, subdued by Vishnuvardhana, I, pt. ii, 495 ; dispersed by Áchagi, *id.* 219, 574.
Malaprabha : *see* Malprabha.
Malaprahárini : modern Malprabha, I, pt. ii, 497.

Malav : reservoir in Ahmadábád district, IV, 19.

Malava, *pl.* Malavaru : a caste of husbandmen, in Dhárwár district, XXII, 140; in Kánara district, XV, pt. i, 175.

Malava or Vikrama era : (B. C. 57), founder of, IX, pt. i, 462 ; I, pt. ii, 311 ; I, pt. i, 67, 124, 465, 467, 469.

Málava : one of the nine kingdoms, I, pt. ii, 403 note 3 ; I. pt. i, 64 ; tribe, *id.* 28 ; its capital, I, pt. ii, 494. *See* also Malwa and Malavas.

Malavalli : village in Mysore, I, pt. ii, 277.

Malavaramarin : slayer of the Malavas or people of the *ghát* country ; title of the Goa Kádamba prince Permádi, I, pt. ii, 569, 570.

Málavas : people of Málwa in Central India and of South-Eastern Rájpútána ; their era and coins ; conquered by the Early Gupta king Samudragupta, I, pt. ii, 311 ; their country falls into the hands of Toramána and in 532-533 A. D. forms part of the kingdom of Vishnuvardhana Yasodharman ; the northern part of their country is held by the Mauryas ; subdued by the Western Chálukya king Pulikeśin II, *id.* 189, 312, 350 ; defeated by Vijayáditya, *id.* 368 ; subjugated by the Ráshtrakúta king Dantidurga, *id.* 389 ; conquered by Govinda III, *id.* 395, 396 ; protected against the Gurjaras by Govinda III, *id.* 400 ; king of, worships Amoghavarsha I, *id.* 402 ; their capital burnt by Hoysala Ereyanga, feudatory of the Western Chálukyas, *id.* 494 ; king of the, made vassal of Vikramáditya II styled also VI, *id.* 219 ; defeated by the Devagiri Yádava Singhana, *id.* 524 ; Krishna claims success over, *id.* 527 ; Malloi of Multan, conquered Malwa, founded Malava era, IX, pt. i, 462.

Málávdi : village in Sátára district, XIX, 520-521.

Málaviká : cousin of the king of Vidarbha, I, pt. ii, 147.

Málavikágnimitra : Sanskrit drama by Kálidás, I, pt. ii, 146.

Málavya : lake at Dholka, built by Siddharája, I, pt. i, 180 note 2.

Malaya : country, I, pt. ii, 216 ; hills, *id.* 442 ; Vikramáditya VI marches through, *id.* 444.

Malayamatidevi : I, pt. ii, 448. *See* Malleyamádevi.

Malaya Parvat : mountain range in Kánara district, XV, pt. i, 4.

Málayas : attack Uttamabhadras, I, pt. ii, 148.

Malayavati : queen of Kuntala Śátakarni S'átaváhana, I, pt. ii, 171.

Malayeśvara : Shiva's attendant, I, pt. ii, 482.

Malcom : Sir John, defeats the Peshwa, Holkar and Nágpur chief at Mahidpur (1817), XVI, 195 ; XII, 254 ; at Mahuli (1817), XVIII, pt. ii, 298 ; Bájiráv surrenders to, *id.* 303 and note 2 ; I, pt. ii, 611 ; IX, pt. i, 60 note 5 ; his notice of Bhats and their mode of revenge, *id.* 210 note 3 ; of Charans as guards or Valávás, *id.* 217 notes 2 and 3, 295 and notes 1 and 2, 482 note 7 ; his notice of Mandu (1820), I, pt. i, 383 ; his remark on Bohorás (1823), IX, pt. ii, 29 note 1 ; his remarks on the condition of Sátára (1824), XIX, 309 ; sequestrates Baroda territory (1828), VII, 241-242 ; visits Pavai in Thána district (1830), XIV, 299 ; opens the Bor pass, XIII, 318 ; his minute on Cutch, V, 166, 265-277 ; rewards Ardeshir Dhanjisha, IX, pt. ii, 198 note 5 ; second sequestration of Baroda by (1832), VII, 244 ; curtails Gáikwár's authority, *id.* 302, 403 ; notice of Sálsette (1833), I, pt. ii, 128.

Malcolm-peth : trade centre, XIX, 214. *See* Mahábaleshvar.

Male : country, subjugated by Vishnuvardhana, I, pt. ii, 496, 499 ; by the Hángal Kadamba Kamadeva, *id.* 563 ; kings of, *id.* 507.

Málegaon : sub-division in Násik district, details, area, aspect, climate, water, history, land revenue, stock, holdings, crops, people, XVI, 345, 349. *Town*, fort, siege (1818), *id.* 450-455 ; XII, 255 ; I, pt. ii, 630 ; military head-quarters at, *id.* 631.

Málegaon : village in Ahmadnagar district, temple at, XVII, 727.

Malek-ul-Tujár : *see* Malik-ul-Tujár.

Male-making : *see* Pumsavana.

Maleo : cape of, east of Cambay, identification of, I, pt. i, 539.

Malepas : people of the *Malenád*, or hilly country, conquered by Rájarája, I, pt. ii, 308, 495.

Málerkotlá : state, I, pt. ii, 346 note 4.

Malet : Charles, chief of the English at Surat (1775), I, pt. i, 402 ; appointed British resident in Poona (1785), XVIII, pt. ii, 268 ; British envoy (1790), XVIII, pt. iii, 409.

Malet : Mrs., tomb of, at Bankot.

Malet Spring : at Mátherán, XIV, 244-245.

Maleus : Mount (in Central India), mentioned by Pliny, I, pt. i, 533.

Málgár : a caste of flower-sellers in Bijápur district, XXIII, 253.

Malgund : village in Dhárwár district, inscription and temple at, XXII, 770 ; I, pt. ii, 440 note 3.

Malhárgad : port in Poona district, XVIII, pt. iii, 258.

Malhári : *see* Pánbhari.

Malhári Koli : sub-division of Kolis in Thána district, XIII, 173.

Malharji Holkar : *see* Malhárráv Holkar.

Malharrav : Honávar chief (1510), helped by the Portuguese, XV, pt. ii, 110, 279, 309.

Malhárráv : son of Khanderáv Gáikwár, retires on a pension to Nadiád, I, pt. i, 412 ; breaks out in rebellion in Káthiáwár ; is captured by Babaji Appaji and Vithal Devaji, *id.* 413.

Malhárráv Gáikwár, His Highness : (1870-1875), his plots and imprisonment, ascends the *gádi*, his vengeance on his enemies, mismanages the government, marries Lakshmibai (1874), attempt to poison Colonel Phayre, his trial (1875), deposed, VII, 278-284 ; substitutes *kámávisdars* for *izardárs*, *id.* 370-371 ; his banks, *id.* 409-410 ; institutes *varishta* court, *id.* 444 ; *see* also I, pt. i, 442-443.

Malhárráv Holkar : Bájiráv Peshwa's officer, plunders Dánta and Vadnagar and exacts tribute from Pálanpur, I, pt. i, 317 ; defeats Dia Bahádur, governor of Mándu, and captures Mándu, *id.* 382 ; founder of the Holkar

family, I, pt. ii, 600; repulsed Portuguese attack on Thána (1739), XIV, 360.
Malhárráv Khuni: Damáji Gáikwár's deputy at Ahmadábád, collects tribute in Gujarát (1740), I, pt. i, 322, 323.
Mali: professional caste of husbandmen in Gujarát said to be Kanbis, religious sects, faith in early beliefs, snake-worship, IX, pt. i, 153, 172; a class of gardeners, converts from the Hindu caste of the same name, IX, pt. ii, 88; a caste of gardeners, I, pt. i, 450; in Cutch, V, 70; in Khándesh, XII, 69; in Thána district, XIII, 61-62; at Mátherán, XIV, 265; in Kánara district, XV, pt. i, 242-244; in Násik, XVI, 47; in Poona district, XVIII, pt. i, 309-310; XVIII, pt. ii, 1; in Sátára district, XIX, 79; in Kolhápur, XXIV, 93; in Káthiáwár, VIII, 143; in Kolába district, XI, 62-63; in Janjira state, *id.* 412; in Ahmadnagar, XVII, 89-91; in Sholápur district, XX, 91; in Ratnágiri district, X, 124.
Máli: apparently Mália in North Káthiáwár, capture of, I, pt. i, 506 and note 5; island, *id.* 509.
Mália (Hatti): town in Káthiáwár, head-quarters of the curious tribe of the Hattis, their founder, VIII, 538.
Mália (Miana): petty state and town in Káthiáwár, VIII, 166, 539-540; IX, pt. i, 126; temple at, I, pt. i, 153; captured by the British (1809), VII, 325.
Máliba: identified with Málwa, expedition against, I, pt. i, 109, 467.
Málik: Sunni *imám*, IX, pt. ii, 125 note 2, 126.
Malik: a caste of Rájpút converts in Gujarát, IX, pt. ii, 66; the name coined by Musalmán governors, *id.* 25; conversion of, by Muhammad Ghazni (1025), *id.* 3 note 3; in Khándesh, XII, 127; in Kaira district, III, 82.
Málika: wife of the Western Chálukya king Vikramáditya VI, I, pt. ii, 449.
Malika Jáhán: mosque of, in Bijápur city, XXIII, 630.
Málik Ahmed Beheri: first Nizámshábi king of Ahmadnagar, reduces the *ghát* and Konkan forts, I, pt. ii, 32; takes Mahuli fort in Thána district (1485), XIV, 320; takes Chákan and Junnar forts, XVIII, pt. iii, 122, 225; captures Chavand and Purandhar forts (1486), *id.* 124, 433; takes Jivdhan fort (1489), *id.* 140; takes Dándá Rajpuri (1490), I, pt. ii, 32; makes the Sidis captain of Janjira fort (1490), XI, 434; defeats Bahmani troops near modern Ahmadnagar, lays siege to Daulatábád; founds Ahmadnagar (1490), XVIII, pt. ii, 220-221.
Malik Ambar: Abyssinian minister of Ahmadnagar, his epithet, IX, pt. ii, 12; sets up Mortiza as king and founds a city at Kharki; defeats the Mughal general Khán-i-Khánán and retakes Ahmadnagar and Berar; his attack on Bassein and Sálsette (1611), XIII, 453; makes Junnar Nizámshábi capital (1605); is defeated by Sháh Jahán (1617) and forced to surrender; his death (1626), I, pt. ii, 624; XIII, 464; his revenue system, I, pt. ii, 38; XVI, 208; XIII, 550 note 4, 553-554 note 3; XVIII, pt. ii, 223, 317-320; XX, 286-287; XI, 143, 169 and note 4; XII, 266-267 note 1.
Malik Báyazid: son and successor of Shujáat Khán, *sultán* of Málwa, with the title of Báz Bahádur (1555-1570), I, pt. i, 369.
Malik Eiaz: Gujarát general, defeats the Portuguese at Cheul (1508), XI, 274; again defeats the Portuguese at Cheul (1522), XIII, 449.
Malikhas: Nabathæan king, I, pt. i, 542, 543.
Maliki: one of the four Sunni schools, IX pt. ii, 126 note 1.
Malik-i-Maidán: the famous Bijápur gun, XVII, 36 note 2, 369 note 1; XXIII, 639-641.
Malik Kabir: Sultán Firuzsháh, deputes Ziá-ud-din Barni to Broach, I, pt. i, 514.
Malik Káfur: slave-general of Alá-ud-din; invades the Dakhan (1306) and takes Rámdeva prisoner (1307), I, pt. ii, 251, 532, 618; XII, 242; is sent to subdue Tailangana and on his way is entertained hospitably at Devagiri (1309), *id.* 251, 533; is sent to Dorasamudra (1310), *id.* 509, 533; returns to Delhi (1311), *id.* 533; is sent against Śamkara whom he puts to death, and fixes his residence at Devagiri (1312), *id.* 251, 533, 619; is summoned to Delhi, poisons Alá-ud-din, and is assassinated (1316), *id.* 533. *See* also I, pt. i, 205, 229; XII, 242; XVIII, pt. ii, 215 note 2; XIX, 225 note 1; destroys Dabhol (1312), X, 327; reduces Cheul (1314), XI, 272; destroys Hoysala power (1312), XV, pt. ii, 91; puts to death Śankardev, son of Rámadev, XVII, 352 note 5; XXI, 361; XXII, 402; XXIII, 396.
Malik Mughis Khilji: minister of Sultán Hoshang (1405-1434), I, pt. i, 359.
Malik Muizzuddin: conquers Gujarát and plunders Kambáyat, I, pt. i, 515.
Malik Mukhil: Gujarát governor, I, pt. i, 230.
Malik Názir: Faruki king (1399-1437) of Khándesh; seizes the fort of Asirgad, builds the town of Burhánpur and Zeinábád; recovers the fort of Thálner from his brother (1417); takes Sultánpur and overruns Nandurbár; is defeated by Alá-ud-din Bahamani (1435); capture of Burhánpur; extent of the Khándesh dominions during his time; his death (1437), *id.* 620-621; his fights with Gujarát and Ahmadnagar kings, XII, 244-245, 454.
Malik Rája: founder (1370-1399) of the Khándesh Fárukis, Thalner and Karanda districts granted to, by Feroz Tughlik (1370), invades Gujarát, is defeated and besieged at Thalner by Muzáfar Sháh (1394), promotes architecture and agriculture, his death (1399), XII, 243-244, 454; I, pt. ii, 620.
Malik Rehan: tomb of, in Bijápur district, XXIII, 617.
Malik Sandal: mosque of, in Bijápur city, XXIII, 631.
Malik Shában: reservoir in Ahmadábád district, IV, 18.
Maliksháhi: the corrected year; the Persian revenue year, IX, pt. ii, 193 note 2.

Malik Tokan: Bahádur Sháha's governor of Diu, fortifies Bassein (1532), defeated by the Portuguese, XIV, 28-29.
Malik Tughán: captain of freebooters (1347), I, pt. i, 230-231.
Malik-ul-Tujár: a Bahmani chief, is sent to subdue the *gháts* and the Konkan (1420), I, pt. ii, 588; seizes Máhim (Bombay) and Sálsette (1429), *id.* 30; is again sent with a considerable force (1451); builds the fort of Chákan; overruns the lands of the Shirke family; is induced to march against Shankar Rái of Khelna; is surrounded and defeated, *id.* 31, 588; *see* also X, 193; XIII, 441; XIV, 226-227; XVIII, pt. ii, 216-217; XXIV, 224, 323; IX, pt. ii, 3 note 1.
Málim: navigator, derivation of the word, XIII, 716.
Malindya: mount mentioned by Varáha Mihira, I, pt. i, 533.
Málingi: town on the Krishna opposite Talakad, I, pt. ii, 497; inscription at (1290), *id.* 509. *See* Jananáthapura.
Malippala: town probably in Nizám's country, I, pt. i, 540.
Malkana: temple of, at Ruddawádi, inscription at, I, pt. ii, 428 note 1.
Malkápur: town in Kolhápur state, temples at, XXIV, 313.
Málkhed: capital of the later Ráshtrakútas, I, pt. i, 120, 514; destroyed by the Chalukya king Tailappa (972), *id.* 519; I, pt. ii, 10, 11, 17, 24; in Nizám's territory, *id.* 200, 396, 403, 450; Ráshtrakútas of, *id.* 299 note 4, 327 note 7, 341 note 2, 386, 423; Ráshtrakúta capital, *id* 382; records of the family of, *id.* 383; burnt by Gunaka Vijayáditya III, *id.* 411; plundered by the Paramára king, *id.* 422; dynasty, *id.* 424, 425; first capital of the Western Chálukyas, *id.* 427, 430; *see* also XV, pt. ii, 84; IX, pt. ii, 2 note 1; XIII, 424, 434. *See* Mányakheta.
Malkungani: an oil-yielding plant common on the *gháts* and in Konkan, XXV, 216.
Malla: brother of Bichana, I, pt. ii, 243.
Malla: Yádava king Krishna's officer, I, pt. ii, 245, 527, 529.
Malla: of Gutta family, I, pt. ii, 452, 580.
Malla: Lingáyat brothers, founders of Kittur, I, pt. ii, 668.
Mallala Mahádevi: *see* Mailala Mahádevi.
Mallali: musical instrument, I, pt. ii, 577.
Mallana: Vira-Ballála II's officer (1203), I, pt. ii, 506.
Mallappa: *desái* of Kittur, resumes possession of his territory from the Maráthás; assists General Wellesly (1803), obtains a *sanad* from the Peshwa (1809); is confirmed in his possessions by General Munro; fictitious adoption by; his death, I, pt. ii, 669-670.
Mallavalli: village grants to the Vira Somnáth temple by the Hángal Kádamba Kámadeva, I, pt. ii, 484.
Mallaya: Jagaddeva's companion in assassinating Vijjana, I, pt. ii, 226.
Mallayan: hill in Belgaum district, XXI, 6; place of interest, *id.* 585.
Malleyamadevi: Western Chálukya king Vikramáditya VI's wife, I, pt. ii, 448.
Malleyasáhani: Billama's officer, I, pt. ii, 520.
Mallideva: Singhana's officer, I, pt. ii, 523.
Mallideva: Yádava king Rámachandra's governor of Huligere (1295-1296), I, pt. ii, 530, 564.
Mallideva: son of Gutta I (1115), I, pt. ii, 579, 580, 581.
Mallidevarasa: Kalachurya Sankama's feudatory (1180), I, pt. ii, 488, 489.
Mallikárjuna: Hindu god, temple of, at Degambe, I, pt. ii, 571.
Mallikárjuna: seventeenth Siláhára king (1156-1160) of Konkan, XIII, 422 note 1; defeated by Kumárapála's general A'mbada, his grants at Chiplun and Bassein, *id.* 426; slain, *id.* 436; *see* also I, pt. i, 185, 186 and I, pt. ii, 24, 539; XIV, 386.
Mallikárjuna: Ratta chieftain, son of Lakshmideva I (1204-1208), I, pt. ii, 551, 556, 557.
Mallikárjuna: Kádamba ruler (1231) also styled Mallideva, I, pt. ii, 564.
Mallikárjuna I: (1132-1145), son of the Hángal Kádamba Tailappa II; feudatory of Someśvara III and Perma Jagadekamalla II, I, pt. ii, 456, 559, 562.
Mallikárjuna: fifth Vijayanagar king (1451-1465), XV, pt. ii, 96 note 4, 100.
Mallikárjuna: hill in Sátára district, caves at, XIX, 11, 521-523.
Mallisetti: *see* Malla.
Mallishena: epitaph of, I, pt. ii, 407.
Mallotus Philippinensis: vegetable poison, XXV, 268; vegetable antidotes to bites of poisonous animals, *id.* 275.
Mallu Adil Sháh: son and successor of Ismail Ádil Sháh; is deposed (1534), I, pt. ii, 642; *see* also XXIII, 413.
Mallugi: Yádava king, I, pt. ii, 235, 517, 519; takes Parnakheta, *id.* 235, 516; at war with Vijjana, *id.* 237; enemy of Bhillama, *id.* 238 and note 2.
Mallu Khán: commandant of Mándu, assumes the title of Kadirsháh Málwi and makes Mándu his capital, indifference of, to the orders of Sher Sháh Sur; does homage to Sher Sháh at Sárangpur (1542), flies to Gujarát and attacks Mándu with Gujarát forces; the defeat of, by one of Sher Sháh's generals, I, pt. i, 368, 369.
Máloji: Mudhol chief (1661), XXIV, 394.
Máloji Bhonsle: Shiváji's grandfather, takes Sháháji to his patron Lukhji Jadhavráv during *Holi* festival; is raised to the command of 5,000 horse with the title of Máloji Rája Bhonsle, XVII, 389; *see* also XVIII, pt. ii, 222-223; I, pt. ii, 591.
Máloji Gáikwár: Dámáji's (1732-1768) uncle, recovers Baroda, VII, 174.
Malprabha: river in Southern Marátha Country, XXI, 12; XXII, 7; XXIII, 11; XXIV, 11; *see* also I, pt. ii, 497, 503, 504, 506, 519, 524.
Malprabha-Gangharvgad: hill spur in Kolhápur state, XXIV, 7.
Malpur: state in Mahi Kántha, V, 417; Rathod chiefship, IX, pt. i, 128.
Málsej or Málshet: pass between Thána and Poona districts, XIII, 320, 403; XVIII, pt. ii, 149.

Malsiras : village in Poona district, temple and fair at, XVIII, pt. iii, 258.

Malsiras : sub-division in Sholápur district, its boundaries, area, aspect, climate, water, soil, stock, holdings, crops and people, XX, 398-400. *Town*, temples at, *id.* 413-414.

Maltecoræ : tribe mentioned by Pliny I, pt. i, 534.

Malthara : village in Poona district, tomb and fair at, XVIII, pt. iii, 258-259.

Malundi : trade centre (1350) north of Málwan, I, pt. ii, 37.

Málva : *see* Málwa.

Málvaceæ : food, oil-yielding and fibrous plants, XXV, 194, 215, 226.

Málvan : sub-division of Ratnágiri district, details of, X. 2, 313-315 ; customs division, its trade, *id.* 185. *Town* and port, its population, trade, manufactures, health, history and fort at, *id.* 346-352 ; *see* also *id.* 172, 177, 186, 198 ; derivation of the name, *id.* 346 note 4 ; fort of, built by Shiváji, I, pt. ii, 68, 69 ; his naval head-quarters, description, *id.* 75 ; taken by the English (1765) and restored, *id.* 106, ceded to the English (1812), *id.* 112.

Málvan : village in Sálsette, XIV, 223.

Málvans : Sávant and Kolhápur ship captains, I, pt. ii, 88 ; pirates, X, 197, 350 and note 9, 351, 378.

Malvi : breed of cattle in Poona district, XVIII, pt. i, 55.

Málwa : I, pt. i, 24, 28 ; Gupta conquest of, *id.* 67 ; conquered by Govinda III, Ráshtrakúta king, *id.* 123, 124 ; its king taken prisoner by Siddharája, *id.* 175 ; annexed to Chaulukya kingdom by Siddharája, *id.* 178 ; its king Ballála defeated by Kumárapála, *id.* 185 ; its king crushed by Visáladeva, *id.* 203 ; incorporation of, to Gujarát by Sultán Bahádur of Gujárát (1526-1536), invasion of, by the emperor Humáyun (1534), *id.* 367 ; under Sher Sháh Sur (1542-1545), *id.* 368 ; under his successor Salim Sháh (1545-1553), becomes independent under Shujáat in 1554, *id.* 369, 510 ; *see* also I, pt. ii, 159, 198, 199, 213, 215, 240, 312, 407, 432, 441, 442, 532, 578 for early history of ; Dámáji Gáikwár's inroad into (1742), VII, 176 ; Bájiráv's expedition in (1724), XIX, 267 ; Udáji Povar's incursion into, *id.* 268 ; Bájiráv's second expedition in (1725), *id.* 270 ; Chimnaji Appá in (1730), *id.* 274 ; ceded (1738) to Bájiráv, *id.* 279 ; Báláji asks the government of (1741), *id.* 284, 285 ; divided between Sindia and Holkar, *id.* 291.

Málwa Dohad : route, shrine of Kalika on, IX, pt. i, p. xi.

Málwa Sultáns : (1400-1570), history of, I, pt. i, 356-371.

Malyah : country included in Sáran or South Gujarát, mentioned by Alberuni, I, pt. ii, 4.

Mama : lady's maid, IX, pt. ii, 96.

Mámala : modern Mával, I, pt. ii, 175.

Mámaláhára : Mámala or hilly Dakhan district, modern Mával, I, pt. ii, 175.

Mámallapuram : town, Pallava inscriptions at, I, pt. ii, 331.

Mambaros : perhaps Mahikshatrap, mentioned by Pliny, I, pt. i, 543, 544.

Mamdápur : village in Bijápur, story, temples, lakes, inscriptions, XXIII, 661-663, 313 ; record at, I, pt. ii, 526.

Mámhal : Arab word for Anáhilváda, I, pt. i, 508, 509 note 3, 511.

Mamjár : caste of Musalmán bracelet-sellers in Bijápur district, XXIII, 290.

Mámlatdár : officer of a district yielding about five lakhs of revenue under the Maráthás, I, pt. ii, 99 ; his duties, XII, 268 ; XIII, 555-556 ; revenue farmer, his powers, had armed messengers, *id.* 559-560, 561, 563 note 4, 564 ; in Poona district under the Peshwás, XVIII, pt. ii, 325 note 2.

Mámo : spirit as maternal uncle, lives in Khijaro tree, his dread, IX, pt. i, 270 and note 3, 284-285.

Mámváni : thirteenth Siláhára king (1060), XIII, 422 note 1, 425 ; *see* also XIV, 8 ; I, pt. ii, 539, 543, 567.

Mán : river in Sholápur district, XX, 4.

Man : bamboo, XXV, 208.

Mán : sub-division of Sátára district, its boundaries, area, aspect, climate, water, soil, stock, holdings, crops and people, XIX, 434-436 ; military post (1464), *id.* 227 ; under the Saif-Ain-ul-Mulk (1551), *id.* 228-229.

Mána : *see* Mauna.

Mána : Ráshtrakúta king, I, pt. ii, 386.

Máua : tribe, support Indrarája of Gujarát, I, pt. ii, 400, 408.

Managoli : in the Bijápur district, inscription at, I, pt. ii, 423 note 5, 503, 521.

Manái : a Sind chief, supposed ancestor of the Kera in Cutch, V, 100 ; brother of the legendary hero Mod, *id.* 132, 233.

Mánáji : brother of Fatehsingh Gáikwár, assumes the government of Baroda, I, pt. i, 410 ; his death, *id.* 411.

Mánáji A'ngria I : (1733-1759), takes Kolába, forms an alliance with Sháhu, his hostility to the English and the Sidi, attacked by Sambháji A'ngria (1738), helped by the Peshwa and the English, captures Elephanta and Karanj, helps the Maráthás at Bassein (1739), attacked by Sambháji a second time (1740), makes peace with Sambháji, his territory attacked by the Peshwa (1747), helped by the Peshwa against the Sidi, XI, 150-152 ; his death (1759), *id.* 154.

Mánáji A'ngria II : (1793-1817), raised to the chiefship by Jaysing, driven from his territory by Jaysing, defeated at Cheul (1796), flees to Mahád, imprisoned by Báburáv A'ngria, again defeated and imprisoned (1799), becomes chief on Báburáv's death (1813), dies (1817), XI, 155-156.

Mánáji Gáikwár : (1789-1793), VII, 198-199.

Manaji Morár or More : Senápati of Rája Sháhu, I, pt. i, 389 ; (1710), XVIII, pt. ii, 242.

Manakatti : village in Dhárwár, inscription at, I, pt. ii, 562 note 8.

Manalarata : Western Ganga prince Permánadi Butugá's feudatory, I, pt. ii, 284 note 4, 421.

Manalkudi : town, family of, I, pt. ii, 334.

Mánalur : village on the Tungabhadra and family, I, pt. ii, 437 and note 4.

Mánánka : early Ráshtrakúta prince; Ráshtrakúta family, I, pt. i, 120.
Mánápur : deserted village in Khándesh, Mánábai's temple at, XII, 456, 104.
Mánapura : city, perhaps Málkhed, grants from, I, pt. i, 120, 132; *see* also I, pt. ii, 438.
Manár (Alang) : village in Káthiáwár, VIII, 356.
Mánas : tribe associated with the introduction of sun-worship, I, pt. i, 142.
Mánasnripa : Chálukya ruler (390 A. D.), XII, 240 note 3.
Mánasollása : Sanskrit work of the later Chálukya king Someśvara, I, pt. ii, 456. *See Abhiláshitarthachintámani.*
Mánávadar : town in Káthiáwár, VIII, 540.
Mánavadharmaśástra : Sanskrit work on Hindu law, I, pt. ii, 298 note 2.
Mánavarman : prince of Ceylon, helps the Pallava king Narasimhavarman I, his war with Chalukya Pulikesi II; obtains help from Narasimhavarman I in his invasion of Ceylon, I, pt. ii, 324.
Mánavas : Sanskrit for men, I, pt. ii, 278 note 1.
Manáváv : táluka in Káthiáwár, VIII, 540.
Mánavya : Chálukya hero, I, pt. ii, 180; race, *id.* 180, 211, 278 and note 1; *gotra, id.* 286, 287 note 4, 290 note 3, 337 and note 1, 339; son of Harita, *id.* 339 and note 7.
Mánbháv : hill in Ahmadnagar, XVII, 4.
Mánbháv : caste of religious beggars, in Khándesh district, XII, 122; in Thána district, XIII, 199; in Násik district, XVI, 73; in Ahmadnagar, XVII, 181-184; in Poona district, XVIII, pt. i, 459; in Sátára district, XIX, 120 122.
Manchanná : Kalachurya Bijjála's minister and rival of Basava, I, pt. ii, 226, 479.
Manchar : market town in Poona district, old reservoir and mosque at, XVIII, pt. iii, 259.
Mancharam : Bráhman of Morvi, converted by Muhammad Begada; Sarod Bohoras claim descent from, IX, pt ii, 58 note 2.
Mancherji Kharsedji : Seth, Dutch broker, IX, pt. ii, 196 note 1; visits Delhi, *id.* 197 note 2.
Mancherpura : a Surat city ward, named after Mr. Mancherji, IX, pt. ii, 196 note 1.
Mánd : maritime island mentioned by Al Idrisi, I, pt. i, 509.
Mand : food plants found on the *gháts*, XXV, 187.
Mándád, Mandagada : creek in Kolába district, XI, 9-10; port, its trade, *id.* 349; stone monuments at, *id.* 473; caves at, I, pt. ii, 174.
Mandagara or Mandagora : mentioned by Ptolemy and Pliny, identified with Mandangad fort in Ratnágiri district, I, pt. i, 541-546; X, 192 note 3, 352; or with a village north of Bánkot, X, 319; or with Mándál in Kolába district, I, pt. ii, 1, 2 note 5, 174.
Mandagas : Sudra class of sun-worshippers, I, pt. i, 142.
Mandai : market in Poona city, XVIII, pt. iii, 313 316.
Mándal : fort and town in Ahmadábád district, IV, 345; expedition against, I, pt. i, 109, 518, 520 and note 2.
Mandali : modern Mándal, Mulanáthadev's temple at, I, pt. i, 161 and note 2; old province, I, pt. ii, 428 note 4, 443.
Mandalika : Chudasama ruler of Junágadh, I, pt. i, 70.
Mandali-Nagara : temple of Muleśvara at, I, pt. i, 161 and note 2.
Mandána : fort in Khándesh, XII, 456.
Mandangad : fort in Ratnágiri district, X, 4, 352; *see* also I, pt. i, 546; and I, pt. ii, 2 note 5.
Mandap : gorge in Sátára district, XIX, 203.
Mandapeshvar : vilage in Thána, remains of a Portuguese Cathedral and College at, XIV, 223-227; caves, I, pt. ii, 9, 12; caves, taken possession of, sculptures destroyed and a Church and the Royal College of Sálsette built at, by the Franciscans (1585), *id.* 56, 57; Portuguese remains at, *id.* 66. *See* Mont Pezier.
Mandapiká : gold canopy, won from Káma the Chedi king and presented to Somanátha, I, pt. i, 163.
Mandara : mountain, Brahma's churning stick, I, pt. ii, 340 note 1.
Mandasor : town in Western Málwa, I, pt. i, 77; inscription of Amsu Varman at, *id.* 81; defeat of Sultán Bahádur of Gujarát at (1534), *id.* 367; inscriptions at (A. D. 473), I, pt. ii, 310; records at, *id.* 312, 426 note 2; treaty of (1818), *id.* 630; *see* also XII, 254, 594.
Mandav : *see* Booth-building.
Mándav : hill range in Káthiáwár, VIII, 9.
Mandavár : Saturday, IX pt. i, 403.
Mandavra : Hindu god, IX, pt. i, 257.
Mandavri : Hindu goddess, temple of, at Muli, worshipped by Parmárs, IX, pt. i, 136.
Mándavya : *see* Mánavya.
Mandelslo : traveller (1623-1639), I, pt. i, 224 note 2; at Ahmadábád (1638), *id.* 279 note 2; his notice of skill and honesty of Surat and Cambay Vaniás, IX, pt. i, 78 note 1; description of Surat Pársis by, IX, pt. ii, 190-191; his description of Dábhol and Jaytápur in Ratnágiri district, X, 330, 341; his notice of Bombay and Bándra, and the saltpans at Uran, XIV, 26, 191; his visit to Bijápur, its artillery, trade and politics; XXIII, 427; his impressions of, *id.* 587.
Mandesar : *see* Mandasor.
Mándev : Bágláu chief (1340), XIII, 440.
Mandeville : traveller (1322-1356); his notice of Cheul, XI, 273 note 3.
Mandhardev : hill in Sátára district, XIX, 523-524.
Mandikeshvar : holy place on the Sarasvati in Baroda state, VII, 619.
Mandisca : vegetable poison, XXV, 270.
Mándla-Borlai : town in Janjira state, XI, 465.
Mándogan : town in Ahmadnagar, temple at, XVII, 727.
Mandrup : town in Sholápur district, XX, 414.
Mánds : tribe identified with Mers, I, pt. i, 140 and note 5, 142 and note 2, 508.
Mándu : town in Central India, expedition against (1394), I, pt. i, 233; (1419), *id.* 237; hill fort, description of, *id.* 352-256; is made

capital of Málwa by Sultán Hoshang, *id.* 358; besieged by Ahmad Sháh of Gujarát (1418-1422), *id.* 359; captured by Muhammad II of Málwa and Muzaffar of Gujarát (1519); besieged by Sultán Bahádur of Gujarát (1526), *id.* 367; local Musalmán chiefs attempt to establish at (1536-1542), Mallu Khán the *sultán* of, *id.* 368; captured by Akbar's general Pir Muhammad (1560); retaken by Sultán Báz Bahadur (1561); re-captured by Akbar's general Abdullah Khán Uzbak (1562); visited by Akbar (1563), *id.* 369; Mughal province (1570-1720), *id.* 370, 371; is given to Muzaffar III of Gujarát by Akbar, *id.* 371; described by Abdul Fazl (1590), Farishtah (1610), Emperor Jehángir (1617), the Reverend Edward Terry (1617), *id.* 371-381; besieged by Khán Jehán Lodi, *id.* 381; captured by Udaji Pavár (1696) and Emperor Bahádur Sháh (1708); Asaph Jah Nizám-ul-Mulk, governor (1717-1721); Rája Girdhar Bahádur, governor (1722-1724); defeated by Chimnáji Pandit and Udáji Pavár; Bájiráv Peshwa, governor of (1734); included in the Pavár territory; Minábái, mother of Ramchandra Pavár, takes shelter in (1805), *id.* 382; under the Maráthás (1720-1820), *id.* 382.

Mandva: state and place of interest in Rewa Kántha, VI, 164; an estate of Chohán group, *id.* 142.

Mandva: place of interest in Káthiáwár, VIII, 541.

Mándva: village in Kolába district, XI, 350.

Mándvi: town and fort in Cutch, its harbour, population, history, palace, light-houses and temples at, V, 237-244; *see* also *id.* 151-153, 157-159.

Mándvi: town in Káthiáwár, VIII, 542.

Mandvi: sub-division of Surat district, II, 271-273; *Town, id.* 298; former seat of the head *mulla* of Daudi Bohoras at, IX, pt. ii, 31 note 4; Sunni Bohora disturbance at (1810), IX, pt. ii, 60 note 4, 198 note 5.

Mandvi: village in Thána, XIV, 227; Bassein copper-plate found at, XIII, 427 note 2, 457; Portuguese remains at, I, pt. ii, 65.

Mane: village in Thána district, XIV, 228.

Mánes: chiefs of Mhaswad, XIX, 231, 527.

Manekji: head of eighty-four *nukhs* or divisions of Sind Lohánas converted to Islám by Eusuf-ud-din, IX, pt. ii, 50-51.

Manekstambha: ruby pillar, worship of, IX, pt. i, 36.

Manekthari Punem: pearl-making fullmoon, observances on, IX, pt. i, 399.

Mánekváda: town in Baroda state, schools and hospitals at, VII, 488, 510.

Mang: early tribe in Gujarát, IX, pt. i, 290, 323-324; depressed class in Ratnágiri district, X, 130; their depredations (1818-1819), *id.* 219; in Koláha district, XI, 73; in Janjira state, *id.* 414; in Khándesh, XII, 119; in Thána district, XIII, 194; musicians, in Kanára district, XV, pt. i, 320; in Násik, XVI, 71; *gárudis*, snake-charmers, *id.* 72; in Ahmadnagar, XVII, 169-172; in Poona district, XVIII, pt. i, 443-444: in Sátára district, XIX, 111-112; in Sholápur district, XX, 171-175; in Belgaum district, XXI, 194-195; in Kolhápur state, XXIV, 111-112. *See* also Madig or Madigar.

Manga: bambu growing in Poona, Malabár, etc., XXV, 187, 208.

Mángad: fort in Kolába district, XI, 350.

Mangal: *see* Mars.

Mangalágauri: worship of, among Deshastha Bráhmans, XXIV, 56.

Mangalapura: *see* Mangrol.

Mangalapuri: identified with Puri, the Konkan Siláhára capital, I, pt. i, 108; charter issued from, by Mangalarasa, I, pt. ii, 374.

Mangalarája: *see* Mangaleśa.

Mangalarája or Mangalarasa: Gujarát Chálukya ruler (698-731), I, pt. i, 56; his plates, *id.* 108-109; at Navsári, *id.* 110; Yuddhamalla, of Gujarát, son of Dharásraya Jayasimhavarman, I, pt. ii, 368; *birudas* or titles of, *id.* 374.

Mangalarasaráya: *see* Mangalarája.

Mangalaváda: town mentioned in a grant, I, pt. ii, 448.

Mangalaveshtaka: *see* Mangalvedhem.

Mangaleśa: (597-608) son of the Western Chálukya king Pulikesi I and brother and successor of Kirtivarman I, I, pt. ii, 181, 328, 335, and note 1, 346 and note 4; various forms of his name, *id.* 346; his *birudas* or titles and epithets, *id.* 347; overthrows the Kalachuri kings Śamkaragana and Buddha and acquires the sovereignty of Lata or the country between the Kim and the Máhi, *id.* 181, 295, 311, 336, 347; captures Revatidvipa with a bridge of boats, *id.* 181, 347 and note 2; endows with a village the cave temple of Vishnu at Bádámi, *id.* 181, 192, 346; his death in the civil war with his nephew Pulikesi II (608), *id.* 182, 329, 347-348; record regarding his reign, *id.* 293, 336 note 3, 338 note 1, 344, 348-349; *see* also I, pt. i, 114; XV, pt. ii, 81; XXIII, 380-381.

Mangalgad: *see* Kángori.

Mangaliśa or Mangalish: *see* Mangaleśa.

Mangaliśvara: *see* Mangaleśa.

Mangalor: identified with Pliny's Nitrias, I, pt. i, 537.

Mangalpuri: old settlement in Sálsette, XIII, 424; capital of Siláhára king Pulashakti, its identification, XIV, 177, 402 and note 2; *see* also I, pt. ii, 17.

Mangal Sakhidás Parikh: guarantee given to (1802), by the resident of Baroda, VII, 259.

Mangalsthán, Mangalthán: present Magáthán, XIV, 177 and note 1; I, pt. ii, 11.

Mángalur: village in the Vengoráshtra country, I, pt. ii, 321.

Mangalvár: ward of Poona city, details of, XVIII, pt. iii, 274.

Mangalvedha: town in Kolhápur state, its history, fort, inscriptions, XXIV, 361-362; action near (1665), XX, 287.

Mangalvedhem: town between Sholápur and Bijápur districts, I, pt. ii, 238, 520.

Mánganga: river in Sátára district, XIX, 16.

Mangaon: sub-division of Kolába district, its boundaries, area, aspect, climate, water, soil, holdings, rental, stock, produce and people, XI, 1, 247-249; included in the old sub-

divisions of Rájpuri and Ráygad, *id.* 159, 186, 196. *Town, id.* 350.
Mangar: feeder of the Kásári in Kolhápur state, XXIV, 9.
Mangela: a caste of fishermen in Thána district, XIII, 147, 719.
Mangi: king killed by Vijayáditya III, I, pt. ii, 411.
Mangifera Indica: Arabic gum and resin plant, XXV, 250; medicinal plant, *id.* 257, 259; sacred plant, *id.* 279, 284, 289; 291.
Mango: in Káthiáwár, VIII, 94; in Ratnágiri district, X, 37, 39; in Khándesh, XII, 26; in Thána district, XIII, 294-295; in Poona district, XVIII, pt. i, 41.
Mangoli: petty division in the Bijápur district, survey of (1844-1845), XXIII, 467-468.
Mangra: reef in Káthiáwár, VIII, 24.
Mángria: pass in Násik district, XVI, 128.
Mángrol or Mangrul: state and town in Káthiáwár, VIII, 240, 542, 545; Velári betelvine cultivators' settlement at, I, pt. i, 113 note 3; Simha era mentioned in an inscription at, *id.* 176; burnt by the Portuguese (1532), I, pt. i, 347.
Mangsoli: village in Kolhapur, cattle fair at, XXIV, 26.
Mangsuli: place of interest in Belgaum district, XXI, 585.
Mangundi: village in Dhárwár, temples and inscriptions at, XXII, 770.
Maniád: river in Násik district, XVI, 10.
Maniár: *see* Shishgar.
Maniar: *see* Manyar.
Mánikádevi: wife of the Goa Kádamba Tribhuvanamala, I, pt. ii, 565, 571.
Manikeri: hill in Belgaum district, XXI, 8.
Mánikgad: hill, in Thána district, XIII, 8; fort, XIV, 228.
Manikpunj: fort in Nasik district, XVI, 441, 456.
Mánikpur: village in Thána district, XIV, 228; a church at, *id.* 37.
Mánikváda: place of interest in Káthiáwár, VIII, 545.
Manikyanandin: Jain writer, I, pt. ii, 407.
Manimangala: Pulakesin II defeated at, I, pt. ii, 322, 326, 358.
Manipur: state, peculiar custom of succession in, I, pt. ii, 346 note 4.
Manja: coasting craft in Thána, XIII, 719.
Manjál: village in Cutch, the ruins of Punvaranogad in the vicinity of, V, 234-237.
Manjarda: village in Kolhápur state, XXIV, 363.
Manjarsumbha: hill, village, fort, pass in Ahmadnagar, XVII, 5, 728.
Manjet: a plant yielding dyes, XXV, 246.
Manjguni: village, in Kánara district, Du Perron's mention of (1758), XV, pt. ii, 138, 330.
Mankatti: village in Dhárwár, temple and inscriptions at, XXII, 771.
Mankeshvar: village in Poona district, temple and remains at, XVIII, pt. iii, 259.
Manki: village and port in Kánara district, its trade, XV, pt. ii, 65, 66, 68, 330.
Mánkir: *see* Málkhed.
Mankni: village in Bijápur, temple, inscription, XXIII, 663.
Mánkoji A'ngria: succeeds to the command of the Marátha fleet (1698), I, pt. ii, 79.
Manmád: town in Násik district, XVI, 457.
Mánmoda Caves: at Junnar, XVIII, pt. iii, 164-184.
Mannaikudi: defeat of the Pándyas at, by the Pallavas, I, pt. ii, 327.
Manneyakere: modern Málkhed, Western Chálukya king Vikramáditya VI reigns at, I, pt. ii, 450 and note 4.
Manoel De Souza: same as Emanuel De Souza, captain of the fleet of Diu, I, pt. i, 349, 350, 351.
Manohar: hill in Kolhápur, XXIV, 5; fort in Sávantvádi state, its history, X, 466-467; rebellion at (1844), *id.* 451.
Manohirgir Gosávi: commander of the troops under the *sarsubhedár* of Khándesh and Báglán, I, pt. ii, 629.
Manoli: old town in Belgaum, temples and remains at, history of, XXI, 585-588; I, pt. ii, 431; inscription of 1222 at, *id.* 523, 558; record at, *id.* 526.
Mánoli: large village in Belgaum district, its history, XXI, 588-589; Marátha district, dispute about, I, pt. ii, 657.
Manor: village in Thána district, Portuguese fort at (1634), XIV, 228-229; taken by the Portuguese (1556), XIII, 452; a Portuguese district (1560), *id.* 455, 456; its defences (1727), *id.* 491; *see* also I, pt. ii, 48.
Manori: village in Thána district, XIV, 229.
Mánpur: identification of, I, pt. i, 545.
Mans: food plant, XXV, 187.
Mánsa: state and town in Mahi Kántha, V, 417, 438; IX, pt. i, 124; taken by Damáji Gáikwár, I, pt. i, 324.
Mánsa: village in Káthiáwár, VIII, 546.
Mansantosh: fort in Ratnágiri district, X, 467; hill in Kolhápur state, XXIV, 5.
Mansar: reservoir in Ahmadábád district, IV, 18.
Mánsarovar: sacred pond in the Himálayás, miraculous power of its water, IX, pt. i, 366.
Mansehra: rock inscription at, I, pt. ii, 142.
Mánsinghráv Pátankar: Kolhápur commander, I, pt. ii, 112.
Manson: Mr., murder of (1885), XXII, 435-436, 787; *see* also XXI, 412.
Mansur: Sufi or freethinker, his full name and title, his crucifixion; followers of, in Gujarát, IX, pt. ii, 35 note 1.
Mansura: in Central Sind, invaded by Muhammad of Ghazni, I, pt. i, 167; kingdom of, in India, foundation and destruction of, IX, pt. ii, 3 note 3 continued on page 4; *see* also I, pt. i, 506, 507, 511, 525.
Mansurgadi: remains of the fort of, in Násik district, XVI, 385 note 1.
Mansuris: followers of Mansur, IX, pt. ii, 35 note 1. *See* Mansur.
Mantarája: king of Kerala, I, pt. ii, 280.
Mánthava: Bahika town, I, pt. i, 534.
Mantigi: village in Dhárwár, inscription at, XXII, 771.

Mantraśástris: proficient in charms, I, pt. i, 161.
Mantravádi: village in Dhárwár, inscriptions at, XXII, 771.
Mantri: private record-keeper under the Marátha government, XIX, 243, 244 note 1; history of the family, *id.* 599-600.
Mantris: revenue agents in Gujarát under the Musalmáns, I, pt. i, 209.
Mantur: in the Mudhol state, inscription at, I, pt. ii, 435 note 10, 553.
Manu: son of the sun, I, pt. ii, 277 note 5; son of Hiranyagarbha Bráhman, *id.* 339; Hindu law giver, *id.* 135; code of laws of, *id.* 316 note 6, 344.
Manufactures; of Surat district, II, 145, 177-180; of Broach, *id.* 438-440; Kaira district, III, 75; of Panch Mahals, *id.* 247; of Ahmadábád district, IV, 116-140; in Cutch, V, 122-128; in Pálanpur, *id.* 300; in Mahi Kántha, *id.* 378; in Rewa Kántha, VI, 56-58; in Cambay, *id.* 198-209; in Baroda state, VII, 154-159; of Káthiáwár, VIII, 149-152; in Khándesh, XII, 75-76; of Kánara district, XV, pt. i, 225-284; of Dhárwár district, XXII, 163-179.
Manure: use of, in Palanpure, V, 293; in Rewa Kántha, VI, 38; in Káthiáwár, VIII, 179; in Kolába district, XI, 94; in Khándesh, XII, 146; in Kánara district, XV, pt. ii, 14-15; in Násik, XVI, 95; in Ahmadnagar, XVII, 249; in Poona district, XVIII, pt. ii, 11, 12, 32; in Sátára district, XIX, 159; in Sholápur district, XX, 215, 228; in Belgaum district, XXI, 244-245; in Dhárwár, XXII, 266-267; in Bijapur district, XXIII, 316; in Kolhápur state, XXIV, 160-161.
Manvar: river in Káthiáwár, VIII, 64.
Mányakheta: modern Málkhed, I, pt. i, 120; capital of Dakhan Ráshtrakútas, *id.* 128, 130, 519; I, pt. ii, 200, 396; founded by the Ráshtrakúta king Govinda III and walled by the Eastern Chálukya king Narendramrigarája-Vijayáditya of Vengi, *id.* 396; beautified by Amoghavarsha I, *id.* 199, 403; Ráshtrakúta capital, *id.* 203, 205, 206, 306, 415, 416, 417, 419, 420, 423. *See* Málkhed and Manneyakere.
Mányapura: town, I, pt. ii, 400.
Manyár: snake in Rátnágiri district, X, 50.
Manyár: caste of Musalmán bangle-sellers in Cutch, V, 127; in Gujarát, Hindu converts, IX, pt. ii, 76-77; in Poona district, XVIII, pt. i, 494; in Sátára district, XIX, 135; in Sholápur district, XX, 200; in Belgaum district, XXI, 207; in Dhárwár, XXII, 234-235; in Kolhápur state, XXIV, 149.
Mapara: caste of corn-weighers, Hindu converts in Gujarát, IX, pt ii, 88.
Mapla Por: building in Bombay island, the present condition of (1894), XXVI, pt. iii, 660-662; the same as the court-house built by President Aungier to serve as a court-house and prison (1671-1676), bought by Aungier, used as a court-house (1720), partly destroyed by fire of 1803, again damaged by fire in 1868, *id.* 662-666.
Már: a land measure in Dhárwár, XXII, 440, 458, 478.
Már: spirit-yeilding plant, XXV, 212.
Mara: Buddhist evil spirit, XII, 492, 572.
Márásárva: king of East Málwa, submits to Govind III, I, pt. i, 123; *see* also I, pt. ii, 198, 397.
Márasimha: Satyavákya-Kongunivarma-Permanadi, Western Ganga prince, I, pt. ii, 305; feudatory of Rashtrakúta Krishna III, *id.* 419, 422, 423; commands an expedition into Gujarát, *id.* 306, 420; subjugates the Pallavas of Nolambavádi, *id.* 306, 332; is expelled from Mányakheta, *id.* 306; his unsuccessful attempt to restore the Ráshtrakúta dynasty (973), *id.* 306, 385, 424; killed in battle by Western Chálukya king Taila II (974), *id.* 307, 332; Kolhápur or Karád Siláhára prince, *id.* 545; rules at Kiligiladurga, *id.* 254, 439, 547; father-in-law of Vikramáditya VI, *id.* 449, 546; his copper-plate grant, *id.* 439, 546; feudatory of the Western Chálukya king Someśvara III, *id.* 456.
Márasingayya: town, I, pt. ii, 494.
Marásthali: Márwár, I, pt. i, 470.
Marátab: *see* Mohbed.
Marátha: caste of cultivators, in Rátnágiri district, X, 122-124; in Sávantvádi, *id.* 414; in Kolába, XI, 412; in Khándesh, XII, 68; in Násik, XVI, 47, 48 note 1; in Poona, XVIII, pt. i, 284-309; in Sátára, XIX, 75-79; in Belgaum, XXI, 126-128; in Dhárwár, XXII, 139-140; in Bijápur, XXIII, 125-127, fighting class in Kánara, XV, pt. i, 192; in Kolhápur, XXIV, 65-85; origin of the name, *id.* 81-85; their surnames, *id.* 65-66, 414; in Sholápur district, XX, 87-91.
Marátha: or Berbera, a division of Abhir country between the Tapti and Bassein, "Introduction to the History of the Konkan," I, pt. ii, p. x.
Marátha Bháts: beggars in Dhárwár district, XXII, 417.
Marátha Bráhmans: believed to be of Persian descent, IX, pt. i, 2, 439, 442 note 6.
Marátha Camp: description of (1790), XXII, 417.
Maratha Chiefs: under the Nizámsháhis, XVII, 388-389
Marátha Gopáls: beggars in Ahmadnagar district, XVII, 184-185.
Maratha Horse: description (1805) of the, XVIII, pt. ii, 287.
Maráthas: of the Dakhan, their rise, XXIII, 424-425; I, pt. ii, 277; their old names, *id.* 143, 277; petty *rájas* of *id.* 30; begin to make themselves conspicuous under the Bijápur kings, *id.* 591; their chiefs become important under Malik Ambar; their greatest family, the Jádhvas of Sindkhed, go over to the Mughals (1621), *id.* 624; their incursions into the Mughal territories (1657-1673), *id.* 625-626; exact for the first time from village officers promises to pay *chauth* (1670), *id.* 625; their attacks on the kingdom of Bijápur, *id.* 653; dissensions among (1697-1700); plunder in the rear of Aurangzib, are joined by his Mánkaris; their independence is formally recognised by the emperor of Delhi (1707), *id.* 597; equip a fleet indepeudent of the Angrias (1707), *id.* 81; obtain a grant of the *chauth* and *sar-*

deshmukhi of the Dakhan (1720), *id.* 626; become the chief power in the Konkan (1735), *id.* 83; invade Sálsette (1737); take Bassein (1739), *id.* 39; allow their Christian subjects full liberty of conscience, *id.* 86; cession of Khándesh to (1752); their compaign against Sávanur (1756), *id* 657; gain Ahmadnagar and Násik (1759-1760), *id.* 627; obtain Bijápur (1760), *id.* 657; their defeat at Pánipat (1761), *id.* 627; defeat the Nizám at Kharda and obtain the districts along the frontier from Purinda to Daulatábád (1795); the last occasion on which all the great Marátha chiefs acted together, *id.* 628; their wars with Haidar and Tipu (1759-1792), *id.* 658-662; complete defeat of the confederates by the English at Assaye and Argaon (1803), *id.* 609. *See* Shivájі, Ráma Rája, Shâhu and the Peshwa. Account of their ascendancy in Gujarát (1760-1802), I, pt. i, 227; raids on Surat (1664), *id.* 284; (1699), *id.* 291; threaten Surat (1700), *id.* 292; enter Gujarát under Dhanáji Jádhav (1705), *id.* 293; plunder Mahudha, enter Ahmadábád and levy tribute (1707), *id.* 295, 296; defeated at Ankleshvar (1711), *id.* 297; plunder the treasure escorted by Muhammad Tabrizi (1713), *id.* 388; yearly raids into Gujarát, *id.* 297; besiege Vadnagar (1725), *id.* 307; quarrels between their leaders Dámaji and Kántáji; under Dámáji expel the Viramgám Kasbátis; under Rangoji are defeated at Dholka by Ratansingh, *id.* 316, 317; defeat Rustam Ali, governor of Surat, *id.* 305; defeated by Khánahzad at Sojitra and Kapadvanj (1725), *id.* 307; compel Mubáriz-ul-Mulk to confirm his predecessor's grants in their favour (1726), *id.* 307; make terms with the viceroy of Gujarát, *id.* 314; driven out of Baroda (1732), *id.* 394; defeat Sher Khán Bábi and capture Baroda (1734), *id.* 314-315; capture Kapadvanj (1736), *id.* 317; expelled from Viramgám fort; call in the aid of Momin Khán; take Viramgám, *id.* 323 324; take Petlád, *id.* 327; engagements with Momin Khán, *id.* 340, 341, 342; their arrangements in Ahmadábád (1758); strike coins of their own at the Ahmadábád mint, *id.* 342; levy tribute in Umeta, Bálásinor, Lunaváda, Visalnagar, and Pálanpur (1758), *id* 343; their supremacy in Gujarát (1760-1819), *id.* 345, 385; help the Rao of Cutch in an expedition against Thatta in Sind (1758), *id* 398; join in a league against the English (1780); driven from their post in Ankleshvar, Hansot and Ámod by the English (1780), *id.* 408; close of their supremacy (1819), *id.* 428 429; their conquests on Thána coast (1737-1739), XIV, 10, 13, 16, 22, 33, 35, 344, 355, 360, 380; *see* also XXVI, pt. i, 133, 160, 181-182, 198, 203, 211-213, 238-242; the East India Company jealous of the growing power of (1769), *id.* 359-360; naval stores not to be sold to (1771), *id.* 360; their alliance (1779) with the French, *id.* 421-426; their rule in Cambay, VI, 221, 226, 231; in Káthiáwár, VIII, 168, 299, 304; in Kánara district (1720-1750), XV, pt. ii, 135-136; their exactions in Ahmadnagar district (1700), XVII, 402; inroads of the, in Násik district (1670-1760), XVI, 190-192; in Belgaum (1648-1680), XXI, 344-375; in Bijápur district, XXIII, 439, 445-446; in Khándesh (1760-1818), XII, 252-254; in Dhárwár (1752 1817), XXII, 443-453; in Násik (1760 1818), XVI. 192-195; their revenue system, XII, 268-271; XVII, 428-432; XVIII, pt. ii, 320-341; their judicial system, XII, 304-305; Munroe's description of the predatory character of their government, XXII, 427-428.

Marátha Vájantri: caste of musicians in Kánara district, XV, pt. i, 315, 316.

Marátha Váni: caste of traders, in Koláha, district, XI, 49-50; in Thána district, XIII, 115; in Sátára district, XIX, 60; in Kolhápur state, XXIV, 87.

Maráthi: language, offshoot of Sanskrit, I, pt. ii, 136.

Maráthi Sidi: *see* Christian Revert.

Marávli: hill in Dhárwár district, XXII, 4.

Marayada: a sacred plant, XXV, 285.

Marco Polo: Italian traveller (1290), I, pt. i, 501, 504; I, pt. ii, 5, 35; mention of Cambay agate trade by, VI, 206; description of Cambay by, *id.* 216; IX, pt. i, 470 note i; his description of ships in the Persian Gulf, XIII, 433; his notice of Bombay, *id.* 434; of Thána and its people, *id.* 438; XIV, 356 note 3; of the Buddhist bowl, *id.* 408; his description of Malabár, XV, pt. ii, 94-95.

Marde: village in Sholápur district, mosque and well at, XX, 414.

Mare Joshi: Mhár priest, X, 130.

Marghum: a food plant, XXV, 189.

Margipanthis: sect. *See* Religious Sects.

Marha: a food plant cultivated on the *ghâts*, XXV, 187.

Marichi: sage, I, pt. ii, 340 note 2.

Marihal: village in Kolhápur state, temples and mosque at, XXIV, 363.

Marimáta: Hindu goddess, IX, pt. i, 323; temple of, *id.* 576.

Marine: Bombay (1754), XXVI, pt. iii, 219-220; reduction in the charges of (1756), *id.* 221-222; marine force (1759), *id.* 224; report on its strength and management, marine orders (1766), *id.* 228-241; comptroller of (1786), *id.* 255-256.

Marine Battalion: raised in Bombay island (1769), XXVI, pt. iii, 158.

Marine Board: formed in Bombay island (1778-1785), XXVI, pt. iii, 252-255; abolished (1786), *id.* 255.

Mariyáne: lordship of Sindigere conferred on, I, pt. ii, 492; second *dandanáyaka*, *id.* 494.

Marjadis: Vaishnav laymen, IX, pt. I, 119, 348, 536.

Marjavel: a sacred plant, XXV, 285.

Marji; Hopeful Musalmán caste, followers of Nasibis, IX, pt. ii, 38.

Mark: a zinc weight in Sávantvádi state, X, 431 note 2.

Markábkhán; Sind ruler of the Samma dynasty, converted to Islám by Eusuf-ud-din, IX, pt. ii, 50 and note 3.

Markand: pass in Násik district, XVI, 130.

Márkándeya : river in Belgaum district, XXI, 11.

Markandeya Puran : IX, pt. i, 532 ; I, pt. ii, 133, 168.

Markets : in Surat district, II, 181 ; in Pálanpur, V, 300 ; in Mahi Kántha, *id.* 379 ; in Káthiáwár, VIII, 243 ; in Kolába district and Janjira state, XI, 120, 430 ; in Khándesh, XII, 217 ; in Thána district, XIII, 58-59, 333-334 ; in Násik district, XVI, 141 ; in Ahmadnagar, XVII, 340-341 ; in Poona district, XVIII, pt. ii, 165-166 ; in Poona city, XVIII, pt. iii, 313-323 ; in Sátára district, XIX, 216-217 ; in Sholápur district, XX, 262 ; in Belgaum district, XXI, 315 ; in Dhárwár district, XXII, 357 ; in Bijápur district, XXIII, 362-363.

Markhadi : pass in Násik district, XVI, 128.

Markianos : geographer (B. C. 400), I, pt. i, 546.

Márkinda : fort in Násik district, XVI, 185 and note 1, 441, 447 ; description of, *id.* 457 ; identified with Mayurkhandi, I, pt. ii, 396.

Marna : a food plant cultivated on the *gháts*, XXV, 187.

Marohæ : tribe mentioned by Pliny, I, pt. i, 534.

Marol : village in Thána district, rock cut cistern and other remains at, XIV, 229 ; remains of a Portuguese Church at, I, pt. ii, 29.

Maroli : village in Thána district, XIV, 229.

Mar-paspoli : a food plant, XXV, 179.

Már Rái : Mátherán forest, XIV, 242.

Marriage : *among Gujarát Musalmáns*, ages of boys and girls in ; betrothals, IX, pt. ii, 162 ; fore-observances in, *id.* 163-164 ; *bari* or *sachak* and *jahez* presents in, procession in, *id.* 165 ; ceremony in, *id.* 166 ; after-observances of, costs of, *id.* 167. *Among Pársis*, observances, turmeric-pounding ceremony, *mándav* ceremony, *adarni* or inviting ceremony, *id.* 233 ; minor observances of, *id.* 233-234 ; observances during four days of, form of invitation to ; song-singing, *id.* 234 and note 1 ; preparations of ; the Sopára procession ; dress of *var-rája* or marriage chief ; procession of the *var-rája*, *id.* 235 ; wedding ceremony, *id.* 236-237 ; giving and accepting presents before, *id.* 233, 235 ; after, *id.* 237 ; occasions of making presents in, the girl's portions of the presents in, *id.* 237 note 1 ; after observances, feast-giving on the first Behram after, cost of, *id.* 238 and note 1 ; modern and earlier forms of, *id.* 238 and note 2, 239 and note 1. Act, *id.* 238, 244. Remarriage of a widow allowed and practised, *id.* 238. *Among Gujarát Hindus*, *viváh*, rites and ceremonies relating to, IX, pt. i, 269 *et seq.* *See* also under all caste names for marriage ceremonies.

Marriott : first collector of the North Konkan, I, pt. ii, 128 ; his revenue system (1818), XIII, 566-567 ; his survey, *id.* 567, 570 ; village rents (1822), *id.* 570.

Mars : Hindu name for the planet is Mangal ; details of the worship of, IX, pt. i, 384, 391, 401-402.

Marsiáhkhán : elegy-singer found among Shiáhs only ; qualifications of, singing of elegies at Muharrum by ; Lakhnau, IX, pt. ii, 133.

Mársinh : Siláhára king (1058), XXIV, 220.

Martin Alonzo de Souza : Portuguese viceroy, defeats the queen of Bhatkal (1542), XV, pt. ii, 273.

Maru : ancient name of Márwár, Rudradáman the overlord of, I, pt. i, 36 and note 4 ; Vatsarája defeated by Dhruva in, 466, 468 ; king of, subjected to Vikramáditya's sovereignty, I, pt. ii, 219.

Máru : caste of, in Rewa Kántha, VI, 24.

Maruk : *Ailanthus excelsa*, timber tree in Poona district, XVIII, pt. i, 49.

Maruladeva : son of Butuga, I, pt. ii, 305.

Marut : IX, pt. i, 348. *See* Vayu.

Márút : angel of high estate, first teacher of magic, his trial in the world, his eternal damnation, IX, pt. ii, 142-143. *See* Magic and Harut.

Máruti : monkey god, XVIII, pt. i, 290.

Marvi Kolis : early tribes in Thána district, XIII, 173.

Márwád : *see* Márwár.

Marwail : fodder plant, XXV, 276.

Márwár : king of, present with Graharipu in the battle with Mularája, I, pt. i, 160 ; chiefs of, attack Lavanaprasád and are defeated, *id.* 199, 200 ; disturbance in (1692), *id.* 289, 464, 532. Vatsaráj driven into, by Dhruva, *id.* pt. ii, 305.

Márwári or Marvádi : caste of Rájpúts in Gujarát Shrávaks, strength, IX, pt. i, 103 and note 1 ; Márwár their original home, movements ; appearance, dress, ornaments ; language, *id.* 103 and note 2 ; food, character, callings, start as shop-keepers and money-lenders, *id.* 104 and note 1 ; customs, *id.* 104-105 ; religion, *id.* 105-110 ; Bráhmans, money-lenders and traders in Kolába district, XI, 45, 48, 104, 411 ; in Thána, XIII, 80, 113-115, 308 ; in Baroda state, VII, 110-111 ; in Khándesh, XII, 56, 59-61, 194 ; money-lenders, in Ratnágiri district, X, 121, 159 ; Bráhmans and traders in Násik district, XVI, 43, 44, 45 ; Bráhmans and money-lenders in Poona district, XVIII, pt. i, 174, 278-279 ; *id.* pt. ii, 99 ; Bráhmans in Sholápur district, XX, 34-35, 85, 86, 242-243 ; in Belgaum district, XXI, 90, 104, 105 ; Bráhmans and traders in Sátára district, XIX, 55, 60-61, 181 ; traders in Dhárwár, XXII, 124-125 ; in Bijápur district, XXIII, 127-129 ; in Ahmadnagar, XVII, 59-61 ; in Kolhápur state, XXIV, 87.

Másálar : caste of beggars in Dhárwár district, XXII, 210-211.

Masalas : orders from Law, IX, pt. ii, 134 note 1.

Masalwáda : local name for Bálásinor and part of Kapadvanj, I, pt. i, 208 note 3.

Masáud Khán : Abyssinian *jáhgirdár* of Adoni, I, pt. ii, 665 ; succeeds Abdul Karim as regent of Bijápur ; applies to Shiváji for aid against Dilir Khan ; retires from office, *id.* 654.

Másavádi : country governed by the Pállavas, I, pt. ii, 333, 435, 437, 440, 465, 497, 501, 502, 523.
Mascarenhas : Don Francisco de, defends Chaul, I, pt. ii, 49.
Mashaikh : grade of *mulla*, IX, pt. ii, 32; religious guide of Momnas, his tomb at Ahmadábad, *id.* 76 note 2; Musalmán priests in Belgaum, XXI, 203-204.
Mashal : torch, uses of, IX, pt. ii, 96.
Mashalchi : caste of light-bearers, IX, pt. ii, 96; in Ratnágiri district, X, 415.
Mash-Hadis : chief *sayad* family in Gujarát, IX, pt. ii, 6 note 1 (5).
Mashki : *see* Pakhali.
Masiso : monthly death ceremony, performed by Bráhmans in Gujarát, IX, pt. i, 50; Vánias, *id.* 95; Kanbis, *id.* 163.
Másiyavádi : country in Dhárwár district, I, pt. ii, 435.
Masjids : mosques, description of, IX, pt. ii, 131; the best specimens of, at Ahmadábád, Cambay, Patan and Rander, *id.* 131 note 1.
Maskat : its trade with Thána coast (1500-1670), XIII, 465; ship building place (1510), *id.* 470; Arabs from, plunder Bándra (1674), *id.* 476; trade centre (1660-1710), *id.* 486; centre of piracy (1810), *id.* 521.
Maskat fishers : their way of fishing, XIII, 359 note 1.
Maskoba : *see* Mhasoba.
Masons : in Cutch, V, 73, 125; in Ratnágiri, X, 125; at Mátherán, XIV, 265; in Kolhápur, XXIV, 20.
Massunda : lake at Thána, XIV, 346, 351, 354, 355.
Mastáni : Bájiráv I's (1721-1740) Musalmán mistress, her tomb at Pábal, XVIII, pt. iii, 264-265; a garden and a gate in Shanvár palace in Poona named after, *id.* 344-345.
Mastáus : Anávala Bráhmans known as, meaning of, IX, pt. i, 4 and note 1.
Mastans : madmen, IX, pt. ii, 34. *See* Rasulsháhi.
Masudi : Arab traveller (915), his notice of Chaul, XI, 271; his mention of Sanján, Sopára and Thána, XII 302 notes 3 and 4, 321, 355; Lár language on Thána coast according to, XIII, 112; his mention of Jhanjha, chief of Chaul, *id.* 424; Persian settlers at Chaul, *id.* 432; his mention of Balhár, king of Lár, *id.* 434 and note 10; his mention of Chitákul and Siddhápur in Kánara, XV, pt. ii, 277, 278, 343; *see* also I, pt. i, 469, 498; IX, pt i, 434 and note 7, 439 note 2, 470 note 2, 498 note 2; IX, pt. ii, 1 note 1, 2 note 1, 183 note 4, 185, 186.
Masulipatam : trade centre (100), 'muslin' derived from, XIII, 415 note 4; embroidered muslins brought from, to Thána (1500-1670), *id.* 466; Hindu colonisers of Java and Cambodia sail from, I, pt. i, 496.
Masur : town in Sátára district, Parashurám Pratinidhi confined in (1806), XIX, 299, 524; surrendered to the British (1818), *id.* 308.
Masur : village in Dhárwár district, fort and inscription at, XXII, 771.
Masura : town in Ratnágiri district, proposed identification of, with Muziris of Ptolemy, X, 352 and note 8.
Masvari : a house tax in Kaira district, III, 171.
Mátádárs : hereditary village officials in Baroda, VIII, 367.
Matag : Hindu goddess, IX, pt. i, 205.
Mataki : a famine plant, XXV, 198.
Máta Meri : she-camel, IX, pt. i, 377.
Mátangas : early hill tribe, defeated by Mangalish (567-610) the Chálukya king, XV, pt. ii, 81; *see* also XXIII, 380 and note 3; Dr. Bhandarkar's view of, I, pt. ii, 293 note 1.
Mátápanthi : sect of Shakti-worshipping Lohánas, IX, pt. ii, 40, 48.
Mátápenai : hill in Rewa Kántha, VI, 6.
Mátar : sub-division of Kaira district, details of, III, 155-158; identified with the Mátri division of Ráshtrakúta Gujarát, I, pt. i, 122 and note 3. *Town, id.* 173.
Matarem : in the island of Java, I, pt. i, 489.
Mátar Mahndha : Mátar and Mahudha in Kaira district made over to the English by Ráoji, Baroda minister, in payment of the subsidiary force at Baroda (1803), I, pt. i, 414.
Mátás : deities or goddesses of North Gujarát, IX, pt. i, p. xxxv; in Cutch, V, 76 note 3; *see* also I, pt. i, 461.
Math : pulse, in Poona district, XVIII, pt. ii, 43; in Sátára district, XIX, 164.
Ma-Thákur : early tribe, in Thána district, XIII, 180.
Matherán : hill, in Thána district, XIII, 6; hill station, its position, the way up, XIV, 230-231; hill top, *id.* 232-233; points, *id.* 233-240; geology, *id.* 240-241; terrace, forests, *id.* 242 243; streams, water-supply, springs pounds, *id.* 243-246; climate, rainfall, thermometer readings, *id.* 246-250; gardening, plants, *id.* 250-253; animals, *id.* 254-259; hill tribes, *id.* 259-264; strangers, visitors, *id.* 264-266; trade, history, *id* 266-268; the season, management, *id.* 268-272; hotels, markets, library, gymkhana, *id.* 272-273; houses, churches, mosque, temples, *id.* 274-275; walks, *id.* 275-282; excursions, *id.* 283-284, 300, 367, 383.
Mathews : Commodore, defeated (1722) by Angria, XI, 149.
Mathews : General, captures the forts of Rájamandrug and Mirján (1782), takes Kodra (1783), Kurmagad and Sadáshivgad and other places in Kánara district, XV, pt. ii, 142, 318, 328, 333, 340, 342.
Mathoe : tribe, I, pt. i, 534.
Mathpati : caste of Lingáyat beadles in Dhárwár, XXII, 186-187.
Mathra : modern Mathura, I, pt. i, 519.
Mathura : place of pilgrimage, IX, pt. i, 119, 157, 168, 176, 220, 549; king of, present at the *svayamvara* or choice-marriage of Durlabhadevi, I, pt. i, 163; Prince Murád confined in (1658), *id.* 282, 533; Yádava lords of, I, pt. ii, 231; king of, killed by the Devagiri Yádava Singhana, *id.* 240, 525.

Máthure : a Vanjári sub-division in Khándesh district, XII, 108, 113.
Mathvádi : a Bhil tribe in Khándesh district, XII, 102.
Máthván : village in Kolába district, monumental pillars at, XI, 351.
Matia or Matia Kanbi : Musalmán caste in Gujarát, settlements of; descendants of Hindu Leva Kanbi converts; followers of Pirána saint Imám Sháh; devotion of, to Sindhsháh Pirzáda of Burhánpur, IX, pt. ii, 66; blind belief of, in the spiritual guide; cultivators, follow Hindu customs, form a distinct body, *id.* 67 68; of Khándesh with Momnas march against Broach, and murder the governor (1691); their defeat and slaughter, I, pt. i, 288. *See* also under Kanbi.
Mátoba : reservoir in Poona district, XVIII, pt. ii, 53-54.
Mátrá : native drug, XI, 122.
Mátra Timba : táluka in Káthiáwár, VIII, 546.
Matri : *see* Mátar.
Matri Gaya : Sidhpur so called, IX, pt. i, 549.
Matrikás : Hindu goddesses, installation of, IX, pt. i, 41; eight images of, in Elephanta caves, XIV, 78-79 and note 1. *See* Mátás.
Mátsya : *Purána*, I, pt. ii, 133, 136, 155, 156, 157, 162, 163, 164, 165, 166, 167, 172, 177.
Matsyanagar : *see* Vairatpur.
Matsyavedha : fish test, IX, pt. i, 58 note 2.
Maues : Northern Kshatrapa king (B. C. 70), I, pt. i, 22.
Maula : lord and master, believed to be the derivation of the name Molesalam, IX, pt. ii, 68.
Maula : a Musalmán class in Khándesh, Hindu converts, XII, 127.
Maulais : followers of Ali. The Upper Indus Valley followers of His Highness the Agha Khán, IX, pt. ii, 36 note 3.
Maulavi : law doctor, position and accomplishments of, IX, pt. ii, 133; duties of, as a doctor of Muhammadan law, as a religious teacher, as a professor, as a spiritual guide, *id.* 134; as a curer of diseases; remuneration of, for several duties, *id.* 135; sometimes a Hafiz or repeater of the *Kuraan* by heart, *id.* 134; representatives of the great preachers of the fifteenth and sixteenth centuries, *id.* 133 note 2.
Maulud : holiday on the 17th of the third month of the Muhammadan year, IX, pt. ii, 140.
Maulud : nativity hymn, IX, pt. ii, 134 note 2; Muhammad-mass carols, *id.* 165.
Mauludias : Arab nativity hymn-singers, IX, pt. ii, 165.
Mauna : Puránic name for the Húnas, I, pt. i, 141 note 2, 143.
Mauryas : of Pátaliputra (B. C. 319-A. D. 500), Andhrabhrityas at first feudatories of, XVI, 182 note 1; their probable rule in Gujarát (B.C. 319-197), I, pt. i, 15; fall of their empire (B. C. 180), *id.* 535; of Chitor, defeated (730), by the Arabs, I, pt. i, 109, 465; feudatory chiefs of Konkan (500 A. D.), I, pt. ii, 282-284; dynasty in the Konkan, *id.* 13, 541; perhaps descendants of the Maurya dynasty of Pátaliputra (322 B. C.), *id.* 284 and note 2; dispersed by the Western Chálukya king Kirtivarman I, *id.* 14, 181, 282, 335, 345 and note 4; overwhelmed by Pulikesin II, *id.* 183, 282-283, 350; destroyed by the Tájikas, *id.* 187, 375; their capital, *id.* 283, 541; Maurya dynasty of Pátaliputra founded 322 B. C., "Introduction to the Early History of the Dakhan," p. ii, *id.* 142, 155, 157, 284 and note 2; duration of the Pátaliputra dynasty, *id.* 162; of Valabhi, *id.* 284; *see* also XI, 141; XIII, 60, 61, 420, 421; XXIII, 380 and note 1; I, pt. i, 15, 106; X, 192.
Mával : lake in Baroda state, VII, 19, 537.
Mával : meaning of, "Introduction to the History of the Konkan," I, pt. ii, p. x, footnote; Western Poona, XVIII, pt. i, 2 and note 1; forest reserves, *id.* 35; survey of, *id.* pt. ii, 461-464.
Mával : sub-division of Poona district, its boundaries, area, aspect, soil, water, climate, crops, people, cultivators, communications, XVIII, pt. iii, 92-94; *see* also, I, pt ii, 175.
Mavalis : Maráthás along the *gháts*, Shiváji's favourite troops, I, pt. ii, 73; XIX, 239; XVIII, pt. ii, 231-232, 235-236; XVI, 200.
Mávchi : a Bhil tribe in Khándesh, XII, 101.
Mavingudda : hill in Kánara district, XV, pt. ii, 316.
Maviukurve : island in Kánara district, XV, pt. ii, 305.
Mavli Dev : worship of, by Konkanas, IX, pt. i, 292.
Mavlis : *See* Mavalis.
Mávulideva : Hángal Kádamba, I, pt. ii, 559.
Máya or Mahámáya : Sakti or Mata so called, IX, pt. i, p. xxxv.
Mayánalladevi : Chaulukya king Karna I's wife, I, pt. ii, 568.
Mávápádar : place of interest in Káthiáwár, VIII, 546.
Máyegaon : village in Ahmadnagar, temple and fair at, XVII, 728.
Mayendirapottaresaru : *see* Mahendravarman I.
Máyideva Pandit : Singhana's governor of the Halasige province, I, pt. ii, 523.
Máyidevarasa : Kalachurya Somesvara's officer, I, pt. ii, 486.
Máyilangái : modern Málingi, I, pt. ii, 497. *See* Jananáthapura.
Máyni : village and lake in Sátára district, XIX, 524, 154; survey of, *id.* 358-359.
Mayor's Court : established (1728) in Bombay island, XXVI, pt. iii, 9; fees of (1728-1774), *id.* 10-12 and note 1; re-established (1753), *id.* 22-29; regulations and powers of (1763-1767, 1769), *id.* 34-41; abolished (1798), *id.* 44.
Mayura : peacock, symbol of the Guptás, I, pt. i, 135.
Mayuradhvaja : banner of the Guptás, I, pt. i, 135.
Mayurakhandi : identified with the hill fort of Markhand, I, pt. ii, 198; modern Márkindan, *id.* 396, 398, 400.
Mayurasarman : identical with Mukkanna Kadamba I, I, pt. ii, 286 note 2, 287 note 1, 561.

Mayuravarman I : Hángal Kádamba, I, pt. ii, 559, 560.
Mayuravarman II : Hángal Kádamba prince and feudatory of the Western Chálukya king Someśvara III (1131), I, pt. ii, 437, 439, 559, 562.
Mayuravarman III : son of the Kádamba king Tailapa II and feudatory of Someśvara III, I, pt. ii, 456.
Mazdayasnian : religion of the Pársis known as, meaning of, IX, pt. ii, 211.
Mazdiashni Zarthostidin or Mazdiashnidin : Pársi's expression for his religion, IX, pt. ii, 213.
Mazgaon : Sidi Kásim's stay at (1677), XI, 439 ; riot of the Sidis at (1680), *id.* 440 ; captured by the Sidi, *id.* 442.
Mazgaon dock : construction of (1769-74), XXVI, pt. ii, 199-200.
Mazun : grade of *mullas*, IX, pt. ii, 32.
McDowall : Lieut.-Colonel, in the Chándod range (1817-1818), I, pt. ii, 630.
Me : depressed class in Cutch, V, 83.
Meadows Taylor : Colonel, historian, XXIII, 396.
Meals : among Gujarát Musalmáns, number and time of, kinds of food served at, IX, pt. ii, 109 ; forms and ceremonies observed at, *id.* 111-112 ; among Pársis, number and time of, kind of food served at, ways of serving at, *id.* 206.
Means of communication : *see* Roads, Railways, etc..
Measles : *see* Gobru.
Measures : *see* Weights and Measures.
Meat : in Bombay island, no force to be used for procuring (1720), XXVI, pt. ii, 74-75 ; high price of (1733-1737), *id.* 75-76 ; imported from Cambay, Fort Victoria and England (1752, 1758, 1767), *id.* 77.
Med : *see* Medh.
Medad : village in Poona district, XVIII, pt. iii, 259.
Medani Rái : commander-in-chief of Muhammad II of Málwa (1512-1530), suppresses the revolt of Muháfiz Khán ; defeats the combination of Muzáffar II of Gujarát and Sikandar Sháh of Delhi ; attempts of Muhammad II of Málwa for the assassination of ; expulsion of, with terrible slaughter by joint forces of Muhammad II and Sultán Muzáffar of Gujarát ; supported by Rána Sanga of Chitor, I, pt. i, 366-367.
Medapala : first capital of Gohils, IX, pt. i, 495 note 4.
Medár : caste of workers in bamboo, in Belgaum, XXI, 173, 174 ; in Dhárwár, XXII, 157 ; in Bijápur, XXIII, 129-130.
Medárket : progenitor of the Buruds, XXIV, 94.
Medha : town in Sátára district, XIX, 525.
Medhs : I, pt. i, 140 ; Báwárij pirates, *id.* 517. *See* Mers.
Mediarem : fifth *Gahambár*, IX, pt. ii, 218.
Medicago sativa : fodder plant, XXV, 277.
Medioshem : second *Gahambár*, IX, pt. ii, 218.
Mediozarem : the first *Gahambár*, IX, pt. ii, 218.
Medleri : village in Dhárwár district, reservoirs at, XXII, 771-772.
Meds : *see* Mers.
Medur : village in Dhárwár district, temples and inscriptions at, XXII, 772 ; record at, I, pt. ii, 527.
Medus Hydaspes : Virgil's phrase for the Jhelum, I, pt. i, 144.
Megalæmidæ : family of birds in Ratnágiri, X, 67.
Megallæ : the Mekalas hill tribe between the Indus and the Jamna mentioned by Pliny, I, pt. i, 532, 533.
Megari : tribe mentioned by Pliny, I, pt. i, 534.
Megasthenes : ambassador of Seleukos Nikator, his account of India, I, pt. i, 532, 533, 534, 535, 536, 537 ; process of founding local Bráhman classes described in, IX, pt. i, 1 note 2, 435 ; (B. C. 300), on Buddhist dialects and nuns, XIV, 135, 139.
Meghaduta : Kálidása's poem, I, pt. ii, 142.
Meghvál : a depressed class in Cutch, V, 82-83, 128.
Megitores : family of birds in Thána district, XIII, 53.
Meguti : temple at Aihole, inscription at, I, pt. ii, 357.
Mehbub-i-Alam : grandson of Sháh Alam, IX, pt. ii, 6 note 1 (5).
Mehdavis : *see* Ghermehdis.
Mehdaviyyah : a Musalmán sect in Pálanpur, V, 291, 318.
Mehdi : Al, twelfth Shiáh *imám*, IX, pt. ii, 125 note 2.
Mehdvi : Musalmán sect in Ahmadnagar, XVII, 377 and note 2.
Mehekri : river in Ahmadnagar district, XVII, 9.
Mehekri : village in Ahmadnagar, Chand Bibi's *mahál* at, view from, XVII, 728.
Meher : wedding gift or dower, IX, pt. ii, 166 and note 1.
Meher : the sun or sun angel, sixteenth day of the Pársi month, seventh month of the Pársi year, IX, pt. ii, 216, 218.
Meherájpanthi : Hindu sect in Gujarát, IX, pt. i, 191.
Meherangan Jasan : *see* Meher Jasan.
Meheri Misl : marriage portion of a girl, IX, pt. ii, 166 note 1.
Meher Jasan : chief festival day, popular in Persia, observances on, IX, pt. ii, 216.
Meherji Rána : high priest of Navsári, converts emperor Akbar, receives grants from Akbar, IX, pt. ii, 190, 197 note 2.
Mehmadábád : sub-division of Kaira district, details of, III, 149-151.
Mehmadábád : town in Kaira district, III, 173.
Mehman : *see* Meman.
Mehmud : *see* Muhammad.
Mehr : northern tribal name, I, pt. i, 87 ; Hinduising of, *id.* 87.
Mehrab : arched niche in a mosque, IX, pt. ii, 131 and note 3.
Mehrán : the Indus, I, pt. i, 510.
Mehrun : lake in Khándesh, XII, 11.

Mehtar: prince, title of the headman of depressed classes, IX, pt. i, 333 note 1; Kumbhár headman, XXIV, 96; sweepers in Bhinmal, I, pt. i, 451.
Mehtar Mahal: Bijápur palace, XXIII, 623-625.
Mehulo: or Mevlo, rain-god, praise-singing by Bhil and other women during holding off of rain, IX, pt. i, 355.
Mehune: village in Khándesh district, XII, 456.
Mehvási: unsettled classes in Ahmadábád district, IV, 2, 186; refractory villages in Kaira, III, 81, 110; in Panch Mahals, *id.* 263; petty chiefs under Baroda, VII, 335-337, 360-362, 438-439.
Meirinho: police officer, I, pt. ii, 52.
Meladi: or Meldi, Hindu goddess, IX, pt. i, 247, 335, 363; famous spirit, *id.* 417.
Melágani: inscription at, I, pt. ii, 305, 322.
Melastomaceæ: an order of plants yielding dyes, XXV, 245.
Melastoma Malabaricum: a plant yielding dyes, XXV, 245.
Molia azadirachta: *nim*, a famine plant, XXV, 196; an oil-yielding plant, *id.* 215, 241; a medicinal plant, *id.* 257, 258; a plant used in religious ceremonies, *id.* 279; sacred plant, *id.* 285; *azedarach*, sacred plant, *id.* 286.
Meliaceæ: an order of oil-yielding plant, yielding dyes, XXV, 215, 241.
Melizeigara or Melizygarus: probably Janjira, I, pt. i, 536, 540, 546; I, pt. ii, 1, 2; identified with Jaygad, *id.* 174; trace of Arab influence in the word, IX, pt. ii, 1 note 1; perhaps Málvan, XIII, 404 note 3; X, 192 note 3, 348 note 4; I, pt. i, 540.
Mello: John de, his mansion near Thána (1739), I, pt. ii, 64.
Melothria: *heterophylla*, sacred plant, XXV, 291, 292; *madraspatana*, vegetable poison, *id.* 265.
Melukote: in Mysore, I, pt. ii, 499.
Melvatteya Vaddaránula: tax, I, pt. ii, 451.
Melvill: Mr., resident at Baroda (1876-1882), VII, 286.
Melvill: Captain, on Kolis, IX, pt. i, 237 note 2; on Bhils, *id.* 295 note 1.
Memadpur: state in Mahi Kántha, V, 428.
Meman: Musalmán caste properly Muamins or Believers: Hindu converts from Sind Lohánas and Káthiáwár Kachhias; sub-divisions of; first conversions of Sind Lohánas by Eusuf-ud-din Kadiri (1421), IX, pt. ii, 50-51; change of the name; arrival of Sind Memans at Bhuj at the invitation of Ráo Khengar (1548-1584); muster strong in Surat (1580-1680); famine of (1813) disperses them to Bombay and other places; settlements of, *id.* 51; appearance of, *id.* 52; character of, *id.* 52-53; dress of, *id.* 53-55; food of, *id.* 55; in inheritance follow the Hindu law, *id.* 56; beliefs and religion of, *id.* 56-57; calling of, *id.* 57; in Cutch, V, 93-94; in Baroda state, VII, 71-72; in Káthiáwár, VIII, 162; in Kolába district, XI, 85; in Thána district, XIII, 240; in Ahmadnagar, XVII, 233; in Poona, XVIII, pt. i, 498; in Sátára, XIX, 138; in Sholápur, XX, 202-203; in Belgaum, XXI, 212; in Dhárwár, XXII, 237; in Kolhápur, XXIV, 150.
Memecylon edule: a plant yielding dyes, XXV, 245.
Memorial pillars: at Sháhápur in Thána district, XIV, 308-312.
Memorial stones: at Borivli, Eksar and Mágáthán in Thána district, XIV, 51, 57-59, 217.
Men: river in Rewa Kántha, VI, 5.
Menander: Baktrian king of India, I, pt. i, 16, 17; his rule in Cutch (142-128 B. C.), V, 129; his conquests in Western India (B. C. 110), I, pt. i, 535, 544, 545; worshipped by the Buddhists as a saint, IX, pt. i, 445, 447 note 7.
Mendan, Mendang: town in Java, built by Bhruvijaya Savelachála of Gujarát, I, pt. i, 489; named after Med sea captains, *id.* 490.
Mendarda: town in Káthiáwár, VIII, 546.
Mendi: plant yielding dyes, XXV, 245.
Menezes: Portuguese commandant of Bassein (1540), XIV, 197.
Mengni: táluka in Káthiáwár, VIII, 546.
Menispermaceæ: an order of poisonous plants, XXV, 264.
Menki: plant used as antidote to snake-bite, XXV, 274.
Menshigudda: hill in Kánara district, XV, pt. ii, 330; XV, pt. i, 4, 5.
Menyanthes cristata: a famine plant, XXV, 201.
Meos: Musalmán, identified with Mers, I, pt. i, 140 and note 8.
Merada: Ratta chieftain, I, pt. ii, 551, 552.
Mercantile classes: *see* Trade under District Name.
Mercenaries: of landowners in Panch Maháls, III, 261; Musalmán, employed by Hindu chiefs, IX, pt. ii, 2 note 3; rise of Arab, against the British (1802); Persian, *id.* 3 note 2; Baluch and Pathan, *id.* 64.
Mercer: Mr., American cotton planter (1840-1846); starts an experimental cotton farm at Kusvugal in Dhárwár, XXII, 288-290, 368-369.
Merchants: *see* Trade under District Name.
Mercury: the planet Budha, details of worship, IX, pt. i, 402.
Merkara: spurious grant of Avinita Kongani at, I, pt. ii, 292 note 10.
Merodipae: family of birds in Ratnágiri, X, 63.
Meroê: capital of Ethiopia according to Pliny, I, pt. i, 542.
Mers: Hindu tribe in Káthiáwár, VIII, 138-139; sun-worshipping foreigners (470-900), passed through Panjáb, Sind and North Gujarát into Káthiáwár, and ruled there (770); allied to Jethvás and Jhálás, descendants of Hunas, I, pt. i, 135-147; known also as Meds, that is Mihiras, IX, pt. i, 492; strange Central Asian tribe, *id.* 493 note 1; said to be Valabhis or Bális; same as Gurjjars; chief traces of, in country near Ajmere in Rájputána, in West Káthiáwar, in Márwár; found settled in Gujarát, Márwár and Sind; importance and power from seventh to eleventh century, *id.* 492; took leading

part in White Huna invasion; Rájpútána Mers, their home, movements; Ajmere Mers, four branches, sameness with Gujars, proved, *id.* 493; divisions of Chohán Mers, *id.* 494 and note 1; Balod Mers, Mars or Mari of Chitor, *id.* 494 and notes 2 and 3; Gohil, *id.* 496 and note 3; Gujarát Mers, called Mhers, class of herdsmen, claim Rájpút descent, clans among, *id.* 285-286. *See* also Mihiras.
Mertha: district, conferred upon Durgádás by the Emperor Aurangzeb (1697), I, pt. i, 290.
Meru Khavas: of Navánagar, his influence with the Jam, IX, pt. I, 147 note 1.
Merulidæ: family of birds in Ratnágiri, X, 72.
Merulinæ: sub-family of birds in Ratnágiri, X, 72.
Merutunga: author of *Prabandhachintámani*, I, pt. i, 151, 152, 155, 156, 196.
Mesæ: tribe mentioned by Pliny, I, pt. i, 534.
Mesána: sub-division in Baroda state, village, VII, 626-627; hospitals in, *id.* 507.
Mesaria: táluka in Káthiáwár, VIII, 546.
Meshri: division of the Vánis in Ahmadnagar district, XVII, 74-76; in Sátára, XIX, 87-88; in Cutch, V, 50-51; in Káthiáwár, VIII, 147-149; in Násik, XVI, 45.
Meshva: river in Gujarát, IV, 7; V, 357; VII, 588.
Mesna ferrea: *Nagchampa*, an oil-yielding plant, XXV, 214; *Nagkesar*, a sacred plant, *id.* 289.
Metals: Thána trade in (810-1260), XIII, 431; (1300-1500), *id.* 445; (1500-1670), *id.* 467; power of, for spirit-scaring, XVIII, pt. i, 549.
Metal work: in Surat district, II, 180; in Baroda state, VII, 157; in Ratnágiri district, X, 188; in Kánara district, XV, pt. ii, 70; in Bijápur district, XXIII, 373-374.
Meteors: falling stars, IX, pt. i, 406.
Methi: an oil-yielding plant, XXV, 217.
Methonia: *gloriosa superba*, vegetable poison, XXV, 270.
Methora: modern Mathura, I, pt. i, 533.
Metrána: village in Baroda state, a Jain temple at, VII, 619.
Meváda: a Bráhman sub-division, in Rewa Kántha, VI, 23; in Gujarát, IX, pt. i, p. xi note 3, 2, 3, 11; in Thána, XIII, 78; a sub-division of the Vaniás, Meshri and Shrávak, in Gujarát, IX, pt. i, 72, 96.
Mevali: state in Rewa Kántha, VI, 149.
Mevas: name of a tribe, I, pt. i, 33.
Mevása: táluka in Káthiáwár, VIII, 546.
Mevundi: village in Dhárwár, XXII, 772.
Mewád, Mewar: origin of the name, I, pt. i, 33; Kumárapála's conquests extend to, *id.* 188; chief of, subdued by Visáldeva, *id.* 203, 532, 533.
Mewás: petty states in the wild west of Khándesh, I, pt. ii, 632.
Meyundi: in Gadag táluka, record at, I, pt. ii, 503.
Mhaisál: village in Kolhápur state, XXIV, 363.
Mhajah: (Mándha?) pass in Konkan hills, I, pt. ii, 77.
Mhalapur: village in Khándesh, dyeing industry at, XII, 456.
Mhángiri: a sailing vessel, in Ratnágiri district, X, 171; in Thána, XIII, 346, 719.
Mhár, Mahar: depressed class in Ratnágiri, X, 129; village servants, copper grant to, *id.* 140, 152, 222; as borrowers, *id.* 161; (1818), *id.* 223 and note 3; (1851), *id.* 240; in Sávantvádi, *id.* 418; in Thána district, XIII, 191-194; introduced by the Maráthás, *id.* 63; village servants, *id.* 529; in Ahmadnagar district, XVII, 172-177; in the Kánara district, XV, pt. i, 378-380; in Násik, XVI, 67; village messengers, *id.* 209; in Poona district, XVIII, pt. i, 439-443; in Sholápur district, XX, 175-180; in Kolhápur state, XXIV, 112-115; in Kolába district, XI, 73; village servants (1882), *id.* 161 and note 3; service of, in Marátha forts, *id.* 173, 414, 452; in Sátára district, XIX, 112-115; in Belgaum, XXI, 192, 193; in Khándesh district, XII, 115-119; *see* Holaya.
Mhar-nachani: a famine plant, XXV, 208.
Mhase: village in Thána district, fair at, XIV, 284.
Mhaske: buffalo-rearing shepherds in Kolába district, XI, 67.
Mhasla: town in Janjira state, perhaps Ptolemy's Musopalle, XI, 465, 432.
Mhasoba: evil spirit, XVIII, pt. i, 290, 553, 554.
Mhasva: lake in Khándesh, XII, 11, 142; place of interest, *id.* 456.
Mhasvad: lake in Sátára district, XIX, 156-157.
Mhaswad: town in Sátára district, market, temples and fair at, XIX, 215, 525-527; the Pratinidhi imprisoned at (1806), I, pt. ii, 609.
Mhat: fodder plant, XXV, 277.
Mhátarás: elders and managers of the cultivators, corresponding to *pátils*, I, pt. ii, 53; village headman under the Portuguese, made *pátils* by Khandoji Mánkar, *id.* 99; *see* also XIII, 552 and note 3.
Mherváda: Mher settlement at, I, pt. i, 136.
Miana: a Musalmán sub-division in Cutch, V, 98, 138, 148; in Káthiáwár, VIII, 154, 166-167; in Gujarát, IX, pt. i, 519, 522.
Miáni: port in Káthiáwár, VIII, 547.
Mián Manju: prime minister of Ibráhim Nizám Sháh (1594); proposes to conclude peace with Bijápur; crowns Ahmad; seeks for Mirza Akbar's son's assistance; a large body of the Dakhanis joins him deserting Yekhlás Khán (1595); attacks the Abyssinians; implores the assistance of the Bijápur and Golkonda sovereigns; enrolled among the nobles of the Bijápur kingdom, XVII, 380-383.
Michael Angelo: copy of his 'Resurrection' at Bassein (1675), XIV, 41.
Micromeria Malcolmiana: oil-yielding plant, XXV, 224.
Middleton: Sir H., chief of the English factory at Surat, sails to Dábhol (1611), I, pt. ii, 36, 39, 120.

Migration : from India to Indo-China, traces of, I, pt. i, 499 ; all district volumes, *see* Census Details under District Name.
Mhira : *see* Mihiras.
Mihiragas : tribe mentioned in *Bhavishya Purán*, I, pt. i, 142 and note 5.
Mihira-Gurjjara : tribe, Sumrás said to belong to, IX, pt. ii, 70. *See* White Huna.
Mihirakula : king of the White Húnás (508-530), I, pt. i, 72, 74, 75, 76, 142 and note 2 ; son of Toramána (500-540), *id.* 146, 465, 496, 497 ; conquered by a Northern Indian king Vishnuvardhana Yasodharman (about A. D. 530), I, pt. ii, 312 ; IX, pt. i, 439, 442, 459, 487 ; great champion of Bráhmans, *id.* 443 note 1 ; Shiv-worshipper, *id.* 442 note 3 ; first leaning to Buddhism, disgust for it, determination to stamp out Buddhism, *id.* 487 ; oppression of Buddhist Śakas, *id.* 413 note 1 ; compact with the invaders, *id.* 444 note 4 ; admitted to be a high caste Hindu, *id.* 442 ; held to be a god, *id.* 501 ; glorified after death, *id.* 502 note 4, 400 note 4, 441.
Mihiras : also called Meds or Mers, IX, pt. i, 473 ; Sanskrit form of Med or Mer, *id.* 479 ; Maitrakas are the same as, *id.* 479, 492 ; leading invading horde, *id.* 439, 455 ; name of fifth century horde, *id.* 434 ; leading element in great White Huna horde, *id.* 461 note 5 ; champions of Bráhmans, *id.* 433 ; respectful name for Gurjjaras, *id.* 479 ; Válas or Bálas of Valabhi are, *id.* 479, 488 ; Sisodias probably are, *id.* 443, 462 ; Talabda Kolis known to have been, *id.* 455 ; Moris of Chitor were, *id.* 440, 461 note 5 ; title, *id.* 471 ; priests known as Magha Bráhmans, *id.* 439, 440 ; their rule in Gujarát (470-1000), I, pt. i, 135-147 ; their conquest of Valabhi (490), *id.* 489, 490 ; king of, his inroads against Dhruva II, *id.* 127 ; defeated by Dhruva's son, I, pt. ii, 409 ; title of respect among Punjáb Gujars, IX, pt. i, 493. *See* Gurjjaras.
Mihireshwar : worship of, started by Maghas, IX, pt. i, 440.
Milburn : his description of Bombay (1803-1808), XXVI, pt. ii, 506-507.
Military : in Bombay island, the position of (1757), XXVI, pt. iii, 131 ; charges, reduction of (1772), *id.* 161-163, 167-169 ; establishment (1768), *id.* 145-148 ; (1770), *id.* 155-166 ; pay (1762), *id.* 139-140 ; regulations (1748), *id.* 108-113 ; strength (1763-1765), *id.* 141, 143-144.
Military artificers : want of, in Bombay island, defects of Indian artificers ; superiority of European artizans ; proposed company of European artizans and engineers (1776), XXVI, pt. ii, 424-430.
Military Service : persons engaged in, and pensioners in Ratnágiri district, X, 105, 130, 143, 160.
Militia : Portuguese, XIII, 458 ; in Bombay island to consist of 260 men (1670), XXVI, pt. iii, 68 ; to be reduced to 300 (1676), *id.* 68-70 ; increased to 600 (1677), *id.* 71-72 ; *vereadores* excused from (1710-1715), *id.* 82.
Milizegyris or Milizigeris : *see* Melizeigara.
Milk-bush : vegetable poison, XXV, 268.
Milkmen : *see* Dudwala and Gavli.
Millet : food plant, XXV, 184 ; cultivation of, in Kaira, III, 46 ; in Ahmadábád, IV, 54 ; in Cutch, V, 105-106 ; in Pálanpur, *id.* 294 ; in Mahi Kántha, *id.* 371 ; in Káthiáwár, VIII, 186-187 ; in Khándesh, XII, 149 ; in Násik district, XVI, 98 ; in Ahmadnagar, XVII, 264-265 ; in Poona district, XVIII, pt. ii, 35.
Mills : spinning and weaving, in Khándesh district, XII, 144, 169, 231 ; in Thána district, XIII, 391 ; at Kurla, XIV, 288.
Milvinæ : family of birds in Ratnágiri, X, 58.
Mimbar : pulpit in a mosque, IX, pt. ii, 131.
Mimusops elengi : oil-yielding plant, XXV, 223 ; yields gums and resins, *id.* 251.
Mina : river in Poona district, XVIII, pt. i, 8.
Minarets : in Ahmadábád, IV, 265.
Minas : foreign tribe, Kasbatis trace descent from, IX, pt. ii, 15 ; class of Dholka Kasbatis, *id.* 64 note 3.
Mindhola : river in Surat district, II, 25 ; in Baroda state, VII, 573, 581.
Minerals : all district volumes, *see* under District Name.
Mines : of gold and silver in Gujarát, I, pt. i, 528.
Minháj-us-siráj : Musalmán historian, I, pt. i, 195 note 4 ; author of the *Tabakat-i-Nasiri*, IX, pt. ii, 38.
Minivets : class of birds in Ratnágiri district, X, 70.
Minnagara : ancient Greek capital, I, pt. i, 15 note 3, 538, 540, 543, 544.
Mins : tribe identified with Mers, I, pt. i, 140 ; name for Yavans, XVIII, pt. ii, 213 note 10.
Mint : at Bágalkot, account of, XXIII, 339-341 ; at Chándor in Násik, XVI, 429 ; in Bombay island, the present building built in 1829, XXVI, pt. iii, 611 ; in Baroda state, VII, 135-136, 420.
Mir : a Musalmán caste, in Gujarát, Hindu converts, IX, pt. ii, 83 ; meaning of the name, *id.* 83 note 1 ; singers and players by profession, followers of Dada Mian, called also Dhobis, Doms, Langhas, Mirasis, *id.* 83 ; in Káthiáwár, VIII, 164 ; in Khándesh district, XII, 128.
Mir : *see* Mihir.
Mir : a *sayad* title, IX, pt. ii, 7.
Mirabilis jalapa : famine plant, XXV, 203.
Mira Dongar : hill in Kolába district, XI, 3, 6.
Miraj (Senior) : state, its description production, people, agriculture, famines, capital, trade, history, land details, justice, instruction, health and places, XXIV, 378-381. *Town*, its details, copper-plates at, *id.* 219, 344 note 1, 381 ; I, pt. ii, 178, 180, 190 ; grants, *id.* 211, 212, 213, 282 note 3, 425 note 2, 434, 435, 467, 538 note 8 ; included in the dominion of Kolhápur Siláháras, *id.* 254 ; charter, *id.* 436 ; retaken by the Bijápur troops from the Maráthás, *id.* 654 ; taken by the Mughals and re-taken by the Maráthás (1730), *id.* 655.
Miraj (Junior) : state, description, people, agriculture, trade, justice, places, XXIV, 382-383.
Mirajgaon : town in Ahmadnagar district, XVII, 728.

Mirán: successor of Murtiza Nizám Sháh, assassinated by his minister Mirza Khán (1588), I, pt. ii, 623.
Miran A'dilkhán: the successor of Malik Názir, his assassination (1441), I, pt. ii, 621.
Mirán Adil Khán: third Fáruki king (1437-1441) of Khándesh, XII, 245.
Mirán Mubárik: fourth Fáruki king (1441-1457) of Khándesh, XII, 245.
Mirán Muhammad I: Fáruki king of Khándesh (1520-1535), defeated by Burhan Nizám of Ahmadnagar (1526), helped by Bahádur of Gujarát, chosen successor to Bahádur, his death (1535), XII, 246; *see* also I, pt. ii, 622.
Mirán Muhammad II: Fáruki king of Khándesh (1566-1576), defeated at Ahmadábád, Khándesh overrun by the Mughals (1572), Burhánpur sacked (1574) by Mortiza Nizám of Ahmadnagar, his death (1576), XII, 246; *see* also I, pt. ii, 623.
Miran Sayad Ali Datar: saint, claims descent from Azud-ud-din, Sami Kasbati, IX, pt. ii, 64; spirit-scaring tomb of, at Unjha, visited by Memans, *id.* 56; and others, *id.* 128; rites of spirit-scaring practised at, *id.* 128-129; leaves of the tree near his tomb are believed to cure diseases, *id.* 128; to favour conception, *id.* 148.
Miras: land held by hereditary tenants, XVI, 209 and note 4; land tenure in Thána, XIII, 564.
Mirási: Mahár land-holders, in Ratnágiri district, X, 129.
Mirát-i-Ahmadi: historical work, I, pt. i, 205; the author of, suppresses the riots at Ahmadábád and is rewarded with the title of Hassan Muhammad Khán (1730), *id.* 310; superintendent of customs, *id* 328, 337; IX, pt. i, 2; first mention of Káthiáwár in, *id.* 259.
Mirát-i-Sikandari: Musalmán history of Gujarát (1536), I, pt. i, 348, 513; mention of the *khants* in Girnár in, IX, pt. i, 241 note 1, 259; *see* also *id.* 8 note 1, 62, 63, 70.
Mirdha: special community of part foreign and part Rájpút descent in Gujarát, IX, pt. ii, 11, 18; derivation of the name of, *id.* 18 note 2; official spies under Native rulers, *id.* 18.
Mir Fakhr-ud-din: obtains the governorship of Junágadh from the viceroy Abheysingh (1730), I, pt. i, 311.
Miri: town in Ahmadnagar district, temple at, XVII, 728-729.
Mirinja: modern Miraj, I, pt. ii, 546, 547; country of, under the rule of Gandaráditya, Kolhápur Siláhára prince, *id.* 255.
Mirjan: old fort in Kánara district, its situation and history, XV, pt. ii, 330-334; port, XV, pt. i, 6.
Mirkhand: author of *Ranzatu-s-safa*, I, pt. i, 168.
Mir Khond: historian, IX, pt. ii, 37 note 5.
Mir Muhammad Látif: minister of A'zamkhán, viceroy of Gujarát (1635-1642), I, pt. i, 298.
Mirror: ancient rock-cut, on Padan Hill in Thána district, XIV, 391.
Mirya: a headland and creek in Ratnágiri town, X, 353.
Mirza: title among Mughals, IX, pt. ii, 9; conferred on the Rao of Cutch by Álamgir II (1757), V, 142.
Mirza A'ziz Kokaltash: Mughal viceroy, I, pt. i, 212.
Mirza Isa Tarkhán: governor of Sorath, afterwards twenty-fourth Mughal viceroy of Gujarát (1642-1644), I, pt. i, 212, 279.
Mirza Khán: Ahmadnagar prime minister (1588), suspected of having concealed in his house the king's uncle Sháh Kásim; taken into king's confidence; advises the king to put to death the surviving males of the family; becomes irksome to the king's company; ensures his safety by deposing the king; takes the king prisoner; commands the king's head to be cut of; makes good his escape; seized near Junnar in the Poona district, XVII, 376-377.
Mirzan: family of, IX, pt. ii, 197 note 2. *See* Kávasji Rustamji.
Mirzan Khosru Beg: title, Kávasji, the first recipient of, IX, pt. ii, 197 note 2.
Mirzas: Timurian princes, shelter given to, by Gujarát Sultán Bahádursháh (1582); many Gujarát Mughal families claim descent from, IX, pt. ii, 9; sons of Sultán Husein of Khurasan, shelter given to, by Changiz Khán (1571); spread over Gujarát, *id.* 10.
Mirza Teman: minister (1780) of Cambay, VI, 229, 230.
Misáar Muhalhil: Arab traveller and writer, I, pt. i, 510 note 1, 516, 517 note 1.
Mishrikot: town in Dhárwár district, XXII, 772; suvey of, *id.* 521-524, 577-581.
Missi: black dentifrice, origin of the use of, IX, pt. ii, 42 note 1; held in high respect, *id.* 52 note 3, 42, 52, 149, 152.
Missionaries: Muhammadan, in Gujarát, IX, pt. ii, 3, 125; Abdullah of the Mustaalian sect, his converts chiefly Bohoras, *id.* 3 note 3, 26, 125; Eusuf-ud-din Kadiri, *sayad*, his converts chiefly Memans, *id.* 50; Imámsháh or Imám-ud-din of the Nazarian sect, his converts chiefly Matia Kanbis and Momnas, *id.* 3 note 3, 40, 66, 76; Muhammad Jaunpuri, *sayad*, chief conversions to Mahdav, faith, *id.* 3 note 3, 62; Muhammad Ali, *mulla*, *id.* 26 note 1; Muin-ud-din Chishti, *id.* 3 note 3, 6 note 1 (4); Nur Satagur, of the Nazarian sect, his converts, chiefly Khojahs, *id.* 38; Sadr-ud-din, *id.* 40; Shams-ud-din, *id.* 39; Sháh Alam, *id.* 3 note 3; Sháh Tahir, *id.* 3 note 3, 125.
Mithgávda or Mithagri: a caste of salt-makers, in Ratnágiri district, X, 125; in Sávantvádi, *id.* 415; in Kánara district, XV, pt. i, 279; in Kolába district, XI, 51; in Thána district, XIII, 116; in Belgaum district, XXI, 128-129.
Mithi Najar: sweet look, children liable to the influence of, IX, pt. i, 427.
Mithi Virdi: place of interest in Káthiáwár, VIII, 508.
Mithra: IX, pt. ii, 216. *See* Meher.
Mithridates I: Parthian king (B. C. 174-136), XIII, 410.
Mithu: *see* Salt.
Mitne Máchhi: caste of fishermen in Thána district, XIII, 148.

Miyágám: village in Baroda state, famous for its swords, VII, 536.
Miyánalladevi: daughter of Jayakeśi, king of the Karnátak, queen of Karna and mother of Siddharája Jayasimha; her regency; her pilgrimage to Somanátha; remits pilgrim tax, I, pt. i, 170-172.
Mobed: Full Priests, higher sacerdotal order of priests; also called *Marátab*, IX, pt. ii, 222; qualifications of; ordination of; religious rules to be observed by; Persian precepts for; disqualification of, *id.* 226.
Mobh: centre tie beam, erection ceremony, IX, pt i, 204; among Pársis, *id.* pt. ii, 206.
Mocca: a famine plant, XXV, 208.
Mochi, Mochigar: caste of shoemakers, I, pt. i, 451; in Cutch, V, 82; in Pálanpur, *id.* 291; in Mahi Kántha, *id.* 367; in Káthiáwár, VIII, 157; in Gujarát, Multani, shoemakers from Multan, arrival of, in Gujarát, from North India, conversion of, during the reign of Muhammad Begada (1459-1513), appearance, dress, occupation of, IX, pt. ii, 77-78; said to be originally Rájpúts of Chámpáner; tribal surnames; local divisions; sections according to callings, IX, pt. i, 192; names of callings, shoemaking, tools, character, *id.* 193; religious sects; customs, *id.* 194-195; in Khándesh, XII, 114, 236; at Mátherán, XIV, 266; in Násik district, XVI, 72; in Ahmadnagar, XVII, 121-124; in Dhárwár district, XXII, 219-221.
Mod: a branch of Samma Rájpúts in Cutch, V, 66.
Mod: a Sind chief, establishes himself in Cutch, V, 132-133.
Modasa: town in Ahmadábád district, IV, 346; capture of (1414), I, pt. i, 236.
Modeganur Kuppade: Kalachurya Someśvara's seat of government, I, pt. ii, 485, 487.
Modh: a sub-caste of Bráhmans in Cucth, V, 45; in Rewa Kántha, VI, 23, 24; in Gujarát, immigrants from Upper India, IX, pt. i, 2; strength and distribution, *id.* 3; sub-classes, *id.* 11-12; in Poona district, XVIII, pt. i, 163; in Káthiáwár, VIII, 146; in Thána district, XIII, 80.
Modhera: town in Baroda state, old buildings at, VII, 608-609; on the Vátrak river, place of great antiquity, gives name to Modhs, IX, pt. i, 11 and note 2, 72 and note 1.
Modh Vánia: caste of traders, in Kathiáwár, VIII, 148; in Thána district, XIII, 112; in Cutch, V, 50; in Gujarát, IX, pt. i, 72.
Modh Vasahika: Jain monastery at Dhandhuka, I, pt. i, 191.
Modi: current form of Maráthi writing, I, pt. ii, 249.
Modies: Pársi family among earlier settlers in Bombay, IX, pt. ii, 195.
Modkal: town in Southern India, laid waste by Malik Káfur, I, pt. ii, 29.
Modogalinga: the Kalingas, I, pt. i, 532, 533.
Modogoulla: probably Mudhol, I, pt. i, 541; same as Mudgal in Bijápur district, XXIII, 378 379.
Modura: modern Madura, I, pt. i, 537.
Mogalan: Shákyamuni's disciple, XIV, 170.
Moger: caste of fishermen in Kánara district, XV, pt. i, 312-313.
Moggaliputto: Buddhist saint, sends missionaries to Mahárattha, I, pt. ii, 143-144.
Moghal: *see* Mughal.
Mogham: vague assessment, land tenure in Thána district, XIII, 565.
Moghlai: revenue charged on certain Baroda villages, VII, 181, 228, 350-351.
Mogra: sweet-scented oil-yielding plant, XXV, 223.
Moha: *Bassia latifolia*, liquor-yielding tree in Poona district, XVIII, pt. i, 49; in Khándesh, XII, 23, 26, 31, 153, 227; in Panch Mahála, III, 247.
Mohábat Khán: sent by Aurangzib to crush Shiváji, his defeat at Sálher and retreat to Aurangábád, I, pt. ii, 594.
Mohagaon Mohgaon; village in Central Provinces, I, pt. ii, 207, 420.
Moha liquor: distillation of, in Thána district, XIII, 395-398; farmed, *id.* 648; in Koláha district, XI, 123; used in Gujarát, IX, pt. i, p. xxx.
Mohamagráma: village identified with Mohgaon, I, pt. ii, 420.
Mohan: place of interest in Rewa Kántha, VI, 164.
Mohan: timber tree in Khándesh, XII, 26.
Mohanpur: state in Mahi Kántha, V, 418.
Mohar: river in Mahi Kántha, V, 357.
Mohartab Khán: *see* Mohtar Khán.
Mohasuli: fine levied for delay in paying revenue, VII, 380.
Mohe: oil-yielding plant, XXV, 213.
Mohgaon: *see* Mohagaon.
Mohiabad: name given to Poona in memory of Kámbaksh's son, XVIII, pt. ii, 240.
Mohit: Turkish seaman's guide (1554), XV, pt. ii, 51, 309, 343.
Moho: pass in Násik district, XVI, 29, 30.
Mohol: town in Sholápur district, XX, 414; its railway traffic, *id.* 267; survey of, *id.* 304-309.
Mo-ho-la-cha, Moholo-cha: Hwan Thsang's name of Mahárashtra, I, pt. ii, 145; *see* also *id.* 184, 353.
Mohorpán: mango-blossom drinking among Rájpúts, IX, pt. i, 140.
Mohota Khokra: place of interest in Káthiáwár, VIII, 547.
Mohtar Khán: *nawáb* of Bhiwndi, ravages Portuguese territory (1690), XIV, 47; his tomb at Kalyán, *id.* 115, 118, 120; I, pt. ii, 41.
Mohtarpha: Marátha shop-tax in Sálsette, I, pt. i, 123.
Moka: timber tree in Khándesh, XII, 26.
Moka Pagina Muvada: state in Rewa Kántha, VI, 150.
Mokása: portion of the *chauth* in Násik, XVI, 207.
Mokásádárs: head revenue collectors under Adil Sháhis (1489-1686), XIX, 230.
Mokha: town in Arabia, its trade with Thána (A. D. 160), XIII, 409 note 2; (1500-1670), *id.* 465, 468, 469; (1660-1710), *id.* 486, 487; Banian traders at (1800-1882), *id.* 520 and note 3.
Mokháda: village in Thána district, XIV, 284.
Mokhdi Ghánta: place of interest in Rewa Kántha, VI, 165.

Mokheráji: Gohil chief of Piram (1347), I, pt. i, 87 note 1, 230.

Mokshakhanda: part of Hemadri's *Chaturvarga Chintámani*, I, pt. ii, 249.

Molasses: making of, in Kánara district, XV, pt. ii, 20, 71; in Dhárwár, XXII, 384-385.

Moleslám: a half Musalmán and half Hindu caste in Baroda, VII, 72; in Gujarát, Rájpút half converts, their conversion in the reign of Muhammad Begada (1459-1513); interpretations of the name of; *thákors* and chiefs; marriages among, IX, pt. ii, 5 note 2, 25 note 1, 68.

Molindæ: Indian tribe mentioned by Pliny, I, pt. i, 533.

Momai: Hindu goddess, IX, pt. i, 200.

Momin: caste of Musalmán cotton weavers, in Thána district, XIII, 385-388; in Ahmadnagar, XVII, 233; in Poona district, XVIII, pt. i, 501-502; in Sátára district, XIX, 144; in Sholápur district, XX, 208; in Dhárwár, XXII, 242; in Bijápur district, XXIII, 299. *See* also Momna.

Momin Khán I: is appointed governor of Surat by Nizám-ul-Mulk (1722), I, pt. i, 303; is made governor of Cambay by Abheysingh (1730), *id.* 311, 313, 315, 316; schemes independence at Cambay (1736), *id.* 317; is appointed fifty-fourth viceroy of Gujarát (1737); assumes the title Nijám-ud-dauláh Momin Khán Bahádur Firuz Jang; asks Jawan Mard Khán Bábi to help him; his disastrous alliance with the Maráthás which gives a final blow to Mughal power in Gujarát, *id.* 318; receives secret instructions to disregard the appointment of Abheysingh fifty-fifth viceroy and to drive his Ráthods from Gujarát, *id.* 319; captures Ahmadábád (1738); is appointed fifty-sixth viceroy (1738-1743), *id.* 320; is honoured with a title and dress by the emperor of Delhi (1742), *id.* 325; his death (1743); his wife seeks protection of Rangoji, *id.* 326; *see* also VII, 169, 174-176; and VI, 222.

Momin Khán II: son of Momin Khán I, I, pt. i, 207; is confirmed as governor of Cambay (1748), *id.* 330-331; at his request Cambay is included in Peshwa's share (1751), *id.* 334; is compelled by Raghunáthráv to pay an annual tribute of Rs. 10,000, *id.* 337, 338; takes Gogha, attacks Jambusar and besieges Borsad (1755), *id.* 339; captures Ahmadábád (1756), *id.* 339; receives compliments and a sword from the emperor of Delhi, *id.* 340; besieged in Ahmadábád, receives help from the *rája* of Idar; Sháh Nur's attempt to make peace between Momin Khán and the Peshwa fails; Ahmadábád and Gogha surrendered to the Peshwa (1758), *id.* 341, 342; oppresses and extorts money from his own followers, *id.* 342; contracts friendship with the English and visits Poona (1759), *id.* 343, 344; receives instructions from Delhi to join in driving the Maráthás out of Gujarát; is defeated (1761), *id.* 345. *Another account of: nawáb* of Cambay (1748-1783), persuades the Peshwa to include Cambay in his share, resists Marátha attack, takes Bhagavantrao prisoner; chief events of his two years' rule (1755-1757); goes to Poona, his letter to the Court of Directors, becomes party to Musalmán revival, his exactions, murders his son, opposes Rághuba, his peace with the English, VI, 225, 230; *see* also XIV, 315.

Momin Khán III: *nawáb* (1789-1823) of Cambay; Marátha extortion; Gáikwár claims on, VI, 231-232.

Momin Khan IV: *nawáb* (1823-1841) of Cambay, VI, 232.

Momin Khán V: *nawáb* (1841-1880) of Cambay, VI, 232.

Momná: caste of Musalmáns, their revolt (1691), I, pt. i, 288; in Cutch, V, 90-91; in Káthiáwár, VIII, 163; properly Momins, that is Believers, IX, pt. ii, 76; offshoot of the main Nazarian stock, *id.* 67; conversion of, by Ismailia *sayads* and Imámsháh of Pirana, *id.* 76 and note 1; divisions of; rising of (1691); appearance and dress of, *id.* 76; religion, customs and community of, *id.* 77; religious disciples of the Pirana *pirs*, *id.* 3 note 3 continued on page 4, 40, 127 note 2; in Khándesh, XII, 126.

Monædes: Munda of Singbhum, I, pt. i, 533.

Monasteries: Shrávak, *see* Apásarás; in Thána district, XIII, 406, 407, 432, 456, 462, 483; Buddhist. in Thána district, XIV, 137; establishment of, *id.* 132; in Dhárwár district, XXII, 755-757.

Monday: sacred to the moon, IX, pt. i, 397; beliefs about, *id.* 400-401; Shravan and Márgashirsh, *id.* 23 note 5; sacredness of, XVIII, pt i, 240.

Money-lenders: classes of, in Surat, II, 185-189; in Broach, *id.* 449; in Kaira district, III, 58; in Panch Mahâls, *id.* 236; in Baroda state, VII, 120, 127, 129-131; in Káthiáwár, VIII, 204; in Ratnágiri district, X, 158; in Sávantvádi, *id.* 428; in Kolába district, XI, 103; in Janjira state, *id.* 426; in Khándesh, XII, 196, 200; in Thána district, XIII, 307-309; in Násik district, XVI, 116, 211; in Ahmadnagar, XVII, 299-300; in Poona district, XVIII, pt. ii, 106, 124-126; in Sátára district, XIX, 181-183; in Kánara district, XV, pt. ii, 28; in Sholápur district, XX, 241-244; in Belgaum district, XXI, 292, 293; in Dhárwár district, XXII, 324-326; in Kolhápur state, XXIV, 194.

Monkey: considered sacred; Hanumán, the god of, fumes from burnt dung of, supposed to drive away spirits, IX, pt. i, 377-378; *langur* and bonnet, in Ratnágiri district, X, 43; at Mátherán, XIV, 259; in Belgaum district, XXI, 68.

Monks: Christian, in Thána district (1498-1681), XIII, 460 note 7; Buddhist, XIV, 139; duties of, *id.* 140 note 1.

Monoglosson: modern Mangrol, I, pt. i, 538.

Monpur: place of interest in Káthiáwár, VIII, 547.

Monsoon: English ship captured by Angria (1707), XV, pt. ii, 134 and note 3.

Montgomery: Lieut.-General, disperses a Bhil gang; is wounded, XVI, 200; disperses a gang of about 100 Bhils under Patharji Náik in the Ráhuri sub-division, XVII, 418.

Month, Months: Hindu, days of, XVIII, pt. i, 238-239; is a lunar month, number of days, beliefs about the first day of, the last day or *amas* of, days of, sacred to the moon, IX, pt. i, 397; of the Pársi year, IX, pt. ii, 215; names of, *id.* 216 and note 2; Bene-Israel, XVIII, pt. i, 513.
Manvel: táluka in Káthiáwár, VIII, 548.
Monypenny: Lieutenant-Colonel, makes an assault on the fort of Airani; XXII, 422-423.
Mooglai erundie: oil-yielding plant, XXV, 221.
Moon: the, a planet, worship, of IX, pt. i, 396-401; offerings, *id.* 409; Musalmán veneration for, IX, pt. ii, 213.
Moor; Lieutenant (1792), describes the fort of Airani, XXII, 649, 709; Hubli, *id.* 760; Motihennur, *id.* 772; Ranebennur, *id.* 783; visits Bijápur, description of the city, of the small gun at, XXIII, 594, 642.
Moore: Commodore, destroys a Marátha ship at Gheria (1774), XIII, 502.
Moors: on Thána Coast, condition of, I, pt. ii, 53, 58; pirates, *id.* 61; traders at Bassein, IX, pt. ii, 15; at Surat, *id.* 15 note 2.
Mophis: river Máhi, I, pt. i, 539.
Mora: Karanja port, XIV, 194.
Mora: fort in the Násik district, XVI, 458, 460.
Moras: *alba*, a food plant, XXV, 173; a fibrous plant, *id.* 235; *Indica*, *id.* 172, 235.
Morbi: state and town in Káthiáwár, VIII, 548-551; IX, pt. i, 126; copper-plate of Jaikadeva at, I, pt. i, 81 87; earliest seat of Jethvás, *id.* 136; grant of Jaikadeva at, *id.* 139; its tribute to the Gáikwár (1758-1803), VII, 317, 319.
Morchopna: táluka in Káthiáwár, VIII, 552.
Mordara: pass in the Násik district, XVI, 129.
Mordhár: range of hills in Kathiáwár, VIII, 11.
Moreh: Elephanta village in Thána district, XIV, 61, 96.
Moreshvar: *see* Morgaon.
Morgad: place of interest in Cutch, V, 244.
Morgaon: market town in Poona district, Ganpati temple and fair at, XVIII, pt. iii, 259-260.
Morgiri: *see* Gunvantgad.
Mori: village in Mahi Kántha, ruins at, V, 439.
Mori: Rájpút clan in Kathiáwár, VIII, 115; peasant proprietors in Gujarát, IX, pt. i, 130.
Morinda: *citrifolia*, a famine plant, XXV, 200; a plant yielding dyes, *id.* 246; *exerta*, *id.* 246; *tomentosa*, *id.* 246; *umbellata*, a famine plant, also yielding dyes, *id.* 200.
Morinda bracelata: plant yielding dyes, XXV, 246.
Moringa: *aptdera*, oil-yielding plant, XXV, 218; *pterygosperma*, *id.* 218; also fodder, *id.* 278.
Moringaceæ: an order of oil-yielding plant, XXV, 218.
Morkhai; tell money, V, 292, 390.
Morkhand; hill fort in Násik district, I, pt. ii, 198; capital of the country ruled by Govinda son of Dhruva, Ráshtrakúta king, I, pt. i, 123.
Moroba Phadnavis: one of Madhavráv's chief ministers, I, pt. ii, 603; kept in confinement, seeks the aid of the English, *id.* 604; joins the ministerial confederacy against Raghunáthráv (1774), tries to make Raghunáthráv Peshwa, confined by Nána (1778), XVIII, pt. ii, 257, 258, 262, 263.
Moro Pandit: *see* Moro Pant Pingla.
Moropant: Maráthi poet, a Karhada Bráhman (1750), X, 114 note 1.
Moro Pant Pingla: also called Moro Pandit, Shiváji's general, defeats the army of Afzul Khán at Jávli (1659), I, pt. ii, 592; is given charge of Rájpuri and Ráygad and captures Máhuli, *id.* 69; goes to burn the Mughal ships at Surat and afterwards to Kalyán, *id.* 70; defeats Mohábat Khán at Sálher (1671), *id.* 594; goes with Shiváji to Junnar and returns to Ráygad (1675), *id.* 70, 594; is appointed Peshwa or *Mukhya Pradhána*, *id.* 594; attacks Janjira but fails (1676), *id.* 71; builds Pratapgad (1656), XIX, 234, 243; takes Máhuli fort (1670), XIV, 220; gains several strongholds north of Junnar (1671), ravages Mughal districts; takes the forts of Aundha and Patta in Akola headed by Shiváji, XVII, 399; XVI, 425; captures the fort of Sáler in Báglán (1672), I, pt. i, 387; demands *chauth* from the Portuguese (1674), XIII, 476.
Morpur: fort in Káthiáwár, VIII, 552.
Mortaba Khán: *see* Mohtar Khán.
Mortaza: *see* Mortiza.
Mortgages: of labour in Káthiáwár, VIII, 213; number of, in Kaira, III, 62; in Panch Mahâls, *id.* 238; in Ahmadábád, IV, 74; in Baroda, VII, 116-118; in Káthiáwár, VIII, 212; in Sátára district, XIX, 188-190.
Mortiza: son and successor of Hussain Nizám Sháh, marches against Revdanda (1570), I, pt. ii, 49; overruns Berar and annexes Khándesh to the Ahmadnagar kingdom (1572); entrusts the management of his government to Salábat Khán; is killed by his son Mirán (1587), *id.* 623; *see* also XIII, 453.
Mortiza Nizám Sháh: killed by the son of Malik Ambar (1631), I, pt. ii, 625, 650.
Moruni: tribe mentioned by Pliny, I, pt. i, 534.
Morva: a fibrous plant, XXV, 236.
Morváda: state in Pálanpur, V, 281, 338; Vághela chiefship, IX, pt. i, 129.
Morvi: *see* Morbi.
Mosalu: party of wife's relations on her father's side going with presents to the husband's house, IX, pt. i, 94.
Mosam: river in Násik, XVI, 10.
Mosques: in Ratnágiri district, X, 320, 330 331 and note 1, 362, 380 note 1; in Sávantvádi, *id.* 464; in Kolába district, XI, 272; in Khándesh, XII, 439, 459, 465, 472; in Kánara district, XV, pt. ii, 108, 270; in Thána district, XIV, 29, 48, 275, 307, 313, 314, 354, 371, 372, 400; in Bijápur city, XXIII, 626-635. *See* Masjids.
Mostyn: Mr., British envoy at Poona (1768-1779), XVIII, pt. ii, 253, 256, 261; *see* also *id.* pt. iii, 406; XIII, 503; I, pt. i, 407.
Mot: water-lift in Khándesh, XII, 145; in Belgaum district, XXI, 241.

Mota: village in Surat district, IX, pt. i, 1, 12 and note 1.
Motacillinæ: family of birds in Ratnágiri, X, 80.
Mota Kotarna: state in Mahi Kántha, V, 429.
Motala: a sub-caste of Bráhmans in Gujarát, IX, pt. i, 1; places of settlements, traditional and legendary account of immigration into Gujarát, *id.* 1, 12 and notes 1 and 2; customs, *id.* 13; in Rewa Kántha, VI, 23.
Motas: Sind Lohánas, IX, pt. ii, 50 note 4, 51.
Mota Saja: place of interest, in Rewa Kántha, VI, 165.
Motásthal: well-irrigation, XVIII, pt. ii, 12-13.
Moths: at Mátherán, XIV, 255.
Motibennur: town in Dhárwár district, XXII, 772.
Motigudda: hill in Kánara district, XV, pt. i, 4, 5; *id.* pt. ii, 334.
Moti Gumbaz: pearl mosque at Bijápur, XXIII, 616-617.
Moti Taláv: reservoir at Sávantvádi, X, 389, 468.
Mottaka: Bráhman settlement in Gujarát, mentioned in a grant, I, pt. i, 127.
Mountains: all district volumes, *see* under District Name.
Mount Calvary: taken charge of by the Franciscans (1585), I, pt. ii, 57.
Mount Mary: Roman Catholic Church at Bándra, destroyed by the Portuguese themselves (1737) and re-built (1761), I, pt. ii, 84.
Mount Pezier: modern Mandapeshvar in Thána district, Portuguese ruins at, I, pt. ii, 66.
Mourning: form of, IX, pt. ii, 170-171.
Mouse Deer: in the Kánara district, XV, pt. i, 102.
Mousopalle: provisionally identified with Karvir, I, pt. i, 542.
Mouza: modern Musa in Arabia, I, pt. i, 543, 545.
Movad: ancestor of Surat and Navsári priests, IX, pt. ii, 221.
Movements: all district volumes, *see* Census Details under District Name.
Mowah: a famine plant, XXV, 201; yielding fermented drinks, *id.* 211; oil-yielding plant, *id.* 213, 219.
Mozaffar: a Gujarát king, invades Somanátha (1390), I, pt. i, 190.
Mozin Beg: invades Cutch (1718), V, 138.
Mragshir: a mansion of the moon, IX, pt. i, 353.
Mrigavarman: Hángal Kádamba, I, pt. ii, 559.
Mrigeśavarman: early Kádamba king, I, pt. ii, 287 note 3; builds a Jain temple, *id.* 288, 291 note 1, 322; also styled Mrigeśa, Mrigeśvara or Mrigeśvaravarman, *id.* 287 note 9; *see* also XV, pt. ii, 79.
Mrityunjaya: death conqueror, name of Shiv, IX, pt. i, 531.
Mrityunjayana Jap: prayers offered to Shiv, IX, pt. i, 531.
Muamon: *see* Memau.
Muazzam: *see* Muazzim.
Muazzam Sháh: Prince Muhammad, I, pt. i, 296, 297. *See* Bahádur Sháh of Delhi.
Muazzim: *sultán*, Aurangzib's son, demands in marriage Pádsháh Bibi the Bijápur king's sister (1676); makes Válva his head-quarters; takes Gadak, Hubli and Dhárwár, I, pt. ii, 654; sent against Shiváji, I, pt. i, 387; ascends the throne as Bahádur Sháh I, pt. i, 296; his death (1712), *id.* 297. *See* Bahádur Sháh.
Mubárak: *see* Mubárik Khán.
Mubárik, Mubarik I: Allá-ud-din's third son, Delhi emperor, marches to the Dakhan (1318), takes Harapala prisoner, and flays him alive, I, pt. ii, 29, 252, 533; *see* also XII, 242; XIII, 438; I, pt. i, 229.
Mubárik Khán: Fáruki king of Khándesh (1535-1566), his claim to Gujarát kingdom, annexes Nandurbár and Sultánpur districts, defeats the Mughals (1561), his death (1566), XII, 246; *see* also I, pt. ii, 621, 623.
Mubariz-Babi: lieutenant of the viceroy of Gujarát, puts down Matia Kanbi revolt, IX, pt. ii, 67.
Mubáriz-ul-Mulk: *see* Sarbuland Khán.
Muchkund: famous sage, X, 345; I, pt. ii, 28.
Muchkundi: river in Ratnágiri district, X, 8; I, pt. ii, 28.
Muckia scabrella: vegetable poison, XXV, 265.
Mucuna pruriens: medicinal plant, XXV, 257.
Muda: form of assessment in Koláha district, XI, 168; in Thána district, a grain measure, XIII, 536, 547, 550 note 2; of 25 *máns*, *id.* 562; 6 to 32 *máns*, *id.* 565 and note 6; divisions of a *muda* (*dhep* system), *id.* 565; equal to four *khandis*, *id.* 565; not uniform, *id.* 565, 574; 6-14 *máns* and 25 *máns*, *id.* 565 note 6, 569 note 6, 574.
Mudábandi: tenure in Thána district, XIII, 536, 550 and note 2; (1845), *id.* 587.
Mudan: hair-cutting or head-shaving or caul, corresponding to *chudakarma* a Vedic rite, rites performed among Bráhmans, IX, pt. i, 35-36; Brahma-Kshatris, *id.* 57; Kayasths, *id.* 61; Rájputs, *id.* 140-141.
Muddebihál: sub-division of Bijápur district, details of, XXIII, 541-542; survey of, *id.* 464-465, 468-497; *Town*, *id.* 663-664; trade centre, *id.* 361.
Muddle Shoal: sunken rock near Ratnágiri, X, 353.
Mudgal: in the Nizám's dominions, I, pt. ii, 527, 533 and note 3; district and fort, taken by Vijayanagar from Bijápur, *id.* 643; *see* also *id.* 245.
Mudgala: *gotra*, I, pt. ii, 240.
Mudgals: early tribe, overrun Cutch, V, 129 note 4.
Mudgiri: village in Kánara district, temple and fair at, XV, pt. ii, 334.
Mudhol: state, description, production, people, agriculture, trade, history, land, justice, instruction, health, places, XXIV, 388-395. *Town*, details, wells, ponds, temple, *id.* 392-393; burnt (1649) by Shiváji, XVIII, pt. ii, 229.
Mudkavi: village in Bijápur district, XXIII, 664.

Mudkebandi: *see* Mudábandi.
Mudliar: a caste of writers in Sholápur district, XX, 45-48; in Belgaum district, XXI, 97, 98; traders in Bijápur district, XXIII, 130-134.
Mudmi: a fibrous plant, XXV, 228.
Mudugala: modern Mudgala, I, pt. ii, 245.
Mudur: village in Dhárwár district, temples and inscriptions at, XXII, 772; *see* also I, pt. ii, 562 note 6.
Muftakhir Khán: assistant to the Mughal viceroy of Gujarát, VII, 176; son of Momin Khán, schemes of Rangoji for the assassination of; unites his forces with Fidá-ud-din Khán, defeats Rangoji and obtains Borsad and Viramgám from him, I, pt. i, 326; fifty-seventh viceroy (1743-1744), appoints Jawán Mard Khán his deputy; the house of, besieged by Jawán Mard Khán; his escape, joins Rangoji and retires to Cambay, *id.* 327.
Mug: pulse variety, in Ratnágiri district, X, 148; in Poona district, XVIII, pt. ii, 43; in Sátára district, XIX, 164.
Mugad: village in Dhárwár district, lake at, XXII, 772.
Mugdhabodha: Bopadeva's treatise on grammar, I, pt. ii, 249.
Mughaira: broker of Hákam, leads an expedition against Debal, I, pt. i, 506; ancestor of Naiata emigrants, IX, pt. ii, 14 note 3.
Mughal Admiralship: conferred on Sidi Sámbal (1670), XI, 437; East India Company desirous of acquiring (1733), XXVI, pt. i, 162-163.
Mughal Camp: description of (1684), XVII, 401-402.
Mughal Court: influence of the Pársis at, Pársi visitors to, IX, pt. ii, 197 and note 2.
Mughals: Musalmáns in Gujarát, derivation of the name, IX, pt. ii, 10 note 3; the two distinct classes of, Persian and Indian or Chughadda; Persian Mughals are descendants of Persian political refugees and merchants and of the Shiáh persuation; Indian Mughals are descendants of the Mughal conquerors of India and Sunni by faith; titles before and after the names of, *id.* 9-10; in Cutch, V, 90; in Ahmadnagar district, XVII, 525-526; in Poona district, XVIII, pt. i, 491-492; in Dhárwár district, XXII, 232; in Bijápur district, XXIII, 288; in Kolhápur state, XXIV, 147; enter Khándesh and sack Burhánpur, but are defeated by the king of Khándesh (1561), I, pt. ii, 623; succeed to the territories of Gujarát in the north Konkan (1572), and attack Daman, Tárápur, and Dáhánu (1582), *id.* 40; besiege Ahmadnagar but are forced to retire (1596), *id.* 624, 649; invade the Dakhan (1600), *id.* 590: besiege Daman, Bassein, and Chaul (1612), *id.* 40; Ahmadnagar surrendered to them (1617), *id.* 624; invade Bijápur, *id.* 650; driven from Purenda by Sháhji Bhonsla (1633), *id.* 591; their peace with Bijápur (1636), *id.* 650; enter into offensive alliance with Shiváji against Bijápur (1664), *id.* 67, 652; attack Shiváji's possessions (1673), *id.* 69, 626; burn Vengurla (1675), *id.* 70; make a raid in the Kalyán district (1683), *id.* 77; take Bijápur (1686), *id.* 655; capture Sambháji at Sangameshvar (1689), *id.* 78; take Ráygad, *id.* 79; decline of the empire of (1708), *id.* 626. *See* also Musalmáns, Akbar, Jehángir, Sháh Jahán and Aurangzeb.
Mugutkhán Hubli: place of interest in Belgaum, XXI, 589; I, pt. ii, 456, 527.
Muháfiz Khán: commandant of Muhammad II of Málwa (1512-1530), the revolt of, suppressed by Medani Rái, I, pt. i, 366.
Muhalhil: Persian traveller (941), his notice of Chenl, XI, 272.
Muhammad: title among *shaiks*, IX, pt. ii, 8.
Muhammad: son of Fazl sails against the Meds of Hind and captures Máli, I, pt. i, 506.
Muhammad: conquers (712) Sind and destroys the Gurjaras, I, pt. ii, 375 note 3; son of Kasim, his conquest of Jaipur, Udaipur and Chitor, IX, pt. ii, 1 note 1 continued on page 2; *see* also I, pt. i, 506; the word "Yaksh" applied to his Syrian horsemen, *id.* 456 note 1.
Muhammad: *sayad*, styled Rajo Shahid, the martyr, arrives in Gujarát, preaches Mahdavi doctrines, is killed in a skirmish with the troops of the viceroy Aurangzib, IX, pt. ii, 6 note 1 continued on page 7, 35 note 1.
Muhammad: son of Abdul Wahhab, IX, pt. ii, 12 note 3.
Muhammad: *sayad* companion of Sayad Muhammad Jaunpuri; Pálanpur and Dakhan Haidarábád Mahdavis claim descent from, IX, pt. ii, 63.
Muhammad I or Muhammad Sháh I: Bahmani ruler (1378-1397), his measures for the relief of Durgádevi famine, XIX, 226; XX, 277; I, pt. ii, 33.
Muhammad II, Muhammad: Bahmani ruler (1482-1518), defeats Bahádur Giláni of Kolhápur, XIII, 443; X, 327.
Muhammad II: of Málwa (1512-1530), son and successor of Násir-ud-din of Mándu; revolt of his commandant Muháfiz Khán crushed by his Rájpút commander-in-chief Medani Rái; combination by Muzáffar II (1511-1526) of Gujarát and Sikandar Sháh of Delhi (1488-1560), baffled by Medani Rái; the attempt of, to crush the power of Medani Rái; siege of Mándu by Sultán Muzáffar of Gujarát (1511-1526); massacre of Rájpúts; capture of Mándu, defeat and capture of, by Rána Sang of Chitor; incurs the wrath of Báhádur Sháh of Gujarát by giving protection to Chand Khán and Kazi-ul-mulk; invasion and capture of Mándu by Báhádur Sháh of Gujarát; surrender and death of, I, pt. ii, 366 367.
Muhammad III: *sultán* of Ahmadábád (1536-1554), tries to spread Islám by force, IX, pt. ii, 5 and note 2; persecutes the Bohoras, *id.* 27 note 1, 58 note 2.
Muhammad IV: Turkish *sultán* (1648-1687), an ambassador from, lands at Surát, I, pt. i, 280.
Muhammadábád: town in Gujarát, I, pt. i, 219 note 3.

Muhammad Aazam Sháh: thirty-ninth viceroy of Gujarát (1703-1705), I, pt. i, 291.

Muhammad Adil Sháh: Bijápur king (1626-1656), parties, rise of the Maráthás, siege of Bijápur (1631), Bijápur limits, rise of Shiváji, condition (1639, 1648), XXIII, 424-428; tomb of, in Bijápur city, *id.* 604-607, 661-663; *another account of*: son and successor of Ibráhim Adil Sháh (1628), I, pt. ii, 649; his change of policy; his alliance with Murtaza Nizám Sháh; sues for peace with the Mughals (1636), *id.* 650; effects a nominal reconciliation between Sháhji and Báji Ghorpade and sends Sháhji again into the Karnátak, *id.* 650; asks Sháhji to suppress the rebellion of Shiváji, *id.* 651; his anger at Shiváji's getting possession of several forts of Bijápur in the Dakhan and the Konkan; his order to Báji Ghorpade to arrest Sháhji and send him to Bijápur, *id.* 651; keeps on good terms with the Mughals; secures the goodwill of Dárá Shikoh but incurs the displeasure of Aurangzeb; his death (1656), *id.* 651.

Muhammad Ali: *pasha* of Egypt, defeats Abdul Wahhab (1812), IX, pt. ii, 12 note 3.

Muhammad Ali: *mulla*, believed to be the first Bohora missionary, works miracles and makes converts in Cambay, shrine of, at Cambay, IX, pt. ii, 26 note 1.

Muhammad Ali: Maisur general attacked by the Marátha troops; captures Pandurang (1776), XXII, 413.

Muhammad Amin: poisons Abu Bakr the leader, and suppresses the riot at Ahmadábád (1681), I, pt. i, 286-287.

Muhammad Amin Khán: Umadut-ul-Mulk, thirty-sixth viceroy of Gujarát (1674-1683), I, pt. i, 285.

Muhammadans: *see* Musalmáns.

Muhammad Bahlol Khán Shirwáni: Mughal general, captures Idar (1679), I, pt. i, 286.

Muhammad Bakir: fifth Shah *imám*, IX, pt. ii, 125 note 2.

Muhammad Begada, Muhammad Sháh Begada: Ahmadábád king (1459-1513), I, pt. i, 243-250; defeats a conspiracy of his nobles (1459); improves the soldiery (1459-1461), *id.* 243-244; helps the king of the Dakhan against the *sultán* of Málwa (1461), *id.* 244-245; his expedition against the pirate *zamindárs* of the hill fort of Barúr and the wharf of Dun or Dahánu; his expedition against Junágadh (1467) and capture of Girnár (1472), *id.* 245; repairs the fort of Jehánpanáh and makes Junágadh his capital under the name of Mustafábad, *id.* 245-246; expedition against Sind and defeat of the Jádejás in Cutch; takes the fort of Jagat or Dwárka and destroys the idol temples, *id.* 246; founds the city of Mehmudábád on the Vátrak; second conspiracy of the nobles (1480) headed by Khudáwand Khán; his war against Chámpáner (1482-1484); captures Pávágad (1484) and makes Chámpáner his capital under the name of Muhammadábád, *id.* 247; invades Somanátha (1490), *id.* 190; places his nephew Miran Muhammad Adilkhan Faruki on the throne of Asir-Burhánpur (1508), *id.* 248; his religious zeal; his death (1513), *id.* 249-250; I, pt. ii, 30, 44; his expedition in Thána district (1465), XIII, 442; finally overthrows (1470) the Chudásmás, VIII, 109 note 2; attacks Junágad, *id.* 160; spreads Islám in Gujarát (1471), IX, pt. ii, 3 note 3, 5 and note 2, 125; receives Imámsháh, *id.* 40; conversions of Bohoras, *id.* 58 note 2; of Rájpúts, *id.* 68; of Multani Mochis, *id.* 77; conversion of Sumra Rájpúts (1473) by, *id.* 70; his conquest of Oka (1480), VIII, 287-289; makes Thána (1480), one of his districts, XIV, 357; his expedition in Khándesh (1499), defeats Miran Adil Khán, XII, 245; I, pt. ii, 622; captures Daulatábád (1500), *id.* 622; destroys (1500) Borsád town and its people, IX, pt. i, 8; takes Bassein (1507), XIV, 28; his expedition of Nagothana and Chaul (1508), XI, 142 and note 8; his hostility and naval fights with the Portuguese (1508, 1509), XIII, 448; supposed by Dr. Wilson to be the conqueror of Sanjan, IX, pt. ii, 187 note 3; trade of Cambay in the reign of, VI, 189; the state of Cambay, *id.* 217.

Muhammad Bidár Bakht: forty-first viceroy of Gujarát (1705-1706), I, pt. i, 294-295.

Muhammad Gáwan, Muhammad Khwája Gáwan: Bahmani minister (1460-1481); his rise; appointed to the government of Bijápur; XXIII, 400-402; suppresses the revolt of Jalal Khán, I, pt. ii, 588; XVII, 355; his expedition into the Konkan (1469), XI, 142; besieges the fort of Vishalgad and encamps at Kolhápur, XXIV, 224; I, pt. ii, 638; captures Vishalgad; takes Goa from the *rája* of Vijayanagar, XXIII, 400-402; XXIV, 224; I, pt. ii, 638; X, 194; his siege and capture of Belgaum, I, pt. ii, 638; takes a large army into the Konkan, *id.* 32-33; appoints one of his officers Khush Kaddam as his deputy to take charge of the newly conquered country, XXIV, 308; his reforms and new administration of Bahamani dominions, XXIII, 400-402; I, pt. ii, 639; his scheme of centralization, XVIII, pt. ii, 217; XIX, 227; his execution, XX, 278; I, pt. ii, 639; XXIII, 402; XVIII, pt. ii, 217; his title of Malik-ul-Tujár or prince of the merchants, XXIII, 402.

Muhammad Ghori: raid of, into Gujarát, I, pt. i, 195 note 4, 512; Sultán Ghazni Khán, son and successor of Sultán Hoshang of Málwa (1434-1436), poisoned by Muhammad, son of Malik Mughis, *id.* 359-360; represses the Karmatians (1175), IX, pt. ii, 3 note 3 continued on page 4, 38.

Muhammadi: Musalmán coin in Násik district, XVI, 459 and note 3; equal to two-thirds of a rupee, I, pt. i, 222 note 2.

Muhammad Jaunpuri: Sayad Mahdavi missionary, comes to Gujarát (1509); claims to be the Imam Mehdi; works miracles; gathers followers, IX, pt. ii, 3 note 3, 62-63.

Muhammad Khan: Ahmadnagar minister, strengthens his position, confines two Abyssinian generals, opposes the entry of Sohail

Khán into the fort (1596); seized by the garrison and delivered to the queen, XVII, 385-386.
Muhammad Khán: son and successor of Sultán Hoshang of Málwa (1405-1434), I, pt. i, 359.
Muhammad Khán Bábi: Musalmán noble in Gujarát, captures (1761) Balasinor, I, pt. i, 345.
Muhammad Khilji: becomes *sultán* of Málwa (1436), his victory over Ráns Kumbha of Chitor (1443); builds his tower of victory, is defeated by Kutb-ud-din Sháh of Gujarát (1453); makes his son Ghiás-ud-din minister, his death (1469), I, pt. i, 362.
Muhammad Kishwar Khán: son of Asad Khán, secures the succession of Ali to the throne of Bijápur (1557), is appointed commander-in-chief and sent to Vijayanagar to negotiate a treaty of alliance, I, pt. ii, 644; killed in hostilities with Ahmadnager, *id.* 645.
Muhammad Kuli: ruler of Cambay (1783-1789), chosen successor, VI, 231.
Muhammad-Muradsháh: *sayad* ancestor of the Mash-hadi *sayad* family, IX, pt. ii, 6 note 1 (5).
Muhammad of Ghazni: invades Gujarát (1025), IX, pt. ii, 2 and note 2; in Gujarát (1023-1025), *id* 64; converts Rájpúts of North Gujarát called Malika (1025), *id.* 3 note 3; expels Karmatians from Multan, *id.* 3 note 3, 38; converts a tribe of Bhatti Rájpúts, *id.* 81; his route to Somnáth Pátan, reduces Mangrol (1024), marches to Somnáth, VIII, 279-280; his expedition to Gujarát, I, pt. i, 164-168, 229, 498, 510, 512, 517, 522 and note 1, 523.
Muhammad Sháh: *pir*, tomb of, at Ahmadábád, IX, pt. ii, 35.
Muhammad Sháh: *see* Ala-ud-din Khilji.
Muhammad Sháh I: (1403-1404), I, pt. i, 234 and note 1.
Muhammad Sháh II: Raushan Akhtar, emperor of Delhi (1721-1748), I, pt. i, 222, 301; sends Mubáriz-ul-Mulk against Hámed Khán and the Maráthás, *id.* 306; his death (1748), *id.* 332; *see* also IX, pt. ii, 197 note 2.
Muhammad Sháh II: Bahmani king (1463-1482); sends his minister Muhammad Gáwan against Sankarrai, XXIV, 224; *see* also I, pt. ii, 638, 639, 640.
Muhammad Sháh III: Gujarát king, his treaty with the Portuguese (1540), XIII, 452.
Muhammad Sháh Tughlik: *see* Muhammad Tughlák.
Muhammad Táj: *maulana*, head of the law doctors of Islám at Ahmadábád, IX, pt. ii, 63.
Muhammad Tughlak or Tughlik: *sultán* of Delhi (1325-1351), I, pt. i, 230, 231; at Asáwal, *id.* 513; quells an insurrection at Broach and Cambay, *id.* 514, 515; in Gondal (1349), *id.* 517; pursues Tághi, *id.* 518; possibly the conqueror of Sanján, re-conquers Gujarát and Thána (1348), IX, pt. ii, 187 note 3; ascends the throne of Delhi (1325); visits Devagiri; fails in his project to make it his capital, I, pt. ii, 510, 533, 620; *see* also XV, pt. ii, 94; XIII, 440; plunders Cambay, (1347), VI, 216; Dakhan subdued by, XII, 242; subdues the Carnatic, XXI, 362; loses Dakhan, XX, 276.
Muhammad Tughlak II: emperor (1391-1393), I, pt. i, 232.
Muhammad Ufi: Musalmán historian (1211), I, pt. i, 195 note 4; IX, pt. ii, 2 note 3.
Muhammad Zaman: *mirza*, finds shelter (1532) under Bahádur Sháh of Gujarát, IX, pt. ii, 9.
Muhspas: or Mobeds, found in Canton (845), IX, pt. ii, 183 note 4 continued on page 185.
Muharram: first month of the Musalmán year sacred to the memory of Hasan and Husain, IX, pt. ii, 136; season of keen grief and self-denial, *id.* 126; ceremonies performed and observances practised in, *id.* 137-139; vows made to *taaziahs* and other institutions of *id.* 128, 129-130; feasts in, *id.* 31 note 3, 114; recital of the Karbala massacre in, *id.* 132; elegy-singing in, *id.* 132; *see* also XIII, 524; festival, observed by Hindus and early tribes, IX, pt. i, 362.
Muharrir: secretary, provincial head accountant under Musalmáns, I, pt. i, 214.
Muhiy-ud-din: of Amroha, IX, pt. ii, 130 note 1. *See* Sheikh Saddo.
Muhtasib: city censor under Musalmán rule, I, pt. i, 214.
Muin-ud-din Chishti: saint, first missionary to settle in India (1165), ancestor of the Chishti *sayad* family in Gujarát, IX, pt. ii, 6 note 1 (4); makes many converts at Ajmir, *id.* 3 note 3; founds Chisht, a Sufi or mystic school, *id.* 8 note 3; reverence of Husaini Bráhmans for, *id.* 22.
Muir: Sir William, Sanskrit texts, IX, pt. i, 434 notes 8 and 9, 435 notes 2 and 3.
Muiz-ud-din: Gujarát governor (1347), I, pt. i, 231.
Muiz-ud-din: son of Sultán Muazim (1684), I, pt. ii, 77.
Muiz-ud-din Bahrám Sháh: *sultán* of Delhi (1194-1205), defeated by Viradhavala, I, pt. i, 201.
Muizz: Al, fourth Fatimite *khalifah* of Egypt, IX, pt. ii, 48.
Mujávar: Musalmán beadle, IX, pt. ii, 128, 131; duties and remuneration of, *id.* 131 note 2, 132; village servant in Ratnágiri district, X, 141.
Mukádam: village headman, XVIII, pt. ii, 315 and note 1, 316. *See* Patel.
Mukái: village goddess, XVIII, pt. i, 290.
Mukani: a famine plant, XXV, 198.
Muksnna Kadamba: identified with Mayuravarman I, I, pt. ii, 561.
Mukarrab Khán: Mughal general, captures Sambháji (1689), XX, 288, 407.
Mukssir: grade of *mulla*, IX, pt. ii, 32.
Mukeri: caste of Musalmán grain-sellers, in Belgaum district, XXI, 212, 213; in Dhárwár district, XXII, 237-238; in Bijápur district, XXIII, 295-296; in Sholápur district, XX, 203-204; in Sátára district, XIX, 138; in Kolhápur state, XXIV, 150.
Mukhis: police headmen, IX, pt. i, 156 and note 1.
Mukhpat: village in Khándesh, a pond and temples at, XII, 457.
Mukhtiár Khán: thirty-seventh viceroy of Gujarát (1683-84), I, pt. i, 287.

Mukhya Pradhán : head manager of the Marátha government, XIX, 244 note 1.
Mukri : *see* Mukeri.
Mukri : a depressed class in Kánara district, XV, pt. i, 374-378.
Muktad : ceremony in honor of the dead, time of holding, observances in, observed as holidays, IX, pt. ii, 218.
Muktáphala : Bopadeva's work, I, pt. ii, 249.
Mukteśvara : temple of, at Chandadámpur, inscription at, I, pt. ii, 527 note 1, 580 note 9, 583 note 5.
Mukti : lake in Khándesh, XII, 11, 140.
Muktias : crown domain officers under Musalmáns, I, pt. i, 299 note 2.
Muktináth : god of salvation, emblem of god Shiv, raised by Rám, IX, pt. i, 12 note 1.
Muktipuri : modern Mota in Surat district, said to be founded by Rám, IX, pt. i, 12 note 1.
Mukundráv Gáikwár : Ánandráv's (1800-1819) brother, VII, 203 ; his death (1851), *id.* 260.
Mula : river in Ahmadnagar district, XVII, 8.
Mulá-Muthá : river in Poona district, XVIII, pt. i, 7-8.
Mulahidah : heretics of Hindustán, led astray by Nur the Turk, IX, pt. ii, 38.
Mulaka : son of Sahajiga, makes grants to Somanátha ; is mentioned in the inscription at Mangrol, I, pt. i, 176.
Mulaka : southern country of the *Puráns*, ruled by Gotamiputra, I, pt. ii, 149.
Mulakgiri : *see* Mulukgiri.
Mulán : pass in Násik district, XVI, 130.
Múlanáthadeva : temple of, at Mandali, I, pt. i, 161 and note 2.
Mularája : Solanki or Chaulukya king (961-996) ; his descent and birth ; kills his maternal uncle and ascends the Chávadá throne ; his fight with Barappa ; his war with Graharipu, ruler of Sorath ; instals his son and retires ; builds temples at Anahilaváda and Siddhapur ; grants villages to Bráhmans, I, pt. i, 131, 139, 153, 156-162, 164, 469, 470 ; founder of the Cháulukya dynasty of Anabilapattana, I, pt. ii, 212, 420, 430, 431 note 1 ; IX, pt. i, 489 note 2 ; is said to have invited Audichya and other Bráhmans to help him in holding a sacrifice, *id.* 6, 7 and note 1 ; *see* also I, pt. ii, 23 ; and XIII, 435, 436.
Mularája : heir-apparent of Bhima I (1022-1064) of Anahilaváda, his mysterious death, I, pt. i, 169.
Mularája II : Chaulukya king (1177-1179), succeeds his father Ajayapála ; disperses the Turushka army, defeats Muhammad Ghori, I, pt. i, 195, 512 ; forces Musalmán captives of war to become low class Hindus, IX, pt. i, 439 note 1, 444.
Mulasamgha : Digambara Jain sect, I, pt. ii, 191.
Mulasthána : sacred place near Broach, mentioned in an inscription, I, pt. ii, 405 ; temple at, *id.* 421.
Mulasthánadeva : god, I, pt. ii, 571.
Mulasvámi : temple of, at Anahilaváda, I, pt. i, 161.
Mulavasatika : Jain temple at Anahilaváda, I, pt. i, 160, 161.
Mulberry : tree, in Pálanpur, V, 295 ; in Surat and Broach districts, II, 40, 442 ; in Kaira district, III, 54 ; in Poona district, XVIII, pt. i, 53 ; *morus indica*, sometimes as a hedge and garden plant found in Dhárwár, XXII, 303-305.
Mul-Dwárka : places of interest near Kodiuár in Kathiáwár, VIII, 552-553 ; IX, pt. i, p. x. *See* also under Kodinár.
Mules : in Poona district, XVIII, pt. i, 65 ; in Belgaum district, XXI, 66
Muleśvara : temple at Mandalinagara, I, pt. i, 161.
Mulgaon : deserted village in Thána district, remains of a temple and images at, XIV, 285 ; silver coins found at, *id.* 400.
Mulgeni : permanent lease, tenure in Kánara district, XV, pt. ii, 180, 182.
Mulgenigárs : permanent lessees in Kanára, XV, pt. ii, 185-186.
Mulgund : town in Dhárwár district, population, temples and inscriptions at, XXII, 772-773 ; survey of, *id.* 524-525, 582-587 ; Jain temple at, I, pt. ii, 201 ; inscription at, *id.* 307, 413, 432, 503.
Mulher : hill fort in Násik district, XVI, 210 note 3, 441, 444 ; details, description, history, *id.* 457-460.
Muli : state in Káthiáwár, VIII, 553-556 ; IX, pt. i, 127.
Mulila Deri : táluka in Káthiáwár, VIII, 556.
Muliyásar : village in Káthiáwár, Kshatrapa inscription at, I, pt. i, 43.
Mulk Ahmad : *see* Málik Ahmad.
Mulkgiri : *see* Mulukgiri.
Mulla : religious and social head of Daudi Bohorás ; chief *mulla* called Dai, his head-quarters at Surat, IX, pt. ii, 31 ; former head-quarters of chief *mullas* from 1785-1893, *id.* 31 note 4 ; his influence and power over the community ; his sources of income ; subordinate grades of, earn their own livelihood, *id.* 32-33. One of the lowest subordinate grades of *mulla*, college at Surat and schools to train youths for the duties of, *id.* 32. One of the lowest orders of religious officers, the Musalmán priest, qualifications, his duties at the mosques, earns his livelihood as a school master and adds to his income by making amulets and dealing in charms, etc., *id.* 132-133 ; in Ratnágiri district, X, 141 ; in Belgaum district, XXI, 209 and note 2.
Mulla Feroz : *see* Peshotan.
Mulla Jamasp : Navsári priest, visits Delhi, IX, pt. ii, 197 note 2.
Mull Káns : *see* Káns.
Mulla Muhammad Ali : Umdát-ut-tujjár, or chief of merchants (1729-1733), raises a disturbance at Surat (1729), fixes his head-quarters at Perim, and afterwards at Athva on the Tápti, I, pt. i, 309 ; builds the fort of Athva (1730), *id.* 310 ; drives Sohráb Khán, governor, out of Surat (1732) ; kept in confinement by Teghbeg Khán, governor of Surat, *id.* 313 ; in correspondence with the Nizám ; letters from Nizám to Teghbeg Khán for the release of ; the assassination of (1734), *id.* 315 ; *see* also II, 110.

Mulnayak : image of chief *tirthankar* in Jain temples, IX, pt. i, 111.
Mulpattás : land grants, XV, pt. ii, 164, 183.
Mulráj : *see* Mularája.
Mulshi Budrukh : market village in Poona district, XVIII, pt. iii, 260.
Multai : grant of Nandaráj (708), I, pt. ii, 377 note 3, 384, 386.
Multán : capital of Húna dynasty, I, pt. i, 143, 459, 509, 518, 528, 545 ; kinghom of, foundation of, by the Karmatians, destruction of, IX, pt. ii, 3 note 3 continued on page 4, 38 ; battle of, *id.* 58.
Multan : reservoir in Ahmadábád district, IV, 19.
Multáni : a Musaulmán class in Khándesh, XII, 127 ; in Násik district, XVI, 78.
Mulukgiri : land-raiding system in Káthiáwár under the Mughals and Maráthás, I, pt. i, 417 ; special rules of, *id.* 418, 421 ; VII, 183 ; its description and history, *id.* 314-322 ; *see* also VIII, 116, 299.
Mum : coasting craft in Thána district, XIII, 720.
Mumbádevi : temple of, in Bombay city, XIII, 474.
Mume-perjerepu-patta : badge of honour, I, pt. ii, 376.
Mummuni : *see* Mámváni.
Muna : lake at Viramgám, I, pt. i, 180.
Munawalli : village in Dhárwár district, inscription at, I, pt. ii, 374 note 3, 433.
Mund : form of assessment in Kolába district, XI, 168 ; in Násik district, XVI, 208 and note 3 ; in Poona district, XVIII, pt. ii, 313 note 1.
Mundagod : *see* Mundgod.
Mundáji Bhonsle : Berár chief (1784), his loyalty to the Peshwa, XVIII, pt. ii, 267.
Mundakallu : village granted by Adityavarman, I, pt. ii, 367.
Mundakeśvara : holy place near Anahilaváda, I, pt. i, 170.
Mundarashtra : country, I, pt. ii, 320.
Mundargi : town in Dhárwár district, details of, fort at, XXII, 773-774 ; trade centre, *id.* 354.
Mundgod : town in Kanára district, history of, XV, pt. ii, 334-335 ; travellers' bungalow and hospital at, *id.* 45, 219 ; *see* also I, pt. ii, 484.
Mundhave : village in Poona district, coffee plantation at (1840-1842), XVIII, pt. iii, 260.
Mundra : town and fort in Cutch, V, 244-245 ; fortified (1730), *id.* 140 ; reduced by Fateh Muhammad (1786-1810), *id.* 150.
Mundulea suberosa : plant for poisoning fish, XXV, 272.
Mung : fodder plant, XXV, 277.
Mungay : oil-yielding plant, XXV, 218.
Mungi Paithan: in Nizám's dominions, Dakhan capital, Pátáne Prabhue supposed to have come from, XIII, 62, 90 ; its trade with Konkan (A. D. 78), *id.* 412 ; Ptolemy's mention of, *id.* 415 ; trade centre (150), *id.* 416 ; treaty of (1740), XIX, 282. *See* Paithan.
Mungoose : *nolio*, natural enemy of the serpent, worship of, IX, pt. i, 378 ; at Mátherán, XIV, 259.
Munhchira : *see* Rafai.
Munh Dhankna : face-hiding, IX, pt. ii, 170.
Munhphoda : *see* Rafai.
Munias : class of birds in Ratnágiri district, X, 83.
Municipalities : *see* all district volumes.
Munim : confidential clerk of Vánia banker, IX, pt. i, 79, 80, 81.
Muni Subhadra : preceptor of Ynddhamalla II's son Narasimha, I, pt. ii, 380.
Munj : fibre plant in Pálanpur state, V, 295.
Munja : Vákpati, Paramára king of Málwa, deprives Chámunda of his marks of royalty, I, pt. i, 162 ; defeated and killed by the Western Chálukya king Taila II and his feudatory the Yádava king Bhillama II, I, pt. ii, 213, 214, 233, 238, 422, 424, 426, 430, 431, 432, 433, 436.
Munja : Sinda feudatory of Vikramáditya VI, I, pt. ii, 450 ; son Sindarája, *id.* 577.
Munjá : the, spirit of a thread-girt and unmarried Bráhman lad, IX, pt. i, 385 ; belief in, XVIII, pt. i, 553, 554, 558.
Munjála : minister of Karna, Chaulukya king, I, pt. i, 170, 171, 172.
Munjaladeva : of Sagara lineage, I, pt. ii, 475.
Munj Mekhala : girdle of *munj* grass, worn at thread ceremony, IX, pt. i, 37.
Munjpur : village in Pálanpur state, a mosque at, V, 342-343.
Munjpur : táluka in Káthiáwár, VIII, 557.
Munro : Sir Thomas, on Haidar's oppressive rule in Kánara, XV, pt. ii, 142 ; appointed collector of Kánara (1799), *id.* 145 ; leaves the district (1800), *id.* 152 ; his revenue system in Kánara, *id.* 158-160 ; his notice of Ankolá (1800), *id.* 259 ; of Gersappa, *id.* 284 ; Haliyál, *id.* 304 ; and other places in Kánara district, *id.* 318, 340, 349 ; conquers the Peshwa's territories (1818), I, pt. ii, 611 ; is appointed commissioner of the districts ceded by Bájiráv (1817), makes Dhárwar his headquarters, wrests country from the Maráthás and captures the forts of Badámi, Bágalkot, Belgaum and Sholapur (1817-1818), *id.* 664-665 ; occupies Dhárwár (1817), reduces Sundur ; points out defects in the Marátha government, takes Navalgund, Gadag, Damba, Hubli and Mishrikot ; his success in South Bijápur, Belgaum and Sholápur ; the secret of his success ; his settlement of the conquered country, impression created by his success, XXII, 427-432 ; *see* also XIII, 449-451 ; XX, 296-300 ; XXI, 398-400, 413 ; XXIV, 350, 351.
Munvalli : village in Dhárwár district, inscriptions at, XXII, 774.
Muos Harmuz : Red Sea port, its trade connection with Thána (A. D. 78), XIII, 410 note 5.
Murád : son of Akbar, invades Ahmadnagar (1576), I, pt. ii, 649 ; appears before Ahmadnagar (1595), his pacific measures, besieges the Ahmadnagar fort, quits the country, XVII, 383-385.
Murád Bakhsh : Prince Muhammad, twenty-ninth viceroy of Gujarát (1654-1657) ; surrender of Kánji Chunvália Koli ; proclaims himself emperor of Gujarát (1657) ;

his transfer to the viceroyalty of Berárt hrough Dárá Shikoh ; collects an army and arranges to meet his brother Aurangzib ; fights a battle with Mahárája Jasvantsing and Kásamkhán, viceroys of Málwa and Gujarát (1658) ; Aurangzib and Murád enter Ujjain, meet Dárá Shikoh at Dholpur and defeat him ; confined by Aurangzib at Mathura (1658), *id.* 281-282.
Muradsing : fibrous plant, XXV, 229.
Muram : pass in Násik district, XVI, 130.
Muráriráv : chief of Guti (1756), brings Hakim Khán to terms, through his influence tries to effect reconciliation with the Peshwa, XXII, 798.
Murar Jagdevrav, Murarpant: Bijápur minister, passes an ass-drawn plough through Poona (1630), XVIII, pt. iii, 339, 403 ; his expedition into Karnátak (1637), XVIII, pt. ii, 225.
Murárráv : Damáji Gáikwár's son, VII, 188.
Murbád : sub-division of Thána district, its boundaries, area, aspect, climate, water, soil, holdings, rental, stock, crops and people, XIII, 2, 690-692 ; its assessment revised (1837), *id.* 582-583 ; survey of (1860), *id.* 604-606 ; *Town*, temples and pond at, XIV, 285-286.
Murdeshvar : port in Kánara district, temple and inscriptions at, XV, pt. ii, 335 ; trade of, *id.* 44, 65, 66, 68.
Murgali : fibrous plant, XXV, 236.
Murgod : town in Belgaum district, headquarters of a petty sub-division, XXI, 589 ; I, pt. ii, 285 notes 3 and 6.
Murhás : level parts of *ghát* country, "Introduction to the History of the Konkan," I, pt. ii, p. x note 1.
Murids : disciples of the Shiáh *mullas ;* of the Sunni *pirzadah* or Murshid ; initiation of, by a *sayad pir*, IX, pt. ii, 127 and note 2.
Muriyi-Kotta : town on Malabár Coast, XIII, 410.
Murkebandi : *see* Mudáhandi.
Murli : a caste of temple-servants, in Poona district, XVIII, pt. i, 476 ; in Sholápur district, XX, 189-190.
Murlidhar Mandir : Násik temple, XVI, 506.
Murraya Kœnigii : oil-yielding plant, XXV, 222.
Mursavirad : monastery in Dhárwár city, XXII, 756.
Murshed Kulikhán : introduces (1637) Todar Mál's revenue system into the Dakhan, XVIII, pt. ii, 225 ; *see* also XVII, 398.
Murshid : an order of teachers in a beggar brotherhood, duties of, IX, pt. ii, 19. Spiritual guide, *id.* 127 and note 2. *See* Pir.
Murtaza Nizám Sháh : assassination of (1629), I, pt. ii, 650.
Murti Manoharji : Hindu god worshipped by Mandvi Khárvás, IX, pt. i, 522.
Murtuza Ali : first Sháh *imám*, IX, pt. ii, 125 note 2.
Murud : a town in Janjira state, XI, 465.
Muruj-uz-zaháb : "Meadows of Gold," work of Al Masudi, I, pt. i, 506 note 8.
Murunda : tribe in Afghanistán, tributary of Samudragupta (370-395), I, pt. i, 64 and note 5 continued on page 65.
Musa : patron saint of the Musa Suhags, used to dress in woman's clothes, famous singer, said to have saved the country from famine by his prayers, tomb of, at Ahmadábád ; *Champa* or *Michelia* tree near the tomb of, IX, pt. ii, 23 and note 2.
Musa : *Sapicutum*, food plant, XXV, 174 ; fibrous plant *id.* 235 ; *Superba*, a famine plant, *id.* 204 ; a fibrous plant, *id.* 235 ; *Ornata*, famine as also fibrous plant, *id.* 204, 235 ; *Parádisiaca*, a food plant, *id.* 417 ; a fibrous plant, *id.* 235 ; *Kela*, plant used in religious ceremony, *id.* 279 ; a sacred plant, *id.* 284.
Musa Bin Ishák : appointed Muhammadan judge by Balhárl (945), I, pt. i, 516 and note 3.
Musala, Musaladatta : Padan hill sage, XIII, 408 ; *see* also XIV, 103, 393, 394.
Musalmáns : defeated by the Devagiri Yádava king Singhana (1210-1247), I, pt. ii, 525 ; under the Delhi emperor invade the Dakhan (1294), *id.* 29, 530-531, 587, 620, extend their power to the Konkan (1312), *id.* 29, 533 ; nobles revolt and establish the Bahamani dynasty (1345-1347), *id.* 587, 620, 637 ; Malik Názir founds the Faruki dynasty of Khándesh, *id.* 620 ; the Bahamanis lose hills and strong places, *id.* 588 ; recover the lost ground (1420-1451), *id.* 30, 31, 32, 588 ; attack the Southern Marátha Country, *id.* 637-639 ; the Gujarát king takes North Konkan, *id.* 30 ; decline of the Bahamani (1481), *id.* 639 ; partition of the Bahamani kingdom (1491), *id.* 33, 589, 621, 640 ; the king of Bijápur loses Goa to the Portugese (1510), *id.* 641 ; the king of Gujarát loses North Konkan to the Portuguese, *id.* 33 ; are not allowed by the Portuguese to exercise their religion within towns, *id.* 60 ; Abyssinians establish themselves at Janjira (1489), *id.* 34 ; in possession of Arnála fort (1530), XIV, 10 ; besiege Bassein (1612), *id.* 31 ; their power wanes with the decline of the Mughal empire (1708), I, pt. ii, 626 ; their rule in Gujarát (1297-1760), I, pt. i, 207-384 ; in Ratnágiri (1312-1660), X, 193 ; in Khándesh (1295-1760), XII, 242-252 ; in Thána, XIII, 550-554 ; in Násik (1295-1760), XVI, 185-189 ; attack Thána (640), I, pt. i, 523 ; Jai Rai, Ráshtrakúta Balhara's ruler in Gujarát partial to (945), *id.* 512, 514, 526, 530 ; settled at Saimur in thousands (945), *id.* 516 ; conquer Gujarát towns (1100), *id.* 518 ; number, occupation and condition of, in Kaira district, III, 36 ; in Panch Mahals, *id.* 226 ; in Surat district, II, 55 ; in Broach district, *id* 376-377 ; in Ahmadábád district, IV, 40 ; in Cutch, V, 88-100 ; in Pálanpur, *id.* 291 ; in Mahi Kántha, *id.* 367 ; in Rewa Kántha, VI, 34 ; in Cambay, *id.* 185 ; in Baroda state, VII, 68-72 ; in Káthiáwár, VIII, 160-167 ; in Ratnágiri district, their composition and sub-divisions, X, 131-134, 171 ; readers and writers (1872), *id.* 284 ; in Sávantvádi state, *id.* 420, 459 ;

in Kolába district and Janjira state, XI, 74-85, 416-421; in Khándesh, XII, 124-128, 331; in Thána district, their history, speech, appearance, house, food, dress, ornaments, calling, earnings, holidays, character, condition, community, religion, customs, prospects, divisions, XIII, 216-246; of the Kánara district, XV, pt. i, 400-411; XV, pt. ii, 3; in Násik district, XVI, 26, 75-84; in Ahmadnagar district, XVII, 214-235; in Poona district, XVIII, pt. i, 481-506; in Sátára district, XIX, 124-147; in Sholápur district, XX, 199-211; in Belgaum district, XXI, 196-226; in Dhárwár, XXII, 222-249; in Bijapur district, XXIII, 282-305; in Kolhápur state, XXIV, 147-151.

Musa Raza: eighth Shiáh *imám*, IX, pt. ii, 125 note 2.

Musa Suhag: caste of beggers, in Gujarát, Hindu converts followers of Saint Musa, dress like married women, remain unmarried, IX, pt. ii, 23 and note 1.

Muscicapidæ: family of birds in Ratnágiri district, X, 71.

Mushaka: country on Malabár Coast (?), I, pt. ii, 281; king of, conquered by Kirtivarman, *id.* 345.

Mushaka Vihára: temple at Pátan, built by Kumárapála, I, pt, i, 190.

Mushika: *see* Mushaka.

Mushrifs: revenue clerks under Gujarát Musalmán kings, I, pt. i, 212, 214.

Mushtiger: caste of husbandmen in Bijápur district, XXIII, 134-137.

Mushtigiri: village in Bijápur district, temples, XXIII, 664.

Musical instruments: of the Ráshtrakútas of Málkhed, of the Rattas of Saundatti, of the Kalachuryas of Kalyáni, of the Kádambas of Hángal and Goa, and of the Western Gangas, I, pt. ii, 327 note 7.

Musicians: in Kolába district, XI, 67; in Kánara district, XV, pt. i, 314-320; in Ahmadnagar district, XVII, 144-145; in Sátára district, XIX, 97-102; in Sholápur district, XX, 144-146; in Kolhápur, XXIV, 100-101.

Musi Kazim: son of the sixth Shiáh *imám* Jafar Sadik, his dispute with his nephew Ismáil for the imámate, his supporters known as Isna-ashari, IX, pt. ii, 30 note 1; seventh Shiáh *imám*, *id.* 125 note 2.

Musiris or Muziris: Muriyi-Kotta (?) on the Malabár Coast, its direct sea trade with Arabia (A. D. 47), XIII, 410, 418; mentioned in *Periplus*, identified with Karangnor in Malabár, XV, pt. ii, 48, 78 note 1, 141, 332.

Muskat: port, 600 Arabs from, ravage Thána Coast (1674), I, pt. ii, 70.

Musla: *see* Bulki.

Muslins: export of (1660), to Europe from Kárwár, XV, pt. ii, 52, 125, 321.

Musopalle: probable identification of, X, 192 note 3. *See* Mhasla.

Mustaalian: division of the great Ismaili sect of Shiáhs in Gujarát called after Almustaali, son of Almustansirbillah, *khalifah* of Egypt (1094), sect represented in India by Bohorás; Abdullah the principal missionary of, IX, pt. ii, 24, 26, 30 note 1; in Thána district, origin of the name, XIII, 223 and note 2.

Mustáfabad: Dabhol so called, I pt. ii, 33.

Mustafabad: Belgaum so called, XXI, 376 note 9.

Mustáphá Khán: head of the Arabs at Sunth, makes the *rája* prisoner (1857); disarmed and shot by Lieutenant Alban, I, pt. i, 441.

Mustapha Khán: Bijápur general at the siege of Bankápur, I, pt. ii, 646.

Musunnipuru: village on the Krishnáverna, I, pt. ii, 369.

Mutasaddi: civil officer under the Musalmáns, I, pt. i, 212.

Mutawalli: mosque guardian, duties of, IX, pt. ii, 131, 132.

Muter: Captain, arrest of (1857), by General Roberts, I, pt. i, 440.

Mutha: river in Poona district, XVIII, pt. i, 8.

Mutha Canals: in Poona district, XVIII, pt. ii, 15-20; water-supply from, XVIII, pt. iii, 328 329.

Mutibas: living on the borders of Aryan settlements, I, pt. ii, 138.

Mutiny: at Ahmadábád, suppression of, by the viceroy (1689), I, pt. i, 288; in Rewa Kántha (1857), VI, 63, 64; share of Khándesh in, XII, 262; of Thána district in, XIII, 525; in Násik district (1857-1859), XVI, 199-204; share of Sátára in, XIX, 316-317; troubles of, in Bijápur, XXIII, 453-454; *desais* in Belgaum, XXI, 409-412; effect of, in Baroda, VII, 278.

Mutiny Act: proclaimed (1754) in Bombay island, XXVI, pt. iii, 121-122.

Mutsadis: clerks of the crown, IX, pt. i, 60. *See.* Kayasths.

Muttage: *see* Muttige.

Muttagi: inscription at, I, pt. ii, 518, 520.

Muttatti: village in Mysore, inscription at, I, pt. ii, 284 note 4.

Muttige: village in Bijápur district, temples and inscription at, XXIII, 664-665; *see* also I, pt. ii, 466.

Muttur: village in Dhárwár district, temple and inscription at, XXII, 774.

Mutu Kumár: police constable, brings (1857) to light the civil and military conspiracy in Belgaum, XXI, 411.

Muválad: caste of Indian-born Arabs in Khándesh, XII, 124, 255; in Gujarát, IX, pt. ii, 11, 15.

Muzaafar Shola: sweet dish, IX, pt. ii, 113.

Muzafari: coin used (1576) in Khándesh, XII, 247.

Muzafarjang: Poona ward, details, XVIII, pt. iii, 274, 279.

Muzafar Sháh: *see* Muzaffar.

Muzaffar: governor of Gujarát, founder of Ahmadábád dynasty (1390-1403); brings Sunni priests to spread Islám, conversion of Patan Shiáh Bohorás to Sunni faith by the priests, IX, pt. ii, 26 note 1, 34; brings more priests (1395), *id.* 3 note 3; encourages the spread of Sunni doctrines, *id.* 27, 58 note

2, 125; *see* also *id.* 188; defeats the chief of Kánthkote (1410), V, 135.

Muzaffar I: of Gujarát (1407-1419), I, pt. i, 210, 234-235; invades Málwa and defeats Sultán Hoshang at Dhár (1407); takes Sultán Hoshang to Gujarát as a prisoner; releases and reinstates him at Mándu (1408), *id.* 358.

Muzaffar II: Ahmadábád king (1536-1550), attacks Somanátha, I, pt. i, 190; settlement of men of letters from Persia and other places in Gujarát in the reign of, IX, pt. ii, 3 note 3; persecutes Mahdavis, *id.* 63, 125.

Muzaffaráhád: port in Gujarát, burned by the Portuguese (1532), I, pt. i, 347.

Muzaffar Jang: Haidarábád ruler (1748-1751), disputes the claims of Násir Jang (1748), deserted by the French, put in irons; his agreement to the three *nawábs*; leaves Pondicherry (1751) with Bussy; marches against the *nawáb* of Kadappa, XXII, 794-797.

Muzaffar Khan: *see* Muzaffar.

Muzaffar Khán Gárdi: Peshwa's captain at, Surat (1758-1759), I, pt. i, 343.

Muzbi: special holiday dish of Arabs, IX, pt. ii, 16.

Muziris: generally identified with Mangalore, I, pt. ii, 3; probable identification of, X, 352 and note 8; with Krangnur, I, pt. i, 537, 546.

Mnzumdár: *see* Pant Amátya.

Mycetoma: disease in Khándesh, XII, 337.

Myiotherinæ: family of birds in Ratnágiri, X, 72.

Mynas: class of birds, in Ratnágiri district, X, 82.

Myos Hormos: port on Arabian Coast near Rás Abu Somer, centre of Indian trade (B. C. 69-A. D. 23), I, pt. i, 536, 543.

Myriceæ: an order of plants yielding dyes, XXV, 249.

Myristica: *attenuata*, jungle *jaiphal*, oil-yielding plant, XXV, 214; *Malabarica*, *id.* 214.

Myristiceæ: jungle *jaiphal*, oil-yielding plant, XXV, 214.

Myrobalans: or *hirdas* in Khándesh, XII, 23; in Thána district, XIII, 30-31; in Kánara, XV, pt. i, 30, 35; export of, XV, pt. ii, 57; in Poona district, XVIII, pt. i, 39, 46; in Sátára district, XIX, 35, 647 note 2; in Belgaum district, XXI, 60.

Myrsineæ: an order of plants used for poisoning fish, XXV, 273.

Myrtaceæ: an order of fibrous plants, XXV, 232.

Myrtaceæ: an order of plants yielding dyes, XXV, 245.

Myrtus communis: a food plant, XXV, 173.

Mysore: copper-plate grants from, I, pt. ii, 277, 298 note 2, 299, 304 and note 1, 318, 377 and note 4, 399, 421, 430, 431, 433, 436, 441, 443, 458, 459 note 3, 466, 468, 470, 473, 478, 491, 492, 495 and note 2, 499, 502, 505, 507, 509, 516, 523, 528, 529 and note 3, 561, 581 note 3.

N

NAAGRAMMA: town in Sind, mentioned by Ptolemy, I, pt. i, 538.

Nabathæa: destruction of the kingdom of (105), I, pt. i, 543.

Nabhága: equalled by Gotamiputra in prowess, I, pt. ii, 149.

Nabud: nonentity, IX, pt. ii, 225. *See* Návar.

Nácharája: lineage of, I, pt. ii, 486.

Nachne-ki-Talái: records, I, pt. ii, 286 note 1.

Náchni: food plant, grown in several districts, XXV, 187; in Ratnágiri district, X, 147; in Sávantvádi, *id.* 425; in Thána District, XIII, 288; in Ahmadnagar district, XVII, 267; in Poona district, XVIII, pt. ii, 40-41; *see* also Rági.

Nád: Kánarese word for district, I, pt. ii, 578.

Nádá: caste of Máng rope-makers in Kolhápur, XXIV, 111.

Nádáchhadi: red thread binding to a pregnant woman's wrist, IX, pt. i, 93.

Nadagi: land tenure in Kánara district, XV, pt. ii, 186.

Nadas: reeds, I, pt. ii, 140.

Nadaviyuppayana Vidu: the Western Chálukya king Vikramáditya VI, reigns at I, pt. ii, 446, 450.

Nadiád: sub-division of Kaira, details of, III, 152-155; town, III, 175; battle near (1412), I, pt. i, 235; given to Khanderáv Gáikwár, VII, 176; Raghunáthráv (1775) at, *id.* 193; Malhárráv of Kadi (1802) permitted to reside at, *id.* 206-207; made over to the British by Rávji Appáji (1803), I, pt. i, 413.

Nádig or Nádigar: caste of barbers in Bijápur district, XXIII, 254-257; in Dhárwár district, XXII, 187-188.

Nádirshah: Persian emperor, invades (1739) Hindustán, I, pt. i, 322; I, pt. ii, 84; XIX, 280; massacre of Delhi by (1739), XXVI, pt. i, 271; his ships in Bombay; his attempt to make Persia a maritime power (1740-1745), *id.* 287 and note 6.

Nadol or Nador: state in Márwár, its chief Kelhana puts a man to death for his wife having offered flesh to a field-god, I, pt. i, 193; copper-plate of, *id.* 183 note 3.

Nador: caste of proprietary husbandmen in Kánara district, XV, pt. ii, 3.

Nadula: modern Nándol, I, pt. i, 198.

Nádur: part of the *Zend Avesta*, IX, pt. ii, 211 note 2 (6).

Nadvat: country mentioned by Pánini, I, pt. ii, 139.

Nág: shrine of, at Angkor in Cambodia, IX, pt. i, 502 note 4.

Naga: *see* Nágás.

Nágabhatta: son of Maheśvaranága, I, pt. ii, 281 note 3.

Nágada: minister of Visáladeva, I, pt. i, 203.

Nágadhvaja: hooded serpent banner, I, pt. ii, 576.

Nágáditya: of the Sinda family, I, pt. ii, 437.

Nágáditya: of Bágadage, I, pt. ii, 577; Sinda princess of Yelburga, closely connected with, *id.* 574, 576.

Nága kings: the, in Khándesh, XII, 486 and note 2; *see* also I, pt. i, 64.
Nágalámbika: sister of Basava and mother of Chenna-Basava, I, pt. ii, 226; incarnation of Párvati, *id.* 479, 480.
Nágamangala: grant, I, pt. ii, 301 note 1, 302.
Nagammasvámin: Bráhman grantee of Chálukya king, I, pt. ii, 191.
Nágámve: village in Dhárwár district, temple and inscriptions at, XXII, 774.
Nágána: temple of, in Mevád, I, pt. i, 133.
Nagánanda: Sanskrit play of Śri Harsha, I, pt. ii, 253 note 1.
Nágane: tribal guardians of the Ráthods, I, pt. i, 452.
Náganna: Hoysála minister, I, pt. ii, 491.
Nágan Ram: Sanján high priest, brings the Sanján fire to Navsári, IX, pt. ii, 186.
Nágaon: town in Koláha district, XI, 351; I, pt. ii, 543.
Nágapanchmi: hill in Belgaum district, XXI, 6.
Nágapur: old town mentioned in inscriptions, possibly modern Nágaon in Thána, not in Koláha, XIV, 402; I, pt. ii, 543.
Nágapura-Nandivardhana: old district in Central Provinces, I, pt. ii, 420.
Nágar: town in the north of Málwa, coins obtained at, I, pt. ii, 311.
Nagar: place of interest in Dharampur state, VI, 257; fort in the Sivalik hills, IX, pt. i, 444.
Nágar: sub-caste of Bráhmans in Gujarát, IX, pt. i, p. xi note 3, xii note 4, 2; strength and distribution, *id.* 3; divisions; claim, Vadnagar as their original seat; places of settlement; sub-divisions named after places of settlement, *id.* 13, 15 and note 2; relations of sub-divisions, *id.* 13; traditions about origin, created by Shiv, to officiate at his marriage; to officiate at his sacrifice; children of a Nág by a Bráhman girl, *id.* 14-15; suggestions as to origin from traditions, *id.* 15 note 1; traces of foreign origin, *id.* 438 and notes 8 and 9; original race believed to be Gujars, *id.* 494, 501 and notes 1 to 6; Vánias, Meshri, called Bam Nágars, claim Vadnagar as their original seat, family deity of, *id.* 73; in Cutch, V, 45; in Rewa Kántha, VI, 22, 24; in Baroda state, VII, 53, 58; in Ahmadnagar district, XVII, 55; in Poona district, XVIII, pt. i, 163; in Sholápur district, XX, 30; in Thána district, XIII, 80; in Káthiáwár, VIII, 144.
Nága Rája: son of Chamunda, Chaulukya king, I, pt. i, 162-163.
Nágarakhanda: section of the Banavási province, territorial possession of the Nágas, situation and origin of the name of, I, pt. ii, 281 note 3; part of the Kadamba territory taken by the Western Chálukyas, *id.* 345 note 4; a village in, granted to the Vira-Somanátha temple by the Western Chálukya king Someśvara IV, *id.* 484; under the Hoysálas of Dorasamudra, *id.* 506; under the Devagiri Yádavas, *id.* 524.
Nagar Devla: village in Khándesh district, temple at, XII, 457.
Nagareśvara: temple of, at Sudi in Dhárwár district, I, pt. ii, 441.
Nágarhál: hill and place of interest in Belgaum district, XXI, 6, 590.
Nágari: leading tribe of Gujars of the North-West Provinces, IX, pt. i, 494.
Nágari characters: the earliest use of, in Southern India, I, pt. ii, 377 note 3.
Nágarika: modern Navsári, I, pt. i, 125.
Nágarji: a class of Musalmán kettle-drummers in Sátára district, XIX, 144-145; in Bijápur district, XXIII, 305.
Nágárjun: twelfth Siláhára king of Thána, XIII, 422 note 1, 425; *see* also I, pt. ii, 15, 539.
Nágárjuna: Hindu god, temple of, in Dhárwár district, I, pt. ii, 422 note 3.
Nágárjuna: aids Kanishka to work out a broader Buddhism, IX, pt. i, 442.
Nágar Kotias: tribe of Bráhmans in Kangra, IX, pt. i, 4 note 2.
Nagarle: town in Mysore, inscription at, I, pt. ii, 306.
Nagarouris: town mentioned by Ptolemy, probably Poona, I, pt. i, 541.
Nagar Párkar: state in Sind, rising in (1857), I, pt. i, 448.
Nagar Patti: suburb of Dhulia, XII, 444.
Nagarseth: or the Mayor of the city, IV, 90, 113; IX, pt. i, 96.
Nagarshah: Pratápsháh's brother-in-law, defeats Pratápsháh and is defeated by the Musalmáns, I, pt. ii, 27.
Nagar-Thatha: capital of Sind (1421), IX, pt. ii, 50.
Nágas: race of, I, pt. ii, 576; figure prominently in the history of Kashmir, spread over the whole of India, defeated by Samudragupta and Skandagupta and Tivararája; uprooted by Dadda I, the Gurjara king; also by the Eastern Chálukya king Narendramrigarája Vijayáditya II, *id.* 281 note 3; foreign tribes vaguely called; admitted as Rájpúts, IX, pt. i, 450 note 2, 458 note 5; priests of, admitted as Bráhmans; considered the best of Bráhmans, *id.* 438, 463 note 2; wild tribe, identified with the Naikdás of the Panch Maháls and the Talábdas of Broach, *id.* 115; tradition connecting Nágar Bráhmans with, IX, pt. i, 115 note 1; in Thána district, XIII, 408.
Nágasárika: modern Navsári, I, pt. i, 125.
Nágasena: Nága chief conquered by Samudragupta, I, pt. ii, 281 note 3.
Nágasri: place of interest in Káthiáwár, VIII, 557.
Nagati: son of Ketarasa the Kádamba, I, pt. ii, 564.
Nágavamsa: race of the hooded serpents, Siudas of Yelburga allotted to, I, pt. ii, 574.
Nágavarddhana: Chálukya prince; king ruling in West Násik; grant of, at Nirpan, I, pt. i, 108, 110, 111, 112; Jayáśraya Tribhuvanáśraya, son of Dharáśraya Jayasimhavarman, brother of Pulakesi II, I, pt. ii, 185, 192, 357; his Nirpan grant, *id.* 345, 352, 357; god or teacher, *id.* 352, 358 note 1, 361, 364 note 3.

Nágavarman : Kánarese poet, I, pt. ii, 343 note 5, 392.
Nágavarman I : Hángal Kádamha, I, pt. ii, 559.
Nágavarman II : Hángal Kádamba, I, pt. ii, 559.
Nágavarmayya : Vikramáditya VI's governor of the Belvola, Purigere, and Banavási provinces, I, pt. ii, 452.
Nágavarmman : Kakka II's maternal grandfather, I, pt. i, 122.
Nágávi : village in Dhárwár district, temple at, I, pt. ii, 422 note 3 ; record of Vira-Ballála II at, *id.* 503, 526 ; inscription at, *id.* 529.
Nagchampa or Chápha : *mesua ferea*, oil-yielding plant, XXV, 214 ; also called Nagkeshar, *id.* 289.
Nagdaun : *crinum asiaticum*, medicinal and poisonous plant, XXV, 256, 270.
Nágdhaniba : place of interest in Káthiáwár, VIII, 557.
Nagdi kanli : a form of tenure in Kolába district, XI, 174 note 2.
Nagdi shirasta : cash rate tenure in Kolába district, XI, 174 and note 2, 178 note 1, 181, 182 and note 5.
Nagdown : *asparagus officinalis*, a food and famine plant, XXV, 180, 204.
Nágeshvar : temple of, in Poona city, XVIII, pt. iii, 337.
Nágeshvári : stream in Kolaba district, XI, 11.
Nágeśvarapandita : Sivnur village granted by Someśvara I to, I, pt. ii, 441.
Nágher : tract of country in Káthiáwár, I, pt. i, 208 note 3 ; origin of the name of, VIII, 5 ; position of, *id.* 8 ; Valabhis at, *id.* 276 ; Mahmud charmed at the climate of, *id.* 280.
Naghera : old town in Cambay, VI, 214 footnote 6.
Nághori : breed of cattle in Poona district, XVIII, pt. i, 57.
Nágkeshar : *see* Nágchampa.
Nágli : food and famine plant, XXV, 187, 208 ; grown in Násik district, XVI, 99 ; in Cutch, V, 106. *See* Nachni.
Náglik : caste of dyers in Dhárwár district, XXII, 158-159 ; in Bijápur district, XXIII, 253.
Nágmandal : snakeland, said to be the old name of Navsári, IX, pt. ii, 186 note 6.
Nagmassad, : a poisonous plant, an antidote to snake-bites, XXV, 267, 275.
Nágmati : river in Káthiáwár, VIII, 64.
Nág Naik : Koli chief (1340) of Sinhgad, opposes Muhammad Tughlak, XVIII, pt. ii, 215, 442.
Nagnes : place of interest in Káthiáwár, VIII, 558.
Nágnur Lake : in Dhárwár district, XXII, 260.
Nágoji Máne : Marátha chief of Mhaswad, surprises and kills Santáji Ghorpade, I, pt. ii, 597.
Nágor : port of, in Afghanistan (?), I, pt. i, 174 note 1.
Nágori : caste of Hindu converts in Gujarát, come from Nágor in Málwa, mostly cart drivers, form a community ; Palanpur section of, have taken to arms, surnames of, fond of giving public dinners, IX, pt. ii, 88.
Nágoshi : *see* Bohors.
Nagothana : place of interest in Kolába district, XI, 352 ; Gujarát kings in possession of, *id.* 142 ; Portuguese at, *id.* 143 ; under Bijápur, kings, *id.* 144 ; Saukuvarbái in possession of *id.* 155 ; Manáji Angria defeated at (1799), *id.* 156 ; plundered by Rámoshis (1840), *id.* 158, 220 ; in hands of *khots*, *id.* 178 ; *khot* residents of, *id.* 182 note 3 ; *khoti* system of, *id.* 203 ; port details, trade, history, old bridge, *id.* 116 ; Siláhára port, *id.* 21 ; south boundary of the kingdom of Gujarát, *id.* 34 ; bridge, *id.* 42 ; port burnt by the Portuguese (1529), *id.* 46 ; *see* also XIII, 443, 450.
Nágpanchmi : Cobrá's fifth, Hindu holiday, IX, pt. i, 23 note 5 ; worship of the Nág or serpent on, *id.* 379 ; observed by the Prabhus in Poona, XVIII, pt. i, 244-245 ; Kunbi festival, *id.* 293.
Nágphani : cliff in Poona district called the Duke's Nose, XVIII, pt. i, 4 ; pass of, XVIII, pt. ii, 153.
Nágphanna, Nágphansi : a famine plant, XXV, 199.
Nágpur : in Násik district, temple at, XVI, 460.
Nágvand : village in Dhárwár district, inscription at, XXII, 774.
Nág worship : legends of, I, pt. i, 502 note 3.
Nahál : a Bhil tribe in Khándesh, XII, 94 ; outbreak of, in the Sátpudás, *id.* 258.
Naban : bathing ceremony, IX, pt. ii, 232.
Nahapána : first Gujarát Kshatrapa, I, pt. i, 24, 29 ; I, pt. ii, 149 ; Kshaharáta, *id.* 155, 166 ; king of foreign descent, a Sáka, *id.* 155 ; dynasty of, *id.* 157, 158 ; Satrap, *id.* 159, 160 ; his or his successors' overthrow by Gotamiputra, *id.* 161, 168 ; his death, *id.* 160 ; Gotamiputra kills his successors, *id.* 160 ; dates of his accession and death, *id.* 168 ; *another account of* : Parthian or Sáka, IX, pt. i, 435 ; his family stock name, his conquests in Málwa, Konkan and the Dakhan, his coins and public works in the Konkan ; is said to be the re-birth of Parnsharam, *id.* 497-498 and note 1 ; elements of his army, *id.* 461 note 2 ; inscriptions of, Junnar the capital of, XVIII, pt. ii, 213 and note 8, *id.* pt. iii, 167 ; inscription, of, in Nána pass, *id.* 224 ; *see* also XII, 239 ; XIII, 411 and note 3, 412 ; XIV, 54, 320 ; *see* also XVI, 182 notes 4 and 5, 571, 573, 574, 576, 578, 611, 614-620.
Nahara : estate in Rewá Kántha, VI, 151.
Nahávand : victory of the Arabs over the Persians at (641), IX, pt. ii, 183.
Nahlwára : Anahilaváda, I, pt. i, 508, 509, 510, 511, 517, 518, 531.
Nahrvára, Nahrwálá : Anahilaváda, I, pt. ii, 24 ; the *rai* of Bhimdeva, I, pt. i, 196, 511, 512 ; *see* also IX, pt. ii, 2 note 1.
Nahush : father of Yayati, I, pt. i, 460 ; Gautamiputra compared to, I, pt. ii, 149.
Náiata : a caste in Gujarát, also called Nawafts, shipmen, came to India in the eighth or ninth century from Arabia, their disappearance from Gujarát, their traces in Ghogha lascars found on the coast of Kánara and the Konkan under the name of Naváiatas ; their

origin; claim to have proselytised one of the Zamorins of Malabár, IX, pt. ii, 14 and note 3, 15 and notes 1, 2; *see* also X, 133 and note 1; and XV, pt. i, 400-403, *id.* pt. ii, 1, 266; husbandmen at Sopára, XIV, 315, settlement of, from Arabia and Persia, *id.* 315 note 1.
Náidu: caste of writers in Belgaum, XXI, 98, 99.
Naigamas: Buddhist merchants, I, pt. ii, 173.
Náik: of Sangameshvar dispossessed of lands, I, pt. ii, 40; petty Konkan chiefs, I, pt. ii, 25.
Náik: early tribe, in Gujarát, IX, pt. i, 290, 324, 325; in Thána district, land allotments to, XIII, 568 and note 2; Rághoji Náik (1860), *id.* 605.
Naikan: *see* Kasban.
Náikda: wild tribe, I, pt. i, 115; in revolt under Rupa and Keval Náiks (1858), *id.* 444; joined by Tatya Topi's broken force, *id.* 445; risings of (1858, 1868), in Panch Maháls, III, 254-258; their origin, occupation, character, religion and customs, *id.* 222-225; in Rewa Kántha VI, 34; rising of (1838), *id.* 62, 64; in Gujarát, IX, pt. i, 290; origin, *id.* 325; lawless habits (A. D. 1826), raids, disturbances (A. D. 1838, 1854, 1857, 1868), *id.* 326; customs, *id.* 327-328; four chiefs, *id.* 328.
Náikidevi: wife of Ajayapála and mother of Mularája II, Chaulukya kings, her fight at Gádáráraghatta, I, pt. i, 195.
Náikvádi: a Musalmán class in Khándesh district, XII, 128; in Násik district, XVI, 83; in Ahmadnagar district, XVII, 228.
Nails: in the tower of silence, IX, pt. ii, 240 note 1.
Naimoto: Chinese for Narmadá river, I, pt. ii, 354.
Náin Pal: slew Ajipal, Kanauj monarch (470), I, pt. i, 120.
Nairne: Rev. A. K., historian, "Introduction to the History of the Konkan," I, pt. ii, p. xiii note 2; *see* also XI, 111.
Náis: barbers, at Bhinmál, I, pt. i, 451.
Naita: *see* Naiata.
Naital: village in Násik district, fair at, XVI, 460.
Náiyad: district in Sorath, I, pt. i, 208 and note 3.
Najamkhan: governor of Cambay (1737-1748), plans an attack on Ahmadábád, VI, 223.
Najis: Musalmán spirit, XVIII, pt. i, 553, 554.
Najm-ud-din: head *mulla* of Daudi Bohoras (1785), (1842), IX, pt. ii, 31 note 4.
Náka: Sinda prince of Yelburga, I, pt. ii, 573, 574.
Nakárchin: *see* Nagárji.
Nakari: lands exempted from assessment in Baroda, VII, 349.
Nakel: common date palm, XXV, 181.
Nákhinda: peak in Thána district, XIV, 231.
Nákhoda: *see* Nákhuda.
Nakhonwat: Nága's shrine in Cambodia, begun in A. D. 825 and completed in A. D. 950, I, pt. i, 499, 500, 504 and note 1.
Nákhuda: Musalmán naval captain in service of the ruler of Somnáth, IX, pt. ii, 2 note 3; IX, pt. i, 520; origin of the word, XIII, 716.
Nakib: office in a mendicant brotherhood, IX, pt. ii, 19. *See* Izni.
Nakimayya: the Western Chálukya king Somesvara II's officer, I, pt. ii, 443.
Nakkabbajja: village on the south bank of the Mahi, I, pt. i, 127.
Naklesvara: temple of Siva at Kárván, I, pt. i, 83 note 1.
Nákri Kunbi: caste of husbandmen in Thána district, XIII, 128.
Nakshatras: lunar asterisms, XXIV, 155 note 1.
Nakshband: caste of mark makers in Gujarát, Hindu converts, beggars, followers of Saint Bahanddin Nakshband, their reverence for fire, IX, pt. ii, 20.
Náktodás: damages by, in Poona, XVIII, pt. ii, 499, 511.
Nakulisá: founder of a Jain sect, shrine of, I, pt. i, 83 and note 1.
Nakulisa Pásupata: sect mentioned, in Somanátha inscription, I, pt. i, 205.
Nal: lake in Káthiáwár, VIII, 68; a place of interest, *id.* 559.
Nál: lake in Ahmadábád district, IV, 16.
Nál: state in Khándesh, XII, 610.
Nalas: Konkan dynasty (630), XXIII, 380 and note 1; XIII, 420; I, pt. ii, 13; subjugated by Kirtivarman I, *id.* 181, 345 note 4; of Nalavádi country in the direction of Bellary and Karnul, *id.* 282, 336.
Nálatwád: village in Bijápur district, temples and inscriptions at, XXIII, 665.
Nalavádi: country of the Nalas, I, pt. ii, 282, 363.
Nalband: caste of Musalmán farriers in Gujarat, Hindu converts, IX, pt. ii, 78; in Khándesh district, XII, 126; in Ahmadnagar district, XVII, 228; in Sátára district, XIX, 136; in Belgaum district, XXI, 208; in Bijápur district, XXIII, 291; in Kolhápur state, XXIV, 149.
Naldurg: fort in Thána district, XIV, 286.
Nalia: estate in Rewa Kántha, VI, 145.
Nalia: port in the Gulf of Cambay, VIII, 27.
Nálieri: tree, its nut an emblem of the family goddess; cocoanut also offered to other goddesses, IX, pt. i, 385.
Naliya: place of interest in Cutch, V, 245.
Nalkántha: district, the hollow between Káthiáwár and the mainland, I, pt. i, 208 and note 3; VIII, 4; fen tract in Dholka and Viramgám tálukás, IX, pt. i, 506.
Nálkote: town in Southern India, burnt by Butuga, I, pt. ii, 419 note 7.
Nal Rája: holds a horse sacrifice near Borsad, IX, pt. i, 8 note 1.
Nal Rája: traditional Malanggad king, in Thána, XIV, 220.
Nál Sáheb: Lord Horseshoe, the cast shoe of the horse of the bridegroom-elect of Husain's daughter, believed to possess power to work cures, imitation horse shoes carried by Dulas or bridegrooms in Muharram, IX, pt. ii, 138. *See* Dulas.

Námados: the Narmada, or Narbada, river, I, pt. i, 539.
Námagranth: part of *Surya Purána,* I, pt. i, 464.
Náma Karma: or naming, the seventh Vedic rite, IX, pt. i, 31 note 3, 34-35.
Namak Chashi: ceremony among Musalmáns, IX, pt. ii, 159.
Námalingánusásana: work of Amarasimha, manuscript of, with the date A. D. 1297, I, pt. ii, 530.
Namazgah: *see* Idgahs.
Namburi: sub-caste of Bráhmans of the Malabár Coast, strange marriage practice among, IX, pt. i, 439 note 1; in Kánara, XV, pt. i, 195, 196.
Námdár Radder: cultivating caste in Kánara, I, pt. ii, 414 note 5.
Námdev: *see* Námdev Shimpi.
Námdev: devotee of Vithoba of Pandharpur, XXIV, 98.
Námdev Niléri: caste of indigo dyers in Dhárwár district, XXII, 157-158.
Námdev Shimpi: caste of tailors in Thána district, XIII, 138; in Ahmadnagar district, XVII, 124-127; in Poona, XVIII, pt. i, 369-371; in Dhárwár district, XXII, 159-160.
Names: choice of, among Gujarát Hindus, IX, pt. i, 34 and note 1, 35 note 1; of children born after performing certain rites, *id.* 367-368; peculiarity of, among Gujarát Musalmáns, among Arabs, IX, pt. ii, 16; Dandi Bohoras, *id.* 31 and note 1; Jaafari Bohoras, *id.* 35; village, 59 note 1, 60; Ghánchis, *id.* 73; Kasbátis, *id.* 65; recommended by the prophet, *id.* 156 note 2; among Pársis, selection of, IX, pt. ii, 229; Persian, Hindu; full, *id.* 229 note 1.
Naming: rites and ceremonies of, among Bráhmans, IX, pt. i, 34-35; Rájpúts, *id.* 139-140; other castes, *id.* 110, 158, 190, 248, 289, 308; Musalmáns, IX, pt. ii, 156-157; practice of giving odd names, *id.* 156 note 2; among Chitpávans in Poona, XVIII, pt. i, 114; Pátáne Prabhus, *id.* 223; Agarváls, *id.* 263; Kunbis, *id.* 298-299; Salis, 363; Tambats, *id.* 376; Rámoshis, *id.* 415.
Namnadios: the Narmada, or Narbada river, I, pt. i, 545.
Nána: *largestrœmia parviflora,* timber tree, in Poona district, XVIII, pt. i, 49; in Khándesh, XII, 26; in Kánara district, *see* XV, pt. i, under Forests.
Nana: (Bálájí Peshwa) offers accommodation to the English at Thána (1757), XXVI, pt. i, 316-317; presents an elephant to the Company (1760), *id.* 346
Nánábhai Narsangji Patel: a Surat landlord, IX, pt. ii, 196 note 4.
Nana bondarah: a dye-yielding plant, XXV, 245.
Nána Darbáre: Bráhman leader (1839) of a Koli rising, XVIII, pt. ii, 307.
Nána Fadnavis: Marátha statesman, kárkún (1762) of Mádhavráv Peshwa (1761-1772), XVIII, pt. ii, 251; is appointed (1763) Fadnavis, *id.* 252; opposes (1774) Raghunáthráv, *id.* 257; jealousy among the Poona ministers, *id.* 258; treaty of Purandhar (1776), *id.* 260; his hate of the English, *id.* 261; fresh dissensions among the ministerial party and Náná's triumph (1778), *id.* 262-263; convention of Vadgaon (1778), *id.* 264-266; Nána crushes a conspiracy (1784) for deposing the Peshwa Mádhavráv, *id.* 267; rivalry between Nána and Mahádji Sindia (1794), *id.* 268-269; Nána's triumph over the Nizám at Kharda (1795), *id.* 270; Náná's conduct towards the Peshwa Mádhavráv, *id.* 270-271; Nána's intrigues to prevent the accession of the last Peshwa Bájiráv, *id.* 271; changes sides and quarrels with Parashurám Bháu and is forced to retire to Mahád, *id.* 272; secures the co-operation of the Nizám, *id.* 273; resumes the duties of prime minister to Bájiráv who shortly afterwards enters into a plot to free himself from Náná's control, *id.* 274; Nána's house plundered and himself confined in Ahmadnagar fort, *id.* 275; Nána set free by Sindia (1798), *id.* 277; Nána induced by Bájiráv to take his post as minister, *id.* 278; his death and character, *id.* 280; *another account of:* cousin of Moroba Fadnavis, one of the chief ministers of Mádhavráv I, I, pt. ii, 603; quarrels with Moroba and retires to Purandhar; soon establishes himself with the help of Haripant Phadke and Sindia (1777), *id.* 604; receives St. Lubin (1777), *id.* 102; throws his rival Sakhárám Bápu into prison (1778), *id.* 605; demands the surrender of Raghunáthráo and Sálsette from the English (1779), *id.* 103; his rivalry with Mahádji Sindia; endeavours to persuade Haidar to restore the territory north of the Tungabhadra; intercedes on behalf of the chief of Nargund with Tipu, *id.* 660; his intrigues to prevent the accession of Bájiráo to the office of Peshwa (1795); determines to forestall Bálobá Tátya, one of Sindia's chief advisers, and himself to seat Bájiráo on the throne; Sindia marches to Poona and Nána retires into the Konkan; wins over Daulatráo Sindia through Sakhárám Ghátge Shirzi Ráo; declares for Bájiráo and becomes his chief minister (1796), *id.* 110, 606; is treacherously arrested by Sindia and confined in the fort of Ahmadnagar (1797), *id.* 606-607, 628; released by Daulatráo Sindia on payment of a large ransom (1798); again becomes Bájiráo's minister, *id.* 607, 628; his breach with the Patvardhan family; incites the *rája* of Kolhápur to attack their possessions; his reconciliation with Parsharám Bháu, *id.* 662; his death (1800), *id.* 607; *see* also XVIII, pt. iii, 8, 231, 253, 275, 333, 409-413; XI, 448, 467; XVII, 407; XXII, 414; XXIV, 345, 346; VII, 196, 199, 201; XIII, 14, 504, 506, 507, 512, 556, 559, 560, 561; XIV, 121, 201, 286; XIX, 298-299; X, 321; I, pt. i, 401, 411.
Nánághát: origin of the name, XIV, 287; pass between Thána and Poona districts, XIII, 316, 321, 403; XVIII, pt. ii, 150-151; old trade route (B. C. 100-A. D. 100), *id.* 211;

I, pt. ii, 29; large cave at, *id.* 144; inscription in a cave at, gives the names of certain members of Sátaváhana royal family, *id.* 147; inscriptions, *id.* 152, 156; XVIII, pt. ii, 212; *see* also XIV, 14, 113, 286-291, 320; I, pt. i, 38; statues in, XVI, 611; XVIII, pt. iii, 218-224.
Nanagol: village in Thána district XIV, 320.
Nanagouna: supposed to be the Kálinadi, I, pt. i, 542.
Nanaguna: river mentioned by Ptolemy, probable identification of, with the Sávitri in Ratnágiri district, X, 320 note 2; *see* also XIV, 291.
Nanaguna: Ptolemy's (A. D. 150) name of the Nána pass, XVIII, pt. ii, 213 note 10; XVIII, pt. iii, 224.
Nának: religious hero of the Sikhs, IX, pt. i, 336, 453.
Nána Khánvelkar: *diwán* of Baroda, VII, 280.
Nának Putras: the Sikhs, pass as Bráhmans, IX, pt. i, 438.
Nanamgola: village, referred to in an inscription at Násik, I, pt. ii, 148.
Nána Pass: *see* Nánághát.
Nána Phadnavis: *see* Nána Fadnavis.
Nána Sáheb: son of Bájiráv II Peshwa, I, pt. ii, 130; Vengaon the birth-place of (1857), XIV, 379.
Nána's Peth: ward in Poona city, XVIII, pt. iii, 274-276.
Nand: island in Rewa Kántha, VI, 6.
Nanda: king, builder of Nandagiri fort, I, pt. ii, 340 note 4.
Nandagiri: modern Nandidurg near Kolár, hill fort, I, pt. ii, 300, 340 note 4; mountain, *id.* 303 and note 3.
Nandagirinátha: hereditary title of the Western Gangas, I, pt. ii, 300.
Nandapadra: identification of, with Nándod, I, pt. ii, 314.
Nandarája: Ráshtrakúta king, I, pt. ii, 377 note 3; grant of, *id.* 384.
Nandarva: sub-division of Rewa Kántha, VI, 124.
Nandas: dynásty, I, pt. ii, 140; kings of the Kuntala country, *id.* 284 note 2.
Nánder: town in Nizám's dominions, battle of (1599), XVII, 390.
Nandgad: place of interest in Belgaum district, XXI, 590; trade centre, *id.* 313.
Nándgaon: sub-division of Násik district, its area, aspect, climate, water, history, land revenue, stock, holdings, crops and people, XVI, 349-353. *Town, id.* 460-461; I, pt. ii, 355.
Nandgiri; hill fort in Sátára district, XIX, 10, 527-528.
Nandi: bull, badge of the religion of Valabha dynasty, I, pt. i, 80; S'iva's, adoration of, I, pt. ii, 477, 478.
Nandi: village in Mysore, inscription at, I, pt. ii, 332.
Nandi: Hindu sage, Nandvánás claim descent from, IX, pt. i, 15.
Nandigráma: village, I, pt. ii, 348.
Nandikeshvar: Mahádev, of Nándod, IX, pt. i, 73.
Nandikeshvar: group of villages in Bijápur district, pond, temples and inscriptions at, XXIII, 665-666.
Nandin: S'iva's bull, I, pt. ii, 226.
Nandin: I, pt. ii, 325. *See* Pallava king Nandivarman the son of Hiranyavarman.
Nandipotarája: I, pt. ii, 325. *See* Nandivarman the son of Hiranyavarman.
Nandipotavarman: I, pt. ii, 189, 374. *See* Nandivarman the son of Hiranyavarman.
Nandipottaraiya: I, pt. ii, 331. *See* Nandivarman the son of Hiranyavarman.
Nandipura: town, Nandivarman besieged at, I, pt. ii, 326.
Nándipuri: modern Nándod, I, pt. i, 4, 85; capital of Gurjjara dynasty of Broach district, *id.* 107; palace of Gurjjara kings, *id.* 111; capital of the Gurjjars, *id.* 113; *see* also I, pt. ii, 314.
Nandisvámin: Bráhman grantee of Chálukya prince, I, pt. ii, 191.
Nandiváli: caste of beggars in Násik district, XVI, 75.
Nandivalli: village in the Panumgal district, I, pt. ii, 377.
Nandivarman: Pallava king (733-747), son of Hiranyavarman, I, pt. ii, 323; his ancestry, *birudas* or titles, *id.* 325 and notes 1 and 2; chosen by the subjects, is besieged in Nandipura by the Dramila princes and rescued by Udayachandra, *id.* 326; put to flight by Vikramáditya II, *id.* 327, 374; his Udayendiram grant, *id.* 319 note 2, 320 note 6, 327; his records at Conjeeveram, *id.* 331.
Nandivarman: Pallava king, son of Skandavarman III; his Kañchipura grant, I, pt. ii, 319 note 2, 320 note 6, 327.
Nandivarman: Pallava king, son of Simhavishnu, I, pt. ii, 331.
Nandivelo: hill in Káthiáwár, VIII, 12.
Nandivraksha: *see* Pálaspiplo.
Nándni: see of the Jain head priest near Kolhápur, XXIV, 136.
Nando: Songhad Rájpút, founder of Patani branch of Parajia Sonis, IX, pt. i, 198.
Nándod: sub-division and place of interest in Rewa Kántha, VI, 97, 165; capital of the Gurjjara dynasty of Broach district, I, pt. i, 107, 108; capital of Rájpipla, *id.* 113. *See* also I, pt. ii, 314; IX, pt. i, p. xii, 13, 72.
Nandoda: a Bráhman sub-division in Rewa Kántha, VI, 23.
Nandol: in Márwár; its chief slain by Lavanaprasáda, I, pt. i, 198.
Nandor: *see* Nándod.
Nandora: caste of Bráhmans and Vanias in Gujarát, IX, pt. i, 13, 72.
Nándos: fort in Ratnágiri district, X, 353.
Nándra: village in Kolhápur, XXIV, 363.
Nándre: village in Khándesh, Hemádpanti well at, XII, 457.
Nandshanker: Mr., on Bhil sub-divisions, IX, pt. i, 295 note 2; on Badva's services during epidemics in Rewa Kántha, *id.* 302 note 1; on Naikda origin, *id.* 325 note 1.

Nándur: village in Násik district, temple at, XVI, 461.
Nandurbár: sub-division of Khándesh, its boundaries, area, aspect, climate, water, soil, holding, survey details, survey results, stock, crops and people, XII, 2, 379-386. *Town, id.* 457-459, 9, 248, 255; English factory (1670) at, I, pt. ii, 625.
Nandvádige: village in Bijápur district, well, temples and inscriptions at, XXIII, 666; *see also* I, pt. ii, 412.
Nandvána: a Bráhman sub-division in Cutch, V, 47; in Gujarát, IX, pt. i, 15.
Náne: market village in Poona district, XVIII, pt. iii, 260.
Nangali: *ghát* in Mysore, I, pt. ii, 299; fortress at, *id.* 496, 499, 501, 505.
Nángám: state in Rewá Kánthá, VI, 144.
Nángarbandi: form of tenure in Thána district, XIII, 531 and notes 2 and 3, 551 note 2, 565; mode of assessment (1845), *id.* 587; (1865), *id.* 617 and note 1.
Náni: river in Ahmadnagar district, XVII, 8.
Nanna: Ratta chieftain, I, pt. ii, 551, 552 and note 8.
Nanniya-Ganga: *biruda* (title) of Satyavakya-Kongunivarma-Permanadi-Butuga, I, pt. ii, 304.
Nannu Mian: name of a vow-receiving *ginn* or spirit, IX, pt. ii, 130.
Nánoli: village in Poona district, caves at, XVIII, pt. iii, 260.
Nánpura: a Surat city ward, named after a Pársi, IX, pt. ii, 196 note 4.
Nánsi: pass in Násik district, XVI, 128.
Naoroz: New Year's day; commonly called *Pátiti*, observances on, IX, pt. ii, 218, 219.
Náos: *see* Boat Offerings.
Naoura: mentioned by Ptolemy, I, pt. i, 546; identification of, with Honávar, XV, pt. ii, 48, 78, 307, 336.
Nápád: village in Kaira district, III, 177; IX, pt. i, 16.
Naphatki: a famine plant, XXV, 197.
Napier Hotel: in Poona cantonment, XVIII, pt. iii, 385.
Nár: stream in Násik district, XVI, 7.
Nárada, Náradji: leader of S'iva's *ganas* or attendants, I, pt. ii, 482; divine sage, I, pt. i, 461.
Náral: *see* Nárel.
Naréna: near Jaipur, ancient capital of Gujarát, I, pt. i, 507, 520. *See* Náráyan.
Nárána: son of the Kalachuri king Kannama, I, pt. ii, 468.
Náranapura: in the Ándhra country, birthplace of Pallava, minister of the Hoysála Vira-Ballála, I, pt. ii, 507.
Nar and Náráyan: names of the god Vishnu, IX, pt. i, 532.
Náransar: Koli place of pilgrimage in Sind, IX, pt. i, 247.
Narasimha: Karnátak king, I, pt. i, 469.
Narasimha: Chálukya prince, I, pt. ii, 212, 380.
Narasimha: Hoysála Yádava king, killed by Bhillama, I, pt. ii, 238.
Narasimha: Pallava king, I, pt. ii, 329 note 5, 331. *See* Narasimhavarman I.
Nárasimha: feudatory of the Chola king, overthrown by Vishnuvardhana, I, pt. ii, 495, 498.
Narasimha: Hindu god, temple of, at Muttagi, inscription at, I, pt. ii, 518 note 2.
Nárasimha: I, pt. ii, 509. *See* Narasimha I, Narasimha II and Narasimha III.
Narasimha I: Hoysála king, son of Vishnuvardhana (1159-1169), I, pt. ii, 493, 499; various forms of his name, his *birudas* (titles) and date, *id.* 500, 501, 505.
Narasimha II: Hoysála king (1224-1234), I, pt. ii, 428 note 4, 491, 493; succeeds his father Vira-Ballála II, *id.* 502, 506; maintains his independent position but loses some territory, *id.* 506; records of his reign, his titles, *id.* 504, 507, 508.
Narasimha III: Hoysála Ballála king of Dvárasamudra (A. D. 1254), I, pt. i, 203 note 3; I, pt. ii, 428 note 4, 508, 509. *See* Vira-Narasimha III.
Narasimha-Bhadradeva: son of Arikesarin I, I, pt. ii, 380. *See* Narasimha the Chálukya prince.
Narasimhagupta: Gupta chief, I, pt. i, 74, 77.
Narasimhapotarája: Pallava king, I, pt. ii, 322 note 7.
Narasimhapotavarman: I, pt. ii, 330. *See* Narasimhavarman II.
Narasimhavarman: *see* Narasimha, the Chola feudatory.
Narasimhavarman I: Pallava king, defeats the Cholas, Keralas, Kalabhras, and Pándyas, and captures and destroys Vátápi I, pt. ii, 322 and note 7; defeats Pulikesin II and conquers Ceylon, *id.* 324, 326, 328, 329 and note 4, 358, 362; variant of his name, *id.* 330.
Narasimhavarman II: son of the Pallava king Parameśvaravarman I, I, pt. ii, 324, 326, 329; founder of the temple of Rájasimheśvara, *id.* 330, 375; his other names, *id.* 330. *See* Rájasimha.
Narasimha-Vishnu: Pallava king Narasimhavarman I, I, pt. ii, 329, 330.
Nárasinga: I, pt. ii, 509. *See* Vira-Narasimha III.
Narasingapottaraiya: *see* Narasimhapotarája.
Naravarman: king of Málwa, at war with Siddharája, I, pt. i, 177; his inscription, *id.* 173, 180.
Naráyan: Bania or Bazána in Jaipur territory, battle of (1192), I, pt. i, 195 note 4; ancient capital of Gujarát, *id.* 527.
Náráyana: Hindu god, gives a standard to the Chálukyas, I, pt. ii, 180; inscription at the temple of, at Ingaleshwar, *id.* 455 note 5, 470 note 2; Hoysála Vira-Ballála acquires sovereignty by the favour of, *id.* 491, 503; the god Vishnu, *id.* 517; stone inscription at the temple of, at Sankeshwar, *id.* 556 note 6.
Náráyana: minister of war and peace; writer of Karka's Surat grant, I, pt. i, 125; writer of Dhruva's Baroda grant, *id.* 126, 511 note 12, 520.

Narayan Bali: memorial service performed to get rid of barrenness in Gujarát, IX, pt. i, 369; among high class Hindus in Sholápur, XX, 522-523.

Náráyangad: hill fort in Poona district, XVIII, pt. i, 5.

Náráyangaon: town in Poona district, details of fort at, XVIII, pt. iii, 260-261.

Naráyan Peth: ward in Poona city, XVIII, pt. iii, 274, 280.

Náráyan Povar; supposed incarnation of the god Náráyan (1830), XIX, 543.

Naráyanpur: place of interest in Khándesh district, XII, 459.

Náráyanráv: fifth Peshwa (1772-1773); succeeds his brother Mádhavráv; changes in the ministry; the Peshwa murdered; perpetrators of the crime, XVIII, pt. ii, 255-256; *see* also I, pt. ii, 604; XVIII, pt. iii, 407-408, XIX, 297-298; I, pt. i, 401; and VII, 191.

Naráyanráv: chief of Mudhol state (1805-1816), XXIV, 394.

Náráyansar: place of interest in Cutch, V, 245-248.

Narbáda: river in Gujarát, its source, course, tributaries, islands, tidal section, and other details, II, 340-348; VI, 4; VII, 14; XII, 9; also known as Reva and Revaji, IX, pt. i, 213; its sacredness, *id.* 549; I, pt. i, 84; its lower valley occupied by wild tribes, *id.* 114; crossed by the Maráthás for the first time (1675), *id.* 198, 387, 444; estuary of, *id.* 513; southern boundary of Mularája's kingdom, I, pt. ii, 23; I, pt. ii, 133, 134; Pulingas living along, *id.* 138; Mahishmati on the banks of, *id.* 140, 183; the northern boundary of the Ráshtrakúta kingdom under Govind III, *id.* 199, 240, 277, 310, 311, 314; boundary line between Northern India and the Dakhan, *id.* 341 and note 2; boundary line of the Maháráshtra proper, *id.* 355 note 3; 359 note 5, 377 note 3; Ráshtrakúta frontier, *id.* 382, 383, 404, 405, 412; Vikrámaditya VI crosses the, *id.* 452; Rámadeva, the Devagiri Yádava general, slain on the banks of the, *id.* 525; crossed by Allá-ud-din, *id.* 530.

Narbherám: Gáikwár's deputy, I, pt. i, 345.

Nardava: hill pass between Ratnágiri district and Kolápur state, X, 166; XXIV, 173, 174.

Nareæ: tribe mentioned by Pliny, I, pt. i, 534.

Naregal: village in Dhárwár district, temples, inscriptions and reservoir at, XXII, 774; *see* also I, pt. ii, 446 note 7, 448 notes 1 and 4, 450 note 4, 457 note 1, 529.

Naregal: town in Dhárwár district, population of, temples and inscriptions at, XXII, 390, 774-775; *see* also I, pt. ii, 376, 438 note 6, 503, 573, 575 note 3.

Narel: cocoa palm, food, liquor and oil-yielding plant, XXV, 180, 212, 221.

Narendra: village in Dhárwár district, XXII, 417, 476; inscription at, I, pt. ii, 568 notes 7 and 8; Peshwa's troops cantoned at (1766), *id.* 659.

Nareyamgal: identified with Naregal, village in the Ron táluka of the Dhárwár district, I, pt. ii, 376, 441 note 6; *agrahára* of, *id.* 458; ruled over by the Sindas of Yelburga, *id.* 572, 575.

Nareyamgal-Abbegere: chief town of the Nareyamgal province, I, pt. ii, 574.

Nárgol: sea-port in Thána district, XIV, 291; sugarcane cultivation at, XIII, 510; *see* also I, pt. ii, 8.

Nargund: town in Dhárwár district, its population, fort, temples and history, XXII, 776-780; survey of, *id.* 529-530; trade centre, *id.* 357; inscription at, *id.* 457; acknowledges the supremacy of Haidar, *id.* 659; siege of (1785), XXII, 414; ceded to the Maráthás by Tipu (1787), *id.* 661; forfeiture (1857) of the state, *id.* 668; XXII, 434-438; XX, 412.

Nargund: hill in Dhárwár district, XXII, 5.

Náring: orange tree, in Poona district, XVIII, pt. i, 49.

Nárli-Pornima: Hindu holiday, as observed among Prabhus in Poona, XVIII, pt. i, 245.

Narmada: *see* Narbada.

Narmadá-Tata-Desa: country on either side of the river Narmadá, I, pt. ii, 134.

Narmaza: the Narbada, valley of, I, pt. i, 510 and note 3.

Nármukhsarovar: *see* Nimbáli.

Náruba Takti: of Karrambha, butchers about 15,000 Bhils in the Gangthari under the orders of Trimbakji Denglia (1806), I, pt. ii, 630.

Naroda: a tribe of Rájpúts in Káthiáwar, VIII, 115; in Pálanpur state, V, 289.

Naro Mahádev: founder of the Ichalkaranji state, XXIV, 238 note 1.

Náro Pandit: deputy of Sadáshiv Rámchandra in Ahmadábád, I, pt. i, 342.

Náropant Chakradev: Poona courtier, restored to liberty (1797), XVIII, pt. ii, 276.

Náro Shankar: Rája Bahádur, builds the Nirmal temple, I, pt. ii, 28; builds the fort of Málegaon, *id.* 631; XVI, 451; active assailant at the siege of Ahmadábád, *id.* 451 note 1.

Narotamdás: Raghoba's agent for negotiating the terms of the treaty of Surat, I, pt. i, 402.

Narpatgir: temple in Poona city, XVIII, pt. iii, 337.

Narsápur: village in Dhárwár district, temple at, XXII, 780.

Narsinga I: seventh Vijayanagar king (1479-1487) in Kánara, XV, pt. ii, 96 note 4; his origin, founder of Seringapatam in Mysore, *id.* 100.

Narsinga II: eighth Vijayanagar king (1487-1508), XV, pt. ii, 96 note 4; Portuguese encroaching upon his territory, *id.* 100-104; sends an ambassador to the Portuguese viceroy, *id.* 271.

Narsing Khanderáv: chief of Vinchur (1801), XVIII, pt. ii, 281.

Narsingpur: village in Poona district, temples and fair at, XVIII, pt. iii, 261.

Narsinh: rising of in Bijápur district (1840), XXIII, 452.

Narsinhgad: island in Kánara district, XV, pt. i, 2.

Narsinh Mehta: Nágar Bráhman saint of Junagad, IX, pt. i, 93 note 1.

Narsipur : town in Pálanpur state, IX, pt. i, 73, 96.
Narsipurá : caste of Vanias, Meshris, IX, pt. i, 73 ; and Shravaks, *id.* 96.
Narsoba : Poona city temple, XVIII, pt. iii, 337 ; temple of, in Bijápur city, XXIII, 636-637.
Narsoba's Vádi : place of pilgrimage, cattle fair at, XXIV, 25.
Narsopant : native agent at Baroda (1843), in collusion with Bába Náphade, efforts to get rid of, VII, 267-269 ; the chief cause of Colonel Outram's removal, *id.* 272 note 2.
Narukot : state in Rewa Kántha, its boundaries, agriculture, trade, history, land administration, justice, police, jail, revenue and finance, instruction, health, places of interest, VI, 171-178 ; Naikda Bhils in revolt in (1858), I, pt. i, 444, 445.
Narushankar : *see* Naro Shankar.
Narva : land tenure in Baroda, account of, VII, 357-359 ; in Káira, III, 88, 105, 111 ; IX, pt. i, 166.
Narvala : *Cratæva religiosa*, sacred plant, XXV, 290.
Nárvekar : caste of traders in Belgaum district, XXI, 105 ; in Dhárwár district, XXII, 125, in Kánara district, XV, pt. i, 183, 184.
Nášakakalpa : work of Jinaprabhusuri, I, pt. ii, 512.
Násardi : river in Násik district, XVI, 8 ; proposed dam of, *id.* 501.
Nasarpur : town in Sind, I, pt. i, 517.
Nasesálárs : bier-bearers among Pársis, dress of, duties of, sources of income of, IX, pt. ii, 239 and note 2.
Násibis : enemies of Ali ; contemptuous term for Sunnis, IX, pt. ii, 38, 47 note 3.
Násik : district, its boundaries, area, sub-divisions, aspect, mountains, rivers, geology, climate, XVI, 1-15 ; minerals, trees, forests, domestic and wild animals, birds and fish, *id.* 16-25 ; population, *id.* 26-89 ; history and census details, *id.* 26-36 ; Bráhmans, *id.* 36-43 ; traders, *id.* 43-46 ; husbandmen, craftsmen and manufacturers, *id.* 46-54 ; bards and actors, servants, labourers, *id.* 54-60 ; unsettled tribes, *id.* 60-67 ; depressed classes, *id.* 67-72 ; beggars, *id.* 72-75 ; Musalmáns, *id.* 75-85 ; Pársis, Christians, Jews, village communities, movements, *id.* 85-89 ; agriculture, husbandmen, holdings, crops, soil, field tools, irrigation, manure, fallows, crops and famines, *id.* 89-113 ; capital, *id.* 114-124 ; capitalists, investments, bankers, *id.* 114-115 ; currency, moneylenders, interest, account books, grain advances, land mortgages, etc., *id.* 115-124 ; trade, *id.* 125-180 ; early routes, roads, passes, and railways, *id.* 125-133 ; bridges, ferries, post offices and telegraph, *id.* 133-136 ; railway and road traffic, trade system, markets and fairs, *id.* 136-140 ; crafts, *id.* 140-180 ; history (B. C. 200-1859), *id.* 181-204 ; land administration, *id.* 205-303 ; acquisition, administrative staff, *id.* 205-207 ; history, *id.* 207-211 ; under the British (1818-1840), land revenue (1818-1840), *id.* 211-216 ; survey (1840-1870), *id.* 216-256 ; revision survey (1870-1880), *id.* 256-290 ; survey results, season reports (1850-1882), land revenue (1850-1882), *id.* 290-303 ; justice, under the Marátbás (1760-1818), under the British (1818-1883), civil courts, registration, magistracy, criminal classes, police and crimes, *id.* 304-320 ; revenue and finance, land and other revenue, excise, assessed taxes, balance sheets (1870-1871 and 1881-1882), *id.* 321-325 ; local funds and municipal revenue, *id.* 326-328 ; instruction : schools, school returns, town and village schools, newspapers, libraries and societies, *id.* 329-336 ; health : climate, diseases, hospitals, vacciuation, births and deaths, *id.* 337-344 ; sub-divisional details, *id.* 345-413 ; places of interest, *id.* 414-663. *Sub-division,* its area, aspect, climate, water, history, land revenue (1842-1878), stock, holdings, crops and people, *id.* 374-381, survey and revision survey (1844-45, 1874), *id.* 223-226, 270-274. *Town,* description, view, climate, hills, natural drainage, *id.* 461-467 ; divisions, sub-divisions, suburbs, *id.* 468-473 ; population, daily life, livings, details, *id.* 473-491 ; houses, wood-carving Hingne's mansion, *id.* 492-496 ; roads, gates, trade, markets, shops, *id.* 496-499 ; management, municipality, night-soil depôt, water-supply, drainage, *id.* 500-502 ; temples, introductory details, *id.* 503-521 ; bathing places, holy pools, *id.* 522-526 ; pilgrims, ceremonies, ascetics, *id.* 527-531 ; Musalmán remains, other objects of interest, history, *id.* 532-537 ; neighbourhood, Dasra pavement, Tapovan, Govardhan-Gangapur, waterfall, old burial mound, Someshvar's temple, *id.* 537-541 ; Pandu Lena Caves, *id.* 541-639 ; Northern Chálukya capital, I, pt. i, 112 ; ancient Panchavati, I, pt. ii, 136, 140 ; inscription in the caves at, *id.* 147, 279 note 1 ; Ushavadátá's principal inscription at, *id.* 148, 173, 176 ; inscriptions of Gotamiputra Sátakarni and Pulumáyi at, *id.* 149, 152, 157, 159, 166, 175, 177 ; district about, under Jayasimha, *id.* 185 ; grant at, *id.* 192 ; district, *id.* 298 note 2 ; records at, *id.* 317, 355, 374, 385, 396, 398, 430, 431 note 2, 437, 512, 513, 514, 515 ; plundered by Amritráo (1802), *id.* 608, 609 ; Ráma at, Buddhism at, XVI, 181 ; Nakansk of, XIV, 166 ; caves at, similar to those at Ambivli, *id.* 9 ; cattle from, *id.* 19 ; inscription of Nargol in the cave of, *id.* 291 ; caves at, *id.* 53, 54, 320, 340 ; XIII, 409 note 1, 411 note 3, 412, 413, 414, 415, 464 ; mentioned by Kátyáyana, I, pt. ii, 140.
Nasik-Trimbak : place of pilgrimage, IX, pt. i, 12 note 1, 119, 549.
Násikya : *see* Násik, I, pt. ii, 140.
Nasirábád : sub-division of Khándesh, its boundaries, area, aspect, climate, water, soil, holdings, survey details, survey results, stock, crops and people, XII, 2, 386-392. *Town,* *id.* 459.
Násir-ud-din : Abdul Kádir, son and successor of Ghias-ud-din Khilji (1502-1512), poisons his father, becomes *sultán,* subjects his mother Khurshid to indignities and torture, I, pt. i, 365. *See* Abdul Kádir.

Nasir-ud-din Kabáchah: *sultán* (1246-1266), deputes his general to attack Nahrwála, I, pt. i, 512, 519.

Nasmyth: Captain D., destroys the fort of Bet in Káthiáwár (1859), I, pt. i, 447.

Nasrápur: old sub-division of Thána district, surveyed (1785-1786), XIII, 558, 560 and note 3; condition (1835), *id.* 578; assessment revised (1836), *id.* 579-581; results, *id.* 584-585; survey begun (1852), *id.* 590-591; survey assessment introduced (1856), *id.* 594-596.

Nasrat Khán: companion of Alaf Khán in the Gujarát expedition, I, pt. i, 205; plunders Cambay, *id.* 515.

Nasratpur: place of interest in Khándesh district, XII, 460.

Nasvádi: state in Rewa Kántha VI, 146.

Nat: caste of tumblers in Gujarát, wandering tribe of Hindu converts from the tribe of the same name, performers of acrobatic feats, peculiar names of their women who take part in the performances, IX, pt. ii, 88-89; in Káthiáwár, VIII, 159.

Natatores: family of birds in Ratnágiri, X, 96-99; in Thána district, XIII, 53.

Natchni: a famine plant, XXV, 208.

Náteputa: town in Sholápur district, temples and ponds at, XX, 414-415; survey of, *id.* 331-334.

Náth: caste of beggars in Khándesh district, XII, 123.

Náthdvar: place of pilgrimage, IX, pt. i, 119, 549; chief shrine of Vallabhacharya at, *id.* 536; shrine of Shrináthji at, *id.* 549.

Native Christians: in Kánara district, XV, pt. i, 380-396; in Thána district, XIII, 379.

Native Physicians: in Poona district, XVIII, pt. iii, 69-71, 288-289; in Násik district, XVI, 340.

Natives: of Bombay not allowed the use of carts and chairs (1784), XXVI, pt. ii, 6-8.

Natural Salts: in Poona district, XVIII, pt. i, 13, 30.

Naulakheshwar: shrine of, at Bhinmál, I, pt. i, 452.

Nauraspur: suburb of Bijápur, XXIII, 579, 586, 667; capital removed (1600) to, *id.* 423.

Nauras Tára: name given (1700) to Parli fort in Sátára district, XIX, 251, 538.

Náusári: *see* Navsári.

Naushahro: town in Sind, I, pt. i, 538.

Naushervan, Naushirvan: Persian king (531-579), I, pt. ii, 14; called the just, his treaties and interchange of presents with the rulers of India and Sind; his embassy to Pulikesi II, IX, pt. ii, 183 note 4; *see* also XIII, 421.

Navaghani: *see* Noghan.

Naváiat, Naváyat: *see* Naiata.

Navaiyat: *see* Naiata.

Navakhandaprithivi: earth composed of nine parts, I, pt. ii, 403 note 3.

Navalgund: hill in Dhárwár district, XXII, 4. *Sub-division*, its boundaries, area, aspect, soil, hills, climate, water, stock, crops and people, *id.* 642-644, survey of, *id.* 490-492, 531-532; *see* also I, pt. ii, 406 note 4, 497, 503. *Town*, its history, XXII, 405, 429, 780-782; seat of the Bahmani province (1454), I, pt. ii, 638; siege of, raised by Colonel J. Munro (1817), *id.* 664.

Navalpur: state in Khándesh, XII, 611.

Navánagar: state in Káthiáwár, its description, soil, pearl fisheries, ports, money-lenders and history, VIII, 560-569; IX, pt. i, 126. *Town*, VIII, 569; I, pt. i, 226; founded by Jám Rával (1548), V, 136; VIII, 112; revolt of the Jám crushed by Ázam Khán, viceroy (1640), *id.* 279; chiefship of, usurped by Raisingji, captured and annexed and the name changed into Islámnagar by Kutb-ud-din (1664), *id.* 283; restored to Tamáchi, son of Raisingji; the city remains in the hands of the Mughals till 1707, *id.* 285; quarrels of the *jám* of, with the *ráo* of Cutch, ejects Baroda agents (1807); British arbitration, *id.* 425; *jám's* death, *id.* 427. Jám Jesáji of, in trouble with the British, Kánhoji expels Arabs from, VII, 217; attacked by Fate Muhammad (1808), *id.* 324; Colonel Smith halts on its frontier, *id.* 326; former seat of the head *mulla* of Daudi Bohoras, IX, pt. ii, 31 note 4.

Navánagar: old name of Kalyán, in Thána district, XIV, 114.

Navápur: forest in Khándesh, XII, 21. *Town*, *id.* 460; in British possession (1818), XII, 256.

Navápur: sea-port in Thána district, XIV, 291.

Navar: new comrade; under-priest; the purifying ceremony of; also called novice, ordination of, IX, pt. ii, 223-225.

Navaritte: traveller (1670), his description of Dábhol, X, 330.

Navasári: *see* Navsári.

Nava-Siddhas: shrine of, at Kukkanur, inscription at, I, pt. ii, 456 note 2.

Navibandar: port in Káthiáwár, VIII, 241, place of interest, *id.* 579.

Navigation: in Surat, II, 12, 26, 27; early, in Thána district, XIII, 403 note 1, 711 note 2.

Navil Tirth: or peacock's pool, in Belgaum district, XXI, 12 and foot-note 2. *See* Sogal.

Navilugunda: province ruled by Barma (1187), I, pt. ii. 465.

Navkird: fresh tillage, a tenure in Thána district, XIII, 544 note 2.

Navlákh Umbre: village in Poona district, Hindu and Musalmán remains in, legend of, XVIII, pt. iii, 261-262.

Navli: village in Thána district, XIV, 292.

Navli: village in Dhárwár district, XXII, 782.

Navraspur: town in Bijápur district, XXIII, 567; Ibráhim removes his capital (1602) to, *id.* 423, 579; Mughal army under Ázaf Khán at (1631), *id.* 586.

Navratra: ten days of Ashvin, IX, pt. i, 23 note 5; Hindu holiday, XVIII, pt. i, 249-250.

Navsári: division of Baroda state, VII, 2-10; agriculture in, *id.* 77-82; roads, *id.* 143; trade, *id.* 149-151; capital, *id.* 106-121; health, *id.* 495-496. *Sub-division*, *id.* 560-562; schools in, *id.* 475, 479; 487; hospitals, *id.* 505-506. *Town*, *id.* 562-569; library at, *id.* 493; capital of the Gujarát branch of the Chálukyas of Bádámi, invasion of, by the Tájikas, repulsed by Avanijanásraya Puli-

kesin, *id.* 187-188, 316, 375, 376; copper-plate grants from, of Sryásraya Siláditya, *id.* 187, 360 note 3, 364; of Avanijanásraya Pulikesin, *id.* 316, 336 note 3, 375, 376; of the Ráshtrakútas, *id.* 197, 199, 201, 202, 203, 383, 405, 415, 416; granted to Rámachandra of Devagiri by the Delhi emperor, *id.* 532; inscription of Siláditya at, capital of Jayasimhavarmman, I, pt. i, 107; copper plate of Jayabhata at, *id.* 108; capital of Pulakesi; destruction of the Chálukya kingdom of, *id.* 110; the great Arab invasion, repulsed by Pulakesi Janasraya at, *id.* 117; graut of, Karka I at, *id.* 124, 125; copper-plate grants found at, *id.* 128; Indra's copper-plates at, *id.* 128, 130; grant of Chálukya king Pulakeśi Janásraya at, *id.* 149, 468; meaning of the name of, settlement of Pársis in, IX, pt. ii, 186 note 6; fire-temple built by Chauga A'sa in, Sanján fire brought to, *id.* 188; religious disputes among the priests of, *id.* 192; Tátá Madresa in, *id.* 204; Zend and Pehelvi scholarship established in, *id.* 194; centre of Gujarát under Devagiri kings (1309), XIII, 438; under Musalmán control, *id.* 441; manufacture, *id.* 486.

Navy: Portuguese, XIII, 458; Shiváji's, XVIII, pt. ii, 229, 231.

Navzot: initiation of a child into the mysteries of the Zoroastrian faith; ceremony and rites relating to, IX, pt. ii, 231-232.

Nawábs: of Sachin, creation of (1784), I, pt. ii, 107; of Surat and Broach, I, pt. i, 214; of Surat (1733-1746), II, 116; (1746-1759), *id.* 122; (1759-1800), *id.* 129; (1800-1876), *id.* 154; of Broach, *id.* 469-472; of Cambay (1730-1880), VI, 221-233; of Sávanur, their ancestor takes service in Bijápur and after the fall of Bijápur enters the service of the Mughals and obtains an assignment of twenty-two *máháls*, I, pt. ii, 665; *see* also XXII, 792-804.

Nawáit: *see* Náiata.

Nawalgund: *see* Navalgund.

Nawmasa: ninth-month celebration or first pregnancy rites, IX, pt. ii, 149.

Naw Shahid: nine martyrs, the shrine of, at Surat, IX, pt. ii, 129.

Náyakvádi: village servants (1828) in Thána district, XIII, 574.

Náyaladevi: daughter of Gogi, married to Vesuga the Yádava king, I, pt. ii, 233, 514.

Náyaniká: Sátavábana's queen, mentioned in an inscription, I, pt. ii, 147; statue of, at Nánághát, XIV, 288.

Náyarkhanda: Prákrit name of Nágarakhanda, I, pt. ii, 281 note 3, 292, 369.

Nayarum: part of the *Zend Avesta*, IX, pt. ii, 211 note 2 (16).

Náydongri: railway station in Násik district, XVI, 638.

Náyer: warlike class in Kánara district, XV, pt. i, 194-197.

Náyiladevi: *see* Náyaladevi.

Náyimma, Nayivarman: Kolhápur or Karhád Siláhára prince, I, pt. ii, 254, 545.

Nazar: son of Khalifah Almustansir-billáh, supporters to his claims to the succession are called Nazarians after him, IX, pt. ii, 30 note 1, 37.

Nazar Ali Khán: governor of Baroda, retakes the fort of Broach from the Matiás and Momnás (1691), I, pt. i, 288.

Nazar Ali Khán: nephew of Momin Khán, viceroy of Gujarát (1738-1743), I, pt. i, 325.

Nazarian: division of the great Ismáili sect of Shiáhs called after Nazar, son of Almustansir-billáh, *khalifah* of Egypt (1036-1095), IX, pt. ii, 30 note 1; Nazár's cause is espoused in Persia by Hassan Sabáh, missionary and political emissary of the Fatemite *khalifah* of Egypt (1094); becomes powerful in Persia, *id.* 37; change in the doctrines of (1163), *id.* 37, 48; transfer of the imámate from the Fatimites to Hasan Ala Zikri-his-salam, the fourth successor of Hasan Sabáh, *id.* 48; Alp-Zikri-his-salam believed to have sent the first Nazarian missionary to India, *id.* 38; sect represented in India by the Khojáhs, *id.* 30 note 1; conversions made in Gujarát and other parts of India by missionaries of the sect, *id.* 38-41; changes made in the doctrines by missionaries to suit Hindu ideas, *id.* 40, 48.

Nazr: son of Kinánah, one of the ancestors of the prophet; one of the Náiata families claims descent from, IX, pt. ii, 14 note 3.

Neacyndon: tribe Melkynda of Ptolemy and Nelkynda of the *Periplus*, I, pt. i, 537.

Nearchus: Alexander's admiral (B. C. 325); his voyage, XIII, 404 note 3; I, pt. i, 536.

Nectarinidæ: family of birds in Ratnágiri, X, 68.

Nedamari: son of Pulikesin II, I, pt. ii, 361 note 2.

Negli: *Potygala chinensis*, a famine plant, XXV, 194.

Negro Slaves: imported by the Portuguese, I, pt. ii, 54.

Nehang Khán: Abyssinian minister of Ahmadnagar, his release, takes the Ahmadnagar fort, sends for Bahádur Sháh, confined, again restored to power, his scheme of seizing queen Chánd, retires to Junnar, XVII, 382, 386.

Nehar: in Thána, surveyed (1785-86) and again in 1793-1794, XIII, 558.

Nehr: place of interest in Pálanpur, V, 343.

Nekadi: purest class of Gujars among the Ajmer Gurjjaras, IX, pt. i, 494.

Nek Álam Khán: Nizám's lieutenant at Broach, I, pt. i, 324; governor of Broach, dies (1754), *id.* 338.

Neknám Khán Bahádur: the title of Hamidbeg, governor of Broach, I, pt. i, 339; supports Sayad Achchan at Surat (1759), *id.* 343.

Nek Sát Khán: a title, meaning of, Sorabji the first recipient of, IX, pt. ii, 197 note 2.

Nelevidu: fixed places of abode, or capital, I, pt. ii, 440, 441 note 1.

Nelkunda: early trade centre in Kánara district, XV, pt. ii, 48 and note 3; mentioned by Pliny under the name of Nelkynda Kallada, I, pt. i, 546.

Nemáditya: minister of war and peace of Karka I, I, pt. i, 125.

Neminátha : stone temples of, on Satrunjaya, Abu and Girnár hills, I, pt. i, 177, 202.
Nemnuk : allowance, VII, 354 ; disbursements of, *id.* 421.
Nengiyur : village near Hangal in the Dhárwár district, I, pt. ii, 377.
Nennapa : grantee iu Dhruva II's Bagumra grant, I, pt. i, 131.
Nepál : inscription of Amsuvarman in, I, pt. i, 81 ; introduction of Hinduism in, IX, pt. i, 451 ; people of one caste in, in ancient ages, division into four castes, *id.* 436 ; king of, feudatory of Singhana the Devagiri king, I, pt. ii, 525 ; king of, subdued by Somesvara III, I, pt. ii, 221 ; conquest of, *id.* 431.
Nepalese : their stock converted to Hinduism by Bráhmans, IX, pt. i, 451.
Neptunia oleracea : a famine plant, XXV, 199.
Neral : village with railway station in Thána district ; Kotaligad fort near, XIV, 210 ; Mátherán distant from, *id.* 230 ; water-stream, *id.* 243 ; climb to Peb fort from, *id.* 298 ; Tungi fort near, *id.* 370.
Neráli : fort in Belgaum district, siege of (1799), XXI, 391.
Nerang : cow's urine, purifying uses of, IX, pt. ii, 208, 223, 224 ; prayer, *id.* 208 note 2, 241.
Nerangdin : bull's urine, purifying use of, IX, pt. ii, 223 and note 2, 232.
Neriosangh, Nerioshang : priest (720), grandson of Shápur Sheheriar, translates the *Zend Avesta* into Sanskrit, IX, pt. ii, 221, 211 note 1.
Nerinm : *odorum kaner*, a poisonous and sacred plant, XXV, 266, 289 ; *oleander*, *id.* 256.
Nerla : town in Sátára district, XIX, 528.
Nera : valleys, XVIII, pt. i, 2 note 1.
Nerur : place of interest in Ratnágiri district, X, 467 ; copper-plate grant from, I, pt. ii, 185, 189, 295, 336 note 3, 337 note 2, 338 note 1, 344, 347, 348, 351, 352, 356, 365 and note 2, 367, 370 note 5, 371, 372, 373.
Nerwer : tribe of Bhils, IX, pt. i, 497.
Nes : temporary hamlets of Chárans in Káthiáwár, VIII, 11.
Nesak : class of Chárans in Cutch, IX, pt. i, 488.
Nesargi : place of interest in Belgaum district, XXI, 591 ; I, pt. ii, 555 ; stone inscription at, *id.* 557.
Nestorian Christians : in Thána district, XIV, 322 ; receive four Friars (1320), *id.* 356 ; *see also* I, pt. ii, 6.
Netaji Palkar : Shiváji's general, ravages the Mughal districts (1662), appears burning and plundering near Ahmadnagar, XVII, 399 ; defeats a body of Mughal horse under Shaista Khán (1664), I, pt. ii, 593.
Netrang : sub-division of Rewa Kántha, VI, 98.
Netráni : island in Kánara district, XV, pt. i, 3 ; probably Nitrias of Pliny (A. D. 77), Kanathra of Ptolemy (A. D. 150), and Kaineitai of the *Periplus* (A. D. 247), XV, pt. ii, 48 note 3, 335 ; Collecalia breeds on, *id.* 337.
Netravati : river mentioned in the *Periplus*, I, pt. i, 542.
Nets : stake, in Thána, XIII, 56-58 ; Ambiga's way of fishing with, XV, pt i, 301-302 ; in Poona district, XVIII, pt. i, 89-91.
Nettapodinæ : family of birds in Ratnágiri, X, 97.
Neva : caste of traders in Khándesh district, XII, 58.
Nevásá : subdivision of Ahmadnagar district, its area, aspect, rivers, climate, rainfall, cultivation, irrigation, crops, people, roads, railway, markets, crafts, survey changes, XVII, 615-621 ; survey of, *id.* 494-504. *Town*, Dnyanoba's pillar at, *id.* 729-730.
Nevra : village in Ratnágiri district, temple at, X, 354.
Newall : Lieutenant-General, besieges Sholápur (1818), XX, 291-298 ; Dhárwár garrison yields to, blockades Navalgund, XXII, 427-429.
Newberry : English traveller, his description of Bijápur city (1583), XXIII, 420.
New English Company : in Surat (1700-1707), II, 100-102.
New Jhánsi Barracks : at Kirkee, near Poona city, XVIII, pt. iii, 385.
Newport : Captain, his mention of a *desái* having 400 *halis*, in Surat district, IX, pt. i, 5 note 2.
Newsári : town in Persia ; Navsári called after, IX, pt. ii, 186 note 6.
Newspapers : in Surat district, II, 259 ; in Broach district, *id.* 530 ; in Kaira, III, 139 ; in Panch Maháls, *id.* 289 ; in Ahmadábád, IV, 217 ; in Ratnágiri, X, 291 ; in Khándesh, XII, 334 ; in Thána district, XIII, 662 ; in Násik district, XVI, 334 ; in Ahmadnagar district, XVII, 581 ; in Poona city, XVIII, pt. iii, 331 ; in Sátára district, XIX, 415 ; in Sholápur district, XX, 385 ; in Belgaum district, XXI, 488 ; in Dhárwár district, XXII, 620 ; in Bijápur district, XXIII, 523 ; in Kolhápur state, XXIV, 284.
New United Company : formation of (1702), XIII, 485.
Nezas : bamboo lances used by Phadális, IX, pt. ii, 150.
Nhágori : caste in Cutch, V, 51.
Nhávi : caste of barbers, in Ratnágiri district, X, 127 and note 1, 142 ; in Sávantvádi, *id.* 415 ; in Kolába district, XI, 67 ; in Janjira, *id.* 413 ; in Khándesh district, XII, 77 ; in Thána district, XIII, 143 ; in Násik district, XVI, 56 ; in Ahmadnagar district, XVII, 146-147 ; in Poona district, XVIII, pt. i, 380-383 ; in Sátára district, XIX, 102 ; in Sholápur district, XX, 143-144 ; in Belgaum district, XXI, 151 ; in Kolhapur state, XXIV, 101-102. *See* Nádig.
Nher : village in Sátára district, storage lake at, XIX, 528-529.
Niayish : portion of the original *Zend Avesta*, IX, pt. ii, 212 note 1.
Nib : *Indigofera tinctoria*, a dye-yielding plant, XXV, 242.
Nibandhas : commentaries on the *Smritis*, I, pt. ii, 228.
Nicholas Ufflet : traveller (1610), describes the country from Agra to Surat, I, pt. i, 224 note 2.

Nicol and Co.: Messrs., remains of, at Vasind, in Thána, XIV, 375.
Nicolo Conti: Italian traveller, notices that Indians never used compass in navigation, XIII, 725; (1420-1440), visits Vijayanagar, XV, pt. ii, 99; his description of Cambay, I, pt. i, 220 note 2.
Nidagundi: *see* Nidgundi.
Nidasingi: *see* Nidshingi.
Nidgundi: village in Dhárwár district, temples and inscriptions at, XXII, 782-783; *see* also I, pt. ii, 403, 443 note 1, 574.
Nidnegal: village in Dhárwár district, temple at, XXII, 783.
Nidshingi: village in Dhárwár district, inscriptions at, XXII, 783; *see* also I, pt. ii, 564 note 4.
Niebuhr: German traveller (A. D. 1763), notices Vánia skill and character, IX, pt. i, 78 note 1; his account of the Pársis, IX, pt. ii, 195; describes Bombay, XIII, 499, 500 note 1, 520; describes Elephanta caves, XIV, 59 note 1, 65 note 1, 80, 87, 92 note 1, 93, 135 note 10.
Nigamasabhá: town corporation under the Andhrabhrityas or Sátaváhanas, I, pt. ii, 176.
Nigdi: village in Sátára district, tomb of Raghunathsvámi at, XIX, 529.
Nigela sativa: *Piper nigrum*, a food plant, XXV, 173.
Niger seed: tillage of, in Poona, XVIII, pt. ii, 45; in Sátára district, XIX, 165.
Nigboj: village in Ahmadnagar district, reservoirs at, XVII, 730.
Nightjars: class of birds, in Ratnágiri district, X, 63; in Khándesh, XII, 34.
Nihśankamalla: king of Anahillapataka, I, pt. i 204.
Nijhardev: place of interest in Khándesh, XII, 461; hot spring at, *id.* 13.
Nijikabbe, Nijiyabbe: wife of Pittuga the Ratta chieftain, I, pt. ii, 552.
Nikitin: Athanasius, Russian traveller (1470), describes Dabhol, I, pt. ii, 31, 35; X, 327; his impressions of trade and riches of, Cheul, XI, 273; his account of slave trade in Janjira, *id.* 433 note 1; his notice of pirates, XIII, 447; remarks (1470) that people sailed from Persia to India in *Tavas*, *id.* 718; spells Pulu as Pilu (1470), XIV, 401; his visit to the Dakhan (1474), XV, pt. ii, 100; visits Junnar, XVIII, pt. iii, 225; his visit to Navlákh Umbre, *id.* 262.
Niklanki: looked for tenth incarnation, the coming Mahdi explained to Shaktipanthis as, IX, pt. ii, 40, 48.
Nikolass: of Damascus, an envoy of Herod, mentioned by Strabo, I, pt. i, 535.
Nikumbha: *see* Nikumbhavansás.
Nikumbhallasakti Prithivivallabha: prince of the Sendraka family in charge of Láta (654), I, pt. ii, 311; grant of, *id.* 360, 363; *see* also I, pt. i, 55-56, 111.
Nikumbhavansás: early rulers in Khándesh, (1000-1216), XII, 241; governing at Pátna (1153, 1207), I, pt. ii, 460, 521; in Násik district, XVI, 186.
Nilagiri: fortress at, I, pt. ii, 496.
Nilakantha or Nilakantheśvara Mahádeva: Kumárapála's royal god, I, pt. i, 189; image of, *id.* 163.
Nilalochaná or Nilamba: sister of the Kalachurya Vijjana or Bijjala and wife of Basava, I, pt. ii, 226, 479.
Nilári: indigo-dyers. *See* Rangári.
Nildongri: hill at Sopára in Thána district, the ruins of a Portuguese fort on, XIV, 339; figures from Musalman temple near, *id.* 417; *see* also XIII, 490.
Nilgár: caste of indigo-dyers in Bijápur district, XXIII, 257-258.
Nilgund: village in Dhárwár district, temple and inscription at, XXII, 782; *see* also I, pt. ii, 426, 429.
Nili: queen of Graharipu, I, pt. i, 160.
Nilkanth: bird, held sacred, worship of, IX, pt. i, 157, 173, 175, 220, 382. *See* Kingfisher.
Nilkanth: pleasure-house at Mandu, visited by Akbar in 1574 and by Jehángir in 1617, I, pt. i, 356; inscriptions, *id.* 370-371.
Nilkantheshvar: temple of, in Násik (1747), XVI, 505; shrine of, *id.* 511.
Nilkanth Lingáyat: *see* Koshti.
Nilkanth Mahádev: shrine of, near Bhinmál, I, pt. i, 455.
Nilkund: pass in Kánara district, XV, pt. ii, 40, 337.
Nilva: Indian millet variety in Khándesh, XII, 149.
Nilvala: place of interest in Káthiáwár, VIII, 580.
Nim: *Melia azadirachta*, a famine, dye-yielding and sacred plant, XXV, 196, 241, 279, 285.
Nimá: caste of Meshri Vánias, Shamláji, family deity of, IX, pt. i, 73; Shrávak, *id.* 96 and note 1; in Rewa Kántha, VI, 24.
Nimb: village in Sátára district, XIX, 529; Gáikwár (1751) at, *id.* 293.
Nimb: an oil-yielding plant, XXV, 215; in Khándesh, XII, 26.
Nimbadevarasa: subordinate of Gandaráditya, I, pt. ii, 548.
Nimbáli: tank near Bhinmál, I, pt. i, 453.
Nimbargi: village in the Nizám's dominions, inscription at, I, pt. ii, 438 note 2.
Nimbargi: village in Bijápur district, temple at, legend of, XXIII, 667-668.
Nimbárka: founder of *Sanakadi Sampradaya*, IX, pt. i, 533.
Nimbavana: battle at, between the followers of Parameśvaravarman II and Udayachandra, I, pt. ii, 326.
Nimbáyat: village in Násik district, XVI, 639.
Nimdari: village in Poona district, temple and fair at XVIII, pt. iii, 262.
Nimgaon: village in Poona district, temple of Khandoba and fair at, XVIII, pt. iii, 262.
Nimgaon Ketki: market town in Poona district, XVIII, pt. iii, 262.
Nimghoria Bhairav: shrine of, near Bhinmál, I, pt. i, 454.
Nimsod: village in Sátára district, XIX, 529.
Nimtána: test system of land assessment, XVIII, pt. ii, 319 note 2.

Ninama : tribe of Bhils in South Udepur, IX, pt. i, 295 note 2.
Nipáni : town in Belgaum district, trade centre, history of the *desáis* of, lapse of, XXI, 313, 591-596, 407 ; chief of, joins Sindia against the Patvardhans, I, pt. ii, 662 ; accompanies General Wellesley as commandant of the Peshwa's troops, is rewarded by Bájiráv II with the title of Sar-Lashkar ; does not act cordially against the English (1817), and is confirmed in the possession of his *saranjám* ; attempts are made to introduce a supposititious child, the *saranjám* is resumed on the death of the chief (1839), *id.* 670.
Niphád : sub-division of Násik district, its area, aspect, climate, water, history, land-revenue, stock, holdings, crops and people, XVI, 357-364 ; survey of (1871), *id.* 257-260. *Town*, *id.* 639.
Nir : place of interest in Khándesh, XII, 460.
Nirá : river in Dakhan, I, pt. ii, 357 ; XVIII, pt. i, 8 ; XIX, 16 ; XX, 4.
Nira Canal : in Poona district, XVIII, pt. ii, 20-24.
Niralgi : village in Dhárwár district, record at, I, pt. ii, 444, 454, 561 note 7.
Nirali : caste of weavers, in Násik district, XVI, 53 ; in Ahmadnagar district, XVII, 127-128 ; in Poona district, XVIII, pt. i, 353-355 ; indigo-dyers in Sholápur district, XX, 123-124.
Niravadya or Niravadya Udayadeva Pandita : house pupil of Pujyapáda, spiritual adviser of Vinayáditya the Chálukya king, I, pt. ii, 191 ; *see* also *id.* 373.
Nirdhi : caste of Musalmán Bhils in Khándesh, XII, 105.
Nirgrantha : Jain sect, I, pt. ii, 288.
Nirgunda : in Mysore, inscription at (1250), I, pt. ii, 495 note 2, 502.
Nirihullaka : chieftain of a wild tribe, I, pt. i, 114, 115 ; grant of, *id.* 58 note 1.
Nirilli : *mahájanas* of, mentioned in a record at Niralgi, in Dhárwár district, I, pt. ii, 444.
Nirmal : a sacred place in Thána district, XIV, 292 ; the garden of Sopára, *id.* 314 ; history of, *id.* 325 ; Vajirgad near, *id.* 373 ; temple at, I, pt. ii, 28. *Lake*, XIII, 2.
Nirmaldas : ascetic of Surat, founder of the sect of Vaishnav *matias*, IX, pt. i, 168.
Nirmali : a plant the seeds of which are used to clear muddy water, XXV, 252 ; in Khándesh, XII, 149.
Nirpan : village in Násik district, grant of Nágavarddhana Tribhuvanásraya at, I, pt. i, 108, 110 ; grant at, I, pt. ii, 345, 349, 352, 357, 358 note 1, 360 note 3.
Nirupama : father of Karka II, the Ráshtrakúta king, I, pt. ii, 207.
Nirupama : *biruda* (title) of Dhruva, son of Subhatunga, I, pt. ii, 409 ; brother of Khattiga and father of Kakka II, *id.* 423 ; of Dhruva I and Dhruva II, I, pt. i, 126.
Nirupamadeva : king mentioned by a Kánarese poet Pampa, I, pt. ii, 380.
Nirvánepan : hill in Belgaum district, XXI, 6.
Nirvangni : village in Poona district, temple at, legend of, XVIII, pt. iii, 263.
Nisbat : meaning of the term, IX, pt. i, 442 note 6 continued on page 443.
Nisháda : country including Bánsda, Dharampur and North-East Thána, I, pt. i, 36 and note 9.
Nishadas : original settlers of the *Rámáyana*, IX, pt. i, 10.
Nishánigudda : hill in Kánara district XV, pt. ii, 337 ; *see* also *id.* pt. i, 5.
Nishkramana : or home-leaving, eighth Vedic rite, IX, pt. i, 31 note 3 ; performance of rite during girding ceremony, *id.* 37.
Nisni : pass between Thána and Kolába districts, XIII, 320 ; XI, 6, 115.
Nisottar : a medicinal plant, XXV, 255.
Nissankamalla : *biruda* (title) of the Kalachurya Sankama, I, pt. ii, 486.
Niśśankapratápa Chakravartin : Hoysála title, I, pt. ii, 507, 508, 509.
Nitimárga-Kongunivarma-Permanadi : Ganga king, I, pt. ii, 303 note 2.
Nitra : identified with Mangalore, I, pt. i, 542 ; indentified by some with Nivti, X, 192 note 3, 354 and note 2.
Nitrates : found in a well in Násik, XVI, 13.
Nitre-making : in Násik district, XVI, 179.
Nitrias : *see* Nitra.
Nittasingi : village managed by Tárádevi, I, pt. ii, 448.
Nityamvarsha Rattakandarpa : son of Jagattunga Ráshtrakúta, I, pt. i, 130.
Nityavarsha : *biruda* (title) of Indra III, the Ráshtrakúta, I, pt. ii, 203, 415, 416 note 5; of Khottiga, *id.* 422.
Nityavinita : Pallava king, I, pt. ii, 331.
Nityavinitcśvara : temple of, mentioned in an inscription in a temple of Conjeeveram, I, pt. ii, 331.
Nival : a dye-yielding plant, XXV, 248.
Nivartana : land measure, I, pt. ii, 150.
Nivdungya Vithoba's Temple : in Poona city, XVIII, pt. iii, 338.
Nivrittinátha ; father of Jnánadeva, I, pt. ii, 250.
Nivti ; town in Ratnágiri district, fort, history of, X, 354 ; I, pt. ii, 112.
Nivul kanta : a poisonous plant, an antidote to snake-bite, XXV, 275.
Niwal : a poisonous plant, XXV, 268.
Nizám : Chin Kilich Khán, appointed governor of Bijápur (1707), XXIII, 440 ; Mughal governor of the Dakhan, gives a *jáhgir* at Bálki to Chandrasen Jádhav (1713), I, pt. ii, 598 ; declares war with Sháhu (1713), *id.* 599 ; governor of Málwa, crosses the Narbada, defeats the imperial army and brings under his sway Ahmadnagar, Gangthari and Khándesh (1720), *id.* 626-627 ; given the title of Nizám-ul-Mulk, appointed governor of Bijápur a second time (1722), XXIII, 440 ; becomes master of the Dakhan (1727) ; revives the quarrel between Sháhu and Sambháji of Kolhápur (1727) ; war with and defeat by Sháhu (1727) ; incites Trimbakráo Dábháde to march against Bájiráv to depose him from his superiority (1731), I, pt. ii, 600 ; shares the revenues of the Southern Marátha Country with the Maráthás, appoints a new *subhedár* to the Bijápur

Karnátak and the fort of Belgaum, *id.* 656; his death (1748), *id.* 627. *Salábat Jang*, successor of Nizám-ul-Mulk, invades the Poona districts (1751); comes to terms with the Peshwa and confirms a cession of territory promised by his brother Gazi-ud-din (1752), *id.* 601-602, 627. *Nizám Ali*; declares war with the Peshwa and is defeated by Sadáshiv Bháu at Udgir (1760), *id.* 602, 627; sides with Raghunáthráv, burns Poona, and is defeated at Rákshas Bhuvan (1763), *id.* 603, 627, 658; levies contributions as far as Athni and Miraj (1774); alliance with the Peshwa against Haidar (1776); his forces bought off by Haidar, *id.* 658-659; forms an offensive alliance with the Maráthás against Tipu (1786), *id.* 660; enters into an offensive alliance with the Maráthás and the English against Tipu (1789), *id.* 661; his troops take Kopal (1790), *id.* 662; defeated by the Maráthás at Kharda (1795), surrenders his minister, XVII, 407-409.

Nizám Ali: *see* under Nizám.

Nizamaluco: Portuguese name of the Nizáms of Ahmadnagar, I, pt. ii, 34.

Nizámpur: town in Kolába district, XI, 353; Sambháji defeated at, I, pt. ii, 78; survey and *khoti* system at, XI, 205-207; plundered by Rámoshis (1840), *id.* 158.

Nizámpur: place of interest in Khándesh, XII, 248, 460.

Nizámpurkál: river in Kolába district, XI, 10.

Nizám Sháhis: rulers in Dakhan (1489-1637), founded by Malik Ahmad Beheri (1489), Ahmadnagar their capital founded (1494); Burhan Nizám (1508-1553), account of their kingdom according to Barbosa (1510), Husain Nizám Sháh (1553-1565), Murteza Nizám Sháh (1565-1588), Ismael Nizám Sháh (1588-1590), Burhán Nizám Sháh II (1590-1594), Ahmad II (1594-1595), Chánd Bibi's regency (1595-1599), Báhádur Nizám Sháh (1596-1599), fall of Ahmadnagar (1599), their institutions, Malik Ambar's regency (1607-1626), Fatteh Khán's regency (1626-1632), fall of Daulatábád (1632), Sháháji regent (1632), end of the dynasty (1636), XVII, 358-398; history of the dynasty, I, pt. ii, 621-625; *see* also XVIII, pt. ii, 219-224; XX, 278-287; XIX, 227 note 5; I, pt. i, 221.

Nizám-ud-din: Shaikh, ancestor of the Chishtis, IX, pt. ii, 8 note 2.

Nizám-ul-Mulk: governor of Gujarát (1351), I, pt. i, 231.

Nizám-ul-Mulk: Asafjah, Viceroy of Ujjain (1720), retires to the Dakhan, defeats and kills Sayad Diláwar Khán; retires to Aurangábád, battle of Bálápur in the Berárs and death of Alam Khán, deputy viceroy of the Dakhan, *id.* 301; appointed prime minister of the empire (1721), *id.* 302; his disagreement with Haidar Kuli Khán (1722), *id.* 303; appointed fifty-first viceroy of Gujarát (1722); appoints Hamid Khán deputy viceroy and Momin Khán governor of Surat, *id.* 303; defeats Rustam Ali, *id.* 390; sends Sayads Mithan and Achhau to Surat to avenge Mulla Muhammad Ali (1748), *id.* 331; favours Sambháji of Kolhápur, XIX, 256-257; becomes independent, seeks Marátha aid, *id.* 266-267; connives at Bájiráv's incursions, his alarm at the Maráthá power, his policy, negotiation with Bájiráv (1728), his interview with Bájiráv, *id.* 271-275; restored to favour and ordered to drive Maráthás from Gujarát and Málwa, commits breach of faith with Peshwa, Bájiráv's plans of conquest during the absence of at Delhi, takes Peshwa's petition to Delhi, *id.* 279-284; *see* also VII, 168, 169, 172-173, 175; XX, 290; XXI, 379; XII, 252; XVIII, pt. ii, 243; also under Nizám.

Nizám-ul-Mulk Bhairi: Bahamani minister (1481-1486), his origin, XVII, 355 and note 9, 356.

Noghan: Ahir ruler of Surashtra, attacked and slain by Siddharája, I, pt. i, 176.

Nokarsi: grand feast among Shrávaks, IX, pt. i, 103.

Nolambádhirája: Pallava king, I, pt. ii, 332.

Nolamba Kulántaka: *biruda* (title) of the Western Ganga prince Márasimha (967-968), I, pt. ii, 305.

Nolamba-Pallava-Bommanayya: Pallava chief (1040), I, pt. ii, 333, 437.

Nolambas: territories of, conquered by the Chola king Rájarájadeva, I, pt. ii, 308.

Nolambavádi: country, I, pt. ii, 298 and notes 2 and 3; of the Pallavas in the direction of Bellary, *id.* 306, 318 and note 13; passes out of the hands of the Pallavas into those of the Pándyas, *id.* 319 and note 1, 333, 434, 443, 452, 453, 456, 459; province, ruled by Vijaya Pándyadeva, *id.* 472, 486; Pándyas of, *id.* 495, 496; seized by Vishnuvardhana, *id.* 497; ruled over by Vishnuvardhana, *id.* 499, 501, 505, 524, 577.

Nolinom: the ninth of Shravan Sud, IX, pt. i, 23 note 5.

Nolio: *see* Mungoose.

Nonambavádi: *see* Nolambavádi.

Nonbar: caste of husbandmen in Kánara district, XV, pt. i, 251, 252.

Nondhs: registers. *See* Book Account.

Nuno Da Cunha: Portuguese viceroy in India, I, pt. i, 349, 351.

Nora: mangrove island in Káthiáwár, VIII, 29.

Noronha: D. Afonso de, Portuguese viceroy (1554), XIV, 42.

Noronha: Signior, Portuguese officer of the Maráthás (1780), XIV, 56.

Norris, Sir William: ambassador of the New Company at Surat (1700), XXVI, pt. i, 122; waits on Auzangzeb at Panhála (1701), XXIV, 314.

Northern Circars: province in Madras, corresponds to Kalinga, I, pt. ii, 139, 140; southern limit of the province of the Aryans previous to the seventh century before Christ, *id.* 141.

Northern India: conquest of, by Timur (1398-1400), I, pt. i, 357; I, pt. ii, 341 note 2.

Nosra: Hindu goddess, shrine of, between Ajmer and Pushkar, IX, pt. i, 483.

Nossa S. da Conceição: chapel of, in Poona, XVIII, pt. iii, 338.

Nossa Senhora des Angustias: image of, at Dáhánu in Thána district, XIV, 54.
Nossa Senhora do Parto: church of, at Sanján in Thána district, XIV, 304.
Nossa Senhora dos Remedios: name of the Portuguese church of Remedi, I, pt. ii, 65.
Notonia grandiflora: a plant used as an antidote to snake-bites, XXV, 274.
Noura: *see* Nowohar.
Nousaripa: modern Navsári, I, pt. i, 539.
Novroji: son of Rustam Mánck, goes to England (1723), receives honor from the Court of Directors; buys Nowroji Hill, his family is known as Shet Khándán family, IX, pt. ii, 196 note 3.
Nowohar: village in the province of Tháua, I, pt. ii, 543.
Nowroji Hill: at Mazagaon in Bombay, property of Shet Khándáu family, IX, pt. ii, 196 note 3.
Nripasimha: *biruda* (title) of Kirtivarman II, I, pt. ii. 376.
Nripati Trinetra: *biruda* (title) of Govind IV, I, pt. ii, 416.
Nripatunga: *biruda* (title) of Amoghavarsha I, I, pt. ii, 199, 200, 401; of Govinda IV, *id.* 416; of Kakka II, *id.* 423.
Nrisimha: *see* Narasimha I, Narasimha II and Narasimha III.
Nufna: word possessing special powers, IX, pt. ii, 143.
Nuh: Noah, given as the first ancestor of the Chudásamma, I, pt. i, 139.
Nuji: stream in Kánara district, XV, pt. i, 6.
Nukhs: clans of Bhátias, IX, pt. i, 117 and note 6.
Nulambavádi: *see* Nolambavádi.
Numeninæ: family of birds in Ratnágiri, X, 92.
Numerals: ancient (B. C. 100) in Nánághát, XIV, 289 and note 2.
Nummulitic rocks: in Surat district, II, 30.
Nunneries: Buddhist, in Thána district (B. C. 150), XIII, 406.
Nuno da Cunha: Portuguese general, captures Daman, Bahádur Sháh of Gujarát makes treaty with (1531), XIII, 451; slain in a scuffle at Diu, *id.* 452.
Nuns: Buddhist, at Kánheri (A. D. 100-600), XIV, 138.
Nur Baksh: tribe of the Hindu Kush, identical with the Khojahs, IX, pt. ii, 36 note 3.
Nur Jehán: wife of emperor Jehángir, at Mándu, I, pt. i, 375.
Nurmadi-Chola: Chola king, I, pt. ii, 433 *See* Ka Rájarája-Rájakesarivarman.
Nurmadi-Taila: I, pt. ii, 428, 459. *See* Taila III and Tailapa II.
Nur Satagur or Nursháh: Ismáilia missionary, is believed to have been sent to India by Ala Zikri-his-Sálam, comes to Patan in Gujarát in the time of Solanki Bhim II (1179-1242), works miracles and makes many converts, is said to have converted the ruler secretly to his faith; marries a daughter of the Hindu governor of Navsári, is killed by one of his disciples, IX, pt. ii, 38; is described by the third Ismáilia missionary Sadrud-din as the incarnation of the prophet, *id.* 40; of Brahma, *id.* 48.
"Nur the Turk:" probably Nur Satagur, believed to have converted the Mulahidah, IX, pt. ii, 38.
Nur-ud Din: *see* Nur Satagur.
Nur-ud-din Muhammad Ufi: author of *Jami-ul-Hikayat* (1211), I, pt. i, 512.
Nurulah: *sayad*, IX, pt. ii, 27 note 1.
Nusaripa: modern Navsári, XIV, 320.
Nusks: original parts of the *Zend Avesta*; names and contents of, IX, pt. ii, 211 and note 2.
Nutmeg: tree in Poona district, XVIII, pt. i, 46.
Nuttal: Captain (1857-1859), forms a Koli corps, his skirmishes with the Bhils, XVII, 419; XVI, 200, 204 and note 2.
Nuzhat-ul-Akhbar: historical work, IX, pt. ii, 50 note 2.
Nuzhat-ul-Mushtak: work of Al Idrisi, I, pt. i, 508 note 10.
Nyáhál Peth: a ward of Poona city, details of, XVIII, pt. iii, 274, 275.
Nyáyádhish: superintendent of justice in the Marátha government, XIX, 243-244.
Nyáyakumda Chandrodaya: commentary on the *Laghiyastraya*, I, pt. ii, 407.
Nyáyashástri: expounder of Hindu law in the Marátha government, XIX, 243.
Nyctagineæ: an order of famine plants, XXV, 203.
Nyctanthes arbartristis: *parijatak*, an oil-yielding, dye-yielding and sacred plant, XXV, 223, 247, 290.

O

OARTS: gardens in Bombay island, revenue of (1724), XXVI, pt. iii, 329-330; farmed (1724), *id.* 330-333; (1743), 340-343; Company's, farmed (1752), *id.* 463-465; again farmed (1759), *id.* 466; (1775), 472-74.
Oat: food plant, XXV, 187.
Oath-taking: Pátáne Prabhu ceremony, XVIII, pt. i, 212.
Obeidullah: surnamed Al Mahdi (872-934), missionary of Abdullah Maimun, founds the Fatemite Khilaphat dynasty in Egypt (910), revealed *imám*, IX, pt. ii, 37, 47, 48.
Obeli: modern Hubli (1547), XXII, 407.
Obollah: port in the Persian Gulf, Abuláma of the Karle inscriptions (A. D. 100-200) identified with, XIII, 413 note 4, 421 note 2; its trade (A. D. 250, 810-1260), with Thána coast, *id.* 418, 429, 433; *see* also XVIII, pt. ii, 213; Ptolemy's Apologos, its trade with Broach (150 A. D.), I, pt. i, 545.
Observances: religious, of the Pársis, IX, pt. ii, 219-220.
Observatory: in Poona, XVIII, pt. i, 19.
Occupations: all district volumes, *see* Census Details under District Name. *See* also under the castes concerned.
O-che-lo: Chinese name of the Arhat Achára, I, pt. i, 79; I, pt. ii, 354.
Ochro-carpus longifolius: dye-yielding plant, XXV, 241.

Ocimum: *basilicum, gratissimum, pilosum, sanctum*, oil-yielding plants, XXV, 224.
Ocymum sanctum: sacred plant, XXV, 279, 284, 287, 288, 292.
Od: town in Kaira district, III, 177.
Od: caste of pond diggers, in Cutch, V, 82; in Káthiáwár, VIII, 158.
Odambari: a tribe in Cutch, V, 130.
Oderic, Odoricus: French Friar (1321-1324), black lions in Thána according to, XIII, 44 note 1; his visit to Thána and account of its religion, *id.* 251; his account of the conquest of Thána by the Turks, *id.* 439; *see* also XIV, 356 and note 7; his account of the Pársis, IX, pt. ii, 189 note 1; *see* also I, pt. ii, 5, 29.
Odhni-ndána: ceremony among Musalmáns, performance of, IX, pt. ii, 162 note 1.
Odina: *odier*, plant yielding dyes, XXV, 242; *woodier*, yields gums and resins, *id.* 250; fodder plant, *id.* 278.
Odonbæores: tribe in South Thána mentioned by Pliny, I, pt. i, 534.
Odoricus: *see* Oderic.
Offences: all district volumes, *see* Justice under District Name.
Offerings: made by Gujarát Hindus to gods or goddesses; two kinds of, bloody and bloodless; bloody: names of goddesses to whom, and of classes by whom, made; offering made by high caste Hindus, days sacred for making; animals offered; mode of making the offering, IX, pt. i, 406; special mode of making an offering at the temple of Bahucharaji; mode of making offerings by those who scruple to kill an animal, *id.* 407; offerings made by Early Tribes to gods, goddesses, *khatras* and *paliyás*, mode of making offerings; *id.* 407-408; bloodless: four kinds of; made to Devi or Mata, Shiv's consort; to Ganpati, to Hanuman; to the moon, *id.* 409; to Shiv, *id.* 408; to the spirits of the dead; to the sun; to Vishnu, *id.* 409.
Office-bearers: under the Valabhi administration (A. D. 500-700), I, pt. i, 81, 82; in a brotherhood of beggars, IX, pt. ii, 19. *See* Beggars, Bhandari Izni and Sargnroh; religious, among Guzarát Musalmáns, IX, pt. ii, 132-135. *See* Kazi Khatib, Marsiah Khán, Manlavi, Mujáwar, Mulla and Mutawalli; Portuguese in Thána district, XIII, 455, 459.
Ogilby: English traveller (1670), his account of Cambay, VI, 219; his account of the Pársis, IX, pt. ii, 188 and note 4, 191; his description of Ratnágiri trade, X, 175; describes Dabhol, *id.* 330 note 5; his notice of Jaytápur and Kelshi, *id.* 341, 342; his description of Khándesh, XII, 250 note 4; his account of the siege of Asirgad, *id.* 580; an earthquake at Bassein, XIV, 32 note 1; his mention of Dáhánu, *id.* 54; of Dheri, *id.* 56; of Kelve Máhim, *id.* 199; of Manora fort, *id.* 229 note 1; of Tarápur, *id.* 344; of Chitákul in Kánara, XV, pt. ii, 278; of Aliga, of Sintacora stream, *id.* 279; his description of Bijápur, XXIII, 433-434, 589.
Ohila: Shiva's attendant, I, pt. ii, 482.
Ohjar Támbat: canal in Násik district, XVI, 94.
Oil-pressing: in Ahmadábád district, IV, 134; in Cutch, V, 127; in Káthiáwár, VIII, 260; in Khándesh district, XII, 228; in Kánara district, XV, pt. ii, 71; in Sholápur district, XX, 272; in Belgaum, XXI, 352; in Dhárwár, XXII, 385-386; in Kolhápur state, XXIV, 212-214.
Oil-seeds: cultivation of, in Surat district, II, 63; in Broach district, *id.* 390; in Pánch Maháls, III, 234, 248; in Ahmadábád, IV, 58; in Cutch, V, 106; in Mahi Kántha, *id.* 371; in Ratnágiri district, X, 148; in Khándesh, XII, 152-153; export of, *id.* 222; in Thána district, XIII, 290; in Kánara district, XV, pt. ii, 19; in Ahmadnagar, XVII, 269-270; in Poona, XVIII, pt. ii, 44-46; in Kolhápur state, XXIV, 169-171.
Ojat: river in Káthiáwár, VIII, 64.
Ojhár: village in Poona district, Ganpati's temple at, XVIII, pt. iii, 263 and note 3.
Ojhár Canal: in Ahmadnagar district, XVII, 254-256.
Ojiravangeh: third watch, IX, pt. ii, 214 note 1. *See* Geh.
Okaketu: bird ensign of the Ráshtrakútas, I, pt. ii, 387; of Amoghavarsha I, *id.* 402.
Okellis: modern Ghalla in East Africa, its sea connection with India (A. D. 50), I, pt. i, 537, 543; XIII, 410 note 5.
Okhagir: *see* Okhámandal.
Okhámandal: district in Káthiáwár, VIII, 8; its description, climate, agriculture, trade, domestic and wild animals, population and history, *id.* 580-602; Wághers, earliest settlers in, *id.* 164-165; *see* also VII, 26, 509; pirates of, *id.* 324-325; *zillah*, I, pt. i, 208 and note 3; chiefs of, admit Sundarji Shiváji as resident on behalf of British government, *id.* 425; chiefs of, take to piracy (1816) and are crushed by a British force; the district of, made over to the Gaikwár (1816), *id.* 427: Wághers of, besiege and plunder Dwárka Bárvala and Bet (1859); expedition against Bet; capture of the forts of Bet and Dwárka, *id.* 446-448; *see* also IX, pt. i, 488 note 8.
Olajikabbe: wife of the village accountant Kayana, I, pt. ii, 449.
Old Man of the Mountain: title, IX, pt. ii, 37. *See* Hasan Sabah.
Old Woman's Island: in Bombay harbour, derivation of the name, XXVI, pt. iii, 667; farmed (1764), *id.* 424-427.
Oleaceæ: an order of oil-yielding plants, XXV, 223.
Olea fragrans: an oil-yielding plant, XXV, 223.
Oleander: vegetable poison, XXV, 266.
Oleineæ: an order of dye-yielding plants, XXV, 247.
Ollaiyaka: grantor mentioned in Akálavarsha Krishna's grant at Bágumra, I, pt. i, 128.
Olochacra: a place of trade, probable identification of, with Lohogad in Poona district, X, 192 note 3.
Olokhaira: a city of pirates, provisionally identified with Karád, I, pt. i, 542.

Olpád: sub-division of Surat, II, 267-276; I, pt. ii, 412. *Town, id.* 298; traditional origin of, IX, pt. i, 12 and note 1; I, pt. i, 539.

Omán: east of the Persian Gulf, I, pt. i, 545; I, pt. ii, 14; the king of; country under the, considered a part of India, IX, pt. ii, 184.

Omayyah: ancestor of one of the Náiatia families, IX, pt. ii, 14 note 3.

Omenagar: Ptolemy's name (A. D. 150) for Junnar, XVIII, pt. ii, 213 note 10; spelt Omenogara, I, pt. i, 541.

Omens: beliefs in, among Gujarát Hindus, IX, pt. i, 409-410; two kinds of—good and bad; objects considered as good, *id.* 138, 410-411; as bad, *id.* 138, 411-413; classes believing in —Bháts, *id.* 213; Bhaváyás, *id.* 225; Chárans, *id.* 220; craftsmen, *id.* 178, 181, 182, 185, 191, 194, 196, 200, 205; Hajáms, *id.* 233; husbandmen, *id.* 154, 157, 164, 172, 173, 174, 175; Rájpúts, *id.* 137; among Gujarát Musalmáns, good and bad, belief in, IX, pt. ii, 22, 30, 145 146; among Ratnágiri, Kolis, X, 128 note 1; in Dhárwár population, XXII, 50-51.

Omkáreshvar: Poona temple, XVIII, pt. iii, 338-339.

One Tree Hill: Mátherán Point, XIV, 233, 238, 276, 281.

Onion: food plant, XXV, 179; tillage of, in Khándesh district, XII, 171; in Poona, XVIII, pt. ii, 56.

Onor: *see* Honávar.

Oomri: Nikitin's (1470), probably modern Umbre in Poona district, XVIII, pt. iii, 262 and note 4.

Oomum: oil-yielding plant, XXV, 223.

Oopara: Sopára, port near Bassein, I, pt. ii, 1.

Opaydos Christãos: official in Mandapeshvar, Máhim, Bombay, Karanja, Mount Calvary and Agáshi, I, pt. ii, 57.

Ophelia: *chirta*, medicinal plant, XXV, 261; *multiflora*, medicinal plant, *id.* 262.

Ophioxylou Ranwolfia serpentinum: vegetable poison, common in Konkan, Goa and Bombay, XXV, 267; antidote to snakebite, *id* 274.

Ophir: proposed identifications of, XIV, 317-318 and notes, 417; *see* also XIII, 404-405.

Opium: used by Gujarát Hindus as drug or narcotic, preparations, IX, pt. i, p. xxxiii; by Gujarát Musalmáns, peculiar names of, takers, IX, pt. ii, 110; cultivation of, in Baroda, VII, 97-102; export of, *id.* 152; income of opium and expenditure on opium department, *id.* 420-421; history, cultivation, growth and trade, of, *id.* 429-432.

Opium trade: not to be the monopoly of the Dutch (1748-1749), XXVI, pt. i. 291-292.

Opuntia Dillenii: famine plant, XXV, 199.

Orange: fruit tree, cultivation of, in Poona district, XVIII, pt. i, 49.

Oratæ: the Aparántakas, I, pt. i, 532, 533, 534.

Oratura: probably Suráshtra, I, pt. i, 6.

Orbadarou: identification of, with a town at Abu, I, pt. i, 539.

Orbitai: Makrán tribe, mentioned by Pliny, I, pt. i, 546.

Orchideæ: an order of food plants, XXV, 176.

Ordeal: trial by, among Hindus (1187) with the cobra and red hot arrow, I, pt. ii, 556 and note 5, 571 and note 3; XXI, 360; with boiling oil, among the Uchliss in Poona district, XVIII, pt. i, 468-469, 474-476; in Káthiáwár, VIII, 326-327.

Orioles: class of birds in Ratnágiri, X, 76.

Oriolinæ: family of birds in Ratnágri, X, 76.

Orissa: people of, I, pt ii, 431, 516; I, pt. i, 494.

Orme: historian, his description of the operations with Tulaji Ángria, I, pt. ii, 88.

Ormuz: Persian Gulf, Pársis at, XIII, 247 and note 2; chief port dealing with Thána, *id.* 444, 465; Albuquerque (1610) finds fleet at, *id.* 469 note 3; captured by the English (1622), *id.* 458; I, pt. ii, 64; city of, IX, pt. ii, 183 note 3; ships of, hired by Friars, I, pt. ii, 5; horses imported from, *id.* 35; shipowner of, I, pt. i, 204.

Ornaments: origin of the use of, XVIII, pt. i, 106 note 1, 547-552; of Káthiáwár population, VIII, 201; of Gujarát Hindus, of Bhils, IX, pt. i, 298-299; Bráhmans, *id.* 21, 53; depressed classes, *id.* 340, 346; early tribes, *id.* 312, 314, 317, 318, 320, 321, 323, 329, 330; herdsmen, 267, 286, 288; husbandmen, *id.* 173, 175; Kolis, *id.* 246; Rájpúts, *id.* 132; Vanias, *id.* 76; of Gujarát Musalmáns, of men, of the rich, IX, pt. ii, 101 and note 3; of middle class, *id.* 102; of the poor, *id.* 103; of women, of the rich, *id.* 104 and note 2; of the middle class, *id.* 106; of the poor, *id.* 107; of children, *id.* 108; among Pársis, details and costs of, of men, *id.* 201-202; of women, *id.* 202-203; of children, *id.* 203; investments in Ratnágiri district, X, 158; in Sávantvadi, *id.* 410; of Mátherán tribes, XIV, 261; of castes in Kánara, XV, pt. i, 119, 131, 144, 176, 191, 193, 195, 214, 285, 375, 403; in Násik district, XVI, 30; of the Chitpávans, XVIII, pt. i, 104-107; Velális, *id.* 256; Agarváls, *id.* 262; Kunbis, *id.* 288; Bhadbhunjás, *id.* 319, 372-373; Mhárs, *id.* 440; Musalmáns, *id.* 484; making of, *id.* 372-373; in Sátára district, XIX, 180; in Belgaum, XXI, 95, 113, 199, 292; in Dhárwár, XXII, 65-67; in Bijápur, among Bedars, XXIII, 92; Komtis, *id.* 119; Lingáyats, *id.* 224 note 1.

Orostræ: tribe, I, pt. i, 534.

Orphanage: Christian, founded (1535) by Antonio do Porto, at Thána, Vehár, Bassein and other places, XIII, 461 and note 1; XIV, 1, 25, 376; Hindu, at Pandharpur, XX, 482.

Orrhotha: Sorath mentioned by Kosmas (A. D. 530), I, pt. i, 547.

Orsang: river in Rewa Kántha, VI, 2, 110.

Orsi: Urasa tribe beyond the Indus, I, pt. i, 534.

Ortzery: (Achra?) a harbour on the Konkan Coast, I, pt. ii, 63.

Orygia decumbens: famine plant common in dry places in Dakhan, XXV, 200.

Oryza sativa: food plant, XXV, 186.

Osa: or the frontier, town near Jodhpur, of Mandovad so named, Osváls take name from, IX, pt. i, 97; also called Osia or Osiauagar, *id.* 496 and note 9; I, pt. i, 463.

Osanpur: town on the left bank on the Indus near the confluence, I, pt. i, 538.

Oshám: hill in Káthiáwár, VIII, 10.

Oshtam: a caste of beggars in Belgaum, XXI, 187; in Bijápur, XXIII, 137-141.

Osia: family goddess of Osvals, IX, pt. i, 97.

Osia, Osianagari: *see* Osa.

Osta: son of a priest before ordination so called, IX, pt. ii, 225 note 1.

Ostend Company: (1717-1745), XXVI, pt. i, 258 and note 1, 259; their trade with Macca, *id.* 260.

Osumbhalá: village, identified with Umbhel or Umbher, I, pt. ii, 370; *see* also I, pt. i, 108.

Osvál: caste of traders, I, pt. i, 463, 464; origin of, *id.* 464 note 1; in Khándesh, XII, 59; in Násik district, XVI, 45 and note 4; in Gujarát, were originally Solanki Rájpúts, converted to Jainism, IX, pt. i, 453, 485 and note 6, 496; are said to be descended from Vaisya chief Ama; divisions, *id.* 496-497; Gujar element in, *id.* 485, 499; of Gujarát, Shrávak Vániás, divisions, story of origin, surnames, *id.* 73, 96-97; in Ahmadnagar district, XVII, 76-82; in Cutch, V, 52-53; in Thána district, XIII, 113; in Káthiáwár, VIII, 148.

Osyris Wightiana: food plant common in *gháts*, XXV, 174.

Otári: a caste of casters, in Kolába district, XI, 65; in Ratnágiri district, X, 125; in Ahmadnagar district, XVII, 128-129; in Poona district, XVIII, pt. i, 355-358; in Sátára district, XIX, 88 89; in Sholápur district, XX, 124; in Kolhápur state, XXIV, 96-97; in Khándesh district, XII, 75; in Belgaum district, XXI, 143; in Násik district, XVI, 52.

Otitidæ: family of birds in Ratnágiri, X, 90.

Otter: found in rivers in Káuara, XV, pt. i, 95. *See* Lutrinæ.

Otur: market town in Poona district, fort, temples and fair at, XVIII, pt. iii, 263 264.

Ougeinia Dalbergioides: plants yielding gums and resins, XXV, 251; used for poisoning fish, *id.* 272; as fodder, *id.* 278.

Ounia: same as Huna, I, pt. i, 146.

Ouppara: *Periplus'* Sopára, XIII, 418; XIV, 320.

Our Lady of the Mount: Roman Catholic Church at Bándra, destroyed (1737), I, pt. ii, 84.

Ouroxylon Indicum: plant yielding dyes, XXV, 248.

Ouseley: mentions that Pársi revolt in Persia was followed by great severities, IX, pt. ii, 185 note 4.

Outram: Sir James, his attempts to destroy the tigers in Khándesh (1822), XII, 30; raises a Bhil corps (1825), *id.* 258-259, 317; I, pt. ii, 631; appointed assistant to the Baroda Resident (1835), exposes the roguery of residency clerks (1838), gives up his post, VII, 265-266 and 265 note 1; resident at Baroda (1847-1852), *id.* 268; his famous *khatpat* report, exposes the underhand dealings of residency clerks, recalled, *id.* 268-273.

Ouvidores: Portuguese magistrates, I, pt. ii, 52.

Ovanna: evil-removing salutation, form of, IX, pt. ii, 227.

Ovans: Mr., survey officer of Broach, mentions a Cháran *traga* in Broach (A. D. 1812), IX, pt. i, 218; his notice of Broach Bohoras (1818), IX, pt. ii, 59 note 1; resident at Sátára (1836), XIX, 310-311; confined in Panhála fort (1844), XXIV, 315.

Ovington: European traveller (1689), his notice of Vánia skill, IX, pt. i, 78 note 1; of their mode of mental calculation, *id.* 80, 180 note 1; on the religious persecution of Aurangzeb in Gujarát, *id.* pt. ii, 5 note 3; on the heavy funeral expenses of the Mughals *id.* 171 note 1; his account of the Pársis, *id.* 192; mention of wild animals in Kánara, XV, pt. ii, 132, 323; description of a carved elephant and horse in Elephanta caves, XIV, 92 note 1, 93.

Owa: oil-yielding plant, XXV, 223.

Owl: bird of evil omen, IX, pt. i. 381; in Ratnágiri district, X, 58-60; in Khándesh, XII, 34.

Oxalis corniculata: famine plant, XXV, 196.

Oxen: in Thána district, XIII, 439; in Kánara district, XV, pt. i, 79, 80; in Ahmadnagar district, XVII, 33-34; in Poona district; breeds, use, keep, food, cattle disease, XVIII, pt. i, 55-60; in Sholápur district, XX, 14-15; in Belgaum district, XXI, 67.

Oxenden: Sir George, English ambassador at Raigad (1674), his mention of Ashtami in Kolába district, XI, 265; his visit to Chaul, *id.* 285; deputy governor of Bombay (1676), *id.* 365.

Oxus: river on the north frontier of India, I, pt. i, 144.

Oyer and Terminer and Gaol Delivery: court of, created (1727) in Bombay island, XXVI, pt. iii, 19-20.

Oyster Rocks: in Kánara district, XV, pt. i, 2; islands, *id.* pt. ii, 47, 337.

Oysters: catchers of, in Ratnagiri, X, 91, 101.

Ozene: modern Ujjain, I, pt. i, 37, 540, 543, 545.

P

PA: táluka in Káthiáwár, VIII, 602.

Pábál: town in Poona district, temples and Mastáni's tomb at, XVIII, pt. iii, 264-265; survey of, pt. ii, 384-389, 426-430, 482-483.

Pábar: hill in Ahmadnagar district, XVII, 4.

Pacham: part of *Zend Avesta*, IX, pt. ii, 211 note 2 (7).

Páchham: island in Cutch, V, 13, 165, 248.

Pachhapur: Dodsay village in Belgaum so named, XXI, 376; survey of (1852-1856), *id.* 437-439, 443-445, 448, 450.

Pachhegám : tálnka in Káthiáwár, VIII, 602.
Pachkalshi : caste of Bráhmans in Thána district, their origin, XIII, 61-62 ; account of, *id.* 129.
Páchora : sub-division of Khándesh, its boundaries, area, aspect, climate, water, soil, holdings, survey details, survey results, stock, crops and people, XII, 2, 392-396. *Town, id.* 461.
Pachori : ceremony, rites relating to, IX, pt. ii, 229.
Pachusan : Shrávak holidays, period of, IX, pt. i, 113 ; details relating to, fasting during, *id.* 114 and note 1 ; reading of *Kalpasutra* in, *id.* 114 and note 2 ; *parikraman* ceremony during, *id.* 114-115.
Pádalsa ; place of interest, in Khándesh district, XII, 461.
Padamdurg : fort in Janjira state, XI, 466.
Padamsáli : caste of traders in Kánara district, XV, pt. i, 282-284 ; in Dhárwár district, XXII, 175.
Padan : hill in Thána district, Musala sage at, XIII, 408 ; remains at, XIV, 102-103, 388-396.
Padáv : coasting craft, in Thána district, XIII, 345-346, 720 ; in Kánara, XV, pt. ii, 63 ; *see* Machvá.
Padhariá : early tribe in Gujarát, IX, pt. i, 506.
Padhiar : a class of Rájpúts in Káthiáwár, VIII, 115 ; in Gujarát, IX, pt. i, 130.
Pádhra : caste of lower class Rájpúts, IX, pt. i, 123.
Padiár : caste of servants in Kánara, XV, pt. i, 335.
Pádli : village in Poona district, temple and fair at, XVIII, pt. iii, 265.
Padmagad : fort of, on a small island in Málvan creek, X, 346, 350 ; I, pt. ii, 75.
Padmaladevi : wife of Hoysála Ballála I, I, pt. ii, 493, 494.
Padmaladevi : wife of Hoysála Vira-Ballála II, I, pt. ii, 493, 502.
Padmaladevi : wife of Ratta Kártavirya III, I, pt. ii, 551, 556.
Padmaladevi : wife of Gutta II, I, pt. ii, 579, 582, 583.
Padmale ; pond in Kolhápur, XXIV, 12.
Padmámbike : Purushottamabhatta's wife, I, pt. ii, 482.
Padmanábha : acquires Singhana's favour, I, pt. ii, 248.
Padmanábhayya : Vikramáditya VI's officer, I, pt. ii, 451.
Padmanál, Padmanáladurga : old name of Panhála, XXIV, 313 ; capital of Bhoj II (Shak 1112), *id.* 222 ; *see* also I, pt. ii, 549.
Padmanandi Kundakunda : Áchárya, Mrigeśavarman's preceptor, I, pt. ii, 288 note 6.
Padmapáni : Bodhisattva, XII, 493 ; litany of, *id.* 531 and note 1 ; the figure of, in Kánheri caves, XIV, 176, 187.
Padmapura : city in Káshmir, I, pt. i, 188.
Padma Puran : IX, pt. i, 532.
Padmarasa ; Kalachurya Bijjala's accountant, I, pt. ii, 473.
Padma Sambhava : Guru, Buddhist wizard, IX, pt. i, 437.
Padmávati : wife of Kumárapála, I, pt. i, 188.
Padmávati : Basava's sister, I, pt. ii, 226.
Padmávati : Hindu goddess, I, pt. ii, 490, 538.
Padmávati : Kártavirya III's wife, I, pt. ii, 556.
Padra : sub-division in Baroda territory, VII, 540-544 ; large village near Baroda, history of, *id.* 541-542 ; hospital at, *id.* 505 ; *desai* of, assists Piláji (1724), *id.* 169 ; raises the Bhils against the Mughals, *id.* 174.
Padraka : village near Surat, I, pt. ii, 376.
Padsáli : a caste of weavers in Bijápur district, XXIII, 258-259.
Pád Shah : meaning of the term, IX, pt. i, 78 note 2.
Pádsháh Bibi : Bijápur king's sister, I, pt. ii, 654.
Pádshazan : an early form of marriage among Pársis, IX, pt. ii, 238 note 2.
Padti : caste of husbandmen in Kánara, XV, pt. i, 227, 228.
Paga : reef in Káthiáwár, VIII, 30.
Pages : allotted to *fidalgos, i. e.,* Portuguese noblemen, I, pt. ii, 55.
Pagi : caste of fishermen in Kánara, XV, pt. i, 313.
Pagis : trackers in Pálanpur, V, 308.
Paglás : footprints, the system of tracking culprits by, in Baroda, VII, 469-470.
Pagoda ; a coin, I, pt. i, 219 note 2 ; South Indian coin, origin of the word, XXIII, 406 note 3 ; in Dhárwár district, XXII, 450.
Pagodas : in the Portuguese India, despoiled of their accumulated riches by the Portuguese (1544), I, pt. ii, 59.
Pahádi : caste of husbandmen, in Thána district, XIII, 130 ; in Násik district, XVI, 49 ; in Ahmadnagar district, XVII, 91 ; in Poona district, XVIII, pt. i, 310-313.
Pahádi : village in Sálsette, ruins of a Portuguese church at, XIV, 293.
Pahárkhán Jhálori : governor of Pálanpur, (1744), I, pt. i, 328.
Páhini : mother of Hemachandra, I, pt. i, 191.
Pahládpur : pillar inscription at, I, pt. ii, 318.
Pahlavas : or Parthians, leading horde of foreigners, IX, pt. i, 455 ; conquerors in Western India, *id.* 433 ; joined Kushan horde in Kabul Valley, *id.* 456 ; entrance into India, *id.* 455 ; converted to Buddhism, *id.* 433 ; broken by Gautamiputra, *id.* 448, 453 note 4 ; tribe of, mentioned in the *Mahábhárata id.* 461 note 2 ; I, pt. ii, 173, 149, 155 ; I, pt. i, 35 ; *see* Pallavas.
Pahnavas : *see* Pallavas.
Paijargudd : hill in Belgaum district, XXI, 6.
Paikári : land tenure in Dhárwár, XXII, 448.
Páinu : a mode of Alibág salt rice tillage, XI, 191.
Pair : food plant, XXV, 172 ; sacred plant, *id.* 279, 284, 291.
Paiśáchi : language, form of the Prákrit, I, pt. ii, 170.
Paitamahi : festival of, I, pt. ii, 367.
Paithan : town on the Godávari, I, pt. ii, 147, 509, 533 ; mentioned by Ptolemy and in the *Periplus, id.* 143 ; capital of Pulumáyi, *id.* 158, 166 ; of Sáliváhana, *id.* 587 ; Sáliváhana attacked at, *id.* 161 ; younger Andhrabhritya princes reign at, *id.* 165 ; invaded by

Vikramáditya, *id.* 169-170; exports from, *id.* 174; flourishing town, *id.* 175; Petenikas inhabitants of, *id.* 277; grant at, *id.* 197, 198, 239, 246, 248, 356 note 3, 387, 393, 394, 397, 511, 512, 516, 522, 524, 529; *see* also I, pt. i, 37, 132, 540, 541, 545; XII, 238 and note 6; XIII, 412, 415, 416; mentioned in Kánheri caves, XIV, 147, 286; XVI, 136, 181; XVII, 351; XX, 275; XXIV, 306.

Paithanakas; people or country about Paithan, I, pt. ii, 143.

Pájua: a class of cultivators in Khándesh, XII, 68.

Pákhádis: raised causeways, X, 136.

Pakháli: caste of water-carriers in Gujarát, also called Mashkis and Bhistis, descendants of converts from the Hindu caste of the same name, Sunnis by religion, IX, pt. ii, 89; Musalmán, in Poona district, XVIII, pt. i, 505; in Sátára district, XIX, 145-146; in Sholápur district, XX, 208-209; in Belgaum district, XXI, 223; in Dhárwár district, XXII, 247; in Bijápur district, XXIII, 301.

Pakidari: modern *kavi* on the Mahi, I, pt. i, 539.

Páknák Radder: caste of husbandmen in Dhárwár district, XXII, 142-143.

Pakshaghát: *see* Paralysis.

Pál: *see* Vol.

Pál: state in Káthiáwár, VIII, 602.

Pál: ruined town in Khándesh, XII, 461; its colonization, *id.* 400 note 1.

Pál: *see* Palc.

Pál: hill in Sátára district, XIX, 11; village, Khandobá's temple, fair and history of, XIX, 529-532.

Palaces: at Sátára, XIX, 567; at Bijápur, XXIII, 617-626.

Páladeva: Western Chalukya king Jagadekamallá II's officer, I, pt. ii, 457.

Palai: wrongly separated from Simoundan by Ptolemy, and taken to mean "formerly" instead of understanding "Palaisimoundan" as one word which is a name for Ceylon, I, pt. i, 543.

Palaipatmai, Palaipotamai: modern Pal, near Mahád, I, pt. ii, 174; I, pt. i, 540, 546; XIII, 418.

Palaisimoundan: Ceylon, I, pt. i, 543.

Pálaj: state in Mahi Kántha, V, 429.

Palakkada; Pallava town, I, pt. ii, 318 and note 12; grant from, *id.* 320.

Palakuda: famine plant, XXV, 201.

Pálanpur: Agency, boundaries, division, aspect, V, 281; hills, *id.* 282; rivers, water-supply, *id.* 283-284; geology, climate, *id.* 284; mineral products, trees, domestic and wild animals, birds and fish, *id.* 285-288; population: Hindu and Musalmán, *id.* 289-292; agriculture: arable land, crops, floods and famines, *id.* 293-296; capital: interest, wages, prices, weights and measures, *id.* 297-298; trade: markets, fairs, etc., *id.* 299-300; history, *id.* 301-303; land administration, *id.* 304-305; justice: civil courts, police, jail, infanticide, *id.* 306-309; revenue and finance, *id.* 310-312; instruction: schools, libraries, *id.* 313-314; health, *id.* 315-316; states under, *id.* 317-338; places of interest, *id.* 339-351; *state*, its boundaries, aspect, climate, rivers, V, 317; history, genealogical tree of the reigning family, *id.* 318-324. *Town*, history, population, temples, *id.* 343-344; its tribute to Baroda, VII, 331-332; birth-place of Siddharája, Chalukya king, I, pt. i, 171, 310.

Palanquin-bearer: IX, pt. i, 504-505; at Mátherán, XIV, 270-271. *See* Bhoi.

Páláru: river, forms the northern boundary of the territory of Cholas, I, pt. ii, 277, 326.

Palas: oil-yielding, fibrous, dye and gum-yielding and sacred plant, XXV, 217, 231, 243, 250, 279, 290, 291; in Khándesh, XII, 28; in Poona district, XVIII, pt. i, 50.

Palásda: place of interest in Khándesh, temple at, XII, 462.

Palasdev: market village in Poona district, temple at, XVIII, pt. iii, 265.

Palasgad: the summit of the hill of Mábuli in Thána district, a fort, XIV, 219-220.

Palasige: territorial division, ruled over by the Kadambas of Goa, I, pt. ii, 298 note 2, 358 note 1, 451, 452, 456, 460, 476, 486, 565, 568, 569, 570.

Palásika: Halsi, in Belgaum district, I, pt. ii, 285, 288, 289; capital of the early Kadambas (500-550), XXIV, 218.

Palásni: state in Rewa Kántha, VI, 146-147.

Palaspiplo: tree called *nandivraksha*, its sacredness, worship of, IX, pt. i, 385.

Palásvihir: state in Khándesh, XII, 606.

Palasvihir: pass in Násik district, XVI, 128.

Palav: form of tenure in Ratnágiri district, X, 450.

Palav: boat in Thána district, XIII, 720.

Palaverkadu: modern Pulicat, I, pt. ii, 318 note 12.

Pale: caves in Kolába district, XI, 345-349; *see* also I, pt. ii, 9, 12, 174; XIII, 418; I, pt. i, 546.

Pálegár: *see* Páligars.

Pálgad: fort in Ratnágiri district, X, 354.

Pálghar: village with railway station in Thána district. *See* Navli.

Palgire: village mentioned in a grant from the Karnul district, I, pt. ii, 367.

Palhavas: or Parthians, *see* Pahlavas and Pallavas.

Páli: ancient dialect, I, pt. ii, 136, 177; inscriptions, *id.* 538 note 8.

Páli: chief trade centre of Márwár, IX, pt. i, 16.

Páli: fort in Kolába district, XI, 267; reduced by Malik Ahmad, I, pt. ii, 32.

Páliás: tombstones in Káthiáwár, VIII, 136 note 2; at Ántália, *id.* 370.

Palibothra: Pátaliputra, modern Pátna, I, pt. i, 533.

Pálidevi: mentioned in an inscription at Sangsi in Kolhápur state, I, pt. ii, 286 note 1.

Pálid-vaja: banner of Vinayaditya the Chálukya king of Bádámi, I, pt. ii, 189, 338, 368; of the Ráshtrakútas, *id.* 387, 402.

Páligars: Marátha and Koli Bhil chiefs; their rule in Poona district (1190-1295), XVIII, pt. ii, 214-215; reduce Konkan (1200), X, 193

note 7; the *desai* of Sávantvádi a Páligar, *id.* 439 note 2; their rule in Khándesh, XII, 238; petty Marátha chiefs in Dhárwár district, Haidar levies tribute from (1761), XXII, 444 and note 1.
Pálil: village in Ratnágiri district, X, 355.
Pálimbothra: Pataliputra, I, pt. i, 546.
Palita: IX, pt. ii, 133; *see* Fatliah.
Pálitána: state and town in Káthiáwár, VIII, 603-605; I, pt. i, 186; Gohil Rájpút chiefship, origin of the house, IX, pt. i, 125-126.
Pálivál: a sub-caste of Bráhmans in Gujarát said to have come from Márwár and Rájpútána, IX, pt. i, p. xi note 3, 2, 16; created from local non-Bráhman classes, *id.* 440; in Cutch, V, 47.
Paliyád: táluka in Káthiáwár, VIII, 602.
Paliyás: stones raised in memory of the dead among wild tribes, IX, pt. i, 363-364, 409; guardian stones erected in memory of Cháran *traga* in Káthiáwár villages, *id.* 218 and note 1; memorial stones in Thána district, XIV, 50, 57, 112, 308-312, 337.
Pálkhed: canal in Násik district, XVI, 94.
Palla: or Pallava, lower classes in Madras, IX, pt. i, 445 note 4.
Pallas yel: dye and gum-yielding plant, XXV, 243, 250.
Pallav: dynasty (400-600), their connection with Kánara district, XV, pt. ii, 79 and note 2, 81, 82; in Dhárwár district, driven out by Kadambas and Chalukyas, Conjeeveram their capital, descended from Parthians, XXII, 390 and note 5; in Bijápur district, XXIII, 379, 380 and note 4, 383; I, pt. i, 35, 58; *see* Pallavas.
Pallavádítya-Nolambádhirája: Pallava king (974), I, pt. ii, 305, 306 note 4.
Pallavamalla: *biruda* (title) of Nandivarman, I, pt. ii, 325.
Pallava-Murári: *biruda* (title) of Tribhuvanadhira Nulamba, I, pt. ii, 332, 422.
Pallavas: foreign tribe, non-Hindu, said to be created by Vasistha, a note on, XIII, 411 note 2, 413 and note 7; I, pt. ii, 316-334; Dramila, Dravida or Drávida, their country and Kánchi or Conjeeveram their capital, *id.* 281; their country also called Tonda; Nolambavádi, portions of Belláry and Mysore, their possession in Western India, *id.* 318: their *gotra* and pursnic genealogy; degraded Kshatriyas, origin of their name; Arsacidan Párthians, *id.* 316 and notes 5 and 6, 317 and notes 1 and 3, 318; their pedigrees, *id.* 321, 323; their crest, banner, and family god, *id.* 299 note 4, 319 and notes 2 and 3; destroyed by Gotamiputra (130), *id.* 317; their dynasty firmly established by the middle of the fourth century, *id.* 317; their king captured and liberated by the early Gupta king Samudragupta, *id.* 319; seek to overthrow Kadamba Mayurasarman, *id.* 286; destroyed by Kadamba Mrigeśavarman, *id.* 288; conquered by the Western Chálukya king Kirtivarman I (567-598), *id.* 281; defeated by Pulikesin II, *id.* 282, 329, 350-351; make constant wars with the Western Chalukyas and are called teirh natural enemies, *id.* 316; invade Bádámi, take Nolambavádi, and interrupt the sovereignty of the Western Chalukyas (634-635), *id.* 318-319, 336, 358, 382; defeated by Vikramaditya I, *id.* 186, 342, 362; by Vinayáditya, *id.* 188, 368; by Vikramáditya II, *id.* 189, 374; by Kirtivarman II, *id.* 190, 375, 377; by the Ráshtrakúta king Dhruva, *id.* 197, 393; subjugated by Govinda III, *id.* 198, 395; lose their sovereign power and sink into the position of mere feudatories and officials (977), *id.* 332; subdued by the Western Chálukya kings Someśvara II and Vikramáditya VI, *id.* 333; their country overrun and ruled over by Hoysála Vishnuvardhana, *id.* 496, 499; brought to obedience by the Devagiri Yádava king Singhana, *id.* 525; exist and continue to exercise some kind of power till the thirteenth century A.D., *id.* 333. *See* under Kánchi.
Palli: thanksgiving ceremony; offerings to the water-spirit in, IX, pt. 230, 231.
Pallis: tribe in Madras purified by fire, IX, pt. i, 486.
Pallu: *see* Dowry.
Pallur: *see* Palakkada.
Palmæ: species of food, famine and oil-yielding plants, XXV, 180, 206, 221.
Palmer: Colonel, British resident (1797) at Poona, XVIII, pt. ii, 276, 279.
Palm-tappers: in Kánara, XV, pt. i, 284-295.
Palm-tapping: in Kolába, XI, 134; in Bijápur, XXIII, 111.
Palmyra: town, its trade relations with Thána coast (B.C. 255-600 A.D.), XIII, 410, 411 note 1, 412; Hindus at (A.D. 243), *id.* 413.
Palmyra palm: food plant, XXV, 180; in Poona district, XVIII, pt. i, 53.
Palsána: sub-division in Baroda state, VII, 570-572. *Town*, 572; *see* also I, pt. i, 127 and note 3.
Palshá, Palshe: a sub-caste of Bráhmans in Sátára district, XIX, 55; in Násik district, XVI, 26; in Kolába district, XI, 45; in Thána district, their origin, XIII, 61-62, 63 note 2; account of, *id.* 81.
Palshi: village in Ahmadnagar district, temple at, XVII, 730.
Palshi: village in Sátára district, XIX, 532.
Palu: foot-path in Thána district, XIII, 321.
Palu Mál: site of a Mughal camp in Sátára district, XIX, 528-529.
Palumbinæ: family of birds in Ratnágiri, X, 86.
Pálus: village in Sátára district, XIX, 532.
Pálwára: local name for Godhra, I, pt. i, 208 note 3.
Pámbhar: seed-drill, an agricultural instrument in Khándesh, XII, 144.
Pampa: lake in the Bellary district, I, pt. i, 142.
Pampa: Canarese poet, author of the *Vikramdrjunavijaya* (863), I, pt. ii, 212, 380, 416 note 7; *see* also I, pt. i, 466.
Pampabhárata: *see* Vikramárjunavijaya.
Pampátirtha: modern Hampe in the Belláry district, I, pt. ii, 369.
Pán: betel vine, cultivation of, in Kolhápur, XXIV, 173-174; grows in several districts, XXV, 173; cultivation of, in Kánara district, XV, pt. ii, 11. *See* also Betel-leaf.

Pánádis : water divines, XVIII, pt. ii, 13.
Pánam : river in Rewa Kántha, VI, 4, 121.
Panamalai : in the South Arcot district, inscription at, I, pt. ii, 330.
Panas : food plant, XXV, 172.
Panasa : Osanpur on the left bank of the Indus, I, pt. i, 538.
Pánbhari : Koli tribe in Ahmadnagar district, XVII, 193.
Panchaitan : town in Janjirá state, XI, 466.
Panchaitan Pir : Shiáh shrine in Janjira fort, XI, 435 ; fair at, *id.* 464.
Panchál : a caste of craftsmen, in Kolába district, XI, 65 ; in Khándesh district, XII, 73 ; in Thána district, XIII, 138 ; in Kánara, XV, pt. i, 257, 258 and note 1 ; in Ahmadnagar district, XVII, 133 ; Buddhist element in, XVIII, pt. i, 343 ; in Sholápur district, their origin, division, houses, food, condition, customs, community, XX, 124-134 ; in Belgaum district, XXI, 132, 133, 143, 144 ; in Dhárwár district, XXII, 159 ; in Kolhápur state, XXIV, 97 ; in Bijápur district, XXIII, 141-143.
Pánchála : *zillah* in Sorath, I, pt. i, 208 note 3 ; I, pt. ii, 139; king of, killed by Taila II, *id.* 424, 426, 432 ; humbled by Singhana, *id.* 525.
Panchaladeva : Narasimha's successor (974-975), killed by the Western Chálukya king Taila II, I, pt. ii, 307.
Pánchálesbvar : rock-cut temple, near Poona city, XVIII, pt. iii, 385-386.
Pancham : or Pánchás, meaning of the term, IX, pt. i, 70, 435.
Pancha Mahávratas : five main vows observed by Shrávak *sádhus*, IX, pt. i, 107, 108.
Panchamsáli : caste of Lingáyat husbandmen in Kánara, XV, pt. i, 228 ; in Bijápur district, XXIII, 221-222.
Panchanetreshvar: Násik temple, XVI, 505-506.
Pánchás : *see* Pancham.
Panchásar : small town in Pálanpur, its history, V, 345 ; fall of its Chavda chiefship (696), I, pt. i, 149-150, 155 ; *see* also IX, pt. i, p. IX, 488.
Panchásara Párasnáth : Jain temple of, I, pt. i, 152.
Panchásikha : Mándavya's son, progenitor of the Chalukyas, I, pt. ii, 339 note 7.
Panchasikhi Hariti : son of Hárita, I, pt. ii, 278 note 1, 339.
Panchatantra : book of tales, IX, pt. i, 435.
Pánchávada : tálnka in Káthiáwár, VIII, 606.
Panchavamaharáya : Chola king, Rájarájadeva's military commander, I, pt. ii, 308.
Panchavati : place on the Godávari, I, pt. ii, 135 ; identified with Násik, *id.* 136 ; IX, pt. i, 12 note 1.
Pancháyat : native jury system, in Ahmadábád district, IV, 106 ; in Baroda, VII, 440-441 ; in Poona district, XVIII, pt. iii, 19, 20 ; village council in Sátára district, XIX, 390, 392 ; caste council among Kunbis, a substitute for civil courts, their methods of procedure, XXIV, 96, 266-267 ; called in survey settlement (1821), XIII, 570 ; in Násik district, XVI, 304 and note 2 ; in Belgaum, XXI, 467 ; IX, pt. ii, 244.
Pancháyatan Devs : five house gods, stone *ling* for Mahádev, stone *shaligram* or picture of *Shrináthji* for Vishnu, picture of metal image of *Sakti Bhaváni* or *Máta* as the goddess or mother, *Ganpati*, *Hanumán*, IX, pt. i, p. XXXV, 393.
Panchayats or Panchayets : *see* Pancháyat.
Panchbhág : daily dole, IX, pt. i, 24.
Panchdand : five magic wands, obtained by Vikram, XIV, 319.
Panchganga : river in Kolhápur state, XXIV, 8, 9-10, 305, 307.
Pánchgani : health-resort in Sátára district, description, water-supply, climate, management, high school and nurseries at, XIX, 532-534.
Panchgavya : five products of the cow, names of, used in religious ceremonies, IX, pt. i, 372, 373.
Panch Mahábhutáni : five elements, meaning of, IX, pt. i, 348.
Panch Maháls : district, description, III, 183-190 ; rivers, *id.* 191 ; geology, *id.* 191-194 ; climate, *id.* 195, 196 ; minerals, *id.* 197 ; trees, *id.* 198-201 ; shrubs and plants, *id.* 202-207 ; forests, *id.* 208 ; animals, *id.* 209-212 ; census details, *id.* 213-215 ; Hindu castes, *id.* 216-218 ; Bhils, *id.* 219-221 ; Naikdas, *id.* 222-225 ; Musalmáns, Pársis and Christians, *id.* 226 ; dwellings, communities, *id.* 227 ; migration, *id.* 228, 229 ; soil, irrigation, holdings and stock, *id.* 230-231 ; aboriginal tillage and crops, *id.* 232 ; details of cultivation, *id.* 233, 234 ; bad seasons, *id.* 235 ; capitalists, money-lenders, *id.* 236 ; borrowers, rates of interest, currency, *id.* 237 ; wages, prices, weights and measures, *id.* 238-239 ; roads, *id.* 240 ; bridges, rest-houses, ferries, post and telegraph figures, *id.* 241 ; land trade, *id.* 242-248 ; manufactures, *id.* 249, 250 ; fairs, trade guilds, *id.* 251 ; Panch Maháls under Rájputs, Musalmáns, Maráthás and British, *id.* 252 ; Tatia Topi's raid, *id.* 253, 254 ; Naikda risings, *id.* 255-258 ; acquisition, *id.* 259 ; staff, *id.* 260 ; state of district, *id.* 261 ; revenue system, *id.* 262 ; alienations, *id.* 263 ; revenue survey, *id.* 264 ; waste lands *id.* 265 ; transit dues, *id.* 266 ; seasons, *id.* 267, 268 ; development, *id.* 269 ; civil and criminal justice, *id.* 270-272 ; police and crimes, *id.* 273-276 ; revenue and finance, 277-281 ; local funds and municipalities, *id.* 282, 283 ; schools, libraries, newspapers, *id.* 284-289 ; diseases, hospitals, dispensaries, births and deaths, *id.* 290, 291 ; sub-divisional accounts, *id.* 292-302 ; places of interest, *id.* 303-317 ; rising in, siege of Dohad raised by Captain Buckle's forces, I, pt. i, 439 ; Tatia Topi in, his expulsion from, *id.* 445 ; *see* also I, pt. ii, 382.
Panch Mási : fifth month pregnancy ceremony, IX, pt. i, 93.
Panchmási ; ceremony relating to pregnancy rites in, IX, pt. ii, 227.
Panchratan : five jewels, placed under foundation stone, IX, pt. ii, 205.
Pánch Talávda : place of interest in Káthiáwár, VIII, 606.

Panchtirthi : or five shrines between Bhimnáth and Gopnáth, IX, pt. i, 549.

Panchvati : *see* Panchavati.

Pandæ : the Pándyas, I, pt. i, 532, 534.

Pandai : the Pándyas, I, pt. i, 546.

Pandanaceæ : species of famine, oil-yielding and fibrous plants, XXV, 207, 225, 236.

Pandanus odoratissimus : famine, oil-yielding, fibrous and sacred plant, XXV, 207, 225, 236, 279, 285, 289.

Pandára : hill in Ahmadnagar district, XVII, 4.

Pándárvada : sub-division in Rewa Kántha, VI, 122.

Pándavas : the, spend twelve years in Banavási, I, pt. ii, 278 note 2 ; at Hángal (B.C. 1500), XXII, 389 ; building of the Buddhist caves ascribed to, XIII, 404 note 2 ; XIV, 81 note 1 ; hall of, at Sopára (B.C. 1400), *id.* 316 ; Tungár springs bearing the name of, *id.* 369 ; at Vairatpur, IX, pt. i, 252 note 1, 294 ; described as Ismáilia pontiffs, IX, pt. ii, 48 ; descendants of, at Kanauj, I, pt. i, 519 ; one sprung from to be called Pándya, I, pt. ii, 139.

Pándav Daráh : Buddhist caves near Panhála, XXIV, 317.

Pándavgad : island, fort in Málvan creek, built by Shiváji, X, 351, 355.

Pándavgad : hill fort in Sátára district, its description and history ; caves at, XIX, 534-536 ; taken by the Mughals (1701), *id.* 252 ; Báláji Vishvanáth conceals himself at (1713), *id.* 256 ; taken by Trimbakji Denglia, *id.* 300.

Pándavs : *see* Pándavas.

Pandavvádi : village in Sátára district, XIX, 534.

Pandes : family of, among the early Pársi settlers in Bombay, IX, pt. ii, 195.

Pandhari plate : famine plant, common in India, XXV, 197.

Pándharpeshás : high class villagers in Thána district, XIII, 63 ; tenure of, *id.* 531, 532-534, 532 notes 1 and 3 ; land holders, *id.* 556, 557 ; low rates, 557 note 4 ; in Bájiráv's time, *id.* 560 ; easy rates, 565 ; farmers' rates, *id.* 566 note 2 ; opinions of the collectors and government concerning (1820), *id.* 566 ; lower rate fixed (1837), *id.* 583 ; final settlement, *id.* 534 ; in Kolába district, XI, 172, 433 note 1. *See* also I, pt. ii, 430.

Pandharpur : sub-division of Sholápur district, its area, aspect, climate, water, soil, stock, holdings, crops and people, XX, 400-402 ; survey of, *id.* 328-333. *Town*, *id.* 415-485 ; details of river, *gháts* or landings, *id.* 415-416 ; Vithoba's temple, its worship and history, *id.* 417-431 ; other temples : Pundalik, Vishnupad, Trimbakeshvar, Panchmukhi Máruti, Ganpati, Belichá Mahádev, Kálabhairav and Shákambhari, *id.* 432-439 ; Mallikárjuna, Ambábái, Rámchandra, *id.* 440-447 ; Bábhlya's Mahádev, Chandrabhága, Murlidhar, Dwárakádhish, Chophála, Padmávati, Vyás, Tákpithya Vithobá, Batteshvar Mahádev, Beri's Mahádev, *id.* 448-456 ; Kála Máruti, Támda Máruti, Gáricha Mahádev, Lakhubái, Amriteshvar Mahádev, and Gopálpura temples, *id.* 457-468 ; worship, priests, pilgrims, *id.* 469-481 ; orphanage, foundling home, trade, industries, and history, *id.* 482-485 ; under Vishnuvardhana, I, pt. ii, 185 ; inscription at, *id.* 247 ; records at, *id.* 527 ; action at (1774), XVIII, pt. ii, 257 ; Gangádhar Shástri murdered at (1815), *id.* 295, I, pt. ii, 610 ; *see* also IX, pt. i, 119, 549.

Pándhri : old Poona fort, XVIII, pt. iii, 272-273, 339.

Pandion : kingdom of the Pándyas, I, pt. i, 537, 546.

Panditráo : expounder of Hindu law under the Marátha government, XIX, 244 note 1.

Pandits : at the courts of Gujarát kings, I, pt. i, 180.

Pándivad : snake in Ratnágiri district, X, 49.

Pándri : stream in Kánara district, XV, pt. i, 5.

Pándu : estate in Rewa Kántha, VI, 153.

Pándugad : *see* Pandavgad in Sátára district.

Pándu Lena Caves : near Násik city, description, view, XVI, 541-542 ; caves I and II, inscription I, *id.* 542-544 ; cave III, *id.* 544-549 ; inscriptions 2-5, *id.* 548-561 ; caves IV-VI, inscription 6, *id.* 562-564 ; cave VII, inscription 7, cave VIII, inscription 8-9, cave IX, *id.* 565-567 ; cave X, inscription 10-15, *id.* 567-580 ; cave XI, inscription 16, cave XII, inscription 17, *id.* 580-582 ; caves XIII, XIV, XV, XVI, XVII, inscription 18, *id.* 583-588 ; cave XVIII, inscriptions 19-21, *id.* 589-591 ; cave XIX, inscription 22, cave XX, inscriptions 23-24, *id.* 592-597 ; caves XXI-XXIII, *id.* 598-603 ; inscription 25, cave XXIV, inscription 26-27, *id.* 604-606 ; remarks, palæography, history, order of caves, geography, *id.* 606-639. *See* also I, pt. ii, 355.

Pándu Mehvas : states in Rewa Kántha, VI, 1, 2, 148-154 ; pay tribute to Baroda, VII, 337.

Pándurang Pandit : Peshwa's agent in Gujarát, marches on Cambay and Ahmadábád, makes peace with Momin Khán and Jawán Mard Khán and retires to Sorath (1752), I, pt. i, 335.

Pándurang Pant : *see* Pándurang Pandit.

Pándurangráv Patwardhan : grandfather of the present chief of Sángli, wounded and taken prisoner by Haidar (1776) to Seringapatam, XXIV, 345 ; I, pt. ii, 659.

Pándus : *see* Pándavas.

Pándya : *see* Pándyás.

Pándyadeva : Western Chálukya king Permajagadekamalla II's vassal, I, pt. ii, 319 note 1.

Pándyadevarasa : Kalachurya Someśvara's officer, I, pt. ii, 486.

Pandyádi Jawán Mardi : book of the Indian Khojáh scriptures written by A'gha Abdus Salámsháh, IX, pt. ii, 41, 48.

Pándyas : boundaries of the country of, I, pt. ii, 277, 281 ; monkey soldiers directed to go to their city, *id.* 137 ; their king defeated by Sahadeva, *id.* 133, 142 ; probably not known to Pánini, *id.* 140 ; their territory outlying Aśoka's kingdom, *id.* 146 ; conquered by the Western Chálukya king Kírtivarman I, *id.* 345-346 ; invaded by Pulakesin II, *id.* 183, 282, 350 ; I, pt. i, 111 ; rebel but are subdued by Vikramáditya I, I, pt. ii, 186, 358 note 1, 362 and note 6 ; reduced by Vinayáditya, *id.* 188-189, 368 ; by Vikramáditya

II, *id.* 190, 375 ; defeated by Udayachandra, the general of the Pallava king Nandivarman, *id.* 327 ; reduced by the Ráshtrakúta king Dantidurga, *id.* 194, 389 ; subdued by Krishna III, *id.* 207 ; conquered by Kakka II, *id.* 423 ; their lands absorbed into the Chola kingdom, *id.* 308 ; subdued by the Western Chálukya king Someśvara II, *id.* 333 ; humbled by Hoysála Vishnuvardhana, *id.* 495, 496 ; associate with the Hoysálas against Vikramáditya II also called VI, and are defeated by Sinda Achugi II, *id.* 218-219, 453, 574 ; their chieftain of Nolambavádi rebels and is defeated by Hoysála Vira-Ballála II, *id.* 505 ; by Narasimha II, *id.* 507 ; their Nolambavádi branch do not recognise the sovereignty of the Devagiri Yádava king Bhillama, *id.* 519 ; subdued by Singhana's general Bichana, *id.* 243, 524, 525 ; mentioned by Pliny, I, pt. i, 534.

Panechana, Panchnad : Portuguese sub-division probably Panvel in Thána district, XIV, 44 ; XIII, 456.

Panetha : sub-division in Rewa Kántha, VI, 97.

Pángal : *see* Pangul.

Pángára : *Erythrina indica,* timber tree, in Poona, XVIII, pt. i, 50 ; in Khándesh, XII, 26.

Pangariká : village mentioned in a grant from Karda in Khándesh, I, pt. ii, 423.

Pángul : a class of beggars in Kolába district, XI, 74 ; in Násik district, XVI, 75 ; in Ahmadnagar district, XVII, 185-186 ; in Poona district, XVIII, pt. i, 459-460 ; in Khándesh, XII, 123. *See* Helav.

Panhálá : hill fort in Kolhápur state, XXIV, 6 ; health resort, *id.* 16, 293 ; survey, *id.* 260-263 ; fort details, history, human sacrifices at ; town, details, reservoirs, market, temples, tomb, fair, Paráshar's caves at, *id.* 313-316 ; inscriptions at, *id.* 422-425 ; *see* also I, pt. ii, 76, 254 ; capital of the Kolhápur Siláháras, *id.* 546, 549, 587 ; taken by Anáji Dattu (1659), *id.* 593 ; besieged by Sidi Johár (1660), *id.* 593 ; fight between the Maráthás and the Bijápur army at (1671), *id.* 594 ; Sambháji confined in, *id.* 595 ; *see* also X, 193.

Panicum : *oplismenus colonum, setaria glaneum, Italicum,* fodder plants, XXV, 276 ; *frumentaceum, maliaceum,* food and fodder plants, *id.* 184, 276 ; (*setaria*) *Italicum,* food plant, *id.* 184 ; *pilosum,* food and fodder plants common in India and on the *ghâts, id.* 185, 276.

Pani-lajak : famine plant, XXV, 199.

Pánini : Sanskrit grammarian, I, pt. ii, 135, 138, 139, 140 ; his date, *id.* 141, 142, 171 ; *see* also I, pt. i, 36, 534.

Pánipat : near Delhi, battle of (1761), I, pt. i, 345 ; I, pt. ii, 101, 627 ; VI, 228 ; VII, 184 ; XIII, 497, 498 note 4 ; XVIII, pt. ii, 249 ; XIX, 295.

Panjáb : first Áryan settlement in, I, pt. ii, 135 ; Áryas progressing from, *id.* 137 ; places mentioned by Pánini in, *id.* 138 ; a part of the Persian dominions ; conquest of, by Darius Hystaspes (B. C. 510) : under the Achæmenean dynasty, under the Indo-Skythian ruler, IX, pt. ii, 183 note 4 ; relations of the Pársis of the, with Cambay Pársis, *id.* 186 note 1, 188 note 4 ; *see* also I, pt. i, 526, 527, 534, 545 ; converts from, in the College of Bándra, XIII, 202 ; called Takkadesh, IX, pt. ii, 70.

Panjábi : a caste of weavers in Násik district, XVI, 53.

Pánjan : river in Násik district, XVI, 10.

Pánjarápol : home for animals, IX, pt. i, 115 ; in Poona city, XVIII, pt. iii, 332-333 ; in Ahmadábád district, IV, 114 ; at Bhiwndi and Chembur in Thána district, XIV, 49, 52 ; in Mahi Kántha, V, 396.

Pánjhra : river in Khándesh, XII, 8 ; waterworks, *id.* 140.

Panjim : town in Goa territory, capital of Portuguese India, I, pt. ii, 565.

Panjnigar : a caste of Musalmán writers in Sholápur district, XX, 209 ; in Gujarát, cotton thread starchers, converts from the Hindu caste of the same name, form a separate community, IX, pt. ii, 78 ; Hir, silk starchers, have a monopoly in the art, *id.* 78.

Panjrapol : *see* Panjarápol.

Panjtan : or Pentad of the holy family of Islám consists of *Ali,* the *Lady Fatimah,* her sons *Hasan* and *Husain,* and the *Apostle of God,* IX, pt. ii, 47.

Pánmul : village, under Bijápur, assigned to the author of *Mirat-i-Ahmedi,* I, pt. i, 322.

Pannagálay : another name of Panhála, XXIV, 313.

Pannála-durgádrisimha : Karád Siláhára Jotiga II's title, I, pt. ii, 546.

Pannaledurga : modern Panhála, I, pt. ii, 549.

Pannappeśvara : temple of, mentioned in an inscription from the North Arcot district, Madras Presidency, I, pt. ii, 422.

Pannáya : tax levied by the feudatories of Vikramáditya VI of the Western Chálukyas of Kalyáni, I, pt. ii, 451, 452.

Pánoli : village near Surat, I, pt. i, 328.

Panorama : point at Mátherán, XIV, 231, 232, 233, 234, 236, 279.

Panoti : deadly influence of Shani or Saturn, IX, pt. i, 403.

Pant : of Bávda, shares of, in the Sálahi province and Bhagvantgad, I, pt. ii, 79.

Pant Amátya : superintendent of finance of Marátha government, XIX, 243-244.

Pánthal : rice soil in Ratnágiri district, X, 144.

Panthers : in Ratnágiri district, X, 42, 44 ; in Khándesh, XII, 30 ; at Mátherán, XIV, 259 ; in Belgaum district, XXI, 69 ; in Kánara, XV, pt. i, 92, 94.

Pánthipura, Pántipura : modern Hángal, I, pt. ii, 558, 562, 563 and note 5.

Pánt-lavadi : estate in Rewa Kántha, VI, 147.

Pán Tower : fort in Kelve village in Thána district, XIII, 293.

Pant Pratinidhi : his dispute with the Marátha state about the joint districts near Ratnágiri settled in 1784, I, pt. ii, 106.

Pant Sachiv : general record-keeper of the Marátha government, XIX, 244 note 1 ; surrender of (1818), I, pt. ii, 116 ; his rights over the Konkan villages settled, *id.* 127 ; his conduct at the time of the mutinies (1857), XIX, 317-319.

Pantyá : a caste of messengers in Cutch, V, 101, 102.
Pánungal : modern Hángal in Dhárwár district, XXII, 389 ; I, pt. ii, 377, 298 note 2, 431, 435, 437, 439, 450, 451, 456, 458, 465, 558, 561, 562, 563, 564.
Pánvad : sub-division in Rewa Kántha, VI, 112.
Panvel : sub-division of Thána district, its boundaries, area, aspect, climate, water, soil, holdings, rental, stock, crops and people, XIII, 2, 692-695 ; under Nana (1781), *id.* 508 ; under the English, *id.* 522, 523 ; condition of (1835), *id.* 578-579 ; assessment revised (1837), *id.* 581-582 : results, *id.* 585 ; survey assessment introduced in (1856), *id.* 596-599. *Town* and port, discription, industry and trade, XIV, 293-296 ; Buddhist or Bráhmanic remains at, *id.* 10 ; under Gujarát kings (1508), XIII, 443 ; ceded to Bijápur (1636), *id.* 464 ; trade centre (1500-1670), *id.* 465 ; Marátha horse at, *id.* 503 ; heavy mortality at (1812), *id.* 508.
Pánwála : vegetable boat, in Thána, XIII, 720.
Panwelly : modern Panvel port under the Gujarát kings, I, pt. ii, 30.
Papai : *Carica papaya*, fruit tree in Poona, XVIII, pt. i, 50.
Papaveraceæ : species of oil-yielding plant, XXV, 214.
Pápdi : gardens and fields near Bassein, XIV, 36 ; church at, *id.* 37.
Paper : manufacture of, in Surat district, II, 179, 181 ; in Broach district, *id.* 549 ; in Panch Maháls, III, 250 ; in Ahmadábád district, IV, 133 ; in Cambay, VI, 189 ; in Khándesh, XII, 237, 440, 479 ; in Kolhápur state, XXIV, 214-216 ; in Thána district, XIII, 399-400 ; in Násik district, XVI, 177-179 ; in Poona district, XVIII, pt. ii, 204-206 ; in Dhárwár district, XXII, 388 ; in Bijápur district, XXIII, 375-376.
Paper mill : at Sassu Navghar in Thána, XIV, 305.
Papiki : cape of, identification of, I, pt. i, 539, 544, 545.
Papnas : pomelo in Poona district, XVIII, pt. i, 50.
Pár : pass in Koláha district, XI, 114.
Par : stream in Násik district, XVI, 7.
Pár : river in Surat district, II, 27.
Parabali : a place probably in Sind, I, pt. i, 538.
Parabhus : *see* Prabhus.
Párádá : river, mentioned in an inscription at Násik, I, pt. ii, 148.
Paradas : Parthians, XIII, 411 note 2.
Páradhi : *see* Párdhi.
Páráhánaka : village, granted, its identity with Palsána, I, pt. i, 127 and note 3 ; modern Parona in the Surat district, I, pt. ii, 406.
Parahitarája : *biruda* (title) of a Chálukya chief, I, pt. ii, 380.
Parajia : a Bráhman sub-caste in Cutch, V, 45 ; degraded Bráhmans in Gujarát, IX, pt. i, p. xii note 3, 160.
Parajia Soni : a sub-caste of goldsmiths in Káthiáwár, VIII, 150 note 1.
Parajiyá : *see* Parájia.
Parakesarivarman : another name of the Chola king Rájendra Choladeva, I, pt. ii, 436. *See* Madhurántaka II and Rájendra Choladeva.
Parakesarivarman : brother-in-law of Vikramáditya VI the Western Chálukya king, I, pt. ii, 445. *See* Adhirájendradeva.
Párakh Nima : Bania of Diu (1677), concession in favor of, made by the Bombay Council, XXVI, pt. i, 74-77.
Paralysis : disease, its cure, IX, pt. i, 365.
Parama : village, presented to Gangarája by Vishnuvardhana, I, pt. ii, 500.
Paramabhattáraka : paramount title, I, pt. ii, 474, 475, 488, 518, 523.
Paramadeva : *rája*, identified with Paramára, king of Abu, I, pt. i, 168 note 2.
Paramahansas : order of Shiv ascetics, IX, pt. i, 543.
Paramáras : *see* Parmar.
Paramárdi : *see* Permádi.
Paramardideva : Vikramáditya II, I, pt. ii, 219, 234, 515.
Paramardin : *see* Permádi.
Parameśvara Potarája : Parameśvaravarman II, I, pt. ii, 325.
Parameśvara Potavarman I : I, pt. ii, 324. *See* Parameśvaravarman I.
Parameśvara Potavarman II : *see* Parameśvaravarman II.
Parameśvaravarman I : Vidyavinita the Pallava king, I, pt. ii, 322 and note 8, 323 ; succeeds Mahendravarman II, *id.* 324 note 3, 325 ; defeats Vikramáditya I at Peruvalanallur, *id.* 326, 343 note 2 ; is overthrown by Vikramáditya I, *id.* 362.
Parameśvaravarman II : Pallava king, I, pt. ii, 324 note 1, 325 and note 2, 326.
Parammadeva : Seunachandra II's successor, I, pt. ii, 516.
Paránda : fort, in Nizám's dominions, Nizámsháhi capital (1599), XVII, 390 ; siege of, *id.* 399.
Parántaka I : Chola king (935), I, pt. ii, 299 note 4, 320 note 6, 325 ; copper-plate grants of, *id.* 326, 327. *See* Madiraikondako-Parakesarivarman.
Parántij : sub-division of Ahmadábád district, its boundaries, area, aspect, climate, water, soil, holdings, rental, stock, produce and people, IV, 230-232. *Town, id.* 346 ; ceded to Damáji Gáikwár (1737) by Momin Khán, VII, 175 ; I, pt. ii, 110, 319.
Parántij Kolis : in Ahmadábád district, land administration among, under British rule, IV, 154, 186.
Parasanga : Sindi linear measure of distance, I, pt. ii, 388 ; *see* also I, pt. i, 165.
Parasangæ : Párasáva, a tribe between the Indus and the Jumna, mentioned by Pliny, I, pt. i, 533.
Párásaryá ; Bráhman sub-caste in Gujarát, IX, pt. I, 16.
Parasgad : hill in Belgaum district, XXI, 9 ; sub-division, its boundaries, area, aspect, soil, climate, water, stock, crops, people, *id.* 501-503 ; survey (1849-1850), *id.* 417-421 ; revision survey (1880), *id.* 452-456. *Town, id.* 596-597.

Parasharám Bháu Patvardhán: Peshwa's general sent to the Konkan to cut off the communication of the English army with Bombay (1781), I, pt. ii, 105, 605; sent against Haidar (1776-1779), *id.* 659; takes Dhárwár (1790), *id.* 661-662; obtains most of the districts acquired from Tipu, sent to Bájiráo to make proposals, is sent to prison, *id.* 606; offers to march against the *rája* of Sátára, is released and takes the *rája* prisoner, *id.* 607; is reconciled to Nána Phadnavis (1799), *id.* 662; is defeated and killed by Kolhápur troops, *id.* 607; *another account of:* Sángli chief, destroys (1779) domed tomb of Nurkhán at Shirol, XXIV, 319; engages himself in war against Kolhápur and Haidar; assists the Peshwa's troops against the English; is appointed commander of the Marátha forces, sent to assist the English against Tipu Sultán of Mysore; is engaged in war with Kolhápur; commands the Marátha army in the battle of Kharda; contrives with Nána Phadnavis to place Chimnáji Appa on the Peshwa's *gádi* after the death of Mádhavráv II; is confined but afterwards released; is sent to oppose the Sátára *rája;* Kolhápur king ravages Parashurám's *jágir* and burns Tásgaon; directs his forces against the Kolhápur *rája;* is mortally wounded at Pattankudi village, *id.* 344-347; *another account of:* raises money for the Marátha contingent (1790) near Tásgaon; takes part in the battle of Kharda (1795) and returns to Tásgaon; summonned to Poona after the suicide of Mádhavráo; made prisoner, released on promise of quelling disturbance; his *jágir* village Tásgaon pillaged by the Kolhápur forces; mortally wounded, XIX, 297-299; *another account of:* assembles a large army at Miraj and takes field against Haidar (1777); captures Gokak, XXI, 384, 386; turns his armies against Kolhápur, quarrels with Nána Phadnavis, his villages plundered by the Kolhápur chief at the instigation of Nána; takes all forts between the Ghatprabha and the Malprabha; taken prisoner and cut to pieces; his age, stature and disposition, *id.* 389-390 and note 2; *see* also X, 117; XVIII, pt. ii, 271-273; XXII, 413, 417, 419.

Parasharam Trimbak: (1690-1706), Marátha commander, his rise at Parli, raised to the rank of *pratinidhi,* takes Panhála fort, XXIV, 314; leaves Vishálgad (1701), I, pt. ii, 80; takes Vasantgad and Sátára; receives order from Sháhu to surrender Sátára, released and restored to power; again thrown into confinement; his death, XIX, 249-255, 256.

Parashurám: great Bráhman maker, IX, pt. i, 436, 438; massacres the Kshatriyas, *id.* 55, 56, 177, 183 note 1, 441; said to have purified shipwrecked strangers and made them Bráhmans, *id.* 438; his re-birth in the person of Nahapána; founds a kingdom in Dakhan, *id.* 498 and note 1; legendary story of, X, 355 note 4; ponds dug by, *id.* 326; conquers the Konkan, XIII, 87; *Hindu demigod,* story of, XV, pt. ii, 76 and note 1; *see* also XVIII, pt. i, 99-100; sixth incarnation of Vishnu, I, pt. ii, 26; son of Jamadagni and Renuká, *id.* 282 note 5.

Parashurám: hill pass in Ratnágiri district, X, 167.

Parashurám Naráyan Angle: Sátára banker and temple builder (1710), XIX, 452, 511 note 2, 542.

Parashurám Shrinivás: under restraint of his deputy, Bápu Gokhale sent to enforce submission from; declares against the Peshwa; severely wounded and his estate sequestrated, XIX, 299-300.

Párasikas: probably Syrians, I, pt. ii, 317; defeated by Vinayáditya, *id.* 368.

Párasnáth: twenty-third Shrávak *tirthankára,* IX, pt i, 105; *see* also I, pt. i, 456; XIV, 2, 338; XXIV, 95, 133.

Párasnath temples: in Poona city, XVIII, pt. iii, 340, 341.

Parśuráma: son of Sajjana; finishes the temple of Nemináth, I, pt. i, 177 note 1.

Pardáo: gold and silver coin, value of, XV, pt. ii, 50 note 18.

Pardápur: Pratápsháh's capital, I, pt. ii, 27.

Pardeshi: a caste of labourers in Kolámaking district, XI, 71; in Thána district, XIII, 153; in Násik district, XVI, 57; in Sátára district, XIX, 107; in Sholápur, XX, 161-163.

Pardeshi Bráhmans: in Násik district, XVI, 43; in Ahmadnagar district, XVII, 61-63.

Pardeshi Halváis: confectioners in Ahmadnagar district, XVII, 129-130.

Pardhadi: pass in Násik district, XVI, 131.

Pardhari: place of interest in Káthiáwár, VIII, 606.

Párdhi: caste of hunters, in Khándesh, XII, 113; in Cutch, V, 83; in Násik district, XVI, 59.

Pardhi: spring at Tungar in Thána, XIV, 368.

Párdi: sub-division of Surat district, II, 292-296. *Town, id.* 298; *see* also I, pt. i, 110.

Parel: suburb of Bombay city; derivation of the word, XXVI, pt. iii, 595 and note 1; Portuguese church at, XIII, 474; taken from the Jesuits, *id.* 489; batty grounds in, farmed (1751), XXVI, pt. iii, 447-448.

Párgad: hill in Belgaum district, XXI, 7; place of interest, *id.* 597-598.

Párgaon: village in Poona district, temple and fair at, XVIII, pt. iii, 265.

Pari: fairy, IX, pt. ii, 142 note 1.

Pariah dog: passing of the (1857), in Gujarát, probable belief about, I, pt. i, 433.

Parichera: (fairy-face) daughter of the king of Sonkehr, sent to Alla-ud-din, I, pt. ii, 31.

Parihár: tribe of Agnikula Rájpúts, IX, pt. i, 483; said to be Shiv-sprung, *id.* 449 note 3, 484; called Pritikádwára; Pratihara, the Sanskrit form of, believed to be of Gujar stock; Gájan *máta,* luck or *shri* of, *id.* 484; two layers of, Girásias of Abu and Rákshás, *id.* 439 note 1; *see* also I, pt. i, 465, 468.

Párijátak: dye-yielding and sacred plant, XXV, 247, 290.

Párikh: honorific title among Vániás, meaning of, IX, pt. i, 78, note 2; Cambay Hajám, also so called, *id.* 231.

Parikraman : or *padikamna* ceremony, performance of, during *pachusan*, rites relating to, IX, pt. i, 114, 115.
Parikshámukha : Jain work, I, pt. ii, 407.
Pari-on-ke-Tabak Bharna ; fairy Házráts, IX, pt. ii, 130.
Paris : Musalmán spirits, IX, pt. i, 417.
Párisasetti : officer under the Devagiri Yádava kings Jaitugi I and Singhana, I, pt. ii, 521, 524.
Parisesha Khanda : appendix to Hemádri's *Chaturvarga Chintámani*, I, pt. ii, 249.
Prishad : Vedic school of Bráhmans, I, pt. ii, 148.
Párisishtaparvan : work of Hemachandra, I, pt. i, 193.
Parit : a caste of washermen in Ratnágiri district, X, 127, 142 ; in Sávantvádi, *id.* 415 ; in Kolába district, XI, 67, 413 ; in Thána district, XIII, 143 ; in Násik district, XVI, 56 ; in Ahmadnagar district, XVII, 147-149 ; in Poona district, XVIII, pt. i, 383-384 ; in Sátára district, XIX, 102-104 ; in Sholápur district, XX, 144 ; in Belgaum district, XXI, 152 ; in Dhárwár district, XXII, 188-189 ; in Bijápur district, XXIII, 274-277 ; in Kolhápur state, XXIV, 102.
Paritium tiliaceum : famine and fibrous plant, grows in several districts, XXV, 194, 227.
Pariyá : village in the Surat district, I, pt. ii, 359 and note 5.
Parijala : village, battle of, won by Narasimbavarman I, I, pt. ii, 322, 326, 358.
Páriyátra : portion of the Vindhya range, I, pt. ii, 135, 149.
Pariyaya : village in the Kásákula division, granted, I, pt. i, 110.
Pariyaya : *see* Pariyá.
Parjápur : *see* Pardápur.
Park : Colonel, defeats Tatia Topi, I, pt. i, 445.
Parkher : local name of Baroda, I, pt. i, 208 note 3.
Parkinsania aculeata : fodder plant, XXV, 278.
Parla : a place of interest in Thána district, XIV, 297.
Parlá-Kimedi : grant at, I, pt. ii, 297.
Párli : hill fort and village in Sátára district, XIX, 6, 10 : description, temple and history, the residence of Rámdás, spiritual adviser of Shiváji, *id.* 538-539 ; surprised by Shiváji (1673), *id.* 244 ; captured by the Mughals, (1700), *id.* 251 ; *see* also I, pt. ii, 594.
Parlipur : Yavanaśva's capital, I, pt. i, 119.
Parmár : a Rájpút clan of Málwa, section of Bhinmál Rájpúts, I, pt. i, 468, 469 ; supreme in Marusthali, lose their possessions, *id.* 470 ; *see* also I, pt. ii, 441, 442 ; in Káthiáwár, VIII, 114 ; Agnikula or fire clan Rajpúts in Gujarát, IX, pt. i, 485 ; said to be Indra-raised, *id.* 449 note 3, 485 ; origin of name ; said to be of Gujar stock ; heritage of ; *Sanchair máta*, luck or *shri* of, *id.* 485 ; said to have come from Sind ; their chiefships in Káthiáwár, in Mahi Kántha, in Pálanpur, in Rewa Kántha, *id.* 127-128 ; their family deity Mandavri *máta*, *id.* 136 ; Rájpút converts, conversions believed to have taken place in 1317 ; Gujarát athletes, IX, pt. ii, 68-69.
Parnadatta : Suráshtra governor of Skandagupta, I, pt. i, 69.
Parnakheta : city, captured by the Yádava king Mallugi, I, pt ii, 235, 516.
Parnámipaothi or Parnámi : religious sect in Gujarát, IX, pt. i, 545.
Párner : sub-division of Ahmadnagar district, its area, aspect, soil, rainfall, water-supply, cultivation, crops, people, roads, railway, markets, crafts and survey changes, XVII, 621-626. *Town*, 1874 riots, temples and wells at, *id.* 730-731.
Parner or Parnera : hill in Surat district, II, 298 ; north boundary of the Portuguese district of Daman, I, pt. ii. 54 ; fort taken by Muhammad Begadá (1465), XIII, 442 ; the Mughals at (1560), *id.* 453 ; Shiváji captures and garrisons the fort of (1672), *id.* 478, I, pt. i, 387 ; besieged by the *subhedár* of Bassein (1751), VII, 179 ; taken by Lieutenant Welsh (1780), *id.* 97 ; I, pt. i, 409 ; XIII, 506.
Párol : village in Thána district, temples and remains at, XIV, 297 ; XIII, 429 ; I, pt. ii, 22.
Párola : town and fort in Khándesh district, history, trade and temples at, XII, 462-463 ; confiscated by government from the Jhánsi family (1859), I, pt. ii, 632.
Pár Pár : village in Sátára district, temples and history of, XIX, 539.
Párpas : local name of Pátan, I, pt. i, 208 note 3.
Párpoli : hill pass in Sávantvádi state, X, 166 and note 2, 169, 388, 397, 433 ; trade (1876), *id.* 436 ; *see* also XXI, 305 ; XXIV, 5, 6.
Parridæ : family of birds in Ratnágiri, X, 93.
Párs : south-west provinces of Irán ; Pársis, the people of, IX, pt. ii, 183 note 1.
Parsharám Pant Patvardhan : *see* Parasharám Bháu Patvardhan.
Parsharámbáva : Bharvád saint, IX, pt. i, 271.
Parshuram Trimbak : *see* Parasharám Trimbak.
Parsi Bridge : in Poona city, XVIII, pt. iii, 285.
Pársi-Prakásh : history of the Pársis ; mention of, IX, pt. ii, 186 notes 6, 8, 189 note 3, 190 note 2, 193 note 1, 195 notes 2, 3, 196 notes 2, 3, 198 notes 2, 5.
Pársis : account of, by European travellers and authors, Jordanus (before 1323) ; Friar Oderic (1323), IX, pt. ii, 189 note 1 ; Garcia d'Orta (1535), *id.* 189 ; Mr. Lord (1620) ; Sir Thomas Herbert (1626), *id.* 90 ; Mandelslo (1638), *id.* 190-191 ; Thevenot (1660) ; Ogilby (1670) ; Fryer (1674), *id.* 191 ; Ovington (1690), *id.* 192 ; Niebuhr (1674), *id.* 195 ; Stavorinus (1774), *id.* 195-196 ; Forbes (1783), *id.* 197-198 ; by Musalmán authors, Idrisi (1153), *id.* 187 ; Abul Fazl (1590), *id.* 190 ; driven from Persia (638-641), settled in Ormuz, XIII, 247 ; from Ormuz sail to Diu and Sanján (716), *id.* 248 ; protected by Jadi Rána ; spread to Navsári, Cambay, Broach,

Thána and Chaul, *id.* 250, 432; fight for their Hindu chief (1305); defeated and fled to Bhárut, *id.* 251, 438 and note 4; go to Bánsda, depressed (1300-1400), *id.* 252; immigrants and local converts (1400-1500), *id.* 253; in Kalyán (1533), *id.* 254; encouraged by Akbar (1578); at Surat (1590); rise to importance (1600-1800), *id.* 255; revenue farmers, land proprietors, husbandmen, tavern-keepers, palm-juice drawers (1817-1881), *id.* 256-257; appearance, dress, *id.* 258-260; speech, house, food, life, *id.* 261-262; customs, religion, *id.* 263-273. Towers of silence of: at Dehgám (1306) and Vejalpur, *id.* 249 note 6; at Kalyán (1533), *id.* 254; at Thána (1790), *id.* 256; at Tárápur (1786); at Kalyán (1790), *id.* 256; population in Bombay (1810), *id.* 516 and note 6, 517; traders (810-1260), *id.* 431; Jordanus' account (1320), *id.* 251, 439, 440 and note 1; *see* also XIV, 302; immigrants, "Introduction to the History of the Konkan," I, pt. ii, p. xii, 7; number, occupation and condition of, in Surat district, II, 55-112; in Broach district, *id.* 378; in Kaira district, III, 37; in Panch Maháls, *id.* 226, in Ahmadábád district, V, 42; in Cutch, V, 100; in Rewa Kántha, VI, 35; in Cambay, *id.* 189, 215, 216 note 2; in Ratnágiri district, X, 134, 171; in Kolába, XI, 87; in Khándesh, XII, 128; in Kánara district, XV, pt. i, 411; in Poona district, XVIII, pt. i, 538; in Násik district, XVI, 85; in Ahmadnagar district, XVII, 239; in Sátára, XIX, 147; in Sholápur, XX, 211; in Belgaum, XXI, 229; in Dhárwár district, XXII, 251; in Kolhápur, XXIV, 152.

Parsons: English traveller (1775); his description of Anjidiv and Honávar, XV, pt. ii, 54, 141-142, 256, 312-313; his description of Bombay in 1750, XXVI, pt. ii, 482; on Bombay docks, *id.* 518; *see* also XIII, 501.

Pársvábhyudaya: poem of Jinasena, I, pt. ii, 200, 407.

Pársvanátha: Jain temple of, at Ratanpur near Jodhpur, I, pt. i, 471; at Vardhamánapura, I, pt. ii, 552 note 8.

Partábpur: village in Kaira district, gathering of the rebels at (1857), destruction of, I, pt. i, 443.

Parthava: I, pt. ii, 318; *see* Pahlava and Pallava.

Párthians: Arácidons, I, pt. ii, 317; or Pahlavas, formed separate class of Hindus under their leader Sivaskanda, IX, pt. i, 445; two divisions in, *id.* 459, 456 note 3; dealings of Thána with, XIII, 403; trade connection of, with Thána coast and the rulers of north-west of India (Sindh), *id.* 410-411 and note 2; their rule from Sind to Broach (100), V, 129 note 4; empire of, I, pt. i, 545; *see* also I, pt. i, 543, 544; I, pt. ii, 318; *see* Persians.

Parthivas: Sisupáda described as the protector of, I, pt. ii, 318.

Párunde: village in Poona district, temple and fair at, XVIII, pt. iii, 265.

Párnttha: Parthian (?), a Kshatrapa coin, XIV, 195 and note 3.

Párva: hill pass in Belgaum district, XXI, 306.

Parvári: a caste of musical Mhárs in Khándesh, XII, 122.

Parvata Matha: monastery at Harasur, inscription at, I, pt. ii, 457 note 5.

Párvati: consort of Shiv, I, pt. i, 455; I, pt. ii, 482; IX, pt. i, 35, 220, 338; said to have remained as cuckoo, *id.* 381; *bel* tree considered her home, *id.* 4, 164, 165, 196, 383, 385; image of, in Elephanta cave, XIV, 72, 75, 212, 337, 367.

Párvatibái: wife of Sadásiva Chimnáji Peshwa; reservoir at Bhivpuri built by, XIII, 322.

Parvati Hill: south of Poona city, description, temples, view, rude stone circles at, XVIII, pt. iii, 386-389.

Párvati in a pet: Elephanta sculpture, XIV, 69.

Parvati Lake: in Poona, XVIII, pt. iii, 389-390, 406.

Parviz: Khasru, grandson of Naushirván the Just, his treaties and interchange of presents with the rulers of India and Sind; his portrait in Ajanta caves; his son, the alleged founder of the Udepur family, IX, pt. ii, 183 note 4.

Pasaita: rent-free land in Baroda state, VII, 350; *see* also IX, pt. i, 24. *See* Vartania.

Pasarni: pass in Sátára district, XIX, 201.

Páshán: village near Poona, temple, fair and reservoir at, XVIII, pt. iii, 265-266; *see* also *id.* pt. ii, 28.

Pasipêda: town identified with Besmaid, I, pt. i, 538.

Pasnávada: place of interest in Káthiáwár, VIII, 606.

Pásodi: village headman's emoluments, XVI, 209 and note 5.

Paspalum scrobiculatum: food, poisonous and fodder plant, XXV, 184, 270, 276.

Passage: rates of, to India (1776-1779), XXVI, pt. ii, 11-12; (1785), *id.* pt. iii, 185.

Passage boats: at Bombay, Máhim and Sion farmed (1702-1779), XXVI, pt. ii, 1-4; to Thána farmed (1776, 1778 and 1779), *id.* 9-10.

Passeridæ: family of birds in Ratnágiri district, X, 84.

Passes: all district volumes, *see* under District Name.

Pástar: place of interest in Káthiáwár, VIII, 606.

Pásupata: religious sect, I, pt. i, 83, 190; military character of its followers, *id.* 84.

Pat: fibrous plant, XXV, 228.

Pát: place of interest in Ratnágiri district, X, 467.

Patála: island in the Indus, in Sind, I, pt. i, 533, 534, 535. *Town, id.* 538, 546.

Pátala: subterranean region, I, pt. ii, 576.

Pátálamalla: another name of Karka I, I, pt. i, 124.

Patále: Indus delta, I, pt. i, 536.

Pátalênê: I, pt. i, 537. *See* Pattalene.

Pataleshwar: the Lord of the Under World, I, pt. i, 452.

Pátálganga: river in Thána district, XIII, 11; XIV, 201.

Pátali: Vishvabhu's tree of knowledge, XIV, 331.

Pátáli : caste of temple servants in Kánara, XV, pt. i, 200.
Patalipura : town of the Guttas, I, pt. ii, 578, 579.
Pátaliputra : modern Pátna, I, pt. ii, 407; capital of Aśoka, *id.* 142; of the Maurya dynasty, *id.* 157, 277; Budhist council held in Aśoka's reign at, *id.* 278 note 2, 579; *see* also I, pt. i, 546.
Patal Khánt : leader of the Khant Kolis, said to have conquered Petlád, IX, pt. i, 240.
Pátan : *see* Pattan.
Pátan : *see* Pátan Somnáth.
Pátan : sub-division of Sátára district, its description, area, aspect, climate, water, soil, stock, holdings, crops and people, XIX, 436-438. *Town, id.* 539-540.
Pátáne Prabhus : in Thána district, origin and settlement, XIII, 62 note 2, 89; appearance, language and character, *id.* 91; house, food, dress and ornaments, *id.* 92-101; life and occupation, *id.* 102-104; religion, community, prospects, *id.* 105-108; in Kolába district, XI, 47; in Ahmadnagar, XVII, 65; in Poona district, writers, settlement, appearance, houses, food, calling, customs, religion, holidays, XVIII, pt. i, 193-256; in Sátára district, XIX, 57; in Kolhápur, XXIV, 64.
Pátaners : marauders, plunder Cambay (1720), VI, 220.
Patang : dye-yielding plant, XXV, 243.
Patani Bohorá : *see* Jaafari Bohorá.
Patanjali : Sanskrit grammarian, author of the *Mahábháshya* (B. C. 150), I, pt. ii, 135; his chronological relations with Kátyáyana, *id.* 140, 141; his references to the *Mahábhárata* characters, *id.* 142.
Patankodi : village near Nipani, battle of (1799), XXI, 390.
Pátan Somnáth : *see* Somnáth.
Pátanvádiyá Kolis : *see* Kolis.
Pátanváv : place of interest in Káthiáwár, VIII, 611.
Pátarváda : place in the Bánsda hills; Rám said to have halted at, IX, pt. i, 4.
Pátas : village in Poona district with railway station, temple at, XVIII, pt. iii, 266; reservoir at, *id.* pt. ii, 28.
Pátasthal : channel-watering in Poona, XVIII, pt. ii, 14.
Patavardhana : family name of Konkauastha Bráhmans, I, pt. ii, 244.
Patcha : oil-yielding plant, XXV, 224.
Pátdi : *see* Pátri.
Patel : *see* Pátil.
Patel : family of, among early Pársi settlers in Bombay, IX, pt. ii, 195. *See* Dorabji Nanabhai.
Patelia or Pateliya : class of professional husbandmen in Gujarát, strength and distribution, IX, pt. i, 153, 172; claim Rájput descent, faith in early beliefs, worship of Ghodádev, animal worship by, customs, *id.* 172-174; in Rewá Kanthá, VI, 24.
Páteshwar : hill in Sátára district, caves at, XIX, 540-542.
Patet Pashemáni : confession of sin, IX, pt. ii, 223, 232.
Pateti : day of penitence, observances on, IX, pt. ii, 218. *See* Navroz.
Pátgad : *see* Vágham Chávdágad.
Pathán or Afghán : in Gujarát, derivation of the name of, IX, pt. ii, 10 note 4; titles after the names of, divisions, appearance and character of, mostly soldiers, Sunnis in religion, *id.* 10-11; class of foreign Patháns known as Jindarans, *id.* 8 note 3; in Cutch, V, 90; in Ahmadnagar district, XVII, 226; in Poona district, XVIII, pt. i, 492; in Sholápur district, XX, 197; in Belgaum, XXI, 205; in Dhárwár, XXII, 232; character according to Orme, *id.* 792 note 1; in Bijápur district, XXIII, 288; in Kolhápur, XXIV, 147-148.
Páthantáná : caste of cobblers, a class of Mángs in Kolhápur, XXIV, 111.
Páthardi : town in Ahmadnagar district, XVII, 731-732.
Pathargi Náik : Bhil rebel (1857-59), XVII, 418.
Páthervat : caste of stone hewers in Ratnágiri district, X, 125; in Khándesh, XII, 75; in Thána district, XIII, 138; in Násik district, XVI, 58; in Poona district, XVIII, pt. i, 358; in Sátára district, XIX, 89-92; in Sholápur district, XX, 134; in Kolhápur state, XXIV, 97.
Pátidárs : Gujarát owners of shares of the lands of a village, IV, 156; shareholders among Leva Kanbis, their position and influence, IX, pt. i, 166, and notes 1 and 2.
Patika : Northern Kshatrapa ruler, I, pt. i, 23 and note 1, 33.
Pátil : village headman, I, pt. i, 210; in Baroda, VII, 74-75, 111; in Kolába district, XI, 161, 162, 171, 177; in Janjira, *id.* 452; in Khándesh, XII, 265, 275; in Thána district, XIII, 529; revenue collectors, *id.* 560; pay (1828), unfit to manage the work of collections, *id.* 564 and note 1; the duties of, *id.* 573; help of, in making revenue settlements, *id.* 575; in Násik district (1882), XVI, 206-207; (1818), 209 and note 5; revenue farmers, *id.* 210; in Poona district, XVIII, pt. ii, 311, 313 note 1, 315 and note 1, 316 and note 1.
Pátimár : despatch boat. *See* Phatemári.
Pátuá : village in Khándesh district, temples and caves at, XII, 241, 463-465; Chángadeva founds a *matha* at, I, pt. ii, 244; inscription at, *id.* 298 note 2, 460, 521, 525; record at, *id.* 522, 523; rock temples of, *id.* 619.
Pátna : place of interest in Káthiáwár, VIII, 612.
Pátni Soni : caste of goldsmiths in Cutch, V, 71.
Pátoda : old sub-division of Ahmadnagar district, now included in Násik, survey (1846-47), XVI, 226-230; revision survey (1876), *id.* 274-279.
Pátphalla : cess in Khándesh, XII, 140 note 1.
Pátradavaru : class of dancing girls in Dhárwár district, XXII, 189-191.
Pátrakesarin : I, pt. ii, 407. *See* Vidyánanda.
Pátri : town in Ahmadábád district, its trade and history, IV, 347-348; fort of, given to

Bhávsingh by the Maráthás (1740), I, pt. i, 323-324; *see* also IX, pt. i, 127.
Patrias: dancing girls, I, pt. i, 451 and note 4.
Pataáli: caste of silk-weavers in Kánara, XV, pt. i, 275, 276.
Patta: fort in Ahmadnagar district, XVII, 4, 732; Shiváji's operations against, *id.* 399, 400; *see* also XVI, 424-425, 441, 447.
Pattabandha: coronation, I, pt. ii, 217 note 5, 286, 446; *see* also I, pt. i, 130.
Pattabandhotsava: coronation festival, I, pt. ii, 203.
Pattadad: *see* Pattadakal.
Pattadadal, Pattadakal: old town in Bijápur district, temples and inscriptions at, history of, XXIII, 668-674; Śiva temple at, I, pt. ii, 190; inscriptions at, *id.* 197, 305 and note 2, 370, 371 note 2, 372, 374 note 6, 376, 377, 393, 394, 459 note 4, 460, 462, 573, 575, 348 note 8, 430, 431, 441 note 6, 572.
Pattada-Kisuvalal: modern Pattadakal, I, pt. ii, 305 and note 2, 348 note 8, 572, 575.
Pattah: *see* Patta.
Pattalene: Lower Sind, I, pt. i, 535.
Pattan: sub-division in Baroda state, VII, 596. *Town*, its foundation, the rule of Chávdás, Solankis, Musalmáns and Maráthás at, temples at, *id.* 597-606; schools and hospitals at, *id.* 487, 507; inscriptions at, I, pt. i, 167 note 1, 174, 178, 190; Sahasralinga lake built by Sidharája at, *id.* 179; vacated by Jhálories and Ráthods, and seized by Jawán Mard Khán (1737), *id.* 318, 460 and note 4; *see* also *id.* 231, 232, 235, 181; capital of Gujarát (1094-1143), IX, pt. ii, 26, 38, 62; I, pt. ii, 8. *See* Anahilaváda.
Pattan Somnáth: *see* Somnáth.
Patta Sáli: caste of weavers in Dhárwár district, XXII, 173-175.
Pattávale: I, pt. i, 469.
Patti-Perumála: I, pt. ii, 496.
Patti-Pombuchchapura: modern Hombucha or Humcha, I, pt. ii, 458, 494; Śántara family of, *id.* 568.
Patvardhans: Southern Marátha chiefs, the founder of the family obtains grants (1761-1768), XXI, 381-382; Marátha generals, against Haidar and Tipu (1764-1777), XXII, 411-413.
Patvardhan States: in Southern Marátha Country, I, pt. ii, 657.
Patvegar or Patvekar: caste of Musalmán tassel-twisters in Ahmadnagar district, XVII, 228; in Poona district, XVIII, pt. i, 496-497; in Sátára district, XIX, 146; in Sholápur district, XX, 209-210; in Belgaum district, XXI, 140, 145, 219-220; in Dhárwár district, XXII, 242-243; in Bijápur district, XXIII, 143-145; in Khándesh, XII, 76; in Násik district, XVI, 53; in Satára district, XIX, 92; in Sholápur district, XX, 134.
Patwári: Mughal village officer, I, pt. i, 212.
Paud: petty divisional head-quarters in Poona district, XVIII, pt. iii, 266.
Paulistines: Jesuits so called, establish themselves in every village and town in Portuguese Konkan (1585), I, pt. ii, 56.
Pauna: river in Poona district, XVIII, pt. i, 9.
Paupera: Jayaba, Jawhár chief (1320 ?), XIII, 440 note 5, 703 and note 1.
Pausanias: (170) describes the Cambodia people, I, pt. i, 499.
Pávágad: hill fort in Panch Maháls, its position, history, fortifications and remains, III, 185-191; goddess Káli on, I, pt. i, 206 note 1; taken from and restored to Sindia by the English (1803), *id.* 414; place of pilgrimage, IX, pt. i, p. xi, 186, 333, 341.
Pavai: estate in Sálsette, XIII, 545; condition of (1833), *id.* 578 note 1.
Pavaiya: *see* Paváyá.
Pavála: Buddhist caves in Kolhápur, XXIV, 317.
Pávangad: hill fort in Kolhápur state, made over to the British (1827), XXIV, 6, 315, 316, 317.
Pavár: Gujar surname, I, pt. i, 468.
Pávargad: Káthi head-quarters about the 8th century, V, 131.
Pávas: port in Ratnágiri district, X, 355.
Paváya: caste in Gujarát called *Fatdás* or *Hijdás*, eunuchs, traditional origin, recruitment to, admission rites, IX, pt. i, 506-507; appearance, live as beggars, death rites, *id.* 507; worshippers of goddess Bahucharáji, IX, pt. ii, 82.
Pávettage: village in Karnapuri district, I, pt. ii, 421.
Pavitra: hill in Belgaum district, XXI, 6, 571.
Pavonia odorata: sacred plant, XXV, 289.
Pavoninæ: family of birds in Ratnágiri, X, 87.
Pavra: Bhil tribe in Khándesh, account of, XII, 95-100; inhabit Sátpudás, *id.* 3, 4.
Pávta: pulse in Poona district, XVIII, pt. ii, 43.
Pawangad: Bammagoura identified with, I, pt. i, 540.
Pawn brokers: or *Jansán Sáhukárs* in Surat district, II, 185.
Payanghát: *see* Payin Ghát.
Páyat: mystic verse, worship of, IX, pt. i, 67.
Payin Ghat: lowland Karnátak, XV, pt. i, 2; Báláji Peshwa demands a share in (1756), XVIII, pt. ii, 248.
Payve: Hayve province, I, pt. ii, 282 note 5, 452, 568.
Pázand: old Persian word for Harbad, IX, pt. ii, 222 note 1.
Peacock: carrier of goddess Sarasvati and god Kártikeya, favourite of god Krishna, worship of, IX, pt. i, 247, 381; in Ratnágiri district, X, 87.
Pearl fisheries: in the gulf of Cutch, I, pt. i, 285.
Pearls: found in Káthiáwár, VIII, 93; in Thána creek, XIII, 55; trade in, at Cheul (A. D. 77), *id.* 416 and note 1; found in Sopára creek (810-1260), *id.* 430, 445, 467; fishing of, at Sopára, XIV, 321.
Peas: crop of, in Sátára district, XIX, 164.
Peb: fort in Thána district, temples and caves at, XIV, 297-298.
Pebi: goddess of Peb fort, XIV, 298.
Pedalineæ: species of oil-yielding plants, XXV, 219.

Pedder, Mr. : commissioned to inquire into salt smuggling (1869), his measures to stop this evil, XIII, 374-376; urges (1877) the *naváb* of Janjirá to redress the grievances of the people, XI, 451.
Pedekul : Chálukya district, I, pt. ii, 369.
Pedgaon : town in Ahmadnagar district, temple and history, XVII, 732-733; Mughal head-quarters (1673), *id.* 400 and note 1; I, pt. ii, 626; taken by the Maráthás, *id.* 627.
Pedlers : in Káthiáwár, VIII, 244; in Thána district, XIII, 335; in Khándesh, XII, 218; in Kánara district, XV, pt. ii, 57; in Násik district, XVI, 142; in Ahmadnagar district, XVII, 342; in Poona district, XVIII, pt. ii, 167; in Sátára district, XIX, 218; in Kolhápur state, XXIV, 206.
Pednekar : a Bráhman and Vani sub-division in Kánara district, XV, pt. i, 172, 186.
Pedro de Mello : Colonel, tries to recover Thána, (1738), XIV, 360.
Pehlevi : language, original texts explained in, IX, pt. ii, 211 note 1; commentaries written in, *id.* 212; scholarship for, *id.* 194.
Peint : sub-division of Násik district, its area, aspect, climate, water, soil, revenue, stock, holdings, crops and people, XVI, 2, 381-388; survey settlement introduced into (1865-1866), *id.* 245-248. *Town*, *id.* 689; history of its chiefs, *id.* 384-388; one chief converted to Islám by Aurangzeb, *id.* 190; the state lapses to the British (1878), I, pt. ii, 633.
Pejjunka : Chálukya tax (1102,) I, pt. ii, 451.
Pelár : village in Thána district, inscribed stone from, XIV, 401; remains at, I, pt. ii, 22; XIII, 428.
Pelly : Sir L., special commissioner at Baroda (1875), VII, 283-284, 412.
Pemble : Colonel Charles, appointed commander-in-chief of Bombay forces (1768), XXVI, pt. iii, 145-146.
Pemgad : hill fort in Ahmadnagar district, XVII, 4.
Pen : old Sánkshi, XI, 159, 178, 186, 189, 196, 202; sub-division of Thána district, its boundaries, area, aspect, climate, water, soil, holdings, rental, stock, produce, people, *id.* 1, 242-245. *Town*, people, trade water-works and history of, *id.* 354-356.
Pendára : place of interest in Káthiáwar, VIII, 613.
Pendáris : free-booters, I, pt. ii, 114. *See* Pendhára.
Pendhára or Pendhári : class of Musalmán labourers in Dhárwár district, XXII, 247-248; in Bijápur district, XXIII, 303-304; in Násik, XVI, 59; in Sholápur district, XX, 209; in Belgaum district, XXI, 216; in Khándesh, XII, 79; as Dakhan free-booters, sack villages in Konkan (1817), I, pt. ii, 125; at war with the English, *id.* 630; their raids, in Násik district, XVI, 193; in Khándesh, XII, 254, 313; in Thána district, XIII, 513, 522, 523; XIV, 290; preparation for crushing the power of, XVIII, pt. ii, 298.
Pendur : lake in Ratnágiri district, X, 11.
Penha : Our Lady of, Portuguese Church at Keranj, XIV, 194.
Penicillaria spicata : food and famine plant, grows in several districts, XXV, 185, 208.
Pension Tax : in Bombay island, its origin, XXVI, pt. iii, 304-305.
Pentad : *see* Panjtan.
Penth : town in Násik district, modern Peint, I, pt. i, 110.
Peperine : island on the Pirate coast, mentioned by Ptolemy, I, pt. i, 542.
Pepper : cultivation of, in Kánara district, XV, pt. i, 30; varieties of, XV, pt. ii, 10-11; trade in, from B. C. 1500-1862 A. D., *id.* 47, 49, 51, 52, 54, 114, 124, 130, 132, 135, 137, 143, 151; trade in, at Bhatkal, *id.* 274; at Honávar, *id.* 310, 312; at Kárwár, *id.* 321, 323, 324; East India Company's trade in (1682-1776), XXVI, pt. ii, 97-108.
Perami : I, pt. i, 545.
Peráru : river in Mysore, I, pt. ii, 441.
Perch : land tenure in Baroda state, VII, 356.
Percival, Mr. E. H. : steam mills started at Bhávnagar in consultation with, VIII, 264.
Perdicinæ : family of birds in Ratnágiri, X, 88.
Pereira : General Louis de Mello, his defence of Sopára, XIV, 322.
Perfumes : manufacture of, in Káthiáwár, VIII, 261; Thána famous for (810-1260), XIII, 430; imported from Arabia (1300-1500), *id.* 445; brought (1500-1670) from Ormuz, *id.* 467; manufacture of, in Kolhápur, XXIV, 216-217.
Perimula : Chaul, I, pt. i, 533, 540; *see* also XI, 270 note 2; perhaps Chembur, XIV, 52.
Periplus : the, of the Erythræan sea, account of Egyptian trade with India, I, pt. i, 7, 17, 535, 537, 538, 539; its author a merchant of Alexandria; the chief views about its age, *id.* 542-546; mention of Broach and Áriaka in, I, pt. ii, 1, 174; of Janjira, *id.* 2; calls Dakhan, Dakshinabades, *id.* 133; mention of Paithan in, *id.* 143; mention of the gulfs of Cutch and Cambay and of Káthiáwár in, VIII, 276; of Mandgora, Masura (Muziris), and of Vengurla rocks (Heptanesia), in Ratnágiri district, X, 319, 352, 378; of trade in Khándesh, XII, 206; of Honávar, XV, pt. ii, 48, 307; of Ánjidiv, *id.* 78; of Hog Island, *id.* 316; of Mirján and Netráni Island, *id.* 332, 336; of Parthian trade with Rome, and Parthian rule in Indo-Skythia, XIII, 411 notes 1 and 2; account of foreign trade of Thána, *id.* 415-417 and note 8; mention of Kalyán, Sopára, Chaul and Pál in, *id.* 418; XIV, 119, 320; of Symulla, *id.* 52; of Tagar, XIII, 424; I, pt. ii, 538 note 8, 619; XVII, 351.
Periyála : village, I, pt. ii, 358 note 1.
Permádi : king, I, pt. i, 172 and note 3; of Jimutaváhana lineage and Khachara race, feudatory of the Western Chálukya king, Vikramáditya VI, I, pt. ii, 452.
Permádi : of the Kalachurya family, feudatory of Someśvara III, I, pt. ii, 456, 468, 470, 471.
Permádi : Goa Kádamba prince and feudatory of Taila III, I, pt. ii, 460, 476, 486, 548; called Sivachittee, *id.* 565; his gold coins, *id.* 566; his wife, his other names and

titles, *id.* 569; rules over Palasige and the Konkan, *id.* 570; *see* also I, pt. i, 172 and note 3, 195.
Permádi I: Sinda prince, son of Achugi II (1144), I, pt. ii, 459, 573; Western Chálukya king Jagadekamalla II's feudatory, *id.* 575; besieges Dorasamudra, takes Belupura and drives Bittiga to the pass of Váhadi, *id.* 497; puts to flight Jayakesin II, *id.* 579; *see* also XXIII, 379.
Permádi II: Sinda prince Chávunda II's son, I, pt. ii, 573, 575.
Perma-Jagadekamalla II: Western Chálukya king Someśvara III's successor, destroys the Pallavas, I, pt. ii, 317 note 1, 333; his feudatories, *id.* 494, 516, 555, 562, 575. *See* Jagadekamalla.
Permanadi: Nitimárga Kongunivarma, the Western Ganga king (900), I, pt. ii, 300.
Permánadi-Butuga: Western Ganga prince, I, pt. ii, 284 note 4; brother-in-law and feudatory of Krishna III, *id.* 307 note 1, 402, 441 note 4.
Permanent Settlement: offer of, to Sálsette landholders (1801), I, pt. ii, 124.
Permatti: musical instrument of the Kádambas, I, pt. ii, 560, 566.
Perron, Anquetil Du: *see* Anquetil Du Perron.
Persecutions: of Bohorás, IX, pt. ii, 27 and note 1; of Mahdavis, *id.* 63.
Persia: kingdom of, also called Irán, IX, pt. ii, 183 note 1; its early religious (B. C. 1000), political (B. C. 1729), and commercial (A. D. 545) connection with India; its commercial connection with China (sixth century), *id.* 183 note 4; passed into the hands of the Arabs (641), *id.* 183; XIII, 247 note 3; its early trade with India (B. C. 800), *id.* 404 and note 3; Parthian rule in, *id.* 410; its connection with India (120-600), *id.* 413; Indian ships sail to (A. D. 150), *id.* 417; Hindus found settled in (500), *id.* 420; trade with India (640), *id.* 421; silks, wine, swords and copper brought from and muslins sent to (810-1260), *id.* 430, 431; Bráhman and Buddhist monasteries, and learned Bráhmans in (810-1260), *id.* 432; muslin and gauze sent to (1300-1500), *id.* 445; muslins, betel-nuts cocoanuts and spices sent to (1500-1670), *id.* 466, 467; Bombay trade with (1800-1810), *id.* 518, 520; supposed home of the Chitpávan Bráhmans, XVIII, pt. i, 100 note 2.
Persian: classical language, IX, pt. ii, 204.
Persian Gulf: its early trade connection with India (B. C. 800), XIII, 404 note 3 continued on page 405; its trade with Palmyra (A.D. 60), *id.* 412; with India (A. D. 135-160), *id.* 414; Christian traders from, settled at Kalyán and Sopára (150), *id.* 417; trade with India (250), *id.* 418; timber, spices and silk exported to (500), *id.* 420; ivory sent to (810-1260), *id.* 430; its trade with India (1300-1500), *id.* 440, 444; trade of Chaul with (1530-1670), *id.* 464; trade with (1500-1670), *id.* 465; dates, silks, brocades and horses imported from (1500-1670), *id.* 466, 467, 468; decline of its trade, *id.* 470; trade with (1660-1710), *id.* 486, 487; Bombay trade with (1800-1810), *id.* 519; traders from, settled in Gujarát cities, IX, pt. ii, 2; refugees from, settled in Cambay, *id.* 3 note 2; Musalmáns from, settled in Chaul (915), I, pt. i, 516; no ships to be sold in (1741), XXVI, pt. i, 275; troops sent to (1768), *id.* 354.
Persians: Maráthás believed to be; their connection with Sisodiás or Ghelots, IX, pt. i, 439; Chitpávans held to be the priests of; Maghas said to be Persian priests, *id.* 429, 440 and note 4; mentioned in old caves and Junnar inscriptions (A. D. 100-200), XVIII, pt. ii, 213.
Persik: fort, in Thána district, XIV, 98, 236, 298, 346.
Personal servants: groups of Hindu castes in Surát district, II, 53; in Broach district, *id.* 374; in Káira district, III, 34; in Panch Mahálś, *id.* 218; in Ahmadábád district, IV, 38; in Cutch, V, 76-77; in Pálanpur, *id.* 290; in Máhi Kántha, *id.* 365; in Rewá Kántha, VI, 25.
Peru: guava tree in Poona district, XVIII, pt. i, 50.
Perumáledeva: Vira-Narasimha III's officer, I, pt. ii, 509.
Perur: original name of Belur, I, pt. ii, 519 note 1.
Peruvalanallur: battle of, I, pt. ii, 326, 362.
Peshawar: Kidáras established in, I, pt. i, 144; *stupas* of, *id.* 497, 545.
Peshkash: Marátha contribution, I, pt. i, 216.
Peshotan: son of Mulla Kans, goes to Persia (1768); becomes Kadmi high priest (1802); known as Mulla Feroz, IX, pt. ii, 193 note 2.
Peshwa: head manager of the Marátha government, XIX, 243; origin of the word, XVIII, pt. ii, 222 note 1.
Pestilence: in Cutch, V, 207; in Palánpur, *id.* 315.
Petari: fibrous plant, XXV, 228.
Petenikas: Paithanakas, rulers of Paithan (B. C. 250), XVIII, pt. ii, 213 note 5; associated with the Bhojas, I, pt. ii, 143, 146, 277.
Petesham: third *Gahambár*, IX, pt. ii, 218.
Peth: village in Poona district, XVIII, pt. iii, 266.
Peth: town in Sátára district, trade, fair, XIX, 542-543.
Pethana: *see* Paithana.
Pethapángaraka: village Dakshina, Siva shrine at, I, pt. i, 132, mentioned in a Ráshtrakúta grant, I, pt. ii, 386.
Pethápur: state in, Mahi Kántha, V, 420. *Town*, 439; *see* also IX, pt. i, 129.
Peth Pár: *see* Pár Pár.
Petirgala: probably Panagala or Hongal, I, pt. i, 541.
Petlád: sub-division in Baroda state, VII, 537-540; schools and hospital at, *id.* 486, 504. *Town*, *id.* 539; captured by Rangoji (1744), *id.* 176; I, pt. i, 327; Peshwa's share in, transferred to the Gáikwár (1817), VII, 228.
Petondh: contribution among Khojáhs, IX, pt. ii, 49.
Pett: Mr. Warwick, sent (1669) by the Directors to build ships in Bombay, XXVI, pt. i, 36.

Peucolitæ: people of Pushkálavatí mentioned by Pliny, I, pt. i, 534.
Peya: cattle disease in Ratnágiri district, X, 294.
Peyiya-Sáhani: Bhillama's officer, I, pt. ii, 520.
Phácharia: *táluka* in Káthiáwár, VIII, 612.
Phadáli: caste of spirit musicians, performances of, during Behlim vow offerings, IX, pt. ii, 150-151; during boat offerings, *id.* 153; during the offerings of vows to *ginn*, *id.* 130.
Phadke's Váda: Poona mansion, XVIII, pt. iii, 341.
Phaladivya: ordeal by holding a red-hot arrowhead, I, pt. ii, 571.
Phalangium tuberosum: food and sacred plant, grows in several districts, XXV, 180, 292.
Phalsi: fibrous plant, XXV, 230.
Phaltan: state in Sátára district, XIX, 2; origin of the chiefs of, *id.* 231; reduced by Shiváji (1665) *id.* 238, 619, 621.
Phanas: dye-yielding plant, XXV, 249; fruit tree, in Poona district, XVIII, pt. i, 51.
Phani: coasting craft in Thána district, XIII, 720.
Phaniband: *see* Tákára.
Phanja: famine plant, grows in several districts, XXV, 202.
Phánsepárdhi: *see* Advichincher.
Pharjan: caste of cultivators in Ratnágiri district, X, 124.
Phárkaude: place of interest in Khándesh, XII, 465.
Phaseolus: *aconitifolius, mal, mungo, trilobus,* fodder plants, XXV, 277; *trinervius,* famine plant, 198.
Phάse Párdhi: *see* Advichincher.
Phasianidæ: family of birds in Ratnágiri, X, 87.
Phatána: abusive songs sung at marriages, considered lucky, beliefs in, IX, pt. i, 277, 278 and note 1.
Phatarphod: dye-yielding plant, XXV, 249.
Phatemári: a large vessel, in Ratnágiri district, X, 171; despatch boat, in Thána district, XIII, 347-348, 720; in Kánara district, XV, pt. ii, 64.
Phathursuwa: famine plant, grows in several districts, XXV, 200.
Phayre: Col., resident at Baroda, attempt on his life, VII, 280-283.
Pherozsha: son of Dhanjisha of Surát, enjoys high posts of honor (1825), receives in grant villages from the British government, IX, pt. ii, 198 note 5.
Phipps: the Honourable Mr., President and governor of Bombay (1728), XXVI, pt. ii, 278.
Phiráugoji Narsála: commandant of the fort of Chákan, I, pt. ii, 591, 593.
Phitoda: a camel disease in Cutch, V, 209.
Phœnicians: their trade with Thána coast, XIII, 404 note 3.
Phœnicopteridæ: family of birds in Ratnágiri, X, 97.
Phœnix: *dactylifera,* food plant, XXV, 181; *farinosa,* famine plant, *id.* 207; *sylvestris,* food, famine, liquor-yielding and fibrous plant, *id.* 181, 206, 212, 237.
Phonda: hill fort in Kánara district, attacked and taken by Shiváji (1675), XV, pt. ii, 127 and note 2; under the Mughals, (1695), *id.* 131 note 9; held by the Portuguese (1763), *id.* 140; *see* also I, pt. ii, 70.
Phonda: pass between Ratnágiri district, and Kolhápur, X, 166 note 2, 169, 332, 343, 358; XXIV, 5, 206.
Phonda Savgaon: hill range in Kolhápur, XXIV, 7.
Phond Sávant: a rebel (1844), XXI, 408.
Phond Savant I: Vádi chief (1665), X, 440; recovers the territory south of the Korlai river (1680), I, pt. ii, 76.
Phond Sávant II: Vádi chief (1709-1737), X, 440-441; builds the fort of Bharatgad (1700), I, pt. ii, 79; enters into an alliance with the English against the Angrias (1730), *id.* 88.
Phond Sávant III: Vádi chief (1806-1812), X, 443.
Phond Sávant IV: Vádi chief (1867-1869), X, 447.
Phopali: food plant, grows in several districts, XXV, 181.
Photozincographic office: in Poona cantonment, XVIII, pt. iii, 390.
Phra Tong: apparently Great Lord, I, pt. i, 497.
Phudgi: a class of labourers in Thána, XIII, 153.
Phula, Phulada: king of Cutch, father of Lákha, I, pt. i, 160.
Phuljhar: river in Khάthiáwár, VIII, 64.
Phulka: place of interest in Káthiáwár, VIII, 63, 612.
Phulmáli: caste of flower-sellers, in Poona district, XVIII, pt. iii, 293.
Phulpáda: old Surat, I, pt. i, 539.
Phulthamba: modern Puntámba in Ahmadnagar district, I, pt. ii, 353 note 2.
Phyllanthus emblica: dye-yielding and sacred plant, also used as soap, XXV, 249, 253, 279, 284.
Phyllitæ, Phyllites: Ptolemy's word for Bhils, XIV, 291; XII, 38.
Phyllornithinæ: family of birds in Ratnágiri, X, 75.
Phylloscopinæ: family of birds in Ratnágiri, X, 79.
Physical features: all districts, *see* Description under District Name.
Piaes: native soldiers in the Portuguese service, I, pt. ii, 55.
Piaj: food plant, XXV, 179.
Pial: dye and gum yielding plant, XXV, 242, 250.
Pichάti: a caste of beggars in Belgaum district, XXI, 187.
Pichdi: *táluka,* in Khάthiáwár, VIII, 612.
Pichula: dye-yielding plant, found in several districts, XXV, 241.
Picidæ: family of birds in Ratnágiri, X, 66.
Pick-pockets: in Poona district, XVIII, pt. i, 464-476.
Picnic: caste, Ujáni, IX, pt. i, p. xxvii.
Pictures: among Musalmáns, keeping of, prohibited by the prophet, now common, IX, pt. ii, 93 and notes 1 and 2.

Piedade : Our Lady of, Church at Mandapeshvar dedicated to, XIV, 227.
Pier : at Elephanta, XIV, 61 ; at Kodibág in Kánara, XV, pt. ii, 325 ; in Kolába district, XI, 116, 378.
Pierre Almeyda : Portuguese viceroy, captures Málvan (1746), X, 349.
Pig : in Kánara, XV, pt. i, 80 ; in Belgaum, XXI, 66.
Pigeon Island : in Kánara, XV, pt. i, 3 ; see Netráni.
Pigeons : in Ratnágiri district, X, 85 ; in Khándesh, XII, 36 ; at Mátherán, XIV, 258 ; in Poona district, XVIII, pt. i, 69.
Pila Dhotra : *Argemone mexicana*, flowering tree in Poona, XVIII, pt. i, 51.
Pilaji Gáikwár : son of Takhatábai, Vanirám's enmity to, oppressed, his death (1855), VII, 233.
Piláji Gáikwár : nephew and successor of Dámáji Gáikwár, marches on Surat (1719) ; defeats Musalmáns ; establishes himself at Songad ; is secretly favored by Ajitsingh, I, pt. i, 301, 390 ; marches on Surat and defeats Momin Khán ; levies contribution ; overruns Surat province and builds forts in Rájpipla, *id.* 303, 304, 390 ; obtains Baroda and Dabhoi ; prevents Udáji Pavár from joining his forces with the viceroy at Baroda (1727), *id.* 308, 391 ; negotiates with Mustafid Khán, governor elect of Surat (1730), *id.* 311 ; assassinated (1732), *id.* 313, 394 ; *another account of :* founder of the Gáikwár family, takes Songad (1719), defeats Momin Khán (1720) at Surat, obtains half the *chauth* of Gujarát (1725), his rivalry with the Peshwa, defeated at Bhilápur (1731), murdered at Dakor (1731), VII, 168, 173 ; *see* also I, pt. ii, 600 ; III, 167 ; VI, 221.
Piles : *see* Arsa.
Pilgrimage : chief places of, Bráhmanical, Indian, provincial and local, of Gujarát Hindus, IX, pt. i, 548 ; Vaishnav ; Shaiv ; shrines ; rivers, *id.* 549 ; places outside Gujarát, *id.* 550 ; resorted to by pilgrims, *id.* 168 ; Allahábád or Prayág, *id.* 157, 168, 176, 220 ; Ambáj, *id.* 157, 225, 333, 341 ; Ayodhya or Oudh, *id.* 549 ; Badrikedár, *id.* 157, 549 ; Bahucharáji or Becharáji, *id.* 157, 187, 225, 336 ; Benáres or Káshi, *id.* 119, 157, 164, 168, 175, 213, 220, 225, 549 ; Bet Dwárka, *id.* 10, 119 ; Bhádbhut, *id.* 549 ; Bodhán, *id.* 550 ; Burhánpur, *id.* 168, 170 ; Chánod-Kanyáli, *id.* 28, 549 ; Dakor, *id.* 10, 28, 119, 157, 164, 173 175, 225, 247, 333, 336, 341, 549 ; Dwárka, *id.* 10, 157, 164, 175, 213, 220, 247, 336, 549 ; Gadhada, *id.* 549 ; the Ganges, *id.* 550 ; Girnár, *id.* 9, 220, 241 note 1, 247 ; the Godávari, *id.* 550 ; Gokarn Mahábaleshvar, *id.* 549 ; Gokul, *id.* 9, 119 157, 176, 220, 549 ; Hardvár, *id.* 549 ; Hinglaj, *id.* 247 ; Jagannáth or Puri, *id.* 119, 157, 168, 225, 549 ; the Jamna, *id.* 550 ; Kabirvad, *id.* 549 ; Khed Bráhma or Bráhmá Khed, *id.* 549 ; Mathura, *id.* 119, 157, 168, 176, 220, 549 ; Naransar, *id.* 247 ; the Narbada, *id.* 213, 350, 549 ; Násik Trimbak, *id.* 12 note 1, 119, 549 ; Náthdwár, *id.* 119, 549 ; Navsári, *id.* 168, 170 ; Pánchtirthi, *id.* 549 ; Pandharpur, *id.* 119, 519 ; Pávágadh, *id.* 186, 333, 341 ; Pirána, *id.* 154, 168, 170 ; Prabhás Pátan, *id.* 9, 28, 119, 220, 247 ; Prayág (Allahábád), *id.* 550 ; Rámeshvar, *id.* 549 ; Reváji (*see* Narbada) ; Sámláji, *id.* 549 ; Shiv Kánchi, *id.* 549 ; Shrináthji, *id.* 157, 549 ; Shukaltirth, *id.* 336, 549 ; Shurpán, *id.* 549 ; Sidhpur, *id.* 7, 164, 175, 549 ; Somanáth Pátan (Prabhás Pátan), *id.* 119, 549 ; the Tapti, *id.* 550 ; Tavra, *id.* 549 ; Tirupati, *id.* 549 ; Tulsishyám, *id.* 549 ; Unái, *id.* 157, 336, 341, 350 ; Untadia, *id.* 549 ; Vadtal, *id.* 549 ; Vaidyanath or Devgadh, *id.* 549 ; Varáhrup, *id.* 549 ; Vemal, *id.* 170 ; Vishnukánchi, *id.* 549 ; Vrindávan, *id.* 549 ; shrines of Amba Bhaváni, Bechraji, Hanumán at Gumáudev, Bhimpor and Dabhoda Hingláj, Kálika, Tulja Bhaváni, Unhái, *id.* 549 ; Jains, shrines on Mount Abu, Girnár, Shatrunjaya, other places, *id.* 550 ; among Gujarát Musalmáns ; enjoined by Muslim law as a duty, IX, pt. ii, 127, 171 note 2 ; places of, for Sunnis and Shiahs, *id.* 47, 126, 171 ; for Daudi Bohorás, *id.* 30 ; for Memans, *id.* 56 ; among Lingayats, XXIV, 128.
Pilgrims : Chinese, " Introduction to the Early History of the Dakhan," I, pt. ii, p. ii ; priest or *gor* of, IX, pt. i, 28 ; to Násik and Trimbak, XVI, 9, 527-531, 653-655 ; to Pandharpur, XX, 469-482.
Pillar : Allahábád inscriptions on, of Samudragupta, I, pt. i, 63-65.
Pillar of Victory : set up by Vikramáditya II, I, pt. ii, 375 ; *see* also *id.* 426 note 2.
Pilli dumpa : famine plant, XXV, 204.
Pi-lo-molo : Bhilmál or Bhiumál, I, pt. i, 3, 466.
Pilu : *salvadora persica*, tree, I, pt. i, 449, 456.
Pimpal : famine plant found in several districts, XXV, 204 ; in Khándesh, XII, 26 ; in Poona district, XVIII, pt. i, 51 ; fibrous and sacred plant, XXV, 235, 279, 283, 290, 291 ; Gautama's tree of knowledge, XIV, 330, 412. *See* also Piplo.
Pimpaldara : pass in Nasik district, XVI, 130.
Pimpalgaon Basvant : town in Násik district, XVI, 640.
Pimpalgaon Budruk : village in Khándesh, temple at, XII, 465.
Pimpalner : sub-division of Khándesh, its boundaries, area, aspect, water, soil, holdings, survey details, survey results, stock, crops, people, XII, 2, 396-400. *Town, id.* 465 ; grant from, I, pt. iii, 344 note 6, 358 note 1.
Pimpalvandi : village in Ahmadnagar district, fair at, XVII, 733.
Pimpalvandi : market town in Poona district, XVIII, pt. i, p. ii, 266.
Pimparkheds : place of interest in Khándesh, XII, 466.
Pimpiri : pass in Thána district, XIII, 320.
Pimpládevi : state in Khándesh, XII, 606.
Pimpola Budrukh : village in Sátara district, scene of a supposed incarnation, XIX, 543.

Pimpri : state in Khándesh, XII, 606.
Pimpri Sadr-ud-din : village in Násik district, tomb at, XVI, 639, 445.
Pinak : lotus-eater, name given to an opium-eater, IX, pt. ii, 110.
Pinákapáni : the Hindu god Śiva, I, pt. ii, 323.
Pinchha dhvaja : banner of the Western Gangas, I, pt. ii, 299.
Pinditakávada : Ushavadát founds benefactions at, I, pt. ii, 148.
Pine-apple : food plant, XXV, 180 ; in Kolába district, XI, 98.
Pinellia tuberifera : food plant, XXV, 182.
Pingalika : wife of Gujarát Chaulukya king Jayasimha (1094-1143), I, pt. i, 174.
Pingle : a caste of beggars in Belgaum district, XXI, 188.
Pingli : village in Sátára district, XIX, 543.
Pinjaji Joráji : mutilated by Vaurám of Baroda, VII, 251.
Pinjára : a caste of cotton-carders in Káthiáwár, VIII, 163 ; in Násik district, XVI, 82 ; in Ahmadnagar, XVII, 234 ; in Poona district, XVIII, pt. i, 502 ; in Dhárwár district, XXII, 243 ; in Sátára district, XIX, 146 ; in Belgaum district, XXI, 220 ; in Bijápur district, XXIII, 300.
Pipal : *see* Pimpal.
Pipal Duára : names of a Bhinmal gateway, I, pt. i, 455.
Pipáván : port in Káthiáwár, VIII, 614.
Piper : *betle, nigrum,* food plants cultivated throughout India, XXV, 173.
Piperaceæ : species of food plants, XXV, 173.
Pipit : class of birds in Ratnágiri district, X, 80.
Piplo : pipal tree, emblem of Vishnu ; haunt of spirit Munj, watered to quiet the spirit ; days sacred to its worship ; worshipped by women on no-moon day falling on Monday, IX, pt. i, 385 ; married to a grown-up girl remained unmarried, to *Tulsi* plant ; worship of, by Bhils, *id.* 386; *see* Pimpal.
Pippalanagara : I, pt. ii, 344 note 6 ; *see* Pimpalner.
Pippar : place of interest in Cutch, V, 248.
Piprali : place of interest in Káthiáwár, VIII, 614.
Pir : or Sai, Musalmán saint, *takio* or tomb of, IX, pt. i, 360 ; pass in Kolába district, XI, 115.
Piracy : A'ngriás, X, 338, 339 ; XI, 147, 148 ; in Surát district, II, 234 ; in Káthiáwár, VIII, 328 ; in Gujarát, chief piratical classes, history (B. C. 325 to A. D. 1873), IX, pt. i, 526-527 ; efforts to put down, *id.* 527, 529 ; reduced to order by the British government (A. D. 1873), *id.* 529 ; of the Shivájis (Maráthás) (1700-1701), XXVI, pt. i, 132, 134-135.
Piram : island in the Gulf of Cambay, history of, IV, 348 ; *see* also I, pt. i, 309 ; VIII, 66.
Pir Amin : tomb of, in Bijápur city, XXIII, 578-617.
Pirána : sect, among Kanbis known as Matia, IX, pt. i, 168.
Pirána : village ten miles south-east of Ahmadábád, IX, pt. ii, 76 note 2 ; *Pir, id.* 79, 140 ; saints of, *id.* 66, 67, 69, 74, 125 ; *sayads* of, *id.* 127 note 2, ; tombs at, *id.* 76 note 2 ; *see* also *id.* pt. i, 154, 168, 170.
Pirate coast : of Ptolemy and Pliny (A. D. 150), X, 105 ; probable identification of, places on the, *id.* 192 note 3 ; *see* also XI, 432, 452 ; I, pt. i, 541.
Pirates : in the Indian sea, early (A. D. 247), XIII, 417 ; Cutch, Káthiáwár, and Malabár (600, 920, 1020, 1290, 1340, 1400-1500, 1670, 1695, 1700, 1708, 1757, 1760, 1815-1820), *id.* 433 and note 8, 434, 438, 440, 449, 458, 472, 482, 484, 488, 499, 521 and notes 4 and 5, 711 note 2 ; trouble the Portuguese (1570), I, pt. ii, 61 ; the Portuguese form alliance against (1615), *id.* 62 ; European (1500, 1695, 1700), 471 note 8, 484, 488 ; Marátha (1695, 1700, 1756, 1812), *id.* 484, 488, 521 and notes 4 and 5 ; Maskat and Johásmi (900, 1570, 1695, 1700, 1708, 1760, 1804, 1819), *id.* 433 and note 8, 434, 458, 482, 484, 488, 499, 521 and notes 4 and 5 ; *see* also I, pt. ii, 66, 72, 82, 112 ; on the coast of Kánara district (A. D. 77-1812), oppose the Portuguese (1498), XV, pt. ii, 102 ; from Sangameshvar, defeated by Bijápur and the Portuguese (1584), *id.* 118-119 ; of Malábar, Fryer's account of, encounter with (1673), *id.* 126 and note 6 ; capture the "Monsoon" (1707), *id.* 134 and note 3 ; of Maskat (1775), *id.* 142 ; greatly hinder Kánára trade (1801), *id.* 148, 149 ; Anjidiv, centre of (1775), *id.* 257 ; of Málvan, their power destroyed (1812), *id.* 55 ; European, troubles caused to the Company by their depredations (1696), XXVI, pt. i, 111-119 ; capture Mughal ships, *id.* 111 ; measures against, *id.* 111-113 ; more captures in the Persian gulf and elsewhere, *id.* 116 ; from Malábar, harass Company's trade, *id.* 65-66 ; their appearance near Bombay (1686), *id.* 100-101 ; the Company empowered to condemn them to death (1763), *id.* 351 ; known as Bhavárij, harass Cambay (1000-1300), VI, 188 ; (1500-1600), *id.* 194 ; of Okhá in Káthiáwár, reduced by Colonel Walker (1807-08), VIII, 305.
Pirduka : glass bead necklace, X, 419 and note 3.
Pir Fort : *see* Sadasivgad.
Pirigipa : village on the Mahánadi, I, pt. ii, 347 note 2, 358 note 1.
Piri-Muridi : profession of spiritual tutelage practised by *sayads* and few *shaikhs,* IX, pt. ii, 127 note 2.
Piri-Rawan : shrine of Mulla Muhammad Ali at Cambay IX, pt. ii, 26 note 1.
Piriya-Chattarasa : ancestor of the Sinda prince Ishvara, I, pt. ii, 578.
Pirjádáj : a caste Musalmán priests in Násik district, XVI, 76.
Pirkháni : old rupee in Ratnágiri, X, 426 and note 1, 429.
Pir Muhammad : Akbar's general, enters Khándesh (1531), lays waste the country and sacks Burhánpur, XII, 246 ; in Málwa, drives Sultán Báz Bahadur out of Mándu (1560) ; his defeat and death (1561), I, pt. i, 369.

Pirotan : reef in Káthiáwár, VIII, 25.
Piroz : Muhammadan shipowner of Ormuz, builds a mosque at Somanátha Pátan, I, pt. i, 204.
Pir-Pardi : a place of pilgrimage in Broach district, II, 567.
Pirs : Musalmán saints, in Cutch, Dáwal Sháh, V, 89 ; Sadr-ud-din, *id.* 90, 92, 227 ; Aliyáji, *id.* 328 ; Lakadia, *id.* 232 ; Karakasim, *id.* 249 ; also called *pirzádahs* or *murshids*, spiritual guides, IX, pt. ii, 7 ; religious persons, disciples of, are called *murids*, *id.* 127 ; most of the *sayads* and Faruki *shaikhs* become spiritual guides, *id.* 7, 8 note 2 ; initiation of *murids* by a *sayad pir*, sources of his income, *id.* 127 note 2 ; spiritual guides of Jaafri Bohorás, *id.* 34 ; village, *id.* 60 ; of Khojáhs, *id.* 40 ; of Memans, *id.* 51, 66, 134 note 3 ; Pirána, *id.* 79, 140 ; blind belief in, *id* 67 note 1.
Pirzáda : a Musalmán sect, in Rewa Kántha, VI, 35 ; in Belgaum district, XXI, 203, 204.
Piscatores : order of birds in Thána district, XIII, 54.
Pisces Australes : constellation of, IX, pt. ii, 217 note 1.
Pisháchnis : female spirits, *see* Spirits.
Pisharnáth : god of the Mátherán hill tribes, XIV, 263 ; stream and valley of, *id.* 232, 244, 234.
Pishtapura : modern Pittápuram, I, pt. ii, 280, 350 and note 6.
Pisol : pass in Násik district, XVI, 129 ; fort, *id.* 640.
Pitalkhorá : inscriptions in the caves at, I, pt. ii, 147.
Pithapuri : I, pt. ii, 350 note 6. *See* Pishtapura.
Pithari : famine plant, grows in Poona district, XXV, 200.
Pithecolobium dulce : food and oil-yielding plant, XXV, 154, 217.
Pithi : sweet yellow powder, pregnant women rubbed with, in first pregnancy rites, IX, pt. i, 32.
Pithvo : ancestor of Gujarát blacksmiths, said to have been created by Párvati, IX, pt. i, 190.
Pitpapra : famine plant common in Poona district, XXV, 200.
Pitri Gaya : place of pilgrimage in Northern India, IX, pt. i, 549.
Pitripaksha : fortnight of the *manes*, XVIII, pt. i, 249.
Pittápuram : I, pt. ii, 280, 350 and note 6 ; conquered by Pulikeśin II, *id.* 352.
Pittuga : Ratta chieftain, I, pt. ii, 551, 552.
Pit Vipers : snakes in Poona district, XVIII, pt. i, 83.
Pivala kaner : poisonous plant, XXV, 266.
Pivla potia : variety of wheat in Khándesh, XII, 150.
Piyadasi : Aśoka so called, XIV, 340.
Plague : in Surat (1684-1690), II, 91 ; in Ahmadábád (1618), IV, 218-224 ; in Káthiáwár (1812-1821), VIII, 350-351 ; in Thána district (1690, 1695, 1702), XIII, 482, 484 and note 1 ; XIV, 33 and note 5 ; the Baghdád in Bijápur (1689), XXIII, 437, 524 and note 1, 592 ; in Bombay Island (1686), XXVI, pt. i, 101.
Planets : *grahas*, have friendly or unfriendly influence on every man, IX, pt. i, 392 ; object and form of worship, occasions for, *id.* 392-393 ; daily worship, *id.* 393 ; names and forms of worship of the nine planets, *id.* 393-406.
Sun : *Surya*, his form ; is father of some heavenly beings and of warrior class ; is the eye of god or represents the three gods Brahma, Vishnu, Mahádev ; is one of the Pancháyatan *devs* ; worshipped by all classes, forms of, among high classes, among early tribes, form of addressing him ; his favourite flowers, *id.* 393, 409 ; his every day salutation ; *gáyatri*, or sun-hymn, *id.* 393 ; worshipped to ward off evil influence, to secure good will ; *Surya Vrats* or sun vows, object of taking, form of fulfilment, *id.* 394-395 ; worship of, by Káthis, *id.* 257, 393 ; worship seems to have been started by Maghás, *id.* 438, 440 ; Sunday sacred to him, common beliefs about Sunday, *id.* 396 ; *eclipse* or *grahan* that is seizure, common beliefs about, practices and observances during, *id.* 395-396 ; gifts made during, *id.* 335, 395.
Moon : *Chandra*, *id.* 392 ; a male deity, his form and characteristics, *id.* 396 ; is the lord of all vegetable drugs or *aushadhádhipati*, has more powerful influence on man and diseases, *id.* 397 ; *worship* by different classes, *id.* 396, 397 ; his revolution round the earth, the lunar month, beliefs about the first day of each month, about the last day or *amás* ; days sacred to him ; beliefs and observances on *bright seconds*, *id.* 397-398 ; on *bright fourths* called *Ganesh Chaturthi*, the bright fourth of Bhádarva called *Dagada Choth* held more sacred ; *dark fourths* called *Sankasht Chaturthi*, the dark fourth of *Asvhin* called *Karavda Choth* or *Galka Choth* is held more sacred, *id.* 398 ; on *bright fifteenths* or full-moon called *Punems*, the full-moon of Shrávan, a *Raksha* binding day ; the full-moon of *Aso*, called *Manekthári*, *id.* 399 ; other occasions to worship him ; special mode of *dasatáli* worship, *id.* 400 ; *vows*, *id.* 396 ; the *Chándráyan*, *id.* 400 ; means of warding off his evil influence ; flowers sacred to him, *id.* 400, 409 ; *eclipse*, practices observed during, *id.* 400 ; *Monday* sacred to him, beliefs about and observances on Mondays, *id.* 400-401 ; classes by whom he is worshipped, *id.* 396, 397.
Mars or *Mangal* : origin and form of ; his characteristics ; means adopted to ward off his evil influences ; Tuesday sacred to him, *id.* 401 ; common beliefs about Tuesday, *id.* 402, 384, 391.
Mercury or *Budha* : his origin and form ; his characteristics ; Wednesday sacred to him ; common beliefs about Wednesday, *id.* 402.

Jupiter : called *Guru* or *Brahaspati* his form and characteristics; Thursday sacred to him; common beliefs about Thursday, *id.* 402.
Venus or *Sukra :* his form and characteristics.; Friday sacred to him; warding off evil influence of, *id.* 402.
Saturn or *Shani :* his form and characteristics; very cruel; Saturday sacred to him; common beliefs about Saturdays; means adopted to ward off his deadly influence called *panoti, id.* 403.
Earth or *Rahu :* Prathvi, an element, *id.* 348; a planet, *id.* 392 note 1, 403; worshipped as an element; looked upon as mother; regarded as kings' consort; different occasions for worship of, *id.* 404; worship of, by husbandmen, *id.* 157, 405; causes of earthquake, *id.* 404.
Comet or Ketu : *id.* 392 note 1; his unfriendly influence, *id.* 405.
Stars and meteors considered divine beings, *id.* 406.
Planet-soothing : *see* Grahashanti.
Planet-worship : among Pátáne Prabhus, XVIII, pt. i, 202-203.
Plantain : cultivation of, in Khándesh, XII, 176; in Thána district, the drying of, XIII, 291-292, 395; in Násik district, XVI, 103; in Poona, XVIII, pt. i, 48; in Dhárwár district, XXII, 303.
Plants : spirit-scaring, XVIII, pt. i, 549. *See* also all district volumes under District Name.
Plant-worship : in Gujarát, names of plants worshipped, object and form of worship, IX, pt. i, 382-388.
Plataleinæ : family of birds in Ratnágiri, X, 96.
Pleasure-houses : Portuguese, in Thána district, I, pt. ii, 65.
Pleiades : mothers of mankind, I, pt. ii, 319 note 3, 337 note 4.
Pliny : naturalist and author (A. D. 23-79), his mention of Oratura (Sauráshtra, Káthiáwár), I, pt. i, 6; his description of Indian places and tribes, *id.* 532-534, 536-537; use of Greek coins at Broach, *id.* 538; his Nitrias identified with Nivti fort in Ratnágiri district, I, pt. ii, 2; X, 354; with Netrani island in Kánara district, XV, pt. ii, 48 note 3, 336; his Symulla is Cheul and not Chembur, XIV, 52; mentions three trade routes between India and Egypt, XI, 432; XIII, 410 note 5; trace of Arab influence in his name Zizerus for a place in Konkan, *id.* 404 note 3; his mention of Androi (Dharnikot), *id.* 409 note 3; value of Indian exports to Rome in his time, *id.* 410 note 3; reference to Parthian trade and riches in his work, *id.* 411 note 1; lead coin in Kolába district according to, XI, 139 note 2.
Plithana : modern Paithan, its trade with Broach, I, pt. ii, 619.
Plotinæ : family of birds in Ratnágiri, X, 99.
Ploughs : introduction of, European, in Kaira district, III, 55; size of, in Kaira district, *id.* 44; in Panch Maháls, *id.* 231; in Ahmadábád district, IV, 52; in Pálanpur, V, 293; in Mahi Kántha, *id.* 369; worship among husbandmen in Gujarát, IX, pt. i, 405; in Ratnágiri district, X, 145; in Kolába district, XI, 92; in Khándesh, XII, 137; in Thána district, XIII, 284; in Kánara district, XV, pt. ii, 12-13; in Ahmadnagar district, XVII, 245; in Poona district, XVIII, pt. ii, 8; in Sátára district, XIX, 150; in Dhárwár district, XXII, 257; in Bijápur, XXIII, 310; in Kolhápur state, XXIV, 156.
Plovers : class of birds in Ratnágiri district, X, 90.
Plowden : Mr., appointed to report on the system of levying salt revenue, smuggling of salt in Bombay, recommends the export of salt free of duty to Calcutta, XIII, 374-375.
Plumbagineæ : species of poisonous plants, XXV, 266.
Plumbago : *coccinea, rosea, zeylanica,* poisonous plants, common throughout India, XXV, 266.
Plunder : Shiváji's system for the disposal of, XIX, 241.
Plutarch : his mention of Menandros' rule in India, I, pt. i, 535.
Pluvial formation : in Belgaum district, XXI, 38.
Podicipidæ : family of birds in Ratnágiri district, X, 98.
Pod Vegetables : in Poona district, XVIII, pt. ii, 60-61; in Kolhápur, XXIV, 183.
Pogilli : Mahárája, of the Sendraka family, Vinayáditya's feudatory, I, pt. ii, 189, 281 note 3, 292, 369, 428 note 4; inscription of, at Balagámve, *id.* 292 note 10.
Pogosthemon patchouli : oil-yielding plant, XXV, 224.
Poicha : state in Rewa Kántha, VI, 153.
Poinsar, Poisar : village in Thána district, XIV, 298, 217; Buddhist rock-cut cisterns at, *id.* 51; caves at Magathan, *id.* 216; the church of Málvan affiliated to, church at, *id.* 223; *see* also I, pt. ii, 57, 66.
Pokarn : near Ajmir, I, pt. i, 464. *See* Pushkar.
Pokarn : Sopára pond, XIV, 339; water-works, *id.* 348.
Pokarna : a Bráhman sub-division in Cutch, V, 44; in Káthiáwár, VIII, 146; in Thána district, XIII, 78. *See* also Pushkarna.
Pol : Rathor chiefship in Máhi Kántha, IX, pt. i, 128; V, 412.
Pola : bull day, Kunbi holiday, XVII, 89.
Poládpur : town in Kolába district, XI, 357.
Polalu : probably Holal in the Bellary district, conquered by Vishnuvardhana, I, pt. ii, 497.
Polálva : minister of Vira-Ballála II and of Narasimha II, Vaishnava leader, I, pt. ii, 491, 506, 507.
Polasinda : Sinda prince, Nágáditya's son, I, pt. ii, 577.
Polekesin : I, pt. ii, 343 and note 5, 351. *See* Pulikesin II.
Polemaios : identified with Pulumáyi; his royal seat at Paithan, I, pt. i, 37.
Poleyabbarasi : Sinda prince Nágáditya's wife, I, pt. ii, 577.
Police : all district volumes, *see* Justice under District Name.
Police : Marátha system of, XVI, 317-318; British, *id.* 319.

Police Regulations : in Bombay island (1780), XXVI, pt. iii, 64-67.

Poligárs : petty *rájás*, I, pt. ii, 30. *See* Páligars.

Polishing : in Cutch, V, 125.

Political Agents : in Káthiáwár, list of, VIII, 313 314.

Pollexfen : his experience of Rájpipla Bhils, IX, pt. i, 301.

Pols : house-groups in Ahmadábád city, IV, 294.

Po-lu-kie-che-po : Chinese for Bharuka-Chheva, modern Broach, I, pt. ii, 354.

Polumbum : town, I, pt. ii, 5.

Polyandry : traces of, in Gujarát, among Bharváds, early polyandrous arrangement, IX, pt. i, 270 note 3, 285 ; in India, XVIII, pt. i, 300, 543-546.

Polygala : *arvensis, Chinensis,* famine plant, grows in several districts, XXV, 194.

Polygaleæ : species of famine plants, XXV, 194.

Polygamy : formerly practised among Pársis, now forbidden, IX, pt. ii, 238 ; allowed and practised among Rájpúts, IX, pt. i, 147 ; Kunbis, *id.* 161 ; Patelias, *id.* 174 ; Ghánchis, *id.* 183 ; Mochis, *id.* 195 ; Suthárs, *id.* 206.

Pombuchcha : fortress taken by Vishnuvardhana, I, pt. ii, 496.

Pomponius Melo : (A. D. 43), had not any recent information about India, I, pt. i, 536.

Poncar ; probably Poinsar, the Church of St. Cecilia at, I, pt. ii, 57.

Pongamia glabra : oil-yielding and medicinal plant, XXV, 217, 260.

Ponies : at Mátherán, XIV, 259, 271 ; in Ahmadnagar district, XVII, 36-37 ; in Poona district, XVIII, pt. i, 61-63 : in Sholápur district, XX, 16-17 ; in Belgaum, XXI, 298-300.

Ponnambala : Hoysála king Vira-Someśvara's daughter, I, pt. ii, 493, 508.

Ponnaváda : Honwád in the Bijápur district, I, pt. ii, 440.

Ponsonby : Captain, carries out the survey of the Mátherán hill, XIV, 268 ; spring, *id.* 245.

Pontiffs : of Shravaks taken from Osváls, IX, pt. i, 502.

Poon : fibrous plant, XXV, 229.

Poona : district, I, pt. ii, 298 ; boundaries, XVIII, pt. i, 1 ; sub-divisions, *id.* 1 ; aspect, *id.* 2-3 ; hills, *id.* 3-5 ; rivers, *id.* 69 ; geology, *id.* 9-13 ; climate, rainfall, temperature at, *id.* 13-28 ; mineral products, *id.* 29-30 ; forests, *id.* 31-40 ; trees, *id.* 41-54 ; domestic animals, *id.* 54-69 ; wild animals, *id.* 69-70 ; game birds, *id.* 70-71 ; snakes and snake-charmers, *id.* 71-87 ; fish, *id.* 87-93 ; census details, *id.* 94-96 ; Bráhmans : Chitpavan, Deshastha and others, *id.* 99-184 ; writers, *id.* 184-261 ; traders, *id.* 261-279 ; husbandmen, *id.* 279-313 ; craftsmen, *id.* 313-377 ; musicians, servants, *id.* 378-384 ; shepherds and fishers, *id.* 384-393 ; labourers, *id.* 393-406 ; unsettled tribes, *id.* 407-431 ; depressed classes, *id.* 431-444 ; beggars, *id.* 444-481 ; Musalmáns, *id.* 481-506 ; Bene-Israels, *id.* 506-536 ; agriculture : soils, arable land, holdings, XVIII, pt. ii, 3-6 ; field tools, *id.* 8-10 ; irrigation ; *id.* 12-29 ; gardening, *id.* 31-34 ; crops, *id.* 34-63 ; silk, *id.* 65-76 ; experimental and botanical gardens, *id.* 76-80 ; field plagues, *id.* 80-84 ; famines, *id.* 84-96 ; capitalists, *id.* 97-100 ; bankers, *id.* 100-106 ; money-lenders, *id.* 106-108 ; borrowers, *id.* 108-133 ; slaves, *id.* 133-134 ; wages, *id.* 134-135 ; prices, *id.* 135-138 ; weights and measures, *id.* 138-140, trade : routes (B. C. 100-A. D. 1818), *id.* 141-149 ; passes, *id.* 149-154 ; bridges and ferries, *id.* 154-158 ; railway, *id.* 159-162 ; trade course, trade centres and market towns, *id.* 163-166 ; imports, exports, *id.* 167-170 ; railway traffic, *id.* 170-173 ; brass work, *id.* 173-185 ; silk-weaving, *id.* 185-191 ; gold and silver thread, *id.* 191-196 ; cotton goods, glass bangles, combs, clay figures, paper, tape-weaving, felt and wood turning, *id.* 196-210 ; early history (B. C. 100-A. D. 1290), 210-215 ; Musalmán (1294-1760) : Delhi governors (1318-1347), *id.* 215 ; Bahámanis (1347-1490), *id.* 215-219 ; Nizám Shahis, Adil Shahis and Mughals, *id.* 220-242 ; Maráthás (1720-1817), *id.* 247-301 ; British (1817-1884), *id.* 301-309 ; land revenue : early Hindu system, *id.* 313-316 ; Malik Ambar, *id.* 317-320 ; Marátha, *id.* 320-341 ; the British (1818-1884), *id.* 351-513 ; tenures (1821), *id.* 355-358 ; land-holders, headman, accountant and the twelve servants (1820), *id.* 359-366 ; Mr. Pringle's survey settlement (1829-1836), *id.* 379-411 ; Bhimthadi survey (1838-1839), *id.* 418-419 ; Pábal survey (1841-1842), *id.* 426-430 ; Haveli survey (1841-1842), *id.* 431-432 ; Supa survey (1843-1844), *id.* 437-438 ; Purandhar survey (1847-1848), *id.* 442-444 ; Báramati, Bori, Bráhmanwadi, Junnar, Ambegaon, Purandhar, Khed and Mával survey (1847-1854), *id.* 445-465 ; revision survey (1867-1884), *id.* 470-508 ; survey results (1836-1880), *id.* 508-510 ; revenue statistics (1837-84), *id.* 512 ; agricultural banks (1884), *id.* 512-513 ; justice, XVIII, pt. iii, 1-40 ; early Hindu and under the Maráthás, *id.* 1-10 ; under the British, *id.* 11-24 ; civil suits, small causes court, registration, criminal justice, police, offences and predatory tribes, *id.* 24-40 ; finance, heads of revenue and expenditure, balance sheets (1870, 1882), *id.* 41-47 ; instruction, *id.* 48-65 ; schools and school returns, colleges, private schools, *id.* 48-61 ; libraries, *id.* 61-62 ; Dakshina Prize Committee and other societies, *id.* 62-64 ; newspapers, *id.* 64-65 ; health, *id.* 66-74 ; climate, diseases, *id.* 66 ; hospitals, infirms, vaccination, *id.* 66-69 ; native physicians, *id.* 69-71 ; cat plague, births and deaths, *id.* 71-73 ; sub-divisions and their details, *id.* 74-101 ; places, *id.* 102-476.

City : position, geology, aspect, river Mutha Mula, roads, drives, XVIII, pt. iii, 266-269 ; city description, ward details, *id.* 270-282 ; streets, bridges, houses, population details, *id.* 283-301 ; trade, imports and exports (1881-1884), details of articles, crafts, markets, *id.* 302-322 ; management, municipality, revenue (1858-1883), drainage, roads, water-supply from aqueducts and the Mutha Canal, medical and educational institutions, museum, library,

newspapers, *id.* 323-331 ; objects of interest (1-40), miscellaneous objects, *id.* 331-349 ; cantonment, divisions, aspect, sadar bazár, houses, shops, population, streets, management, garrison, history, *id.* 350-357 ; Kirkee cantonment, suburban municipality, *id.* 358-360 ; objects of insterest outside the city, *id.* 360-401 ; history, *id.* 402-424 ; captured by Mughals (1662), XVIII, pt. ii, 229 ; Mughals surprised (1663) by Shivaji at, *id.* 230 ; restored to Shivaji (1667), *id.* 235 ; taken by Khan Jahán (1685), *id.* 238 ; became capital of the Marátha empire (1750), *id.* 245; XIX, 291 ; destroyed (1763) by the Nizám, XVIII, pt. ii, 252 ; Mahadji Sindia in (1792), *id.* 268-269 ; plundered by Sindia and Sirzirav Ghatge (1797), *id.* 275 ; I, pt. ii, 607 ; plundered by Holkar (1802), XVIII, pt. ii, 282 ; treaty of (1817), *id.* 297 ; XIII, 522 ; XIV, 35, 220 ; I, pt. i, 428 ; I, pt. ii, 664 ; surrendered to the English (1817), XVIII, pt. ii, 301 ; Lingáyats in, I, pt. ii, 478 ; settlers from, into Bombay (1763), XXVI, pt. i, 351.

Poona Hotel : in Poona cantonment, XVIII, pt. iii, 390.

Pope : the, orders conversion to Christianity by force (1594), I, pt. ii, 59.

Pophli : hill, in Thána district, XIII, 7.

Popli : food plant, grows on the *gháts*, XXV, 174.

Poppy : cultivation of, in Kaira, III, 54 ; in Panch Mahals, *id.* 234 ; in Khándesh, XII, 167.

Popsha : cattle disease in Khándesh, XII, 338.

Population : all district volumes, *see* Census Details under District Name.

Population : of the Konkan, history and character of, "Introduction to the History of the Konkan," I, pt. ii, 11-12.

Porbandar : Jethva Rájpút chiefship, IX, pt. i, 127 ; state, town and place of interest in Káthiáwár, VIII, 240, 614-629 ; port, I, pt. i, 524 ; *rána* of, pays tribute to Baroda, VII, 323, 325 ; dispute with the *rája* of (1733), XXVI, pt. i, 265.

Porcupine : Mátheián point, XIV, 232, 233-240, 278, 282.

Porcupine : bird in Kánara, XV, pt. i, 95.

Poros, Porus : Indian king, mentioned by Strabo, I, pt. i, 535, 536 ; wages a great battle with Alexander, I, pt. ii, 5.

Porphyry : (A. D. 300) his mention of Shrámans at Kánheri, XIV, 125 note 4.

Ports : in Rewa Kántha, VI, 51 ; in Cambay, *id.* 238 ; in Gujarát (1513-1515), I, pt. i, 220 and note 2 ; I, pt. ii, 1 ; under Siláháras, *id.* 21 ; of Malabár, attain more importance than the Konkan and Gujarát ports, *id* 64 ; in Surat and Broach district, II, 171, 418 ; in Ahmadábád district, IV, 13, 334, 339 ; in Káthiáwár, VIII, 236-242 ; in Ratnágiri district, X, 356 ; in Kolába district, XI, 126-130 ; in Thána district, XIII, 354-361 ; in Kánara, district, XV, pt. ii, 65-68.

Portuguese : play a grand part in the whole of the East, the objects which they pursued in Asia, their first visit to Calicut (1498), the Venetians join the Egyptians to oppose them, have many encounters with the Musalmán fleet, their first voyage north of Goa (1503), I, pt. ii, 43 ; take the island of Jeran (1508), IX, pt. ii, 183 note 5 ; supply guns and ammunition to Vijayanagar (1510) and secure her friendship, XXI, 367 ; capture Goa on the west coast (1510), I, pt. ii, 641 ; capture Bijápur vessels, *id.* 646 ; destroy vessels in the port of Chaul and near Dábhol (1507), their defeat at Chaul (1508), defeat Egyptian and Gujarát fleets at Diu (1508), defeat Turkish fleet at Diu (1538), *id.* 44 ; protect vessels frequenting Ahmadnagar ports, establish a factory, and build a port at Chaul, *id.* 45 ; destroy Dábhol because the Bijápur king does not acknowledge the supremacy of their fleet, *id.* 45 ; defeated by the Gujarát admiral (1521) ; defeat the Gujarát fleet at Chaul (1527) and take seventy-three Gujarát ships in a battle off Bándra (1528), burn Nágothna, Bassein and Agáshi (1529), defeated at Chaul (1530), Bassein ceded to them and Gujarát ships put under their protection, obtain Diu as the price of the alliance against the Mughals, *id.* 46 ; make treaties with Ahmadnagar and Bijnagar against Bijápur ; obtain Bijápur ports and give protection to Bijápur fleet ; defeat Bijápur troops at Achra (1555), become masters of the Bijápur coast (1560), *id.* 47 ; acquire places in the North Konkan, *id.* 48, 49 ; repulse attacks by the Bijápur and Ahmadnagar kings, *id.* 49 ; take Korlai (1594), *id.* 50 ; their system of administration and decline, *id.* 52-66 ; send out fleets of the north and of the south to protect their ships and possessions from the pirates, *id.* 61 ; trade of the (1565), *id.* 62 ; enter into a, treaty with the emperor Jahangir against the English, the Dutch and the Malabár pirates (1615), *id.* 62 ; prevent native vessels from sailing along the Konkan without their permission, *id.* 63 ; lose commercial superiority and prestige on the Persian Gulf and the Cape of Good Hope routes ; cause of the decline of their power, *id.* 64 ; driven from Jeran (1622) by the English and the Persians, IX, pt. ii, 183 note 5 ; show for some time interest in their Indian possessions, but again neglect them till 1739, I, pt. ii, 64 ; their pleasure-houses near Bassein, *id.* 65 ; remains at Bassein, Lower Chaul, Mándvi, Kelva-Máhim and Marol, *id.* 65 ; churches in Sálsette and Bassein, *id.* 65 ; remains at Mandapeshvar, *id.* 66 ; capture ships from Shiváji's fleet (1670), *id.* 69 ; friction with Bombay Presidency (1676), XXVI, pt. i, 61-65 ; prevent Shiváji from entering into the port of Bombay (1678), I, pt. ii, 71 ; repulse Sambháji's attack on Chaul but lose Karanja (1683), *id.* 77 ; retake Karanja, Santa Cruz, and Asheri (1684), *id.* 78 ; war declared against, by Aurangzeb (1794), *id.* 80 ; burn Marátha ships (1695), *id.* 80 ; fight with the Arab pirates (1712-1720), *id.* 82 ; trouble with, caused by the expulsion of Catholic priests from Bombay (1720), XXVI, pt. i, 61-65 ; their struggle with the Maráthás (1737-1740), *id.* 181-236 ; apply to the Bombay Presidency for aid

(1737), *id.* 184-186, 190-194, 199-201, 206-211, 222-225; *see* also XIX, 279-280; I, pt. ii, 84, 85; their fleet destroyed by Angria (1741); their alliance with the French (1741), XXVI, pt. i, 276; attack the Marátha district near Goa but are defeated (1756), I, pt. ii, 85; *another account of:* affairs of the, in Diu (1529-1536), I, pt. i, 347; send an expedition to South Káthiáwár and sack Tárápur, Bulsár and Surat (1531); burn the ports of Somnáth Pattan, Mangrul, Talaja and Muzaffarábád; destroy Bassein and burn Damán, Thána and Bombay; send an embassy to the court of Humáyun to obtain Diu; treaty with Sultán Bahádur of Gujarát; disputes with Sultán Bahádur (1536), *id.* 347, 348; in Surat (1700-1703), *id.* 292; their rule in Thána, XIII, 403, 428; (1500-1670), *id.* 447-474, 479, 482, 489, 492; land-holders, *id.* 550; *dhep* system, *id.* 550-551; administration, *id.* 552-553; districts, 552 note 2; revenue system, 552 note 10; cesses, *id.* 552-553; condition, *id.* 553; excise, *id.* 553 note 1; districts passed to the Peshwa (1733-1739), *id.* 555; *pándharpeshás*, *id.* 556; rates, *id.* 557; their administration, judicial and revenue, I, pt. ii, 52, 53; their garrisons in Thána district, XIII, 458 note 2; at Bassein and Kelva-Máhim (1727) *id.* 490-491; their land system, *id.* 459; their rule in Bombay island (1500-1662), IX, pt. ii, 195; their rule in Kolába (1507-1660), XI, 143; buildings of, at Chaul (1520-1722), *id.* 279 note 4, 289-290; in Kánara district (1498-1512), XV, pt. ii, 101-104; (1514-1600), *id.* 112-115, 118-119, 124; in Surat district (1608-1658), II, 88; (1658-1707), *id.* 107; (1707-1733), *id.* 115; (1759-1800), *id.* 153; in Ahmadábád, IV, 87 251; in Cambay, VI, 189, 190, 217.

Portuguese Asia: historical work by Faria-e-Souza (1650), I, pt. i, 349.

Portuguese Church: in Bombay, removed, XXVI, pt. iii, 531-532.

Porus: *see* Porus.

Porvád: suburb of Shrimál, IX, pt. i, 73.

Porvád, Porwal: a caste of Vániás in Gujarát, IX, pt. i, p. xi note 3; Meshri, *id.* 73; Shrávaks, *id.* 97; in Rewa Kántha, VI, 24; in Káthiáwár, VIII, 148; in Thána district, XIII, 112, 113; origin of the caste, I, pt. i, 464.

Poseidonios: auther quoted by Strabo, I, pt. i, 535.

Poshitra: port in Káthiáwár, VIII, 32; under Baroda, *id.* 242.

Poshkaráni: Ushavadáta performs ablutions at, I, pt. ii, 148.

Posina: village in Mahi Kántha, temples at, V, 439; north boundary of the Vaghela kingdom in 1297, I, pt. i, 206.

Post: in Musalmán period, I, pt. i, 214.

Postal arrangement: between England, Bombay and Madras (1787-1788), XXVI, pt. ii, 13-16.

Postans: Mrs. (1838), at Bassein, XIV, 35.

Post Offices: all district volumes, *see* Trade under District Name.

Potana: Potala, mart frequented by the Arabs, I, pt. i, 535.

Potarasa: Kalachurya Bijjala's accountant, I, pt. ii, 473.

Potato: cultivation of, in Khándesh, XII, 170; sweet, *id.* 170; in Násik district, XVI, 103 and note 1, 104; in Poona district, XVIII, pt. ii, 55-56.

Potavta: exchange cess in Baroda state, VII, 379.

Potedári: system of making payments through bankers, in Baroda state, VII, 396-399.

Potphugi: stream in Kolhápur state, XXIV, 9.

Potrájá: depressed class in Dhárwár district, XXII, 217.

Pottalakere: modern Daṇṇáyakana-kere in Madras, I, pt. ii, 437.

Potter's Gate Causeway: in Poona city, XVIII, pt. iii, 284.

Pottery: in Ahmadábád, IV, 126; in Baroda state, VII, 157-158; in Ratnágiri district, X, 188, 348; in Kolába district, XI, 133; in Khándesh, XII, 225; in Kánara district, XV, pt. ii, 71; in Sátára district, XIX, 221; in Belgaum district, XXI, 352; in Dhárwár district, XXII, 383; in Kolhápur state, XXIV, 208-210.

Pottinger: Captain Henry (1818), collector of Poona, XVIII, pt. ii, 304; restores peace in Ahmadnagar, I, pt. ii, 631.

Pottinger: Major, attacks (1858) Bhágoji's force near Yeola, XVI, 202.

Poulipoula: identification of, with Phulpádá (old Surat), I, pt. i, 539.

Pouzolzia tuberoza: famine plant, XXV, 204.

Pova: variety of honey-bee in Kolhápur, XXIV, 24, 25.

Povai: village in Sálsette, XIV, 299; purchased (1829) by a Bombay merchant, *id.* 44.

Povaron: Malabars' name for Honávar, XV, pt. ii, 309.

Povárs: of Dhár, origin of, XVIII, pt. ii, 244.

Powers: of Káthiáwár chiefs, VIII, 318 note 1.

Poynad: town in Kolába district, XI, 357; Mánáji A'ngria (1733-1759) confines Yesaji at, *id.* 150.

Poysala, Poysana: I, pt. ii, 490. *See* Hoysála.

Prabal: fort in Thána district, XIV, 300-301, 98; point at Mátherán, *id.* 98.

Prabandhachintámani: historical work dealing with the Chávada kings, references to, I, pt. i, 149 and note 2, 151, 152, 154, 156, 158, 160, 162, 163, 169-174, 176, 178-180, 183-186, 189, 190, 193-195.

Prabandhaśata: work of Rámachandra, Kumárapála's *pandit*, I, pt. i, 190.

Prabánváli: capital of the Dábhol *subhedári*, I, pt. ii, 39.

Prabháchandra: Jain teacher, I, pt. ii, 407, 408 and note 1, 491.

Prabháchandrasiddhántadeva: I, pt. ii, 494. *See* Prabháchandra.

Prabhákarasvámin: Bráhman grantee of the Chálukyás, I, pt. ii, 191.

Prabhákaravardhana: king of Magadha (600-606), I, pt. i, 467, 497; father of Shri Harsha, supposed to be a foreign invader, IX, pt. i, 444 and note 4.

Prabhánvalli : hill path in Kolhápur, XXIV, 5.
Prabhás : or Somnáth Pátan on south coast of Káthiáwár, temple of Somnáth Mahádev at, IX, pt. i, 195; place of pilgrimage, 9, 28, 119, 220, 247, 549; I, pt. ii, 148; Mularája's visit to, I, pt. i, 160; holy place, *id.* 164; inscription at, *id.* 176.
Prabhás Khand : historical work, IX, pt. i, 9.
Prabhás Kshetra : *see* Prabhás.
Prabhás-Pátan : *see* Prabhás.
Prabhritasára : a work of Bálachandra, I, pt. ii, 288.
Prabhus, Parbhus : in Gujarát, *Káyasth*, found chiefly in Baroda; their settlement; *Pátáne*, found in Surat, once enjoyed the monopoly of government service as English writers, IX, pt. i, 68; district of, coinciding with Virát, "Introduction to the History of the Konkan," I, pt. ii, p. x; claim Bhimrája, *id.* 27; employed in high position under the Portuguese but not allowed to perform their religious duties openly; forcibly converted to Christianity, their Christian descendants in Sálsette and Bassein, *id.* 60; in Ratnágiri, X, 118; in Sávantvádi, *id.* 412; Portuguese village clerks, XIII, 552; *Dhruv*, *Káyasth* and *Pátáne*, in Poona district, XVIII, pt. i, 185-256; in Sátára district, XIX, 57; Shiváji's partiality to, *id.* 232; in Kolhápur, theories as to their origin, XXIV, 64-65.
Prabhutavarsha : *biruda* (title) of Govinda II, I, pt. ii, 399 and note 7; of Govinda III, *id.* 199, 401; of Govinda IV, *id.* 205, 416; *see* also *id.* 383, 399; I, pt. i, 126.
Prachanda : noble of Krishna, Dakhan Ráshtrakúta king, I, pt. i, 129; I, pt. ii, 413.
Práchi Kund : sacred place in Káthiáwár, VIII, 630.
Prachitgad : Sahyadri fort in Sátára district, its history and details, XIX, 5, 11, 543-545; XXIV, 4, 5; captured by Rámoshis (1815), I, pt. ii, 610; taken by Chitursing, a *gosávi* (1816), XIX, 300. *See* Uchitgad.
Prajápati : Hindu sage, daughter of, loved by the moon, I, pt. i, 521.
Prajápati : the creator, Kumbhárs also so called, IX, pt. i, 189 note 2, 531.
Prakásha ; place of interest in Khándesh, XII, 466.
Prákrit : dialect, I, pt. i, 533, 534; I, pt. ii, 133, 136, 137, 144, 410 note 1.
Prákrita Prakáśa : Vararuchi's Prákrit grammar, I, pt. ii, 144.
Pralhádha : IX, pt. ii, 48. *See* Bhakta.
Pralhád Niráji : Rájárám's officer, I, pt. ii, 596.
Prameya Kamalamártanda : Prabháchandra's commentary on Mánsikyanandin's *Parikśamukha*, I, pt. ii, 407.
Pranálakadurga : modern Panhálá, I, pt. ii, 549.
Pranava : sacred syllable *om*, I, pt. ii, 227.
Pránlák : old name of Panhála, XXIV, 313.
Prántvel : place of interest in Máhi Kántha, V, 439.
Prárjuna : a tribe tributary to Samudragupta, I, pt. i, 64 and note 3.
Praśántarága : title of Dada II, Gurjjara ruler, I, pt. i, 115. *See* also I, pt. ii, 312 note 7.
Praśasti : poetical eulogium on the Sahasralinga lake written by Śripála, I, pt. i, 180.
Prashnora : division of Nágar Bráhmans, IX, pt. i, 13; called Ahichhatrás, *id.* 15 and notes 1 and 2.
Prasi : Prácyas of Palibothra, I, pt. i, 532, 533.
Prasiddhagad : hill-fort on Kolhápur and Sávantvádi boundary, XXIV, 5; X, 467.
Prssnottaramálá : I, pt. ii, 403. *See* Ratnamáliká.
Prasnottara-ratnamáliká : work on morality, I, pt. ii, 200.
Pratápa Hoysala : I, pt. ii, 500, 501. *See* Narssimha I and Vira-Ballála II.
Pratápamalla : son of Kumárapála's daughter, I, pt. i, 194.
Pratápamalla : second son of Viradhavala, I, pt. i, 203.
Pratáparndra : Tailangana prince, I, pt. ii, 246, 247.
Pratáparudriya : work on poetics, I, pt. ii, 246, 511.
Pratápasimha ; king of Kalumbapattana, receives Kumárapála, builds a temple and issues a coin named after Kumárapála, I, pt. i, 183.
Pratapgad : Sahyadri fort in Sátára district, XIX, 5, 9; fort details, history, *id.* 545, 547; built by Shiváji (1656), *id.* 234; I, pt. ii, 67; XVIII, pt. ii, 227; Afzulkhán murdered at (1659), XIX, 234-237; I, pt. ii, 592; surrenders to the British (1818), XIX, 308, 509.
Pratáppur : village in Khándesh, I, pt. ii, 633.
Pratappuri : Pratápsháh's capital, I, pt. ii, 27.
Pratápráo Gujar : captain under Sultán Mazum, ordered to be arrested by Aurangzib; escapes and joins Shiváji (1670), I, pt. ii, 594; levies *chauth* in Khándesh (1670), *id.* 625; defeats the Mughals at Sálher and falls in an action at Panhála, *id.* 594.
Pratápráv : brother of Dámáji Gáikwár, advances with Deváji Tákpar and exacts tribute and plunders the country; levies tribute from the chiefs in Soráth, dies of small-pox at Kánkar near Dholka (1737), I, pt. i, 317; VII, 174.
Pratápsháh : Bhimrája's son, builds a capital at Marol, and calls it Pratáppuri, I, pt. ii, 27.
Pratápsháh : Báglán chief, XVI, 188, 459 note 1.
Pratápsinh : *rája* of Sátára, installed by the English (1818), I, pt. ii, 611; deposed and sent to Benares (1839), *id.* 612.
Prathampur : place of interest in Rewa Kántha, VI, 166.
Pratham Shákhis : *see* Kánva Bráhmans.
Prath Nagri : local name of Dholka, I, pt. i, 208 note 3.
Pratika : old coin, mentioned in Kánheri caves, XIV, 147 note 2, 177, 178.

Pratinidhi: Marátha officer, creation of the office of, XIX, 249; at Chiplun (1733), I, pt. ii, 82-83; Parsharám Shrinivás imprisoned by Bájiráo at Mhaswad (1806); released by his Telin mistress; defeated and taken prisoner by Bápu Gokhale (1807), *id.* 609.

Pratisthána: old name of Paithana, I, pt. ii, 143, 147, 277, 397; XVII, 351.

Pratyandaka: king of, vanquished by Bhillama V, I, pt. ii, 238, 520.

Pravará: river in Ahmadnagar district, XVII, 7.

Pravarásangam: *see* Toka.

Pravarasena II: Vákátaka Mahárája, I, pt. ii, 279 note 1.

Prayág: near Kolhápur, meeting of the Bhogávati and the Kásári at, XXIV, 10; I, pt. ii, 255.

Práyág: *see* Allahábád.

Práyas-chitta: atonement ceremony, I, pt. ii, 249.

Prayers: enjoined by Muslim law as a duty, IX, pt. ii, 126, 171 note 2; form, number, time and place of reading, *id.* 47, 49, 116, 126 and notes 2, 3, 5; funeral, *id.* 126; written, put in the hand of a dying Daudi Bohora, *id.* 31 and note 2; vow to repeat, *id.* 127; among Pársis, *kusti*, IX, pt. ii, 208 note 1; marriage, *id.* 236 note 1; meal, *id.* 220 note 1; *nerang*, *id.* 208 note 2.

Precious stones: spirit-scaring powers of, XVIII, pt. i, 549-550.

Pregnancy: ceremonies among Gujarát Hindus; *simanta*, *simantonnayana*, that is hair-parting or hair-dividing, more commonly called *kholo-bharvo*, that is lap-filling ceremony, also known as *agharni*; among Bráhmans, IX, pt. i, 31-33; Kanbis, *id.* 161; Rájpúts, *id.* 147-148; Vániás, *id.* 93-94; bards and actors, *id.* 214, 225, 226; craftsmen, *id.* 179, 185, 188, 195, 201, 206; husbandmen, *id.* 154, 170, 176; Kolis, *id.* 250; personal servants, *id.* 230, 234; traders, *id.* 102, 105; 121; writers, *id.* 59, 64, 66, 68; among Gujarát Musalmáns, horror felt at the prospect of leaving no issue, resort to remedies to obtain children, appeals made to saints; *amils* or exorcists asked to cast out spirit of barrenness, IX, pt. ii, 147; visit to shrines and trees possessing issue-giving properties, *id.* 148; caution taken against the baneful influences from the time of conception, *id.* 148-149; rites and ceremonies relating to seventh and ninth month celebration of, *id.* 149-150; performance of a *behlim* vow in, *id.* 150-151; performance of earthen dish rite or *sahnak* in, *id.* 151-152; offerings of grass, boats or *náos*, *id.* 152-153; rite of sex divination by milk in, *id.* 153-154; rites and ceremonies relating to, among Pársis, *panchmásin* ceremony in; *agarni* ceremony in; *ovanna* salutation in, IX, pt. ii, 227; in Kánara district, XV, pt. i, 164, 251, 343; among Pátáne Prabhus, XVIII, pt. i, 219-220; Musalmáns, *id.* 488.

Premaládevi: sister of Kumárapála, married to Krishnadeva, Siddharája's general, I, pt. i, 181.

Premdás Báva: Bharvád saint, IX, pt. i, 271.

Premna: *latifolia*, *serratifolia*, famine plants, XXV, 202, 203.

Prempur: state in Mahi Kánthá, V, 426.

Prescott: Mr., on Bhil sub-divisions, IX, pt. i, 295 note 2; on Bhil appearance, *id.* 296 note 1; on Bhil huts, *id.* 296 note 2; on Bhil character, *id.* 300 note 3; on Naikda raids, *id.* 326 note 2; on Naikda disrespect of Bráhmans, *id.* 327 note 1.

Presents: religious, among Gujarát Hindus, chief days for making, IX, pt. i, 23 note 5; making and receiving of, in betrothal among Pársis, IX, pt. ii, 232-233; on birth, 228; on marriages, before and after, *id.* 233, 235, 237 and note 1; on pregnancy, *id.* 227.

"President:" English East India Company's ship, attacked by some Arab vessels in Sambháji's pay, I, pt. ii, 77.

Presses: cotton, in Násik, XVI, 457; in Khándesh, XII, 232; at Dhulia, *id.* 442; at Jalgaon, *id.* 451; in Dhárwár district, XXII, 374.

Preticulatus anisonema multiflora: dye-yielding plant, XXV, 249.

Price: Mr., chief of the English factory at Surat, Fatehsing's negotiations with (1722), VII, 189-190.

Prices: history of, in Surat district, II, 207; in Broach, *id.* 459; in Kaira district, III, 63; in Panch Mahálś, *id.* 239; in Ahmadábád district, IV, 76; in Cutch, V, 111 112; in Pálanpur, *id.* 297; in Mahi Kánthá, *id.* 375; in Rewa Kántha, VI, 43-44; in Cambay, *id.* 209; in Baroda, VII, 141; in Káthiáwár, VIII, 216-218; in Ratnágiri, X, 163; in Savántvádi, 431; in Bombay island (1741), XXVI, pt. ii, 78-79; in (1747), *id.* 80; Surat high prices committee, *id.* 82-85; in 1779, 1780, 1781, *id.* 89-90; in Kolába district, XI, 107-108; great fall in, after 1825, *id.* 175 and notes 1 and 6; rise in, in 1834-1837, *id.* 182 note 1, 184; high (1854-1866), *id.* 176, 197; low (1872-1876), *id.* 177; (1852-1881), *id.* 214, 428; in Khándesh (1788-1879), XII, 202; in Thána district, XIII, 312-314; high prices (1800-1818), *id.* 562; still high (1820), *id.* 571; doubtful, *id.* 571 note 2; Nasrápur prices (1820), *id.* 571 note 2; (1827-1832), *id.* 576 note 5; cheapness of grain (1830), *id.* 577 note 2; (1831-1833), *id.* 577 note 5; causes of decline in 1836, *id.* 577 note 5, 579; Sálsette high prices (1836), *id.* 584; Bhiwndi yearly prices (1840-1860), *id.* 606 note 1; (1855-1881), *id.* 628-629; in Kánara district, XV, pt ii, 35, 36; in Násik district, XVI, 122 and 123, 210, 211, 213, 265, 272, 273, 281, 282, 303; in Ahmadnagar district (1772-1837), XVII, 322-324, 461 note 6, 465 note 4, 476 note 2; in Poona district, XVIII, pt. ii, 135-138, 373, 374, 376, 415, 438 note 1, 474 note 1, 478 note 1, 479, 512; in Sátára district, XIX, 190-192, 376 note 1; in Sholápur district, XX, 251-252; 312 note 3, 316, 323, 336 and notes 2 and 3, 342 and note 2, 349 and note 1, 354 and note 1; in Belgaum district, XXI,

453, 457, 565; in Dhárwár district, XXII, 338-340, 453 and note 6, 454 and note 1, 455 and note 1, 528 and note 1; in Bijápur district, XXIII, 54-61; of food-grains, *id.* 351-353, 461 and note 1, 465 and note 1, 466 and note 1, 468 note 1, 485 note 2, 492 and note 2, 495 note 2; in Kolhápur state, XXIV, 196-197.

Priests: Pársi, introduction of, from Persia into Dwárka, IX, pt. ii, 183 note 4; trace their descent to Shápur Sheheriar; genealogical tree of, *id.* 221; distribution of, into districts or charges: high priest or *dastur* over a district or charge; secular business followed by; intermarriages among, *id.* 222; dress of, *id.* 201, 222; appearance of; religious functions of, *id.* 222; *kusti* weaving by the women of, *id.* 209, 222; other names of, higher and lower sacerdotal orders of, Herhad and Mobeds, ordination of, *id.* 222-226; schools kept by, *id.* 209; education of the sons of, *id.* 210; religious disputes among the two bodies of, in Navsári, *id.* 192. *See* Herbad, Mobeds.

Primates: order of animals in Ratnágiri district, X, 42.

Principal Sadar Amin: *see* Amin.

Pringle: Mr., his survey and settlement in Poona district, XVIII, pt. ii, 379-393, 396, 397-410.

Prinsep: Mr. James, "Introduction to the Early History of the Dakhan," I, pt. ii, p. iii; tries to decipher the inscriptions in Nánághát chamber (1838), XIV, 291.

Pritamdás: a Bhát poet, IX, pt. i, 213.

Pritchard: Mr. C. B., carries out the system of checking contraband trade proposed by Mr. G. W. Pedder, XIII, 374; prepares the draft Salt Act (1871), *id.* 376; his administration and its results, *id.* 378; introduces a new excise system, *id.* 647.

Prithiráj Chohán: king of Delhi, I, pt. i, 470.

Pritbivimula: Prabhákara's son, I, pt. ii, 334.

Prithivisena: ninth Kshatrapa (A. D. 222), coin of, I, pt. i, 43.

Prithivivallabba: *biruda* (title) of the Western Chalukyas, I, pt. ii, 345 note 1. *See* Prithvivallabba.

Prithivivallabha-Nikumbhallásakti: Sendraka prince (655), I, pt. ii, 292.

Prithivivyághra: Nishâda chief, defeated by the Pallava general Udayachandra, I, pt. ii, 326.

Prithvi: *see* Earth.

Prithviráma, Prithvirám: Ratta prince of Saundatti, feudatory of the Ráshtrakútas, I, pt. ii, 411 note 1, 420, 550, 551; builds a Jain temple (875), *id.* 201; XXI, 356.

Prithvivallabha: I, pt. ii, 181, 182; *biruda* (title) of Govinda III, *id.* 199. *See* Prithivivallabha.

Pritikadwára: other name of Parihár, meaning of the name, IX, pt. i, 484. *See* Parihár.

Pritzler: General, at Tásgaon, engaged in a warfare with the Peshwa (1818), XIX, 302; joins Munro at Nagar Manoli, engaged in the siege of Sholápur, XX, 296-298.

Private Schools: in Surat district, II, 249; in Broach district, *id.* 523; in Kaira district, III, 132; in Ahmadábád district, IV, 209; in Kewa Kántha, VI, 86; in Koláha district, XI, 230-231; in Násik district, XVI, 333, 334; in Poona city, XVIII, pt. iii, 58-60; in Sátára district, XIX, 409; in Sholápur district, XX, 379; in Dhárwár district, XXII, 612; in Bijápur district, XXIII, 518.

Private Secretaryship: to the governor of Bombay created (1789), XXVI, pt. ii, 411.

Prohy: officer in the Surat factory, IX, pt. ii, 196 note 3.

Probyn: Major O., the destruction of tigers in Kbándesh under, XII, 30; the surprise of Khajarsing, *id.* 311; Tulia Náik meets and gives himself up to, *id.* 312-313.

Professions: census details of 1872 of classes in Gujarát following, condition of, IX, pt. ii, 122.

Proklais: near Peshâwar, I, pt. i, 545.

Prola, Proláraja: Kákatiya prince, I, pt. ii, 458 note 2, 462; fights with Tailapa II, I, pt. ii, 222.

Proprietary Husbandmen: in Kánara, XV, pt. ii, 2-3.

Prosopis spicigera: fodder and sacred plant, XXV, 278, 279, 280, 290.

Prospects: of Bráhmans in Gujarát, IX, pt. i, 51; Kolis, *id.* 251; Vánias, *id.* 96; Early Tribes, *id.* 294; of Gujarát Musalmán population in general, IX, pt. ii, 176.

Protagoras: geographer, I, pt. i, 546.

"Protector:" English ship, pursues Ángria's vessels 1756), I, pt. ii, 90.

Prother: Colonel, takes the forts of Karmála, Avchitgad, Songad, Páli, Bharap, Rájmáchi and Kuári (1818), I, pt. ii, 116-117; takes the forts of Tala, Ghosála, Ráygad, Lingána, Kángori, Chandangad, and Mahipatgad (1818), *id.* 117; captures places in Kolába, XI, 156; his visit to the Peshwa's wife, *id.* 267, 316, 345, 376; XIII, 522; XIV, 197; captures Lohogad, XVIII, pt. ii, 303.

Provost Marshal: in Bombay island, duties (1701) of, XXVI, pt. iii, 197-198.

Pryági Prabhu: commandant of the fort of Sátára (1700), XIX, 251.

Pseudostomos: river, possibly the Malprabhá and Krishna, or the Tungabhadra with its tributaries, I, pt. i, 540.

Psittacidæ: family of birds in Ratnágiri, X, 66.

Pterocarpus marsupium: gum-yielding and medicinal plant, XXV, 251, 259.

Pterocarpus santalinus: dye-yielding plant, XXV, 243.

Ptolemy: Egyptian geograhper (A. D. 150), his description of Western India, I, pt. i, 538-542; XI, 138; his mention of Surastrene (Káthiáwár), I, pt. i, 6, 7; of Balai (Valeb, Valabhi), *id.* 78 note 1; of Aberia or Ahir country, *id.* 137; his Symulla identified with Cheul and Chembur, *id.* 533; XI, 136, 270; XIV, 52; his Minnagara identified with Junagad, I, pt. i, 544; his map of India, IX, pt. ii, 1 note 1; his Mandagora identified with Bagmandle and Mandangad fort, X, 319, 352; his Hippokura identified with Ghodegaon in Kolába, Ghodhandar in Thána, with Kolhápur and Karhad, XI, 10; XIV, 99; XXIV, 218, 306, 307; I, pt. ii, 176; his Milizeguris, identified with Janjira and Malvan,

XI, 432; Musopalli with Mhasla, *id.* 465; his description of Thána trade, XIII, 414-415; his mention of Tagar, *id.* 424; I, pt. ii, 538 note 8; calls Bassein creek Binda, XIV, 45, 46; his Dung identified with Dugad and Tungár, *id.* 56, 366 note 1; calls Vaitarni river the Goreh, *id.* 103; his mention of Supara (Sopára), *id.* 320, 333 note 1; his mention of Pulumáyi, *id.* 147; I, pt. ii, 158, 159, 165, 166; of Nánághát, XIV, 291; his mention of Konkan and Konkan places, I, pt. ii, 1, 2; of the Pulindas, on the Narbada, *id.* 138; of Baithana (Paithan), *id.* 143; XVII, 351; of Banavasi, XV, pt. ii, 77, 265; I, pt. ii, 278 note 2; Kánara known to, as Lymirike or Damurike, XV, pt. i, 1 note 2; his mention of Nitra (Netrani island), XV, pt. ii, 48 note 3, 336; of Anjidiv, *id.* 251, 252 and note 2; of Mirjan, *id.* 332; his mention of five places in Bijápur, XXIII, 378; *see* also IX, pt. i, 294.

Ptychotis: *ajowan* and *montana*, oil-yielding plants, XXV, 223.

Puberty Ceremonies: of the Chitpávans, XVIII, pt. i, 140-144; Deshasths, *id.* 159; Kanojas, *id.* 170; Pátáne Prabhus, *id.* 218-219; Kunbis, *id.* 307; Badháis, *id.* 316; Bhávsárs, *id.* 324; Buruds, *id.* 326; Koshtis, *id.* 49; Sális, *id.* 364; Ladhis, *id.* 400-401; Vanjáris, *id.* 430; Kolhátis, *id.* 458; Uchliás, *id.* 473; Bene-Israels, *id.* 531-532.

Puchán: family, hereditary servants of the Pallavas, I, pt. ii, 326.

Puchhi: cess in Pálanpur state, V, 311, 312.

Pucho: *see* Putchuk.

Pudumáyi Vásishthiputra: Andhrabhritya ruler (A. D. 130), XIV, 147; I, pt. ii, 11.

Pujyapáda: Jain preceptor and grammarian, I, pt. ii, 191, 256; author of the Jainendra grammar, *id.* 371.

Pujyapáda: epithet of Jain teachers, I, pt. ii, 373 note 5.

Pulakesi, Pulakesi Janásraya: Avanijanásraya, son of Dharáśraya Jayasimhavarman, younger brother of Vikramáditya I (738-739), I, pt. ii, 187, 376; feudatory, ruler of Láta, vanquishes the Tájikas and annexes the Gurjara territory to Láta, *id.* 187-188, 310, 311, 316, 375; Gujarát Chalukya king at Navsári, I, pt. i, 110; repulses the Arab invasion, *id.* 117.

Pulakesi I: Western Chalukya king, the real founder of the dynasty, establishes his power about 550 in the territory surrounding Bádámi, takes Bádámi from the Kadambas of Banavási and makes it his capital, I, pt. ii, 181, 335-344; various spellings of his name, *id.* 343 and note 4; his genealogy, *id.* 341, 342; his sons, *id.* 328; his younger brother, *id.* 360 note 3; performs sacrifices, *id.* 181, 338 and note 1; described in the Pallava records as defeated by Narasimhavarman I, *id.* 323, 358; his rule in Kánara district, XV, pt. ii, 80-81; in Khándesh, XII, 241 note 1.

Pulakesi II: (609-642), son of the Western Chalukya king Kirtivarman I, "Introduction to the Early History of the Dakhan," I, pt. ii, p. ii, 182, 282, 349-361; various spellings of his name, *id.* 351; civil war with his uncle Mangalesa, *id.* 348, 349; vassals renounce allegiance; subdues various kings and successfully resists an attack by Harshavardhana of Kanauj, *id.* 283, 300, 312, 323, 325 note 3, 341, 350; establishes himself at Bádámi and assumes the regal title of Parameśvara, *id.* 351 and notes 3 and 4; establishes the eastern branch of the Chalukyas at Vengi, *id.* 185, 335 note 1, 352; letters and presents are interchanged between himself and Khosru II of Persia, *id.* 185, 352; Hiuen Tsiang's account of his kingdom, *id.* 184-185, 352-354, 431 note 2; records of his time, *id.* 292, 313 note 1, 337 note 2, 338, 341 note 2, 344 and notes 1 and 6, 345, 355-358, 538 note 8; his reign ends in disaster; is defeated and Bádámi laid waste by the Pallavas, *id.* 322, 358; records for the interval that followed Pulakesi's defeat and the re-establishment of power by Vikramáditya I, *id.* 359-361; his embassy to Naushirván, the subject of one of the Ajanta cave painting, XIII, 247 note 3; IX, pt. ii, 183 note 4; his conquest of Konkan, *id.* 420; his connection with Khándesh, XII, 494; rule in Kánara, XV, pt. ii, 79, 81, 265; in Bijápur, XXIII, 381-382; *see* also I, pt. i, 109, 107, 110, 116, 465.

Pulakeśi Vallabha Satyásraya: *see* Pulakesi II.

Pulanvat: sandy rice soil in Ratnágiri district, X, 144, 204.

Puláo: Musalmán dish, public dinner called after, cost of, IX, pt. ii, 113, 114 and note 2.

Pulashakti: Siláhára king, genealogy of, XIII, 422 note 1; inscription of, at Kanheri cave, *id.* 424; *see* also I, pt. ii, 11, 17; XIV, 148, 173, 177.

Pulicat: town in Madras presidency, I, pt. ii, 318 note 12.

Puligere: old territorial division in the Dhárwár district, I, pt. ii, 307, 373, 418, 428 note 4, 431, 432, 443, 449, 451, 452, 454, 456, 563.

Pulikála: Sinda prince, I, pt. ii, 574, 576, 577.

Pulikara: Sanskrit form of Puligere, I, pt. ii, 304 and note 6, 373.

Pulikaranagara: Lakshmeshwar in the Miraj state, I, pt. ii, 524.

Pulikeshi I, etc.: *see* Pulakesi I, etc.

Pulikesi Janásraya: his grants, I, pt. i, 149. *See* Pulakeśi.

Pulikesin: *see* Avanijanáśraya Pulakeśi; also Pulakeśi I.

Pulikesin II: *see* Pulakesi II.

Pulimat: successor of Gotamiputra, I, pt. ii, 155, 158.

Pulindæ: a tribe referred to by Ptolemy (150 A. D.), XII, 38 note 4.

Pulindas: wild tribe living about the Vindhyas, I, pt. ii, 134, 138, 143.

Puliyappayanavidu: in the Sindavádi province, I, pt. ii, 441 and note 6.

Pullalura: in Conjeeveram *táluka*, defeat of the Chalukya army at, I, pt. ii, 324, 350.

Pullaśakti: Siláhára feudatory of Amoghavarsha (843-844), I, pt. ii, 200, 253, 404, 405 note 1, 539, 541.

Pulomat: I, pt. ii, 158. *See* Pulimat.

Pu-Lo-Ri-She: Hwan Thsang's name of Pulikesin II, I, pt. ii, 184, 353.
Pulses: varieties of, in Kánara district, XV, pt. ii, 18; price of, *id.* 36; cultivation of, in Surat district, II, 63; in Broach district, *id.* 390; in Káira, III, 42; in Panch Mahál s, *id.* 232-234; in Ahmadábád district, IV, 53; in Cutch, V, 106; in Pálanpur, *id.* 294; in Mahi Kántha, *id.* 371; in Ratnágiri district, X, 147-148; in Kolába, XI, 97; in Thána, XIII, 289; in Násik district, XVI, 100; in Ahmadnagar district, XVII, 268-269; in Poona district, XVIII, pt. ii, 42-44; in Kolhápur, XXIV, 168-169.
Pulumáyi or Pulumavi Vásishthiputra: Andhrabhritya ruler (A. D. 130-154), account of, XVI, 620-623, 552-554; mention of, in Pándu Lená caves, *id.* 544, 553, 557, 604, 611; *see* also I, pt. i, 38, 540; XVIII, pt. ii, 213; his dates, I, pt. ii, 158, 159, 168; his charter, *id.* 150, 165; his inscriptions, *id.* 149, 151, 152, 153, 154, 156, 166; regains the lost province, *id.* 160, 161, 165, 167, 170, 175.
Pulu Senála: caves in Thána district, XIV, 10, 301, 401, 287, 290.
Pumsavana: or male-making, a Vedic rite among Gujarát Hindus, IX, pt. i, 31 note 3; performance of, *id.* 32; pregnancy ceremony among Chitpávans, XVIII, pt. i, 145.
Punád: old district, I, pt. ii, 303.
Punádra: state in Mahi Kántha, V, 419; place of interest, *id.* 439.
Punaji Vithal: Peshwa's agent in Gujarát, I, pt. i, 329.
Punarnava: famine plant, XXV, 203.
Punavem: dye-yielding flower, cess on, Thána district, XIII, 552.
Punch houses: in Bombay island, farmed (1760-1763), XXVI, pt. iii, 483-484; (1767), *id.* 490.
Pundarik: Shikhi's tree of knowledge, XIV, 331.
Pundras: a tribe claiming descent from the sons of Viśvámitra, I, pt. ii, 138.
Punems: full moons, sacred to the moon and *mátás*; belief about, IX, pt. i, 398-399.
Punica granatum: dye-yielding plant, XXV, 246.
Punja: minister in Cutch (1741); account of his career, V, 141-145.
Punsavan: *see* Pumsavana.
Punt: proposed identification of, with Ethiopia or India, XIII, 404 and note 3; or with Somali or the Arabian Coast, XIV, 318.
Puntámba: town in Ahmadnagar district, temples at, XVII, 733.
Punvaránogad: *see* Manjal.
Punya Prakásh: Shrávak holy text, IX, pt. i, 102.
Pur: town near Udaipur, I, pt. i, 539.
Pur: village in Poona district, temples, and fairs at, XVIII, pt. iii, 424.
Pur: village in Junnar táluka of the Poona district, Hemádpanti temple of Kukdeshvar at, XVIII, pt. iii, 424-428.
Pura: in Dhárwár, record at, I, pt. ii, 527.
Purab: father of Kánheji A'ngria, XI, 145.
Puradakeri: in Kod *táluka* of the Dhárwár district, I, pt. ii, 460 note 3.
Pura Gáváni: ruler of Cutch (1340-1350), V, 133.
Puragupta: Gupta chief (A.D. 470), I, pt. i, 74.
Purána, *pl.* Puránas, Puráns: *Bhavishya*, I, pt. i, 142, 533, 534, 545; works of legendary lore, sectarian in purpose, names of the, IX, pt. i, 532-533; "Introduction to the Early History of the Dakhan," I, pt. ii, 1-2; references to, *id.* 133, 134, 136, 138, 140, 142, 145, 146, 155, 156, 157, 162, 163, 164, 165, 172, 177, 225, 226, 334.
Purandhar: sub-division of Poona district, its boundaries, area, aspect, water, climate, crops, people, cultivators, and communications, XVIII, pt. iii, 94-98; fort, fortifications, buildings and history, *id.* 428-435; XVIII, pt. i, 5; taken by Shiváji (1647), I, pt. ii, 592; XVIII, pt. ii, 226-227; siege of (1665), *id.* 231-232; in the hands of the Mughals (1667), retaken by Shiváji, I, pt. ii, 594; taken by the Mughals (1705), XVIII, pt. ii, 240; action near (1711), *id.* 241; granted to Báláji by Pant Sachiv, *id.* 242; I, pt. ii, 598; treaty of (1776) between the Peshwa and the English, I, pt. i, 406; I, pt. ii, 102; XIV, 193; XIII, 502; XVIII, pt. ii, 260; the renewal of the treaty of, XIII, 505; the country acquired in the treaty of, restored to the Maráthás, *id.* 508; ceded to the English (1817), XVIII, pt. ii, 297; siege of (1818), *id.* 302; surveyed, *id.* 392, 393-394, 396, 442-444, 457, 502-508; forest reserves, XVIII, pt. i, 36-37.
Purandhare's Váda: Poona mansion, XVIII, pt. iii, 341-342.
Purangad: village in Ratnágiri district, X, 356; exports and imports of, *id.* 186.
Puráni: reader of sacred books, also known as Vyás or Bhatji, his mode of reading or recital, his source of income, IX, pt. i, 24-25.
Puránic gods: under the Chálukyas, I, pt. ii, 192.
Puránic religion: under the Kalachuris, I, pt. ii, 228-229.
Purenda: port of the Bahámani kingdom, held by Khwája Jahán (1511), I, pt. ii, 589.
Puri: *see* Danda Rájpuri.
Puri: *see* Jagannáth.
Puri: ancient name of Broach, I, pt. i, 159.
Puri: Konkan Mauryas of, I, pt. i, 107, 108; Maurya capital, I, pt. ii, 14, 350, 404; identification of, *id.* 16 note 2, 18, 283, 540-541; attacked and reduced by Pulakesi II, *id.* 183 and note 4; capital of the Siláháras of the North Konkan, *id.* 16, 253, 404, 542; *see* also XIII, 420, 423 and note 2, 425, 426; XIV, 6, 96, 355 note 5, 401, 402, 418.
Purigere: old territorial division between Miraj state and Dhárwár district, I, pt. ii, 304 and note 6, 306, 373, 403, 416, 418, 419, 422, 431, 437, 440, 442, 460. *See* Puligere.
Purimat: *see* Pulimat.
Purification: Our Lady of, Churches dedicated to, at Karanja and Uran, XIV, 194, 371.
Purná: river in Gujarát, II, 26; VII, 8, 578, 580, 583.
Purna: Sopára Buddhist apostle, story of, XIII, 404 note 2, 406-408; XIV, 124, 320, 394, 395, 410.

Purneah : minister of Mysore (1799), stations guards at Banavási, Sirsi and Sonda against the attacks of robbers, XV, pt. ii, 266 note 2, 345, 349.
Purohits : priests of Bráhma-Kshatris, degraded Sárasvat Bráhmans, IX, pt. i, 56.
Puru-Ranaparákrama : *biruda* (title) of Kirtivarman, I, pt. ii, 345.
Purushottama : *biruda* (title) of Gunabhara the Pallava king, I, pt. ii, 331.
Purushottamabhatta : Bráhman of Alande in the Kuntala country, I, pt. ii, 482.
Pusesávli : town in Sátára district, XIX, 547-548 ; trade centre, *id.* 216.
Pushkar or Pokarn : holy *thirtha*, IX, pt. i, p. xi note 3 ; place of pilgrimage ; shrine of Brahmá at, *id.* 489, 490 and note 4, 502 note 4 ; lake near Ajmer, *id.* 16 ; I, pt. i, 464.
Pushkarna, Pushpakarn : caste of Bráhmans in Gujarát, also called Pokarna and Pushpákarn, IX, pt. i, p. xi note 3 ; origin ; followers of Vallabhácharya, priests of Bhátiás, *id.* 16 and note 1 ; Gujar element traced in, *id.* 438 note 9, 50, 502 and note 4.
Pushpamal : name of Bhinmál in Dwáparayuga, I, pt. i, 461.
Pushpamitra : *see* Pushyamitra, I, pt. ii, 155.
Pushpávati : river in Poona district, XVIII, pt. i, 9.
Pushti Marga : sect of the Mahárájas otherwise called Vallabhháchari, IX, pt. i, 535 and note 1.
Pushyagupta : Gujarát governor of Chandragupta, I, pt. i, 14.
Pushyamitra : name of a king reigning in the 5th century A. D., I, pt. i, 69 and note 4, 73-74.
Pushyamitra : first king of the Súnga dynasty in the 2nd century B. C., I, pt. ii, 146, 147 ; Brihadratha's general, murders him and founds the Súnga dynasty, *id.* 155.
Pusilávilli : village in the Kásáhrada province, I, pt. ii, 404.
Puskar : *see* Pushkar.
Put : the Hindu hell, Bráhmanic belief about, IX, pt. i, 39 and note 1.
Putchuk : a fragrant root, export of, to Rome (B. C. 50), XI, 284 and note 4, 470.
Putharji Náik : a rebel in Ahmadnagar district, XVI, 200.
Putranjiva Roxburghii : fodder plant, XXV, 278, 286.
Pyal : oil-yielding plant, XXV, 217.
Pygmies : race of, in India, I, pt. i, 532.
Pyke : Captain (1712), finds the Portuguese in Elephanta, XIV, 85 ; his mention of the small elephant in Elephanta caves, *id.* 92 note 1 ; his mention of a horse in Elephanta, *id.* 93.
Pyrard de Laval, François : French traveller (1601-1608), his description of Chaul, XI, 279, 280 ; XVII, 391 ; I, pt. ii, 36 ; his mention of the Portuguese Inquisition at Goa, *id.* 58 ; his notice of Bassein, XIV, 31 note 2 ; his mention of Sanjan, *id.* 302 ; his mention of Honávar, XV, pt. ii, 310.

Q

QUAIL : class of birds in Ratnágiri district, X, 88-89.
Quartz : at Mátherán, XIV, 242 ; in the Poona district, XVIII, pt. i, 29-30 ; rocks in Ratnágiri district, X, 13-15 ; in Belgaum district, XXI, 19-23 ; beds, in Bijápur district, XXIII, 24-27, 33-35 ; shingle beds, *id.* 49 ; tools, *id.* 49, 59 ; slabs, *id.* 55-56.
Quartz powder : used for marking lines and pictures with, note on, XXII, 821-822.
"Queen :" name of a ship, built by Pársi carpenters, IX, pt. ii, 192 note 3.
Quench-longing : ceremony, XVIII, pt. i, 145.
Quilon : port in Malabár, trade centre, XIII, 429, 444 ; I, pt. ii, 3 note 9, 341 note 2.
Quit-rent : in the Portuguese provinces in India, I, pt. ii, 53 ; reduced one half (1720) in Bombay island, XXVI, pt. iii, 301-302.
Qwan-shái-yin, Qwan-tsen-tsái : Avalakiteshvar, one of the Bodhisattvas, XIV, 207 note 1.
Qwan-yin : *see* Qwan-shái-yin.

R

RABA'RI : class of herdsmen in Gujarát, IX, pt. i, 264 ; Gujar element in, *id.* 499 ; meaning of name, origin, surnames, subdivisions, appearance, dress, cattle rearing by, religion, customs, *id.* 286, 289 ; in Cutch, V, 80 ; in Pálanpur, *id.* 287, 290 ; in Baroda, VII, 61 ; in Káthiáwár, *id.* VIII, 137.
Rabi : alluvial soil in Ratnágiri district, X, 145.
Rabi : late season, XVIII, pt. ii, 3.
Rabi-ul-Akhir : *see* Rabi-us-sáni.
Rabi-ul-Awwal : third month of the Musalmán year, holidays in, IX, pt. ii, 140 ; sermon dinners given on first twelve days of, *id.* 114.
Rabi-us-Sáni : fourth month of the Musalmán year, holiday in, IX, pt. ii, 140 ; feast in, *id.* 114.
Rabkavi : town in Sángli state, fort, trade centre, temples at, XXIV, 363, 365.
Race-course : Poona, XVIII, pt. iii, 390-391.
Ráchamalla : Western Gangá prince, son and successor of Ereyappa, killed by Butuga, I, pt. ii, 304 and note 4, 419.
Rachamalla Permanadi : Satyavákya-Konguniyarma (978), Western Gangá prince, I, pt. ii, 307 and note 7.
Ráchbhara : a caste of Musalmán heddle fillers in Sholápur district, XX, 210.
Rachcha Ganga : Maruladeva's son, I, pt. ii, 305.
Ráchevár : *see* Konger.
Ráchias : envoy of Claudius (A. D. 41-54), I, pt. i, 536.
Racolets : Franciscan sect, Ogilby's mention of, as inhabitants of Tárápur, XIV, 344.
Radder : a caste of husbandmen in Dhárwár, XXII, 141-142.
Raddi : the Sanskritised form of Rátta the contraction of Ráshtrakúta, I, pt. i, 119 ; I, pt. ii, 383. *See* Reddi and Ratta.
Raddi : a caste of labourers, in Poona district, XVIII, pt. i, 404-406 ; in Sholápur district, XX, 163 ; in Bijápur district, origin, divi-

sions, appearance, language, houses, food, dress, calling, religion, customs, XXIII, 145-155, 386 note 7; in Kolhápur state, XXIV, 93; in Belgaum district, XXI, 129.

Rádhá Bái: wife of Fatesing Gáikwár, threatens to become *sati*, allowed to adopt a son, VII, 230; her quarrel with Sayájiráv II, *id.* 232; life pensions, *id.* 243.

Rádha-Krishna: form of Vishnu, IX, pt. i, 118.

Rádhanpur: state in Pálanpur, boundaries, area, climate, rivers, history and genealogical tree of its chiefs, V, 325-328; town, history, trade, *id.* 345-347; disloyalty of the *nawáb* of, I, pt. i, 441; grant of Govind III at, *id.* 123; plate from, *id.* 466; grant of, *id.* 468; grants from, I, pt. ii, 196 and note 3, 197, 198 note 2, 209, 396, 398; grant of, to Fateh Khán Baluch, IX, pt. ii, 17.

Rádhá-Vallabhi: *see* Religious Sects.

Radi: caste in Belgaum, *see* Raddi.

Radish: tillage of, in Khándesh, XII, 171; in Poona district, XVIII, pt. ii, 57.

Rae: town in Media, Zoroaster born at, IX, pt. ii, 211.

Raeka: estate in Rewa Kanthá, VI, 152.

Rafái: caste of beggars in Gujarát, meaning of the name of, other names of, followers of Sayad Ahmed Kabir, ways of begging, Sunnis in religion, IX, pt. ii, 23-24.

Raffles: Sir Stamford, his description of Jává, I, pt. i, 489-491.

Rafia-ud-Daraját: grandson and successor of the emperor Farrukhsiyar (1719), his murder by the *sayads*, I, pt. ii, 301.

Ráfizi: contemptuous term for Shiáhs, IX, pt. ii, 47 note 3.

Rafugár: a caste of Musalmán cloth-darners, in Poona district, XVIII, pt. i, 494-495; in Sholápur district, XX, 20.

Rághav: *khavás* of Navánagar, IX, pt. i, 236; Bharvád *bhagat*, *id.* 269.

Rághoba: Peshwa, *see* Raghunathráv.

Ragho Ballál: Shiváji's agent, murders the Javli *rája* (1653), XIX, 233.

Rághoji: Marátha deputy, assassination of, at Ahmadábád (1756), I, pt. i, 339.

Rághoji Angria I: (1759-1793), succeeds Mánáji, drives the Janjira troops, his rule, XI, 154-155, Forbes' (1771) mention of, tribute to Peshwa, confines Sadáshivráo Bháu (the pretender), *id.* 264, I, pt. ii, 102.

Rághoji Angria II: (1817-1839), succeeds Mánáji, tries to free himself from Bivalkar, his rule under Bivalkar, *id.* 156-157.

Rághoji Bhangria: Koli freebooter (1844 1848), once a police officer, appears in Panvel, Captain Giberne in pursuit of, sentenced to death, XIII, 636-637; XVIII, pt. ii, 307-303; makes raid on Márwári Vánis, cuts the noses of Marwáris, caught at Pandharpur and hanged, XVII, 417-418.

Rághoji Bhousla: (1735-1753) *Sena Saheb Subha* (1735), XIX 276; makes an incursion to the north, Avji Kávre defeated, meditates revolution, his subsequent intrigues, his authority to levy contributions north of the Narbada disputed, his reconciliation with Bájiráv, his rivalry with the Bráhman party (1740), incites Dámáji, bought over, prevents Báláji's succession as Peshwa, *id.* 280-283; VII, 176; joins with Dámáji in attacking the Peshwa (1743), I, pt. i, 395; overtaken and defeated in Bengal by Báláji Peshwa, sends agents to Peshwa for reconciliation (1744), XIX, 285-287; receives his footing in Bengal, called to Sátára, *id.* 290-291.

Rághoji Náik: Koli outlaw (1860) in Thána district, XIII, 605.

Ragho Shankar: Marátha leader, sent to subdue Kolis (1753), I, pt. i, 338.

Raghu: Kadamba king, I, pt. ii, 286.

Raghu Náik: third Sondá chief (1618-1638), genealogy of, XV, pt. ii, 120 note 3; his accession, *id.* 123; his grant to the temple of Madhukeshvar at Banavási in Kánara, *id.* 264, 266.

Raghunáthdás: *rája*, Nizám's minister, I, pt. i, 333.

Raghunáth Ráo: younger brother of the Pehswa Báláji Bájiráo, with Dámáji Gáikwár captures Ahmadábád and firmly establishes Marátha supremacy in Gujarát (1754); drives the forces of Ahmad Sháh Abdáli from the Punjáb (1758); aspires to rule the state and keeps on good terms with the English, I, pt. ii, 98, 602; with the help of the Nizám defeats his nephew Mádhav Ráo's army and takes charge of the government, *id.* 603; pursues Haidar across the Tungabhadra and makes a treaty at Bednur (1766), *id.* 659; retires from court and raises a force, but is defeated (1768), and kept in custody, *id.* 603, 628; is released; keeps on good terms with his other nephew Náráyan Ráo for a time; is again placed in confinement; is believed to be implicated in the murder of Náráyan Ráo (1772-1773); assumes charge of the government and defeats the ministerial army at Pandharpur (1774), *id.* 604; seeks British help but refuses to surrender Bassein, Sálsette, and the Bombay islands, *id.* 100; by the treaty of Surat cedes Sálsette and other possessions to the English (1775), *id.* 101, 604; invites Haidar, who favoured his cause, to take possession of the Southern Marátha Country up to the Krishna (1776), *id.* 659; by the treaty of Purandhar his cause is given up by the English (1776), *id.* 604; leaves Surat to join Sadáshiv Bháu, the impostor, but is compelled to take shelter at Tárápur, *id.* 102; promises to cede Khánderi and Bassein to the English for their help to make him Peshwa (1778), *id.* 103; by the treaty of Sálbái he is provided for (1782), *id.* 605; retires to Kopargaon, *id.* 628; *another account of*: Báláji Bájiráv Peshwa's brother, called also Raghunáthráv, levies tribute in Gujarát, takes possession of Rewa and Mahi Kántha districts and marches on Surat (1752), I, pt. i, 334; takes Ahmadábád (1753), *id.* 336-337; compels Momin Khán to pay tribute; appoints Shripatráv his deputy at Ahmadábád and collects tribute from Limbdi and Wadhwán chiefs, *id.* 337; acts as guardian of his nephew Mádhavráv, is joined in his

intrigues by Jánoji Bhonsle and Govindráv Gáikwár, is defeated by the young Peshwa at Dhárap (1768) and confined at Poona, *id.* 399-400; is invested with the robe of Peshwa by the titular king of Sátára; reinstates Govindráv Gáikwár in the title and estates of Dámáji Gáikwár (1774); sets out for Gujarát and attacks the city of Baroda (1775), *id.* 401-402; opens negotiations with the English through Mr. Gambier, the chief at Surat *id.* 401; joins Govindráv Gáikwár (1775); sends an agent to negotiate with the Bombay council; flies to Cambay and through the help of Mr. Malet goes to Surat *viâ* Bhávnagar, *id.* 402; reception of, by the *nawáb* of Cambay, *id.* 403; abandoned by the English after the treaty of Purandhar (1776); takes refuge at Surat, *id.* 406; at Bombay; a fresh alliance of, with the English (1778), *id.* 407; handed over to Sindia, flies to Broach (1779), *id.* 408; receives a pension and goes to Kopargaon (1782), *id.* 410; *another account:* leads an army into Gujarát (1754), XVIII, pt. ii, 246; in North India (1756), *id.* 248; quarrels with Sadásivráv and becomes the head of civil affairs (1759), *id.* 249; becomes regent of Mádhavráv I, *id.* 250; refuses to cede Sálsette to the English, *id.* 251; quarrels with Mádhavráv and retires to Násik, *id.* 251; is supported by the Nizám, regains power and keeps Mádhavráv in confinement, *id.* 251; his unpopular measures; is defeated by Mádhavráv at Dhodap and is kept in confinement, *id.* 253; intrigues with Haidar Ali and the Nizám, *id.* 254; is released and placed in charge of the young Peshwa Náráyanráv, *id.* 254; his share in Náráyanráv's murder, *id.* 255-256; becomes Peshwa, *id.* 256; is opposed by the ministers, *id.* 257; is helped by the English and signs the treaty of Surat, *id.* 259; the English attempt to restore him to power, *id.* 263-266; Sindia keeps him in power, his flight to Surat, *id.* 266; treaty of Sálbái; fixes his residence at Kopargaon; his death, *id.* 267; *see* also XXVI, pt. i, 400-405; XIX, 296; VII, 177, 179, 182, 185-186, 191-196; XIII, 498, 501-503, 505; I, pt. i, 334, 336, 337, 398-400.

Raghunáth Sávant: (1869), ruler of Sávantvádi, X, 447.

Raghunáth Svámi: religious teacher, tomb of, at Nigdi in Sátára district, XIX, 529.

Rághvendrácharya: Vaishnav pontiff, XXIV, 63.

Rági: food plant cultivated on the *gháts*, XXV, 187; in Kolába district, XI, 96; in Sátára district, XIX, 162; in Belgaum district, XXI, 252; in Dhárwár district, XXII, 274.

Ráhada: another name of Ghaghada, the Chavadá king, I, pt. i, 154, 155.

Rahánjur: Rándir, capital of Lárdes, I, pt. i, 507 and note 11, 513.

Ráhapa: king conquered by Krishna I, I, pt. ii, 391.

Ráhátá: town in Ahmadnagar district, XVII, 733-734.

Rahimatpur: town in Sátára district, details of, mosque and inscriptions at, XIX, 548-549; trade centre, *id.* 214.

"Ráhime:" Musalmán pilgrim ship, burnt by the Portuguese (1614), II, 77.

Rahim-ki-bázár: town in Sind, the minister of Cutch builds a fortress at (1745), V, 140; plundered by Khosás (1819), *id.* 163.

Rahma, Rahmi: Ruhmi, apparently Burma and Sumátra, I, pt. i, 527, 528.

Raht: spine of Indra, I, pt. i, 119, 133.

Ráhtod: derived from Ráshtrakúta, I, pt. ii, 198, 384.

Ráhtod Ráshtraśyena: image of, brought from Karnátak Sevji, now in Mevad, I, pt. i, 133.

Ráhtor: *see* Ráhtod.

Ráhu: earth, IX, pt. i, 392 note 1, 403. *See* Planet (Earth).

Ráhudi: pass in Násik district, XVI, 130.

Ráhudvádi: pass in Nasik district, XVI, 129.

Ráhula: Shákyamuni's son, inscription of, in Kánheri cave, XIV, 170.

Ráhuri: sub-division of Ahmadnagar district, its area, aspect, soil, water-supply, climate, rainfall, cultivation, irrigation, crops, people, roads, railways, markets, crafts, survey, changes, XVII, 626-632, 489-494, 540-541. *Town*, *id.* 734.

Raichor, Raichur: town in the Nizam's dominions, I, pt. ii, 441 note 6; laid waste by Malik Káfur, *id.* 29, 533; fort, *id.* 638; taken by Asad Khán, general of Bijápur, *id.* 642; taken by Vijáyanagar from Bijápur, *id.* 643.

Rai Dán: *jám*, (1454), Sind ruler of the Samma dynasty, IX, pt. ii, 50. *See* Markab Khán.

Raidi: place of interest in Káthiáwár, VIII, 630.

Raids: in Thána district (1817), Pendhari, XIII, 522; Koli, *id.* 524; gang, *id.* 526; arm protection against, *id.* 563 note 4; Marátha, in Kánara district, XV, pt. ii, 135 and note 6, 137, 146 and note 8.

Rái-ispand: mustard, burning of, at the door to prevent demons from entering, IX, pt. ii, 155.

Ráika: caste of shepherds in Mahi Kántha, V, 366.

Raikot: fort and a place of interest in Khándesh, XII, 466.

Rail pattern: Buddhist in Kanheri caves, XIV, 166; in Kondivti caves, *id.* 203, 205, 206, 207, 208.

Rails: class of birds in Ratnágiri district, X, 94.

Railway: all district volumes, *see* under District Name.

Raima: caste of Jadeja Musalmáns in Cutch, V, 140.

Raimurdha: seaport in Thána district, saltpans at, XIV, 301; water-works, *id.* 55.

Rain: god Indra presides over, IX, pt. i, 348, 351; signs showing beginning of South-West rain; expectation of, *id.* 351; sure fall of, on the 1st of Vaishakh, *id.* 351-352; good and seasonable fall of; heavy downpour of; partial failure of, *id.* 352; complete failure of, *id.* 352-353; contrivances for determining whether the year will be wet or dry, used by better classes of husbandmen, *id.* 343, 354; by Bráhmans, by chiefs of Native States, *id.* 354; by early tribes, *id.* 354-355; crow and Indian crane or Sáras believed to know

whether year will be wet or dry, *id.* 353; Thnveria test, *id.* 354; signs showing famine, *id.* 353; rites and observances during holding off of, prayers and offerings made to rain god, to *joginis*, to Mahádev; leaving waste the village or town; Mehulo or Mevlo, that is, rain god praise singing by Bhil women, sacrifices, *id.* 307 note 1, 311, 355-356.

Rainfall: in Surát district, II, 36; in Broach, *id.* 353; in Kaira, III, 14; in Panch Mahâls, *id.* 195; in Cutch, V, 18; in Pálanpur, *id.* 284; in Mahi Kántha, *id.* 358; in Rewa Kántha, VI, 10; in Cambay, *id.* 182; in Káthiáwár, VIII, 86 89; in Ratnágiri, X, 23; in Sávantvádi, *id.* 399; in Kolába district, XI, 15; (1852-1881), *id.* 214, 243, 246, 248, 250, 404; in Khándesh, XII, 14; in Thána district (1860-1880), XIII, 17, 628, 629; at Mátherán, XIV, 249; in Kánára district, XV, pt. i, 13, 17, 18; in Násik district, XVI, 3, 14, 303; in Ahmadnagar district, XVII, 12, 14; in Poona district, yearly and monthly rainfall and rain days (1856-1872), XVIII, pt. i, 14-18; in Sátára district, XIX, 20-25; in Sholápur, XX, 5-7; in Belgaum district, XXI, 40-43, 45; in Dhárwár district, XXII, 14-16, *id.* 272; in Bijápur district, XXIII, 14-15; in Kolhápur, XXIV, 16, 17, 400-405; scarcity of (1737, 1742, 1755) in Bombay island, XXVI, pt. iii, 519-521.

Rainha Da Pimenta: pepper-queen (1623), Gersappa queen so called by the Portuguese, XV, pt. ii, 124.

Raipur: place of interest in Cutch, V, 248.

Ráiri: or Ráygad, *rája* of, I, pt. ii, 31; district in charge of the Abyssinians, *id.* 34; fort, *id.* 40; surprised by Shiváji, *id.* 67; Shiváji's capital, *id.* 68; taken by the English (1765) and restored on payment of Rs. 80,000 (1766), *id.* 106. *See* Ráygad.

Ráis: petty Konkán chiefs, I, pt. ii, 25.

Rái Sánkli: *táluka* in Káthiáwár, VIII, 635.

Ráis Bhára: Samma chief of great Cutch, I, pt. i, 518.

Raisinghji: usurps the chiefship of Navánagar, is defeated and slain (1664), I, pt. i, 283.

Raisinghji: *rája* of I'dar, joins Fakhr-ud-daulah, I, pt. i, 329, 331.

Raivata: legendary king, I, pt. i, 8.

Raivataka: Girnár hill, I, pt. i, 177.

Ráj: famine plant, XXV, 208.

Rája: Bhillama I's son, I, pt. ii, 513 and note 3, 514.

Rája A'li, Rája A'li Khán: successor of Mirán Muhammad of Khándesh (1576-1596), I, pt. ii, 623; XII, 247.

Rájab: sixth month of the Musalmán year, holiday in; preaching the sermons during first eleven nights of, IX, pt. ii, 140; feast given on the last Wednesday of, *id.* 114.

Rájabhakti: sect of king-worshippers, its text and beliefs, IX, pt. i, 441 note 1.

Rájáditya: Chola king, I, pt. ii, 322 note 8; at war with the Ráshtrakúta Krishna III, is treacherously slain by Butuga, *id.* 305, 322 note 8, 421.

Rájágharatta: title conferred on Cháhada by Kumárapála, I, pt. i, 187.

Rájagi: I, pt. ii, 513 and note 3. *See* Rája.

Rájahamasa: Prachanda's grandfather, I, pt. i, 129.

Rája Jaysing: Mughal general, (1665) sent against Shiváji; blockades Sinhgad; Shiváji in the camp of; Shiváji co-operates with; in want of means to garrison forts in Dakhan, XVIII, pt. ii, 231-234; I, pt. ii, 593.

Rájakesarivarman: Chola king, inscription of, I, pt. ii, 322 note 7; makes friendly overtures to Vikramáditya VI, *id.* 444. *See* Vira-Rájarájadeva I.

Rájala: Kalachurya Kannama's son, I, pt. ii, 469.

Rája Mahendri: Pliny's Dandagnda identified with, by General Cunningham, I, pt. i, 533.

Rájamalla: Pallava king, I, pt. ii, 303 note 7, 307 note 7, 328 note 3. *See* Ráchamalla.

Rájamandri: province in Madras, Ala-ud-din pretends to serve the *rája* of, IX, pt. ii, 2 note 3.

Rajanya: the name under which non-Aryan rulers were admitted as Kshatriyas, IX, pt. i, 445 note 6.

Rájapitámaha: title of Silábára kings, I, pt. i, 185; XIII, 436, 437 note 1; Mallikárjuna's title, conferred on Ambada, I, pt. ii, 24.

Rájápur: town in Ratnágiri district, its population, trade, communication, buildings, municipality, water-supply, history, fort and factory, X, 357-362; trade (1649), *id.* 175; (1818), *id.* 177; (1880), *id.* 180, 358; Portuguese victory at, *id.* 195 note 7; ancient district, I, pt. ii, 29, 39; port, plundered by Shiváji (1660-61), *id.* 68, 70; XVIII, pt. ii, 228; flourishes under Shiváji, I, pt. ii, 72; Musalmán governor of, offers the trade of the town to the English East India Company (1649-1650), *id.* 120; English factory at, given up (1664), re-established (1674), given up (1681), and again re-established between A. D. 1698 and A. D. 1708; French factory established in, (A. D. 1670); description of, *id.* 121; grant at, *id.* 253.

Rájápur: on the Ghod river in the Ahmadnagar district, Maráthás surprised by Bussy at (1751), I, pt. ii, 627; XVII, 404.

Rájápur: pass in Násik district, XVI, 130.

Rájapuri: *see* Puri.

Rajapuri: creek, I, pt. ii, 173, 174.

Rajapuri: taken by the Maráthás (1731), XXVI, pt. i, 164. *See* Danda Rájápuri.

Rájarája, Rájarájadeva: Chola king (A. D. 1006), I, pt. ii, 308, 341 note 2, 491. *See* Ko-Rájarája-Rájakesarivarman, Nurmadi Chola and Rájendra.

Rájárám: Shiváji's second son, Sátára king (1689-1700), I, pt. ii, 76; is imprisoned at Ráygad, sends his family to Vishálgad and moves about the country, *id.* 79; regent of the Marátha empire, his plans against the Mughals, *id* 596; escapes from Jinji and arrives at Vishálgad, *id.* 596; makes a plundering expedition through the Gangthari, Báglán, Khándesh, Berár, and levies *chauth*, *id.* 597; his death at Ráygad, *id.* 597. *See* also XVIII, pt. ii, 239; XXIV, 226.

Rájárám II : seventh *rája* of Kolhápur (1866-1870), his minority and education ; his visit to Europe ; his death, XXIV, 244, 248.
Rája Sekharavilása : work of the poet Shadakshari, I, pt. ii, 437 note 6.
Rájasimha : Pallava king, son of Parmeśvaravarman I, I, pt. ii, 329.
Rájasimha : Indravarman, the Western Ganga prince, I, pt. ii, 297.
Rájasimhapallaveśvara : Pallava king, I, pt. ii, 330. *See* Rájasimha.
Rájasimheśvara : temple of S'iva, built by Narasimhavarman II at Kañchi, inscription at, I, pt. ii, 327 note 8, 328, 330, 375.
Rájasthánik Court : a final court of appeal in Káthiáwár (1882), VIII, 117, 310.
Rájataramgini : chronicle of Káshmir, "Introduction to the Early History of the Dakhan," I, pt. ii, p. i ; Sanskrit work, *id.* 281 note 3, 293 note 1, 449 note 3 ; Káshmir history, IX, pt. i, 438, 439, 440 note 4.
Rájatrinetra : *biruda* (title) of Kakka II, I, pt. ii, 423.
Rájavula : Northern Kshatrapa, I, pt. i, 23.
Rájbái : famous Bharvad *sati* of Viramgám, account of her self-sacrifice, IX, pt. i, 358, 359.
Rájdair : fort in Khándesh, XII, 466.
Rajder or Rájdhair : fort in Násik district, XVI, 441 ; its natural strength, *id.* 442 note 3 ; captured by the English (1818), *id.* 196.
Rájendra : Chola king, I, pt. ii, 433. *See* Ko-Rájarája Rájakesarivarman, Nurmadi Chola and Rája-Rájadeva.
Rájendra : original appellation of the Eastern Chalukya Kulottunga Chodadeva I, I, pt. ii, 445.
Rájendra Choda : Dravila king, I, pt. ii, 416 note 6.
Rájendra Chola or Choladeva : I, pt. ii, 341 note 2, 436. *See* Ko-Parakesarivarman.
Rájendra Choladeva : Chola king, I, pt. 436. *See* Madhurantaka II.
Rájendrapura : conquered by Vishnuvardhana, I, pt. ii. 497.
Rájendravarman : Western Ganga king, I, pt. ii, 297.
Raje Shirke : surname of the Shirke family, I, pt. ii, 86.
Rájgad : sub-division in Rewa Kántha, VI, 17.
Rájgad : fort in Bhor state captured (1711) by Sháhu, XVIII, pt. ii, 240.
Rájgor : a caste of degraded Bráhmans in Gujarát, called Rájgurus, priests to Rájpúts and Káthis, IX, pt. i, 16-17 and note 1 and 2 ; in Cutch, V, 43-44 ; in Káthiáwár, VIII, 145.
Ráji : father of Mularája, I, pt. i, 156, 157 ; marries Lákha's sister Ráyáji ; is slain by Lákha, *id.* 160.
Rajib : food plant, XXV, 181.
Rajiga : king of Vengi, deposes the king of Kañchi and usurps the power, is defeated by Vikramáditya VI, I, pt. ii, 217, 445.
Rájkot : State and town in Káthiáwár, details of, VIII, 630-635 ; IX, pt. i, 126.
Rájkot : fort in Ratnágiri district, X, 351.
Rájkot : Cheul citadel, destroyed by the Peshwa, XI, 150 ; remains of, *id.* 365.
Rájkumár College : at Rájkot in Káthiáwár, opened in 1870, VIII, 310 ; object of, *id.* 348-349.
Rájmáchi : fort in Poona district, XVIII, pt. iii, 435-437 ; XVIII, pt. i, 4 ; I, pt ii, 592 ; known as the Konkan Darvájá, XIII, 6 ; taken by Kanhoji (1713), XI, 146 ; given to the Peshwa, *id.* 151 ; I, pt. ii, 88 ; A'ngria's power as far as, XIII, 489 ; Mr. Hornby proposes to garrison it (1781), *id.* 508 ; a foot pass, *id.* 322 ; XVIII, pt. ii, 152 ; imposter Sadáshiv Chimnaji defeated (1776) at, *id.* 261.
Rájmándurg : hill fort in Kánara district, XV, pt. i, 3 ; *id.* pt. ii, 138 ; captured by General Mathews (1783), *id.* 142, 333.
Rájo : -*sayad*, of Bukhara, IX, pt. ii, 18.
Rájo Shahid : *see* Sayad Muhammad.
Rájpar ; state in Rewa Kántha, VI, 152.
Rájpipla : State in Rewa Kántha, VI, 1, 2 ; its boundaries, aspect, rivers, hills, *id.* 91-93 ; climate, trees, population, soil and crops, roads, trade, manufactures, administrative sub-divisions, *id.* 94-98 ; history : early Hindu, Musalmán ascendancy (1390-1720) ; Marátha interference (1720-1820) ; British supervision (1820-1879) ; family tree of its chiefs, *id.* 99-110 ; *see* also I, pt. i, 226 ; origin of the house of, IX, pt. i, 125-126 ; Gaikwár in alliance with the *rája* of, VII, 169 ; tribute reimposed on, *id.* 185 ; tributary, *id.* 332, 334.
Rájpur : *táluka* in Káthiáwár, VIII, 636.
Rájpuri : in Kolába district, comes into British possession (1818), XI, 159 ; *khots*, *id.* 178 ; condition, revenue system, and assessment (1837), *id.* 183, 184, 185 note 1, 189 note 1, 197 ; revenue survey (1863), *id.* 204-205 ; creek, *id.* 402 ; Abyssinian settlement at, I, pt. ii, 7 ; remains at, *id.* 41 ; fort taken by the Sidis, *id.* 79 ; the capital of Thána Siláháras, XIV, 402 and note 2.
Rájpuri : village in Sátára district, caves at, XIX, 550.
Rájpút : Strength ; chiefships (1891), IX, pt. i, 123 ; divisions, clans and sub-clans, *id.* 123, 124 and note 1 ; history of the chief tribes, *id.* 124, 129 ; appearance ; speech ; house *darbár*, *id.* 130 ; dress, *id.* 131-132 ; Character ; calling ; *id.* 133 ; condition ; food, *id.* 134 ; daily life, *id.* 134-135 ; religion—Shiv worshippers, worship Hindu gods and goddesses, names of tutelary goddesses, *id.* 136-137 ; early beliefs—spirit-worship, Bhuvás, ways adopted to drive out evil spirits good and bad omens, *id.* 137-138 ; customs and birth-rites, *id.* 138 ; *Chhathi* worship, four baths, sun-worship, *id.* 139 ; naming, *id.* 139-140 ; *mohorpán* or mango blossom-drinking ; *botan* ; *mudan* or hair clipping, *id.* 140 ; thread-girding, *id.* 141 ; marriage ; intermarriages among clans, explanation of practice of female infanticide, marriageable age, *id.* 141 ; betrothals, *id.* 141-142 ; marriage contracts, *id.* 17 note 2 ; invitation or *lagan patrika*, *id.* 143 ; ceremonies of *manak stambh* or ruby pillar-fixing, *id.* 143-144 ; of *Chakvadhávani*, of Ganpati and gotraj in-

stallation, of *rándel*, of *gotardo bharvo*, *id.* 144 ; observances and rites in sword-marriage, *id.* 145-146 ; in marriage when the bride-groom goes personally, *id.* 147 ; visits to the shrines of tutelary goddesses, *id.* 136 ; position of women after marriage, *golis* or female attendants, *khavás* or male slaves, *id.* 147 ; pregnancy, *rakhadi* or guard-binding, *agharni* or lap-filling, *id.* 147-148 ; Death, dead body, bier, *id.* 148 ; widow, religious part of ceremonies, mourning aud rites during first ten days after death, *id.* 149 ; eleventh day rites, performance of a *shrádda* thirteenth day rites, *id.* 150 ; fifteenth day rites, monthly rites during the year after anniversary rites ; community, *id.* 151 ; foreign or Gujar origin traced in Agnikula tribes, Chohan, Parmár, Parihára Solanki, *id.* 449, 450, 480, 483-487 ; in Chavadás, *id.* 480 and note 4, 488-489 ; in Sisodiás, *id.* 443, 452, *id.* 495-496 ; in other Rájpúts, *id.* 444, 446 note 4, 482, 494-495, 500 ; claim Bhimrája, I, pt. ii, 27 ; their clan of Ráthods connected with Ráshtrakútas, *id.* 384 ; in Káthiáwár, VIII, 109-115 ; patrimony, *id.* 115 ; Bhásjads, *id.* 115 ; Bahárvatia, *id.* 116-117 ; distribution and character, *id.* 117 ; dress, daily life, customs aud religion, *id.* 118-121 ; in Cutch, V, 57-69 ; in Pálanpur, *id.* 289 ; in Mahi Kántha, *id.* 364 ; in Rewa Kántha, VI, 24 ; in Kolhápur state, XXIV, 85-86 ; in Kánara district, XV, pt. i, 193, 194 ; surnames of, XIII, 61 note 3 ; husbandmen in Násik district, XVI, 48 ; in Ahmadnagar district, XVII, 91-92 ; in Belgaum district, XXI, 129-131 ; in Dhárwár district, XXII, 143-144 ; in Bijápur district, XXIII, 155-160 ; labourers in Poona district, XVIII, pt. i, 401-404 ; messengers in Ratnágiri district, X, 128.

Rájpútána : establishment of the kingdom of the Scythians in, I, pt. ii, 158 ; Ráshtrakútas connected with, *id.* 384.

Rájpút Companies : raised (1684) in Bombay island, XXVI, pt. iii, 76-77.

Rájugi : *see* Shrirája.

Rájula : place of interest in Káthiáwár, VIII, 636.

Ráj-ul-Mulak : special rules for conducting the *mulakgiri* or land-raiding system, I, pt. i, 418.

Rájur : hills in Ahmadnagar district, XVII, 4. *Town*, *id.* 734.

Rájur : village in Poona district, old stones and Musalmán remains at, XVIII, pt. 437-438.

Ráj Vasna : sub-division in Rewa Kántha, VI, 112.

Rakam : basis of assessment of the Bijápur government, XXII, 440, 441, 442, 443, 447 note 3.

Rakanoj : place of interest in Cutch, V, 249.

Rakhadi : *see* Guard-binding.

Rákháich : son of Ráji and Lákha's sister Ráyáji, I, pt. i, 160.

Rakhasji : village in Bijápur district, XXIII, 674.

Rakishon : *see* Rákshasbhuvana.

Ráksha : division of Parihár Rájpúts, I, pt. i, 465.

Rákshas : hill in Kanara district, XV, pt. i, 4, 5.

Rákshasas : wild tribe infesting the forest of Dandakáranya and disturbing the religious rites of Bráhman sages, I, pt. ii, 137 ; wild tribes met by the Áryas, *id.* 137.

Rákshasbhuvana : village on the river Godavari, the Nizám defeated by the Peshwa at (1763), I, pt. ii, 627 ; XVII, 406 ; XVIII, pt. ii, 252.

Rákshasgudda : hill in Kánara district, XV, pt. ii, 316.

Rákshi Dongar : basalt dyke at Sopára, XIV, 342, 417.

Rakshita : Buddhist missionary to Banavási (B. C. 242), XV, pt. ii, 77, 264 ; I, pt. ii, 278 note 2.

Raktapura : town, identified with the modern Lakshmeśvara in the Miraj state, I, pt. ii, 304 note 6, 368, 373 ; camp of Vijayáditya at, *id.* 373 ; camp of Vikramáditya II, *id.* 376.

Rála : food plant, XXV, 184 ; grown in Poona district, XVIII, pt. ii, 41 ; in Sátára, XIX, 163.

Rallidæ : family of birds in Ratnágiri, X, 93.

Rám : hill pass between Ratnágiri and Belgaum districts, X, 166, 388, 392 ; XXI, 306.

Rám : king of Ayodhya ; incarnation of Vishnu, IX, pt. i, p. xxxvi, 530, 531 ; I, pt. ii, 28, 135, 142 ; followers of, IX, pt. I, 530 ; hero of the epic *Rámáyana*, *id.* 531 ; said to have created Anávala Bráhmans, *id.* 4 ; worships god Shiv at Saras ; raises a *ling* or stone home known as Siddhnath ; builds a well known as Rámkund ; offers a sacrifice near Bodhán ; asks Hanumán to bring Bráhmans from Kolhápur to help at the sacrifice ; raises emblem of god Shiv known as Muktináth at Mota ; founds a village, Muktipuri (Mota) for the Kolhápur Bráhmans or Motalas, *id.* 4, 12 note 1, 292, 313, 332, 345, 383 ; not alluded to by Patanjali and Pánini, I, pt. ii, 142 ; rivalled by Gotamiputra in exploits and prowess, *id.* 149 ; supposed ancestor of the Chudásamma clan, I, pt. i, 139.

Ráma : son of Kholeśvara, Singhana's minister (1240), in charge of Ambá, I, pt. ii, 524, 525 ; leads an expedition to Gujarát, is killed, *id.* 240, 242.

Ráma : Western Chálukya king Someśvara's officer, I, pt. ii, 465.

Ráma : Purushotama's son called Ekantada Rámayya, I, pt. ii, 482.

Rámachandra : *pandit* in Kumárapala's court, writes the *Prabandhaśata*, I, pt. i, 190 ; Jain scholar ordered by Ajayapála to sit on a red-hot sheet of copper, *id.* 194.

Rámachandra Paránjpe : *subhedar* of Ratnágiri, releases the imposter Sadáshiv Bháu, I, pt. ii, 102.

Rámadev : Devagiri Yádava king, I, pt. ii, 529, 530. *See* Rámchandra.

Rámadeva : *see* Kholeśvara's son Ráma.

Rámaji Mahádev : Peshwa's *sarsubhedár* of Thána (1760-1772), his water-works at Kalyán, Ganesh gate near the mansion of, at Kalyán, XIV, 115-117 ; the civil court at Thána the

mansion of, *id.* 352; the Sangameshvar Mahádev temple at Uran built by, *id.* 371.
Rámájipant: Báláji Peshwa's general, I, pt. ii, 90; takes Anjanvel and Dábhol and all the forts north of Vijayadurga (1756), *id.* 92.
Rámá Kámáti: citizen of Bombay Island, his supposed treasonable correspondence with Angria, tried and condemned (1720), XXVI, pt. i, 144-148.
Rámakirva: Koli outlaw, plunders, both below and above the Sahyádris (1830), XVII, 417.
Rámalinga: temple of, at Deur, I, pt. ii, 521 note 5; inscription at, *id.* 558 note 7.
Rámánand: founded Rámánandi religious sect, IX, pt. i, 534.
Rámánandi: *see* Religious Sects.
Ra Mandlik: last Chudásama ruler of Junágadh, becomes Muslim, raised to a saint, IX, pt. i, 125.
Rámanka: *taluká* in Káthiáwár, VIII, 638.
Rámánuj, Rámánujácharya: South Indian Bráhman, founded *Shri Sampradaya* cult of Vaishnav creed in the twelfth century, IX, pt. i, 533; Vaishnav reformer, converted Vishnuvardhana, XV, pt. ii, 89; his life, reforms, spread of his sect, followers, their mode of life, initiation ceremony, XX, 36-38; XXIII, 149-150; XXIV, 134.
Rámapuri: old territorial division, mention in a Sángli grant, I, pt. ii, 417.
Rámarája: I, pt. ii, 524. *See* Kholeśvara's son Ráma.
Ramás: state and place of interest in Mahi Kántha, V, 426, 439.
Rámatirth: Ushavadáta founded benefaction at, I, pt. ii, 148.
Rámáyana: Sanscrit epic, IX, pt. i, 531; I, pt. ii, 135, 136, 137, 138; corruption of the, *id.* 141; uncertainty of the date of the, *id.* 142; reference to certain countries in passages of the, *id.* 142, 344; mention of Gokarn in, XV, pt. ii, 298.
Ramazán: ninth month of the Musalmán year, month of fasting, IX, pt. ii, 115, 126, 141, 171 note 2; first fast of, *id.* 161; holidays in, *id.* 140; feasts in, *id.* 31 note 3, 127; recital of prayers in, *id.* 126, 132, 135, 136. *See* I'd.
Rámbágh: a place at Mátherán, XIV, 276.
Ramban: food-plant, XXV, 183.
Rambhájí Nimbálkar: Marátha noble (1715-1727), Nizám-ul-mulk takes him into his service, XX, 290; the founder of the Nimbálkar family of Karmála in Sholápur; gets Karmála in exchange for his estates in Poona (1727), *id.* 412-413; *see* also I, pt. ii, 598.
Rámchandra: Devagiri Yádava king (1271-1310), I, pt. ii, 519; wrests the kingdom from his cousin A'mana, his epithets and titles, the extent of his empire, *id.* 247, 528; the records of his time, *id.* 25, 247, 511, 529; his minister Hemádri, *id.* 248, 530; is defeated by Allá-ud-din Khilji and compelled to pay tribute (1294), *id.* 250-251, 530-531; neglects to send tribute regularly; is defeated and taken prisoner to Delhi by Malik Káfur (1307); is released and presented with the district of Navsári, *id.* 251, 532; entertains Malik Káfur (1309); his death, *id.* 533; his rule in Thána district, XIII, 437-438; mentioned in Thána inscriptions, XIV, 387, 396, 418; in North Kánara, XV, pt. ii, 92 note 1, 93; his rule in Sátára district, XIX, 225 note 1; *see* also XVII, 352 and note 5; XVIII, pt. ii, 214 note 3, 215 note 2; XX, 275 and note 3.
Rámchandra Appa Sáheb: Parashurám Bháu's son, XXIV, 347.
Rámchandra Basvant: Baroda *kárbhári*, confined in Poona (1751), effects his escape, his intrigues to obtain his master's release, VII, 179.
Rámchandradeva: *see* Devagiri Yádava king, Rámchandra.
Rámchandra Ganesh: Peshwa's commander, defeated and slain at Dugad in Thána (1780), XIV, 56; I, pt. ii, 105.
Rámchandra Malhár: administrative (1753) reforms of, XVIII, pt. ii, 250.
Rámchandra Naik: second Sonda chief (1598-1618), his family tree, XV, pt. ii, 120 note 3, 123.
Rámchandra Pant, Rámchandrapant Bávdekar: founder of the Bávda Amátya family (1689-1729); defends Vishálgad and Rángna against the Mughal forces, XXIV, 226, 293; suspected of leaving the Sátára fort unprovided, XIX, 249-253; tries to place Sambháji on the throne, *id.* 255.
Rámdás Svámi: Shiváji's spiritual guide (1608-1681), XVIII, pt. ii, 228-229; XIX, 238; his letter to Sambháji, *id.* 245; his descendant, the chief of Cháphal, *id.* 460; his temple at Parli, *id.* 537, 538; *see* also XXIV, 294.
Rámdé: converted Tuwar Rájpút, spreads Islám in Cutch and Káthiáwár, IX, pt. ii, 40.
Rámde Pir: legend of, IX, pt. I, 544 and note 2; spreads the Bij or Márgi sect, *id.* 347, 375.
Rámdepotrá: a Sodha Rájpút sub-division in Cutch, V, 67.
Rámdev: *see* Rámchandra.
Rámdharan: caves in Kolába district, XI, 377.
Rámdurg: state in Southern Marátha Country, description, people, trade, history, land, justice, instruction, health, XXIV, 396-399.
Rámeshvar: place of pilgrimage near Cape Comorin, IX, pt. i, 549.
Rámeshvar: Cheul temple, XI, 272; (1623-1628), *id.* 282, 308-310.
Rámeshvar: hot springs at Vajrábái in Thána district, XIV, 374.
Rámeshvar: *see* Nárushankar's Temple.
Rámeshvar: Poona temple, XVIII, pt. iii, 342.
Ráмеśvar: I, pt. ii, 198; *tirth* on the Tungabhadra, temple of Parameśvara at, *id.* 377; sacred place, *id.* 397.
Ráмeśvara: temple of, at Hulihalli, inscription at, *id.* 582 and note 1.
Rametta: poisonous plant, XXV, 268.
Rámgad: fort in Ratnágiri district, X, 362.
Rámi: island of the Jáva group, I, pt. i, 528.
Ramiar: Pársi priest, son of Shápur, IX, pt. ii, 221.

Rámji Bhángria : Koli robber (1825) in Thána, XIII, 524; as police officer, receives present from villages, asks for discharge, his subsequent outlawry, XVII, 416-417.
Rámkánta : *Acacia ramkanta*, a tree in Poona district, XVIII, pt. i, 51.
Rámkund : Rám's well, near Saras, origin of, IX, pt. i, 12 note 1.
Rámkund : Sopára reservoir, XIV, 320, 340.
Rámnavmi : Rám's birth-day, a holiday, a day of fast, IX, pt. i, 23 note 5; Hindu holiday, XVIII, pt. i, 242-243.
Rámoshi : unsettled tribe, in Poona district, origin, settlement, divisions, surnames, appearance, language, special language, food, dress, ornaments, occupation, religion, holidays, customs, community, XVIII, pt. i, 409-425; *id.* pt. iii, 34-39; enlisted by Báji Ráo II to shut up the *ghâts*; invade the Kalyán district, I, pt. ii, 116; in Ratnágiri district, X, 129, 219; in Kolába, XI, 71; plunder, *id.* 158, 220; in Thána district, XIII, 177; let loose on the Konkan by the Peshwa, *id.* 522; at Prabal fort in Thána district; their proclamation (1828), XIV, 300; in Násik district, XVI, 72; in Ahmadnagar district, XVII, 209; in Khándesh, XII, 105; in Sátára district, XIX, 108-109; in Belgaum district, XXI, 174 and 175; in Kolhápur, XXIV, 107.
Rámoshi Rising : of 1826, in Poona and Ahmadnagar districts, XVIII, pt. ii, 306-307.
Ramparda : táluka in Káthiáwár, VIII, 638.
Rám Pátil : the Koli captain of Janjira (1490), XI, 435.
Rámphal : *Anona reticulata*, a fruit-tree in Poona district, XVIII, pt. i, 51.
Rámpur : place of interest in Káthiáwár, VIII, 637.
Rámpura : state in Mahi Kántha, V, 429.
Rámpura : Chávada Rájpút estate in Rewa Kántha, IX, pt. i, 124; VI, 145; place of interest, *id.* 167.
Rám.áj : stream in Kolába district, XI, 9.
Rám Rája : king of Sátára, appoints (1699) Khanderáv Dabháde to collect *chauth* and *sardeshmukhi* in Baglán, I, pt. i, 388. *See* Rájárám.
Rám Rája : king of Sátára, entrapped by Tárábái and made a prisoner (1751), I, pt. ii, 603; set at liberty and allowed to live in Sátara (1761), *id.* 603; his death (1777), *id.* 604.
Rám Rája : Vijayanagar king (1542-1565), Burhan Nizám attacks Bijápur with the aid of (1549); renews alliance with Burhan (1553), his alliance with the king of Bijapur (1559); Nizám Sháh acknowledges the superiority of; attacks the Ahmadnagar fort; overthrown at Tálikot (1565), XVII, 366-370; XV, pt. ii, 114-116.
Rámráv Náráyan : Rájmáchi commandant, surveys Vásra (1795-96), XIII, 558.
Rámráv Shástri : adviser of the Peshwa; decides in favor of Sayájirav, son of Dámáji by his second wife, I, pt. i, 400.
Ramri : island off the coast of Arakan, I, pt. ii, 347 note 2.
Ramsay : the Honourable Mr. Andrew, President and Governor of Bombay (1788), XXVI, pt. ii, 490.
Rámsej : hill fort in Násik district; its history, XVI, 64, 642, 441, 442 note 3, 447; Dindori villages attached to (1826), *id.* 210 note 3.
Rám Seu : hill range near Bhinmal, I, pt. i, 456.
Rám Shástri : Poona judge (1761-1773), XVIII, pt. ii, 253; his opinion for the atonement of Náráyanráv's murder; retires, *id.* 256; produces the proof of Raghunáthráv's knowledge of the plot against Náráyanráv, *id.* 257; I, pt. ii, 603; XVIII, pt. iii, 8, 408; XIX, 296.
Rámsing : Malám, a skilful artist, V, 143; his works in the Cutch palace, *id.* 216; visits Holland (1750), XIII, 521.
Rámsnehi : *see* Religious Sects.
Rám Taláv : hot spring in Khándesh, XII, 467.
Ramtil : oil-yielding plant, XXV, 219.
Rám-tirth : holy pool near Honávar, XV, pt. ii, 307.
Rámtirth : village in Belgaum district; holy river at, XXI, 598-599.
Ramusio : Italian geographer (1550); his mention of Bhatkal (Baticala) kings, XV, pt. ii, 273
Ran : encircles Cutch and Káthiáwár, its area, boundaries, bed, islands, routes, products and history, V, 11-16; VIII, 23, 77-78, 69-77; mention of, I, pt. i, 538.
Ráua : of Chitor, supposed to have given sun-face to the religious *gurus*, I, pt. i, 464.
Rána : title of Udepur family, IX, pt. i, 495 note 5.
Rááná : ancestor of Navsári priests, IX, pt. ii, 221.
Ranagraha : Gurjjara prince (A. D. 639), brother of Dadda II; his copper-plate grant (A.D. 641), I, pt. i, 115; I, pt. ii, 314.
Ranajaya : *biruda* (title) of Rájasimha the Pallava king, I, pt. ii, 329, 330, 331.
Ránaka : chieftain, title of the Vaghelas, I, pt. i, 199.
Ránakadevi : daughter of a potter sought in marriage by Siddharája, I, pt. i, 176.
Ranarága : second Chálukya prince, I, pt. ii, 181, 243 note 2; son of Jayasimha I, Chálukya king, *id.* 340, 342, 343; father of Pulakesin I, *id.* 329 note 4.
Ranarangabbima : probably Tailapa, I, pt. ii, 233.
Ranarasika : Vikramáditya I, I, pt. ii, 329 and notes 4 and 5, 343 note 2, 361.
Ranásan : state in Mahi Kántha, V, 420.
Ránáváv : place of interest in Káthiáwár, VIII, 639.
Ranavigraha : *biruda* (title) of Samkaragana, son of Kokkala, the king of Chedi, I, pt. ii, 203, 414.
Ranavikrama : *biruda* (title) of Pulikesin I, I, pt. ii, 343.
Ranavikránta : *biruda* (title) of Mangalesa of Vátápi, I, pt. ii, 347; *biruda* (title) of Buddhavarman, son of Jayasimhavarman, the Chálukya prince of Gujarát, *id.* 359.
Ran-bhendy : fibrous plant, XXV, 227.
Ranchod : Bhagat's Panth. *See* Religious Sects.

Ranchodji : image of Vishnu at Dákor, IX, pt. i 118.
Ranchodji : Diwán, his local history of the Káthis, extract from, IX, pt. i, 262.
Randákhurd : village in Ahmadnagar district, waterfall, XVII, 734.
Rándel Máta : Hindu goddess, IX, pt. i, p. xxxvi, 122.
Rander : town in Surat district, II, 299; Rábanjir or Rahánjur, capital of Lar, mentioned by Al Biruni, I, pt. i, 513, 520; a place of great trade (1507), XIII, 448, 449 note 1; plundered by the Portuguese (1530). id. 451.
Rándhia : táluka in Káthiáwár, VIII, 639.
Randhikpur : sub-division in Rewa Kántha, VI, 116.
Randia dumetorum : plant used as soap and for poisoning fish, fodder plant also, common everywhere, XXV, 252, 272, 278.
Randpar : place of interest in Ratnágiri district, X, 362.
Randullah Khán : Bijápur general, I, pt. ii, 39; defeated by the Mughals (1629), id. 650; plunders Ráybág, XXIV, 318; mosque at Rahimatpur built in honour of, XIX, 548-549.
Ránebennur : táluka in Dhárwár district, I, pt. ii, 578; sub-divisional details, boundaries, area, aspect, soil, hills, climate, water, stock, crops and people, XXII, 644-646; survey of, id. 502-505, 555-559. Town, id. 783-784.
Rangaon : place of interest in Khándesh, XII, 468.
Rangapatáka : wife of Kálakála Narasimha Vishnu, the Pallava king, I, pt. ii, 330.
Rangári : a caste of dyers in Ratnágiri district, X, 125; in Kolába district, XI, 65; in Khándesh, XII, 76; in Thána district, XIII, 133; in Sátára district, XIX, 92-93, 143-144; in Sholápur district, XX, 134-135; in Kolhápur, XXIV, 97.
Rangarika : district, mentioned in an inscription at Udepur, I, pt. i, 187.
Rángna : fort on the border of Sávantvádi and Kolhápur, besieged by Shâhu, I, pt. ii, 81; X, 467; XXIV, 5, 293; description and history of, id. 319; pass, id. 6; X, 166.
Rango Bapuji : Pratapsinh's agent (1857), a rebel. XIX, 317-318.
Rangoji : is appointed agent by Dámáji Gáikwár in Gujarát; defeats Kántáji at Anand Mogri (1735), I, pt. i, 316, 317; agrees to aid Momin Khán on condition of receiving half the revenues of Gujarát (1737), id. 318, 394; again appointed deputy by Dámáji to collect tribute in Gujarát (1741), id. 323, 325; defeated by Muft Khir Khan and Fidá-ud-din; deserted by Sher Khán Bábi; is taken prisoner, his escape (1743), id. 326, 395; captures and demolishes the fort of Petlád; employed by the Musalmáns in the quarrels regarding the viceroyalty of Gujarát (1743-1744), id. 327, 395; imprisoned by Khanderáv Gáikwár; is released by Umábái and appointed her agent (1745), id. 329, 396; expels Trimbakráv from Ahmadábád and himself collects the Marátha share of the city revenues, id. 329; takes shelter with Sher Khán Bábi in Kapadvanj; besieged at Kapadvanj by Fakr-ud-daulah; requests Holkar to come to his help; the siege raised at the approach of Holkar; his interview with Jawán Mard Khán at Ahmadábád (1747), id. 330; captures Borsad and forces Hariba to leave the country, id. 331; deserted by his allies and imprisoned (1747), id. 332; see also VII, 174-177.
Rángoli : quartz powder, note on, XXII, 821-822.
Rangrez : a caste of Musalmán dyers, said to be converts from Hindu Khatri or weaver caste, Sunnis in religion, IX, pt. ii, 79; I, pt. ii 451; in Ahmadnagar, XVII, 229; in Poona district, XVIII, pt. i, 495; in Sholápur district, XX, 200; in Dhárwár district, XXII, 243-244; in Kolhápur, XXIV, 149.
Ránigám : táluka in Kháthiáwár, VIII, 640.
Rani Mahâls : forests in Baroda, VII, 28, 117-118.
Ranishkar : ruler of the Panjáb; seems to have adopted the religion of the Magi, IX, pt. ii, 183 note 4.
Ráni's Lake : in Mahi Kántha, V, 357.
Rani Tunk Hill : in Pálanpur, V, 282.
Ránjangaon : deshmukhi villages in Ahmadnagar district, old reservoir at, XVII, 734.
Ránjangaon : village in Poona district, Ganpati's temple at, XVIII, pt. iii, 438; plundered by the Mughals, XVIII, pt. ii, 246.
Rankále : pond in Kolhápur, XXIV, 12, 161; legend of, 305-306, 309.
Ran-Kela : famine and fibrous plant, common on the ghâts, XXV, 204, 235.
Rankine : Professor, suggests the form of Tulsi Lake in Thána, XIV, 364.
Ranmalji : Navánagar jám (1664), I, pt. i, 283.
Rannadevi : daughter of Govinda III, I, pt. ii, 394.
Ránojiráv Sinde : founder of the Sindia family, I, pt. ii, 600; helps the prince of Idar, I, pt. i, 315; built a temple of Yamái on Jotiba's Hill, in Kolhápur, XXIV, 299.
Ranpur : place of interest in Káthiáwár, VIII, 639.
Ranshil : see Bhimáshankar.
Ranu : sub-division in Baroda state, VII, 544.
Ránubái : a gosávi goddess, in Sávantvádi, X, 419; in Khándesh, XII, 51.
Ranvára : light-house and shoal in Káthiáwár, VIII, 19.
Ránvata : see Abhir.
Ránvati : dialects in Khándesh, XII, 53.
Ránvatia : land tenure in Baroda, VII, 352.
Ranzan : pass in Sátára district, XIX, 205.
Ráo Náik Nimbálkar : Phaltan chief, XIX, 231.
Ráos of Cutch : Bhármal I, V, 136; Bhármal II, id. 156-162; Bhojráj, id. 137; Desal I, id. 137; Desal II, id 162; Godji I, id. 137; Godji II, id. 143-146; Khengár I, id. 135; Khengár II, id. 137; Khengár III, id. 172; Lákha or Lákhpatji, id. 140-142; Prágmalji I,

id. 137 ; Prágmalji II, *id.* 172 ; Prithiráj, *id.* 149-151 ; Ráyadhan I, *id.* 137, 138 ; Ráyadhan II, *id.* 147-149, 152-155 ; Tamáchi, *id.* 137.

Ráos of Murbád : are Knnbis, XIII, 124.

Rapithavan : midday ceremony among Pársis, performed on the *Ardibehesht* day, IX, pt. ii, 219.

Rapithavangeh : second watch, IX, pt. ii, 214 note 1.

Raptores : family of birds in Ratnágiri, X, 54-60 ; in Thána district, XIII, 48-49.

Rarungæ : tribe mentioned by Pliny, I, pt. i, 534.

Rasálgad : fort in Ratnágiri district, X, 4, 362.

Rasátala : division of Patála, I, pt. ii, 576.

Rásenanagar : city, camp of Vijayáditya at, identified with Rásiyana of the Ráshtrakúta grant of A. D. 807, modern Rásin in the Karjat *táluka* of the Ahmadnagar district, I, pt. ii, 371-372, 399.

Ras Fartak : town in Arabia, I, pt. i, 536.

Rashid-ud-din : Arab geographer (1310), I, pt. i, 501 ; translated *Al-Biruni*, *id.* 508, 514 note 9, 518, 529, 531 ; I, pt. ii, 4 ; his mention of the area of Gnjarát, XIII, 437.

Rashnád : *taluka* in Káthiáwár, VIII, 640.

Ráshtrakúta : *see* Ráshtrakútas.

Ráshtrakútas : Dakhan dynasty, I, pt. ii, 194-210, 382-425 ; origin of their name, *id.* 178, 383-385 ; said to be Reddis, *id.* 22 note 2, 143, 383 ; their earliest trace, probably Rahtods, and thus connected with Rájpútána and Kanauj ; Lattanur, their original town, *id.* 384 ; another explanation of the name, *id.* 384-385 ; their early kings, *id.* 296, 385-386 ; crest of the Ráshtrakútas of Mánapura, *id.* 386 ; crest, banner, family god, and hereditary title of the Málkhed family of, *id.* 299 note 4, 387 ; their insignia, *id.* 338 note 7, 387 ; their musical instrument, *id.* 327 note 7, 387 ; their Puránic genealogy, *id.* 341 note 2, 383 ; overwhelm the Western Chalukyas of Bádámi, succeed them (757), and extend their territory, *id.* 336, 340, 341 note 1, 382 ; identified with the Balháras, *id.* 209 ; Dantidurga is the real founder of the family, *id.* 194, 389 ; establishment of an independent family of Ráshtrakútas in Láta, *id.* 392 ; overlords of the Konkan, *id.* 10, 16, 22, 392 ; kept back by the kings of Valabhi, *id.* 382 ; Govinda III places the power of the dynasty on a really firm footing, *id.* 197-199, 395 ; Láta placed in charge of a prince of the family, *id.* 23, 382, 397 ; annex all the territory to the north as far as the Sábarmati and pnsh on to the frontier of Sind, *id.* 383 ; become natural enemies of the Eastern Chalukyas, *id.* 316 note 5 ; Násik is probably their first capital, *id.* 396 ; Málkhed is made their capital, *id.* 403 ; their Gujarát branch, *id.* 400, 408, 413 ; extent of their territory, *id.* 382, 383, 396 ; religion under them, *id.* 208, 406-407 ; their dominions pass into the hands of the Western Chálukya of Kalyáni (973-974), *id.* 23, 207-208, 424, 426, 542 note 4 ; *see* also Dakhan branch of the (760-973), XX, 275 ; XVII, 351 ; XVIII, pt. ii, 214 and note 2 ; XIX, 224 ; XXI, 353-354 and note 2 ; XXII, 392 ; XXIII, 386 and note 7 ; XXIV, 218 ; XIII, 423-425, 434 ; their family tree, XV, pt. ii, 83-85 and note 1 ; IX, pt. ii, 2 note 1 ; *another account of* : I, pt. i, 119 ; dynasty of (743-974), *id.* 119-134 ; their origin and name, *id.* 119-120 ; their early dynasty (630-972), *id.* 120 ; Gujarát branch of the, overthrows Chalukya kingdom, I, pt. i, 117 ; their conquest of Gujarát (750-760), *id.* 465 ; their grants, *id.* 466, 506, 512 and note 1 ; in Gujarát, *id.* 525, 526, 527 ; IX, pt. i, 48 and note 4 ; their dominions, I, pt. i, 529 ; their towns, *id.* 530 ; *see* also Dantidurga, Krishna I, Govinda II, Dhruva, Govinda III, Amoghavarsha I, Krishna II, Jagattunga II, Indra III, Amoghavarsha II, Govinda IV, Krishna III, Jagattunga III, Khottiga, Kakka II, and Indra IV.

Ráshtrikas : Sanskrit for Prákrit Ráshtrakas, I, pt. ii, 143 ; Kshatriya tribe, *id.* 178.

Rásin : old town in Ahmadnagar district, temple at, XVII, 734-735 ; I, pt. ii, 399.

Rásiyana : territorial division, I, pt. ii, 398 ; may be identified with Rásin, *id.* 399.

Rás Mála : (Forbes') historical work, IX, pt. ii, 2 note 3, 3 notes 1, 2, 3, 5 note 2, 15 note 3, 25 note 1, 26 note 2, 29 note 1, 58, 64 note 3, 68 ; I, pt. i, 146, 153.

Rasores : order of birds, in Ratnágiri, X, 87-89.

Rasti : group of villages in Kaira (1802), III, 81.

Rástia : Poona ward, details of, XVIII, pt. iii, 274, 275.

Rastias : Marátha nobles, XIX, 298-299 ; *váda* of, in Poona city, XVIII, pt. iii, 342.

Rastikas : country to which Aśoka sent his ministers of religion, I, pt. ii, 143 ; province to which Asoka appointed religious ministers, *id.* 146 ; supposed to be Maráthás, *id.* 277.

Rasti Mahals : districts in Baroda state, VII, 28, 117, 439.

Rásubái : hill in Belgaum district, XXI, 6.

Rasulnagar : name given by Aurangzib to Visalnagar, I, pt. i, 286.

Rasulpnra : place of interest in Khándesh, XII, 468.

Rasulsháhi : a caste of beggars in Gnjarát, followers of the prophet ; also called *mastáns*, Suunis in religion, IX, pt. ii, 24.

Rat : Ganpati's carrier called *Undar Mama*, killing of, considered a sin in Gujarát, worship of, IX, pt. i, 379.

Ratajuna : old name for Ratajan, village in Ahmadnagar district, XVII, 352.

Rátambi : *Garcinia purpurea*, fruit tree in Poona district, XVIII, pt. i, 51.

Ratangad : fort in Kolába district, XI, 378.

Ratangad : fort in Násik district, XVI, 642.

Ratangad : hill fort in Ahmadnagar district, XVII, 3, 735-736.

Ratanlál Pandit : Mr., his note on Sárika, I, pt. i, 463 note 1.

Ratanmál : name for Bhinmal in *Tretáyuga*, I, pt. i, 461.

Ratanmál : hills in Rewa Kántha, VI, 2.

Ratanpur : town near Jodhpur, I, pt. i, 471.

Ratanpur : town in Central Provinces, proposed identification of, with the Ráshtrakúta Lattanur, I, pt. ii, 385.
Ratanpur : town in Rewa Kántha, the Maráthás gain a victory at (1705), tomb of Bába Ghor at, VI, 167; see also VII, 167; IX, pt. ii, 12; Rájpút chief of, sends troops against the Pársi settlers of Variáv, heroic defence of the Pársi female-warriors, IX, pt. ii, 186 note 9.
Ratanpur Dhámanka : táluka in Káthiáwár, VIII, 640.
Ratansingh Bhandári : deputy viceroy of Gujarát (1733-1737), I, pt. i, 314; receives Dolka; defeats Sohráb Khán at Dholi near Dhandhuka, id. 315-316; enmity of, with Momin Khán, id. 316, 319; his attempts to oppose the Gáikwár, id. 317; defends Ahmadábád, id. 319; leaves Ahmadábád, id. 320. See also VII, 174-175.
Ratansuri : Jain priest, converts king Jaychand and his followers to his faith, IX, pt. i, 97.
Ratanvadi : village in Ahmadnagar district, temple at, XVII, 736.
Rata Ráyadhan : chief of Cutch (1365), V, 134.
Ratha : see Ratta.
Rathestár : warrior, a class of the old Persian community, IX, pt. ii, 31.
Rathod : a class of Rájpúts, driven from Kanauj by Mahomedans, establishment in the deserts of Márwár, received the fief of Sámetra from Anahilaváda sovereign, take the fort of Idar; chiefships in Mahi Kántha, in Rewa Kántha, IX, pt. i, 128; a class of Rájpúts in Káthiáwár, VIII, 115; their history, id. 283; chief, at Idar, I, pt. i, 217 note 3; dynasty identified with Ráshtrakútas, their origin, id. 119; chiefs in Khándesh (A. D. 800), XII, 241; rulers in Ratnágiri (A. D. 1000), X, 193; Dakhan rulers (A. D. 300-970), trace of, in Násik, XVI, 184; the Malkhet, XIV, 126.
Ráthor : caste of Rájpút converts, take wives of Hindu birth, some have reverence for Swamináráyan, observe mostly Hindu customs, IX, pt. ii, 69.
Ratl : pound (troy), I, pt. i, 531.
Ratnáditya : Chávada king, I, pt. i, 154, 155.
Ratnágar : hill range near Bhinmal, I, pt. i, 456.
Ratnágar : the sea, meaning of, IX, pt. i, 349.
Ratnágiri : district, boundaries, sub-divisions, aspect, hills, X, 1-5; rivers, creeks, id. 6-11; geology, id. 12-19; water-supply, hot and intermittent springs, climate, id. 20-28; minerals, forests, trees, id. 29-40; animals, birds, fish, id. 41-103; original settlers, colonists, population in 1820, 1835, 1846, 1852 and 1872; census details of 1872, dress, food, id. 104-110; details of Hindus, Musalmáns, Pársis and Christians, id. 111-135; villages, houses, communities, movements, id. 136-143; soil, irrigation, holdings, stock, crops, cultivators, bad seasons, id. 144-153; capitalists, currency, classes who save, investments, money-lending, interest, id. 154-160; borrowers, land transfers, labour mortgage, wages, prices, weights and measures, id. 160-165; communications, tolls, bridges, rest-houses, ferries, shipping, light-houses, post, telegraph, id. 166-174; trade (247-1880): traders, exports and imports, course of trade, details of sea-trade, customs divisions, id. 175-187; industries, id. 188-191; history: early Hindus, Musalmáns, Maráthás (1660-1818); British (1818-1880), id. 192-199; acquisition, changes and staff, tenures, history of land revenue settlement, season reports, id. 200-265; judicial changes, staff, civil and criminal justice, civil court statistics, arbitration court, registration, criminal justice, staff, offences, police, jails, id. 266-274; balance sheet, local funds, municipalities, id. 275-281; schools, pupils, education, statistical returns, school of industry, town and village education, libraries, newspapers, id. 282-291; diseases, hospitals, native practitioners, cattle disease, vaccination, id. 292-295; sub-divisions, id. 296-316; places of interest, id. 317-384. Town, climate, X, 24; customs division, exports and imports of, id. 184; port details, water-supply, population, trade, manufactures, management, buildings, burning and burial grounds, history, fort, light-house, id. 363-368; see coast town, I, pt. ii, 388-467; caves at, id. 9; fort, id. 39; rebuilt by Shiváji id. 68; head-quarters of the Southern Konkan, id. 128.
Ratnágiri : town in the southernmost parts of the Bellary district, I, pt. ii, 363.
Ratnágiri : estate near Navasári, Mullá Jamasp receives the grant of, IX, pt. ii, 197 note 2.
Ratnágiri : river in Ratnágiri district, X, 8.
Ratnakośa : Sanskrit work, I, pt. ii, 134.
Ratnamálá : poetic history of Gujarát, I, pt. i, 149 note 2, 150, 151, 157; I, pt. ii, 409 note 1.
Ratnamáliká : see Prasnottara Ratnamáliká.
Ratnapála : king, slain by Perumáladeva, I, pt. ii, 509.
Ratnapur : Kalachuri branch of, I, pt. ii, 296 note 5.
Ratrávali : dramatic play, I, pt. ii, 139.
Ratnávate : Tamluk, port on the Hugli, I, pt. i, 499.
Ratrakas : people of Maharáshtra, I, pt. ii, 143.
Rats : plague of, in Bombay (1771), XXVI, pt. i, 364; in Ahmadnagar district, XVII, 280, 281; in Poona district, XVIII, pt. ii, 82-84, 502, 508; in Sátára, XIX, 388; in Sholápur district (1878-1882), XX, 238, 364; in Belgaum district, XXI, 289; in Dhárwar district (1879), XXII, 318; in Bijápur district, XXIII, 336-337, 500; at Mátheran, XIV, 258.

Ratta: progenitor of the Ráshtrakútas, I, pt. ii, 194, 387.

Ratta: a caste of Kánarese husbandmen in Kánara, XV, pt. ii, 84.

Rattagiri: village mentioned in the grant from Madras, I, pt. ii, 364.

Rattajjuna: village mentioned in a grant from Rádhanpur, I, pt. ii, 398.

Ratta-Kandarpa: *biruda* (title) of Govinda IV and Khettiga, I, pt. ii, 387, 416, 422.

Rattapádi: province mentioned in the Chola record, I, pt. ii, 431, 436.

Rattapalli: village of Ratehalli in Dhárwár district, I, pt. ii, 504.

Rattapáti: country of the Ráshtrakútas, I, pt. ii, 298 note 3, 341 note 2; country of the Rattas or Ráshtrakútas, *id.* 387, 431, 433.

Rattarája: South Konkan Siláhára chieftain, feudatory of the Western Chalukya king Satyáśraya, I, pt. ii, 414 note 1, 433, 538; his grant, *id.* 426.

Rattas: hold political supremacy in the Dakhan; assume the name of Ráshtrakúta, I, pt. ii, 143; name derived from the Ráshtrakútas, *id.* 384; name used for the Ráshtrakútas, *id.* 339, 424, 426; of Saundatti, *id.* 143, 384 note 4, 549-558; the title of the first branch is supreme lord of Kandharapura and probably belongs to the Reddi caste, *id.* 550; the second branch represents the Ráshtrakútas, *id.* 425; their crest and banner, *id.* 299 note 4, 552; their musical instrument, *id.* 329 note 7, 552; Prithvirámа, the founder of the first branch, is raised to the rank of feudatory by Krishna III, *id.* 420, 552; their hereditary territory, *id.* 546; the boundaries of the Kundi province fixed by Kartavirya I, of the second branch, *id.* 549, 553; feudatories of the Western Chalukyas, *id.* 437, 439, 443, 450, 451, 458, 498, 552, 553, 554, 555; Kalachurya feudatories, *id.* 498, 555; independent, *id.* 519, 555, 556, 557; reduced by Bichana the general of the Devagiri Yádava king Singhana, *id.* 243, 524, 558; their rule in Belgaum district (850-1250), their inscriptions, administration and genealogy, XXI, 354-358; *see* also XVIII, pt. ii, 213 note 1.

Rattavádi: kingdom of the Ráshtrakútas of Málkhed conquered by the Chola king Rájarájadeva, I, pt. ii, 308.

Rattehalli: *see* Rattihalli.

Ratthas: branch of Kshatriyas from whom the Ráshtrakútas descended, I, pt. ii, 194.

Rattiga: country mentioned in an inscription at Bálmuri, I, pt. ii, 308.

Rattihalli: village in Dhárwár district, temple, inscriptions and history of, XXII, 390, 412, 784; records at, I, pt. ii, 523, 529.

Rattis: Ráshtrakútas known as, I, pt. ii, 143.

Ratus: heads of creation, IX, pt. ii, 211 note 2 (8).

Ratushtai: part of the *Zend Avesta*, IX, pt. ii, 211 note 2 (8).

Raul: original title of Mewar chiefs, IX, pt. i, 495 note 5.

Raul or Raval: caste of tape-weavers, in Thána district, XIII, 133; in Poona district, XVIII, pt. i, 358-361; in Sholápur district, XX, 135-136; in Sátára district, XIX, 93; in Kolhápur district, XXIV, 97; in Násik district, XVI, 53; in Ahmadnagar district, XVII, 209-211; in Belgaum district, XXI, 75; in Bijápur district, XXIII, 160.

Raula: hill in Ahmadnagar district, XVII, 4.

Raulia: peak in Khándesh, story of, XII, 12 note 2.

Raushanias: *literally* "people of light," the Chaks so called, IX, pt. ii, 39.

Ráuttaráya: *see* Perumáledeva.

Ráuzan: gorge in Sátára district, XIX, 205.

Rauzat-us-safá: Musalmán historian, I, pt. i, 168, 512 note 3, 523 and note 1.

Rav: village in Cutch, inscriptions, a stone well and a temple at, V, 249; I, pt. i, 204.

Rávad Chincholi: village in Khándesh, temple at, XII, 468.

Rával: title, I, pt. i, 215 and note 2.

Rával: Jain, goes to Káthiáwár and founds the town of Navánagar, V, 135, 136.

Rával: town in Káthiáwár, VIII, 641; tomb at, *id.* 21.

Raval: a caste of Bráhmans in Gujarát, IX, pt. i, 17; priests of Bhils, duties, *id.* 304, 305.

Ravaleyanáyaka: Bijjala's officer, I, pt. ii, 460.

Ravalia: or Rával, a low class in Gujarát, divisions of, appearance, means of livelihood, customs, IX, pt. i, 508-509; in Káthiáwár, VIII, 159; *see* also Jagaria.

Rávaliavadar: place of interest in Káthiáwár, VIII, 640.

Rávan: demon king of Ceylon, IX, pt. i, 12 note 1; I, pt. ii, 135; tradition of, Kánara coast under, builds five temples, XV, pt. ii, 76; Gokarn the scene of the austerities of, *id.* 291; the Gokarn temple built by, *id.* 290; temple built by, at Shiveshvar fort, *id.* 341; builder of the silver temple of Somnáth, I, pt. i, 190, 454 note 1.

Ravania: village officer in Cambay, VI, 237.

Rávan under Kailás: Elephanta sculpture, XIV, 70.

Raváyets: collection of opinions of the Persian priests on doubtful religious questions, IX, pt. ii, 189; compilation of, *id.* 189 note 3; writings in Persian of authoritative customs, *id.* 212 and note 3; Persian precepts, *id.* 226; mention of Pársi settlements in Navsári and other places in, *id.* 189; reference to the year of moving the Sanján fire to Navsári in, *id.* 88 note 1, 190 note 3, 238.

Ravel: perhaps Ránder, I, pt. i, 220 note 2.

Ráver: petty division in Khándesh, survey (1856) settlement, XII, 405-406. *Town*, *id.* 249, 255, 468.

Ravikirti: poet, composer of the Aihole inscription and builder of Jain temples, I, pt. ii, 191, 194, 357.

Ravipanthis: *see* Religious Sects.

Ravivár: Sunday, IX, pt. i, 393.

Ravivarma, Ravivarman: early Kadamba king (A. D. 520), XV, pt. ii, 79; I, pt. ii, 288 and note 7; his war with the Pallava king, *id.* 289, 291 note 1, 322.

Rávji: son of Mánekji the head of Sind Lobanás, converted to Islám by Eusuf-ud-din, called Ahmed after conversion, IX, pt. ii, 51.
Rávji Apáji: Baroda minister, brought with his brother Bábáji Ápa to Baroda (1793) by Govindráv Gáikwár, I, pt. i, 412; both the brothers receive from the Bombay government the assistance of an auxiliary force under Major Walker, take the fort of Kadi by storm and compel Mulhárráv to surrender, *id.* 412; his interview with governor Duncan at Cambay, *id.* 412; death of Rávji Ápa (1803), *id.* 414; VII, 200, 202-205, 293-294.
Rávlya-Jávlya: forts in Násik district, XVI, 441, 447, 642.
Rawla: food plant, XXV, 184.
Ráya: minister of Rachamalla the Western Ganga king, and promoter of the Jain religion, I, pt. ii, 499.
Ráyadevarasa: feudatory of Vira-Ballála II, I, pt. ii, 506.
Ráyáji: sister of Lákha, married to Raji, I, pt. i, 160.
Ráyakvál: a class of Bráhmans in Gujarát, IX, pt. i, 2; derivation of name, origin of, sub-division, claim descent from Saiyngava Rishi, *id.* 17; Vánias, Meshri, *id.* 73 and note 1.
Ráyan: tree, IX, pt. i, 360; close to the tomb of Báva Ghor at Ratanpur, its use in ordeals, *id.* 361.
Ráyana: village accountant, father-in-law of Vikramáditya VI, I, pt. ii, 449.
Ráya Náráyana: *biruda* (title) of the Devagiri Yádava kings, I, pt. ii, 517.
Ráyappa Sángoli: village watchman (1820) in Belgaum, XXI, 404-405.
Ráyarájaguru: royal preceptor of the Devagiri Yádava king Krishna, I, pt. ii, 527.
Ráyarájapura: Talakád, pillaged by Vishnuvardhana, I, pt. ii 496.
Ráya-rekha: a land measure in Dhárwár district, XXII, 407, 440 and note 2.
Ráyaśettipura: record at, I, pt. ii, 508.
Ráyathala: class of Bráhmans in Gujarát, IX, pt. i, 17.
Ráybág: hill in Kolhápur, XXIV, 4; pond, *id.* 12; town, temples, tomb, 318-319; survey of, *id.* 257; I, pt. ii, 457 note 2, 557; under the Delhi emperor (1347), XXI, 362.
Raygad: fort in Kolába district, its description, approaches, the way up, XI, 357-359; hill top, objects, *id.* 360-362; history, *id.* 367-376, 442; centre of Vijayanagar power in Konkan, *id.* 142; taken by Shiváji (1648), I, pt. ii, 592; Shiváji crowned at (1674), *id.* 594; XIII, 476; Rájárám imprisoned in, I, pt. ii, 79; captured by the Mughals (1690), *id.* 79; XI, 145; XVIII, pt. ii, 239; XIX, 249; made over to the Sidi (1699), XI, 146; Rajárám dies at (1700), I, pt. ii, 597; retained by the Sidi (1732), XI, 150; taken by the Maráthás (1735), I, pt. ii, 83, 600; its commander rises in rebellion and is put down (1772), *id.* 100; Peshwa Bájiráv sends his family to (1817), XI, 156; taken by the English (1818), *id.* 159; I, pt. ii, 117; XVIII, pt. ii, 297. *See* Rairi.
Rayghar: village in Khándesh, a ruined fort and temples at, XII, 468.
Ráykaran: Anahilaváda king (A. D. 1300), flees to Biglán, takes shelter with Rámdev of, Devgiri (1306), XVI, 187.
Raziah: *sultánah* (1237-1240), IX, pt. ii, 12, 38.
Readers and Writers: details of, in Kolába, XI, 231, 232; in Thána, XIII, 657; in Násik district, XVI, 330; in Ahmadnagar district, XVII, 576-577; in Sátára district, XIX, 410; in Sholápur, XX, 380-381; in Belgaum district, XXI, 484; in Dhárwár district, XXII, 613-614; in Bijápur district, XXIII, 519-520.
Reading Rooms: in Kaira, III, 139; in Panch Maháls, *id.* 289; in Kolába, XI, 235; in Khándesh, XII, 335; in Thána district, XIII, 662; in Belgaum district, XXI, 489; in Dhárwár district, XXII, 621.
Readymoney: Hirji Jivanji, visits China (1756), IX, pt. ii, 195 note 2.
Reagaon: village in Khándesh, temple at, XII, 468.
Rechanayya: Rechana Kalachurya Sankama's officer, I, pt. ii, 487, 489.
Reclamations: of waste land in Ratnágiri district, I, pt. ii, 33; in Thána district, XIII, 281-283.
Recolets: Friars, at Tárápur, XIII, 460 note 7; monasteries of, at Tárápur, *id.* 483.
Recorder's Court: established (1798) in Bombay island, XXVI, pt. iii, 44-47.
Recruits: bad treatment of, on board (1686-87) of Company's ships, XXVI, pt. iii, 78-80.
Reda: pass in Sátára district, XIX, 205.
Redájiji: image of, at Govalkot fort in Ratnágiri, X, 336.
Reddi: Kánarese caste name, I, pt. i, 119; Telugu farmer, I, pt. ii, 383-84; tribe or caste, *id.* 550; Ráshtrakútas probably descended from, XXI, 354 note 2, 355; XVIII, pt. ii, 213 note 1, 214 note 2.
Redi: village near Vengurla in Ratnágiri district, I, pt. ii, 181, 347; fort, history and construction of, X, 369-371.
Red Sea: trade with, XIII, 410, 414, 416, 715; I, pt i, 535, 536.
Redshanks: class of birds in Ratnágiri district, X, 93.
Reeves: Mr., commissioner in the Kolhápur rising (1844), XXIV, 242.
Reforms: of Aurangzib, I, pt. i, 283; (1863-1882), in Káthiáwár, VIII, 309-312; Báláji II's (1740-1761) administrative, XVIII, pt. ii, 250; Shiváji's (1839-1848), XIX, 312; introduced by Máhmud Gáwán (1478), XXIII, 402; by Yusuf Adil Sháh (1489-1510), *id.* 409-410.
Refugees: in Gujarát, I, pt. i, 1.
Regan: state in Rewa Kantha, VI, 146.
Registration: all district volumes, *see* Revenue and Finance under District Name.
Regulations: first published with vernacular translations in Bombay (1757), XXVI, pt. i, 318-319.
Rehbáris: herdsmen at Bhinmal, I, pt. i, 451.
Rehekuri: village in Ahmadnagar district, temple and pond at, XVII, 736.

Rehen : Musalmán foreign tribe, Kasbátis trace descent from, IX, pt. ii, 15 ; class of Dholka Kasbátis, *id.* 64 note 3.

Rehvar : sub-division of Rájpúts, in Mahi Kántha, V, 355, 418 note 1 ; in Gujarát, origin of ; derivation of name, IX, pt. i, 128 and note 2 ; minor estates in Mahi Kántha, *id.* 128-129.

Reinaud : French writer ; Parthian trade with India (B. C. 255-A. D. 235) according to, XIII, 410 ; his mention of the Chinese compass, *id.* 756 ; his notice of Dravir, I, pt. ii, 4 ; date of the *Periplus* according to, I, pt. i, 542-543.

Rekha : standard rent in Kánara district, XV, pt. ii, 157 ; *jhadti*, assessment scrutiny, *id.* 155.

Rekhánasht : untaxed waste lands in Kánara district, XV, pt. ii, 171.

Relacao : supreme court of the Portuguese, I, pt. ii, 52.

Relic Chamber : Sopára *stupa*, XIV, 328.

Relic Mound : at Sopára, XIII, 419.

Relics : in Kanheri caves, XIV, 142, 145, 146, 167, 175 note 1 ; at Sopára, *id.* 336 ; Gautama's, at Sopára, *id.* 404-405 ; XIII, 409 ; in Kondivti caves, *id.* 204, 206.

Relief Act : Dakhan Agriculturists', working of, in Ahmadnagar district, XVII, 319-320 ; in Poona district, XVIII, pt. ii, 129-133 ; in Sátára district, XIX, 188.

Relief Houses : famine (1877), in Poona district, XVIII, pt. ii, 92-93.

Religion : Musalmán, two forms of—Sunni and Shiah, origin and points of difference between the two forms, IX, pt. ii, 47-48, 125-126 ; *imáms* of, *id.* 125 note 2, 126 ; schools of, *id.* 126 note 1 ; schisms from Sunni, Mahdavi, *id.* 6 note 1, 35 note 1 ; and Wahhábis, *id.* 12 and note 1, 13 ; divisions of Shiahs—the Isna-Asharis and Ismáilis, further sub-divisions of Ismailis into—Nazarians and Mustaalians, *id.* 30 note 1 ; spread of the faith in Gujarát by missionaries and Musalmán rulers, *id.* 3-5, 125 ; leading beliefs and practice of, *id.* 126-130 ; religious buildings, *id.* 130-132 ; religions officers, *id.* 132-135 ; holidays, *id.* 136 141 ; early beliefs, *id.* 142-146 ; *of the Pársis*, different names of, IX, pt. ii, 211, 213 ; meaning of, *id.* 211 ; explanation of, 185 ; the sacred books of, *id.* 211, 212 ; leading beliefs in, *id.* 212-213 ; fire temples, *id.* 213-215 ; sacred fires—*Atesh Dádghan*, *id.* 213, *Aderan*, *id.* 213-214, *Atesh Behram*, *id.* 214-215 ; objects of veneration—*Amshaspánda* and *Yazads*, *id.* 215-216 ; high festival days—*Jasans*, *id.* 216-217 ; season festivals—*Gahambárs*, *id.* 217-218 ; *Gáthás*, *Muktád* holidays, *id.* 218 ; leading high days, *id.* 218-219 ; observances, *id.* 219-220 ; early beliefs, *id.* 220 ; Brahmanical in Gujarát, early beliefs, religious beliefs, IX, pt. i, page xxxiv ; worship of gods and goddesses ; *Pancháyatan Dev* worship ; *Sakti* worship in her various forms, *id.* p. xxxv ; *Mátás* or worship of goddesses, *id.* pp. xxxv-xxxvi ; trinity or *trimurti* worship, *id.* p. xxxvi, 531 ; guardian or *dev* worship by early tribes, *id.* p. xxxiv ; sun worship ; fire worship ; spirit worship, *id.* p. xxxv ; *Jain*, *id.* 105-110 ; followed by different classes, bards and actors, *id.* 213, 220, 225, 226 ; Bráhmans, *id.* 30-31 ; craftsmen, *id.* 178, 179, 181, 182, 185, 186, 189, 191, 194, 196, 200, 205 ; depressed classes, *id.* 332-333 ; Bhangias, *id.* 335 336 ; Dhedas, *id.* 341, 345 ; early tribes, *id.* 292 293 ; Bhils, *id.* 301-305, 312, 314, 319, 322, 323 ; herdsmen, Bharváds, *id.* 268-269 ; Rabáris, *id.* 288 ; husbandmen, Kanbis, *id.* 156-157, 154, 164, 168, 172, 173, 175 ; Káthis, *id.* 257 ; Kolis, *id.* 247 ; Rájpúts, *id.* 136-137 ; traders, Vániás, *id.* 89 ; Shrávaks, *id.* 105-110 ; writers, *id.* 56, 61, 64 ; Portuguese in Thána, XIII, 460-463 ; of Mátherán tribes, XIV, 263 ; see also census details under District Name.

Religious beggars : in Surat and Broach districts, II, 55, 376 ; in Kaira, III, 35 ; in Panch Mahals, *id.* 226 ; in Cutch, V, 83-88 ; in Pálanpur, *id.* 291 ; in Mahi Kántha, *id.* 367 ; in Ratnágiri district, X, 131.

Religious Beliefs : in Gujarát, IX, pt. i, p. xxxiv ; animal worship, *id.* 372-382 ; disease worship, *id.* 365-372 ; element worship, *id.* 348-358 ; epidemic scaring, *id.* 413-415 ; grain worship, *id.* 389-392 ; hill worship, *id.* 388-389 ; offerings, *id.* 406-409 ; omens, *id.* 409-413 ; planet worship, *id.* 392-460 ; plant worship, *id.* 382-388 ; spirit possession, *id.* 415-425 ; stone worship, *id.* 362-365 ; tomb worship, *id.* 358-362 ; witchcraft, *id.* 425-430.

Religious Sects : in Gujarát, chief object of modern Hindu worship, the trinity or *trimurti*—Brahma, Vishnu in his incarnation of Rám and Krishna, Shiv, IX, pt. i, p. xxxvi, 531 ; epics and *purâns* furthering worship of Vishnu and Shiv, *id.* 531 533 ; growth of sectarianism, religious founders or apostles, *id.* 532-533 ; Vishnuites or Vaishnav sects, worshippers or followers of Vishnu—chief cult Vallábhachári, *id.* p. xxxvi, 530, 533, 535 ; Shaivs, worshippers or followers of Shiv, *id.* 541 ; minor sects or cults called " ways," that is *margs* or *panths*, *id.* p. xxxvi, 530 ; census details (A. D. 1872), *id.* 530.

Bijpanthis : or Bijmargis, *id.* p. xxxvi, 530 ; beliefs ; Rámde Pir, object of worship ; initiatory ceremony ; pecular features ; saints, *id.* 544-545 ; followers among Bajániás, *id.* 503 ; Bhois, *id.* 505 ; Cháraus, *id.* 220 ; Dhedás, *id.* 341 ; Golás, *id.* 185 ; Hajáms, *id.* 233 ; Káchhiás, *id.* 154 ; Kanbis, *id.* 156 ; Kolis, *id.* 247 ; Mochis, *id.* 194 ; Rabáris, *id.* 288 ; Sathvaras, *id.* 175 ; Sindhvás, *id.* 346.

Dádupanthis : Vishnav sect, branch of the Rámánandi school, *id.* p. xxxvi, generation ; doctrines ; divisions—*Viraktas*, *Nágas*, *Vistardháris* ; holy texts ; chief shrine of the sect at Naraina, *id.* 548 ; followers among Kanbis, *id.* 156, 168, 548.

Godiapanthis : followers among Luhárs, *id.* 19.

Haribáva : followers among Dheds, *id.* 341.

Imámsháhi : or *Piráná* sect, generation ; observances ; religious books ; *kákas* or shrine managers, *id.* 546-547 ; followers

among Golás, *id.* 185; Káchhiás, *id.* 154; Kanbis, *id.* 167.

Jainism : id. 69, 105-110; followers in Shrávak Vániás, Mevádas, Narsipurás, Nimas, Osváls, *id.* 96; Porváds, Shrimális, *id.* 97; Ummads, *id.* 98; Márwáris, Porwád and Osvál, *id.* 103; Bhávsárs, *id.* 179.

Kabirpanthis : Vaishnavs of the Rámanandi cult, *id.* p. xxxvi; 530; founded by Kabir; Kabir's philosophy, tenets of faith; moral code; rules of conduct; *guru* or spiritual guide; *gádis;* pontiffs; temples; branches of the sect, *id.* 539-540; followers among Bhangiás, *id.* 336; Bháts, *id.* 213; Bhávsárs, *id.* 178; Chárans, *id.* 220; Dhedas, *id.* 341; depressed classes, *id.* 332; Dhobis, *id.* 229; Ghánchis, *id.* 182; Golás, *id.* 185; Káchhis, *id.* 154; Kádiyás, *id.* 186; Kanbis, *id.* 156; Kolis, *id.* 247; Luhárs, *id.* 191; Mális, *id.* 172.

Kuber Panth : doctrine, ascetics; followers among Luhárs, *id.* 548.

Lakshmangar's Panth : doctrine, ascetics; followers among Hajáms, Kanbis, Kolis, Kumbhárs, *id.* 548.

Lalbegs : followers of, among Bhangiás, *id.* 336.

Mádhaváchari : Brahma sampradáya of Vaishnav creed, *id.* 530, 534, followers among Darjis, *id.* 181.

Mádhavgarnis : or *Mádhavgar's Panth,* tenets; *gurus,* their duties; *id.* p. xxxvi, 546; followers among Bráhmans, Hajáms, Kanbis, *id.* 156.

Márgipanthis : see Bijpanthis.

Meherájpanthis : see Parnámipanthis.

Nának : followers among Bhangiás, *id.* 336.

Parnámipanthis or *pranámis :* also called *Meherájpanthis, id.* p. xxxvi, 530; feature; temples; book of faith; *gurus, id.* 545; followers among, Bháts, *id.* 213; Darjis, *id.* 181; Kadiyás, *id.* 186; Mochis, *id.* 194; Kanbis, *id.* 156; Suthárs, *id.* 205.

Piránás : see Imámsháhi.

Radha Vallabhi : id. p. xxxvi; object of worship, holy books, *id.* 548; followers among Darjis, *id.* 181.

Rámánandis : or *Rámavats,* also known as *Veragis,* Vaishnav sect, *id.* p. xxxvi, 530; worship Rám; initiation; chief seat of the sect at Benáres; *mathas* or monastic houses; *sadhus;* moral tenets, *id.* 534; followers among, Bhangiás, *id.* 336; Bharváds, *id.* 268; Bhávsárs, *id.* 178; Bhois, *id.* 505; Darjis, *id.* 181; Dhedas, *id.* 341; Ghánchis, *id.* 182; Golás, *id.* 185; Hajáms, *id.* 233; Kadiyás, *id.* 186; Kanbis, *id.* 156, 168; Kansárás, *id.* 187; Luhárs, *id.* 191; Mochis, *id.* 194; Rabáris, *id.* 288; Sathvárás, *id.* 175; Suthárs, *id.* 205.

Rámánujas : Vaishnav sect, doctrine, called Visishtádvaita; *sádhus;* initiation; chief see or *gádi* at Dwárka, *id.* 534; followers among Bháts, *id.* 213; Chárans, *id.* 220; Dhobis, *id.* 229; Kanbis, *id.* 164; Lohánás, *id.* 122; Mális, *id.* 172; Máthur Kayásths, *id.* 64; Rájpúts, *id.* 136; Sindhvas, *id.* 346.

Ramsnehi : Vaishnav sect, worship Rám, *id.* p. xxxvi, 530; doctrine, *sádhus, id.* 534-535; followers among, Ghánchis, *id.* 182; Kolis, *id.* 247.

Ranchhod Bhagat's Panth : doctrine, *id.* 548.

Ravipanthis : Vaishnav sect, object of worship, *id.* 547.

Sáktás : or *Vámámargis, id.* p. xxxvi; devotees of Sakti or the creative energy; sacred texts; divisions—*Dakshináchári*s, *Vámáchári* or *Vámamargi, Kaulamárga,* form of worship, *id.* 545-546.

Santram Panth : doctrine, chief *gádi* and temple at Nadiád, *id.* p. xxxvi, 547.

Shaivs or smárts : worshippers of Shiv also called Shivites, *id.* p. xxxvi, 530; worship Shiv under his various names; worship Shiv's phallic emblem called *ling; Svayambhu* and *jyotir* sacred emblems; elaboration of worship *shodash puja;* worship on *Shivrátris, id.* 541; worship placed on its modern footing by later Shankaráchāryas; four seats or *gádis* established by Shankar; *achāryas* or religious heads; moral code of Shankar school, *id.* 541-542; orders of *sádhus* or ascetics—*Dandis* or *Sanyásis, id.* 542; *Paramahansas, Aghoris, Yogis, id.* 543; *Jangamas, Urahvabáhus, A'kasa Mukhis, id.* 544; followers among Bráhmans, *id.* 30; Bháts, *id.* 213; Bhavayas, *id.* 225; Bhávsárs, *id.* 178; Bhois, *id.* 505; Brahmakshatris, *id.* 56; Chárans, *id.* 220; Darjis, *id.* 181; Ghánchis, *id.* 182; Golás, *id.* 185; Káchhiás, *id.* 154; Kanbis, *id.* 56, 164; Kansárás, *id.* 187; Luhárs, *id.* 191; Mális, *id.* 172; Máthur-Kayasths, *id.* 64; Rájpúts, *id.* 136; Saláts, *id.* 196; Sathvárás, *id.* 175; Sonis, *id.* 200; Suthárs, *id.* 205.

Sváminaráyens : Vaishnav sect, *id.* p. xxxvi, 530; growth, *id.* 536-537; tenets of faith; religion; doctrines, sees or *gádis* of the sect, *id.* 537; four orders—*Brahmacháris, Sádhus, Pálás* and *Satsángis;* their duties; initiation, *id.* 538; position of women, a special feature in, *id.* 539; followers among, Bháts, *id.* 213; Bhávsárs, *id.* 178; Bráhmans, *id.* 30; Chárans, *id.* 220; Darjis, *id.* 181; depressed classes, *id.* 332; Dhedás, *id.* 341; Ghánchis, *id.* 182; Golás, *id.* 185; Káchhiás, *id.* 154; Kadiyás, *id.* 186; Kanbis, *id.* 156, 164; Kolis, *id.* 247; Luhárs, *id.* 191; Mális, *id.* 172; Mochis, *id.* 194; Rájpúts, *id.* 136; Sompura Saláts, *id.* 196; Sáthvárás, *id.* 175; Sonis, *id.* 200; Suthárs, *id.* 205.

Udási : beliefs, *mahant* or head; followers among, Uda Kanbis, *id.* 547-548.

Vallábháchári : or Vallábhácharys, Vaishnav sect, called sect of the *Mahárájas* or *Pushti-Márga,* propagated by Vallabha, *id.* p. xxxvi, 530, 533; generation and growth; articles of creed, element of love for the deity; forms of worship; worship the image of Krishna in temples or *mandirs, id.* 535; eight daily services or *darshans;* chief seats or *gádis;* initiation; holy books; spiritual heads, *id* 535-536; followers in Meshri Vaniás, *id.* 69, 70, 71, 74, 89; Bhátiás, *id.* 118; Lohánás, *id.* 120; among Bháts, *id.* 213; Bhois, *id.* 505; Bráhmans (*abotis*), *id.* 4; Girnárás, *id.* 9; Guglis, *id.* 9; Push-

karnás, *id.* 16; Brahmakshatris, *id.* 56; Chhipas, *id.* 179; Darjis, *id.* 181; Ghánchis, *id.* 182; Káchhiás, *id.* 154; Kanbis, *id.* 156; Káyasths, *id.* 61, 67; Khatris, *id.* 189; Luhárs, *id.* 191; Mális, *id.* 172; Rájpúts, *id.* 136; Sáthvárás, *id.* 175; Sonis, *id.* 200; Suthárs, *id.* 205.
Váma Margis: *see* Sháktás.
Remádevi: senior wife of the Hoysála king Vira-Balláta II, I, pt ii, 488, 493, 501, 502.
Remains: Buddhistic (50), I, pt. ii, 1; at Atgaon, Párol, Wálkeshvar in Bombay, and Lonád, *id.* 22; Musalmán, at Kalyán, Bhiwndi, Lánja and Rájpuri, *id.* 41; Portuguese, at Bassein, Chaul, Mándvi, Kelvá-Máhim and Marol, *id.* 65; and at Mandapeshvar, *id.* 66; Elephanta, XIV, 61, 90-93, 94-97; Goregaon, *id.* 101, 388-396; Kalyán, *id.* 396-399; Kanheri, *id.* 189; Karanja, *id.* 192; Lonád, *id.* 212; Nánághát, *id.* 287-290; Sanján, *id.* 303; Atgaon, *id.* 307-312; Sonávli, *id.* 313; Thána, *id.* 349; Vehár, *id.* 379; Hemadpanthi, in Poona district, XVIII, pt. ii, 214 note 4.
Remedies: Our Lady of, church dedicated to, at Poinsar in Thána, XIV, 298, 386; I, pt. ii, 65; burnt by Kákáji, *id.* 80.
Remington: Mr., officiating resident of Baroda, VII, 267.
Remmádevi: *see* Remádevi.
Renadál: near Kolhápur, record at, I, pt. ii, 527, 528.
Renávi: village in Sátára district, temple at, XIX, 549-550.
Rend-bhatti: Portuguese still-cess, XIII, 553.
Rend-dáru: Portuguese liquor-cess, XIII, 553.
Rend-doli: Portuguese net-cess, XIII, 553.
Rend-másli: Portuguese fish-cess, XIII, 553.
Renuká: mother of Parasuráma, the destroyer of the Kshatriyas, I, pt. ii, 282 note 5.
Reservoirs: in Káthiáwár, VIII, 68; in Kolába, XI, 11, 12; in Násik district, XVI, 95; in Poona district, XVIII, pt. i, 9; XVIII, pt. ii, 24-28; in Belgaum district, XXI, 240, 241; in Dhárwár district, XXII, 258-263; in Bijápur district, XXIII, 312-314.
Residency: at Sangam (1805), in Poona city, XVIII, pt. ii, 287.
Residents: English, appointed to collect the revenues of Belapur, Kalyán and Karanja (1781), I, pt. ii, 105; at Baroda, Fatesing asks for a resident (1780), VII, 197; list of (1802-1882), *id.* 288.
Rest-houses: all district volumes, *see* Trade under District Name.
Restoration: Angria's *grab*, I, pt. ii, 94.
Resurrection: day of, Musalmán belief in, IX, pt. ii, 126.
Reva or Reváji: Narbada river, I, pt. i, 467; I, pt. ii, 350, 389.
Revágiri: hill in Sátara district, XIX, 12.
Revakabbe: wife of Palikála the Sinda prince, I, pt. ii, 577.
Revali: Hindu goddess, temple of, at Vadáli, healing shrine of, IX, pt. i, 366.
Revana: the Western Chálukya king Someśvara IV's officer, I, pt. ii, 465.
Revan Siddh: a saint at Renavi in Sátára district, XIX, 549-550.
Revarasa: lord of Máhishmatipura, feudatory of the Western Chálukya king Someśvara I and of Jagadekamalla II, I, pt. ii, 439, 457.
Revarasa: *see* Revana.
Revári Canal: in Sátára district, XIX, 151-152.
Revas: port in Kolábá district, XI, 378; taken by A'ngria (1733), *id.* 150.
Revati, Revatidvipa: island identified with Redi near Málvan, I, pt. ii, 181, 182 and note 5, 345, 347 and note 2, 349, 355, 358 note 1.
Revatikshetra: traditional name of Cheul, XI, 269, 270 note 1.
Revatimitra: present with Mularája in the battle with Graharipu, I, pt. i, 160.
Revdanda: Portuguese Cheul, village in Kolábá district, XI, 299; I, pt. ii, 48; Portuguese remains at, *id.* 65; sieges of (1570, 1592), XVII, 371-372, 379-380; proposed cession of, to the French, I, pt. ii, 102-103; lapses to the British (1840), XI, 159, 190; its assessment revised (1852), *id.* 192-193; revenue survey of (1857), *id.* 198-200.
Reve Gujar: a caste of cultivators in Khándesh, XII, 18-21.
"Revenge:" English frigate, beats off Shiváji's fleet (1679), I, pt. ii, 72; falls in with the Marátha fleet (1774), *id.* 101.
Revenue: land, its history and management under the British and under native rule; all district volumes, *see* under District Name.
Revenue: of Bombay island farmed (1676), XXVI, pt. iii, 271; details of (1737), *id.* 308-313; improvements in (1753-55), *id.* 374; of villages farmed (1747-1772, 1779-1786), *id.* 430.
Revenue Department: of the Bombay Government formed (1778), XXVI, pt. iii, 398.
Revenue Farmers: in Thána district, *deshmukhs* and *deshpándes*, XIII, 553, 554; revenue farming introduced by the Maráthás, *id.* 557-558; farming extended to *tálukás* and *pránts*, *id.* 559; farmers unrestricted, *id.* 559 note 5; could raise the rental, *id.* 560; their settlement with husbandmen, *id.* 560; their tyranny, *id.* 561; stipendiary officers as revenue farmers (1817), *id.* 563; result of farming, *id.* 563 note 5; disorders, *id.* 565; *talátis* appointed, *id.* 566 and note 5, 553 554; Maráthás, *id.* 553-562; British, *id.* 562; British changes (1818), *id.* 566-569; effect, *id.* 568 note 2; village accountants (1824), *id.* 571; (1828), *id.* 575-576.
Reverts: from Christianity in Thána district, XII, 117, 201 note 2, 202-203; *see* also Christian Reverts.
Revolt: of Matia Kanbis and Momnas at Broach, IX, pt. ii, 66, 76; Pársi (648), IX, pt. ii, 185 note 4; at Mándvi (1810), *id.* 198 note 5.
Revti Nakshtra: Star-chamber, IX, pt. i, 352.
Rewá: state in Central India, inscription, I, pt. ii, 277 note 5.
Rewádi: *see* Rewandi.
Rewa Kántha Agency: political division, its boundaries, area, aspect, mountains, rivers,

geology and climate, VI, 1-10; minerals, trees, forests, animals, birds and fish, *id.* 11-18; population, *id.* 19-37; census details, *id.* 19-22; Hindus and Rájpúts, *id.* 22-26; Bhils, Kolis, Christians, communities and movements, *id.* 27-37; agriculture, *id.* 38-40; interest, wages, weights and measures, *id.* 41-45; trade, *id.* 46-58; roads, ferries, post, imports and exports, and manufactures, *id.* 46-58; history, early Hindus up to 1484, Musalmán supremacy (1484-1700), local revival (1700-1730), Marátha supremacy (1730-1820), British supervision (1820-1879), Náikda rising (1838), the mutinies (1857), Náikda rising (1868), *id.* 59-66; land administration, management, staff, assessment, revenue survey, cesses, surveys, boundary disputes, *id.* 67-76; justice, civil and criminal, crime, courts of award, police and jails, *id.* 77-82; revenue and finance, *id.* 83-85; instruction, schools, readers and writers, libraries, *id.* 86-88; health, diseases and dispensaries, *id.* 89-90; states, *id.* 91-156; places of interest, *id.* 157-170; tribute to the Baroda state, VII, 332-337.

Rewandi: village in Ratnágiri district, north of Málvan, I, pt. ii, 347 note 2.

Rewásvámi: Bráhman grantee, I, pt. ii, 191.

Reynal: Abbé, European writer (A. D. 1760), IX, pt. i, 78 note 1.

Rhamnaceæ: species of fibrous and dye-yielding plants, XXV, 231, 242.

Rhan-amb: gum-yielding plant, grows throughout India, XXV, 250.

Rhea: fibrous plant, XXV, 234.

Rheumatism: wind complaint, its cure, IX, pt. i, 358, 365.

Rhita: oil-yielding plant, also used as soap, XXV, 216, 252.

Rhizophoreæ: species of dye-yielding plants, XXV, 244.

Rhynchocarpa fœtida: famine plant, grows in several districts, XXV, 200.

Riayat Khán: minister of Azám Khán, Gujarát viceroy (1635-1642), I, pt. i, 278.

Ribda: place of interest in Káthiáwár, VIII, 641.

Rice: most sacred of grains, offerings of, to gods and goddesses; worship of, IX, pt. i, 391; cultivation of, in Surat, II, 65; in Broach, *id.* 406; in Káira, III, 47; in Panch Maháls, *id.* 233; in Pálanpur, V, 294; in Mahi Kántha, *id.* 370; in Bánsda state, VI, 247 footnote 3; in Rátnágiri, X, 147; varieties of, *id.* 147 note 1; in Sávantvádi, *id.* 424, 425 note 1; in Kolába, XI, 95-96; in Khándesh, XII, 150; in Thána district, XIII, 287, 288, 429, 465, 466 note 1, 501; trade in, XIV, 113; in Kánara district, sprouted rice, rice-planting, varieties of, XV, pt. ii, 16-18, 30; price of, *id.* 36; export of, *id.* 50, 53, 57-58; Portuguese tribute in, *id.* 110, 114, 133; in Násik district, XVI, 99; in Ahmadnagar district, XVII, 267; in Poona district, XVIII, pt. ii, 36-37; in Sátára district, XIX, 162; in Belgaum district, XXI, 248-250, in Dhárwár district, XXII, 275-277; in Bijápur, XXIII, 321; in Kolhápur state, varieties of, XXIV, 165 and note 1; in Bombay island its supply to Bombay from Kánara, Surat, Sind, Mangalore and Bengal (1676-1743), XXVI, pt. ii, 17-67; discussion as how best to provide to the poor (1744), *id.* 31-53; its supply to the troops (1744), *id.* 53-54.

Rice-washing: Bene-Israel marriage ceremony, XVIII, pt. i, 517.

Richikas: Southern Country, Sugriva sends his followers to, I, pt. ii, 135.

Ricinus communis: oil-yielding and medicinal plant, common in India, XXV, 220, 255.

Rifáis: chief *sayad* family in Gujarát, IX, pt. ii, 6 note 1 (3).

Rihal: Persian coin, IX, pt. ii, 233.

Ring-worm: disease in Khándesh, XII, 337.

Riot: Broach (1857), IX, pt. ii, 198 and note 3; survey (1852), in Khándesh, XII, 261; in Surat district, II, 155-157; in Broach, *id.* 476-477; at Cambay (1094-1143), VI, 215; in Thána district, XIII, 456, 523, 524, 525; between the Hindus and Musalmáns at Bhiwndi (1837) in Thána, XIV, 47; at Karanja in Thána, *id.* 193; in Kánara (1830), owing to high taxes or to Bráhman intrigues, XV, pt. ii, 152, 165; in Násik district (1843, 1857), XVI, 199-204.

Rishabhadev: first Jain *tirthankara*, XIV, 319.

Rishi Panchemi: Seer's fifth, Hindu holiday IX, pt. i, 23 note 5, 390; mention of, in the legend of Purna, XIII, 406, 408; *see* also I, pt. ii, 162.

Rising: at Daulatábád, headed by Bahrám Khán aided by a Yádava chief and the *rája* of Báglán, the rebels defeated by the Bahamani king Muhammad Sháh (1366), I, pt. ii, 620; against Báji Ráo II, Rámoshi chiefs headed by a *gosávi* seize Prachitgad (1816), in Khándesh (1817), *id.* 610; of Bhils in Khándesh, Ahmadnagar, and the Nizám's country, quelled (1859), *id.* 632; at Kittur (1824), XXI, 401-404; (1829), *id.* 404-405; in Kolhápur (1844), *id.* 407-408; in Sávantvádi (1844), *id.* 408-409; Narsimh's, in Bijápur (1840) XXIII, 452-453.

Ristikas: supposed to be Maráthás, I, pt. ii, 277.

Rites: heathen, prohibited by the Portuguese (1581), I, pt. ii, 59; field, by husbandmen, IX, pt. i, 157, 405; by early tribes, *id.* 405.

Rivea hypocrateriformis: famine plant, grows in several districts, XXV, 202.

Rivers: abode of Varuna, IX, pt. i, 349; sacred days for bathing in, *id.* 29, 349; offerings to; burning and after-death rites on the banks of, worship of after child-birth, *id.* 349; during flood, by a pregnant woman; sacred rivers—the Ganges, Godavari, Jamna, Narbada, Sarasvati, Tápti; religious importance of, *id.* 350. *See* also all district volumes under District Name.

Roads: all district volumes, see Trade under District Name.

Road-side Trees: in Kánara, XV, pt. i, 31; in Poona district, XVIII, pt. i, 40-41; in Kolhápur, XXIV, 25.

Road-Traffic: in Násik district, XVI, 140.

Robbers : bands of, in Kolába district, put down (1834-1854), XI, 175 ; in Thána (1817), protection of armed messengers to officers against, XIII, 563 and note 4, 569 ; (1825-1844), *id.* 572 note 6 ; at Chandod in Násik district, XVI, 211.

Robber's Caves : at Mahábaleshvar, XIX, 510.

Roberts : General, puts down the rising of the *thákors* in Mahi Kántha (1857), I, pt. i, 439, 443.

Robertson : Captain Henry Dundas, first collector of Poona (1818), XVIII, pt. ii, 304.

Robin : birds in Ratnágiri, district, X, 76.

Rockhill : author of *Life of Buddha*, IX, pt. i, 434 note 1, 437 note 1.

Rock Temples : in Ratnágiri, X, 371 ; Shaivite, in Poona district, XVIII, pt. ii, 214 note 4.

Rodas : Portuguese coins, XIV, 350 note 2.

Rodda : conquered by Vishnuvardhana, I, pt. ii, 497.

Rodentia : order of animals in Ratnágiri district, X, 45.

Roe, Sir Thomas : traveller, on the oppressions of Mughal provincial governors (1615-1618), I, pt. i, 217 note 2 ; his description of Toda country, *id.* 222 note 1 ; passes through Khándesh, his reception at Burhánpur by prince Parviz (1616), I, pt. ii, 625 : *see* also XII, 249.

Roha : sub-division of Kolába district, its boundaries, area, aspect, climate, water, soil, holdings, rental, stock, produce and people, XI, 245-247. *Town, id.* 378-379 ; plundered by Rámoshis, *id.* 158 ; old Rájpuri, *id.* 159, 186, 196, 220.

Rohan : medicinal plant, XXV, 258 ; in Khándesh, XII, 26.

Rohar : place of interest in Cutch, V, 250.

Rohidas : Chamár religious teacher, IX, pt. i, 333.

Rohing : medicinal plant, XXV, 258.

Rohini : daughter of Prajápati, loved by the moon, I, pt. i, 521.

Rohini : wife of Hiranya, the Pallava king, I, pt. ii, 325.

Rohini Nakshatra : Star-chamber, IX, pt. i, 351, 352.

Rohisa : place of interest in Káthiáwár, VIII, 641.

Rohisala : *táluka* in Káthiáwár, VIII, 642-643.

Rojhi : light-house in Káthiáwár, VIII, 19, 25.

Rojmal : cash book, contents of, IX, pt. i, 83.

Roller : the Indian, in Ratnágiri, X, 64.

Rolt : President and Governor of Bombay (1677), XXVI, pt. i, 78.

Roman element : in the architecture of Java and Cambodia, I, pt. i, 496.

Romans : as chief traders in the Persian Gulf (545), IX, pt. ii, 185 note 4 ; in India as traders, XIII, 410, 417.

Rome : appealed to, against the violence of the Inquisitors, I, pt. ii, 61 ; Indian spices in, XIII, 410 note 3.

Ron : sub-division of Dhárwár district, its boundaries, area, aspect, soil, climate, water, stock, crops and people, XXII, 646-647. *Town, id.* 785 ; inscription at, I, pt. ii, 419 note 2, 477, 497, 503, 529, 573, 574, 576.

Ropla : petty division in Sholápur district ; survey, XX, 321-324.

Rori : town in Sind, I, pt. i, 143.

Rosa : oil-yielding plant, XXV, 222.

Rosaceæ : species of oil-yielding plants, XXV, 222.

Rosary : Our Lady of the, Church of, at Thána (1605), XIV, 358.

Rose : Sir Hugh, suppresses the mutiny (1857) in Khándesh, XII, 263.

Rose : Mr., assistant collector (1839), suppresses Koli rising in Poona district, XVIII, pt. ii, 307.

Rose-apple : fruit tree in Poona district, XVIII, pt. i, 46.

Roselle : fibrous plant, XXV, 227.

Rosha : grass oil in Khándesh, XII, 23.

Rosh Hosána : Bene-Israel feast day, XVIII, pt. i, 513.

Roshmal : fort in the Satpuda hills built by Bhausingh of Maltwar, surprised by Deváji son of Jaugar, Bhil Náik of Chikli, I, pt. ii, 633.

Rotation : of crops, in Káthiawár, VIII, 180 ; in Khándesh, XII, 147 ; in Násik district, XVI, 97 ; in Ahmadnagar district, XVII, 259-261 ; in Poona district, XVIII, pt. ii, 30-31 ; in Belgaum district, XXI, 245.

Rothia trifoliata : famine plant, XXV, 197.

Roti : village in Poona district, temple and fair at, XVIII, pt. iii, 439.

Rot-puja : form of worship among the Bráhmans in Khándesh, XII, 51.

Rottlera tinctoria : dye-yielding, medicinal and poisonous plant, XXV, 248, 258, 268.

Rough Tail : snakes in Poona district, XVIII, pt. i, 72-73.

Rowee : fibrous plant, grows in Konkan, XXV, 232.

Royal Asiatic Society : Bombay Branch of the, I, pt. ii, 544.

Royal College : of Sálsette, built at Mandapeshvar, I, pt. ii, 56.

Royal Family Hotel : Poona, XVIII, pt. iii, 392.

Royal Insignia : of the Chalukyas, I, pt. ii, 341 note 1.

Rozabág : burial-place of the Ahmadnagar princes, I, pt. ii, 622.

Rozi : place of interest in Káthiáwár, VIII, 643.

Rubiaceæ : species of famine and dye-yielding plants, XXV, 200, 246.

Rubia cordifolia : dye-yielding plant, XXV, 246.

Rudd : Lieutenant, suppresses Koli rising in Poona district (1839), XVIII, pt. ii, 307.

Ruddavádi : old country, I, pt. ii, 298 note 3, 428 note 1 ; *agrahára* of, *id.* 449 and note 4.

Rudder : Maráthi word for, derived from Arabic *sukkan*, XIII, 722.

Rudra : lord of the Tailangas, slain by Jaitrapála, I, pt. ii, 239, 522.

Rudra : prayer-book, XV, pt. ii, 290-291 and note 1.

Rudra : *see* Shiv.

Rudradáman : fourth Kshatrapa (143-158), coins and inscriptions of, I, pt. i, 6 note 2,

13, 34-36, 80 note 1; his kingdom, *id.* 540. *another account of:* Chashtana's grandson (150), I, pt. ii, 159; chosen as their lord by men of all castes, *id.* 160; drives away the Satavāhanas and gets himself crowned as Mahákshtrapa, *id.* 161, 170; his Junagad inscription, *id.* 157; his minister, *id.* 317; reduces Andhra power, XVI, 183; mention of, in Pándu-Lena caves, *id.* 617, 619, 624; conquers North Konkan, XIII, 417; *see* also X, 192; XII, 240.
Rudradása: grant of, I, pt. ii, 294.
Rudradeva: I, pt. ii, 239; inscriptions of, *id.* 462, 522. *See* Rudra.
Rudráditya: minister of Munja, king of Málwa, I, pt. ii, 213, 432.
Rudragana: Traikutaka king, son of Indravarman, first king after the revival of Traikutaka power, I, pt. ii, 295 note 1; *see* also I, pt. i, 58 and note 1.
Rudramá: female ruler of Tailangana, I, pt. ii, 246, 247.
Rudramahálaya: great shrine of Rudra at Siddhapura, I, pt. i, 161; built by Siddharája, *id.* 179, 180.
Rudramálá: building at Sidhpur in Baroda state, I, pt. i, 172; story of its erection, VII, 616-617.
Rudrasena: seventeenth Kshatrapa (256-272), coins of, I, pt. i, 47; Viradáman's son, drives away the Traikutakas and restores the Western Kshatrapa power, I, pt. ii, 294.
Rudrasena I: Kshatrapa (203-220) coins and inscription of, I, pt. i, 42-43.
Rudrasena III: twenty-fifth Kshatrapa (378-388), coins of, I, pt. i, 51.
Rudrasena IV: twenty-fourth Kshatrapa (348-376), coins of, I, pt. i. 50-51.
Rudrasimha I: seventh Kshatrapa (181-196), coins and inscription of, I, pt. i, 41-42.
Rudrasimha II: twenty-first Kshatrapa (308-311), coins of, I, pt. i, 49.
Rudraswámin: Bráhman grantee, I, pt. ii, 191.
Rudri: prayer to Shiv, IX, pt. i, 531.
Ruháni: divine magic, *see* Magic.
Rui: liquor-yielding, fibrous and sacred plant, XXV, 211, 232, 279, 282, 290, 291; in Poona district, XVIII, pt. i, 51; marriage with, *id.* 560.
Ruins: of Valabhi, I, pt. i, 78, 79. Portuguese, I, pt. ii, 27.
Ruk: a giant bird on the sea, XIII, 433.
Rukdi: village in Kolhápur, temple and *darga* at, XXIV, 317-318.
Rukmanibái Dispensary: in Thána, XIII, 668.
Rukmávati: river in Cutch, V, 127.
Rukn-ud-Din Amir: ruler of Ormuz, I, pt. i, 204.
Ruknuddin-Khur Sháh: ancestor of His Highness the Aghá Khán, IX, pt. ii, 41.
Rulers: Musalmán, of Gujarát, spread Islám in Gujarát by persecution; Mahmud Ghazni or Ghaznavi (1025), IX, pt. ii, 3 note 3, 81; emperor Alá-ud-din (1297), *id.* 82; governor Alifkhán (1297-1317), *id.* 3-5, 125; Muzaffar I (1395), *id.* 3 note 3, 125; Sultán Ahmad (1414-1420), *id.* 5 and note 2, 25 note 1, 125; Mahmúd Begada (1459-1513), *id.* 3 note 3, 5 and note 2, 68, 70, 77, 125; Muzaffar II (1513-1526), *id.* 125; Mahmud II (1536-1547), *id.* 5 and note 2; emperor Jahángir (1618), *id.* 5 and note 3, 125; emperor Aurangzib as viceroy of Gujarát (1648), *id.* 5 and note 3, 125.
Rumadesa, Rumála: I, pt. i, 490; South Panjáb, *id.* 491, 509 note 5.
Rum Distillery: at Bhandup, XIV, 44.
Rumi: I, pt. i, 527. *See* Rahma.
Rumi Khán: officer of Sultán Bahádur of Gujarát (1536), I, pt. i, 349, 350, 351.
Ruminantis: an order of animals in Ratnágiri, X, 46.
Rumis: Mamelukes, Sabayo (1509) hopes to defeat the Portuguese with the help of, XV, pt. ii, 108, 109 and note 1.
Rumla: country of Sind, I, pt. i, 520 and note 1.
Rundha: sub-division in Rewa Kántha, VI, 98.
Rundhvál: caste of Bráhmans in Gujarát, IX, pt. i, 18.
Rupál: state in Mahi Kántha, V, 424.
Rupa Náik: leader of Náikda Bhils; surrender of (1869), I, pt. i, 446.
Rupa Sundari: wife of Jayaśekhara, gives birth to a son in the forest, I, pt. i, 150, 151.
Rupa: silver, quarries of, near Bhinmál, I, pt. i, 455.
Rupen: river in Baroda state, VII, 229, 607-608.
Rupgad: ruined fort in Baroda state, VII, 585.
Rupmati: same as Rupmani, wife of Báz Bahádur of Málwa (1555-1570); her pavilion at Mándu, I, pt. i, 353, 356, 371; captured by Adam Khán Atkah at Sárangpur, commits suicide (1562), *id.* 369, 371.
Rupshi Sha: minister (1750) in Cutch, V, 141, 142.
Ruriddhá: circle of villages, I, pt. ii, 413.
Russel: Mr., English resident at Poona (1811), XVIII, pt. ii, 289.
Rustam Ali Khán: marches on Jodhpur with Shujáat Khán and captures it (1723), I, pt. i, 303; governor of Surat, asks Piláji Gáikwár's aid against Hámid Khán and Kántáji; defeats Hámid Khán at Arás; his severe defeat and death by the Maráthás near Ahmadábád (1723), *id.* 305, 390; *see* also VII, 169-170.
Rustam Meherbán: of Persia, makes copies of the *Vandidád*, IX, pt. ii, 189 note 2.
Rustampura: a Surat city ward, IX, pt. ii, 196 note 1.
Rustampura: a Pársi colony in the Panch Maháls, IX, pt. ii, 200.
Rustamráv: Maráthá leader in the army of Abdul Aziz, I, pt. i, 328; assists Jawán Mard Khán (1744), VII, 176.
Rustom: Persian hero, IX, pt. ii, 136.
Rustom Mánek: of Surat, leading English broker, visits Delhi, IX, pt. ii, 196 and notes 1 and 3, 197 and note 2.
Rustum Zamán: Bijápur officer in charge of Miraj and Panhála, allows Shiváji to plunder up to the gates of Bijápur, I, pt. ii, 652.

Rutaceæ : species of oil-yielding plants, XXV, 222.
Ruticillinæ : family of birds in Ratnágiri, X, 77.

S

Sabæns : settled (B.C. 200), at Sofále in Thána, XIV, 313; *see* also I, pt. i, 535.
Sabalaessa : mouth of the Indus, I, pt. i, 538.
Sábaliá : *see* Dúdwalá.
Sabana : town mentioned by Ptolemy, I, pt. i, 538.
Sabaras : aboriginal tribe on the banks of the Tápti and Narmadá, I, pt. ii, 134, 138 and note 3.
Sábar Kántha : sub-division of Mahi Kántha, V, 355.
Sábarmati : river in Gujarát, VII, 22; VI, 181; III, 4; IV, 5; V, 356; *see* also I, pt. ii, 383; I, pt. i, 159, 198, 206; floods of (1683, 1739), *id.* 287, 322, 511, 517; bridge on the, IV, 83.
Sabayo : title of Yusuf Ádil Sháh (1489-1510), XV, pt. ii, 105, 254; title of the Bijápur kings, origin of the word, XXIII, 404 and note 1.
Sabayo : Shábaz, Portuguese sub-division (1500-1670), XIII, 456.
Sabdaliya : or Chandal, women mentioned by Al Idris, I, pt. i, 531.
Sabdánuśasana : grammatical work of Hemachandra, I, pt. i, 193.
Sábdárnava Chandriká : Somadeva's commentary on Pujyapáda's Sanskrit grammar, I, pt. ii, 256, 549.
Sabian : religion of early Arabs, IX, pt. ii, 1 note 1.
Sábiins : *see* Seveners.
Sabiria : upper Sind, I, pt. i, 537. *See* Abiria.
Saccharum : *mimja*, fibrous plant, XXV, 238; *officinale*, liquor-yielding plant, *id.* 212; *officinarum*, food and fodder plant, *id.* 185, 277; *spontaneum*, fibrous plant, *id.* 237.
Saccopetalum tomentosum : fodder plant, XXV, 277.
Sachai : family goddess of Visas, IX, pt. i, 98.
Sachin : state in Surat district, its area, climate, production, population, dwellings, villages, crops, wages and prices, roads, ferries, manufactures, history, land administration, justice, registration fees, police, revenue and finance, duties, cesses, instruction and health, VI, 258-264; IX, pt. ii, 12; village, VI, 265.
Sachin Nawábs : origin of, XI, 448.
Sáchora : a Bráhman sub-division in Cutch, V, 46; in Gujarát, IX, pt. i, p. xi, note 3, 18.
Sacrifice : holding of, by Krishna at Dwárka, by Rám at Patarváda, IX, pt. i, 4; by king Mulraj, *id.* 7 and note 1; by Nal Rája at Borsad, *id.* 8 note 1; *Játars* among Bhils, *id.* 306-307; Vedic, XVIII, pt. ii, 212; of a buffalo at Dasara in Poona district, XVIII, pt. i, 61; among Musalmáns, IX, pt. ii, 158.
Sadalgi : village in Belgaum district, sugar-making at, XXI, 599-600.
Sádar : a caste of husbandmen in Dhárwár district, XXII, 145; in Kánara district, XV, pt. i, 239, 240.
Sadárat : Mughal department of justice, I, pt. i, 213.
Sadáshiv : Poona ward, details of, XVIII, pt. iii, 274, 280-281.
Sadáshiv : other name of Shiv, IX, pt. i, 541.
Sadáshiv Bháu, Sadáshivráv : Chimnáji Apa's son and cousin to Báláji Bájiráv Peshwa (1749-1761); assists Báláji Peshwa in his scheme of usurping the sole power; quarrels with Báláji; is reconciled and becomes the Peshwa's minister; reforms the civil administration; character; enmity with Gopikábái, Báláji's wife; quarrels with Raghunáthráv; attempts on his life, XVIII, pt. ii, 245-249; XVIII, pt. iii, 338; leads an expedition into the Bombay Karnátak (1746), I, pt. ii, 656; XIX, 287; suppresses the revolt of Yamaji Shivdev at Sángola, *id.* 292; I, pt. ii, 601; resolves to take Goa (1756), *id.* 88; falls in the battle of Pánipat (1761), *id.* 602.
Sadáshiv Bhau Mánkeshvar : *see* Sadásiv Mankeshvar.
Sadáshiv Chimnáji : imposter, marches through the Konkan, is defeated, taken prisoner and put to death (1776), I, pt. ii, 101-102.
Sadáshiv Chimnáji Bhán : *see* Sadáshiv Bhán.
Sadáshivdev Ráy : eleventh Vijayanagar king (1542-1573), XV, pt. ii, 96 note 4, 115-116, 258, 263, 265, 299.
Sadáshivgad : hill fort in Sátára district, description, temple and fair at, XIX, 511, 8, 11; built by Shiváji (1676), I, pt. ii, 1, 595; surrendered to the British (1818), XIX, 308.
Sadáshivgad : port in Kánara district, its description, history, fort and trade (1874-1882), XV, pt. ii, 338-340, 65-67; *id.* pt. i, 2, 3, 5; the fort said to have been built by Shiváji, *id.* pt. ii, 133 note 1; head-quarters of the Sonda chief (1715), *id.* 134; Portuguese attempt on (1747), *id.* 136 and note 7; captured (1752) by them, *id.* 137; taken (1763) by Hyder's general, *id.* 140; taken by the English, taken back by Tipu (1784), *id.* 143; origin of the name, *id.* 279.
Sadáshiv Keshav : *sarsubhedár* of the Konkan, I, pt. ii, 109; Marátha *mámlatdár*, his survey (1788-89) in Thána district, XIII, 558, 559; districts surveyed, *id.* 559 note 3; his rates changed, *id.* 560, 556 note 2.
Sadáshiv Khanderáv : Bhor *kárbhári* (1857), restored to office, XIX, 319.
Sadáshiv Mankeshvar : Bájirav II's agent (1808), employed in conducting affairs with the Resident, XVIII, pt. ii, 288; quarrels with Khusruji (1813), *id.* 291; chief adviser, *id.* 295; I, pt. ii, 609.
Sadáshiv Náik : founder (1499) of Bednur family, XV, pt. ii, 101.
Sadáshiv Náik : fifth Sonda chief (1674-1697), XV, pt. ii, 120 note 3, 130, 132, 339, 342, 348.
Sadáshiv Raghunáth : Marátha *mámlatdár*, his survey (1793-94) in Thána district, XIII, 558.

Sadáshiv Ramchandra: Peshwa's general, besieges and takes the town of Ahmadábád from Momin Khán (1758); helps the *Ráv* of Cutch, I, pt. i, 340, 341, 342; besieges Bálásinor (1758) and levies tribute, *id.* 343, 398; defeats the chief of Dhrángadhra at Halvád and captures him, *id.* 344; appointed viceroy of Ahmadábád by the Peshwa (1760), *id.* 344.

Sadáshivráv: *see* Sadáshiv Bháu.

Sadávarts: alms-houses, money of members of merchant guilds spent on, IV, 112.

Saddleback Hill: *see* Makrandgad.

Saddo: *sheikh*, name of a vow-receiving genius, origin of, IX, pt. ii, 130 and note 1.

Sadhara Jesangh: work of Ráo Sáheb Mahipatrám Ruprám, I, pt. i, 180 note 2.

Sadharo Jesingh: another name of Siddharája, I, pt. i, 173.

Sadhus: or *friars* in Gujarát, Bijpanthi, IX, pt. i, 544; Kabirpanthi, *id.* 539; 540, Madhavgars, *id.* 546; Parnamis, *id.* 545; Rámánandis, *id.* 534; Ramanujs, *id.* 534; Ramsnehi, *id.* 535; Sváminaráyans, *id.* 538; ascetics, Dádupanthi, *id.* 548; Lakshmangarpanthi, *id.* 548; Kuberpanthi, *id.* 548; Shaiv, *id.* 542; Shrávak, *id.* 106. *See* Ascetics.

Sádhvis: nuns, Shrávak ascetics, IX, pt. i, 108.

Sadi: village in Baroda state, VII, 544.

Sadia: class of Musalmán carriers in Cambay, VI, 185.

Sádik: *pir*, son of Pir Dádu, IX, pt. ii, 41.

Sadinoi: tribe mentioned by Ptolemy, I, pt. i, 540, 542.

Sadi Sambati: bandits in Kánara district, (1801), XV, pt. ii, 150-151.

Sadola: tree in Khándesh district, XII, 27.

Sadr: Mughal judge, I, pt. i, 213.

Sádra: town in Mahi Kántha, V, 439; schools, and hospitals at, VII, 487, 508; (Sháhdaráh), military post of the Mughals (1674), I, pt. i, 285, 433.

Sadra: sacred shirt of the Pársis, IX, pt. ii, 201, 227; clothing the child with, *id.* 231. *See* Navzot.

Sadr-ud-din: *pir*, third Ismáilia missionary, adopts Hindu names, IX, pt. ii, 38 note 7; said to have converted Brahma-kshatris, *id.* 39; founds the first *khánah* or Khojah religious lodge; tests the faith of his followers; starts the first tythe-gathering wallet; engrafts incarnations on the Ismáilia faith to present it in an inviting form to Hindus; introduces himself as incarnation of Brahma, *id.* 40; gives his name to the fourth *bhakta*; adopts the name of Satpanth for his new faith, *id.* 48.

Sadrye: pass in Thána district, XIII, 320.

Saela: state in Káthiáwár, VIII, 643-645; IX, pt. i, 127; fort, supposed to be built by Sidharája, I, pt. i, 180 note 2.

Saer: gum-yielding plant, XXV, 250.

Sáfán: Táfán, principality next to Konkan of the Arab travellers, I, pt. i, 527.

Safand: part of the *Zend Avesta*, IX, pt. ii, 211 note 2 (13).

Safar: second month of the Musalmán year, holidays in, IX, pt. ii, 139-140.

Safdar Jang: son of Kamál Khán, the protector of the Bijápur king Yusuf Ádil Khán, assassinated (1510), I, pt. ii, 641.

Safdar Khán, Safdar Muhammad Khán: successor of Teghbeg Khán (1746), governor of Surat, I, pt. i, 330; expelled by Sayad Achchan, *id.* 331; retires to Sind, *id.* 332; brought back to Surat by the Dutch and other merchants, *id.* 333; VII, 177-178.

Safed Chandan: oil-yielding plant, XXV, 224.

Safed Ran-phal: food plant, XXV, 178.

Safflower: tillage of, in Poona district, XVIII, pt. ii, 46; in Násik district, XVI, 172-175; in Kaira, III, 52; in Sátára district, XIX, 165; in Khándesh district, XII, 153, 164.

Safran: food plant, XXV, 177.

Sagala-Vasahika: temple at Cambay, I, pt. i, 190.

Sagapa: mouth of the Indus, I, pt. i, 538.

Sagar: caste of professional husbandmen in Gujarát, claim Rájpút descent, their surnames; saints among, their faith in early beliefs, customs, IX, pt. i, 174-175.

Sagara: Puranic hero, I, pt. ii, 149; king, *id.* 284 note 4; lineage, *id.* 475.

Sagarababrasi: wife of Kammara the Sinda prince of Bágadage, I, pt. ii, 576.

Sagararasa: son of Kalachuri king Sankama, I, pt. ii, 468.

Sagarchakravarti: *lit.* ruler of the sea, another word for Gavandi, XXII, 146.

Ságardvipi: a Bráhman sub-division in Khándesh district, XII, 53.

Ságargad: fort in Kolába district, built by Kánhoji Ángria, I, pt. ii, 96; XI, 6, 146, 151, 155, 156; description, view, remains, walks, *id.* 254, 379-383.

Sagar-Gavandi: a caste of masons in Sholápur district, XX, 97-101.

Sagargota: oil-yielding and medicinal plant, XXV, 217, 218, 258.

Ságbára: state in Rewa Kántha, VI, 98; mountain range, *id.* 3; forest tract, I, pt. i, 388.

Ságtála: sub-division in Rewa Kántha, VI, 117.

Sah: rulers in Cutch (78 A. D.), XII, 239 and note 4, 240 note 1.

Sahadeva: the youngest of the Pándu princes, visits Dakshinápatha in his career of conquest, XV, pt. ii, 77; I, pt. ii, 133; subdues the Pándyas and other tribes and visits Kishkindha, *id.* 142.

Sahadev Joshi: a caste of astrologers, in Ahmadnagar district, XVII, 186-187; in Poona district, XVIII, pt. i, 461-463.

Sahajánand Svámi: founder of Sváminaráyan sect, his life and works, IX, pt. i, 537.

Sahajiga: father of Mulaka, mentioned in the inscription at Mangrol, I, pt. i, 176.

Sahajigeśvara: temple at Prabhása, I, pt. i, 176.

Sahamyapura: village on the bank of the Vihige, I, pt. ii, 372.

Sahárais: of Aror in the north of Sind, rule over south Panjáb and North Sind I, pt. i, 496; Buddhists, overthrow of, by usurping Brahmanist Chách (642), *id.* 497-498.

Saháran : Tánk ancestor of the Gujarát sultáns, converted to Islám by Firuz Tughlak, IX, pt. ii, 70.
Sahas : Kshatrap kings of Saurashtra (140-380 A. D.), conquer Cutch, V, 130.
Sáhasánka ; another name of the Ráshtrakúta king Govinda, IV, I, pt. ii 205, 416.
Sahasra Arjuna : ancestor of the Central India Kalachuris, I, pt. ii, 293 ; lineage, *id.* 410.
Sahásrabáhu Arjuna : *see* Sahasra Arjuna.
Sahasralinga : lake at Pátan, built by Siddharája, I, pt. i, 177, 179 ; VII, 600.
Sáhib Khán : Ahmadnagar minister (1576), enters into a plot against Changiz Khán, his crimes, put to death, XVII, 372-373.
Sáhifat-us-Salát : prayer book of the Dáudi Bohorás, IX, pt. ii, 30 note 1.
Sahnak : also called Bibí-kí-sahnak and Kandúri, fulfilment of vow by women to the Lady Fátimah, description of, IX, pt. ii, 151-152.
Sáhu : Turk ancestor of the Gujarát sultáns, converted to Islám by Firuj Tughlak, IX, pt. ii, 70.
Sahya : the Sahyádris, I, pt. ii, 149, 537.
Sahyádri Khand : a Sanskrit work, date of, I, pt. ii. 27 ; X, 114 note 2, 115, 372 ; XVIII, pt. i, 99-101, 171.
Sahyádris : range of hills, I, pt. ii, 133, 136 ; inscriptions in the cave temples on, *id.* 147 ; chain on the north-east of Násik, *id.* 355 ; mountains, *id.* 537 ; in Ratnágiri district, X, 3 ; geological formation of, *id.* 16 ; in Khándesh district, XII, 5 ; in Thána district, XIII, 4-6 ; in Kánara district, XV, pt. i, 1 ; in Násik district, XVI, 2 ; in Ahmadnagar district, XVII, 3-6 ; in Poona district, XVIII, pt. i, 3-4 ; in Sátára district, XIX, 3.
Sai : Shahid, IX, pt. i, 360.
Sajad : endemic form of small-pox, IX, pt. i, 368.
Saiad-kaka : small-pox uncle, Hindu god, IX, pt. i, 368 ; his other names Balio or Baliákáka, his dwelling place, his nature, *id.* 369, 370. *See* Small-pox.
Saiads : rulers at Delhi in the name of Farukhshir, I, pt. ii, 626.
Saib : a caste of courtezans in Kánara district, XV, pt. i, 325, 326.
Saif-Ain-un-Mulk : Bijápur general (1551), suspected of treachery, tries to become independent, XIX, 228-229 ; XX, 283.
Saikalgar : a caste of Musalmán blacksmiths in Násik district, XVI, 81 ; in Khándesh, XII, 126 ; in Bijápur, XXIII, 301 ; in Ahmadnagar district, XVII, 234 ; in Dhárwár district, XXII, 244 ; in Poona district, XVIII, pt. i, 496 ; in Sholápur district, XX, 210 ; in Sátára district, XIX, 146 ; in Belgaum district, XXI, 220-221.
Sailáhára : *See* Siláhára.
Sailing Vessels : in Kánara district, canoes, *machvas, padávs, phatemaris*, XV, pt. ii, 60-65.
Sailors : in Gujarát, *Hindu* Khárvas, IX, pt. I, 519, 521 ; Kolis, *id.* 519, 521, 524 ; Máchhia, *id.* 520 ; Mahomedan, Bhadelas, *id.* 519 ; Kábavaliyas, *id.* 522 ; Miánás, *id.* 519 ; Vaghers, *id.* 519, 523 ; form the most trusted portion of every Indian crew, *id.* 241 note 3 ; Gujar, *id.* 499 ; on the Thána coast at the time of Siláháras (810-1260), XIII, 433 ; Indian, their skill (1300-1500), *id.* 447 ; (1500-1670), *id.* 471 ; (1800-1882), *id.* 521 ; in Káthiáwár, VIII, 153 ; Abyssinian and Arab, I, pt. ii, 62.
Saimhalaka : tribal name mentioned in the Allahábád pillar inscription, I, pt. i, 64 and note 5.
Saimur : identified with Chembur, XIV, 52 ; with Cheul, *id.* 321 ; XIII, 424, 429 ; XI, 271 and note 1, 272 note 5 ; southern boundary of Balhára kingdom, I, pt. ii, 388 ; IX, pt. ii, 2 note 1 ; I, pt. i, 507, 508, 509, 510, 513, 516, 520, 523, 528, 529.
Saiu : Hajam saint of Márwár, IX, pt. i, 233.
Saindhava : king, destroyed by the army of the Tájikas, I, pt. ii, 187, 375 and note 4.
Saints : living and dead, appeals of women to, for children, IX, pt. ii, 147 ; belief in, *id.* 17, 22 ; vows made to, *id.* 128 ; worship of, *id.* 12 ; Abyssinian, *id.* 12 ; of Ahmadábád, *id.* 76 ; of Ajmer, *id.* 6 note 1 (4), 22 ; of Baghdád, *id.* 56 ; of Cambay, *id.* 26 note 1 ; of Gilan, *id.* 6 note 1 (2) ; of Gotarka, *id.* 17 ; Hindu-Musalmán, of Northern India, *id.* 17 ; Madársháh, *id.* 82 ; Músa, *id.* 23 ; Nakshband, *id.* 20 ; of Pirána, *id.* 66, 67, 69, 74, 125 ; of Rafáis, *id.* 6 note (3) ; of Syria, *id.* 22 ; tombs of Musalmán, famous tombs of Bává Ghor, Dariyásha, worship of, IX, pt. i, 360-361 ; of Bijpanthi sect, *id.* 545. *See* Tomb-worship.
Saint-wheel : worship of, among Shravaks, IX, pt. i. 115. *See* Siddhachakra Puja.
Śaiva Faith ; I, pt. ii, 435, 442 ; revival of, under the Kálachurya Bijala, *id.* 477, 481, 482, 484 ; site called Muktitirtha, *id.* 580.
Sáiván : name for Bassein district under the Portuguese, XIII 455, 456, 457 ; Portuguese garrison (1727) at, *id.* 490.
Saivas : sect of, I, pt. ii, 464 ; ordinary, distinguished from Lingáyats, *id.* 477, 478.
Saivism : revival of, I, pt. ii. 406 note 5 ; religion of the Valabhi kings, I, pt. i, 83.
Saiyngava : *rishi* ; his excommunication ; Rayakváls claim descent from, IX, pt. i, 17.
Sájgaon : village in Khándesh, temple at, XII, 469.
Sájgaon : village in Thána district, temple and fair at, XIV, 301.
Sajiri : sacred plant, XXV, 291.
Sajjana : Siddharája's viceroy in Suráshtra, builds a temple at Girnár, his inscription, I, pt. i, 176-177.
Sajjana : potter, hides Kumárapála, I, pt. ii, 182 ; is rewarded by Kumárapála with seven hundred villages, *id.* 184.
Sajjangad : *see* Parli.
Sajod : place of early sanctity in Broach district ; Sajodra Bráhmans take name from, IX, pt. i, 1, 18.
Sajodrá : caste of Bráhmans and cultivators in Gujarát ; origin of, IX, pt. i, 1, 18, 152.
Saka : era (A. D. 78), founded by Sáliváhana, I, pt. ii, 157, 158, 169, 294, 335 and note 2, 337 and note 3 ; effaced by Western Chalukya king Vikramaditya VI, *id.* 447, 566 ; I, pt. i, 29.

Sakæa : Pausanias' (170) name for Cochin China, I, pt. i, 499.
Sakakala : Sáka era, I, pt. ii, 169.
Sákambhari : the Sámbhar lake in Rájpútána, goddess at, I, pt. i, 158 and note 1.
Sakanripakála : era of the Sáka king, I, pt. ii, 169.
Sákapadra : probably Sákin ear Tulsi, I, pt. ii, 11.
Sákaria : *táluka* in Káthiáwár, VIII, 645.
Sákarkolu : pumpkin, seeds of, worship of, in Gujarát, IX, pt. i, 386.
Sákár Páthar : plateau in Poona district, XVIII, pt. i, 5 ; health resort, XVIII, pt. iii, 439.
Sakas : or Skythians, conquerors in Western India, IX, pt. i, 433 ; two hordes of, Su Sakás and Yuechis or Kusháns ; their entrance into India, *id.* 455, 461 ; were same as Kusháns, *id.* 456 note 3 ; converted to Buddhism, *id.* 433 ; played leading part in first spread of Buddhism, were great friends of Gautama Buddha, *id.* 445 and note 5 ; their overthrow, *id.* 448 ; defeated by Guptas, *id.* 443 note 1 ; beaten by Gautamiputra, by king Sagara, *id.* 448, 453 note 4, 439, 441, 443 note 1, 446, 449, 450, 461 and note 2 ; I, pt. ii, 149 ; masters of Maháráshtra, *id.* 155 ; inroads of the, *id.* 158 ; foreign tribe, *id.* 167, 168, 170, 173, 317 and note 3 ; I, pt. ii, 155, 158 and note 1 ; I, pt. i, 22, 67 note 2, 499.
Sakasaka : king Sakasena, I, pt. ii, 167.
Sakasena : king, I, pt. ii, 153, 154, 156 ; wrongly identified with Siva S'ri, *id.* 167.
Sakastene : land of the Sakas, I, pt. i, 142 note 5.
Sakhaji Angria : (1731-1733) succeeds Kánhoji as chief of Kolába, attacks Janjira (1731), defeats Ghazi Khán and destroys Rájkot; sues for peace (1733), XI, 149, 150.
Sákhar : stream in Kolába district, XI, 8 ; defeat of Peshwa at, 155.
Sakhárám Bápu : Peshwá's minister, I, pt. ii, 603 ; VII, 191 ; Poona minister (1761-1778), appointed chief minister by Raghunáthráv, XVIII, pt. ii, 251 ; removed from the office, *id.* 254 ; leading member of the ministry, his influence, *id.* 257-258 ; refuses to record his opinion in writing to restore Raghunáthráv ; kept under restraint, *id.* 262-264, 263 note 3.
Sakhárám Divánji : nephew of Rávji Appáji, receives a double share from Gáikwár, VII, 208 ; is persuaded to help the English ; Sitárám, the Baroda minister, tool in the hands of, *id.* 212 ; British advances to pay the mutinous *sibandi* of, *id.* 215.
Sakhárám Ghátge Shirzi Ráo : Poona noble, (1796), joins Sindia's army, wins over Sindia to Nána's side, and at Sindia's orders arrests Baloba Tátya, I, pt. ii, 606 ; levies money from the people of Poona ; illtreats Mahádaji Sindia's widows ; his arrest by the Sindia, *id.* 607 ; *another account of* : Bájiráo under the charge of, XVIII, pt. ii, 273 ; made Sindia's minister, attacks Muzaffar, arrested, *id.* 275-277 ; destroys Báloba, plunders Dakhan, summoned to Málwa, *id.* 280-281. *See* also XXIV, 234 and note 1 ; XVIII, pt. iii, 412-413.
Sakhárám Hari : *see* Sakhárám Bápu.
Sakhupathár : *see* Sákar Pathár.
Sakínah : Lady, daughter of Husain, bride-elect of Kásim, IX, pt. ii, 138.
Saklapuri : a Bráhman sub-division in Kánara district, XV, pt. i, 134-135.
Sakran-mon : sweet-curd ceremony, IX, pt. i, 58.
Sáksa : fortress, perhaps Sankshi, taken by the Portuguese (1540), I, pt. ii, 48.
Sakti : the creative energy, mother of all creation ; called *Máyá* or *Mahámáyá prakriti*, her worship under different names in Gujarát, IX, pt. i, p. xxxv, 530, 545.
Saktivarman : Chálukya-Chandra, restores the Eastern Chálukya sovereignty (1003), I, pt. ii, 308 note 5, 347 note 2.
Sakunika Vihara : at Broach (1143 A. D.), I, pt. i, 186.
Sakurbái : dispensary at Chinchni in Thána, XIII, 667.
Sakvárbái : widow of Sháhu, applies to Dámáji Gáikwár and Rághoji Bhonslé against the Peshwa (1748), I, pt. i, 396 ; declares Rám Rája an impostor, XIX, 288-290 ; declares for Sambháji of Kolhápur ; forced by the Peshwa Báláji to perform the rite of *sati*, I, pt. ii, 600.
Sakyas : un-Indian Buddhist converts, claim Buddha's relics, IX, pt. i, 446 note 1.
Sal : dye-yielding plant, XXV, 248.
Sala : mythical ancestor of the Hoysálas, propitiates the goddess Padmávati, I, pt. ii, 490, 491, 492.
Salábat Jang : Nizám, succeeds Nizám-ul-Mulk (1748), is attacked by the Peshwa (1751), confirms the cession of territory made to the Maráthás by his brother Gázi-ud-din (1752), I, pt. ii, 627 ; combines with the Peshwa against the *nawáb* of Sávanur (1756), *id.* 657, 666. *See* Nizám.
Salábat Khán : Ahmadnagar minister (1519-1589), sends an army to invade Bijápur dominions, attempt for his displacement, released, defeated at Paithan, allowed to retire, XVII, 373-378 ; his tomb at Ahmadnagar, *id.* 705-706 ; *see* also I, pt. ii, 623.
Salábat Khán : claimant (1811) to the chiefship of Junágad, I, pt. i, 425.
Salai : *Boswellia thurifera*, frankincense in Poona district, XVIII, pt. i, 52 ; in Khándesh, XII, 27.
Salami : ancient tenure in Baroda, VII, 340.
Sálana : identified with Sáliváhana by Hemachandra, I, pt. ii, 169.
Salangoi : Sálankáyana, tribe probably on the western coast, mentioned by Stephanos (450), I, pt. i, 546.
Salaries : increase of, to civil and military officers (1768) in Bombay, XXVI, pt. iii, 388-89 ; inadequacy of, to writers, petition for increase of (1768), *id.* 389-90 ; revision of (1789), *id.* 402-404.
Salaries and allowances : to the governor and other officials in Bombay (1711-1727), XXVI, pt. iii, 284-85.
Salat : caste of stone-workers, in Gujarát, three classes of : Somparás, Kumbhárs, Ta-

labdakolis; Somparás said to be originally Bráhmans, IX, pt. i, 195-196; Rájpút origin of Kumbhár Salats; early beliefs, religious sects, *id.* 196; customs, *id.* 197; a class of masons in Cutch, V, 73; in Káthiáwár, VIII, 151; converts from the Hindu caste of the same name, IX, pt. ii, 79.

Salaya: port in Káthiáwár, trade of, VIII, 27, 250, 645.

Sálbái, Salbye: treaty of, between the English and the Peshwa (1782), I, pt. ii, 605, 628, 660; XIII, 508, 509; XIV, 35, 193; XVIII, pt. ii, 267; I, pt. i, 410; VI, 230.

Saldanha: Antonio de, Portuguese admiral, destroys (1532) Thána coast, XIII, 451.

Saldanha: Manuel de, attacks (1675) Bombay, XIII, 478.

Sale: Mr., his *Preliminary Discourse to the Kuraán*, IX, pt. ii, 1 note 1.

Sáler: hill fort between Baroda territory and Násik district, its original name, fair at, captured by Moro Trimal (1672), VII, 7, 584-586; I, pt. i, 387; I, pt. ii, 625, 626; XVI, 441, 442 note 3, 458, 459.

Sálgirah: child's first birth-day among Musalmáns, IX, pt. ii, 159 and note 4.

Sálgogah: *zillah* in Sorath, I, pt. i, 208 and note 3.

Sálher: *see* Saler.

Sáli: a caste of weavers, in Ratnágiri district, X, 125; in Thána district, XIII, 134; in Násik district, XVI, 53; in Ahmadnagar district, XVII, 130-131; in Sátára district, XIX, 93; in Sholápur district, XX, 137; in Belgaum district, XXI, 145-147; in Dhárwár district, XXII, 172-178; in Bijápur district, XXIII, 277-279; in Kolhápur state, XXIV, 95; in Poona district, XVIII, pt. i, 361-365; in Kolába district, XI, 65, 412; in Khándesh district, XII, 75, 229, 234.

Saliks; name for Ceylon, known to Ptolemy, I, pt. i, 543.

Salim-i-chisti: *sheikh*, tomb of, at Fatehpur Sikhri, IX, pt. ii, 147.

Salim Sháh: (1545-1553), Sher Sháh Sur's successor, I, pt. i, 369.

Salix tetrasperma: fodder plant, XXV, 278.

Sáliváhana: amorous verses attributed to, I, pt. ii, 144; same as Sátaváhana, defeats the king of Ujjayini, *id.* 161; Prákrit corruption of Sátaváhana, legends about his era, his birth, defeats Vikramáditya, his identification with Pulumáyi, his ignorance of phonetic rules of Sanskrit, *id.* 169-170, 175, 587.

Saliva Tikkama: Devagiri Yádav general (1277), XV, pt. ii, 91.

Sálivoge: village on the north-east of Banavási, I, pt. ii, 309, 369.

Saliyaputta: province, bordering on Aśoka's kingdom, I, pt. ii, 146.

"Salkh": scarification, performance of, in Arabia, IX, pt. ii, 160 note 3 continued on page 161.

Salotgi: village in Bijápur district, temple at, legend of, XXIII, 674-675; inscriptions at, I, pt. ii, 206, 418, 420, 427 note 3, 536.

Sálsette: island, in Thána district, XIII, 2; sub-division, its boundaries, area, aspect, climate, water, soil, holdings, rental, stock, crops, people, *id.* 2, 685-689; rent system, *id.* 547; leasehold villages (1882), *id.* 545-550; Portuguese, *id.* 552; Maráthás, *id.* 555 note 3; *havaldárs* (1741), *id.* 556; rates, *id.* 557; condition (1774), *id.* 558, 562; British management (1774-1819), *id.* 562-563; residents and factors (1774), *id.* 562; revenue system (1798), *id.* 562; changes (1801-1811), *id.* 562; condition (1774-1819), *id.* 562, 563; compared with other parts, *id.* 566; improvements in Pavai, Virár and Goregaon (1833), *id.* 578 note 1; condition (1836), *id.* 584; survey assessment (1861), *id.* 608-609; included in Kápardikadvipa, I, pt. ii, 567; ruled over by the North Konkan Siláháras, *id.* 544; by Achyutanáyaka, officer of Rámachandra of Devgiri, *id.* 529; cave temples, *id.* 9, 404-541; stronghold of Buddhism, *id.* 12; district, seized by Bhim Rája, *id.* 27: its occupation and possession by Gujarát, *id.* 29; its independence of Gujarát, *id.* 37; its possession by the Portuguese, *id.* 46; supports the Goa and Bassein establishments; its condition and revenue system under the Portuguese, *id.* 53; Christian descendants of Parbhus in, *id.* 56; dispute about its cession, *id.* 63; its intended conquest by the English, *id.* 64; Portuguese churches at, *id.* 65; its division into seven districts, *id.* 100; its condition (1818), *id.* 122-3; proposal to establish a Chinese colony in, *id.* 123; *khots*, offer of permanent settlement (1801), customs duties abolished (1803) and administration of justice in, *id.* 124; invasion of, by the Maráthás (1737), XIV, 16; cession of, refused (1760), to the English, XVIII, pt. ii, 251; Portuguese attempt to retake (1774), XXVI, pt. i, 375; expedition against and capture of, by the Company (1774), *id.* 377-391; its settlement (1774), *id.* 397-400.

Salshi: district in South Ratnágiri, I, pt. ii, 68; divided among the Pants of Bávda, the Sávants and the Angriás, *id.* 79.

Salt: *mithu* or *sabras*, meaning of; beliefs about; gift of, by the dying; use of, in spirit-scaring rites, IX, pt. i, 349; manufacture of, in Ahmadábád district, IV, 116-124; in Cutch, V, 21; in Káthiáwár, VIII, 92-93, 262; in Ratnágiri, X, 190; receipts and expenditure of, *id.* 276; pans, *id.* 348; in Sávantvádi, *id.* 438, 455; manufacture of, in Kolába district, XI, 134, 135, 226; in Janjira, *id.* 431; in Khándesh, XII, 237, 322; in Sátára district, XIX, 30-31; in Kánara district, XV, pt. ii, 58; receipts and charges, *id.* 206; price, trade in, *id.* 72-74.

Saltangar, Saltankar: a caste of Musalmán tanners, in Ahmadnagar district, XVII, 132-133; in Solápur district, XX, 136, 210; in Poona district, XVIII, pt. i, 505; 366-367.

Salter: hill, in Poona district, XVIII, pt. i, 4.

Salt industry: in Bombay (1680-1819), XXVI, pt. ii, 164-175; farmed (1751), *id.* 170.

Salt-lands : in Kolaba district, XI, 90-91.
Salt-making : works, in Thána district, XIII, 363-365 ; *shilotris*, *id.* 365 ; workers, *id.* 365-366 ; process, *id.* 366-369 ; trade, *id* 369-372 ; excise, *id.* 372-374 ; smuggling, *id.* 374-376 ; changes, *id.* 376, 377 ; results, *id.* 378 ; receipts, *id.* 651, 317, 429.
Salt Marsh Trees : in Kolába district, used as fuel, XI, 26.
Saltpetre : in Ahmadábád district, IV, 125 ; making of, in Dhárwár district, XXII, 388 ; in Bijápur district, XXIII, 61 ; making of, *id.* 376-377 ; in Ahmadnagar district, XVII, 350 ; in Bombay island for gunpowder from Rájápur (1676), XXVI, pt. iii, 186 ; house for (1762-64), *id.* 190-191.
Salt-tasting : also called *botan* and *namak chashi*, rites relating to, IX, pt. ii, 159.
Salt-works : in Cambay, VI, 208.
Sálukika : family mentioned in a grant from Khándesh district, I, pt. ii, 399.
Salutes : to the governor and other officers (1784) in Bombay, XXVI, pt. iii, 183-184.
Saluvankuppam : village, I, pt. ii, 331.
Sálnva-Tikkamadeva : Yádava king Rámchandra's commander (1277-1280), I, pt. ii, 529, 530.
Salva : mythic king of Mrittikávati, attacks and plunders Dwárka, I, pt. i, 10 and note 1.
Salva, Salvan : hill between Ratnágiri district and Kolhápur ; geological formation of, X, 14 ; XXIV, 8.
Salvas : tribe mentioned by Ptolemy, I, pt. i, 534 ; by Katyáyana, I, pt. ii, 139.
Salvation : Onr Lady of, Church at Karanja, XIV, 194.
Sálveya : descendant of Sálva, form mentioned by Katyáyana, I, pt. ii, 139.
Sálvi : caste of handloom weavers in Gujarát, claims Kanbi stock, IX, pt. i, 197.
Sama : *see* Samma.
Sama : a caste of Hindu converts in Gujarát, origin of, probably a Turk tribe, IX, pt. ii, 69.
Sama : a food plant, XXV, 184.
Sámádaskat : acknowledgment book, contents of, IX, pt. i, 83. *See* Books (Account).
Samádhi : mental absorption, IX, pt. i, 360 ; practised by Núr Satágur, IX, pt. ii, 38.
Samadhiala : *táluka* in Káthiáwár, VIII, 646-647.
Samadhigata-Panchamahásábada : title of the Gurjjars, I, pt. i, 113.
Samádhs : tombs raised over the remains of Hindu ascetics, sacred days for worship of, IX, pt. i, 360.
Samagár : a caste of cobblers in Dhárwár district, XXII, 221.
Samagi : *see* Satáni.
Samandár : town near Kanauj, mentioned by Al Idrisi, I, pt. i, 519.
Samangad : hill range in Kolhápur, XXIV, 7 ; *fort*, description, history, *id.* 319 ; copper-plate grant found at, *id.* 219 ; grant from (753-754), I, pt. i, 467, 122 ; I, pt. ii, 190, 195, 377 and note 3, 378, 384, 387, 390, 538 note 8.
Sámanta : feudatory, title of the Gurjjars, I, pt. i, 113.
Samantabhadra : Jain writer, I, pt. ii, 406, 408.
Sámantadhipati : title of Jayabhata III, Gurjjara king, I, pt. i, 113 and note 6.
Sámantasimha : Chávada king, defeated and slain by Mularája, I, pt. i, 157.
Samara : king of Suráshtra, at war with Kumárapála, I, pt. i, 186 and note 1.
Samarasimha : Chohán chief, daughter of, married to Bhim II (1179-1242), I, pt. ii, 197.
Samarchhanta : the holy drop, death ceremony among Khojas, IX, pt. ii, 46.
Sámarkha : town in Kaira district, III, 178.
Samastabhnvanásraya : *biruda* (title) of the Chálukya king Vijayáditya, I, pt. ii, 370 ; of the Kalachurya Bijjala, *id.* 474 ; of the Kalachurya Sovideva, *id.* 484 ; Yádava epithet, *id.* 518, 521, 527.
Samatata : Ganges delta province, tributory to Samndragupta (370-395), I, pt. i, 64 and note 2.
Samávartana : home-returning, Vedic rite, IX, pt. i, 31 note 3 ; performauce of, *id.* 38.
Sámba : son of Mallugi, the Yádava prince, I, pt. ii, 237.
Sámba : son of Krishna, Samás trace descent from, IX, pt. ii, 69.
Sambal : appointed Mughal admiral (1670), XI, 437 ; his quarrel with Sidi Kasim, removed from his command (1677), *id.* 439.
Sámbar : wild elk in Kánara district, XV, pt. i, 99-100.
Sámba Sampradaya : *see* Vaishnav.
Sámbhai Náik : object of Bajánias' veneration, IX, pt. i, 503, 504.
Sambháji : Shiváji's son, deserts him (1679), I, pt. ii, 71, 595 ; returns to his father ; plots against him, besieged at Panhála by Janárdan Pant Sumant ; is joined by Hambir Ráo Mohite, enters Ráygad (1680), *id.* 76, 595 ; revenges himself savagely on his opponents, putting to death Rájárám's mother ; members of the Sirke family plot against him, puts to death Annáji Dattu and Báláji Auji (1681), *id.* 595 ; lays siege to Janjira (1682), successfully opposes the Mughals ; builds the fort of Belápur, is defeated by the Sidis, plunders Portuguese villages and prepares to fortify Elephanta, besieges Chaul and takes Karanja (1683), *id.* 77 ; retires to Vishálgad, invests Bassein, spends his time in sensual pleasures, and is captured by the Mughals and put to death (1689), *id.* 78, 79, 596 ; *see* also XIX, 245-249 ; X, 195 note 8 ; *another account of* : second Marátha ruler (1680-1689) ; his dissipation ; oppression ; associates himself with the rebel prince Sultán Akbar ; is surprised by Takarrib Khán ; is disgraced ; his insolence and execution, XVIII, pt. ii, 238-239 ; *another account of* : besieges Chaul and Janjira, XI, 285, 441, 145 ; plunders Burhánpur, XII, 251 ; XIII, 479 ; gives Karanja to the Portuguese, XIV, 193 ; builds fortification at Panvel, *id.* 296 ; fights with the Portuguese at Anjidiv, XV, pt. ii, 130, 131, 256, 349 ; XXIV, 314 ; capture and execution of, XX, 288.
Sambháji II : second Kolhápur *rája* (1712-1760), Tárábái is (1712) confined and the administration conducted by Rámchandra

Pant Amátya; Chin Kuli Khán the first Nizám, with a view to weaken the Marátha power supports Sambháji against Sháhu of Sátára; Sambháji is defeated by the *pratinidhi* and driven to Panhála; Tárábái and Bhawánibái taken prisoners to Sátára; treaty with Sháhu (1730), XXIV, 227-229; Rája of Kolhápur, XIX, 255, 257, 272, 273; defeated by the *pratinidhi*, I, pt. ii, 600.
Sambháji Angria: supported by the Portuguese (1737), XIII, 492; carries away Bombay craft (1740), *id.* 496; XI, 149-152.
Sámbhar: expedition of Kumárapála's general Chábada against, I, pt. i, 187, 188.
Sambhu: Śaiva ascetic, I, pt. ii, 380.
Sámbráni: village in Kánara district, history, XV, pt. ii, 132, 146, 304, 340 and note 8, 349.
Sambuk: Arab passenger-boat in Thána district, XIII, 470 note 1, 721.
Sámda: *thákor* of, conspires (1857), I, pt. i, 441.
Sametshikhar: death-place of Párasnáth in Kolhápur, XXIV, 133.
Samgameśvara: capital of a Chálukya prince, I, pt. ii, 224; town in the Konkan, probably Sangameshwar, *id.* 467; local idol, *id.* 478.
Samgár: *see* Chámbhár.
Samghuráma: mentioned by Hiuen Tsiang, I, pt. ii, 335.
Samgitaratnákara: treatise on music by Sárngadhara, I, pt. ii, 243.
Sami: town in Pálanpur state, V, 300, 347; grant of, to Fateh Khán Baluch, IX, pt. ii, 17.
Sami: tree, *see* Khijáro.
Samipadraka: village, gift of, entered in a grant found at Navsári, I, pt. i. 125; I, pt. ii, 314.
Samkama: *see* Sankama.
Śamkara: last Devagiri Yádava king, Deváládevi offered in marriage to, I, pt. i, 205; rules Navsári, XIII, 438; marches to the relief of the fort of Devagiri, but is defeated, I, pt. ii, 250-251, 531; succeeds his father (1309), *id.* 251, 530; withholds the annual tribute, is defeated and put to death by Malik Káfur (1312), *id.* 251, 533.
Sámkara: Jaitugi I's governor of Tardavádi (1196), I, pt. ii, 521.
Samkarácharya: *see* Shankarácharya.
Samkaragana: Kalachuri prince of Western India, father of Buddha, I, pt. ii, 181, 295 and note 3; his father, *id.* 385; overthrown by Mangaleśa (602), *id.* 311, 347.
Samkaragana: Ranavigraha, son of Kokkala Kalachuri, king of Chedi, I, pt. ii, 203, 414.
Samkaragráma: battle at, I, pt. ii, 326.
Samkaraguru: supposed author of *Prasnottararatnamálika*, I, pt. ii, 200.
Samkarana: *see* Samkaragana, father of Buddha.
Samkshepa-Śariraka: Vedántic work, I, pt. ii, 212.
Samla: *táluka* in Káthiáwár, VIII, 647.
Samláji: old temple in Mahi Kántha, V, 440; place of pilgrimage, IX, pt. i, 549.
Samma: Rájpút tribe, I, pt. i, 138; probably of Turk origin, Chudásamas an off-shoot of, IX, pt. i, 125; Jádejas, the last representatives of, adopted Islám, *id.* 126; masters of Cutch after the fall of the Chauras, *id.* 517; conquer Cutch (1320), V, 132; a Musalmán sub-division in Cutch, *id.* 93; rulers in Sind (1351-1531), IX, pt. ii, 50.
Sammatiya: Buddhist school, I, pt. i, 79.
Sampagádi: possibly modern Sampgaon, I, pt. ii, 570 and note 1.
Sampakarasa: of the Gutta family, I, pt. ii, 487, 581 and note 3.
Sampgaon: sub-division of Belgaum district, its boundaries, area, aspect, soil, climate, water, stock, crops and people, XXI, 503-505; survey (1852), *id.* 434-437; place of interest, *id.* 600; inscription at, I, pt. ii, 436 note 1, 439 note 1, 556, 566, 567, 568, 569, 571.
Samprati: grandson of Aśoka, I, pt. i, 15.
Sámrádev: or Siniario, god of wild tribes, IX, pt. i, 363.
Samri: tree, *see* Shami.
Samsám-ud-Daulah: Dauran Nasrát Jang Bahádur, forty-eighth viceroy of Gujarát (1716-1719), I, pt. i, 300.
Samshergudd: hill in Belgaum district, XXI, 9.
Samudraghosha: Pallava musical instrument, I, pt. ii, 327 and note 7, 374-375.
Samudragupta: early Gupta king (370-395), his conquest, I, pt. ii, 280, 281 note 3, 311 and note 3; Eran inscription of, *id.* 286 note 1; restores the *Aśvamedha* or horse-sacrifice, *id.* 290 note 3, 320 note 2, 320 note 1; Allahábád pillar inscription of, *id.* 293, 317; father of Chandragupta II, *id.* 361 note 3; *see* also I, pt. i, 62-65, 67; pillar inscriptions of, IX, pt. i, 470 note 6; his victories, *id.* 448.
Sámudri-Máta: Hindu goddess, chief shrine of, at Sundri, family goddess of Kapols, IX, pt. i, 71; of Sorathiyas, *id.* 74.
Samundarphal: medicinal plant, XXV, 256.
Sámvargad: fort in Kánara district, XV, pt. ii, 340-341.
Samvat: Vikram era, I, pt. i, 204.
Samvatasimha: king (1278) of Bhinmál, I, pt. i, 471.
Samvatsaras: of the planet Jupiter, I, pt. ii, 288 note 1; cyclic years, list of, *id.* 432 note 8.
Sámvedi Bráhmans: in Thána district, XIII, 82; XIV, 315.
Samydaceæ: species of poisonous plants, XXV, 265.
Samyn: ancestor of the Pallavas, I, pt. ii, 317.
San: Bombay hemp, cultivation of, in Khándesh, XII, 163.
Sána: hill in Káthiáwár, VIII, 12; caves, 647.
Sánabhoga: village accountant, I, pt. ii, 449 and note 5.
Sanadh: a caste of Bráhmans in Gujarát, IX, pt. i, 4 note 2.
Sanadi Koravár: a caste of robe-makers in Dhárwár district, XXII, 162-163.

Sanads : title-deeds in Kánara district, furnished the revenue history to Sir T. Munro, XV, pt. ii, 156 and footnote 1.
Sanakadi Sampradaya : *see* Vaishnav.
Sanakánika : name of a province on the frontier of Samudragupta's kingdom, I, pt. i, 64 and note 3, 65.
Sanála : *tálnka* in Káthiáwár, VIII, 647.
Sánand : sub-division of Ahmadábád district, details of, IV, 238-240. *Town, id.* 353.
Sanaphulla : founder of the Southern Konkan branch of the Siláháras, entrusted with the government of the Konkan, I, pt. ii, 253 and note 3, 392 ; favoured by the Ráshtrakúta Krishna I, *id.* 536, 537.
Sanchair : *máta*, luck of Parmárs, IX, pt. i, 485.
Sanchi Stúpa : Gupta inscription on, I, pt. i, 66.
Sanchnimakta : an Alibág survey, XI, 191.
Sanchor : an old gate of Bhinmál, I, pt. i, 449.
Sand : in Kánara district, XV, pt. i, 20 ; in Poona district, XVIII, pt. i, 30 ; in Sátára district, XIX, 30 ; in Dhárwár district, XXII, 26.
Sandábur : commercial town on the Western Coast mentioned by Arab travellers, I, pt. i, 510 ; old port, XIV, 81 note 2.
Saudalias : Chandala, menials, I, pt. i, 530.
Sandalpur : the site of an ancient city in Kaira, III, 178.
Sandalwood : trade in, at Sopára (B. C. 150), XIII, 406, 408 ; in Kánara district, export of, XV, pt. ii, 47, 54, 58 ; carving, *id.* 70, 306 ; in Poona, XVIII, pt. i, 44.
Sandanes : of the *Periplus*, I, pt. i, 44 note 2.
Sandanes : envoy, I, pt. i, 542, 543.
Sandanes : king of Kalyán, I, pt. ii, 1 ; I, pt. i, 546 ; sends Greek ships to Broach, XIV, 119.
Sandápur : apparently Goa, I, pt. i, 509.
Sandarája : son of the Kalachurya king Kannama, I, pt. ii, 468.
Sandhan : old town in Cutch, V, 240 ; an Arab settlement (700-800) at, *id.* 131 note 5 ; I, pt. i, 509.
Sandhier : village south of the river Kim, I, pt. ii, 359 and note 5.
Saudhiyara : modern Sandhier, I, pt. ii, 359.
Sandhubhúpa : ruler of, defeated by Dantidurga, I, pt. ii, 389.
Sandhya : twilight prayer, IX, pt. i, 31.
Sándor : church near Bassein, XIV, 37, 402.
Sand Pipers : class of birds in Ratnágiri district, X, 92.
Sandrocottos : Chandragupta, I, pt. ii, 277.
Sand Snakes : in Poona district, XVIII, pt. i, 80.
Sand Spits : class of birds in Ratnágiri district, X, 19.
Sandstone Ridges : to the north of Belgaum, XXI, 7 ; beds, in Bijápur district, XXIII, 24-25 ; working of, *id.* 56-57.
Sandur : Randir, I, pt. i, 509, 520.
Sanes : village in Káthiáwár, VIII, 647.
Sángali : *see* Sángli.
Sangam : village in Bijápur district, temple, flight to and absorption of Basav at, fair at, XXIII, 675.
Sangameshvar : sub-division of Ratnágiri district, details of, X, 2, 303-305. *Town*, trade, fires, history and temples of, *id.* 371-373 ; *náik* of, *id.* 341 ; caves at, I, pt. ii, 9, 37 ; head-quarters of Asad Khán, *id.* 39 ; Sambháji captured (1689) at, *id.* 78, 108, 596.
Sangameshvar : village in Khándesh district, Hemádpanti temple at, XII, 469.
Sangameshvar : Lingáyat place of pilgrimage in Bijápur, XXIV, 119, 120 ; on the confluence of the Malaprabha and the Krishna, favourite shrine of Basava, I, pt. ii, 227.
Sangameshwar : town, *see* Sangameshvar.
Sangam-Máhuli : village in Sátára district, I, pt. ii, 334 note 2. *See* Máhuli.
Sangamner : sub-division in Ahmadnagar district, its area, aspect, water-supply, climate, rainfall, cultivation, irrigation, crops, people, roads, railways, markets, crafts, survey changes, XVII, 632-640 ; survey of, *id.* 487-489, 538-540. *Town, id.* 736-738 ; grants at, I, pt. ii, 231, 232, 430, 433, 511, 512, 513, 514.
Sangau : a notorious pirate, IX, pt. i, 525.
Sangana : ruler of Vanthali, killed by Viradhavala, I, pt. i, 200.
Sangana-Basaveśvara : inscription in the temple of, at Hirúr, I, pt. ii, 436 note 1.
Sanganians : pirates from Cutch and the Gulf of Cambay, harass Thána coast (1760), XIII, 499 note 1, 711 note 2 continued on pages 713 and 714.
Sangar : caste of weavers in Ratnágiri, X, 125 ; in Kolába district, XI, 65 ; in Thána district, XIII, 134 ; in Poona district, XVIII, pt. i, 365-366 ; in Sátára district, XIX, 93-94 ; in Sholápur district, XX, 137 ; in Kolhápur state, XXIV, 97-98.
Sangavadla : village in Gujarát, I, pt. i, 187.
Sanghadáman : tenth Kshatrapa (222-226) ; coins of, I, pt. i, 43-44, 546.
Sanghadia : a caste of turners in Káthiáwár, VIII, 152 note 1.
Sanghár : caste of pirates in Cutch, V, 69, 95-97 ; in Káthiáwár, VIII, 165-166 ; Hindu and Mahomedan in Gujarát, IX, pt. i, 519, 525, 526.
Sangharama : *stúpa* mentioned by Hiuen Tsiang, I, pt. ii, 354.
Sanghs : pilgrims going in bands, IX, pt. i, 550.
Sanghvis : leaders of *sanghs*, IX, pt. i, 550.
Sangit Mehel : Bijápur palace, XXIII, 626.
Sangli : state in Southern Marátha Country, description, production, people, agriculture, famine, capital, trade, fairs, history, land details, justice, instruction, health places, XXIV, 324-377. *Town*, details, fort, chief's residence, *id.* 365-367 ; copper-plate grant at, *id.* 219 ; I, pt. ii, 199 note 3, 203, 204, 205, 209, 342 note 1, 414 and note 5, 416 and note 5, 417, 431, 554.
Sangola : sub-division of Sholápur district, its boundaries, area, aspect, climate, water, soil, stock, holdings, crops and people, XX, 402-404. *Town, id.* 485 ; rising of Yamáji

Shivdev (1750) against the Peshwa at, *id.* 290; XIX, 292.
Sangrahni: dysentery and diarrhœa, its cure, IX, pt. i, 365.
Sangreji: sand, IX, pt. ii, 223 note 1.
Sangsi: village near Báwada in Kolhápur state, fragmentary inscription at, I, pt. ii, 286 note 1.
Sangur: village in Dhárwár district, temples, and inscriptions at, XXII, 785; record at. I, pt. ii, 527.
Sánikatta: salt works in Kanára district, XV, pt. ii, 72-73, 341.
Sanjala: village in Rewa Kántha, temple and fair at, VI, 168.
Sanján: old village in Thána district, early history of, remains at, XIV, 301-304; identified with the Sindan of Arab writers, I, pt i, 509, 520; Pársis settle at (716), IX, pt. ii, 185, 221; XIII, 248, 249; Siláháras rule at (810-1260), *id.* 423, 425, 428; trade centre (900-1000, 1100), *id.* 429, 430, 432; chief of, defeated by Álap Khán (1312), *id.* 438; IX, pt. ii, 187; attacked by the Abyssinians (1559), I, pt. ii, 48; emporium of trade (1598), XIV, 30; under the Maráthás, *id.* 555 note 3; surveyed (1793-1794), *id.* 558; Marátha cesses, *id.* 560; (1838), *id.* 585; cost and profit of tillage in (1845), *id.* 588; survey assessment (1866), *id.* 619-620; holy fire of Behram taken to Bharut hills (1315), to Bánsda, *id.* 187; to Navsári (1419), *id* 188; to Surat (1733), retaken to Navsári (1736), *id.* 192; taken to Bulsár (1741), to Udváda (1742), *id.* 193, 185 note 2; temple for, at Sanján, *id.* 185; at Navsári, *id.* 188.
Sanjár: name borne by the *jáms*, I, pt. i, 139.
Sanjeli: state in Rewa Kántha, VI, 1, 2, 155-156.
Sankagávunda: village headman, I, pt. ii, 482.
Sankama: Kalachurya king, I, pt. ii, 227-228, 465; son of Bijjala, *id.* 469; Nisaankamalla (1177-1181), *id.* 471, 477, 486, 487, 488; recognised sovereign of Vira-Ballála II, *id.* 502, 576, 581.
Sankaráchárya: *see* Shankaráchárya.
Sankaradeva: *see* Samkara.
Sankaragana, Sankarana: father of Buddhavarmman, Kalachuri prince, I, pt. i, 114.
Sankaravarman: Kashmir king (890), I, pt. i, 3, 468.
Sankasht-Chaturthi: trouble-cleaning fourth, worship of the moon on, IX, pt. i, 398.
Sankeshvar: town in Pálanpur state, temples and fair at, V, 300, 347.
Sankeshwar: large village in Belgaum district, the *math* of Shankaráchárya at, XXI, 600-602; seized by Bahádur Gilani (1493), *id.* 366; stone inscription at, I, pt. ii, 556 and note 6.
Sankh: Broach chieftain, claims Cambay; is defeated by Vastupála, I, pt. i, 200 and note 2.
Sankhachúda: serpent king, saved by Jimútavahána from Garuda, I, pt. ii, 253 and note 1, 536.
Sankha-Jinálaya, Sankha-Jinendra: Jáin temple near Pulikara, I, pt. ii, 373, 358 note 1.
Sankhanpur: village sixty miles north-east of Ahmadábád, temple of goddess Behechra at, IX, pt. ii, 21, 82.
Sankhavarman: son of the Kalachurya Sandrája, I, pt ii, 468.
Sánkheda: sub-division in Baroda territory, VII, 555-558. *Village*, ravaged by Kanhoji, *id.* 199; Ganpatráo Gáikwar *jághirdár* of *id.* 206; the chiefs of, *id.* 336; grant from, I, pt. ii, 295, 313 note 4, 314; I, pt. i, 118.
Sankheda Mehvás: state in Rewa Kántha, VI, 1, 2; its area, boundaries, history and subdivisions, *id.* 140-148; Chohan estates in, IX, pt. i, 125.
Sankh-há-ra: Egyptian king, sends an expedition to Punt (B. C. 2500), XIII, 404 note 3.
Sankráji Náráyan Gaudekar: ancestor of the present *pant sachiv*, I, pt. ii, 597; Tarábái's chief adherent, commits suicide (1711), *id.* 598.
Sankrant: Hindu holiday, IX, pt. i, 23 note 5.
Sankshi: old fort in Kolába district, description, tomb, the remains of a town at, history of, XI, 383-388; under the Gujarát kings (1540), taken by Burhan Nizám Sháh (1540), *id.* 142, 143; XIII, 443, 452; came into British possession (1818), XI, 159; *khots* of, *id.* 178; condition, high assessment at (1837), *id.* 182 and notes 3, 5, 6 and 7, 183 and notes 2, 3; survey (1837, 1858), *id.* 189, 201-203, 220.
Sankuvarbái: wife of Jaysing Ángria; captures Nágothna (1793), XI, 155; takes Khánderi (1799), *id.* 156, 327.
Sánoli: Saonli, near Baroda, burning place of Piláji Gáikwár (1732), I, pt. i, 313.
Sanosra: village in Káthiáwár, VIII, 648.
Sansári Jangam: a caste of traders in Ahmadnagar district, XVII, 82-85.
Sanseviera zeylanica: fibrous plant, XXV, 236.
Sansi: near Dhárwár, action at (1776), between the Maráthás and Hyder, XXII, 413.
Sansi: *see* Sansya.
Sanskára: sixteen observances, kept by Chitpávans, XIII, 76.
Sanskrit College: in Poona city (1821-1851), XVIII, pt. iii, 49, 51.
Sanskrit Schools: in Baroda, VII, 488-489.
Sansya: or Sansis, race of plunderers in the Punjáb, Vághris said to have sprung from, IX, pt. i, 510.
S'anta: I, pt. ii, 559. *See* S'antivarman II.
Santa Cruz: hill, near Asheri, retaken by the Portuguese (1684), I, pt. ii, 78.
Santa Cruz: Church of, at Nirmal in Thána district, XIV, 293.
Santa Cruz: Poona tombs, XVIII, pt. iii, 392.
Santáji Ghorpade: Shiváji's officer under Hasáji Mohita, I, pt. ii, 594; commander-in-chief of the Maráthás, *id.* 596; his rupture with his lieutenant Dhanáji Jádhav; is surprised and killed by Nágoji Máne, *id.* 597. *See* also XIX, 249.
S'antakarna: *see* S'atakarni, I, pt. ii, 155.

Santalaceæ: species of food, famine and oil-yielding plants, XXV, 174, 204, 224.
S'antaladevi: wife of the Hoysála king Vishnuvardhana, disciple of the Jain Prabháchandra, I, pt. ii, 491, 493, 494.
Sántalige: old territorial division, I, pt. ii, 298 note 2, 306 and note 5, 430, 433, 437, 439, 443, 449, 450, 452, 454, 456, 476, 489, 505, 506 and note 1, 562, 563, 577.
Sántali Mandala: old territorial division, I, pt. ii, 583, 506 note 2.
Sántalpur: state in Pálanpur, V, 281, 332; Jádeja Rájpút chiefship, IX, pt. i, 126.
Santalum album: famine and oil-yielding plant, XXV, 204, 224.
Santama: Kalachurya king, I, pt. ii, 468.
Sántara: family of Patti-Pombuchchapura in Mysore, I, pt. ii, 458.
Santasama: see Santama.
S'antaya: see S'antivarman II, the Hángal Kádamba.
Santeya-Bágevádi: modern Hire-Bágewádi, I, pt. ii, 527.
Santhál: early tribe in Kánara district, XV, pt. i, 298 footnote 1.
Santharo: vow of fasting to death, taken by Jain *sádhus*, IX, pt. i, 114 note 1.
Sánthli: *táluka* in Káthiáwár, VIII, 648.
S'antideva: Jain teacher of Vinayáditya, I, pt. ii, 491, 492.
Sántikas: a Konkan tribe, identified with Sadinoi of Ptolemy, I, pt. i, 44 note 2, 540.
S'antinátha: Jain *tirthankara*, I, pt. i, 192.
S'antiváhana: Southern king, I, pt. ii, 171.
Santivaravarman: see S'antivarman I.
S'antivarman: chieftain, I, pt. ii, 411 note 1; Ratta chieftain of Saundatti, *id.* 428; feudatory of the Western Chálukya king Taila II (980), *id.* 552, 553.
S'antivarman I: Hángal Kádamba, I, pt. ii, 559, 286, 287 and note 9.
S'antivarman II: Hángal Kádamba prince and feudatory of Vikramáditya VI (1075-1089), I, pt. ii, 450, 559, 561.
Santoshgad: see Táthávade.
Santram: holy man, or *bhágat*, founder of Santrampanth, his temple at Nadiád, IX, pt. i, 154, 547.
Santrámpanthi: see Religious Sects.
Sántu: minister of Chálukya king Karna, builds a Jain temple, I, pt. i, 170; Siddharája's minister, *id.* 172; attacks an army of Bhils, *id.* 178.
Sántuvasahi: Jain temple, built by Santu, Karna's minister, I, pt. i, 170.
Sanwa: food plant, XXV, 184.
Sanyásis: Shaiv, see Dandi.
Saon: food plant, XXV, 184.
Sapádalaksha: name of the Ajmir kings, I, pt. i, 157.
Sapádalaksha: Sámbhár territory, I, pt. i, 184. *See* Sewálik.
Sapádalakshiya: name of Chohans, I, pt. i, 157.
Sapara: mouth of the Indus, I, pt. i, 538.
Saphád: village in Konkan, cave at, I, pt. ii, 11.
Sapindaceæ: species of famine and oil-yielding plants, XXV, 197, 216.
Sapindi-Shrádh: memorial service in honour of seven generations of ancestors, XVIII, pt. i, 154, 157.
Sapindus: *detergens, laurifolius, mukorossi, saponaria* trees, fruits of, used as soap, XXV, 252; *emarginatus, trifoliatus*, oil-yielding plants, also used as soap, *id.* 216, 252.
Sapinolus trifoliatus: tree used to poison fish, XXV, 272.
Sap-Kanda: famine plant, grows on the *gháts*, XXV, 207.
Sápor: the Sassanian, his wars with Constantine, with emperor Julian, IX, pt. i, 473 and note 5.
Sapotaceæ: species of famine and oil-yielding plants, XXV, 201, 213, 219, 223.
Sappalig: a class of musicians in Kánara district, XV, pt. i, 314, 315.
Sapsan: vegetable antidote to snake-bite, XXV, 275.
Saptakholla: district, I, pt ii, 547.
Saptakotiśvara: family god of the Goa Kádambas, I, pt. ii, 566 and note 7.
Saptapadi: principal part of Chitpávan marriage ceremony, XVIII, pt. i, 212.
Saptaságar: holy village in Belgaum district, XXI, 602.
Saptaśati: work composed by Hála, I, pt. ii, 171.
Saptashring: hill and temple in Násik district, reservoirs and fairs at, XVI, 643-646.
Saptavarman: a minister mentioned in Taranatha's *History of Buddhism*, I, pt. ii, 171.
Sara: small town in Káthiáwár, mosque and an inscription at, VIII, 648.
Sárábhai: Native agent at Baroda, misuses his power, VII, 265.
Saraca Indica: sacred plant, XXV, 279, 285.
Sarafdar: village in Káthiáwár, history of, VIII, 649.
Saraganes: the Shátkarnis, XIII, 417; I, pt. i, 543; the younger and the elder, *id.* 546.
Sáragvála: old port in Ahmadábád district, IV, 353.
Saráj-ud-din: *maulvi*, preaches *jehád* or religious war in Ahmadábád (1857), I, pt. i, 434.
Sárákachchha: circle of villages mentioned in a Paithan grant, I, pt. ii, 397.
Sarambal: village in Sávantvádi state, a large lake at, X, 467.
Sarandib or Sarandip: Ceylon, I, pt. i, 516; dependency of the Gujarát kingdom, rubies imported (1025) from, to Somnáth, I, pt. i, 168.
Saráng: boat-captain, XIII, 716.
Sárangadeva: Vághela king (1275-1296), I, pt. i, 203; succeeds Arjunadeva, his inscriptions, *id.* 204-205, 206.
Sarangpur: town near Ujjain, I, pt. i, 368; battle of (1422), *id.* 207 note 1.
Sarània: caste of arms-cleaners in Káthiáwár, VIII, 158.
Saraostus: probably Suráshtra, I, pt. i, 6, 535.
Saras: village, centre of Motála Bráhmans; origin of name; Siddhanáth or *ling* stone-home of Shiv raised by Rám near, IX, pt. i, 12 and note 1.

S'árasamgraha: Jain mathematical work, I, pt. ii, 200.
S'arasgad: fort in Kolába district, I, pt. ii, 32. *See* Páli.
Sarasi: Sanskrit word for large lake in use in Dakhan in Patanjali's time, I, pt. ii, 140.
Sárasvat: sub-caste of Bráhmans, in Gujarát, IX, pt. i, 1 note 1, p. xi note 3; created for performing sacrifice, *id.* 438, 440; derivation of name; abound in Punjáb, spread in Cutch, Káthiáwár and Gujarát; sub-divisions of, in South Káthiáwár, *id.* 18 notes 1 to 6; priests of Brahma-Kshatris in South Gujarát; condition; prospect, *id.* 19; in Thána district, XIII, 78, 83-85; in Cutch, V, 43; in Káthiáwár, VIII, 146; in Kánara district, XV, pt. i, 139-168; in Dhárwár district, XXII, 98.
Sarasvati: deity, Brahma's daughter, her chief place of worship in Punjáb, IX, pt. i, 19.
Sarasvati: well of talent near Dhara in Gujarát, I, pt. i, 180, 511, 521.
Sarasvati: river in Panjáb, gives name to Sárasvat Bráhmans, IX, pt. i, 18.
Sarasvati: river in Gujarát, held sacred at Siddhpur; death-rites performed on the banks of, IX, pt. i, 350; V, 283, 356; VII, 23; I, pt. i, 161, 173; I, pt. ii, 135; VIII, 63.
Sarasvati: river in Ahmadnagar district, XVII, 8.
Sarasvati: under-ground stream in Kolhápur, XXIV, 9.
Sarasvati-Gachchha: author of *Pattávali*, I, pt. ii, 288 note 6.
Sarasvati Kanthábharana: a Sanskrit work, I, pt. ii, 171.
Saravda: a caste of religious beggars in Ratnágiri district, X, 131.
Sárbán: a caste of Musalmán camel-drivers, in Sholápur district, XX, 201; in Bijápur district, XXIII, 293; in Kolhápur, XXIV, 149.
Sartana: town identified with Sarwan, I, pt. i, 539.
Sarbhon: place in Ámod *táluka* of Broach, Govind III, halts at, I, pt. i, 123.
Sarbuland Khán: Khán Bahádur Mubáriz-ul-mulk Diláwar Jang; appointed deputy viceroy of Gujarát (1712-1713), robbed on his way to Gujarát (1713), I, pt. i, 297; appointed fifty-second viceroy (1723-1730); his deputy defeated (1724), *id.* 304; ordered to proceed in person with a strong army to Gujarát (1725), *id.* 306; is compelled to pay tribute to the Maráthás (1726), *id.* 307; makes alliance with the Peshwa, extorts tribute in Sorath, and marries the daughter of Jhála Pratápsingh whom he exempts from tribute (1728), *id.* 308; grants formally to the Peshwa one-fourth and one-tenth share of the revenue of the province (1729), *id.* 309; levies tribute in Káthiáwár (1730), *id.* 310; defeats the new viceroy at Adálaj and retires (1730), *id.* 311; advances (1725) towards Bhuj, V, 139; *see* also VII, 169, 171-172.
Sardárs: in Baroda state, VII, 200; their rise, were military officers, paid in money, *id.* 290-293; court for, established, *id.* 459; in Janjira state, their privileges, their disaffection against the *nawáb* (1855), XI, 449-451; of Poona, their authority maintained by Elphinstone, XVIII, pt. ii, 305.
Sardesáis: known only in Konkan (1818), I, pt. ii, 34; of Kudál, chiefs of Sávantvádi, *id.* 68.
Sardeshmukhi: Marátha tribute, right to the levy of, in Bijápur territory granted (1656), XVIII, pt. ii, 234; exacted in eastern and northern Dakhan by Marátha chiefs (1690), *id.* 239; Shâhu sends Chandrasen Jádhav to collect it (1712), *id.* 241; XIX, 256; exacted by Khanderáv Dábháde (1715), *id.* 260; grant of, obtained by Báláji Vishvanáth in the name of Sháhu (1719), *id.* 261-262; XVI, 192; XVIII, pt. ii, 243; I, pt. ii, 655; levied by Udáji Povár in Málwa (1723), XIX, 268; Holkar and other chiefs empowered by the Peshwa to collect it (1725), *id.* 270; granted to the Peshwa in Gujarát (1726), *id.* 273; VII, 171 and note 1; levied by the Peshwa in Málwa (1736), XIX, 278.
Sardeshmukhs: only two families of in Konkan (1818), I, pt. ii, 34.
Sardeshpandegiri: five per cent. on the revenue, Marátha exaction, promised to Bájiráv (1736), XIX, 278.
Sardhár: town in Káthiáwár, its history, VIII, 649.
Sardhar, Sardhári: a dyke in Káthiáwár, VIII, 12; said to have been built by Siddha ája, I, pt. i, 180 note 2.
Sárekari: caste of palm-juice drawers, in Kolába district, XI, 71.
Sargaras: Bhil messengers at Bhinmál, I, pt. i, 451.
Sárgargota: *Cæsalpinia handucella*, timber tree in Poona district, XVIII, pt. i, 52.
Sar-Gurah: office of a head teacher in a beggar brotherhood, IX, pt. ii, 19.
Sarhind: town in Panjáb, head-quarters of the high priest of Memans at, IX, pt. ii, 57.
Sarika: demon, destroys Bhinmál, I, pt. i, 462, 463.
Sáriputra: Shákyamuni's disciple, a *stupa* raised over him at Kánheri, XIV, 170.
Sarisabis: town, mentioned by Ptolemy, perhaps in Nizám's territory, I, pt. i, 540.
Sarjekot: fort, near Málvan, in Ratnágiri district, X, 352, 373; built by Shivaji, I, pt. ii, 69.
Sarjeráv Ghátge: *see* Sakharam Ghatge Shirzi Ráo.
Sarkárgeni: land tenure (1807), in Kánara district, XV, pt. ii, 184.
Sarkárs: Gujarát districts under Ahmadábád *sultáns* so-called, I, pt. i, 209, 218-219.
Sarkhej: village and reservoir in Ahmadábád district, I, pt. i, 438; IV, 18.
Sarkhel: Ángria's title, XI, 146.
Sarkhot: over-*khot*, revenue contractor in Thána district (1818), XIII, 538.
Sárnáth: *stupa* of, near Benares, XIV, 136, 170.

Sárngadhara: author of the *Samgitaratnákara*, I, pt. ii, 243.
Sarnobat: chief captain of the Marátha army, XIX, 243.
Sarodi or Dákuji: caste of beggars in Janjira state, XI, 415.
Saronda: village in Thána district, XIV, 305.
Sarpánmalik: *see* Sherif-ul-mulk.
Sarpátil: over-headman in Thána district, XIII, 538; (1828), *id.* 572.
Sarpatoli: snake in Ratnágiri district, X, 49.
Sarru: dye-yielding plant, XXV, 241.
Sársa: town in Kaira, III, 178.
Sarson: oil-yielding plant, XXV, 214.
Sarsubhedár: Marátha provincial officer in Thána district, XIII, 555-556; in Poona district, XVIII, pt. ii, 325 note 2; in the Konkan, I, pt. ii, 99.
Sarsut: the river Sarasvati mentioned by Al Biruni, I, pt. i, 510, 521.
Sartha: native place of Bopadeva's father, I, pt. ii, 249.
Sárthipura: sub-caste of Bráhmans in Gujarát, IX, pt. i, 19.
Sarusa: apparently the river Sarasvati, but perhaps the Sábarmati, I, pt. i, 510.
Sarva: village in Káthiáwár, its history, VIII, 650.
Sarva: *see* Amoghavarsha.
Sarvade Joshi: a caste of religious beggars in Poona district, XVIII, pt. i, 460-461.
Sarvadevácharya: royal family priest; Chinchuli village granted to, by Seunachandra II, I, pt. ii, 515.
Sarvaiyás: Rájputs, probably Chudásamás, IX, pt. i, 129.
Sárvajanik Sabha: political association at Poona, XVIII, pt. iii, 64; at Ahmadnagar, XVII, 581; at Násik, XVI, 335-336.
Sarvajnabhúpa: all-knowing king, title of Someśvara III, I, pt. ii, 221.
Sarvajnátman: author of the *Samkshepaśáriraka*, I, pt. ii, 212.
Sarvákshadalana: Pulumayi's lieutenant in Govardhana, I, pt. ii, 150.
Sarvamangalásatta: village, Druva's camp at, I, pt. ii, 404.
Sarvanátha: of Uchchakalpa, Kalachuri feudatory prince, I, pt. ii, 293.
Sarvaria: a sub-caste of Bráhmans, in Dhárwár district, XXII, 96-97; in Thána district, XIII, 85.
Sarvavarman: minister of Sátavúhana, propitiates the god Kartikeya for a new grammar, I, pt. ii, 170-171.
Sarvva: Ráshtrakúta or Gurjjara king, his coins, I, pt. i 87. *See* Amoghavarsha.
Sarvvamangala: village in Gujarát, I, pt. i, 126.
Saśakapura: *see* Sasápura.
Sasan: village in Káthiáwár, origin of the name, VIII, 650-651.
Saśapura: identified with Angadi in Mysore, I, pt. ii, 490 note 3; birth-place of Vinayáditya, *id.* 492.
Sásashtkar: a sub-caste of Bráhmans in Kánara district, XV, pt. i, 136, 139; Vaishnav Shenvis in Ratnágiri, X, 411.
Sásati: Sálsette, I, pt. ii, 529, 567.
Sáshtikar: *see* Sasashtakar.
Sássanians: Persian dynasty (226-650), I, pt. ii, 14; revival of Persian power under, IX, pt. ii, 183 note 4; their trade with Thána coast (500), XIII, 419; destruction of, *id.* 421; imitation of their architecture in Elephanta caves, XIV, 82.
Sassoon Asylum: in Poona, XVIII, pt. iii, 342-343.
Sassoon Hospital: in Poona, XVIII, pt. iii, 392-393.
Sassoon Point: at Mahábaleshwar, XIX, 506.
Sassu Navghar: village in Thána district, XIV, 305.
Sásvad: town in Poona district, details of, XVIII, pt. iii, 439-440.
Sátakani: I, pt. ii, 153. *See* Sátakarni.
Sátakarni: Andhra dynastic name, I, pt. i, 37, 38, 49; Sri, Sátavàhana king, mentioned in an inscription at Nánághát, I, pt. ii, 147; Gotamiputra, his inscriptions and the extent of his rule, *id.* 149; his and his wife's charters, *id.* 150; his wife and capital, *id.* 151; Gotamiputra Sriyajna, mentioned in an inscription, *id.* 152; his coin, *id.* 153; Chaturapana Yanna, *id.* 153, 155, 156. *See* Gotamiputra and Haritiputra, *id.* 277; *see* also I, pt. i, 541, 546.
Satána: town in Násik district, temples at, XVI, 646-647.
Satáni: a caste of beggars in Dhárwár district, XXII, 211.
Satanones: *táluka* in Káthiáwár, VIII, 651.
Sátára: district, its boundaries, sub-divisions, aspect, hills, rivers, geology and climate, XIX, 1-27; production, *id.* 28-42: iron, limestone, salt, forests and forest management, domestic and wild animals, snakes, fish and birds, *id.* 28-42; population, *id.* 43-147: census details, dress, communities, *id.* 43-50; Bráhmans, writers, traders, husbandmen, *id.* 51-79; craftsmen, musicians and servants, *id.* 79-104; shepherds, labourers, unsettled tribes, depressed classes, beggars, *id.* 104-124; Musalmáns, Christians and Pársis, *id.* 124-147; agriculture, husbandmen, soil, holdings, field tools, irrigation works, wells, manure, crops, famines, *id.* 148-177; capital, saving classes, investments, money-lenders, interest, borrowers, land and service mortgage, prices, weights and measures, *id.* 178-193; trade: roads, passes, railways, *id.* 194-209; bridges, post and telegraph, trade centres, markets, fairs, *id.* 209-218; imports and exports, *id.* 219-220; crafts, *id.* 220-223; history: early (B. C. 200-A. D. 1294), Bahmanis (1347-1489), Adil Shahis (1489-1686) and their institutions, *id.* 224-230; Maráthás, Shiváji (1627-1680) and his institutions, *id.* 230-245; Mughals (1686-1720), Maráthás (1720-1848), British (1848-1857), *id.* 245-319; land and its administration: staff, tenures, history of, under the British, *id.* 320-350; survey (1853-1863), season reports (1849-1883), *id.* 350-389; justice: civil and criminal, under the Maráthás, under the British (1849), *id.*

390-395; civil courts and suits, registration, magistracy, police, offences, jails, *id.* 395-402; finance, *id.* 403-408; instruction: staff, cost, private schools, school details, liabraries and newspapers, *id.* 409-415; health: hospitals, vaccination, cattle disease, births and deaths, *id.* 416-422; sub-divisional details, *id.* 423-446; places of interest, *id.* 446-616; states, *id.* 617-624; copper-plate inscriptions in, I, pt. ii, 298 note 2, 390, 544, 546, 548, 577; Lingáyats in, *id.* 478.

Sub-division, its boundaries, area, aspect, climate, water, soil, stock, holdings, crop, and people, *id.* 438-440; survey of, *id.* 367, 369.

Town, its description, climate, divisions population, management, water-supply, markets, gardens, objects, fort and history, *id.* 551-580; trade centre, *id.* 214; reservoir at *id.* 157-158; fort of, built, *id.* 226; used as a prison, *id.* 244; Diláwar Khán the Bijápur regent imprisoned in (1591), I, pt. ii, 590; taken by Shiváji (1673), *id.* 594; XIX, 244; head-quarters of the Marátha government (1697), I, pt. ii, 597; captured by Aurangzeb (1700), XIX, 250-251; taken by the Maráthás (1705), *id.* 253; taken by Sháhu (1707), *id.* 254; Tárábái imprisoned (1734) in, *id.* 276; Chandásáheb imprisoned in (1741), *id.* 283; ceases to be Marátha capital, *id.* 291; Rám Rája imprisoned (1750) in, *id.* 292; disturbance at (1798), *id.* 298-299; surrendered to the British (1818), *id.* 303, 313-316; *see* also I, pt. ii, 601, 603, 607; proclamation (1818) of, *id.* 665; XVIII, pt. ii, 302; annexation of (1848), I, pt. ii, 613; copper-plate inscription and grants at, *id.* 71, 185, 338, 351, 352, 356.

Sátára Rajás: (1818-1848), the state of Bijápur under the, XXIII, 598-599.

Satárkár: a caste of husbandmen in Kánara district, XV, pt. i, 240-242.

Sátarur: Armativala rules at, I, pt. ii, 505.

Sátaváhana: prince mentioned in an inscription, I, pt. ii, 147.

Sátaváhana: dynasty, I, pt ii, 147-148, 151, 154, 158; identified with the Andhrabhrityas, *id.* 156; chronology of, *id.* 157-168; blood relationship of Kshatrapas with, *id.* 161; their rise, *id.* 165; dates of the later, *id.* 168; political and literary traditions about, *id.* 169-172; religious, social and economic condition of Mahárásbtra under, *id.* 173-176; foreign princes, their establishment in the Dakhan, *id.* 194. *See* Andhrabhrityas.

Satavari: food plant, XXV, 180.

Sataves: principal star of the West, is supposed by Dr. Geiger to be the star "Vega," IX, pt. ii, 217 note 1.

Sátavli: village in Ratnágiri district, identified with Dobetala of Barbosa, remains at X, 373; I, pt. ii, 37.

Satbán: son of Rásal, king of Hindustán, that is Kanauj, I, pt. i, 519.

Sátenhalli: village in Dhárwár district, temples and inscriptions at, XXII, 785; I, pt. ii, 563.

Sateraka: counsellor of the queen of Vasishthiputra Sátakarni, I, pt. ii, 153.

Sáthamba: state in Mahi Kántha, inscription at the town of, V, 423, 442.

Sathi: *see* Chhathi.

Sáthod: place of interest near Dabhoi, IX, pt. i, 13.

Sáthodra: division of Nágar Bráhmans, IX, pt. i, 13, 15 and note 2.

Sáthvára: caste of professional husbandmen in Gujarát, surnames; faith in early beliefs, bird-worship among; places of pilgrimage, customs, IX, pt. i, 175-176; in Káthiáwár, VIII, 143.

Sati: suppression of, by Lord William Bentinck; beliefs regarding, woman sacrificing herself; famous *satis* of Gujarát, IX, pt. i, 358; story of Rajbái, famous *sati* of Bharvád caste, *id.* 358-359; account of widow-burning in Gujarát, *id.* 359-360; *devdi* or masonry platform over the burning spot; daily and annual worship of the *devdi*, *id.* 360; suppression of, in Sátára (1840), XIX, 312.

Sátin: variety of honey bee in Kolhápur state, XXIV, 24.

Sátivli: hot spring in Thána district, XIII, 15, 16; XIV, 342

Satiyaputa: king of Southern India, I, pt. ii, 277.

Satka: evil spirit of Bhinmál, I, pt. i, 457.

Satlásan: state in Mahi Kántha, V, 425.

Satmála: mountain range in Khándesh and Násik districts, XII, 5; XVI, 2, 5; Ajanta and other caves in, I, pt. ii, 355, 619.

Satmasa: seventh-month celebration during first pregnancy among Gujarát Hindus, IX, pt. ii, 149.

Sát Mazli: palace at Bijápur, XXIII, 617-619.

Satodar Vávdi: *táluka* in Káthiáwár, VIII, 651.

Satpanth: name given by Pir Sadr-ud-din to his new faith, IX, pt. ii, 48.

Sátpatti: a village in Thána district, XIV, 305.

Sátpudas: hills in Khándesh, XII, 4; forests, *id.* 19.

Satrap: Persian word for Kshatrapa, I, pt. ii, 155; I, pt. i, 21.

Satrumalla: *biruda* or title of the Pallava Mahendravarman I, I, pt. ii, 328; of Gunabhara the Pallava king, *id.* 331.

Satrunjaya: Jain hill in Káthiáwár, I, pt. i, 78, 79 note 3, 164 note 5, 177, 186; Hemácharya's visits to, *id.* 189, 199; temple of Neminátha on, *id.* 202.

Sat-svarup: lineal descendant of Vallabhachárya, establishes seven bishoprics or *gádis* of Vallabhacháryan sect, IX, pt. i, 537.

Sattalige: district, *see* Sántalige.

Satti: pass, in Násik district, XVI, 128.

Sattiga: Western Chálukya king Satyásraya, I, pt. ii, 432.

Sattigaṇa Chatta: *see* Kundamarasa.

Sattikkara: village mentioned in a Karnul grant, I, pt. ii, 369.

Sattima: Western Chálukya king Satyáśraya, I, pt. ii, 432.

Sattúru : inscription at, I, pt. ii, 501.
Sátu : food-plant, cultivated throughout India, XXV, 189.
Saturday : Shanivár ; other names of ; beliefs about, IX, pt. i, 403 ; sacredness of, XVIII, pt. i, 241.
Saturn : *Shani*, a planet ; worship of, IX, pt. i, 403 ; influence of, I, pt. ii, 400.
Satvái : Hindu goddess, XVIII, pt. i, 291.
Satwin : medicinal plant, XXV, 259.
Satyadeva : Vikramáditya VI's feudatory, I, pt. ii, 450.
Sátyaki : branch of the Yadu race, I, pt. ii, 194, 383.
Satyasamdha : *biruda* or title of the Pallava king Gunabhara, I, pt. ii, 331.
Satyasena : Chálukya king, I, pt. i, 51.
Satyáśraya : *biruda* or title of Pulikeśin I, I, pt. ii, 181, 343 ; of Kirtivarman I, *id.* 345, 358 note 1 ; of Pulikeśin II, *id.* 182, 351, 357 note 1 ; of Vikramáditya I, *id.* 361 ; of Vikramáditya II, *id.* 374 ; of Kirtivarman II, *id.* 376, 377.
Satyáśraya : progenitor of the Western Chálukyas of Kalyáni, I, pt. ii, 211, 339.
Satyáśraya : Western Chálukya king (997-1008), succeeds his father Taila II, I, pt. ii, 213, 332 ; his *birudas*, *id.* 432 ; his feudatories, *id.* 254, 432-433 ; records of his time, *id.* 431, 432, 433, 434 note 5.
Satyáśraya-Dhruvarája-Indravarman : appointed governor of the Konkan by Kirtivarman I ; stationed at Revatidvipa by Pulikeśin II ; victories of, I, pt. ii, 345, 355, 356.
Satyavakya-Kongunivarma-Permanadi : Western Ganga king (A. D. 870) ; also known as Satyavakya-Kongunivarman Rajámalla Permanadi, I, pt. ii, 303 and note 7.
Satyavakya-Kongunivarma-Permanadi : Western Ganga king (A. D. 910), I, pt. ii, 304.
Satyavakya - Kongunivarma - Permanadi-Butuga or Butayya : Western Ganga king (A. D. 940) ; his *birudas* (or titles) ; kills Rachamalla and acquires the Gangavádi province ; marries a daughter of Amoghavarsha Vaddiga and receives as her dowry the Puligere district, I, pt. ii, 304 and notes 1 and 4.
Satyavakya-Kongunivarma-Permanadi-Marasimha : Western Ganga king (A. D. 963-974) ; son of Butuga ; his *birudas* (or titles), I, pt. ii, 305.
Satyavakya-Kongunivarma-Rachamalla-Permanadi : Western Ganga king (A. D. 978), I, pt. ii, 307.
Satyavarman : Western Ganga king, son of Devendravarman ; Chicacole grants of, I, pt. ii, 297.
Satyavarman : Hángal Kadamba king, I, pt. ii, 559.
Satyayug : first cycle of Hindu chronology, I, pt. i, 461.
Saubha : name of a country, perhaps Svabhra, I, pt. i, 10 and note 1.
Saud : Wahhábi leader, IX, pt. ii, 12 note 3.
Saudágar : a caste of Musalmán traders in Dhárwár district, XXII, 238 ; in Bijápur district, XXIII, 289.
Saudágar Gumbaz : merchant's tomb at Junnar, XVIII, pt. iii, 150-152.
Saunágars : school of the, I, pt. ii, 140.
Saundatti : town in the Belgaum district, inscriptions, fort and history of, XXI, 602-607 ; I, pt. ii, 431 ; Rattas of, *id.* 143, 299 note 4, 327 note 7, 411, 420, 425, 428, 437, 439, 443, 450, 451, 455, 458, 476, 498, 519, 524, 546, 549, 550, 551, 556, 571 ; Jain temple at, *id.* 201, 213 ; inscriptions at, *id.* 202, 411 note 1, 552, 553, 554, 555, 557.
Saur : gum-yielding plant, XXV, 250.
Sauraseni : the Prákrit language, I, pt. ii, 136.
Sauráshtra : ancient name of Káthiáwár, VIII, 272, 277 ; king of, destroyed by the army of the Tájikas, I, pt. ii, 187, 375 and note 6 ; afflicted by an Arab army, I, pt. i, 109 ; tribe of Káthiáwár, *id.* 534.
Saurs : tribe in Sind, I, pt. i, 533.
Sausara : king of Suráshtra, I, pt. i, 186 and note 1.
Sautas : tribe conquered by Govind III, Ráshtrakúta king, I, pt. ii, 396.
Sauvira : or modern I'dar, XIV, 318.
Sauvira : Upper Sind and Multán, I, pt. i, 537, 545.
Sáva : food-plant, XXV, 184 ; cultivation of, in Poona district, XVIII, pt. ii, 41 ; in Sátára district, XIX, 162.
Savadhavatti : Saundatti, I, pt. ii, 550.
Savái Suti : one and-a-quarter remission, XIII, 532 note 1 ; *see* Suti.
Sával : pass in Násik district, XVI, 128.
Sávaladevi : wife of the Western Chálukya king Vikramáditya VI, I, pt. ii, 448.
Sávaladevi : wife of Kalachurya Sovideva, I, pt. ii, 471, 484.
Savali : village in Baroda, tombs of Dhanáji and Piláji at, VII, 537 ; Damáji burns his father's body at, *id.* 174 ; restored to Peshwa (1791), *id.* 199 ; ceded to the British (1817), exchanged, *id.* 226-227.
Savandhavatti : modern Saundatti, I, pt. ii, 550.
Sávant Rising : (1858-1859) in Kánara district, XV, pt. ii, 152-153.
Sávants : hereditary *deshmukhs* of Kudál, I, pt. ii, 39 ; Marátha chiefs of Sávantvádi, make a temporary alliance with Shiváji but soon return to their fealty to Bijápur ; enter into a treaty with Bijápur and the Sidis against Shiváji ; submit to Shiváji (1661), *id.* 68 ; share in the Sálshi province, *id.* 79 ; help Tárábái (1710), *id.* 81 ; plunder Vengurla (1780), *id.* 107 ; negotiate with Sindia and retain their possessions (1793), *id.* 108 ; take the forts Nivti and Ráiri (1803), *id.* 112 ; their treaties with Kolhápur, X, 198 ; family tree of, *id.* 447 ; *see* also XVIII, pt. ii, 228-229.
Sávantvádi : state in Ratnágiri district, its boundaries, sub-divisions, aspect, rivers, geology and climate, X, 387-400 ; production, minerals, trees, forests, domestic and wild animals, birds and fish, *id.* 401-406 ; population : census details, food, dress, *id.* 407-411 ; Bráhmans, writers, husbandmen,

traders, depressed classes, beggars, Musalmáns and Christians, *id.* 411-422; agriculture: soil, irrigation, holdings, stock and crops, *id.* 423-427; capital, investments, currency, land transfers, labour-mortgage, wages, prices, weights and measures, *id.* 428-432; trade, roads, bridges, rest-houses, post offices, exports and imports, toys, fairs, *id.* 433-438; history: early Hindus (500-1500), Bijápur rule (1500-1627), the Sávants (1554-1884), *id.* 439-447; land, its administration, tenures, peasant holders, survey rates, *id.* 448-451; civil and criminal justice, registration, police, *id.* 452-454; revenue and finance, *id.* 455-457; instruction, readers and writers, library, *id.* 458-459; health, diseases, hospitals, vaccination, births and deaths, *id.* 460-462; places of interest, *id.* 463-469; rises in importance, I, pt. ii, 67, 663; rising in, XXI, 408-409. *Town,* population, trade, lake, fort and sub-divisions of, X, 467-469.

Savanur: state in Dhárwár district, description, production, people, agriculture, capital, trade, history, land, justice, finance, schools, XXII, 410-411, 442-443, 792-806; *nawáb:* origin of the, XXI, 377; XXIII, 439, 441; deprived of his Belgaum possessions, XXI, 380-381; the fort of Belgaum passes into the hands of, I, pt. ii, 656; Majid Khán throws off his dependence on the Mughals, cedes a large portion of the territory to the Peshwa (1747); his son Abdul Hakim Khán incurs the displeasure of both the Peshwa and the Nizám and cedes to the Peshwa additional territory (1756), *id.* 656-657, 666-667; is defeated by Haidar, (1764), *id.* 658, 667; taken by Haidar (1776), *id.* 659; the *nawáb* of, enters into a close alliance with Haidar (1779), XXI, 384; I, pt. ii, 659, 667; taken by Tipu; practically annexed by the Peshwa (1787), *id.* 667; revenue of twenty-five villages assigned to the *nawáb* of, *id.* 667-668; the name of the *nawáb* of, is entered in the list of first class *sardárs, id.* 668. *Town, id.* 229 note 1, 441 note 6, 665; its history, *id.* 665; founded by Abdul Rauf Khán (1700), *id.* 666.

Savásha: a caste of Bráhmans in Kolhápur, XXIV, 63; in Sátára, XIX, 55.

Savati-Gandhahasti-Basadi: Jain temple at Śravana-Belgola built by Lakshmadevi, wife of the Hoysala Vishnuvardhana, I, pt. ii, 495.

Savati Gandavárana Jinálava: Jain temple at Sravana Belgola built by Lakshmadevi, wife of the Hoysála Vishnuvardhana, I, pt. ii, 495.

Sávda: sub-division of Khándesh, boundaries, area, aspect, climate, water, soil, holdings, survey details, survey results, stock and crops, people of, XII, 2, 400-409. *Town, id.* 261, 469.

Savdi: village in Belgaum district, a tomb at, XXI, 607.

Savdi: village in Dhárwár district, temples at, XXII, 785.

Sáve: coarse grain in Dhárwár district, XXII, 274.

Sávgaon: village in Kolhápur, battle at (1808), XXIV, 235.

Sávidar: gateway of Bhinmál, I, pt. i, 450 note 1.

Savimale: country, I, pt. ii, 298; place of trade in Western India in the sixth century, identified with Savanur, *id.* 299 note 1, 439, 492; plundered by Vishnuvardhana, the Hoysála king, *id.* 496, 499.

Sávitri: wife of Brahma, said to be a Gurjjara maiden, I, pt. i, 464; IX, pt. i, 15, 502.

Sávitri: river, dividing the Konkan into North and South, "Introduction to the History of the Konkan," I, pt. ii, p. x, 28, 33; X, 6, 297; XI, 10, 11.

Sávla: pass in Thána district, XIII, 322; XVIII, pt. ii, 152.

Savri: silk cotton tree in Poona district, XVIII, pt. i, 52.

Sávta: timber mart in Thána district, XIV, 306.

Savváse: a sub-caste of Bráhmans in Dhárwár district, XXII, 97.

Sawa: *see* Sava.

Sawanihnigars: news-writers under the Mughals, I, pt. i, 214.

Sawantvadi: *see* Sávantvádi.

Saw-gins: in Belgaum district, XXI, 328-336.

Saw-mills: steam, in Kanára district, XV, pt. ii, 74; in Ratnágiri district, X, 189, 288-289.

Saxicolinæ: sub-family of birds in Ratnágiri, X, 76.

Sayad: Musalmán trader, arrest of, at Cambay in the thirteenth century, I, pt. i, 202.

Sayad: title among Musalmáns, IX, pt. ii, 7.

Sayad Achchan: paymaster at Surat, aspires to the governorship of Surat, seeks Marátha help (1747), I, pt. i, 396; takes the city of Surat and gets the merchants to sign a deed addressed to the emperor and the Nizám that he should be appointed governor (1748), *id.* 331-332; makes over one-third of Surat revenue to the Maráthás, *id.* 332; oppresses influential persons, surrenders the citadel to the Habshi and withdraws to Bombay and thence to Poona (1750), *id.* 333; receives the governorship of Surat from the Peshwa and establishes himself in the government (1758), *id.* 343; receives a body-guard from the Peshwa (1759), *id.* 399.

Sayad Imám-ud-Din: Ismáiliáh missionary in Gujarát during the reign of Máhmud Begada (1459-1513), I, pt. i, 288.

Sayad Jelál Bhukhári: chief law officer or *sadr-us-sudur* under the Mughals for the whole of India (1642-1644), I, pt. i, 279.

Sayad Miththan: marches on Surat and returns unsuccessful, his suicide, I, pt. i, 331.

Sayads: Musalmán class; descendants of Fatimah and Ali; their dislike to intermarry with other communities, IX, pt. ii, 6 note 1, 7; arrival and settlement of, in Gujárat;

the ten chief families of, *id.* 6 note 1; appearance, titles before or after their names, condition, religion—Sunnis and Shiahs, Shiah *sayads* form a distinct community, *id.* 7-8; beggars of Bukhári stock, *id.* 8 note 1; of Mahdavi faith, *id.* 6 note 1 continued on page 7.

Sayads: brothers Hassan Ali and Abdullakhán, king-makers at Delhi, I, pt. i, 297, 301.

Sayad Shahji: preceptor of Matias of Khándesh and Momnas of Gujárat, his suicide, I, pt. i, 288.

Sayaji Gáikwár I: (1771-1778) son of Dámáji Gáikwár; collects tribute in Sorath (1759), I, pt. i, 342, 398, 344; sent to Mangalvedha, VII, 179; enthroned (1771), *id.* 188; I, pt. i, 400, 401; his grant to the British, VII, 195; eldest son of, killed at Bhilapur (1731), *id.* 173.

Sayaji Gáikwár II: (1819-1847) account of his administration, VII, 230-268, 300-304, 385, 388, 399-400.

Sayaji Gáikwár III: adopted by Jamnábái (1875); the present *Mahárája* of Baroda; account of his administration, VII, 283-286.

Sáyan: village near Kamlej, I, pt. i, 130.

Sáyana, Sáyanáchárya: codifies civil and religions laws, I, pt. ii, 229; *Rigveda* commentator (1370), XV, pt. ii, 96 note 3, 262 note 3.

Sáyer: land customs under Mughals, I, pt. i, 213.

Sáykheda: town in Násik district, XVI, 647.

Sáyván: stockaded fort of the Portuguese on the Vaitarna river, I, pt ii, 48; built by Shiváji, *id.* 71.

Sázantion: town, possibly Rutlám, I, pt. i, 540.

Sazgaran: food plant cultivated in several districts, XXV, 185.

Scansores: class of birds in Thána district, XIII, 49.

Scarcity: *see* Famine.

Scharan: a quadruped in the Konkan, mentioned by Alberuni, I, pt. ii, 4.

Scherpi: rats in Thána, mentioned by Odoricus, I, pt. ii, 5.

Schiefner: translator of the *Ratnamáliká* from the Thibetan language, I, pt. ii, 201.

Schistose Rocks: in Bijápur district, XXIII, 18; in Ratnágiri, X, 13; in Savantvádi, 391.

Schleichera trijuga: medicinal plant, XXV, 261.

Scholarship: centres of, Zend and Pehlevi, IX, pt. ii, 194.

School: Protestant charity, in Bombay, funds raised for (1719), XXVI, pt. iii, 535; established (1753-54), *id.* 537-538; state of (1754-1771), *id.* 536-541.

Schools: of the Sunni division, IX, pt. ii, 126 note 1.

Schools: in Káthiáwár, VIII, 311, 347, 348; in Kánara district, XV, pt. ii, 210, 211, 213-216; in Kolába district, XI, 230, 232-235; in Janjira, *id.* 459-460; in Khándesh district, XII, 329-330; in Thána district, XIII, 216, 500; town and village, *id.* 660-661; in Násik district, XVI, 329; in Ahmadnagar district, XVII, 574-581; in Sholápur district, XX, 381-384; in Belgaum district, XXI, 481-488; in Dhárwár district, XXII, 612-619; in Bijápur district, XXIII, 518-523; for orphans, at Chaul and Dabhol, I, pt. ii, 33. All district volumes *see* Instruction under District Name.

Schultzen: Dutch writer (1650), describes Honávar in Kánara district, XV, pt. ii, 124, 310; describes Anjidiv (1658), *id.* 255.

Schweinfurth: African traveller, concludes that the Hindus were the first sailors in the Indian Ocean, XIII, 715.

Scirpus Kysoor: food plant, common throughout India, XXV, 184.

Scitamineæ: species of food, famine, fibrous and dye-yielding plants, XXV, 174, 204, 235, 249.

Scobie: Colonel, marches against Bet (1859), I, pt. i, 447.

Scolopacidæ: family of birds in Ratnágiri district, X, 91.

Scolopacinæ: sub-family of birds in Ratnágiri district, X, 91.

Scorfula: *see* Kanthmal.

Scott: Colonel Caroline Frederick, appointed engineer general of all Indian settlements (1733), XXVI, pt. ii, 304.

Sculptures: in Elephanta caves, reflections on, XIV, 83.

Scythians: identified with Sakas, I, pt. ii, 158; settlement of, in Cutch, defeated by Vikram (56 B. C.), V, 129; drive the Andhras from North Konkan (A. D. 150), XIII, 411.

Sea: abode of Varuna, water-god; also called *Ratnágar*; churned during Vishnu's second incarnation; days sacred for sea-bath; sea-bath held cleansing on no-moon day, on no-moon Monday during intercalary month; worship of, by different classes on different occasions; salt, its use, IX, pt. i, 349.

Sea: Our Lady of the, church atUtán in Thána district, XIV, 372.

Seafarers: chief classes of, in Gujarát, distribution, IX, pt. i, 519; Máchhis, *id.* 519-520; Dhimars, *id.* 620; Khárvás, *id.* 520-522; Kábávaliyás, *id.* 522; Vághers, *id.* 522-523; *Kolis*, *id.* 523-524; Sanghars, *id.* 525-526; festival in South Gujarát, *id.* 524-525; piracy, *id.* 526-529.

Sea Fisheries: in Kolába district, XI, 474; in Thána district, XIII, 55-56.

Seal: Valabhi, I, pt. i, 80.

Seamen: in Ratnágiri district, earnings of, X, 170, 172; in Kánara, XV, pt. ii, 60, 61, 63; on Thána coast, Hindu, early, XIII, 403, *id.* 711-715; (A. D. 150-247), *id.* 417; (810-1260), *id.* 433; (1320-1442), *id.* 447; (1508), *id.* 471 and note 4; (1820), *id.* 521; (1882), *id.* 716; names of, *id.* 716.

Seamen's Wages: in Bombay island (1769), XXVI, pt. iii, 241-242; regulations about (1771), *id.* 242-243.

Sea of Fars: the Indian Ocean, I, pt. i, 516, 518.

Sea Snakes: in Poona district, described, XVIII, pt. i, 81.

Sea Trade: in Ratnágiri district, X, 170, 172; early, sixteenth, seventeenth, eighteenth, and nineteenth centuries, *id.* 174-178; (1819-

1879), *id.* 181-183; in Kolába district, XI, 126-130; of Thána district, XIII, 342-363; prehistoric, *id.* 404 note 3; (B. C. 25-A. D. 150), *id.* 410, 412; (A. D. 150), *id.* 416; (250), *id.* 418; (550), *id.* 420; (810-1260), *id.* 429-431; (1300-1500), *id.* 444-447; (1530-1670), *id.* 464-468; (1660-1710), *id.* 485-488; (1800-1812), *id.* 514, 518-520; in Baroda, VII, 149-150.
Sea View: name of Kánheri cave LVIII, XIV, 186.
Sebbi: modern Chabhi, I, pt. ii, 307.
Secretariat: Bombay, accommodated in a building north of the Cathedral, now occupied by Kemp and Co. (1764-1829), in the old Secretariat (1829-1874), in the present buildings since 1874, XXVI, pt. iii, 611-12; provided in the Fort House (1668-1758), in the warehouses adjoining the marine yard (1758-1764), *id.* 613-614.
Securinega obovata: poisonous plant, also used for poisoning fish, XXV, 269, 272.
Sedbál: village in Kolhápur, inscription at, XXIV, 219.
Sedimentary Rocks: in Bijápur district, XXIII, 47-48.
Sefareh-el-Hendi: Sopára in Thána, XIII, 404 note 3.
Sefareh-el-Zinge: Sofála in Africa, XIII, 404 note 3.
Segat: oil-yielding plant, XXV, 218.
Segváh: fort in Thána district, XIV, 98; discription of, *id.* 306.
Sehra: flower-sheet, IX, pt. ii, 159, 165.
Seif-ein-ul-Mulk: Bijápur noble, is harshly treated by Ibráhim Adil Sháh, rebels, and is defeated by the brother of the king of Vijayánagar, I, pt. ii, 590.
Seif-ud-din: chief *mulla* of the Dáudi Bohorás (1797), IX, pt. ii, 31 note 4.
Seja: tenant-held villages, IX, pt. i, 166.
Sejak: leader of Gohils, IX, pt. i, 125.
Sejakpur: village in Káthiáwár, ruins at, founded by Sejak (1236), VIII, 651.
Sejja: bedstead given on the twelfth day after death, IX, pt. i, 50.
Selára: family name among the Maráthás, traced to Siláháras, I, pt. ii, 256.
Seláravádi: village with railway station in the Poona district, I, pt. ii, 257.
Selbári: mountain range in Násik district, XVI, 5.
Seleucus Nikátor: general of Alexander the Great, I, pt. ii, 155; I, pt. i, 532.
Seleyaballiya-koppa: a village, halt at of Someśvara IV, Chalukya king, I, pt. ii, 484.
Self-sacrifice: in the Konkan, Masudi's account of (915), XI, 271 note 4.
Sell: pass in Násik district, XVI, 129, 130.
Sella-Vidyádharas: North Konkan Siláháras, I, pt. i, 129.
Sembolala: village south of Pulikara, I, pt. ii, 373.
Semicarpus anacardium: oil-yielding, dye-yielding, gum-yielding, and poisonous plant, XXV, 216, 242, 250, 264.
Seminary: Jesuit, establishment of, at Bassein (1548), I, pt. ii, 56.
Semmenatty: famine plant, XXV, 195.
Semulla, Semylla: I, pt. ii, 2; identified with Chembur or Chaul, *id.* 174; I, pt. i, 546.
Sena I: also called Kálasena, Ratta chieftain, I, pt. ii, 551, 553.
Sena II: also called Kálasena, Ratta chieftain (1102-1121), I, pt. ii, 455, 551, 554.
Sena-khas-khel: hereditary title of the Gáikwárs, meaning of, conferred on Piláji by Bájiráo (1731), VII, 173; said to be conferred on Dámáji (1763) by Sátára *rája*, *id.* 186; Govindráv recognized as, by Rághuba (1773), *id.* 101; obtained by Sayájiráv (1776), *id.* 184; assumed by Govindráv (1793), *id.* 199.
Senánanda: Prithivivallabha, Sendraka prince, I, pt. ii, 366.
Senánandarája: I, pt. ii, 186. *See* Senánanda.
Senapati: chief captain of Marátha army, XIX, 244 note 1; authorised to levy tribute in Gujarát (1717), VII, 167.
Senápati Bhatárka: *see* Bhatárka.
Sendrakas: ruling race, identified with the Marátha name Sinde, I, pt. ii, 186, 189, 369; family, XV, pt. ii, 82; dynasty, I, pt. ii, 292 and note 10; feudatory family under the Chalukyas of Bádámi, *id.* 361, 369 note 3; possibly Nágas, *id.* 281 note 3; chief, I, pt. i, 55; grant, *id.* 111.
Sendur or Rásuhai: hill in Belgaum district, temple on, XXI, 607.
Senja: or simple villages in Káira, III, 106.
Seuna: plant in Poona district, XVIII, pt. ii, 64.
Sepoy: pay and regulations (1759), in Bombay island, XXVI, pt. iii, 133-135.
Sequestrations: of Baroda territories, by the British, for the discharge of debts (1828), VII, 241-242; in 1830, *id.* 244-245; of Petlád (1839), *id.* 248-249.
Sericulture: experimental (1828-1884), in Ahmadnagar district, XVII, 277-280.
Serpent: cobra or *nag*, form of worship, cures of snake-bite, IX, pt. i, 379-380.
Servants: personal, among Gujarát Hindus, three classes of; strength and distribution, IX, pt. I, 228 and note 1; accounts of the three classes of, *id.* 228, 236; staff of, in a Musalmán house, IX, pt. ii, 96-97; personal, in Kolába district, XI, 67, 413; in Khándesh district, XII, 77; village, *id.* 265; personal, at Mátherán, XIV, 265; in Kánara, XV, pt. i, 326-335; in Ahmadnagar district, XVII, 145-149; in Sholápur district, XX, 143-144; in Poona district, XVIII, pt. i, 379-384; in Dhárwár district, XXII, 183-189.
Service: Musalmán classes of Hindu converts connected with: *see* Behrúpias, Bhánds, IX, pt. ii, 80; Bhattis, Bhawayyás, Gandhraps, *id.* 8; Kamálias, Madaris, *id.* 82; Mirs or Mirásis Sipáhis, *id.* 83; Táshchis, Turki Hajáms, *id.* 84; government and private, followed by Musalmáns, *id.* 122.
Service Mortgage: *see* Labour Mortgage.
Sesamum: grain, seeds of, emblem of Vishnu, worship of, offerings of, on Makár Sankraut day, IX, pt i, 391; cultivation of, in Kolába district, XI, 97; in Poona district, XVIII, pt. ii, 46; in Khándesh district, XII, 152.

Sesamum Indicum: oil-yielding plant, XXV, 219.
Sesbania: *ægyptiaca*, famine plant, XXV, 197; *grandiflora*, sacred plant, *id.* 292.
Sesekreienai: burnt islands, near Vengurla, I, pt. i, 546; also called Vengurla rocks, XV, pt. ii, 48 note 3; I, pt. ii, 1; X, 378.
Sesha: king of serpents, I, pt. ii, 169, 281.
Seshás: I, pt. ii, 389; possibly Nágas, *id.* 403 note 3.
Sesodia or Sisodia: a clan of Rájpúts, called Gohils, or Gehlots, said to be foreigners of Mihira tribe of the Gujar or White Húna, horde, IX, pt. i, 443, 452, 495-496; the premier Hindu family in India; Bálá, their oldest name; Bappa, their founder, *id.* 494 notes 2 and 3, 495; of Udaipur, their Persian connection, *id.* 439; *rána*, the title of the honored family of, *id.* 495 note 5; of Gujarát, representatives of the Mevad house of Udaipur, traditional settlement of in Gujarát, the present chiefships, *id.* 129.
Sessions: quarter, in Bombay island, to be presided over by the governor and council (1728), XXVI, pt. iii, 9; (1753), *id.* 22-29.
Setæ: tribe of Mewár, I, pt. i, 533.
Setarzan: early form of marriage among Pársis, IX, pt. ii, 238 note 2.
Sethia Indica: famine plant, XXV, 195.
Seton Kerr: Mr., resident at Baroda, VII, 271.
Settlement: of Shahu's territory (1720), XIX, 263-266; of Bijápur (1818), XXIII, 451.
Settlements: of the Aryas in the Dakhan, I, pt. ii, 135-137; in Dandakaranya, *id.* 138; Pársi, in Diu (about 700), IX, pt. ii, 184; in Sanján (716), *id.* 185; in Cambay (900-1100), *id.* 186 and note 1; in Cheul (966); in Navsári (1142), *id.* 186; in Variáv, *id.* 186 and notes 1 and 9; in Ankleshvar (1258); in Broach (1300); in Chandravati (15th century), *id.* 189; in Thána, Vánkánir, *id.* 186; in Bombay (before and after 1666), *id.* 195, 199 note 1; Indian, in Persia, Arabia and Africa; foreign, in Thána, XIII, 60-65, 403, 404 note 3.
Settlers: Portuguese, lands in Sálsette granted to, I, pt. ii, 53.
Setubandha: poem, attributed to Kálidása, I, pt. ii, 144.
Setudgar: part of *Zend Avesta*, IX, pt. ii, 211 note 2 (2).
Setudtar, Setud Yashts: part of *Zend Avesta*, IX, pt. ii, 211 note 2 (1).
Setuvina-Bidu: town in Mysore, I, pt. ii, 458 and note 2.
Seuna: country, I, pt. ii, 247, 284, 433, 443, 445, 460, 511, 520.
Seuna: king, army of, pursued and destroyed by Vira-Ballála II, I, pt. ii, 504 and note 2, 516, 517. *See* Seunachandra II.
Seunachandra I: son of Dridhaprahára and founder of Seunapura, I, pt. ii, 231, 512.
Seunachandra II: Yádava prince (1069), XIV, 387; I, pt. ii, 235, 236, 284; feudatory of the Western Chálukya king Someśvara II, *id.* 443, 515; assists Vikramáditya VI to the throne, *id.* 445; elevates the Yádava sovereignty, *id.* 515, 516, 518.
Seunadeśa: country, ruled by Seunachandra I, the Yádava king, I, pt. ii, 231; Yádavas of, *id.* 236, 420, 425, 430, 433, 435, 436, 437, 457, 501; named after Seunachandra I, *id.* 512.
Seunadeva: of the Yádava family, feudatory of the Western Chálukya king Jagadekamalla II, I, pt. ii, 457, 515; his *biruda*, *id.* 516.
Seunapura: town, founded by Seunachandra I, I, pt. ii, 231, 512 and note 4.
Sevalakuraaa: word inscribed on coins found at Kolhápur, probably the name of the governor, I, pt. ii, 152.
Sevana: kings of, I, pt. ii, 511; possibly Seunachandra II, *id.* 515; Mallugi's father, *id.* 517, 519.
Sevener: division of the Shiáhs, also called Sábuns and Ismáilis, IX, pt. ii, 47. *See* Ismaili.
Seven Mothers: guardians of the Chálukyas, I, pt. ii, 180.
Sevuna: king, humbled by Narasimha II, I, pt. ii, 507.
Sevya, Sevyarasa: son of the Sinda prince Polasinda and feudatory of the Western Chálukya king Someśvara II, I, pt. ii, 437, 577.
Sewalik: hills possibly near Ajmir, I, pt. i, 157; king of, *id.* 194.
Sewant: a caste of Hindu servants in Sátára district, XIX, 102-104.
Sewri: famine plant, XXV, 197.
Sex Divination: by milk, ceremony of, IX, pt. ii, 153-154.
Shaâbán: eighth month of the Musalmán year, holiday in, IX, pt. ii, 115, 140. *See* Shab-i-barát.
Shábáz: old Portuguese province, XIII, 456; captured by the Sidis (1682), *id.* 479; state of its defences, *id.* 491.
Shab-i-barát: night of record, falls on the 14th of Shaâbán, IX, pt. ii, 115, 140.
Shachi: Indra's wife, image of, in Ajanta caves, XII, 493.
Shadakshari: poet, author of the *Rájaśekhara-vilása*, I, pt. ii, 437 note 6.
Shadhs: beggars at Bhinmál, I, pt. i, 451.
Shaer: ancestor of the Udvada priests, IX, pt. ii, 221.
Sháfaii: Sunni *imám*, IX, pt. ii, 125 note 2, 126; Sunni school, *id.* 126 note 1.
Shag: *see* Cormorant.
Shah: honorific title of Vania, meaning of, IX, pt. i, 78 note 2; title among *sayads*, IX, pt. ii, 7.
Sháháb-ud-Din Ghori: defeat of (1178), by Jaichand, I, pt. i, 229; IX, pt. ii, 39.
Shahábuddin Khán: Mughal general, defeats Sambháji (1684), I, pt. ii, 78.
Sháh Abdul Hassan: Bijápur noble, called to her council by Chánd Bibi, I, pt. ii, 647; frees the state from its difficulties, is blinded and put to death by Diláwar Khán, *id.* 647-648.
Sháháda: sub-division of Khándesh, boundaries, area, aspect, climate, water, soil, holdings, history, survey details, survey results, stock, crops and people of, XII, 2, 409-413. *Town*, *id.* 469.

Shahádat: night of the martyrdom, the ninth night of the Muharram, IX, pt. ii, 129.

Sháháji: eighth *rája* of Sátára (1839-1848), his loyalty, his reforms, adopts a son, his death, XIX, 312-313; justice under, *id.* 391-394.

Shahaji: *rája* of Kolhápur (1821-1837), XXIV, 238-240.

Shahaji Bhonsle: (1594-1665), Shiváji's father; his marriage with Jijabai; succeeds (1629) to his father's estate of Poona and Supa: breaks his connection with the Nizámshahi and goes over to the Mughals; leaves Mughal service and sides with Bijápur; on the fall of Ahmadnagar overruns the country and seizes places of strength; weighs himself against money; is humbled (1637) by the Mughals; is confirmed in his estates in Poona and Supa; leads an expedition into the Karnatic; visits Poona (1649); much respected by his son Shiváji; his death, XVIII, pt. ii, 223-231; XXIV, 81; Karád under, XIX, 232; seizes (1632) Násik and other places for Ahmadnagar, XIII, 464; retreats to the hill-fort of Mahuli (1635); enters the service of Bijápur (1637), XI, 143 and note 7; deserts Malik Ambar (1621), XVII, 393; becomes regent (1632); manages the Ahmadnagar country; submits to Sháh Jahan and enters the Bijápur service (1636), *id.* 397-398; *another account:* sets up a king at Ahmadnagar; overruns the Gangthari and Poona districts and drives the Mughals from Purandhar (1633), I, pt. ii, 590-591; overruns the North Konkan, *id.* 38; takes service under the Bijápur king and receives the *jahagir* of Poona and Supa (1637), *id.* 39, 590-591; goes with Randulla Khán and extends the limits of the Bijápur kingdom to the Bay of Bengal, *id.* 650-651; arrested by Báji Ghorpade of Mudhol and imprisoned, *id.* 592, 651; XIV, 220.

Sháh Álam: saint, learned man of Mahmud Begada's reign, IX, pt. ii, 3 note 3, 76, 148; shrine of, at Ahmadábád, *id.* 56.

Sháhámat Khán: forty-fifth viceroy of Gujarát (1713), I, pt. i, 297; defeats the Marátha invaders at Ankleshvar (1711), VII, 167.

Shahánushahis: Kushán dynastic name, I, pt. i, 64 and note 5.

Shábápur: sub-division of Thána district, its boundaries, area, aspect, climate, water, soil, holdings, rental, stock, crops and people, XIII, 2, 683-685. *Town,* temples, ponds, and history of, remains near, XIV, 306-312.

Sháhápur: Bijápur suburb, XXIII, 577.

Shábápur: town in Kolhápur state, schools, temples and churches at, XXIV, 367.

Shahapur: town in Belgaum district, built in 1559, XXI, 371.

Shahazan: royal marriage, marriage of a maid, IX, pt. ii, 238 and note 1.

Sháh-Bandar: harbour master, village officer under the Mughals, I, pt. i, 212.

Shah-Bandar: town in the Indus delta, I, pt. i, 538.

Shahbaz-Garhi: rock inscription at, I, pt. ii, 142.

Shah Bhikan: Hajrat, son of Saint Sháh-i-Álam, the tomb of, on the Sáharmati near Ahmadábád, I, pt. i, 337 note 1.

Shah Budágh Khán: appointed commandant of Mándu (1568); builds Nilkantha, I, pt. i, 370.

Sháhdádpur: town near Haidarábád (Sind), I, pt. i, 538.

Sháh Husain Kaderi: Bijápur minister (1663), tomb of, at Bhiwndi, XIV, 47.

Sháhi: Kushán name, I, pt. i, 64 and note 5.

Sháh Jahán: Mughal emperor (1625-1658), defeats Malik Ambar (1621-1623), XVII, 393-394, 376, 398; favors the Portuguese, I, pt. ii, 40; calls on Bijápur to deliver the Ahmadnagar forts and show no favour to Sháhji Bhonsle, besieges Bijápur, forces the king of Bijápur to come to terms and annexes to the Mughal territory the country north of the Bhima (1636), *id.* 590-591, 650; admits Shiváji into the imperial service and causes the release of Shahji from imprisonment, *id.* 651; introduces revenue settlement in Khándesh, XII, 249; cedes the province of Kalyán-Bhiwandi to Bijápur, XIV, 47; stays at Mándu; is defeated, his brother Sháh Parwiz retreats to Mándu (1621-1622), I, pt. i, 381; his death (1666), *id.* 284; XIV, 380.

Shahji: *sayad pir*, descendant of Imám-ud-din (1691); spiritual head of Matids, commits suicide, IX, pt. ii, 69.

Shah Madar: Musalmán saint, IX, pt. ii, 82.

Shah Najaf: Shiah place of pilgrimage, place of Ali's martyrdom, IX, pt. ii, 47, 126.

Sháh Nawáz: tomb of, in Bijápur city, XXIII, 617.

Sháh Nawáz Khán Safávi: thirty-first viceroy of Gujarát, joins prince Dára in his rebellion against Aurangzeb (1659), I, pt. i, 282.

Sháh Nur: Hassan Kuli Khán Bahadur, viceroy of Oudh, sets out for Macca; his unsuccessful attempt to arrange matters between Momin Khán and the Peshwa, I, pt. i, 341.

Shahpur: *táluka* in Káthiáwár, VIII, 651.

Shah Ramzan Mahi Savar: *see* Kanboba.

Shah Tahir: Ismailian courtier-missionary, preceptor of Muzaffar II, IX, pt. ii, 3 note 3, 125.

Sháh Tahir: minister of Burhán Nizám (1508-1553), XI, 435, 464, 466; his visit to the Gujarát king, XVII, 364-365; his death, *id.* 367.

Sháhu: Marátha ruler (1707-1749), his imprisonment, release, marriage, arrives at Poona, is established at Sátára; Ángria becomes tributary to, appoints Bálá̇ji Vishvanáth as his Peshwa; receives three imperial grants of *chauth, sardeshmukhi* and *svaráj*, Bajiráv and Báláji, the second and third Peshwas, invested by; his death, XVIII, pt. ii, 239-245; *another account of:* taken prisoner at Raygad (1690), I, pt. ii, 79, 596; released by the Mughals (1708), *id.* 655; XVII, 403; plunders Khándesh, XII, 251; adopts the founder of the present Akalkot state, XVII, 403, XX, 489; defeats the army of Tárábai and is formally seated on the throne (1708), I, pt. ii, 598; lays siege to Rángna and builds

the Harnai fort (1707-1713), *id.* 81; takes the fort of Panhála (1708), XXIV, 314; appoints Khanderáv Dábháde *senápati*, I, pt. i, 389; obtains a grant of *chauth, sardeshmukhi* and *svaráj* in the Dakhan (1719), I, pt. ii, 655; XX, 290; XIX, 262-263; his attempts at order, I, pt. ii, 599; obtains Miraj, Tasgaon and Athni by treaty with the *rája* of Kolhápur (1731), *id.* 656; settles the terms of agreement between the Peshwa and Dábháde (1732), I, pt. i, 393; his friendly relations with the Bombay government (1739), XXVI, pt. i, 217-219; makes the Peshwa the head of the Marátha confederacy (1749), XXIV, 229; his death, I, pt. ii, 600; his ministers, XIX, 259.

Sháhu: adopted son and successor of Rama Rája of Satára, I, pt. ii, 604.

Shahu: Pratapsimha's adopted son (1857), XIX, 317, 319.

Sháhuka: *táluka* in Káthiáwár, VIII, 652.

Shaik: caste of Musalmáns of the regular class, in Gujarát, IX, pt. ii, 6; also include local converts, *id.* 8 note 3; meaning of the name, origin, branches, appearance, titles before and after the names of, *id.* 8 and notes 2 and 3, 9; Telia division of, in Rádhanpur, *id.* 8 note 2; in Cutch, V, 89; in Ahmadnagar, XVII, 226; in Poona district, XVIII, pt. i, 491; in Sholápur district, XX, 197-198; traders and soldiers in Belgaum district, XXI, 204; in Dhárwár district, XXII, 231; in Bijápur district, XXIII, 288; in Kolhápur, XXIV, 148.

Shaik: title among Musalmáns, IX, pt. ii, 8.

Shaikhda: caste of Hindu converts, devotees of the Pirána saints, also called Shaikhs, form a distinct community, IX, pt. ii, 69-70.

Shaikhji: pirate on the Ratnágiri coast (1733), I, pt. ii, 82.

Shaikhsallás: tombs of Musalmán saints in Poona city, XVIII, pt. iii, 339, 343-344.

Shaikh-ul-Jabal: title assumed by Hasan Sabáh, IX, pt. ii, 37.

Shaikh-Zeinudin: sage of Daulatábád, I, pt. ii, 620.

Shailáhára: Sanskritised form of the Maráthi surname Selar, I, pt. ii, 15 note 4.

Sháistah Khán: twenty-sixth viceroy of Gujarát (1646-1648), I, pt. i, 280; twenty-eighth viceroy of Gujarát (1652-1654); his expedition against the Chunvália Kolis, *id.* 281; Mughal general (1662-1664) in Poona; surprised and wounded by Shiváji, I, pt. ii, 593; takes the fort of Chakan, XVIII, pt. iii, 122, 404; XVIII, pt. ii, 229-230; *subhedár* of Surat (1671), XXVI, pt. i, 47.

Shaivites: religious sect, worshippers of Shiv, IX, pt. i, p. xxxvi, 530, 541; places of pilgrimage, *id.* 549.

Shaiv Nágas: Shaivite mendicants, attack General Goddard (1778), XIV, 135 note 10.

Shaivs: religious sect in Gujarát, IX, pt. i, 530, 541, 542.

Shaiv Temples: the ten great, XVIII, pt. ii, 211 and note 1.

Shakespeare: Sir Richmond, resident at Baroda, I, pt. i, 443; VII, 274-275.

Shakra: god Indra, XIII, 406.

Shaks: tribe mentioned in *Vishnu Purána*, XIII, 413 and note 7. *See* Sakas.

Sháktas: devotees of Sakti, the creative energy, IX, pt. i, 545-546. *See* Religious Sects.

Shakuna Sáli: a caste of weavers in Dhárwár, XXII, 177-178.

Shákyamuni: Gautama Buddha, image of, at Sopára in Thána district, XIV, 412; statue of, in Ajanta caves, XII, 483, 499 note 1, 501.

Shálás: lecture-halls in Kánheri caves, I, pt. ii, 10.

Shales: in Ratnágiri, X, 14-15.

Shaley Beds: in Bijápur district, XXIII, 27, 33, 35-37.

Sháli: stream in Kolhápur state, XXIV, 9.

Sháligrám: black round stone representing Vishnu, IX, pt. i, 362; origin of, *id.* 387; daily worship of, *id.* p. xxxv; XIII, 105 note 2.

Shaliváhan: or Kanaksena, that is, Kanishka, IX, pt. i, 125, 443 note 1; founder of the Shaka era (A. D. 78), XVII, 351. *See* Kanishka.

Shalu: food and fodder plant cultivated throughout India, XXV, 186, 276.

Shama: food plant common throughout India, XXV, 184.

Shamans: priests and medicine-men of the foreign conquerors; their admission among Bráhmans, IX, pt. i, 436.

Shambu: other name of Shiv, IX, pt. i, 531.

Shambhu: fourth *rája* of Kolhápur (1812-1821), XXIV, 237.

Shambhudev Hill: in Poona district, temple on, XVIII, pt. iii, 440.

Shambhurám: Nágar Bráhman, supporter of Momin Khán at the siege of Ahmadábád, is taken prisoner by Damaji and sent in chains to Baroda, I, pt. i, 342.

Shami: *Prosopis spicigera*, tree, also called *aparajita*, regarded as Shiv's wife; also known as *vijayádevi*, held sacred; reason why; worship on Dasara day chiefly by Rájpúts, marriage of a man with, object of the marriage, *id.* 386; held to be the abode of a saint, *id.* 362; a sacred plant, XXV, 279, 280; XVIII, pt. i, 52.

Shámia Aliks: beggars at Bhinmál, I, pt. i, 451.

Shámil: extra levy on land in Kánara under Musalmáns, XV, pt. ii, 155.

Shámla Dev: Hindu god, worship of, in Gujarát, IX, pt. i, 292, 314, 319, 363; family deity of Nimas, *id.* 73, 96.

Shamonámir: tomb of, at Arag in Kolhápur state, XXIV, 293.

Shamoola: fodder plant, XXV, 276.

Shámrájpant: Shiváji's minister (1655), XVIII, pt. ii, 227, 228.

Shamsher Bahádur: heriditary title of the Gáikwár, title conferred on Damáji by Sháhu after the battle of Bálápur (1720), I, pt. i, 389; VII, 168, 176.

Shamshergad: hill fort in Belgaum district, XXI, 607.

Sháms-ud-din Altamsh: *sultán*, I, pt. i, 174 note 1; takes the fort of Mándu and drives away its Hindu chief (1234), *id.* 357.

Shams-ud-din : second Ismáilia missionary, also known as Chote, works miracles, makes conversions chiefly from Cháks, IX, pt. ii, 39 and note 3.
Shani : *see* Saturn.
Shanivár : Saturday, IX, pt. i, 403.
Shankaldev : Yádava ruler (1312), XII, 242.
Shankar : doer of good, other name of Shiv, IX, pt. i, 531 ; XIII, 406.
Shankar : *see* Samkara.
Shankaráchárya : founder of the Smárt sect, XV, pt. i, 121 note 2 ; I, pt. ii, 28 ; his date, *id.* 212 ; is credited with the authorship of *Prasannottara Ratnamálikà, id.* 200 ; his *Vedántasutrabhashya, id.* 246 ; places Vedic worship on modern footing, his work on philosophy, seats or sees of Shaivite sect established by, IX, pt. i, 533, 541-542 ; turns Elura and Elephanta caves into Bráhmanic caves, XIV, 135 ; temple of, at Nirmal in Thána district, *id.* 292 and note 3, 325. *See* also I, pt. i, 84 ; XXIV, 134.
Shankaráchárya : title of Smárt pontiffs of Dwárka, IX, pt. i, 542 ; at Sankeshvar, XXIV, 60.
Shankargand : Chellketan chief (860-870), XV, pt. ii, 84.
Shankarji : governor of Viramgám (1753), I, pt. i, 338.
Shankarji Keshav : *sarsubhedár*, builds temples at Nirmal in Thána district (1750), XIV, 292, 325, 367, 373.
Shankar Náráyan : temple and story of, XV, pt. ii, 292-293.
Shankar Rái : *rája* of Khelna, defeats the Musalmán army, I, pt. ii, 31.
Shankráji Malhár : Syed Husain Ali's clerk (1716), XIX, 260.
Shankráji Náráyan : appointed *pant sachiv* (1697), XIX, 618 ; supports Tárábái, *id.* 255 ; XVIII, pt. ii, 240 ; is filled with remorse and commits suicide, *id.* 241.
Shanmukha : Shivá's son, I, pt. ii, 479.
Shánti : quieting ceremonies, details of, IX, pt. i, 413-414 ; performance of, to stay epidemics, *id.* 368, 413 ; for other occasions, *id.* 413 ; spirit-quieting ceremonies, *id.* 416 ; *planet-soothing, id.* 42-43 ; use of trees in ; Ambo, *id.* 382 ; Ankdo, *id.* 383 ; Limdo, *id.* 385 ; Sopári, *id.* 387 ; quieting rites, XVIII, pt. i, 140-143, 152.
Shántivarma II : Kádamba chief (1088), XV, pt. ii, 88.
Shanvár : ward of Poona city, details of, XVIII, pt. iii, 274, 279-280.
Shanvár Váda : Peshwá's palace in Poona city, XVIII, pt. iii, 344-346 ; *id.* pt. ii, 287.
Shápur Sheheriar : first Pársi priest to settle in Sanján with his family (716), is claimed as ancestor by all Gujarát priests except those of Cambay, IX, pt. ii, 221.
Sharad : cold season, XV, pt. i, 11.
Shárada Pith : throne of learning, Dwárka seat established by Shankar, IX, pt. i, 542.
Sharákati : share villages in Thána, number of, XIII, 539 and note 3, 540, 544.
Sharanpur : Christian settlement near Násik city, XVI, 85-87, 537, 543.
Sharivar : *Amshaspand* ; fourth day of the Pársi month, sixth month of the Pársi year, IX, pt. ii, 217, 218.
Sharivar Jasan : chief festival day among Pársis, IX, pt. ii, 217.
Sharmistha : wife of Yayáti, I, pt. i, 460.
Sharva : an animal, I, pt. i, 508.
Shásanas : land grants in Kánara district, XV, pt. ii, 164.
Shashthadeva I : Goa Kádamba prince (1007-1008), feudatory of the Western Chálukya king Jayasimha II, I, pt. ii, 436, 565, 567.
Shashthadeva II : Sivachitta, the Goa Kádamba king (1246-1257), I, pt. ii, 565, 571 ; makes grant to Goveśvara, *id.* 572.
Shasthi Pujan : destiny worship, corresponding to *játakarma*, the sixth Vedic rite, worship of goddess Shasthi or mother sixth, IX, pt. i, 33.
Shástri : or divine ; qualifications, authority on Hindu law till A. D. 1827 ; *vidyárthis* or pupils of, IX, pt. i, 26-27 ; head religious officer in Ratnágiri, X, 141.
Shástri : river in Ratnágiri district, X, 8, 303.
Shatakarni : Hindu dynasty (B. C. 200-A. D. 300), XVIII, pt. ii, 212 and note 1 ; I, pt ii, 10 ; XIX, 224 ; XX, 275 ; their rule in Thána, XIII, 409 ; driven from Konkan (A. D. 50-100), *id.* 411 ; king of, defeated by Rudradáman (A. D. 178), *id.* 417 ; Thána coast again lost to (247), *id.* 418. *See* Andhrabhritya.
Shatánand : capital of Mallikárjun, I, pt. ii, 24.
Shátaváhana : king, statue of, at Nánághát in Thána district, XIV, 288.
Shataváhans : *see* Andhrabhritya.
Shatrunjaya : hill in Kathiáwár, VIII, 12 ; description, *id.* 147 note 1 ; inscriptions on, Gujjara occurs among the tribe names given in inscriptions, IX, pt. i, 499 note 3 ; Jain shrines on, *id.* 9, 550.
Shatrunji : river in Káthiáwár, VIII, 62.
Shatshashti : old district included in Thána, I, pt. ii, 543 ; Salsette, *id.* 544, 567.
Shaving ceremonies : of the Chitpávans, XVIII, pt. i, 116 ; Gujaráti Bráhmans, *id.* 164 ; Kanojs, *id.* 168 ; Dhruv Prabhus, *id.* 187, 206-207 ; Pátáne Prabhus, *id.* 225-226 ; Velális, *id.* 257 ; Brahma-Kshatris, *id.* 267 ; Gujaráti Vánis, *id.* 275 ; Kunbis, *id.* 300 - Páhadis, *id.* 311 ; Beldárs, *id.* 317 ; Bhávsárs, *id.* 323 ; Chámbhárs, *id.* 330 ; Gaundis, *id.* 332 ; Jingars, *id.* 341 ; Kumbhárs, *id.* 350 ; Salis, *id.* 363 ; Nhávis, 381 ; Bhois, *id.* 388 ; Kolis, *id.* 393 ; Lodhis, *id.* 399 ; Rajpúts, *id.* 403 ; Rámoshis, *id.* 415 ; Vanjáris, *id.* 429 ; Dhors, *id.* 433 ; Uchliás, *id.* 471 ; Bene-Israels, *id.* 518, 530 and note 2.
Shaw : Mr. A. N., collector ; encourages cotton experiments in Dhárwár (1840-1842), XXII, 287-289, 368.
Shawwál : tenth month of the Musalmán year, its first day is the Ramázán I'd holiday, IX, pt. ii, 141. *See* Ramázán I'd.
Shearer : Mr. W. (1866-1876), his cotton experiments in Dhárwár, XXII, 296-300 ; appointed superintendent of the cotton farm,

id. 305-306; agricultural instructor in the College of Science, Poona, XVIII, pt. ii, 8 note 1.
Shedbal: village in Belgaum district, a temple with inscription at, XXI, 607; I, pt. ii, 548 note 6.
Shedhi: river In Kaira district, III, 4.
Sheep: in Ratnágiri, X, 40; in Khándesh district, XII, 29; in Kánara district, XV, pt. i, 80; in Poona district, XVIII, pt. i, 65-67; in Sholápur district, XX, 17-18; in Belgaum district, XXI, 68; in Ahmadnagar district, XVII, 37-39; in Dhárwár district, XXII, 37.
Shehedmakhi: opium-eater, IX, pt. ii, 110.
Shekhdár: Marátha petty divisional officer, XII, 269, 271; XVIII, pt. ii, 326.
Shel: moist land in Ratnágiri district, X, 423.
Shelgaon: village in Khándesh district, remains of a *matha* at, XII, 470.
Shell-bracelet: manufacture of, in Káthiáwár, VIII, 261.
Shell-games: among Parbhu girls, XIII, 104 note 1.
Shell-lime: manufacture of, at Kurla in Thána district, XIV, 211.
Shell-money: sowing of, at the gate of Anahilaváda, I, pt. i, 163, 164 and note 1.
Shemti: a dye-yielding plant, XXV, 242.
Shenala: lake in Thána district, XIII, 13.
Shendivadar: *táluka* in Káthiáwár, VIII, 652.
Shendri: fibrous and dye-yielding plant, XXV, 226, 248.
Shendurni: town in Khándesh district, Hemadpanti temple at, XII, 470.
Shenshahis: a division of the Pársi community, meaning of, IX, pt. ii, 193 note 2, 194.
Shenvi: a caste of Bráhmans in Gujarát also called Sárasvats, said to have been shipwrecked strangers purified with fire by Parasharám, IX, pt. i, 436, 438; in Ratnágiri district, X, 116; peculiarities in dialect of, *id.* 116 note 6; in Sávantvádi, *id.* 411; in Kolába district, XI, 45, 46; in Thána, XIII, 85; in Násik district, XVI, 41; in Ahmadnagar district, XVII, 63-64; in Poona district, XVIII, pt. i, 175-180; in Sátára district, XIX, 56; in Sholápur district, XX, 38-40; in Belgaum district, XXI, 90-92; in Kolhápur state, XXIV, 63; in Dhárwár district, XXII, 98; in Bijápur district, XXIII, 89; in Kánara district, XV, pt. i, 139, 168; influence (1797) of, at Sindia's court, XVIII, pt. ii, 276; district of the, coinciding with the Konkan, "Introduction to the History of the Konkan," I, pt. ii, p. x.
Shenvi: title of respect in Cutch, IX, pt. i, 438.
Shepherds: in Kolába district, XI, 67, 68, 414; in Kánára district, XV, pt. i, 295-300; in Ahmadnagar district, XVII, 149-153; in Poona district, XVIII, pt. i, 384-387; in Sátára district, XIX, 104-105; in Sholápur district, XX, 146-151; in Dhárwár, XXII, 179-182; in Kolhápur state, XXIV, 102-103.
Sher: weight in Ratnágiri district, X, 164; in Sávantvádi, *id.* 432.
Shera: place of fair in Panch Maháls, III, 317.
Sheri: state lands, in Thána district, XIII, 564; in Násik district, XVI, 209 and note 3.
Sherif-ul-mulk: Bijápur governor, defeats Venkatappa of Bednur (1608), XV, pt. ii, 122, 123, 258, 277, 317, 331, 342.
Sheri Thikán: a special tenure in Ratnágiri district, X, 259.
Sherkhán Babi: governor of Baroda; defeat of; capture of Baroda, I, pt. i, 314; deputy governor of Sorath (1738), *id.* 321; allows Rangoji to escape to Borsad and joins Khauderáv, Dámáji's brother, *id.* 326; joins Rangoji and marches against Fakhr-ud-daulah; wounded in the battle of Kapadvanj, *id.* 330; dispute of, with his Arab mercenaries at Bálásinor, *id.* 338; dies (1758) at Junágadh, *id.* 343.
Shero-gár: a caste of husbandmen in Kánara district, XV, pt. i, 225-226.
Sher Sháh Sur: revolt of, in Bengal, I, pt. i, 368; emperor (1542-1545), *id.* 368-369; IX, pt. ii, 9.
Sherzi: Bijápur bastion, XXIII, 569-570.
Sheth: headman of a mercantile community, IX, pt. i, 103.
Shethe: *see* Kunkari Valánju.
Shetia: headman among Vánis, in Ratnágiri, X, 118, 142, 191.
Shetiyár: a caste of traders in Bijápur district, XXIII, 160-163.
Shetsandi: village watchman in Kolhápur state, XXIV, 274.
Shetuji: commander of the Ahmadábád garrison (1753), suffers a defeat, I, pt. i, 338.
Shevga: *Moringa pterygosperma,* food plant in Poona district, XVIII, pt. i, 52.
Shevak: caste of priests in Gujarát, IX, pt. i, 19; Gujar element in, *id.* 500; at Bhinmal, I, pt. i, 450, 464; in Cutch, V, 47.
Shevgad: hill pass in Ratnágiri district, X, 166.
Shevgaon: sub-division of Ahmadnagar district its area, aspect, water-supply, climate, rainfall, cultivation, irrigation, crops, people, roads, railway, markets, crafts and survey changes, XVII, 640-645; survey of, *id.* 520-524. *Town, id.* 738.
Shevtya: pass in Kolába district, XI, 5, 114.
Shia, Shiah: one of the two forms of the Musalmán faith, IX, pt. ii, 125; etymological meaning of, *id.* 47 note 1; origin and points of difference of, 46-47, 125-126; *imáms,* 125 note 2; divisions of, into Isnáásharis or twelvers, and seveners also called Ismáilians or Ismáilis (765), *id.* 30 note 1, 47; further sub-divisions of seveners or Ismáilis into Nazárians and Mustaálians (1094); Nazárians represented in India by Khojahs, Mustaálians by Bohorás, *id.* 30 note 1; spread of, in Gujarát, chiefly by Ismáili missionaries, *id.* 24, 125; Musalmán sect in Belgaum district, XXI, 202 and note 1; state religion, in Ahmadnagar (1531), XVII, 365.
Shiál: *see* Koli.
Shial Bet: island in Káthiáwár, history of VIII, 66, 652-653.

Shiáni: ancient capital of Limbdi state in Káthiáwár, VIII, 653.
Shibádi: a sailing vessel in Ratnágiri district, X, 171.
Shibar: large *phátimári*, a sailing vessel in Thána district, XIII, 348-349.
Shibi: puranic king, famous for his charity, version of the life of in Ajanta caves, XII, 536 and note 1, 562.
Shiddápur: *see* Siddhápur.
Shidgad: pass between Thána and Poona districts, XIII, 321; XVIII, pt. ii, 151.
Shidodi: fibrous plant, XXV, 233.
Shield: manufacture of, in Cutch, V, 127.
Shiggaon: town in Dhárwár, district, XXII, 785; inscription at, I, pt. ii, 529.
Shihanagar: village in Káthiáwár, VIII, 653.
Shikandar Adil Sháh: Bijápur king (1672-1686), minority; factions; the Mughals besiege Bijápur (1679); overthrow of the kingdom of, XXIII, 431-435, 591 and note 3.
Shikári: a caste of hunters, in Khándesh, XII, 79; in Belgaum district, XXI, 175-177.
Shikárpur: village in Cutch, a fort and temples at, V, 250.
Shikárpur: *táluka* in Mysore, I, pt. ii, 277.
Shikhar-Shingnápur: hill in Sátára district, XIX, 11.
Shikotri: Shikotar, Hindu goddess, IX, pt. i, 336, 363, 520; a famous spirit, *id.* 417.
Shikshapátri; sacred book of Matia Kanbis, IX, pt. i, 168.
Shilangi: a caste of husbandmen in Kánára district, XV, pt. i, 252, 253.
Shiledárs: self-horsed Marátha cavaliers; pay of, under Shiváji, XIX, 240-241.
Shi-lo-o-t'ie-to: Chinese for Siláditya, I, pt. ii, 353.
Shilotri: salt-marsh reclamation tenure in Thána district, XIII, 534, 544 and note 2, 545, 551 and note 4, 553 and note 2, 561 note 7; in Sálsette (1836) *id.* 584 note 5.
Shilotridárs: gap wardens in Kolába district, XI, 90, 91, 166-168, 168 note 2, 195.
Shilvant: a caste of Lingáyat traders, in Dhárwár, XXII, 125-126; in Bijápur district, XXIII, 221; origin of the name of, XXIV, 123 note 1.
Shimga: Hindu holiday, as kept by Shenvis, XVIII, pt. i, 254-255; by Kunbis, *id.* 292-293, by Rámoshis, *id.* 414.
Shimogga: district in Mysore, I, pt. ii, 561.
Shimpi: a caste of tailors, in Ratnágiri district, X, 126, 142; in Sávantvádi, *id.* 415; in Kolaba district, XI, 66, 413; in Khándesh district, XII, 73; in Thána district, XIII, 138-139; in Kánara district, XV, pt. i, 268; in Násik district, XVI, 50, 51; in Poona district, XVIII, pt. i, 367-371; in Sátára district, XIX, 94-95; in Sholápur district, XX, 140; in Belgaum district, XXI, 147-148; in Dhárwár, XXII, 159-161; in Bijápur district, XXIII, 163-169; in Kolhápur, XXIV, 98.
Shimti: gum-yielding plant, XXV, 250.
Shinda, Shinde: caste of cultivators, in Ratnágiri district, X, 124; in Kolába district, XI, 71; son of a Kunbi woman by Bráhman father so styled, IX, pt. i, 442 note 6; in Kolába district, XI, 71.
Shindi: liquor-yielding tree in Khándesh district, XII, 27.
Shindigár: a caste of palm-juice sellers in Belgaum district, XXI, 167.
Shinga: hill in Poona district, XVIII, pt. i, 5.
Shingaru: literally a foal, a table land in Nánághát so called, XIV, 287.
Shingnápur: holy village in Sátára district, temples and fair at, XIX, 580-587.
Shingnápur: old name of Kavlápur near Sángli, XXIV, 360.
Shinguti: famine plant, XXV, 201.
Ship-building: at Bassein, Surat and other ports on the Western Coast (1530-1620), I, pt. ii, 36; at Surat (1759-1800), II, 146, 180; in Ratnágiri district, X, 172; at Agáshi and Bassein, XIV, 1, 31; in Kánara district, XV, pt. i, 22; in Bombay (1672-1778), XXVI, pt. ii, 187-196; cost of (1776), *id.* 194-195.
Shipil: canoe in Thána district, XIII, 721.
Shipman: Sir Abraham, commissioned to take possession of Bombay, XXVI, pt. i, 10; lands (1662) at Anjidiv; his death (1666), *id.* 11; XIII, 472; XV, pt. ii, 256, 251.
Shipping: in Ahmadábád district, IV, 84; in Cutch, V, 114-117; investments in, in Ratnágiri, X, 158; in Kánara district, XV, pt. ii, 27-28; of the East India Company, half to load directly at Bombay without going to Surat (1684), XXVI, pt. iii, 581.
Shiprak: Andhrabhritya founder (300 B. C.), XII, 239 and note 1.
Ships: the English and the Dutch, frequent the ports of Dábhol, Chaul and Bassein without hindrance, I, pt. ii, 63; in Bombay, description of, by Grose (1750), XXVI, pt. ii, 522-524; by Forbes (1766-1770), *id.* 524; by Parsons (1775), *id.* 525; list of Bombay ships (1736-1857), *id.* 526-529; not to be built for country powers (1765), XXVI, pt. i, 352.
Shipwrecks: in Bombay, list of (1826-1872), XXVI, pt. ii, 532-533.
Shir: pass in Násik district, XVI, 129.
Shiral: fibrous plant, XXV, 230.
Shirála: town in Sátára district, grove and fair at, XIX, 587-588.
Shiráli: port in Kánara district, XV, pt. ii, 341; imports and exports of, *id.* 65, 66, 68.
Shirápur: village in Ahmadnagar district, water-fall at, XVII, 739.
Shirávati: river in Kánara district, XV, pt. i, 4, 7.
Shirazis: chief *sayad* family of Gujarát, IX, pt. ii, 6 note 1 (6).
Shirhatti: town in Kolhápur, its history, fort, monasteries and fair, XXIV, 367-371.
Shirin: picture of, in Ajanta caves, IX, pt. ii, 183 note 4.
Shiris, Shirish: sacred plant, XXV, 291; in Khándesh district, XII, 27.
Shirke: Konkan chiefs, I, pt. ii, 31; Marátha chiefs, *id.* 72; their state put an end to by the Peshwa (1768), *id.* 86; X, 194.
Shirke: surname among Kunbis, XIII, 63 note 4.

Shirol : town in Kolhápur state, survey details, XXIV, 256-257 ; temples and mosque at, *id.* 319-320.
Shiroli : village in Kolhápur, temple and fair at, XXIV, 320.
Shirpur : sub-division of Khándesh district, its boundaries, area, aspect, climate, water, soil, holdings, history, survey details, survey results, stock, crops and people, XII, 2, 413-417. *Town, id.* 470.
Shirsári : pass in Násik district, XVI, 130.
Shirsuphal : reservoir at, in Poona district, XVIII, pt. ii, 26-27.
Shirval : village in Sátára district, caves at, XIX, 588.
Shirve : peak in Kánara district, XV, pt. ii, 303, 341.
Shirvegudda : hill in Kánara district, XV, pt. i, 4, 5.
Shirzekhán : Mughal general (1686), at Sátára, defeated by Hambirráv, XIX, 246-247.
Shirzi Ráo Ghátge : *see* Sakhárám Ghátge Shirzi Ráo.
Shishahgar : a caste of glass-makers, Hindu converts, found chiefly in Kaira district, make glass bottles, etc., IX, pt. ii, 89 ; Musalmáns in Khándesh, XII, 126.
Shist : standard rent in Kánara district, XV, pt. ii, 157.
Shiul : modern Cheul, XI, 275 note 3.
Shiv : or Rudra, god or deity worshipped by Shaivs ; third member of Hindu trinity, IX, pt. i, p. xxxvi, 531 ; worshipped under the names Máhádev, Sadáshiv, Shambhu, Shankar, *id.* 531, 541 ; form, *id.* 541 ; nature, euphemistic epithets ; healing powers ; praised as greatest of the physicians ; is given name of Mrityunjaya ; *Rudri* and *Mrityunjayanajap* prayers, *id.* 531 ; worship of *ling* emblem, *id.* p. xxxv, 531, 541 ; elaboration of worship ; *Shivrátris* or great nights of worship, *id.* 541 ; worshipped by Rám at Saras ; *ling* or stone home of, at Siddhnáth, *id.* 12 note 1 ; of Hátakeshvar at Vadnagar, *id.* 14 ; worship of, by women on *Rishi Panchmi, id.* 23 note 5 ; *Nandi* the bull, his carrier, *id.* 374 ; is lord of serpents, *id.* 379 ; Mondays sacred to him ; is represented with a crescent moon on his fore-head, *id.* 397, 400 ; his ill-treatment by his father-in-law ; *Pálas piplo* worshipped by, *id.* 381, 385 ; offerings to the stone image of ; his pet flowers, *id.* 408-409 ; *Bel* tree leaves are favourite offerings to, *id.* 383 ; Nágar Bráhmans said to have been created by, *id.* 14 ; devotion to the worship of, among strangers, *id.* 433, 440 ; worshipped at Sopára (100-400 A. D.), XIII, 406 ; titulary deity of the Siláháras (810-1260), *id.* 424 ; image of, at Elephanta, XIV, 75, 76, 130 note 10 ; at Mandapeshvar, *id.* 224 ; at Sopára, *id.* 337 ; Elephanta sculpture in Thána district, XIV, 66-67, 76.
Shivachari : caste of Lingáyat weavers in Bijápur district, XXIII, 259.
Shiváji : founder of the Marátha power (1627-1680), his birth ; early life under Dádáji Kondadev, manager of his father's estates ; takes Torna, Rájgad, Chákan, Kondhána, Supa and Poona ; plunders a Bijápur caravan ; captures Rájmáchi and Lohogad forts and most places of strength in the Konkan ; enters the Mughal service ; his schemes for possessing himself of the whole of the *Ghátmátha ;* murders the *rája* of Jávli ; builds Pratápgad ; insults Aurangzeb ; plunders Junnar and Ahmadnagar ; strengthens his cavalry ; the repulse of his army against Janjira ; enters into a treaty with the Sávants of Vádi ; assassinates Afzulkhán ; takes some of the Kolhápur forts, levies contributions along the banks of the Krishna, and spreads terror over the whole country ; his respect for Rámdás Svámi, his religious guide ; his conduct towards Báji Ghorpade of Mudhol ; fits out a navy ; his conduct towards his father ; changes his capital from Rájgad to Ráygad ; extent of his power ; his wars with the Mughals ; his defence of Sinhgad ; takes the title of *rája ;* plunders Ahmadnagar ; his success against Bijápur ; burns Vengurla and plunders Barcelor ; Dilerkhán, the Mughal general, lays siege to Purandhar ; gallant conduct of the besieged ; Shiváji proposes to enter the Mughal service ; his interview with Jaysing and Dilerkhán ; gives up several forts to the Mughals ; levies *chauth* and *sardeshmukhi ;* assists the Mughals in their attack on Bijápur ; visits Delhi ; escapes from Delhi ; the districts of Poona, Chákan and Supa restored to him ; surprises Sinhgad and Purandhar ; his coronation at Ráygad ; his appearance ; death ; extent of his territory at the time of his death, XVIII, pt. ii, 223-238.
Another account of : founder of the Marátha empire (1627-1680) ; associates with Máwalis and thinks of establishing himself as an independent chief ; takes the fort of Torna (1646) ; builds Ráygad (1647) ; obtains Chákan and Kondána ; surprises Lohogad and Rájmáchi (1648), I pt. ii, 591-592 ; extends his operations into the Konkan ; takes several forts including Ráiri or Ráygad ; arranges for the revenue management of the country ; and appoints Ábáji Sondev *subhedár* of Kalyán, *id.* 67, 592 ; is obliged to remain quiet owing to the confinement of his father at Bijápur, *id.* 592, 651 ; applies for aid to Sháh Jahán, *id.* 651 ; storms Jávli and reduces the fort of Vásota (1653) ; storms the fort of Rohira and kills the *deshmukh* of the Hardas Máwal, *id.* 592 ; builds the forts of Birvádi, Lingána and Pratápgad, *id.* 67, 592 ; plunders Junnar (1657), *id.* 592 ; obtains Aurangzeb's permission to take possession of the whole Konkan and is joined by the Sávants (1658), *id.* 68 ; stabs Afzulkhán and takes Vasantgad, Rangna and Kelna (1659), *id.* 592-593 ; is besieged at Panhála by Sidi Johár (1660) ; plunders Rájápur and burns Dábhol (1660), *id.* 68 ; Áli Ádil Sháh marches in person against him and he surrenders Panhála and many other forts (1661), *id.* 593 ; plunders Rájápur and captures Dánda-Rájápur ; makes Málvan his naval head-quarters and builds several forts in the Konkan, *id.* 68 ; surprises and kills

Báji Ghorpade at Mndhol and transfers his head-quarters from Rájgad to Ráiri (1662), *id.* 593; plunders Surat (1663) and Barcelor (1654), *id.* 68; surprises and wounds Shaista Khán at Poona (1664), *id.* 593; submits to Jaysing (1665); goes to Delhi (1666); his escape from Delhi (1667), *id.* 69, 593-594; drives the Mughals from Kalyán; opens communication with Snltán Mázum; attempts the conquest of Goa and Janjira (1668); sends a large force up the coast (1670), *id.* 69; Mohábat Khán sent against him (1671), *id.* 594; takes several forts in the Dakhan and sacks Húbli (1672), *id.* 594; is crowned (1674), *id.* 70, 594; his chief ministers, *id.* 594; sends a force to Bassein to demand *chauth* from the Portuguese (1674), *id.* 70; recovers several forts in the Konkan then held by Bijápur (1675) and builds several other forts, *id.* 594-595; sends a large fleet to meet the Mughal fleet (1675), *id.* 70; his invasion of the Karnátak (1678), *id.* 71, 595; enters into an alliance with Bijápur against the Mughals, *id.* 595; sends a large fleet to burn the Musalmán fleets then in Bombay (1678), *id.* 71; his son Sambháji deserts (1679), *id.* 71, 595; takes Khánderi or Kennery and fortifies it (1679), *id.* 71-72; enters into treaty with the English (1679), *id.* 72; his death (1680) *id.* 72; condition of the Konkan under him, *id.* 72-73; his forts, *id.* 73-75; the excnt of his territory, *id.* 595; his possessions in Belgaum district, XXI, 375-376; his infantry, institutions, fort establishment, ministers, XIX, 239-244; the building of Násik hill forts ascribed to, XVI, 442; admitted to the Kshatriya caste, XIII, 411 note 3; IX, pt. i, 442; *see* also XVII, 399-400; XXIII, 426-427, 430-433; XV, pt. ii, 52, 125, 127, 321, 322, 299, 258, 317.

Shiváji II: son of Rájárám, I, pt. ii, 597; first Kolhápur *rája* (1700-1712); Tárábái's administration of government; Aurangzeb marches against Panhála and Vishálgad and receives Sir William Norris, English ambassador in Panhála; Aurangzeb moves to Ahmadnagar and Pant Amátya retakes Panhála which becomes the capital of Kolhápur; release of Sháhu and his successful struggle with Tárábái for sovereignty; dies in 1712, XXIV, 226-227.

Shiváji III: third Kolhápur *rája* (1760-1812); Jijibái, widow of Sambháji II; adopts the son of Sháháji Bhonsle of Khanvat under the name of Shiváji and manages the state; establishment of the family of Patvardhans by the Peshwa; English expedition against the maritime possessions of Kolhápur terminated by the capture of Málvan and a treaty (1766); human sacrifices to Ambábái by Jijibái; her death (1772); Yashvantráv's management of the state affairs; revolt of the chiefs of Bávda, Kágal and Vishálgad, (1777); Mahádji Sindia is sent by the Peshwa against Kolhápur authorities who agree to pay fifteen lákhs of rupees; Parashrám Bháu captures Rangna; Ratnákarpant's administration; successful expedition headed by the *rája* against the *desái* of Sávantvádi; second treaty with the British Government (1792); war with Parasharám Bháu Patvardhan; war with *sar desái* of Sávantvádi and chief of Nipáni; third treaty with the British government; his death, XXIV, 230-237.

Shiváji IV: sixth *rája* of Kolhápur (1837-1866), XXIV, 240-243.

Shiváji V: eighth *rája* of Kolhápur (1870-1883), XXIV, 244-245.

Shivajogi: a caste of comb-makers in Dhárwár district, XXII, 178.

Shivalli: a class of Bráhmans in Kánara district, XV, pt. i, 136.

Shivan: *Gmelina arborea,* tree in Poona district, XVIII, pt. i, 52.

Shivappa Náik: Bednur chief (1648-1670); takes Mirjan fort; fortifies Honávar; his revenue system, XV, pt. ii, 122-125, 307, 332.

Shivar: village in Násik district, memorial stones and posts at, XVI, 647.

Shivbara: state in Khándesh district, XII, 606.

Shiveshvar: village in Kánara district, old fort of, its history, XV, pt. ii, 341-342; captured by Shiváji (1673), *id.* 127, 128; mention of, by Hamilton (1720), *id.* 135; Portuguese church at (1735), *id.* 136.

Shivgad: hill fort in Kolhápur state, XXIV, 5; pass, *id.* 5-6.

Shivganga: river in Poona district, XVIII, pt. i, 9.

Shivites: *see* Shaivites.

Shivkanchi: place of pilgrimage near Conjeveram, IX, pt. i, 549.

Shivkorbái: famous Nágar Bráhman *sati*, IX, pt. i, 358.

Shivne: market village in Poona district, XVIII, pt. iii, 440.

Shivner: Junnar hill-fort in Poona district, details, hill-top, upper hill, Musalmán remains, view, flying-arch, mosque, XVIII, pt. iii, 153-163; caves (I-L), *id.* 184-201; taken by Malek-ul-Tujar (1451), I, pt. ii, 588; captured by Malik Ahmad Beheri, XVIII, pt. ii, 219; birth-place of Shiváji, Shiváji's attempt to take it fails, I, pt. ii, 594; falls into the hands of the Maráthás (1760), *id.* 602; survey of, XVIII, pt. ii, 384-389.

Shivo: a Dhed saint, IX, pt. i, 341.

Shivpur: village in Bijápur district, XXIII, 676.

Shiv Purán: *see* Garud Purán.

Shivrái: copper coinage of Shiváji, XIII, 306.

Shivráj: *rája,* commandant of Mándu (1658), I, pt. i, 382.

Shivrám Gárdi: Gáikwár's officer (1801), VII, 204-205, 317.

Shivrátri: Shivrátra or Shiv's night, day sacred to make offerings to Shiv; *Maha,* IX, pt. i, 409, 541; Hindu holiday, XVIII, pt. i, 254.

Shivsingh: *rája* of I'dar, sends Sajan Singh to help Momin Khán at the siege of Ahmadábád by the Maráthás (1757), I, pt. i, 341.

Shivta: *see* Páthantána.

Shoes: making of, in Ahmadábád district, IV, 140; in Cutch, V, 128; in Kolába district,

XI, 135; foreign trade in, at Sopára (810-1230), XIII, 430; Spanish, import of, in Thána district (1500-1670), *id.* 467 and note 5; making of, in Bijápur district, XXIII, 374-375.

Sholápur: district, its boundaries, sub-divisions, aspect, hills, rivers, geology and climate, XX, 1-8; minerals, forests and their management, domestic and wild animals, fish and birds, *id.* 9-22; population, census details, Bráhmans, writers, traders, husbandmen, craftsmen, and other castes, communities and movements, *id.* 23-213; agriculture, husbandmen, holdings, soil, field, tools, irrigation, crops and famines, *id.* 214-238; capital, capitalists, investments, money-lending, borrowers, service, mortgage, land transfers, interest, currency, wages, prices, weights and measures, *id.* 239-253; trade, roads, railways, bridges and ferries, post and telegraph, trade-centres, markets, carriers, imports and exports, *id.* 254-268; crafts, *id.* 269-274; history, early period (B. C. 90-A. D. 1294), Báhmanis (1347-1489), Durgádevi Famine (1396-1407), Dámájipant's famine (1460), under Bijápur and Ahmadnagar (1489-1720), under the Maráthás (1720-1818), *id.* 275-300; land, its management and staff, survey (1839-1858), revision survey (1859-1874), season reports and alienated villages, *id.* 301-366; justice, Civil Courts and suits; registration, magistracy, police, crime and jails, *id.* 367-373; revenue and finance, *id.* 374-378; instruction, staff, cost, readers and writers, school returns, libraries and newspapers, *id.* 379-385; health, diseases, hospitals, vaccination, cattle disease and births and deaths, *id.* 386-390; sub-divisional details, *id.* 391-406; places of interest, *id.* 407-510.

Sub-division, its boundaries, area, aspect, climate, water, soil, stock, holdings, crops and people, *id.* 404-406; survey (1840-1841), *id.* 309-317; revision survey (1870-1871), *id.* 341-346.

Town, its position, appearance, walls and gates, divisions, suburbs, streets, population, houses, trade, cotton mill, management, water, climate, temples, cantonment, fort and history, *id.* 485-502; divided between Ahmadnagar and Bijápur (1508), *id.* 278; siege (1510) of, *id.* 279; (1524), *id.* 279-280; promised as Ismael Adil Sháha's sister's dowry, invaded unsuccessfully by Burhan Nizám Sháh in 1524, 1528 and 1531; taken by Burhan Nizám (1542), I, pt. ii, 570, 623; XX, 282; restored (1543) to Bijápur, *id.* 282; taken and strengthened by Burhan Nizám (1551), *id.* 282; sieges (1553, 1557), *id.* 283-284; ceded to Bijápur as the dowry of Chánd Bibi (1562), *id.* 284, I, pt. ii, 645; sieges of (1590, 1594), *id.* 592; XX, 285, 286; taken by Malik Ambar (1623), XX, 287; passes to Bijápur (1636), *id.* 287; to the Mughals (1668), *id.* 287; taken by Aurangzeb's son Azam (1685), I, pt. ii, 595; passes to Nizam-ul-mulk (1723), XX, 290; besieged and taken by General Munro (1818), *id.* 296-300; I, pt. ii, 612.

Shopkeepers: Vánias, their start in life, IX, pt. i, 78-79 and note 3; in Ratnágiri district, X, 181; in Káthiáwár, VIII, 244; in Kolába district, XI, 120; in Khándesh district, XII, 218; in Thána district, XIII, 335; in Kánara district, XV, pt. ii, 56-57; in Násik district, XVI, 142; in Ahmadnagar district, XVII, 342; in Sátára district, XIX, 218; in Belgaum district, XXI, 315; in Dhárwár district, XXII, 358; in Bijápur district, XXIII, 364; in Kolhápur, XXIV, 206.

Shorpáraga: Sopára in Thána district, XIV, 320.

Shráddha: offering to the manes, I, pt. ii, 249; memorial rites among Hindus, performance of, on the 10th, 11th, 12th and 13th days after death; monthly rites; yearly rites; caste dinners given as part of mind rites on 11th, 12th and 13th days after deaths, yearly rites; *sejja* giving on the 12th; special mind rite in the month of Bhádarva, IX, pt. i, 50; satisfying the wishes of the spirits of the dead, *id.* 348, 409; details of the rites among Bráhmans, *id.* 50-51; Rájpúts, *id.* 149-151; husbandmen and Kanbis, *id.* 163, 174, 175, 176; craftsmen, *id.* 181, 183, 186, 188, 192, 195, 201, 206; Bháts, *id.* 214; herdsmen, *id.* 285, 289; *see* also XVIII, pt. i, 232-234.

Shrávak: caste in Western India, traces of Gujar element in, IX, pt. i, 496; Vániás, *id.* 69, 70, 96-103; Marváris, *id.* 103-105; religion, Jainism, two leading sects, Digambaras and Shvetambars, distinction between the two sects, *id.* 105; *gachhas* or subsects in Shvetambars, *id.* 105, 106, 109 and notes 1 and 2; Shripujyas or spiritual heads of *gachhas*, *id.* 109-110; three classes of ascetics—Sadhus, *id.* 106, 108; Sádhvis, *id.* 108; Gergis, *id.* 108-109; religious buildings, temples or *dehras*, description, images, image installation, *id.* 110, 111 and notes 1 and 2; ministrants, worship, *id.* 111-113; monasteries or *apasaras*, *id.* 113; *holidays*, Pachusan, *id.* 113-115; *Siddha Chakrapuja* or saint-wheel worship; *pánjrápol* or animal home, *id.* 115; places of pilgrimage, *id.* 350; in Cutch, V, 52-53; in Káthiáwár, VIII, 147-148; in Southern India, despoiled (1000), I, pt. ii, 437 note 5. *See* Jains.

Shrávanur: old name of Sávanur in Dhárwár district, XXII, 793.

Shrávasti: Sewet near Benares, XIII, 406; merchants of, visit Sopára (A. D. 400), XIV, 124, 320.

Shridepathár: plateau in Poona district, XVIII, pt. i, 5.

Shrigaud: a caste of Gujarát Bráhmans, their origin, I, pt. i, 161; in Gujarát, IX, pt. i, 2; strength and distribution, *id.* 3, 19; in Poona district, XVIII, pt. i, 163; in Thána district, XIII, 78.

Shrigonda: sub-division of Ahmadnagar district, its area, aspect, water, soil, climate, cultivation, crops, people, roads, railway, markets, and survey changes, XVII, 645-650. *Town*, temple, *id.* 739-740.

Shri Harsha: king of Magadha (610-642), father of, conquered the Gurjjaras, I, pt. i,

467; defeats the Húnas, Gurjjaras, Látas and king of Sind and Málava, *id.* 497; drives away White Húnas, *id.* 500; defeated by Dantidurg, I, pt. ii, 194.
Shrikes: an order of birds in Ratnágiri district, X, 69-71.
Shrimál: town, capital of the Gurjjar kingdom, now Bhinmál; Shrimális take name from, IX, pt. i, 16 note 1, 19, 73.
Shrimáli: a caste of Gujarát Bráhmans, I, pt. i, 450, 462 and note 2; their origin, *id.* 44; in Thána district, XIII, 78; in Ahmadnagar district, XVII, 55; in Poona district, XVIII, pt. i, 163; in Sholápur district, XX, 30; in Káthiáwár, VIII, 145; in Gujarát, IX, pt. i, 2; strength and distribution, *id.* 3, 19; a caste of Vániás (Meshri), derivation of the name; seem to be Gurjjars, formerly Solanki Rájpúts, *id.* 73, 496, 499; Vágheshvari, the family goddess of, *id.* 73; Shrávaks, sub-divisions, distribution, said to have been created by goddess Mahálakshmi, origin of, sub-divisions, minor divisions, *id.* 97, 98; I, pt. i, 463; in Cutch, V, 46, 52; in Kolába district, XI, 48; in Thána district, XIII, 112; meaning-making of the name of, I, pt. i, 458; brought back to Bhinmál (1694), *id.* 464.
Shrimál Mahátmya: legendary account of Shrimál, I, pt. i, 461.
Shrimantgad: fort in Kolhápur state, details, temple and ponds at, XXIV, 371-372.
Shrinagar: Shrimál, I, pt. i, 461.
Shrinagar: town in Káthiáwár, was formerly the capital of the Jethvas, VIII, 653.
Shrináthji: picture of, represents Vishnu, IX, pt. i, p. xxxv; shrine of, at Nathdwára, *id.* 157, 549.
Shrine, shrines: of Abdul Kádir Giláni at Baghdád, IX, pt. ii, 56; of Ali and Hussain, *id.* 47; of Miran Sayadali at Unjha, *id.* 56, 128; of Naw Shahid at Surat, *id.* 129; of Pir-i-Rawan at Cambay, *id.* 26 note 1; of Sháh A'lam at Ahmadábád, *id.* 56; of Shams-ud-din at Uch, *id.* 39; of Sindsáh at Navasári, *id.* 66; miniature, of Karbala martyrs, *id.* 128; vows made to visit, *id.* 128; spirit-expelling element in the, of Miran Sayad Ali, *id.* 128-129; of North Gujarát, IX, pt. i, p. ix; Shaivite, *id.* 541, 549; Vaishnav, *id.* 549; Mátá, *id.* 549; Jain, *id.* 550; of goddess Bakucharáji, of goddess Reváli and tomb of Dátár Pir visited by sick persons, *id.* 366; at Gokarn in Kánara district, XV, pt. ii, 291-298.
Shringeri: town in Mysore, monastery at, XV, pt. i, 131.
Shringeri: village in Dhárwár district, old weir at, XXII, 785-786.
Shripál: mythical Jain king, said to have married the princess of Soparaka, XIV, 319.
Shripat Ráo: son of Parashrám Trimbak, opposes the appointment of Báji Ráo as Peshwa, I, pt. ii, 599.
Shripatráv: deputy of the Peshwa in Gujarát, negotiates with Momin Khán for the release of Bhagvantráv; is recalled, I, pt. i, 338.
Shripujyas: spiritual heads of Shrávak *gachhas* IX, pt. i, 106, 109; selection; successor's selection, initiation; dress, daily life, *id.* 109-110.
Shripunj: another name of Jágsom, the restorer of the sun temple at Bhinmál, I, pt. i, 460, 462 and note 3.
Shri Rámeshvar: temple near the hot springs at Akloli in Thána district, XIII, 16.
Shristhának: old name for Thána, chief town of the Siláhárás (810-1260), XIII, 423, 425, 428; XIV, 355, 356, 418, 195; I, pt. ii, 18.
Shrivaishnav; a caste of Bráhmans in Dhárwár district, XXII, 98-100.
Shrivardhan: town in Janjira state, birthplace of Báláji Vishvanáth, XI, 146, 425, 467; south boundary of the Nizám Sháhi Konkan, I, pt. ii, 34.
Shrivraksha: *see* Bel.
Shroff: coin-tester in Vánia banker's shop, IX, pt. i, 79, 81.
Shron Aparánta: the Konkan, XIII, 407 and note 1.
Shuddha Sáli: a caste of weavers in Dhárwár district, XXII, 175-177.
Shujáat Khán: Kártalab Khán, thirty-eighth viceroy of Gujarát (1684-1703), I, pt. i, 287; his campaign in Jhálaváda and Sorath and storming of the fort of Thána, *id.* 288; captures Jodhpur (1722), *id.* 303.
Shujáat Khán: one of Sher Sháh Sur's generals in Málwa; defeats Kádir Khán at Mándu; appointed commandant of Mándu, I, pt. ii, 368-369; recovers Málwa (1554), *id.* 369.
Shujait Khán: (1724), deputy of the viceroy of Gujarát, VII, 169.
Shujá-ud-Daulah: *nawáb* of Lucknow, negociates with the Peshwa, I, pt. i, 341.
Shukarvár: Friday, IX, pt. i, 402.
Shuklatirth: island in the bed of the Narbada in Rewa Kántha, VI, 6; place of pilgrimage, IX, pt. i, 549.
Shukra: *see* Venus.
Shukravár: ward of Poona city, details of, XVIII, pt. iii, 274, 282-383.
Shukravár Váda: in Poona city, XVIII, pt. iii, 346.
Shurpán: place of pilgrimage, on the Narbada, IX, pt. i, 549.
Shurpárak; Sopára, mentioned in the *Mahábhárata*, XIII, 404; chief city of the Siláháras (810-1260), *id.* 423; XIV, 316, 319, 320, 321, 385, 387, 417.
Shute: sailors of Somanáth, I, pt. i, 204.
Shvetámbars; white-robed, religious sect of Shrávaks, also called Tappás; form of image worshipped by their priests, IX, pt. i, 105; sub-sects or *gachhas* in, *id.* 105, 109 and notes 1 and 2, 110.
Shyhar: *see* Shihár.
Siam: Bráhman influence in, IX, pt. i, 437; introduction of Bráhman and Buddhist details into literature and architecture of, *id.* 441.
Sibor; perhaps Cheul, XI, 270; possibly Sopára, XIV, 320.
Sida: *acuta, carpinifolia*, fibrous plants, XXV, 228.

Siddápur: in the Dhárwár *táluka*, record of 1158 at, I, pt. ii, 459 note 4, 569.
Siddápur: sub-division of Kánara district, villages, aspect, climate, water, soil, stock, survey details, people, XV, pt. ii, 247-248; schools, rest-houses and dispensaries in, *id.* 45, 215, 219. *Town, id.* 342.
Siddhabhatta: grantee in Indra's grant of 914, I, pt. i, 131.
Siddha Chakra Puja: saint-wheel worship among Shrávaks, IX, pt. i, 115.
Siddhachakravartin: title of Siddharája, I, p. i, 173.
Siddhagiri: religious teacher of the Buruds of Kolhápur, XXIV, 94.
Siddhahema: treatise on grammar by Hemachandra, I, pt. i, 180.
Siddha Hemachandra: I, pt. i, 191. *See* Siddhahema.
Siddhánta: work of the astronomer Brahmagupta of Bhinmál, I, pt. i, 467. *See* Brahma Siddhánta.
Siddhántaśiromani: Bháskaráchárya's work, taught in a college founded by Changadeva, I, pt. ii, 244, 526.
Siddhapayya: Kalachurya Bijjalá's governor of the Hánumgal province, I, pt. ii, 476.
Siddhappa: temple of, in the Dhárwár district, inscription at, I, pt. ii, 460 note 3.
Siddhapur: ruins of, in Kánara district, XV, pt. i, 321, 342-343.
Siddhapur: town in Gujarát. *See* Sidhpur.
Siddharája, Sidhraj: Chálukya king (1094-1143), I, pt. i, 156, 161, 162; succeeds Karna; regency of his mother; intrigues regarding his succession; remission of pilgrim-tax; his wars with the kings of Sauráshtra, Málwa, and Sind; his era; his religious leanings and architectural buildings, *id.* 171-181; his shrine at Siddhpur, IX, pt. i, 445; overpowers Barbara and his followers and forces them to become Hindus, *id.* 443-444, 485; Gujarát Solanki, XIII, 436; called king of kings, I, pt. ii, 24; king of Anahilaváda, IX, pt. ii, 186 note 5; gives justice to Musalmán traders of Cambay, *id.* 2 note 3; gives patronage to Bohora missionary; said to have embraced Islám, *id.* 26 note 2.
Siddhas: demi-gods, pictures of, in Elephanta caves, XIV, 73 and note 1.
Siddheśvar: temple of, at Nirmal, in Thána district, XIV, 293; at Kembhávi in the Nizám's dominions, inscription at, I, pt. ii, 440 note 8.
Siddhnáth: *ling* or stone home raised by Rám in honour of god Shiv near the village of Saras near Surat, IX, pt. i, 12 note 1.
Siddhpur: *see* Sidhpur.
Siddiki: section of *sheikhs,* claim descent from Abu Bakar Siddik, IX, pt. ii, 8 and note 3.
Sidenur: village in Dhárwár district, with a temple and inscription at, XXII, 786.
Sidgad: fort in Thána district, XIII, 523; XIV, 312, 98.
Sidhgad: fort in Ratnágiri district, X, 373.
Sidhoji: *see* Sidoji Gujar.
Sidhpur: sub-division in Baroda state, its area, aspect, climate, water-supply, soil, assessment and population, VII, 615-616; schools and hospital at, *id.* 487, 508. *Town,* remains at, Rudra Málá and other buildings, its holiness, place of pilgrimage, *id.* 616 619; also called Matri Gaya, IX, pt. i, 519; shrine at, *id.* p. ix; former seat of the head *mulla* of Daudi Bohras at, pt. ii, 31 note 4; Vanarája's image at, I, pt. i, 152; Mularája's grants at, *id.* 161; Jain temple at, *id.* 172; Rudramahálaya temple at, *id.* 179; Kumárapála's visits to, *id.* 183; Ahmadsháh's march against, *id.* 237.
Sidhráj, Sidhraj Jaisingh: *see* Siddharája.
Sidhsar: Buddhist caves in Káthiáwár, VIII, 10.
Sidhtek: village in Ahmadnagar district; Ganapati's temple at, XVII, 739.
Sidi Ali Kapodhan: Turkish admiral (1554), lands at Anjidiv, XV, pt. ii, 252, 273, 278.
Sidi Johár: Bijápur general, besieges Shiváji in Panhála (1660), I, pt. ii, 593; XXIV, 225, 314.
Sidi Kasim: captures Marátha forts; his defeat (1686), XXVI, pt. i, 100-101; invades Bombay, XIV, 27.
Sidi Merich: governor in Cutch, his banishment (1780), V, 147, 148.
Sidi Rahman: provided for by the Maráthás, I, pt. ii, 83.
Sidis: Musalmáns of special community, of part foreign descent, also called Habashis, origin, divisions, language, character of, IX, pt. ii, 11; special form of worship among, dance of, men of position and power among, rulers, *id.* 12; of Janjira, arrival and settlement at Surat of, *id.* 3; Abyssinians, said to have taken possession of Janjira (about 1489), 1, pt. ii, 34; their districts invaded by Shiváji (1658); unite with Bijápur and Savants against Shiváji, *id.* 68; abandon Dánda-Rájápur and take refuge in Janjira, put the state under the protection of the Mughals (1670), *id.* 69; destroy the fortifications of Dánda-Rájápur, take several of the ports in the neighbourhood, and treat people with cruelty (1672); blockade the Karanja river and lay waste villages along the Nágothna river (1673), *id.* 70; their fleet plunders the coast, and carries the inhabitants away as slaves (1677-78), *id.* 71; their alliance with the English broken; take Underi (1680), *id.* 72; renew the struggle for the possession of Khánderi and burn Apta (1680), *id.* 76; make raids on the Marátha territory and defeat Sambháji's fleet in Bombay harbour (1682), *id.* 77; obtain a *sanad* from Aurangzeb and take the districts of Suvarndurg and Anjanvel and the forts of Rájpuri and Ráygad, *id.* 79; attack Bassein, threaten Sálsette and ravage the country about (1692), *id.* 80; lose some places to the Maráthás (1713), *id.* 82; take Govalkot (1733), *id.* 83; enter into a formal alliance with the English, *id.* 83, 88; their alliance with the English dissolved (1784), *id.* 107; receive revenues of Surat from Aurangzeb (1660), II, 89, 117; live in the Gir province in Káthiáwár, VIII, 11; capture the port of Jáfarábád, *id.* 161; down-

fall of (1733), XXVI, pt. i, 161 ; *another account of:* origin, XI, 433 ; constitution, *id.* 434 ; in Ahmadnagar and Bijápur service, *id.* 435 ; appointed Mughal admirals, *id.* 436 ; in wars with the Maráthás, *id.* 437-442 ; quarrel with the English and driven out of Surat, *id.* 443-446 ; take Jáfarábád, *id.* 447 ; internal affairs, *id.* 448-452 ; people, *id.* 420-421 ; in South Kolába, their changes in the revenue demands, *id.* 171 and note 3; the Peshwa recovers Ráygad from them (1735) and changes their rates, *id.* 172 ; division of lands between the Sidi and the Peshwa, *id.* 173 and note 6 ; winter in Bombay harbour (1672-1680), XIII, 475 ; their struggle with Shiváji (1675-1680), *id.* 478 ; attack Bassein (1690), *id.* 481 ; decline of their power (1735), *id.* 492 ; independence of, granted by the Peshwa (1762), *id.* 498 ; settlement of, and element in other castes of Thána, XIII, 64 ; pirates on Thána coast (1700), *id.* 488 ; defeat Shamrajpant (1657), XVIII, pt. ii, 228 ; Maráthás destroy the state of (1761), *id.* 250 ; levy contributions from Shahu's districts, Marátha intrigues for the ruin of, XIX, 277 ; Kasim and Sambal's flects in Bombay, XXVI, pt. i, 66-72 ; their quarrel, *id.* 73 ; Masat and Saut, advances to, by the Company (1735), *id.* 175-176; station garrison at Sion (1737), *id.* 178.

Sidi Sambhal : chief of Janjira, burns Jaytápur (1676), I, pt. ii, 71.

Sidi Yákut : commandant of Janjira, offers to become a vassal of the emperor through the governor of Surat and receives the title of Yákut Khán from the emperor with an annual subsidy of 1½ lákhs payable from the port of Surat, I, pt. i, 285.

Sidiyanurudivi : village in the Santalige province mentioned in the Mysore inscription, I, pt. ii, 306 and note 5.

Sidney Point : at Mahábáleshwar, XIX, 504.

Sidnurle : stone inscription at, I, pt. ii, 529.

Sidoji Gujar : Marátha admiral, dies (1698) and is succeeded by Kanhoji, XI, 146 ; *see* also IX, pt. i, 499 note 2.

Sidoji Ráo : *desái* of Nipáni, distinguishes himself in the Peshwa's service and is made *sarlashkar* (1803) ; does not act cordially against the English (1817) ; is confirmed in his *saranjam* ; dies (1839), I, pt. ii, 670 ; (1799-1818), engaged in the siege of Nerali, XXI, 391 ; rewarded, summoned to Poona (1813), *id.* 396-397.

Sigerdis : perhaps Ságaradvipa or Cutch, I, pt. i, 16.

Sigertis : Cutch, mentioned by Strabo, I, pt. i, 535.

Sigerus : probably Janjira, mentioned by Pliny, perhaps Cutch, I, pt. i, 535, 536, 540.

Sigihalli : experimental farm (1831-1836) at, in Dhárwár district, XXII, 287.

Siharakhi : probably modern Serkhi near Baroda, I, pt. ii, 399.

Sihi Jagapura : palace of, supposed to have been erected by Siddharája, I, pt. i, 180 note 2.

Sihor : old city in Ahmadábád district with the remains of an old temple, IV, 353.

Sihor, Sihur : town near Bhávnagar in Káthiáwár, famous for a fountain of leprosy-healing waters, history, IX, pt. i, 7 and note 2 ; an old village, I, pt. i, 64 note 5, 161 ; reservoir at, *id.* 180 note 2 ; is famous for brass and copper work, snuff and mortar, and numerous dyes, VIII, 654-655 ; is also called Simhapura, I, pt. ii, 196.

Sihora : state in Rewa Kántha, VI, 150.

Sihukura : village granted by Vinayáditya, I, pt. ii, 369.

Sikalgar : *see* Saikalgar.

Sikandar : emperor, said to have destroyed fire temples, by Bedani (1504), IX, pt. ii, 188 note 4.

Sikhakai : used as soap, XXV, 252.

Sikhi : (second Buddha) image of, at Sopára in Thána district, XIV, 331, 413.

Sikhs : their home-earth in South-East Panjáb, IX, pt. i, 453 note 3.

Sikra : a village in Cutch, remains at, V, 250-251.

Silabhanjapati : Silabhanja country is an example of the case where *pati* is used in the sense of country, I, pt. ii, 298 note 3.

Siladitya : king of Malwa (640), had for his nephew a king of Valabhi, I, pt. i, 79.

Siladitya : king of Kanyakubja (Kanauj), his son's son-in-law, the king of Valabhi (640), I, pt. i, 79 ; the court of, visited by a Chinese traveller (640), I, pt. ii, 353 and note 3.

Siladitya : Sryasraya, Gujarát Chalukya king (669-691), son of Dharasraya Jayasimhavarman, his Nausari grant, I, pt. ii, 364, 370, 360 note 1, 363 ; I, pt. i, 56, 108.

Siladitya I : Valabhi king (594-609) ; is also called Dharmaditya ; stops the progress of Mangalesh (605), I, pt. ii, 336 ; respects Buddhism, I, pt. i, 91.

Siladitya II : Valabhi king, probably retires early from the world, I, pt. i, 91.

Siladitya III : Valabhi king (671), his grants, I, pt. i, 92.

Siladitya IV : Valabhi king (691), probably referred to in the grant of Jayabhata III, I, pt. i, 117.

Siladitya V : Valabhi king (722), probably defeated by Jayabhata III, I, pt. i, 117.

Siladitya VI : Valabhi king (760), acquires Godrahaka, I, pt. ii, 315, 382.

Siladitya VII : Valabhi king, surnamed Dhruvabhatta (A. D. 766), grant of, IX, pt. i, 13.

Silæ : tribe east of the Indus mentioned by Pliny, I, pt. i, 534.

Silaganasuri : Jain priest, notices the royal marks on the boy Vanarája, I, pt. i, 151.

Siláháras : of the Southern Konkan, I, pt. ii, 25-26, 213, 535-538 ; their origin ; various forms of the name ; their hereditary title and banner ; southern branch seems to be the oldest of the three branches ; connected with the kings of Simhala or Ceylon, *id.* 536 ; their genealogical tree, *id.* 537 ; the founder of the family Sanaphulla appointed governor of Konkan by Krishna I (754-782), *id.* 392, 537 ; the last prince of the family Rattarája

becomes feudatory of the Western Chalukya king Irivahedanga Satyasraya and the power of the family dies with him, *id.* 433, 537-538 ; extent of their territory, *id.* 538.

Siláháras : of Northern Konkan, I, pt. ii, 15-25, 538-544 ; their family tree, *id.* 15, 539 ; various forms of the name, legend about their origin ; suggestion as to their identity with Silar Afridis, *id.* 15 and note 4 ; their hereditary title and banner, *id.* 16, 174, 299 note 4, 538 note 8 ; worshippers of S'iva, *id.* 17 ; their capital, *id.* 16 and note 2, 19, 540, 541 ; under Amoghavarsha, Pullaśakti acquires the feudatory government (843-844), *id.* 17, 541 ; continue under the Ráshtrakútas to the close of the tenth century, *id.* 16, 404, 405, 406 ; Aparajit assumes independence, *id.* 16, 426 ; quarrels with the Kolhápur or Karád branch, *id.* 19 and note 1, 543, 567 ; Jayakesin I, the Kadamba prince, wrests Goa from them (1059), *id.* 216, 543, 567 ; feudatories of the Western Chalukyas of Kalyáni, *id.* 430, 450, 498 ; their power in abeyance, *id.* 544 ; restored by Vijayaditya Silahara, king of Karád or Kolhápur, *id.* 25, 524, 544, 548, 570 ; claim independence and make Thána their capital, *id.* 24, 544 ; their rule put an end to by the Devagiri Yádavas, *id.* 240 ; their possessions, *id.* 16 ; condition of their kingdom, *id.* 21 ; I, pt. i, 527; Konkan rulers (810-1260), XI, 141 ; claim descent from Jimutavahana, IX, pt. i, 15 note 1 ; their administration, I, pt. ii, 21 ; North Konkan rulers (810-1260), XIII, 60 ; origin and genealogical table, *id.* 421, 422 and note 1 ; political status, Puri, Tagar, religion, 423 and notes 2 and 4 ; details of kings, land-grant stones, *id.* 423-427 and notes ; ministers, language, administration, roads, forts, coinage, *id.* 428 ; perhaps the Balharas, *id.* 434 and note 10 ; suggested origin of the name, *id.* 730 ; mention of, XIV, 8, 127, 290, 302, 355, 385, 386, 387, 388, 401, 402, 419.

Siláháras : of Karad or Kolhápur, I, pt. ii, 544-549 ; extent of their territory, *id.* 544 ; their family tree, *id.* 545 ; their hereditary title, banner and family goddess, *id.* 546 ; hold temporarily the North Konkan, *id.* 546-547 ; their marriage connection with the Western Chalukyas, *id.* 217-218, 449, 546, 547 ; reinstate the North Konkan Siláháras, *id.* 25, 544, 548, 570 ; Western Chalukya feudatories, *id.* 452, 456, 458, 460 ; Kalachurya feudatories, *id.* 475 ; under Bhoja II assume independence, *id.* 549 ; Kolhápur kings, XIX, 224 ; XXIV, 219-223 ; records of A. D. 1026 and 1095, I, pt. ii, 298 note 2.

Silana : *táluka* in Káthiáwár, VIII, 654.

Silaprastha : perhaps Sitha in Jhálávàda, king of, present with Mularája in the battle with Graharipu, I, pt. i, 160 and note 2.

Siláras : original form of Siláháras, I, pt. ii, 536. *See* Siláháras.

Silháras : I, pt. ii, 10. *See* Siláháras.

Silicious Limestone Beds : in Bijápur district, XXIII, 28-32.

Siliaátem : worship of small-pox goddess on, IX, pt. i, 368.

Silk : trade of Thána coast in, with the Parthians, (B. C. 255 - A. D. 235), XIII, 412 ; imported from Persia and China (810-1260), *id.* 430 ; from Venice, Persia and China (1300-1500), *id.* 444 ; imported and locally manufactured (1500-1670), *id.* 466-467 and note 2 ; manufacture of, at Thána, mentioned by an Italian traveller, I, pt. ii, 37 ; attempts to grow, in Khándesh district, XII, 180 ; experiments of the cultivation of (1875-1882), in Poona district, XVIII, pt. ii, 64-76 ; manufacture of, in Ahmadábád district, IV, 135 ; in Thána district, XIV, 347 ; in Dhárwár district, XXII, 375-377; culture in the Konkan (1845), XXVI, pt. iii, 593 ; manufacture of, in Surat, II, 179 ; industry in Násik (1290), XVI, 182 and note 6.

Silk Waistcloth ; weaving of, in Bijápur district, XXIII, 371.

Silk-weaving : in Thána district, weavers, XIII, 378-379 ; trade, *id.* 380 ; sorting, *id.* 380-382 ; appliances, *id.* 382 ; bleaching, *id.* 382 ; mordanting, *id.* 382-383 ; materials, *id.* 382-384 ; warping, *id.* 384 ; weaving, *id.* 384-385 ; in Násik district, manufacturers, description of silk-dyeing, sizing, warping, weaving, appliances, articles, XVI, 143, 155-162 ; in Kolába district, XI, 132, 278, 279 ; in Ahmadábád district, IV, 135-139 ; in Cutch, V, 126 ; in Poona district, workmen, tools, process, articles, XVIII, pt. ii, 185-191.

Silk Worms : rearing of, in Kaira district, III, 54 ; in Dhárwár district, XXII, 42 ; details of, *id.* 304-305.

Silli : place in Kaira district with a reservoir, III, 178.

Silsilát-ut-Tuwárikh : a work written (851-852) by the merchant Sulaiman, I, pt. i, 505 note 2.

Silveira : James de, Portuguese captain, burns the ports of Pattan-Somnáth, Mangrul, Talája and Muzáfarábád ; Thána, Bassein ; and Bombay, I, pt. i, 347.

Silver Casket : in Sopára *stupa*, XIV, 334.

Silver Thread : the making of, in Násik district, XVI, 162-167.

Sim : country near Ujjain, king of, imprisoned by Siddharája, I, pt. i, 179.

Simadia-dev : worship of, IX, pt. i, 292, 313, 363.

Simal : timber tree in Khándesh district, XII, 27.

Simanta : *see* Pregnancy.

Simanti : marriage ceremony in Khándesh district, XII, 65.

Simantonnayan : hair-parting, Vedic rite, IX, pt. i, 31 note 3.

Simario : *see* Sámrádev.

Simha : maternal uncle of king Visaladeva, worships the servant of a Jain monastery, I, pt. i, 202.

Simha : era, I, pt. i, 176, 204.

Simha ; *see* Singhana.

Simha : lord of the Santali Mandala, I, pt. ii, 579, 583.

Simhala : Ceylon, I, pt. ii, 368 ; king of, made tributary of Chálukya crown, *id.* 189 ; is

subdued by king Krishna III, *id.* 207; submits to Vikramáditya, *id.* 215; kings of, connected with Siláhára family, *id.* 536.
Simhala: *see* Singhana.
Simhalánchhana: lion crest on the seals of the Kádambas, I, pt. ii. 560, 566.
Simhana: *see* Singhana.
Simhapura: modern Sihur, I, pt. ii, 196.
Simharája: *see* Singhana.
Simhasena: twenty-sixth Kshatrapa, coin of, I, pt. i, 51.
Simhavarman: Kadamba king, mentioned in a Mysore grant, I, pt. ii, 290.
Simhavarman I: Pallava king, I, pt. ii, 321, 324.
Simhavarman II: son and successor of the Pallava king Vishnugopavarman, I, pt. ii, 321.
Simhavishnu: Pallava king, defeats the Malaya, Kalabhra, Málwa, Chola, Pándya, Simhala and Kerala kings, I, pt. ii, 324 and note 1, 325, 328.
Simhirája: Yádava prince, grand-father of Bhillama, I, pt. ii, 516, 517.
Simpson: reservoir at Mátherán, XIV, 235, 244, 245, 276.
Simuka: Satavåhana king, mentioned in an inscription, I, pt. ii, 147, 154, 156; dates of his accession and death, *id.* 166; Ándhrabhritya founder (B. C. 130), XVI, 611, 612, 613, 614.
Simulla: modern Chaul, I, pt. i, 533; XI, 270 note 5.
Simylla: modern Chaul, I, pt. i, 540; mentioned by Ptolemy, XIV, 320.
Sina: river in Ahmadnagar and Sholápur districts, XVII, 9; XX, 4.
Sinclair: Mr. W. F., detached for the arrest of Bhagoji (1874), XVII, 420; XI, 253.
Sinclair: Sir John (1800), at the siege of Sungdal in Belgaum district, XXI, 394.
Sind, Sindh: mentioned by Megasthenes (B. C. 300), I, pt. i, 533; Scythian kingdom established in (A. D. 150), I, pt. ii, 158; mention of Parthian rule in (A. D. 250), XIII, 404 note 3, 411 note 2; conquered by Chudasamas (560), I, pt. i, 139; rulers of, connected by treaties with Naushirvan the Just (531-579), IX, pt ii, 183 note 4; king of, defeated by the father of Shri Harsha (606), I, pt. i, 467; Sámantabhadra said to have made a missionary tour to (800), I, pt. ii, 407; considered to be beyond Indian limits by Arab travellers, sea trade of, with Broach (900-950), I, pt. i, 509, 513; fire temples found in (916), IX, pt. ii, 186; parts of, belonged to the Gabres (950), *id.* 188 note 4; conquered by the Sumras (1069), I, pt. i, 517; ruler of, humbled by Singhana (1230), I, pt. ii, 525; expedition against, by the *Ráo* of Cutch (1758), I, pt. i, 342; people of, invade Cutch (1762), V, 143-146, 164.
Sinda: *see* Sindas.
Sinda: perhaps Vadnagar, I, pt. i, 546.
Sindabur: identified with Goa, I, pt. i, 517, 521; with Sanján, I, pt. ii, 4 and note 7; with Chitakul starting point for voyages to Aden, XV, pt. ii, 51; arrival of Ibn Batuta at, *id.* 97, 252, 308; mention of, *id.* 278; identified with Siddhapur, *id.* 343.
Sindagi: *see* Sindgi.
Sindan: in Cutch, conquest of, and Jama mosque founded at, I, pt. i, 506; IX, pt. ii, 1 note 1, 2 note 1; mentioned by Ibni Haukal, I, pt. i, 523.
Sindan: St. John or Sanjan, mentioned by Al Biladuri (892), I, pt. i, 507, 508, 509; by Al Istakhri as exporting shoes to Baghdád, *id.* 514, 516; by Al Idrisi, *id.* 521. *See* also 528, 529, 530; I, pt. ii, 4.
Sindarája: son of Bhima of the Sinda race, I, pt. ii, 577.
Sindas: of Yelburga, I, pt. ii, 572-576; their territory, *id.* 572; said to be of the Nága race, *id.* 281 note 3; their genealogical list, *id.* 573; possibly descended from Pulikála, *id.* 574; their crest and banner, *id.* 299 note 4; Chálukya feudatories, *id.* 443, 452, 458, 460, 462, 477, 497, 498; their intermarriage with Kalachuryas, *id.* 463; Kalachurya feudatories, *id.* 485, 488, 576; chiefs, XXII, 401; XXIII, 392-394, 389; of Bágadage, their crest, banner and hereditary title, I, pt. ii, 576, 577; Chálukya feudatories, *id.* 450, 577; of Halavar, their crest, banner, hereditary title and genealogy, *id.* 578, 579; feudatories of the Kalachuryas, *id.* 476, 577-578.
Sindavadi, Sindavádi Nád: country ruled over by the Sindas of Yelburga, I, pt. ii, 572, 298 note 3, 441 and note 6.
Sindavamśa: Sinda race, I, pt. ii, 576.
Sindavne: pass in Poona district, XVIII, pt. ii, 154.
Sinde: modern Marátha name for Sendraka, I, pt. ii, 186.
Sinde: village in Poona district, caves at XVIII, pt. iii, 440-441.
Sindelwan: food plant, common in the Konkan, XXV, 176.
Sinderbur: food plant, XXV, 176.
Sinderwani: food plant, XXV, 176.
Sindgi: sub-division in Bijápur district, its boundaries, area, aspect, soil, climate, water, stock, crops and people, XXIII, 542 544; survey of, *id.* 484-491. *Town,* temples and rising (1824) at, *id.* 676-677; trade centre, *id.* 360; inscriptions at, I, pt. ii, 455, 503.
Sindh: *see* Sind.
Sindhábur: *see* Sindabur.
Sindhdi: lake in Cutch, V, 11.
Sindhia: *see* Sindia.
Sindhshah: probably Núr Satágur, shrine of, at Navsári, IX, pt. ii, 66.
Sindhu: identified with Sind, afflicted by Arab army, I, pt. i, 109.
Sindhu: the river Indus, I, pt. ii, 576, 577; I, pt. i, 189.
Sindhudurg: fort near Málvan in Ratnágiri district, Shiváji's temple at, history of, I, pt. ii, 75; X, 349-351; becomes centre of piracy under Kolhápur (1713), *id.* 373; its name changed to Fort Augustus (1765), I, pt. ii, 106.
Sindhuka: corruption of Siśnka, I, pt. ii, 156.
Sindhurája: killed by Siddharája, I, pt. i, 175, 179.
Sindhuvalli: records at, I, pt. ii, 308.

Sindhvá : a depressed class in Gujarát, IX, pt. i, 321 ; other names, Rájpút surnames, occupation, religion, *id.* 346-347.
Sindia : orgin of the family, XVIII, pt. ii, 244; XIX, 268 ; admitted as Kshatriya, IX, pt. i, 442 ; Nimáji gained over to his side by Sháhu, I, pt. ii, 598 ; Ránoji of Kanarkhed rises to note, *id.* 600 ; given (1750) a share in the revenue in the Málwa, XIX, 291 ; Máhádji, one of the commanders of the Marátha army at Vadgaon (1778), connives at the arrest of Sakhárám Bápu by Nána Phadnavis, XIII, 504, 512 ; I, pt. ii, 605 ; his unsuccessful attack on Sinor (1781), I, pt. i, 409 ; decorates the Peshwa with the insignia of the office of *vakil-i-mutálik* and tries to supplant Nána Phadnavis, I, pt. ii, 605-606 ; his death (1794), *id.* 606 ; Daulat Ráo, succeeds Máhádji (1794); determines to put Chimnáji on the throne, XIX, 298 ; is won over by Nána Phadnavis to his side ; obtains Ahmadnagar as a reward for help ; imprisons Nána at Ahmadnagar, I, pt. ii, 606-607, 628 ; his quarrels with the widows of Máhádji (1798-1800) ; arrests Shirzi Ráo and releases Nána and Báloba Tátya with the help of Yashvant Ráo Holkar; drives the widows of Máhádji to Málwa, *id.* 607 ; attacks the Patvardhan *jáhgir*, *id* 662 ; defeats Yashvant Ráo Holkar at Indor (1801) ; sends a large force to help the Peshwa against the Holkar ; the Peshwa intrigues with him against the Holkar and the English, *id.* 608 ; views the treaty of Bassein with dissatisfaction and is defeated by the English at Assaye and Argaon (1803), *id.* 609 ; his treaty at Sirji Anjangaon, I, pt. i, 414 ; was granted the proceeds of the Ahmadábád farm, VII, 201 ; claim of, on Baroda, *id.* 205 ; danger to Baroda state from, *id.* 208-210.
Sindiápura : state in Rewa Kántha, VI, 143.
Sindia's Tomb : at Vánavdi, near Poona, XVIII, pt. iii, 393-394.
Sindigere : in Asandi district in Mysore, inscription at, I, pt. ii, 492 and 2, 494, 495, 497, 498, 499.
Sindinagara, Sindinera : that is Sinnar in the Násik district, I, pt. ii, 437, 512 note 4 ; capital of Bhillama III, *id.* 514 ; birth-place of Dhádiyappa, *id.* 513, 514.
Sindkheda : town in Khándesh, mentioned by Hawkins, XII, 470, 248.
Sindságar : branch of the Indus, I, pt. i, 517.
Sindu : Debal port, mentioned by Kosmos, I, pt. i, 547.
Sindura-Lánchhana : elephant crest, I, pt. ii, 552 and note 3.
Sindva : fort in Khándesh district, XII, 256, 594.
Singa I : Sinda prince of Yelburga, I, pt. ii, 573 ; also called Simha, *id.* 574.
Singa II : I, pt. ii, 443 ; Sinda prince of Yelburga, *id.* 573 ; feudatory of the Western Chálukya king Someśvara II, *id.* 574.
Singaldip : Ceylon, I, pt. i, 512.
Singamale : conquered by Vishnuvardhana, I, pt. ii, 497.
Singana : *see* Singa II.
Singanadevarasa : (1045) feudatory of the Western Chálukya king Someśvara I, I, pt. ii, 439.
Singaváda : river in Káthiáwár, VIII, 63.
Singayya Devananáyaka : Yádava king Mahádev's officer (1264), I, pt. ii, 528.
Singhæ : tribe mentioned by Pliny, I, pt. i, 534.
Singhana : another name of Jayasimha III, the Western Chálukya prince, I, pt. ii, 453.
Singhana : Kalachurya king, son of Bijjala, I, pt. ii, 471, 477 ; succeeds his brother (1183), *id.* 489.
Singhana I : same as the Yádava prince Sevana or Simhirája, I, pt. ii, 235, 236, 516, 517.
Singhana II : Devagiri Yádava king (1210-1247), I, pt. ii, 252, 519 ; succeeds his father, *id.* 239, 522 ; his epithets and titles, *id.* 243, 522-523 ; his feudatories and officials, *id.* 523-524 ; his capitals, *id.* 520 ; his conquests and defeat of the Musalmáns, *id.* 240-243, 506, 524-525, 549, 557, 558, 583 ; his treaty with Lavanaprasáda of Gujarát (1232), *id.* 241, 525 ; his chief astrologer, *id.* 244, 526 ; his treaty, I, pt. i, 198, 199 ; conquers Panhala, I, pt. ii, 587 ; *see* also XV, pt. ii, 91, 92 and note 1 ; XXIV, 314.
Singhar : a Sind prince, grandson of Sumra, extends his sway (1069), I, pt. i, 517 ; overruns Cutch, V, 132.
Singhavarman : another name of Simhavarman I, I, pt. ii, 320 note 6.
Singnápur : holy place in Sátára, place of pilgrimage of Kolhápur Chámbhárs, XXIV, 110.
Singpur : state in Khándesh district, XII, 610.
Sinh : Káthiáwár dynasty of Kshatrapas so called (A. D. 78-A. D. 328), XIII, 411.
Sinhadatta : a king mentioned in an inscription of Vada in the Thána district, XIV, 373.
Sinhanadeva : *see* Singhana.
Sinhasth : sacred Hindu year, IX, pt. i, 550.
Sinhdev : a Devagiri Yádava (1100), conquers Konkan, X, 193 ; mention of, in the inscription at Khidrapur in Kolhápur, XXIV, 302.
Sinhgad : hill fort in Poona district, XVIII, pt. i, 5 ; its description and history, XVIII, pt. iii, 441-446 ; name given (1647) to Kondhána by Shiváji, XVIII, pt. ii, 226 ; surprised (1670) by Shiváji's army, *id.* 235-236 ; siege (1700-1703) of, *id.* 239-240 ; surrendered (1817) to the English, *id.* 297 ; siege (1818) of, *id.* 302 ; garrisoned by the Mughals ; stormed and taken by Tanaji Malusara for Shiváji (1671), I, pt. ii, 594 ; given to the Peshwa by Pant Sachiv, *id.* 601 ; death of Rájárám at, XXIV, 266.
Sinnar : sub-division of Násik district, its boundaries, area, aspect, climate, water, history of land revenue, stock, holdings, crops and people, XVI, 364-369 ; measured and assessed (1783), *id.* 208 and note 5 ; survey of (1843-1845), *id.* 222-223 ; revision survey (1874), *id.* 264-270. *Town*, temples and history of, *id.* 647-649 ; founded by the Chandor Yádav king Dhridhaprabar, *id.* 186.
Sinor : sub-division in Baroda state, its boundaries, area, aspect, climate, water, soil, revenue, products and places of interest, VII, 552-555 ; hospital and schools in, *id.* 505, 486. *Town*, its history, *id.* 554-555 ; attacked by Sindia (1781), I, pt. i, 409.

Sinthon, Sinthos : mouth of the Indus, I, pt. i, 538, 544.

Sion Causeway : in Thána district, built (1798-1803), I, pt. ii, 124; XIII, 322, 512, 517, 562.

Sipáhi : caste of Musalmán soldiers, in Gujarát, of mixed origin, partly immigrants and partly Rájpút converts, mostly husbandmen, Sunni in religion, IX, pt. ii, 83-84; name coined by Musalmán governors for Rájpút and other converts, *id.* 25; in Thána district, XIII, 243-244; in Káthiáwár, VIII, 163.

Sipáh Salár : title of Asad Khán, I, pt. ii, 642.

Sipala : Sopára in Thána district, noticed by Du Perron, XIV, 322.

Sipraka : founder of the Andhrabhrityas, overthrows the Kánvas, I, pt. ii, 155; corrupted form of Simuka, *id.* 156.

Sipu : river in Pálanpur, V, 283.

Siras : *Albizzia lebbek*, a tree in Poona district, XVIII, pt. i, 53.

Sirdi : fodder plant, XXV, 277.

Sirgaon : fort in Thána district, XIV, 11, 98, 312.

Sirgod : village in Dhárwár district, temples and inscriptions at, XXII, 786.

Sirbatti : captured by Hari Pant, the Peshwa's general (1787), I, pt. ii, 661.

Sirimalaga : modern Sirnál in the Bijápur district, I, pt. i, 541.

Siripalla : unidentified town, mentioned by Ptolemy, I, pt. i, 540.

Siri Ptolemaios : Sri Pulumáyi, Andhra king, I, pt. i, 37.

Sirisena : I, pt. ii, 167. *See* Sakasena.

Sirisha : Krakuchchhandá's tree of knowledge, XIV, 331.

Sirishapadraka : Sisodra, village near Ankleśvar, I, pt. i, 115; I, pt. ii, 314 and note 2.

Sirius : star, IX, pt. ii, 217 note 1. *See* Teshtar.

Siriyádevi : daughter of the Kalachurya Bijjala and wife of the Sinda prince Chavunda II, I, pt. ii, 470, 477, 573, 576.

Siriyadevi : wife of the Hangal Kádamba S'antivarman II, I, pt. ii, 559, 561.

Siriyála : S'iva's attendant, I, pt. ii, 482.

Sirji Anjangaon : treaty (1803) of, between Sindia and the British, I, pt. ii, 629; XII, 253, 590.

Sirkeer : class of birds in Ratnágiri district, X, 68.

Sirohi : chief of, head of Devra Rájpúts, I, pt. i, 465.

Siro Polimios : mentioned by Ptolemy as governor of the Northern Province, identified with Pulumáyi, I, pt. ii, 158.

Siroptolemaios : Sri-Pulumáyi, I, pt. i, 541.

Sirozah : 30 days or calendar of the Pársis, IX, pt. ii, 212 note 1.

Sirpur : town in Central Provinces, inscriptions at, I, pt. ii, 425.

Sirsangi : in Belgaum district, XXI, 360; origin of *desais* of, *id.* 371.

Sirsi : sub-division of Kánara district, villages, climate, water, stock, soil, survey details and people of, XV, pt. ii, 243-246; travellers' bungalows in, *id.* 45. *Town*, description, fair, temple and fort of, *id.* 343-345; trade centre, *id.* 56; condition (1801), *id.* 151; schools, library and hospital in, *id.* 215, 216, 218, 219.

Sirul Khán : governor of Janjira (1707-1734), defends Janjira against the attack of the Maráthás, XI, 443; tomb of, *id.* 464.

Sirur : a village in the Dhárwár district, temples and inscriptions at, XXII, 786; Amoghavarsha's inscription at, I, pt. i, 124; other inscriptions I, pt. ii, 200, 387, 401 notes 2 and 3, 405, 412 note 8, 436 note 2, 529, 538 note 8.

Sirur : sub-division in Poona district, its boundaries, area, aspect, water, climate, crops, stock, people, cultivators, communications, XVIII, pt. iii, 8-101. *Town*, details, Colonel Wallace's tomb (1809) and inscription at, *id.* 446-448; head-quarters of the Poona subsidiary force (1813), I, pt. ii, 610.

Sirur : village in Ahmadnagar district, temple at, XVII, 739.

Sirur : village in Bijápur district, temples and inscriptions at, XXIII, 677-678.

Sisáng Chándli : *táluka* in Káthiáwár, VIII, 655.

Sisoda : town, Sisodiyás take name from, IX, pt. i, 464.

Sisodani Ráni : queen of Kumárapála, I, pt. i, 188.

Sisodiyá : *see* Sesodiá.

Sisodra : village in the Ankleśvar district, I, pt. i, 115.

Sissu : oil-yielding plant, XXV, 217.

Sistán : *see* Yezdstán.

Sisuka : founder of the Andhrabhritya dynasty (B. C. 73), uproots the Kánvas and Sungas, I, pt. ii, 163. *See* Simuka.

S'isupála : Párthiva or Pahlava king, I, pt. ii, 318.

Sitá : wife of Ráma, I, pt. ii, 28, 135; IX, pt. i, p. xxxvi; believed to have been purified by walking on live charcoal, *id.* 356; Asopalav tree worshipped by, *id.* 383.

Sitábaldi : near Nágpur, inscription at, I, pt. ii, 425, 450.

Sitá Gumpha : Násik temple, XVI, 515.

Sitala : epidemic small-pox, IX, pt. i, 368.

Sitala-Máta : small-pox mother, goddess Sitala, her form as described in books, worship of, in Gujarát, IX, pt. i, 368.

Sitáphal : custard apple, tree in Poona district, XVIII, pt. i, 53.

Sitárám : becomes prime minister at Baroda, VII, 209; plan to seize, goes on pilgrimage, *id.* 211; begs support, his disgrace, his *pagas* taken (1809), *id.* 214-216; Takhatábhái the ally of, confined; Peshwa's intervention; his restoration, his mischiefs, *id.* 221-224; his *nemnuk* increased, allowed to return to private life, *id.* 235.

Sitha : village in Káthiáwár, temples at, VIII, 656; king of, feudatory to Mularája, I, pt. i, 160.

Sitikond : village in Dhárwár district, inscriptions at, XXII, 786.

S'iva : god, I, pt. ii, 468, 469; new mode of worshipping, *id.* 226, 477, 484; Parasuráma acquires the seven Konkans by the boon of, *id.* 282 note 5; family god of the Pallavas, *id.* 319 and note 3, 359; of the Ráshtrakútas,

id. 387; of the Thána Siláhárás, *id.* 17; of the Guttas, *id.* 578, 580; temple of, at Ellora, *id.* 391; temple of, *id.* 538; built by the Gutta prince Vira-Vikramáditya II, *id.* 583; grant to, *id.* 572; is traditionally supposed to be the father of Kádamba Mayuravarman I, *id.* 560; Trilochana-Kádamba springs from a drop of sweat from the forehead of, *id.* 566; union of, with the Sindhu, *id.* 577.

Sivabhaktas: S'iva-worshippers, sect established by Bijjala, I, pt. ii, 477.

Sivachitta: Goa Kadamba king (1147-1175), the father of Naikidevi, I, pt. i, 173 and note 3, 195.

Sivachittachattayadeva: I, pt. ii, 571. *See* Shashthadeva II.

Sivadatta: Abhira prince, mentioned in a Násik cave inscription, I, pt. ii, 177.

Sivadhári: Govinda III allots land to, I, pt. ii, 198.

Sivagupta: inscription of, at Sirpur in Central Provinces, I, pt. ii, 425.

Siváji: *see* Shiváji.

Sivakumára: Kadamba prince, I, pt. ii, 288.

Sivamára I: Western Ganga king (713), I, pt. ii, 301 note 1.

Sivamara II: Western Ganga king (807), I, pt. ii, 301 note 1.

Sivánanda Kumárapáleśvara: temple of, at Kalambapattana, I, pt. i, 183.

Sivára: in Mysore, inscriptions at, I, pt. ii, 302.

Sivaratha: Kadamba prince, I, pt. ii, 289.

Sivári: a caste of Musalmán servants in Bijápur district, XXIII, 304.

Sivarpatna: in Mysore, inscriptions at, I, pt. ii, 302.

Sivasakti: priest of the god Kalleśvaradeva of Kittur, I, pt. ii, 571.

Sivasána: king of, conquered by Hammuka, I, pt. i, 163.

Sivaskanda: of Kánchipura, leader of Pahlavas, IX, pt. i, 445; admitted to the sacred clan of Rishi Bháradvája, *id.* 442.

Sivaskandavarman: Pallava king, grant of, I, pt. ii, 279 note 1, 319 note 2, 320 and note 2.

Sivaskandha: Andhrabhritya king, successor of Siva Sri, I, pt. ii, 156; dates of his reign, *id.* 168.

Siva Sri: successor of Pulimat, I, pt. ii, 156; his reign and death, *id.* 166; dates of his reign, *id.* 168.

Sivasvati: end of the reign of, I, pt. ii, 165.

Sivrájpur: in Gujarát, success of the Náikdás at (1858), I, pt. i, 446.

Sivunúr: village in Dhárwár district, I, pt. ii, 441 and note 6.

Siwana: town in the bend of the Luni, I, pt. i, 538.

Siwani Vákátaka: records at, I, pt. ii, 286 note 1.

Siyájiráv Gáikwár: *see* Sayáji Gáikwár.

Siyaka Harsha: Paramára king of Málwa, plunders Malkhed (971 ?), I, pt. ii, 422, 432.

Siyalára: *see* Siláháras.

Skambhtirth: word "Cambay" derived from, VI, 211-212.

Skanda: twenty-seventh Kshatrapa, I, pt. i, 51.

Skanda: name of Amoghavarsha, Dakhan Ráshtrakúta king, I, pt. i, 126.

Skanda: *see* Kártikeya.

Skandagupta: seventh Gupta king (454-470), his inscription at Bhitári and Girnár, I, pt. i, 69; at Junágadh, *id.* 73, 74; his coins, *id.* 70-71, 80 note 1, 86; defeats the Nágas, I, pt. ii, 281 note 3; the enemies of, called in the Hunás, IX, pt. i, 447.

Skandagupta: Gupta king (A. D. 190), his inscription on Alláhábád pillar, XIII, 409 note 1.

Skanda Purána: contains legends of Bhinmal, I, pt. i, 461.

Skandasena: vassal of the Pallava king Mahendrapotarája, I, pt. ii, 328.

Skandavarman I: Pallava king, one of the successors of Ashok, I, pt. ii, 320, 321, 324.

Skandavarman II: Pallava king, I, pt. ii, 320 note 6, 321.

Skandavarman III: Mahárája, son of Singavarman, I, pt. ii, 320 note 6.

Skirt-wearing: Bene-Israel ceremony, XVIII, pt. i, 531.

Skunks: at Mátherán, XIV, 256.

Skythænus: founder of the Manichæan doctrines, his knowlege of Buddhism, XIV, 125 note 4.

Skythia: Sind, I, pt. i, 544.

Skythians: *see* Scythians.

Slaves: in Thána, the Africans or Sidis imported by the Portuguese, XIII, 64, 460 and note 3; imported from Sophála (810-1260), *id.* 431; (1300-1500), *id.* 446; from Abyssinia (1500-1670), *id.* 468, 483 and note 4, 552 and note 6; *Akarmashes* were formerly slaves, *id.* 142; Portuguese trade in, in India, I, pt. ii, 54, 56, 71; trade in, in Baroda prohibited, VII, 270; in Cutch, V, 169 note 3; in Kolába district, XI, 140, 216; in Ahmadnagar district, XVII, 320-321; in Poona district, XVIII, pt. ii, 133-134, 354; in Dhárwár district, XXII, 463; in Kánara district, XV, pt. ii, 151-152; in Bombay island (1677-1780), XXVI, pt. ii, 255-262; for the king (1683), *id.* 255; rules for the treatment of (1752), *id.* 260-262; price of (1762-1763), *id.* 263-264. See Arabs, Page 24

Small Arms and Ammunition Factory: at Kirkee, XVIII, pt. iii, 394-396.

Small Causes Court: in Kaira, III, 118; in Poona city and cantonment, XVIII, pt. iii, 27-29; at Hubli and Dhárwár, abolished (1875), XXII, 602.

Small-pox: includes *Gobru* or measles and *Achhabda* or chicken-pox; *Sitala*, epidemic form of Sitala Máta its goddess, day sacred for her worship, rites and form of worship, offerings made to, safeguards against attack of, performance of *Shánti* ceremony in an attack of, IX, pt. i, 368; *Saiad*, endemic form of, *Saiad Káka*, god of, *id.* 368, 369; days sacred for his worship, peculiar treatment in an attack of, safeguards to protect the child from the gaze of people, *id.* 369; rules and forms to be observed by the parents, *id.* 369-370; places where image of the god is kept, famous small-pox gods, *id.* 370; form of worship by the mother of the

child, *id.* 370-371 ; vows taken in an attack of, *id.* 371 ; special offerings to the god, *id.* 371-372 ; *Gobru* and *Achhabda*, ceremonies in an attack of, *cattle-pox* plague, *id.* 372, 382 ; in Ratnágiri district, X, 292 ; details of, in Khándesh district, XII, 338 ; outbreaks of, in Kánara district, XV, pt. ii, 218 ; details of, in Násik district, XVI, 339 ; goddess, XVIII, pt. i, 224-225 ; in Kolhápur state, XXIV, 287 ; vaccination against (1788), XXVI, pt iii, 563 ; brought in by Europeans, *id.* 563-564 note 1.

Smárt Bhágvat : a caste of Deshasth Bráhmans in Dhárwár district, XXII, 90-92.

Smilax ovalifolia : food plant, grows in several districts, XXV, 179.

Smith : General, commander of Báji Ráo II's subsidiary force, marches on Poona and pursues Báji Ráo II (1817-18), I, pt. ii, 611 ; *see* also XVII, 414-415 ; XVIII, pt. ii, 296, 299 ; XIX, 300-303 ; XX, 293-295.

Smithia Sensitiva : sacred plant, XXV, 291.

Snake-bird : the Indian, in Ratnágiri district, X, 99.

Snake-bite : cure of, IX, pt. i, 364.

Snake-charmers : in Poona district, XVIII, pt. i, 83-87.

Snake People : marriage of, with Bráhmans, IX, pt. i, 435.

Snakes : in Poona district, XVIII, pt. i, 71-83 ; in Kaira district, III, 20 ; in Panch Maháls, *id.* 212 ; in Ratnágiri district, harmless colubrine, X, 48 ; venomous colubrine, *id.* 49 ; viperine, *id.* 50 ; in Kolába district, XI, 36 ; in Janjira, *id.* 407 ; in Thána district, XIII, 47-48 ; at Mátherán, XIV, 256 ; in Kánara district, XV, pt. i, 106-107 ; in Ahmadnagar district, XVII, 39-41 ; in Sátára district, XIX, 39 ; in Belgaum district, XXI, 85 ; in Dhárwár district, XXII, 42 ; in Bijápur district, XXIII, 67-68 ; in Kolhápur state, XXIV, 33-34.

Snuff : manufacture of, in Ahmadábád district, IV, 134.

Soap : manufacture of, in Kaira, III, 76 ; in Panch Maháls, *id.* 250 ; in Rewa Kántha, VI, 57 ; in Ahmadábád district, IV, 134 ; in Káthiáwár, VIII, 261-262.

Soapnuts : in Kánara district, XV, pt. i, 30, 35.

Sobhanarasa : feudatory of the Western Chálukya king Satyásraya, I, pt. ii, 432.

Societies : public, founded by the natives in the Násik district, XVI, 335-336.

Society of Jesus : Portuguese colleges and schools in India made over to (1551), I, pt. ii, 59.

Socotra : Hindu colonization of, XIII, 404 note 3, 714 ; Thána trade with (810-1260), *id.* 429, 434 ; (1500-1670), *id.* 465 ; (1670-1800), *id.* 487.

Sodha : a Rájpút clan in Cutch, V, 66-67.

Sodhala : chief secretary of Singhana, I, pt. ii, 243.

Sodhali Váv : step-well at Mangrol, I, pt. i, 176.

Sodha Parmárs : Rájpút tribe, entered Gujarát in the thirteenth century, I, pt. i, 217 note 3.

Sodre : Vincent, sails along the coast as far as Cambay (1503), I, pt. ii, 43.

Sœlas : Musalmán hymns, IX, pt. ii, 151.

Sofále : old village in Thána district, XIV, 313.

Sogal : village in Belgaum district, a water-fall near, XXI, 608 ; inscription at, I, pt. ii, 428, 553.

Sog-uthána : grief-lifting ceremony among Musalmáns, IX, pt. ii, 170.

Sohada : ruler of Málwa, defeated by Lavanaprasada, I, pt. i, 198.

Sohail Khán : Bijápur general (1595-1599) sent to Sháhdurg, XVII, 383 ; blockades Ahmadnagar (1596), his retreat, *id.* 385-386.

Sohani : Hángal Kádamba Kámadeva's general killed in battle with Vira-Balláls II, I, pt. ii, 563.

Sohráb Ali, Sohráb Khán : governor of Surat (1730), I, pt. i, 310 ; confirmed in the appointment ; driven out of Surat (1732) ; settles at Bhávnagar, *id.* 313 ; appointed governor of Viramgám (1735) ; is defeated at Dholi by Ratansingh Bhandári, *id.* 315-316 ; *see* also VII, 177.

Soideva : officer of Jaitugi I, his rule in Khándesh, I, pt. ii, 521.

Soil : varieties of, in Surat, II, 31-59 ; in Broach, *id.* 389 ; distribution of, in Kaira, III, 43 ; in Panch Maháls, *id.* 230 ; distribution and varieties of, in Ahmadábád district, IV, 49-50 ; varieties of, in Pálanpur, V, 293 ; Mahi Kántha, *id.* 369 ; in Rewa Kántha, VI, 38 ; in Cambay, *id.* 183 ; in Káthiáwár, VIII, 175 ; in Kolába district, XI, 89 ; in Janjira, *id.* 424 ; in Khándesh, XII, 11, 138 ; in Násik district, XVI, 13, 91 ; in Ahmadnagar district, XVII, 242-243 ; in Poona district, XVIII, pt. ii, 3, 5 ; in the Sátára district, XIX, 149 ; in Sholápur district, XX, 219, 221 ; in Belgaum district, XXI, 38, 236, 237 and footnote 1 ; in Dhárwár district, XXII, 254, 256 ; in Bijápur district, XXIII, 50, 308-309 ; in Kánara district, XV, pt i, 10 ; XV, pt. ii, 4-5.

Sojitra : village in Baroda, VII, 540 ; schools at, *id.* 486 ; hospital, *id.* 504 ; battle of (1725), I, pt. i, 307.

Sokhoda : village in Baroda, a Gujaráti school at, VII, 535.

Sola : famine plant, grows in Bengal, XXV, 198.

Soladaganda : *biruda* of Baddiga the Chálukya king, I, pt. ii, 380.

Solaki : *see* Solanki.

Solaknáth : hill in Sátára district, XIX, 12.

Solanaceæ : species of famine and poisonous plants, XXV, 202, 268.

Solankis : I, pt. i, 156, 191 ; Rájpúts, their settlements, *id.* 464 ; their kingdom, *id.* 465 ; their change of faith (743), *id.* 463 and note 2, 468 ; of Anahilaváda, section of the Bhinmál empire, *id.* 469 ; dynasty of (961-1242), *id.* 526 ; Chálukya, tribe of Agnikula Rájpúts, IX, pt. i, 483 ; said to be Brahma-created, *id.* 449 note 3, 483 ; history of origin ; *Keonj Máta*, the guardian or luck of ; *Anahilpur* their heritage, *id.* 485 ; believed to be of Gujar stock, *id.* 483 ; evidence in support of the belief, *id.* 485, 487 ; powerful successors of Chávadás in the sovereignty of Gujarát ; present chief houses of, in Rewa Kántha and

Bánsoda, *id.* 129; goddess, *id.* 205. *See* Agnikulas; in Cutch, V, 68; in Káthiáwár, VIII, 110; Rájpút converts, IX, pt. ii, 70.
Solanum: *Jacquinii nigrum, torvum*, famine plants, XXV, 202.
Soldados: Portuguese soldiers, I, pt. ii, 55.
Soldiers' Institute: Poona, XVIII, pt. iii, 396.
Soleiman: prophet, knowledge of the great *Náme Ismi Aázam* first possessed by, dominion of, over men, *genii*, winds, birds and beasts, uttering the name of, casts out demons, cures the sick and raises the dead, IX, pt. ii, 143.
Solesi Koli: early tribe in Thána district, XIII, 174.
Solla: son of Udaya Vania, minister of Karna, I, pt. i, 170.
Soln Appáji: Anegundi minister (1508-1542), introduces the unit of land assessment in Dhárwár (1530), XXII, 440-441.
Soma: the moon, I, pt. ii, 339; the son of Atri, I, pt. ii, 511; builds the gold temple of Somanátha, I, pt. i, 190.
Soma: *see* Siláhara king Someśvara.
Soma: Hangal Kadamba king (1161-1162), feudatory of Bijjála, I, pt. ii, 475. *See* Sovideva.
Soma: Hoysála king, son of Narasimha II, I, pt. ii, 507. *See* Vira-Someśvara, Someśvara and Sovideva.
Soma: vedic plant, IX, pt. ii, 228 note 1.
Somachandra: Hemachandra's name after his consecration, I, pt. i, 191.
Somadeva: author of the *Kathasaritsagara*, I, pt. ii, 170.
Somadeva: author of the *Yasastilaka*, I, pt. ii, 207.
Somadeva: *see* Someśvara.
Somadeva: author of the *Sabdarnava Chandrika*, I, pt. ii, 549.
Somadeva: Chálukya prince of Samgameśvara, grants a village, I, pt. ii, 224.
Somadeva: Kalachurya Someśvara's officer, I, pt. ii, 486.
Somadeva: Kadamba ruler of the Panumgal province, I, pt. ii, 564 and note 6.
Somáditya: Mularájá's ancestor, I, pt. i, 157.
Somaladevi: wife of Hoysála Vira-Someśvara, I, pt. ii, 493, 508.
Somáli Coast: the holy land of Punt located on, XIII, 404 note 3; Sophir Coast identified with, XIV, 318.
Somana: Kalachurya Sankama's officer, I, pt. ii, 487.
Somanátha: god Shiv, temple of, at Alande, I, pt. ii, 482; grants to, *id.* 569, 581.
Somarája: son of Sahajiga, builds a temple at Prabhása, I, pt. i, 176.
Somaśarmman: Bráhmanic king of Cambodia (610), held daily *Mahábhárata* readings in temples, I, pt. i, 499.
Somavamśa: lunar race, I, pt. ii, 339, 383, 389, 490, 512, 569, 578.
Someshvar: last Siláhára king of Thána (1249-1260), XIII, 422 note 1; his grant, *id.* 427 and note 3; defeated by the Devagiri Yadava king Mahádev, I, pt. ii, 247; inscriptions of, *id.* 21; XIV, 356, 388.
Someshvar: Poona temple, XVIII, pt. iii, 346.
Someshvargudd: hill in Belgaum district, XXI, 9; temple on, *id.* 609.
Someśvara, Soma: poet, author of *Kirtikaumudi*, I, pt. ii, 213, 241, 525 note 5; of *Vastupálacharita*, I, pt. i, 174, 199, 202.
Someśvara: king of the Hoysála Ballálas of Dvárasamudra (1252), I, pt. i, 203 note 3; *see* Soma.
Someśvara: Kalachurya king, son of Bijjála; his father abdicates his throne in his favour, I, pt. ii, 464, 484, 507, 508; wife of, makes a grant of a village, *id.* 227.
Someśvara: shrine at Somanáth Patan, rebuilt by Kumarapála, I, pt. i, 189 and note 2; god, grant of land to, I, pt. ii, 227; inscriptions at the temple of, at Kalasapur, *id.* 417 note 1; at Lakshmeshwar, *id.* 455 note 6; at Kallukeri, *id.* 528 and note 2.
Someśvara I: Western Chálukya king (1044-1068), succeeds his father; his *biruda*, I, pt. ii, 214, 438; his wives and sons; records of his reign, *id.* 438; his feudatories, *id.* 439; his aunt and two of his wives hold government; makes Kalyána his capital, XV, pt. ii, 86; I, pt. ii, 215, 427, 428, 440; provinces of, *id.* 435, 439-440; his capital burnt by the Chola king, *id.* 350 note 8; his successful wars with the Cholas of Káñchi, the Paramáras of Málwa, and the Kalachuris of Dáhala, *id.* 214-215, 441; drowns himself in the Tungabhadrá, *id.* 215-216, 442.
Someśvara II: Western Chálukya king (1069-1076), I, pt. ii, 229; claims to have levied tribute from the Chera, Chola, Pandya and Pallava kings, *id.* 333; rules Belvola and Purigere under his father, *id.* 440; appointed prince regent, *id.* 215, 442; succeeds his father; his *biruda* and records of his reign, *id.* 216, 442; his feudatories, *id.* 443, 453, 454, 492, 515, 561, 574, 577; falls into evil courses and is abandoned by his brothers, *id.* 216, 444; enters into an alliance with Rajiga against his brother Vikramáditya VI; is defeated and taken prisoner, *id.* 217, 445, 446, 447.
Someśvara III: Western Chálukya king (1126, 1138-39), succeeds his father, I, pt. ii, 221, 455; his *biruda* and title, *id.* 221, 455; records of his time, *id.* 455; his feudatories, *id.* 456, 470, 498, 562; is represented as the author of the *Abhilashitarthachintámani* or *Mánasollása*, *id.* 221, 456.
Someśvara IV: (1183-1189), I, pt. ii, 223; his *biruda*; is also called Vira-Someśvara; revives the Western Chálukya sovereignty, *id.* 463, 489; secures the help of Brahma, *id.* 464; establishes himself at Annigere in the Dhárwár district, XV, pt. ii, 90; I, pt. ii, 223, 465; secures Kalyána the capital, *id.* 465; laves the feet of Ekántada Rámayya, *id.* 487; his feudatories and officials, *id.* 465-466, 518, 563; Bhillama defeats his general Brahma, *id.* 502, 556, 582; is driven back into the extreme south-west of his dominions, and with him the dynasty of the Western Chalukyas of Kalyáni comes to an end, *id.* 466.

Someśvarabhatta: Western Chálukya king Someśvara II's officer, I, pt. ii, 443.

Someśvaradeva: Yádava king Krishna's preceptor (1251), I, pt. ii, 527.

Someśvara-pandita: Sivunur village granted by Someśvara I to, I, pt. ii, 441.

Someśvara temple: at Cheul in Kolába district, XI, 301.

Som Gadalya: Bene-Israel feast day, XVIII, pt. i, 513-514.

Somnáth: place of pilgrimage in Káthiáwár, VIII, 607-611; IX, pt. i, 119; original temple of, believed to have been of wood, I, pt. i, 79 note 3; Arjuna's visit to, XIII, 404; legendary origin, early history, description, and destruction of, by Muhammad of Ghazni (1024), I, pt. i, 164-168, 521-523, 512, 229 and note 1; Miyanalladevi's pilgrimage to, *id.* 172; Kumárapála's pilgrimage to, *id.* 187, 190; rebuilding of a new shrine at, by Kumárapála, *id.* 189; Lavánaprasáda grants a village to, *id.* 200; Thána trade with (810-1260), XIII, 429; ruler of, had several Musalmáns under him (1264), IX, pt. ii, 2 note 3; house-tax imposed in, for the maintenance of a mosque at, I, pt. i, 204; destroyed by the Mahomedans (1297), *id.* 205; forms part of Gujarát (1310), I, pt. ii, 4, 25; XIII, 437; burned (1532) by the Portuguese, I, pt. i, 347; Arab references to, I, pt. i, 507, 508, 510, 529, 531; modern temple of, built by Ahilyábai Holkar (1800), IX, pt. i, 19 and note 2; place of pilgrimage of several Gujarát Hindu castes, *id.* 9, 28, 119, 220, 247, 549; inscription in Bhadrakáli's temple at, I, pt. i, 81.

Sompara: only true class of *saláts* or masons in Gujarát; their distribution; said to be originally Bráhmans; defiled in their Bráhmanic purity by a Jain merchant, IX, pt. i, 195-196; great Gurjjara builders, *id.* 499; I, pt. i, 464.

Sompura: a sub-caste of Bráhmans in Cutch, V, 48; in Káthiáwár, VIII, 146; in Thána district, XIII, 78.

Somthan: pass in Násik district, XVI, 131.

Somvanshi A'rya Kshatri: *see* Jingar.

Somvár: ward of Poona city, details of, XVIII, pt. iii, 274-275.

Somvati Amás: religious no-moon day, IX, pt. i, 23, note 5.

Sonai: market town in Ahmadnagar district, XVII, 739.

Sonápur: becomes the burial ground (1760) of Bombay island, XXVI, pt. iii, 577-578.

Sonár: a caste of goldsmiths, in Ratnágiri, X, 125, 142; in Sávantvádi, *id.* 415; in Kolába district, XI, 66; in Janjira, *id.* 413; in Khándesh district, XII, 71; in Thána district, XIII, 63, 139-140; in Kanára district, XV, pt. i, 257; in Násik district, XVI, 50, 486; in Ahmadnagar district, XVII, 133-137; in Poona district, XVIII, pt. i, 371-374; in Sátára district, XIX, 95-96; in Sholápur district, XX, 138; in Belgaum district, XXI, 148; in Dhárwár district, XXII, 161-162; in Kolhápur, XXIV, 98-99; at Bhinmál, I, pt. i, 450. *See* Soni.

Sonar Darri: shoal in Káthiáwár, VIII, 22.

Sonári: *see* Malhárgad.

Sonári: village in Sholápur district, temple at, XX, 502-503.

Sonária: reservoir in Ahmadábád district, IV, 19.

Sonávli: village in Thána district, temple of Sumpeśvar at, XIV, 212, 213.

Sonda: town in Kánara district, fort, Honalli and Terbidi monasteries, inscriptions and history of, XV, pt. ii, 345-349; chiefs (1555-1763), *id.* 120 and note 3, 121, 123, 130, 132-133, 134, 136-137; present representative of, *id.* 349 note 10.

Sonepur: in Bijápur district, battle at (1597), XXIII, 421.

Songad: sub-division of Baroda state, its boundaries, area, aspect, soil, produce, climate and water, VII, 583-584; village and fort, its description, *id.* 584-585, 7; captured by Piláji Gáikwár (1719), continues to be the head-quarters of the Gáikwárs (1719-1766), *id.* 169, 170; I, pt. i, 304, 390, 330; burnt by Bápuji Náik (1742), VII, 176; Dámáji leaves it (1751) for the Dakhan, *id.* 179.

Songad: fort, the citadel of Mandu, captured by Humayun (1534), I, pt. i, 356, 367-368.

Songad Bagatnu: village in Káthiáwár, sun-temple at, VIII, 657.

Songara Rájpúts: resisted by Solankis, I, pt. i, 451 notes 3 and 4.

Songiri: fort in Kolába district, XI, 388.

Sonhaddeva: Nikumbhavansa ruler (1206), establishes a college for the study of astronomy, XII, 241.

Soni: a caste of gold and silversmiths in Gujarát, six divisions of—*Trágads* claim a part-Bráhman origin, IX, pt. i, 197; *Parajiás*, their two branches, claim Rájpút origin and said to have come from Persia, *id.* 197 and note 1; origin of the two branches of Garána and Patani, distribution, *id.* 197-198; Shrimális, originally Shrimali Vánias, two divisions in; *Meváda* originally Meváda Vániás; *Marus* said to have come from Márwár; Gujjar said to belong to the Gujjar Vánia stock, names of other classes following the craft of, *id.* 198; divisions of, according to work, *Sonis, Jadiás, Pachchigars; dukán* or shop; tools; daily life, character, *id.* 199; religious sects; family goddesses, *id.* 200; holy men or *Bhagats* among; customs, *id.* 201-202; in Cutch, V, 51, 70; in Káthiáwár, VIII, 150; Musalmán in Gujarát, converts from the Hindu caste of the same name; have a bad name for mixing gold or silver with cheaper metals, IX, pt. ii, 79.

Sonkehr; *rája* of, made tributary (1436) by Alla-uddin II, I, pt. ii, 31.

Son Koli: caste of fishermen in Thána, XIII, 148-149; derivation of the 1st part of the name, *id.* 407 note 1. *See* Koli.

Sonots: a tribe, trace of the word Húnas in, I, pt. i, 465.

Sonpat: on the Godávari, battle of (1597), XII, 247; XVII, 386.

Soothsaying: early belief among Rájpúts, IX, pt. i, 137; in Ahmadnagar district, XVII, 56, 61, 64, 66, 90, 96, 140; among Gavandis in Bijápur, XXIII, 100.

Sopara: procession in fore-marriage observances, IX, pt. ii, 235.

Sopara: village in Thána district, its situation and description, XIV, 314-316; history, *id.* 316-323; Brahma hill or Vakál, Nirmal, *id.* 323-325; Buddhist relic mound: shape, tradition about, how opened, masonry, stone, copper, copper images of Buddhas, copper casket, coins, stones drilled and undrilled, silver casket, stone casket, crystal casket, gold casket, relics, found at, *id.* 325-336; Chakreshvar temple, Bráhmanical images (A. D. 900-1200), Sopára creek, miscellaneous objects of interest, *id.* 336-339; Ashoka edict at (VIII), *id.* 339-340; Rámkund, temple remains (Bráhmanic and Jain), Gas village, Vájirgad, Rákshi Dongar, basalt dyke, inscribed stones, *id.* 340-342, 355, 356 note 7, 373, 382, 386, 387, 403-418; the glaze of the casket of, *id.* 411; oldest historical place in Thána district, XIII, 403, 404 note 3; seat of a kingdom (B. C. 300), *id.* 406; Purna, Buddha's missionary preaches at, *id.* 407; Buddha's legendary visit to, *id.* 408; skill of its craftsmen (A. D. 160), *id.* 409, 412; Ushavadáta's rest-houses at, *id.* 411 note 3; Ptolemy's mention of, *id.* 415; Christian traders settled at (150), *id.* 417; mentioned in the *Periplus*, *id.* 418; chief place of Thána Siláháras (810-1260), *id.* 423; Indian mart (900-1300), *id.* 429; pearls found at (810-1260), *id.* 430; Balhara king rules over (916), *id.* 434; under Gujarát *sultáns* (1300-1500), *id.* 443; chief Thána port (1300-1500), *id.* 444; system of trade at, from pre-historic times, *id.* 446; Portuguese defences at (1727), *id.* 490; mentioned in a Kárle inscription (100-200) XVIII, pt. ii, 213 and note 8; Southern Mauryan capital, I, pt. i, 14, 38; *see* also I, pt. ii, 1, 2, 16, 21.

Sopáraka: Sopára, XIV, 319.

Sopáraya: Sopára, XIV, 320.

Sopári: betel palm, betel-nuts used in all sacrifices, IX, pt. i, 387.

Sorab: perhaps modern Sopara, XIV, 322; port under Gujarát kings, I, pt. ii, 30.

Soráb: in Mysore, grant at (692), I, pt. ii, 309, 369 and note 5; inscription at, *id.* 529.

Sorabji Kavasji: renders great service to the English (1760); visits Delhi; said to have been taught watch-making by a European; mends a clock for the Mughal emperor; receives the title of Nek Sat Khan and other high distinctions from the emperor, IX, pt. ii, 197 note 2.

Soráb Khán: *see* Sohráb Khán.

Sorath: old name for Káthiáwár, rulers of (315 B. C.-1300 A. D.), VI, 213 note 1; chief of, owes allegiance to Gollas, I, pt. i, 143; annexed to the Chaulukya kingdom of Anahilaváda, *id.* 176; name and extent, *id.* 208 and notes 1 and 3, 209; land-raid system of the Maráthás in, *id.* 418-419; becomes a Muslim territory, IX, pt. i, 125; *sub-division* in Káthiáwár, VIII, 4, 6, 294; Dámáji levies contributions in (1736), VII, 174-175; under the Peshwa, *id.* 318.

Sorathiyá: sub-caste of Bráhmans in Gujarát, IX, pt. i, 20; of Vánias Meshri, a class of great commercial enterprise are known as Chhápariás, *id.* 74 and note 1; in Cutch, V, 50; in Káthiáwár, VIII, 149; in Kolába district, XI, 48.

Sorathiyá: a class of husbandmen in Thána district, XIII, 130-131.

Soratur: village in Dhárwár district, temples and inscriptions at, XXII, 786; I, pt. ii, 504, 520, 421.

Sorcery: belief in, IX, pt. ii, 56.

Sorghum saccharatum: food plant, cultivated throughout India, XXV, 186.

Sorghum vulgare: food, famine and fodder-plant, grows in several districts, XXV, 186, 208, 276.

Sorpáraga, Sorparaka: modern Sopára, I, pt. ii, 148; sea port mentioned in the *Periplus*, I, pt. ii, 174, 176.

Soshios: looked-for son of Zarathustra, IX, pt. ii, 213.

Soter Megas: possibly a Yaudheya leader, I, pt. i, 19.

Soubara, Soubáráh: modern Sopára, XIV, 321; I, pt. ii, 4.

Souboutton: unidentified town of Ptolemy, I, pt. i, 541.

Sougir: town in Khándesh district, XII, 470; crops and revenue settlement (1862) of, *id.* 366-368.

Souparu: modern Sopára, I, pt. i, 540.

Souppara: modern Sopára, I, pt. ii, 174; I, pt. i, 546.

Sousikana: town, not the Kamigara of Ptolemy, I, pt. i, 538.

Souter: Sir Frank, Bhágoji surprised by police under, XII, 262; XVI, 203-204; XVII, 419; captured the rebel chief of Nargund, (1858), XXII, 437.

Southerland; Serjeant, his murder (1676) by the Portuguese at Bándra, XXVI, pt. i, 61.

Southern India: notices of, in ancient Indian literature and inscriptions, I, pt. ii, 138.

Southern Marátha Country: Jainism flourished in, I, pt. ii, 191; the chiefs of, kept at peace by General Wellesley (1803), *id.* 663; wrested from the Maráthás by Colonel T. Munro (1817), *id.* 664-665.

Southern Skythians: notice of, by Dionysios Periegetes, I, pt. i, 537.

South Kánara: Tulu, one of the seven Konkans, I, pt. ii, 282 note 5.

Sov: village in Kolába district, XI, 388; hot spring at, *id.* 13.

Sovanayya; Kalachurya Sankama's officer, I, pt. ii, 487.

Sovarasa: Kalachurya Bijjala's accountant, I, pt. ii, 473.

Sovideva: Kalachurya king (1167-1177), I, pt. ii, 471; succeeds his father, *id.* 227, 484; his *birudas*, epithets and titles; his queen Bávaladevi sings in the presence of an influential assembly and obtains his consent to grant land to the god Someśvara and fourteen Bráhmans, *id.* 227, 484; his other seat of government, *id.* 485; his feudatories, *id.* 485-486.

Sovideva: Western Chálukya king Jagadekamalla II's officer, I, pt. ii, 458.

Sovideva: Hángal Kádamba feudatory of Bijjala, I, pt. ii, 475. *See* Soma.

Sovidevarasa: Hángal Kádamba (A. D. 1173), feudatory of Someśvara, I, pt. ii, 486.

Soyarábái: Rájáram's mother, put to death by Sambháji (1680), XIX, 245.

Soyimarasa: Hángal Kádamba prince (A. D. 1067-68) and feudatory of the Western Chálukya king Someśvara I, I, pt. ii, 439.

Soymida febrifuga: medicinal plant, XXV, 258.

Soyrábái; Shahu's mother, was taken prisoner (1690), XVIII, pt. ii, 239.

Spangles: manufacture of, in Surat, II, 180.

Sparrows: in Ratnágiri district, X, 84.

Spells: beliefs in, among Mochis of Gujarát, IX, pt. i, 194.

Spencer: Mr., chief of the English factory and governor of the castle of Surat, I, pt. i, 343; visits (1756) Poona, XVIII, pt. ii, 247-248.

Spentomad: third Gáthá day among Pársis, IX, pt. ii, 218.

Sphinx: Mátherán Point, XIV, 233.

Spices: Indian, prehistoric foreign trade in, XIII, 404 note 3; Roman passion for (B. C. 25-A. D. 150), *id.* 410 and note 3; sent to Rome by the Parthians, *id.* 411 note 1; brought to Thána from Malabár Coast (810-1260), *id.* 430; (1300-1500), *id.* 445; (1500-1670), *id.* 467; cultivation of, in Kolhápur, XXIV, 174-175; gardens of, in Kánara district, XV, pt. ii, 5-11; export of, *id.* 50, 58.

Spider: beliefs about, in Gujarát, IX, pt. i, 380.

Spies: Shiváji's system of, XIX, 240; Mádhavráv Peshwa's system of, XVIII, pt. ii, 253, 254.

Spirits: belief in, among Gujárat Hindus, classes, males called *bhuts* and females called *pisháchnis*, further classed into *gharna bhuts* or *pisháchni* that is family spirits, and *bahárna bhuts* or *pisháchni* that is outside spirits; the quiet family spirits, their wishes; the troublesome family spirits, their mischief, IX, pt. i, 416; names of the chief male and female outside spirits; Musalmán spirits *jin* and *paris*, their abode, *id.* 417; unfriendly spirits, *id.* 356, 363, 377, 379, 416; food, *id.* 417; favourite haunts, *bábul* tree, *id.* 383; 417; *amli* tree, *id.* 382, 417; days most favourable for spirits entering human bodies, occasions for entering bodies, *id.* 417; greatest spirit day, observances on, *id.* 349, 417; possession or seizure, signs showing possession, *id.* 415, 416, 417; people liable to; Bráhmans believed to be spirit-proof; women open to, during their monthly sickness, in pregnancy, in child-bed, *id.* 416; children apt to be seized by a spirit, *id.* 416; by *paris*, *id.* 417; safeguards against attacks of, on a woman in child-bed, on a second wife by the spirit of the husband's former wife, *id.* 416; on children, *id.* 417; safeguards against second attack, satisfying spirits, *id.* 423; five kinds of offerings made to, *id.* 423-424; performances of the memorial rites at holy places; days for performing rites, *id.* 424; going to pilgrimages with the possessed, *id.* 425; scaring powers, in *adad* grain, *id.* 383; in dung of cat, dog, *id.* 377; donkey, *id.* 376; goat, *id.* 377; horse, *id.* 376; monkey, *id.* 378; in fire, *id.* 356; in leaves of *khákharo*, *id.* 385; *piplo*, *id.* 386; in salt, in water, *id.* 349; beliefs, causes of the beliefs weakening, *id.* 425; beliefs in, among Kolis, *id.* 247; Rájpúts, *id.* 137; early tribes, *id.* 292, 301; quieting of troublesome family spirits among high caste Hindus, *id.* 416; among early and wild tribes, *id* 416-417; exorcism, preliminary modes adopted in, *id.* 417-418; exorcist or spirit-scarer, his other names; mode of gaining spirit-scaring power, rites to be observed by high class Hindu exorcists, by low caste Hindu exorcists, by Musalmán exorcists; Hindu method of gaining control over a spirit on the dark fourteenth of A'so, *id.* 418; tests to ascertain the presence of a spirit; grain test used by Hindu exorcists, *id.* 419; lamp reflection test called *hájrát* practised by Musalmán exorcists, *id.* 419-420; dislodging, by mild measures, by harsh measures, *id.* 420; devices used to make the possessed sway his body, *id.* 421; to make him speak, 421-422; modes of confining a spirit into a bottle, into a lemon, *id.* 422; signs that the spirit has left; spirit-possessed exorcist, *id.* 423; process adopted by exorcists employed by Rájpúts to dislodge spirits, *id.* 137-138; evil, belief in, among Pársis, IX, pt. ii, 213; possession, belief in; employment of exorcists to drive out, *id.* 220; scarers, *id.* 205 and note 1, 206 and note 1; earth, *id.* 206; place, belief in, *id.* 205; water, *id.* 206, 216; belief in, among Musalmáns, *id.* 30, 142, 147; religious men *sayads* or *mullas* called to cast out, *id.* 142; Ámils or exorcists asked to cast out spirit of barrenness, *id.* 147; casting out of, at the shrine of Mirán Sayad Ali at Unjah, *id.* 128-129; Aláchhála-treatment resorted to by Meman women to cast out, *id.* 56; vows made to, *id.* 128; evil, Gujarát means of subduing, *id.* 145; cautions against the baneful influences of, during pregnancy, *id.* 148-149; during childhood, *id.* 155 and note 1; belief in, among the Kánarese, XV, pt. i, 218, 219, 223, 225, 233, 247, 248 and footnote 1, 249, 251 and footnote 1, 292, 300, 319, 365, 388; belief in, in Bijápur district, XXIII, 114-115, 123, 199, 218, 273; Jain belief in, XXIV, 139-140, 415-421; belief in, in Dhárwár district, XXII, 813-817; in Poona district, XVIII, pt. i, 106 note 1; fear of, *id.* 112; possession by, *id.* 144 and note 1; 163, 168, 291-292, 334, 345, 362, 367, 429, 433, 441-442, 470, 553-559, 173, 427; basis of the rule in favour of child-marriage, and against widow-marriage, *id.* 539-542; classes of, *id.* 553-554; in Sholápur district, XX, 44; worship of, in Thána district, XIII, 65; in Belgaum district, XXI, 118, 119.

Splitgerbera scabrella: fibrous plant, XXV, 234.

Spondias mangifera: gum-yielding plant, XXV, 250.

Sponia Wightii: fibrous and gum-yielding plant, XXV, 234, 251.

Spooner : Mr., commissioner of customs (1844), opposed to raising salt duty, XIII, 373.
Sports : Dasara in Sátára city, XIX, 565-566, 658-659.
Spotted Deer : in Kánara district, XV, pt. i, 100-101
Spray-bows : in the Ghatprabha river, XXI, 11 and note 2.
Springs : abode of water-god Varuna, IX, pt. i, 349 ; chief hot spring of Unái in Surat district, *id.* 350 ; hot, in Ratnágiri district, X, 21 ; intermittent, *id.* 22.
Squirrels : at Mátherán, XIV, 258.
Sramaka : governor of Govardhana, I, pt. ii, 150.
Sravana Belgola : records at, I, pt. ii, 306, 500, 505 ; epitaph at, *id.* 407 ; inscription at, *id.* 420, 424, 498, 501, 502, 507 and note 3 ; Jain temples at, *id.* 495.
Sreshthagiri : mountain ruled over by king Gotamiputra, I, pt. ii, 149.
Sribhara : *biruda* or title of Rájasimha (Narasimhavarman II) the Pallava king, I, pt. ii, 329, 330, 331.
S'ri Bhavana : identified with Sarbhon near Broach, I, pt. i, 123 ; Govind, III's halt at, I, pt. ii, 198, 395.
S'ri Chápa : dynasty mentioned by the astronomer Brahmagupta, I, pt. i, 467.
S'ri Devi : installed the Chavada king Vanarája and was considered by him as his sister, I, pt. i, 152.
Sridhara : *biruda* of Nandivarman, I, pt. ii, 325 ; Kalachurya Bijjala's officer, I, pt. ii, 475.
Śri Gaudá : *see* Shrigauda.
Śri Gundi : a sacred place in Bombay island, description of, by Moor (1800-1810), meaning of the word, XXVI, pt. iii, 667-668.
Śri Gupta : *see* Gupta.
Śri Harsha : *see* Shri Harsha.
S'ri Harshacharita : life of S'ri Harsha, I, pt. i, 467.
Sriharshapura : *see* Harashapura.
S'ri Jayatasihadeva : king of Bhinmál, mentioned in a Bhinmál inscription, I, pt. i, 470.
Srikaranádhipa : chief secretary, office of, under Singhan, I, pt. ii, 243, 248, 530 and note 1.
Srikaranaprabhu : I, pt. ii, 248. *See* Srikaranádhipa.
Srikhetaka : I, pt. ii, 404, 413. *See* Khetaka.
S'ri Lakshmi : name of a gate of Bhinmál, I, pt. i, 449.
S'ri Mála : identified with Bhinmál, I, pt. i, 160.
Srimantgad : hill fort close to Lakshmeshwar, I, pt. ii, 504.
Srinagara : city in Káthiáwár, capital of the Yádava dynasty, I, pt. ii, 231 ; Dridhaprahára establishes himself at, *id.* 512 ; seat of Jethva power, I, pt. i, 138.
Srinidhi : *biruda* of Narasimha the Pallava king, I, pt. ii, 331.
Srinilaya : province probably in Sátára district, I, pt. ii, 356, 357.
Sripála : Siddharája's poet-laureate, I, pt. i, 180.
Sriparvata : holy place mentioned in the Araleshwar inscription, I, pt. ii, 284 note 4.
Sriparvata : mountain. *See* Srisaila.
Sripati : Bhaskarácharya's brother, I, pt. ii, 244.
Sripat Iyarasa : Vikramáditya VI's minister of peace and war for Kánarese district, I, pt. ii, 452.
Sri-prithivivallabha : *biruda* of Pulikesin I, I, pt. ii, 343 and note 6.
Sripujyapáda : *see* Pujyapáda.
S'ri Pulimai : king Pulumai mentioned by Ptolemy (150), I, pt. ii, 11.
Sripura : modern Sirur, I, pt. ii, 196.
Srípurusha, Srípurusha Prithiví Kongani : Muttarasa (762-777), Western Ganga king, I, pt. ii, 301 note 1, 302, 303.
Sríraja : Yádava king, son of Bhillama, was succeeded by Vaddiga, I, pt. ii, 231.
Srirangam : in the Trichinopoly district, Vira-Somesvara's rule over, I, pt. ii, 508.
Sríśaila : hill, I, pt. ii, 286 note 4, 480.
Sríśaila : Karnul territory, I, pt. ii, 389 ; king of, subdued by Dantidurga, *id.* 194 ; kingdom, *id.* 403 note 3.
Sríśatakarni : *see* S'átakarni.
Sristhala-Siddhapura : Bráhmans at, troubled by *rákshasas* or demons, I, pt. i, 174.
S'rivallabha : secondary name of Govinda III, I, pt. ii, 195, 394 ; of Krishna I, *id.* 390, 419 note 1.
Srivallabha Senánandarája : Sendraka prince, I, pt. ii, 292 ; marries his sister to Kirtivarman I, *id.* 345, 356.
S'rivardhana : town, captured by the Yádava king Bhillama, I, pt. ii, 238, 520.
Srívatsa : *gotra*, I, pt. ii, 482.
Sriyambátaka : village, grant of, mentioned in the Mahákuta pillar inscription, I, pt. ii, 348.
Srongdzan-Gambo : (640-698), founder of Tibetan power and civilization, overruns Tarim valley and Western China, I, pt. i, 501.
Srutakirti : *senápati* of Kákusthavarman, saves the life of the king, I, pt. ii, 287.
S'ryáśraya Siladitya : (669-691), his plates ; I, pt. i, 107-108 ; Yuvarája (691-692), *id.* 110, 111, 112 ; Jayasimha's son, rules Southern Gujarát as his father's regent, I, pt. ii, 187.
St. Peter : Church of, at Bándra, XIV, 16, 24, 25.
Stambha : leader of the confederacy against Govinda III, I, pt. ii, 395 ; *see* also, I, pt. i, 123.
Stambhatirtha : modern Cambay, I, pt. i, 123 ; granted to Srigaudás by Mularája, *id.* 161 ; temple at, repaired by Kumárapála, *id.* 190.
Stamps : receipts from, *see* Revenue and Finance in all district volumes under District Name.
St. Andrew : Church of, at Bándra, XIV, 15, 16, 22, 23, 26 ; in Poona, XVIII, pt. iii, 396.
St. Anne : Roman Catholic Church at Bándra, destroyed (1737) by the Portuguese themselves, I, pt. ii, 84 ; XIV, 18, 22, 27 ; chapel in Poona, XVIII, pt. iii, 396.
St. Anthony : church and lake in Thána district, at Málvan, XIV, 223 ; at Máne, *id.* 228 ; at Thána, *id.* 351, 358.
Stars : reading of, by Husaini Bráhmans, IX, pt. ii, 22 ; considered divine beings ; vows made to, by Gujarát Hindus, IX, pt. i, 406 ; Pársi veneration for, IX, pt. ii, 213.

Staunton: Captain, marches (1817) on Poona, XVIII, pt. ii, 301-302.
Stavorinus: Dutch traveller (1774), describes the Surat Pársis, IX, pt. ii, 195-196.
St. Barbara: Franciscan tower at Cheul, XI, 296.
St. Bonaventura: Portuguese church at Yerangal, I, pt. ii, 65.
St. Cecilia: Portuguese church at Poncar, I, pt. ii, 57.
St. Dominique: Church of, at Karanja, XIV, 194; at Thána, *id.* 360.
Steamers: in Ratnágiri, X, 170, 365; in Kánara district, XV, pt. ii, 59-60, 319, 326.
Steam Factories: in Ahmadábád district, IV, 131; in Sholápur district, XX, 270-271.
Steam-ferries: at the Carnac wharf, Bombay, XI, 116; at Alibág, *id.* 255; at Jánjira, *id.* 429; in Thána, XIII, 330.
Steam-presses: in Káthiáwár, VIII, 253-254.
Stephanos: of Byzantium, geographer, I, pt. i, 546.
Stephegyne parviflora: fodder plant, XXV, 278.
Sterculia: *colorata, fœtida*, fibrous plants, XXV, 229; *guttata, urens, villosa*, fibrous and gum-yielding plants, *id.* 229, 250.
Sterculiaceæ: species of famine and fibrons plants, XXV, 195, 229.
Stersospermnm chelonoides: sacred plant, XXV, 290.
Sterninæ: sub-family of birds in Ratnágiri, X, 98.
Stevenson: Colonel, in pursuit of Dhundia Vágh, XXI, 392-393; drives him from Mysore, XXII, 421; goes to Kundgol, *id.* 423-424; moves to Gár Dhond to help General Wellesley in the Dakhan, I, pt. ii, 608, 609; stations his army at Pureuda (1802); takes Asirgad and Burhánpur from Sindia, *id.* 629; XVIII, pt. ii, 283.
Steveson: Rev. Dr., assigns Elephanta caves to the eighth century, XIV, 82; his notice of Nánághát inscriptions, *id.* 291; his interpretation of the legend of Parashurám, I, pt. ii, 26.
Stewart: Captain James (1778), English commander, takes Bor *ghát* and encamps at Khandála; killed, XVIII, pt. ii, 263-264.
St. Francis: Church of, at Karanja, XIV, 194; at Thána, *id.* 360.
St. George's Hospital: in Bombay island, located in a house near the present Cooperage (1672-1700), a building for, on the site of the Great Western Hotel (1700-1745); proposals for a new building (1767-1792), (1814-1828), XXVI, pt. iii, 595-599, 601-606; this building sold (1862), removed to officers' quarters (1876), *id.* 606; the present building opened in 1892; its description, *id.* 606-608.
Sthánaka: modern Thána, I, pt. ii, 542, 543, 544, 548.
Sthánakamandala: Thána, prince of, reinstated by the Karád Śiláhára Vijayáditya, I, pt. ii, 570.
Sthánakundúra: Tálgund, a tank built at, by Kákusthavarman, I, pt. ii, 287.
Sthanik: *see* Pátáli.
Stháuugúdhapura: modern Tálgund, Bráhmans established in, I, pt. ii, 561.
Stiávarapalliká: identified with Chhárolí, I, pt. ii, 392.
Sthaviras: life of, by Hemachandra, I, pt. i, 193.
Sthiramati: name of a Bodhisattva, constructed the Bappapadiyavihára, I, pt. i, 79 and note 1, 85.
Stilbite: stone in Poona district, XVIII, pt. i, 30.
Stilts: class of birds in Ratnágiri, X, 93.
Stimulants and Narcotics: in use in Gujarát, fermented and distilled drinks, *tadi* or toddy, *mahuda* liquor, IX, pt. i, pp. xxix-xxx; drinking classes, *id.* pp. xxx-xxxii; hemp preparations, *bháng, yakudi, gánja, id.* pp. xxxii-xxxiii; *opium, tobacco, betel-nut, tea* and *coffee, id.* pp. xxxiii-xxxiv; stimulants among Musalmáns, IX, pt. ii, 110.
Stints: class of birds in Ratnágiri, X, 92.
Stiora: piosonous plant, XXV, 268.
St. Jerome: Church of, at Cáshi in Thána district, XIV, 51.
St. John: Dr., first admiralty judge in Bombay island, XXVI, pt. i, 84.
St. John the Baptist: Church of, at Karanja, XIV, 194; at Thána, *id.* 351, 355.
St. John the Evangelist: Church of, at Márol in Thána district, XIV, 229.
St. John's Peak: at Sanján, XIV, 304.
St. Joseph: Convent of, at Bándra, XIV, 15, 21, 23.
St. Lubin: French adventurer, lands at Collaby (1777), well received by Nána Phadnávis, dismissed from Poona (1778), I, pt. ii, 102, 103; *see* also XVIII, pt. ii, 261 and note 3, 262; XXVI, pt. i, 408-410; XI, 286, 287 note 2.
St. Martin: identifies some of Pliny's tribes with Rajpút tribes, I, pt. i, 534; identifies Posipeda with Besmaid, *id.* 538; Auxoamis with Suni, *id.* 539.
St. Mary Isles: in Kánara district, Vasco da Gama lands at, XV, pt. ii, 101, 271 and note 2.
St. Mary's Church: in Poona, XVIII, pt. iii, 396-397.
Stock: agricultural, all district volumes, *see* Agriculture under District Name.
Stockings: spinning of, at Anjidiv (1775), XV, pt. ii, 54, 138, 141, 251, 256, 257.
Stone: disease in Khandesh district, XII, 337.
Stone Casket: Sopára *stúpa*, XIV, 365.
Stones: worship of, *consecrated* stones, forms of gods and goddesses as stones worshipped by high caste Hindus in Gujarát; varieties used in making idols; *sháligrám* stone representing Vishnu, stone *ling* representing Shiva, consecration of; treated as a god after consecration, IX, pt. i, 362; daily worship of *id.* 363; stones worshipped by low and wild tribes, *id.* 362, 363; dwellings and names of gods and goddesses worshipped; dwellings of the dead, stones or cairns raised in memory of the dead *Khatras*, form of, days and details of worship, *id.* 363; *Páliyás, Khámbhiyás, Chirás*, literal meaning of, form of; object

and for whom raised, setting up of; days for setting up; days and details of worship, *id.* 363-364; famous stones, *id.* 364-365; for building, in Kaira, III, 15; in Panch Mahâls, *id.* 198; in Cutch, V, 22; in Pálanpur, *id.* 285; in Mahi Kántha, *id.* 360; in Khándesh district, XII, 225; in Ratnágiri district, X, 401; in Sátára district, XIX, 221; in Poona district, XVIII, pt. i, 29; in Surat district, II, 38; for building, in Ahmadábád district, IV, 22; in Rewa Kántha, VI, 11; in Káthiáwár, VIII, 91-92, 262, 355; in Dhárwár district, XXII, 25-26; in Belgaum district, 53, 54; in Bijápur district, XXIII, 54-61; inscribed, found in Thána district, XIII, 420, 425 notes 5 and 6, 426 and notes 2, 3 and 4, 427 and notes 1, 2 and 3, 437; memorial, *id.* 429 note 1, 433; precious, *id.* 413, 416 and note 1, 430, 445, 467 note 10; memorial carved, in Kánara district, XV, pt. ii, 275, 276.

Stone Vessels: making of, in Dhárwár district, XXII, 383.

Stone-work: in Sholápur district, XX, 273.

Storks: class of birds in Ratnágiri district, X, 94.

Storms: in Ratnágiri, X, 23, 231; at Bassein in Thána district, XIV, 1, 31.

St. Patrick's Church: in Poona, XVIII, pt. iii, 397.

St. Paul's Church: in Poona, XVIII, pt. iii, 397-398.

St. Peter: Church of, at Bándra in Thána district, XIV, 16, 24, 25.

St. Petersburg: dictionary, I, pt. ii, 278 note 2.

Strabo: Roman geographer (B. C. 50-A. D. 20), his date for the conquests in India of Eucratides, I, pt. i, 16; Cutch and Sauráshtra conquered by Menander (B. C. 120) according to, *id.* 17; Greek coins at Barygaza in his time, *id.* 535; great increase of trade between India and Egypt, *id.* 536; his mention of pirates of Suvarndurg (B. C. 50-A. D. 20), I, pt. ii, 1; mentions Sigerdis which may be identified with Jánjira, XI, 432; his mention of Indian trade with the Parthians (B. C. 30), XIII, 411 note 1, 412.

Strachey: Mr. E., appointed to negotiate settlement between Bájiráv Peshwa and the Patvardhans, XXIV, 349.

Strakútaka: identified with Traikutaka, I, pt. ii, 178.

Strangers: settlements of, in Gujarát, I, pt. i, 1.

Streets: improvement of, in Bombay (1787), XXVI, pt. ii, 493-494.

Strigidæ: family of birds, in Ratnágiri district, X, 58.

Strikes: among craftsmen in Káthiáwár, VIII, 266.

Strychnos: *colubrina*, poisonous plant, antidote to snake-bite, XXV, 267, 275; *potatorum*, plant used as soap, *id.* 252; *nux-vomica*, piosonous plant, *id.* 267.

St. Sebastian: Church of, at Mátherán, XIV, 229.

St. Stanislaus: Orphanage of, at Bándra in Thána district, XIV, 15, 21, 25.

St. Thomas the Apostle: Church of, at Páhádi in Thána district, XIV, 293; at Sopára, *id.* 322.

Stuart: Lieutenant, mortally wounded (1858) near Nándgaon, XVI, 200.

Stupa: Buddhist relic mound, in Thána district, XIV, 169-171, 325 note 4; Elephanta, *id.* 60, 94, 388; Kalyán, *id.* 397, 398, 399; Kánheri, *id.* 180-184; Kondivti, *id.* 204; Sopára, *id.* 325-336, 405, 406, 410; XIII, 408, 412; of As'oka, I, pt. ii, 354; at Kolhápur, *id.* 538 note 8.

Sturninæ: sub-family of birds, in Ratnágiri district, X, 82.

St. Valentine's Peak: at Mahálakshmi in Thána district, XIV, 218.

St. Xavier's Church: in Poona, XVIII, pt. iii, 398.

Styraceæ: species of dye-yielding plants, XXV, 247.

Suæda Indica: famine plant, grows in the Konkan, XXV, 203.

Suár: as caste of cooks and beggars in Pálanpur, V, 290.

Suaratarataæ: tribe mentioned by Pliny, I, pt. i, 532, 534.

Suari: Sávaras of Central India, a tribe mentioned by Pliny, I, pt. i, 533.

Sub-aërial formations: in Ratnágiri, X, 19; in Sávantvádi, *id.* 398; in Belgaum district, XXI, 37; in Bijápur district, XXIII, 50.

Subah: province, I, pt. i, 211.

Subahdár: Mughal viceroy, I, pt. i, 211.

Subáhu: Yádava king, said to have divided his whole kingdom among his four sons, I, pt. ii, 231, 512.

Subára: modern Surat, Arab references to, I, pt. i, 508, 509, 514, 516; perhaps Sopára, *id.* 523 note 4, 529; XIV, 321.

Subhadra: Krishna's sister, I, pt. i, 9, 10.

Subhakesi: king of the Karnátaka, gave his granddaughter in marriage to Karna, I, pt. i 170.

Subhánji Pol: *killedár* of Kaira, Gáikwár's guarantee for the respect of, VII, 253.

Subhatavarman: king of Málwa, turned back by Lavanaprasáda, I, pt. i, 198.

Subhatunga: Akalavarsha of Gujarát branch of Málkhed Ráshtrakútas, recovered his paternal kingdom by defeating the army of Vallabha, I, pt. ii, 408, 409; I, pt. i, 126.

Subhatunga: *biruda* or title of Krishna I, pt. ii, 390; of Krishna II, *id.* 410.

Subhedár: Marátha district officer, XIII, 555-556, 561; XI, 170; XVIII, pt. ii, 325 note 2.

Suboji-nimaz: morning prayer among Musalmáns, IX, pt. ii, 49.

Subsidiary force: establishment of, at Poona (1813) and Sirúr by the English, I, pt. ii, 610; in Baroda (1805), VII, 212-213; (1817), *id.* 226, 298; territory assigned to the Company for the maintenance of, *id.* 391.

Succession Act: Pársi, IX, pt. ii, 238, 244; administration of justice under, *id.* 244.

Suchianas: oil-yielding plant, common throughout India, XXV, 214.

Sudágri: caste of husbandmen in Thána district, XIII, 116.

Sudaria: Shudras, husbandmen mentioned by Ibni Khurdadbah, I, pt. i, 530.

Sudarsána : ancient lake near Girnár, I, pt. i, 35, 36, 69.
Sudása : northern Kshatrapa king, his coins, I, pt. i, 23.
Sudasna : state in Mahi Kántha, governed by a Parmár Rájpút chief, IX, pt. I. 127; V, 422-423. *Town*, temple and fair at, *id.* 442; attacked by the Gáikwár, VII, 329.
Suddhakkumbadi : ancestor of Prachanda, I, pt. i, 129.
Sudhágad : *see* Bharap.
Súdi : village in Dhárwár district, temples and inscriptions at, XXII, 786; grant from, I, pt. II, 302 note 2, 303 note 7, 419; inscription at, *id.* 434, 435 note 4, 441 and note 6, 477; records at, *id.* 573, 576.
Sudir : a caste of husbandmen in Kánara district, XV, pt. i, 236-237.
Suez : ships built at, I, pt. ii, 45; trade to, from India, stopped (1777), XXVI, pt. i, 407-408.
Sufárah : *see* Supára.
Sufli : low divine magic among Gujarát Musalmáns, IX, pt. ii, 143.
Sugandhavarti, Sugandhavartin : modern Saundatti, I, pt. ii, 143, 439, 550.
Sugar : manufacture of, in Khándesh district, XII, 226; in Baroda, VII, 80-81, 90; in Kolhápur, XXIV, 179-180; in Thána district, XIII, 391-395.
Sugarcane : cultivation of, in Surat, II, 66; in Broach, *id.* 408; in Kaira, III, 54; in Panch Mahála, *id.* 233; in Ahmadábád district, IV, 58; in Cutch, V, 107; in Pálanpur, *id.* 295; in Mahi Kántha, *id.* 377; in Ratnágiri district, X, 148; Mauritius variety, *id.* 148 note 1; varieties and growth of, in Khándesh district, XII, 167-169; cultivation of, in Thána district, XIV, 300; XIII, 290-291; newly introduced in Sálsette (1788), *id.* 510 and note 6, 511; cultivation of, in Kánara district, XV, pt. ii, 19-20; in Násik district, XVI, 101; in Ahmadnagar district, XVII, 273-274; experiments of growing Mauritius variety in Poona district, XVIII, pt. ii, 51-55; crop of, in Sátára district, XIX, 166-168; in Belgaum district, XXI, 251-252; in Dhárwár district, XXII, 278-280; in Kolhápur state, area, varieties, and other details, XXIV, 175-180.
Sugar-eating : Bene-Israel marriage ceremony, XVIII, pt. i, 516.
Sugar Factory : in Thána district, XIV, 35, 36, 40.
Suggaladevi, Suggale : wife of the Western Chálukya king Jayasimha II, I, pt. ii, 435.
Sugríva : monkey king, I, pt. ii, 135; met by Ráma, *id.* 142.
Suhágans : married women who have never lost their husbands, IX, pt. ii, 163.
Suhuka : *see* Chánka.
Suidæ : boars, etc., in Ratnágiri district, X, 45.
Suigám : Chohan Rájpút chiefship, IX, pt. i, 125; state and place of interest in Pálanpur, V, 281, 336, 348.
Suits : civil, in Kánara district, XV, pt. ii, 196-198; in Belgaum district, XXI, 268-269; for other districts *see* Justice under District Name.
Sujna : oil-yielding plant, XXV, 218.
Suka Bhádar : river in Káthiáwár, VIII, 63.
Sukeli : pass in Kolába district, XI, 115.
Suketuvarma : Mauryan king (A. D. 400), XIII, 420; king of the Konkan mentioned in an inscription from Váda, I, pt. ii, 14; I, pt. i, 107; XIV, 373.
Sukhtara : or Socotra island off the coast of Africa, V, 68 note 3.
Suklatirtha : place on the Narbada, Chamunda retired at, to die, I, pt. i, 162.
Sukoth : Bene-Israel feast day, XVIII, pt. i, 514.
Sukrita Sankirtana : Sanskit work on Chávada kings, I, pt. i, 149 and note 2, 154, 156, 159 note 3, 171, 194, 195, 196; represents Barappa as the general of the king of Kananj, I, pt. ii, 431 note 1.
Súktimuktávali : anthology of select verses from Sanskrit poets, I, pt. ii, 245.
Sul : village in Dhárwár district, temple at, XXII, 786.
Sulaimán : Arab merchant and traveller; author of *Silsilat-ut-Tawárikh*, I, pt. i, 498, 505 and note 2, 525, 526, 527, 530; his remarks on the Konkan king (850), XIV, 58; his mention of Balhara of Thána, XIII, 434; I, pt. ii, 22, 387, 388; traveller (851), mentions the partiality to Arabs of the Ráshtrakúta king, IX, pt. ii, 2 note 1.
Sulaimán : Yaman priest of the Shiah Bohorás, IX, pt. ii, 27.
Sulaimán : Turkish admiral, lays siege to Diu (1538), XIII, 452.
Sulaimán Fáras : saint of Turki Hajams, IX, pt. ii, 85.
Sule, *pl.* Suleru : a caste of courtezans in Dhárwár district, XXII, 192.
Suleimán : I, pt. ii, 4. *See* Sulaimán.
Sulimán : early Arab traveller (840), X, 132. *See* Sulaimán.
Sulliyúr : village on the bank of the river Aradore mentioned in a Mysore grant, I, pt. ii, 377.
Sultán Akbar : Aurangzib's fourth son, revolts against his father, joins the Maráthás (1681), and accompanies Sambháji to the siege of Jánjira (1682), I, pt. ii, 76-77; goes to Vengurla to leave the country but is prevailed on to return (683), *id.* 77; goes to Vishálgad with Sambháji and retreats; goes with Sambháji to invest Bassein; abandons Sambháji and goes to Persia in an English ship (1688), *id.* 78.
Sultángang : near Mongir, *stúpa* at, I, pt. i, 51.
Sultani Khatiks : *see* Bakar Kasái.
Sultankar : *see* Saltangar.
Sultan Lád : a caste of Musalmáns in Kánara district, XV, pt. i, 410.
Sultán Mázum, Sultan Muazim : governor of the Dakhan, confirms Shiváji in his *jágir* of Poona, Supa and Chákan and retains the forts of Purandhar and Sinhagad, I, pt. ii, 594; XVIII, pt. ii, 235; Aurangzib's son afterwards emperor Bahádur Sháh, sacks

villages between Ráygad and Vengurla, I, pt. ii, 77.
Sultánpur: one of the chief towns under the Goudál state, VIII, 657.
Sultánpur: place in Khándesh ceded to Mubarik, XII, 244, 246, 255, 259; its history, remains, *id.* 471.
Sultán Sikandar: son and successor of Áli Ádil Sháh, I, pt. ii, 653.
Sumant: foreign minister of the Marátha government, XIX, 244 note 1.
Sumárgad: fort in Ratnágiri district, X, 4, 373.
Sumati: counseller of Mádhavasena, I, pt. ii, 147.
Sumátra: Hindu settlements of, I, pt. i, 493; Rahma or Ruhmi identified with, *id.* 527, 528.
Sumda: a Musalmán sub-division in Cutch, V. 99.
Sumersing: Peshwa Náráyanráv's murderer, XVIII, pt. ii, 255-256.
Sumra: chief of Sind, I, pt. i, 139, 160, 517; IX, pt. i, 126.
Sumras: Sind tribe of Rájpút origin, converted by Mahmud Begada (1473), said to belong to the Mihira Gurjara stock; call themselves descendants of Arab tribe, IX, pt. ii, 70.
Sun: called Surya, a planet, IX, pt. i, 392, 393-396; veneration for the, among Pársis, IX, pt. ii, 213; image of, at Sopára in Thána district, XIV, 337. *See* Planet (Sun).
Sunáhdev: *see* Rám Taláv.
Sunda: hill range near Bhinmál, I, pt. i, 456.
Sunda Máta: shrine of, at Bhinmál, I, pt. i, 455, 456.
Sundara Pándyadeva: took Śrirangam from Someśvara, I, pt. ii. 508. *See* Jatávarman.
Sundarji: Lohána convert, grandson of Mánekji, his Muhamedan name Adam, head of the converted Lohána community, IX, pt. ii, 51.
Sundarji Desai: guarantee granted to, in 1801, VII, 259.
Sundar Náráyan: Násik temple, XVI, 503-504.
Sundarvádi: *see* Sávantvádi.
Sunday: Ravivár, other name of; is sacred to the sun, IX, pt. i, 393; beliefs about, *id.* 396; sacredness of, XVIII, pt. i, 239-240. *See* Planet (Sun).
Sundrái: port in Káthiáwár, VIII, 64, 242.
Sundri: village of, near Thána; shrine of Samudrimáta at, IX, pt. i, 71, 74.
Sun Feast Day: IX, pt. ii, 216. *See* Meher Jasan.
Sunga: dynasty, I, pt. ii, 146; Puránic dynasty, *id.* 155.
Sungabhrityas: Kánvas or servants of the Sungas, I, pt. ii, 163.
Sungas: duration of the, I, pt. ii, 162; uprooted by Śisuka, *id.* 163.
Sunghiri: island in Kánara district, XV, pt. ii, 328, 350.
Sunguiceers: pirates from Sangameshvar, I, pt. ii, 88.
Sung-Yun: Chinese pilgrim (A. D. 519), notices the use of leather in Tibet, IX, pt. i, 437, 454; his notice of the Gandhára family (520), I, pt. i, 74, 75; his surprise at dragons, *id.* 502.
Sunkeri: suburb of the town of Kárwár in the Kánara district, a church at, XV, pt. ii, 350.
Sunmukh: one of the ceremonies of marriage, XII, 66.
Sunn: sacred plant, XXV, 290.
Sunnágár: a caste of lime-sellers in Dhárwár district, XXII, 126.
Sunnah-wal-Jamáat: the prophet, IX, pt. ii, 3 note 3.
Sunni: one of the two forms of Musalmán faith, IX, pt. ii, 125; origin and points of difference of, *id.* 46-47, 125-126; *imáms* of, *id.* 125 note 2, 126; schools of, *id.* 126 note 1; schisms of, Mahdavi, *id.* 6 note 1, 35 note 1, and Wahhábi, *id.* 12 and note 1, 13; spread of, in Gujarát, by Sunni Musalmán rulers, *id.* 125; Musalmán sect in Belgaum, XXI, 202.
Sunt, Sunta: food plant, XXV, 174.
Sun Temple: at Bhinmál, I, pt. i, 455; description of, *id.* 459-460; history, *id.* 460-461; dates, *id.* 463.
Sunth: state in Rewa Kántha, its area, boundaries, aspect, rivers, hills, climate, soil and produce, population, sub-divisions, history, development and family tree of its chiefs, VI, 131-136. *Town, id.* 169; Arab outbreak at, I, pt. i, 441.
Sun-worship: among Húnas, I, pt. i, 142 and notes 2 and 5.
Supa: sub-division of Kánara district, villages, aspect, climate, water, soil, stock, survey details, people, XV, pt. ii, 235-238; village, dispensary, temple, history, *id.* 44, 146, 219, 350-351; forests, XV, pt. i, 34, 36.
Supa: in Poona district, reservoir at, XVIII, pt. ii, 28; granted (1720) in *jágir* to Chimnáji Apa, *id.* 243; survey, *id.* 437-438, 496-499; surprised by Shiváji (1647), I, pt. ii, 591; inscriptions at, XVIII, pt. iii, 448-449.
Supára: *see* Sopára.
Supárem: *see* Supára.
Supe: village and a place of interest in Ahmadnagar district, XVII, 740.
Supedi: one of the chief towns of the Gondál state, a fair at, VIII, 658.
Supera: Sopára, XIV, 321.
Suphárak: Sopára, Bodhisattva of, XIV, 316.
Supratika: Vikramáditya I's elephant, I, pt. ii, 322 note 8.
Surabára: town mentioned by Ibni Haukal, apparently Surat, I, pt. i, 514, 516.
Surabara: Supára, I, pt. i, 523.
Surabáya: Sorabára, Surat, I, pt. i, 507 and note 3, 514.
Surabáya: Sopára, XIV, 321.
Surábhái: Pirána tomb of, IX, pt. ii, 76 note 2. *See* Pirána Tombs.
Suradhenupura: in Mysore, copper-plate grant from, I, pt. ii, 301 note 1; charter from, *id.* 302.
Suræ: tribe mentioned by Pliny, I, pt. i, 533.
Suragi: beggar. *See* Satáni.

Súrah-i-Ar-Rehmán: holy book of the Musalmáns, IX, pt. ii, 162.

Surah-I-Yásin: chapter of the *Kurán* read to a dying Khojáh, IX, pt. ii, 46.

Surájiráo: Nimbálkar (1820), his depredations at Yával put down, XII, 257, 479.

Surajmaka: oil-yielding plant, XXV, 219.

Surajmal: claimant to the Lunáváda *gádi* or chiefship, I, pt. i, 441.

Surajpul: gateway of Bhinmál, I, pt. i, 450 note 1.

Suramára: battle of, I, pt. ii, 322, 358; defeat of Pulikesin II at, *id.* 326.

Suran: food-plant cultivated throughout India, XXV, 182.

Surapála: brother-in-law of Jayaśekhara and maternal uncle of Vanarája, I, pt. i, 150, 151.

Suráshtra: ancient division of Gujarát, I, pt. i, 6, 35, 36, 135; lord of, taken prisoner by Siddharája, *id.* 175; kingdom of, *id.* 535; Verával, *id.* 547; ruled by Gotamiputra, I, pt. ii, 149; conquered by Rudradáman, *id.* 160; subjugated by Gotamiputra, *id.* 161; Kathiáwár, *id.* 284, 515; XVI, 183 and note 2, 630; Muhammad makes peace with the inhabitants of, I, pt. i, 506.

Surastra: village, mentioned by Ptolemy which is perhaps Verával, I, pt. i, 538.

Surastrene: Suráshtra, I, pt. i, 15-16, 537, 538; V, 130; XIII, 414.

Surat: district, its area, boundaries, aspect and hills, II, 1-4; rivers, *id.* 5-28; lakes, geology, *id.* 29-35; climate, rainfall, *id.* 36-37; minerals, trees, *id.* 38-42; domestic and wild animals, birds, fish and fisheries, *id.* 43-46; population, *id.* 47-55; village communities and movements of the people, *id.* 56-57; soil, marsh reclamations, agricultural stock, aboriginal tillage, field produce, area under cultivation, irrigation, details of cultivation and years of scarcity, *id.* 59-68; early history (1194-1573), *id.* 69-72; under Mughal rule (1573-1733), *id.* 73-115; under independent governors (1733-1759), *id.* 116-127; English ascendancy (1759-1876), *id.* 128-158; roads, bridges, rest-houses, ferries and railways, landing stages and light-houses, *id.* 160-165; trade by sea and land and traders with Surat, *id.* 166-177; manufactures, *id.* 177-180; markets or *hál-wáras*, *id.* 181; capitalists, forms of investments and classes of money-lenders, *id.* 182-189; traders, artizans and cultivators, as borrowers, *id.* 190-193; aboriginal tribes, as borrowers, *id.* 194-200; relations between creditors and debtors, *id.* 201; rates of interest, currency, transfers and sale value of land, *id.* 202-205; rates of wages, prices, and weights and measures, *id.* 206-210; acquisition of land, administrative changes and condition of district, *id.* 211-213; *garásias'* exactions, *id.* 214; *desáis'* or revenue contractors' powers, exactions and relation with Government and cultivators, *id.* 215-219; mode of land settlements at different times from the commencement of the British rule, *id.* 216-226; village establishment, *id.* 226; administration of the civil and criminal justice, *id.* 228-232; piracy and police statistics, *id.* 233-237; revenue and finance, *id.* 238-245; Local Funds and Municipalities, *id.* 246-248; instruction, libraries, newspapers, post and telegraph statistics, *id.* 249-260; chief diseases, dispensaries, vaccination, cattle-disease, and vital statistics, *id.* 261-266; sub-divisional accounts, *id.* 267-296; places of interest, *id.* 297-334.

City, origin of name, *id.* 70, 71; sacked by Musalmáns, *id.* 69; story of Gopi, the founder, *id.* 70; thrice burnt by Portuguese, *id.* 71; fort built, *id.* 71; taken by Akbar, *id.* 72; plundered by Malik Ambar, *id.* 74; famine of 1731, *id.* 81; plundered by Shiváji, *id.* 89; taken by the English, *id.* 126; revenues, *id.* 93, 135; administration of the city, *id.* 92, 142-145; the *nawáb* pensioned and complete surrender of Surat to the English, *id.* 154; aspect and condition at different times (1514), *id.* 71; (1590), *id.* 73; (1608-1620), *id.* 79, 82; (1670-1707), *id.* 90; (1759-1780), *id.* 131; (1800-1876), *id.* 315-317; population at different times, *id.* 80, 82, 90, 134, 319; inner wall, *id.* 308; suburbs, *id.* 309-313; outer wall, *id.* 314; houses, public buildings and places of interest, *id.* 321-330; governors of (1628-1657), *id.* 81; (1658-1707), *id.* 91; (1707-1733), *id.* 110; rival of Cambay (1700), VI, 195; mention of, XIV, 322, 344, 347; trade in coloured goods (1733-1737), XXVI, pt. ii, 113-114.

Surat Athavisi: old province in Gujarát, II, 1 note 1, 92 note 6; plundered by the Maráthás (1780), I, pt. i, 409.

Suratvál: see Rájpút.

Śúrávalundúr: battle at, fought by Udayachandra, I, pt. ii, 326.

Surbakri: hills in Pálanpur, V, 282.

Surbáráh: mouth of the Tápti, I, pt. i, 523.

Surbárah: Sopára, XIV, 321.

Súrchand: *rája*, governor of Navsári, his daughter married to Núr Satágur, IX, pt. ii, 38.

Sureśvara: pupil of Samkaráchárya mentioned in a Vedantic work, I, pt. ii, 212.

Surgad: fort in Kolába district, XI, 267; temples at, *id.* 388-390.

Surgána: group of states in Khándesh, I, pt. ii, 633; XII, 611-613.

Suri: sage, title conferred on Hemachandra, I, pt. i, 191.

Suri: tribe mentioned by Pliny, I, pt. i, 534.

Suribán: village in Dhárwár district; Mr. Manson's murder at (1858), XXII, 787.

Suringee: dye-yielding plant, grows in several districts, XXV, 241.

Surnames: *see* under caste concerned.

Surnis: general record-keeper of the Marátha government, XIX, 243.

Surpáli: village in Belgaum district, temple and fair at, XXI, 607-608.

Surpan: holy place in Rewa Kántha, VI, 169.

Surparaka: modern Sopára, visited by Sahadeva, I, pt. ii, 142; capital of the Northern Konkan, *id.* 143; I, pt. ii, 543.

Sursi: sub-division of Rewa Kántha, VI, 111.

Survey: of land by Todarmal (1575), I, pt. i, 223; of Kaira (1820-1826 and 1863-1867), III, 98, 101, 108, 112; of Panch Mahals (1871-1874), *id.* 264; in Baroda, VII, 368-370, 381; of Kolába district, XI, 176, 181, 186, 189, 191, 192, 193; (1857-1866), *id.* 200-209; (1872), *id.* 210; results, *id.* 211; in Kánara district (second century), XV, pt. ii, 155; (1822), *id.* 162; (1848), *id.* 168; (1862-1882), *id.* 177-181, 224-225, 226 note 1, 228-231, 233-234, 235-237, 239-243, 244-246, 247; of the Násik district, in Sinnar (1771), XVI, 208 note 5; revenue survey introduced (1838-39), *id.* 211, 214; in plain or *desh* villages (1840-1841), *id.* 214, 216-230; in hill or *dáng* villages (1840-1860), *id.* 214-217, 230-245; in Peint, Málegaon, Báglán, Jáykheda, and Abhona (1865-1869), *id.* 245-257; revision survey in plain and hill villages (1871-1880), *id.* 257-291; survey results, *id.* 291-295; of the Ahmadnagar district (1825-1828), XVII, 450; (1838-1848), *id.* 471; hill survey (Akola) (1848), *id.* 483-486; plain survey (1848, 1853), *id.* 487, 528; survey results, *id.* 529-538; revision survey, *id.* 538, 547; Mr. Pringle's, of the Poona district, XVIII, pt. ii, 379-410; thirty years' revenue survey, *id.* 410-411, 412-415, 418-422, 426-432, 437-438, 442-464; revision survey, 470-475, 477-508; results, *id.* 508-510; of the Sátára district, Tásgáon, Khatáv, Máyni, Koregaon, Khánápur, Wái, Sátára, Jávli, Tásgaon, Karád, Helvák, Válva (1853-1863), XIX, 350-383; results, *id.* 383-384; 417-460; of the Sholápur district Mohol, Mádha, Sholápur, Bársi, Ropla, Karmala, Pandharpur, Náteputa, (1839-1858), XX, 304-334; revision (Mádha, Sholápur, Pandharpur, Bársi, Karmála, 1869-1874), *id.* 334-358; revised settlement reduced (1874), *id.* 358-360; results, *id.* 360-361; details, in Dhárwár district, XXII, 459-460, 486-527, 529-588; of the Bijápur district, Indi, XXIII, 460-464; Muddebihál, *id.* 464-465, 468-469; Hippargi, *id.* 465-467; Mangoli, *id.* 467-468; Bádámi, *id.* 469-471; Bágalkot, *id.* 471-473; Hungund, *id.* 473-476; Bijápur, *id.* 476-480; Chimalgi, *id.* 481; revision survey, Indi, Bijápur, Bágevádi, *id.* 484-491; Bágevádi, Muddebihál, *id.* 492-494; Muddebihál, *id.* 495-497; survey results, *id.* 497. All district volumes, *see* Land under District Name.

Survey: marine, between the Maldives and Madagascar (1772-1775), XXVI, pt. i, 374-375; of the West Coast (1788), XXVI, pt. ii, 12-13; of Bombay City: (1747), XXVI, pt. iii, 416-417; of Bombay islands (1772-1780), *id.* 420 and note 5, 421.

Surya: name of a Bhinmál gate, I, pt. i, 449.

Súrya: god, I, pt. ii, 340 note 2; I, pt. i, 461. *See* Planet (Sun).

Surya Puran: I, pt. i, 464, 465.

Suryáji: Marátha commander at the battle of Sinhgad (1670), XVIII, pt. ii, 235-236.

Suryavalokana: sun-gazing, the ninth Vedic rite, IX, pt. i, 31 note 3.

Súryavamsa: solar race, I, pt. ii, 569, 583; puranic genealogy of, *id.* 340 note 2.

Suryavanshi Lád: butcher. *See* Khatik.

Suryavanshi Váni: *see* Lád Váni.

Suryavrat: sun-vow, nature of, performances of, IX, pt. i, 394. *See* Sun.

Suryayantra: three-cornered sun copper-plate, worship of, IX, pt. i, 393. *See* Planet (Sun).

Sus: Skythian tribe, XIII, 411 note 2.

Susa: in Persia, resemblance of Kárli pillars to the capitals of, XIII, 413.

Sutaldev: a Gabri chief, IX, pt. ii, 188 note 2.

Sutar, Suthar: a caste of carpenters in Gujarát, six divisions of; distribution, origin of divisions; claim descent from Vishvakarma; trace of Rájpút origin in some divisions; social position, IX, pt. i, 202; two classes, town and village; town, tools, daily life, *id.* 203; house-building; Gajjárs or house-builders, *id.* 203; other works of; village remuneration and work; religious sects; goddesses, *id.* 205; customs, *id.* 205-220; in Cutch, V, 71-72; in Káthiáwár, VIII, 150; in Ratnágiri, X, 125, 141; in Sávantvádi, *id.* 415; in Koláha district, XI, 242 note 1, 413; in Khándesh district, XII, 72, 127; in Kánara district, XV, pt. i, 263; in Násik district, XVI, 51, 484; in Ahmadnagar district, XVII, 137-140, 234; in Sátára district, XIX, 96; in Sholápur district, XX, 139-140, 201; in Kolhápur, XXIV, 99.

Sutgatti: village in Belgaum district, has a travellers' bungalow, XXI, 609.

Sutherland: Mr., resident at Baroda (1837), VII, 265-266.

Suti: tenure in Thána, XIII, 531-532; meaning of, *id.* 532 note 1; same as *mirás*, *id.* 564 and note 3.

Sútradhárin: architect, constructed a temple at Degamve near Sampgaon, I, pt. ii, 569.

Sutrápáda: place of interest in Káthiáwár, a reservoir and temples at, VIII, 658-660.

Sutras: grammatical rules of Pánini, I, pt. ii, 138-140.

Suvál: coasting craft in Thána district, XIII, 720.

Suvarnagarudadhvaja: banner of the Devágiri Yádavas, I, pt. ii, 517; of the Siláháras, *id.* 538-544; of the Rattas, *id.* 552.

Suvarnakáras: Buddhist goldsmiths, I, pt. ii, 173.

Suvarnamukha: benefactions founded at, by Ushavadáta, I, pt. ii, 148.

Suvarnavarsha: another name of Karka I, I, pt. i, 124.

Suvarnavarsha: *biruda* of Govind IV, the Ráshtrakúta king, I, pt. ii, 205, 416, 417 note 1.

Suvarnavarsha Karkarája: Gujarát Ráshtrakúta king, I, pt. ii, 383; his Baroda grant, *id.* 387, 399, 400.

Suvarna-Vrishabha-Dhvaja: banner of the Kalachuryas, I, pt. ii, 469.

Suvarndurg: in Ratnágiri district, haunt of pirates, I, pt. ii, 1, 2; fort built by Shiváji, *id.* 39, 68; description of the fort, *id.* 75; district taken by the Sidis, *id.* 79; Angria's depôt at, *id.* 79; its capture by the English (1755), *id.* 91; taken by the English for the

Peshwa, *id.* 111; costoms division, X, 183; fort, history, *id.* 338-340; XI, 146.
Snviśakha: Palhava, son of Kalaipa and minister of Rudradáman, settles in Káthiáwár (150), I, pt. ii, 317.
Suvrittinátha: installation of, in Sakunika Vihára, I, pt. i, 186.
Suwáli: an old seaport in Surat, II, 332.
Svabhra: name of country, I, pt. i, 10 note 1, 36 and note 3.
Svabhravati: *see* Sábarmati.
Svámi: a class of pontiffs, in Dhárwár district, XXII, 52-55; at Daungur near Bangalore, I, pt. ii, 437 note 6.
Svámidatta: king of Kottura, mentioned in an Allahábád pillar inscription, I, pt. ii, 280.
Svámikarája: Ráshtrakúta king mentioned in a Mullai grant, I, pt. ii, 386.
Svámi Mahásena: favourite god of the Kadambas and the Chalukyas, I, pt. ii, 287 and note 1, 290 and note 3, 338. *See* Kártikeya.
Svamin: title attached to Brahman writers on sacrifical rites, I, pt. ii, 191.
Svamin: probably Kartikeya the god of war, I, pt. ii, 338.
Svami Náráyan: a religious sect in Gujarát, IX, pt. i, 536-539; its theory of religion, XIV, 130 note 7; fights with Vaishnav *Vairágis*, *id.* 135 note 10; temples of, in Kaira, III, 180.
Svamirája: Chalukya king in the Konkan, slain by Mangaleśa, I, pt. ii, 347.
Svámitva: farmer's share system, XIII, 530.
Svaráj, Svarájya: personal sovereignty, grant of, by the Mughals to Sháhu of a greater portion of the old Bijápur dominions (1719), I, pt. ii, 655; imperial grant for home-rule, XIX, 262, 265; XVIII, pt. ii, 243 and note 1.
Svargárohana: heaven-climbing, a Vedic rite, IX, pt. i, 31. *See* Death.
Svargárohanaprásáda: shrine on Satrunjaya in honour of Vastupála, I, pt. i, 202.
Svayambhuva Manu: mind-born, son of Bráhman, I, pt. ii, 278 note 1, 339.
Svayamvara: bridegroom-choosing of Durlabhadevi, I, pt. i, 162-163; of Chandralekha, I, pt. ii, 218, 546.
Śvetopata: Jain sect, I, pt. ii, 288.
Swallows: in Ratnágiri district, X, 61; at Mátherán, XIV, 257; in Khándesh district, XII, 34.
Swanston: Captain, captures Trimbakji Denglia (1818), XVI, 198; his description of the Achla fort, *id.* 414.
Swat: valley to the north of Panjáb, I, pt. i, 468.
Swedes: visited Surat thrice between the years 1746-1765 and maintained a factory there for a time, II, 149.
Sweet Potatoes: growing of, in Poona district, XVIII, pt. ii, 57.
Swiftlet: Netráni Edible-nest, frequents Kánara district, XV, pt. ii, 336.
Swifts: class of birds, in Ratnágiri district, X, 62.
Swiss Recruits: in Bombay island (1752), XXVI, pt. iii, 116; clothing expenses of (1755), *id.* 122.
Sword-marriage: among Rájputs, IX, pt. i, 145.
Syádváda: Jain doctrine, I, pt. ii, 200, 406.
Syagrus: Rás Fartak in Arabia, I, pt. i, 536.
Sydros: town mentioned by Ptolemy, I, pt. i, 538.
Syed: a Musalmán sub-division in Cutch, V, 88-89; in Rewa Kántha, VI, 35; in Thána, XIII, 230; in Sholápur district, XX, 198; in Násik district, XVI, 75-76; in Ahmadnagar, XVII, 226; in Poona district, XVIII, pt. i, 490-491; in Dhárwár district, XXII, 230-231; in Bijápur district, XXIII, 287; in Kolhápur, XXIV, 148; in Belgaum district, XXI, 203-204; children of, brought up as Christians under the Portuguese, I., pt. ii, 60.
Syed Hussain Ali: Mughal governor (1715) of the Dakhan, XIX, 260, 261.
Syenite: rock in Ratnágiri district, X, 394; in Bijápur district, XXIII, 19; slabs, *id.* 54.
Syer: Sir William, Bart., appointed first Recorder (1798) in Bombay island, XXVI, pt. iii, 45; death of (1802), *id.* 50.
Sykes: Colonel, remarks on Chálukyas, toleration, I, pt. ii, 12; his mention of the authority of Bráhmans at the king's court, IX, pt. i, 434 note 2, 436 note 4.
Sylveira: Heitor de, Portuguese admiral, his stay in Bombay, burns Bassein (1530), XIII, 450.
Sylviadæ: family of birds in Ratnágiri district, X, 76.
Symbols: carved in Padan hill in Thána district, XIV, 389-391, 102.
Symplocos: *paniculata*, *racemosa*, dye-yielding plants, XXV, 247; *spicata*, sacred plant, *id.* 286.
Symulla: Chaul, XIII, 410 and note 6, 414, 415; XIV, 52.
Synagogue: in Poona, XVIII, pt. iii, 398-399, constitution of, *id.* pt. i, 535-536.
Syphilis: spread of, in Khándesh district, XII, 337.
Syphilitic Eruptions: *See* Visphotak.
Syrastrene: country mentioned by the author of the *Periplus*, which is possibly Suráshtra, I, pt. i, 544.
Syria: country, "Introduction to the Early History of the Dakhan," I, pt. ii, p. ii.

T

TAAWI'Z: amulet, use of, IX, pt. ii, 133.
Taáziahs: miniature shrines of the martyrs of Karbala, IX, pt. ii, 128; vows paid to, during Muharram, *id.* 128, 129-130; show of, in Gujarát during Muharram, *id.* 138-139; first making of (1400), *id.* 139 note 1.
Tabakát-i-Násiri: historical work, IX, pt. ii, 38, 65; mention of Bhima II in, I, pt. i, 196.
Tában: king of Táfak (Panjáb ?), mentioned by Al Idrisi, I, pt. i, 527.
Tabari: Arab writer (838-932), Porbandar (Baroda) conquered (776) by the Arabs according to I, pt. i, 524; includes Basra in India, IX, pt. ii, 183 note 4.

Tabarruk: morsel of sacred food, IX, pt. ii, 140.
Tabáshir: bambu pith, exported from Thána (810) to foreign countries, XIII, 430 and note 15; (1300-1500), *id.* 15; *see* also XIV, 356 and note 1.
Tabssô, Tabasoi: probably Pandharpur, I, pt. i, 541.
Tabassi: Ptolemy's (150 A.D.), probably Buddhist ascetics of Ajanta, XII, 38 note 4, 239 note 6.
Tabi: the Tápti, I, pt. i, 510.
Tábuts: or *Tájiás*, models of the tombs of Hassan and Hussain at Karbala; held sacred by some Hindus; offerings made to, IX, pt. i, 137, 362; offerings of vows and presents to, by Pársis, IX, pt. ii, 220.
Taccaceæ: species of food-plants, XXV, 178.
Tacca pinatipida: food-plant, XXV, 178.
Tacla: *cassia tora*, food-plants, XXV, 198, 243.
Tad: *borassus flabelliformis*, food and fibrous plant, XXV, 180, 237; in Poona district, XVIII, pt. i, 53.
Tadi: palm-juice, IX, pt. ii, 207, 209.
Tadigaipádi: province not yet identified, I, pt. ii, 341 note 2.
Tadi-Málingi: records at, I, pt. ii, 308.
Tadorninæ: family of birds in Ratnágiri, X, 97.
Tadri: river in Kánara district, XV, pt. i, 3, 5, 6.
Tadri: town and port in Kánara district, XV, pt. ii, 351-352; its trade, *id.* 65, 66, 67; visited by Fryer (1676), *id.* 129.
Tadvi: a caste of Musalmán Bhils in Khándesh district, XII, 104, 128; plunder the district, *id.* 259-260.
Táfak: the Panjáb, I, pt. i, 526, women of, *id.* 527.
Tafán: apparently the Panjáb, I, pt. i, 527.
Tag: *crotolaria juncea*, a fibrous plant, XXV, 231, 290; cultivation of, in Ratnágiri district, X, 149.
Tág: pass in Násik district, XVI, 130.
Tagadur: copper-plate grant at, I, pt. ii, 301 note 1.
Tagar, Tagara: city mentioned by Ptolemy in the second century, I, pt. ii, 538 note 8; original seat of the Siláharas, *id.* 16, 253, 536, 546; Dakhan metropolis (B. C. 200-A. D. 612), XIII, 409; a great commercial mart, *id.* 412, 415, 416, 419; XII, 240; XVI, 136; XVII, 351; I, pt. ii, 174, 619; various identifications: Dr. Bhagvanlal identifies it with Junnar in Poona district; Wilford with Devagiri or Daulatabad; Dr. Burgess with Roza near Devagiri; Yule with Kulburga; Fleet with Kolhápur; Grant Duff with a town north of Bhir; Dr. Bhandarkar suggests its identification with Darur or Dharur in Nizám's dominions, XIII, 419, 423 and note 4, 424; XII, 238; XVI, 181 note 2; I, pt. i, 540-541; 545; I, pt. ii, 3, 16, note 4, 17, 174, 538 note 8, XVIII, pt. ii, 211, note 2.
Tagarapura: *see* Tagara.
Tagarapuraparameśvara: hereditary title of the Siláharas, I, pt. ii, 538.
Ta-Gaz-Gaz: tribe of Turkish rulers of Kushan (10th century), IX, pt i, 470, note 2.
Tagetes patula: gul-jafri, dye-plant, XXV, 247.
Tághi: rebellious Gujarát noble, I, pt. i, 513, 518.
Tahajjud: midnight prayer of Musalmáns, IX, pt. ii, 126 note 3.
Táhákari: village in Ahmadnagar district, temple at, XVII, 740.
Tai: caste of Musalmán weavers in Gujarát, take their name from Tai, are of mixed origin, partly foreign Musalmáns, partly Hindu converts, said to have been taught the art by prophet Idris, Balsár Tais claim Arab descent, IX, pt. ii, 80; in Káthiáwár, VIII, 163; in Thána district, XIII, 225, 242-243.
Tái Bái: wife of the chief of Nipáni, passes off a widow's child as her own, I, pt. ii, 670.
Taila I: Kadamba prince Tailapa I.
Taila I: Western Chálukya prince of Kalyáni, I, pt. ii, 378, 379.
Taila II: A'havamalla Núrmadi, Western Chálukya king (973-997), I, pt. ii, 379; his *biruda* and titles, records of his time, *id.* 428-434; marries the Ratta princess Jákaladevi, *id.* 425; overthrows the Ráshtrakúta Kakka II (973), *id.* 18, 207-208; 306, 385, 424, 426, 542 note 4; acquires the whole Ráshtrakúta kingdom, *id.* 431; restores the Chalukya power, *id.* 190, 211, 336 and note 2, 342, 427; his enemy Muñj killed by the Yádav Bhillama, *id.* 433, 552, 553, 233, 576; his general Barapa defeated and slain by Mulráj of Gujarát, XIII, 435; I, pt. i, 158, 159; his expeditions, I, pt. ii, 212-213; slain by Bhoja, *id.* 214; *see* also I, pt. i, 120, 131, 519; X, 193 note 1; XII, 241; XIII, 425.
Talia III: brother and successor of the Western Chálukya king Jagadekamalla II, I, pt. ii, 457 and note 3; his *biruda* and records of his reign, *id.* 459 and notes 3 and 4; his feudatories and officials, *id.* 460, 472, 473, 474, 484, 494, 501, 564, 575; his capitals and the date of his death, *id.* 461, 484, 494, 501, 564, 575.
Tailaha: *see* Tailama.
Tailakhali: Sálva tribe, I, pt. i, 534.
Tailama: Hángal Kádamba feudatory of the Western Chálukya king Jagadekamalla II, I, pt. ii, 458, 559, 562.
Tailang: a sub-caste of Dravid Bráhmans: *see* Telang.
Tailanga, Tailangana: country, king of, defeated by the Yádava king Mahádeva, I, pt. ii, 246, 528; king of, defeated by Jaitrapá'a, *id.* 239, 522; Sivaśri's coin found in, I, pt. ii, 166; later Satavábanas in, their dates, *id.* 168, 246.
Taliang Nhavi: a caste of barbers in Poona district, XVIII, pt. i, 381-383.
Tailapa: *see* Taila II.
Toilapa I: Hángal Kádamba, I, pt. ii, 559, 561.
Tailapa II: Hángal Kádamba, feudatory of the Western Chálukyas Vikramáditya VI and Someśvara III, I, pt. ii, 456, 559, 561, 562.

Tailapa II, Tailapadeva : *see* Taila III.
Tain : village in Baroda, tank at, VII, 20, 554.
Tai Telin : mistress of Parashurám Shrinivás Pratinidhi, rescues her master (1807), XIX, 299-300 ; Jangli Jaygad under (1810), *id.* 469.
Táj Bávdi : Bijápur well, XXIII, 637.
Tájiás : *see* Tábuts.
Tájika : branch of astrology, I, pt. ii, 188.
Tájikas : Arabs, their expedition in Gujarát (778), I, pt. i, 149 ; army of, vanquished by Pulakeśi, I, pt. ii, 187, 310, 316, 375.
Tajkhan Sálár : mosque of, at Ahmadábád, IX, pt. ii, 62.
Tájpur, Tájpuri : state in Mahi Kántha, V, 427 ; captured by mutineers (1858), I, pt. i, 438.
Tájul Maásir : historical work, I, pt. i, 512, 519 and note 4.
Táj-ul-Mulk : Gujarát governor (1320), I, pt. i, 230.
Taka : *see* Toka.
Takárá : a caste of Musalmán stone masons in Khándesh, XII, 127 ; in Ahmadnagar district, XVII, 187, 234 ; in Poona district, XVIII, pt. i, 503.
Tákári : village in Sátára district, cave, temple and fair at, XIX, 589.
Takarib Khán : Mughal officer, captures Sambháji, I, pt. ii, 596 ; XVIII, pt. ii, 238, 239 note 1 ; XXIV, 226.
Takbandi : tenure in Kolába district, XI, 170. *See* also under Toka.
Takbir : call to prayer, IX, pt. ii, 154, 155.
Takhatábái : Anandráv Gáikwár's wife ; her plans to seize the *diván* and resident, VII, 211 ; assists Kánhoji (1812), *id.* 217-218 ; Sitárám's relations with, *id.* 220 ; Fatesing quarrels with, *id.* 224 ; her hope about the succession of her son to the *gádi*, *id.* 230 ; her quarrel with Sayájiráv II, *id.* 233 ; *see* also I, pt. i, 426.
Taki Abu Jaáiár : ninth Shiah *imám*, IX, pt. ii, 125 note 2.
Takio : tomb of Musalman saint, called *pir*, or *sái*, IX, pt. i, 360 ; famous tombs of Báva Ghor, of Dariyasha, history of their origin ; occasions to ask for intercession and help of these and other saints ; general and special offerings made to the tombs ; days and ways for making offerings, *id.* 361 ; persons by whom visited, *id.* 360.
Takiyyah : Shiáh doctrine of concealment, literally fear or caution, IX, pt. ii, 126 note 2.
Takkadeśa : tract of country (Panjáb), I, pt. i, 3, 468 ; called after the tribe of Takshaks, IX, pt. ii, 70.
Takkas : Tanks, said to be of the same race as Agnikulas, IX, pt. i, 497 and note 1.
Takki : *see* Afzulpur.
Takkola : Ráshtrakúta Krishna III kills the Chola Rájáditya at, I, pt. ii, 419.
Takla : medicinal and sacred plant, XXV, 254, 291, 292.
Tákli : village in Ahmadnagar district, temple at, XVII, 740.
Tákli : village in Sholápur district, XX, 503.
Tákli Budruk : village in Khándesh, temple at, XII, 472.
Takmak : hill in Thána district, XIII, 6 ; fort, XIV, 98, 219, 342-343.
Táks : Rájpút rulers (800-1200) of Asirgad, XII, 241 and note 7 ; driven by Chohánš, *id.* 242.
Takshaka : hooded serpent, I, pt. ii, 577.
Takshaks : tribe in the Panjáb represented by the Tanks, IX, pt. ii, 70.
Tákve Budrukh : market, village, in Poona district, temple and fair at, XVIII, pt. iii, 449.
Tal : hill pass in Thána district, XIII, 320 ; opened for wheeled traffic (1830), I, pt. ii, 129.
Tala : *see* Talagad.
Tála : manuscript of Amarakośa written on the leaves of, is preserved in the Dakhan College Library, I, pt. ii, 248.
Talabda : a Koli sub-division, I, pt. i, 115 ; *see* Koli.
Talagad : fort in Kolába district, its description, history, XI, 391-395 ; captured by Shiváji (1646), *id.* 144 ; captured by the Peshwa (1735), I, pt. ii, 83 ; XI, 445 ; taken by the British, *id.* 156.
Tálah : capital of the Konkan mentioned by Alberuni, I, pt. ii, 4.
Talaja : fort of, in Cambay, VI, 228-229.
Talaja : hill in Káthiáwár, VIII, 12 ; fort, *id.* 241 ; town, *id.* 660-662 ; port burned by the Portuguese (1532), I, pt. i, 347.
Talakád : place in Mysore, inscription at, I, pt. ii, 302 and note 1, 439, 492 ; taken by the Hoysala Vishnuvardhana, *id.* 495, 496, 498, 499, 501, 505.
Talakádu-Gonda ; Hoysala Vishnuvardhana's *biruda* (title), I, pt. ii, 494.
Talakhba : a Mhár idol, X, 418.
Talan : special dish among Hijdás, IX, pt. ii, 21.
Talan Tezi : *see* Tera.
Tálapadeva : Chálukya king, I, pt. ii, 587.
Tálapurumshaka : village granted by Krishna III, I, pt. ii, 420.
Talátis : village accountants appointed in 1814 in Kaira, III, 94 ; in Baroda state, VII, 75, 367 ; in Thána district (1882), XIII, 529 ; (1820), 566 and note 5, 569, 573, 575.
Talavanapura : *see* Talakád.
Talavda : river in Sávantvádi state, X, 389.
Talávia : a wild tribe of Surat, their immigration in Panch Mahála (1876), III, 227.
Talavna : pond in Sávantvádi state, X, 389.
Talbi : lake near Bhinmál, I, pt. i, 453.
Tale : mineral in Panch Maháls, III, 197 ; in Mahi Kántha, V, 360 ; in Ratnágiri district, X, 30 ; in Sávantvádi, *id.* 401 ; in Kánara district, XV, pt. i, 10.
Talegaon : a market town in Kolába district, remains, temples and ponds at, XI, 390-391.
Talegaon Dábháde : town in Poona district, reservoir and temples at, XVIII, pt. iii, 449-450 ; death (1590) of Salábat Khán of Ahmadnagar at, XVIII, pt. ii, 222 ; destroyed by the Mughals (1751), *id.* 246 ; action near (1779), *id.* 264-265 ; I, pt. ii, 605.

Talegaon Dhamdhere: town in Poona district, temples at, XVIII, pt. iii, 451; Nizám's troops routed by the Maráthás at (1751), I, pt, ii, 627.
Talekkád: Western Ganga capital, I, pt. ii, 299.
Tale Sap: lake in Cambodia, I, pt. i, 499, 504.
Talghát: Ferishta's name for the Konkan, "Introduction to the History of the Konkan," I, pt. ii, p. ix.
Talghát; *see* Tal.
Tálgund: town in Mysore, inscription at, XV, pt. ii, 84; I, pt. ii, 287 and note 1, 291, 322, 430, 435 and note 10; record at, *id.* 473, 561.
Talhari Kunbi: caste of husbandmen in Thána district, XIII, 124-128.
Tálikot: town in Bijápur district, mosques and temple at, XXIII, 678 679; limestones at, *id.* 37-38, 58; battle of (1565) between Rám Ráj of Vijayanagar and the Musalmán confederation of Ahmadnagar, Bijápur, Bidar and Golkonda; complete defeat and death of Rám Ráj, I, pt. ii, 645; XXIII, 417, 646; XV, pt. ii, 116 and note 4; XVII, 370; XXI, 371; XXII, 408.
Talismans: use of, to secure speedy delivery, IX, pt. ii, 155.
Talkhat: hill pass in Kolhápur state, XXIV, 6.
Tal-konkan: low lands, "Introduction to the History of the Konkan," I, pt. ii, p. ix.
Taloda: sub-division of Khándesh district, its boundaries, area, aspect, climate, water, soil, holdings, survey details, survey results, stock, crops and people, XII, 2, 417-421. *Town*, *id.* 472.
Taloja: old sub-division (1840) in Thána district, XIII, 528, 602 note 1; survey assessment in (1859), *id.* 602-604; divided between Kalyán and Panvel (1861), 528.
Taloja: sub-caste of Bráhmans in Thána district, XIII, 78.
Talpat: state lands in Gujarát, acquired from small *zamindárs* by Ahmadsháh (1411-1443), I, pt. i, 215; in Baroda state, VII, 344-346, 348.
Talsána: *táluka* in Káthiáwár, VIII, 662.
Tálukdárs: land proprietors in Panch Mahála, III, 262; in Káthiáwár, VIII, 318; Rájpút, IX, pt. i, 123.
Talupáka: old province, I, pt. ii, 334.
Talvádi: a class of palm-tappers in Thána district, XIII, 643.
Talvár: *see* Bed.
Talvárkop: deserted village in Belgaum district, temple and a holy pool at, XXI, 609.
Tamáchi: son of Raisingji, restored to Navánagar (1673), I, pt. i, 285.
Tamáchi: name borne by *jams*, I, pt. i, 139.
Tamághua: words with special magical powers, IX, pt. ii, 143.
Tamal: *xanthochymus*, dye-plant, XXV, 241.
Tamar: probably Devgad, X, 333.
Tamara: *dactylifera*, food-plant, XXV, 181.
Támaramuge: village granted by Kirtivarman II, I, pt. ii, 377.
Tamarind, Tamarindus Indica: fruit-tree, used in famine and in medicine, XXV, 198, 225; in Khándesh, XII, 27; in Poona district, XVIII, pt. i, 45.
Tamariscineæ: species of dye-plants, XXV, 240.
Tamarix: *articulata, dioca, gallica, Indica*, dye-yielding plants, XXV, 240, 241.
Támasvádi: village in Khándesh district, temple at, XII, 473.
Támbánagri: local name of Cambay, I, pt. i, 208 note 3.
Tambapanni: modern Ceylon, province outlying Asoka's dominion, I, pt. ii, 146.
Támbat: caste of coppersmiths in Kolába district, XI, 66; in Khándesh, XII, 127, 224; in Thána district, XIII, 140-141; in Násik district, XVI, 26, 52, 80, 145; in Ahmadnagar district, XVII, 139-140; in Poona district, XVIII, pt. i, 374-376; in Sátára district, XIX, 146-147; in Sholápur district, XX, 140-142; in Kolhápur, XXIV, 99. *See* also Kásár.
Támbdi Jogeshvari: Poona temple, XVIII, pt. iii, 346.
Tambi: village in Sátára district, XIX, 589.
Tamboli: caste of betel-leaf sellers, in Ratnágiri district, X, 128; in Khándesh district, XII, 62; in Thána district, XIII, 112; in Násik district, XVI, 59; in Ahmadnagar district, XVII, 235; in Poona district, Hindu, XVIII, pt. i, 273; Musalmán, *id.* 499; in Sátára district, XIX, 61-63; in Sholápur district, XX, 142, 210-211; in Belgaum district, XXI, 214, 215; in Dhárwár district, XXII, 126, 240-241; in Kolhápur state, XXIV, 88.
Támbra Barani: apparently the Tápti, I, pt. i, 510.
Támbrapuri: village in Belgaum, I, pt. ii, 527.
Tambut: fodder-plant, XXV, 276.
Tameri: hill pass in Belgaum district, XXI, 306.
Támhal: Anhilváda, I, pt. i, 516.
Tamhána, Tamhini: pass in Kolába district, XI, 6, 115; in Poona, XVIII, pt. i, 4.
Tamil: non-Aryan language, I, pt. ii, 137; people, XIII, 415; ousted by Gangarája, I, pt. ii, 499; chronicle, *id.* 300.
Tamkane: village in Sátára district, caves at, XIX, 589.
Tamluk: port on the Hugli, migrations of the Yavans from, in the first century, I, pt. i, 499, 533.
Támraliptakas: a tribe from Tamluk on the Lower Ganges, I, pt. i, 533.
Támraparni: river and valley in Belgaum district, XXI, 7, 11.
Tamruj: *Elædendron Roxburghii*, a poisonous plant, XXV, 264; used as antidote to snake-bite, *id.* 274.
Tána: modern Thána, expedition against, by Usmán, I, pt. i, 505, 508, 509, 523, I, pt. ii, 4.
Tána: town in Káthiáwár, battle at (1794), VIII, 662.
Tánah: *see* Tána.
Tánáji Málusra: Shiváji's friend, present at the meeting of Shiváji with Afzul Khán, I, pt. ii, 592; storms the fort of Sinhgad, his death, *id.* 594; XVIII, pt. ii, 235-236; *see* also *id.* 230; XIX, 236.

Tandassir: famine plant found in Gujarát and Sholápur, XXV, 195.
Tándav: Shiva's dance, representation of, in Elephanta caves, XIV, 75; at Jogeshvari and Mandapeshvar caves, *id.* 111-112, 224, 285.
Tándel: boat-captain, XIII, 716.
Tandul: famine plant, XXV, 186.
Tandulja: the Nizám defeated in the battle (1763) of, VII, 186. *See* Rakishon.
Tándulvádi: fort in Thána district, XIV, 11, note 3, 98, 343.
Tangdi: village in Belgaum district, XXI, 609.
Tanjápuri: modern Tanjore, besieged by Bútuga, I, pt. ii, 419 note 7.
Tanjore: town in Madras, taken by the Rashtrakúta Krishna III, I, pt. ii, 419; grant at, *id.* 301 note 1.
Tanká: coin, worth $\frac{1}{100}$ of a rupee, I, pt. i, 222 note 2.
Tánka: country, part of the modern Broach district, I, pt. i, 467 and note 7; its king subdued by Dantidurga, I, pt. ii, 195, 389.
Tankara: town in Káthiáwár, agates found near, VIII, 662-663.
Tankari: a port in Broach district, II, 569.
Tankha: land-rent as fixed by Todar Mal in Dakhan, XVIII, pt. ii, 318 note 2, 325.
Tánks: Hindu converts, land-holders, said to represent the tribe of Takshaks, the family of the *sultáns* of Gujarát belonged to, IX, pt. ii, 70.
Tanna: modern Thána, kingdom of, I, pt. ii, 5.
Tanners: in Thána district, XIV, 20.
Tanning: in Cutch, V, 128; in Khándesh district, XII, 236.
Tánsa: river in Thána district, XIII, 9.
Tantalidæ: family of birds in Ratnágiri, X, 96.
Tánthikontha: village on the Krishna, grant of, I, pt. ii, 334.
Tantia Topi: *see* Tatia Topi.
Tantrik: proficient in *tantras* (charms), branch of learning, I, pt. i, 161.
Tanvána: a village near Bhuj in Cutch, a fair and a pond at, V, 251.
Tape-weaving: in Thána district, XIII, 401; in Poona district, XVIII, pt. ii, 207-208; in Násik district, XVI, 170; in Belgaum district, XXI, 344.
Tápi: river Tápti, not included in Dakhan in the *Vayupurána*, I, pt. ii, 133, 134.
Tapioca: poisonous plant, XXV, 270.
Tapodhan: sub-caste of Bráhmans in Gujarát IX, pt. i, 3, 20; in Thána district, XIII, 86.
Tappas: groups of villages in Kaira district, III, 81.
Taprobane: Ceylon, I, pt. i, 543.
Tápti: river in Khándesh and Gujarát, XII, 6; VII, 576-580, 582-583; its course, tidal sections, bed, tributaries, islands, ferries, navigation, irrigation and floods (1727-1876), II, 6-24; *see* also I, pt. i, 514, 523; I, pt. ii, 282 note 5, 310, 353 note 2, 359, 525.
Tar: food-plant, XXV, 207; yields toddy, *id.* 212; a fibrous plant, *id.* 237. *See* Tad.
Tárábái: Rájárám's widow, regent of the Marátha kingdom, I, pt. ii, 597; retakes Panhála (1710) and makes Kolhápur her residence and the capital of the younger branch of the family of Shiváji, *id.* 81, 598; her intrigues; Dámáji Gáikwár joins her (1751), *id.* 601; VII, 178; her rebellion (1754), I, pt. ii, 602; her death (1761), *id.* 603; *another account of*: widow of Rájárám (1689-1700), puts her son Shiváji on the Kolhápur throne and assumes administration; confines her husband's second widow Rájabái with her son Sambhájі; takes her abode in Panhála; disowns Sháhu's claims to the Marátha territories; collects forces to meet Sháhu but being defeated flees into the Konkan; retakes Panhála; is confined for a time after her son's death (1712); again taken prisoner, XXIV, 226-227, 228; *see* also XVIII, pt. ii, 239-241, 245, 247.
Tárabái: daughter of Khanderáo Gáikwár, married to the *rája* of Sávantvádi (1880), VII, 279, 285.
Tárádevi: wife of Jogamarasa, I, pt. ii, 406 note 5, 448.
Tarafs: ancient Musalmán word for a territorial division, I, pt. ii, 42.
Táragadh: hill citadel of Ajmir, IX, pt. ii, 6, note 1 (7).
Tarakágáhara: village granted by a Chálukya queen, I, pt. ii, 365.
Tárakeśvara: temple of, at Hángal, inscription at, I, pt. ii, 505 note 3, 563 note 3.
Taram: literally a class or variety, a form of tenure in Dhárwár district, XXII, 478 and note 3, 479.
Táránád: district ruled over by the Hoysálas, I, pt. ii, 505.
Táránáth: author of the history of Buddhism, I, pt. ii, 171.
Tarappa: boat used in Thána district, XIII, 720.
Tárápur: town and port in Thána district, its trade and history, XIV, 343-345; customs division, its trade, XIII, 358; seized by Bhimrája I, pt. ii, 27; destroyed by the Portuguese (1531), I, pt. i, 347; XIII, 451; Portuguese fort at (1533), *id.* 456; I, pt. ii, 66; place of trade (1500-1670), XIII, 465; attacked by the Abyssinians (1559), I, pt. ii, 48; Dominican and Franciscan monasteries at (1695), XIII, 483; Hamilton's mention of, *id.* 485; Portuguese defences at (1727), *id.* 491; taken by the Maráthás (1739), *id.* 493; plundered by Kolis (1817), *id.* 522.
Tárápur: town near Cambay, Raghunáthráo goes (1753) to, I, pt. i, 337.
Taras: town in Dhárwár district, XXII, 787; survey and revision survey of, *id.* 510-512; 551-555.
Tarav: river in Rewa Kántha, VI, 92.
Taráwih: night prayers during Ramazán, IX, pt. ii, 126.
Tarbiyatkhán: Mughal commander, mines Sátára fort (1700), XIX, 251.
Tarbuj: *cucumis melo*, oil-yielding plant, XXV, 218.
Tardavádi: territorial division, I, pt. ii, 298 notes 2 and 3; governed by officers of the Western Chálukyas of Kalyáni, *id.* 367, 431, 440, 443, 456, 458, 460, 470; governed by Kalachurya officers, *id.* 473, 485; by an officer of the Devagiri Yádavas, *id.* 521.

Targála : caste of players, in Mahi Kántha, V, 365 ; *see* Bhavaya.
Targaon : village in Sátára district, XIX, 590 ; survey of, *id.* 372-375.
Targol : sub-division of Rewa Kántha, VI, 112.
Targollah : the fruit of *tar* tree, XXV, 207, 212.
Tárikh-i-Alái : historical work of Amir Khusrao, I, pt. i, 515 note 6 ; IX, pt. ii, 65.
Tárikh-i-Firuzsháhi : work of Zia-ud-din Barni, I, pt. i, 514, 515, 517.
Tárikh-i-Kámil : work of Ibni Asir, I, pt. i, 522 note 4.
Tarikh-i-Maásumi : historical work, IX, pt. ii, 50 note 3 ; written in 1600 A. D., I, pt. i, 517 and notes 7, 8 and 10.
Tárikh-i-Mubárakshábi : notices Asáwal (1403-1504), I, pt. i, 513.
Tárikh-i-Sorath : mention of the Káthis in, IX, pt. i, 259, 414.
Tárikh-i-Tabari : historical work, IX, pt. ii, 14 note 3.
Tárikh-i-Táhiri : written in A. D. 1521, I, pt. i, 139, 517 note 12, 518.
Taringa : village in Mahi Kántha, Jain temples at, V, 442.
Tarizakát : customs duty levied by the Mughals, I, pt. i, 213 note 1.
Tárla : village in Sátára district, temple at, XIX, 590.
Tarli : river in Sátára district, XIX, 14-15.
Tar-mar : *Borossus flabelliformis*, famine plant, XXV, 207.
Tartariyeh-Dirham : Indo-Sassanian silver coin used in Western India (500-1100), I, pt. i, 469 and note 2, 519 and note 8.
Tarwar : *Cassia auriculata*, a famine plant, XXV, 198, 243.
Tasar : average commutation rate of rentals of the farmed villages in Kolába district, XI, 183, 197, 206 and note 1.
Tasar Farokht : commutation sale system in Kolába district, XI, 172 note 2.
Tasar Silk : experiments of, in Poona district, XVIII, pt. ii, 67-76.
Táschi : a caste of Musalmán kettle-drummers in Belgaum district, XXI, 226 ; in Dhárwár district, XXII, 249 ; in Bijápur district, XXIII, 305; in Gujarát, guild of, IX, pt. ii, 84.
Tásgaon : sub-division of Sátára district, its boundaries, area, aspect, climate, water, soil, stock, holdings, crops and people, XIX, 440-442 ; survey of, *id.* 351-356. *Town,* temples and history of, *id.* 590-593 ; trade centre, *id.* 216 ; assigned to Shábu (1730) by the treaty with Kolhápur, I, pt. ii, 656 ; attacked and pillaged (1798) by the *rája* of Kolhápur, XIX, 299 ; XXI, 389 ; lapse of, to the British (1848), *id.* 409.
Tasobai : ridge in Poona district, XVIII, pt. i, 5.
Tasu : a division of the land measuring rod, XIII, 558 note 4.
Tásu : river in Thána district, XIV, 122, 364.
Tátárkhán : *sultán* of Gujarát, confines his father at Asáwal (1403), I, pt. i, 513.
Tathágata : name for Buddha, meaning of the term, XII, 481 note 1.
Tathaváde : hill fort in Sátára district, description, temples and history of, XIX, 11, 593-597 ; taken by Shiváji (1665), *id.* 238 ; taken by the Mughals (1689), *id.* 249.
Ta-Thsin : Chinese for Dakshina, I, pt. ii, 133.
Tátia Topi : rebel, enters (1858) the Panch Maháls, III, 253 ; I, pt. i, 441 ; corresponds with the chiefs of Jamkhandi and Nargund ; is defeated at Chhota Udepur, *id.* 445 ; approach of, in Khándesh, XII, 262 ; *see* also VII, 274.
Tattihalla : stream, in Kánara district, XV, pt. i, 5 ; bridge on, XV, pt. ii, 43.
Tattooing : rational explanation of the origin of the practice, XVIII, pt. i, 552.
Tátya Makaji : Koli dacoit (1879), in Poona district, XVIII, pt. i, 38.
Táv : fever, its cause and cure in Gujarát, IX, pt. i, 365.
Tavadrum : *Erythroxylon monogynum*, a famine plant, XXV, 195.
Távandi : village in Belgaum district, Jain temple and fair at, XXI, 609.
Távareyaghatta : mountain pass of Távare, I, pt. ii, 433.
Tavernier : English traveller (1641-1660), Cambay harbour silted up in the time of, VI, 220 ; notices the skill of Surat and Cambay Vanias in trade, IX, pt. i, 78 note 1 ; his notice of Burhanpur, XII, 250 note 4, 589 ; of Chopda, *id.* 438 ; of Dháyata, *id.* 441 ; of Bijápur kingdom, XXIII, 427-428 ; Virgin Mary worshipped as Sita by the natives of Bassein at the time of, XIV, 32 note 2.
Taverns : licensed, opened in Bombay island, authorized rates at (1770), XXVI, pt. iii, 490-493.
Távi : village and petty state in Káthiáwár, VIII, 663.
Tavlái : village in Khándesh district, stepwell at, XII, 473.
Tavra : place of pilgrimage on the Narbada, IX, pt. i, 549 ; festival, period of its occurrence ; stones representing Shiv brought from the banks of the Narbada during ; beliefs about, *id.* 362, 549.
Tawakkul : resignation, IX, pt. ii, 7, 8.
Tax : in Gujarát under the Mughals, on tobacco, I, pt. ii, 53 ; on houses and shops, *id.* 99, 100 ; on grazing, wood-cutting, trades, and fishing, *id.* 123 ; thirty-six taxes levied in the Northern Konkan, *id.* 125 ; conservancy, levied in Bombay (1757), XXVI, pt. i, 320 ; XXVI, pt. ii, 454 ; levied to meet prison charges (1743), XXVI, pt. iii, 22 ; miscellaneous, in Baroda state, VII, 420, 432-436 ; paid to the religious head by Dáudi Bohorás, IX, pt. ii, 32-33 ; by Khojáhs, *id.* 49 and note 2 ; by Memans, *id.* 57, 126 and note 4, 141 note 3.
Taxila : town in the north-west of India, I, pt. i, 490, 491, 546.
Taxila : Takshasila tribe, I, pt. i, 534.
Tayalúr : place in Mysore, inscription at, I, pt. ii, 318 note 14, 332.
Táyghát : track in Sátára district, XIX, 203.
Taylor : Captain, killed in the rising at Ahmadábád (1857), I, pt. i, 438.
Taylor : Reverend J. S., on the origin of Borsad Bráhmans, IX, pt. i, 8 note 1 ; his derivation

of 'Koli,' *id.* 237 notes 1 and 2; on Gujarát Dhedas, *id.* 339 note 1, 340 note 2, 341 note 1, 343 note 2; his work at Kolhápur (1870), XXIV, 151-152.
Tázeás: *see* Taáziáhs.
Tazjyat-ul-Ansár: work of Abdullah Wassáf, (1300), I, pt. i, 518.
Teak: growth of, in Ratnágiri, X, 32, 36, 297; in Khándesh district, XII, 27; trade, in Thána district, XIII, 418, 431 and note 8, 466, 509, 510 and note 2; in Poona district, XVIII, pt. i, 52.
Teal: class of birds in Ratnágiri district, X, 97, 98.
Tebumlaára: village, grants of lands in, made by Vikramáditya, Chálukya king I, pt. ii, 365 note 1.
Teerowra: Tirawade, I, pt. ii, 548 note 1.
Teething: Pátáne Prabhu ceremony, XVIII, pt. i, 225.
Tegbakht or Tegbegkhan: first independent *Nawáb* of Surat, means taken to increase revenue by, struggles with the English and Sidhis, II, 116-120; defeats the forces of Mominkhán and contrives (1733) to become governor of Surat, I, pt. i, 313; cruelties of, at Surat, *id.* 315; kills Mulla Muhammad Ali, *id.* 331; dies (1746), *id.* 330. *See* also XI, 443-444.
Tegur: village in Dhárwár district, XXII, 787.
Tehengrighatchah: Indian Bráhman, sent back from Persia to convert his countrymen, IX, pt. ii, 183 note 4.
Tej: town in Cutch, mentioned as the capital of Cutch by Abul Fazl (1582); said to have been the metropolis of Sauráshtra, V, 251, 129 note 3.
Tejahpála: minister of the first two Vághelá chieftains and famous temple-builder, I, pt. i, 199; accompanies Viradhavala in the expedition against the rulers of Vanthali, defeats Ghughula, chief of Godhra, *id.* 201.
Tejara: village in Cutch, pond, memorial stones and a beautiful temple of Mahádev at, V, 251.
Tejgad, sub-division of Rewa Kántha, VI, 112.
Tejirája: Tejimayya or Tejugi, the Western Chálukya king Someśvara IV's officer, I, pt. ii, 465; Kalachurya Sovideva's officer, *id.* 485.
Tejpura: state in Mahi Kántha, V, 428.
Tejugi: *see* Tejirája.
Telang: sub-caste of Bráhmans in Gujarát, appearance, customs, religion, IX, pt. i, 51; in Thána district, XIII, 85; in Násik district, XVI, 43; in Poona, XVIII, pt. I, 180-183; in Sátára district, XIX, 56; in Sholápur district, XX, 40-41; in Belgaum district, XXI, 92; in Dhárwár, XXII, 100-101; in Kolhápur state, XXIV, 63, 64.
Telangsi: village in Ahmadnagar district, temple at, XVII, 740.
Telegraph: all district volumes, *see* Trade under District Name.
Teli: a caste of oil-pressers in Ratnágiri district, X, 125, 142; in Sávantvádi, *id.* 415; in Kolába district, XI, 67; in Janjira state, *id.* 412; in Khándesh district, XII, 75; in Thána district, XIII, 134-135; Musalmán in Násik district, XVI, 82; in Ahmadnagar district, XVII, 140-141; in Poona district, XVIII, pt. i, 376-377; in Sátára district, XIX, 96-97; in Sholápur district, XX, 143; in Kolhápur, XXIV, 99.
Telia Shaikh: caste of Musalmán beggars in Rádhanpur, IX, pt. ii, 8 note 2. *See* Shaikhs.
Telingana: Andhras of, I, pt. i, 533; princes of, I, pt. ii, 533.
Telingas: Telugus, tribe mentioned by Megasthenes, I, pt. i, 534.
Telnal: place of interest in Máhi Kántha, V, 442.
Teluga: *see* Tailanga.
Telugu Banjig: a caste of traders, in Kánara district, XV, pt. i, 183; in Dhárwár district, XXII, 126-129.
Telugu Oshnámaru: a caste of traders in Dhárwár district, XXII, 129-130.
Telugus: *see* Telingas.
Telunga: country, kings of, uprooted and established by Singhana, I, pt. ii, 244, 522, 524-525 and note 1.
Tembhurni: *Diospyros melanoxylon*, timber tree in Poona district, XVIII, pt. i, 53.
Tembhurni: town in Sholápur district, temples at, XX, 503.
Temblái: Hindu goddess, younger sister of Mahálakshmi of Kolhápur, temple, Mahálakshmi's yearly visit, he-buffalo offering, XXIV, 311-312.
Temperature: all district volumes, *see* Climate under District Name.
Temple: Sir Richard, in Káthiáwár, VIII, 223.
Temples: Jain, *see* Dehrás; in Gujarát; of brick and wood up to ninth century, I, pt. i, 79 and note 3; fire, for the holy fire of Behrám, at Sanján, IX, pt. ii, 185; at Navsári, *id.* 188; Kadmi, in Bombay, *id.* 193 note 2; description of, in Gujarát, *id.* 213; the chief, *id.* 214-215; worship in, *id.* 215; list of Atesh Behráms, *id.* 247; of Agiáris, *id.* 247-251.
Temple Servants: in Kánara district, XV, pt. i, 198-201.
Ten: village near Bárdoli in Gujarát, I, pt. ii, 361 note 1.
Tená: village in the Navsári division, I, pt. ii, 203.
Tenants: four classes of, in Ratnágiri district, X, 205; *Khot's* lower, *id.* 209-213.
Tenants-at-will: in Kánara district, XV, pt. ii, 187.
Tenevalege: Yádav capital, XVIII, pt. ii, 214 note 3; Bhillama reigns at, I, pt. ii, 520 and note 5.
Tenná: village identified with modern Tena, I, pt. i, 130; I, pt. ii, 203, 415.
Tenri: a medicinal plant, XXV, 255.
Tenuirostres: family of birds in Thána district, XIII, 49, 50.
Tenures; of land, in Baroda state, VII, 340-346, 355, 362; in Ratnágiri district, X, 203-213; special, *id.* 259-262; in Sávantvádi, *id.* 449; in Kolába district, (1882), XI, 162-168; in early Hindu, *id.* 168-169, 174 note 2; in Thána district, XIII, 530-550; early Hindu, 550-551; (1817), 564-565; British, *id.* 566;

(1828), *id.* 574-575; in Poona district, XVIII, pt. ii, 313 note 1, 355-359; in Sátára district, XIX, 322 328; in Dhárwár district, XXII, 462; kinds of, in Kolhápur, XXIV, 249-250.
Tephrosia suberosa: a poisonous plant, XXV, 272.
Tera: town near Lakhapat in Cutch, V, 252; allotted to one of the sons of Rao Rayadhan I, *id.* 138; Ghulam Shah marched on (1762), *id.* 144.
Tera: holiday on the thirteenth day of Safar, IX, pt. ii, 139.
Teravan: village, I, pt. ii, 223, 224.
Teravátaka: identified with Teravan, I, pt. ii, 223, 467.
Terbidi Math: Sonda Vaishnav monastery in Kánara district, XV, pt. ii, 120, 346-348.
Terdal: town in Sángli state, wall, gates, temples and inscriptions, XXIV, 372-377; inscriptions and records at, I, pt. ii, 431, 548, 554, 556.
Terekhol: river in Sávantvádi state, X, 388; southern boundary of the Konkan, "Introduction to the History of the Konkan," I, pt. ii, p. ix.
Terem: *Colocasia antiquorum*, food-plant, XXV, 182.
Tereyúr: invaded by Hoysala Vishnuvardhana, I, pt. ii, 496.
Terminalia: *bellerica, catappa chebula, paniculata* and *tomentosa*, dye-yielding plants, XXV, 244; *bellerica, catappa chebula*, oil-yielding plants, *id.* 218; *bellerica*, yields gum, *id.* 251; *chebula*, medicinal plant, *id.* 259.
Terns: family of birds in Ratnágiri district, X, 98.
Territorial Divisions: under the Valabhis, their identification with the present, I, pt. i, 82 and note 4.
Territorial limits: of Gujarát under Musalmáns, I, pt. i, 207 and note 1, 208.
Terry: Mr., European Traveller (A. D. 1618), notices Vania honesty, IX, pt. i, 78 note 1; on the condition of North-West Gujarát, I, pt. i, 221 note 1, 224 note 2; chaplain to Sir T. Roe, *id.* 376.
Terváda: state in Pálanpur, V, 281, 337.
Terwan: village in Ratnágiri district, copper-plate grant from, I, pt. ii, 466; granted to a Bráhman, *id.* 467.
Teshtar: star "Sirius," IX, pt. ii, 217 note 1.
Tesuka: misreading for Vesuka, I, pt. ii, 233.
Tetal: is probably Yethal tribe, I, pt. i, 145.
Tetranidæ: family of birds in Ratnágiri, X, 88.
Tevur, Tewar: town near Jabalpur, I, pt. ii, 214; capital of the Kalachuri family, *id.* 225, 380, 527. *See* Tripura.
Thacker: Major, at the battle of Kirkee, (1817), XIX, 301.
Thackeray: Mr., political agent (1824), killed in the Kittur disturbance, XXIV, 238; XXI, 401-403; monumental obelisk of, at Dhárwár, XXII, 705.
Thaga: appearance of, in Konkan, I, pt. ii, 126.
Tháhiriká: old province in South Gujarát, I, pt. ii, 364.
Thakar: a caste of beggars in Kánara district, XV, pt. i, 354.
Thákardas: Rájpút Koli chiefs, IX, pt. i, p. ix, 239; petty chiefs in Pálanpur, V, 289, 290.
Thákarias: Ibni Khurdadbah's royal tribe, I, pt. i, 130 and note 10.
Thakkar: title. *See* Thákur.
Thákors: large land-holders in Broach district, II, 481; in Kaira district, III, 83, 113; in Panch Maháls, *id.* 261; petty chieftains, I, pt. i, 215 note 2.
Thákur: *see* Bhát.
Thákur: title of the Lohánas; Hálár Khojáhs addressed by the title of, IX, pt. ii, 39.
Thákur: unsettled tribe in Ratnágiri district, X, 130; in Sávantvádi, *id.* 420; in Násik district, XVI, 26, 63, 64; in Ahmadnagar district, XVII, 212; in Poona district, XVIII, pt. i, 425 426; in Sátára district, XIX, 107-108; in Kolába district, XI, 72; in Thána district, XIII, 177-181, 523; at Mátherán, XIV, 259, 266.
Thal: town and fort in Kolába district, XI, 151, 395; seized by Bhimrája, I, pt. ii, 27; capture and recapture of, by the Sidi and Manaji A'ngria (1747), XXVI, pt. i, 285-286.
Thal: pass in Násik district, XVI, 129.
Thal: land system in Poona district, XVIII, pt. ii, 313-317; in Dhárwár district, XXII, 441.
Thálner: old town in Khándesh, its history, XII, 473-477, 248, 255.
Thalutæ: identified with Támraliptakas, I, pt. i, 533.
Thán: state in Káthiáwár, VIII, 663, I, pt. i, 180 note 2; fort, head-quarters of the Káthis, stormed by Shujaat Khán (1692), *id.* 388.
Thána: district, its boundaries, sub-divisions, aspect, hills, rivers, lakes, geology, hot springs, climate, XIII, 1-19; minerals, trees, forests, and forest administration, domestic and wild animals, birds and fish, *id.* 20-59; population: recent settlers, religion, census details, Bráhmans, writers, husbandmen, manufacturers, craftsmen, early tribes, and other castes, *id.* 60-279; agriculture: soil, reclamation, hill tillage, holdings, field tools, crops, bad seasons, *id.* 280-304; capital: exchange bills, currency, investments, service mortgage, wages, prices, weights and measures, *id.* 305-315; trade: roads (600-1781), passes, causeways, railways, ferries, post and telegraph, *id.* 316-331; brokers, trade centres, markets, fairs, shop-keepers, imports and exports, railway returns, *id.* 332-341; sea trade, vessels, ports, *id.* 342-363; crafts, *id.* 363-402; history; Aśoka's edicts (B. C. 225), Nahapán (A. D. 78), Parthians (B. C. 225-A. D. 235), Palhavs (A. D. 120-600), Trikutakas (420), Mauryas (550), *id.* 403-422; Siláháras (810-1260), Gujarát Solankis (943-1150), Devagiri Yádavas (1270-1300), *id.* 423-438; Musalmáns (1300-1500), *id.* 438-447; Portuguese (1500-1670), *id.* 447-447;

Maráthás (1670-1800), English (1800-1882), *id.* 475-526 ; land administration : acquisition, changes, staff, tenures, *vatan* settlement, history, survey results, season reports, *id.* 527-629 ; justice : civil courts and suits, registration, Magistracy, crime, gang robberies, pirates, police and jails, *id.* 630-640 ; revenue and finance, *id.* 641-654 ; instruction, private and girls' schools, readers and writers, school returns, libraries, reading rooms and newspapers, *id.* 641-662 ; health : diseases, hospitals and dispensaries, vaccination, births and deaths, *id.* 663-670 ; sub-divisional details, *id.* 671-697 ; places of interest, XIV, 1-419.

Town, its suburbs, municipality, remains, the jail, old churches, English graves, dispensaries, mosques, markets and history, XIV, 345-361 ; early trade connection of, with Persian Gulf, IX, pt. ii, 183 note 4 ; Pársi settlement in, *id.* 186 ; Khalif Umar sends a fleet to ravage (638-639) the coast of, *id.* 183 note 4 ; capital of the North Konkan under the Siláháras, I, pt. ii, 16, 24, 542 ; Siláhára port, *id.* 21 ; its decay as a port, *id.* 7, 33 ; Siláhára princes of, reinstated by their Karád relatives, *id.* 548-570 ; Siláhára dynasty of, destroyed by the Devagiri Yádava king Mahádeva, *id.* 247 ; copper-plate grants from, *id.* 247, 248, 529, 543 ; martyrdom of four friars at, 5 ; capital of the Konkan province of the Gujarát Musalmán kingdom, *id.* 33 ; burnt (1532) by the Portuguese, I, pt. i, 347 ; pays tribute to the Portuguese, I, pt. ii, 46 ; Portuguese fort at, *id.* 66 ; taken by the Maráthás (1737), *id.* 84 ; XXVI, pt. i, 182 ; taken by the English (1774), I, pt. ii, 85, 100, 101 ; I, pt. i, 401, 523, 524, 527, 534 ; XXVI, pt. i, 377-384 ; Marátha designs against (1779-80), *id.* 424-429 ; condition of, I, pt. ii, 108 ; Trimbakji Dengle imprisoned in the fort of, (1815), *id.* 610.

Thánádars : officers in charge of military posts under the Mughals, I, pt. i, 210.

Thánás : fortified outposts under the Mughals, I, pt. i, 210 ; groups of villages in Baroda, VII, 363, 367.

Thanavi, Thánawa ; village near Kávi, I, pt. ii, 404.

Thánesar : town in Northern India, I, pt. ii, 135.

Thánga : hill range in Káthiáwár, VIII, 9.

Thánges : Kulkarnis' messengers in Thána district, XIII, 538.

Thánkar Koli : early tribe in Thána district, XIII, 174.

Tharád : state under Pálanpur, its description, V, 328-331, 281 ; Vághela chiefship, IX, pt. i, 129. *Town,* its description, V, 348 ; exemption of, from paying tribute to the British Government from 1825, *id.* 303.

Thar and Párkar : district in Sind, I, pt. i, 538.

Thásra : sub-division of Kaira, III, 146-149. *Town, id.* 178.

Thatcher : Lieutenant, sent against Bhágoji (1857), XVI, 199. *See* also XVII, 418 ; holds Sankheda in Gujarát (1858), I, pt. i, 444.

Thavá : sub-division of Rewa Kántha, VI, 98.

Thengoda : town in Násik district, XVI, 649.

Theophila : town, identification of, with Tháu in Káthiáwár, I, pt. i, 539.

Theophilus : Indian Bishop, sent to Constantinople, XIV, 322 note 2.

Theriophonium Dalzellii : a famine plant, XXV, 208.

Thespesia populnea : fibrous, medicinal and sacred plant, XXV, 226, 260, 289.

Theur : village in Poona district, XVIII, pt. iii, 451-452 ; death of Mádhavráv Peshwa (1761-1772) at, XVIII, pt. ii, 254.

Thevenot : traveller (1660-1666), in Cambay, VI, 219 note 5 ; describes the Pársis, IX, pt. ii, 191 ; his mention of Dábhol, X, 330 ; his account of Cheul, XI, 285 note 2 ; of Burhánpur, XII, 250 note 4, 590 and note 2 ; of the Portuguese at Honávar, XV, pt. ii, 125 note 3, 311 ; his travels from Surat to Aurangábád, XVI, 190 and note 2.

Thevetia neriifolia : a poisonous plant, XXV, 266.

Thiba : pass in Kolába district, XI, 6, 115.

Thika : *see* Tika.

Thilsongti : king of Tibet (878-901), I, pt. i, 501.

Thisrong : king of Tibet (803-845), I, pt. i, 501.

Thobhan Bárot : a Bhát poet, IX, pt. i, 213.

Thok, Thokábandi : *see* Toka.

Thom : apparently great lord, I, pt. i, 497.

Thor : *Euphorbia neriifolia,* vegetable antidote to snake-bite, XXV, 275, 289.

Thori : caste of broom-sellers in Káthiáwár, VIII, 159 ; wandering tribe in Gujarát, IX, pt. i, 509-510 ; IX, pt. ii, 90.

Thorla champa : an oil-yielding plant, XXV, 214.

Thorla tacla : a famine plant, XXV, 198.

Thread : gold and silver, making of, in Khándesh, XII, 233.

Thread : sacred, worn by classes other than Bráhmans, IX, pt. i, p. xiv note 1.

Thread-girding : called *upanayana,* Vedic rite, ceremonies of, among Bráhmans, IX, pt. i, 36-39 ; Rájputs, *id.* 141 ; in Kánara, among Shenvis, XV, pt. i, 152-154 ; among Kushasthalis, *id.* 170 ; among Bávkule Vánis, *id.* 174 ; among Nayers, *id.* 196 ; among Kongers, *id.* 198 ; among Chetris, *id.* 343 ; among Jains, *id.* 234 ; XXIV, 140-141 ; among Deshasthas, *id.* 48-50 ; among the Chitpávans, XVIII, pt. i, 116-120 ; Govardhans, *id.* 162 ; Gujarát Bráhmans, *id.* 164 ; Kanojs, *id.* 169 ; Shenvis, *id.* 177 ; Tailangs, *id.* 182 ; Dhruv Prabhus, *id.* 187-189 ; Pátáne Prabhus, *id.* 226-228 ; Velális, *id.* 258 ; Jingars, *id.* 341 ; Shimpis, *id.* 368.

Thrush : class of birds, in Ratnágiri district, X, 72 ; at Mátherán, XIV, 257.

Thugaon : village in Ahmadnagar district, temple at, XVII, 740.

Thunderstorm : in Poona district, XVIII, pt. i, 14 and note 1 ; in Belgaum district, XXI, 39 and note 1.

Thur : hill range, near Bhinmál, I, pt. i, 456.
Thúrnávi : modern Thanavi or Thánawa, I, pt. ii, 404.
Thursday : Guruvár or Brahaspatvár, day sacred to Jupiter, beliefs about, IX, pt. i, 402 ; sacredness of, XVIII, pt. i, 240.
Thuverio : thorny milkbush, IX, pt. i, 354.
Thymelaceæ : poisonous plant, XXV, 268.
Thyphinæ : species of poisonous plants, XXV, 183.
Tiagli : village in Kánara district, XV, pt. ii, 352.
Tiastenes : identified with king Chastana, I, pt. ii, 159 ; I, pt. i, 37, 540.
Tiatoura : modern Chándor, I, pt. i, 540.
Tibet : ceases to acknowledge the overlordship of China (729), spreads its power to the Yangtsekiang valley (750), confederacy formed by the king of China with Indian chiefs and Arabs against it (787), I, pt. i, 501.
Tickar : a food plant, XXV, 175.
Tidgundi : in the Bijápur district, I, pt. ii, 450 ; copper-plate grant from, *id.* 553, 577.
Tieffenthaler : German missionary and traveller (1750), his description of Thána population, XIII, 499 ; in Cambay, VI, 225 ; his mention of Nivti fort in Ratnágiri, X, 354 note 3 ; of Cheul, XI, 286, 353 ; of Bándra, XIV, 27 note 6 ; of Kalyán, *id.* 120; of Kelve Máhim, *id.* 199 ; of Sháhápur, *id.* 306 ; of Tárápur, *id.* 345 ; of Sáler and Mahuli fort in Násik, XVI, 459.
Tigadahalli : inscription at, I, pt. ii, 509.
Tiger : worship of, on Vághbáras day ; guarding against ravages of, IX, pt. i, 378 ; in Khándesh district, XII, 30 ; in Thána district, XIII, 44 ; (1774, 1788), *id.* 501, 510 ; at Mátherán, XIV, 259 ; at Tungar, *id.* 370 ; in Kánara district, XV, pt. i, 81-92 ; in Belgaum district, XXI, 69.
Tiger-god : worship of, by Thákurs, XVIII, pt. i, 426.
Tigler : caste of husbandmen in Kánara district, XV, pt. i, 255.
Tigulas : Tamil people, I, pt. ii, 499.
Tijái : one-third rental system of Sálsette, XIII, 547.
Tika : old tenure in Poona district, XVIII, pt. ii, 313 note 1 ; in Násik district, XVI, 208 and note 5.
Tikar : village in Káthiáwár, history of, VIII, 664.
Tikka : of the Kádamba stock, father-in-law of Vikramáditya VI, I, pt. ii, 448.
Tikona: peak, in Poona district, XVIII, pt. i, 5.
Til : *Sesamum Indicum*, an oil-yielding plant, XXV, 219.
Tilaksundari : princess of Sopára, XIV, 319.
Tilakvádi : sub-division in Baroda state, details of, village, VII, 558.
Tiláre : stream in Belgaum district, XXI, 13.
Tilári : river in Sávantvádi, X, 389 ; geological formation of the bed of, *id.* 392.
Tilari : a caste of husbandmen in Belgaum district, XXI, 131.
Tiláts : chiefs of Ker Rájpúts in Cutch, their customs, V, 100.
Tilavadi : timber tree in Khándesh, XII, 27.
Tilawalli : village in Dhárwár district, I, pt. ii, 281 note 3 ; inscription at, *id.* 240, 438 note 3, 440 note 1, 524 note 1.
Tilbhándeshvar : Násik temple, XVI, 509.
Tiles : making of, in Kánará district, XV, pt. i, 20 ; in Poona district, XVIII, pt. i, 31 ; in Sholápur district, XX, 9 ; in Belgaum district, XXI, 54 ; in Dhárwár district, XXII, 27.
Tiliaceæ : species of famine and fibrous plants, XXV, 195, 230.
Tinospora cordifolia : medicinal plant, XXV, 261.
Tilolá : a caste of cultivators in Khándesh, XII, 68.
Tilse : village in Thána district, XIV, 361.
Tilvan : pass in Násik district, XVI, 130.
Timalinæ : family of birds in Ratnágiri, X, 73.
Timána : old village in Káthiáwár, remains, temples and history of, VIII, 664.
Timba : state in Máhi Kántha, V, 428.
Timber : trade and prices of, in Surat, II, 43, 162 ; trade of, in Khándesh, XII, 22 ; export of, *id.* 223 ; in Thána district, XIII, 27-29 ; with Gedrosia (250), *id.* 418 ; with the Persian Gulf (810-1260), *id.* 431 ; with Malabár Coast (1300-1500), *id.* 445 ; in Sálsette (1500-1670), *id.* 455 ; at Bassein (1500-1670), *id.* 465 ; I, pt. ii, 36 ; in Kánara district, XV, pt. i, 20 ; XV, pt. ii, 58 ; first notice of, in Bombay island (1694), XXVI, pt. i, 105 ; in Poona district, XVIII, pt. i, 38-39.
Timbi : *táluka* in Káthiáwár, VIII, 665.
Timmaya : Hindu corsair, surprises the Portuguese at Anjidiv, XV, pt. ii, 308, 254 ; defeated by the Portuguese, *id.* 101 ; helped by the Portuguese to attack the Chief of Bhatkal, *id.* 105 ; induces Albuquerque to attack Goa, *id.* 107, 108, 109 ; proves a very useful ally to the Portuguese, *id.* 111 ; takes Cintacora and Gersappa, *id.* 279, 309, 332 ; Gasper calls him a foreign Moor, *id.* 102 note 2.
Tim Ráj : son of Rám Ráj of Vijayanagar, I, pt. ii, 645.
Timulla : modern Chaul, XIII, 414 ; XIV, 52.
Timur : his rigorous rule in Persia and Upper India, IX, pt. ii, 188 and note 3 ; his invasion of India, *id.* 188 note 4.
Tinái : pass between Goa and Haliyal in Kánara district, XV, pt. ii, 39 and note 1, 40, 351.
Tinamidæ : family of birds in Ratnágiri, X, 89.
Tinnevelly : district in Madras, the rule of the Pándyas in, I, pt. ii, 277.
Tin-working : in Dhárwár district, XXII, 382.
Tipparasa : Yádava king Maháдeva's officer (1269), I, pt. ii, 528.
Tippoja : architect, builds the temple at Degámve, I, pt. ii, 569.
Tippoo Sultán : *see* Tipu Sultán.
Tippúr : place in Mysore, inscription at, I, pt. ii, 309 and note 1 ; given to Gangarája by Vishnuvardhana, *id.* 500.
Tipu Sultán : son of Haidar Ali of Mysore, succeeds Haidar, reigns over Kánara, ruins the trade of Kánara, XV, pt. ii, 55 ; forces the native Christian population of

Kánara to become Musalmáns, *id.* 143; defends Honávar, *id.* 315; Sadáshivgad garrisoned by, *id.* 258, 340; Kumárgad restored to, *id.* 328, 329; wages the third Mysore War, *id.* 145; *another account of* (1782-1799): besieges Nárgund (1785), XXII, 414; at war with the Maráthás (1786-1787), *id.* 415-416; at war with the English and the Maráthás (1790-1792), 417-418; *see* also I, pt. ii, 660-662; XXI, 385-388; XXIII, 679-680; XXIV, 150.

Tir: fourth month of the Pársi year, IX, pt. ii, 218.

Tiranhu: name of the Pandu Lena Cave hill, in Násik district, XVI, 633.

Tiraváda: modern Tirvádi in Kolhápur state, I, pt. ii, 547, 548; place of residence of Gandaráditya, Siláhára ruler of Kolhápur, *id.* 255.

Tirde: village in Ahmadnagar district, XVII, 740.

Tirgár: a caste of Musalmán arrow-makers, I, pt. i, 451; in Ahmadnagar district, XVII, 229; in Násik district, XVI, 49.

Tirgul: sub-caste of Bráhmans in Poona district, XVIII, pt. i, 184; in Ahmadnagar district, XVII, 64; in Sátára district, XIX, 56; in Sholápur district, XX, 41-43; in Belgaum district, XXI, 92; in Dhárwár district, XXII, 101; in Bijápur district, XXIII, 90; in Kolhápur, XXIV, 64.

Tirhut: birth-place of Śrigaudas, I, pt. i, 161, 456 note 1.

Tiripangalida: town, probably Tikota in Kurdunwád state, I, pt. i, 541.

"Tirkati": European ship, XIII, 718.

Tirlápur: village in Dhárwár district, XXII, 788.

Tirmali: a caste of beggars in Sátára district, XIX, 122; in Ahmadnagar district, XVII, 211-212; in Poona district, XVIII, pt. i, 463, 464.

Tirmizis: chief *sayad* family in Gujarát, IX, pt. ii, 6 note 1.

Tirthakalpa: work, I, pt. i, 176; written by Jinaprabhásuri, *id.* 182 note 1.

Tirthakhanda: part of Hemádri's *Chaturvarga Chintámani*; treats of pilgrimages to holy places, I, pt. ii, 249.

Tirthankars: patron saints of Shrávaks, IX, pt. i, 102, 105, 110; images of, set in the Shrávak Dehras, *id.* 111; *see* also I, pt. i, 451 note 3.

Tirthas: holy bathing places, *literally* fords and crossings, IX, pt. i, 548; at Násik, XIV, 522-525.

Tirthvalá: bather's priest, his daily life, IX, pt. i, 29.

Tirukally: poisonous plant, XXV, 268.

Tirukkalukkunram: inscription at, I, pt. ii, 318 note 3, 322 note 7, 419, 421.

Tirumakudlu-Narasipur: *táluka* in Mysore, I, pt. ii, 284 note 4.

Tirupanatara: place near Cochin, mentioned by Pliny, I, pt. i, 533.

Tirupati: place of pilgrimage in Gujarát, temple of Báláji at, IX, pt. i, 549.

Tisi: oil-yielding plant, XXV, 215.

Tit: class of birds in Ratnágiri district, X, 80.

Titles: among Mughals, IX, pt. ii, 9; Patháns, *id.* 11; *sayads*, *id.* 7; *shaikhs*, *id.* 8, 22, 39.

Titvála: village in Thána district, XIV, 56, 361.

Tiundha: Násik town sub-division, XVI, 472, 535.

Tivarája: conquers the Nágas, I, pt. ii, 281 note 3.

Tivas: timber tree in Khándesh, XII, 28.

Tivili: musical instrument of the Ráshtrakutas of Málkhed, I, pt. ii, 387.

Tivra (North and South): hill passes between Ratnágiri district and Kolhápur state, X, 166, XXIV, 5.

Tiwar: gum-yielding plant, XXV, 251.

Tobacco: cultivation of, in Surat, II, 67; in Broach, *id.* 408; in Pálanpur, V, 295; in Baroda, VII, 89-90, 97; used as stimulant by Hindus and Musalmáns, IX, pt. i, pp. xxxiii-xxxiv; use of, among Musalmán population, IX, pt. ii, 110-111; cultivation of, in Khándesh district, XII, 165-166; in Thána district, XIV, 113; in Násik district, XVI, 101; in Ahmadnagar district, XVII, 274; in Poona district, XVIII, pt. ii, 50; in Sátára district, XIX, 166; in Sholápur district, XX, 231; in Belgaum district, XXI, 252, 253; in Dhárwár district, XXII, 277-278; in Bombay island, farmed (1720), XXVI, pt. iii, 363; (1733), *id.* 364; (1736), *id.* 364 and note 1, 365-366; (1745), *id.* 366; imported from Surat (1724-25), *id.* 363; (1730), *id.* 364; revenue from the farm of (1748-1778), *id.* 498; conditions of the farm (1773), *id.* 499-500.

Toda: *táluka* in Káthiáwár, VIII, 665.

Toda Girás: ready-money payment, I, pt. i, 216, 227 and note 1.

Todar Mal: *rája*, said to have first introduced the Bháts as securities, IX, pt. i, 209 note 2; revenue system of (1530-1590), XII, 266; *see* also XIII, 553, 554 note 2; XV, pt. ii, 155; XVII, 398; XVIII, pt ii, 225.

Toddy: *tádi*, juice of wild date plam *khajuri*, process of drawing, drinking classes, IX, pt. i, pp. xxix and note 1, xxx.

Togochchedu: grant from, I, pt. ii, 369.

Toka: old tenure in Thána district, XIII, 531, 550 and note 2, 551 note 5; unmeasured plot, *id.* 565; assessment, *id.* 565; *taka* probably for *toka*, *id.* 565 note 7; (1828), *id.* 574; in Murbad (1837), *id.* 583 note 1; in Kolába district, XI, 170 and note 3.

Toka: town in Ahmadnagar district, temples at, XVII, 740-741; I, pt. ii, 353 note 2; meeting of the Pravará and the Godávari at, *id.* 627.

Tokar: a food plant, XXV, 187, 208.

Tokre Koli: *see* Koli.

Tolachkod: village in Bijápur district, pond, temple, legend of, XXIII, 679-680.

Tôll-bars: in Káthiáwár, VIII, 224; in Kolába district, XI, 115-116; in Thána district, XIII, 323-324; in Kánara district, XV, pt. ii, 42; in Násik district, XVI, 134-135; in Ahmadnagar district, XVII, 334; in Poona district, XVIII, pt. ii, 159; in Sátára district, XIX, 208; in Sholápur district, XX, 258; in Belgaum district, XXI, 350-352; in Dhárwár district, XXII, 347; in Bijápur district, XXIII, 357.

Tombs worship: in Gujarát, of *sati* tombs, IX, pt. i, 358-360; of *samádhs* raised over Hindu ascetics, details of, *id.* 360; of the *takio* of a Musalmán saint called *pir* or *sái*; of Báva Ghor; of Dariyásha, *id.* 360-361; of *tábuts* or *táziás* during Muharram festival, details of worship and offerings made to, *id.* 362. *See* Shrines.

Tonas: marriage songs among Musalmáns, IX, pt. ii, 164.

Tonda: Tondai, Tondira, Tundira, Tundáka, old district round Conjeveram, I, pt. ii, 318; Pallava rulers of, *id.* 496.

Tondai: *see* Tonda.

Tondsimán: Karunakara, Pallava chief and general of the Eastern Chalukya Kulottungachodadeva I, I, pt. ii, 333.

Tondanúr: modern Tonnur, near Seringapatam, Vira-Ballála III's place of retirement, I, pt. ii, 510.

Tondapur: village in Khándesh district, Hemádpanti pond and temple at, XII, 477.

Tondira: *see* Tonda.

Tone: Mr., visited (1796) Poona, XVIII, pt. ii, 274.

Toni: canoe, derivation of the word, XIII, 721.

Tonnúr: *see* Tondanur.

Tooria: oil-yielding plant, XXV, 214.

Toparon: port between Broach and Vengurla, mentioned by Ptolemy, I, pt. ii, 1; proposed identification of, X, 192 note 3, 333 note 1.

Topasses: Eurasian soldiers in Bombay island (1760), increase of pay to, XXVI, pt. iii, 138-139.

Toradav: mortgage system in Kánara district, XV, pt. ii, 31.

Toragale: Torgal, territorial division of Kuntala, I, pt. ii, 298 note 2, 431, 465, 523; taken by Ali Adil Sháh (1573), *id.* 645.

Toragaleva-Devarasa: probably identical with Devarája, I, pt. ii, 528.

Tora Gara: *see* Garásia.

Toragare: territorial division, I, pt. ii, 435, 440.

Toramáns: king (471), perhaps of Húna descent, I, pt. i, 72, 74-75; overthrows Budhagupta, *id.* 136, 146, 465, 496; foreign invader, conquers Málwa between A.D. 484-510, I, pt. ii, 312.

Toramara: country, I, pt. ii, 369.

Toran: pass in Násik district, XVI, 129.

Toranagal-Brahmadeva: inscription at the temple of, at Sirúr, I, pt. ii, 436 note 2.

Torgal: *see* Toragale.

Torgal: town in Kolhápur state, citadel, temple, XXIV, 320-321.

Torke Nádor: a caste of husbandmen in Kánara district, XV, pt. i, 224.

Torkhede: village in Khándesh district, grant at, I, pt. ii, 395, 399, 401, 409.

Torki: famine plant, XXV, 197.

Torna: hill fort in Bhor state, captured by Shiváji (1646), XVIII, pt. ii, 226; I, pt. ii, 591.

Torriano: Major, his defence of Honávar (1783-1784), XV, pt. ii, 143, 313-315.

Torvi: village in Bijápur district, Adil Shahi remains and temples at, XXIII, 680-681; water-works at, *id.* 579-580.

Totanince: family of birds in Ratnágiri, X, 92.

Tovarsyaghatta: *see* Távarcyaghatta.

Tower of Silence: Dokhma, IX, pt. ii, 239, 240; description of, foundation ceremony, opening ceremony, *id.* 240 note 1; beliefs about the first body to be laid in, *id.* 195 note 3, 240 note 1; list of, *id.* 240 note 1, 252-254; at different places in Thána district, XIV, 110, 119, 291, 304, 305, 344, 354, 366, 371; in Poona, XVIII, pt. iii, 399.

Town Ditch: in Bombay island, outside the wall (1739-1745), XXVI, pt. ii, 283-291.

Town Hall: of Bombay, part of Mapla Por used as (1677-1720), Ráma Kámáti's house in the Bazár Gate used as (1720-1786); this Town Hall sold (1786), accommodated in Hornby's house, the present Great Western Hotel (1786), transferred to part of the Marine House (1788), accommodated in Hornby's house (1800-1811), XXVI, pt. iii, 614-616; money raised by lotteries to build the present Town Hall (1814), *id.* 616-626; one more lottery (1820); the site given by the Company, completed by the Government at the total cost of over six lákhs, *id.* 626-643; old, sold (1786), *id.* pt. ii, 487-488.

Townsend: Mr., Political agent at Kolhápur (1844), XXIV, 247.

Town Wall: of Bombay island (1710-1717), XXVI, pt. ii, 277; finished (1718), *id.* 436.

Toyimadeva: Kádamba feudatory of Jayasimha II, I, pt. ii, 435, 437, 560, 564.

Toys: wooden, making of, in Belgaum district, XXI, 350-352.

Trade: all district volumes, *see* under District Name.

Trade Companies: in Dhárwár district, XXII, 352-353.

Trade-guilds: in Surat, II, 321; in Broach, *id.* 441, 442; in Kaira, III, 76; in Panch Maháls, *id.* 251; in Cutch, V, 122; in Mahi Kántha, *id.* 379; in Baroda, VII, 160-162; in Ratnágiri district, X, 191.

Traders: all district volumes, *see* Population under District Name.

Trades Union: in Poona district, XVIII, pt. ii, 173.

Trágá: self-sacrifice practised in Gujarát, rites of, resorted to by Bháts, instances of, IX, pt. i, 210-212; by Chárans, *id.* 218; in Kaira district, III, 120; in Káthiáwár, VIII, 136 note 1, 326.

Traikutakas: kings of Central and South Gujarát and North Konkan, I, pt. ii, 13; charter issued from the camp of the, driven by the Kshatrapas, retire to Central India and assume the name of Haihaya and Kalachuri, *id.* 294; finally destroy the power of the Kshatrapas and regain possession of their capital (249-250), *id.* 294, 295; their era

(249-250) comes to be called Káláchuri or Chedi era, *id.* 178-179, 294; their coins, *id.* 295; *see* also I, pt. i, 55-57; 110, 113, 114; XIII, 419.
Trailokyamahádevi: Haihaya princess, wife of Chálukya king Vikramáditya II, builds a S'iva temple, I, pt. ii, 90, 296, 374, 377, 414 note 4.
Trailokyamalla: *biruda* (title) of Someśvara I, I, pt. ii, 214, 438; of Tailapa II or Taila III, *id.* 222, 459.
Trailokyeśvara: temple of S'iva at Pattadakala built by Trailokyamahádevi, wife of Vikramáditya II, I, pt. ii, 190, 374, 377.
Training College: in Káthiáwár, VIII, 346; in Poona city, XVIII, pt. iii, 55-56.
Trambaksarovar: lake near Bhinmál, I, pt. i, 453. *See* Talbi.
Trambávati: legendary town, Cambay supposed to be derived from VI, 212, 213, 214.
Tránjipura: town, Shimhirája, the Yádava king, brought an elephant from, I, pt. ii, 516.
Tranqueira: Portuguese word for a stockaded fort, I, pt. ii, 48.
Transit Duties: in Káthiáwár, VIII, 338-340; reduced (1855-1858) in Panch Mahals, III, 266, 282; abolished in Kolába, XI, 182 and note 1; in Poona district (1867), XVIII, pt. ii, 411-412. *See* also Customs.
Transoxiana: country, Turkish rule in (560 A.D.), I, pt. i, 139.
Trap: formations, in Surat district, II, 29; Dakhan, in Ratnágiri district, X, 13, 15-17; in Sávantvádi, *id.* 395; in Poona district, XVIII, pt. i, 12-13; flows and beds, in Bijápur district, XXIII, 43-44, 59-60.
Trápaj: town in Káthiáwár, history of, VIII, 665, 666.
Trapdykes: in Ratnágiri, X, 17; in Sávantvádi, *id.* 393.
Trappaga: boat used at Broach at the time of the *Periplus*, I, pt. i, 545.
Travancore: state, I, pt. ii, 277, 282 note 5; Pándyas of, I, pt. i, 534.
Travellers' Bungalows: all district volumes, *see* Trade under District Name.
Treasury Committee: of Bombay presidency formed (1755), XXVI, pt. iii, 374-375.
Treaty: between Singhana and Lavanaprasáda, conditions of, I, pt. i, 200; between Rámadeva, king of Devagiri and Alla-ud-din Khilji, I, pt. ii, 251; between the Peshwa and the Mughals (1760), *id.* 627; of partition between Sátára and Kolhápur (1730), *id.* 82, 656; between the English and the Sidis (1733), *id.* 83; with the Maráthás (1739), *id.* 97; of Surat, *id.* 101; of Purandhar, *id.* 103; of Sálbai (1782), *id.* 106; between the Pant Pratinidhi and the Peshwa (1784), *id.* 106; between the Maráthás and Tipu (1787), *id.* 661; of Mahád (1796), *id.* 110; of Bassein (1803), *id.* 111; of Poona (1817), *id.* 115, 611; with the *jáhgirdárs* (1818), *id.* 612; between the Angria and the English (1822), *id.* 127; of marriage between Charles II and Catharine of Braganza, XXVI, pt. i, 1-9.
Tree: near the grave of Saint Mirán at Unjáh, disease-curing powers of the, IX, pt. ii, 128; issue-giving property in the, near the tomb of Saint Sháh Alam at Ahmadábád, near the grave of Saint Mirán at Unjáh, jasmine and rose bushes at the shrines of certain saints, *id.* 148.
Trees: in Poona district, XVIII, pt. i, 41-54; in Surat, II, 39, 41; in Broach, *id* 355, 408; in Cutch, V, 23; in Pálanpur, *id.* 285; in Mahi Kántha, *id.* 360; in Rewa Kántha, VI, 12, 14; in Cambay, *id.* 183; in Baroda state, VII, 34-43, 379; in Kolába district, XI, 23-26; in Khándesh, XII, 23-28; fruit, *id.* 176-177, 599; in Thána district, XIII, 21-23; forest, *id.* 23-27; at Matherán, XIV, 252; Sopára *stupa*, *id.* 326 and note 1; in Kánara district, XV, pt. i, 60-79, 426, 446; in Násik district, XVI, 16; in Ahmadnagar district, XVII, 22-27; in Sholápur district, XX, 13; in Belgaum district, XXI, 62-64; in Dhárwár district, XXII, 33-35; in Bijápur district, XXIII, 60-64.
Tree-snakes: in Poona district, XVIII, pt. i, 77.
Trepenjyo: term of scorn among Khojás, IX, pt. ii, 44.
Treronidæ: family of birds in Ratnágiri district, X, 85.
Tretáyuga: second cycle of Hindu chronology, I, pt. i, 461.
Trewia nudiflora: fibrous plant, XXV, 228.
Treyauna: old district in Gujarát, I, pt. i, 111.
Trial by Ordeal: *see* Ordeal.
Trianthema pentandra: famine plant, XXV, 200.
Tribes: early or aboriginal, in Gujarát, also called *káli paraj* or dusky race, IX, pt. i, p. x; chief classes of, census details, *id.* 290; origin, language, appearance, food, occupation, *id.* 290; social position, religion, object of worship, their *devasthán* or godyard, *id.* 292; powers over spirits, *bhagats* among, *id.* 293; customs, community, prospects, *id.* 294; accounts of the chief classes, *id.* 294-330; Indian, mentioned by Ptolemy, I, pt. i, 535; forest, in Poona district, XVIII, pt. i, 37-38.
Tribhog Abhyantara-Siddhi: levy of one-third of the revenues, I, pt. ii, 440, 448.
Tribhuvanácharya: *see* Gunda Anivaritacharya.
Tribhuvanadhira Nulamba: Pallava king, I, pt. ii, 332, 421.
Tribhuvanamalla: *biruda* (title) assumed by the Western Chálukyas, I, pt. ii, 211; of Western Chálukya king Vikramáditya V, *id.* 434; of Vikramáditya II or VI, *id.* 216, 445, 447; of Someśvara IV, *id.* 463; of Kalachurya Bijjala, *id.* 470, 471, 474; of Hoysála Vishnuvardhana, *id.* 492, 493, 494; of Nársimha I, *id.* 500; of Vira-Ballála, *id.* 501.
Tribhuvanamalla: Pandya feudatory of Vikramáditya VI, I, pt. ii, 452.
Tribhuvanamalla: Goa Kádamba prince, I, pt. ii, 565, 571.
Tribhuvanapála: great-grandson of Bhima I (1022-1064) and father of Kumárapála, murdered by Siddharája, I, pt. i, 182; representative of Anahilaváda Solankis, *id.* 203.
Tribhuvanapálavasati: temple at Báhadapura, I, pt. i, 186.

Tribhuvanáśraya-Nágavardhana: Nirpan grant of, I, pt. ii, 357, 359 note 1.
Tribulus terrestris: famine plant, XXV, 196.
Tributes: of Baroda state in Káthiáwár, history of, VII, 314-319.
Trichinopoly: district in the Madras presidency, I, pt. ii, 508. *Town,* surrendered (1741) to the Maráthás, XIX, 283.
Trichosanthes palmata: fruit tree, XXV, 281.
Trident: rock-cut, Buddhist, at Padan in Thána district, XIV, 390.
Trigonella fœnum-græcum: an oil-yielding plant, XXV, 217.
Trigonella Indica: a famine plant, XXV, 197.
Trikadiba: island mentioned by Ptolemy, I, pt. i, 542.
Trikalingas: Telanga country, king of, killed by Jaitugi, I, pt. ii, 239, 522.
Trikam: Sind Mukhi, devotee of Pir Sadr-ud-din, IX, pt. ii, 40.
Trikúta: town, I, pt. ii, 179; in Aparánta (Konkan), *id.* 294; kingdom, *id.* 403 note 3; perhaps Junnar, I, pt. i, 57, 58 note 1; XIII, 419.
Trikutakas: dynasty of (A. D. 420), XIII, 409. *See* Traikutakas.
Trikúteśvara: god, inscription in the temple of, at Gadag, I, pt. ii, 432 note 7, 506 note 3, 518 note 4, 520.
Trilochana: Kadamba founder, sprung from a drop of sweat of the god S'iva after the conquest of Tripura, also called Jayanta, I, pt. ii, 286 note 2, 342, 566.
Trilochana: Pallava king, attacked by Vijayáditya, I, pt. ii, 340.
Trilochanapála: king of Látadésa, I, pt. ii, 340 note 1, 412 note 5, 431.
Trimalkop: village in Dhárwár district, XXII, 788.
Trimbak: pond near Bhinmál, I, pt. i, 462.
Trimbak: town in Násik district, aspect, water-supply, fairs, temples, pilgrims, forts, history, siege (1818), XVI, 649-660, 210 note 3, 414, 441, 447; fort, surprised by the Maráthás (1751), I, pt. ii, 627.
Trimbakeshwar Mahádev: shrine of, I, pt. i, 454.
Trimbakji Dengle or Denglia: Báji Ráo II's chief adviser, I, pt. ii, 609; commissions Nároba Takti, *pátil* of Karrambha, to clear the Gangthari of Bhils, *id.* 630; takes Chatursing prisoner (1812), *id.* 114, 610; in the zenith of his power (1813-1814), *id.* 610: murders Gangádhar Shástri (1814), *id.* 610; his imprisonment in and escape from the fort of Thána (1815-16), *id.* 115, 610; levies men and stirs the country (1817), *id.* 610; is surrendered to the English by the Peshwa and is imprisoned in the fort of Thána (1818), *id.* 119, 610; *another account of*: appointed *sarsubhedár* of Ahmadábád, assassinates the Shástri, shut up in Thána fort, escapes, I, pt. i, 427, 428; VII, 219. 221-223, 225; *see* also XIII, 521, 522, 523; XVI, 195, 198; XVIII, pt. ii, 292, 294, 295; XIX, 300; XX, 292.
Trimbak Pandit: deputy of Khanderáv Gáikwár at Ahmadábád; his intrigues with Fakhr-ud-daulah, I, pt. i, 329.
Trimbakráv Dábháde: son and successor of Khanderáo Dábháde (1720), I, pt. i, 389; advances with an army to Cambay (1725), *id.* 306, 391; his jealousy of the interference of the Peshwa in Gujarát affairs; intrigues of, against the Peshwa; intercourse of, with the Nizám; confederacy with Piláji, Kántáji, and Udáji to rescue the Maratha *rája* from the Bráhman minister; defeat of the allies by the Peshwa (1731), and death of, in battle, *id.* 312, 392-393; *see* also I, pt. ii, 600; XIX, 267, 273-274.
Trimbakráv Mámá: commander of the army of the regency; defeated by Raghunáthráo near Pandharpur (1774), I, pt. ii, 604; XX, 291.
Trimbak Vináyak: Marátha *mámlatdár*, his survey (1771-1772) in Thána district, XIII, 558.
Trimurti: Hindu trinity, IX, pt. i, p. xxxvi; sculpture at Elephanta, XIV, 63-66.
Trinetra: god S'iva, I, pt. ii, 580, 581.
Trinetra: Kadamba king, I, pt. ii, 342. *See* Jayant.
Tringalvádi: fort in Násik district, caves at, XVI, 441, 445, 660.
Tringinæ: family of birds in Ratnágiri, X, 92.
Trinity: or *Trimurti*, Brahma, Vishnu and Shiv, worship, IX, pt. i, p. xxxvi, 531, 532.
Triparavata: modern Murgod in the Parasgad *táluka* of the Belgaum district, I, pt. ii, 285 note 6.
Tripitakas: Buddhist scriptures in Kanheri caves, XIV, 170.
Tripura: modern Tevur in Central Provinces, I, pt. i, 57 note 4; I, pt. ii, 225, 240; capital of the Kalachuri dynasty, *id.* 179, 181, 380, 418, 527; capital of the Chedi country, *id.* 225, 240.
Tripura: demon killed by S'iva, I, pt. ii, 286 note 2, 566; 380 note 1.
Tripurántaka: religious benefactions of, I, pt. i, 205.
Tripurushaprásáda: Mahádeva's temple at Anahilaváda, I, pt. i, 161; new temple of, *id.* 169.
Triraśmi: mount, modern Tiranhu, Ushavadáta builds a cave on, I, pt. ii, 148.
Trisáshthi Salákápurushacharitra: lives of sixty-three Jain saints, compiled by Hemachandra, I, pt. i, 193.
Trisirápalli: modern Trichinopoly, inscription at, I, pt. ii, 331.
Triticum æstivum: food and famine plant, XXV, 189, 208.
Triumpheta: *angulata, rotundi folia,* fibrous plants, XXV, 230.
Trivádi: family name among Gujarát Bráhmans, I, pt. ii, 245.
Triváti: musical instrument of the Rattás, I, pt. ii, 522.
Triveni Sangam: holy confluence of the Ganges, the Jumna and the Saraswati at Alláhábád, place of pilgrimage, XIV, 66 and note 1.
Trombay: island in Bombay harbour, Portuguese remains at, XIV, 363; sea trade of, XIII, 359, 360.

Tropidonotus stolatus: a species of snakes in Poona district, XVIII, pt. i, 77.
Tropina: Tirupanatara, near Kochin, mentioned by Pliny, I, pt. i, 533.
Tsa-Ta-li: Kshatriyas, mentioned by Hwan Thsang, I, pt. ii, 184.
Tudáka: country, I, pt. ii, 189.
Tuesday: day sacred to Mars, other names of, beliefs about, IX, pt. i, 401-402; sacredness of, XVIII, pt. i, 240.
Tufaceous Deposits: in Bijápur district, XXIII, 50.
Tughlik: name borne by *jáms*, I, pt. i, 139.
Tughlikhpur: people of, said to have acknowledged Yazdan and Ahrimán; *maghs* of, are believed by Professor Dawson to be the relics of the old Upper India Pársis; infidels of, are believed by Wilford to be Manichæan Christians, IX, pt. ii, 188 note 4.
Tuhfat-ul-Kirám: historical work, I, pt. i, 139, 538.
Tukáji: Kánoji A'ngria's father, founder (1643) of the family, XI, 145; distinguishes himself in Shiváji's fleet, I, pt. ii, 87.
Tukáji Holkar: *see* Tukoji Holkar.
Tukárám: Marátha Váni saint (1608-1649), XVIII, pt. iii, 404; XVIII, pt. ii, 231.
Tuklu: a food-plant, XXV, 173.
Tukoji Holkar: Marátha general (1763-1797), sent to Málwa by Mádhavráo Peshwa (1769), XVIII, pt. ii, 253; favours Raghunáthráo (1778), *id.* 262; opposes English expedition to Poona (1779), *id.* 264; his expedition against Tipu (1786-1787), XXII, 415-416; his death (1797), XVIII, pt. ii, 274; *see* also I, pt. ii, 604.
Tul: food-plant, XXV, 172.
Tuláji A'ngria: (1748-1755), succeeds his brother Sambháji, twice attacks English fleets, captured at the siege of Gheria (1755), XI, 153-154.
Tulapur: village in Poona district, its history, XVIII, pt. iii, 452; Aurangzeb's camp at (1689), XVIII, pt. ii, 238; Sambháji executed at (1689), *id.* 239; I, pt. ii, 596.
Tulas: *see Tulsi.*
Tulava Bráhmans: said to have been made by Parshurám, IX, pt. i, 436.
Tolia Náik: unruly Bhil chief (1867-1876), XII, 312-313.
Tuling: hill at Sopára in Thána district, XIV, 339, 342.
Tulja Bhavani: Hindu goddess, shrine of, in the Nizám's territory, IX, pt i, 549.
Tulja Caves: at Junnar, XVIII, pt. iii, 201-204.
Tullock: Colonel, surveyed the site of the Tulsi lake, XIV, 364, 378.
Tulshibág: Poona city temple, XVIII, pt. iii, 347.
Tulsi: sweet basil plant, held sacred by all classes, XXV, 279, 284, 287, 288; chiefly by Chárans, IX, pt. i, 220; by depressed classes, *id.* 332, 333; Bhangias, *id.* 336; Dhedás, *id.* 341; by Vaishnav Khatris, *id.* 387; regarded as Vishnu's consort; worship of, marriage of, with the image of Vishnu on the bright eleventh of *Kártik*, *id.* 387-388; other occasions for worship; sin-cleansing power of leaves, *id.* 388; leaf put in the mouth of the dead, *id.* 47, 94, 161, 388; offered to Vishnu, *id.* 409.
Tulsi: lake in Thána district, XIII, 12; constructed for water-supply in Bombay, XIV, 363-366.
Tulsi: peak in Kánara district, XV, pt. i, 3.
Tulsi: stream in Kolhápur state, XXIV, 9, 10.
Tulsibái: queen mother of Holkar, beheaded on the bank of the Shipra (1817), XVI, 195.
Tulsi-bij: an oil-yielding plant, XXV, 224.
Tulsirám: form of Lakshmi and Krishna, IX, pt. i, 266.
Tulsishám: hill in Káthiáwár, VIII, 12; place of pilgrimage, origin of the name, *id.* 666-667; IX, pt. i, 549.
Tulu: country conquered by the Hángal Kádamba Kamadeva, I, pt. ii, 563; kings of, conquered by Vishnuvardhana, *id.* 495, 496, 499.
Tu-Lu-H'o-Po-Tu: Chinese name of Dhruvapatu, Valabhi king, I, pt. i, 79.
Tuluva: one of the seven Konkans created by Parashuram, I, pt. ii, 282 note 5, 308.
Tuluvaladevi: Gutta princess, married to Ballála, son of Simha, of the Sántalimandala, I, pt. ii, 579, 583.
Tuluvas: people of Tuluva, defeated by Hoysala Vishnuvardhana, I, pt. ii, 496.
Tumba: famine plant, XXV, 203.
Tumbe: a poisonous plant, XXV, 265.
Tumbige: inscription at, I, pt. ii, 432.
Tuminkatti: village in Dhárwár district, XXII, 788.
Tun: *cedrela toona,* a dye-yielding plant, XXV, 241.
Tuna: port of Anjar in Cutch, V, 252; Fateh Muhammad's attempt to establish a harbour at (1802), *id.* 151, 211; taken by the British (1813), *id.* 158; a lighthouse at, VIII, 18, 23.
Tundáka: *see* Tonda.
Tundás: literally beliefless epicures, Khojáhs so called, IX, pt. ii, 44.
Tundira: *see* Tonda.
Tundírapurai: name of Káñchi, capital of the Pallava kings, I, pt. ii, 318.
Tundis: old trade centre in Tamil country, mentioned in the *Periplus*, XV, pt. ii, 48 and note 3.
Tung: peak in Poona district, XVIII, pt. i, 5.
Tunga: river in Mysore territory, I, pt. ii, 441.
Tungabhadrá: river in Dhárwár and Kánara districts, XXII, 5-6; XV, pt. i, 7; I, pt. ii, 186, 198; the southern boundary of the Ráshtrakúta kingdom under Govinda III, *id.* 199, 216, 217; Someśvara I, the Western Chálukya king of Kalyáni, drowns himself in, *id.* 215-216, 217, 377, 395, 396, 442, 444, 445, 454, 500, 580, 582 note 4, 659.
Tungár: hill in Thána district, temple at, proposed site for a sanitarium, XIV, 366-369; *see* also XIII, 6; mentioned in *Puránás*, I, pt. ii, 28.
Tungbhadra: see Tungabhadra.
Tungi: fort in Thána district, XIV, 98, 370.
Tungjái: hill in Kolhápur state, XXIV, 8.
Tuni, Tunna: medicinal plant, XXV, 258.
Tunnel: in Sátára, XIX, 560.

Tupat Komti: *see* Komti.
Tupkoty: fibrous plant, XXV, 228, 230.
Tur: pulse variety, food-plant, XXV, 153; cultivation of, in Ratnágiri district, X, 148; in Násik district, XVI, 100; in Poona district, XVIII, pt. ii, 43-44; in Sátára district, XIX, 163.
Tural: village in Ratnágiri district, hot springs at, X, 21.
Turanmal: hill in Khándesh district, XII, 4; legends of, *id.* 238.
Turannes boas: possible identification of, with Rájápur, X, 192 note 3, 360 note 2; XV, pt. ii, 48 note 3.
Turashkas: Turks, I, pt. i, 189; Musalmán kings of Dalhi, I, pt. ii, 509, 525; army of, dispersed by Mularája II in childhood, I, pt. i, 195 and note 4.
Turi: caste of drummers in Gujarát, strength, IX, pt. i, 207, 225; origin, object of worship, custom, *id.* 225-227; in Káthiáwár, VIII, 157.
Turk Bábi: Musalmán sub-division in Kánara district, XV, pt. i, 400, 411.
Turkheda: town in Khándesh, fort at, XII, 477.
Turki Hajám: caste of barbers in Gujarát of mixed origin, two divisions of: Jokháris and Hajáms, duties of, character, Sunnis by religion, honour saint Sulaimán Fáras, IX, pt. ii, 84-85.
Turks: immigrants into India, route by which they entered India, aid to Bráhmans, IX, pt. i, 455; beaten by Sri-Harsha, *id.* 448; Gujars suggested to be, *id.* 469; defeat the White Húnas, I, pt. i, 497; their territories in India bordered on Kumárapalá's kingdom (1143), *id.* 189; their conquests in Thána district (1300-1500), XIII, 438, 439; defeat the Portuguese (1586), I, pt. ii, 45.
Turmeric: *see* Halad.
Turmeric Pounding: ceremony among Pársis pertaining to marriage, IX, pt. ii, 233.
Turmeric rubbing: ceremony among Pátáne Prabhus, XVIII, pt. i, 198-199.
Turturinæ: family of birds in Ratnágiri, X, 86.
Turushkas: *see* Turashkas.
Tushásps: Yavana governor of Aśoka in Suráshtra, I, pt. i, 14.
Tut: mulberry tree in Poona district, XVIII, pt. i, 53; XXV, 173.
Twelvers: divisions of Shiáhs, IX, pt. ii, 47. *See* Isnaashari and Shiáh.
Two-headed Snake: in Poona district, XVIII, pt. i, 80.
Two Sisters: tomb of the, in Bijápur city, XXIII, 614.
Tylophora: *asthmathica*, medicinal plant, XXV, 256; *fasciculata*, poisonous plant, *id.* 267.
Tyndis: Kadalundi, the mart of the Tamil country, mentioned in the *Periplus*, I, pt. i, 546.
Typhonium: *bulbiferum*, food-plant, XXV, 183; *bulbiferum* and *divaricatum*, famine plants, *id.* 207.
Tyre: its probable trade connection with India (B. C. 588), XIII, 404 note 3.
Tytler: Mr. Fraser, his settlement of the Dángs, in Násik district and reports (1841-1860), XVI, 205 note 1, 217, 230-245, 424.

U

UBAIDULLAH-IBNI ZIAD: besieges and slaughters the holy martyrs of Karbala, IX, pt. ii, 138.
Ubatna: cosmetic rub, IX, pt. ii, 163, 164.
Uben: river in Káthiáwár, VIII, 164.
Uccha: probably Uch.
Uch: in the Panjáb, Pársi settlement in (1184); connection of the Pársis of, with those of Cambay, IX, pt. ii, 186 note 1, 188 note 4.
Uchad: state in Rewa Kántha, VI, 146.
Uchchangidurg: in the Bellary district of the Madras Presidency, I, pt. ii, 285 note 5.
Uchchangidurg: in the Chitaldurg district of Mysore, a Kadamba inscription connected with, I, pt. ii, 285 note 5.
Uchchangidurg: capital of Nolambavádi, I, pt. ii, 319 and note 1, 486; fortress at, reduced by Hoysala Vishnuvardhana, *id.* 496; taken by Hoysala Vira, Ballála II, *id.* 505; hill fort at, *id.* 456; probably identified with Uchchangidurg in the Bellary district, *id.* 319.
Uchchangigiri: lord of, I, pt. ii, 285 note 5, 564. *See* Uchchaśringi.
Uchchaśringi: identified with Uchchangidurg in the Chitaldurg district of Mysore; one of the capitals of early Kadambas, I, pt. ii, 285 and note 5.
Uchitgad: fort in Ratnágiri district, X, 373.
Uchla, Uchlia: a caste of pick-pockets in Poona district, origin, disguises, special language, modes of stealing, admittance into the caste, initiation ceremony, appearance, dress, houses, food, ornaments, character, caste rules, customs, oil ordeal, religion, XVIII, pt. i, 464-476; in Sátára district, XIX, 122-123. *See* also Bhamta.
Ucla: a timber tree, XXV, 125.
Uda: *see* Udaya.
Udachavva: Hindu goddess, image of, at Hire-Handigol in Dhárwár district, I, pt. ii, 422 note 3.
Udaipur, Udepur: in Rájpútána, *rána* of, premier Hindu prince in India, head of Gohils, IX, pt. i, 125; his divine power, *id.* 436 note 1, 441 note 1; conquest of, by Arabs, IX, pt. ii, 1 note 1; family of, said to have sprung from the son of Khosru Parviz, 183 note 4.
Udáji Chawhán: seizes the fort of Battis Shirála and is won over by Sháhu by the grant of the *chauth* of Shirála and Karád, I, pt. ii, 599; XIX, 257.
Udaji Pavar: Marátha officer, XIX, 268; captures (1696) Mandu, I, pt. i, 382; his incursions into Málwa, VII, 168; sent by the Peshwa as a check against the Gaikwár; defeats Piláji; joins a league against the Peshwa; captured (1731); his death, *id.* 171, 172, 173, 174; *see* also I, pt. i, 14, 302.
Udaleśvara: temple, mentioned in an inscription from Bhadresar, I, pt. i, 172.

Udambara: Hindu sage, Udambaras of Gujarát take name from, IX, pt. i, 20.
Udambara: a town in Gujarát, Bráhmans said to have come from Márwár and Rájpútána to, IX, pt. i, 2; Kumárapála takes shelter at, I, pt. i, 182.
Udambara: Kanakamuni's tree of knowledge, XIV, 331, 412.
Udar: timber tree, XXV, 19.
Udási: Hindu religious sect in Gujarát, IX, pt. i, 547.
Udaya: minister of Chaulukya king Karna and builder of the temple Udaya-Varáha, I, pt. i, 170; minister during Siddharája's minority, *id.* 172.
Udayachandra: one of Kumárapála's leading *pandits*, I, pt. i, 190.
Udayachandra: of the Puchán family, renders to his hereditary master Nandivarman Pallava various services, I, pt. ii, 326-327.
Udayachandramangala: modern Udayendiram, I, pt. ii, 327.
Udayadevapandita: *see* Niravadyapandita, I, pt. ii, 191.
Udayáditya: successor of Bhoja, inscription of, at Udepur, I, pt. i, 164.
Udayaditya: Kumárapála's inscription in the temple of, at Udayapura near Bhilsa, I, pt. i, 185.
Udayaditya: brother of Hoysala Vishnuvardhana, I, pt. ii, 493, 500.
Udayaditya: officer of Someśvara II, I, pt. ii, 443.
Udayaditya: Ganga chief of Banavási (1075), XV, pt. ii, 87.
Udayáditya-Ganga-Permádi, Bhuvanaikavira: Western Ganga prince and feudatory of Vikramáditya VI, I, pt. ii, 428 note 4, 452.
Udayápitya-Vira-Kálarasa: of the Bána race, I, pt. ii, 486.
Udayagiri Caves: near Bhilsa, Gupta inscriptions at, I, pt. i, 65-66.
Udayamati: queen of Bhima I, builds a step well at Anahilaváda, I, pt. i, 169; persuades her son Karna to marry Miyanalladevi, *id.* 171.
Udayana: Siddharája's minister, helps Kumárapála, I, pt. i, 183; appointed minister by Kumárapála, *id.* 184; mortally wounded in the fight with the king of Suráshtra, *id.* 186.
Udayana: Sábara king, slain at Nelveli by Udayachandra the Pallava general, I, pt. ii, 326.
Udayana: king, mentioned by Táranáth in his *History of Buddhism*, I, pt. ii, 171.
Udayapura: near Bhilsa, inscription of Udayáditya at, I, pt i, 164; Kumárapála's inscription in the temple at, *id.* 185; grant to the god of, *id.* 187, 194 note 4.
Udayasimhadeva: Chohán king, captures Bhinmál, I, pt. i, 470.
Udaya Varáha: temple at Karnávati, I, pt. i, 170.
Udayendiram: in the North Arcot district, Madras, grant from, I, pt. ii, 299 note 4, 319 note 2, 320 note 6, 322, 324 note 1, 325 note 4, 327, 351.
Udbhata: S'iva's attendant, I, pt. ii, 482.
Udepur: *see* Udayapura.
Udepur: early capital of Rewa Kántha, VI, 169; VII, 334.
Udgir: a village about 160 miles east of Ahmdanagar, battle of, between the Maráthás under Sadáshivráo Bháu and the Nizám (1760), I, pt. ii, 627; XVII, 404; XVIII, pt. ii, 249; XXIII, 441.
Udha: a timber tree, XXV, 137.
Udhali Budruk: village in Khándesh district, temple at, XII, 477.
Udhali Khurd: village in Khándesh district, temple at, XII, 477.
Udid: *see* Urid.
Udrak: timber tree, XXV, 29.
Udras: tribe, subdued by Sahadeva, I, pt. ii, 142.
Udul: timber tree, XXV, 70.
Udváda: village of, fifteen miles south of Balsár, Sauján fire finally remains at, IX, pt. ii, 185 note 2, 193.
Ufflet: Nicholas, English merchant (1611), describes Gujarát, I, pt. i, 224 note 2, 449 and note 2.
Ughad: Márwár astrologer, father of Bhadli, IX, pt. i, 351.
Ugradauda-Lokáditya-Parameśvaravarman I: Pallava king, contemporary of Vikramáditya I, I, pt. ii, 291 note 1, 329, 330. *See* Parmeśvaravarman I.
Ugrasena: legendary Yádava chief of Dwárka, I, pt. i, 9.
Ugrasená: king of Palakka, mentioned in an Allahábád pillar inscription, I, pt. ii, 280.
Ugravarman: successor of the Pallava king Arkavarman, I, pt. ii, 331.
Ujalváv: village in Káthiáwár, VIII, 667.
Ujáni: caste picnics in Gujarát, IX, pt. i, p. xxvii.
Ujjain, Ujjayini: city in Málwa, I, pt. ii, 139, 583; I, pt. i, 174; visited by Kumárapála in his exile, *id.* 183, 513 note 9; Kshatrapas of, I, pt. ii, 153; satraps at, *id.* 157, 160, 161, 169, 170; Dantidurga's charity at, *id.* 195; Akalavarsha-Krishnarája conquers his enemies at, *id.* 414; king Vikramáditya of, *id.* 578, 579, 580, 581, 582, 583 584; conquest of, by Arabs (724); appanage of Chitor, IX, pt. ii, 1 note 1 continued on page 2; former seat of the head priest of the Daudi Bohorás, *id.* 31 note 4; Yashavantráv Holkar defeats Sindia's troops at the battle of (1801), XVIII, pt. ii, 281.
Ujjánta: Júnágad hill, possibly conquered by the Arabs, IX, pt. ii, 1 note 1 continued on page 2. *See* Girnár.
Ujli: stream in Kánara district, XV, pt. i, 5.
Ujli Varan: bright coloured race in Gujarát, chief classes, IX, pt. i, p. x; divisions: upper class called Bráhman Vania, lower class called Ghánchi Gola, *id.* p. xxv; object of worship; beliefs, *id.* p. x; settlements, *id.* pp. xi-xii; castes, *id.* pp. xii-xiv; language, *id.* p. xv.
Ukardi Notarvi: dung-hill asking ceremony among Gujarát Bráhmans, IX, pt. i, 42.
Ukund: village in Dhárwár district, temple and inscribed copper-plates at, XXII, 788.
Ulabalandaperumál: temple at Conjevaram, inscription at, I, pt. ii, 331.

Ulamas: Musalmán learned men of Ahmadábád, drew up a charge of apostacy against Sayad Muhammad, IX, pt. ii, 63.
Ulandi: small boat in Ratnágiri district, X, 171.
Ulavi: *see* Ulvi.
Ulavi: high magic among Musalmáns, IX, pt. ii, 143.
Ulhás: river in Thána district, XIII, 10.
Ullu: timber tree, XXV, 104.
Ulmus Integrifolia: timber tree, XXV, 132.
Ulpár: a village in Surat, Suraha is confounded with, by Ibn Haukal and Al Istakhri, XIV, 321.
Ulugh Khán: brother to Alá-ud-din, sometimes by mistake is called A'lp Khán, conquers Gujarát (1295-1297), IX, pt. ii, 187 note 3; I, pt. i, 229, 512, 515. *See* A'lp Khán.
Ulvi: village in Kánara district, roads, remains, temple and fair at, XV, pt. ii, 56, 90, 352-354; Basava takes refuge at, I, pt. ii, 227, 480; Lingáyat place of pilgrimage, XXIV, 119, 120.
Uma: or Umia, Kanbi goddess, IX, pt. i, p. xxxvi; temple of, at Unja, *id.* 164, 165, 226.
Umábái: widow of Khánderáv Dábháde and mother of Yashavantráv Dábháde; goes to Gujarát to avenge Piláji's death and marches upon Ahmadábád, I, pt. i, 314, 393; intrigues of, against the Peshwa; recognises Dámáji as her agent in Gujarát (1736), *id.* 394; causes Rangoji to be set at liberty and re-appoints him her agent in Gujarát (1745), *id.* 329, 396; dies (1748), *id.* 332, 396; *see* also VII, 174-176, 179.
Umad: caste of traders in Rewa Kántha, VI, 24.
Umadi; state in Mahi Kántha, V, 429.
Umáji Náik: Rámoshi freebooter (1827) in Thána district, XIII, 634-635; in Poona district, XVIII, pt. ii, 307.
Umá-maheshwar: Násik temple, XVI, 505.
Umán: Persian Gulf, I, pt. i, 505, 523.
Umar: (634-643), son of Khattáb, second Khalifáh, his prejudice against India, IX, pt. ii, note 1, 125; founds the city of Basra, sends fleets to ravage the Thána coast, *id.* 183 note 4; suffers death as a martyr, *id.* 136; *see* also I, pt. i, 505 and note 5, 513, 523.
Umar-Al-Fárúk: ancestor of the Fáruki *shaikhs*, IX, pt. ii, 8.
Umar Cheyam: astronomer, directed by Jalál-ud-din Malik Sháh, king of Persia, to make a calendar, IX, pt. ii, 193 note 2.
Umarda: place in Káthiáwár, founded about 200 years ago, VIII, 667.
Umardaki: river in Pálanpur, V, 317.
Umar Ibnal Khattáb: *see* Umar.
Umarkhádi Jail: in Bombay island, built (1799-1802), XXVI, pt. iii, 56-57.
Umbar, Umar, Umari: timber tree, XXV, 131; in Khándesh district, XII, 28; in Poona district, XVIII, pt. i, 53; believed to be the resting place of sage Bhrigu, worshipped during *Navrátri* holidays, IX, pt. i, 388.
Umbará: village in Láta country, I, pt. ii, 416.
Umbarda: pass between Kolába district and Bhor state, XI, 5, 114.
Umbarda: pass in Násik district, XVI, 128.
Umbargaon: a town in Thána district, Portuguese tower and fire temple at, XIV, 370; sea trade at, XII, 357; survey assessment introduced at (1864), 614-616.
Umbelliferæ: order of food-plants, XXV, 160.
Umbhel, Umbher: village near Surat, I, pt. ii, 370.
Umbraj: trade centre in Sátára district, XIX, 215; village and a place of interest, *id.* 597.
Umeta: state in Rewa Kántha, VI, 151; town, copper-plate grant from, I, pt. i, 113 note 6, 117; I, pt. ii, 312 note 7.
Umia: *see* Uma.
Ummad: a caste of Vániás, Mesbri, IX, pt. i, 74; Shráváks, take name from Humda, their spiritual head, *id.* 98.
Umrala: place of interest in Káthiáwár, VIII, 667.
Umreth: town in Kaira district, III, 178.
Umro Patkar: Káthi leader, marriage of his daughter with a Rajpút chief of Dhánk, IX, pt. i, 252.
Umvárá: identified with Umra, I, pt. i, 130.
Una: place of interest in Káthiáwár, a celebrated inscription at, VIII, 667.
Unábdev: place of interest in Khándesh district, XII, 477; hot springs at, *id.* 12.
Unad: son of Lakha, the Samma Rájpút chief of Sind, V, 132.
Unái: goddess among Gujarát Hindus, IX, pt. i, p. xxxvi.
Unai: place of pilgrimage in Surat district, II, 333; hot springs at, their sacredness, IX, pt. i, 157, 336, 341, 350, 549; fair at, VII, 170, 581-582.
Unáva: village in Baroda state, temple at, VII, 619.
Unch: river in Baroda, VII, 13.
Uncha Kotra: place of interest in Káthiáwár, ancient capital of the Vajas, VIII, 668.
Unchaya: *táluka* in Káthiáwár, VIII, 669.
Unchhali: falls in Kánara district, XV, pt. ii, 352.
Und: river in Káthiáwár, VIII, 63.
Undarau: apparently Vindhya mountain, I, pt. i, 517.
Underi: Henery island on Kolába coast, taken and fortified by the Sidis (1680), XI, 145, 440-441; I, pt. ii, 72; XIII, 479; defended by the British against Maráthás, (1733), XXVI, pt. i, 163-170; taken (1759) by Angria, XI, 155; lapses (1840) to the British, *id.* 159, 190; revenue survey (1857), *id.* 200-201; *see* also *id.* 215.
Undi: oil-yielding tree in Ratnágiri district, X, 37, 39.
Undikavátiká: a village granted to a Bráhman by Abhimanyu, Ráshtrakúta king, I, pt. ii, 386.
Undirkheda: place of interest in Khándesh district, a beautiful temple at, XII, 477.
Undivana Koshthaka: modern Urrukkádu near Conjevaram, I, pt. ii, 325.

Und Sarvaiya : ancient sub-division of Káthiáwár, VIII, 5.
Unevál : caste of Gujarát Bráhmans come from Márwár and Rájputána, IX, pt. i, 2, 20.
Ungulata : order of animals in Ratnágiri district, X, 45.
Unhále : village in Ratnágiri district, sacred intermittent spring at, X, 22, 131.
Unheri : in Kolába district, hot springs at, XI, 13.
Unikankan : *see* Kurubar.
United Service Library : in Poona Cantonment, XVIII, pt. iii, 399-400.
Unja : village in Baroda state, temple at, VII, 620; tradition regarding the foundation of, IX, pt. i, 164 ; shrine of Miran Sayad Ali at, IX, pt. ii, 56, 128, 148.
Unkal : village in Dhárwár district, temples and inscriptions at, XXII, 788.
Unona pannosa : a timber tree, XXV, 2.
Unsettled Tribes : in Poona district, XVIII, pt. i, 406-431 ; in Pálanpur, V, 291; in Mahi Kántha, *id.* 366, 367; in Kolába district, XI, 71-72; in Khandesh district, XII, 79-114 ; in Ahmadnagar district, XVII, 188-214 ; in Sátára district, XIX, 108-109 ; in Sholápur district, XX, 163-169.
Untadia : place of pilgrimage in Baroda territory, IX, pt. i, 549.
Untdi : *táluka* in Káthiáwár, VIII, 669.
Untiavadar : *táluka* in Káthiáwár, VIII, 669.
Upakeságaccha : author of *Pattavali*, I, pt. i, 469.
Upanayana : *see* Thread girding.
Upar : a caste of grindstone-makers in Kolhápur, XXIV, 99-100.
Uparavata : Viradhavala's horse, I, pt. i, 201.
Uplea Kamal : food-plant, XXV, 143.
Upleta : a town in Gondál state in Káthiáwár, palace and dispensary at, VIII, 669.
Uppaliká : territorial division mentioned in a Karda grant, I, pt. ii, 423.
Uppár : a caste of salt-makers in Belgaum district, XXI, 148, 149 ; in Kánara district, XV, pt. i, 280-281.
Uppinakatte : given to flames by the Sinda prince Achugi II, I, pt. ii, 574.
Uppu Nádor : a caste of husbandmen in Kánara district, XV, pt. i, 228.
Upri : Bijápur tower, XXIII, 638-639.
Upris : yearly tenants in Ratnágiri district, X, 203, 210; non-hereditary tenants in Násik district, XVI, 209; in Khándesh district, XII, 266.
Upton : Colonel, special envoy deputed (1776) by the Calcutta government to negotiate with ministers in Poona, I, pt. i, 406 ; XIII, 502; concludes the treaty of Purandhar, XVIII, pt. ii, 259-260.
Upupidæ : family of birds in Ratnágiri district, X, 69.
Uraizis : chief *sayad* family in Gujarát, IX, pt. ii, 6 note 1 (7).
Uran : town in Thána district, municipality and custom house at, XIV, 371-372; a stone grant found at, *id.* 32; a Silahára town, I, pt. ii, 16, 21 ; sea trade of, XIII, 360-361 ; distilleries, *id.* 395-397, 423, 428, 456, 528 ; survey assessment (1866), *id.* 620-621.
Uraps or Varaps : sub-caste of the Agris, Christian reverts in Thána district, XIII, 117, 201 note 2.
Uras : death-day fairs, IX, pt. ii, 56 ; yearly meetings in honor of saints, *id.* 133 note 2 ; at Bhiwndi in Thána district, XIV, 48.
Urchan : battle of (1544), between Ibrahim and Burhan Nizám, XXIII, 415.
Urdhva Báhu : order of Shiv ascetics, IX, pt. i 544.
Urid, Udid : a fodder plant, XXV, 277.
Urmodi : river in Sátára district, XIX, 14.
Urostigma : *Bengalense, benjamineum, cordifolium, dasycarpum, infectorium, nitidum, religiosum, retusum,* timber trees, XXV, 129, 130.
Urpattan : Olpád, origin of the name, IX, pt. i, 12 note 1.
Urrukkádu, Urrukkáttukkotta : village near Conjevaram, I, pt. ii, 325.
Urticaceæ : order of timber trees, XXV, 126.
Uruli : village in Poona district, Cornets Hunter and Morrison captured at (1817), XVIII, pt. iii, 452-453.
Urun-Islámpur : town in Sátára district, XIX, 597-600.
Urn-Ranavikránta : *biruda* of Mangaleśa, I, pt. ii, 347.
Uruvupalli : village in the Mundaráshtra country, I, pt. ii, 320.
Usas : *see* Oswáls.
Usha : daughter of Bánásur, dedicates herself to perpetual virginity, XIV, 81.
Ushavadáta : son of Dinika and son-in-law of Nahapan ; was the Konkan and Dakhan viceroy of his father-in-law Nahapan (A. D. 100), XII, 239 note 7; XVIII, pt. ii, 213 and note 8; XIV, 54; built rest-houses and alms-houses, *id.* 320 ; his public works and gifts, I, pt. i, 25-26 ; XVI, 614-615 ; his probable conversion to Buddhism, XIII, 411 and note 3 ; his inscriptions, I, pt. ii, 148, 149, 154, 157, 173, 176 ; XVI, 571, 573, 574, 576, 578.
Usman ; third Khalifáh (643-655), sends a special officer to India, I, pt. i, 505 note 5.
Usman : governor of Bahrein and Persian Gulf, sends (636) a plundering expedition to Hindustán, I, pt. i, 505, 513, 523; *see* also XIV, 355.
Usnai : rent and cesses in Kolába district, XI, 190.
Ustvat : second Gáthá day among Párais, IX, pt. ii, 218.
Usutri : *see* Malalu.
Utan : port and town in Thána district, XIV, 372 ; three land-grant stones found at, about 1835, *id.* 418-419.
Utbah : governor of Basrah, sent to India by Umar, I, pt. i, 505 note 5 ; IX, pt. ii, 1 note 1.
Utegar : a caste of shepherds in Koláha district, XI, 67.

Uthamna : rising from mourning, ceremony relating to, observances in, among Pársis, IX, pt. ii, 242.

Uthlápát : sweet rice land in Kolába district, XI, 190.

Uthman : lawful heir of the prophet according to Sunnis, IX, pt. ii, 125, 136.

Uthmán-ath-Thákafi : *see* Usman, governor of Bahrein.

Utkal : sub-division of Gaud Bráhmans, IX, pt. i, 1 note 1.

Utkala : Orissa, I, pt. ii, 142 ; king of, defeated by Mallugi, the Yádava king, *id.* 235, 516.

Utkalas : people of Orissa, defeated by Mularája, I, pt. ii, 431.

Utricularia Albocærulea : plant with purple flowers, I, pt. ii, 28.

Utsarpini : Jain age, I, pt. i, 193.

Uttamabhadras : Kshatriyas, king of, relieved by Ushavadáta from an attack of the Málayas, I, pt. ii, 148.

Uttamapurushas : Jain saints, I, pt. i, 451 note 3.

Uttamiyar : female demon killed by Párvati, I, pt. i, 455.

Uttara-Purána : latter half of the *Máha Purána* compiled by Gunabhadra, I, pt. ii, 407, 411.

Uttara Rámacharita : Sanskrit drama by Bhávabhuti, I, pt. ii, 136.

Uttaráyana Samkránti : the winter solstice, I, pt. ii, 466.

Uttar Bhudargad : hill spur in Kolhápur, XXIV, 23.

Uttungabhuja : father of Nanda, comes from Upper India and settles to the south of the Godávari, I, pt. ii, 340 note 4.

Uzain : identified with Ujjaini ; expedition against, I, pt. i, 109, 467.

V

VACCINATION : Pátáne Prabhu ceremony, XVIII, pt. i, 224-225 ; Beni Israel ceremony, *id.* 531 ; in Surát district, II, 265 ; in Broach district, *id.* 533 ; in Kaira district, III, 141 ; in Panch Maháls, *id.* 291 ; in Ahmadábád district, IV, 227 ; in Cutch, V, 208-209 ; in Pálanpur, *id.* 316 ; in Mahi Kántha, *id.* 396 ; in Rewa Kántha, VI, 90 ; in Baroda territory, VII, 270, 512 ; in Káthiáwár, VIII, 354 ; in Ratnágiri district, X, 295 ; in Sávantvádi, *id.* 461 ; in Kolába district, XI, 238 ; in Janjira state, *id.* 460 ; in Khándesh district, XII, 340 ; in Thána district, XIII, 668-669 ; in Kánara district, staff, details, cost, XV, pt. ii, 220 ; in Násik district, XVI, 343 ; in Ahmadnagar district, XVII, 584-585 ; in Poona district, XVIII, pt. iii, 69 ; in Sátára district, XIX, 418 ; in Sholápur district, XX, 388 ; in Belgaum district, XXI, 491, 492 ; in Dhárwár district, XXII, 623-624 ; in Bijápur district, XXIII, 526 ; in Kolhápur state, XXIV, 288 ; a pamphlet on (1803), published in Bombay island, XXVI, pt. iii, 564.

Vacha, Vachania : land tenure in Baroda state, VII, 351.

Váchaspatimisra : author of the *Bhámati*, a commentary on *Vedantasutrabhashya*, I, pt. ii, 245.

Vachha : lord of the Agra race, said to have started Chandravansa and Vachha clans ; said to be head of Sámbhar Chohána, IX, pt. i, 450.

Vachhya : Rájpút clan founded by lord Vachha, IX, pt. i, 450.

Vachran : goddess of the Gujarát *sutárs*, IX, pt. i, 205.

Vád : *táluka* in Káthiáwár, VIII, 669.

Vad : *Ficus Bengalensis*, a timber tree, XXV, 129 ; in Khándesh district, XII, 24 ; in Poona district, XVIII, pt. i, 54 ; Indian fig, believed to be the emblem of Shiv ; worship of, by women on full moon days, object of the worship, IX, pt. i, 388.

Váda : religious discussion, I, pt. i, 181.

Váda : sub-division of Thána district, its boundaries, area, aspect, climate, water, soil, holdings, rental, stock crops and people, XIII, 675-678. *Town, id.* 528 ; XIV, 372 ; inscription of Suketuvarman at, XIII, 420 ; I, pt. i, 107.

Vadádra : Bráhman sub-caste in Gujarát, said to be immigrants from Upper India, IX, pt. i, 2, 20.

Vádágám : state in Mahi Kántha, V, 425.

Vadagra : superior quality salt prepared in Ahmadábád district, IV, 117.

Vadal : *táluka* in Káthiáwár, VIII, 670.

Vádál : pass in Násik district, XVI, 130.

Vadáli : ancient town in Mahi Kántha, has a revenue and police-station, V, 442.

Vadáli : *táluka* in Káthiáwár, VIII, 670.

Vadáli : canal in Násik district, XVI, 94.

Vadapadraka : village identified with Baroda, I, pt. i, 125 ; I, pt. ii, 399.

Vadar, Vaddar : a caste of wood-cutters and quarrymen in Ratnágiri, X, 128 ; in Kolába district, XI, 72 ; in Janjira state, *id.* 414 ; in Khándesh district, XII, 114 ; in Thána district, XIII, 181-182 ; in Násik district, XVI, 64, 65 ; in Ahmadnagar district, 141-145 ; in Poona district, XVIII, pt. i, 426-428 ; in Sátára district, XIX, 97 ; in Sholápur, district, XX, 167-169 ; in Belgaum district, XXI, 177 ; in Bijápur district, XXIII, 210-213 ; in Kolhápur, XXIV, 31, 108-109 ; in Kánara district, XV, pt. i, 347, 348 ; in Dhárwár district, XXII, 197-198.

Vadaran : *see* Goli.

Vadávali : sub-division in Baroda, its boundaries, area, aspect, water, soil, occupancy, and population, VII, 607, 608.

Vaddar : *see* Vadar.

Vaddáravula : tax of Chángadevayya, I, pt. ii, 450, 451.

Vaddi : pass in Kánara district, XV, pt. ii, 39, 40, 354.

Vaddiga : Amoghavarsha, the Ráshtrakúta king, successor of Govinda IV, I, pt. ii, 414 note 1, 418 ; his *biruda*, epithet, and titles, *id.* 418 ; his wife, *id.* 296, 418.

Vaddiga : Yádava chief of Seunadeśa, feudatory of the Ráshtrakúta king Krishna III, I, pt. ii, 231, 232, 420, 513 ; successor of Bhillama III, *id.* 234, 231, 515.

Váde ; market town in Poona disrict, temple at, XVIII, pt. iii, 453-454.

Vadenpur : village in Dhárwár district, inscription at, XXII, 788.
Vade Padel : village in Ratnágiri district, caves at, I, pt. ii, 9.
Vadgaon : a village in the Mával *táluka* of the Poona district, convention of 1779 signed at, XVIII, pt. iii 453 ; XVIII, pt. ii, 265-266 ; XIV 201 ; XIII, 318, 504, 505; I, pt. ii, 103, 605 ; convention of, disallowed by the Bombay council, I, pt. i, 407.
Vadgaon : a village in the Khed *táluka* of the Poona district, temple at, XVIII, pt. iii, 453.
Vadgaon : town in Kolhápur state, its history, temples at, XXIV, 321.
Vadgaon : a village in Khándesh district, temple at, XII, 478.
Vadgaon Amba : an important market town in Khándesh district, a temple and a well at, XII, 478.
Vadgaon Darya: a village in Ahmadnagar district, caverns at, XVII, 741.
Vadhávan : a petty Bhil state in Khándesh district, XII, 606.
Vadhávo : presents, giving of, during pregnancy ceremony among Pársis, IX, pt. ii, 229.
Vadhel : Rajpúts of Ráthod clan in Káthiáwár, VIII, 110 ; drive the Chavadás from Dwárka, IX, pt. i, 129.
Vadhias : village in Pálanpur state, original seat of the Chávadas, V, 349-350 ; I, pt. i, 149, 150.
Vadhrira : village identified with Berdi, I, pt. ii, 420.
Vadhvan : a city in Gujarát, ancient capital of Chápa dynasty, I, pt. i, 138, 139, 180 note 2, 186, 469 ; Jhala Rájpút chiefship, IX, pt. i, 127, 488.
Vádi : meaning of the word, I, pt. ii, 298 note 3.
Vadi : Sávantvádi, insurrection in (1844-1845), I, pt. ii, 129.
Vadi : estate in Rewa Kántha, VI, 98.
Vadi : wandering caste of mill-sellers in Káthiáwár, VIII, 159.
Vádia : family among early Pársi settlers in Bombay, IX, pt. ii, 195. *See* Lavji Nasarvanji Vádia.
Vádi Machál : hill fort, in Kolhápur, XXIV, 4.
Vádi Narsinh : town in Kolhápur, temples and fair at, XXIV, 321, 322.
Vádiráj : Vaishnav *guru* (1582), XV, pt. ii, 346-347.
Vádi Ratnágiri : *see* Jotibá's hill.
Vádla : hot spring in Khándesh district, XII, 13.
Vadnagar : town in Baroda territory, fairs and temple at, VII, 623-624 ; hospitals at, *id.* 508 ; dynastic seat, IX, pt. i, p. ix ; original seat of Nágar Bráhmans, *id.* 13, 15 ; said to have been founded by Kanaksen, *id.* 15 and note 1 ; identified with Anarttapura, *id.* 13 note 2 ; installation of Shiv's *ling* under the name of Hatakeshvar at, *id.* 14 ; besieged by Antáji Bháskar, again by Kantaji, burnt (1725), I, pt. i, 370, 467, 546.
Vadnagara : sub-caste of Nágar Bráhmans, IX, pt. i, 13, 15.
Vadod : a tribute paying *táluka* in Káthiáwár, VIII, 670.
Vad Pornima : Hindu holiday, XVIII, pt. i, 243-244.
Vadsar : Káthi chief of Jasdan, model landlord, IX, pt. i, 254.
Vadshighat : hill in Sholápur district, XX, 2.
Vadtál : village in Kaira district, head-quarters of the Svámi Náráyan sect, III, 178-180 ; IX, pt. i, 537, 549.
Vádugi : *see* Vaddiga the Yadava chief.
Vaduj : town in Sátára district, XIX, 600.
Vágabhava : *see* Báhada.
Vagad : province in Cutch, V, 2, 131, 138.
Vágadh : a village near Rádhanpur, I, pt. i, 208 note 3.
Vagatores : birds in Thána district, XIII, 53.
Vághbhata : Sanskrit medical author, I, pt. ii, 249.
Vageshankar Gavrishankar : Mr., *naib diván* of Bhávnagar ; his collection of articles found in Valabhi, I, pt. i, 78 note 1.
Vaggayá : a caste of beggars in Dhárwár district, XXII, 212-213 ; ministrants at the fair of Gudguddápur, *id.* 721.
Vagghachchha : modern Vághodia near Baroda, I, pt. i, 125.
Vaghácháрathár : Tiger's Terrace, hill in Thána district, XIII, 5.
Vághad : a village in Násik district, reservoir at, XVI, 95.
Vágham Chávdagud : a village in Cutch, temples at, V, 252-253.
Vághandevi : goddess of the Chodhras, IX, pt. i, 378.
Vagharia : pass in Násik district, XVI, 129.
Vaghavri : a tribute paying táluka in Káthiáwar, VIII, 670.
Vághbáras : tiger's twelfth, worship of tiger on, IX, pt. i, 378.
Vagh Dev : tiger god, worship of, by early tribes in Gujarát, IX, pt. i, 292, 319, 322 ; worshipped by Poona Kunbis, XVIII, pt. I, 291.
Vághe : *see* Vaghya.
Vaghela : a town near Pálanpur, V, 350 ; I, pt. i, 465.
Vághela Rájpúts : in Cutch, V, 68-69, 132, 133, 138 ; in Káthiáwár, VIII, 115, 284. *See* Vághelas.
Vághelas : branch of the Chalukyas of Anahiláváda, help the last Chalukya king and succeed him, I, pt. i, 196-197 ; their rule and genealogy, *id.* 198-206 ; Rájpút rulers of Gujarát (1240-1304) after the Solankis, *id.* 526 ; I, pt. ii, 525 and note 4, 582 note 1 ; existing chiefships, IX, pt. i, 129 ; Chamunda their family deity, *id.* 136 ; Shakti-worshippers, worship the horse on Dasara day, worship picture of *koyel* or cuckoo ; pacification of flood-spirits by, *id.* 137 ; rulers of Cambay, VI, 215 ; IX, pt. ii, 2 note 3.
Vagher : a caste of sea-farers and pirates on the Gujarát coast, IX, pt. i, 519 ; name, divisions—Hindus and Musalmáns ; settlements, surnames, *id.* 522 ; origin, appearance, language, character, occupation, religion, *id.* 523 ; Musalmán pirates in Cutch, V, 97 ; in Káthiáwár, VIII, 154, 164-165, 305, 307 ; revolt of, *id.* 308 ; disturbances of (1857-1867), *id.* 364-365.

Vaghera : pass and fort in Násik district, XVI, 128, 660, 661, 441.
Vágheri : hill in Ratnágiri district, a well-known land mark for seamen, X, 469.
Vagheshvari : goddess of Shrimal, family deity of Meshri Shrimali Vániás, IX, pt. i, 73, 200 and note 3.
Vaghili : village in Khándesh district, temples at, XII, 478.
Vágnakhs : tiger's claws, Shiváji murders (1659) Afzulkhán with, XIX, 236 and note 1.
Vághoba : see Vagh Dev Kunbis, XVIII, pt. i, 291.
Vaghoba : hill in Sholápur district, XX, 2.
Vághod : village in Khándesh district, mosque at, XII, 478.
Vághodia : a village north of Baroda, I, pt. i, 125.
Vagholi : a village near Sopara in Thána district, XIV, 514, 322; an inscribed stone at, *id.* 419.
Vághotan : a small village and port on the Vijaydurg river in Ratnágiri district, X, 374.
Vághpur : a village in Ahmadábád district, tombs at, IV, 354.
Vághri : a caste of hunters in Gujarát, strength, meaning of name, history, origin, IX, pt. i, 486, 510-512; divisions, *id.* 512; origin of divisions, appearance, dress, huts, food, means of livelihood, *id.* 513; religion, chief holidays, saints among ancestors, *id.* 514; take pride in the chastity of women, ordeal to prove woman's chastity, *id.* 514-515; vow-making by, fulfilment of, *id.* 516-517; customs, marriage, *id.* 517; birth, death, *id.* 518; in Cutch, V, 82; in Káthiáwár, VIII, 158; in Thána district, XIII, 182.
Vághvihir : pass in Násik district, XVI, 128.
Vághya : a caste of beggars in Sholápur district, XX, 188-189; in Poona district, XVIII, pt. i, 476-477.
Vágjái : hill in Kolhápur, XXIV, 8.
Vagjhipur : village in Baroda state, place of pilgrimage, VII, 591.
Vágra : village in Broach district, I, pt. i, 129 and note 3.
Váhadhasimha : son of Udayasimha, I, pt. i, 471.
Váhadi : mountain pass, Bittigo driven as far as, I, pt. ii, 459, 497, 575.
Váhágaon : gorge in Satára district, XIX, 202.
Vabi Pujan : book worship on last day of the year, details of ceremony among Gujarát Vanias, IX, pt. i, 82.
Vabista Mathra : part of the *Zend Avesta*, IX, pt. ii, 211 note 2 (3).
Vaibhale : a village in Khándesh district, temple at, XII, 478.
Vaidarbha : *see* Vidarbha.
Vaidhrat : day for making charitable gifts to Bráhmans, IX, pt. i, 23 note 5 continued on page 24.
Vaidisa : Besnagar Samantabhadra's visit to, I, pt. ii, 407.
Vaids : *see* Vaidyas.
Vaidu : a caste of medicine hawkers in Ratnágiri district, X, 129; in Násik district, XVI, 65; in Ahmadnagar district, XVII, 212-214; in Poona district, XVIII, pt. i, 477-479; in Sátára district, XIX, 123-124.
Vaidyanath : place of pilgrimage in Bengal, IX, pt. i, 549.
Vaidyas : native physicians in Poona district, XVIII, pt. iii, 69-71; in Baroda, VII, 499-501; in Ratnágiri district, X, 294.
Vaijánones : a tribute paying *táluka* in Káthiáwár, VIII, 684.
Vaijayanti : probably Buzantion of the Greek geographers, probably Banavási; may be identified with Vijaydurg, I, pt. ii, 174-175; Kadamba king of, conquered by Kirtivarman I, *id.* 281, 285, 345.
Vairág : town in Sholápur district, trade centre, XX, 503.
Vairagad : fort mentioned by Ferishtah, I, pt. ii, 620.
Vairagi : a caste of religious beggars in Káthiáwár, VIII, 155. *See* Bairagi.
Vairamegha : *biruda* of Dantidurga, I, pt. ii, 389 note 5, 399 note 7.
Vairát : *rája* of Matsyanagar, gave shelter to the Pándavas, IX, pt. i, 294.
Vairátapur : modern Hangal, I, pt. ii, 558.
Vairátgad : Sahyadri spur in Sátára district, XIX, 6; hill-fort, fort details, a great banian tree at the foot of, *id.* 9, 601.
Vairatpur : or Virát, supposed to be Dholka, Pándavs take refuge at, IX, pt. i, 252 note 1, 294.
Vairisimha : Chávada king (A. D. 845) mentioned in *Prabandhachintámani*, I, pt. i, 154, 155.
Vaiságra : village at the foot of the Náná pass in Thána district, XIV, 287.
Vaisha : a caste of artificers and domestics mentioned by Ibni Khurdadbah, I, pt. i, 530.
Vaishákhara : a division in Thána district, surveyed (1771-72), XIII, 558.
Vaishnav : creed or sects, in Gujarát, four cults or *sampradayas—shri, sanakadi, sambha, Brahma*; generation, IX, pt. i, 533; followers of Vishnu called, *id.* p. xxxvi, 530; places of pilgrimage, *id.* 549; Hoysalas converted to, I, pt. ii, 491.
Vaishnava Bráhmans : in Kolhápur state, XXIV, 60; *see* Mádhva Bráhmans.
Vaishnava Cave : at Bádámi, completed (578), I, pt. ii, 346.
Vaishnavi : one of the divine mothers (Pleiades), I, pt. ii, 337 note 4.
Vaishya Vani : traders in Kánara district, XV, pt. i, 180, 181; in Poona district, XVIII, pt. i, 279; in Sholápur district, XX, 86.
Vaitál Dev : worship of, IX, pt. i, 292.
Vaitarná : river, rises near Trimbak in the Násik district, runs through the Thána district and falls into the Arabian Sea, XVI, 7; forms the boundary of the Portuguese district of Bassein and Daman, I, pt. ii, 54, 71; perhaps Ptolemy's Goaris (A. D. 150), its sanctity, course, tributaries, XIII, 8-10.
Vaitarni : river in the infernal regions, IX, pt. i, 372.
Vaiti : early tribe in Thána district, XIII, 182.
Vajai Máta : patron goddess of Bajániás, IX, pt. i, 503.

Vajantra : pass in Poona district, XVIII, pt. ii, 151.
Vájantri : a caste of musicians in Ratnágiri district, X, 415 ; in Kolhápur, XXIV, 111. *See* Ghadse.
Vajas : Rájpút branch of Ráthod clan, IX, pt. i, 129 ; were much harassed by *girásias* and sought the protection of Bhávnagar, VIII, 110.
Vájasneya : section of Mádhyandin Bráhmans in Kolhápur state, XXIV, 62.
Vajifa : land held at quit-rent in Baroda, VII, 351.
Vajirgad : fort in Thána district, remains at, XIV, 373.
Vajjada I : North Konkan Siláhára king, I, pt. ii, 539. *See* Vajjadadeva.
Vajjada II : North Konkan Siláhára king, I, pt. ii, 539. *See* Vajjadadeva II.
Vajjadadeva I : seventh Thána Siláhára king, son of Goggi, I, pt. ii, 15, 17 ; XIII, 422 note 1, 424.
Vajjadadeva II : ninth Thána Siláhára king, son of Aparájita, I, pt. ii, 15, 18, 542 note 6 ; XIII, 422 note 1, 425.
Vajra : Kalachurya king Bijjala's son, I, pt. ii, 471, 477.
Vajrábai : hot springs in Thána district, XIII, 16, 509, 510 ; XIV, 373-374.
Vajradeva : *see* Vajra.
Vajragad : peak in Poona district, XVIII, pt. i, 5.
Vajrahasta : Ganga king, his Parla-kimedi grant, I, pt. ii, 297.
Vajrata : paramount king of Northern India, defeated by Vinayáditya, I, pt. ii, 368, 378, 389.
Vajreshvari : temple of, at Gunj in Thána district, XIV, 105.
Vajrin : ruler of Mangalaveshtaka, slain by Bhillama, the Devagiri Yádava king, I, pt. ii, 520.
Vakal : village in Baroda state, VII, 578.
Vakal : Sopára hill in Thána district, XIII, 408, 409.
Vákátaka : *see* Vindhyashakti.
Vakeśvara : village, Shiva's temple at, I, pt. ii, 334.
Vakhár : business office of a Vania banker, IX, pt. i, 79.
Vakhátnáth : saint or *pir*, of Pátan, IX, pt. i, 247.
Vakhatsingh : fifty-ninth or the last viceroy of Gujarat appointed by the imperial court, I, pt. i, 332.
Vakhtapur : estate in Rewa Kántha, VI, 151.
Vakil ; deputy of Khoján *imáms*, IX, pt. ii, 41.
Vakil-ul-Mutlak : title bestowed (1792) on the Peshwa, XVIII, pt. ii, 268-269 ; XIX, 298.
Vakkal : caste of husbandmen in Kánara district, XV, pt. ii, 3-4.
Vakkaleri : Western Chalukya record from, I, pt. ii, 316, 322, 376 ; copper-plate grant of Kirtivarman II from, *id.* 327, 330, 374, 377, 378, 427 and note 3.
Vakkund : village near Sampgaon in Belgaum district, temple at, XXI, 609.
Vaktápur : state in Mahi Kántha, V, 427.
Vaktrittvottejak Sabhá : Poona elocution society, XVIII, pt. iii, 64-65.
Vákyapadiya : work on Sanskrit grammar, I, pt. ii, 406.
Vál : pulse variety in Poona district, XVIII, pt. ii, 44.
Vala : ancient Valabhipur, state and town in Káthiáwar, its old history, VIII, 670-675 ; IX, pt. i, 20 ; I, pt. i, 506.
Valabhdás Mánikchand : Baroda merchant, his family imprisoned by Vánirám, commits suicide (1834), VIII, 248.
Valabhi : city in Suráshtra or Káthiáwár, modern Vala or Valeh, capital of Valabhi dynasty, I, pt. i, 78 and note 1 ; history, *id.* 78-106 ; Mihira or Gurjjara conquest of (490), *id.* 489 ; its kings succeed the early Guptas in Káthiáwár, referred to as a *tirtha* or sacred place, I, pt. ii, 515, 284 and note 4 ; its king anointed by Vishnuvardhana-Yashodharman to the rule of Káthiáwár, *id.* 526, 382 ; defeated by Harshavardhana (606-648), *id.* 314 note 1 ; Godhra owned by, *id.* 315, 382 ; at war with Dadda III (706), *id.* 316 ; stops the progrss of the Western Chalukya king Mangaleśa, *id.* 336 ; irregularities in the succession of the rulers of, *id.* 346 note 4 ; Ráshrakútas kept back by the kings of, end of the dynasty, *id.* 382 ; dynastic seat, IX, pt. i, p. ix ; called Valabhipur, *id.* 125, 488, 495 ; ruined by Arabs, *id.* 125, 496 ; I, pt. i, 506, 524, 525.
Valabhipur : Gujarát capital, XV, pt. i, 117 note 1. *See* Valabhi.
Valabhis : Hindu kings in Káthiáwár, VIII, 274-277 ; I, pt. i, 516 ; supposed by Dr. Bhagvanlal to be Gurjjars ; by Dr. Hultzsch to be Maitraks and therefore Gurjjars, IX, pt. i, 479, 492 ; admitted as Rájpúts, *id.* 480, 486, 488 ; Bhatárka, their founder (480), *id.* 479, 492 ; Balas or Valas, rulers of Valabhi are Maitrakas and therefore Gurjjaras, *id.* 125, 479, 488, 492, 495-496 ; ancestors of Gohils or Sisodias, *id.* 29-30, 125, 129, 492, 494 note 2, 495 ; their administration (500-700), I, pt. i, 81.
Valáhaka : province, mentioned by Jinaprabhásuri, I, pt. i, 78.
Valahi : Valabhi, mentioned by Jinaprabhásuri, I, pt. i, 78.
Válákhiyá : *see* Koli.
Valalan : *see* Mudliar.
Valam : a sub-caste of Bráhmans in Gujarát, IX, pt. i, 20.
Vála Matra : a Káthi out-law in Gir hills, IX, pt. i, 254.
Valamdás Báva : Bharvád saint, IX, pt. i, 271.
Váland : a caste of barbers in Cutch, V, 76.
Válá Ráning : Káthi out-law, IX, pt. i, 254.
Válás : tribes of Rájpúts claim to belong to Káthiáwár, VIII, 110, 114 note 3. *See* Valabhis.
Valasna : Rathor chiefship in Mahi Kántha, IX, pt. i, 128 ; V, 427.
Valáti : inner uplands in Ratnágiri district, X, 151 note 1.

Valaváda: probably Válvá in Kolhápur state, I, pt. ii, 548, 549.
Válával: village in Savantvádi state, X, 469.
Valavas: guards to travellers and goods, Bháts used as, their devotion to duty and self-sacrifice, IX, pt. i, 210 note 1; Charáns used as, 217 and note 3.
Valavàta: modern Válavdem, I, pt ii, 255.
Válavdem: place of residence of Gandaráditya the Kolhápur Siláhára ruler, I, pt. ii, 255.
Valeh: modern name of Valabhi, town, its site examined (1872), I, pt. i, 78 and note 1.
Valentia: Lord, his visit to Sálsette (1803), I, pt. ii, 123; his journey from Panvel to Khandála, XIII, 303; his visit to Elephanta, XIV, 88; to Khopivli, *id.* 201; his notice of the painting of a saint at Mandapeshvar, *id.* 223 note 1, 227; his notice of Panvel and Thana, *id.* 295, 361; at Poona, XVIII, pt. iii, 414-419.
Valermani: timber tree, XXV, 37.
Valhár: a caste of beggars in Kolhápur, XXIV, 118.
Válhe: village in Poona district, supposed birth-place of the poet Válmik, XVIII, pt. iii, 454.
Valipattana: stronghold founded by Dhammiyara, Silahara king of the Southern Konkan, I, pt. ii, 537.
Válkhel: a caste of Bráhmans in Cutch, a trace of Bábika Bráhmans in, created by Brahma to live in Bet Dwarka, IX, pt. i, 439 note 5.
Vallabha: title or epithet of the kings of the Western Chalukya family, I, pt. ii, 181, 190, 324, 326, 344, 351, 377; epithet of Buddhavarman of the Gujarát branch of the Western Chalukyas of Bádámi, *id.* 359; epithet assumed by the Ráshtrakúta king, Dantidurga, *id.* 389; by Amoghavarsha I, *id.* 199, 408 and note 4, 409; *see* also I, pt. i, 127, 525.
Vallabha or Vallabhácharya: founder of Vallabhácháryan cult of Vaishnav sects, his life, teachings, descendants and works, IX, pt. i, 533, 535-536.
Vallabhácharí: Vaishnav religious sect otherwise called Vallabhácháryan or Pushti Marga, IX, pt. i, p. xxxvi, 535.
Vallabhákula: title of Vallabhacharya *Satsvarup*, IX, pt. i, 536.
Vallabharája: Chaulukya king (A. D. 1010), son of Chámunda; marches against Málwa, dies of small-pox, I, pt. i, 162.
Vallabhendra: epithet of Pulikeśin II, used in the Eastern Chalukya records, I, pt. ii, 351.
Vallabhgad: hill and fort in Belgaum district, XXI, 6, 609-610.
Vallam: village in Madras, inscription on a rock-cut Śaiva temple at, I, pt ii, 328.
Valle: Dela, Italian traveller, visits Mandu (1623), I, pt. i, 381; *see* Dela Valle.
Vallúr: town, passed through by Vishnuvardhana, I, pt. ii, 496, 498.
Vallúraka: *see* Valúraka.
Vallurikà: village granted to a Bráhman by Krishna II, I, pt. ii, 413.
Válmik: reputed author of the Rámáyan, XXIV, 106.
Válo: guinea worm, its cure, IX, pt. i, 365.
Válpapri: food plant, XXV, 153.
Valsang: town in Sholápur district, dyeing and weaving industries at, XX, 503-504.
Valtar: a system of compensation in Mahi Kantha, V, 390.
Valúraka: village in the Nizám's dominions, cave monastery at, I, pt. ii, 149, 175, 391 note 6.
Válvá: sub-division of Sátára district, its boundaries, area, aspect, climate, water, soil, stock, holdings, crops, people, XIX, 442-444; survey of, *id.* 380-383. *Town*, history, *id.* 601-602; Sultán Muazzam at (1685), *id.* 246; I, pt. ii, 654; surrendered to the British (1818), *id.* 308.
Válva: *dumála* village in Kolhápur, history, mosque and fair at, XXIV, 322.
Vámana: great-grandfather of Hemádri, I, pt. ii, 248.
Vámanasthali: modern Vanthali in Káthiáwár, I, pt. i, 160.
Váman Dvadashi: Hindu holiday, XVIII, pt. i, 248-249.
Váman Pandit: Marátha poet, his works, died (1673), XIX, 534.
Vámarási: Pandit in Kumárapála's court, insults Hemachandra, loses his annuity, I, pt. i, 163.
Vambhori: a great market town with a railway station in Ahmadnagar district, XVII, 741.
Vana: a tribute paying *táluka* in Káthiáwár VIII, 675.
Vanálá: a separate tribute-paying *táluka* in Káthiáwár, VIII, 675.
Vanant: star of the south, identified with the star "Fowalhaut," IX, pt. ii, 217 note 1.
Vana-parvan: third book of the *Mahábhárata*, I, pt. ii, 278 note 2.
Vanarája: Chávada king (720-780), born and bred in forest, founded Anahilaváda; his installation, his image, his successors, I, pt. i, 150, 151-152, 153, 155, 512.
Vanavása: Banavási province, XV, pt. ii, 261 note 2; perhaps the scene of the Pándavas' exile, *id.* 264 note 4; Moggaliputto sends missionaries to, I, pt. ii, 143-144, 278 note 2, 346, 370. *See* Banavási.
Vandan: hill-fort in Sátára district, XIX, 9; Bajába Purandhare imprisoned in (1788), *id.* 297.
Vandhásurchauka: fortress at, subdued by Vishnuvardhana, I, pt. ii, 496
Vandidád: original part of the *Zend Avesta*, IX, pt. ii, 211 note 2 (20); preserved portion of the *Zend Avesta*, *id.* 212 note 1; original copy of, said to have been lost, *id.* 189 note 2; Herbad Mahyar brings copy of, from Yezd to Uch, *id.* 186 note 1, 188 note 4, 189 note 2; copies of, made in Cambay, *id.* 189 note 2; Zend and Pehlevi copy of, is left in India by the Persian priest Jamaap, *id.* 194; code, *id.* 226; XIII, 252 note 3, 253 note 2.
Vandiga: *see* Vaddiga, the Yádava chief.
Van-Dindori: grant of Govind III at, I, pt. i, 123, 466, 468.
Vanellinæ: family of birds in Ratnágiri district, X, 91.

Vanga : eastern Bengal, I, pt. i, 124, 468 ; I, pt. ii, 281 ; king of, brought under subjection, *id.* 219 ; conquered by Kirtivarman I, *id.* 345 ; by the Gurjara king, *id.* 400 ; king of, worships the Ráshtrakúta king Amoghavarsha I, *id.* 402.

Vangadhra : a tribute-paying *táluka* in Káthiáwár, VIII, 676.

Vangalia : mentioned by Ptolemy, Vengurla rocks (?) in Kánara district, XV, pt. ii, 48 note 3, 336.

Vangaon : village in Thána district, XIV, 53.

Vángni : a village near Karjat in Thána district, fort and buildings at, XIV, 375.

Vanguiera : *edulis,* food plant, XXV, 162 ; *spinosa,* food and timber plant, *id.* 87, 162.

Vanhalli : a village in Dhárwár district, a temple of Ishvar with an inscription at, XXII, 786.

Váni : village in the Násik district, temples, inscriptions and reservoir at, XVI, 661-662.

Váni, Vániá : class of traders in Gujarát, two main sections of Bráhmanic or Meshri and Jain or Shrávak, social ties between the two sections ; main divisions of, names, strength and distribution, IX, pt. i, 69 ; social position ; sub-divisions into Visás, Dasás, and Pánchás, meaning of the terms, *id.* 70, 435 ; Meshri, leading classes, *id.* 70-74 ; appearance, *id.* 74 ; speech, house, food, dress, *id.* 75 ; ornaments, *id.* 76 ; character, proverbs, *id.* 76 and notes 1 and 2, 77 and notes 1 and 2 ; occupation—miscellaneous, *id.* 77 ; of traders, shopkeepers, poor Vania or village trader's start in life, *id.* 78 ; money-lender's start in life, *id.* 78 and note 3 ; European travellers' notice of Vania skill and character, *id.* 78 note 1 ; honorific titles of *Sháh* and *Párekh, id.* 78 note 2 ; business of rich merchants, *id.* 79 ; as bankers, *id.* 71-82 ; book-worship or *vahipujan, id.* 82 ; account books, *id.* 82-88 ; daily life, *id.* 88 ; religion, adherents of Vallabhácharya sect, Mahárájás, religious heads of the sect, *id.* 69, 70 ; customs—birth, *chhathi pujan, báran balians* worship, *id.* 89 ; betrothals, presents given on, *id.* 89-90 ; marriage age, the marriage day, *mandwa* making ceremony, *id.* 90 ; *chori* or marriage altar, presents given on the marriage day procession, *id.* 91 ; marriage service, *id.* 92-93 ; pregnancy, *panchmasi* ceremony, *id.* 93 ; *simant* ceremony, *id.* 93-94 ; death, bier *daghus,* widow, funeral rites, *id.* 94-95 ; Community or *Mahajan, id.* 95 ; prospects, *id.* 96 ; Shravaks, main divisions of, *id.* 96-98 ; appearance, food, *id.* 98 ; character, *id.* 99 ; customs—birth, *id.* 99 ; *chhathi* worship, naming, *mudan,* betrothal, *id.* 100 ; marriage, *id.* 100-101 ; pregnancy, death, *id.* 102 ; community, *id.* 103 ; religion, *id.* 105-110 ; foreign element traced in Osváls, Shrimális, *id.* 452-453 ; Gujar element in Osvals, Shrimalis, *id.* 496, 497, 499 and note 3 ; a caste of traders in Kolába district, XI, 48 ; in Janjira state, *id.* 411 ; in Ratnágiri district, X, 118 ; in Sávantvádi, *id.* 413 ; in Khándesh district, XII, 56, 59-61 ; in Thána district, XIII, 112-115, 432, 524 ; at Mátherán, XIV, 265 ; at Sopára, *id.* 315 ; in Sátára district, XIX, 51-58, 59-61 ; in Baroda state, VII, 57-59 ; in Poona district, XVIII, pt. i, 273-279.

Vani-Dindori : grant found at, I, pt. ii, 196 note 3, 197, 198 note 2, 199.

Vaniram Aditram : minister at Baroda ; intrigues against Gopal Atmárám (1833), VII, 240 ; hates Bháskarráv (1836), *id.* 236 ; dismissal of, demanded by the Bombay government (1839), *id.* 250-251.

Vanjára, Vanjári : a caste of carriers in Rewa Kántha, VI, 25 ; in Káthiáwár, VIII, 159 ; in Sátára district, XIX, 109 ; in Ratnágiri district, X, 131 ; in Kolába district, XI, 73 ; in Janjira state, *id.* 414 ; in Khándesh district, XII, 41, 69, 106-113 ; wandering traders, *id.* 218 ; cattle stealers and gang robbers, *id.* 314 ; in Thána district, XIII, 118, 131 ; in Násik district, XVI, 62 ; in Poona district, XVIII, pt. i, 428-431 ; in Sholápur district, XX, 169 ; in Kánara district, XV, pt. ii, 200 ; in Ahmadnagar district, XVII, 162-163 ; *see* also I, pt. ii, 80.

Vanjha : caste of weavers in Káthiáwár, VIII, 152 ; in Cutch, V, 74.

Vankal : family goddess of Nandvána Bráhmans at Virani, in Márwár, IX, pt. i, 16.

Vankaner : Jhala Rájpút chiefship in Káthiáwár, IX, pt. i, 127 ; chief of, defeats Názar Ali Khán (1705), I, pt. i, 295 ; Pársi settlement in, in the the 8th century, IX, pt. ii, 186. *Town,* VIII, 676-679.

Vankápura : modern Bankápur, I, pt. ii, 411.

Vankeśvara : *see* Vakeśvara.

Vánki, Vankika : creek near Balsár, I, pt. i, 125.

Vanknis : private record-keeper in the Marátha government, XIX, 243.

Vankund : forest pool near Bhinmál, I, pt. i, 454.

Vanniyar : fire-sprung Rájpúts, outside tribes raised to be Rájpúts under the name of, IX, pt. i, 449-450 ; fire castes in Madras, the, name, *id.* 486.

Vanod : a tribute-paying *táluka* in Káthiáwár ; temple of a *máta* at, VIII, 679.

Vanta : private lands of Gujarát chiefs, VII, 340, 344, 346 ; I, pt. i, 215.

Vanthali : town in Káthiáwár, VIII, 679-682 ; I, pt. i, 136 ; Chudásamas settle at, *id.* 139 ; capital of Graharipu, *id.* 160 ; its rulers killed by Viradhavala Vaghela, *id.* 200-204 ; *see* also IX, pt. i, 125.

Vanva : food plant, XXV, 168.

Váphgaon : market village in Poona district, XVIII, pt. iii, 453.

Vaphla : village in Sholápur district, inscription at, XX, 504.

Vappa : *see* Bappa.

Vappuka : king, slain by the Ráshtrakúta king Krishna III, I, pt. ii, 420.

Vappuvanna : fourth North Konkan Siláhára king, I, pt. ii, 17, 539 ; XIII, 422 note 1, 424.

Varád : lake in Ratnágiri district, X, 11.

Varadá : river in Vidarbha, I, pt. ii, 147.

Váradapallika : village in the Lat province, I, pt. i, 130.

Varáh ; village in Dhárwár district, inscriptions at, XXII, 788.

Varáha : wild boar coin, I, pt. i, 219 note 2.
Varáha : king, contemporary of Govinda III, I, pt. ii, 395.
Varáha : Hindu god, third incarnation of Vishnu in the form of a boar, I, pt. i, 451.
Varáha-lánchchana : Chalukya crest, I, pt. ii, 338.
Varáha Mihira : astronomer, I, pt. i, 533, 534, 540 ; contemporary of Vararuchi, I, pt. ii, 144 ; author of the *Brihatsamhita*, *id.* 310, 431 note 2.
Varáha Rup : a village near Junagad in Káthiáwár, a temple at, VIII, 682 ; IX, pt. i, 549.
Varáhi : state in Pálanpur, history of its Jat chiefs, V, 281, 334-335.
Várahi : one of the Pleiades, I, pt. ii, 337 note 4.
Varáhsiddha : a tribe said to have established colonies in Gujarát, IX, pt. i, 8 note 1.
Varal : a village in Káthiáwár, a battle at, VIII, 683.
Varalatta : one of the seven Konkans, I, pt. ii, 282 note 5 ; tribe, I, pt. i, 534.
Vara Mudrá : giving position of Sopára image of Buddha, XIV, 330, 331, 412.
Váránasi : Benares, I, pt. ii, 284 note 4.
Varandha ; pass between Kolába district and Bhor state, XI, 5, 114 ; XIX, 201.
Varangaon : town in Khándesh district, temple at, XII, 478.
Vararuchi : author of the *Prákrita Prakása*, one of the nine gems of the court of Vikramáditya, the contemporary of Varáha Mihira and Kálidása, I, pt. ii, 144, 171.
Varashfal : astrological statement of year's events, IX, pt. i, 27.
Varát : rent-draft, cheque, XIII, 561.
Varáta kings : dispersed by Vishnuvardhana, I, pt. ii, 496.
Varda : river in Kánara and Dhárwár districts, I, pt. ii, 658 ; XV, pt. ii, 265 and note 5 ; XV, pt. i, 7 ; XXII, 6.
Vardangad : *see* Vardhangad.
Vardhamánapura : modern Vadhván, I, pt. i, 176 ; Jain temple at, I, pt. ii, 552 note 8.
Vardhangad : hill fort in Sátára district, XIX, 12, 461 ; fort details, history, *id.* 602-604 ; built by Shiváji (1676), I, pt. ii, 595.
Vardhangad-Machhindragad : Mahádev hill spur in Sátára district, XIX, 7-8.
Vardhári : sub-division in Rewa Kántha, VI, 124.
Vardhman : Jain merchant, said to have defiled the Bráhmanic purity of Sompara Salats, IX, pt. i, 195-196.
Varelatæ, Varetatæ : *see* Varalatta.
Vargs : estates in Kánara district, XV, pt. ii, 166, 182.
Vargund : timber tree, XXV, 102.
Varhádi : cotton variety in Khándesh district, XII, 160, 161, 220, 231.
Varhádi : breed of cattle in Poona district, XVIII, pt. i, 57.
Vari : river in Baroda state, VII, 8.
Vari : grain, cultivation of in Ratnágiri district, X, 147 ; in Kolába district, XI, 96 ; in Thána district, XIII, 289.
Variáv : village near Surat in Baroda state, VII, 578-579 ; school at, *id.* 487 ; Pársi settlement in, IX, pt. ii, 186 and notes 1 and 9 ; heroic defence by the Pársi female warriors of, against the troops of the Ratanpur chief, *id.* 186 note 9.
Variávi : modern Variáv near Surat, I, pt. i, 128 ; I, pt. ii, 310, 412.
Varibhokar : pond in Khándesh district, XII, 11.
Varik : *see* Nhávi.
Várkaris : Phandharpur pilgrims, XX, 471-473.
Varkas : upland soil in Ratnágiri, X, 145 ; in Sávantvádi, *id.* 423.
Varkeda : village in Khándesh district, XII, 479 ; opposition to the British at (1844), *id.* 260.
Varkute : village and a place of interest in Sholápur district, temple at, XX, 504.
Varli : wild tribe mentioned by Pliny, I, pt. i, 534 ; in Gujarát, IX, pt. i, 290, 328, 329 ; in Khándesh, XII, 100, 601 ; in Násik district, XVI, 26, 64 ; in Thána district, XIII, 182-189.
Várna : river in the Sátára district and the Kolhápur state, XIX, 15 ; XXIV, 8, 9.
Varnoli : estate in Rewa Kántha, VI, 153.
Varnol Mál : state in Rewa Kántha, VI, 151.
Varnu : village in Cutch, temple at, V, 253.
Varosha : stream at Mátherán, XIV, 244, 300.
Varosha : Mátherán forest, XIV, 239.
Varshásan : charitable annual grant, VII, 350.
Varsoda : Chavda Rájpút chiefship in Mahi Kántha, IX, pt. i, 124 ; V, 420.
Varsoddharas : seven flowing streams, names, worship of, during marriage rites, IX, pt. i, 41.
Varsoli : wart disease, its cure, IX, pt. i, 365.
Varsoli : stream in Kolába district, XI, 8.
Vartaniás : police subordinates of Mughal *havaldárs*, I, pt. i, 212.
Vartej : town in Káthiáwár, was formerly a a roadstead, VIII, 683.
Varthema : Italian traveller (1503-1508), describes Cambay, I, pt. i, 220 note 2 ; his mention of Dábhol, X, 328 ; places Cheul in Gujarát, XI, 142 note 8, 273 ; XIII, 443 ; his notice of Calicut boats, *id.* 470 ; of Begada's fight with the *jogis*, XIV, 135 note 10 ; his description of Bijápur, XXIII, 406-407, 583 ; the king of Vijayanagar, XV, pt. ii, 50, 103-105 ; his notice of Anjidiv, *id.* 254 ; of Bhatkal, *id.* 272 and note 2 ; of Chitakul, *id.* 278.
Vártikas : aphorisms of Kátyáyána, I, pt. ii, 139, 140.
Varubenná : river in the Avaretiká province, I, pt. ii, 356.
Varugad : hill fort in Sátára district, XIX, 11 ; fort details, history, *id.* 604-606.
Varuna : village in Mysore, inscription at, I, pt. ii, 380.
Varuna : water god, deity presiding over earth water, IX, pt. i, 348 ; five abodes of, the sea, river, pond, spring, well, *id.* 349 ; *see* also I, pt. ii, 347 ; XIII, 406.
Varvar, Varvaraka : *see* Barbaraka.
Vasai : Bassein district, I, pt. ii, 29.
Vásaka : or camp, the word occurs in Gurjjar grants, I, pt. i, 113.

Vaśan: state in Rewa Kántha, VI, 144.
Vasant: spring season, XV, pt. i, 11.
Vasantapriyarája: vassal of Mahendrapotarája, I, pt. ii, 328.
Vasantasena: king of Nepál, I, pt. i, 84.
Vasantgad: hill fort in Sátára district, XIX, 7, 11; surprised (1659) by Shiváji, XVIII, pt. ii, 228; XIX, 238; taken (1699) by Aurangzib, *id.* 250; taken (1706) by the Maráthás, *id.* 253; action near (1807), *id.* 300; Trimbakji Denglia imprisoned in (1815), *id.* 300; surrendered to the British (1818), *id.* 308, 461.
Vásantikádevi: goddess Padmávati, family goddess of the Hoysalas, I, pt. ii, 490.
Vasavad: a tribute-paying *táluka* in Káthiáwár, a fort at, VIII, 684.
Vasco da Gama: Portuguese statesman, comes to India (1498), XV, pt. ii, 101-102; anchors at Anjidiv, XIII, 470; XV, pt. ii, 252-253, 278, 308; stops at the island of Bhatkal, *id.* 271.
Vashala: village in Thána district, rock-cut temple at, XIV, 375.
Váshishthiputra: *see* Vásisthiputra.
Váshishti: river in Ratnágiri district, X, 6-8.
Vásind: village in Thána district, XIV, 375.
Vásingapura: a fort at, erected by Siddharája, I, pt. i, 180 note 2.
Vasishtha: *rishi*, his foreign allies, IX, pt. i, 447 and note 6; *see* also I, pt. i, 461.
Vásishthi: mother of Pulumáyi, I, pt. ii, 149; wife of Gotamiputra S'átakarni, *id.* 151.
Vasishthiputa or putra: identified with S'átakarni prince Chatarapana (185 A. D.), I, pt. ii, 153-154, 167; XII, 484 and note 3.
Vasisthiputra: Andhrabhritya king (133-162), I, pt. ii, 10; XVIII, pt. ii, 213.
Vasna: Rathor chiefship in Mahi Kántha, IX, pt. i, 128; V, 425.
Vasna: river in Sátára district, XIX, 15.
Vaso: town in Baroda state, Rustam Ali's death at (1725), VII, 170; tomb of Rustam Ali at, *id.* 539.
Vásota: hill fort in Sátára district, fort details, history, XIX, 606-608, 9; captured by Shiváji (1653), *id.* 233; taken by Tái Telin, Parashurám Pant Pratinidhi's mistress (1807), I, pt. ii, 609; XIX, 299-300; Pratapsinh (1810-1839) imprisoned at (1817), *id.* 301; siege of (1818), *id.* 306-307.
Vásra: a division in Thána district, surveyed (1795-96), XIII, 558.
Vassilief: traveller, luxurious life of the monks of Kánheri according to, XIV, 137.
Vasteriox: husbandman, a class of the old Persian community, IX, pt. ii, 213.
Vastu: *see* Vástu Shanti.
Vastupála: minister of Lavanaprasáda Vághelá, I, pt. ii, 241; builds magnificent Jain temples, I, pt. i, 199 and note 2, 200, 201, 202 and note 1; governor of Cambay (1241), VI, 215.
Vastupálacharita: life of Vastupála by Someśvara, I, pt. i, 199.
Vastu-shánti: house consecration ceremony, XX, 524-527; IX, pt. i, 204.
Vásudev: a caste of beggars in Khándesh district, XII, 124; in Násik district, XVI, 75; in Ahmadnagar district, XVII, 187-188; in Poona district, XVIII, pt. i, 479-480; in Sátára district, XIX, 124; in Sholápur district, XX, 191; in Belgaum district, XXI, 188, 189; in Kolhápur, XXIV, 118; in Thána district, XIII, 199.
Vasudeva: Kushán king (A. D. 123-150), defeated by the Yaudheyas, I, pt. i, 37.
Vásudeva: Chohán king (780), mentioned in the *Hammiramaháhávya*, I, pt. i, 157.
Vásudeva: one of the names of Krishna, I, pt. ii, 142.
Vásudeva: grandfather of Hemádri, I, pt. ii, 248.
Vásudevas: Jain saints, I, pt. i, 451 note 3.
Vasudev Balvant Phadke: his organization of a gang of robbers; their dacoities, captured by Colonel Daniell at Deveh Nadige (1879), XIII, 637-638, 526; *see* also XVIII, pt. iii, 38, 424; XXIII, 645-646.
Vásuki: Nága king, I, pt. ii, 576-577.
Vasurna: state in Khándesh district, XII, 606.
Vasváya: *literally* a settler, artizans in a village community so called, IV, 106.
Vatan: service tenure in Thána district, XIII, 534, 537-539.
Vatanagara: district in the vicinity of Násik, I, pt. ii, 398.
Vatandárs: in Baroda, VII, 362-363; Kanbi, in Gujarát, IX, pt. i, 156.
Vatapadrapura: probably Baroda, I, pt. i, 183.
Vátápi: identification of, with modern Bádámi in Bijápur district, I, pt. ii, 280 and note 3, 351 note 1, 356, 538 note 8; destroyed by Narasimhavarman I, *id.* 326; taken by Mahámalla, the Pallava king, *id.* 328, 329 note 4; captured by and capital of Pulikeśin I, *id.* 181, 189, 344, 345; adorned by Kirtivarman I, *id.* 345; installation of the gods Bráhma, Vishnu, and Maheśvara at (699), *id.* 371.
Vátápi: Bádámi demon, story of, XXIII, 378.
Vatápikonda: taker of Vátápi, ëpithet of Narasimhavarman I, the Pallava king, I, pt. ii, 322.
Vátápipura: *see* Vátápi.
Vatavrikshadhvaja: banner of the Guttas, I, pt. ii, 578.
Vátegaon: village in Sátára district, temples at, XIX, 608, 609.
Vaterica Indica: timber tree, XXV, 15.
Vathira: king of, conquered by Kirtivarman I, I, pt. ii, 281, 345.
Vat Puja: fig-tree worship among Deshastha Bráhmans in Kolhápur, XXIV, 56.
Vátrak: river in Mahi Kántha, V, 357.
Vátrak Kántha: sub-division in Mahi Kántha, V, 353.
Vatsa: *gotra*, I, pt. ii, 482.
Vatsarája: king of Ujjain, I, pt. i, 466, 468; Gurjjara king, his success in Bengal, *id.* 527; defeated by Dhruva, I, pt. ii, 393, 197; contemporary of Govinda III, *id.* 395.
Vatsavitri: Hindu holiday, worship of banian tree on, IX, pt. i, 47.

Vatayáyana : author of the *Kámasútras*, I, pt. ii, 171.
Vattaraka : village, modern Watargon in Thána district, XIV, 385 and note 1.
Vatvad : hill in Thána district, XIII, 4.
Vaupell : Mr. (1837), his description of Kánheri caves, XIV, 164 ; of Sopára, *id.* 323.
Vautha : village in Ahmadábád district, fair at, IV, 354.
Vaux's tomb : in Surat, II, 334.
Vav : Chohan Rájpút chiefship in Pálanpur, IX, pt. i, 125 ; V, 333-334, 281, 350.
Vává : caste of traders in Cutch, V, 56.
Vavania, Vavanya : a small port in the gulf of Cutch, was formerly in a flourishing state, VIII, 412, 684 ; V, 211.
Vavdi Dharvala : *táluka* in Káthiáwár, VIII, 683.
Vavdi Mehoti : village under Pálitána state in Káthiáwár, VIII, 684.
Vavdi Rájgar : village in Káthiáwár, VIII, 683.
Vavdi Vachani : village in Káthiáwár, VIII, 683.
Vavulatalla : territorial division mentioned in the Karda grant, I, pt. ii, 423.
Vayada : a caste of Bráhmans in Gujarát, IX, pt. i, 21 ; of Vanias, sub-divisions, special feature of marriage rites, *id.* 74 ; Vanias in Cutch, V, 48, 50.
Vayajalladeva : manager of Tripurushaprásáda temple at Anahilaváda, I, pt. i, 161.
Vayu : element, *see* wind, Marut, deity presiding over wind, IX, pt. i, 348.
Vayu Puran : Hindu religious book, I, pt. ii, 133, 134, 156, 165, 177.
Vazen : perhaps Vásind, I, pt. ii, 49.
Veadors : Portuguese officers, factors, I, pt. ii, 52, 53.
Vedant : a Bráhman sub-division in Cutch, V, 47 ; in Gujarát, IX, pt. i, 21.
Vedánta Kalpataru : commentary on Váchaspatimisra's *Bhámati*, I, pt. ii, 245.
Vedántasutrabhháshya : S'amkaráchárya's work, I, pt. ii, 246.
Vedashála : Vedic school in Ratnágiri district, X, 290.
Vedasiras : same as S'iva S'ri mentioned in *Bhágvata*, I, pt. ii, 155.
Vedganga : river in Kolhápur state, XXIV, 8, 9, 10, 11.
Vedic Rites : names of, practised by Gujarát Bráhmans, IX, pt. i, 31 and note 3.
Vedic Sacrifices : performance of (B. C. 100), XVIII, pt. iii, 220.
Vedisri : S'átakarni king (B. C. 100), XIV, 288 ; XVIII, pt. ii, 212 ; XVI, 612, 614 ; XVIII, pt. iii, 220.
Vegávati : river near Conjevaram, I, pt. ii, 326.
Vegetables : at Mátherán, XIV, 250 ; varieties of, in Kánara district, XV, pt. ii, 21 ; in Násik district, XVI, 105 ; bulb, fruit, pod, leaf, in Kolhápur, XXIV, 180-184.
Vegu : *see* Bhansáli.
Vehár : lake in Thána district, XIII, 11-12, 425 note 6, 461 ; XIV, 375-378 ; remains at, *id.* 379.
Vehárgaon : village in Poona district, cave, details and inscriptions at, XVIII, pt. iii, 454-464 ; *see* also under Karle.
Vehela : pass in Násik district, XVI, 128.
Vehergaon : spur in Poona district, XVIII, pt. i, 5.
Vehestoast : fifth Gáthá Day, IX, pt. ii, 218.
Veholi : village in Thána district, hot spring at, XIV, 379.
Vejalketha : an ancient historical town in Káthiáwár, VIII, 685.
Vejanand Bhasariyo : Cháran saint, IX, pt. i, 272.
Vejápur : village in the Mahi Kántha, I, pt. ii, 359 note 3.
Vejayanti : *see* Banavási.
Vekria : a tribute-paying *táluka* in Káthiáwár, VIII, 685.
Vel : river in Poona district, XVIII, pt. i, 7.
Veláchha : sub-division in Baroda state, VII, 577-578. *Town, id.* 578.
Velali : caste of writers in Poona district, XVIII, pt. i, 256-257.
Velápa Rái : former servant of the Vijayanagar king, independent ruler of Bankápur, defends himself with much vigour against the Musalmáns of Bijápur (1573), I, pt. ii, 645.
Velápur : village in Sholápur district, temple and inscriptions at, XX, 504.
Velápura : Belápura, modern Belur in Mysore, I, pt. ii, 298 ; historical authority of the Hoysalas first connected with, *id.* 491 and note 2, 498.
Velas : town in Janjira state, birth-place of Báláji Janardan *alias* Nana Phadnavis, XI, 467.
Vellore : town in the North Arcot district, Madras, inscription at, I, pt. ii, 332, 419, 421.
Vellúra : village in the Nizám's dominions, I, pt. ii, 391 note 6.
Velneshvar : village in the Ratnágiri district, a large fair at, X, 374.
Velo : Koli *sádhu*, IX, pt. i, 247.
Velugráma, Velugráme : territorial division in the vicinity of Belgaum, I, pt. ii, 298 note 2, 460 ; seat of government of the Rattás, *id.* 550, 556, 557 ; ruled over by the Goa Kádambas, *id.* 568, 570.
Velúrppádi : village granted by Krishna III, I, pt. ii, 422.
Vena : Royal *rishi*, caused a confusion of castes, IX, pt. i, 434 and note 9.
Venefars : perhaps Vanjáris (1670), traders in Konkan according to Ogilby, X, 176.
Veneration : objects of, among Pársis, IX, pt. ii, 213, 215-216.
Venetians : carriers of Indian goods, join Egyptians against the Portuguese (1500), I, pt. ii, 43.
Vengainádu : Vengi territory of the Eastern Chálukyás, I, pt. ii, 341 note 2.
Vengaon : village in Thána district, birthplace of Nána Sáheb (1857), XIII, 525 ; I, pt. ii, 130 ; XIV, 379.
Vengi : boundaries and identification of, I, pt. ii, 280 ; Vishnuvardhana, brother of Pulakesi II, founds the family of Eastern Chálukyás at (about 617), *id.* 185, 277, 335 note 1, 352 ; subjected by the Pallavas (733-747), *id.*

326-327; king of, attends on the Ráshtrakúta king Govind III as his servant and builds the wall of Málkhed, *id.* 198, 396, 402-403; conquered by Amoghavarsha I, *id.* 199, 402; territory, overrun by Krishna II, *id.* 412; conquered by Vikramáditya II also styled VI, *id.* 215, 442; king of, seizes the throne of Káñchi and is defeated by Vikramáditya II, *id.* 217, 234, 445, 525; king of, subdued by the Cholas (1012), *id.* 308.
Vengoráshtra: country, I, pt. ii, 321.
Vengurla: sub-division of Ratnágiri district, details of, X, 2, 315; port, *id.* 170; trade (1660), *id.* 175; trade (1879), *id.* 178; customs division, exports and imports of, *id.* 187. *Town,* position, population, trade, communications, management, history, rocks, light-house at, *id.* 374-379; Dutch factory at, I, pt. ii, 63; burnt by Shiváji (1664), XVIII, pt. ii, 231; I, pt. ii, 168; burnt by Mughals (1675), XI, 439; I, pt. ii, 70; sacked by Sultán Mauzim (1684), *id.* 77; plundered, by the Sávants (1780), *id.* 107; ceded to the English, *id.* 112, 347 note 2.
Vengurlem: I, pt. ii, 181, 185. *See* Vengurla.
Venkáji: half brother of Shiváji, I, pt. ii, 595.
Venkáji: Sháhaji's (1848) adopted son, XIX, 313.
Venkatadri: brother of Rám Ráj, I, pt. ii, 645.
Venkatappa Náik: Bednur chief (1610), defeats the Bijápur forces, XV, pt. ii, 122, 123; takes Chandavar, *id.* 277; captures Gersappa and Honávar, *id.* 284, 310.
Venkati Yesav Rái: officer of the Bijápur government (1753), I, pt. ii, 645.
Venkatráo: chief of Nargund, is pressed for an increased tribute by Tipu; applies for aid first to the English and then to the Peshwa; capitulates; is thrown into prison and his daughter taken into Tipu's harem (1785), I, pt. ii, 660; seeks assistance (1785) of Poona court, pressed by Tipu, force from Poona to the relief of, XXII, 414.
Venktápur: river in Kánara district, XV, pt. i, 7, 8.
Venugráma: I, pt. ii, 298 note 2; province, *id.* 431, 527; lost by the Goa Kádambas, *id.* 571; seat of government of the Rattas, *id.* 550, 556, 557. *See* Velugráma or Belgaum.
Venupura: Belgaum, seat of government of, the Rattas, I, pt. ii, 550, 557.
Venus: *Shukra,* planet, details of worship of, IX, pt. i, 402; the observation of the transit of, taken in Bombay (1768), XXVI, pt. i, 356-357.
Verar: goddess among Gujarát Hindus, IX, pt. i, 205, 247, 363.
Verás: cesses in Kaira district, III, 87, 107, 111; in Panch Maháls, *id.* 266; in Ahmadábád district, IV, 157; in Cutch, V, 179; in Pálanpur, *id.* 311-312; in Mahi Kántha, *id.* 387; in Rewa Kántha, VI, 85; in Cambay, *id.* 238; in Káthiáwár, VIII, 319.
Verat: an ancient town of Chávada Rájpúts in Káthiáwár, VIII, 687.
Verával: ancient sea-port in Káthiáwár, famous for onions, VIII, 685-686, 238; inscription of, I, pt i, 81, 176, 203, 204, 521 547.
Verbenaceæ: an order of timber trees and food plants, XXV, 107, 168.
Vereadores: chosen by the people annually (1742) in Bombay Island, XXVI, pt. iii, 520; abuse of power by, the extent of their power publicly proclaimed (1775), *id.* 421-423.
Verisálji: of Rájpipla, rebels againt the Mughals, I, pt. i, 294.
Versova, Vesava: a small village and port in Sálsette, its description; a fort at, XIV, 379-381; taken by the Arabs (1700), XXVI, pt. i, 128; taken by the Maráthás (1739), *id.* 203; taken by the English (1774), *id.* 384-385; I, pt. i, 401; XIV, 193; I, pt. ii, 101, 128; mention of, *id.* 54, 66; XIII, 484, 485, 491, 493, 501, 509, 514.
Verul: I, pt. ii, 391. *See* Ellora.
Vesáva: *see* Versova.
Veskars: village gate-keepers (1828) in Thána district, XIII, 574.
Vessels: engaged in the Indian trade, Egyptian (B. C. 2500), XIII, 404 note 3; Arab (B. C. 1500), *id.* 716; Phœnician (B. C. 1100-850), *id.* 716; Greek (A. D. 62-100), *id.* 417 note 6; Roman (A. D. 78), *id.* 410 note 5; early Hindu (A. D. 250), *id.* 419; Arab (600-1000), *id.* 432, 433; Chinese (1290), *id.* 433 note 3; pirate of Káthiáwár (700-1300), *id.* 433-434; of Socotra (1290), *id.* 434; of the Malabár coast (1290), *id.* 434; of the Bombay harbour (1290), *id.* 434, 438; (1500), *id.* 449; of Maskat (1600-1800), *id.* 488, 521 note 4; of Bet in Káthiáwár (1812-1820), *id.* 521 note 5; Arab, Persian, and Chinese (1300-1500), *id.* 447; Portuguese vessels (1500), *id.* 470 and note 9, 469-470, 471 and notes 1-3; Dutch and English (1600-1615), *id.* 471 and note 3; *building of,* at Agáshi (1500), *id.* 465 note 4, 468; at Goa (1510), *id.* 469; at Surat (1600), *id.* 469 note 4; at Bombay (1735-1800), 500 and note 3, 517, 518 and note 1; names of vessels, *id.* 717-721; passed from Asia to Europe, *id.* 723-724; from Europe to Asia, *id.* 722-723; names held in common, *id.* 723; number and tonnage of, in Surat district, II, 177; in Broach district, *id* 413-418; in Káthiáwár, VIII, 226-233; in Ratnágiri district, X, 170-172; names of, *id.* 172 note; in Kolába district, XI, 124-125; in Janjira state, *id.* 429.
Vessels: copper and brass, making of, in Poona district, XVIII, pt. i, 375.
Vesu, Vesuga, Vesugi or Vesuka: Yádava king, son of Bhillama II, his various names, I, pt. ii, 233, 234, 514; succeeds Vádugi, *id.* 515.
Vetal: leader of evil spirits, XVIII, pt. i, 291, 553; I, pt. ii, 169; image of, on Yashavantgad in Ratnágiri district, X, 371; temple of, in Poona city, XVIII, pt. iii, 347-348.
Vetál: ward in Poona city, details of, XVIII, pt. iii, 274, 278-279.
Vetál Circle: near Parvati hill, Poona, XVIII, pt. iii, 388 and note 1.
Vetálgad: fort in Ratnágiri district, X, 378.

Vetasvat: country containing *vetas* or canes mentioned by Pánini, I, pt. ii, 139.
Veth: unpaid labour levied from agriculturists in Kolába (1825), XI, 187, 188 and note 1.
Vetravati: river, modern Betva, I, pt. ii, 142.
Vetugideva: Chálukya prince, I, pt. ii, 224.
Vevji: village in Thána, XIV, 370.
Viara: sub-division in Baroda; its details, VII, 581-582; village, *id.* 582; hospital at, *id.* 506.
Viarála: lake in Thána district, XIII, 12.
Vibhuti: cowdung ash, Bráhmans' sacred dust, IX, pt. i, 373.
Vicar General: of Bombay island, appointment of (1770), XXVI, pt. iii, 533-534; at Bassein during Marátha rule, I, pt. ii, 86.
Vicars Apostolic: freed from the jurisdiction of the Inquisition of Goa (1673), I, pt. ii, 61.
Viceroys: Portuguese, prohibit all heathen rites, I, pt. ii, 59; engage in illicit trading, *id.* 52.
Vichana: southern viceroy of the Devagiri Yádava king Singhana, reduces the Western Chálukyas, Rattas, and Kádambas, I, pt. ii, 523, 524, 527, 555, 558.
Vichárašreni: historical work, I, pt. i, 149 and note 2, 152, 154, 155, 156, 162, 170, 171, 183, 204.
Vichávad: *táluka* in Káthiáwár, VIII, 688.
Vichhia: town and trade centre in Káthiáwár, VIII, 688.
Vicia hissuta: a food plant, XXV, 152.
Vidarbha: modern Berar and east Khándesh, I, pt. ii, 134; the first A'ryan province in the south; Sugriva sends his followers to, *id.* 135; first settlement of A'ryas in, *id.* 141; country mentioned in the *Rámáyana*, *id.* 142; ruled by Bhojas, *id.* 143 and note 2; separate kingdom in the time of the Šungas, *id.* 146; ruled by Gotamiputra, *id.* 149; XVI, 183 and note 2; *see* also *id.* 631.
Videnúrapalliká: village in Kuluhára district, I, pt. ii, 333.
Vidhatra: form of Brahma, beliefs about, IX, pt. i, 33.
Vidišá: Besnagar near Bhilsa, I, pt. i, 65, 66; I, pt. ii, 142; capital of Agnimitra, *id.* 147.
Vidur: a Bráhman sub-caste in Khándesh district, XII, 53; in Ahmadnagar district, XVII, 64; in Poona district, XVIII, pt. i, 184-185; in Sholápur district, XX, 43-44; in Bijápur district, XXIII, 90.
Vidyádharás: class of demi-gods, I, pt. ii, 253, 536; ancestors of North Konkan Siláháras, I, pt. i, 129; pictures of, in Ajanta caves, XII, 493 and note 3.
Vidyánanda: Jain writer, I, pt. ii, 407-408.
Vidyanátha: author of the *Pratáparudriya*, I, pt ii, 246.
Vidyarthis: pupils of the *shastri*, training devotion to the *shastri*, IX, pt. i, 26-27.
Vidya-Sála: Sanskrit college at Bhinmál, I, pt. i, 453 and note 1.
Vigna catiang: food plant, XXV, 153.
Vigne: traveller (A. D. 1840), Gujar immigration into Cashmere according to, IX, pt. i, 481.
Vigraharája: king of Ajmir, I, pt. i, 157.
Viháras: monasteries of Buddha and A'rya-Tárádevi at Dambal, I, pt. ii, 452; in Konkan, I, pt. ii, 10; in Khándesh, XII, 482 note 3, 483.
Viharoli: village in Thána district, ponds and Portuguese remains at, XIV, 381-382.
Vihat Devi: Vaghris' guardian goddess, story of her quarrel with Bhagawan, IX, pt. i, 511 and note 1, 512; shrine of, offerings of sacrifices at, *id.* 515-516.
Vihige: Sarambal, river in Sávantavádi state, I, pt. ii, 372.
Vihirgaon: *see* Viharoli.
Vijámbá: great-granddaughter of Kokkalla I, I, pt. ii, 296.
Vijámba: wife of Indra III, I, pt. ii, 203 and note 3, 204, 414 note 5, 415.
Vijápur: four different towns of the name in Gujarát, I, pt ii, 359 note 3.
Vijápur: sub-division in Baroda, details of, VII, 627. *Town*, *id.* 627-628; hospital at, *id.* 508.
Vijaya: Sátavahana king (202-208), I, pt. ii, 168.
Vijaya: son of the king of Lás in Bengal, mythical conqueror of Ceylon (B. C. 540), XIV, 317.
Vijayabhattáriká: wife of Chandráditya, the brother of Vikramáditya I, I, pt. ii, 185, 186, 365, 366.
Vijayabuddhavarman: Pallava king, grants of, I, pt. ii, 319 and note 2.
Vijayadevi: *see* Shami.
Vijayáditya: mythical Chálukya king, comes from the north, attacks Trilochana-Pallava and loses his life, I, pt. ii, 340-341.
Vijayáditya: Western Chálukya king of Bádámi (696-733), assists his grandfather in a southern campaign and his father in the northern campaign, and acquires the signs of Ganga and Yamuná, is appointed *yuvarája* or prince regent, *id.* 189, 368, 370-371; taken prisoner; escapes and contrives to tranquilise disturbances in his country, *id.* 189, 370-371; succeeds his father, his *biruda*, epithets, and titles, *id.* 370; his temple of Vijayešvara, *id.* 371; records of his time, *id.* 189, 337 note 2, 338, 369, 371, 372, 373, 374, 399, 419 note 2; ancestor of the Western Chálukyas of Kalyáni, *id.* 379, 427; *see* also I, pt. i, 150; XV, pt. ii, 82; XXIII, 385.
Vijayáditya: Karád Siláhára feudatory of Taila III, I, pt. ii, 460; assists the Kalachurya Bijjala in overthrowing the Western Chálukyas, *id.* 475; reinstates the Siláháras of Sthánaka or Thána, *id.* 544, 548, 570; (1142-1154), his inscriptions, XXIV, 222.
Vijayáditya I: Goa Kádamba prince, feudatory of Taila III, I, pt. ii, 460, 486, 565, 568.
Vijayáditya II: Narendramrigarája, Eastern Chálukaya king, I, pt. ii, 281 note 3; wages war with the Gangas and the Ráshtrakútas, *id.* 303, 396; helps Govinda III, in fortifying a town, *id.* 402.
Vijayáditya II: Vishnuchitta the Goa Kádamba (1158-1172), I, pt. ii, 565, 476, 489, 569; helped by Vijayáditya of Karád, *id.* 570.

Vijayáditya III: Gunaka, Eastern Chálukya king (844-888), conquered the Gangas, I, pt. ii, 303, 412, 420 note 3.

Vijayádityadeva: *see* Vijayáditya of Bádámi.

Vijayamahádevi: Chálukya Chándráditya's wife, I, pt. ii, 366.

Vijayanagar: in the Bellary district, I, pt. ii, 431; dynasty of, *id.* 175, 209; history of the dynasty (1330-1580), XV, pt. ii, 95-118; kingdom of, founded by an officer of the Ballál kings, *id.* 637; maritime possessions of, attacked and Goa taken (1470); Belgaum lost (1472), *id.* 638-639; Mudgal and Ráichur fall into the hands of the Musalmáns; intrigues and revolutions at, *id.* 642; king of, joins the confederacy formed by the kings of Ahmadnagar and Golkonda against Bijápur (1536), *id.* 643; treaty with John de Castro against Bijápur (1547), *id.* 46-47; alliance with Ahmadnagar against Bijápur; king of, regains Sholápur, Mudgal and Raichur (1541); treaty with Bijápur, *id.* 643; wife of the king of, adopts Ali Adil Khán of Bijápur as her son; insolent conduct of the king of, leads to the formation of a Musalmán confederacy and the subversion of the kingdom, *id.* 644-645. *See* also XXII, 402-407, 408; XXIII, 396 and note 7, 418; XXI, 362, 371; XI, 142 and note 1, 272.

Vijayanandivarman: eldest son of Chandavarman, I, pt. ii, 333.

Vijaya-Náráyana: god at, apparently, Belúr, I, pt. ii, 505 note 4.

Vijayapandita: learned Jain, rewarded (733) by Vikramáditya II, I, pt. ii, 191.

Vijaya-Pándya, Vijaya-Pándyadeva: Pándya feudatory of Jagadekamalla II under the Kalachurya Bijjala, I, pt. ii, 458, 463, 472; Kalachurya Someśvara's feudatory, *id.* 486; *see* also *id.* 564, 577.

Vijayapura: identified with Bijápur near Parántij, I, pt. i, 108, 110; *see* also I, pt. ii, 359 and note 3.

Vijayapura: modern Bijápur city, I, pt. ii, 450.

Vijayarája: Chálukya prince, his grant, I, pt. i, 108, 110, 112; *see* also I, pt. ii, 188, 359.

Vijayáraka: I, pt. ii, 222, 255; *see* Vijayáditya, Śiláhára prince of Karád.

Vijayárka: Goa Kádamba king, I, pt. i, 172 note 3.

Vijaya Śáha or Vijayasena: fifteenth Kshatrapa (238-249), coins of, I, pt. i, 46-47, 49; brother of Viradáman, I, pt. ii, 294; *see* also I, pt. ii, 177.

Vijaya-Siva-Mándhátrivarman: Kádamba king, I, pt. ii, 290.

Vijayaskandavarman: Pallava king of Káñchi, I, pt. ii, 319.

Vijaya Skandhávára: victorious camp of Vira-Balláladeva II, I, pt. ii, 505.

Vijayavarma: early Chálukya king (A. D. 472), XV, pt. ii, 80.

Vijayavarman: Hángal Kádamba king, I, pt. ii, 559.

Vijayavarman, Vijayavarmarája: *see* Vijyarája.

Vijaydurg: creek in Ratnágiri district, X, 9; port, customs division, trade, exports and imports of, *id.* 185, 378-380; fort, its description and history, *id.* 380-383; I, pt. ii, 39, 74, 75; rebuilt by Shiváji, *id.* 68; Ángria's head-quarters (1713), *id.* 79; XI, 147; attacked by the Dutch (1724), *id.* 149; captured by the English (1756), I, pt. ii, 89-94; X, 196; XXVI, pt. i, 304-305; consequent security to French and Dutch ships (1758), *id.* 320-321; surrenders to the British (1818), I, pt. ii, 118.

Vijayeśvara: temple of god Śiva now known as Sangameśvara at Pattadakal, I, pt. ii, 371 and note 2, 377.

Vijaygad: fort in Ratnágiri district, X, 383.

Vijjal: Jain king of Kalyán (1156-1167), XXIV, 119.

Vijjalá: queen of Hoysála Vira-Someśvara, I, pt. ii, 508.

Vijjala: *see* Vijjana, Bijja, Bijjana, and Bijjala.

Vijjaladeva: Ajayapála's door-keeper and murderer, I, pt. i, 195.

Vijjalaráyacharita: account of Vijjala written by a Jain, I, pt. ii, 225.

Vijjana: Kalachurya king, I, pt. ii, 222, 223, 225, 226, 227, 237, 256, 470. *See* Bijjala.

Vijli: lightning, IX, pt. i, 358.

Vijnáneśvara: author of the *Mitakshará*, I. pt. ii, 219, 229.

Vikatgad: *see* Pele.

Vikkayya: *see* Vikrama, Sindá prince.

Vikram: mythical king (B. C. 56), XIV, 319.

Vikram III: king of Ujjain (400-500), VI, 213.

Vikrama: Sindá prince, nephew and feudatory of Kalachurya Someśvara, I, pt. ii, 485, 488, 573, 576.

Vikrama: Hangal Kádamba prince, I, pt. ii, 559.

Vikramadeva: Sindá prince, I, pt. ii, 463. *See* Vikrama.

Vikramáditya: king of Ujjyini, nine gems of the court of, I, pt. ii, 144; defeated by Saliváhana, *id.* 169-170.

Vikramáditya: ancestor of the Guttas of Guttal, I, pt. ii, 578, 579, 580, 581, 582, 583.

Vikramáditya: name of Chandragupta II, I, pt. i, 65, 67.

Vikramáditya I: Western Chálukya king of Bádámi (655-680), I, pt. ii, 193, 323; succeeds his father, *id.* 186, 361; his *birudas*, epithets and titles, *id.* 329, 361; his charger, *id.* 322 note 8, 361; his contemporary, *id.* 291 note 1; defeated by Pallava Parameśvaravarman I, *id.* 326; his conquests, *id.* 186, 327, 342, 358 note 1, 361-363; establishment of a Western Chálukya branch in Gujarát in the reign of, *id.* 186-187; spurious Chálukya grant, *id.* 188; records of his time, *id.* 282, 328 note 3, 351, 352, 359 and note 1, 363-367; probably referred to under the name of Áditya in the *Samkshepaśáriraka*, *id.* 212. *See* also I, pt. i, 56, 107, 110, 111, 112; gives Láta to his brother Jayasimha, *id.* 117. *See* also XXIII, 383-384; XV, pt. ii, 8.

Vikramáditya I: Western Chálukya king of Kalyáni (1009-1011), succeeds his uncle, I, pt. ii, 213. *See* Vikramáditya V.

Vikramáditya II: Western Chálukya king of Kalyáni (1076-1126), I, pt. ii, 229; declines the honour of prince regent; is employed by his father to fight his battles, *id.* 215; quarrels with his brother; submission of Jayakeśi of Goa to; his alliance with the Chola prince, *id.* 216; defeats his brother Someśvara II and Rájiga; his coronation, *id.* 217; rebellion of his brother Jayasimha, *id.* 218; invasion of his dominions by Hoysála Vishnuvardhana, *id.* 218-219; his patronage of learning, *id.* 219, 221, 228, 237. *See* Vikramáditya VI.

Vikramáditya II: Western Chálukya king of Bádámi (733-746), succeeds his father, I, pt. ii, 189, 374; his *birudas*, epithets and titles, *id.* 374; marries two uterine sisters of the Kalachuri family, *id.* 190, 225, 374, 414 note 4; his family foe, *id.* 316; his conquests, *id.* 189-190, 327 and note 8, 374-375; sets up a pillar of victory on the shore of the southern ocean, *id.* 375; confers the badge of honour called *Mume-perjerspu-patta*, and the name of Tribhuvanácháraya upon the architect Gunda, *id.* 376; records of his time, *id.* 327, 372, 375-376. *See* also XV, pt. ii, 82; XXIII, 385-386.

Vikramáditya III: Western Chálukya prince, one of the ancestors of the Western Chálukyas of Kalyáni, I, pt. ii, 378, 379.

Vikramáditya IV: father of Taila II, founder of the Western Chálukya dynasty of Kalyáni, I, pt. ii, 378; marries a princess of Chedi, *id.* 296, 379-380, 427.

Vikramáditya IV: *see* Vikramáditya VI, Kalyáni Chálukya king.

Vikramáditya V: Western Chálukya king of Kalyáni (1009 and 1011), succeeds his uncle, his *biruda*, his records, I, pt. ii, 333, 426, 434 and note 3, 435, 458 note 2. *See* Vikramáditya I, Western Chálukya king of Kalyáni.

Vikrámáditya VI: Western Chálukya king of Kalyáni (1076-1126); governor under his father, I, pt. ii, 440, 444 note 2; deposes his brother Someśvara II and seats himself on the throne, *id.* 445; his *biruda* and the various forms of his name, *id.* 445-446; his coronation, *id.* 446; supersedes the use of the Śaka era, *id.* 447; his conquests, *id.* 333, 442; records of his reign, *id.* 282 note 3, 339, 358 note 1, 425, 428 note 4, 448; his wives appointed to manage districts, *id.* 448-449; his brother Jayasimha III rebels, *id.* 449; his feudatories and officers, *id.* 450-452, 493, 498, 515, 547, 553, 554, 561, 562, 568, 574, 577, 580; Hoysala Vishnuvardhana invades his dominions, *id* 453, 497, 500; his life, written by Bilhana, *id.* 180. *See* Vikramáditya II, Western Chálukya king of Kalyáni; *see* also XV, pt. ii, 87, 262 and note 1; X, 193, XXIII, 550.

Vikrama Era: commencing B. C. 58, said to be founded by Vikramáditya, the mythical king of Ujjain, I, pt. ii, 579; its early name Málav, *id.* 311.

Vikramánka: Hangal Kádamba prince, I, pt. ii, 559.

Vikramánkadevacharita: life of Vikramáditya II, also styled VI by Bilhana, I, pt. ii, 180, 278 note 2, 281 note 3, 309, 335 note 1, 440 and note 7, 441 and notes 7 and 8, 444 and note 5, 449 note 3, 450 note 5, 452 note 4.

Vikramapura: town founded by Vikramáditya II, the Western Chálukya king of Kalyáni, I, pt. ii, 219; Akkádevi's seat of government, *id.* 435; improved by the founder, *id.* 450 and note 5.

Vikramapura: modern Kannanur, built by Hoysála Vira-Someśvara, I, pt. ii, 508.

Vikramárjunavijaya: work by Kanarese poet Pampa, I, pt. ii, 380.

Vikramasimha: Paramára king of Chandrávati, joins the king of Sámbhara and is dethroned by Kumárapála, I, pt. i, 185, 188.

Vilas: princes, made steadfast allies of the Chálukya crown by Vinayáditya (696), I, pt. ii, 189, 368.

Viláyti ambi: a timber tree, XXV, 91, 10.

Viláyti babul: timber tree, XXV, 66.

Vilivá yakura: identified with Baleocuros, I, pt. ii, 158, 176.

Viliváyakurasa: word inscribed on coins found at Kolhápur, probably name of the governor, I, pt. ii, 152.

Village communities: in Bijápur district, XXIII, 75-77; in Surat district, II, 56; in Broach district, *id.* 381-388; in Kaira district, III, 39; in Panch Mahals, *id.* 227; in Ahmadábád district, IV, 46; in Cutch, V, 101-102; in Mahi Kántha and Pálanpur, *id.* 368; in Rewa Kántha, VI, 35; in Baroda, VII, 74; in Káthiáwár, VIII, 171, 172; in Ratnágiri: village officers, the *khots*, *pátils*, etc., village servants, the Mhars, the *sipais*, etc., X, 137-142; in Sávantvádi, *id.* 421; in Kolába district, XI, 87; in Janjira, *id.* 423; in Khándesh, XII, 131-134, 267; in Thána district, XIII, 275; in Násik district, XVI, 33, 87, 88; in Kánara, XV, pt. i, 412-415; in Ahmadnagar district, XVII, 48-49; in Poona district, XVIII, pt. i, 96-98; in Sátára, XIX, 48-50; in Sholápur, XX, 211-213; in Belgaum, XXI, 232-234; in Dhárwár, XXII, 49-50; in Kolhápur, XXIV, 40-42.

Village deities: in Kánara district, XV, pt. i, 146 and footnote 1.

Village goddesses: in Dhárwár district, Durgava and Dayamava, temples, images, worship, fair, XXII, 807-812.

Village Officers: (1882) in Thána district, XIII, 529; (1817), *id.* 563-564; how paid (1828), unfit to manage local funds (1845), *id.* 564 note 1, 573 note 2, 573-574, 575; in Kolába district (1882), XI, 161 and notes 1 and 2, 162; in Kánara district, XV, pt. ii, 190; Mughal, in Gujarát, I, pt. i, 212; in Poona district, XVIII, pt. ii, 311, 360-361; in Násik district (1882), *id.* 206-207; (1818), *id.* 209 and note 5; in Belgaum district, XXI, 416; in Kaira district, III, 87.

Village Servants: in Kolába district (1882), XI, 161 and note 3, 162; in Thána district (1882), XIII, 529; (1817), *id.* 563-564;

(1828), *id.* 573-574; in Kánara district, XV, pt. ii, 190; in Násik district (1882), XVI, 207; in Poona district, XVIII, pt. ii, 312, 361-366; in Belganm, XXI, 416-417.

Villana: ruler of Mangalvedhem, killed by Bhillama V, I, pt. ii, 238.

Vilvalangara: modern Villivalam, I, pt. ii, 326.

Vimala: general of Bhima I, subdues Dhandhuka, chief of A'bu, and builds Jain temples on A'bu, I, pt. i, 169.

Vimala: Jain author, I, pt. ii, 200.

Vimaláditya: Chálukya prince, I, pt. ii, 211, 399.

Vimalavasahi: group of Jain temples on A'bu, I, pt. i, 169 and note 1.

Vimaleshvar: temple of, at Nirmal in Thána district, XIV, 293.

Vinápoti: mistress of Vijayáditya, I, pt. ii, 372.

Vinayáditya: Western Chálukya king of Bádámi (680-696), I, pt. ii, 296; succeeds his father, *id.* 367; date of the commencement of his reign, *id.* 365 note 3, 367 note 4; his *birudas*, epithets and titles; his conquests; acquires the *pálidhvaja* banner and other insignia of sovereignty from some paramount king of Northern India, *id.* 188-189, 362, 368; records of his time, 342, 360 note 1, 368-370, 428 note 4; identified with Yuddhamalla I, *id.* 380 note 6; his spiritual adviser, *id.* 191; probably referred to under the name of Aditya in the *Samkshepasáriraka*, *id.* 212; *see* also I, pt. i, 56, 110; his inscriptions, *id.* 111; XV, pt. ii, 81-82; XXIII, 384-385.

Vinayáditya: first historical person in the family of the Hoysálas of Dorasamudra (1048), I, pt. ii, 491, 493; said to owe his rise to a Jain teacher named S'antideva, *id.* 492; feudatory of Someśvara I, *id.* 439; feudatory of the Chola king, *id.* 492; (1047-1076), XV, pt. ii, 85 note 3.

Vinayáditya Mangalarája: copper-plate grant at Balsár of, I, pt. i, 108.

Vináyak Parshurám Bivalkar: (1817-1840), minister of Kolába state, XI, 156-157.

Vináyakráo: Amrutráo's son, placed on the throne of the Peshwa (1802), I, pt. ii, 608.

Vincent: antiquarian, I, pt. i, 542; I, pt. ii, 1; XIII, 712.

Vincent le Blanc: French geographer (1567-1578), his mention of Bhatkal, XV, pt. ii, 274.

Vinchur: town in Násik district, XVI, 662; chief of, exercises civil powers, *id.* 308 note 3.

Vinchurkar: Vithal Shivdev, distinguishes himself at the siege of Ahmadábád (1753); accompanies the Marátha army in the fatal expedition of Pánipat; raised to high rank by Raghunáthráo, I, pt. ii, 633.

Vindhya: mountain in Rewa Kántha, VI, 2; northern limit of Dadda I's Gurjjara kingdom, I, pt. i, 115; its king, *id.* 163; southern boundary of Kumárapála's kingdom, *id.* 189, 468, 517; abode of the Pulindas and Śabaras, I, pt. ii, 138; countries mentioned in the *puránás* as situated on the, *id.* 139.

Vindhyashakti: ruling dynasty (600 A. D.) in Khándesh district, XII, 240 and note 5, 485 and note 1, 543 and note 1.

Vindhyavasini: goddess, IX, pt. i, p. xxxvi; shrine on the river Nágmátá close to Navánagar, chief temple of, at Chhaya near Porbandar, worshipped by Jethvas, *id.* 136.

Vindhyávat: mountain, I, pt. ii, 149.

Vindiri: village in Konkan, I, pt. ii, 347 note 2.

Vindu: the Vindhya mountains, I, pt. i, 510.

Vines: growth of, in Násik district, XVI, 102; in Poona district, XVIII, pt. ii, 62-63; in Ahmadnagar district, XVII, 274-276.

Vingavalli: Chálukyas conquered at, by Amoghavarsha I, I, pt. ii, 402.

Vinhukadadutu, Vinhupaduchutu: family name of king Haritiputra Śatakarni, I, pt. ii, 278.

Vinján: a ruined town in Cutch, the site of Kanchiba Páttan in the vicinity of, temples at, V, 253.

Vinkar: a caste of weavers in Násik district, XVI, 53, 485.

Vipashyi: first Buddha, image of, at Sopára, XIV, 331, 413.

Vipers: snakes in Poona district, XVIII, pt. i, 81-82.

Vir: spirit, a hero, IX, pt. i, 426.

Vir: caste of beggars in Poona district, XVIII, pt. i, 480-481.

Vir: village in Poona district, temple and fair at, XVIII, pt. iii, 454.

Vira: village in Cutch, old temples at, V, 253.

Vira-Ballála: *see* Ballála II.

Vira-Ballála II: *see* Ballála II.

Vira-Ballála III: *see* Ballála III.

Vira-Bhadra: S'iva's attendant, I, pt. ii, 482; images of, at Elura and Elephanta caves, XIV, 73.

Vira-Bhoja: *see* Bhoja II.

Vira-Bijjarasa: feudatory of Singhana, I, pt. ii, 523.

Vira-Bukkanna: *see* Bukka.

Viráchárya: author of the *Sárasamgraha*, a Jain mathematical work, I, pt. ii, 200.

Viradáman: thirteenth Kshatrapa (A. D. 236-238), coins of, I, pt. i, 46; I, pt. ii, 294.

Viradhavala: Vághela king (1233-1238), I, pt. i, 179, 196, 197; his father abdicates in his favour; his expeditions against Vanthali, Bhadreśvara and Godhra, and his treaty with the Sultán of Delhi, *id.* 200-201, 206, son of Lavanaprasáda, I, pt. ii, 241, 525 and note 6; king of Anahilapattana, *id.* 242.

Vira-Ganga: *biruda* of the Hoysála kings Ereyanga and Vishnuvardhana, I, pt. ii, 492.

Vira-Gonkarasa: of the Bána race, Kalachurya Someśvara's officer, I, pt. ii, 486, 488, 489.

Vira-Korchavarman: *see* Vira-Kurchavarman.

Vira-Kurcha: Pallava king, I, pt. ii, 324.

Vira-Kurchavarman: Pallava king, I, pt. ii, 322.

Vira-Mahádeva: *see* Mahádeva the Yádava king.

Vira-Mahendra: Pallava king Mahendrádhirája, at war with the Western Ganga Ereyappa (930-940), I, pt. ii, 304, 332, 379.

Viramati: Jain nun, brings up Vanarája, I, pt. i, 151.

Virama Visala : *see* Visaladeva.
Viramgám : sub-division of Ahmadábád district, details of, IV, 235-237. *Town, id.* 354 ; Muna lake at, I, pt. i, 180 note 2 ; disturbance at (1734), *id.* 314 ; Sher Khán Bábi appointed governor of, *id.* 315 ; expulsion of the Maráthás from, by Bháv Singh, *id.* 323 ; besieged by the Maráthás ; surrendered by Bháv Singh, *id.* 323, 324 ; given by Rangoji to the Musalmáns, *id.* 326, 513, 518 ; *see* also VII, 174-176.
Virampura : state in Rewa Kántha, VI, 146.
Vira Narasimha III : Hoysála king (1254-1290), I, pt. ii, 493 ; succeeds his father Vira-Someśvara, his various names, records of his time, his titles, *id.* 509.
Vira-Náráyan : temple of, at Gadag, I, pt. ii, 426 note 3.
Vira-Náráyana : title of Amoghavarsha I, I, pt. ii, 199 ; *biruda* of Govinda IV, *id.* 416 ; of Kakka II, *id.* 423 ; of Kalachurya Áhavamalla, *id.* 488.
Vira-Pandyadeva : Someśvara III and Jagadekamalla II's governor of the Nolambavádi province, I, pt. ii, 456, 458.
Virár : village in Thána district, XIV, 382-383.
Vira-Rájendradeva I : Chola king ; *see* Rájakesarivarman.
Vira-Rámachandra : *see* Rámchandra the Yadava king.
Vira-Rámadevarasa : Kalachurya Someśvara's officer, I, pt. ii, 486.
Vira-Rámanátha : Hoysála prince, son of Vira-Someśvara, I, pt. ii, 493 ; holds local authority under the Pándyas, *id.* 508.
Vira-Saivas : Śaiva champions, the Lingáyat sect so called, I, pt. ii, 477, 478.
Viraśarman : preceptor of Mayuraśarman, founder of the Kádamba family, I, pt. ii, 286.
Vira-Satyáśrayadeva : son of Govindaráya, I, pt. ii, 467.
Virasenabhattáraka : teacher of Jinasena, I, pt. ii, 407 note 4.
Virasimha : Pallava king, I, pt. ii, 324.
Virasimha : Chalukya king, I, pt. ii, 340 note 3.
Vira-Somanátha : image of, set up at Ablúr by Ekántada Rámayya, I, pt. ii, 483.
Vira Someśvara : *see* Someśvara IV, the Western Chalukya.
Vira-Someśvara : Hoysála king (1234-1235 and 1253), I, pt. ii, 493 ; succeeds his father Narasimha II ; his various names and records, *id.* 507 ; marries the Chálukya princess Devalamahádevi, *id.* 466 ; takes the Chola kingdom ; his earliest and latest dates ; his titles ; fights against the Yádava king Krishna of Devagiri, *id.* 508.
Virat : a division of Abhir, "Introduction to the History of the Konkan," I, pt. ii, p. x.
Virat : *See* Vairatpur.
Viráta : Puranic king, I, pt. ii, 278 note 2.
Virátakot, Virátanagara or Virataiakot : another name of Hangal, XXII, 389 ; *see* also I, pt. ii, 504, 558 and notes 6 and 7.
Viráta-Parvan : fourth book of the *Mahábhárata*, I, pt. ii, 278 note 2.
Virátnagari : old name of Wái, XIX, 224 note 3, 614.
Vira-Vághela : *see* Viradhavala.
Viravarman : successor of Skandavarman I, the Pallava king, I, pt. ii, 321.
Vira-Vikramáditya I : Gutta prince, Mallideva's son, I, pt. ii, 579, 581, 582, 583.
Vira-Vikramáditya II : Gutta prince and feudatory of the Western Chálukya king Someśvara IV, I, pt. ii, 466 ; son of Joyideva I of the Gutta family, *id.* 489 ; ruler of Banavási, *id.* 520 ; Gutta feudatory, holds Banavási province, *id.* 524, 578 ; Áhavaditya, Gutta prince, son of Gutta II (1182 and 1213), *id.* 579, 581 ; feudatory of the Kalachurya king Áhavamalla, *id.* 582, 583.
Viráwáh : town in Sind, the post of the Cutch chief driven from (1760), V, 142 ; Gadji repairs to (1762), *id.* 143 ; Cutch Girásiás take refuge at (1819), *id.* 163.
Vir Ballál : Hoysála chief (1192-1211), XV, pt. ii, 91 and note 1.
Virdel : sub-division of Khándesh district, boundaries, area, aspect, climate, water, soil, holdings, survey details, survey results, stock, crops, and people of, XII, 2, 424-430.
Virgal : monumental tablet, I, pt. ii, 563.
Virgin Mary : image of at Mandapeshvar, XIV, 223.
Virhoi : timber tree, XXV, 18.
Virpur : sub-division of Bálásinor state in Rewa Kántha, VI, 137, 146. *Town*, a mosque at, *id.* 170 ; Siddharája builds a fort at, I, pt. i, 180 note 2 ; an independent state at, during Musalmán occupation of Gujarát, *id.* 206.
Virpur : state and town in Káthiáwár, VIII, 688-689.
Virsen : Abhir king (419 A. D.) of Násik, XII, 240. *See* also I, pt. ii, 177.
Viruli : cattle disease in Khándesh district, XII, 337.
Virúpáksha : temple of Śiva at Pattadakal, built by Lokamahádevi, wife of Vikramáditya II, I, pt. ii, 374.
Virupáksha : sixth Vijayanagar king (1465-1479), XV, pt. ii, 96 note 4, 100.
Virvav : *táluka* in Káthiáwár, VIII, 689.
Visala : *see* Visáladeva, the Vághela king.
Visaladeva : ruler of Chandrávati near Mount Abu, vassal of Sárangdeva Vághela (1275-1296), I, pt. i, 204.
Visáladeva : Vághela king (1243-1261), I, pt. i, 206 ; defeats his brother and Tribhuvanapála Solanki ; refuses to acknowledge an overlord and lessens the miseries of a three years' famine, I, pt. i, 203 ; defeated by Krishna and overthrown by Mahádev the Yádava king, I, pt. ii, 244, 246, 528.
Visáladeva : son of Viradhavala, *ráná* of Dholka, I, pt. ii, 242, 525 and notes 8 and 9.
Visalanagara : town in East Gujarát, fortifications of, repaired by Visáladeva, I, pt. i, 203.
Visaldev : king of Ajmir, I, pt. ii, 24.
Visápur : peak in Poona district, XVIII, pt. i, 5 ; fort, details, history, XVIII, pt. iii, 254-256.
Visa : section in Vania castes, meaning of, IX, pt. i, 70, 435.

Visavadar: village in Káthiáwár, Hothal Padmini's cave near, VIII, 690-691.
Visávar: village in Káthiáwár, temples near, VIII, 691.
Vishálgad: hill fort in Kolhápur state, XXIV, 4, 6, 293; mosques, fair, tradition of the building of, water-supply, inscription and history of, *id.* 322-323; Malik-ul-Tujár defeated by the *rája* of (1453), I, pt. ii, 31; captured by Bahmani troops (1469), *id.* 32; surprised by Shiváji (1659), XVIII, pt. ii, 228; surrendered and its name changed to Sákhkháralana (1701), I, pt. ii, 80.
Vishálgad: hill pass in Ratnágiri district, X, 166.
Vishálgad: fort in Thána district, XIV, 383.
Vishálgad Panhála: hill range in Kolhápur, XXIV, 6-7.
Vishamasiddhi: *see* Vishnuvardhana I.
Vishaya: district, I, pt. ii, 21, 398.
Vishnu: the preserver, second member of Hindu Trinity or *trimurti*, worship of, in his incarnations of Rám and Krishna, IX, pt. i, p. xxxvi, 530, 531; cursed by Vranda, marriage with Vranda in her form of *tulsi*, *id.* 387-388; bloodless offerings made to, in his form of Krishna, *id.* 409; *asopalav* leaves offered to, *id.* 383; sesame seeds, the emblem of, *id.* 391; worship of image as Ranchhodji and Rádhákrishna, *id.* p. xxxv, 118, 136, 213, 362; synonyms of, I, pt. ii, 142; idol of, *id.* 181; the family god of Chálukya and Ráshtrakúta dynasties, *id.* 338, 359, 387; Adam represented as, IX, pt. ii, 40.
Vishnu: minister of Kapardin I, I, pt. ii, 541.
Vishnu: minister of Pullasakti, I, pt. ii, 404.
Vishnu: minister of Kapardin II, I, pt. ii, 406.
Vishnu: *see* Hoysála king Vishnuvardhana.
Vishnubali: guardian-pleasing, fourth Vedic rite, IX, pt. i, 31 note 3.
Vishnubhatta-Somayájiu: saint, gives shelter to the queen of Vijayáditya, I, pt. ii, 340.
Vishnudása: chief, father of Chandragupta's (396-415) feudatory, I, pt. i, 65.
Vishnugopa: Pallava king of Kañchi, his grant, I, pt. ii, 319 note 2, 320 and note 6, 321 and note 2, 280, 317, 324; conquered and afterwards liberated by Samudragupta, the early Gupta king, about the middle of the fourth century A. D., *id.* 319; *yuvarája*, brother of Simhavarman I, the Pallava chief, *id.* 321.
Vishnugopa: Ganga king (A. D. 351), I, pt. ii, 300.
Vishnugopavarman: *see* Vishnugopa, Pallava king.
Vishnuhára: god, grant made to the temple of, at Kandukura by the Pallava general Vishnuvarman, I, pt. ii, 321.
Vishnuites: religious sect in Gujarát, followers of Vishnu, divisions—followers of Rám, chief sects; followers of Krishna, chief sects, IX, pt. i, 530, 533, 535.
Vishnu Kanchi: place of pilgrimage, IX, pt. i, 549.
Vishnupálita: Sátakarni lieutenant in Govardhana, I, pt. ii, 150.
Vishnu Puran: Hindu religious book, IX, pt. i, 532; I, pt. ii, 155, 162, 164; proofs of the careless preparation of, *id.* 165.
Vishnurája: Vishnuvardhana III (709-746), I, pt. ii, 326.
Vishnusimha: Pallava king, I, pt. ii, 324.
Vishnuvamsa: race of Vishnu, Bhillama II said to come of, I, pt. ii, 511 and note 7.
Vishnu-vamsodbhava: Devagiri Yádava epithet, I, pt. ii, 517.
Vishnuvardhana: Hoysála prince (1117-1137), various forms of his name, I, pt. ii, 494; his *birudas*, *id.* 492, 494; his titles, *id.* 498; feudatory of the Western Chálukya king Someśvara III, *id.* 456, 498; of the Western Chálukya king Vikramáditya VI, *id.* 452, 497, 498; his conquests, *id.* 495-497, 499; invades Vikramáditya VI's dominions, *id.* 218-219, 497; is pursued by the Sindas, *id.* 459, 497, 575; his war with the Kádambas of Hangal, *id.* 562, 569; presents Gangarája with territory for his services, *id.* 499-500; makes a successful night attack upon the forces of Vikramáditya VI, *id.* 500; Puránic genealogy of the family probably devised in his time, *id.* 490; his wife's religion, *id.* 491; *see* also XV, pt. ii, 88-89, 92.
Vishnuvardhana: Varika prince, feudatory of Samudragupta, I, pt. ii, 311-312.
Vishnuvardhana I: brother of Pulakesi II, Western Chálukya king, I, pt. ii, 185, 193, 349; appointed to rule over Sátára and Pandharpur, *id.* 185; establishes at Vengi the Eastern Branch of the Chálukyas, *id.* 185, 352; his grants, *id.* 338, 351, 356, 410 note 1. *See* Kubja-Vishnuvardhana.
Vishnuvardhana II: Eastern Chálukya king, I, pt. ii, 369 note 5.
Vishnuvardhana III: Eastern Chálukya king (709-746), I, pt. ii, 327.
Vishnuvardhana IV: Eastern Chálukya king (764-799), I, pt. ii, 296.
Vishnuvardhana Rájarája I: Eastern Chálukya king (1022-1063), grant of, I, pt. ii, 340.
Vishnuvardhana Vijayáditya: imaginary progenitor of the Chálukyas, I, pt. ii, 339.
Vishnuvardhana Vijayáditya: Western Chálukya prince (1064-1074), son of Someśvara I, I, pt. ii, 428 note 4, 440, 444; governor of Nolambavádi; his *birudas*, *id.* 454 and note 6.
Vishnuvarman: Kádamba king, I, pt. ii, 290.
Vishnuvarman: *see* Vishnugop, Pallava king.
Vishnuvarman: Hangal Kádamba, I, pt. ii, 559.
Vishopáka: village, I, pt. i, 169.
Vishrámbág Palace: in Poona city, XVIII, pt. iii, 348, 349.
Vishrámgad: fort in Kolába district, XI, 397.
Vishrámgad: name given by Shiváji to Pattah, XVII, 400.
Vishvabhu: third Buddha, image of at Sopára, XIV, 331, 413.
Vishvadev: universal lord, fire so considered, IX, pt. I, 356.
Vishvakarma: divine architect, I, pt. i, 461, 462; IX, pt. i, 202.

Vishva Karma : Elúr cave temple, I, pt. ii, 9.
Vishvakarma : title of a book about Sutár caste, IX, pt. i, 202, note 1.
Vishvámitra : royal *rishi*, or warrior-sage, IX, pt. i, 434 and note 9, 447 and note 6 ; I, pt. i, 461.
Vishvámitri : river in Baroda, VII, 14-18.
Vishveshvar : god Śiva, great Shaivite temple of, at Benaras, IX, pt. i, 549.
Visnagar : sub division in Baroda, details of, VII, 621. *Town*, its origin, fairs, public buildings and temples at, *id.* 621-622 ; hospital at, *id.* 527 ; *see* also IX, pt. i, 13.
Visnagara : sub-caste of Nágar Bráhmans, IX, pt. i, 13, 15.
Visnnusvámi : founder of Sámba *sampradáya* cult of Vaishnáv sects, IX, pt. i, 533, 535.
Visparad, Visparatu : preserved portion of the *Zend Avesta*, IX, pt. ii, 212 note 1, 226 ; copy of, made at Ankleshvar, *id.* 186.
Visphotak : syphilis, its cure, IX, pt. i, 365.
Visroda : state in Mahi Kántha, V, 428.
Vistashp : Nusks, original part of the *Zend Avesta*, IX, pt. ii, 211 note 2 (11) ; preserved portion of the *Zend Avesta*, *id.* 212 note 1.
Visvakarman : writer of the Hallegere grant, I, pt. ii, 301 note 1.
Visva Saha, Visvaśena : the last Kshatrap king (A. D. 292), I, pt. ii, 177 ; twentieth Kshatraps (294-300), his coins, I, pt. i, 48-49.
Viśvasimha : eighteenth Kshatrapa, I, pt. i, 272-278 ; coins of, *id.* 47.
Visvavaráha : father of Grahári, I, pt. i, 139.
Visvavarman : the son or younger brother of Naravarman the Málava (A. D. 423), I, pt. ii, 312.
Vita : town in Sátára district, XIX, 609-610 ; trade centre, *id.* 216.
Vital Statistics : *see* Births and Deaths.
Vitárája Jayabhata : title of Jayabhata I, Gurjjára ruler, I, pt. i, 115 ; I, pt. ii, 312 note 2.
Vitarája : Jain *tirthankara*, I, pt. i, 195.
Vitex : *alata*, *altissima*, *bicolor*, *leucoxylan*, *negando*, timber trees found in Southern Marátha Country and Konkan, XXV, 108, 109.
Vithal Deváji : Gáikwár's officer, captures Malhárráv Gáikwár (1803), I, pt. i, 413 ; appointed *subha* in Káthiáwár, *id.* 426.
Vithalgad : *táluka* in Káthiáwár, VIII, 689.
Vithalpant : Anegundi or Bahmani revenue officer (1343-1490) his unit of measurement, XXII, 440 and note 3, 459 note 3, 650 and note 2.
Vithalráv Bháu : Baroda minister (1810), VII, 216, 235-236.
Vithalráv Diwanji : Baroda minister, his career, VII, 206, 216, 230, 236, 239-240, 242, 321, 322, 324, 326.
Vithal Shukdev : lieutenant of Raghunáthráv in Gujarát, settles peace with Jawán Mard Khán (1753), I, pt. i, 337.
Vithalvádi : in Thána district, temple and an old pond at, XIV, 383.
Vithoba : Hindu god, XIII, 524 ; shrine of, at Pandharpur, IX, pt. i, 549, worship, service and history, XX, 417-432, 473 note 2 ; at Násik, XVI, 512.
Vithoji Holkar : murder of (1802), XVIII, pt. iii, 15 note 2, 413.
Vitis Vinifera : grape tree, XXV, 150.
Vitolia : early tribe in Gujarát, IX, pt. i, 290, 329-330.
Vittarasa : the father of Somaládevi, I, pt. ii, 508 ; Yádava king Mahádeva's officer (1270), *id.* 528.
Viverridæ : civet cat, etc., in Ratnágiri district, X, 45.
Vizagapatam : grants from, I, pt. ii, 297.
Vizárat Mal : Ángria's title, IX, 146.
Vizaydurg : *see* Vijaydurg.
Voddiyavva : daughter of prince Dhorappa, married to Vaddiga, the Yádava prince, I, pt. ii, 231.
Voddiyavva : wife of Bádagi, I, pt. ii, 513.
Vohorvu : word Bohora derived from, IX, pt. ii, 24.
Vohukhshathra : fourth Gátha day, IX, pt. ii, 218.
Vol : meaning forced contributions, levied by powerful landowners, in Gujarát, I, pt. i, 216, 227 and note 1.
Vologesocerta : Parthian mart (A. D. 60), XIII, 412.
Vora : state in Rewa Kántha, VI, 144.
Vovla : an estate in Sálsette, XIII, 545, 546.
Vows : among Gujarát Musalmáns, offerings of, allowed by the law of the prophet ; forms of, IX, pt. ii, 127-128 ; made by Indian Musalmáns to saints, to visit shrines of note, *id.* 128-129 ; to Táaziáhs and other institutions of the Muharram, *id.* 129-130 ; to genii, fairies and spirits, *id.* 128, 130 ; called *Goths* among Pársis, offerings of ; objects of ; names of, *id.* 230-231 ; among Gujarát Hindus ; marriage, IX, pt. i, 45, 46 ; moon, *id.* 400 ; sun, *id.* 394 ; made to Tajias, *id.* 137, 362 ; of walking over live coal as a cure for cattle plague and sickness, *id.* 357 ; taken in saints' honor, *id.* 361 ; by barren women, *id.* 367 ; when child is attacked by small-pox, *id.* 370-371 ; during epidemics, *id.* 414 ; taken by Vághris, *id.* 515-517.
Voyagers : Hindu, prehistoric, XIII, 711-715 ; in Palestine (B. C. 700), Persia (B. C. 480), Carthage (B. C. 300), Rome (B. C. 250), Greece, Germany, England (B. C. 200-60), *id.* 403 and note 1 ; in Egypt, Alexandria, Constantinople and Jáva (A. D. 150), *id.* 414 and note 3, 417 note 1 ; in Persia, Alexandria, Ceylon, Jáva, and China (A. D. 500), *id.* 420 and note 5 ; in Persia and Arabia (650-900), *id.* 432 and note 6, 711 note 2 ; in Ormuz, Aden, Zanzibár and Malacca (1300-1500), *id.* 446 and note 7, 712 ; in the Persian Gulf, Mokha, East Africa, Malacca, Sumátra, Cong and Bassora (1500-1700), *id.* 468 and note 10, 488 ; in Maskat, Red Sea, Batávia, Yemen, the Somáli Coast, Holland and England (1760-1811), *id.* 520 and note 3 ; in the Persian Gulf, Arabia, Africa and the Bay of Bengal (1882), *id.* 350, 716, 730 note 1.
Vranda : wife of demon Jálandhar, cursed by Vishnu, Vishnu's consort in the form of Tulsi, IX, pt. i, 387.
Vrata Khanda : the work of Hemádri, I, pt. ii, 136, 230, 231, 232, 234, 236, 244 ; part

of Hemádri's *Chaturvarga Chintámani*, an exposition of religious fasts and observances, *id.* 249; introduction to, *id.* 268-275, 445, 511, 512, 513.
Vriatrasur: domon, IX, pt. i, 9.
Virhimukhagráma: village granted to a temple by Mangaleśa, I, pt. ii, 348.
Vriji: ruler of Málwa, is said to have introduced new divisions into old castes, IX, pt. i. 469 note 3.
Vrijjis: Central Asian tribe identified with Sakas, I, pt. i, 456 note 1.
Vrindávan: place of pilgrimage, IX, pt. i, 549.
Vrishabha: S'iva's bull, I, pt. ii, 227.
Vrisbadhwaja: bull standard, used by Mihirakula, IX, pt. i, 442.
Vultures: at Mátherán, XIV, 257.
Vulturidæ: family of birds in Ratnágiri district, X, 54.
Vyághralánchhana: tiger crest, I, pt. ii, 576.
Vyághra Mrigalánchhana: crest of a tiger and a deer, I, pt. ii, 577.
Vyághramukha: king of Gurjjárás, said to belong to Sri Chápa dynasty, IX, pt. i, 488 and note 3, I, pt. i, 467.
Vyághrapálli: Vághela, the home of Vaghelás, I, pt. i, 198.
Vyághrarája: Chápa king (628 A. D.), I, pt. i, 138 note 1.
Vyághrarája: king of Mahá-Kántara (350 A. D.), subdued by the Guptás, I, pt. ii, 280.
Vyághrarata: Varika prince, I, pt. ii, 312.
Vyághrása: village identified with Vágra, in Broach district, I, pt. i, 129 and note 3; or with Wághás in Kaira, I, pt. ii, 413.
Vyaj-Vahi: interest book, IX, pt. i, 84.
Vyankatesh: god, XII, 58.
Vyankantráv: becomes chief of Mudhol (1817), XXIV, 394.
Vyas: Bráhman sub-caste in Gujarát, origin of, IX, pt. i, 21.
Vyásji: island in the Narmada in Rewa Kántha, VI, 6.
Vyatipáts: days of certain combinations of stars, IX, pt. i, 23 note 5 continued on page 24.

W

WAÁZ*: Musalmán sermon, IX, pt. ii, 134 note 2, 169.
Wadageri: village in the Nizám's dominions, I, pt. ii, 446; inscription at, *id.* 450 note 1.
Wadder: *see* Vadar.
Wádhel: Rajput tribe, Musalmán prisoners of war enrolled among, by Mularaj II (A. D. 1177-1179), IX, pt. i, 444.
Wadhwán: state and town in Káthiáwár, VIII, 261, 691-701; fortifications at, capital of Dharanivaraha (914), I, pt. ii, 383.
Wádiás: Pársi boat builders, IX, pt. i, 205.
Wafát: Musalmán holiday on the twelfth day of the third month, IX, pt. ii, 140.
Waganti, Wagatti: a food and sacred plant, XXV, 145, 291.

* For many words sometimes written with the initial "w" the reader is referred to "v," the more correct form.

Wages: in Bombay island (1717-1768), XXVI, pt. ii, 252-253; *hamáls'* (1768), *id.* 253-255; artificers' (1772), *id.* 389-391; history of, all district volumes, *see* Capital under District Name.
Waghdás: name possessing special magical powers, IX, pt. ii, 143.
Wághili: village in Khándesh, inscription at, I, pt. ii, 284, 515; record at, *id.* 518.
Wághria: castrator, at Bhinmál, I, pt. i, 451.
Wagra: sub-division of Broach district, II, 539-541. *Town, id.* 569.
Wagtail: class of birds in Ratnágiri district, X, 80.
Wahabi, Wahhábi: Musalmán sect in Gujarát; dissenters, known as Gheir Mukallid or Ahl-i-Hadith, IX, pt. ii, 12; schism from Sunni faith, *id.* 13; origin and rise of sect in Arabia, the chief leaders and the government of, duties of, *id.* 12 note 3; brought into India (1821), their rise to importance (1857), spread of their doctrines in Gujarát, chiefly by Maulavi Liákat Ali, among Sunni Bohorás, *id.* 13, 61, 175; doctrines of, *id.* 13, 61, 128; in Thána district, XIII, 225; in Poona district, XVIII, pt. ii, 308; in Sholápur district, XX, 201; in Belgaum district, XXI, 411; in Kolhápur state, XXIV, 150-151.
Wai: sub-division of Sátára district, its boundaries, area, aspect, climate, water, soil, stock, holdings, crops and people, XIX, 444-446. *Town*, temples, old bridge, caves and history, *id.* 610-615; trade centre, *id.* 213-214; military post (1464), *id.* 227; under a Bijápur *mokásádar* (1648), *id.* 232; Shirzekhan the Mughal general defeated at (1686), *id.* 247; surprised by Rámchandrapant (1696), *id.* 250; Nána Fadnavis at (1795), *id.* 298.
Waikumba: timber tree, XXV, 78.
Waingi: a food plant, XXV, 167.
Waite: Sir Nicholas, chairman of the New or English Company, XXVI, pt. i, 121; his false allegations against the old or London Company at Surat, *id.* 122; dismisses the broker Rustam, IX, pt. ii, 196 note 3; governor of Bombay (1708), XIX, 254.
Wáizapur: village in Gujarát, rebels (1857) hanged at, I, pt. i, 443.
Wájha: a caste of Musalmán weavers in Thána district, XIII, 243.
Wake: Mr., president and governor of Bombay (1742-1750), arrives in Bombay, XXVI, pt. i, 252; retires (1750), XXVI, pt. iii, 370.
Wákiáthnigár: news-writer under the Mughals, I, pt. i, 214.
Walá: town in Káthiáwár, I, pt. ii, 284, 312; *see* Vala.
Wálan Kund: sacred fish-pool in Koláha district, XI, 37, 358, 397-398.
Walena: timber tree, XXV, 21.
Wali: a Musalmán saint, IX, pt. ii, 62.
Wali: name of a child in *akika* or naming sacrifice, IX, pt. ii, 158.
Wali Báwa: Musalmán saint, temple of, at Kendur in Poona district, XVIII, pt. iii, 232.

Walid : Al, Umayyad Khalifáh, IX, pt. ii, 1 note 1.
Walimah : marriage dinner among Arabs, IX, pt. ii, 16.
Walker : Colonel, sent to Baroda as an arbitrator (1802), I, pt. i, 412 ; decides in favour of Rávji Appáji, VII, 204-205 ; induces Colonel Murray to accept Gáikwár's aid, *id.* 212 ; resident at Baroda, I, pt. i, 413. 414 ; VII, 293-297 ; his reforms in Baroda, *id.* 215-216 ; interferes in the affairs of Káthiáwár, *id.* 320 ; his settlement of Baroda affairs, *id.* 322-325 ; settles the Káthiáwár tribute question, I, pt. i, 416, 422, 423 ; his proposed administration for the unsettled villages of Ahmabad district, IV, 149 ; on the existence of the practice of *sati* in Káthiáwár (1807), VIII, 121 note 1 ; on the changed condition of Káthiáwár in 1808 and 1835, *id.* 167, 246 ; his account of the Kathis, IX, pt. i, 252, 253, 257 note 1 ; his derivation of Molesalam, IX, pt. ii, 68.
Walker : Captain, quiets the disturbances in the Násik district (1857), XVI, 202.
Wallace : Colonel (1844), takes Rangna and Vishálgad, XXIV, 242 ; defeats the Náikdás, (1858), I, pt. i, 446 ; Resident at Baroda, VII, 272, 275.
Wallurg : timber tree, XXV, 133.
Wallursi, Walsura : timber tree, XXV, 44.
Walton : Mr. Rienzi, Bombay Municipal Engineer, designed Tulsi lake, XIV, 365 ; Malabár Hill reservoir, *id.* 366 ; and Vehar new outlet works, *id.* 378.
Walukeshvar : temple in the island of Bombay, XIII, 429 and note 1 ; remains at, I, pt. ii, 22.
Wálwa : *see* Valva.
Wal-wangi : food plant, XXV, 167.
Wanesi, Wanisa : *táluka* south-east of Baroda territory, I, pt. ii, 360, 361 note 1.
Wani : a village in the Násik district, copper-plate grant at, I, pt ii, 387, 391, 398.
Wansa : timber tree, XXV, 167.
Wáundev : deity of village Bohorás, IX, pt. ii, 61.
War : timber tree, XXV, 129.
Wara : town near Thatha, seat of the Memans, IX, pt. ii, 51.
Warblers : class of birds in Ratnágiri district, X, 78-79.
Warda : *see* Varda.
Wardhá : town in Central Provinces, grant and plates at, I, pt. ii, 192, 195, 197, 199, 201, 202, 203, 205, 206, 207, 414 note 5, 420.
Warehouses : for the Company built in Bombay (1672), XXVI, pt. ii, 433 ; two more bought (1760), *id.* 462 ; purchase of, in Bombay for military stores (1766), *id.* 473-474.
Wárna : *see* Varna.
Warrak : caste of Musalmán paper-makers in Ahmadnagar district, XVII, 229.
Warras : timber tree, XXV, 105.
Warts : *see* Varsoli.
Wart Snakes : in Poona district, XVIII, pt. i, 81.
Waruna, Warvansh : timber tree, XXV, 5.
Warungud : timber tree, XXV, 16.
Watch Towers : in Thána district, built by the Portuguese, XIII, 456, 457, 491 ; at Mandapeshvar and Thána, XIV, 226, 351.
Water : or *ap*, an element, two kinds of, earth and sky ; deities or gods presiding over ; running water pure ; standing water defiled ; used in various religious purposes, removes outward impurity, cleanses from sin ; used in every-day worship ; water dropping over Shiv's *ling*, offered in all Shraddha services ; object, IX, pt. i, 348 ; used in cases of spirit seizures ; gift of ; five abodes of the water-god Varuna—the sea, rivers, ponds, springs, wells, *id.* 350 ; form and details of worship, *id.* 349 351 ; details of rain worship, *id.* 351 353 ; veneration for, among Pársis, IX, pt. ii, 213 ; spirit, angel, 216, 217.
Water-carriers : at Mátherán, XIV, 265.
Water falls : in Kánara district, XV, pt. ii, 284-288, 328 329, 352 ; in Ahmadnagar district, XVII, 720, 730, 734 ; at Mahábaleshwar, XIX, 506-507 ; in Belgaum district, XXI, 11, 556-561, 608.
Water-pot : worship of, among the Komtis, XX, 54.
Water Works : all district volumes, *see* Irrigation under District Name.
Wathen : Mr., archæologist, I, pt. i, 120 ; I, pt. ii, 199, 247, 254 ; brought to light an inscription at Miraj, *id.* 178.
Watson : Colonel J. W., his history of the Káthis, IX, pt. i, 257-260 ; similarity between Káthiáwár Kolis and the Rájpúts according to, *id.* 237 note 2 ; his notice of Khants and their customs, *id.* 240 notes 3 and 4, 241 note 1 ; of Valakiyas, *id.* 245, note 1 ; his opinion that the Jethvas are Medhs, I, pt. i, 145 ; identifies Pilomolo with Bhinmál, *id.* 466 ; his notice of Bohorás, IX, pt. ii, 25 note 2.
Watson : Admiral James, captures the fort of Vijayadurg (1755), XI, 152-153, 447 ; X, 196 ; XIII, 497 ; I, pt. ii, 95 ; a monument erected in honour of, by the Company, in Westminister Abbey, *id.* 95.
Watson : Captain John, reduces the fort of Sindhudurg (1765), X, 351 ; in joint command of the expedition against Thána (1774) ; wounded in the siege ; captures Thána, XXVI, pt. i, 378, 384 ; I, pt. ii, 101 ; XIV, 360.
Watson : General, succeeds Mr. Melvill as the resident of Baroda (1882), VII, 286.
Wawali, Woula : timber tree, XXV, 132.
Wax : Kánara forest produce, XV, pt. i, 30 ; export of, XV, pt. ii, 58.
Wazifah : land grants, I, pt. i, 212 ; land held on religious tenures by Hindus, confiscation of, by an order of Aurangzeb between 1671 and 1674, *id.* 285.
Weather : tests to find out dry or wet year among better class husbandmen, IX, pt. i, 353-354 ; among early tribes, *id.* 354-355.
Weather-wagers : in Káthiáwár, VIII, 211-212.
Weaver Bird : in Ratnágiri district, X, 83.
Weavers : in Bombay island, wages of, advances to, encouragement (1731-1740), XXVI, pt. ii,

137-141; in Cambay, VI, 192 note 5; in Baroda, VII, 154-156; in Ahmadnagar district, XVII, 348-350; in Poona district, XVIII, pt. ii, 185-191, 196-198; XVIII, pt. iii, 296-297; in Sátára district, XIX, 202; in Sholápur district, XX, 270; in Belgaum district, XXI, 336-342; in Bijápur district, XXIII, 369-373; in Kolhápur, XXIV, 211-212.

Weaving: cotton and silk in Bombay island (1672-1762), XXVI, pt. ii, 131-142; of stockings (1683), *id.* 134-135. *See* all District Volumes under Crafts.

Webb: Colonel, grave of at Málvan, X, 352.

Weber: Professor, on the early entrance of the Pallavas into India, I, pt. ii, 317.

Wedderburn: Sir W., his proposal to establish arbitration courts in Thána district, XIII, 633.

Wednesday: Budhvar, sacred to Mercury, other name of, beliefs about, IX, pt. i, 402; *see* also XVIII, pt. i, 240.

Week Days: their sacredness, beliefs about, XVIII, pt. i, 239-241; among the Bene-Israels, *id.* 513

Wega: star, IX, pt. ii, 217 note 1.

Weights and Measures: all district volumes, *see* Capital under District Name.

Wellesley: Sir Arthur, captures Supa and the adjoining province in the Kánara district and returns to Mysore (1799), XV, pt. ii, 146, 351; captures the chief of Bilgi (1799), *id.* 276; visits Haliyal and Sambráni, *id.* 304, 340; drives out banditti from Sirsi (1800), *id.* 345; pursues Dhundia Vágh (1800); crosses the Tungabhadra; takes the forts of Airani and Ránebennur; passes through Haveri and Devagiri; crosses the Varda and arrives at Savaur; defeats Dhundia at Kundagol; passes through Kalas, Lakshmeshvar and Shirhatti; takes Dambal and Gadag; passes through Dhárwár, Belgaum and Bijápur, XXII, 421-425; XXI, 391-396; XXIII, 446-447; marches to Poona to place Bájiráv on the throne, XXII, 426, 649, 651, 802; I, pt. ii, 608; on his way halts at Akluj (1803), XX, 407; reaches Poona (1803) after a march of 60 miles in thirty-two hours, XVIII, pt. ii, 283 and note 1; his observations on the condition of the country round Poona, and the Peshwa's administration, *id.* 284-287; his estimate of Bájiráv's character, *id.* 288 note 2; XVIII, pt. iii, 414; takes Ahmadnagar from Sindia and restores it to the Peshwa (1803), XVII, 411-412; I, pt. ii, 629; defeats the Maráthás at Assaye (1803), *id.* 629; disperses the free-booters about Akalkot (1804), XX, 292; improves the way to Bor Ghát (1804), XIII, 318; checks the aggressions of Kolhápur against the allies of the English, XXIV, 235.

Wellesley Bridge: in Poona, named after General Wellesley, XVIII, pt. ii, 154-155; XVIII, pt. iii, 400-401.

Wellington: Duke of, *see* Wellesley.

Wells: abodes of the water-god Varuna, IX, pt. i, 349; worship of, by women after child-birth, *id.* 351; ceremonies before sinking, among Hindus, *id.* 350; among Pársis, IX, pt. ii, 205, 206; number of, in Surat district, II, 29, 34-36; in Kaira district, III, 43; in Baroda, VII, 375; in Káthiáwár, VIII, 67, 68, 178-179; in Kolába district, XI, 13; in Khándesh district, XII, 143; in Poona district, XVIII, pt. ii, 12-13; in Sholápur district, XX, 227-228; in Násik district, XVI, 13, 95, 502; in Ahmadnagar district, XVII, 250-251; in Sátára district, XIX, 158; in Belgaum district, XXI, 241-242; in Dhárwár district, XXII, 266, 700-702, 752; in Bijápur district, XXIII, 11-12, 314-315; in Kolhápur, XXIV, 11-12.

Welsh: Lieutenant, captures the forts of Párnera, Indergad and Bágvada (1780), I, pt. i, 409; XIV, 108.

West: Colonel E. W., suppresses the mutiny in Kánara district, XXI, 410; tutor of Rájárám II (1866-1870) of Kolhápur, accompanies him to Europe, XXIV, 244; his notice of Kanheri caves, XIV, 164, 174; I, pt. ii, 153; his proposed identification of Vijayapur, mentioned in Kaira grant, I, pt. i, 110.

Westergaard: Professor, his notice of *Kavirahasya*, I, pt. ii, 208; suggests a probable reason of the arrival of the Pársis to India, IX, pt. ii, 183 note 4; his mention of the Pársi settlement at Sanján (716), *id.* 185 note 5; his notice of the remains at Ankleshwar, *id.* 186 note 7; of the copy of *Vandidad*, *id.* 189 note 2, 194 note 1; his meaning of the word *Zend*, *id.* 211 note 1.

Western Chalukyas: (550-760 and 973-1184), *see* Chalukyas.

West Násik: connected with South Gujárát under the Chálukya rule, I, pt. i, 110.

Whale Reef: the, in Janjira state, XI, 467.

Wheat: used in religious ceremonies, sacred to Ganpati and Mangal offerings, worship of, IX, pt. i, 391; cultivation of, in Cutch, V, 106; in Pálanpur, *id.* 294; in Mahi Kántha, *id.* 370; in Khándesh, XII, 150; in Thána district, XIII, 289, 444; in Kánara district, XV, pt. ii, 36; in Násik district, XVI, 98; in Ahmadnagar district, XVII, 265-267; in Poona district, XVIII, pt. ii, 38-39; in Sátára district, XIX, 162; in Sholápur district, XX, 231; in Belgaum district, XXI, 250-251; in Dhárwár district, XXII, 274-275; in Bijápur district, XXIII, 320-321; in Kolhápur, XXIV, 166; in Broach district, II, 405; in Kaira district, III, 47; in Panch Maháls, *id.* 233; in Ahmadábád district, IV, 54; quantity of, required for Bombay island till 1743, its price (1743), quantity of, imported (1776-1781), XXVI, pt. ii, 67-70.

Wheel: Shákyamuni's emblem, XII, 491 and note 6.

Wheels: cart, making of, at Panvel in Thána district, XIV, 294.

Whip Snakes: in Poona district, XVIII, pt. i, 77-78.

White: Colonel, ascertained the price of the gold flowers at Sopára, XIV, 332 note 1.

White Húnas or Huns: foreigners, I, pt. i, 142-146, 459; in North Sind and South Panjáb, *id.* 496; defeat of, by Sassanians and Turks

(550-600), *id.* 497; settle in Yannang with Tibatans and Kedarites, *id.* 501; *another account of:* great fifth century horde, its complexity, IX, pt. i, 434, 455, 456; were known as Yetas or Ephthalites, 455, 456, 458, 461, 463, 471, 472; Khazars, forming part of, *id.* 472-476; *history* (of fifth century White Hunas who entered India), passed from northern settlements in Kirgiz, overtook Juan-Juan in Oxus Valley, *id.* 472; crossed Oxus and passed South to India, united with other bodies of White Húnas, *id.* 473, 474-476; referred to in India by complimentary title of Mihiras or Maitrakas, *id.* 471, 473; Gujars proved to be Khazars and therefore same as White Húnas, *id.* 434, 475-477; were great champions of Bráhmans, *id.* 433; settlements along Konkan Coast, *id.* 438, 439 note 1; Mihirakula (A. D. 480-530), their great leader, *id.* 439, 441, 442, 443 note 1, 444 note 4, 594; fire-reverencing element in, *id.* 447; opposed Buddhism and favoured Bráhmanism, *id.* 449, 453, 469, 155; struggles of the Persians with, IX, pt. ii, 183 note 4. *See* also Khazars, Gujars and Huns.

Wholliaru: *see* Holayar.

Widow: rites, among Gujarát Bráhmans, IX, pt. i, 50; Rájpúts, *id.* 149; Shrávaka, *id.* 102; Vánias, *id.* 95.

Widow-burning: stopped in Mahi Kántha (1835), V, 391.

Widow-marriage: among Gujarát Hindus, called *natra*, different forms of, among Kolis, IX, pt. i, 249-250; allowed, among bards and actors, *id.* 213, 221, 226; Bráhmans, Audichyas of Vagad, *id.* 7; Bhojaks, *id.* 8; Jethimal Modhs, *id.* 12; Parajiyas, *id.* 16; Rajgors, *id.* 17; Káthiáwár Sarasvats, *id.* 18; Tapodhans, *id.* 20; Vyas, *id.* 21; craftsmen, *id.* 179, 181, 183, 185, 186, 188, 189, 190, 192, 195, 197, 201, 206; herdsmen, *id.* 285, 286, 289; husbandmen, *id.* 154, 163, 170, 172, 174, 175; Káthis, *id.* 257; Lohanas, *id.* 122; personal servants, *id.* 230, 234; among Pársis, IX, pt. ii, 239 and note 1; among Rámoshis, XVIII, pt. i, 423; origin of the rule against, *id.* 540-542; among Pátharvats, XIX, 90.

Wigeon: class of birds in Ratnágiri district, X, 97.

Wild Animals: all district volumes, *see* Production under District Name.

Wild Ass: in Cutch, V, 30-31; in Káthiáwár, VIII, 105.

Wild Citron: tree in Poona district, XVIII, pt. i, 49.

Wild Date-palms: in Káthiáwár, VIII, 95-96; in Poona district, XVIII, pt. i, 48.

Wild Dog: in Kánara district, XV, pt. i, 94.

Wild Tribes: in Thána district, XIII, 567; condition (1818), *id.* 567-568; (1836), *id.* 580 and note 2; (1842), *id.* 586.

Wilford: antiquarian, Bhátia settlements in Sind and to the east of Ganges according to, IX, pt. i, 116 note 7; some Bhatti tribes, claim to descend from Shálivábana, *id.* 117 note 1; his *pandits* admit Kshatriyás becoming Bráhmans, *id.* 436 note 10, 442 note 6 continued on page 443; Behrám Gor (436) of Persia founds a kingdom in India, IX, pt. ii, 183 note 4 continued on page 184; Pársis become (1315) Hindus and Musalmáns, *id.* 187 note 4; wrongly holds that the infidels of Tujhlikpur whom Timur defeated (1398) were Christians, *id.* 188 note 4; identifies Tagar with Devagiri, I, pt. i, 541.

Williams: Mr., resident at Baroda (1827), gains Sayájiráv's assent to his reforms, VII, 239-240; appointed political commissioner in Gujarát, *id.* 244; his notice of Gujarát Kolis (1820), IX, pt. i, 244.

Willoughby: resident at Baroda, VII, 239; his account of Kolis, IX, pt. i, 237 note 2.

Wilson: Professor H. H., his translation of the *Vishnupuráṇa,* "Introduction to the History of the Konkan," I, pt. ii, p. ix, 8, 282 note 5, 287 note 4.

Wilson: Dr., first physician in Bombay (1676), XXVI, pt. iii, 543.

Wilson: Dr. John, traces the 'Jethvas' to 'Jats' or 'Jits,' I, pt. i, 145; his derivation of the word 'Kanbi,' IX, pt. i, 154 note 1; his description of Kolis, *id.* 237 note 1; of Bhils, *id.* 294 note 1; his origin of the word 'Bhangia,' *id.* 334 note 1; the probable date of the arrival of Pársis in India, IX, pt. ii, 185 note 3; identifies Muhammad Sháh of the Kissah-i-Sanjan with Muhammad Begáda, *id.* 187 note 3; his notice of the Elephanta caves, XIV, 88, 388; his derivation of 'Marátha,' XXIV, 81.

Wind: or *Vayu*, an element, IX, pt. i, 348; its god, beliefs about; wind complaints and their cure; current beliefs regarding direction of, *id.* 358.

Wise: Major, sent against Tátya Makáji, a Koli rebel (1879), XVIII, pt. iii, 39.

Witches: *Dakens*, belief in, of Gujarát Hindus, powers of bewitching, IX, pt. i, 292, 425-426; women suspected to be, *id.* 426; ways adopted to find out a witch, *id.* 302-303, 426; found among low caste Hindus and early tribes; head-quarters of witchcraft in Gujarát, *id.* 426; mischief by witch glance, by influence and effect of *mithi-najar* or sweet-look, *id.* 427; chief guards against evil-eye, *id.* 427-428; ascertaining sickness caused by evil eye, *id.* 428; seizure signs, means to drive out, *id.* 429; other ways of mischief; their supernatural powers bring gain as well as trouble to them, *id.* 430; among Pársis, IX, pt. ii, 220. *See* also XVII, 56, 61, 64, 90, 96, 200-201.

Wiwarana: timber tree, XXV, 113.

Wodehouse: H. E. Sir Philip, governor of Bombay (1875), VIII, 223.

Wojhár: *see* Ojhár.

Wolf: in Khándesh, XII, 31; in Kánara district, XV, pt. I, 94.

Wood-apple: fruit tree in Poona district, XVIII, pt. i, 47.

Wood-ash Tillage: in Poona district, XVIII, pt. ii, 30; in Sátára district, XIX, 159; in Belgaum district, XXI, 245; in Kolhápur, XXIV, 163.

Wood-carving: by Surat Sutárs, IX, pt. i, 205, and note 1; in Thána district, XIII, 399; in

Násik district, XVI, 53, 493-496; in Kánara district, XV, pt. ii, 70.
Wooden Bracelets: manufacture of, in Ahmadábád district, IV, 130.
Wooden Toys: manufacture of, in Belgaum district, XXI, 350-352.
Wood-pecker: bird in Khándesh district, XII, 35; in Ratnágiri district, X, 66.
Woodrow: Mr. G. M., conducts (1876-1877) experiments on *tasar* silk, XVIII, pt. ii, 71.
Wood-turning: in Násik district, XVI, 154; in Poona district, XVIII, pt. ii, 209-210.
Wood work: in Ahmadábád district, IV, 130; in Cambay, VI, 191 foot-note 6; in Koláha district, XI, 133 134; in Sholapur district, XX, 273; in Dhárwár district, XXII, 384; in Surat district, II, 180.
Woollen Goods: trade in (1703-1719), in Bombay island, XXVI, pt. ii, 129-130.
Wool-working in Kolába district, XI, 132-133; in Thána district, XIII, 445, 467, 510.
Worship: chief objects of modern Hindu, in Gujarát; trinity or *trimurti*—Brahma, Vishnu, Shiv, IX, pt. i, p. xxxvi, 531, 532, animal, *id.* 372 382; book, *id* 82; disease, *id.* 365-372; healing shrines, *id.* 366; small-pox, *id* 368; elements, *id.* 348 358; fire, *id.* 356; ponds, *id.* 350; rain, *id.* 351; rivers, *id.* 349; sea, *id.* 349; springs, *id* 350; water, *id.* 137, 348; wells, *id.* 350; wind, *id.* 358; *gotraj* or family goddess, *id.* 31, 32, 36, 39; grain, *id.* 389-392; hill, *id.* 388 389; planet, *id.* 392 406; comets, *id* 405; earth, *id.* 403; Jupiter, *id.* 402; Mars, *id.* 401; Mercury, *id.* 402; Moon, *id* 396; Saturn, *id.* 403; Stars, *id.* 406; Sun, *id.* 393; Venus, *id* 402; plant, *id.* 382-388; Saint wheel, *id.* 115; spirit, *id.* 137-138; stone, *id.* 362-365; tomb, *id.* 358-362; among Musalmáns in Gujarát, Muslim form of, IX, pt. ii, 126 note 5; form of, among Khojáhs, *id.* 48; saint *id.* 12; fire, *id.* 20; in Poona district, of the goddess Shashthi, XVIII, pt. i, 113, 300, 350, 471; of the sun, *id.* 115; of boundary, *id.* 129; of guests, *id.* 133; of Ganesh, *id* 199-201; of ancestors, *id.* 201; of planets, *id.* 202; of clothes, *id.* 211; of daily-worship, *id* 235-238; of animals, *id.* 294; of trees, *id.* 208, 294; of tombs, *id.* 413; Buddhist, XIV, 141.
Wowli: timber and food tree, XXV, 91, 164.
Wrecks: on the Konkan coast of the steamer "Outram" (1871), X, 23. 342; of the steamer "Johnston Castle" (1865), *id.* 347; of the steamship "Jeddo" and "Di-Vernon," XI, 254.
Wrestling Houses: in Dhárwár district, XXII, 818 820.
Wrightia: *tinctoria*, food and timber tree, XXV, 100, 166: *tomentosa*, *id.* 100.
Writers: chief classes of, names, strength and distribution in Gujarát, IX, pt. i, 55 68; in Surat district, II, 52; in Broach district, *id.* 372; in Kaira district, III, 30; in Panch Mahálss, *id* 216; in Ahmadábád district, IV, 35; in Cutch, V, 48-49; in Pálanpur, *id.* 289; in Mahi Kántha, *id.* 363; in Kolaba district, XI, 46-47; in Poona district, XVIII, pt. i, 185-261.
Wud: timber tree, XXV, 36.
Wumb: timber tree, XXV, 52.
Wumb-asphal: food plant, XXV, 150.
Wundi: timber tree, XXV, 12,
Wutma: timber tree, XXV, 127.
Wuzú: ablution, before prayer, among Musalmáns, IX, pt. ii, 126 note 5.

X

XANTHOCHYMUS PICTORIUS: timber and food tree, XXV, 11, 146.
Xavier: St Francis, Portuguese missionary, arrives in India (1544 A. D.), changes nature of Christian observances, establishes a Jesuit seminary at Bassein (1548); sends missionaries to Thána and Chaul and is made Patron Saint of Bassein and Chaul, I, pt. ii, 56; XIII, 200, 201, 461; XIV, 40, 41, 42; XI, 295; Chapel of, at Chaul, XI, 298.
Xeque: the, sent an embassy, offering a tribute to the Gujarát prince (1400-1500), I, pt. ii, 37.
Xerxes: Hindus in the army of (B. C. 480), XIII, 403 note 1.
Ximenia Americana: a food plant, XXV, 149.
Xoana: town identified by Yule with Siwana, in Sind, I pt. i, 538.
Xodrake: a city probably in Mewár, I, pt. i, 539.
Xylia dolabriformis: a timber tree, XXV, 65.

Y

YA'AKÚB: Sayad Budha, ancestor of the Uraizi Sayad family, IX, pt. ii, 6 note 1 (7).
Yachi: capital of Karájang or Yunnan (1290), I, pt. i, 501, 504.
Yádava Chakravartin: title of Rámachandra Yádava, I, pt. ii, 529.
Yádava Kingdom: at Dwárika, establishment of, I, pt. i, 8.
Yádavakula Ambaradyumani: suns in the sky, which is the family of the Yadavas, I, pt. ii, 490.
Yádava-Náráyana: I, pt. ii, 501; *biruda* of Bhillama, I I, *id.* 514; *biruda* of Seunadeva, *id.* 516; *biruda* of the Yádavas of Devagiri, *id.* 517.
Yádavapura: modern Melukote in Mysore, Vishnuvardhana rules at, I, pt. ii, 499.
Yádavas: of Devagiri, I, pt. ii, 16, 230, 252, 511-534; their Puranic genealogy; claim to belong to the Lunar race, *id.* 512; their crest and banner, *id.* 299 note 4. 517; their *birudas*, *id.* 517; their early history, *id.* 230-236; Dridhaprahára, founder of the family, *id.* 231, 512; Chandor, their first capital, *id.* 512; their connection with the Ráshtrakútas, Chálukyas and Siláháras by marriage, *id.* 231-234, 513; Seunachandra II lifts up the family, *id.* 515; feudatories of the Ráshtrakútas, *id.* 420; of the Western Chálukyas of Kalyáni, *id.* 430, 433, 436, 437, 443, 457; Bhillama makes himself master of the whole country north of the Krishna and founds the city of Devagiri, *id.* 238, 466, 520; at war with the Hoysalas for the possession of the Chálu-

kya dominions, *id.* 504; Singhana assumes the full paramount epithets and titles, *id.* 523; Musalmán invasions commence and the dynasty falls, *id.* 235-252, 530, 549, 555, 557, 558, 583; Hoysalas of Dorasamudra, *id.* 237, 490; their connection with Ratnágiri district, X, 193; with Sávantvádi, *id.* 439; with Kolába district and Janjira, XI, 141, 272, 432; with Thána (1150-1310), XIII, 423, 427; with Khándesh (750, 1200), XII, 241, 242; with Poona, XVIII, pt. ii, 214 and note 3; *see* also XIV, 387; theory of the home-coming of, from Central India, IX, pt. i, 446 note 4.

Yádavas: mythical dynasty of Dwarka, destruction of, I, pt. i, 521.

Yadu: the race from which the Ráshtrakútas are said to have sprung, I, pt. ii, 194; lineage of, *id.* 490; race of, promoted by Vishnuvardhana, *id.* 495.

Yadu: the founder of Yaduvamsa, I, pt. ii, 512.

Yádvád: town in Belgaum district, history of, weaving industry at, XXI, 611; survey of (1851-1852), *id.* 425-427.

Yahudi: *see* Bene-Israel.

Yá-Jabbár: word having special powers, IX, pt. ii, 143.

Yajanasila: Bráhman, cut the channel of Gautama's lake near Bhinmál, I, pt. i, 461.

Yajmans: patrons of Bráhman priests, IX, pt. i, 23.

Yajñasena: king of Vidarbha, defeated by Agnimitra, I, pt. ii, 147.

Yajnashri Shatakarni: Andhrabhritya king (133-162), son of Chatarapana, defeated by Rudradamana, I, pt. i, 38; XVIII, pt. ii, 213; XVI, 593, 597, 623; I, pt. ii, 10, 156, 166, 167, 168; his inscriptions at Kanheri and Sopára, XIV, 147, 167, 320, 332; his coins, I, pt. ii, 161.

Yajnasvámin: Bráhman grantee of Chálukya prince, I, pt. ii, 191.

Yájnavalkya: Hindu sage, Jambu Bráhmans claim descent from, IX, pt. i, 10.

Yajur Veda: one of the four Vedas, Gujarát Bráhmans followers of, IX, pt. i, 2; *see* also I, pt. i, 534; White Yajurved its part, I, pt. ii, 207.

Yajurvedi: sub-caste of Bráhmans in Thána district, XIII, 86; in Násik district, XVI, 37-39; in Khándesh district, XII, 52.

Yáklar: caste of temple servants in Bijápur district, XXIII, 173-176.

Yaksha: king of Bhinmal, his pond, I, pt. i, 454, 456 and note 1; statue of, described, *id.* 456-458; high day of, *id.* 458, 465.

Yakshas: Buddhist and Bráhmanic demi-gods, images of, at Ajanta and Elephanta, XII, 493 and note 3; XIV, 73 note 1; belief in the existence of, in Western India (A. D. 100-400), XIII, 406; Musalmáns or Persians probably meant by, in Cutch legends, X, 133 note 7, 235, 236 note 1.

Yákub Khán: a converted Koli (1732) officer of the Sidi, his treachery, XI, 443.

Yakudi: or Majam. *See* Stimulant.

Yákut: Sidi, admiral of Bahádur Gilání (1493), XI, 434.

Yakut Dábuli: tomb of, in Bijápur city, XXIII, 616.

Yakut Khán: Sidi Sambal so called, becomes Mughal admiral (1670), XI, 437.

Yalawál: in Mysore, inscription at, I, pt. ii, 433; record at, *id.* 523.

Yalawatti: in the Hángal *táluka*, Dhárwár district, inscription at, I, pt. ii, 558 notes 5 and 7, 562 and note 2.

Yaligára-Karibasappa: inscription on the premises of, I, pt. ii, 558 note 5, 562 note 2.

Yálige: in the Nizám's dominion, record at, I, pt. ii, 527.

Yalisirur: village in Dhárwár district, temples and inscription at, XXII, 788-789.

Yam: god of death, IX, pt. i, 377.

Yam: growing of, in Poona district, XVIII, pt. ii, 56; in Khándesh, XII, 171.

Yamáji Shivdeo: Marátha rebel (1750), XX, 290.

Yaman: province of, in Arabia, IX, pt. ii, 3; ancient seat of the head priest of the Bohorás in, *id.* 27, 33.

Yamkanmardi: town in Belgáum district, fort of, XXI, 610.

Yammiganur: in the Kod *táluka* of Dhárwár, I, pt. ii, 281 note 3.

Yamuná: the Jamna in United Provinces, I, pt. ii, 338 note 7, 371, 387, 416; emblem of, insignia of the Ráshtrakútas, *id.* 387, 396; *see* also I, pt. i, 533.

Yan: holy valley in Kánara district, limestone rocks and cave-fissure in, legend of, XV, pt. ii, 354-356.

Yánemarasa: lord of Mahishmati, Vikramáditya VI's feudatory, I, pt. ii, 451.

Yápaniyas: Jain sect, I, pt. ii, 288, 290.

Yasádaman I: fourteenth Kshatrapa (A. D. 239), coins of, I, pt. i, 46.

Yasádaman II: twenty-second Kshatrapa (A. D. 320), coins of, I, pt. i, 49.

Yasáji Kank: Shiváji's general (1663), XVIII, pt. ii, 230.

Yasastilaka: a Jain work by Somádeva, I, pt. ii, 207.

Yashna: portion of the *Zend Avesta*, IX, pt. ii, 212 note 1.

Yashto: portion of the *Zend Avesta*, IX, pt. ii, 212 note 1.

Yashvantgad: fort in Ratnágiri district, X, 384.

Yashvant Malhar Chitnis: minister of Sátára *rája*, rewarded (1857), XIX, 319.

Yashvantráv: minor son of Trimbakráv Dábhade made *senápati* by Bájiráv Peshwa (1731), I, pt. i, 393, 396.

Yashvantráv Holkar: (1802), overruns almost the whole of Málwa; defeated by Ghátge; arrives near Poona; his brother Vithoji dragged to death in Poona; his vow of vengeance against Bájiráv; his nephew imprisoned at Asirgad; marches to Poona by the Rájvári pass and is camped between Loni and Hadapsar; is opposed by the Peshwa assisted by Sindia; his triumph and Bájiráv's flight; plunders Poona; treaty of Bassein; is driven to Chándor in Násik, XVIII, pt. ii,

280-283; *see* also *id.* pt. iii, 414; XIII, 512; I, pt. ii, 110, 628; XIV, 35.
Yashvantráv Sinde: Kolhápur minister (1772-1782), defeats the rebel chief of Kágal and drives off Peshwa's officer (1777), XXIV, 231; destroys the fort of Kágal (1780), *id.* 300; his death (1782), *id.* 233.
Yasna: Pársi ceremony during ordination of Návar, IX, pt. ii, 225; of Marstab, *id.* 226.
Yaśodharman: king of Málwa, I, pt. i, 76, 77; defeats Huns, *id.* 143; defeats Mihirakula the famous White Hun conqueror at Kárur near Multán (530), *id.* 496; *see* also IX, pt. i, 444. 448, 453; pillar of victory set up at Mandasor by, I, pt. ii, 426 note 2.
Yaśodhavala: Kumárapála's viceroy, I, pt. i, 187; set on his uncle's throne by Kumárapála, *id.* 189.
Yasoráta: son of Vyághrárata, Varika prince of Málwa, I, pt. ii, 312.
Yaśovarman: king of Málwa (1133-1143), I, pt. i, 160, 172, 173, 174; his war with Siddharája, taken prisoner and kept in a cage, *id.* 177-178, 496.
Yaśovarman: Chálukya prince, I, pt. ii, 211, 380; marries a sister of a ruler of the Ganga country, *id.* 399, 433, 434. *See* Daśavarman.
Yaswád: word having special magical powers, IX, pt. ii, 143.
Yathrem: the fourth *Gahambár*, IX, pt. ii, 218.
Yaudheya: Kshatriya tribe, I, pt. i, 19 and note 3; defeated by Rudradaman (A. D. 143-158), account of, *id.* 36-37, 64 and note 3, 138.
Yaungal: village in Dhárwár district, XXII, 789.
Yával: town in Khándesh district, fort at, old paper and indigo trade of, XII, 479.
Yavanas: Greeks, conquerors in Western India, IX, pt. i, 433; mainly Baktrian Greeks, join Kushans in Kábul Valley, entrance into India, *id.* 455; converted to Buddhism, *id.* 433; broken by Gautamiputra, *id.* 448; I, pt. ii, 149, 155; *see* also *id.* 155, 173, 317; I, pt. i, 12, 119, 160, 456 note 1; migration of, to Indo-China (100), *id.* 499; mentioned in Junnar inscriptions (A. D. 100-200), XVIII, pt. ii, 213 and note 10.
Yavanasva: Yavana prince of Parlipur, I, pt. i, 119.
Yavani: handmaids of the Indian drama, I, pt. i, 545.
Yavteshvar: hill and village in Sátára district, temple at, XIX, 551, 562, 615.
Yá-Wadúdo: word having special powers, IX, pt. ii, 143.
Yayáti: king, son of Nahush, asks boon from the sun, I, pt. i, 460 and note 2; equalled by Gotamiputra in prowess, I, pt. ii, 149, 340 note 2.
Yayati Kesari: line of Yavanas, brought Bráhmans to Orissa, IX, pt. i, 440-441.
Yazads: the worshipfuls; veneration for; days and months named after, XI, pt. ii, 215, 216; angels, prayers recited in honour of, *id.* 206.
Yazatas: angels, IX, pt. ii, 211 note 2 (1), 217 note 1.
Yazdezard: Sháh of Persia, defeated by the Arabs (638, 641), IX, pt. ii, 183, 185; his son takes the Persians to China, *id.* 183 note 4; *see* also I, pt. ii, 14.
Year: Bene-Israels' calculation of the, XVIII, pt. i, 512.
Yedaráve: in the Nizám's dominions, inscriptions at, I, pt. ii, 447 note 3.
Yedur: village in Belgaum district, temple and fair at, a favourite halting place, XXI, 611.
Yekdare: village in Ahmadnagar district, caves at, XVII, 741.
Yekdi, Yekaddi: timber tree, XXV, 8.
Yekhlas Khán: leader of the Abyssinian officers at Bijápur; associates with Chánd Bibi in the regency during the minority of Ibráhim A'dil Sháh II; seized and blinded by Diláwar Khán, I, pt. ii, 647.
Yelawatti: village in the Banavási province, I, pt. ii, 278 note 2.
Yelburga: in the Nizám's dominions, I, pt. ii, 504; Sinda family of, *id.* 477, 488, 498, 547, 569, 572, 573, 577, 578.
Yelguri: village in Bijápur district, XXIII, 681.
Yelival: village in Dhárwár district, XXII, 789.
Yellamma Hill: in Belgaum district, temple fairs and legend of the goddess; barbarous practices at the fairs, XXI, 9, 612-614.
Yellápur: sub-division of Kánara district, villages, aspect, climate, water, soil, stock, survey details and people of, XV, pt. ii, 238-243. *Town, id.* 356; travellers' bungalow, school and hospital at, *id.* 44, 216, 219.
Yellur: village in Dhárwár district, inscriptions at, XXII, 789.
Yellurgad: fort in Belgaum district, XXI, 614.
Yelur: village in Sátára district, XIX, 615-616.
Yelvatti: fort in Kolhápur state, description, wells, temples, history and inscriptions, XXIV, 377-378.
Yemen: Indian trade with (200 A. D.), I, pt. i, 535; XIII, 417; Hindus settled in (1763), *id.* 520; Bene-Israel people come from, I, pt. ii, 7.
Yemnur: village in Dhárwár district, Musalmán tomb and a large fair at, XXII, 789-790.
Yenna: river in Sátára district, XIX, 14; falls of, at Mahábaleshvar, *id.* 506-507.
Yeola: sub-division of Nasik district, area, aspect, water, history, land revenue, stock, holdings, crops and people of, XVI, 354-357. *Town,* population and manufacturers of, *id.* 662-663.
Yerad: village in Sátára district, temple at, XIX, 616.
Yerangal: village in Thána district, XIV, 383; Portuguese church at, I, pt. ii, 65; XIII, 457.
Yeravda Central Jail: near Poona city, XVIII, pt. iii, 40, 401-402.
Yerguppi: village in Dhárwár district, XXII, 790.
Yerindi: timber tree, XXV, 42.

Yerla: river in Sátára district, XIX, 15; canals, *id.* 152-153.
Yerrul: timber tree, XXV, 65.
Yerulá: *see* Ellorá.
Yesáji: son of Kánhoji Angria, XI, 149; appointed governor of Kolába fort (1733), defeated by Mánáji, *id.* 150.
Yesdejard III: *see* Yazdezard.
Yeshwantrao Holkar: *see* Yashvantráv Holkar.
Yesodharmman: I, pt. i, 143. *See* Yaśodharman.
Ye-ta-i-li-to: Ephthalite, ruling class of White Húnas, "Jethwa" derived from, I, pt. i, 145; IX, pt. i, 458 note 7.
Yetas, Ye-tha: leading mixed horde of foreigners, Oxus Valley White Húnas known as, IX, pt. i, 472; also known as Ephthalites, *id.* 455; also known as Khazars and Mihiras, *id.* 461; White Huna of Khazar race known as, *id.* 456; *see* also I, pt. i, 75, 142, 145.
Yetti: timber tree, XXV, 50.
Yeur: in the Nizám's dominions, I, pt. ii, 457; inscriptions at, *id.* 425 note 2.
Yevat: village in Poona district, temple and fair at, XVIII, pt. iii, 454.
Yevur: inscription tablet at, I, pt. ii, 178, 180, 181, 190, 211.
Yezd, Yezdstán: town of, in Persia, IX, pt. ii, 186 note 1, 189 note 2.
Yimtal: Arabic name for Nádur, IX, pt. ii, 211 note 2 (6).
Yir: Mátherán sprite, XIV, 263.
Yoga: Bráhman donee, I, pt. i, 126.
Yogarája: Anahilaváda chief (805-841), I, pt. i, 124; mounts funeral pyre, *id.* 154, 155.
Yogaśástra: work compiled by Hemachandra, I, pt. i, 193.
Yogeshvari: Chitpávan goddess, XVIII, pt. i, 100.
Yogesvara: writer of Govind's Kávi grant, I, pt. i, 126.
Yogis; order of Shaiv ascetics, IX, pt. i, 542; different grades of, *id.* 543-544; *see* also Jogis.
Yojana: three miles, I, pt. i, 510, 521.
Young: Mr., deputy governor of Bombay, recalled (1669) to Surat and tried, XXVI, pt. i, 36-37.
Yuan-Yuán: Central Asian horde, occupy Balkh (380), I, pt. i, 144. *See* Juan Juan.
Yuchin: leader of Oxus Valley White Húnas, attacks Persia (500), IX, pt. i, 472.
Yuddhamalla: of a branch of the Chálukyas, I, pt. ii, 212.
Yuddhamalla: *biruda* of Mangalarasa, son of Dharasraya Jayasimhavarman, I, pt. ii, 374.
Yuddhamalla I: Chálukya chief of the Sapádalákha country, I, pt. ii, 380; identified with Satyáśraya-Vinayáditya, *id.* 380 note 6.
Yuddhamalla II: son of Baddiga Soladaganda Chálukya, I, pt. ii, 380.
Yuddhásura-Nandarája: Ráshtrakúta king, I, pt. ii, 386.
Yudhisthira: another name of Dharmarája, the Pándava, I, pt. ii, 142; his test for admission as Bráhmans, IX, pt. i, 437; Khoja saint of the third epoch or *yuga*, IX, pt. ii, 48.
Yuechi or Yuetchi: Central Asian tribe, driven by the Avárs into the Kábul Valley (B. C. 50), one of the Medh tribes, I, pt. i, 144; word Yaksha applied to *id.* 456 note 1; called Baktrians owing to their settlement in Baktria, IX, pt. i, 463 note 4; the *Great* and the *Little* known as Kushana and Kedarites.
Yugapurusha: representative man of the present age, I, pt. ii, 580.
Yugs: cycles of Hindu chronology, I, pt. i, 461.
Yukávihára: louse temple, built by Kumárapála (1143-1174), I, pt. i, 193.
Yukzan: early form of marriage among Pársis, IX, pt. ii, 238 note 2.
Yule: Sir H., antiquarian, quoted, I, pt. i, 499, 504, 537, 538, 539, 540; his remarks on Buddha's bowl, XIV, 403; his notice of Konkan-Tána, I, pt. ii, 3, 4.
Yunnan: settlement in, of Thisrong and his successor Thi-tsong-ti, I, pt. i, 501.
Yusuf Adil Khán or Sháh: believed to be the son of an emperor of Constantinople, I, pt. ii, 32; governor of Daulatábád, made governor of Bijápur on the death of Muhammad Gáwán, avails himself of the weakness of the Báhamani kings and declares himself king of Bijápur (1489); assists his former sovereign Muhammad Sháh Báhamani II to put down the rebellion of Bahádur Gilání; joins Muhammad Sháh in an expedition against Kásim Barid; betrothes his daughter to Muhammad Sháh's son Ahmad and thus establishes his equality with his former king, *id.* 640; takes steps to improve the Konkan, *id.* 33; died (1510), *id.* 640; *another account of:* (1489-1510); his early life, becomes independent and fixes on Bijápur as his capital; his wars with Vijayanagar; changes the state religion, his character and reforms, XXIII, 404-410; *see* also XVII, 357 note 2, 360; XIX, 227-228; XXI, 366 note 2; X, 195, 327.
Yúsuf bin Sulaimán: high priest of Shiáh Bohorás, settles at Sidhpur, IX, pt. ii, 27 note 2.
Yusufzai: children of Joseph, IX, pt. i, 463 note 4.
Yuvanáshva: king of Turanmál, mentioned in the *Mahábhárata*, XII, 238.
Yvons: Mr., Englishman in the Peshwa's service (1790), XXII, 417.

Z

ZAFAR KHA'N: Khilji governor of Gujarát, restores order in Gujarát (1318), I, pt. i, 230; appointed governor; his death (1371), *id.* 231; accompanied by Musalmán missionaries, IX, pt. ii, 3 note 3.
Zafar Khán: governor of Gujarát (1391-1411), attacks I'dar (1391), defeats the *ráo* of Junágadh (1394), destroys Somnáth twice (1394, 1398), I, pt. ii, 232-233; confined by his son Tátár Khán at Asáwal, *id.* 513; first king of Ahmadábád, IX, pt. ii, 5; *see* also VI, 217.
Zahir: *pir*, Bhangia saint, *chhadi* procession in honor of, IX, pt. i, 336 note 1; origin, *id.* 524-525.
Zain Khán: *see* Zein Khán.

Zain-ul-A'bidin : fourth Shiáh *imám*, IX, pt. ii, 125 note 2.
Zakariyah : prophet, IX, pt. ii, 127.
Zakariyya : Háji Meman of Bombay, instance of his secret charity, builds a mosque in Bombay named after him, IX, pt. ii, 52 note 4.
Zakát : *literally* 'purification,' a Musalmán religious tax, I, pt. i, 213 note 1 ; paid to the head *mulla*, IX, pt. ii, 33, 49, 126 note 4.
Zamenis fasciolatus : a species of snake in Poona district, XVIII, pt. i, 76.
Zamindárs : land-holders in Gujarát under the Mughals, I, pt. i, 215, 216 note 1 ; three classes of, *id.* 226 ; in Koláha district, XI, 170, 182 ; in Thána district, *deshmukhs* and *deshpándes*, XIII, 540 note 1, 553 ; holders of *izáfat* villages, *id.* 565 note 1 ; Mr. Marriott an advocate of the *zamindári* system, 566 note 11 ; numerous in Kalyán, their emoluments and duties (1828), 572-573.
Zamorins : of Malabár, proselytisation of one of the, by Naiatas, IX, pt. ii, 15 note 1 ; of Calicut in alliance with Muhammad Begáda (1500), XIII, 448.
Zamotika : father of Kshatrapa Chastana, I, pt. i, 31.
Zamzam : the well of the *Kaába*, holy water of, IX, pt. ii, 171.
Zand : *see* Zend.
Zanjira : *see* Janjira.
Zanthoxylum : *Rhetsa*, *triphillum*, timber trees, XXV, 30, 31.
Zanzibár : Indian trade with (1300-1500), XIII, 444 ; Hindus found in (1300-1500), *id.* 446.
Zarathustra : *see* Zoroaster.
Zarekari : *see* Jhara.
Zaris : vows or offerings to, IX, pt. ii, 128.
Zarmanokhegas : S'ramanácharya, accompanied an embassy to Rome from Broach (A. D. 23), I, pt. i, 536.
Zarthostno Diso : anniversary of the death of Zoroaster, a chief Pársi holiday, IX, pt. ii, 219.
Zarus : food plant, XXV, 160.
Zea Mays : food and famine plant, XXV, 186, 208.
Zehneria umbellata : food plant, XXV, 160.
Zein Khán : Báhamani chief, I, pt. ii, 589 ; he and his brother Khwájá Jahán hold Purenda, Sholápur and eleven districts of the Báhamani kingdom about 1485 ; they quarrel and are supported by Yusúf A'dil Khán and Ahmad Sháh respectively, *id.* 589 ; *see* also XX, 278-279.
Zein-ud-din : head *mulla* of Dáúdi Bohorás, IX, pt. ii, 31 note 4.
Zenana : private apartments of Rájpút women, IX, pt. i, 133 ; inmates of, *id.* 147.
Zend : meaning of, XIII, 271 note 3 ; IX, pt. ii, 211 note 1 ; language of the Pársi holy books, *id.* 204 ; commentary or translation, *id.* 204 note 1 ; language of the early fragments, *id.* 212.
Zend Avesta : sacred books of the Zoroastrians, literal meaning of ; *nusks* or parts of, IX, pt. ii, 211 and note 2 ; preserved portions of, *id.* 212 note 1 ; education of laymen's sons in, *id.* 209-210 ; of the sons of the priests in, *id.* 210, 212 and note 2, 226 ; Sanskrit translation of, *id.* 221.
Zérogerei : town mentioned by Ptolemy, identified with Dhár in Central India, I, pt. i, 540.
Ziárat : feast on the third day after death among Musalmáns, IX, pt. ii, 169.
Zia-ud-din Barni : annalist of Muhammad Tughlak's reign and author of *Tarikh-i-Firuz-Sháhi* (1325), I, pt. i, 513, 514, 517, 518.
Zichás : women dying in child-birth, IX, pt. ii, 150.
Zilhaji : twelfth month of the Musalmán year, holidays in, IX, pt. ii, 141.
Zimmis : infidels, Jaziah tax collected from, I, pt. i, 213.
Zizera, Zizerus : old name of Janjira, XI, 432 ; I, pt. ii, 2 ; XIII, 410 note 6.
Zizyphus : *jujuba*, *rugosa*, food plants, XXV, 149 ; *jujuba xylocarpus*, timber trees, *id.* 49, 50.
Zohak : sorcerer, discomforted by Faredun, IX, pt. ii, 216, 220 note 1.
Zoroaster : the prophet of the Pársis, IX, pt. ii, 211 ; brings the true religion from Ahuramazd, *id.* 213 ; his religious connection with India in mythic times, *id.* 183 note 4 ; his miracles, *id.* 211 and note 2 (13), 219.
Zoroastrians : or Mobeds, Magha Bráhmans said to be, IX, pt. I, 440 and note 4 ; followers of Zoroaster, IX, pt. ii, 211, 212, 215, 225.
Zoakalés : king Za Ságal or Za Asgal or Za Hakalé, I, pt. i, 543.
Zubeir : ancestor of one of the families of Náiatas, IX, pt. ii, 14 note 3.
Zuhr : noon prayer among Musalmáns, IX, pt. ii, 126 note 3.
Zulfikarkhán : Aurangzeb's general in the Dakhan, attacks Rájárám at Jálna (1700), XX, 289 ; XIX, 252 ; supports Sháhu (1707-1709), *id.* 253-255 ; captures and loses Sinhgad (1707), XVIII, pt. ii, 240 ; XVIII, pt. iii, 444 ; defeated by Khanderáo Dábháde near Burháupur (1716), I, pt. i, 388.

FINIS.